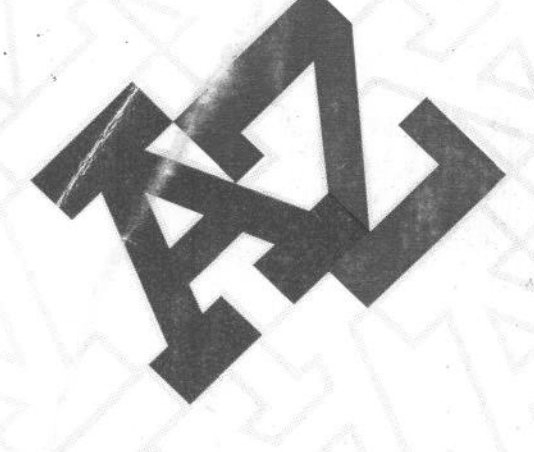

A-Z SURREY

CONTENTS

Key to Map Pages	2-3
Map Pages	4-199
Large Scale Town Centres: Croydon, Dorking, Epsom, Guildford & Kingston upon Thames	200-203
Postcode Map	204-205
Road Map Pages (1:250,000 / 4 miles to 1 inch)	206-207
Index to Streets, Towns, Villages, Stations & selected Places of Interest	208-302
Index to Hospitals & Hospices	303-304

REFERENCE

Motorway M3

Primary Route A31

Under Construction

A Road A22

Proposed

B Road B2236

Dual Carriageway

One-way Street

Traffic flow on A Roads is also indicated by a heavy line on the driver's left

Junction Names SUNBURY CROSS

Restricted Access

Pedestrianized Road

Track & Footpath

Residential Walkway

Railway — Level Crossing — Tunnel

Stations: National Rail Network

Heritage Station

Underground Station

Croydon Tramlink — Stop — Tunnel

The boarding of Tramlink trams at stops may be limited to a single direction, indicated by the arrow

Built-up Area STATION VIEW

Local Authority Boundary

Posttown Boundary

Postcode Boundary (Within Posttown)

Map Continuation 86 — Large Scale Town Centre 203

Airport

Car Park (Selected)

Church or Chapel

Fire Station

Hospital

House Numbers (A & B Roads only) 69 63

Information Centre

National Grid Reference 520

Park & Ride Artington P+

Police Station

Post Office

Toilet:

without facilities for the Disabled

with facilities for the Disabled

Disabled facilities only

Viewpoint

Educational Establishment

Hospital or Hospice

Industrial Building

Leisure or Recreational Facility

Place of Interest

Public Building

Shopping Centre or Market

Other Selected Buildings

SCALE

Map Pages 4-199

1:19,000 3⅓ inches (8.47cm) to 1 mile 5.26cm to 1km

0 ¼ ½ ¾ Mile

0 250 500 750 Metres 1 Kilometre

Map Pages 200-203

1:9,051 7 inches (17.78cm) to 1 mile 11.05cm to 1km

0 ⅛ ¼ ⅜ Mile

0 100 200 300 400 500 Metres

Fairfield Road, Borough Green, Sevenoaks, Kent TN15 8PP
Telephone: 01732 781000 (Enquiries & Trade Sales)
01732 783422 (Retail Sales)

www.a-zmaps.co.uk

Edition 5 2007

KEY TO MAP PAGES

HENLEY-ON-THAMES

Sonning Common

Wargrave

Caversham

Twyford

Woodley

READING

Winnersh

Sindlesham

Shinfield

M4

Arborfield Cross

Arborfield Garrison

Wick Hill

Eversley

Eversley Cross

Yateley

Hartley Wintney

Hook

COOKHAM

BURNHAM

MAIDENHEAD

SLOUGH

Iver Heath

UXBRIDGE

Hillingdon

HAYES

Southall

Bray

Langley

West Drayton

Yiewsley

Oakley Green

Eton Wick

Eton

Datchet

Colnbrook

Harmondsworth

Harlington

Cranford

HESTON

4

5

Poyle

6

7

8

9

WINDSOR

Old Windsor

Wraysbury

Stanwell Moor

London - Heathrow Airport

Hatton

Windsor Great Park

Cranbourne

Hythe End

13

Stanwell

Ashford

Feltham

Shurlock Row

14

Binfield

15

16

Winkfield

17

18

19

Englefield Green

20

Egham

21

STAINES

Hanworth

22

23

Dowlesgreen

Priestwood

Winkfield Row

North Ascot

Cheapside

Virginia Water

Thorpe

Laleham

Sunbury

Upper Halliford

West Molesey

Wokingham

30

31

BRACKNELL

32

South Ascot

33

Ascot

Sunningdale

34

35

36

37

Chertsey

38

Shepperton

39

Walton-on-Thames

Eastheath

Easthampstead

Sunninghill

Addlestone

Weybridge

Crowthorne

Bagshot

Windlesham

Burrowhill

Ottershaw

Row Town

Hersham

Little Sandhurst

48

49

50

51

Lightwater

52

West End

53

Chobham

54

55

56

57

Sandhurst

CAMBERLEY

Sheerwater

West Byfleet

Byfleet

Cobham

Frogmore

Frimley

Bisley

Knaphill

Pyrford

Hawley

Fox Lane

68

69

70

Frimley Green

71

72

Brookwood

73

74

Woking

75

Ripley

76

77

Ockham

Farnborough

Mytchett

Worplesdon

Send

Send Marsh

West Horsley

Little Bookham

Pondtail

88

89

90

91

Ash Vale

92

93

94

West Clandon

95

East Clandon

96

East Horsley

97

Effingham

Fleet

Church Crookham

Fairlands

Burpham

Crookham Village

Aldershot

Normandy

Wood Street Village

GUILDFORD

LARGE SCALE GUILDFORD

202

Ewshot

108

Hale

109

Weybourne

Ash

Flexford

110

Tongham

111

112

113

Onslow Village

114

Chilworth

115

Shere

Gomshall

116

117

Crondall

Shalford

Littleton

Albury

Abinger Hammer

Bentley

Puttenham

The Sands

Farncombe

Wonersh

Peaslake

FARNHAM

128

Wrecclesham

129

130

131

132

133

134

135

136

Holmbury St. Mary

137

Millbridge

Tilford

Elstead

Godalming

Busbridge

Bramley

Shamley Green

S

U

R

Frensham

Milford

Thorncombe Street

Rowly

Ewhurst

148

149

150

Thursley

151

Witley

152

153

Hascombe

154

155

156

157

Churt

Cranleigh

Walliswood

Headley Lindford

Arford

Beacon Hill

Hindhead

Dunsfold

Chawton

168

Bordon

169

Headley Down

170

Grayshott

171

Grayswood

172

173

Chiddingfold

174

Alfold Crossways

175

176

Cox Green

177

Rowhook

Whitehill

Alfold

Rudgwick

Selborne

Haslemere

Ifold

Loxwood

Greatham

188

189

190

191

192

Plaistow

193

194

195

Slinfold

Liphook

Northchapel

Liss

Fernhurst

Billingshurst

Wisborough Green

PETERSFIELD

ALTON

Kingsley

LONDON
LARGE SCALE KINGSTON 203
LARGE SCALE CROYDON 200
LARGE SCALE EPSOM 201
LARGE SCALE DORKING 201
SCALE
0 1 2 3 4 Miles
0 1 2 3 4 5 Kilometres
Surrey County Boundary
Surrey Postal Boundary

A
B
C
D
E
F
G
1
2
3
4
5
6
7
8
9
94
495
96
78
77
74
DORNEY COMMON
COMMON ROAD
ETON
NORTH FIELD
Common Ditch
Bell Farm
ETON GREAT COMMON
Crown Farm
The Bungalow
ETON WICK
Eton Wick Rec. Grd.
Boveney Ditch
B3026
WICK
SOUTH VIEW
RELIEF ROAD
Colenorton Brook
Depot
Farrer Theatre
Stamford
Cress Brook
ROASTHILL LANE
BOVENEY ROAD
SOUTH FIELD
Folly Bri.
Cemy.
Games Ct.
Masters' Field
College
Boveney Court Farm
LOCK PATH
Boveney
Boveney Court
SOUTH BUCKS
WINDSOR and MAIDENHEAD
Water Jump
Athens
MEADOW
Boveney Lock
Weir
ROYAL WINDSOR RACECOURSE
Parade Ring
Long Bri.
Upper Hope
Cuckoo Weir
Grand Stand
Recreation Ground
ETON
SOUTH MEADOW
HIGH STREET
DORNEY LAKE
Dorney Lake Rowing Centre
RIVER THAMES
Windsor Racecourse Yacht Basin
Toll
Bird Sanctuary
Clewer St. Andrew
The Brocas
Mill Stream
Works
Elizabeth Bri.
Leisure Cen.
Pleasure Grd.
Deadwater Ait
Windsor Bri.
Ruddles Pool
THE WILLOWS
WILLOWS LODGE
SUTHERLAND GRANGE
CLEWER VILLAGE
Clewer St. Stephen
Play. Fld.
BARRY AVENUE
Alexandra Gds.
Windsor & Eton Central
MAIDENHEAD ROAD
A308
WINDSOR ROAD
WHITELEY
SAWYERS CL.
WINWOOD
BUCKLAND CR.
Cemy.
Youth Cen.
Comm. Cen.
Rec. Grd.
Schs.
Tennis Cts.
Fitness Club
WINDSOR & ETON ROAD
A332
STOVELL RD.
MAIDENHEAD RD.
Games Ct.
Spts. Cen.
Sch.
ARTHUR ROAD
OXFORD
ALBERT
BEXLEY ST.
CLARENCE ROAD
VANSITTART
DEDWORTH
Playing Field
Schools
LONGMEAD
TESTWOOD
CLIFTON
HAYSE
Sch.
B3025 ROAD
VALE
CLARENCE RD.
DEDWORTH ROAD
B3024
Super store
Dedworth Green
Windsor
Clewer Green
Clewer New Town
Convent
Play. Fld.
GOSLAR WAY
A308
Sports Ground
Clewer Within
Mun. Offs.
Comm. Cen.
OSBORNE RD.
FRANCES RD.
HOSP.
Household Cavalry Museum
Clewer Hill
THAMES HOSPICECARE
Windsor Girls' Sch.
IMPERIAL B3175 ROAD
SL4
WESTMEAD
UPCROFT
PERRYCROFT
WASHINGTON DR.
ILLINGWORTH
ST. LEONARD'S ROAD
B3022
CEMETERY
Windsor & Eton FC (Stag Meadow)
Spital
Tennis Cts.
Playing Fld.
Moat
Bourne Ditch
Park Pale
Queen Mary's Plantation
Arklow Cott.
KING'S ROAD
Reservoirs (covered)
Water Tower
St. Leonardshill
ST. LEONARD'S HILL
FAIRLAWN PARK
Ash Plantation
Withy Cover
Miniature Rifle Range
Queen Annes Gate Cott.
St. Leonard's Farm
St. Leonard's
LEGOLAND
Main Entrance
Lodge
Crown Cotts.
Diningroom Close
Spital Meadow
Cavalry Exercise Grounds
Government Lodge
Windsor (Legoland)
Paddockhill Copse
Palatine Gate
New Cover
DRIVE
A332
ROAD
Review Ground
QUEEN ADELAIDE'S RIDE
ST. LEONARD'S ROAD
B3022
Flemish Farm
CONSORT'S
Fish Pond
Forest Park
PRINCE CONSORT'S DRIVE
Bromley Hill
Star Clump
Park Pale
SHEET STREET
QUEEN ANNE'S RIDE
WINKFIELD ROAD
High Standing Hill
Flemish Farm

18

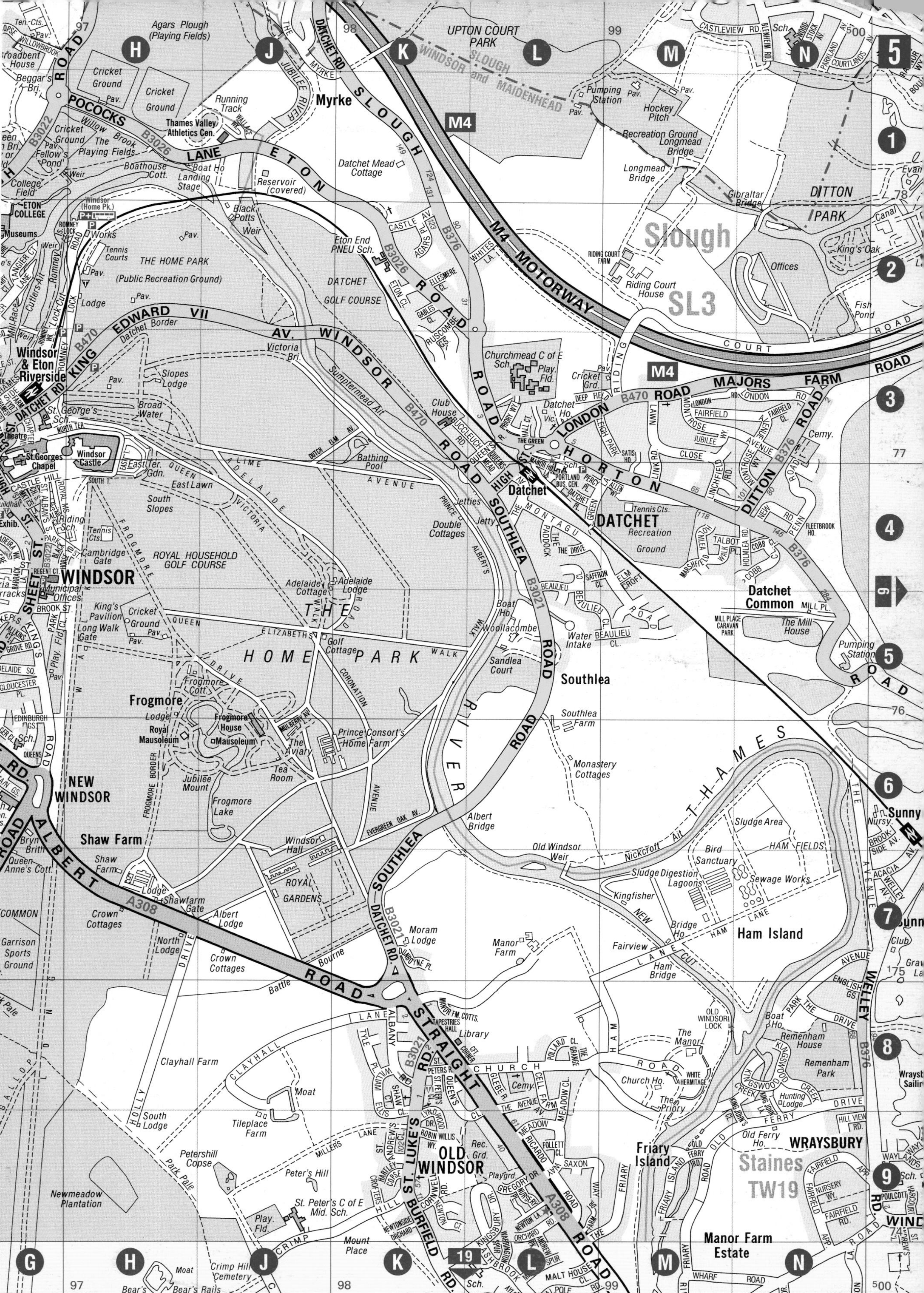

5
97
98
99
500
G
H
J
K
L
M
N
1
2
3
4
5
6
7
8
9
78
77
76
75
74
Agars Plough
(Playing Fields)
UPTON COURT
PARK
WINDSOR and MAIDENHEAD
SLOUGH
CASTLEVIEW RD.
BLENHEIM RD.
WOODSTOCK AV.
PARKLAND AV.
COURTLANDS AV.
Broadbent House
Beggar's Bri.
Cricket Ground
Cricket Ground
Pav.
POCOCKS
LANE
B3026
B3022
ROAD
Running Track
Thames Valley Athletics Cen.
Cricket Ground
Willow Brook
The Playing Fields
Fellow's Pond
Boathouse Cott.
Boat Ho
Landing Stage
Weir
College Field
ETON COLLEGE
Museums
JUBILEE RIVER
Myrke
MYRKE
DATCHET RD.
SLOUGH
ETON
ROAD
M4
Pumping Station
Pav.
Hockey Pitch
Recreation Ground
Longmead Bridge
Longmead Bridge
Gibraltar Bridge
DITTON
PARK
King's Oak
Offices
Fish Pond
Canal
Slough
SL3
RIDING COURT FARM
Riding Court House
M4 MOTORWAY
COURT
ROAD
Datchet Mead Cottage
Reservoir (covered)
Black Potts Weir
Eton End PNEU Sch.
B3026
CASTLE AV.
AGARS PL.
B376
WHITES LA.
ELLESMERE CL.
ETON CL.
GABLES CL.
RUSCOMBE GS.
DATCHET GOLF COURSE
Windsor (Home Pk.)
Works
Tennis Courts
THE HOME PARK
(Public Recreation Ground)
Lodge
Pav.
ROMNEY LOCK
ROMNEY LOCK RD.
Weir
Lock Cut
Cutlers Ait
KING EDWARD VII AV.
B470
Datchet Border
WINDSOR ROAD
Victoria Bri.
Sumptermead Ait
Windsor & Eton Riverside
DATCHET RD
St. George's Sch.
NORTH TER.
Theatre
St. Georges Chapel
Windsor Castle
CASTLE HILL
Slopes Lodge
Broad Water
Churchmead C of E Sch.
Play. Fld.
Cricket Grd.
Pav.
DEEP FIELD
RIDING
M4
B470
LONDON ROAD
MAJORS FARM ROAD
LONDON RD
FAIRFIELD
MONTROSE
JUBILEE
CLOSE
AVENUE
Cemy.
Club House
BUCCLEUCH RD.
QUEENS RD.
Datchet Ho.
Vic.
THE GREEN
MANOR HO.
Sch.
PORTLAND BUS. CEN.
DATCHET PL.
HIGH ST.
Datchet
HORTON
LINK RD.
SATIS HO.
LINCHFIELD RD.
DITTON ROAD
B376
PENN RD.
FLEETBROOK HO.
DITCH ELM AV.
Bathing Pool
LIME AVENUE
ADELAIDE
QUEEN
East Ter. Gdn.
East Lawn
South Slopes
SOUTH T.
VICTORIA
Jetties
Jetty
PRINCE ALBERT'S
Double Cottages
THE MONTAGU
PADDOCK
THE DRIVE
Tennis Cts.
DATCHET
Recreation Ground
TALBOT
HOLMLEA RD.
COBB CL.
Datchet Common
MILL PL.
MILL PLACE CARAVAN PARK
The Mill House
Pumping Station
ROAD
Riding Sch.
Tennis Cts
Cambridge Gate
FROGMORE
ROYAL HOUSEHOLD GOLF COURSE
WINDSOR
Municipal Offices
SHEET ST
BROOK ST
KING'S
PARK ST.
Play. Fld
Adelaide Cottage
Adelaide Lodge
THE WALK
BEAULIEU
SAFFRON CL.
ELM CROFT
Boat Ho.
Woollacombe
Water Intake
BEAULIEU CL.
King's Pavilion
Long Walk Gate
Cricket Ground
Pav.
QUEEN ELIZABETH'S WALK
Golf Cottage
HOME PARK
Sandlea Court
Southlea
SOUTHLEA ROAD
B3021
GROVE RD.
GLOUCESTER PL.
EDINBURGH GS.
DRIVE
Frogmore Cott.
Frogmore
Lodge
Royal Mausoleum
Frogmore House
Mausoleum
MULBERRY AV.
CORONATION
Prince Consort's Home Farm
The Aviary
Tea Room
Southlea Farm
Monastery Cottages
RIVER
THAMES
NEW WINDSOR
Jubilee Mount
Frogmore Lake
FROGMORE BORDER
AVENUE
EVERGREEN OAK AV.
Albert Bridge
Old Windsor Weir
Nickcroft Ait
Sludge Area
HAM FIELDS
Bird Sanctuary
Sludge Digestion Lagoons
Sewage Works
Sunny
Nursy.
BROOKSIDE AV.
ACACIA AV.
WELLEY
Shaw Farm
Shaw Farm
Lodge
Shawfarm Gate
Windsor Hall
ROYAL GARDENS
SOUTHLEA
Kingfisher
NEW CUT
Bridge Ho.
HAM LANE
Ham Island
ALBERT
Bryn Brith
Queen Anne's Cott.
COMMON
Garrison Sports Ground
Crown Cottages
A308
Albert Lodge
North Lodge
DRIVE
Crown Cottages
Moram Lodge
DATCHET RD.
B3021
SUNNYMEAD PL.
Manor Farm
Fairview
Ham Bridge
Club
175
ENGLISH GS.
AVENUE
Bourne
Battle
ROAD
LANE
ALBANY
TYLE PL.
STRAIGHT
MANOR FM. COTTS.
TAPESTRIES HALL
Library
POLLARD CL.
THE GRANGE
HAM
OLD WINDSOR LOCK
The Manor
Boat Ho.
PARK
THE DRIVE
Remenham House
Remenham Park
B376
Wraysbury
Clayhall Farm
CLAYHALL
Moat
CHURCH ROAD
Cemy.
GLEBE RD.
CELL FARM AV.
MEADOW CL.
THE AVENUE
Church Ho.
WHITE HERMITAGE
The Priory
KINGSWOOD CREEK
Hunting Lodge
DRIVE
HILL VIEW RD.
HOLLY
South Lodge
Tileplace Farm
ELLIS
SHAW
WILLIAM CT.
ST. PETERS CL.
LYNWOOD
ROBIN WILLIS WY.
MEADOW
FOLLETT CL.
RICARDO
SAXON WAY
FRIARY
Friary Island
OLD FERRY
FERRY
Old Ferry Ho.
WRAYSBURY
Petershill Copse
MILLERS LANE
Peter's Hill
ST. ANDREW'S CL.
HARTLEY
CROFTERS
ST. LUKE'S RD.
CORNWELL RD.
OLD WINDSOR
Rec. Grd.
Playgrd.
GREGORY DR.
NURSERY
Staines
TW19
FAIRFIELD
NURSERY WY.
FAIRFIELD RD.
POULCOTT
Sch.
WAYLANDS
Park Pale
Newmeadow Plantation
St. Peter's C of E Mid. Sch.
Play. Fld.
CRIMP HILL
NEWTONSIDE ORCHARD
NEWTON CT.
KINGSBURY DR.
NEWTON LA.
ORCHARD RD.
A308
ROAD
FARM
THE
Mount Place
BURFIELD RD.
19
ASHBROOK
MALT HOUSE CL.
WALPOLE RD.
Manor Farm Estate
WHARF ROAD
LA.
Sch.
Moat
Crimp Hill Cemetery
Bear's Rails
GALLOP

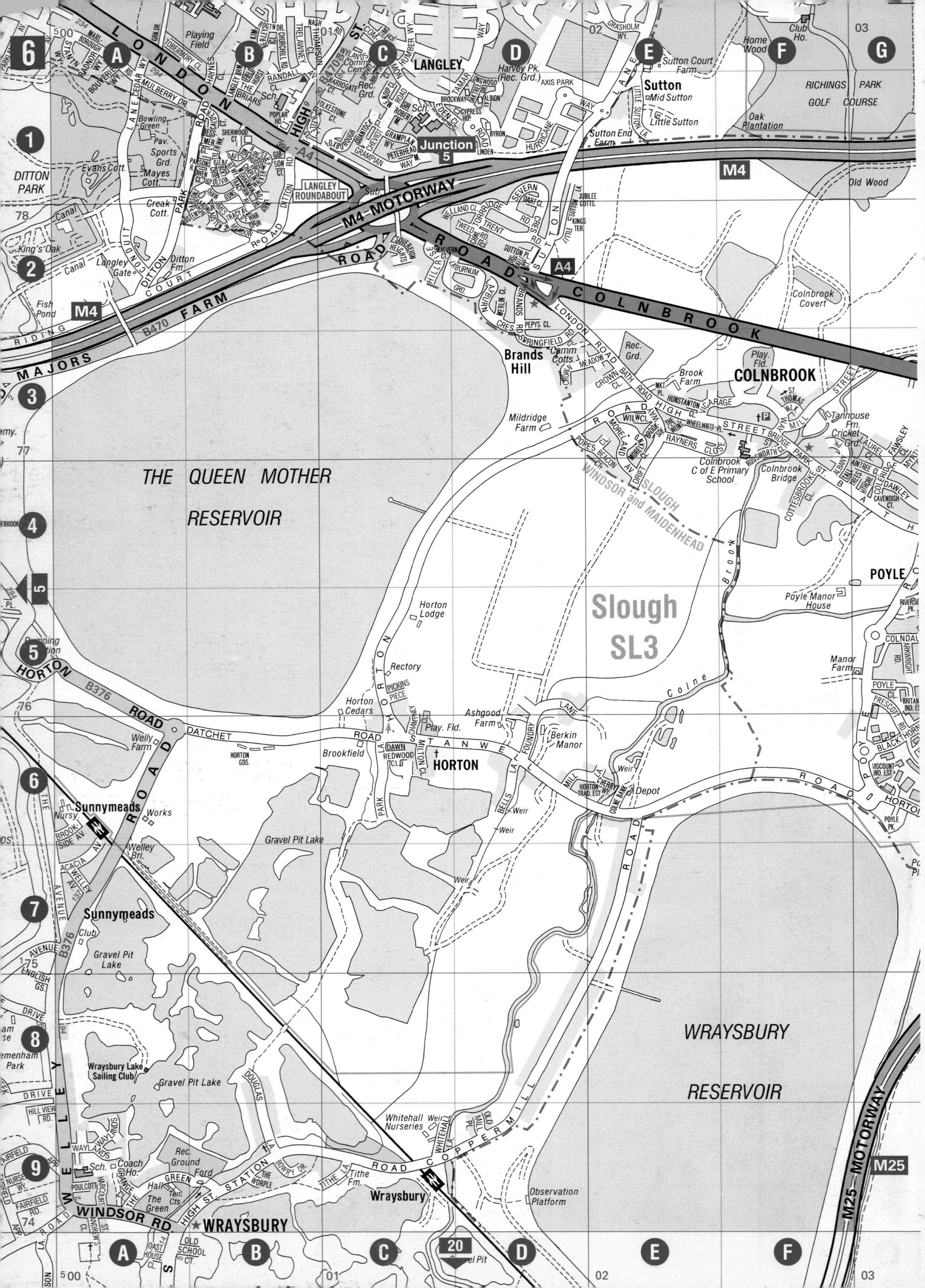
LONDON ROAD
LANGLEY
Playing Field
Sutton
Mid Sutton
Little Sutton
Sutton Court Farm
Home Wood
Club Ho.
RICHINGS PARK GOLF COURSE
Oak Plantation
Old Wood
Harvey Pk. (Rec. Grd.)
AXIS PARK
Junction 5
M4
M4 MOTORWAY
LANGLEY ROUNDABOUT
DITTON PARK
Evans Cott.
Mayes Cott.
Creak Cott.
King's Oak
Canal
Langley Gate
Ditton Fm
Fish Pond
RIDING COURT ROAD
MAJORS FARM ROAD
B470
A4
COLNBROOK
Colnbrook Covert
Brands Hill
Camm Cotts.
Rec. Grd.
Brook Farm
Play. Fld.
Mildridge Farm
Tanhouse Fm.
Cricket Grd.
Colnbrook C of E Primary School
Colnbrook Bridge
WINDSOR and MAIDENHEAD
SLOUGH
THE QUEEN MOTHER RESERVOIR
POYLE
Poyle Manor House
Manor Farm
Slough SL3
Horton Lodge
Rectory
Horton Cedars
Ashgood Farm
Berkin Manor
HORTON
Brookfield
Play. Fld.
Welly Farm
HORTON ROAD
B376
DATCHET ROAD
STANWELL ROAD
Sunnymeads
Works
Welley Bri.
Gravel Pit Lake
Weir
Depot
Colne
Brook
Sunnymeads
Club
Gravel Pit Lake
Wraysbury Lake Sailing Club
Gravel Pit Lake
Whitehall Nurseries
Rec. Ground
Ford
Coach Ho.
Sch.
Hall
The Green
Tithe Fm.
Wraysbury
WRAYSBURY
WINDSOR RD.
HIGH ST.
STATION ROAD
COPPERMILL ROAD
WELLEY ROAD
Observation Platform
WRAYSBURY RESERVOIR
M25 MOTORWAY
M25
Gravel Pit
20
5
A B C D E F G
1 2 3 4 5 6 7 8 9
500 01 02 03
78 77 76 75 74

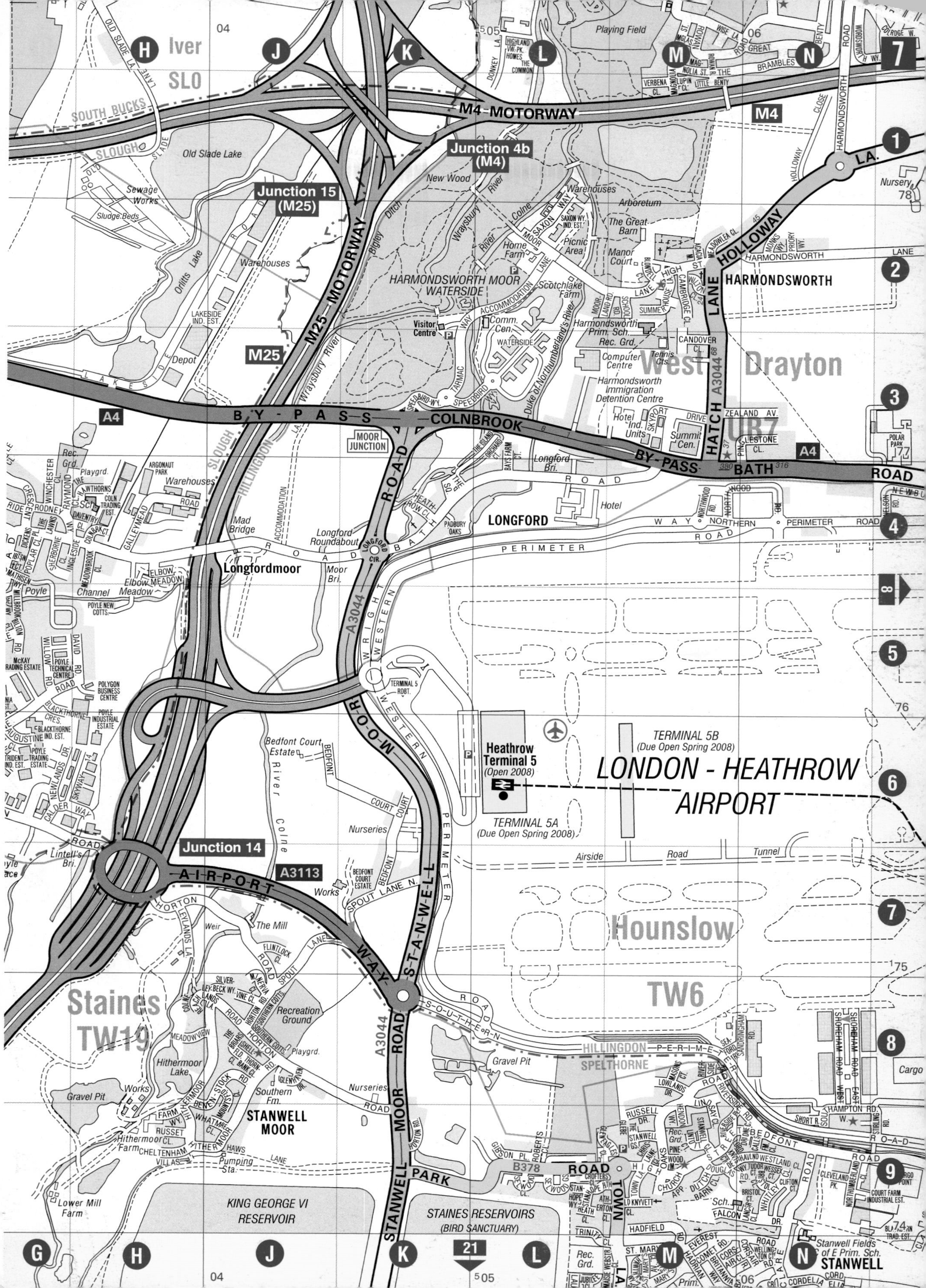

7
Iver
SLO
SOUTH BUCKS
SLOUGH
M4 MOTORWAY
M4
Playing Field
Old Slade Lake
Junction 4b
(M4)
Junction 15
(M25)
Sewage Works
Sludge Beds
New Wood
Warehouses
Arboretum
The Great Barn
Manor Court
Home Farm
Picnic Area
Nursery
HARMONDSWORTH MOOR WATERSIDE
HARMONDSWORTH
Orlitts Lake
LAKESIDE IND. EST.
Depot
M25
M25 MOTORWAY
Visitor Centre
Comm. Cen.
WATERSIDE
Scotchlake Farm
Harmondsworth Prim. Sch.
Rec. Grd.
Tennis Cts.
CANDOVER CL.
Computer Centre
West Drayton
Harmondsworth Immigration Detention Centre
Hotel Ind. Units
Summit Cen.
UB7
HATCH LANE
HOLLOWAY
A3044
A4
BY-PASS COLNBROOK
BY-PASS BATH ROAD
MOOR JUNCTION
ZEALAND AV.
POLAR PARK
Longford Bri.
Hotel
LONGFORD
PERIMETER
NORTHERN PERIMETER ROAD
ARGONAUT PARK
Warehouses
Playgrd.
Rec. Grd.
COLN TRADING EST.
Mad Bridge
Longford Roundabout
LONGFORD CIR.
Longfordmoor
Moor Bri.
Elbow Meadow
Channel
Poyle
POYLE NEW COTTS.
McKAY TRADING ESTATE
POYLE TECHNICAL CENTRE
POLYGON BUSINESS CENTRE
POYLE INDUSTRIAL ESTATE
BLACKTHORNE IND. EST.
POYLE TRADING ESTATE
TRIDENT IND. EST.
WRIGHT WESTERN
TERMINAL 5 ROBT.
MOOR
Bedfont Court Estate
River Colne
Heathrow Terminal 5
(Open 2008)
TERMINAL 5B
(Due Open Spring 2008)
TERMINAL 5A
(Due Open Spring 2008)
LONDON - HEATHROW AIRPORT
Nurseries
Junction 14
A3113
AIRPORT WAY
Lintell's Bri.
BEDFONT COURT ESTATE
Works
SPOUT LANE N.
STANWELL
PERIMETER
Airside Road Tunnel
The Mill
Weir
Hounslow
TW6
Staines
TW19
Recreation Ground
Playgrd.
Hithermoor Lake
Gravel Pit
Southern Fm.
Nurseries
STANWELL MOOR
SOUTHERN ROAD
HILLINGDON
SPELTHORNE
Gravel Pit
Cargo
Hithermoor Farm
Pumping Sta.
STANWELL MOOR ROAD
A3044
PARK ROAD
B378
TOWN LANE
KING GEORGE VI RESERVOIR
STAINES RESERVOIRS
(BIRD SANCTUARY)
Lower Mill Farm
Rec. Grd.
Sch.
Stanwell Fields C of E Prim. Sch.
STANWELL
COURT FARM INDUSTRIAL EST.
1
2
3
4
5
6
7
8
9
G
H
J
K
L
M
N
21
04
505
06
76
175
74
78

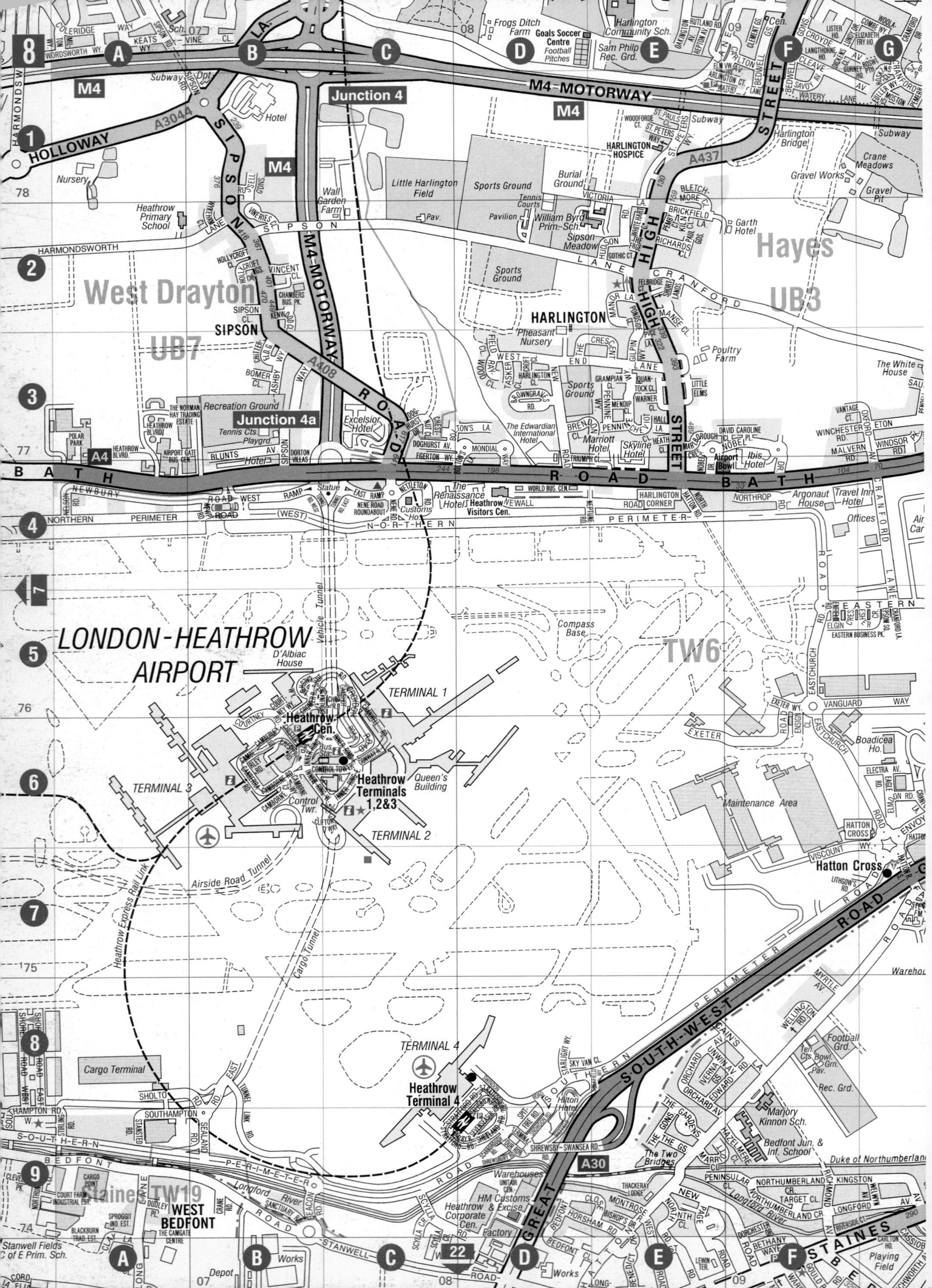8
M4
M4-MOTORWAY
Junction 4
Junction 4a
HOLLOWAY
A3044
SIPSON
SIPSON LANE
HARMONDSWORTH
West Drayton
UB7
A408
Heathrow Primary School
Nursery
Little Harlington Field
Sports Ground
Burial Ground
HARLINGTON HOSPICE
William Byrd Prim. Sch.
Sipson Meadow
HARLINGTON
Pheasant Nursery
HIGH STREET
A437
Hayes
UB3
Harlington Bridge
Crane Meadows
Gravel Works
Gravel Pit
Poultry Farm
The White House
Frogs Ditch Farm
Goals Soccer Centre
Football Pitches
Harlington Community Sch.
Sam Philp Rec. Grd.
Recreation Ground
Tennis Cts.
Playgrd.
Excelsior Hotel
The Edwardian International Hotel
Marriott Hotel
Skyline Hotel
Airport Bowl
Ibis Hotel
A4
BATH ROAD
NORTHERN PERIMETER ROAD
Renaissance Hotel
Heathrow Visitors Cen.
Customs Ho.
Travel Inn Hotel
Argonaut House
Offices
LONDON-HEATHROW AIRPORT
D'Albiac House
Vehicle Tunnel
Compass Base
TW6
TERMINAL 1
TERMINAL 2
TERMINAL 3
Heathrow Cen.
Heathrow Terminals 1,2&3
Queen's Building
Control Twr.
EASTERN PERIMETER ROAD
VANGUARD WAY
EXETER RD.
Boadicea Ho.
Maintenance Area
HATTON CROSS
Hatton Cross
Airside Road Tunnel
Heathrow Express Rail Link
Cargo Tunnel
SOUTHERN PERIMETER ROAD
GREAT SOUTH-WEST ROAD
A30
TERMINAL 4
Heathrow Terminal 4
Cargo Terminal
Hilton Hotel
Warehouses
HM Customs & Excise
Heathrow Corporate Cen.
Factory
Works
Depot
Longford River
STANWELL ROAD
STAINES ROAD
WEST BEDFONT
Staines TW19
Stanwell Fields C of E Prim. Sch.
Marjory Kinnon Sch.
Bedfont Jun. & Inf. School
The Two Bridges
Football Grd.
Rec. Grd.
Duke of Northumberland
Playing Field
22
7

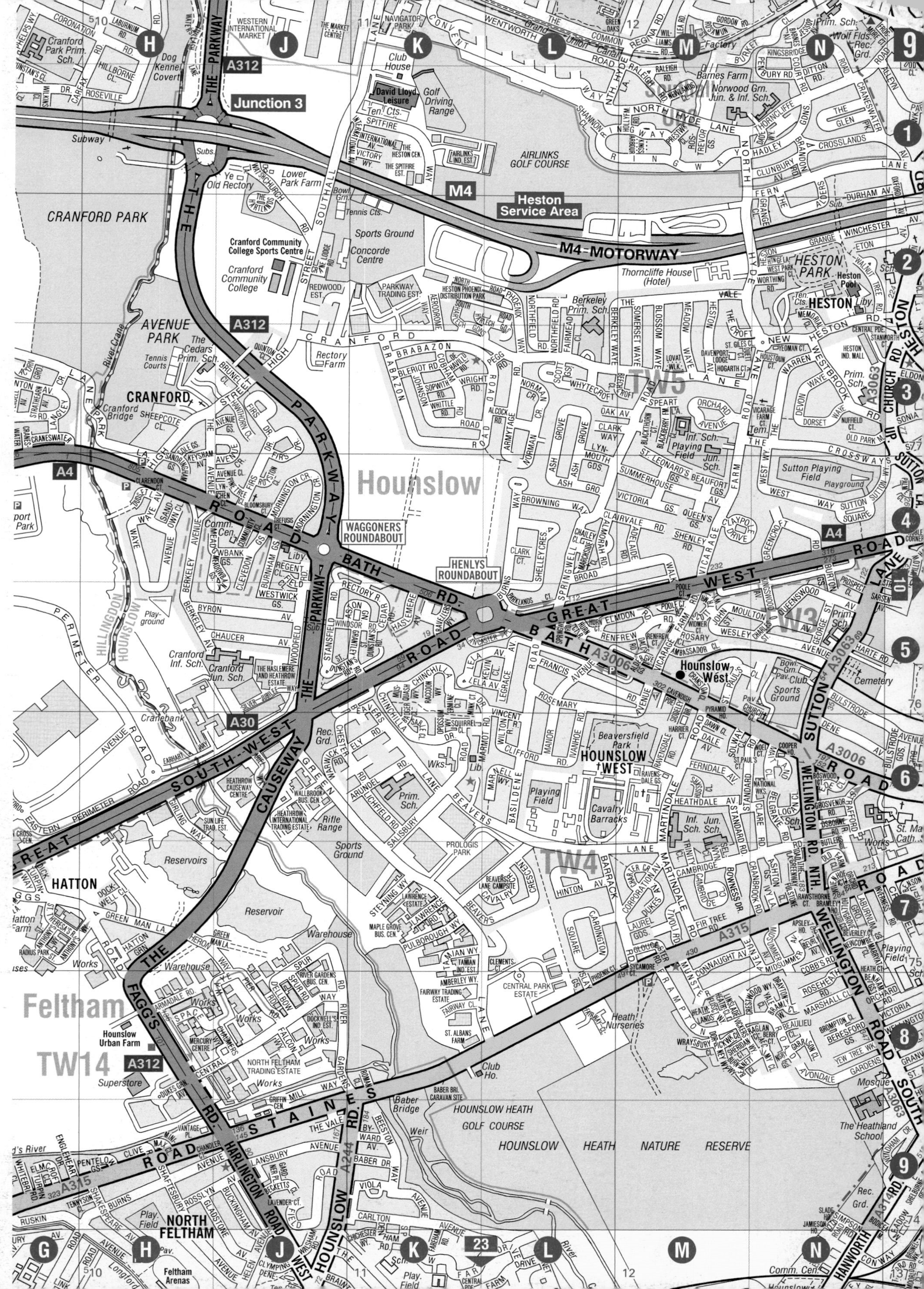

9
H
J
K
L
M
N
CORONATION
LABURNUM RD.
WESTERN INTERNATIONAL MARKET
THE MARKET CENTRE
NAVIGATOR PARK
CONVENT
WENTWORTH
Grand Union Canal
THE COMMON
GREEN OAKS
REGINA RD.
GORDON RD.
Factory
Prim. Sch.
Wolf Flds. Rec. Grd.
Cranford Park Prim. Sch.
HILLBORNE CL.
ROSEVILLE
CARFAX
Dog Kennel Covert
A312
THE PARKWAY
Junction 3
Club House
David Lloyd Leisure
Golf Driving Range
Ten. Cts.
SPITFIRE
INTERNATIONAL AV.
VICTORY WY.
THE HESTON CEN.
THE SPITFIRE EST.
AIRLINKS IND. EST.
AIRLINKS GOLF COURSE
Subway
Subs.
Ye Old Rectory
Lower Park Farm
M4
Heston Service Area
M4 MOTORWAY
NORTH HYDE LANE
RALEIGH
Barnes Farm
Norwood Grn. Jun. & Inf. Sch.
HORNCLIFFE
THE GLEN
CROSSLANDS
CLUNBURY AV.
HADLEY
BRANDON
FERN
DURHAM AV.
WINCHESTER
CRANFORD PARK
Bowl. Grn.
Tennis Cts.
Sports Ground
Concorde Centre
Cranford Community College Sports Centre
Cranford Community College
REDWOOD EST.
PARKWAY TRADING EST.
HESTON PHOENIX DISTRIBUTION PARK
Thorncliffe House (Hotel)
HESTON PARK
Heston Pool
HESTON
Liby.
Berkeley Prim. Sch.
A312
AVENUE PARK
The Cedars Prim. Sch.
Tennis Courts
Rectory Farm
CRANFORD
BRABAZON
TW5
NEW HESTON RD.
HESTON IND. MALL
Prim. Sch.
A3063
CHURCH RD.
CRANFORD
Cranford Bridge
SHEEPCOTE CL.
River Crane
PARKWAY
Hounslow
Inf. Sch.
Playing Field
Jun. Sch.
Sutton Playing Field
Playground
A4
BATH ROAD
WAGGONERS ROUNDABOUT
HENLYS ROUNDABOUT
GREAT WEST ROAD
A4
10
Comm. Cen.
Liby.
BROWNING WAY
CLARK CT.
TW3
Prim. Sch.
HILLINGDON
HOUNSLOW
PERIMETER
Play-ground
BYRON AV.
CHAUCER AV.
Cranford Inf. Sch.
Cranford Jun. Sch.
THE HASLEMERE AND HEATHROW ESTATE
A3006
Hounslow West
Bowl. Grn. Pav.
Club
Sports Ground
Cemetery
SUTTON LANE
A3063
Cranebank
A30
SOUTH WEST
CAUSEWAY
Rec. Grd.
Wks.
Prim. Sch.
Lib.
Beaversfield Park
HOUNSLOW WEST
Playing Field
Cavalry Barracks
A3006
ROAD
EASTERN PERIMETER ROAD
HEATHROW CAUSEWAY CENTRE
WALLBROOK BUS. CEN.
HEATHROW INTERNATIONAL TRADING ESTATE
Rifle Range
Sports Ground
PROLOGIS PARK
Inf. Sch.
Jun. Sch.
WELLINGTON RD. NTH.
Works
St. Mary Cath.
Reservoirs
HATTON
TW4
BEAVERS LANE CAMPSITE
GREEN MAN LA.
Hatton Farm
Reservoir
Warehouse
MAPLE GROVE BUS. CEN.
A315
Works
Warehouse
RIVER GARDENS BUS. CEN.
CENTRAL PARK ESTATE
Playing Field
Feltham
FAIRWAY TRADING ESTATE
ST. ALBANS FARM
Heath Nurseries
Hounslow Urban Farm
DOCKWELL'S IND. EST.
TW14
A312
Superstore
NORTH FELTHAM TRADING ESTATE
Works
Club Ho.
Mosque
The Heathland School
A3063
WELLINGTON ROAD SOUTH
STAINES ROAD
Baber Bridge
BABER BRI. CARAVAN SITE
HOUNSLOW HEATH GOLF COURSE
Weir
HOUNSLOW HEATH NATURE RESERVE
A244
HOUNSLOW RD.
HARLINGTON ROAD
A315
Play. Field
NORTH FELTHAM
Rec. Grd.
A314
23
G
H
J
K
L
M
N
Feltham Arenas
Play. Field
Comm. Cen.
HANWORTH
River

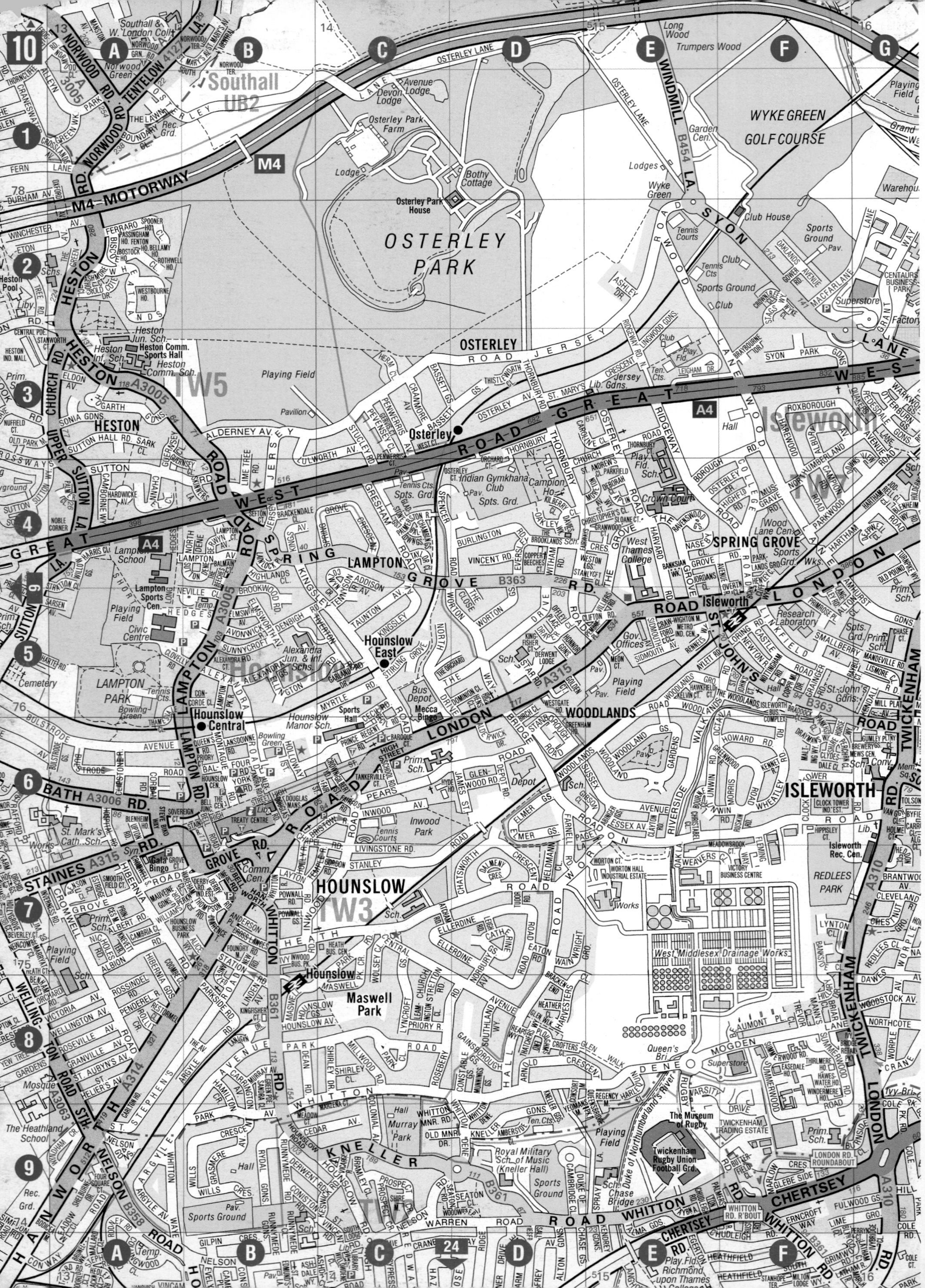

10
A
B
C
D
E
F
G
1
2
3
4
5
6
7
8
9
Southall UB2
Southall & W. London Coll.
Norwood Green
M4 MOTORWAY
M4
OSTERLEY LANE
Osterley Park Farm
Lodge
Bothy Cottage
Osterley Park House
OSTERLEY PARK
Long Wood
Trumpers Wood
WINDMILL LA.
WYKE GREEN GOLF COURSE
Wyke Green
Club House
Sports Ground
Lodges
Playing Field
Warehouse
SYON LANE
Superstore
CENTAURS BUSINESS PARK
Factory
HESTON
Heston Pool
Heston Comm. Sports Hall
Heston Comm. Sch.
TW5
OSTERLEY
JERSEY ROAD
Osterley
GREAT WEST ROAD
A4
Isleworth
TW7
Indian Gymkhana Club
Crown Court
West Thames College
SPRING GROVE
LAMPTON
Lampton School
Lampton Sports Cen.
Civic Centre
LAMPTON PARK
Cemetery
GROVE RD.
B363
LONDON ROAD
Hounslow East
Hounslow Central
A3005
A315
Bus Depot
Mecca Bingo
WOODLANDS
Research Laboratory
BATH RD.
A3006
STAINES RD.
Treaty Centre
Gala Bingo
HOUNSLOW
TW3
Inwood Park
Depot
ISLEWORTH
Isleworth Rec. Cen.
REDLEES PARK
West Middlesex Drainage Works
Worton Hall Industrial Estate
Hounslow
Maswell Park
A314
B361
A310
TWICKENHAM RD.
Superstore
The Museum of Rugby
Twickenham Rugby Union Football Grd.
TWICKENHAM TRADING ESTATE
Royal Military Sch. of Music (Kneller Hall)
Murray Park
KNELLER RD.
WHITTON ROAD
Sports Ground
TW2
CHERTSEY RD.
LONDON RD. ROUNDABOUT
The Heathland School
Mosque
HANWORTH RD.
NELSON RD.
A3063
B358
24
Richmond upon Thames College

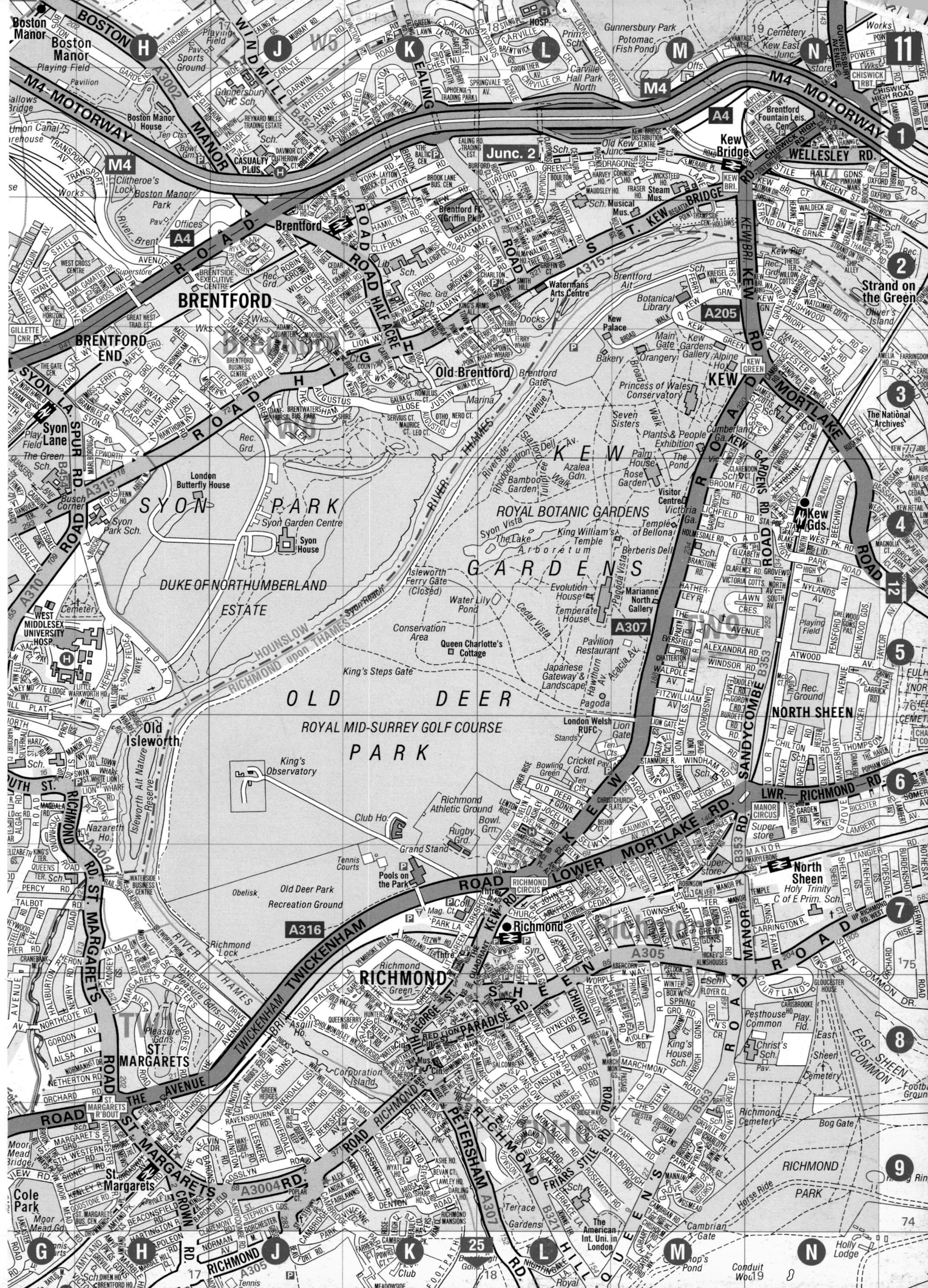
11
Boston Manor
Boston Manor Playing Field
M4 MOTORWAY
Gunnersbury Park
Potomac (Fish Pond)
Cemetery
Kew East Junc.
CHISWICK RBT.
Junc. 2
Kew Bridge
WELLESLEY RD.
Brentford Fountain Leis. Cen.
Boston Manor House
Clitheroe's Lock
Boston Manor Park
Brentford
Brentford FC (Griffin Pk.)
Steam Mus.
Musical Mus.
Strand on the Green
Oliver's Island
Kew Pier
BRENTFORD
BRENTFORD END
Waterman's Arts Centre
Brentford Ait
Botanical Library
Kew Palace
Old Brentford
Brentford Gate
Marina
Syon Lane
KEW
KEW GREEN
Princess of Wales Conservatory
Seven Sisters
The National Archives
London Butterfly House
SYON PARK
Syon Garden Centre
Syon House
Syon Park Sch.
Busch Corner
KEW
Palm House
Rose Garden
Plants & People Exhibition
Visitor Centre
Victoria Ga.
ROYAL BOTANIC GARDENS
Syon Vista
The Lake
King William's Temple
Temple of Bellona
Arboretum
Berberis Dell
Kew Gds.
GARDENS
DUKE OF NORTHUMBERLAND ESTATE
Isleworth Ferry Gate (Closed)
Water Lily Pond
Evolution House
Temperate House
Marianne North Gallery
Conservation Area
Queen Charlotte's Cottage
Pavilion Restaurant
Japanese Gateway & Landscape
Pagoda
King's Steps Gate
OLD DEER PARK
ROYAL MID-SURREY GOLF COURSE
West Middlesex University Hosp.
NORTH SHEEN
Old Isleworth
London Welsh RUFC
Lion Gate
King's Observatory
Richmond Athletic Ground
Rugby Grd.
Grand Stand
Pools on the Park
Isleworth Ait Nature Reserve
Nazareth Ho.
Obelisk
Old Deer Park Recreation Ground
RICHMOND CIRCUS
LOWER MORTLAKE RD.
LWR. RICHMOND RD.
North Sheen
Holy Trinity C of E Prim. Sch.
Richmond
Richmond Lock
TWICKENHAM ROAD
RICHMOND
Richmond Green
Pesthouse Common
East Sheen Cemetery
EAST SHEEN COMMON
Christ's Sch.
King's House Sch.
ST. MARGARETS
Corporation Island
Richmond Cemetery
Bog Gate
RICHMOND PARK
St. Margarets
Cole Park
Moor Mead Bridge
The American Int. Uni. in London
Cambrian Gate
Horse Ride
Terrace Gardens
Holly Lodge
Conduit Wood
Bishop's Pond
25

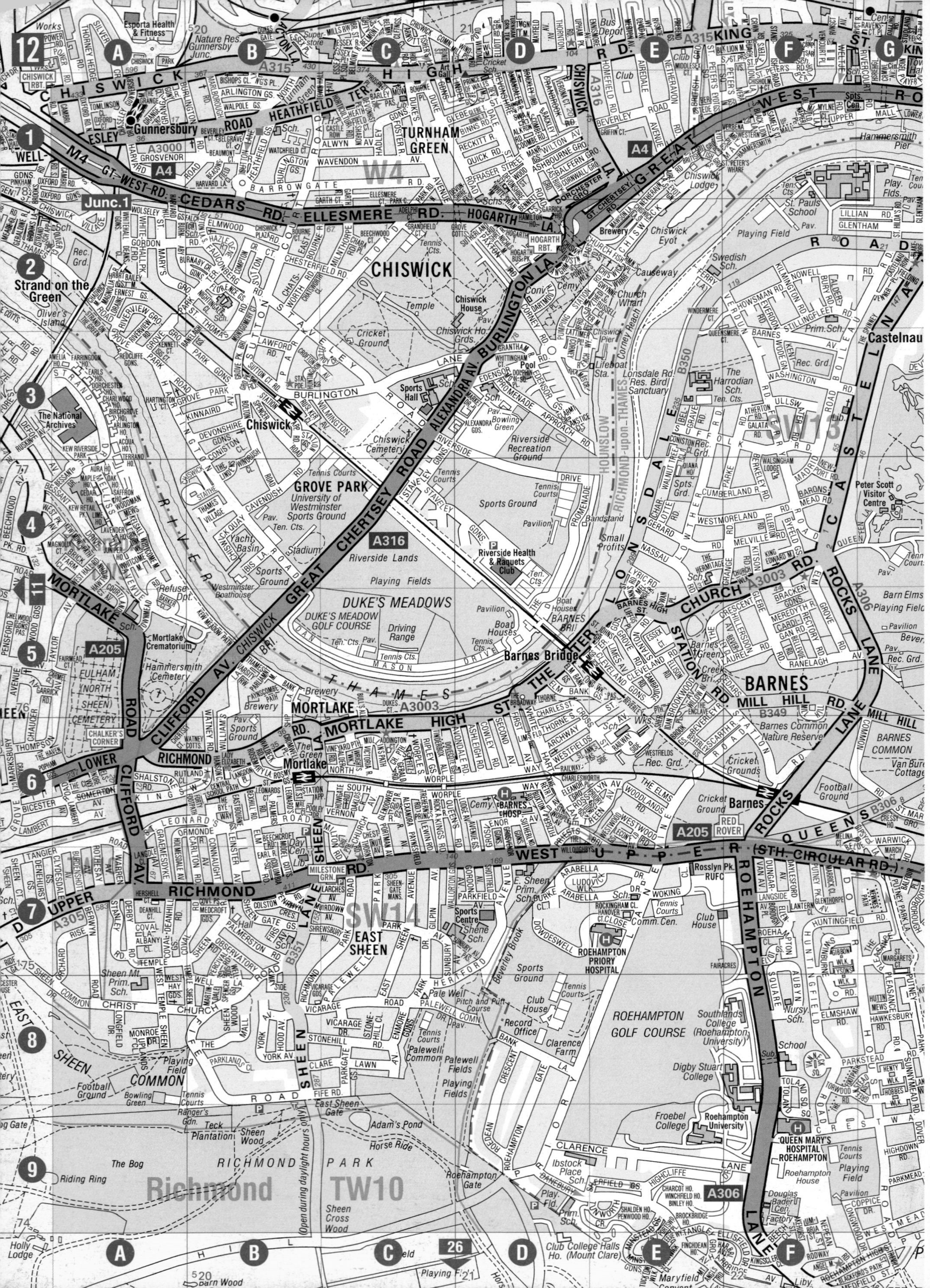
12
A
B
C
D
E
F
G
1
2
3
4
5
6
7
8
9
11
26
CHISWICK
TURNHAM GREEN
W4
Gunnersbury
CHISWICK HIGH RD.
KING ST.
GREAT WEST RD.
A315
A316
A4
A3000
M4
GT. WEST RD.
Junc.1
CEDARS RD.
ELLESMERE RD.
HOGARTH LA.
HOGARTH RBT.
HEATHFIELD TER.
BURLINGTON LA.
BURLINGTON ROAD
Chiswick
Chiswick House
Chiswick Ho. Grds.
Temple
Cricket Ground
Chiswick Cemetery
Riverside Recreation Ground
GROVE PARK
University of Westminster Sports Ground
Sports Ground
Riverside Health & Raquets Club
Riverside Lands
Playing Fields
DUKE'S MEADOWS
DUKE'S MEADOW GOLF COURSE
Driving Range
Barnes Bridge
Strand on the Green
Oliver's Island
The National Archives
Kew Riverside Park
Mortlake Crematorium
Hammersmith Cemetery
FULHAM (NORTH SHEEN) CEMETERY
CHALKER'S CORNER
MORTLAKE
Mortlake
MORTLAKE HIGH ST.
RICHMOND RD.
LOWER RICHMOND RD.
CLIFFORD AV.
GREAT CHERTSEY ROAD
ALEXANDRA AV.
A205
A3003
A306
A305
B350
B349
B351
B306
THAMES
RIVER
HOUNSLOW
RICHMOND-upon-THAMES
Corney Reach
Chiswick Eyot
Chiswick Pier
Lifeboat Sta.
Hammersmith Pier
Brewery
Church Wharf
Causeway
Swedish Sch.
St. Pauls School
Playing Field
Castelnau
Lonsdale Rd. Res. Bird Sanctuary
The Harrodian Sch.
SW13
Peter Scott Visitor Centre
BARNES
Barnes
Barnes Common Nature Reserve
BARNES COMMON
Barn Elms Playing Fields
CASTELNAU
ROCKS LANE
LONSDALE RD.
CHURCH RD.
MILL HILL RD.
STATION RD.
THE TERRACE
UPPER RICHMOND RD. WEST
UPPER RICHMOND RD. (STH. CIRCULAR RD.)
QUEENS RIDE
RED ROVER
Rosslyn Pk. RUFC
EAST SHEEN
SW14
SHEEN LANE
Milestone Grn.
Sports Centre
ROEHAMPTON PRIORY HOSPITAL
ROEHAMPTON GOLF COURSE
Southlands College (Roehampton University)
Digby Stuart College
Froebel College
Roehampton University
QUEEN MARY'S HOSPITAL ROEHAMPTON
Roehampton House
ROEHAMPTON LANE
Palewell Common
Palewell Fields
Playing Fields
Beverley Brook
Record Office
Clarence Farm
EAST SHEEN COMMON
Football Ground
Bowling Green
Tennis Courts
Ranger's Gdn.
Teck Plantation
Sheen Wood
East Sheen Gate
Adam's Pond
Horse Ride
The Bog
Riding Ring
RICHMOND PARK
Richmond
TW10
Sheen Cross Wood
Roehampton Gate
Open during daylight hours only
Holly Lodge
Ibstock Place Sch.
Douglas Bader Cen.
Club College Halls Ho. (Mount Clare)
Maryfield Convent
Esporta Health & Fitness
Nature Res. Gunnersby Junc.
Bus Depot
Barn Wood

H
J
K
L
M
N
HAMMERSMITH RD.
HAMMERSMITH FLYOVER
TALGARTH ROAD
WEST CROMWELL RD.
WEST KENSINGTON
Hammersmith
HAMMERSMITH
Barons Court
West Kensington
EARL'S COURT
Earl's Court
A4
A3220
Earls Court Exhibition Building
Gibbs Green School
Hammersmith Cemetery
The Queen's Club
CHARING CROSS HOSP.
Riverside Studios
West Brompton
WEST BROMPTON
Brompton Cemetery
OLD BROMPTON RD.
A3218
REDCLIFFE
FINBOROUGH
SW10
A304
Chelsea FC (Stamford Bridge)
Fulham Broadway
FULHAM BROADWAY
FULHAM ROAD
DAWES ROAD
A3219
LILLIE ROAD
FULHAM PALACE ROAD
A219
NORTH END ROAD
Fulham Pools
Normand Park
Fulham Cross Sec. Sch.
Fulham Cemetery
FULHAM
SW6
WALHAM GREEN
Eel Brook Common
Parsons Grn.
PARSONS GRN
KING'S RD.
WANDSWORTH BRIDGE RD.
A217
A308
SANDS END
Gas Works
SOUTH PARK
HURLINGHAM PARK
Hurlingham Stadium
Running Track
Hurlingham
The Hurlingham Club
Fulham FC (Craven Cottage)
Stevenage Wharves
Blakes Wharves
Eternit Wharf
LONDON WETLAND CENTRE
Barn Elms
Barn Elms Athletic Track
Barn Elms Schools Sports Centre
Boat House
BISHOP'S PARK
Moat Garden
Fulham Palace
Old Barnes Cemetery
Putney Cemetery
LOWER RICHMOND
B349
B306
Putney Pier
Putney Bri.
RIVER THAMES
HAMMERSMITH and FULHAM
WANDSWORTH
Hurlingham Wharf
Trinidad Wharf
Fulham Wharf
Solid Waste Transfer Station
Fitness Club
Wandsworth Town
WANDSWORTH GYRATORY
A3209
WANDSWORTH BRIDGE
WANDSWORTH PARK
PUTNEY BRIDGE ROAD
PUTNEY HIGH ST.
Putney
PUTNEY
SW15
WANDSWORTH
A205
UPPER RICHMOND ROAD
East Putney
PUTNEY HILL
WEST HILL
A3
WANDSWORTH HIGH ST.
ARMOURY WAY
GARRATT LA.
BUCKHOLD RD.
A218
MERTON RD.
King George's Park
Wandle Rec. Cen.
Elliott Sch.
PUTNEY HEATH
TIBBET'S RIDE
ROYAL HOSP. FOR NEURO-DISABILITY
G
1
2
3
4
5
6
7
8
9
27

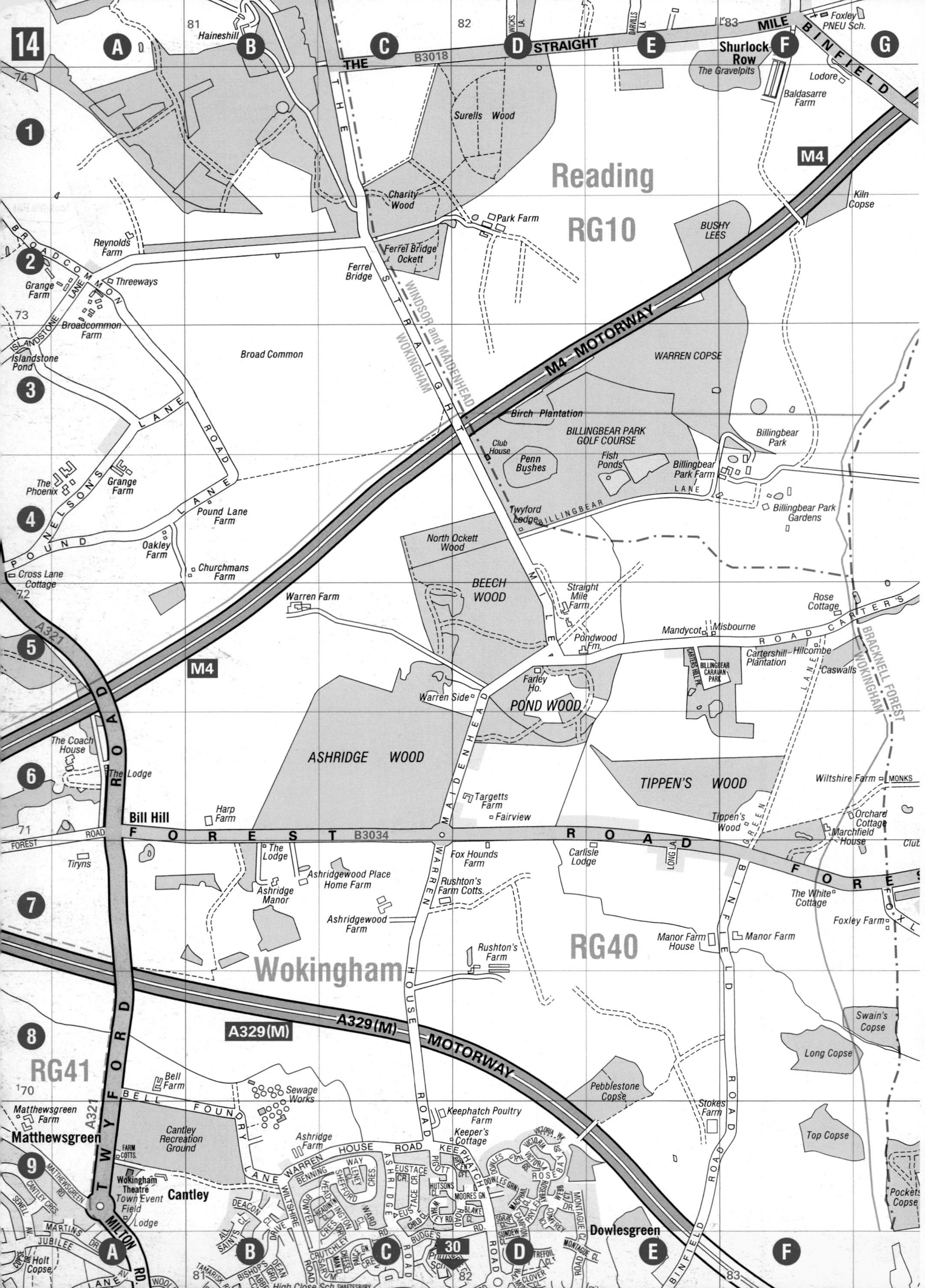
THE STRAIGHT MILE
B3018
Haineshill
Shurlock Row
The Gravelpits
Foxley
PNEU Sch.
BINFIELD
Lodore
Baldasarre Farm
Surells Wood
Reading
RG10
M4
Kiln Copse
Charity Wood
Park Farm
BUSHY LEES
Reynolds Farm
Ferrel Bridge Ockett
Ferrel Bridge
BROADCOMMON
Threeways
Grange Farm
Broadcommon Farm
ISLANDSTONE
Islandstone Pond
Broad Common
WINDSOR and MAIDENHEAD
WOKINGHAM
M4 MOTORWAY
WARREN COPSE
Birch Plantation
BILLINGBEAR PARK GOLF COURSE
Billingbear Park
Club House
Penn Bushes
Fish Ponds
Billingbear Park Farm
The Phoenix
Grange Farm
NELSON'S LANE
POUND LANE
Pound Lane Farm
Twyford Lodge
BILLINGBEAR LANE
Billingbear Park Gardens
North Ockett Wood
Oakley Farm
Churchmans Farm
Cross Lane Cottage
BEECH WOOD
Straight Mile Farm
Warren Farm
Rose Cottage
CARTER'S ROAD
Mandycot
Misbourne
Pondwood Fm.
A321
Cartershill Plantation
Hilcombe
Caswalls
BILLINGBEAR CARAVAN PARK
BRACKNELL FOREST
Farley Ho.
Warren Side
POND WOOD
MAIDENHEAD
The Coach House
ASHRIDGE WOOD
TIPPEN'S WOOD
The Lodge
Wiltshire Farm
MONKS
Targetts Farm
Fairview
Harp Farm
Bill Hill
Tippen's Wood
Orchard Cottage
Marchfield House
Club
FOREST ROAD
B3034
Tiryns
The Lodge
Fox Hounds Farm
Carlisle Lodge
LONG LA.
Ashridgewood Place Home Farm
Ashridge Manor
Rushton's Farm Cotts.
The White Cottage
Foxley Farm
Ashridgewood Farm
Manor Farm House
Manor Farm
RG40
Rushton's Farm
Wokingham
WARREN HOUSE ROAD
A329(M)
A329(M) MOTORWAY
Swain's Copse
Long Copse
RG41
TWYFORD ROAD
Bell Farm
BELL FOUNDRY LANE
Sewage Works
Pebblestone Copse
Stokes Farm
BINFIELD ROAD
Matthewsgreen Farm
Keephatch Poultry Farm
Keeper's Cottage
Top Copse
Cantley Recreation Ground
Ashridge Farm
Matthewsgreen
FARM COTTS.
KEEPHATCH
DOWLES GRN.
Wokingham Theatre
Town Event Field
Lodge
Cantley
MATTHEWSGREEN RD.
Pockets Copse
DEACON
WILTSHIRE
EUSTACE CR.
HUTSONS CL.
MOORES GN.
BLAKE CL.
ROSE
Dowlesgreen
MARTINS
JUBILEE
MILTON RD.
Holt Copse
ALL SAINTS CL.
BISHOP'S
DEAN
CRUTCHLEY
BUDGE'S
SUNDEW
TREFOIL
MONTAGUE CL.
TAMARISK
High Close Sch
SHAFTESBURY
CLOVER
30
81
82
83
74
73
72
71
70
A
B
C
D
E
F
G
1
2
3
4
5
6
7
8
9

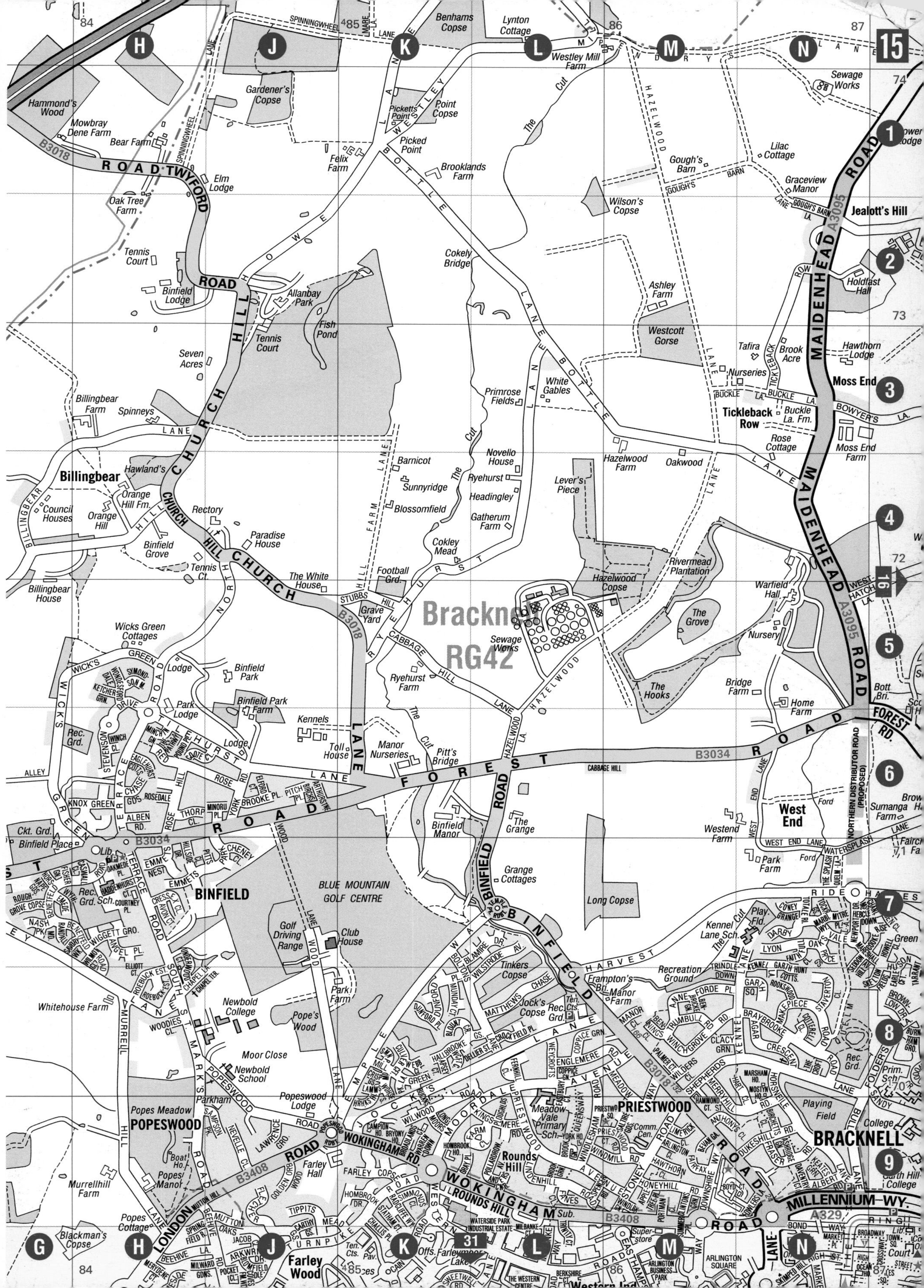
15
Bracknell
RG42
Hammond's Wood
Mowbray Dene Farm
Bear Farm
Gardener's Copse
Benhams Copse
Lynton Cottage
Westley Mill Farm
Sewage Works
Picketts Point
Point Copse
Picked Point
Felix Farm
Brooklands Farm
Lilac Cottage
Gough's Barn
Graceview Manor
Jealott's Hill
Wilson's Copse
Elm Lodge
Oak Tree Farm
Tennis Court
Binfield Lodge
Allanbay Park
Fish Pond
Seven Acres
Cokely Bridge
Ashley Farm
Holdfast Hall
Westcott Gorse
Tafira
Brook Acre
Hawthorn Lodge
Nurseries
Moss End
Primrose Fields
White Gables
Tickleback Row
Buckle La. Fm.
Rose Cottage
Moss End Farm
Billingbear Farm
Spinneys
Billingbear
Hawland's
Council Houses
Orange Hill
Orange Hill Fm.
Rectory
Barnicot
Sunnyridge
Blossomfield
Novello House
Ryehurst
Headingley
Gatherum Farm
Hazelwood Farm
Oakwood
Lever's Piece
Binfield Grove
Paradise House
Cokley Mead
Rivermead Plantation
Billingbear House
Tennis Ct.
The White House
Football Grd.
Grave Yard
Hazelwood Copse
Warfield Hall
The Grove
Wicks Green Cottages
Binfield Park
Ryehurst Farm
Nursery
The Hooks
Bridge Farm
Home Farm
Park Lodge
Binfield Park Farm
Kennels
Toll House
Manor Nurseries
Pitt's Bridge
Rec. Grd.
West End
Westend Farm
Park Farm
Binfield Manor
The Grange
Binfield Place
BINFIELD
BLUE MOUNTAIN GOLF CENTRE
Grange Cottages
Long Copse
Golf Driving Range
Club House
Kennel Lane Sch.
Recreation Ground
Tinkers Copse
Frampton's Br.
Manor Farm
Whitehouse Farm
Newbold College
Park Farm
Pope's Wood
Jock's Copse
Moor Close
Newbold School
Parkham
Popeswood Lodge
Popes Meadow
POPESWOOD
PRIESTWOOD
Meadow Vale Primary Sch.
Playing Field
College
BRACKNELL
Rounds Hill
Farley Hall
Murrellhill Farm
Popes Manor
Popes Cottage
Blackman's Copse
Farley Wood
Waterside Park Industrial Estate
Arlington Square
Garth Hill College
TWYFORD ROAD
CHURCH HILL
CHURCH LANE
FOREST ROAD
MAIDENHEAD ROAD
BINFIELD ROAD
WOKINGHAM ROAD
LONDON ROAD
MILLENNIUM WY.
B3018
B3034
A3095
B3408
A329
16
31

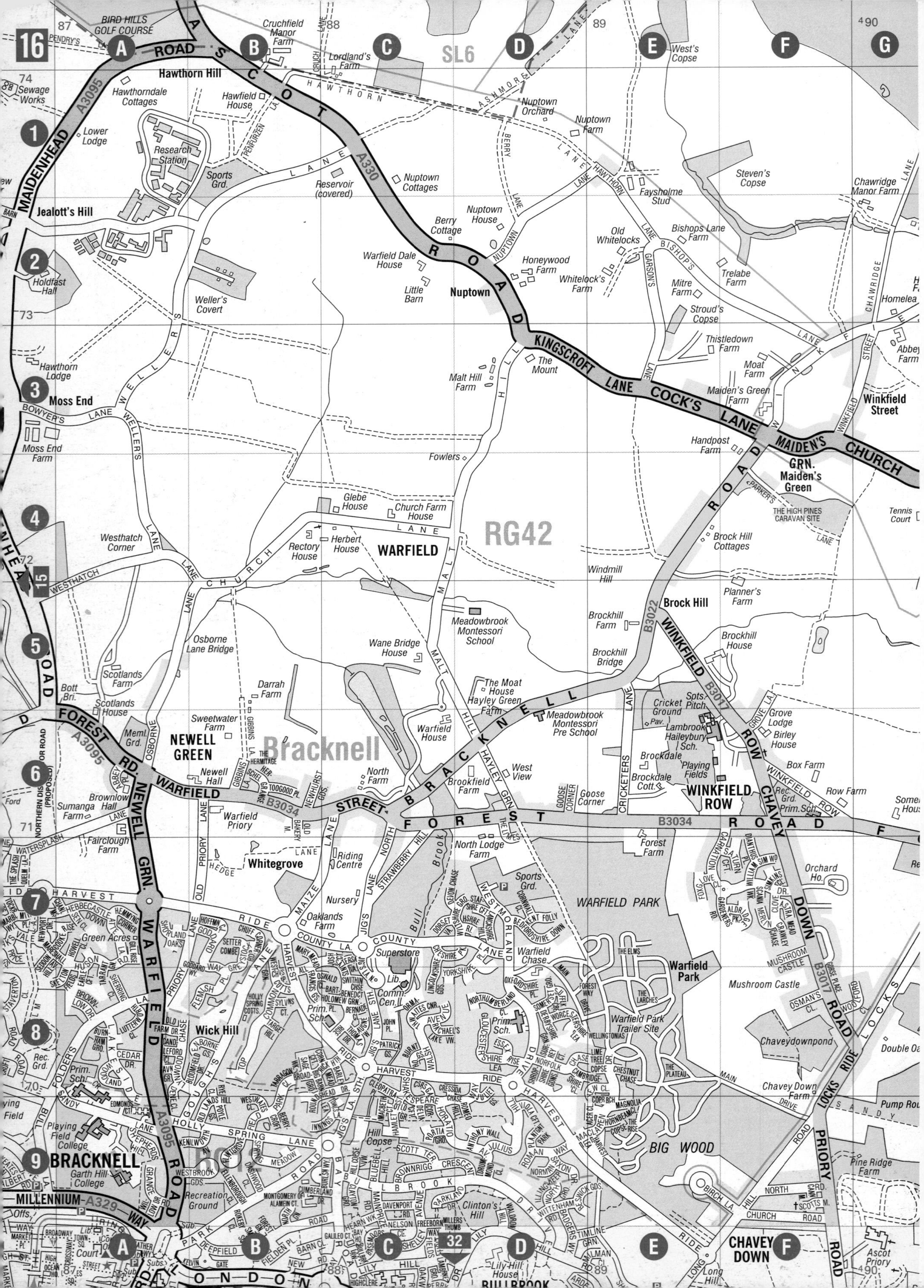

16
BIRD HILLS GOLF COURSE
PENDRY'S LA.
Cruchfield Manor Farm
Lordland's Farm
SL6
West's Copse
Hawthorn Hill
Sewage Works
Hawthorndale Cottages
Hawfield House
HAWTHORN
ASHMORE LANE
Nuptown Orchard
Nuptown Farm
Lower Lodge
Research Station
Sports Grd.
Reservoir (covered)
Nuptown Cottages
Steven's Copse
Chawridge Manor Farm
MAIDENHEAD ROAD
A3095
ASCOT ROAD
A330
Jealott's Hill
Berry Cottage
Nuptown House
Faysholme Stud
Bishops Lane Farm
Old Whitelocks
Holdfast Hall
Warfield Dale House
Honeywood Farm
Whitelock's Farm
Little Barn
Nuptown
Mitre Farm
Trelabe Farm
Weller's Covert
Stroud's Copse
Homelea
Thistledown Farm
Hawthorn Lodge
KINGSCROFT LANE
COCK'S LANE
The Mount
Malt Hill Farm
Moat Farm
Maiden's Green Farm
Moss End
BOWYER'S LANE
WELLER'S LANE
Winkfield Street
Moss End Farm
Handpost Farm
MAIDEN'S GRN.
CHURCH
Fowlers
Maiden's Green
Glebe House
Church Farm House
THE HIGH PINES CARAVAN SITE
Tennis Court
Westhatch Corner
RG42
Rectory House
Herbert House
WARFIELD
Brock Hill Cottages
CHURCH LANE
WESTHATCH
Windmill Hill
Planner's Farm
Brock Hill
Meadowbrook Montessori School
Brockhill Farm
Osborne Lane Bridge
Wane Bridge House
Brockhill House
Brockhill Bridge
Scotlands Farm
Bott Bri.
Darrah Farm
The Moat House
Hayley Green Farm
Scotlands House
Sweetwater Farm
Warfield House
Meadowbrook Montessori Pre School
Cricket Ground
Spts. Pitch
Lambrook Haileybury Sch.
Grove Lodge
Birley House
FOREST RD.
A3095
Meml. Grd.
NEWELL GREEN
Bracknell
Newell Hall
North Farm
Brookfield Farm
West View
Brockdale
Playing Fields
Brockdale Cott.
Box Farm
WINKFIELD ROW
Row Farm
Brownlow Hall
Sumanga Farm
WARFIELD STREET
B3034
Warfield Priory
BRACKNELL
FOREST ROAD
B3022
B3017
Goose Corner
Rec. Grd. Prim. Sch.
Fairclough Farm
WATERSPLASH
North Lodge Farm
Forest Farm
Riding Centre
Whitegrove
CHAVEY DOWN ROAD
Orchard Ho.
HARVEST RIDE
Sports Grd.
WARFIELD PARK
Nursery
Oaklands Farm
Green Acres
COUNTY LA.
Superstore
Warfield Chase
Warfield Park
Lib.
Comm. Cen.
Mushroom Castle
Prim. Sch.
Wick Hill
Warfield Park Trailer Site
Chaveydownpond
Double Oak
Rec. Grd.
Prim. Sch.
Chavey Down Farm
Pump Roa
Playing Field College
LOCKS RIDE
BIG WOOD
BRACKNELL
Garth Hill College
Recreation Ground
Pine Ridge Farm
MILLENNIUM WAY
A329
Clinton's Hill
NORTH RD.
CHURCH ROAD
CHAVEY DOWN
PRIORY ROAD
Court
LONDON
32
Lily Hill House
BULLBROOK
Long Hill
Ascot Priory
87
88
89
490
74
73
72
71
170
15

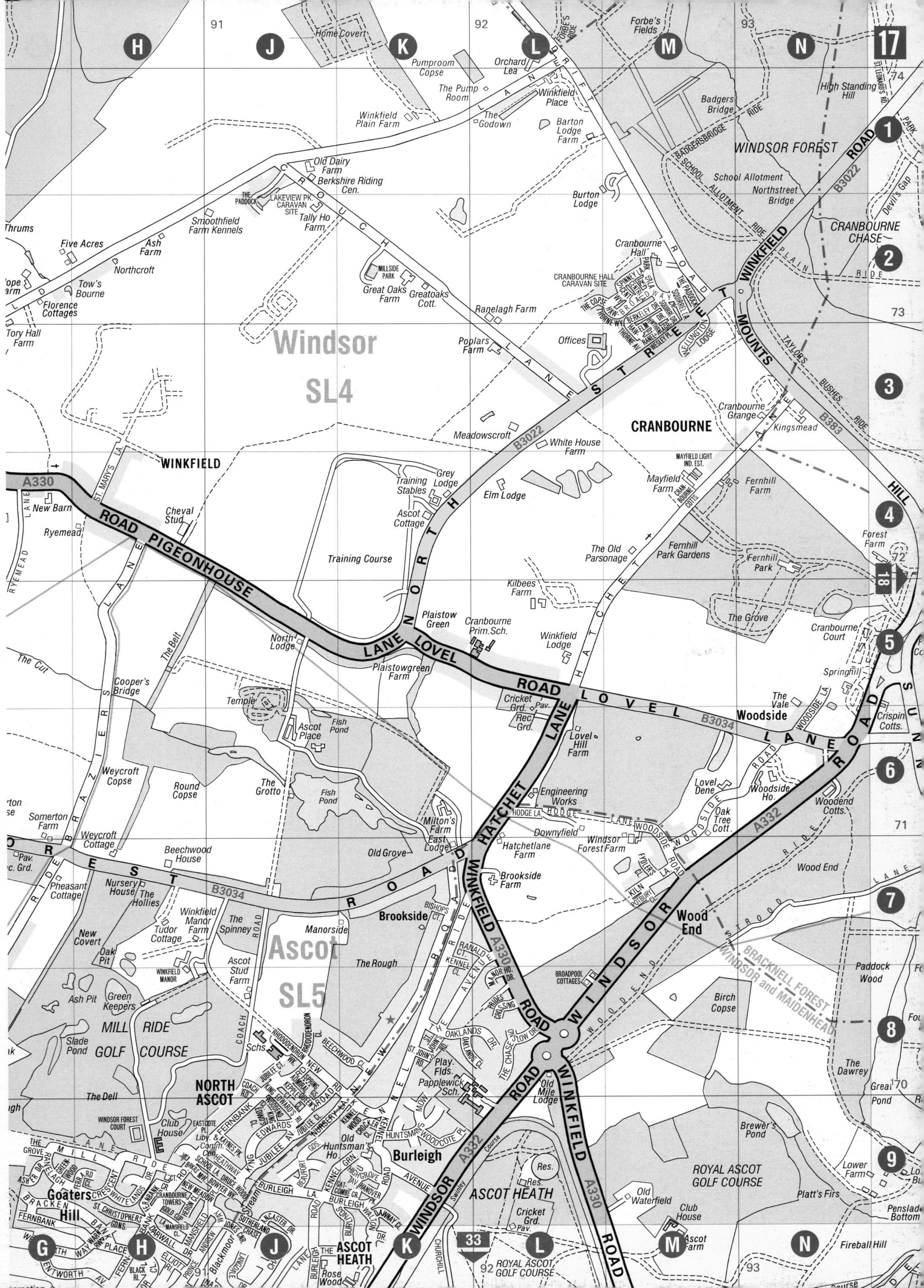
Windsor
SL4
WINKFIELD
CRANBOURNE
WINDSOR FOREST
Ascot
SL5
NORTH ASCOT
Burleigh
Goaters Hill
ASCOT HEATH
Woodside
Wood End
MILL RIDE GOLF COURSE
ROYAL ASCOT GOLF COURSE
Training Course
PIGEONHOUSE ROAD
LOVEL ROAD
LOVEL LANE
HATCHET LANE
NORTH STREET
WINKFIELD ROAD
WINDSOR ROAD
FOREST ROAD
MOUNTS HILL
BRACKNELL FOREST
WINDSOR and MAIDENHEAD
A330
A332
B3022
B3034
B383
18
33

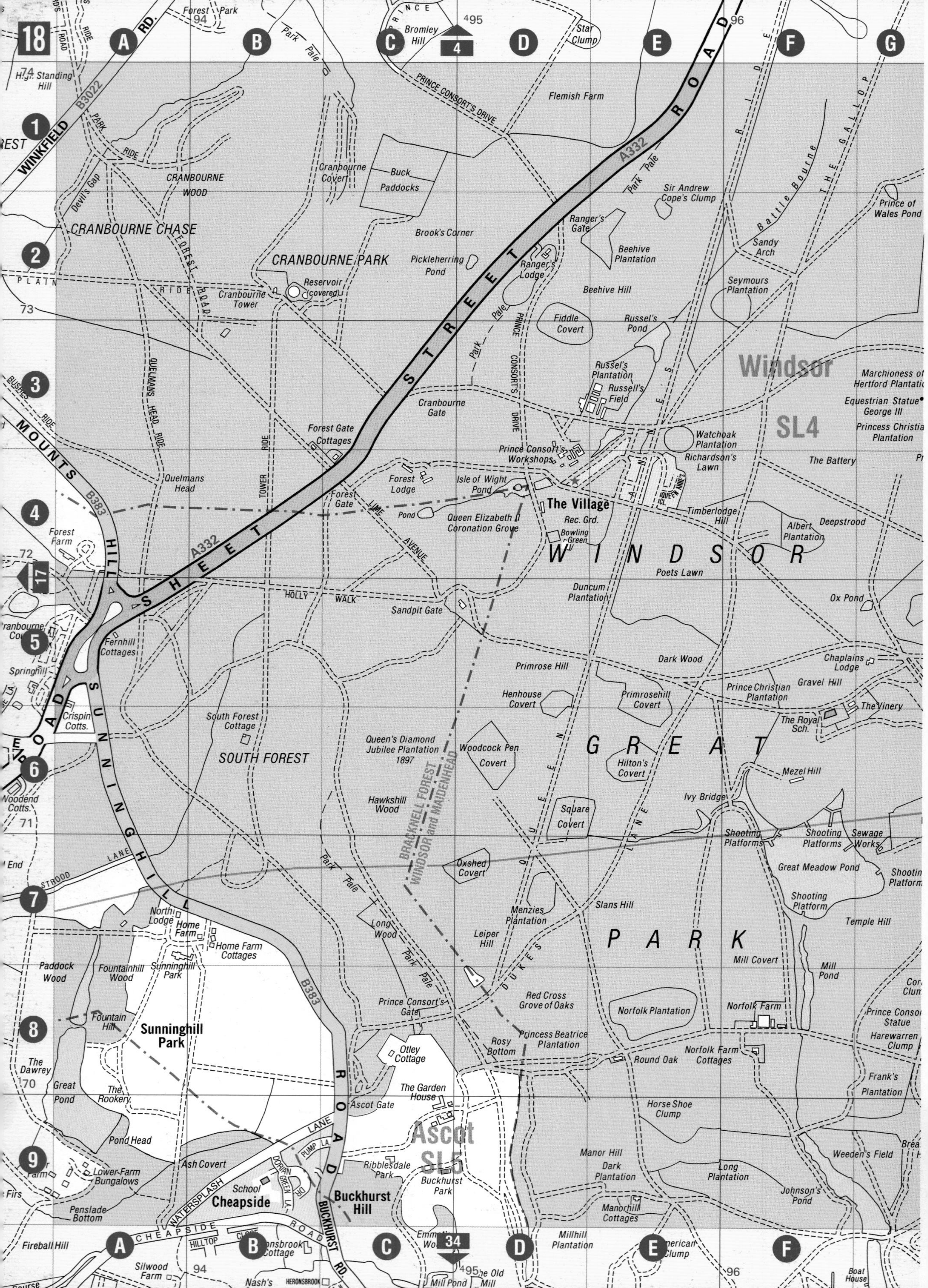

Windsor
SL4
WINDSOR GREAT PARK
Ascot
SL5
CRANBOURNE CHASE
CRANBOURNE WOOD
CRANBOURNE PARK
SOUTH FOREST
SHEET STREET ROAD
A332
WINKFIELD RD.
B3022
MOUNTS HILL
B383
SUNNINGHILL ROAD
BUCKHURST RD.
CHEAPSIDE ROAD
WATERSPLASH LANE
STROOD LANE
PRINCE CONSORT'S DRIVE
QUEEN ANNE'S RIDE
DUKES LANE
QUELMANS HEAD RIDE
FOREST ROAD
TOWER RIDE
LIME AVENUE
HOLLY WALK
PLAIN RIDE
BUSHES RIDE
PARK RIDE
THE GALLOP
Park Pale
Battle Bourne
BRACKNELL FOREST
WINDSOR and MAIDENHEAD
Forest Park
Bromley Hill
Star Clump
Flemish Farm
High Standing Hill
Devil's Gap
Cranbourne Cover
Buck Paddocks
Brook's Corner
Pickleherring Pond
Reservoir (covered)
Cranbourne Tower
Ranger's Gate
Ranger's Lodge
Beehive Plantation
Beehive Hill
Sir Andrew Cope's Clump
Sandy Arch
Seymours Plantation
Prince of Wales Pond
Fiddle Covert
Russel's Pond
Russel's Plantation
Russell's Field
Marchioness of Hertford Plantation
Equestrian Statue George III
Princess Christian Plantation
Cranbourne Gate
Forest Gate Cottages
Watchoak Plantation
Richardson's Lawn
The Battery
Prince Consort's Workshops
Quelmans Head
Forest Lodge
Isle of Wight Pond
The Village
Forest Gate
Pond
Queen Elizabeth II Coronation Grove
Rec. Grd.
Bowling Green
QUEEN ANNE'S CL.
Timberlodge Hill
Albert Plantation
Deepstrood
Forest Farm
Poets Lawn
Duncum Plantation
Ox Pond
Sandpit Gate
Fernhill Cottages
Dark Wood
Chaplains Lodge
Primrose Hill
Prince Christian Plantation
Gravel Hill
Henhouse Covert
Primrosehill Covert
The Viner
The Royal Sch.
Springhill
Crispin Cotts.
South Forest Cottage
Queen's Diamond Jubilee Plantation 1897
Woodcock Pen Covert
Hilton's Covert
Mezel Hill
Woodend Cotts.
Hawkshill Wood
Ivy Bridge
Square Covert
Shooting Platforms
Sewage Works
Oxshed Covert
Great Meadow Pond
Shooting Platform
End
North Lodge
Home Farm
Home Farm Cottages
Long Wood
Slans Hill
Menzies Plantation
Temple Hill
Leiper Hill
Paddock Wood
Fountainhill Wood
Sunninghill Park
Mill Covert
Mill Pond
Red Cross Grove of Oaks
Norfolk Plantation
Norfolk Farm
Prince Consort's Gate
Prince Consort Statue
Fountain Hill
Princess Beatrice Plantation
Harewarren Clump
Rosy Bottom
Otley Cottage
Round Oak
Norfolk Farm Cottages
The Dawrey
Great Pond
The Rookery
The Garden House
Frank's Plantation
Ascot Gate
Horse Shoe Clump
Pond Head
Manor Hill
Dark Plantation
Weeden's Field
Ash Covert
Ribblesdale Park
Long Plantation
Lower Farm Bungalows
PUMP LA.
DORIAN DR.
GREEN LA.
Buckhurst Park
Johnson's Pond
Firs
School
Cheapside
Buckhurst Hill
Manorhill Cottages
Penslade Bottom
Fireball Hill
HILLTOP
CLOSE
Millhill Plantation
American Clump
Silwood Farm
Nash's
HERONSBROOK
Mill Pond
The Old Mill
Boat House
Course
495
94
96
74
73
72
71
70
4
17
34
A B C D E F G
1 2 3 4 5 6 7 8 9

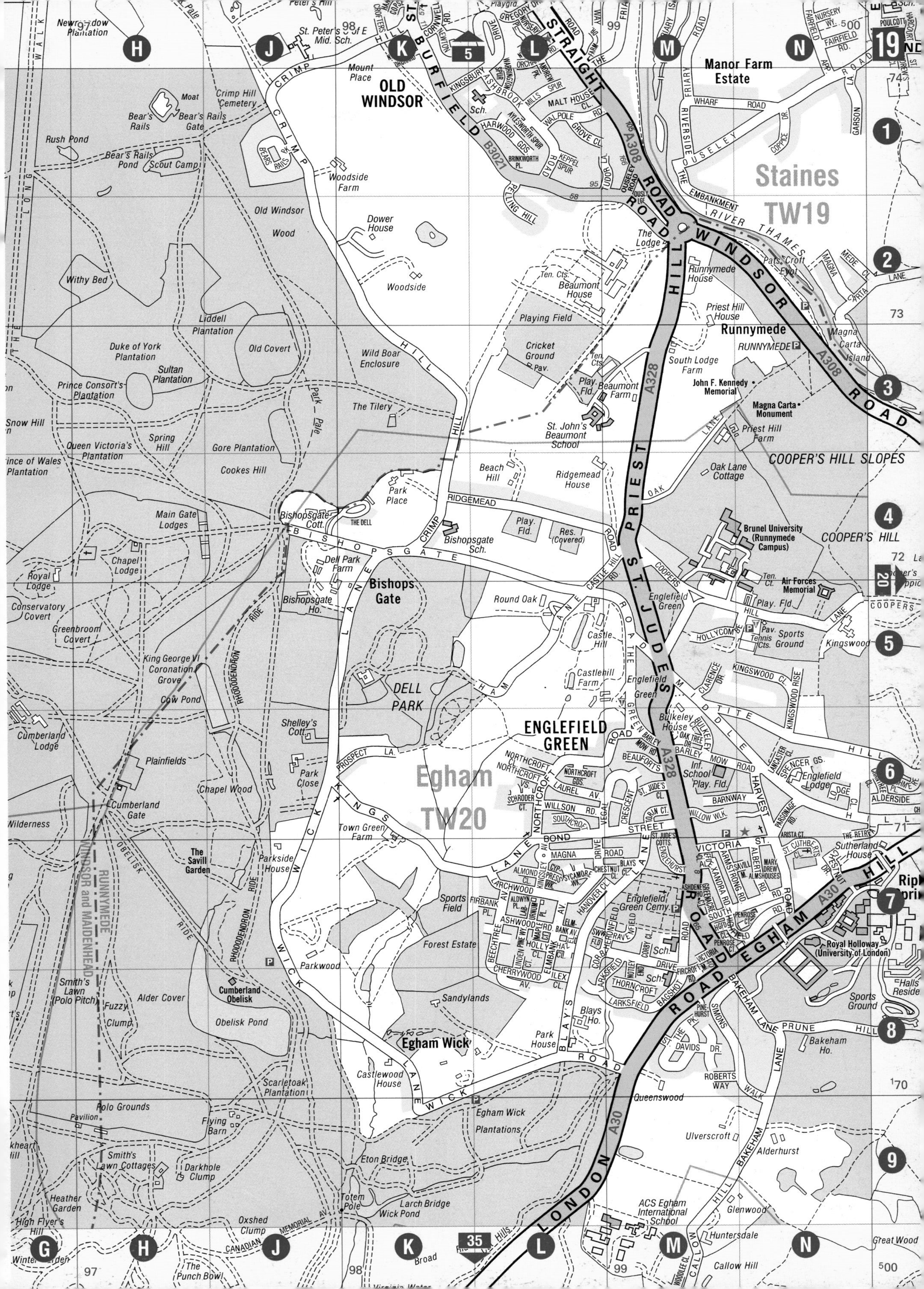

19
20
5
35
H
J
K
L
M
N
G
1
2
3
4
5
6
7
8
9
97
98
99
500
74
73
72
71
70
OLD WINDSOR
Staines
TW19
Egham
TW20
ENGLEFIELD GREEN
Bishops Gate
DELL PARK
Egham Wick
Runnymede
Manor Farm Estate
New Meadow Plantation
St. Peter's C of E Mid. Sch.
Mount Place
Crimp Hill Cemetery
Moat
Bear's Rails
Bear's Rails Gate
Rush Pond
Bear's Rails Pond
Scout Camp
Woodside Farm
Old Windsor Wood
Dower House
Woodside
Withy Bed
Liddell Plantation
Duke of York Plantation
Old Covert
Sultan Plantation
Prince Consort's Plantation
Wild Boar Enclosure
The Tilery
Snow Hill
Spring Hill
Queen Victoria's Plantation
Gore Plantation
Cookes Hill
Prince of Wales Plantation
Main Gate Lodges
Bishopsgate Cott.
THE DELL
Park Place
Chapel Lodge
Royal Lodge
Dell Park Farm
Bishopsgate Ho.
Bishopsgate Sch.
Conservatory Covert
Greenbroom Covert
King George VI Coronation Grove
Cow Pond
Cumberland Lodge
Shelley's Cott.
Plainfields
Park Close
Chapel Wood
Cumberland Gate
Wilderness
The Savill Garden
Parkside House
Town Green Farm
Sports Field
Forest Estate
Parkwood
Cumberland Obelisk
Obelisk Pond
Smith's Lawn (Polo Pitch)
Fuzzy Clump
Alder Cover
Sandylands
Castlewood House
Egham Wick Plantations
Scarletoak Plantation
Polo Grounds
Pavilion
Flying Barn
Smith's Lawn Cottages
Darkhole Clump
Eton Bridge
Heather Garden
Totem Pole
Larch Bridge
Wick Pond
High Flyer's Hill
Oxshed Clump
CANADIAN MEMORIAL AV.
Broad
The Punch Bowl
The Lodge
Beaumont House
Ten. Cts.
Runnymede House
Priest Hill House
Playing Field
Cricket Ground
Pav.
South Lodge Farm
RUNNYMEDE
John F. Kennedy Memorial
Magna Carta Monument
Magna Carta Island
Pats Croft Eyot
Beaumont Farm
Play. Fld.
St. John's Beaumont School
Priest Hill Farm
COOPER'S HILL SLOPES
Beach Hill
Ridgemead House
Oak Lane Cottage
Brunel University (Runnymede Campus)
COOPER'S HILL
Air Forces Memorial
Res. (Covered)
Round Oak
Castle Hill
Englefield Green
Castlehill Farm
Sports Ground
Tennis Cts.
Kingswood
Bulkeley House
Englefield Lodge
Inf. School
Englefield Green Cemy.
Sch.
Royal Holloway (University of London)
Sutherland House
Blays Ho.
Park House
Bakeham Ho.
Sports Ground
Halls Reside
Queenswood
Ulverscroft
Alderhurst
Glenwood
ACS Egham International School
Huntersdale
Callow Hill
Great Wood
RIVER THAMES
THE EMBANKMENT
WHARF ROAD
RIVERSIDE
OUSELEY
STRAIGHT ROAD
A308
WINDSOR ROAD
ST. BURFIELD
B3021
KINGSBURY
ASHBROOK
MALT HOUSE CL.
WALPOLE RD.
GROVE CL.
HARWOOD GDS.
BRINKWORTH PL.
KEPPEL SPUR
TUDOR LA.
PELLING HILL
PRIEST HILL
A328
ST. JUDES ROAD
CRIMP HILL
RIDGEMEAD
BISHOPSGATE ROAD
CASTLE HILL RD.
COOPERS HILL LANE
HOLLYCOMBE
KINGSWOOD CL.
KINGSWOOD RISE
MIDDLE HILL
BARLEY MOW ROAD
HARVEST RD.
SPENCER GS.
ALDERSIDE
NORTHCROFT
LAUREL AV.
WILLSON RD.
BOND STREET
MAGNA ROAD
VICTORIA ST.
BARNWAY
WILLOW WLK.
PROSPECT LA.
KINGS LANE
WICK LANE
WICK ROAD
BLAY'S LANE
ROAD
EGHAM HILL
A30
LONDON ROAD
BAKEHAM LANE
PRUNE HILL
ROBERTS WAY
DAVIDS DR.
CALLOW HILL
RHODODENDRON RIDE
OBELISK RIDE
RUNNYMEDE
WINDSOR and MAIDENHEAD
THE LONG WALK
BAGSHOT RD.
LARKSFIELD
THORNCROFT
CHERRYWOOD AV.
ASHWOOD RD.
BEECHTREE AV.
FIRBANK PL.
LARCHWOOD
ALMOND CL.
HANOVER CL.
CHESTNUT CL.
BLAYS CL.
CRESCENT
MAGNA
MEDE CL.
LANE
GARSON
COPPICE DR.
FAIRFIELD RD.
NURSERY WY.

WRAYSBURY
Wraysbury
WRAYSBURY RESERVOIR
Gravel Pit
Gravel Pits
Observation Platform
Ankerwycke Farm
Ankerwycke Priory
Magna Carta Island
Longfield Farm
Watts Hill Cottages
HERON LAKE
British Disabled Water-Ski Association
Junction 13
M25 MOTORWAY
TW19
Cambridge Kennels
The Moor
Moor Farm
STAINES ROAD
WINDSOR ROAD
A308
A30
B376
HYTHE END
Hythe End Bridge
Dearsley Island
Wraysbury Hall
Bellweir Lock
Runnymede Bridge
Runnymede Pleasure Ground
RIVER THAMES
COOPER'S HILL SLOPES
COOPER'S HILL
Langham's Pond
Cooper's Hill Coppice
RUNNYMEDE
RUNNYMEDE PARK
Langham Farm
A30 BY-PASS
EGHAM
Egham
Glanty
Queensmead Lake
Church Lammas Quarry
Church Lammas
The Lammas Rec. Grd.
Hollyhock Island
Holm Island
London Stone
Church Island
Water Works
Gas Works
THE CAUSEWAY
Superstore
Pooley Green
Egham Sports Centre
Garden Centre
Manorcroft Prim. Sch.
EGHAM HYTHE
The Magna Carta Sch.
Playing Field
THORPE LEA
Ripley Springs
Royal Holloway (University of London)
Halls of Residence
Sports Ground
Sports Centre
Egham TW20
Milton Park
Research Laboratories
Rusham Crossing
Milton Park Cottages
Crown Cottages
Great Fosters
Moat
Whitehall Farm
Great Wood
Black Lake Farm
Crabtree Corner
Works
Nursery
THORPE IND. PARK
THORPE BY-PASS
M25
36

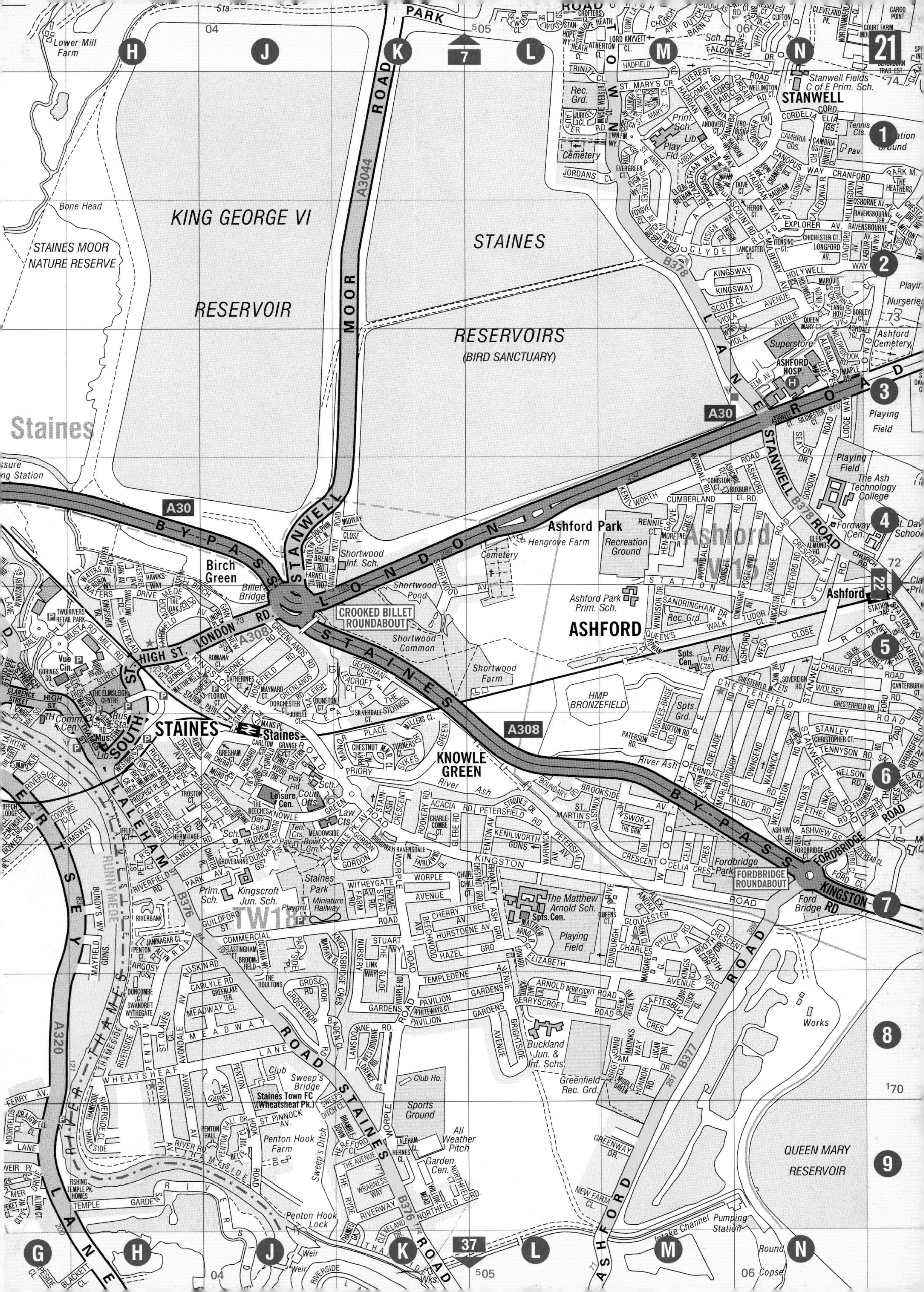

21
7
H
J
K
L
M
N
1
2
3
4
5
6
7
8
9
22
37
G
04
505
06
Lower Mill Farm
STANWELL
Stanwell Fields C of E Prim. Sch.
Rec. Grd.
Cemetery
KING GEORGE VI
RESERVOIR
STAINES
RESERVOIRS
(BIRD SANCTUARY)
STAINES MOOR NATURE RESERVE
Bone Head
MOOR ROAD
A3044
Staines
A30
Superstore
ASHFORD HOSP.
Ashford Cemetery
Playing Field
The Ash Technology College
Fordway Cen.
BYPASS
STANWELL
LONDON ROAD
Birch Green
Billet Bridge
CROOKED BILLET ROUNDABOUT
Shortwood Inf. Sch.
Shortwood Pond
Shortwood Common
Shortwood Farm
Cemetery
Hengrove Farm
Ashford Park
Recreation Ground
Ashford Park Prim. Sch.
Ashford
TW15
ASHFORD
HMP BRONZEFIELD
STAINES ROAD
A308
STAINES
KNOWLE GREEN
Leisure Cen.
Two Rivers Retail Park
Vue Cin.
The Elmsleigh Centre
Comm. Cen.
Bus Sta.
Mus.
Lib.
River Ash
BYPASS
FORDBRIDGE ROUNDABOUT
Fordbridge Park
KINGSTON RD.
Ford Bridge
TW18
Staines Park
Miniature Railway
Prim. Sch.
Kingscroft Jun. Sch.
The Matthew Arnold Sch.
Spts. Cen.
Playing Field
RUNNYMEDE
LALEHAM ROAD
B376
THAMES
THAMES SIDE
A320
Staines Town FC (Wheatsheaf Pk.)
Sweep's Bridge
Club
Club Ho.
Sports Ground
All Weather Pitch
Garden Cen.
Penton Hook Farm
Penton Hook Lock
Sweep's Ditch
Buckland Jun. & Inf. Schs.
Greenfield Rec. Grd.
Works
QUEEN MARY RESERVOIR
Intake Channel
Pumping Station
Round Copse
ASHFORD ROAD
B377
CHERTSEY LANE
Weir

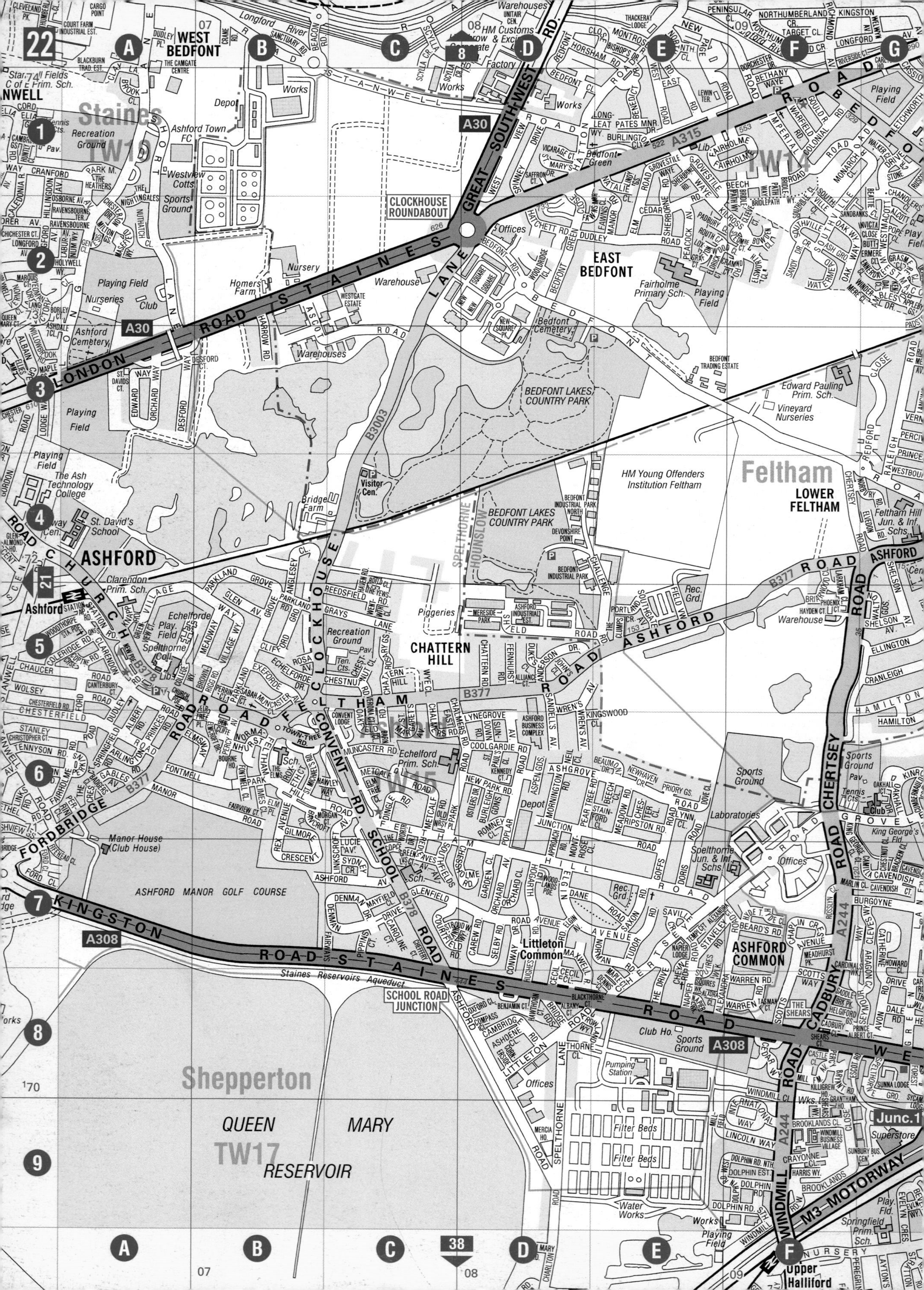
22
WEST BEDFONT
Staines
TW18
Ashford Town FC
Westview Cotts.
Sports Ground
CLOCKHOUSE ROUNDABOUT
A30
A315
TW14
EAST BEDFONT
Fairholme Primary Sch.
BEDFONT LAKES COUNTRY PARK
Edward Pauling Prim. Sch.
Vineyard Nurseries
HM Young Offenders Institution Feltham
Feltham
LOWER FELTHAM
Feltham Hill Jun. & Inf. Schs.
Visitor Cen.
Bridge Farm
The Ash Technology College
St. David's School
ASHFORD
Clarendon Prim. Sch.
Ashford
Echelforde Play. Field
Spelthorne Coll.
Recreation Ground
CHATTERN HILL
B377
Echelford Prim. Sch.
TW15
Manor House (Club House)
ASHFORD MANOR GOLF COURSE
A308
Staines Reservoirs Aqueduct
SCHOOL ROAD JUNCTION
Littleton Common
ASHFORD COMMON
Sports Ground
Laboratories
Spelthorne Jun. & Inf. Schs
Offices
A244
Shepperton
QUEEN MARY RESERVOIR
TW17
Filter Beds
Water Works
Pumping Station
Springfield Prim. Sch.
M3 MOTORWAY
Junc.1
Superstore
Upper Halliford
8
21
38

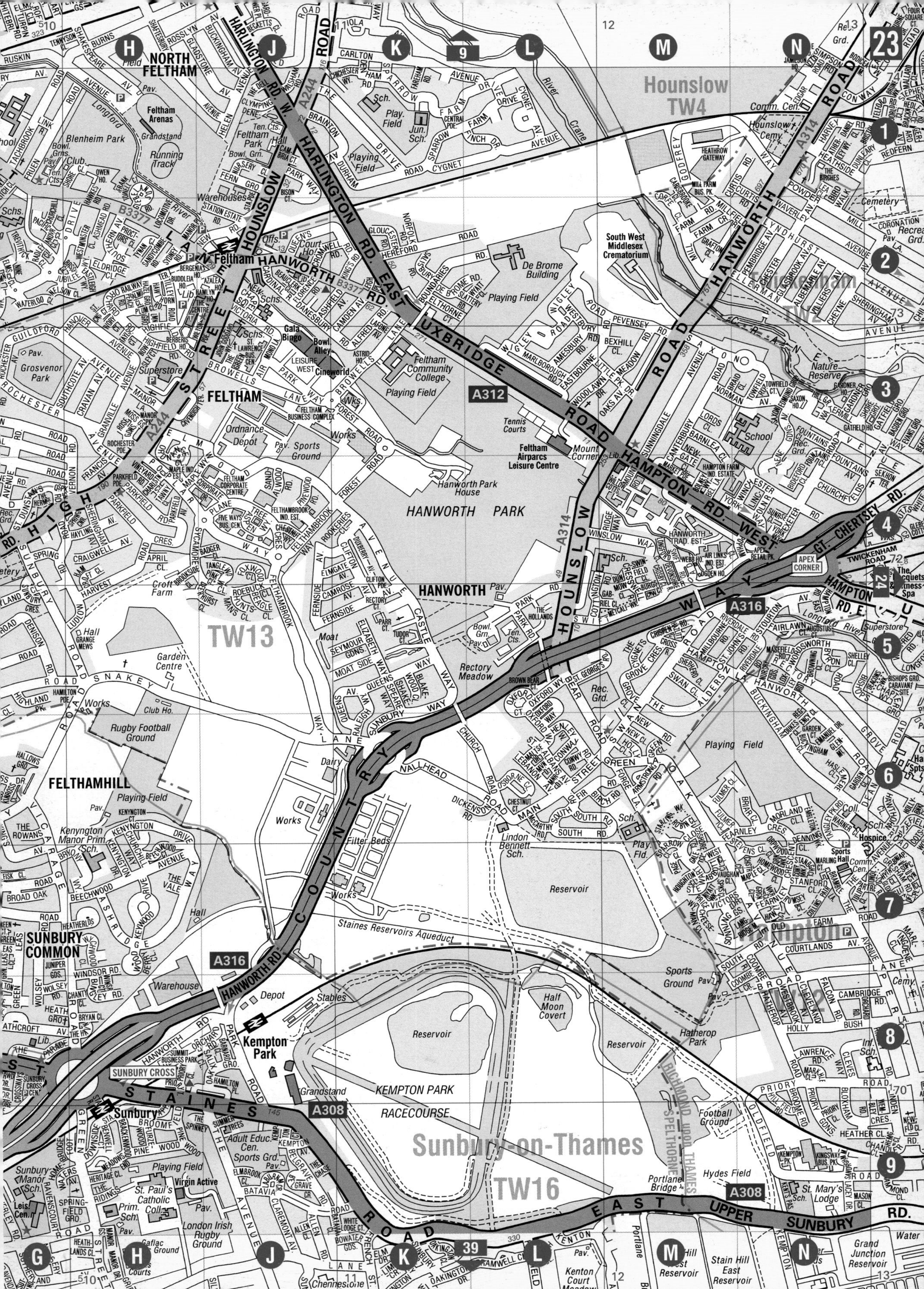

23
NORTH FELTHAM
Hounslow TW4
Feltham Arenas
Blenheim Park
Running Track
Feltham Park
Warehouses
Feltham
HANWORTH RD.
HARLINGTON RD. W.
HARLINGTON RD. EAST
A244
HOUNSLOW ROAD
HIGH STREET
South West Middlesex Crematorium
De Brome Building
Playing Field
Gala Bingo
Bowl. Alley
Cineworld
Feltham Community College
UXBRIDGE ROAD
A312
HANWORTH ROAD
A314
Twickenham TW2
Nature Reserve
School
Grosvenor Park
Superstore
FELTHAM
Ordnance Depot
Pav. Sports Ground
Tennis Courts
Feltham Airparcs Leisure Centre
Mount Corner
HAMPTON RD. WEST
Hanworth Park House
HANWORTH PARK
HANWORTH TRAD. EST.
HAMPTON FARM IND. EST.
APEX CORNER
GT. CHERTSEY RD.
TWICKENHAM ROAD
24
HAMPTON RD. E.
A316
SWIFT WAY
HANWORTH
TW13
Croft Farm
Rectory Meadow
Garden Centre
SNAKEY LANE
Rugby Football Ground
Club Ho.
FELTHAMHILL
Playing Field
Kenyngton Manor Prim. Sch.
COUNTRY WAY
Works
Filter Beds
Dairy
Reservoir
Lindon Bennett Sch.
Staines Reservoirs Aqueduct
SUNBURY COMMON
A316
HANWORTH RD.
Warehouse
Depot
Stables
Half Moon Covert
Sports Ground
Hampton
TW12
Hatherop Park
Kempton Park
SUNBURY CROSS
Grandstand
KEMPTON PARK RACECOURSE
STAINES ROAD
A308
Sunbury
Sunbury-on-Thames
TW16
Football Ground
RICHMOND UPON THAMES
SPELTHORNE
Hydes Field
Portlane Bridge
UPPER SUNBURY RD.
EAST
Adult Educ. Cen.
Sports Grd.
Playing Field
Virgin Active
St. Paul's Catholic Coll.
Sunbury Manor Sch.
London Irish Rugby Ground
Grand Junction Reservoir
Stain Hill East Reservoir
Kenton Court Meadow
St. Mary's Lodge
39
9
G H J K L M N
1 2 3 4 5 6 7 8 9
10 11 12 13

24
WHITTON
Whitton
Twickenham
TW1
TW2
TW4
TW12
Feltham
STRAWBERRY HILL
Strawberry Hill
TEDDINGTON
Teddington
Fulwell
HAMPTON HILL
HAMPTON
Hampton
BUSHY PARK
CHERTSEY ROAD
GREAT CHERTSEY ROAD
A316
STAINES ROAD
A305
TWICKENHAM RD.
UXBRIDGE ROAD
A312
HAMPTON ROAD
A313
WELLINGTON RD.
A311
HIGH STREET
SIXTH CROSS ROAD
B358
WALDEGRAVE ROAD
A309
STANLEY ROAD
CHURCH ROAD
B360
UPPER SUNBURY ROAD
A308
THAMES ST.
HAMPTON CT. ROAD
KNELLER RD.
HOSPITAL BRIDGE RD.
B361
HEATH ROAD
THE GREEN
STRAWBERRY VALE
PARK ROAD
CHESTNUT AVENUE
HOSPITAL BRIDGE ROUNDABOUT
WHITTON RD. R'BOUT
Twickenham Cemetery
Kneller Gdns.
Richmond upon Thames College
Harlequins RUFC & Harlequins RLFC (Stoop Meml. Grd.)
Fulwell Park
TWICKENHAM GOLF COURSE
FULWELL GOLF COURSE
STRAWBERRY HILL GOLF COURSE
The Racquets & Fitness Spa
Waldegrave Sch. for Girls
St. James's Catholic Primary School
University of Surrey (St. Mary's) College
Stanley Jun. & Inf. Schs.
Bus Garage
Hampton Comm. Coll.
Hampton School
The Lady Eleanor Holles Sch. (Jun. Dept.)
The Lady Eleanor Holles Sch. (Senior Dept.)
Carlisle Park
Clarendon Sch.
Hampton & Richmond Borough FC
Hampton Open Air Pool
Canal Plantation
Upper Lodge Mews
National Physical Laboratory
Bushy House
Round Plantation
Willow Plantation
Waterhouse Woodland Garden
River Lodge
Broom Clumps
Teddington Lodge
Radnor Gardens
Grand Junction Reservoir
Water Works
Filter Beds
Nature Reserve
Heathfield Jun. & Inf. Schs.
Bridge Farm Nursery
23
10
40

25
Riding Ring
St. Margarets
Cole Park
Twickenham
TWICKENHAM
Marble Hill Park
Marble Hill House
Orleans Ho. Gallery
River Thames
Glover's Island
Petersham Meadows
Petersham Farm
Petersham Common
Royal Star & Garter Home
The American Int. Uni. in London
Richmond Gate
Bishop's Pond
Conduit Wood
Holly Lodge
Sawyer's Hill
(Open during daylight hours only)
Saw Pit Plantation
Kidney Wood
Jubilee Plantation
RICHMOND PARK
Sidmouth Wood
King Henry VIII Mound
Queen Elizabeth's Plantation
Pembroke Lodge (Cafeteria)
Oak Lodge
Whiteash Lodge
Pond Slade
Ham Cross Plantation
Ham Bottom
Ham Cross
Ham Gate
High Wood
Coronation Plantation
The Flat
Gallows Pond
King's Clump
Kingston Gate
PETERSHAM
Petersham Park
Sudbrook Park
Sudbrook Park (Club Ho.)
The Wilderness
Richmond Golf Course
Ham House
Polo Ground
The German Sch. London
The Russell Sch. (Juniors)
The Russell Sch. (Infants)
Strathmore Sch.
The Copse
Grey Court School
Ham Green
TW10
HAM
Meadlands Prim. Sch.
Ham Common
The Cassel Hosp.
Ham Gate Avenue
Ham Lands Nature Reserve
Thames Young Mariners Base
Ham Fields
Ham Riverside Lands
Teddington Lock
Teddington Weir
Teddington Studios
Lensbury Club
Teddington
TW11
Kingston upon Thames
HMP Latchmere House
St. George's Industrial Estate
YMCA Sports Grd.
The Tiffin Girls' Sch.
Tiffins Girls Comm. Spts. Cen.
Fern Hill Prim. Sch.
KT2
Rec. Grd.
RC Prim. Sch.
Sports Ground
Recreation Ground
Trowlock Island
Steven's Eyot
The Avenue Centre
Canbury Gardens
KINGSTON UPON THAMES
Collis Prim. Sch.
Bushy Park
Warren Plantation
Half Moon Plantation
East Molesey
Leg-of-Mutton Pond
Oval Plantation
Thatched Cottage
KT1
Hampton Wick
HAMPTON WICK
Hampton Wick Royal Cricket Ground
Kingston
Kingston Hospital
Norbiton
Park Hill Sch.
Fitness Club
Superstore
The Rotunda Cen.
A305 A307 A310 A308 A238 B321 B352 B353 B358 B359 B351
11
203
41
26
H J K L M N G
1 2 3 4 5 6 7 8 9

26
A
B
C
D
E
F
G
12
Riding Ring
Sheen Cross Wood
Roehampton Gate
Roehampton House
Playing Field
SAWYER'S HILL
(Open during daylight hours only)
Polo Field
Playing Field
Barn Wood Pond
RICHMOND PARK
Club College Halls Ho. (Mount Clare)
Maryfield Convent
Roehampton Recreation Cen.
ROEHAMPTON
ROEHAMPTON HIGH ST.
A306
Saw Pit Plantation
Jubilee Plantation
Queen's Ride
Duchess' Wood
Deer Pen
White Lodge Plantation
Queen Mothers Copse
The Royal Ballet School
Pen Ponds
Leg of Mutton Pond
Queen Elizabeth's Plantation
Horse Ride
Victory Plantation
Killcat Corner
RICHMOND PARK GOLF COURSE
Kingsfarm Plantation
Hyde Park Nursery
Lawn Plantation
Richmond
Treebox Wood
SPANKERS HILL WOOD
TW10
Pen Ponds
DEER PARK
King George V Jubilee Plantation
Pond Plantation
Playing Fields
Beverley Brook
Chohole Gate
Silver Hill
STAG LANE
Putney Vale Crematorium
PUTNEY VALE CEMETERY
Superstore
Tercentenary Plantation
(Open during daylight hours only)
Horse Ride
Robin Hood Gate
Beverley Bridge
ROEHAMPTON VALE
KINGSTON
Newlands Hall
PUTNEY VALE
Queen's Mere
Kingston University (Roehampton Vale Centre)
Playing Fields
Memorial Gardens
War Memorial
A3
ROBIN HOOD
Pond Slade
Prince Charles's Spinney
Gibbet Wood
Peg's Pond
Thomson's Pond
Broomfield Hill
Broomfield Hill Wood
WANDSWORTH
MERTON
Silent Pools
Stag Bog
WIMBLED
ISABELLA PLANTATION
KINGSTON VALE
Playing Fields
Gravelly Ride
Horse Exercise Ring
WIMBLEDON COMMON & LONDON SCOTTISH GOLF COURSE
Gravelly Hill
High Wood
Still Pond
Deer Fold
RICHMOND upon THAMES
Walkden Hall
Robin Hood Prim. Sch.
Horse Exercise Area
White Cottage
COMMO
Coronation Plantation
Kingston University (Kingston Hill)
(KINGSTON BY-PASS)
Tennis Courts
Subway
Farm Bog
Farm Ravine
Dann's Pond
Coronation Plantation
COOMBE PARK
Horse Ride
Warren Farm
Caesar's Camp
Ladderstile Gate
Canbury Sch.
Playing Fields
Fishpond Wood
Gallows Pond
King's Clump
Warren House
Mill Corner
ROYAL WIMBLEDON GOLF COURSE
Shadwell Wood
The Warren
KT2
COOMBE HILL GOLF COURSE
KINGSTON upon THAMES
COOMBE WOOD GOLF COURSE
COOMBE
Club House
Playing Field
Tennis Courts
The Rowans Sch.
Kingston upon Thames
Rokeby Sch.
Holy Cross Preparatory RC Sch.
Marymount International School
The Wolfson Rehabilitation Cen.
COPSE HILL
COOMBE WOOD GOLF COURSE
Tennis Cts.
KINGSTON HOSPITAL
Coombe Hill Jun. & Inf. Schools
NEW VICTORIA HOSPITAL
COOMBE LANE FLYOVER
Sports Grd.
Playing Field
St. Matthew's C of E Prim. Sch.
SW20
COTTENHAM PARK
COOMBE LANE WEST
A238
KT1
New Malden
KT3
MALDEN GOLF COURSE
Wimbledon College Playing Fields
Norbiton
Coombe Girls Sch.
42
Club House
Coombe Brook
(KINGSTON BY-PASS)
BEVERLEY WAY
Tennis Courts Sports Ground
Civil Service Sports Ground
520
21
22
71
72
73
25

27
H
J
K
L
M
N
WEST HILL
PUTNEY HEATH
ROYAL HOSP. FOR NEURO-DISABILITY
13
A219
TIBBET'S CORNER
A3
Scio Pond
King's Mere
Seven Post Pond
PUTNEY HEATH
ROEHAMPTON LANE
Wimbledon Windmill Museum
Club House
Manor Cottage
Southfields
SOUTHFIELDS
King George's Park
Mecca Bingo
Earlsfield
A217
A218
SW18
Wimbledon Park Athletics Track
WIMBLEDON PARK
WIMBLEDON PARK GOLF COURSE
Aorangi Park
Museum
Wimbledon All England Lawn Tennis & Croquet Club
Indoor Ten. Cts.
Cricket Ground
Wimbledon Park
PARKSIDE HOSP.
SW19
Buddhist Temple
Horse Ride
Ricards Lodge High Sch.
Bishop Gilpin C of E Prim. Sch.
Carriage Cleaning Shed
SUMMERSTOWN
Superstore
Wimbledon Cemetery
Football Grd.
B235
The Priory C of E Sch.
Cannizaro House
Cannizaro Park
Rushmere Pond
WIMBLEDON
Wimbledon High Sch.
Esporta
Wimbledon
CENTRE COURT
THE BROADWAY
SOUTH WIMBLEDON
South Park Gardens
Lady Jane's Wood
The King's Club
King's Coll. Sch.
Wimbledon Coll.
Ursuline Prep. Sch.
Dundonald Rd.
Dundonald Prim. Sch.
Recreation Ground
B285
A238
South Wimbledon
MERTON HIGH ST.
Merton Park
A24
MERTON
WORKS
A219
B281
G
H
J
K
L
M
N
43
Wimbledon Chase
Morden
1
2
3
4
5
6
7
8
9
28

28
A
B
C
D
E
F
G
1
2
3
4
5
6
7
8
9
EARLSFIELD
Earlsfield
HMP WANDSWORTH
WANDSWORTH CEMETERY
SW18
Wandsworth Common
WANDSWORTH COMMON
Wandsworth Common
BALHAM
Balham
SW12
TRINITY ROAD
A214
A24
BALHAM HIGH ROAD
BEDFORD HILL
NIGHTINGALE LANE
BELLEVUE RD.
ST JAMES'S DR.
BURNTWOOD LANE
EARLSFIELD ROAD
GARRATT LANE
THE CENTRAL LONDON GOLF COURSE
SPRINGFIELD UNIVERSITY HOSPITAL
Burntwood School
Garratt Green
Garratt Park
STREATHAM CEMETERY
UPPER TOOTING
Tooting Bec
Tooting Bec
Tooting Graveney Common
Athletic Ground
TOOTING BEC ROAD
SW17
UPPER TOOTING ROAD
SUMMERSTOWN
Wimbledon Stadium (Greyhound)
Lambeth Crematorium
LAMBETH CEMETERY
A217
Tooting Leisure Cen.
Tooting Broadway
ST. GEORGE'S HOSPITAL
TOOTING
Haydons Road
HAYDONS ROAD
A218
Wandle Meadow Nature Park
TOOTING GRAVENEY
FURZEDOWN
Furzedown School
MITCHAM LANE
TOOTING HIGH STREET
COLLIERS WOOD
Colliers Wood
COLLIER'S WOOD
Tooting
MERTON
MERTON HIGH STREET
A238
MERANTUN WAY
A24
WESTERN ROAD
A236
LONDON ROAD
A217
Mitcham
CR4
Lavender Park
Cemetery
STREATHAM ROAD
A216
STREATHAM VALE
Streatham Vale Park
Lonesome
SW19
44
27
29

BROCKWELL
PARK
SE24
SE21
The Mansion
Knight's Hill
TULSE HILL
Tulse Hill
WEST DULWICH
STREATHAM HILL
Streatham Hill
STREATHAM
Streatham
STREATHAM PARK
West Norwood Crematorium
Cemetery
West Norwood
WEST NORWOOD
SE27
SW16
SE19
STREATHAM COMMON
Streatham Common
Norwood Grove Recreation Ground
Playing Fields
NORWOOD PARK
NORWOOD NEW TOWN
Biggin Wood
NORBURY PARK
NORBURY
Norbury
Norbury Manor Business & Enterprise Coll. for Girls
Thornton Heath
CR7
Kensington Avenue Prim. School
David Livingstone Prim. Sch.
Powerleague Soccer Centre
School Playing Fields
Sports Ground
Tooting Bec Lido
Football Pitch
COMMON
WANDSWORTH
LAMBETH
CROYDON
HMP BRIXTON
A23
A205
A215
A204
A2199
A214
A216
B221
B273
B272
CHRISTCHURCH ROAD
STREATHAM COMMON NORTH
CROWN DALE
BRIXTON HILL
STREATHAM HIGH ROAD
NORWOOD ROAD
KNIGHTS HILL
THURLOW PARK RD.
CROXTED ROAD
POYNDERS RD.
KINGS AVENUE
TOOTING BEC ROAD
GARRAD'S RD.
GREYHOUND LA.
LONDON RD.
BEULAH HILL
GREEN LANE
NORBURY AV.
45
31
32

Wokingham Theatre
Cantley
Dowlesgreen
A329(M) MOTORWAY
14
Holt Copse
The Holt School
Rectory
Bowling Club
Comm. Cen.
High Close Sch. (Barnardo's)
Suffolk Lodge
Wokingham
Council Offs.
WOKINGHAM
King George V Playing Field
Cricket Grd.
Leisure Cen.
Carnival Pool
RG41
Recreation Ground
Waterloo Crossing
Starlane Crossing
The Knoll Farm
Superstore
Wokingham
East Lodge
Wood's Farm
Britton's Farm
Lock's House
Big Wood House
Piggery
Chapel Green
Chapel Green Cottages
Chapel Green Farm
Lucas's Hospital (Almshouses)
Ludgrove Sch.
Long Patch
Pearce's Farm
Holme Green
Little Grange Nursery
Holme Park
Holme Grange School
Sutton Cottages
Ham Bridge
Luckley-Oakfield School
Playing Fields
RG40
Water Hill Farm
Kirkwood
Holme Grange Farm
Gardeners Green
Redlake
Dairy Cottage
Trench's Bridge
Sutton Court Farm
Woodcray Manor Farm
Birchin Inhams
Watley's Copse
Heathlands Farm
Rouse's Pond
The Throat
Gorrick Cottage
Gorrick
Honeyhill
Long Thatch
The Paddocks
Woodcray Cottages
GORRICK PLANTATION
Offices
Pickeridge House
The Walled Garden
Pinewood House
Pine Wood
Silverstock Bog
St. Sebastian's C of E Primary School
WOKINGHAM WITHOUT
Queen's Mere
Heath Lake
Kingsmere House
King's Bridge
Pineridge Farm
Bigshotte Park
Hatch Ride Prim. Sch.
Crowthorne
Ravenswood Village
Club House
The Green
48

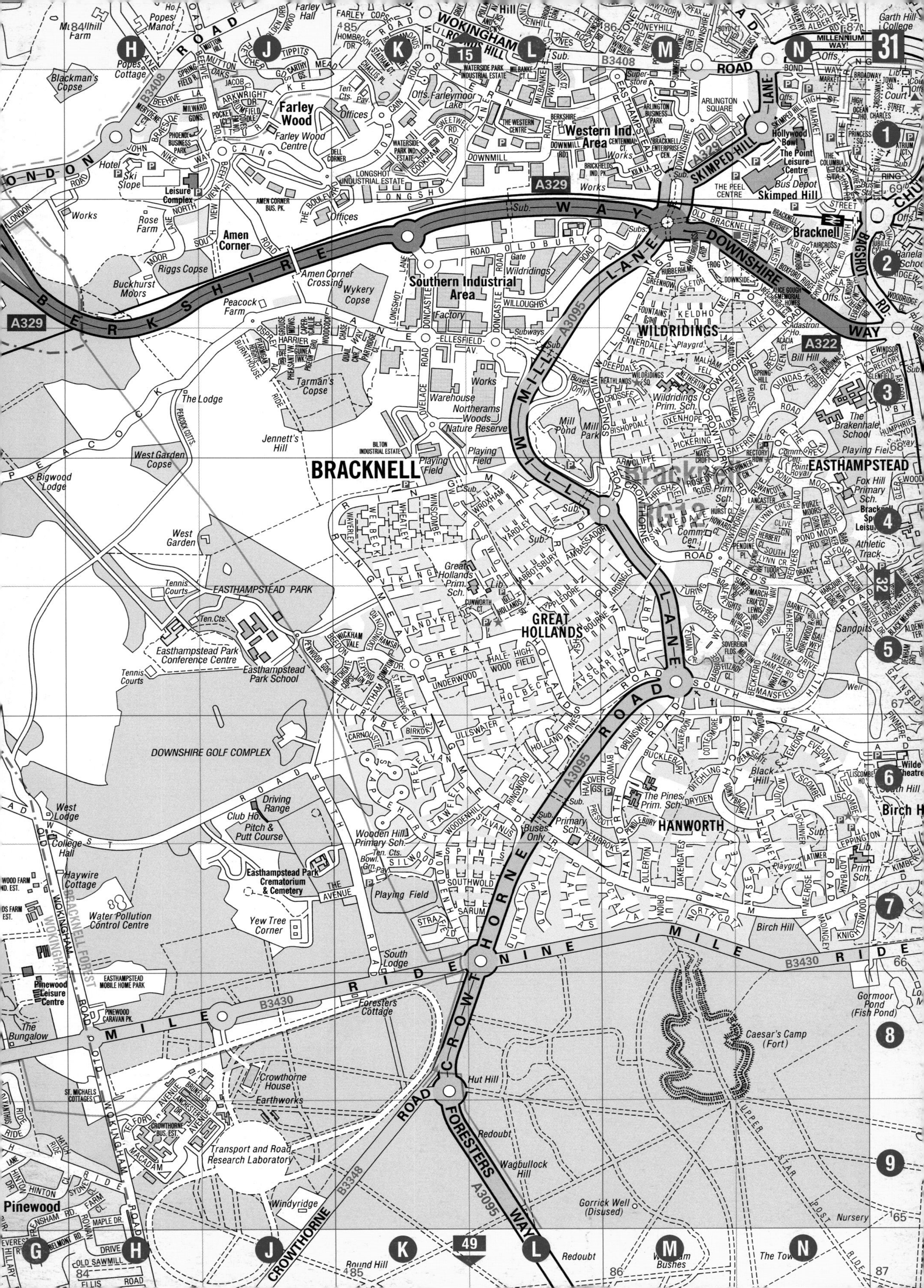

31
15
49
32
H
J
K
L
M
N
G
1
2
3
4
5
6
7
8
9
84
85
86
87
65
66
67
68
69
BRACKNELL
WOKINGHAM
LONDON ROAD
BERKSHIRE WAY
A329
B3408
A3095
A322
B3430
B3348
MILLENNIUM WAY
SKIMPED HILL LANE
DOWNSHIRE WAY
MILL LANE
CROWTHORNE ROAD
NINE MILE RIDE
FORESTERS WAY
PEACOCK LANE
OLD WOKINGHAM ROAD
WEST ROAD
SOUTH ROAD
RINGMEAD
GREAT HOLLANDS ROAD
SOUTH HILL ROAD
UPPER STAR POST RIDE
Farley Wood
Farley Wood Centre
Farleymoor Lake
Western Ind. Area
Southern Industrial Area
Amen Corner
Amen Corner Crossing
Wykery Copse
Riggs Copse
Buckhurst Moors
Rose Farm
Peacock Farm
Tarman's Copse
Jennett's Hill
Northerams Woods Nature Reserve
West Garden Copse
West Garden
Bigwood Lodge
The Lodge
EASTHAMPSTEAD PARK
Easthampstead Park Conference Centre
Easthampstead Park School
DOWNSHIRE GOLF COMPLEX
Driving Range
Pitch & Putt Course
Easthampstead Park Crematorium & Cemetery
Yew Tree Corner
Water Pollution Control Centre
West Lodge
College Hall
Haywire Cottage
Pinewood Leisure Centre
EASTHAMPSTEAD MOBILE HOME PARK
The Bungalow
South Lodge
Foresters Cottage
Crowthorne House
Earthworks
Transport and Road Research Laboratory
Windyridge
Hut Hill
Redoubt
Wagbullock Hill
Gorrick Well (Disused)
Caesar's Camp (Fort)
Gormoor Pond (Fish Pond)
Nursery
Round Hill
Pinewood
WILDRIDINGS
Wildridings Prim. Sch.
Mill Pond
Mill Park
GREAT HOLLANDS
Great Hollands Prim. Sch.
EASTHAMPSTEAD
Fox Hill Primary Sch.
Athletic Track
Sandpits
HANWORTH
The Pines Prim. Sch.
Black Hill
Birch Hill
Wooden Hill Primary Sch.
Playing Field
Bracknell
Skimped Hill
The Point Leisure Centre
Hollywood Bowl
Bus Depot
THE PEEL CENTRE
ARLINGTON SQUARE
The Brakenhale School
Leisure Complex
Ski Slope
Hotel
Popes Cottage
Blackman's Copse
Garth Hill College
Wilde Theatre

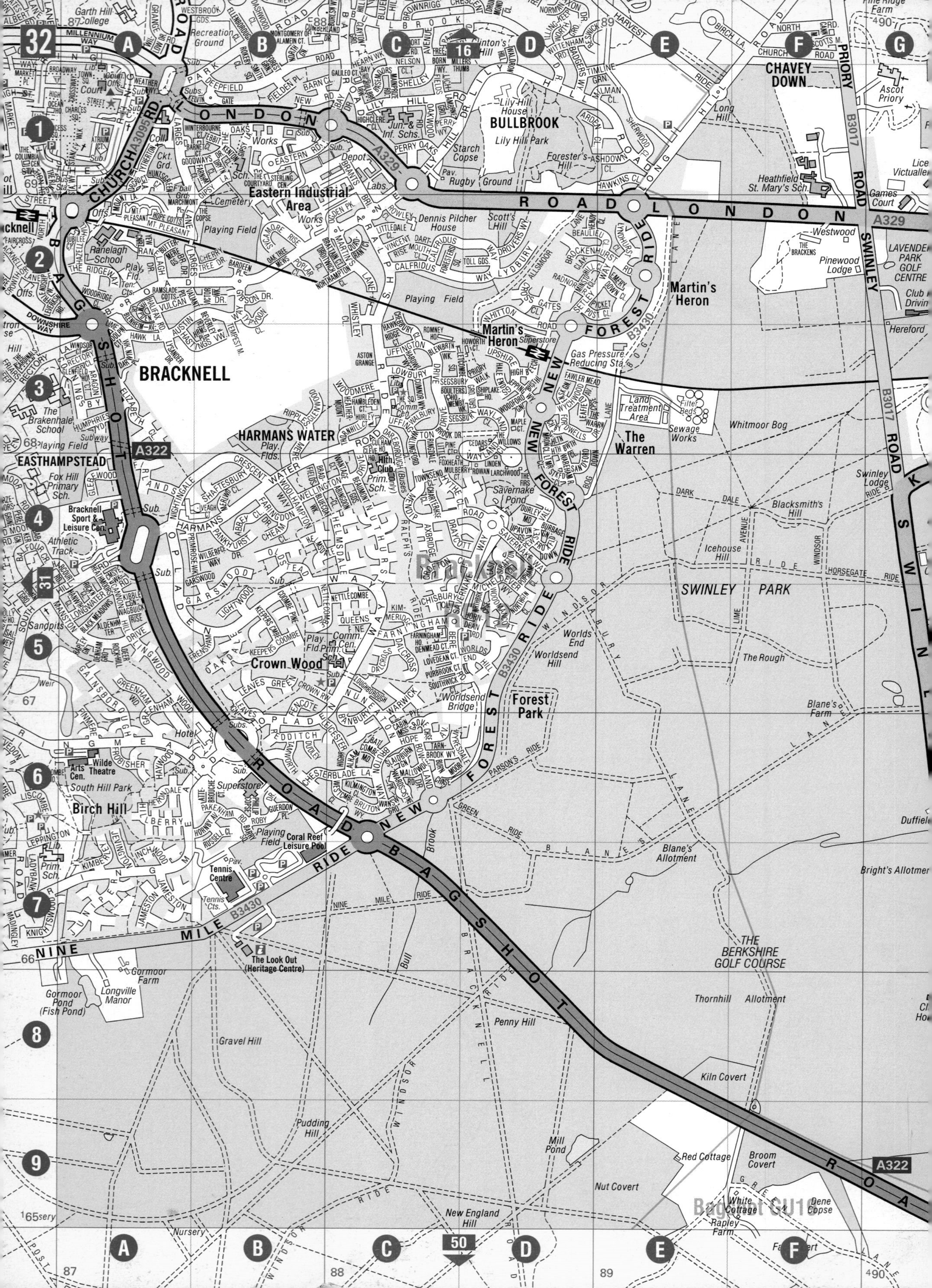

32
16
31
50
A
B
C
D
E
F
G
1
2
3
4
5
6
7
8
9
87
88
89
490
69
68
67
66
65
BRACKNELL
BULLBROOK
CHAVEY DOWN
EASTHAMPSTEAD
HARMANS WATER
Crown Wood
Birch Hill
Martin's Heron
Forest Park
SWINLEY PARK
Eastern Industrial Area
Lily Hill Park
Lily Hill House
Starch Copse
Forester's Hill
Scott's Hill
Dennis Pilcher House
Long Hill
Ascot Priory
Heathfield St. Mary's Sch.
Westwood
The Brackens
Pinewood Lodge
LAVENDER PARK GOLF CENTRE
Games Court
Hereford
Land Treatment Area
Filter Beds
Sewage Works
The Warren
Whitmoor Bog
Gas Pressure Reducing Sta.
Superstore
Swinley Lodge
Blacksmith's Hill
Icehouse Hill
The Rough
Blane's Farm
Blane's Allotment
Bright's Allotment
Worlds End
Worldsend Hill
Worldsend Bridge
Savernake Pond
Ranelagh School
The Brakenhale School
Fox Hill Primary Sch.
Bracknell Sport & Leisure Cen.
Athletic Track
Sandpits
Wilde Theatre
Arts Cen.
South Hill Park
Coral Reef Leisure Pool
Tennis Centre
The Look Out (Heritage Centre)
Gormoor Farm
Longville Manor
Gormoor Pond (Fish Pond)
Gravel Hill
Penny Hill
Pudding Hill
Mill Pond
Nut Covert
New England Hill
Kiln Covert
Red Cottage
Broom Covert
White Cottage
Rapley Farm
Dene Copse
THE BERKSHIRE GOLF COURSE
Thornhill
Allotment
Garth Hill College
Recreation Ground
Playing Field
Cemetery
Rugby Ground
Pine Ridge Farm
LONDON ROAD
A329
A322
A3095
B3430
B3017
BAGSHOT ROAD
CHURCH RD.
NEW FOREST RIDE
NINE MILE RIDE
SWINLEY ROAD
PRIORY ROAD
MILLENNIUM WAY
DOWNSHIRE WAY
WINDSOR RIDE
BRACKNELL LANE
Bagshot GU19

17
34
51
92
93
91
G
H
J
K
L
M
N
1
2
3
4
5
6
7
8
9
Goaters Hill
ASCOT HEATH
ROYAL ASCOT GOLF COURSE
Royal Ascot Golf Course
Fireball Hill
Lower Farm
Old Waterfield
Club House
Ascot Farm
Rose Wood
ASCOT TOWERS
THE LINKS
WINDSOR ROAD
A332
WINKFIELD ROAD
A330
ASCOT RACECOURSE
New Mile Course
Straight Course
The New Mile Course (Disused)
The Old Mile Course
Sunninghill Lodge
Tetworth Hall
Silver Stand
New Stand
Grand Stand
Playgrd.
HIGH STREET
A329
LONDON ROAD
KINGS RIDE
A332
Timber Yard
Englemere Pond (Nature Reserve)
The House in the Wood
Milcote
Woodstock
HEATHERWOOD HOSPITAL
THAMES HOSPICECARE Offices
Ascot Heath House
Bowledge Hill
Stables
Englemere
Larklands
Queen's Hill Lodge
Index House
Ascot Hill Ho.
Ascot Wood
ASCOT
St. George's Sch.
Nutfield
Victory Field
Ascot
STATION HILL
BROCKENHURST
Prince Albert's Bridge
KINGS YARD
King's Ride House
Highbury
KINGS RIDE PARK
Factory
South Ascot Village Sch.
Rec. Grd.
SUNNINGHILL
Coombe Meadows
WINDSOR and MAIDENHEAD
BRACKNELL FOREST
Kings Ride Farm
Swinley Court
Whiteladies Park
Resr. (covered)
Ascot SL5
Pinehurst
Hurstleigh
Lucombe
SOUTH ASCOT
Maryland
St. Mary's Sch. Ascot
Erollston
Hewarth
Gilmuire
Playing Field
A330 ROAD
DEVENISH RD.
B3020
Hotel
Lowood House
Forest Ridge
King's Beeches
West Lodge
Cedar House
Broadlands
Clock House
KINGSRIDE
NINE MILE RIDE
Buttersteep Hill
Tower Court
Tower Hill
Buttersteep Cott.
Buttersteep House
Clavering
Berroc End
Golf Club Cotts.
Club Ho.
Tree Tops
Bodens Ride
Swinley Edge
Earleywood Chace
SWINLEY FOREST GOLF COURSE
Hurst Lodge (School)
Play. Fld.
Earleywood Pines
Broadlands Farm
Chaceside
Playing Field
Earleywood Lodge
Keeper's Cottage
The Belt
Earlywood
Earlywood Orchard
Little Stream
Richmond Nurseries
Garden Centre
White Stones
Heathlands
Fairway
Winklands Allotment
Fern Hill
Windlesham GU20
Lavershot Hall
Lavershot Court
Dukeshill Allotment
SWINLEY FOREST GOLF COURSE
Combe Edge
Winklands
The Devil's Highway (Course of Roman Road)
Windlesham Moor
Windlesham Hall Fm.
Windlesham Hall
Lodge
Braids
Green Lanes
Merrywood
A30
LONDON ROAD
SUNNINGHILL ROAD
BAGSHOT ROAD
Woodhay House
Roundwood
Heathfield Ho.
BRACKNELL FOREST
SURREY HEATH
Laboratories
Dukeshill Nursery
Windlesham Ct.
Snow's Ride
SWINLEY

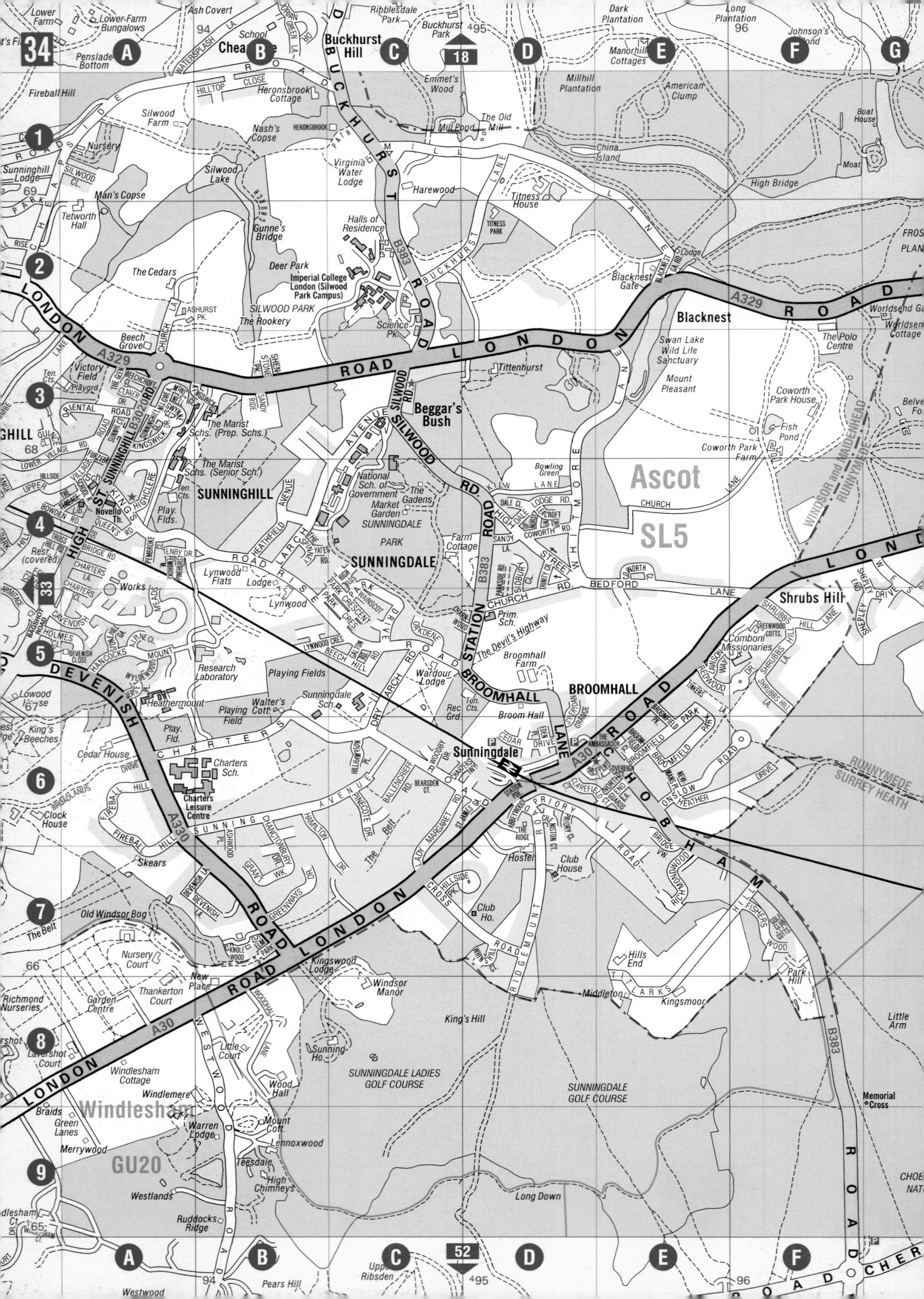

Buckhurst Hill
18
Cheapside
Silwood Park Campus
Imperial College London (Silwood Park Campus)
SILWOOD PARK
Blacknest
LONDON ROAD
A329
Beggar's Bush
SUNNINGHILL
SUNNINGDALE
Ascot
SL5
Shrubs Hill
BROOMHALL
Sunningdale
33
DEVENISH ROAD
A330
Charters Sch.
Charters Leisure Centre
A30
SUNNINGDALE LADIES GOLF COURSE
SUNNINGDALE GOLF COURSE
Windlesham
GU20
Long Down
RUNNYMEDE
SURREY HEATH
WINDSOR and MAIDENHEAD
B383
B3020
52
Memorial Cross

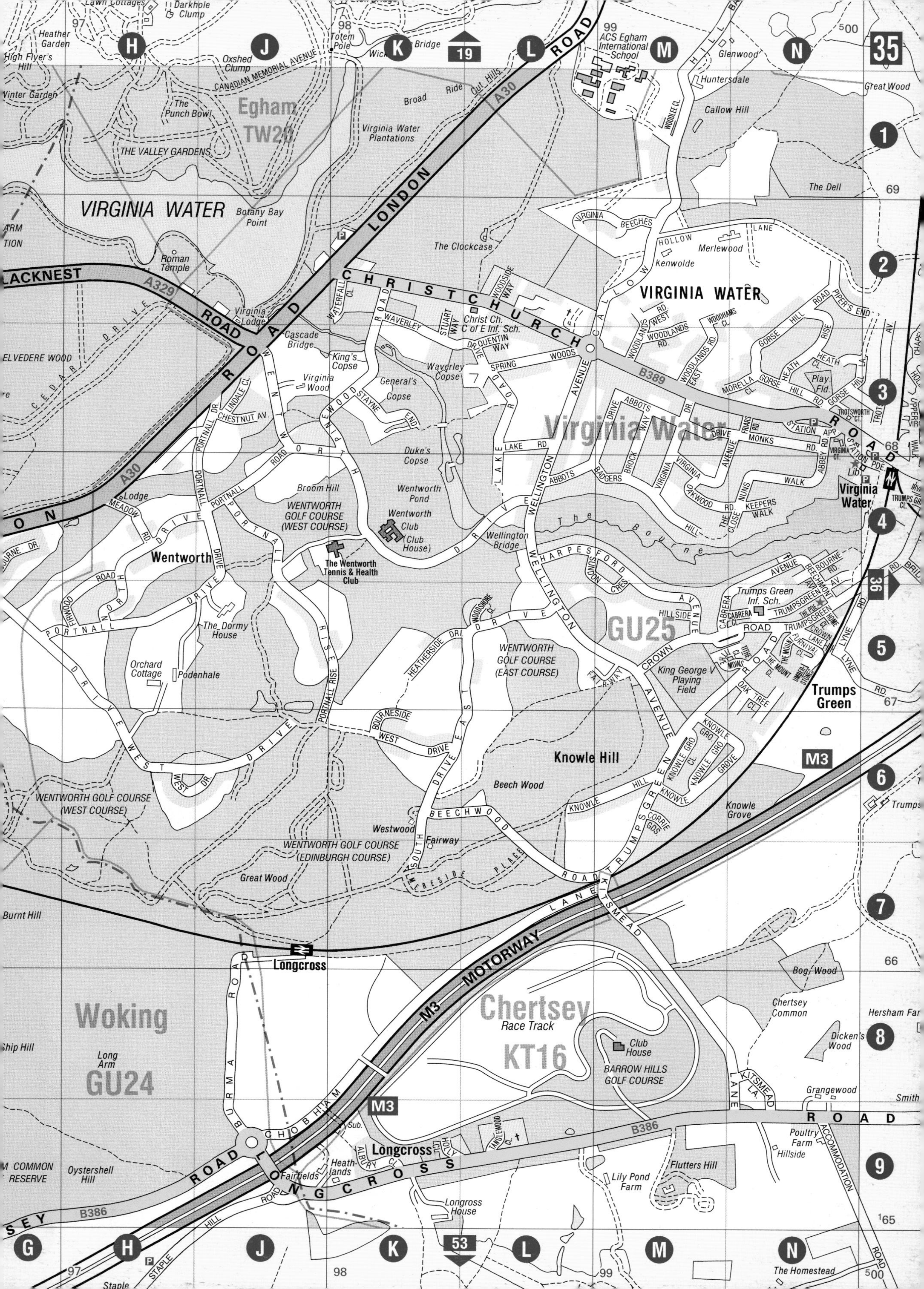

36
20
54
35
Egham
TW20
Virginia Water
GU25
Chertsey
KT16
VIRGINIA WATER
THORPE
LYNE
Stroude
Stroude Farm
Stroude Crossing
Stroude Hill
Whitehall Farm
Great Wood
Luddington House
Black Lake Farm
Nursery
Crabtree Corner
Works
Thorpe Ind. Park
Egham Bus. Village
Crabtree Office Village
Sky Business Cen.
Cemetery
Spring Farm
Inf. Sch.
Sch.
Play. Fld.
Ten. Cts.
Hall
Coldharbour
Offices
Eastly End
Manor Lake
Water Gardens
Playing Field
Woodcock Farm
Longside Lake
ST. ANN'S HEATH
Home Farm
St. Ann's Park
Hurst Farm
Tennis Courts
Playing Field
Thorpe Green
St. Ann's Lake
John Battleday Waterski
Britannia
Junction 2 (M3)
Junction 12 (M25)
Anchor Copse
St. Ann's Hill
St. Ann's Hill Park
The Dingle
Monk's Grove
Hill Cottages
Ruxbury Farm
St. Ann's Court
Druidswood
The Grange
Chilseygreen Farm
Sewage Disposal Works
Refuse Pulverising Plant
Junior Sch.
Waterloo Bri.
Pond
Trumps Green
Redlands
Lyne Farm
Lyne Grove Cotts.
Nursery
Lyne Hill House
Elm Farm Caravan Park
Lyne Place Manor
Trumps House
Trumps Farm
The Rough
Merrywood Farm
Almner Priory
Almner's Farm
Silver Birch Caravan Site
Piggery
Lyne Copse
Club
Pantiles Farm
Rec. Grd.
Hersham Copse
Fangrove Park
Fan Grove
Playing Field
Great Cockcrow Railway
Cockcrow Hill
Lynwood Farm
Trys Hill Farm
Pavilion
Hardwick Cott.
Hardwick Court Farm
Hersham Farm
Lyne & Long Cross C of E Inf. Sch.
Fan Court Farm
Lyne Farm
Arbon Grove
Silverlands
Abraham Cowley Unit
Runnymede BMI Hosp.
St. Peter's Hospital
Chertsey South
Grangewood
Smith's Cotts.
Trys Hill
Nursery
Silverlands Farm
France Farmhouse
FOXHILLS GOLF COURSE
Botleys Park
Fox Hills
Home Wood
Oracle Pk.
M25
M3
M25 MOTORWAY
M3 MOTORWAY
THORPE BY-PASS
B388
B389
B386
A320
MILL HOUSE LANE
THORPE LANE
CHRISTCHURCH RD.
SANDHILLS
LANE GREEN ROAD
HURST ROAD
LYNE LANE
LYNE CROSSING ROAD
RUXBURY ROAD
ST. ANN'S HILL ROAD
ALMNERS ROAD
HARDWICK LANE
LONGCROSS ROAD
HOLLOWAY HILL
GUILDFORD ROAD
STONEHILL ROAD
LYNE BRIDGE ROAD
TRUMPS MILL LANE
HARROW BOTTOM RD.
VILLAGE ROAD
GREEN LANE
WATERY LANE
OLD COACH RD.
NORLAND

37
QUEEN MARY RESERVOIR
Penton Hook Lock
Penton Hook Island
Penton Hook
Penton Hook Marina
Yacht Basin
Fleet Lake
Main Entrance
Laleham Reach
PENTON PARK
LALEHAM
Laleham C of E Prim. Sch.
Manor Farm
Youth Centre
Rec. Grd.
Staines
TW18
Laleham Nurseries
LALEHAM GOLF COURSE
LALEHAM BURWAY
Club House
Reservoir
Laleham Park
Camping Site
Pumping Station
Pavilion
Gravel Pit
Works
Mountbatten Pavilion
Beomonds Farm
Thorpe Park
Abbey Lake
ABBEY MEAD
Burway Ditch
Abbey River
M3 MOTORWAY
Abbey Bridge
Chertsey Abbey (Rems.)
Abbey Chase
Abbey Chase Farm
Shepperton
TW17
Abbeyfields Park
Chertsey Lock
Chertsey Bridge
RIVER THAMES
SPELTHORNE
RUNNYMEDE
Hamperstone Bridge
Playing Field
Cricket Grd.
Chertsey Town FC Grd.
Gogmore Farm Park
River Bourne Health Club
CHERTSEY
Eastworth
Play. Fld.
Sir William Perkins's Sch.
HANWORTH TRADING ESTATE
Salesian Sch.
Chertsey Meads
Marina
Dockett Moorings
Riversleigh Farm
The Range
Dockett Point
Fordwater Trading Estate
Tennis Courts
The Runnymede Centre
Philip Southcote Sch.
Woburn Park Farm
Woburn Park
Pannells Farm
M25 MOTORWAY
Addlestone Moor
ABBEY MOOR GOLF COURSE
Addlestone Cemy.
Club Ho.
Hatch Farm
Woburn Hill
Addlestone KT15
WOBURN PARK
Athletic Grd.
Running Track
St. George's College
Tennis Courts
Cricket Ground
Woburn Bri.
St. George Gate Offices
Victory Park
Rec. Grd.
Sports Grd.
Addlestone
Superstore
Junction 11
Woodside Farm
Simplemarsh Farm
St. Augustine's Nurs. Home
Ham Moor
STAINES ROAD
CHERTSEY LA.
ST. ANNS ROAD
LONDON ST.
BRIDGE ROAD
CHERTSEY BRIDGE RD.
GUILDFORD ST.
EASTWORTH RD.
WEIR RD.
FORDWATER RD.
CHERTSEY RD.
WOBURN HILL
WEYBRIDGE ROAD
SHEPPERTON ROAD
LALEHAM RD.
ASHFORD ROAD
LITTLETON LANE
21
38
55

38
A
B
C
D
E
F
G
07
08
09
22
QUEEN MARY RESERVOIR
Water Works
Works
Playing Field
DOLPHIN EST.
HARRIS WY.
BROOKLANDS
Springfield Prim. Sch.
NURSERY
Upper Halliford
M3
CHARLTON
Manor Farm
Halliford House Rec. Grd.
Playing Field
Caravan Site
Spts. Grd.
Nursery
Refuse Transfer Station
STIRLING AVENUE
HAZELWOOD GOLF CENTRE
1
2
3
4
5
6
7
8
9
69
68
67
66
65
LALEHAM STUDIOS
River Ash
Shepperton Film Studios
The Green
NEW ROAD
LITTLETON
Littleton Fm.
Play. Fld.
Laleham Nurseries
Nurseries
Squire's Bridge
SHEPPERTON GREEN
Shepperton TW17
Rec. Grd.
M3 MOTORWAY
Driving Range
Club House
Grange Farm
UPPER HALLIFORD
SUNBURY GOLF COURSE
UPPER HALLIFORD BY-PASS
UPPER HALLIFORD RD.
A244
LALEHAM RD.
B376
Staines Road Farm
Nurseries
Saxon Prim. Sch.
Play. Fld.
Shepperton
River Ash
Gaston Bridge
CUCKOO POUND
Watersplash Farm
37
Gravel
Pool End
Playing Field
Prim. Sch.
Lib.
B3366
GREEN LANE
GASTON BRIDGE ROAD
The Bradbury Cen.
Thamesmead School
Rec. Grd.
River Ash Estate
The Swan Sanctuary
Gravel Pit
Shepperton Marina
SHEPPERTON
RENFREE WAY
CHERTSEY RD.
B375
Mead Farm
Sleigh Farm
Lords Bri.
Halliford Mere Lake
Cemetery
War Close
Cricket Ground
Las Palmas Estate
RUSSELL RD.
Lower Halliford
Bishop Duppas Pk.
WALTON LANE
WALTON BRIDGE RD.
The Range
DOCKETT EDDY LANE
Desborough Sailing Club
Playing Field
DESBOROUGH ISLAND
Thames Meadow
Marina
Cowey Sale
WALTON BRI.
BRIDGE ST.
DOCKETT MOORINGS
DOCKETT EDDY
Works
SPELTHORNE
ELMBRIDGE
Walton Channel
Desborough
Play. Fld
A3050
TOWPATH
PHARAOH'S ISLAND
Shepperton Lock
Lock Island
RUNNYMEDE
Weybridge KT13
Dockett Point
HAMM COURT
HAMHAUGH ISLAND
Whittets Ait
Hamhaugh Point
Thames Lock
Play. Fld.
Tennis Courts
Engine River
Greenlands Farm
Broadwater Farm
PORTMORE PARK
Hamm Court Farm
Broad Water
The Bull Dogs
WEYBRIDGE
Golf Course
St. James C of E Prim. Sch.
OATLANDS DR.
OATLANDS PARK
MEADOWLANDS PARK
River Wey
A317
WEYBRIDGE RD.
Ham Moor
HIGH ST.
MONUMENT HILL
56
OATLANDS
Oatlands Park

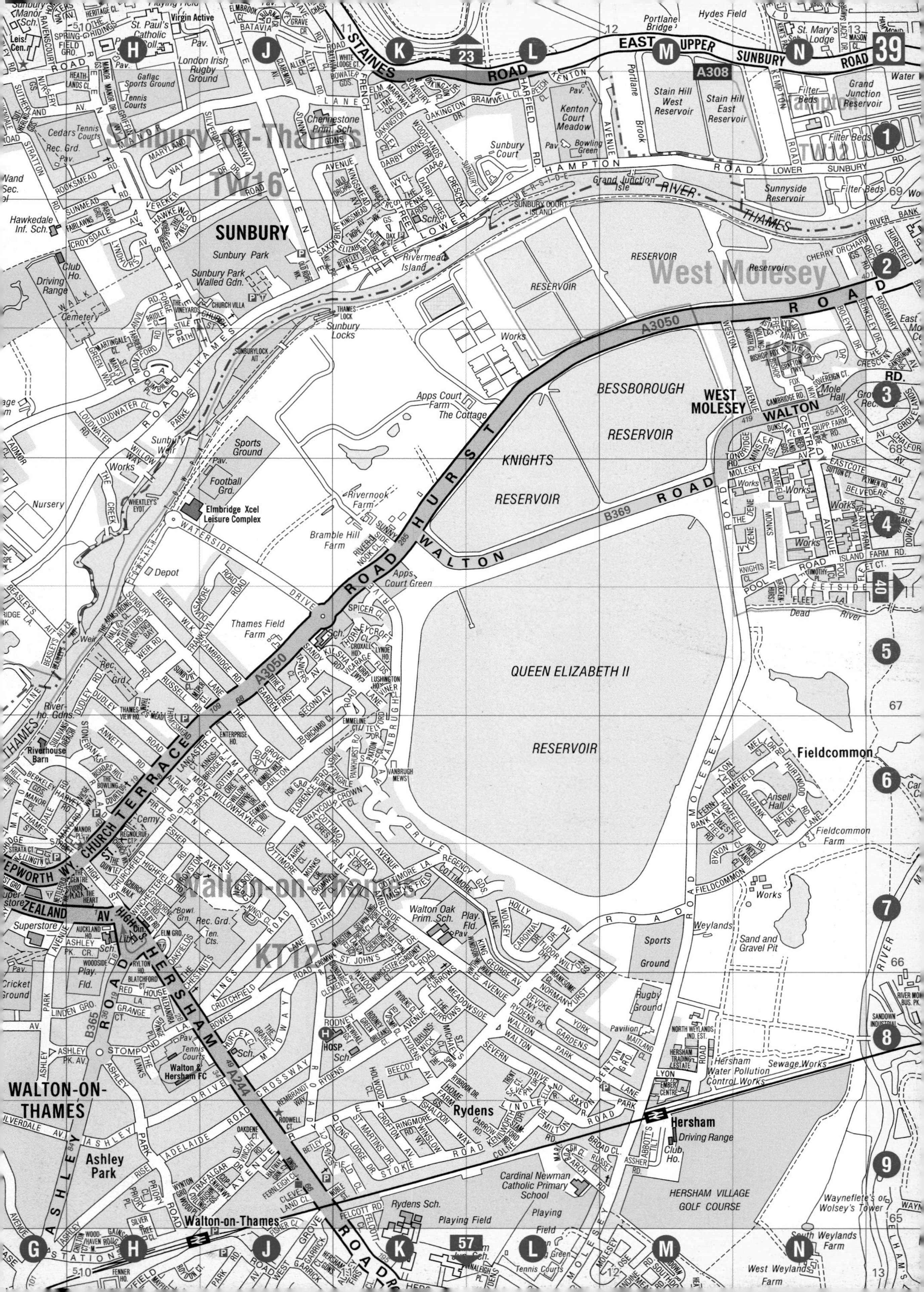

39
23
40
57
Sunbury-on-Thames
TW16
SUNBURY
Sunbury Park
Sunbury Park Walled Gdn.
West Molesey
WEST MOLESEY
Walton-on-Thames
WALTON-ON-THAMES
KT12
TW12
Hampton
Fieldcommon
Rydens
Hersham
Ashley Park
STAINES ROAD
UPPER SUNBURY ROAD
EAST
A308
HAMPTON ROAD
LOWER SUNBURY RD.
HURST ROAD
A3050
WALTON ROAD
B369
MOLESEY ROAD
CHURCH TERRACE
HERSHAM ROAD
A244
B365
ASHLEY RD.
RIVER THAMES
St. Paul's Catholic Coll.
Virgin Active
London Irish Rugby Ground
Gaflac Sports Ground
Chennestone Prim. Sch.
Stain Hill West Reservoir
Stain Hill East Reservoir
Grand Junction Reservoir
Filter Beds
Kenton Court Meadow
Sunbury Court
Grand Junction Isle
Sunnyside Reservoir
Sunbury Court Island
Hawkedale Inf. Sch.
Driving Range
Club Ho.
Cemetery
Rivermead Island
Thames Lock
Sunbury Locks
Sunbury Lock Ait
RESERVOIR
Reservoir
Works
BESSBOROUGH RESERVOIR
KNIGHTS RESERVOIR
QUEEN ELIZABETH II RESERVOIR
Apps Court Farm
The Cottage
Sports Ground
Football Grd.
Elmbridge Xcel Leisure Complex
Sunbury Weir
Nursery
Wheatley's Eyot
Rivernook Farm
Bramble Hill Farm
Apps Court Green
Thames Field Farm
Depot
Weir
Riverhouse Barn
Mole Hall
Dead River
Ansell Hall
Fieldcommon Farm
Weylands
Sand and Gravel Pit
Rugby Ground
Pavilion
North Weylands Ind. Est.
Hersham Trading Estate
Hersham Water Pollution Control Works
Sewage Works
Embercourt Centre
Hersham Driving Range
HERSHAM VILLAGE GOLF COURSE
Cardinal Newman Catholic Primary School
Playing Field
Rydens Sch.
Walton Oak Prim. Sch.
Walton & Hersham FC
Superstore
Cricket Ground
Walton-on-Thames
Wayneflete's or Wolsey's Tower
South Weylands Farm
West Weylands Farm
Sandown Industrial
River Mole Bus. Pk.

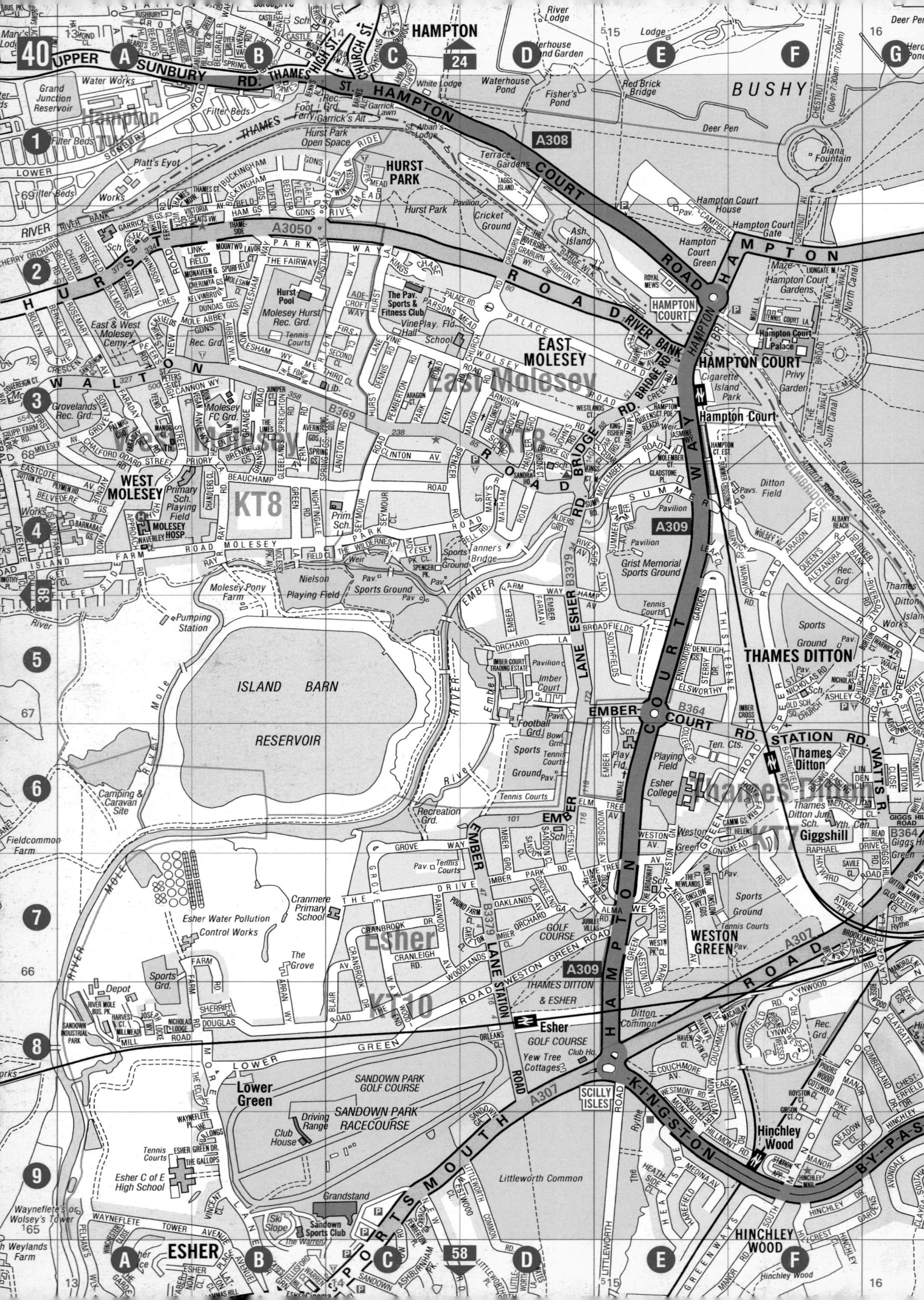

40
HAMPTON
24
UPPER SUNBURY RD.
THAMES ST.
HAMPTON COURT ROAD
A308
BUSHY
Grand Junction Reservoir
Water Works
Filter Beds
Platt's Eyot
Garrick's Ait
Hurst Park Open Space
HURST PARK
Tagg's Island
Ash Island
Hampton Court House
Hampton Court Gate
Hampton Court Green
HAMPTON COURT
Hampton Court Palace
Privy Garden
Diana Fountain
Deer Pen
A3050
HURST ROAD
WALTON ROAD
B369
EAST MOLESEY
East Molesey
West Molesey
WEST MOLESEY
KT8
Molesey Hurst Rec. Grd.
Hurst Pool
Molesey Hosp.
Grovelands Rec. Grd.
Molesey FC Grd.
Cigarette Island Park
Ditton Field
A309
Grist Memorial Sports Ground
Nielson Playing Field
Molesey Pony Farm
Pumping Station
ISLAND BARN RESERVOIR
River Mole
River Ember
Camping & Caravan Site
Fieldcommon Farm
Esher Water Pollution Control Works
Cranmere Primary School
The Grove
Esher
KT10
EMBER LANE
ESHER ROAD
HAMPTON COURT WAY
B364
EMBER COURT RD.
STATION RD.
THAMES DITTON
Thames Ditton
Esher College
Imber Court
Imber Court Trading Estate
Weston Green
WESTON GREEN
KT7
Giggshill
A307
PORTSMOUTH ROAD
KINGSTON BY-PASS
Esher
THAMES DITTON & ESHER GOLF COURSE
Ditton Common
Yew Tree Cottages
SCILLY ISLES
Lower Green
SANDOWN PARK GOLF COURSE
SANDOWN PARK RACECOURSE
Driving Range
Club House
Grandstand
Sandown Sports Club
Littleworth Common
Hinchley Wood
HINCHLEY WOOD
Esher C of E High School
Wayneflete's or Wolsey's Tower
ESHER
58
39
A B C D E F G
1 2 3 4 5 6 7 8 9

41
42
25
203
59
Hampton Wick
HAMPTON WICK
KINGSTON UPON THAMES
Kingston
Norbiton
NORBITON
Berrylands
BERRYLANDS
Surbiton
SURBITON
LONG DITTON
Cockcrow Hill
SOUTHBOROUGH
TOLWORTH
Chessington
HOOK
KT1
KT5
KT6
KT9
HAMPTON COURT PARK
HAMPTON COURT PALACE GOLF COURSE
Club House
The Long Water
Farm Cottages
The Rick Pond
Stud House
The Royal Paddocks
Bushy Lodge
Hampton Wick Pond
Oval Plantation
Half Moon Plantation
Leg-of-Mutton Pond
Thatched Cottage
Hampton Wick Royal Cricket Ground
The King's Field
Tennis Courts
Pav.
War Mem.
The Wilderness
Parkfield
Raven's Ait
Seething Wells
Halls of Residence
Long Ditton Recreation Ground
Kingston Cemetery
Kingston upon Thames Crematorium
Athletics Centre
Kingstonian FC (Kingsmeadow)
Indoor Bowls Club
Hogsmill River
Sewage Works
Waste Disposal Centre
Surbiton Cemetery
The Fairfield Recreation Ground
Kingston Univ.
County Hall
Guildhall
The Rotunda
The Bentalls Centre
Tiffin Sch.
Leisure Cen.
Mus.
Lib.
Surbiton Hosp.
Tolworth Hosp.
Alexanda Millennium Green
Recreation Ground
Tolworth Rec. Cen.
Playing Field
Sports Ground
Cemetery
Manor Ho.
SURBITON GOLF COURSE
Pavilion
Chessington Equestrian Centre
Corinthian Casuals FC Grd. Club
King George's Field
KINGSTON BY-PASS
ESHER BY-PASS
PORTSMOUTH ROAD
HAMPTON COURT ROAD
BRIGHTON ROAD
UPPER BRIGHTON ROAD
LONDON ROAD
CAMBRIDGE RD.
KINGSDOWNE RD.
EWELL ROAD
HOOK ROAD
DITTON ROAD
HOOK RISE SOUTH
RIVER THAMES
A307
A308
A309
A3
A243
A240
A2043
A3210
B3363
B3364
B3370
B359
A310
RICHMOND upon THAMES
KINGSTON upon THAMES
G
H
J
K
L
M
N
1
2
3
4
5
6
7
8
9

42
A
B
C
D
E
F
G
1
2
3
4
5
6
7
8
9
26
60
41
COOMBE LA.
Coombe Hill Jun. & Inf. Schools
COOMBE
COTTEN
Norbiton
Kingston upon Thames
KT1
Indoor Bowls Club
Kingstonian FC (Kingsmeadow)
Athletics Centre
Comm. Cen.
Sludge Beds
Recreation Ground
Sewage Works
Berrylands
KINGSTON ROAD
A2043
Islamic Cen.
Rec. Grd.
Retail Park
Corpus Christi Catholic Prim. School
New Malden
Coombe Girls' Sch.
Theatre
Club House
Sports Ground
Club Ho.
MALDEN GOLF COURSE
Coombe Brook
Beverley Brook
Wimbledon College Playing Fields
Tennis Courts Sports Ground
Civil Service Sports Ground
Raynes Park Sports Ground
Bowling Green
A3
KINGSTON BY-PASS
Sports Ground
Golf Driving Range
BEVERLEY PARK
Emanuel School Playing Field
Blagdon House
Superstore
Raynes Pk. High Sch.
Sports Cen.
NEW MALDEN
Comm. Cen.
The Malden Cen.
The Crescent
B282
BURLINGTON
SHANNON CORNER
SHANNON CNR. RETAIL PK.
WEST BARNES
B283
COOMBE ROAD
HIGH ST.
MALDEN RD.
FOUNTAIN ROUNDABOUT
KT3
Coombe Boys Sch.
MALDEN JUNC.
University of London Athletic Ground
Running Track
Motspur Park
WEST BARNES LA.
BBC Sports Ground
The Sir Joseph Memorial Playing Field
MOTSPUR PARK
Gas Works
Green Prim.
Recreation Ground
Pavilion
Tennis Courts
Study Sch.
Club House
Bowling Green
Hogsmill River
BERRYLANDS
KT5
Grand Avenue Prim. Sch.
Surbiton
Alexandra Millennium Green
MALDEN ROAD
ASM Ten. Cen.
MANOR PARK
Bowling Green
Sports Field
Richard Challoner School
Malden Manor Prim. Sch.
Malden Manor
OLD MALDEN
Liby
B284
A2043
Malden Green
Worcester Park
Sports Grd.
CENTRAL ROAD
Worcester Park
KT4
Playing Field
Tennis Courts
Community Centre
Maori Sports Ground
Knollmead Prim. Sch.
RIVERHILL MOBILE HOME PARK
Nursery
Riverhill
Cricket Ground
Sports Ground
Linden Bridge School
Shadbolt Park
WORCESTER PARK
Superstore
Tennis Courts
TOLWORTH
Bowl. Alley
TOLWORTH JUNCTION
Tolworth
Government Offices
Sports Ground
Tennis Courts
Sports Ground
A240
KINGSTON RD.
OLD MALDEN LANE
WORCESTER PARK RD.
King George's Field Playing Field
Corinthian Casuals FC Club
KT9
Tolworth Court Bridge
Wandgas Athletic Ground
Dancer Dick Wood
Cuddington Prim. Sch.
Play. Fld.
EPSOM and EWELL
SUTTON
Cuddington Recreation Ground
King George's Field
Auriol
520
21
22

43
MERTON
MERTON PARK
WORPLE RD.
KINGSTON ROAD
Raynes Park
Wimbledon Chase
NELSON HOSP.
SW20
SW19
BUSHEY MEAD
PRINCE GEORGE'S PLAYING FIELD
David Lloyd Leisure & Lloyds Lanes Raynes Park
Messines Playing Field
Joseph Hood Recreation Ground
CANNON HILL COMMON (Recreation Ground)
Cannon Hill
RAYNES PARK
South Merton
Mostyn Gardens
Morden
Morden Hall
MORDEN
Morden South
Mosque
MORDEN PARK
Merton College
Morden Park Pool
Raynes Park Playing Fields
School Playing Fields
Sports Centre
North East Surrey Crematorium
MORDEN CEMETERY
Merton & Sutton Joint Cemetery
Old Blues Rugby Football Grd.
Sports Ground
St. John Fisher RC Prim. Sch.
Hatfield Prim. Sch.
Aragon Prim. Sch.
King George's Field
THE WOODSTOCK
St. Helier
Recreation Ground
Risley Sports Ground
Playing Fields
ROSE HILL ROUNDABOUT
ROSEHILL
Rosehill Recreation Ground
Sutton Junior Tennis Centre
Sutton Common
Sutton Cemetery
Glenthorne High Sch.
Mayflower Park
Refuse Destructor
Dorchester Prim. Sch.
ST. ANTHONY'S HOSP.
St. Raphael's Hospice
Sutton
SM3
SM1
NORTH CHEAM
Superstore
Fairlands Pk.
Cheam Park Farm Jun. Sch.
Westbourne Prim. Sch.
Hallmead Day Cen.
BENHILTON
CHEAM COMMON RD.
A2043
LONDON ROAD
STONECOT HILL
EPSOM ROAD
SUTTON COMMON ROAD
REIGATE AVENUE
OLDFIELDS
ST. DUNSTAN'S HILL
LONDON ROAD
CENTRAL ROAD
MORDEN ROAD
MORDEN HALL RD.
GREEN LANE
ROSE HILL
ANGEL HILL
TUDOR DRIVE
GRAND DRIVE
MARTIN WAY
CANNON HILL LANE
A24
A217
A238
A298
A239
B279
B286
B278
B2230
27
44
61
QUEEN VICTORIA
Cheam Leisure Cen.
Collingwood Road Recreation Ground
G
H
J
K
L
M
N
1
2
3
4
5
6
7
8
9
23
24
25
26
65
66
67
68
69

44
43
28
62
A
B
C
D
E
F
G
1
2
3
4
5
6
7
8
9
26
27
28
29
69
68
67
66
165
MERTON
Deen City Farm
SW19
THE TRAMLINK
WESTERN ROAD
A236
Lavender Park
Liberty Prim. Sch.
Gas Works
Cemy.
Mitcham
Lonesome
Lonesome Prim. Sch.
St Mark's C of E Academy
South London Crematorium
Streatham Park Cemetery
Sports Ground
Playing Field
Beehive Bridge
COMMONSIDE EAST
COMMONSIDE WEST
LONDON RD.
MITCHAM
Blue Houses Bridge
Cricket Green
The Canons Leisure Centre & Lib.
Sports Ground
Running Track
MADEIRA RD.
A239
CRANMER RD.
Cranmer Bri.
CROYDON ROAD
MITCHAM
MITCHAM GOLF COURSE
COMMON
Club House
Mitcham Junction
WINDMILL RD.
Depot
Beddington Lane
Traq Motor Racing
Hundred Acre Bridge
MORDEN HALL PARK
Morden Hall
Morden Cottage
Phipps Bridge
River Wandle
MORDEN HALL RD.
A297
Belgrave Wlk.
Morden Lodge
MORDEN ROAD
Ravensbury Park
Melrose Sch.
Playing Field
Liongate Enterprise Park
A217
LONDON ROAD
Mitcham Park
Prim. Sch.
Watermeads
Tooting & Mitcham United FC (Imperial Fields)
Stand
Poulter Park
Bennett's Hole
Bishopsford House
Depot
WORKS
THE WILLOW BUSINESS CENTRE
Willow Lane Bri.
CARSHALTON ROAD
A237
LONDON ROAD
Mill Green
Resr.
BEDDINGTON CORNER
Irrigation Bridge
Comm. Hall
Nature Reserves
CENTRAL ROAD
ST. HELIER AVENUE
Morden
SM4
Bishopsford Comm. Sch.
Moreton Green
BISHOPSFORD ROAD
Playing Fields
Open Space
ST. HELIER
Hill Ho. Comm. Cen.
Bingo
Sutton Arena Leisure Centre
St. Helier Open Space
Carshalton
SM5
ROSEHILL
Rosehill Park East
Greenshaw Wood
ST. HELIER HOSPITAL
QUEEN MARY'S HOSPITAL FOR CHILDREN
B278
WRYTHE LANE
B2230
Spts. Cen.
High Sch.
Sutton
SM1
BENHILTON
Royston Park
Sports Cen.
Muschamp Prim. Sch.
Limes Grn.
THE WRYTHE
Rushy Meadow Prim. Sch.
Carshalton Coll.
CARSHALTON
Carshalton Athletic FC
Carshalton
NORTH ST.
NIGHTINGALE RD.
B277
HACKBRIDGE RD.
HACKBRIDGE
Hackbridge
Mile Road Bridge
Wallington
SM6
FELNEX TRADING ESTATE
Wilderness Island
Wandle Bri.
BEDDINGTON
The Grange
Boating Lake
Manor Gdn.
Grammar Sch.
LONDON RD.
Westcroft Leisure Cen.

45
NORBURY
Norbury
29
SW16
A23
Cannons Health Club
Harris Academy Merton
Recreation Ground
William Morris Primary Sch.
Donnelly Green
Sherwood Park
Thornton Heath
THORNTON HEATH
CR7
Thornton Heath Pond
Gala Bingo
Mitcham Common
Playing Fields
Croydon Athletic FC Grd.
Croydon Crematorium
CROYDON CEMETERY
The Archbishop Lanfranc Sch.
Mayday University Hosp.
Ecclesbourne Jun. & Inf. Schs.
Queen's Rd. Cemy.
46
A236
MITCHAM ROAD
BRIGSTOCK ROAD
LONDON ROAD
A235
B266
B273
B272
Therapia Lane
Lombard Roundabout
BROAD GREEN
A213
A222
ST. JAMES'S RD.
WHITEHORSE RD.
WELLESLEY RD.
West Croydon
Beddington Sewage Treatment Works
Factory
Bus Depot
Ikea Ampere Way
Valley Leisure Park
Cinema
Megabowl Croydon
PURLEY WAY
CR0
CROYDON
WANDLE PK.
Wandle Park
Waddon Marsh
WADDON
Reeves Cnr.
Centrale
Church St.
George St.
Wellesley Rd.
200
ROMAN WAY
OLD TOWN
CROYDON FLYOVER
BEDDINGTON
Carew Manor & Dovecote
A232
63
DUPPAS HILL RD.
Duppas Hill
Waddon
1
2
3
4
5
6
7
8
9
G
H
J
K
L
M
N
30
31
32
65
66
67
68
69

46
UP. NORWOOD
A
B
C
D
E
F
G
1
2
3
4
5
6
7
8
9
45
64
33
34
35
SE19
SE20
SE25
CR0
CR7
Beaulieu Heights
Cypress Inf. Sch.
Playing Field
Bowling Green
Tennis Courts
Athletic Grounds
Cypress Jun. Sch.
Spurgeon's College
South Norwood Lake
Orchard School Sports Centre
Nursing Home
Tennis Cts.
Betts Pk.
ANERLEY
ANERLEY ROAD
ELMERS END ROAD
CROYDON RD.
A213
A215
A212
A214
A222
A232
B266
B243
Bromley Junction
Birkbeck
Beckenham Crematorium
Thornton Heath
Grangewood Park
SOUTH NORWOOD
High Sch.
SOUTH NORWOOD HILL
PORTLAND ROAD
PENGE RD.
MANOR RD.
WHITEHORSE
Crystal Palace FC (Selhurst Park)
Norwood Junc.
Priory Sch.
Tennis Courts
Recreation Ground
Harrington Rd.
Blind Corner
Pitch & Putt Course
SOUTH NORWOOD COUNTRY PARK
South Norwood Country Park Visitors Cen.
Playground
Croydon Sports Arena
Croydon FC Grd.
Ryelands Prim. Sch.
Swim. Pools
Temple
Arena
Croydon Golf Driving Range
Elmers End
Play. Fld.
St. Chad's Cath. Prim. Sch.
Heavers Farm Centre
Heavers Farm Prim. Sch.
Heavers Meadow
Norbury Brook
Works
Wks.
Selhurst
SELHURST
SELHURST ROAD
Brit. Sch.
WOODSIDE
Brickfields Mdw.
Prim. Sch.
Lupin Bri.
Gloucester Rd. Junc.
Cottage Bri.
Cottage Junc.
Training Cen.
Davidson Prim. Sch.
Woodside
Blackhorse La.
Bowl. Green
Pav.
Tennis Courts
Ashburton Park
Ashburton Playing Fields
Ashburton Learning Village & Comm. Sch.
Play. Flds.
SHIRLEY OAKS BMI HOSPITAL
WOODSIDE GREEN
SPRING LANE
LONG LANE
LOWER ADDISCOMBE ROAD
MORLAND ROAD
SHIRLEY ROAD
Addiscombe
ADDISCOMBE
Recreation Grd.
Playing Field
Shirley Oaks
CROYDON
High Sch.
Lunar Ho.
YMCA
Gov. Offs.
East Croydon
Thtre
Wellesley Rd.
George St.
Fairfield Halls
Mag. Courts
CHERRY ORCHARD ROAD
ST. JAMES'S ROAD
WELLESLEY ROAD
PARK LANE
CHEPSTOW ROAD
ADDISCOMBE ROAD
BARCLAY R.
FAIRFIELD RD.
PARK HILL
200
Lebanon Rd.
Sandilands
Sandilands Junc.
Park Hill
Jun. & Inf. Schs.
Coombe Cliff (CETS)
Trinity School Playing Field
Tennis Courts
Sports Ground
Bowling Green
SHIRLEY PARK GOLF COURSE
Club House
Sports Cen.
Trinity Sch.
Playing Field
SHIRLEY
Hall Grange
Coloma Convent Girls Sch.
Shirley Windmill
Oaks Farm
Coombe Farm
COOMBE PARK
LLOYD PARK
Cambridge Tutors Coll.

47
BECKENHAM
Beckenham
BR3
ELMERS END
EDEN PARK
PARK LANGLEY
UPPER ELMERS END
MONKS ORCHARD
SPRING PARK
WEST WICKHAM
West Wickham
BR4
Bromley
BR2
SHORTLANDS
LANGLEY PARK
LANGLEY PARK GOLF COURSE
Kelsey Park
Elgood Playing Field
Kelsey Park Sports College
Crease Park
Langley Court (Research Labs)
Langley Park Schools
Sports Centre
THE BETHLEM ROYAL HOSPITAL
Edenham High Sch.
Parkfields Recreation Ground
Crouch Oak Wood
Cold Shaw
High Broom Wood
High Broom Wood
Nurses' Home
Caravan Park
Oak Lodge Prim. Sch.
Blake Recreation Ground
West Wickham Pools
Hawes Down Jun.& Inf. Schs.
Glebe Sch.
Sparrow's Den Playing Fields
Spring Park Wood
Miller Pond
Benson Prim. Sch.
Shirley High Sch.
Foxes Wood
Pinewoods
Glade Wood
Monks Orchard Prim. Sch.
Amida Leisure Cen.
BECKENHAM HOSPITAL
Beckenham Road
Clock Ho.
The Spa
Cinema
Theatre Cen.
Bishop Challoner Sch.
THE SLOANE HOSP.
Superstore
Eden Park
West Wickham
Clock House
Bandstand
Putting Green
Recreation Ground
Beau Lodge
Club House
The Rookery
Wickham
Lodge
Weir
BECKENHAM RD.
HIGH STREET
RECTORY RD.
BROMLEY RD.
MANOR RD.
WICKHAM ROAD
HAYES LANE
SOUTH EDEN PARK RD.
ELMERS END ROAD
UPPER ELMERS END
LINKS WAY
WICKHAM ROAD
HIGH STREET
GLEBE WAY
STATION ROAD
BECKENHAM ROAD
CROYDON ROAD
CHURCH ROAD
ADDINGTON RD.
A222
A234
A214
A232
A2022
B230
B251
H
J
K
L
M
N
G
1
2
3
4
5
6
7
8
9
36
37
38
39
65
66
67
68
69

NINE MILE RIDE
B3430
Kingsmere House
King's Mere
Club House
Wokingham
RG40
HEATH RIDE
HOLLYBUSH RIDE
Queen's Bri.
Jack's Bri.
LOWER
A321
WOKINGHAM ROAD
Pineridge Farm
NEW ACRES MOBILE HOME PARK
PINE RIDGE MOBILE HOME PARK
30
Ravenswood Village
Annie Lawson Sch.
The Green
HEATHERMOUNT GARDENS
Oaklands Inf.& Jun. Schools
EAST BERKSHIRE GOLF COURSE
Club House
Roman Road (course of)
THE DEVIL'S HIGHWAY
ROMAN RIDE
The Devil's Highway
Blencathra
Heath Pond
Simons Wood
Armholes
Rhododendron Corner
The Ridges
Puckswood House
WELLINGTONIA AVENUE
B3348
FINCHAMPSTEAD RIDGES
St. Anthonys Cottage
WOKINGHAM
BRACKNELL FOREST
DUKES RIDE
WELLINGTONIA ROUNDABOUT
WELLINGTON BUSINESS PK.
Crowthorne
The Wellington College Sports Club
Sports Area
Cricket Ground
Playing Field
Derby Field
WELLINGTON COLLEGE
Chaucer Woods
Benson House
Anglesey
Lockwood
Pollock Bridge
Heatherways
Edgbarrow Star
Russets
Spout Pond
Fisher's Copse
Sandhurst Lodge
Beech Hill
Ambarrow Hill
Smallbrook Bottom
Edgbarrow Hill
Rosina Cottage
Moor Green Farm
Foxglade
Hall Farm
Hilton Cottage
Grove Farm House
Coalpit Copse
Ambarrow Wood
Yonder
AMBARROW FARM COURTYARD
Ambarrow Farm
Grove Farm
SANDHURST ROAD
New Scotland Hill Prim. Sch.
Eagle House School
LITTLE SANDHURST
Play. Fld.
Perry Bridge Farm
Perry's Bridge
Horseshoe Lake Watersports Centre
HIGH STREET
Long Down
Hurts Hill
Scotland Hill
Mill Farm
Pavilion
Riverside
Mill Bridge
Church Farm
BLACKWATER VALLEY GOLF COURSE
Driving Range
Club House
Sean Devereaux Park
Blackwater River
Yateley Bridge
Trilakes Country Park
YORKTOWN ROAD
Sandhurst
LAKESIDE BUSINESS PARK
Yateley
Depot
Yateley Green
Yateley Industries
THE YATELEY LAKES
SANDHURST
BRACKNELL FOREST
HART
READING ROAD
GU46
B3272
Village Hall
Yateley Manor Sch. Play. Flds.
YATELEY
St. Peter's C of E Jun. Sch.
Yateley Inf. Sch.
Playing Fld.
Yateley School
Hall
Lib.
Comm. Centre
Jun. & Inf. Schs.
Yateley Hill
Clark's Farm
Works
Pond Fm.
DARBY GREEN
68
A B C D E F G
1 2 3 4 5 6 7 8 9
81 82 83
65 64 63 62 61

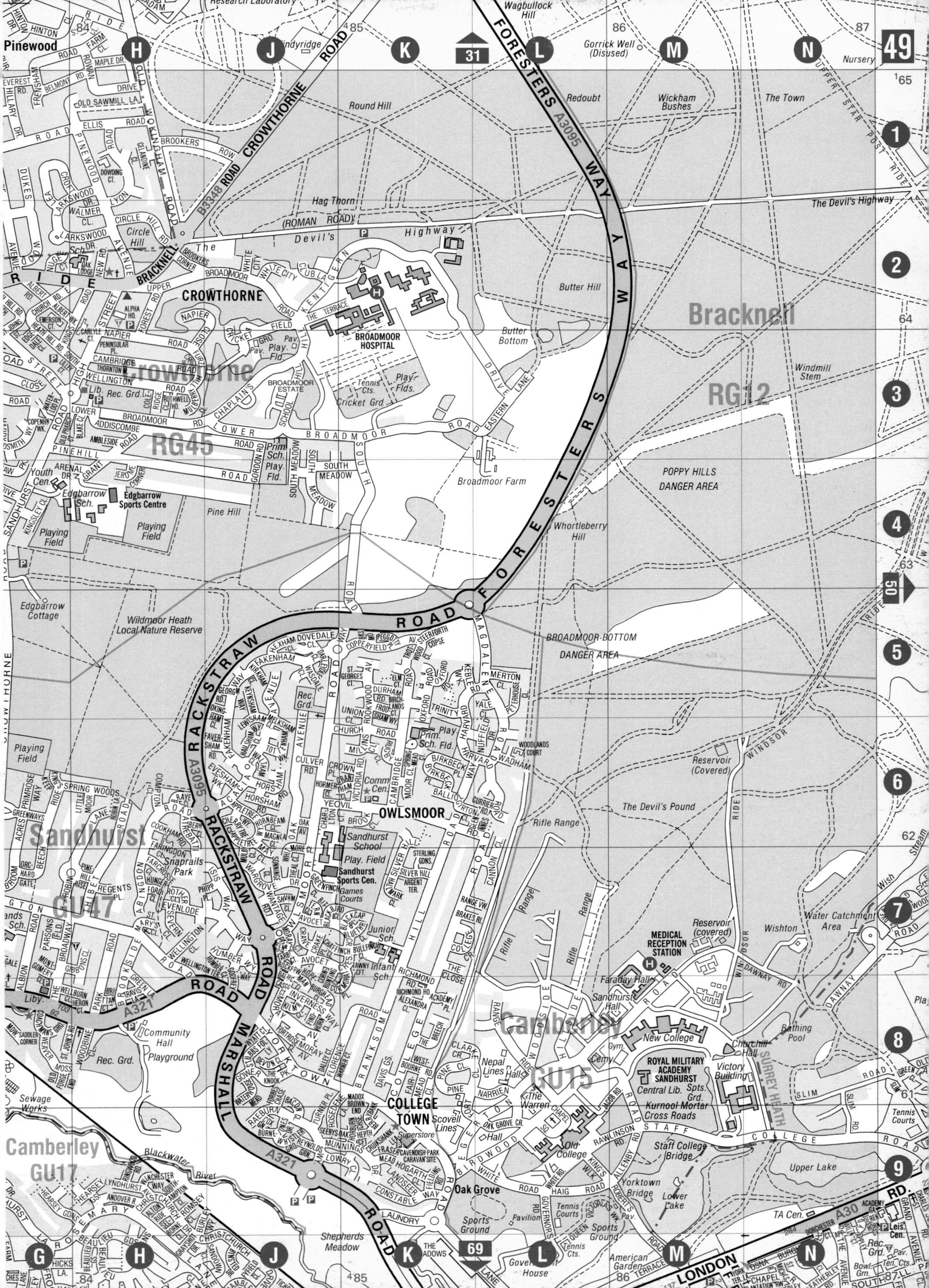
49
31
50
69
H
J
K
L
M
N
G
1
2
3
4
5
6
7
8
9
Pinewood
Research Laboratory
Wagbullock Hill
Gorrick Well (Disused)
Nursery
Windyridge
Round Hill
Redoubt
Wickham Bushes
The Town
FORESTERS WAY
A3095
CROWTHORNE ROAD
B3348
Hag Thorn
(ROMAN ROAD)
The Devil's Highway
Circle Hill
Butter Hill
Bracknell
RG12
CROWTHORNE
Crowthorne
BROADMOOR HOSPITAL
Butter Bottom
Windmill Stem
Cricket Grd.
Play. Flds.
BROADMOOR ESTATE
RG45
LOWER BROADMOOR ROAD
POPPY HILLS DANGER AREA
Broadmoor Farm
Edgbarrow Sch.
Edgbarrow Sports Centre
Pine Hill
Playing Field
Whortleberry Hill
Edgbarrow Cottage
Wildmoor Heath Local Nature Reserve
RACKSTRAW ROAD
BROADMOOR-BOTTOM DANGER AREA
Reservoir (Covered)
The Devil's Pound
Rifle Range
OWLSMOOR
Sandhurst
Sandhurst School
Sandhurst Sports Cen.
Snaprails Park
GU47
MEDICAL RECEPTION STATION
Reservoir (covered)
Wishton
Water Catchment Area
Faraday Hall
Sandhurst Hall
Camberley
New College
Churchill Hall
Bathing Pool
ROYAL MILITARY ACADEMY SANDHURST
Victory Building
Central Lib.
Kurnool Mortar Cross Roads
GU15
Nepal Lines
The Warren
Old College
Staff College Bridge
Upper Lake
Lower Lake
Yorktown Bridge
Community Hall
Playground
Rec. Grd.
Sewage Works
Blackwater River
Camberley GU17
MARSHALL ROAD
A321
COLLEGE TOWN
Scovell Lines
Superstore
Oak Grove
Sports Ground
Shepherds Meadow
Government House
American Garden
LONDON RD.
A30
TA Cen.
Tennis Courts

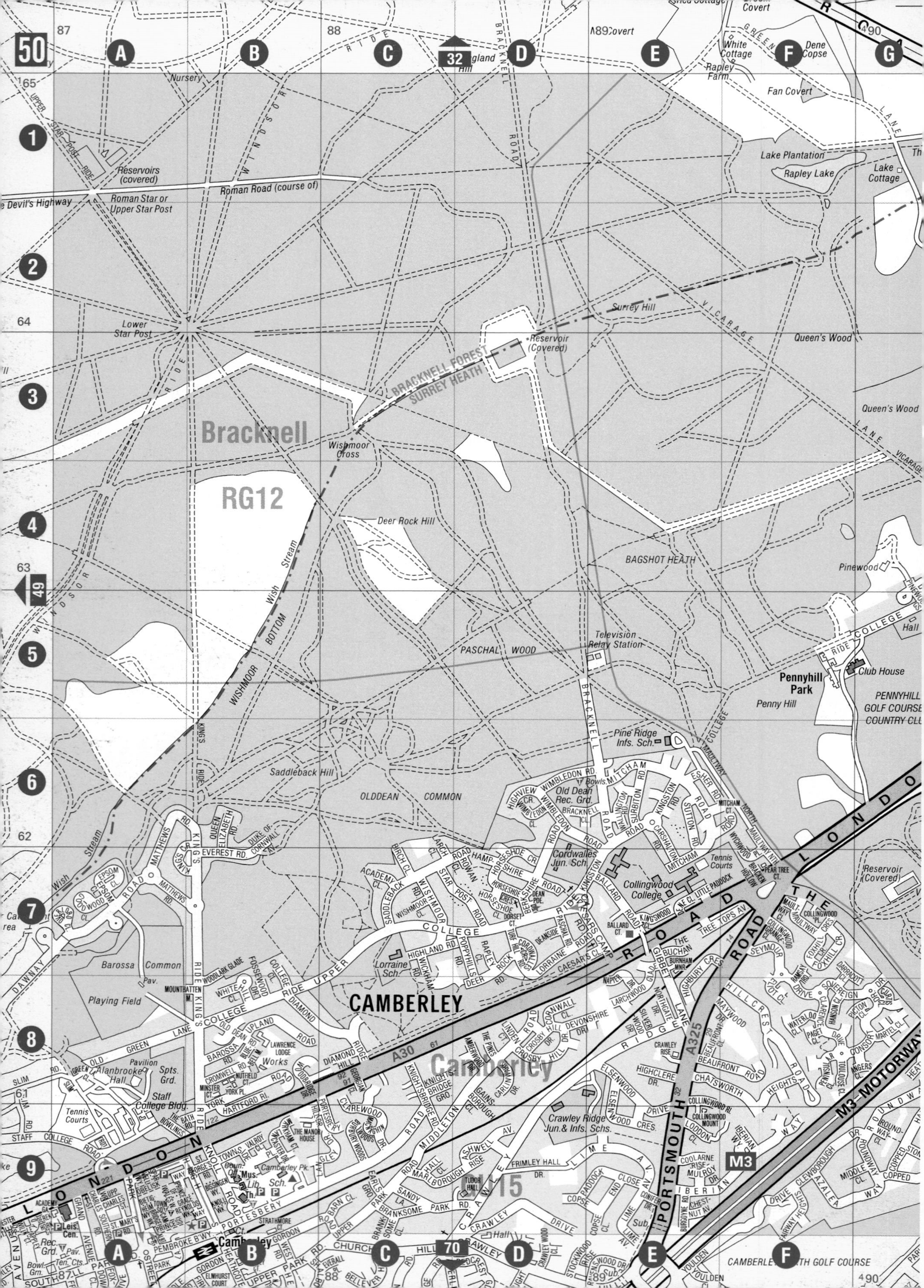

50
87
88
A
B
C
D
E
F
G
32
49
70
1
2
3
4
5
6
7
8
9
65
64
63
62
61
Nursery
Covert
White Cottage
Dene Copse
Rapley Farm
Fan Covert
Lake Plantation
Rapley Lake
Lake Cottage
Reservoirs (covered)
Roman Road (course of)
Devil's Highway
Roman Star or Upper Star Post
Lower Star Post
WINDSOR RIDE
UPPER STAR POST RIDE
BRACKNELL ROAD
Surrey Hill
VICARAGE LANE
Queen's Wood
Reservoir (Covered)
BRACKNELL FOREST
SURREY HEATH
Bracknell
Wishmoor Cross
RG12
Deer Rock Hill
BAGSHOT HEATH
Pinewood
COLLEGE RIDE
Hall
Wish Stream
WISHMOOR BOTTOM
Television Relay Station
PASCHAL WOOD
Club House
Pennyhill Park
Penny Hill
PENNYHILL GOLF COURSE COUNTRY CLUB
Pine Ridge Infs. Sch.
KING'S RIDE
Saddleback Hill
OLDDEAN COMMON
Old Dean Rec. Grd.
Bowls
Cordwalles Jun. Sch.
Collingwood College
Tennis Courts
Reservoir (Covered)
Barossa Common
Playing Field
Lorraine Sch.
CAMBERLEY
Camberley
A30
LONDON ROAD
A325
PORTSMOUTH ROAD
M3
M3 MOTORWAY
Alanbrooke Hall
Pavilion
Spts. Grd.
Staff College Bldg.
Tennis Courts
STAFF COLLEGE ROAD
Works
Crawley Ridge Jun.& Infs. Schs.
Camberley Pk.
Mus.
Lib.
Sch.
Th.
Leis. Cen.
Rec. Grd.
Camberley
GU15
CAMBERLEY HEATH GOLF COURSE
490

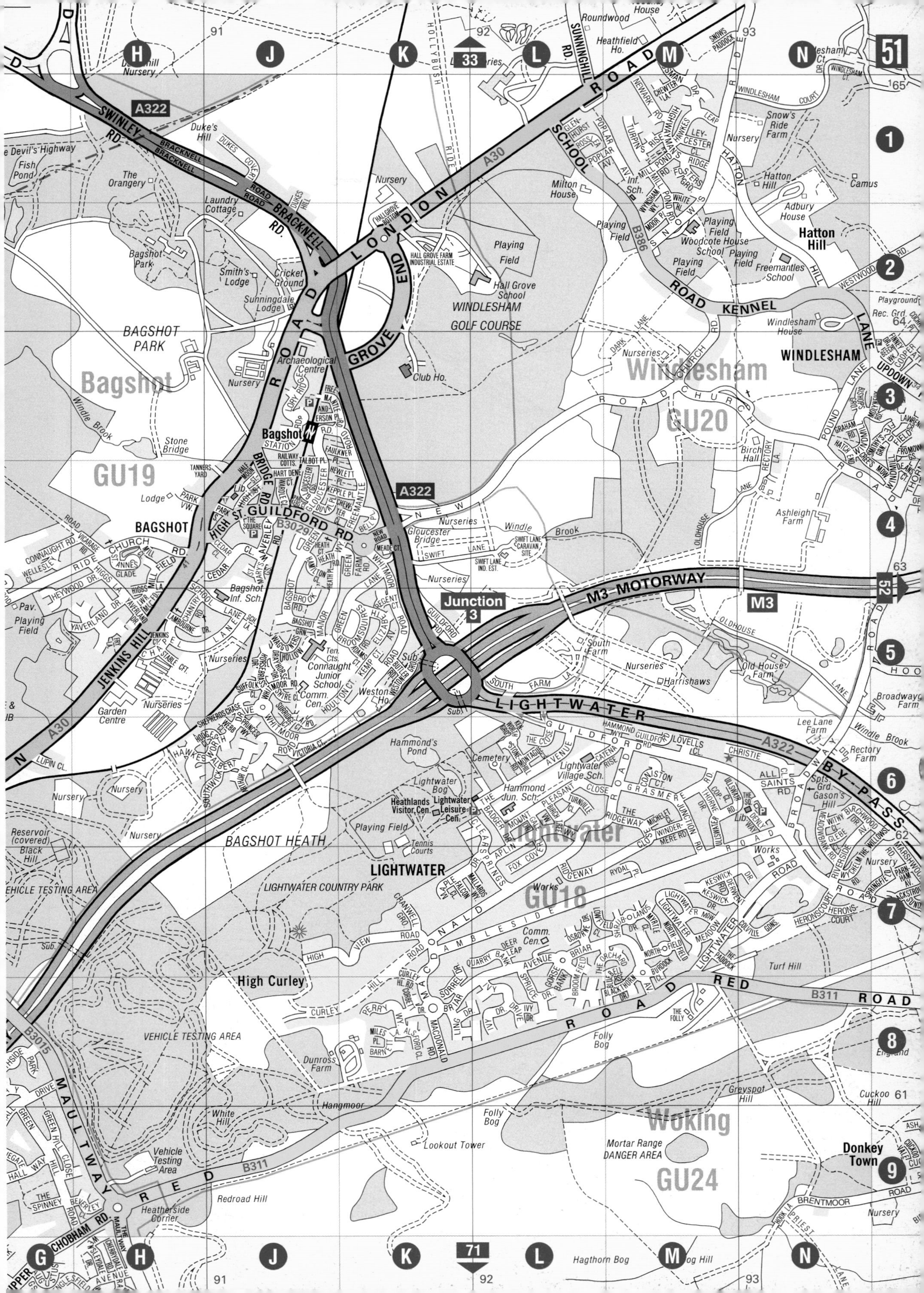

Bagshot
BAGSHOT
BAGSHOT PARK
GU19
Windlesham
WINDLESHAM
GU20
Lightwater
LIGHTWATER
GU18
Woking
GU24
High Curley
BAGSHOT HEATH
LIGHTWATER COUNTRY PARK
WINDLESHAM GOLF COURSE
M3 MOTORWAY
Junction 3
A322
A30
B386
B3029
B311
B3015
SWINLEY RD.
BRACKNELL ROAD
LONDON ROAD
GUILDFORD RD.
LIGHTWATER BY-PASS
RED ROAD
KENNEL LANE
SCHOOL ROAD
SUNNINGHILL RD.
JENKINS HILL
MAULTWAY
CHOBHAM RD.
MACDONALD ROAD
AMBLESIDE ROAD
Bagshot Station
Archaeological Centre
Hall Grove School
Club Ho.
Woodcote House School
Freemantles School
Bagshot Inf. Sch.
Connaught Junior School
Lightwater Village Sch.
Hammond Jun. Sch.
Heathlands Visitor Cen.
Lightwater Leisure Cen.
Hatton Hill
Donkey Town
Turf Hill
Folly Bog
Greyspot Hill
Cuckoo Hill
Mortar Range DANGER AREA
Lookout Tower
Hangmoor
White Hill
Vehicle Testing Area
VEHICLE TESTING AREA
Redroad Hill
Heatherside Corner
Hagthorn Bog
Dunross Farm
Hammond's Pond
Lightwater Bog
Old House Farm
Harrishaws
South Farm
Lee Lane Farm
Rectory Farm
Broadway Farm
Ashleigh Farm
Birch Hall
Windlesham House
Snow's Ride Farm
Milton House
Adbury House
Camus
Roundwood
Heathfield Ho.
Duke's Hill
The Orangery
Laundry Cottage
Bagshot Park
Smith's Lodge
Sunningdale Lodge
Cricket Ground
Stone Bridge
Windle Brook
Fish Pond
Reservoir (covered)
Black Hill
Garden Centre
Nurseries
Cemetery
Weston Ho.
33
71
91
92
93
61
62
63
64
65
52
H J K L M N G
1 2 3 4 5 6 7 8 9

Windlesham
GU20
Valley End
WINDLESHAM
Lightwater
GU18
GU24
WEST END
Donkey Town
Penny Pot
Brick Hill
Sparrow Row
M3 MOTORWAY
CHERTSEY ROAD
BAGSHOT ROAD
GUILDFORD ROAD
LIGHTWATER BY-PASS
RED ROAD
WINDSOR ROAD
WINDLESHAM ROAD
HIGHAMS LANE
HALEBOURNE LANE
RYE GROVE
PENNYPOT LANE
WINDLEMERE GOLF COURSE
Coworth-Flexlands School
Valley End C of E Infants Sch.
Holy Trinity C of E Prim. School
Gordon's School
Chobham Place Wood
Heathpark Wood
Halebourne Copse
Manor Farm Wood
Sandpit Hill
Westwood Lodge
Updown Hill House
Ribsden Holt
Leech Pond
Westcroft Park
Windlesham Park
Woodlands Farm
Twelve Oaks
Broadwaygreen Farm
Rectory Farm
Manor Farm Cottages
Brooklands Farm
Hookstone Green
Pankhurst Farm
Brook Place
Holly Farm
Little Barn
Lovelands Farm
Beldam Bridge Farm
Hatchgate Farm
Rosedene Farm
Rounce Farm
Scott's Farm
Grove Farm
Poultry Farm
Buckstone Farm
Shrubb's Farm
Manx Farm
Biddle Farm
Home Farm House
Steep Acre Farm
Higher Park Farm
Halebourne House
Pembroke House
Russell Hill
The Old Vicarage
Westley Green Fm.
Shergolds Stud Fm.
Valley Wood Place
Chobham Place
Walk End
The Laurels
The Oaks
New England
Cuckoo Hill
A319
A322
B386
B311
B383
34
72
51

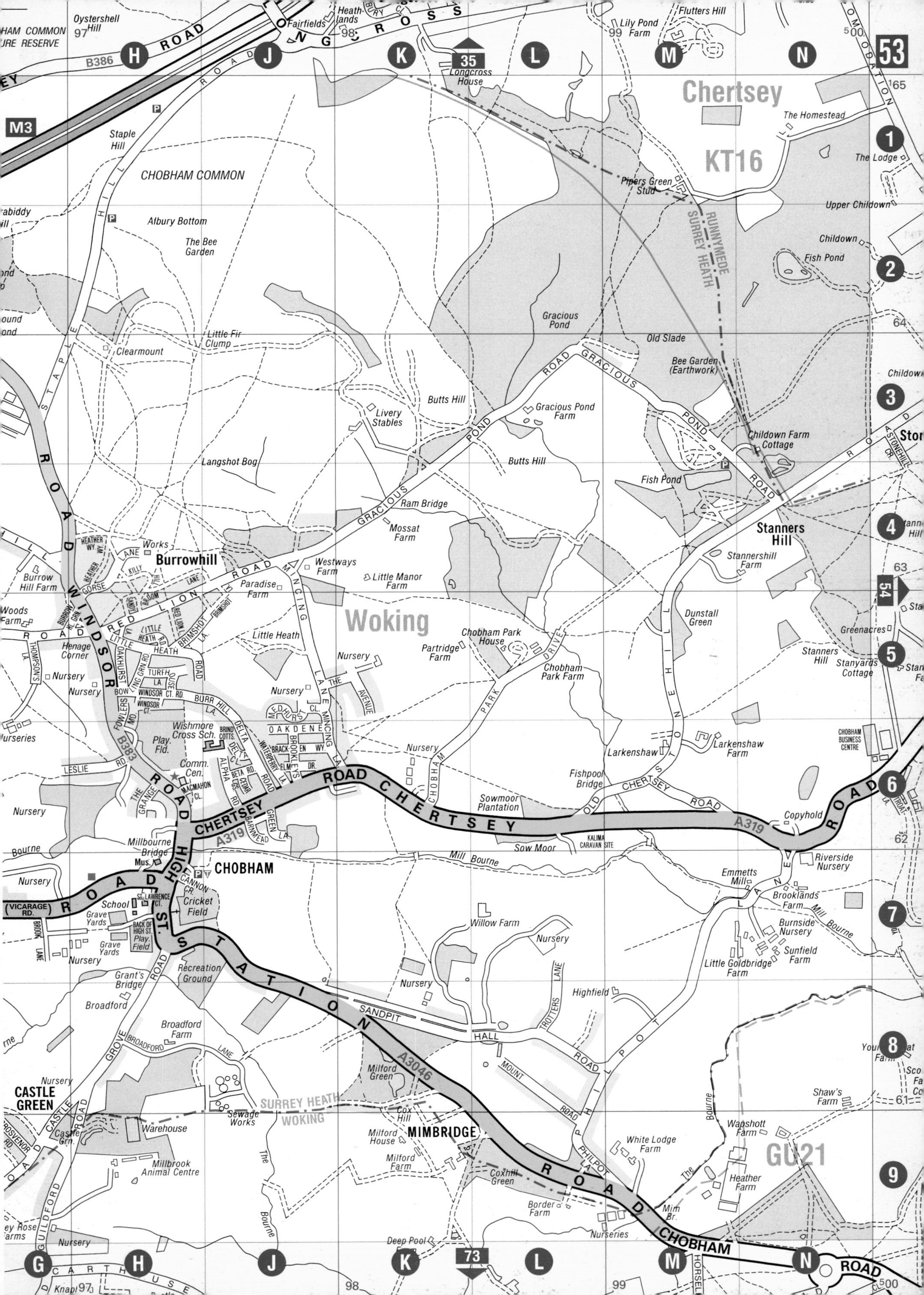
Oystershell Hill
Fairfields
Heathlands
LONGCROSS
Flutters Hill
Lily Pond Farm
B386
ROAD
M3
35
Longcross House
Chertsey
The Homestead
KT16
The Lodge
Staple Hill
CHOBHAM COMMON
Pipers Green Stud
RUNNYMEDE
SURREY HEATH
Upper Childown
Childown
Fish Pond
Albury Bottom
The Bee Garden
Gracious Pond
Little Fir Clump
Clearmount
Old Slade
Bee Garden (Earthwork)
STAPLE HILL
Butts Hill
Livery Stables
Gracious Pond Farm
Childown Farm Cottage
Langshot Bog
Butts Hill
Fish Pond
GRACIOUS POND ROAD
Ram Bridge
Mossat Farm
Stanners Hill
WINDSOR ROAD
Works
Burrowhill
Westways Farm
Little Manor Farm
Stannershill Farm
Burrow Hill Farm
RED LION ROAD
Paradise Farm
MINCING LANE
Woods Farm
Woking
Dunstall Green
54
Little Heath
Chobham Park House
Greenacres
Henage Corner
Partridge Farm
Stanners Hill
Stanyards Cottage
Nursery
Chobham Park Farm
CHOBHAM PARK DRIVE
STONEHILL
Nurseries
Wishmore Cross Sch.
OAKDENE
CHOBHAM BUSINESS CENTRE
Play. Fld.
Larkenshaw
Larkenshaw Farm
LESLIE RD.
Comm. Cen.
B383
Fishpool Bridge
OLD CHERTSEY ROAD
Sowmoor Plantation
CHERTSEY ROAD
A319
Copyhold
Millbourne Bridge
Mus.
CHOBHAM
Sow Moor
KALIMA CARAVAN SITE
Mill Bourne
Riverside Nursery
Emmetts Mill
Brooklands Farm
School
Cricket Field
HIGH ST.
Willow Farm
Burnside Nursery
Grave Yards
Play. Field
Nursery
Sunfield Farm
Little Goldbridge Farm
Recreation Ground
STATION ROAD
Grant's Bridge
Broadford
Highfield
SANDPIT HALL ROAD
TROTTERS LANE
Broadford Farm
A3046
MOUNT ROAD
PHILPOT LANE
Milford Green
CASTLE GREEN
SURREY HEATH
WOKING
Sewage Works
Cox Hill
Shaw's Farm
Warehouse
MIMBRIDGE
Wapshott Farm
Milford House
White Lodge Farm
GU21
Millbrook Animal Centre
Milford Farm
Coxhill Green
Heather Farm
Border Farm
Mim Br.
Nurseries
Nursery
Deep Pool
CHOBHAM ROAD
73
CARTHOUSE
97
98
99
500
65
64
63
62
61
G H J K L M N
1 2 3 4 5 6 7 8 9

FOXHILLS GOLF COURSE
36
FOXHILLS GOLF COURSE
Club House
Foxhills Country Club
Tennis Courts
Fox Hills
Foxhills Lodge
Dower House
Budds Cottage
North Lodge
The Lodge
Upper Childown
Childown
ACCOMMODATION ROAD
Botleys Park
Botleys Mansion
Homewood Park Open Space
Home Wood
Offices
Church Farm
Oracle Pk.
Chertsey South
ST. PETERS
Kitchenride Corner
Kitchenride Cotts.
Penny Farthing Cottage
FOXHILLS
Playground
Ether Hill
Stonehill Cottage
Stone Hill
Childown Lodge
Merlewood
Stonehill
QUEENSWOOD GOLF COURSE
Coach House
Queenwood House
Club House
The Paddock
Ten Acres
Rec. Grd.
Bowling Green Pav.
Tennis Courts
OTTERSHAW
MURRAY ROAD
B3121
GUILDFORD RD.
A320
A319
CHOBHAM ROAD
Timber Hill
The Common
Meath School
Chertsey
KT16
Brox
Bousley Farm
Otterhill Nursery
Fern Hill
Stanners Hill
Hawks Hill
Hawks Hill Cottage
Timber Hill
South Lodge
Home Farm
Ottershaw Park
Playing Field
Tennis Courts
Play. Fld.
The Mansion
Miniature Rifle Range
Ottershaw Park
Hill Crest
Brox Copse
Brox Wood
Bourne Rise Farm
Holly Farm
Beyond
Stanyards
Greenacres
GU24
Timber Hill Cotts.
Long Copse
Stanyards Cottage
Stanyards Farm
Berwin Park
CHOBHAM BUSINESS CENTRE
CHERTSEY ROAD
Samson's Wood
RUNNYMEDE
SURREY HEATH
Little Blackmole Pond
Sandpit Plantation
Bramshill
Gable Cottage
Great Wood
ANNINGSLEY PARK
Beech Hill Clump
Great Blackmole Pond
The Wey Farm
Summerhill
Halls
The Warren
Groves Farm
Birch Wood
FAIROAKS AIRPORT
Woking
Decoy Plantation
Bridge House
Thatch Cottage
Ware Copse
Anningsley Park
Tennis Court
The Bourne
Old Farm
Dunford Ho.
Dunford Bridge
Bonsey's Bridge
McCLAREN TECHNOLOGY CENTRE
The Cottage
Hoyt Wood
The Bourne
GUILDFORD ROAD
Tennis Courts
Durnford Farm
Timber Yard
The Hoyte
Hoyte Lodge
Club House
GU21
Bonseys Cotts.
Pinewood Cotts.
Young Stroat Farm
Scotchers Farm
Scotchers Farm Cotts.
Danewell
Anthonys
New Houses
NEW ZEALAND GOLF COURSE
SHEERWATER
LANE
Gutter
Danewell Hill
A245
WOODHAM ROAD
HORSELL COMMON
Danewell House
Tennis Courts
Sheerwater Recreation Ground
Running Track
Play. Fld.
The Bishop David Brown Sch.
Broadmere Prim. Sch.
Basingstoke Canal
WOODHAM HALL ESTATE
74
CHERTSEY A320
53

55
ADDLESTONE
Addlestone
KT15
NEW HAW
WOODHAM
ROW TOWN
Rowhill
West Byfleet
KT14
WEST BYFLEET
BYFLEET
Weybridge
Junction 11
M25
M25-MOTORWAY
Golf Course
Central Veterinary Laboratory
Dartnell Park
Addlestone Junction
Byfleet & New Haw
West Byfleet
Ham Moor
Electricity Switching Station
Surrey Golf & Fitness
Garden Centre
Crockford Bridge Farm
Sports Ground
Recreation Ground
Tins Wood
Old Wood
The Moat
West Hall
Broadoaks
Woodham Lock
Scotland Bri. Lock
Brooklands Business Park
Brooklands Industrial Estate
Sheerwater Bri.
37
56
75

56
A
B
C
D
E
F
G
1
2
3
4
5
6
7
8
9
38
55
76
WEYBRIDGE
OATLANDS
OATLANDS PARK
BROOKLANDS
ST. GEORGE'S HILL
WHITELEY VILLAGE
BYFLEET
West Byfleet KT14
Weybridge KT13
Ham Moor
Black Boy Bri
Weybridge Lock
Wey Meadows
Cemetery
Heathside School
Playing Fields
Brooklands College
Weybridge
Play. Fld.
Conduit Hill
Weybridge Junc.
Nine Arches Bridge
Seven Arches Bridge
Works
Mercedes-Benz World
Brooklands Museum
Wet Circle
Handling Track A
Handling Track B
David Lloyd Leisure
The Heath
Churchfields Rec. Grd.
The Green
Oatlands Sch.
Walton Leigh Sch.
Cleves School
Haine's Bri.
Tennis Courts
Club
Warren Pond
Sports Ground
Recreation Ground
Club House
ST. GEORGE'S HILL GOLF COURSE
Blue Barn Farm
Plough Bridge
Plough Bridge Farm
Foxholm Covert
Cobham Bus Museum
Silver Mere
Silvermere
SILVERMERE GOLF COURSE
Club House
Driving Range
Silvermere Farm Estate
Home Farm
Thirty Acre Wood
The Hangers
Queen Anne's Cottage
St. George's Nursing Home
Lodge
Hotel
Feltonfleet Sch.
Play. Fld.
Pains Hill
Manor Farm
Manor Farm Estate
Byfleet Mill
Bluegates Hole
Weymede
Horizon Business Village
Seven Hills Estate
Walton Firs Scout Camp
Manor Pond
Strawberry Hill
Beards Hill
Golf Course
The Bull Dogs
St. James C of E Prim. Sch.
WEYBRIDGE RD.
A317
A3050
A245
A3
B373
B374
B365
B372
HIGH ST.
MONUMENT HILL
QUEENS ROAD
ST. GEORGE'S AVENUE
HEATH ROAD
HANGER HILL
(CAENSWOOD HILL)
BROOKLANDS ROAD
SEVEN HILLS ROAD
BYFLEET ROAD
PORTSMOUTH RD.
PAINSHILL
PARVIS RD.
SOPWITH DR.
WELLINGTON WAY
CLUB ROAD
WEST ROAD
CAVENDISH ROAD
GOLF ROAD
OLD AVENUE
EAST ROAD
WARREN LANE
ELLESMERE RD.
BURWOOD ROAD
GODOLPHIN ROAD
OATLANDS DR.
OATLANDS AVENUE
BAKER STREET
CHURCHFIELDS AV.
BEECHWOOD AV.
CONVENT LANE
MILL LANE
REDHILL ROAD
WHITE KNIGHTS RD.
SOUTH RD.
BROOKS CL.
YAFFLE ROAD
ABBOTSWOOD DR.
RODONA ROAD
RAVENSCROFT RD.
LINDEN RD.
CHESTNUT AV.
KELVEDON AV.
OCTAGON ROAD
NORTH AV.
WEST AV.
CRANLEY RD.
ALBURY RD.
PATMORE RD.
ERISWELL CRES.
FOXHOLES
HALL PLACE DR.
WALTON COMMON
ELLESMERE RD.

39
77
58
HERSHAM
Walton-on-Thames
Walton-on-Thames
KT12
Burhill
Esher
KT10
WEST END
Hersham Green
Burwood Park
Cobham
KT11
COBHAM
Fairmile
Hersham Village Golf Course
Cardinal Newman Catholic Primary School
Playing Field
Rydens Sch.
Bell Farm Jun. Sch.
South Weylands Farm
West Weylands Farm
Wayneflete's Wolsey's Tower
Hersham Riverside Park
Burhill Inf. Sch.
Burvale Cemetery
Burvale Farm
Kennels
Upper Common
Rabbit Lane House
Nurseries
Southwood Manor Farm
Winterhouse Farm
Garson Farm
Recreation Ground
Albany Bridge Hall
WEST END COMMON
Claremont Landscape Gardens
Claremont Lake
Horseshoe Clump
BURHILL (Old) GOLF COURSE
Riverside Farm
Practice Ground
Burhill Park
Burhill Club House
BURHILL (New) GOLF COURSE
Winterdown Wood
The Homewood
Winterdown
Black Pond
Dick Turpin's Cottage
Norwood Farm
ACS Cobham International School
Upper Court
FAIRMILE COMMON
Middle Pond
Hollybush Cottages
Notre Dame Preparatory & Senior Schools
Golf Driving Range
The Fairmile
Chestnut Lodge Farm
Hook's Corner
Chippings Farm
Randalls Cotts.
Old Common
Superstore
Cobham Bridge
Reed's Sch.
Cricket Ground
RIVER MOLE
QUEENS ROAD
HERSHAM BY-PASS
ESHER ROAD
A244
A317
A307
A3
A245
B365
STONY HILL
BURWOOD ROAD
BURHILL ROAD
BLACKHILLS
ELVEDON ROAD
ESHER BY-PASS
PORTSMOUTH ROAD
FAIRMILE LANE

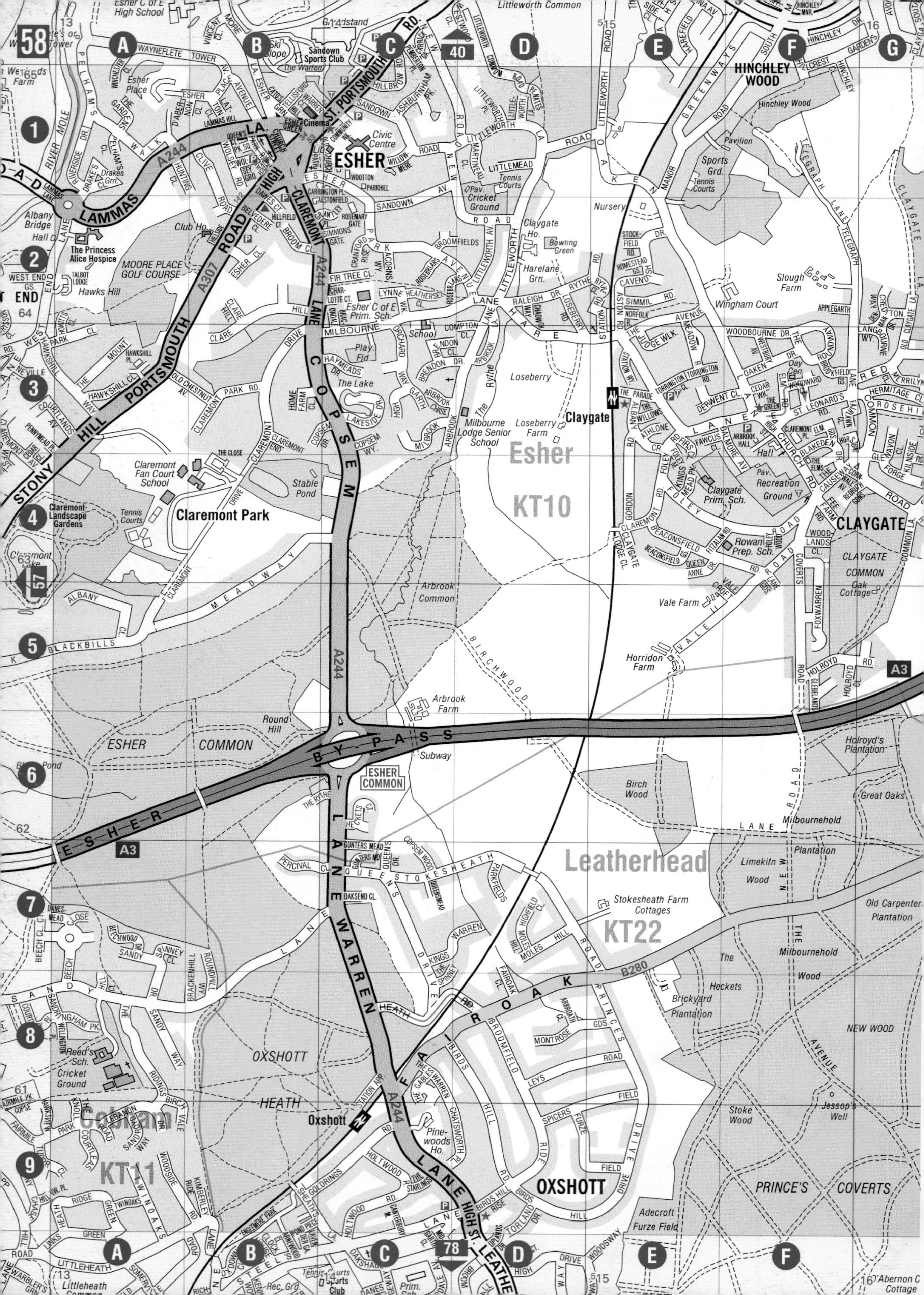

58
40
57
78
ESHER
CLAYGATE
OXSHOTT
HINCHLEY WOOD
Cobham
Esher
KT10
Leatherhead
KT22
KT11
Claremont Park
Claremont Landscape Gardens
Claremont Fan Court School
Moore Place Golf Course
The Princess Alice Hospice
Sandown Sports Club
Esher Common
Oxshott Heath
Arbrook Common
Claygate Common
Prince's Coverts
Milbournehold Wood
Stokesheath Farm Cottages
Reed's Sch.
Rowan Prep. Sch.
Claygate Prim. Sch.
Milbourne Lodge Senior School
Esher C of E Prim. Sch.
Esher C of E High School
Claygate
Oxshott
A244
A307
A3
B280

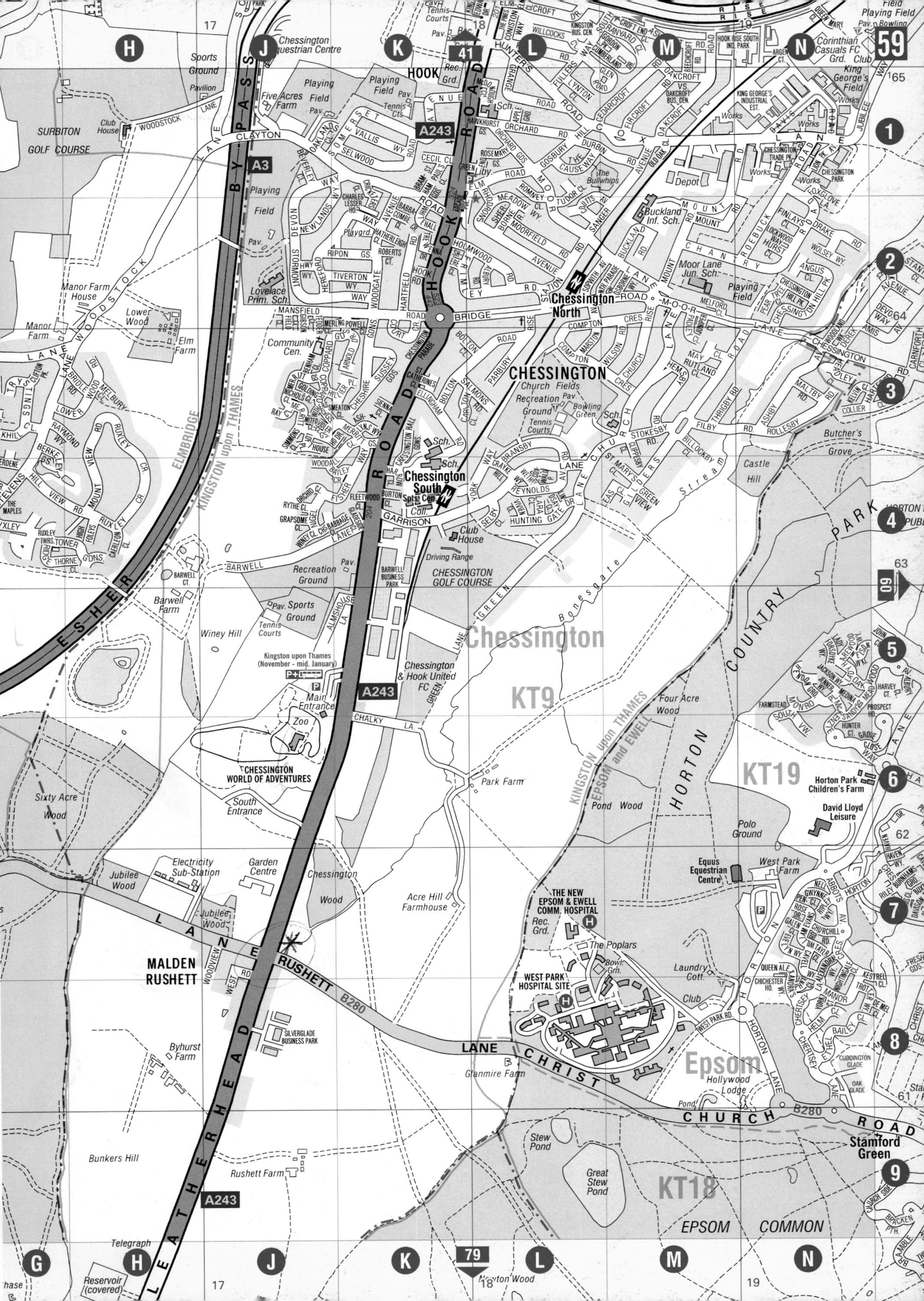

59
HOOK
CHESSINGTON
Chessington North
Chessington South
Chessington
KT9
KT19
KT18
Epsom
EPSOM COMMON
HORTON COUNTRY PARK
SURBITON GOLF COURSE
CHESSINGTON GOLF COURSE
CHESSINGTON WORLD OF ADVENTURES
MALDEN RUSHETT
ESHER BY-PASS
LEATHERHEAD ROAD
HOOK ROAD
A3
A243
B280
41
60
79

60
Chessington
KT9
Hogsmill River
KINGSTON upon THAMES
KINGSTON ROAD
A240
42
Cuddington Recreation Ground
Beverley Brook
King George's Field
Auriol Park
Riverview C of E Prim. Sch.
Dragons Hlth. Club
Sports Ground
STONELEIGH
Stoneleigh
RUXLEY LANE
B284
Epsom & Ewell High Sch.
West Ewell Inf. Sch.
Playing Field
Ewell Ct. Park
BEGGAR'S HILL
KT17
CHESSINGTON ROAD
B2200
Butcher's Grove
HORTON PARK COUNTRY CLUB (PUBLIC) GOLF COURSE
HORTON COUNTRY PARK
Gt. Wood
59
Driving Range
Hook Road Arena
The Harrier Cen.
Hogsmill River
Chamber Mead
WEST EWELL
ORGAN CROSSROADS
LONDON ROAD
EWELL BY-PASS
A24
St. Ebba's Farm Cottage
Cemetery
Playing Field
Playing Fields
Ewell West
Bourne Hall Mus.
Ewell Castle Jun. Sch.
Ewell Castle Senior Sch.
KT19
ST. EBBA'S
EWELL
Hatch Furlong
Horton Farm
HORTON
David Lloyd Leisure
Gibraltar Rec. Grd.
Epsom
Ewell East
Priest Hill Cotts.
Nescot Sports Centre
NESCOT (North East Surrey College of Technology)
Southfield Park Prim. Sch.
Sports Ground
Glyn Tech. Sch.
Supermarket
Sewage Wks.
Youth Cen.
LONGMEAD BUSINESS CEN.
NONSUCH TRAD. EST.
EPSOM BUS. PK.
A24
Sports Club
Stamford Green Prim. Sch.
Court Recreation Grd.
201
Rainbow Leisure Centre
EAST ST.
EPSOM RD.
REIGATE ROAD
Wallace Fields Jun. Sch.
Alexandra Rec. Grd.
Playing Field
CHURCH ROAD WEST
B280
Stamford Green
Kingswood Ho. Sch.
Epsom
HIGH ST.
UP. HIGH ST.
ALEXANDRA ROAD
A2022
KT18
Ashley Centre
EPSOM
St. Joseph's Cath. Prim. Sch.
80
The Downs Farm

61
NORTH CHEAM
43
Worcester Park
KT4
SM3
SM1
SM2
SM7
SUTTON
CHEAM
CHEAM PARK
NONSUCH PARK
Mansion House
Oak Plantation
Cheam Recreation Ground
Cheam Leisure Cen.
QUEEN VICTORIA
MALDEN ROAD
A2043
A24
A232
A217
A240
B2230
B2218
B283
ST. DUNSTAN'S HILL
HIGH ST
CHEAM ROAD
EWELL RD.
BELMONT RISE
BRIGHTON ROAD
COTSWOLD RD.
SUTTON LANE
BURDON LANE
THROWLEY WAY
ST. NICHOLAS WAY
Collingwood Road Recreation Ground
Sutton United FC
West Sutton
Perrett's Field
Seears Park
Water Wks.
Sutton Ckt. Grd.
Cheam
David Lloyd Leisure Cen.
Nonsuch High Sch.
Harefield Bri. Playing Field
Warren Fm.
Sports Club
Rugby Football Grd.
Sports Ground
Sutton
BELMONT
Belmont
Overton Grange Sch.
SUTTON HOSPITAL
THE ROYAL MARSDEN HOSP. (SUTTON)
EAST EWELL
Priesthill
Sports Centre
Priest Hill
LA Fitness
CUDDINGTON GOLF COURSE
BANSTEAD DOWNS
BANSTEAD DOWNS GOLF COURSE
Gally Hills Tumuli
Banstead
Golf Course
Club House
Reservoir (covered)
North Looe
The Looe
North Looe Farm
Banstead
81
The Cutting
WINKWORTH
HMP
62
29
63
64
65
23
24
525
26
H
J
K
L
M
N
G
1
2
3
4
5
6
7
8
9

A
B
C
D
E
F
G
44
82
61
1
2
3
4
5
6
7
8
9
26
27
28
29
Carshalton Athletic FC
Wrythe Rec. Grd.
Playing Field
Carshalton Coll.
Carshalton
CARSHALTON
SM1
A232
CARSHALTON ROAD
RUSKIN ROAD
HIGH ST.
ACRE LA.
WALLINGTON GRN.
LONDON RD.
MANOR ROAD
CROYDON
Westcroft Leisure Cen.
The Grove
Council Offices
Studio Thtre.
Boating Lake
Manor Gdn.
Grammar Sch.
St. Philomena's School
Heritage Cen.
Benhill Rec. Grd.
WESTMEAD
Manor Park
SUTTON
Sutton
Super-store
BRIGHTON ROAD
THROWLEY
The Frying Pan
CARSHALTON PARK
CARSHALTON WAR MEMORIAL HOSP.
GROSVENOR AVENUE
Wallington
BOUNDARY RD.
PARK LA.
Carshalton Beeches
GORDON RD.
Stanley Pk. Rec. Grd.
High Sch.
Play. Fld.
STANLEY PK. RD.
B271
B278
A237
WOODCOTE ROAD
Little Holland Ho.
Resrs (covered)
Tennis Cts.
SM2
THE CROSSWAYS
CARSHALTON BEECHES
CARSHALTON ON THE HILL
Offices
Banstead Mobility Cen.
ORCHARD HILL
Carshalton
SM5
Woodcote Green
High Sch. for Girls
Play. Fields
WOODCOTE GREEN
Nursery
SUTTON HOSPITAL
THE ROYAL MARSDEN HOSP. (SUTTON)
Play. Fld.
Seaton House Sch.
White Lodge
Biological Research Labs.
Diamond Riding Centre
OAKS TRACK
TELEGRAPH TRACK
LITTLE WOODCOTE ESTATE
Club Ho.
Driving Range
Oaks Sports Cen.
OAKS SPORTS CENTRE GOLF COURSE
THE OAKS PARK
WOODMANSTERNE LANE
Little Woodcote Farm
Little Woodcote Fm. Cotts.
LITTLE WOODCOTE
Old Lodge Farm
A2022
WOODMANSTERNE LA.
HMP DOWNVIEW
HMP HIGHDOWN
Fairlawn
REIGATE and BANSTEAD
SUTTON
Hunters Field Farm
Fairlawn Farm
Nursy.
April Cott.
Woodland Craft Centre
South Lodge
Lower Pillory Down
WOODCOTE PARK GOLF COURSE
The Oaks Farm
Caravan Park
Banstead
Rose Cott.
Hylands Nurseries
SM7
CROYDON A2022
Ruffet Wood
Hillside Cotts.
Sports Ground
Barn Grove
Nursing Ho.
Woodmansterne Primary Sch.
Big Wood
Playground
Coulsdon
CR5
New Lodge Farm
Woodcote Grove House
Orford Ho.
Woodcote Grove
Woodcote Farm
Club Ho.
CARSHALTON ROAD
COTSWOLD RD.

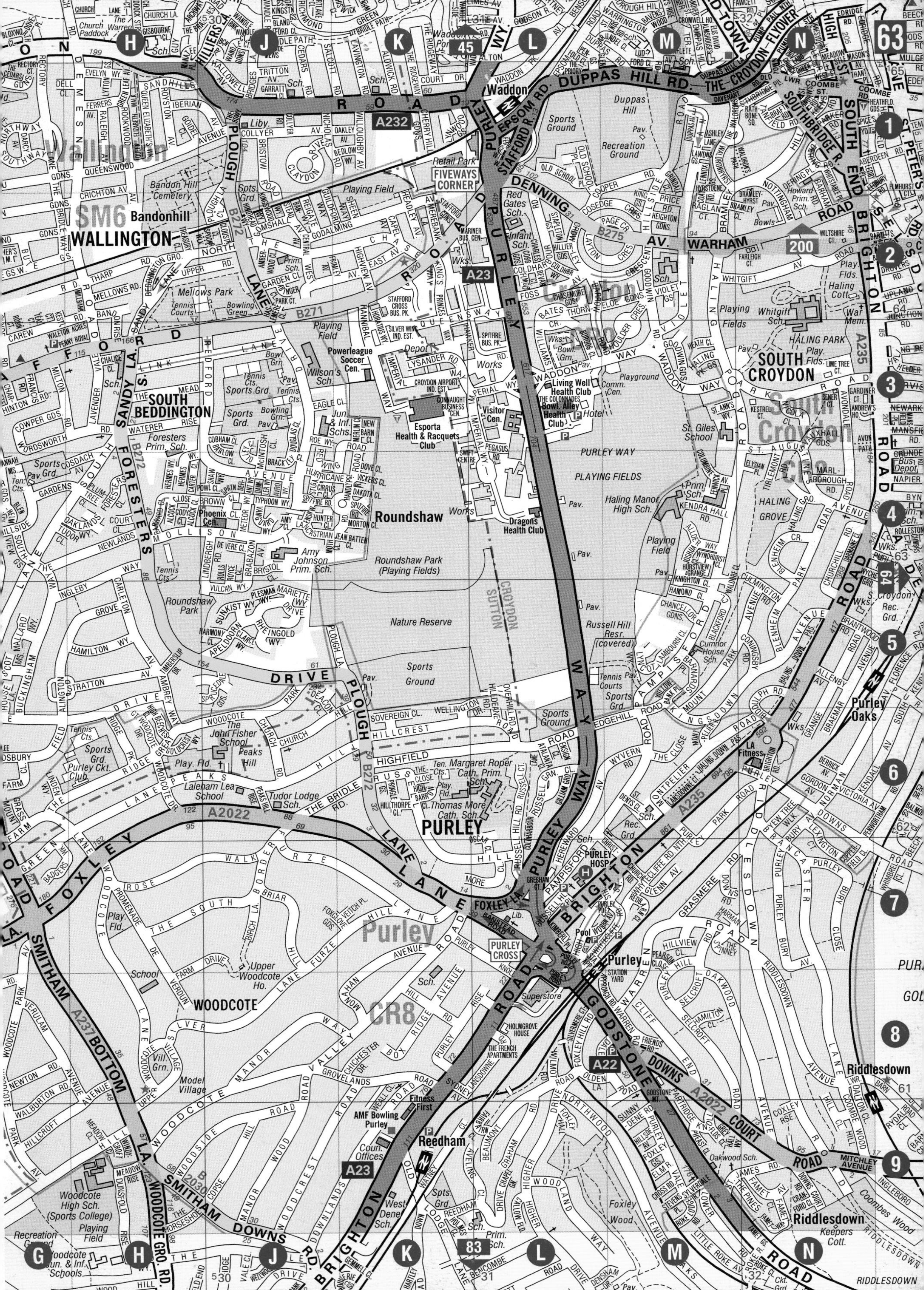

63
H
J
K
45
L
M
N
Waddon
DUPPAS HILL RD.
THE CROYDON FLYOVER
A232
ROAD
Duppas Hill
Recreation Ground
Sports Ground
Wallington
SM6
Bandonhill
WALLINGTON
Bandon Hill Cemetery
FIVEWAYS CORNER
Retail Park
Playing Field
PLOUGH LANE
B272
PURLEY WAY
A23
DENNING AV.
B275
WARHAM
200
STAFFORD R.
EPSOM RD.
Mellows Park
B271
STAFFORD RD.
Croydon
SOUTH BEDDINGTON
SANDY LA. S.
FORESTERS DRIVE
Foresters Prim. Sch.
Roundshaw
Roundshaw Park (Playing Fields)
Amy Johnson Prim. Sch.
Roundshaw Park
Nature Reserve
Sports Ground
CROYDON
SUTTON
Esporta Health & Racquets Club
Powerleague Soccer Cen.
Wilson's Sch.
Living Well Health Club
Bowl. Alley Health Club
Visitor Cen.
Dragons Health Club
PURLEY WAY PLAYING FIELDS
Haling Manor High Sch.
Playground
Russell Hill Resr. (covered)
SOUTH CROYDON
South Croydon
Whitgift Sch.
HALING PARK Play. Flds.
Playing Fields
St. Giles School
HALING GROVE
A235
BRIGHTON ROAD
SOUTH END
1
2
3
4
5
6
7
8
9
64
Purley Oaks
DRIVE
The John Fisher School
Peaks Hill
Laleham Lea School
Tudor Lodge Sch.
Sports Grd.
Purley Ckt. Club
A2022
FOXLEY LANE
PURLEY
Margaret Roper Cath. Prim. Sch.
St. Thomas More Cath. Sch.
PURLEY HOSP
Purley
PURLEY CROSS
Superstore
CR8
WOODCOTE
Upper Woodcote Ho.
Model Village
SMITHAM BOTTOM
A237
GODSTONE ROAD
A22
DOWNS COURT ROAD
A2022
Riddlesdown
MITCHLEY AVENUE
Coombes Wood
Fitness First
AMF Bowling Purley
Reedham
A23
BRIGHTON
West Dene Sch.
Foxley Wood
83
Woodcote High Sch. (Sports College)
Playing Field
Recreation Ground
SMITHAM DOWNS RD.
Woodcote Jun. & Inf. Schools
G
H
J
K
L
M
N
Keepers Cott.
RIDDLESDOWN

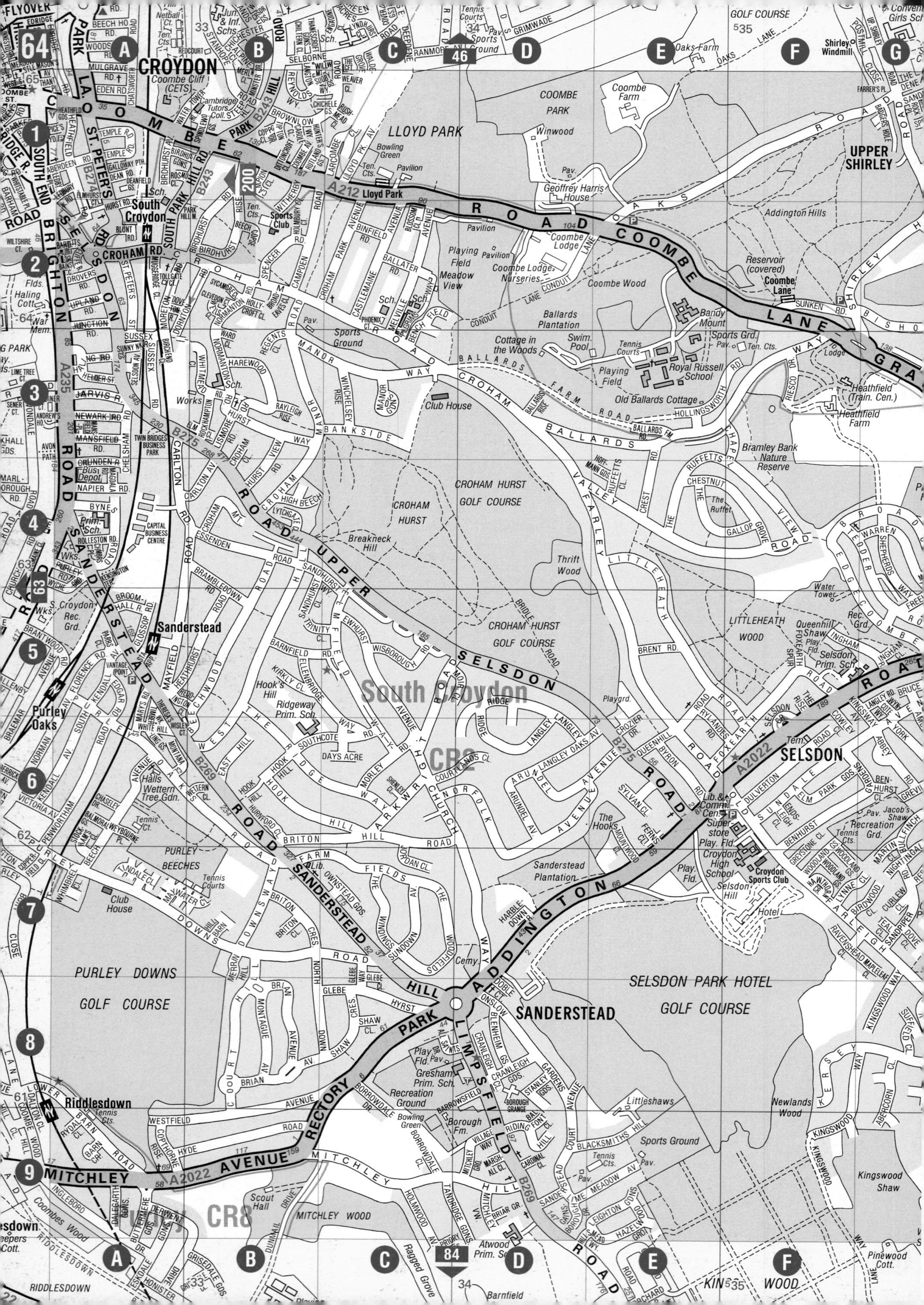
64
A
B
C
D
E
F
G
46
CROYDON
Coombe Cliff (CETS)
Cambridge Tutors Coll.
South Croydon
CROHAM RD.
COOMBE ROAD
COOMBE LANE
A212
Lloyd Park
LLOYD PARK
COOMBE PARK
Coombe Farm
Oaks Farm
GOLF COURSE
Shirley Windmill
UPPER SHIRLEY
Winwood
Geoffrey Harris House
Addington Hills
Coombe Lodge
Coombe Lodge Nurseries
Coombe Wood
Reservoir (covered)
Coombe Lane
Ballards Plantation
Bandy Mount
Sports Grd.
Cottage in the Woods
Swim. Pool
Playing Field
Royal Russell School
Old Ballards Cottage
Heathfield (Train. Cen.)
Heathfield Farm
Bramley Bank Nature Reserve
Playing Field Meadow View
Pavilion
Sports Club
Sports Ground
Club House
BALLARDS WAY
BALLARDS FARM ROAD
CROHAM ROAD
CROHAM HURST GOLF COURSE
CROHAM HURST
Breakneck Hill
Thrift Wood
LITTLEHEATH WOOD
Water Tower
Queenhill Shaw
Selsdon Prim. Sch.
UPPER SELSDON ROAD
B275
South Croydon
CR2
SELSDON
A2022
Lib. & Comm. Cen.
Croydon High School
Croydon Sports Club
Selsdon Hill
Hotel
Jacob's Shaw
Recreation Grd.
BRIGHTON ROAD
A235
SANDERSTEAD ROAD
B269
Sanderstead
S. Croydon Rec. Grd.
Purley Oaks
Hook's Hill
Ridgeway Prim. Sch.
DAYS ACRE
Halls Wettern Tree Gdn.
PURLEY BEECHES
Club House
PURLEY DOWNS GOLF COURSE
Sanderstead Plantation
The Hooks
ADDINGTON ROAD
SANDERSTEAD HILL
SANDERSTEAD
Cemy.
SELSDON PARK HOTEL GOLF COURSE
Newlands Wood
Kingswood Shaw
Littleshaws
Sports Ground
Gresham Prim. Sch.
Recreation Ground
Borough Fm.
LIMPSFIELD ROAD
RECTORY PARK
MITCHLEY AVENUE
Riddlesdown
Coombes Wood
Scout Hall
MITCHLEY WOOD
MITCHLEY HILL
CR8
Atwood Prim. Sch.
Ragged Grove
Barnfield
84
KINGS WOOD
Pinewood Cott.
RIDDLESDOWN
63
1
2
3
4
5
6
7
8
9

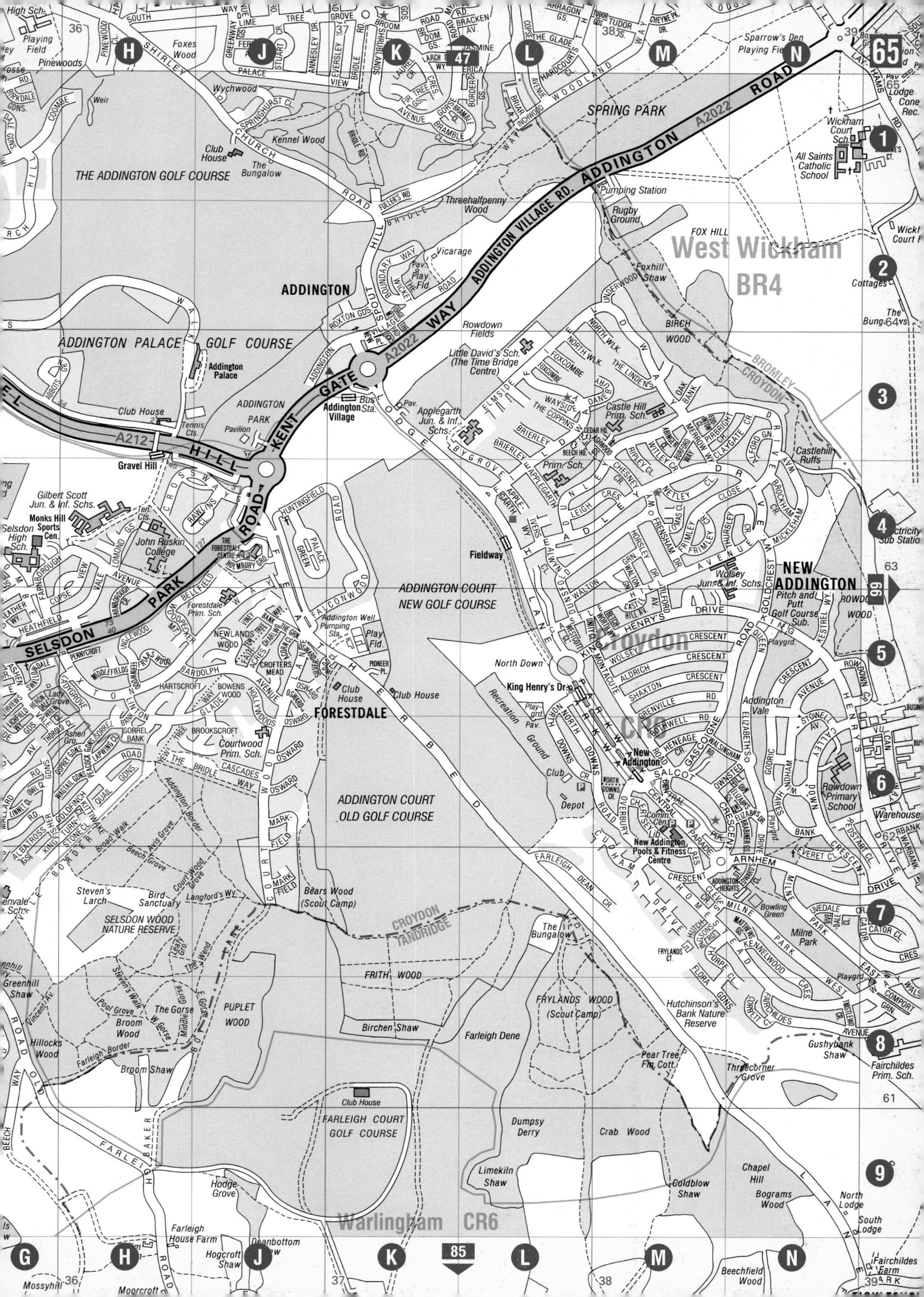

H
J
K
L
M
N
47
36
37
38
39
THE ADDINGTON GOLF COURSE
Kennel Wood
Club House
The Bungalow
Foxes Wood
Wychwood
SPRING PARK
ADDINGTON ROAD
A2022
Wickham Court Sch.
All Saints Catholic School
Pumping Station
Rugby Ground
Threehalfpenny Wood
FOX HILL
West Wickham
BR4
Foxhill Shaw
BIRCH WOOD
ADDINGTON
ADDINGTON PALACE GOLF COURSE
Addington Palace
ADDINGTON PARK
Addington Village
KENT GATE
ADDINGTON VILLAGE RD.
Rowdown Fields
Little David's Sch. (The Time Bridge Centre)
Applegarth Jun. & Inf. Schs.
Castle Hill Prim. Sch.
Castlehill Ruffs
A212
HILL
Gravel Hill
Gilbert Scott Jun. & Inf. Schs.
Monks Hill Sports Cen.
Selsdon High Sch.
John Ruskin College
SELSDON PARK ROAD
Fieldway
Wolsey Jun. & Inf. Schs.
NEW ADDINGTON
Pitch and Putt Golf Course
ROWDOWN WOOD
ADDINGTON COURT NEW GOLF COURSE
Addington Well Pumping Sta.
Forestdale Prim. Sch.
Club House
FORESTDALE
North Down
King Henry's Dr.
Croydon
CR0
Recreation Ground
Depot
New Addington
New Addington Pools & Fitness Centre
Rowdown Primary School
Addington Vale
Courtwood Prim. Sch.
ADDINGTON COURT OLD GOLF COURSE
Bears Wood (Scout Camp)
Steven's Larch
Bird Sanctuary
SELSDON WOOD NATURE RESERVE
CROYDON
TANDRIDGE
The Bungalow
FRITH WOOD
FRYLANDS WOOD (Scout Camp)
Milne Park
Bowling Green
Greenhill Shaw
PUPLET WOOD
Broom Wood
Birchen Shaw
Farleigh Dene
Hutchinson's Bank Nature Reserve
Pear Tree Fm. Cott.
Threecorner Grove
Gushybank Shaw
Fairchildes Prim. Sch.
Hillocks Wood
Broom Shaw
Club House
FARLEIGH COURT GOLF COURSE
Dumpsy Derry
Crab Wood
Limekiln Shaw
Coldblow Shaw
Chapel Hill
Bograms Wood
North Lodge
South Lodge
Hodge Grove
Farleigh House Farm
Hogcroft Shaw
Warlingham CR6
Beechfield Wood
Fairchildes Farm
85
1
2
3
4
5
6
7
8
9
61
62
63
64
65
66
G
H
J
K
L
M
N

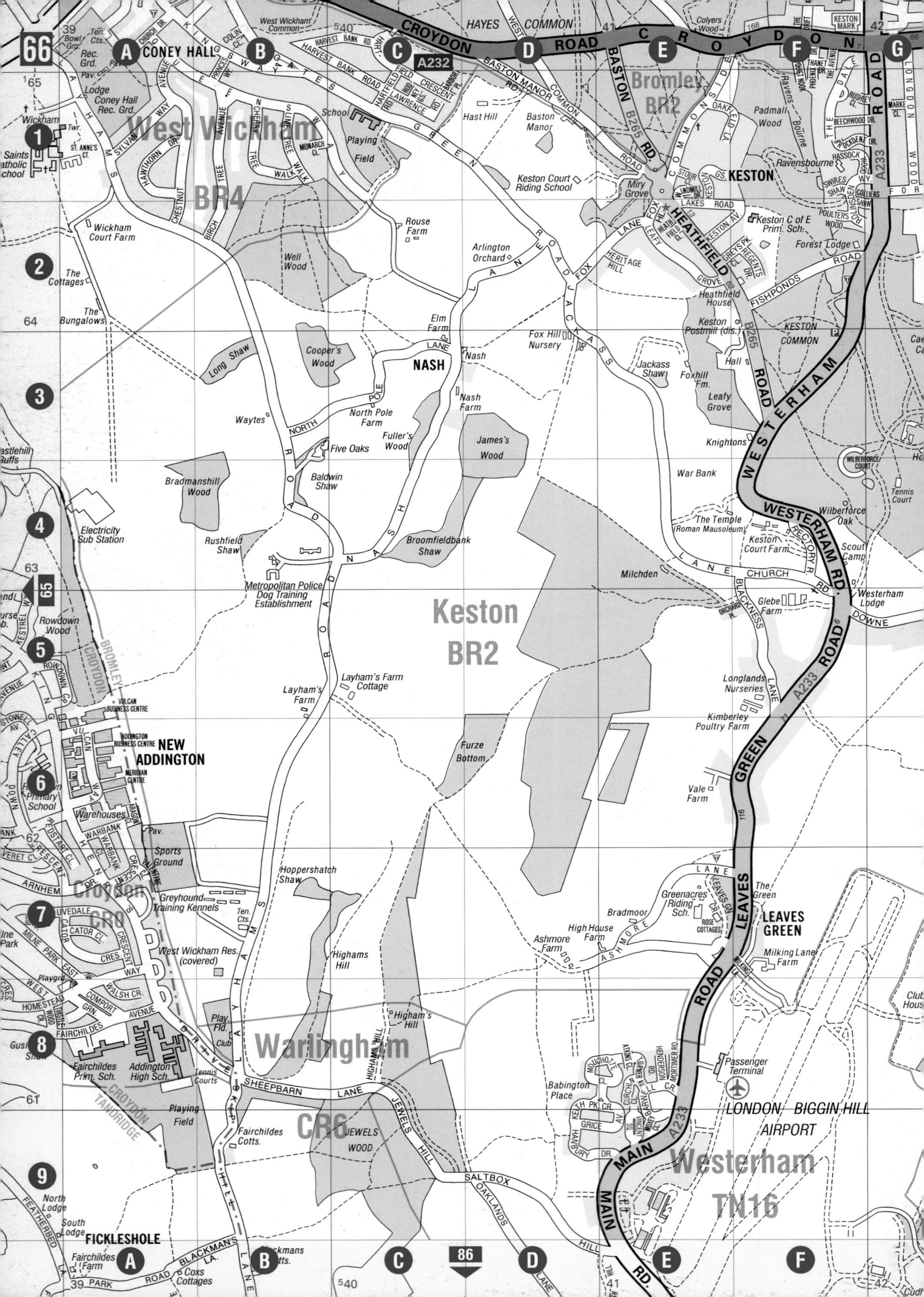
66
CONEY HALL
West Wickham
BR4
CROYDON ROAD
A232
HAYES COMMON
Bromley
BR2
KESTON
NASH
Keston
BR2
WESTERHAM ROAD
A233
NEW ADDINGTON
Croydon
CR0
Warlingham
CR6
LEAVES GREEN
LONDON BIGGIN HILL AIRPORT
Westerham
TN16
FICKLESHOLE
65
86

KESTON MARK
FARNBOROUGH
Orpington
BR6
Farthing Street
DOWNE
HAZELWOOD
Sevenoaks
TN14
GREEN STREET GREEN
HIGH ELMS COUNTRY PARK
HIGH ELMS GOLF COURSE
WEST KENT GOLF COURSE
CUCKOO WOOD
FARNBOROUGH COMMON
HIGH STREET FARNBOROUGH
SHIRE LANE
NORTH END LANE
HIGH ELMS ROAD
CUDHAM ROAD
LUXTED ROAD
SNAG LANE
CUDHAM LANE
The Princess Royal Uni. Hospital
Darrick Wood School
Down House and Darwin Museum
Christmas Tree Farm
Downe Bank Nature Reserve
High Elms Nature Cen.
Luxted
A21
A232
A223
B2158
87

68
48
88
YATELEY
DARBY GREEN
Cricket Hill
Yateley Common
YATELEY COMMON COUNTRY PARK
BLACKBUSHE AIRPORT
LONDON ROAD
A30
Hartford Bridge Flats
PENNY HILL CARAVAN PARK
Forest Lodge
GIBRALTAR BARRACKS
Parade Grd.
HORNLEY COMMON
Minley
MINLEY LANE
A327
B3013
West Minley Farm
YATELEY HEATH WOOD
MINLEY WOOD
Minley Manor
Water Tower
Minley Warren
Home Farm
Minley Farm
Pump House
Lower Minley Cottages
Linklater's Cottages
Blackbushes Farm
Oak Grove
Strip Plantation
Lichett Plain
BLACKBUSHES ROAD
Mallards Copse
Moor Copse
Tobridge Copse
Brook House
Fleet
GU51
GU17
M3
M3-MOTORWAY
Sewage Works
Broomhurst Farm
Broomhurst Wood
Practice Area
Ancels Copse
Bramshot Copse
New Plantation
The Bungalow
Island Copse
The Thorns
RSPB GREAT BRAMSHOTT RESERVE
Elvetham Heath Nature Reserve
ANCELLS BUSINESS PARK
Westfields Jun. & Inf. Schs.
Yateley School
Newlands Prim. Sch.
Heathlands Cemetery
Wyndham's Pool
Thriftswood
Hill Farm
Leafy Oak Farm
Cottage Farm
Hayward's Cottage
Picnic Area
Frogmore Community College
Potley Hill Prim. Sch.
Two Oaks Farm
Playing Field
Clark's Farm
Pond Fm.
READING ROAD
Blackwater Lodge
Grange Cottage
Works
BLACKBUSHE BUSINESS PARK

Oak Grove
49
Upper Lake
Yorktown Bridge
Lower
Shepherds Meadow
Government House
American Garden
Superstores
MARSHALL A321 ROAD
FROGMORE
BLACKWATER
Blackwater
YORK TOWN
GU47
GU15
Frogmore Inf. & Jun. Schs.
LONDON ROAD
A30
HAWLEY ROAD
BLACKWATER VALLEY A331 ROAD
Blackwater Park
Sewage Works
Filter Beds
Krooner Park (Football Grd)
Crabtree Park
Camberley Indoor Bowling Club
Superstore
Camberley
Starve Acre
Hawley Hill
HAWLEY
HAWLEY PARK
Hawley Park Farm
North Lodge
The Wood
Sports Ground
Almshouses
Hawley Prim. Sch.
Hawley Bridge
Hawley Place Sch.
All Saints Cottages
Junc. 4
Warehouse
HAWLEY COMMON
FOX LANE
Fernhill Sch.
Fernhill Prim. Sch.
M3 MOTORWAY
M3
Landing Stage
HAWLEY LAKE
Farnborough Grange Inf. Sch.
Hawley Lane
Farnborough Town FC
Grange Jun. Sch.
Pinewood Inf. Sch.
Running Track
Hawley Lake Stream
Guillemont Jun. Sch.
Farnborough
GU14
Manor Inf. & Jun. Schs.
Oak Farm Comm. Sch.
FARNBOROUGH
Sixth Form Coll. Farnborough
Playing Field
COVE
Cove Inf. Sch.
Cove Sch.
Cove Jun. Sch.
Recreation Ground
St. Bernadette Catholic Prim. School
Clodden Hole
WEST HEATH
QUEEN ELIZABETH PARK
Farnborough Main
LINK ROAD
Junc. 4a
A327
FARNBOROUGH RD.
A325
FLEET ROAD
89
70
The Watchetts Jun. Sch.
Bristow Inf. Sch.
Adult Educ. Cen.

70
A
B
C
D
E
F
G
87
88
89
90
50
Camberley
CAMBERLEY HEATH GOLF COURSE
CRAWLEY HILL
CAMBERLEY
TEKELS PARK
GU15
M3 MOTORWAY
M3
Camberley Heath Golf Course
Club House
HEATHERSIDE
FRIMLEY RIDGE
Carwarden House School
Ravenscote Jun. Sch.
Watchetts Rec. Grd.
Cricket Ground
Bowling Green
Tennis Courts
Putting Green
Watchetts Lakes
The Watchetts Jun. Sch.
Kings International College
Bristow Inf. Sch.
Southcote Park Nursery
Warren Wood
Camberley
Tomlinscote Sports Cen.
Tomlinscote Sch. and Sixth Form College
Tomlin's Pond
Playing Field
Jackpond Hill
FRIMLEY FUEL ALLOTMENTS
Reservoir (covered)
FRIMLEY PARK HOSPITAL
Frimley Park
FRIMLEY
PORTSMOUTH ROAD
CHOBHAM ROAD
FRIMLEY BY-PASS
A331
A325
B3411
B311
B3012
B3015
69
Prim. Sch.
Frith Ho.
Loen
The Grange
Ling Cottage
Factory
Comm. Cen.
Frimley
Sandringham School
FRIMLEY GREEN
Frimley Green Recreation Ground
Frimley C of E Jun. Sch.
St. Cross
Richmond Hill
Little Ingestre
Lakeland House
Four Acres
DEEPCUT
Dunedin
Toad Hall
Longwood
Wharfenden Lake
Lakeside Country Club
Frimhurst Cottages
Frimhurst
Frimhurst Farm
Deepcut Bridge
Frimley Aqueduct
Corry Hill
Frimley Lodge
The Drake Pavilion
Frimley Lodge Park
The Old Mill
Quainton
Cross Farm Inf. Sch.
Cross Fm.
Football Ground
Cemetery
BLACKWATER VALLEY ROUTE
Blackwater River
Farnborough
FARNBOROUGH GREEN
GU14
Farnborough North
Farnborough Hill School
Playing Field
North Farnborough Inf. Sch.
FARNBOROUGH STREET
Recreation Ground
St. Michael's Abbey
Sixth Form Coll. Farnborough
FARNBOROUGH ROAD
HAWLEY LA.
Warehouse
FRIMLEY BUSINESS PARK
RUSHMOOR
Mytchett Rec. Grd.
GUILDFORD ROAD
STURT ROAD
FRIMLEY GREEN ROAD
FRIMLEY ROAD
UPPER CHOBHAM ROAD
OLD BISLEY ROAD
FRITH HILL ROAD

51
91
92
93
H
J
K
L
M
N
G
1
2
3
4
5
6
7
8
9
72
60
59
58
57
56
Woking
GU24
WESTEND COMMON
(DANGER AREA)
PIRBRIGHT COMMON
CHOBHAM RIDGES
SURREY HEATH
GUILDFORD
Hagthorn Bog
Dog Hill
Great Bottom
Strawberry Hill
Brock Hill
Strawberry Bottom
Peatmoor Pond
Cockadobbin
Bending Oak
Straight Oak
Round Butt
Dean's Bottom
Colony Bog
Trulley Brook
Loveland's Hill
Stickle Down
High Hoglees
DANGER AREA
Hog's Back
Mainstone Bottom
Stickledown Range
Bisley Ranges
Hog Lees
Clock Tower
Running Deer Range
Cheylesmore Range
Mainstone Hill
PIRBRIGHT RANGES DANGER AREA
Cow Moor
BISLEY CAMP
(National Rifle Association)
No 1 Range
No 2 Range
No 3 Range
No 4 Range
Smith Range
Loyd Range
Running Track
Sports Ground
Pirbright Camp
Parade Gd.
Alexander Barracks
Elizabeth Barracks
Parade Ground
Lord Roberts Centre
Cowshot Mnr. Bri.
New Pond
BASINGSTOKE CANAL
Pirbright Junction
Stanley Pool
Manyuema
Furze Hill Camping Ground
Aruwimi Wood
Furzehill Place
Furze Hill
Mazamboni Farm
Stoney Castle Camping Ground
Holy Island
Ruwenzori Hill
FURZEHILL COTTS.
GRANGE RD.
CHURCH LA.
West Hall Farm
Hodge Brook
Pirbright Common
Hodge Bottom
Curzon Bridges
GOLE ROAD
B3012
STANLEY HILL
B3405
VAPERY
Club H.
MAULTWAY
B3015
DEEPCUT BRIDGE ROAD
Colony Gate
MINORCA AVENUE
MINORCA RD.
AISNE ROAD
Ten. Cts.
Pavilion
Sports Ground
DETTINGEN CRES.
DETTINGEN
Comm. Cen. GARDENS
Miniature Rifle Ranges
Blackdown Hill
NEWFOUNDLAND
BLACKDOWN
RLC Museum
Parade Ground
Tennis Courts
Sports Ground
Princess Royal Barracks
Tennis Court
Devil's Pound
Old Windmill Hill
Porridgepot Hill
Tennis Courts
BRUNSWICK ROAD
BASINGSTOKE CANAL
Frimley Lock
Heatherhurst Grange
Lodge Hill
GAPEMOUTH ROAD
Gapemouth Plantation
Rangelands Poultry Farm
Pine Ridge Golf Course
Club House
Driving Range
BISLEY ROAD
THE RIDGEWOOD CEN.
Heather Ridge Inf. Sch.
Playing Field
HEATHER RIDGE ARC.
Heatherside Corner
Redroad Hill
THE SPINNEY
B311
Pav.
Sports Ground
Running Track
JEFFERSON RD.
PIRBRIGHT CAMP
Parade Grnd.
UNION
PARLIAMENTARY RD
GEORGE ST
ARGYLE ST.
LOTHIAN RD.
MOORE RD.
ADAIR WLK.
GREENWOOD
NORTH
SOUTH
BEECH
COOPERS HILL DR.
SLADE
HERONS
ELCHO ROAD
QUEEN'S
Priest Lane
Hook La.

BISLEY
BISLEY COMMON
HMP COLDINGLEY
GU24
Miles Green
Staffordlake
KNAPHILL
Woking
BROOKWOOD
Brookwood
PIRBRIGHT
Bisley Camp
Cowshot Common
CHOBHAM GOLF COURSE
WEST HILL GOLF COURSE
WOKING PRIORY HOSPITAL
Brookwood Cemetery
Military Cemetery
Pirbright Common
GOAL FARM GOLF COURSE
Grindstone Handle Corner
Long Siberia Range
Short Siberia Range
Century Range
Bisley Ranges
Shorts Range
Cheylesmore Range
Basingstoke Canal
GUILDFORD ROAD
BAGSHOT ROAD
CONNAUGHT ROAD
BROOKWOOD LYE RD.
DAWNEY HILL
GRANGE ROAD
SCHOOL LANE
QUEENS ROAD
LUCAS GREEN ROAD
SURREY HEATH
GUILDFORD
WOKING
A322
A324
B3012
B3405
52
71
92

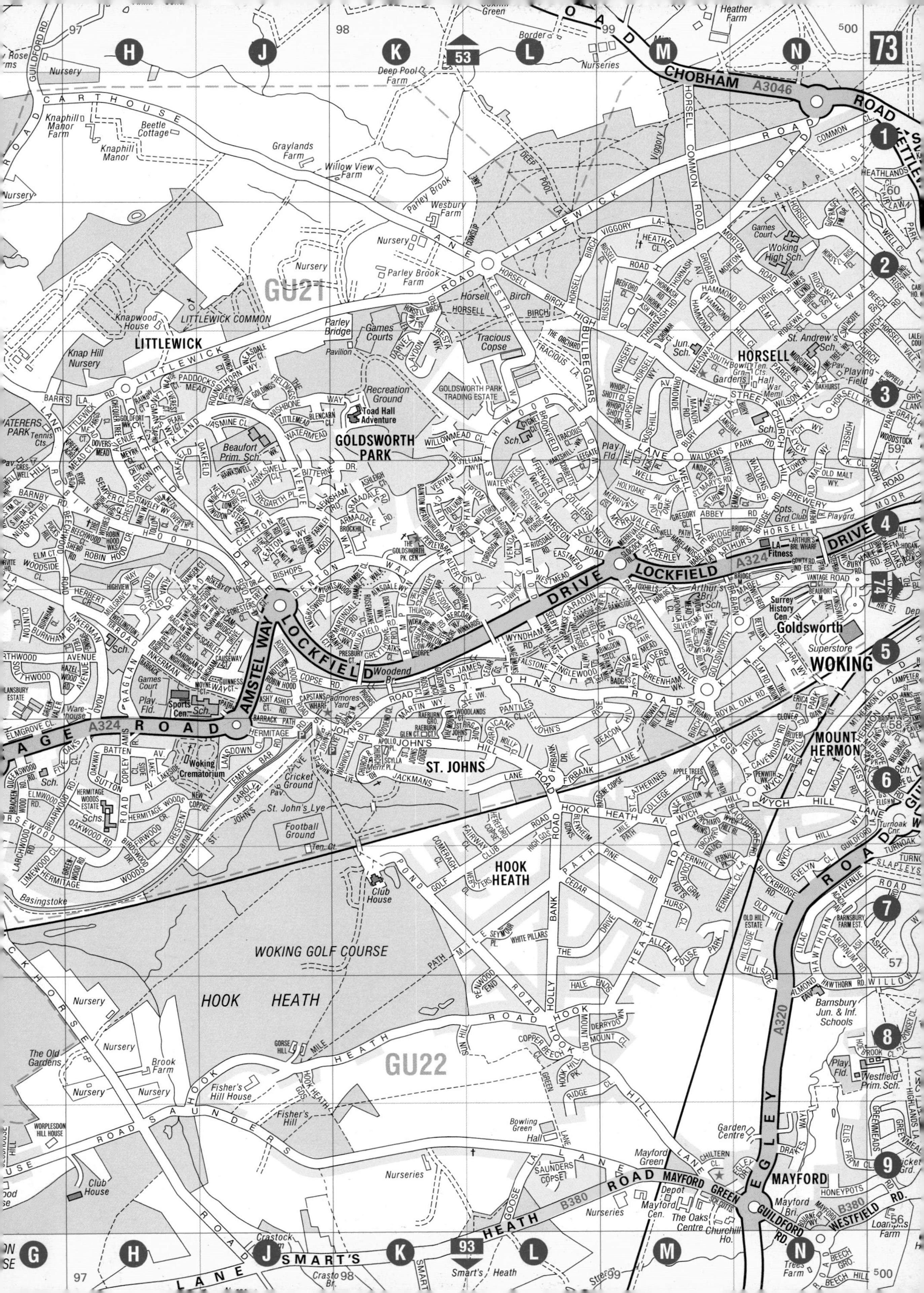

H
J
K
L
M
N
53
74
93
97
98
99
500
1
2
3
4
5
6
7
8
9
G
GU21
GU22
LITTLEWICK
LITTLEWICK COMMON
Knap Hill Nursery
Knapwood House
Knaphill Manor Farm
Knaphill Manor
Beetle Cottage
Graylands Farm
Willow View Farm
Parley Brook
Wesbury Farm
Parley Brook Farm
Deep Pool Farm
Heather Farm
Nurseries
Nursery
CHOBHAM ROAD
A3046
CARTHOUSE
LITTLEWICK ROAD
HORSELL COMMON ROAD
HORSELL
Woking High Sch.
St. Andrew's Sch.
Games Court
Jun. Sch.
Playing Field
Parley Bridge
Games Courts
Pavilion
Tracious Copse
GOLDSWORTH PARK TRADING ESTATE
Recreation Ground
Toad Hall Adventure
GOLDSWORTH PARK
Beaufort Prim. Sch.
THE GOLDSWORTH PK. CEN.
WATERERS PARK
Tennis Cts.
LOCKFIELD DRIVE
A324
AMSTEL WAY
LA Fitness
Surrey History Cen.
Goldsworth
Superstore
WOKING
MOUNT HERMON
ST. JOHNS
ST. JOHN'S ROAD
Woking Crematorium
Sports Cen.
Games Court
Play. Fld.
Cricket Ground
St. John's Lye
Football Ground
Club House
Basingstoke
Canal
HOOK HEATH
WOKING GOLF COURSE
HOOK HEATH ROAD
The Old Gardens
Brook Farm
Fisher's Hill House
Fisher's Hill
SAUNDERS ROAD
Bowling Green
Hall
Garden Centre
Mayford Green
MAYFORD
Mayford Cen.
The Oaks Centre
Churchill Ho.
Depot
SMART'S HEATH ROAD
B380
Smart's Heath
Crastock
Barnsbury Jun. & Inf. Schools
Westfield Prim. Sch.
EGLEY ROAD
A320
GUILDFORD RD.
WESTFIELD RD.
Loampits Farm
Turnoak Cnr.
WORPLESDON HILL HOUSE

HORSELL COMMON
SHEERWATER
WEST BYFLEET GOLF COURSE
GU21
GU22
WOKING
MAYBURY
KINGFIELD
OLD WOKING
WESTFIELD
CARTBRIDGE
HOEBRIDGE (PUBLIC) GOLF COURSE
Pyrford Common
Shey Copse
Monument Hill
Roundbridge Farm
Hoebridge Farm
Sewage Works
Oldhall Copse
Broad Mead
Broadmead Cut
River Wey Navigation
Riverdale Farm
Mill Moor
Sports Ground
Westfield Common
Loampits Farm
Woking FC (Kingfield Stadium)
David Lloyd Leisure
Kingfield Green
Woking Leisure Cen.
Pool in the Park
WOKING PARK
St. John the Baptist Catholic Comp. Sch. Woking
Woking College
Hoe Bridge Sch. (Pre-Preparatory)
New Monument School
Basingstoke Canal
Horsell Moor
Woking
Civic Cen.
Big Apple
Lion Retail Park
Mosque
Piggery
Club Ho.
Barnsbury Jun. & Inf. Schools
Westfield Prim. Sch.
Cricket Grd.
Nurseries
Little Moorlane Farm
Cartbridge House
Ashburton House
Hipley Bri.
Grave Yard
Play. Fld.
Running Track
Recreation Ground
Woodham Hall Estate
Kingsway Bus. Pk.
Sheerwater Bus. Cen.
Genesis Business Park
Woking Business Park
Monument Bus. Cen.
Maybury Est.
Hockering Estate
Elmbridge Estate
Tennis Courts
CHOBHAM RD.
SHORES ROAD
WOODHAM LANE
CHERTSEY ROAD
KETTLEWELL HILL
CHOBHAM RD.
VICTORIA WAY
MAYBURY HILL
GUILDFORD RD.
KINGFIELD ROAD
WYCH HILL LA.
HIGH STREET
BROADMEAD ROAD
SEND ROAD
WOKING RD.
OLD WOKING RD.
WESTFIELD ROAD
LOOP RD.
VICARAGE RD.
CARTERS LANE
HOCKERING RD.
PYRFORD ROAD
WOKING ROAD
A245
A320
A3046
A247
B380
B381
B382
A B C D E F G
1 2 3 4 5 6 7 8 9
54
73
94

75
WEST BYFLEET
55
West Byfleet KT14
Cannons Health & Leisure Club
Byfleet Lawn Tennis Club
TRADITIONS GOLF COURSE
RIDGWAY
PYRFORD
Woking
PYRFORD GREEN
PYRFORD GOLF COURSE
WISLEY GOLF COURSE
WISLEY
Sanway
M25
M25 MOTORWAY
The Royal Horticultural Society Gardens (Wisley Gardens)
PYRFORD VILLAGE
Newark Priory (Remains of)
River Wey
GU23
Dunsborough Park
RIPLEY
PORTSMOUTH ROAD
RIPLEY BY-PASS
A3
OCKHAM PARK
OCKHAM ROAD
Papercourt Sailing Club
Sewage Works
76
95

76
56
96
75
A
B
C
D
E
F
G
1
2
3
4
5
6
7
8
9
West Byfleet
BYFLEET
KT14
Byfleet Mill
Manor Farm Estate
Manor House
The Island
WOKING
Common Meadows
The Hangers
Queen Anne's Cottage
Queen Anne's Hills
Nursery
Park Barn Farm
Foxwarren Park
Red Hill
Home Farm
Driving Range
SILVERMERE GOLF COURSE
Thirty Acre Wood
REDHILL
St. George's Nursing Home
Hotel
Lodge
SEVEN HILLS RD. SOUTH
Feltonfleet Sch.
Play. Fld.
PAINSHILL
Pains Hill
A3
Long Orchard Farm
Belt Wood
Highlands Farm
ROAD
Heyswood Girl Guide Camp
The Broom
PAINSHILL PARK
Gothic Temple
Chinese Bridge
Grotto
The Lake
Waterwheel
Wheel Island
Tower Hill
Gothic Tower
Buxton Wood
Clearmount
M25 MOTORWAY
M25
WISLEY INTERCHANGE
Oak Pollard
Red Hill
WISLEY
Sports Ground
Tennis Courts
Wisley Common
Woolger's Wood
Junction 10
Pond Farm
Cockcrow Hill
Redhill Bottom
Chatley Wood
Sandpit Hill
Chatley Farm
RIVER MOLE
Chatley Cott.
The Bogs
Wren's Nest
WISLEY COMMON
Hut Hill Cottage
Hut Hill
Currie's Clump
OCKHAM COMMON
Breach Hill Wood
Chatley Heath
Telegraph Hill
Chatley Heath Semaphore Tower
Lodge Copse
Aberconway House
Stable Yard
Garden Cen.
Bolder Mere
ELMBRIDGE
GUILDFORD
Hatchford Wood
The Royal Horticultural Society Gardens (Wisley Gardens)
Battleston Hill
Oakham Village Green
Fellside Cottages
Woodside Cottage
Elm Cottage
HATCHFORD MANOR
Hatchford Park
Little Bridge
Nurseries
ELM CORNER
Wilderness Farm
Hunt's Copse
THE GARDENS
Hatchford End
Highfield Farm
Hatchford
Woking
GU23
Wisley Airfield (disused)
Tennis Courts
Orchard Farm
Hazeldene Farm
El. Sub. Sta.
Bridge End Farm
MARTYR'S GREEN
Pound Farm
May's Green
HYDE LA.
HATCH LA.
Little Upton Cottages
The Lodge
Upton Farm
Tanner's Copse
Old Rectory Farm
Bridge End
Trullibber Copse
Tankards
Chimneys
Church End
Chestnut Farm
Appstree Farm
Pavilion Recreation Ground
Chaffers Copse
OCKHAM ROAD
B2039
OCKHAM
Alms Heath
SCHOOL LA.
Hook Wood
Ockham Park
OCKHAM PARK
Guileshill Lodge
Tennis Court
Stumps Grove
Stumpsgrove Cottages
GUILESHILL LANE
REACH
NORTH
Blackmoor Farm
Guileshill Farm
LONG
Slade Farm
Ridings Copse
Slade Cottage
BARNSTHORNS WOOD
DRIFT GOLF COURSE
07
08
09
56
57
58
59
60

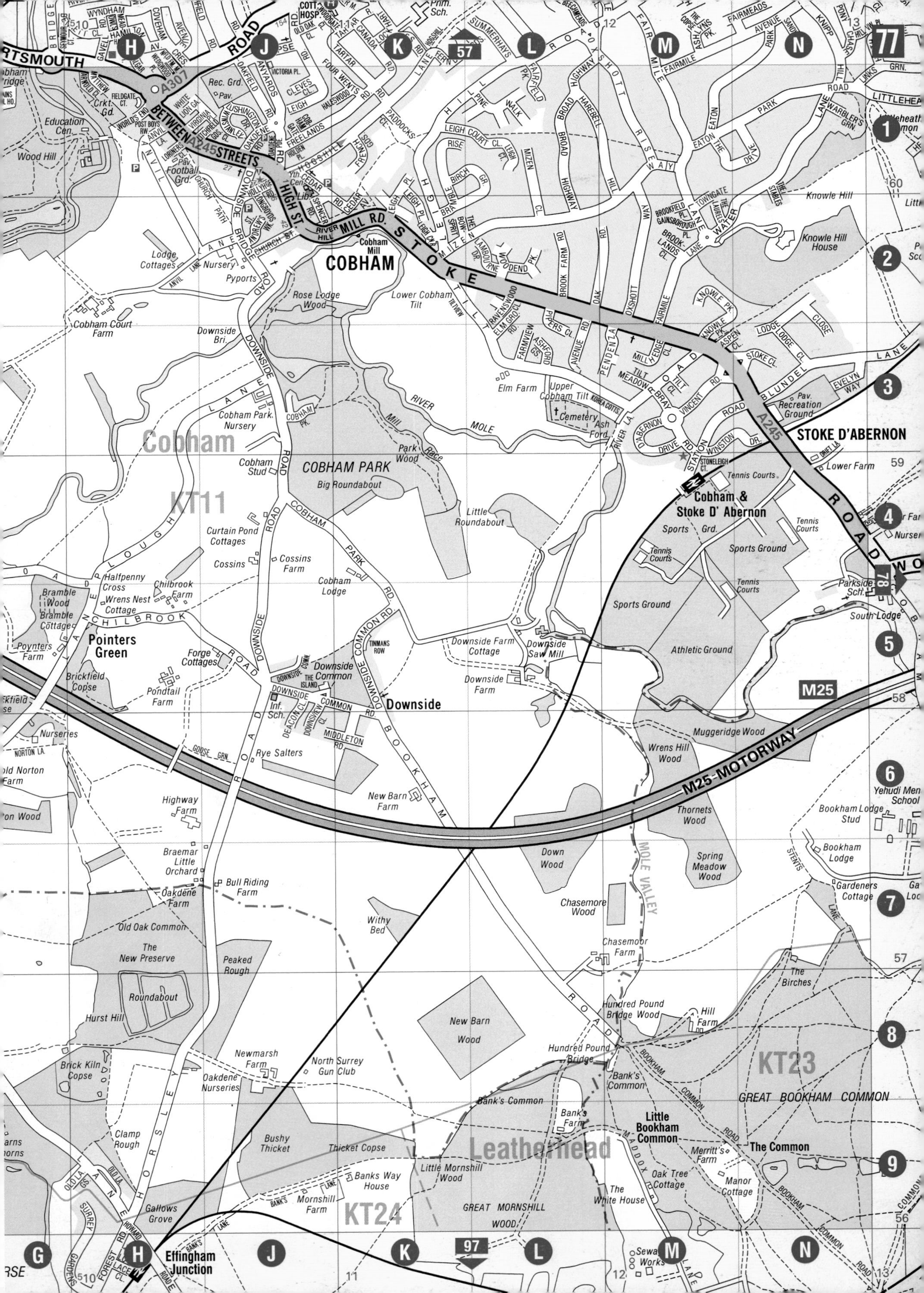

PORTSMOUTH ROAD
A307
BETWEEN STREETS
A245
HIGH ST.
MILL RD.
STOKE ROAD
COBHAM
Cobham Mill
Rec. Grd.
Pav.
Crkt. Gd.
Education Cen.
Wood Hill
Football Grd.
Lodge Cottages
Nursery
Pyports
Rose Lodge Wood
Lower Cobham Tilt
Cobham Court Farm
Downside Bri.
DOWNSIDE ROAD
Cobham Park Nursery
COBHAM PARK
Big Roundabout
Park Wood
RIVER MOLE
Mill Race
Little Roundabout
Cobham
KT11
Cobham Stud
Curtain Pond Cottages
Cossins
Cossins Farm
Cobham Lodge
COBHAM PARK RD.
Halfpenny Cross
Wrens Nest Cottage
Chilbrook Farm
CHILBROOK ROAD
Bramble Wood
Bramble Cottage
Poynters Farm
Pointers Green
Forge Cottages
Brickfield Copse
Pondtail Farm
Nurseries
NORTON LA.
Old Norton Farm
Downside Farm Cottage
Downside Saw Mill
Downside Farm
Downside Common
Downside
Inf. Sch.
DOWNSIDE COMMON RD.
MIDDLETON RD.
Rye Salters
GOOSE GRN.
New Barn Farm
Highway Farm
BOOKHAM ROAD
Braemar
Little Orchard
Bull Riding Farm
Oakdene Farm
Old Oak Common
The New Preserve
Roundabout
Peaked Rough
Hurst Hill
Withy Bed
Brick Kiln Copse
Newmarsh Farm
Oakdene Nurseries
North Surrey Gun Club
Clamp Rough
Bushy Thicket
Thicket Copse
Gallows Grove
HORSLEY ROAD
New Barn Wood
Banks Way House
Mornshill Farm
KT24
Little Mornshill Wood
GREAT MORNSHILL WOOD
Leatherhead
Effingham Junction
Elm Farm
Upper Cobham Tilt
Cemetery
Ash Ford
RIVER LA.
STOKE D'ABERNON
Recreation Ground
Lower Farm
Cobham & Stoke D'Abernon
Tennis Courts
Sports Grd.
Sports Ground
Athletic Ground
Parkside Sch.
South Lodge
Knowle Hill
Knowle Hill House
Muggeridge Wood
Wrens Hill Wood
Thornets Wood
M25
M25 MOTORWAY
Down Wood
Spring Meadow Wood
Chasemore Wood
MOLE VALLEY
Chasemoor Farm
Hundred Pound Bridge Wood
Hundred Pound Bridge
Bank's Common
Bank's Farm
Little Bookham Common
Hill Farm
The Birches
KT23
GREAT BOOKHAM COMMON
The Common
Merritt's Farm
Oak Tree Cottage
Manor Cottage
The White House
BOOKHAM COMMON ROAD
Sewage Works
Yehudi Menuhin School
Bookham Lodge Stud
Bookham Lodge
Gardeners Cottage
OXSHOTT ROAD
OXSHOTT RISE
FAIRMILE LANE
BLUNDEL LANE
WATER LANE
57
97
78
G H J K L M N
1 2 3 4 5 6 7 8 9

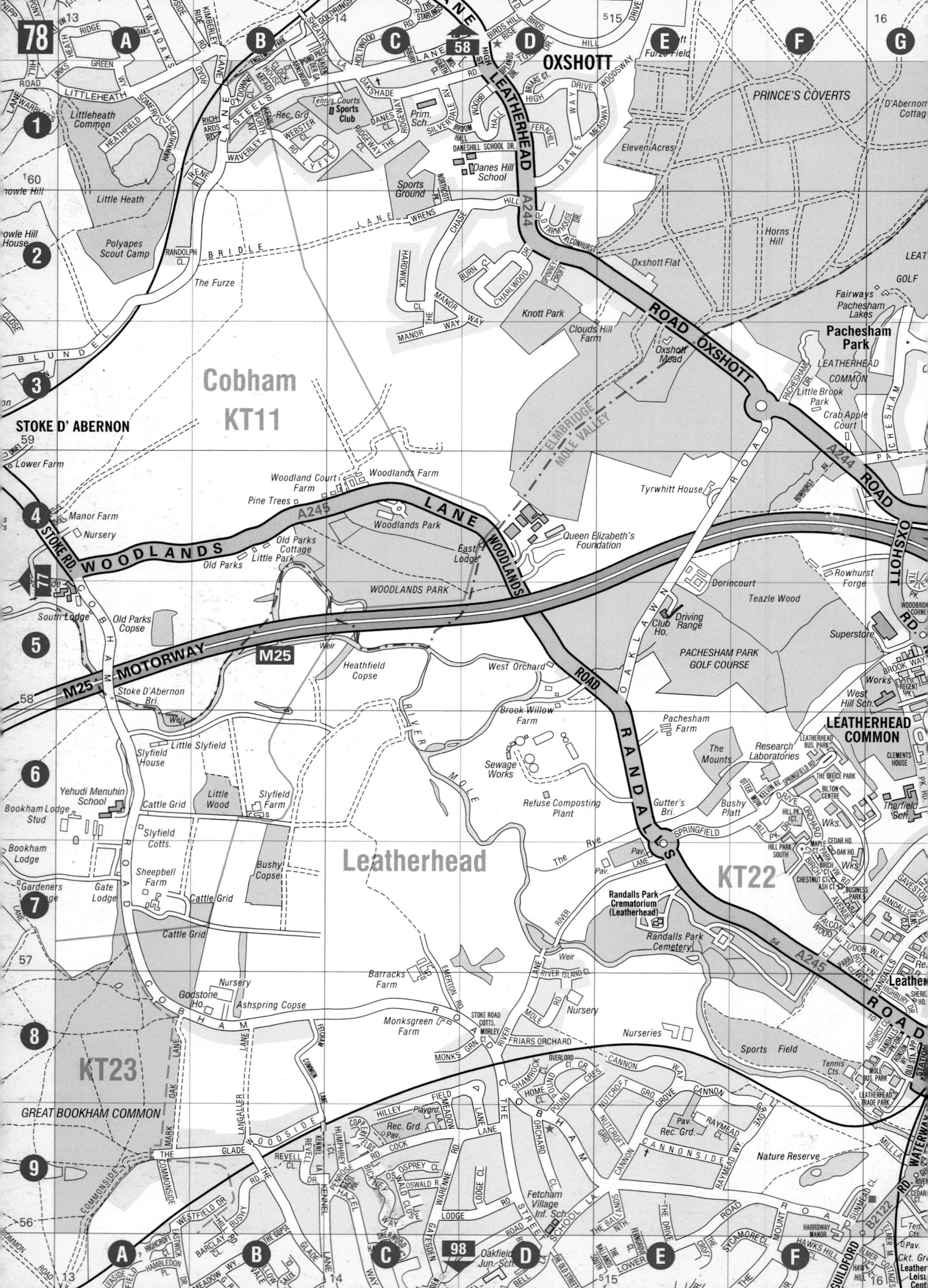
OXSHOTT
Cobham
KT11
STOKE D' ABERNON
Leatherhead
KT22
KT23
LEATHERHEAD COMMON
GREAT BOOKHAM COMMON
PRINCE'S COVERTS
Pachesham Park
PACHESHAM PARK GOLF COURSE
Littleheath Common
Little Heath
Polyapes Scout Camp
The Furze
Danes Hill School
Sports Ground
Knott Park
Clouds Hill Farm
Oxshott Mead
Oxshott Flat
Horns Hill
Eleven Acres
ELMBRIDGE MOLE VALLEY
Woodlands Farm
Woodland Court Farm
Pine Trees
Manor Farm
Nursery
Woodlands Park
Queen Elizabeth's Foundation
Old Parks Cottage
Little Park
Old Parks
East Lodge
WOODLANDS PARK
Old Parks Copse
South Lodge
M25 MOTORWAY
Heathfield Copse
West Orchard
Stoke D'Abernon Bri.
Little Slyfield
Slyfield House
Yehudi Menuhin School
Bookham Lodge Stud
Little Wood
Slyfield Farm
Cattle Grid
Slyfield Cotts.
Sheepbell Farm
Bushy Copse
Gate Lodge
Brook Willow Farm
Sewage Works
Refuse Composting Plant
Pachesham Farm
The Mounts
Research Laboratories
Bushy Platt
Gutter's Bri.
Randalls Park Crematorium (Leatherhead)
Randalls Park Cemetery
Tyrwhitt House
Dorincourt
Teazle Wood
Driving Range
Club Ho.
Rowhurst Forge
Superstore
West Hill Sch.
Therfield Sch.
Barracks Farm
Monksgreen Farm
Nursery
Godstone Ho.
Ashspring Copse
Nurseries
Sports Field
Nature Reserve
Fetcham Village Inf. Sch.
Oakfield Jun. Sch.
RANDALLS ROAD
OXSHOTT ROAD
LEATHERHEAD ROAD
WOODLANDS LANE
COBHAM ROAD
OAKLAWN ROAD
A244
A245
M25
B2122
58
77
98

H
J
K
59
L
M
N
17
18
19
Stew Pond
Telegraph Hill
LEATHERHEAD ROAD
A243
Reservoir (covered)
Chessington
KT9
KINGSTON upon THAMES
MOLE VALLEY
Newton Wood
THE FOREST
EPSOM COMMON
Epsom
KT18
EPSOM and EWELL
The Wells
THE CRESCENT
SPA DRIVE
WELLS HO.
WELLS
THE GREENWAY
COMMON SIDE
WARNEYS CL.
WOODLANDS ROAD
160
1
2
3
4
5
6
7
8
9
D'Abernon Ho.
EPSOM GAP
ASHTEAD COMMON
NATIONAL NATURE RESERVE
RHEAD
COURSE
Newton Wood
A24
DORKING RD.
BROADHURST
OVERDALE
CULVERHAY
Caen Wood
The Oaks
The Rye
Ashley Court
Hillthorpe
Paddock Lodge Stables
WOODS
Wood Field
ASHTEAD GAP
KINGSTON ROAD
A243
Trevona
Junction 9
Ashtead
KT21
ASHTEAD
LOWER ASHTEAD
Ashtead
ST. STEPHEN'S AV.
CRADDOCKS AV.
WOODFIELD LA.
BRAMLEY WAY
MEAD END
FOREST CR.
AVENUE
PETERS RD.
CHAFFERS
DEVITT CL.
CRAIGWELL
The Cottage in the Park
ASHTEAD PARK
ASHTEAD PARK
Island Pond
80
M25
M25-MOTORWAY
The Rye
LINKS
WARWICK GDNS.
TAYLOR
BROOKERS
RICHBELL CL.
SKINNERS
GLEBE RD.
CHURCH
OAKFIELD RD.
Rec. Grd.
Lib.
Tennis Courts
CLAVERTON
Ckt. Grd.
Hall
GREVILLE PK. AV.
POUND
THE STREET
EPSOM
RECTORY LA.
PARK LA.
ROOKERY HILL
Pav.
Playing Field
City of London Freemen's Sch.
Barnett Wood
HARRIOTTS
BARNETT WOOD
FARM
GLADSTONE RD.
OLDFIELD GDS.
HIGHFIELDS
SOUTH VIEW RD.
THE MEAD
Playing Field
Tennis Cts.
CRAMPSHAW
ALEXANDER GODLEY CL.
RALLIWOOD
OAKEN LANE
COPPICE LANE
GRAY'S
CHALK LANE
WARREN
Play. Field
Convent
St. Peter's Catholic Prim. Sch.
OTTWAYS LANE
TALEWORTH RD.
Prim. Sch.
ASHTEAD CAPIO HOSP.
WHITE LODGE
A24
A243
Junc. 9
BY-PASS RD.
PLOUGH INDUSTRIAL ESTATE
St. Andrew's Catholic Sec. Sch.
Downsend School
LEATHERHEAD ROAD
Chase Farm Stud
Playing Field
Milner Ho.
Offices
ERMYN WAY
THE CEDARS
GREEN LA.
STAG LEYS
KINGSTON ROAD
A245
Leatherhead Trinity Prim. School
Fairfield
Play. Fld.
Tennis Courts
St. John's Sch.
B2122
KNOLL R'BOUT
KNOLL ROUNDABOUT
BY-PASS ROAD
BULL HILL
LERET WY.
EPSOM
STATION R.
LEATHERHEAD HOSP.
Care Home
Woodlands Sch.
Leatherhead Trinity Prim. School
Rec. Grd.
A24
Epsom
KT18
Stane Street
PEBBLE LANE
M25-MOTORWAY
M25
HIGHLANDS RD.
B2033
REIGATE ROAD
HEADLEY ROAD
Highdale
LEATHERHEAD
Leatherhead FC Ground
Spts. Grd.
Thorncroft Manor
CHURCH ST.
DORKING RD.
B2450
B2430
Highlands Farm
99
G
H
J
K
L
M
N
56
57
58
59

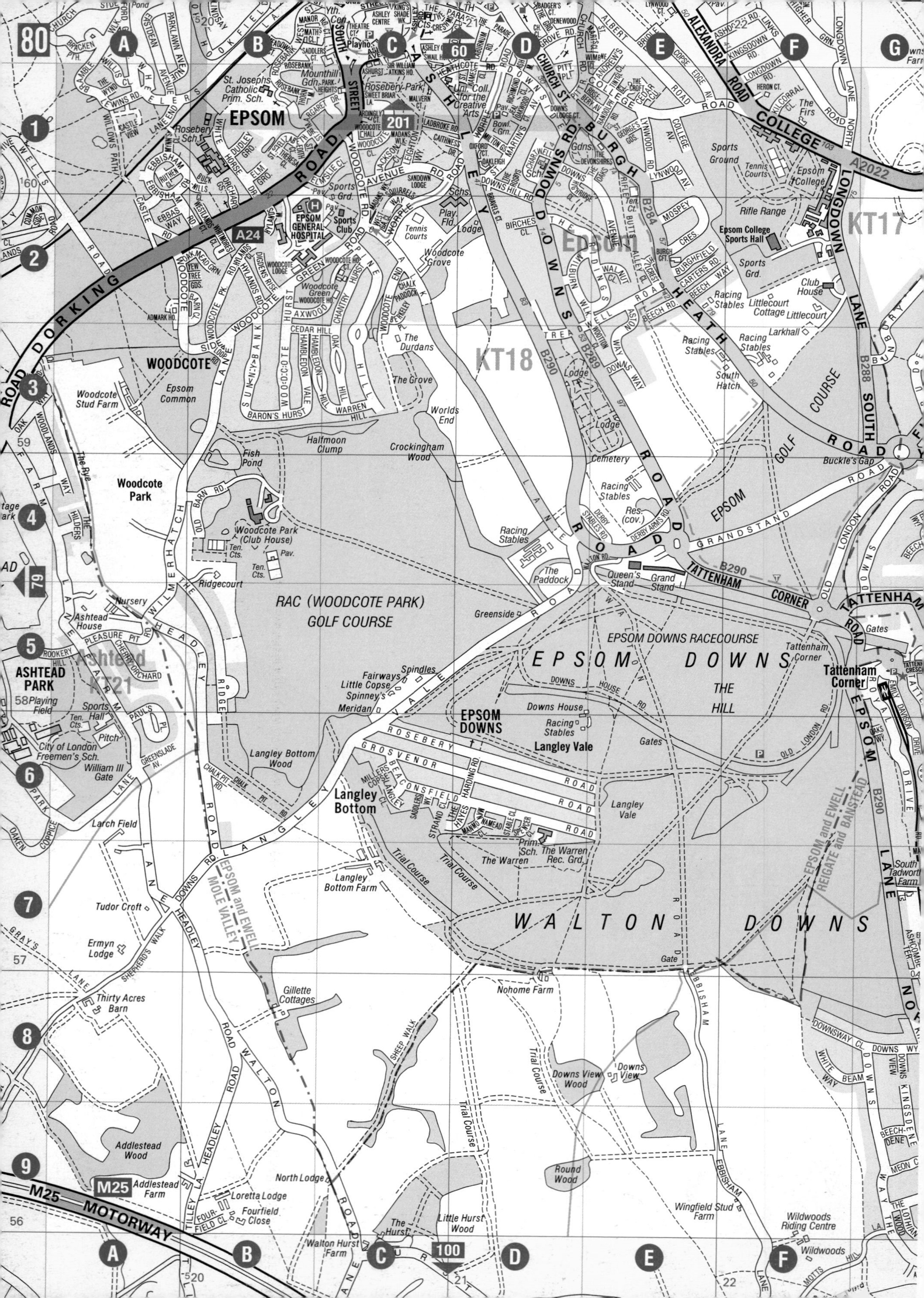

EPSOM
Epsom
KT18
KT17
KT21
WOODCOTE
Woodcote Park
Woodcote Park (Club House)
Epsom Common
Woodcote Stud Farm
Halfmoon Clump
Crockingham Wood
Fish Pond
Ridgecourt
RAC (WOODCOTE PARK) GOLF COURSE
EPSOM DOWNS RACECOURSE
EPSOM DOWNS
THE HILL
EPSOM DOWNS
Langley Vale
Langley Bottom
Langley Bottom Wood
Langley Bottom Farm
WALTON DOWNS
Tattenham Corner
Queen's Stand
Grand Stand
The Paddock
Racing Stables
Cemetery
Epsom College
Epsom College Sports Hall
Sports Ground
Rifle Range
EPSOM GOLF COURSE
Buckle's Gap
South Hatch
Worlds End
The Grove
The Durdans
Woodcote Grove
EPSOM GENERAL HOSPITAL
St. Josephs Catholic Prim. Sch.
Uni. Coll. for the Creative Arts
Rosebery Park
Mounthill Gdns.
ASHTEAD PARK
City of London Freemen's Sch.
William III Gate
Larch Field
Ashtead House
Nursery
Tudor Croft
Ermyn Lodge
Thirty Acres Barn
Gillette Cottages
Addlestead Wood
Addlestead Farm
Loretta Lodge
Fourfield Close
North Lodge
The Hurst
Little Hurst Wood
Walton Hurst Farm
Nohome Farm
Downs View Wood
Downs View
Round Wood
Wingfield Stud Farm
Wildwoods Riding Centre
Wildwoods
Trial Course
Greenside
Downs House
The Warren
DORKING ROAD
A24
COLLEGE ROAD
A2022
BURGH HEATH ROAD
B284
DOWNS ROAD
B290
B289
TATTENHAM CORNER
GRANDSTAND ROAD
LANGLEY VALE
HEADLEY ROAD
WALTON ROAD
EBBISHAM LANE
EPSOM LANE
LONGDOWN LANE SOUTH
B288
M25 MOTORWAY
EPSOM and EWELL
MOLE VALLEY
REIGATE and BANSTEAD
60
201
79
100
A B C D E F G
1 2 3 4 5 6 7 8 9

Banstead
SM7
Tadworth
KT20
BANSTEAD
NORK
NORK PARK
Great Burgh
TATTENHAM CORNER
BURGH HEATH
Tadworth Park
TADWORTH
KINGSWOOD
Furze Hill
Epsom Downs
Kingswood
Tadworth
REIGATE ROAD
BRIGHTON ROAD
WINKWORTH ROAD
FIR TREE ROAD
TATTENHAM WAY
TATTENHAMS WAY
WATERHOUSE LANE
OUTWOOD LANE
HIGH STREET
GARRATTS LANE
HOLLY LANE
BONSOR DRIVE
A240
A217
A2022
B2221
B2219
B2217
B2032
B2220
B290
B291
B284
B2218
RUFFETT WOOD
Pages Acre
Lambert's Shaw
Perotts Wood (Nature Reserve)
Canons Farm Cottages
Canons Farm
Reads Rest Cottages
Ambrose Cottages
Lunch Wood
Sports Ground
Perrotts Farm
Aberdour School
Canons Wood
Superstore
Tattenham Way Recreation Ground
Tumble Beacon
The Beacon Sch.
Nork Park Farm
Park Wood
Round Wood
Playing Field
Banstead Athletic FC Grd. & Epsom & Ewell FC
Marbles Pond
Lonesome Ponds
Garden Farm
Millennia Ho.
Masonic Hall
Training Cen.
Kingswood House
Workhouse Pond
Lady Neville Rec. Grd.
Cricket Grd.
Mint Farm
Nursing Home
Beecholme Recreation Gnd.
Rifle Range
The Cutting
H
J
K
L
M
N
G
1
2
3
4
5
6
7
8
9
61
82
101

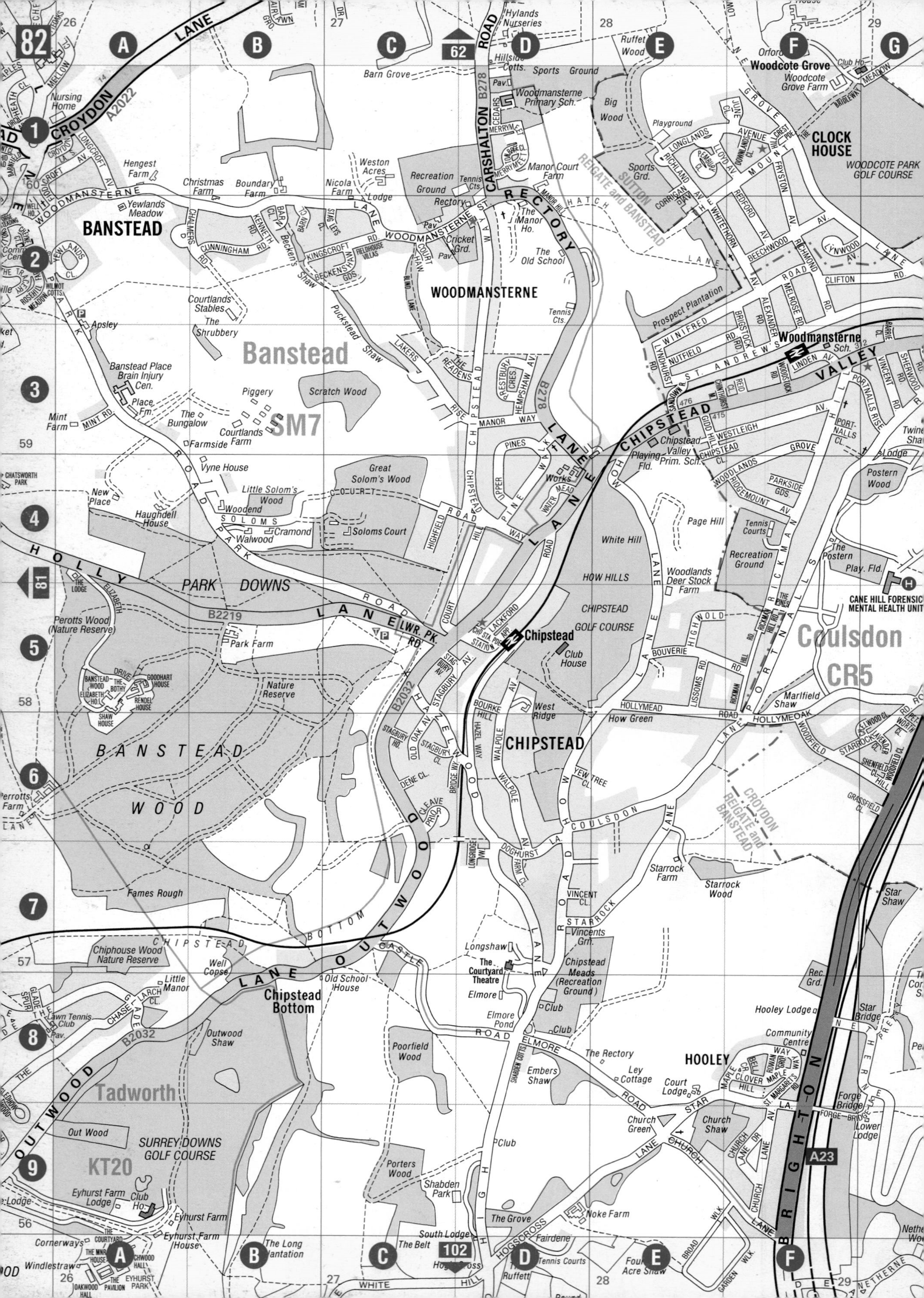
BANSTEAD
Banstead
SM7
WOODMANSTERNE
Woodmansterne
CLOCK HOUSE
WOODCOTE PARK GOLF COURSE
Woodcote Grove
PARK DOWNS
BANSTEAD WOOD
CHIPSTEAD
Chipstead
CHIPSTEAD GOLF COURSE
HOW HILLS
Coulsdon
CR5
CANE HILL FORENSIC MENTAL HEALTH UNIT
Chipstead Bottom
Tadworth
KT20
SURREY DOWNS GOLF COURSE
HOOLEY
The Courtyard Theatre
REIGATE and BANSTEAD
SUTTON
CROYDON
Hylands Nurseries
Recreation Ground
Great Solom's Wood
Scratch Wood
Perotts Wood (Nature Reserve)
Chiphouse Wood Nature Reserve
Starrock Wood
Porters Wood
Poorfield Wood
Out Wood
Fames Rough
HOLLY LANE
CHIPSTEAD VALLEY
RECTORY LANE
CARSHALTON ROAD
WOODMANSTERNE LANE
OUTWOOD LANE
BRIGHTON ROAD
A23
B2032
B2219
B278
A2022
62
81
102

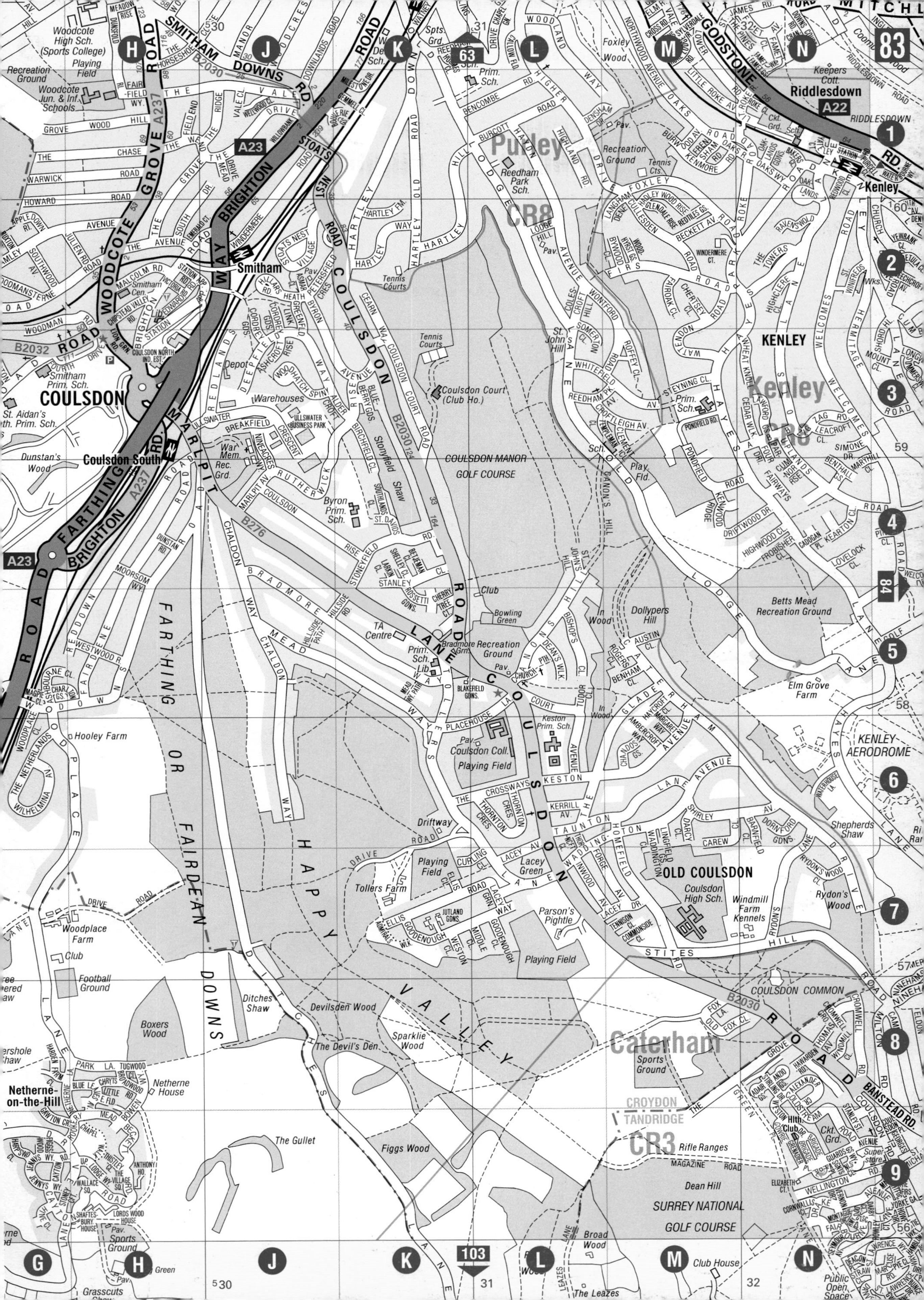

83
H
J
K
L
M
N
63
84
103
G
1
2
3
4
5
6
7
8
9
30
31
32
59
58
57
56
COULSDON
Smitham
Coulsdon South
Purley
CR8
KENLEY
Kenley
CR3
Riddlesdown
OLD COULSDON
Caterham
Netherne-on-the-Hill
CROYDON
TANDRIDGE
A23
A22
A237
B2030
B2032
B276
BRIGHTON ROAD
BRIGHTON WAY
WOODCOTE GROVE ROAD
SMITHAM DOWNS RD.
STOATS NEST ROAD
COULSDON ROAD
MARLPIT LANE
FARTHING WAY
FARTHING OR FAIRDEAN DOWNS
HAPPY VALLEY
GODSTONE ROAD
RIDDLESDOWN RD.
BANSTEAD RD.
COULSDON COMMON
COULSDON MANOR GOLF COURSE
SURREY NATIONAL GOLF COURSE
Coulsdon Court (Club Ho.)
Woodcote High Sch. (Sports College)
Woodcote Jun. & Inf. Schools
Smitham Prim. Sch.
Reedham Park Sch.
Keston Prim. Sch.
Coulsdon Coll.
Coulsdon High Sch.
Byron Prim. Sch.
Recreation Ground
Playing Field
Betts Mead Recreation Ground
Bradmore Recreation Ground
KENLEY AERODROME
Hooley Farm
Woodplace Farm
Tollers Farm
Elm Grove Farm
Windmill Farm Kennels
Netherne House
Devilsden Wood
Sparklie Wood
The Devil's Den
Figgs Wood
The Gullet
Boxers Wood
Ditches Shaw
Dean Hill
Rifle Ranges
Broad Wood
Dunstan's Wood
Dollypers Hill
Rydon's Wood
Shepherds Shaw
Parson's Pightle
Lacey Green
Foxley Wood
Stonyfield Shaw
Warehouses
Ullswater Business Park
Depot
Sports Ground
Football Ground
Club House
The Leazes
Public Open Space

84
MITCHLEY AV.
RIDDLESDOWN
Purley
CR8
Playing Field
Riddlesdown High Sch.
Scout Hall
MITCHLEY WOOD
64
Ragged Grove
Atwood Prim. Sch.
Barnfield Shaw
LIMPSFIELD
KINGS WOOD
Pinewood Cott.
Kingswood Shaw
A22
GODSTONE
Kenley
Ansley Berry Shaw
South Croydon
CR2
Dipsley's Shaw
B269
Sports Ground
Riding School
Kingswood Lodge
KENLEY
Rec. Grd.
Warehouse
Gasholder Sta.
Warlingham Sch.
Hamsey Green Jun. Sch.
Hamsey Green Inf. Sch.
Playing Field
Hamsey Green
Hamsey Grn. Play. Fld.
Kenley
CR8
Kenley Prim. Sch.
Warlingham Court Farm
Batts Farm
Kenley House
Tithepit Shaw
KENLEY COMMON
Whyteleafe Rec. Grd.
Putting Grn.
Sunnycroft Farm
83
Whyteleafe
Upper Warlingham
HILLBURY
B270
Tennis Courts
Sports Ground
WARLINGHAM
THE GREEN
CROYDON
TANDRIDGE
WHYTELEAFE
Joysons Hill
Sports Field
KENLEY AERODROME
Bryngwyn Farm
Whyteleafe FC Grd.
Reservoir (covered)
Coxes Wood
Whyteleafe
Flintfield House
Whyteleafe South
CR3
Blize Wood
Shepherds Shaw
Rifle Range
Little Manor
Little Wold
Windmill Shaw
Cottershill Shaw
MANOR PARK
WAPSES LODGE ROUNDABOUT
CATERHAM
Viaduct Lodge
Nursery
Cloisters
Playing Field
Audley Prim. Sch.
St. Francis Catholic Prim. Sch.
Sunnydown School
Burntwood Hill
Round Shaw
Birchwood House Farm
North Downs Farm
Caterham
de Stafford School
Sports Cen.
CR3
Recreation Ground
Stony Hill
Birchwood House
BIRCH WOOD
BANSTEAD ROAD
B2030
B2208
Caterham-on-the-Hill
BY-PASS
A22
CATERHAM
104
Westway Common
The Bushes
Worlds End
Public Open Space

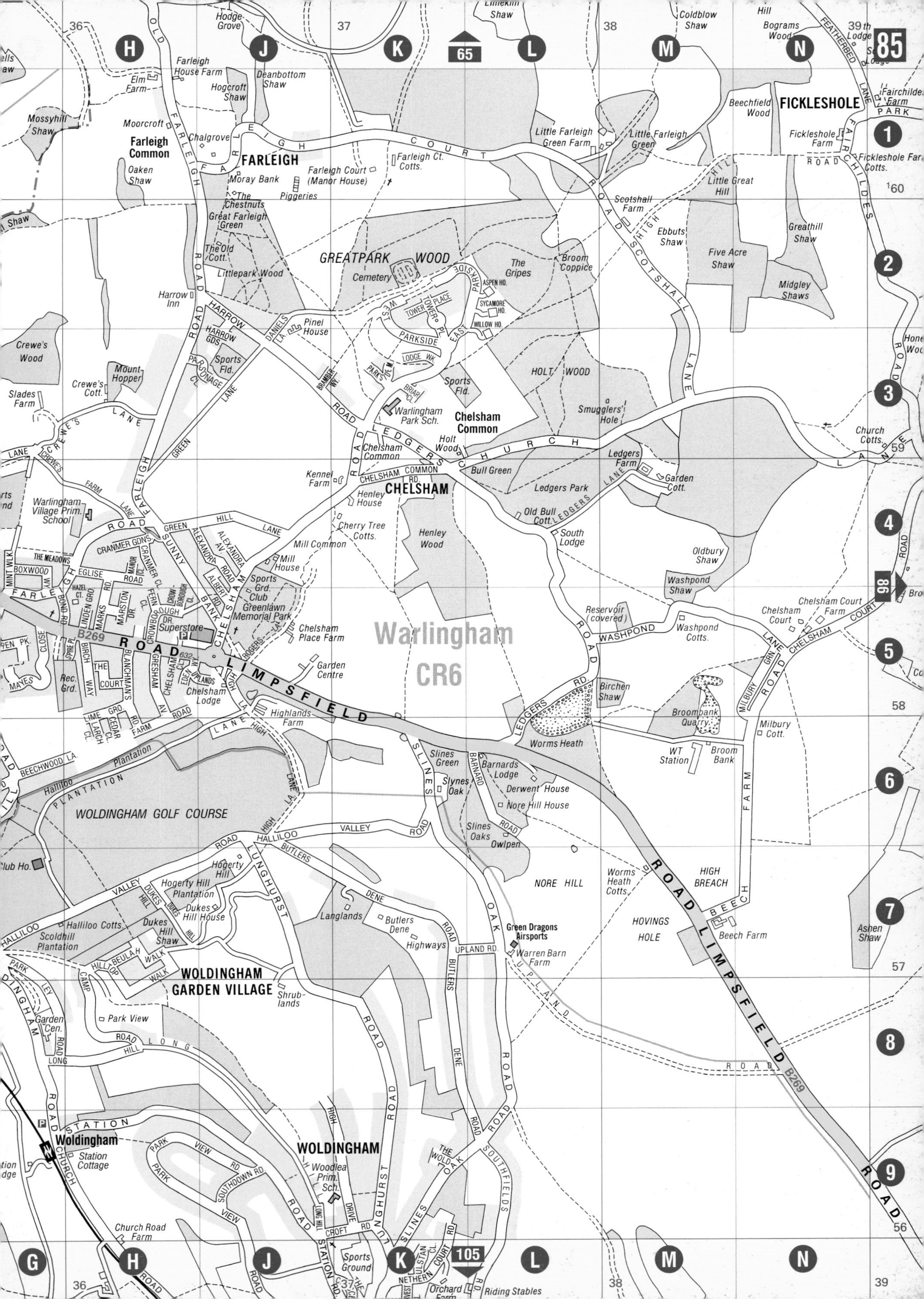
FARLEIGH
Farleigh Common
FICKLESHOLE
GREATPARK WOOD
Chelsham Common
CHELSHAM
HOLT WOOD
Warlingham
CR6
WOLDINGHAM GOLF COURSE
WOLDINGHAM GARDEN VILLAGE
WOLDINGHAM
NORE HILL
HIGH BREACH
HOVINGS HOLE
Woldingham
LIMPSFIELD ROAD
B269
Farleigh House Farm
Hogcroft Shaw
Deanbottom Shaw
Hodge Grove
Mossyhill Shaw
Elm Farm
Moorcroft
Chalgrove
Oaken Shaw
Moray Bank
Farleigh Court (Manor House)
Farleigh Ct. Cotts.
Piggeries
The Chestnuts
Great Farleigh Green
The Old Cott.
Littlepark Wood
Little Farleigh Green Farm
Little Farleigh Green
Scotshall Farm
Little Great Hill
Beechfield Wood
Fickleshole Farm
Fickleshole Farm Cotts.
Ebbuts Shaw
Five Acre Shaw
Greathill Shaw
Midgley Shaws
The Gripes
Broom Coppice
Cemetery
Harrow Inn
Crewe's Wood
Mount Hopper
Crewe's Cott.
Slades Farm
Pinel House
Sports Fld.
Warlingham Park Sch.
Smugglers' Hole
Holt Wood
Bull Green
Ledgers Farm
Garden Cott.
Ledgers Park
Old Bull Cott.
South Lodge
Church Cotts.
Kennel Farm
Henley House
Cherry Tree Cotts.
Mill Common
Mill House
Henley Wood
Oldbury Shaw
Washpond Shaw
Warlingham Village Prim. School
Sports Grd. Club
Greenlawn Memorial Park
Superstore
Chelsham Place Farm
Garden Centre
Chelsham Lodge
Highlands Farm
Reservoir (covered)
Washpond Cotts.
Chelsham Court
Chelsham Court Farm
Birchen Shaw
Broombank Quarry
Worms Heath
WT Station
Broom Bank
Milbury Cott.
Rec. Grd.
Slines Green
Slynes Oak
Barnards Lodge
Derwent House
Nore Hill House
Slines Oaks
Owlpen
Club Ho.
Hogerty Hill
Hogerty Hill Plantation
Dukes Hill House
Halliloo Cotts.
Scoldhill Plantation
Dukes Hill Shaw
Langlands
Butlers Dene
Highways
Green Dragons Airsports
Warren Barn Farm
Worms Heath Cotts.
Beech Farm
Ashen Shaw
Shrublands
Park View
Garden Cen.
Station Cottage
Woodlea Prim. Sch.
Church Road Farm
Sports Ground
Riding Stables
Orchard Farm
Plantation
Halliloo Plantation
HARROW ROAD
FARLEIGH ROAD
FARLEIGH COURT ROAD
SCOTSHALL LANE
CHURCH LANE
LEDGERS ROAD
CHELSHAM COMMON RD.
GREEN HILL LANE
WASHPOND LANE
CHELSHAM COURT ROAD
HALLILOO VALLEY ROAD
LUNGHURST ROAD
BUTLERS DENE ROAD
UPLAND RD.
SLINES OAK ROAD
SOUTHFIELDS ROAD
STATION ROAD
CHURCH ROAD
PARK VIEW RD
SOUTHDOWN RD.
LONG HILL ROAD
FARM ROAD
BEECH FARM ROAD
HIGH LANE
PLANTATION LANE
BEECHWOOD LA.
CREWE'S LANE
FARM LANE
SUNNY BANK
ALEXANDRA AV.
ALEXANDRA ROAD
CRANMER GDNS.
CRANMER CL.
EGLISE ROAD
BOXWOOD WY.
MINT WLK
THE MEADOWS
LINDEN GRO.
MARKS RD
MARSTON DR.
CROMBOROUGH DR.
BIRCH WAY
THE COURT
BLANCHMAN'S ROAD
GRESHAM AV.
LIME GRO.
CEDAR CL.
LARCH CL.
PARKSIDE
TOWER PLACE
LODGE WK
DANIELS LA.
FEATHERBED LANE
FAIRCHILDES ROAD
HONE WOOD ROAD
MILBURY GRN.
UPLANDS
ROGERS LA.
36
37
38
39
1
2
3
4
5
6
7
8
9
56
57
58
59
60
H
J
K
L
M
N
G
65
86
105

86
FICKLESHOLE
LONDON BIGGIN HILL AIRPORT
South London Aero Club
BIGGIN HILL
Warlingham
CR6
TATSFIELD
Tatsfield Green
MOLLARDS WOOD
MAIN ROAD
A233
Fairchildes Farm
Coxs Cottages
Blackmans Cotts.
Fickleshole Farm Cotts.
Skid Hill House
Skid Hill Farm
Honeyoak Wood
Church Cotts.
Broom Lodge Farm
Owls Wood
Cony Crook
White Bank
Cowyard Shaw
Beddlestead House
Forge Cott.
Beddlestead Farm
Culver Keys
Beddlestead Farm Cotts.
Lumberdine Wood
Ashen Shaw
Kitchen Grove
Cheverells Farm
Cheverells
PITCHERS WOOD
Works
Pitchers Copse Farm
Wireless Station
Jerry Reddins Shaw
Round Wood
Cherry Tree Shaw
Shepherds Shaw
Longlands Shaw
Glengarry
Sports Field
Furze Corner
Beaver Water World
Beacon Shaw
Clarkslane Shaw
Clarks Lane Farm
Norheads Farm
Norheads Farm Cotts.
Long Coppice
Oaklands Jun.Sch.
Oaklands Inf.Sch.
Jugg Hill
Airport Industrial Estate
Biggin Hill Business Park
Concorde Business Pk.
Cemetery
Recreation Ground
Library
Hall
Parsons Shaw
Farley Kennels
Isle Shaw
Gorsey Down Farm
Kingscote
Cedar Lodge
Lusted Hall Farm
Home Wood
Paynesfield Coppice
Limehouse Bottom
Colegates
Tatsfield Prim. Sch.
Playing Field
Church Farm
Club House
GOLF
NORTH DOWNS PARK WOOD
BROMLEY
TANDRIDGE
B2024
B269
CLARKS LANE
LIMPSFIELD RD.
Paygate
66
85
106
39
540
41
42
60
59
58
57
56

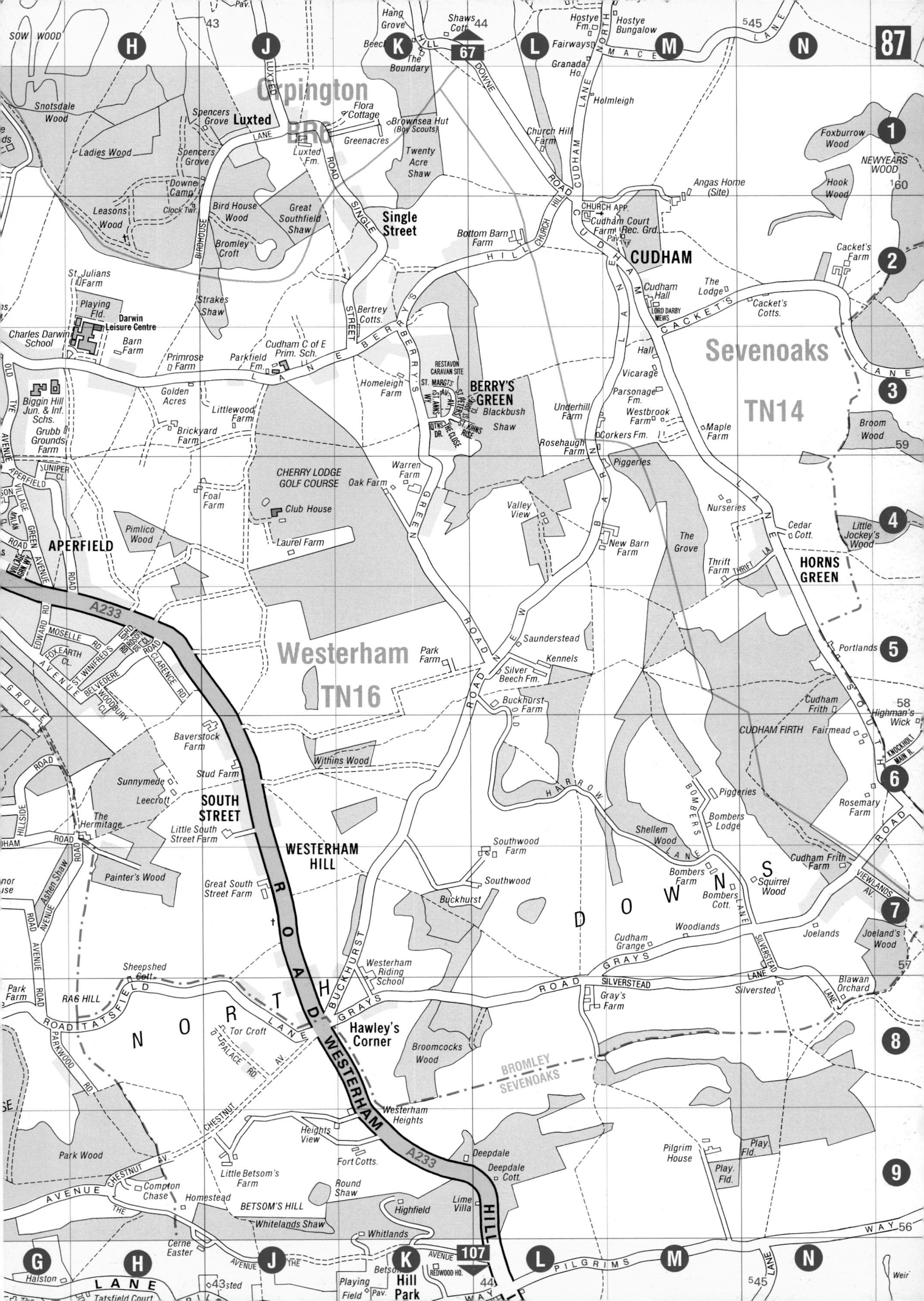

Orpington
BR6
Westerham
TN16
Sevenoaks
TN14
Luxted
Single Street
CUDHAM
BERRY'S GREEN
APERFIELD
HORNS GREEN
SOUTH STREET
WESTERHAM HILL
Hawley's Corner
CUDHAM FIRTH
NORTH DOWNS
BETSOM'S HILL
RAG HILL
Hill Park
BROMLEY
SEVENOAKS
A233
WESTERHAM ROAD
WESTERHAM HILL
PILGRIMS WAY
GRAYS ROAD
SILVERSTEAD LANE
CUDHAM LANE NORTH
CUDHAM LANE SOUTH
CHURCH HILL
BERRYS HILL
BERRYS GREEN ROAD
NEW BARN LANE
HARROW
BOMBERS LANE
CACKET'S LANE
MACE LANE
LUXTED ROAD
SINGLE STREET
BIRDHOUSE
DOWNE ROAD
TATSFIELD LANE
CHESTNUT AVENUE
PARKWOOD RD
Snotsdale Wood
Ladies Wood
Leasons Wood
Spencers Grove
Downe Camp
Bird House Wood
Great Southfield Shaw
Bromley Croft
Strakes Shaw
Flora Cottage
Brownsea Hut (Boy Scouts)
Greenacres
Luxted Fm.
Twenty Acre Shaw
Hang Grove
Shaws Cott.
The Boundary
Hostye Fm.
Hostye Bungalow
Fairways
Granada Ho.
Holmleigh
Church Hill Farm
Angas Home (Site)
Church App.
Cudham Court Farm
Rec. Grd.
Bottom Barn Farm
Foxburrow Wood
Newyears Wood
Hook Wood
Cacket's Farm
The Lodge
Cudham Hall
Lord Darby Mews
Cacket's Cotts.
St. Julians Farm
Playing Fld.
Darwin Leisure Centre
Charles Darwin School
Barn Farm
Primrose Farm
Parkfield Fm.
Cudham C of E Prim. Sch.
Bertrey Cotts.
Restavon Caravan Site
Homeleigh Farm
Blackbush Shaw
Underhill Farm
Hall
Vicarage
Parsonage Fm.
Westbrook Farm
Corkers Fm.
Maple Farm
Broom Wood
Biggin Hill Jun. & Inf. Schs.
Grubb Grounds Farm
Golden Acres
Littlewood Farm
Brickyard Farm
Rosehaugh Farm
Piggeries
Cherry Lodge Golf Course
Club House
Oak Farm
Warren Farm
Foal Farm
Pimlico Wood
Laurel Farm
Valley View
New Barn Farm
Nurseries
The Grove
Cedar Cott.
Little Jockey's Wood
Thrift Farm
Saunderstead
Kennels
Silver Beech Fm.
Park Farm
Buckhurst Farm
Portlands
Cudham Frith
Highman's Wick
Fairmead
Baverstock Farm
Withins Wood
Stud Farm
Sunnymede
Leecroft
The Hermitage
Little South Street Farm
Painter's Wood
Great South Street Farm
Shellem Wood
Bombers Lodge
Rosemary Farm
Southwood Farm
Southwood
Buckhurst
Cudham Frith Farm
Squirrel Wood
Bombers Farm
Bombers Cott.
Woodlands
Joelands
Joeland's Wood
Cudham Grange
Sheepshed Cott.
Westerham Riding School
Gray's Farm
Silversted
Blawan Orchard
Tor Croft
Broomcocks Wood
Westerham Heights
Heights View
Fort Cotts.
Park Wood
Little Betsom's Farm
Compton Chase
Homestead
Round Shaw
Highfield
Lime Villa
Deepdale
Deepdale Cott.
Pilgrim House
Play. Fld.
Whitelands Shaw
Whitlands
Cerne Easter
Halston
Playing Field
Redwood Ho.
Weir
Tatsfield Court
43
44
545
160
59
58
57
56
67
107
H
J
K
L
M
N
G
1
2
3
4
5
6
7
8
9

M3 MOTORWAY
Broomhurst Wood
Elvetham Heath Nature Reserve
Elvetham Heath
NORTH HANTS GOLF COURSE
Practice Area
Club House
Ancells Business Park
68
The Bungalow
Island Copse
Great Bramshot Farm
RSPB GREAT BRAMSHOT RESERVE
Little Bramshot Farm
FLEET ROAD
COVE ROAD
A3013
MINLEY RD.
B3013
Ancells Fm. Nature Reserve
Fleet
FLEET POND
(Nature Reserve)
Landing Stage
FLEET COMMUNITY HOSPITAL
Stockton Ho. Sch.
GU51
FLEET
KINGS ROAD
B3010
PONDTAIL
Pyestock
COBY TECHNOLOGY PARK
The Harlington Cen.
Fitness First
Oakley Park
Pav.
Cricket Grd.
READING RD. NTH.
READING ROAD
ALDERSHOT ROAD
A323
NORRIS HILL ROAD
BASINGSTOKE CANAL
Pyestock Hill
Pyestock Wood
Norris Hill West
Norris Hill East
Heatherside Inf. Sch.
Heatherside Junior Sch.
Fleet Inf. Sch.
Velmead Jun. Sch.
Fleet
Court Moor School Playing Field
GU52
Gelvert Bottom
Miles Hill
Miles Copses
Hussar Copses
Norris Hill Copse
Brock's Hill
Aunt's Pool
Aunt's Pool Hill
TWESELDOWN RACE COURSE
Tweseldown Hill
Parade Ring
Grandstand
Long Hill Copse
Cocked Hat Wood
Long Hill
Long Valley
Bickley Oaks
Bickley Moor
Outridden Hill
Chestnut Copse
Outridden Copse
RUSHMOOR
HART
GRANGE ESTATE (Caravan Site)
Rec. Grd.
CHURCH CROOKHAM
SOUTH ROAD
BEACON HILL
POTTERS IND. PARK
Sports Ground
Depot
Crookham Jun. Sch.
Tweseldown Inf. Sch.
Queen Elizabeth Barracks
Parade Grd.
Soanes Copse
Wood Copse
FLEET BUSINESS PARK
108
Greendane Copse
Bickley Copse
The Old Horns

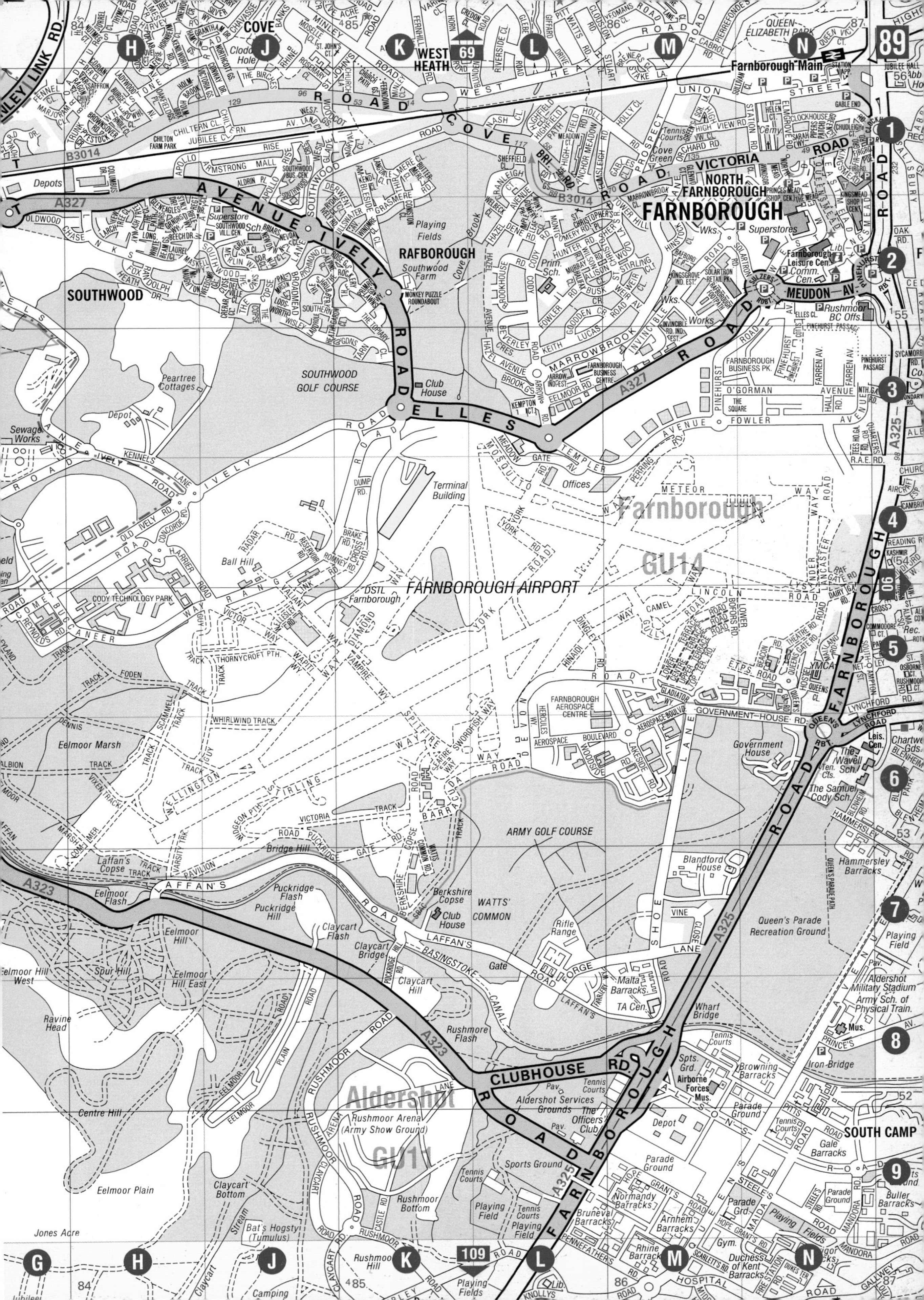

89
FARNBOROUGH
NORTH FARNBOROUGH
Farnborough Main
COVE
WEST HEATH
RAFBOROUGH
SOUTHWOOD
Farnborough
GU14
FARNBOROUGH AIRPORT
DSTL Farnborough
CODY TECHNOLOGY PARK
Terminal Building
SOUTHWOOD GOLF COURSE
Peartree Cottages
Sewage Works
Ball Hill
Eelmoor Marsh
Eelmoor Flash
Eelmoor Hill
Spur Hill
Ravine Head
Centre Hill
Eelmoor Plain
Jones Acre
Claycart Bottom
Bat's Hogsty (Tumulus)
Aldershot
GU11
Rushmoor Arena (Army Show Ground)
Rushmoor Bottom
ARMY GOLF COURSE
WATTS' COMMON
Government House
Queen's Parade Recreation Ground
Aldershot Military Stadium
Army Sch. of Physical Train.
Airborne Forces Mus.
SOUTH CAMP
Gale Barracks
Buller Barracks
Normandy Barracks
Bruneval Barracks
Arnhem Barracks
Rhine Barrack
Duchess of Kent Barracks
Browning Barracks
Malta Barracks
Hammersley Barracks
FARNBOROUGH AEROSPACE CENTRE
Aldershot Services Grounds
The Officers' Club
Farnborough Leisure Cen.
Rushmoor BC Offs.
Superstores
A327
A323
A325
B3014
IVELY ROAD
AVENUE
ELLES ROAD
VICTORIA ROAD
FARNBOROUGH ROAD
CLUBHOUSE RD.
LAFFAN'S ROAD
BASINGSTOKE CANAL
MEUDON AV.
LYNCHFORD ROAD
GOVERNMENT HOUSE RD.
QUEEN'S RBT.
69
109
90
H J K L M N
G H J K L M N
1 2 3 4 5 6 7 8 9
84 85 86 87

FARNBOROUGH STREET
FARNBOROUGH
St. Michael's Abbey
FARNBOROUGH PARK
GU14
Farnborough Coll. of Technology
Farnborough
SOUTH FARNBOROUGH
Salesian Coll.
South Farnboro' Jun. Sch.
South Farnboro' Inf. Sch.
King George's Field
Knellwood War Memorial Old People's Home
MYTCHETT
Mytchett Rec. Grd.
Mytchett Prim. Sch.
Leisure Park
Coleford Farm
The Jigsaw School
Linsford Business Park
Linsford Farm
Comm. Centre
MYTCHETT FARM CARAVAN PARK
Grove Farm
GROVE FARM PARK
Frimley Lodge Park
The Drake Pavilion
The Old Mill
Four Winds
Quainton
Camberley
Potters Pool
Playing Field
Basingstoke Canal Centre
GU16
Open Air Theatre
Camping Ground
Mytchett Place
Royal Army Medical Corps Museum
Mytchett Lake
Keogh Barracks
Holly Lodge Prim. Sch.
Carrington Recreation Ground
North Camp
Ash Vale
Ash Vale Junc.
Little Mytchett Flash
Sub-Machine Gun Range
Pistol Ranges
Scarp Hill
DANGER AREA
Great Bottom
Greatbottom Flash
Automatic Target Range
Furze Hill
Fox Hill West
ASH VALE
Steel Hill
Rifle Range No.1
Rifle Range No.2
Rifle Range No.3
Rifle Range No.4
Stony Hill
Pistol Range
ASH
Surprise Hill
Coronation Gardens
LAKESIDE PARK
The Gold Spring Lakes
Gold Farm
Hollybush Park
Aldershot Stubs
HOLLYBUSH INDUSTRIAL ESTATE
Lille Barracks
Marlborough Park
Marlborough Inf. Sch.
NORTH CAMP
Normandy Barracks
Ramillies Park
Sewage Works
GU11
Military Mus.
Hammersley Barracks
Wavell Ho. Playing Field
Sports Cen.
Running Track
Aldershot Military Stadium
Army School of Physical Training
Silvester Bridge
MONS BARRACKS
St. Omer Barracks
Parade Ground
SOUTH CAMP
Clayton Barracks
Buller Barracks
Alpine Ski Centre
Ash Lock
Gasworks
NORTH TOWN
Military Cemetery
Peaked Hill
Goose Green
The Samuel Cody Sch.
Chartwell Gds.
Leis. Cen.
BLACKWATER VALLEY ROUTE
A331
A325
A3011
B3411
B3165
B3166
B3206
LYNCHFORD ROAD
FARNBOROUGH ROAD
ALEXANDRA ROAD
MYTCHETT ROAD
FRIMLEY ROAD
VALE ROAD
BASINGSTOKE CANAL
Blackwater River
RUSHMOOR
SURREY HEATH
GUILDFORD
70
89
110
A B C D E F G
1 2 3 4 5 6 7 8 9
87 88 89 490
56 55 54 53 52

Gapemouth Plantation
GAPEMOUTH ROAD
Hodge Bottom
Stoney Castle Camping Ground
Mazamboni Farm
Holy Island
Ruwenzori Hill
HILL
GRANGE
FURZEHILL COTTS.
71
Rangelands Poultry Farm
Pirbright Common
Hodge Brook
West Hall Farm
No. 1 Range
Reservoir (Covered)
Longdown Hill
DANGER AREA
Vines Farm
Hazelac Hill
OLD GUILDFORD ROAD
No. 2 Range
Stoney Castle Ranges
Mortar Range
Woking
Tunnel Hill
ROAD
DANGER AREA
Emperor's Hill
Bowling Hill
SURREY HEATH
GUILDFORD
Mortar Range
GU24
Chair Hill
PLACE
Frimley Ridges
Hangman's Hill
Bush Bottom
ADMIRAL'S ROAD
RAILS
Mytchett Gate
Double Clump
Kiln Hill
Bridge Hill
The Bungalow
Rails Farm
Spur Hill
CLEYGATE COMMON
Scragley Hill
Oldfield Wood
PIRBRIGHT COMMON
Crown Prince Hill
Sheep Hill
Peat Moor
DANGER AREA
92
Romping Downs
Westwind
Foxholes Bottom
Peatmoor Pond
Ash Ranges
Long Hill
HENLEY
5
Henley Park Ranges
Lookout Hill
Longhill Bottom
Henleypark Lake
CLEYGATE COMMON
Peatmoor Hill
BADGER WALK
Pit Hill
Slyfield Wood
Bastion Hill
ROAD
HENLEY PARK
FOX HILLS
Whitepatch Hill
The Glen
Engineering Works
Guildford
Dukes Hill
Henley Park Farm
Whitepatch Bottom
Vine Farm
Henleypark Farm
GU3
WYKE COMMON
A324
Kiln Copse
Ricochet Hill
Withybed
Dolleyshill
DOLLEYSHILL CARAVAN PARK
HUNTS HILL ROAD
Hunts Hill
Normandy Hill
Normandy Lodge Farm
NORMANDY
Hunts Hill Farm
Cricket Grd.
Woodlands
Elm Hill
Normandy Common
NORMANDY COMMON LANE
Anchor Copse
ANCHOR CL.
Orchard Dene
Roughs Farm
Football Field
Normandy Pond
Rand's Plantation
PIRBRIGHT ROAD
SCHOOL LANE
A323
Fair View Farm
Gravelpit Hill
Slade Cottage
Sandpit Farm
NORMANDY
Wyke Prim. Sch.
GUILDFORD ROAD
WYKE CROSS
MARINERS DR.
GLAZIERS
UPPER PINEWOOD RD.
Wyke Heath Farm
111
NIGHTINGALE
KIRRIEMUIR GS.
Elstowe
PINEWOOD
ELM HILL
GUILDFORD RD.
WYKE
North Wyke Farm
WEST
MANOR FM. LANE
Manor Farm
ROAD

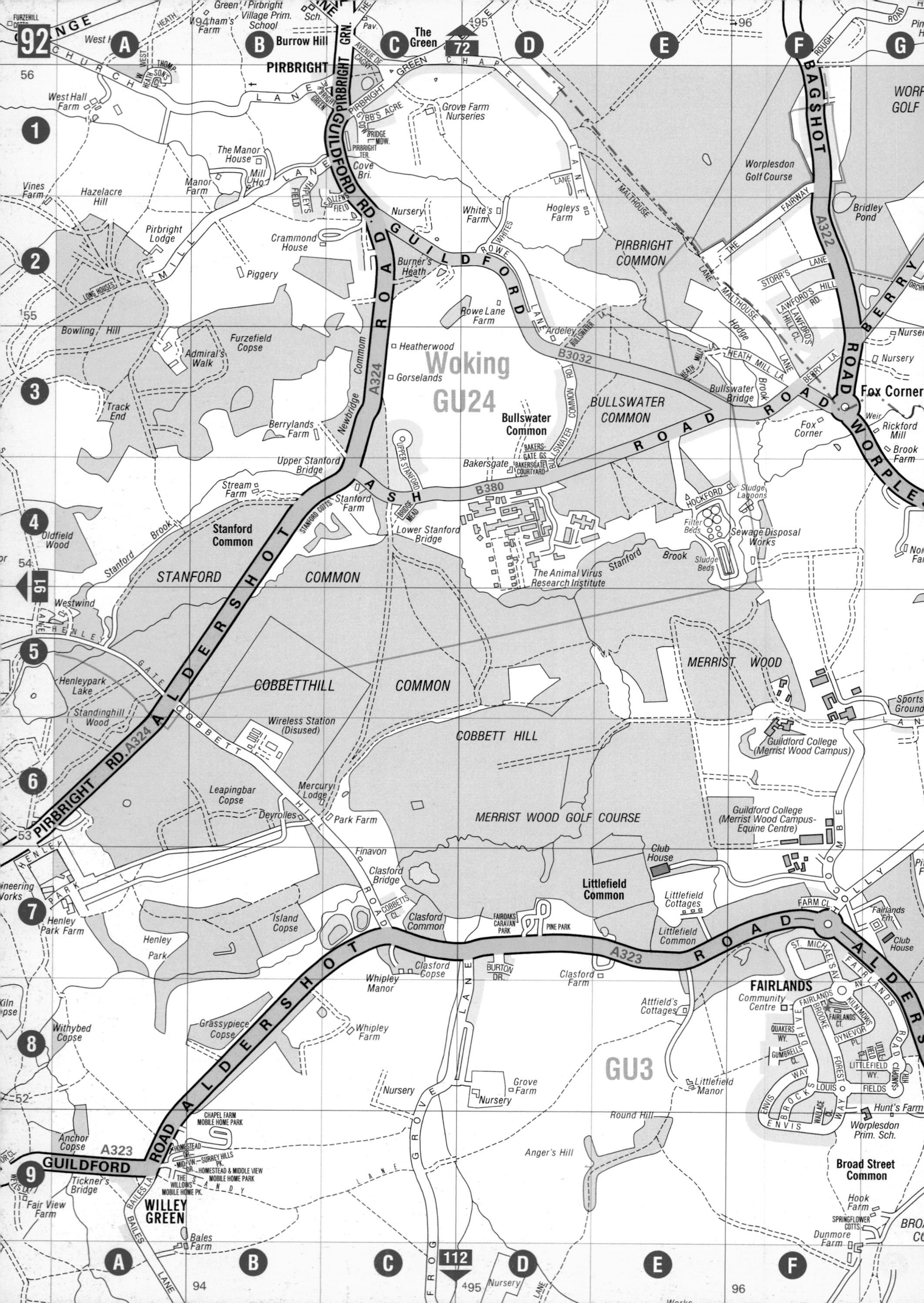

PIRBRIGHT
Burrow Hill
The Green
72
Pirbright Village Prim. School
CHURCH LANE
West Hall Farm
The Manor House
Mill Ho.
Manor Farm
Vines Farm
Hazelacre Hill
Pirbright Lodge
MILL LANE
Piggery
Crammond House
Cove Bri.
Nursery
Grove Farm Nurseries
White's Farm
Hogleys Farm
Worplesdon Golf Course
Bridley Pond
PIRBRIGHT COMMON
Burner's Heath
Rowe Lane Farm
Bowling Hill
Furzefield Copse
Admiral's Walk
Heatherwood
Gorselands
Woking
GU24
Ardeley
BULLSWATER COMMON
Bullswater Common
Bullswater Bridge
Fox Corner
Rickford Mill
Brook Farm
Track End
Berrylands Farm
Upper Stanford Bridge
Bakersgate
Stream Farm
Stanford Farm
Lower Stanford Bridge
Stanford Common
Oldfield Wood
Stanford Brook
STANFORD COMMON
The Animal Virus Research Institute
Sewage Disposal Works
Sludge Lagoons
Filter Beds
Sludge Beds
91
Westwind
Henleypark Lake
Standinghill Wood
COBBETTHILL COMMON
MERRIST WOOD
Wireless Station (Disused)
COBBETT HILL
Guildford College (Merrist Wood Campus)
Sports Ground
Leapingbar Copse
Mercury Lodge
Deyrolles
Park Farm
MERRIST WOOD GOLF COURSE
Guildford College (Merrist Wood Campus-Equine Centre)
Finavon
Clasford Bridge
Club House
Littlefield Common
Littlefield Cottages
Henley Park Farm
Island Copse
Clasford Common
Fairoaks Caravan Park
Pine Park
Henley Park
Clasford Copse
Whipley Manor
Clasford Farm
Attfield's Cottages
FAIRLANDS
Community Centre
Fairlands Fm
Withybed Copse
Grassypiece Copse
Whipley Farm
GU3
Nursery
Grove Farm
Littlefield Manor
Hunt's Farm
Worplesdon Prim. Sch.
Anchor Copse
Round Hill
Anger's Hill
Broad Street Common
GUILDFORD ROAD
ALDERSHOT ROAD
A323
A324
PIRBRIGHT RD.
GUILDFORD RD.
ASH ROAD
B380
B3032
BAGSHOT ROAD
A322
WORPLESDON ROAD
COBBETT HILL ROAD
GROVE LANE
FROG LANE
SANDY LANE
BAILES LANE
WILLEY GREEN
Tickner's Bridge
Fair View Farm
Bales Farm
Hook Farm
Dunmore Farm
112
94
495
96
52
53
54
55
56

H
J
K
L
M
N
73
MAYFORD GREEN
MAYFORD
Club House
Crastock Farm
Crastock Br.
Crastock Manor
Nursery
Berryhill Nursery
Woking
GU22
SMART'S HEATH ROAD
LANE SMART'S HEATH
B380
Smart's Heath
Hoe Stream
KEMISHFORD
MARTLANDS IND. EST.
Depot
The Oaks Centre
Churchill Ho.
Nurseries
GUILDFORD RD.
Elm Trees Farm
Green Lane Farm
Beech Hill
BEECH HILL
Loampits Farm
Bridley Manor Farm
Bridley Manor
Prey Heath or Pray Heath
Kemishford Bridge
PREY HEATH ROAD
Worplesdon
PREY HEATH CL.
WOODPECKER WAY
MAYBOURNE RISE
PYLE HILL
Wingstone
Bonnieshott Wood Farm
Burdenshott Hill
BURDENSHOTT HILL
Nursery
Havering Farm
WOKING
GUILDFORD
Bridley Copse
Blanketmill Farm
Rye Farm
RYE ROAD
White Lodge
Hockley Lands
Nursery
Whitmoor Pond
GU4
Gooserye
GOOSE RYE
Rickford Common
Perryhill Cottage
Upper Jordan
Gooserye Cottage
Whitmoor Hatch
JORDAN HILL
Woodcorner Farm
Heather Court
THE WATCHINGTAN
Poor Jack's Wood
Whitmoor Wood
Whitmoor House
Whitmoor Farm
WHITMOOR LANE
Cox's Farm
Cricket Grd.
Tennis Ct.
THATCHERS LA.
CHURCH LANE
WORPLESDON
Perry Hill
Vine House
COOMBE LA.
Perry Hill Farm
ST. MARYS GDN.
Maryland
WHITMOOR COMMON
The Old Cottage
Mount Pleasant
SHAMROCK COTTS
Hurst View
Willow Grange
Nursery
A320 WOKING ROAD
GUILDFORD ROAD
A332
Rectory
Greenacre
WORPLESDON ROAD
Sudpre
Britten's Pond
CLAY LANE
SUTHERLAND AV.
Guildford
Field Research Station
Rifle & Pistol Range
PITCH PLACE
SALT BOX ROAD
Stringer's Common
Stringers Common
JACOBS WELL
Tangley Place Farm
TANGLEY LANE
GRANGE ROAD
BURDEN WAY
Gunners Farm
Bullens Hill Farm
Stringer's Farm
Stoke Hill
ROKER PARK PUBLIC GOLF COURSE
KEENS LANE
Queen Elizabeth Park
MOORFIELD
Abattoir
SLYFIELD IND. EST.
OPUS PARK
Frosbury Farm
Smallholding
Chittys Common
Liddington Hall Farm
Works
BELLFIELDS
GU1
GU2
Esporta Health & Fitness
Play. Fld.
SLYFIELD GREEN
Guildford Children's Centre
Christ's College
Christ's Coll. Ski Centre
Stoke New Cemetery
Jun. Sch.
Inf. Sch.
Sch.
Weyfield Prim. Sch.
Sewage Works
A323
Rydeshill Lodge
Liddington Lodge
Holly Farm
Ryde's Hill
Rydeshill
STOUGHTON
STOUGHTON ROAD
A322
113
G
H
J
K
L
M
N
Rec. Grd.
Stoke Cemy.
Depot
1
2
3
4
5
6
7
8
9
94
97
98
99
500
52
53
54
55
56

94
74
93
114
A
B
C
D
E
F
G
1
2
3
4
5
6
7
8
9
CARTBRIDGE
SUTTON GREEN GOLF COURSE
GU22
PYLE HILL
SEND
Crickets Hill
SUTTON GREEN
Sutton Park
SUTTON PARK
Sutton Place
Send Hill
Cemetery
JACOBS WELL
Burpham Court Farm Park
Bower's Lock
Bower's Mill
River Wey Navigation
Guildford
BURPHAM
Superstore
SLYFIELD INDUSTRIAL ESTATE
Refuse Site
GU1
SLYFIELD GREEN
Sewage Works
Stoke Lock
ABBOTSWOOD
George Abbot School
Merrow Common
A3
A247
A3100
B2234
LONDON ROAD
SEND ROAD
CLAY LANE
NEW INN LANE
MERROW PARK

Papercourt Sailing Club
Industrial Estate
SEND MARSH
Woking
Grove Heath
Grove Heath Farm
Willow Farm
Loveland's Copse
Ryde Farm
Roborow
Roborow Wood
Hangover Ho.
Hungry Hill Cottage
Hungry Hill
Garlick's Arch Copse
Garlick's Arch
BURNTCOMMON
Oldlands
Oldlands Copse
Three Bridges
The Paddocks
Nursery
GU23
Sheppardsgrove Copse
Brambleride Copse
Tithe Barns
Tythebarns Farm
Depot
Sussex Farm
Holride Farm
August Hill
Cedarwood
Oak Ride Farm
Blendon
Highcotts Wood
The Oaks
Hazelhurst Cottage
Southernwood
HMP SEND
Dedswell Manor Farm House
Dedswell Manor Farm
Humphreys Copse
Fish Pond
Martin Furze
FRITHYS WOOD
WEST CLANDON
Birch Farm
Buttinham Copse
Clandon
Cuckoo Farm
Cammocks Wood
Withybed Plantation
Norcote Wood
Home Farm
GU4
CLANDON PARK
Summers
Club House
Clandon Regis
NEW PARK
CLANDON REGIS GOLF COURSE
EAST CLANDON
Old Manor Farm
New Manor House
Fullers Hill
Fullers Farm
Clandon C of E Infant Sch.
Ashley Park
The Queen's Royal Surrey
Blake's Lane Farm
RIPLEY BY-PASS
A3
B2215
B368
A247
A246
PORTSMOUTH ROAD
CLANDON ROAD
THE STREET
EPSOM ROAD
GROVE HEATH ROAD
TITHE BARNS LANE
HUNGRY HILL LANE
RIPLEY ROAD
GREEN LANE
GRANGE
LIME GROVE
MEADOWLANDS
75
115
96

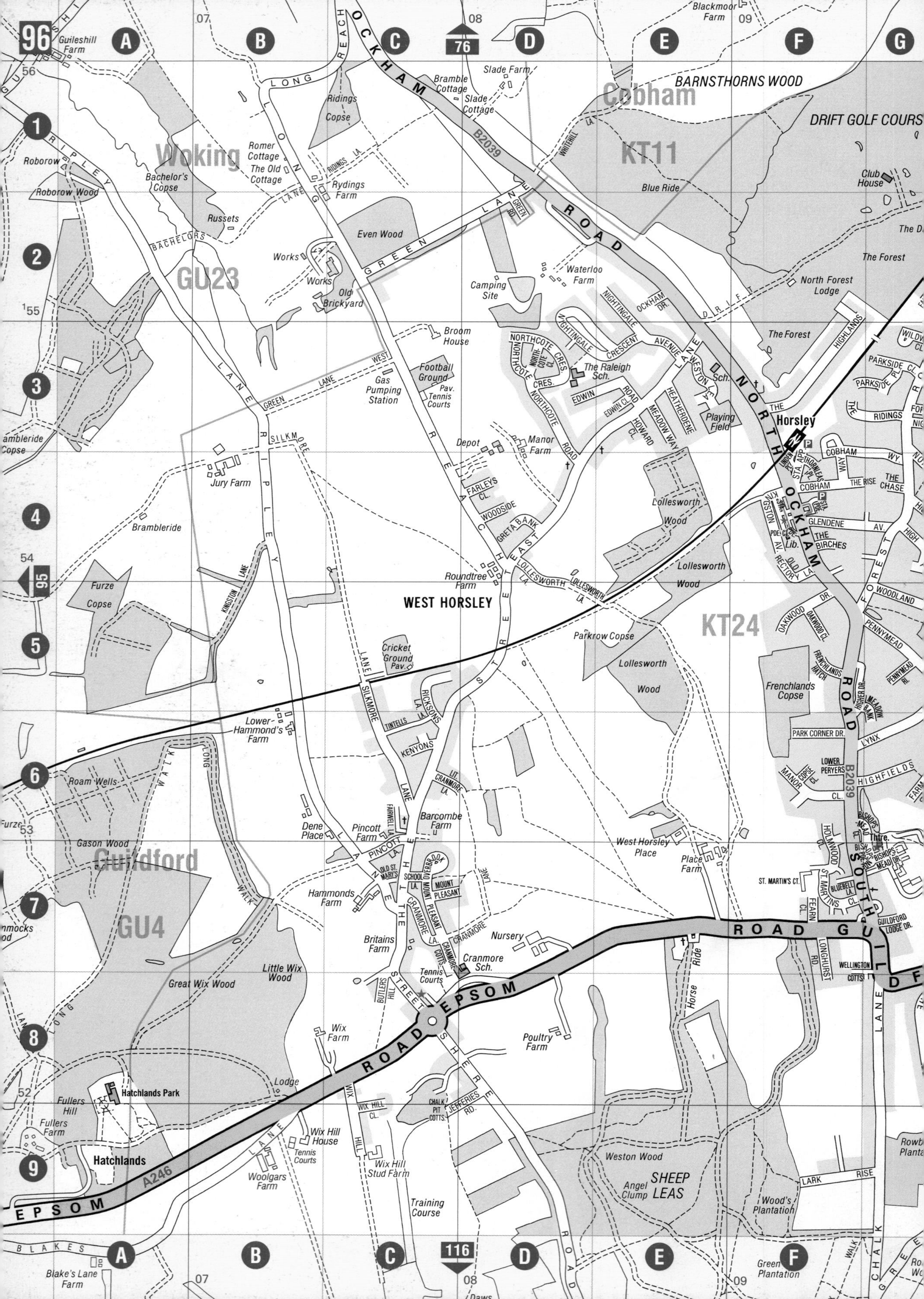

Guileshill Farm
Woking
GU23
Cobham
KT11
KT24
Guildford
GU4
WEST HORSLEY
Horsley
Hatchlands
Hatchlands Park
BARNSTHORNS WOOD
DRIFT GOLF COURSE
OCKHAM ROAD NORTH
OCKHAM ROAD SOUTH
B2039
A246
EPSOM ROAD
GUILDFORD ROAD
RIPLEY LANE
LONG REACH
GREEN LANE
EAST LANE
THE STREET
SHERE ROAD
LOLLESWORTH LA.
SILKMORE LANE
Roborow Wood
Bachelor's Copse
Romer Cottage
The Old Cottage
Rydings Farm
Ridings Copse
Even Wood
Bramble Cottage
Slade Farm
Slade Cottage
Blue Ride
Club House
The Forest
North Forest Lodge
Waterloo Farm
Camping Site
Old Brickyard
Broom House
Football Ground
Gas Pumping Station
The Raleigh Sch.
Playing Field
Manor Farm
Jury Farm
Brambleride
Furze Copse
Lollesworth Wood
Roundtree Farm
Parkrow Copse
Cricket Ground
Frenchlands Copse
Lower-Hammond's Farm
Roam Wells
Gason Wood
Dene Place
Pincott Farm
Barcombe Farm
West Horsley Place
Place Farm
Hammonds Farm
Britains Farm
Cranmore Sch.
Nursery
Little Wix Wood
Great Wix Wood
Wix Farm
Poultry Farm
Fullers Hill
Fullers Farm
Wix Hill House
Woolgars Farm
Wix Hill Stud Farm
Training Course
Weston Wood
SHEEP LEAS
Angel Clump
Wood's Plantation
Green Plantation
Blake's Lane Farm
76
95
116

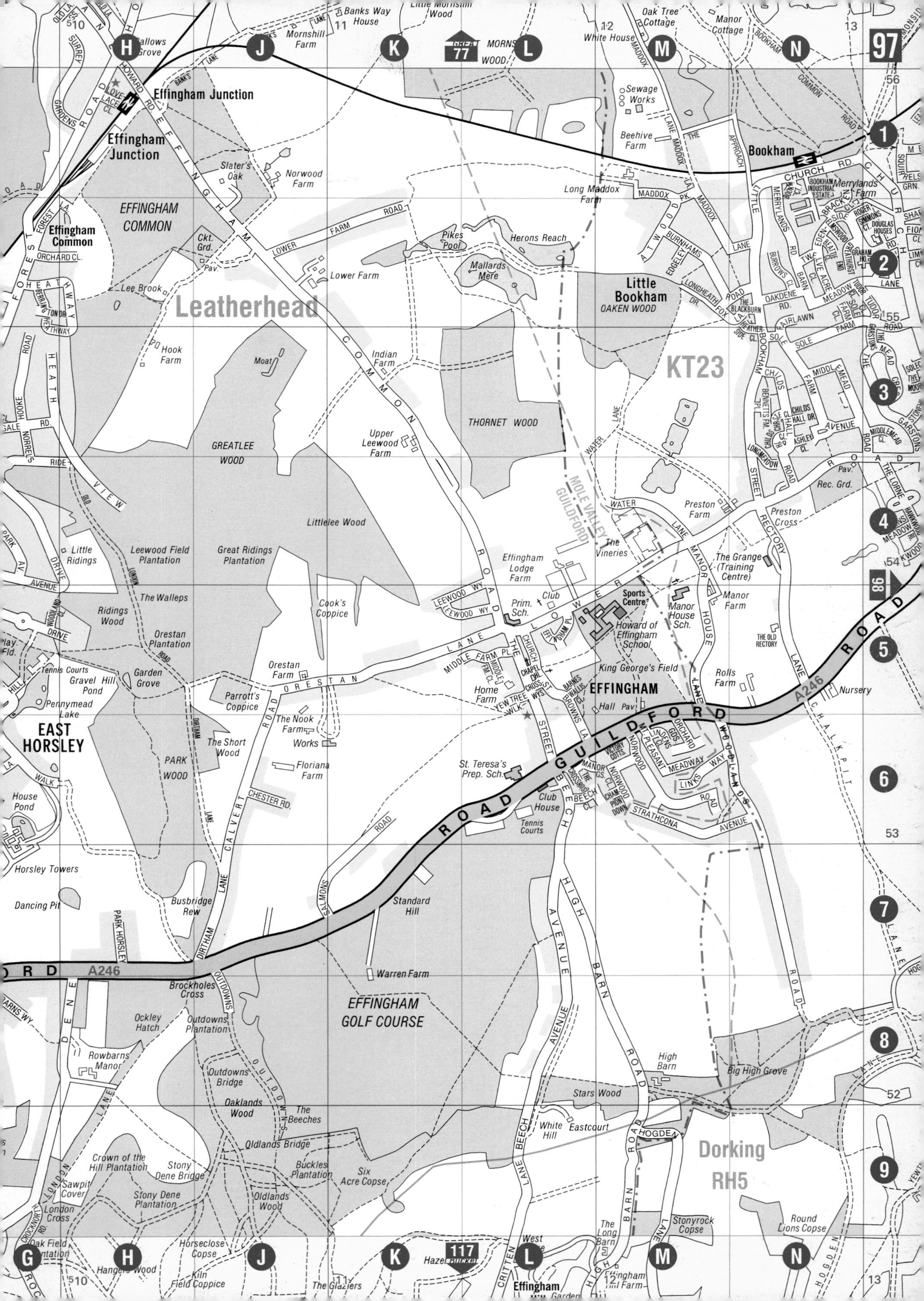
Effingham Junction
Effingham Junction
Effingham Common
EFFINGHAM COMMON
Leatherhead
Gallows Grove
Banks Way House
Mornshill Farm
GREAT MORNS WOOD
77
White House
Oak Tree Cottage
Manor Cottage
Sewage Works
Beehive Farm
Bookham
Slater's Oak
Norwood Farm
Long Maddox Farm
Merrylands Farm
Pikes Pool
Herons Reach
Mallards Mere
Lower Farm
Lee Brook
Little Bookham
OAKEN WOOD
KT23
Hook Farm
Moat
Indian Farm
Upper Leewood Farm
THORNET WOOD
GREATLEE WOOD
Littlelee Wood
Preston Farm
Preston Cross
Rec. Grd.
Pav.
Little Ridings
Leewood Field Plantation
Great Ridings Plantation
Effingham Lodge Farm
The Vineries
The Grange (Training Centre)
MOLE VALLEY
GUILDFORD
Sports Centre
Manor House Sch.
Manor Farm
Prim. Sch.
Club
Howard of Effingham School
THE OLD RECTORY
The Walleps
Ridings Wood
Cook's Coppice
Orestan Plantation
King George's Field
Rolls Farm
Nursery
Tennis Courts
Gravel Hill Pond
Garden Grove
Orestan Farm
Home Farm
EFFINGHAM
Hall
Pennymead Lake
Parrott's Coppice
The Nook Farm
Works
EAST HORSLEY
The Short Wood
PARK WOOD
Floriana Farm
St. Teresa's Prep. Sch.
Club House
Tennis Courts
House Pond
Horsley Towers
Dancing Pit
Busbridge Rew
Standard Hill
A246
Warren Farm
Brockholes Cross
Ockley Hatch
Outdowns Plantation
EFFINGHAM GOLF COURSE
Rowbarns Manor
Outdowns Bridge
High Barn
Big High Grove
Stars Wood
Oaklands Wood
The Beeches
White Hill
Eastcourt
Oldlands Bridge
Crown of the Hill Plantation
Stony Dene Bridge
Buckles Plantation
Six Acre Copse
Dorking
RH5
Sawpit Cover
Stony Dene Plantation
Oldlands Wood
London Cross
The Long Barn
Stonyrock Copse
Round Lions Copse
Oak Field Plantation
Horseclose Copse
Hangers Wood
Kiln Field Coppice
The Glaziers
Hazel Bucket
117
West
Effingham
Effingham Hill Farm
GUILDFORD ROAD
LOWER FARM ROAD
EFFINGHAM COMMON ROAD
ORESTAN LANE
CALVERT ROAD
HIGH BARN ROAD
BEECH AVENUE
RECTORY LANE
CHALK PIT LANE
MANOR HOUSE LANE
WATER LANE
LITTLE BOOKHAM STREET
CHURCH RD.
HOWARD RD.
FOREST ROAD
HEATHWAY
OLD LANE
DIRTHAM LANE
OUTDOWNS
STRATHCONA AVENUE
WOODLANDS ROAD
ORCHARD GDS.
CHESTER RD.
SALMONS ROAD
HOGDEN LANE
G H J K L M N
1 2 3 4 5 6 7 8 9
56 55 54 53 52
10 11 12 13
98

FETCHAM
GREAT BOOKHAM
Leatherhead
KT22
KT23
NORBURY PARK
Polesden Lacey
Fetcham Downs
GUILDFORD ROAD
LEATHERHEAD ROAD
YOUNG
A246
B2122 (HAWK'S HILL)
COBHAM ROAD
Bockets Farm Park
Hawk's Hill
Cherry Orchard Farm
Elmer Water Works
The Junipers
The Crown of the Hill
The Hazels
Roaringhouse Farm
Denshire Hill
The Scrubs
Walnut Tree Clump
Updown Wood
Saw Mill
Norbury Farm
Druids Grove
BEECHY WOOD
Bookham Wood
South Bookham Sch.
Kenilworth Riding Stables
Goldstone Farm
Phoenice Park Cottage
Phoenice Farm
North Lodge
Connicut Wood
Chapel Wood
Crabtree Cotts.
Preserve Copse
Camping Site
Cooksfield Wood
Chapelhill Wood
Freehold Wood
The Terrace
Polesden Farm
Cherrytree Copse
Bagden Farm
Old Dene
Old Dean Cottages
West Humble Chapel (Remains of)
Chapel Cottage
Chapel House
Chapel Farm Animal Trail
Chapel Hill
Round Copse
Tanner's Hatch (Youth Hostel)
Dorking Wood
Old Dean Cottage
Ashleigh Grange
Ashcombe
Ashcombe Wood
Yewtree Farm
Yewtree Shaw
Prospect Lodge
Belcham's Copse
Bagden Wood
Long Bottom
Nursery
Merrylands Farm
The Dawnay Sch.
Jun. Sch.
Inf. Sch.
Keswick
Oakfield Jun. Sch.
Fetcham Village Inf. Sch.
Rec. Grd.

78
97
118

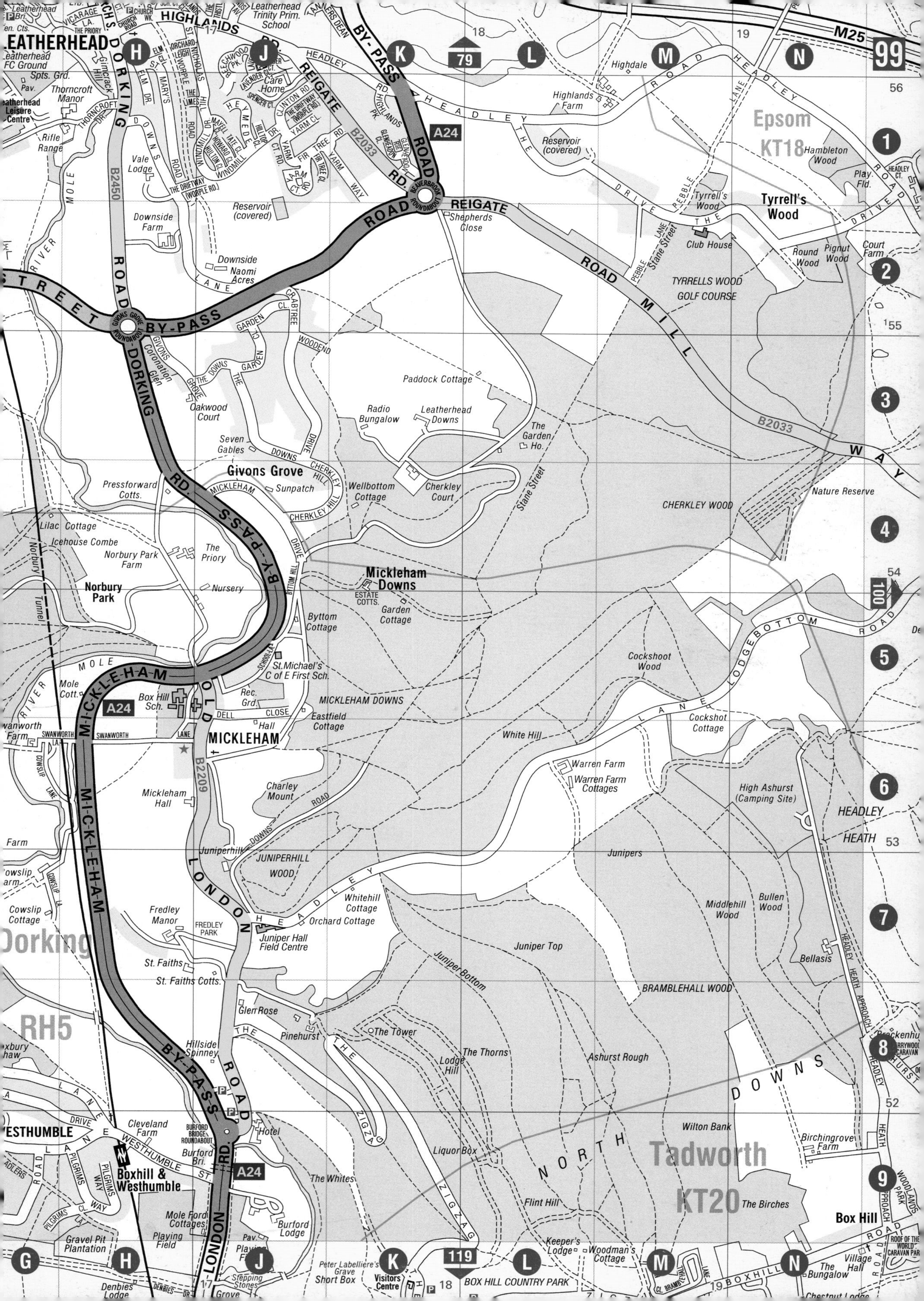
99
LEATHERHEAD
MICKLEHAM
Givons Grove
Mickleham Downs
Norbury Park
Tyrrell's Wood
Epsom KT18
Tadworth KT20
Dorking RH5
WESTHUMBLE
Boxhill & Westhumble
Box Hill
HEADLEY HEATH
NORTH DOWNS
BOX HILL COUNTRY PARK
TYRRELLS WOOD GOLF COURSE
CHERKLEY WOOD
MICKLEHAM DOWNS
JUNIPERHILL WOOD
BRAMBLEHALL WOOD
79
100
119

M25 MOTORWAY
Epsom
KT18
HEADLEY
Tot Hill
NOWER WOOD
GREAT HURST WOOD
WALTON PARK WOOD
SANDHILL WOOD
WALTON ON THE HILL
Walton Heath
HEADLEY HEATH
NORTH DOWNS
Betchworth
RH3
Box Hill
Headley Park Farm
Headley Park
Hook Wood
Court Farm
Oyster Hill
Great Hurst Wood
Costal Wood
Tumber House
Tunbarr
Hayes Cotts.
Kingsbarns
Manor House
Heath Farm
Goodman's Furze
Cricket Ground
Great Hayes
White Lodge
Dean Wood
Frith Park
Frith Park Farm
Hedgecroft
STURT HOUSE PRIORY HOSP.
Herring Grove
Queen's Wood
Headley Grove Farm
Headley Grove
Little Heath Cottages
Walton Oaks
The Hermitage
Pebble Coombe
Fraser Heath
Headley Plantation
Headley Reservoir (covered)
Boidier Hurst Scout Camping Site
Heath Plantation
White's Wood
Dawcombe Wood
Dewriding Plantation
Round Wood
Lady Hill
Harebeating Brow
Prestige Farm
Brackenhurst
Batchelor's Rough
Holly Rough
Betchworth Hills Wood
Betchworth Hills
Poor's Field
Kemp's Farm
Kemp's Farm Cottages
Wildecroft
Quarry
Betchworth Clump
Dorking Lime Works
Boxhill Nurseries
Fort (dismantled)
Village Hall
The Bungalow
Glebe House
Betchworth
Addlestead Farm
Loretta Lodge
North Lodge
Walton Hurst Farm
The Hurst
Wingfield Stud Farm
Wildwoods Riding Centre
Wildwoods
Twistwood
Edes Barn Cottages
Police Training School
Mere Pond
Ebbisham Farm
Walton Manor
Walton Manor Farm
Bramley Sch.
Recreation Ground
Club House
Prim. Sch.
Comm. Cen.
Rectory
Subway
Nature Reserve
REIGATE and BANSTEAD
MOLE VALLEY
B2033
B2032
B2220
Pilgrims' Way

101
TADWORTH
KINGSWOOD
KINGSWOOD GOLF COURSE
BANSTEAD HEATH
WALTON HEATH GOLF COURSE
WALTON HEATH
Tadworth
KT20
LOWER KINGSWOOD
MUGSWELL
Coulsdon CR5
MOGADOR
MARGERY
NORTH DOWNS
Reigate RH2
BRIGHTON ROAD
A217
M25 MOTORWAY
Junction 8
REIGATE HILL INTERCHANGE
REIGATE HILL
DORKING ROAD
MILL ROAD
NEW ROAD
B290
B2032
B2220
B2032
81
102
121
Colley Hill
The Saddle Knob
Juniper Hill
Queen's Park
Reigate Hill
Pilgrims' Way
Chussex Plain
Workhouse Pond
Sports Ground
Hedge Corner
Castle House
Dowding Lodge
Heath Farm
Red Lodge
High Bank
Stables
Rookery Cottages
Kingswood Prim. Sch.
Recreation Ground
Council Yard
Kingswood Manor
Kingswood Knoll
Natural Gas Pressure Reducing Station
Mogador Cottages
Wayside Farm
Dent's Farm
Margery Wood
Margery Ho.
Reservoir (covered)
Margery Hall Nursery
Margery Farm
Margery Hall Pig Farm
Two Acre Wood
Margery Hall
Water Tower
Pilgrims Holt
Four Acre Upper Woods
Fort (dismantled)
Rock Farm
The Beeches
Mount Hill
Conybury Hill
Buckland Hills
White Cottage
Thistle Hill
Underhill Farm
Northland Shaw
Bushy Shaw
Clifton's Shaw
Colleyland Shaw
Dowde's Farm
Quarry Orchard
Broadleas
Hotel
Club House
Grub Wood
Beechen Copse
Merton Vean
Sandy Crest
Millfield Wood
Mill House
May Cottages
Old Farm House
Lilac Cottage
Furzefield Copse
Corner Cottage
Gatwick Wood
Home Field Farm
Lovelands Mead
Ishstar Gate
Majority Plantation
Grove Shaw
Catsbrain Shaw
Wellfield Shaw
Warren Cotts.
Woodcot Cottages
Kingswood Warren
Walton Heath Sports Club
Hockey Ground
The Gallops
G H J K L M N
1 2 3 4 5 6 7 8 9
23 24 25 26
52 53 54 55 56

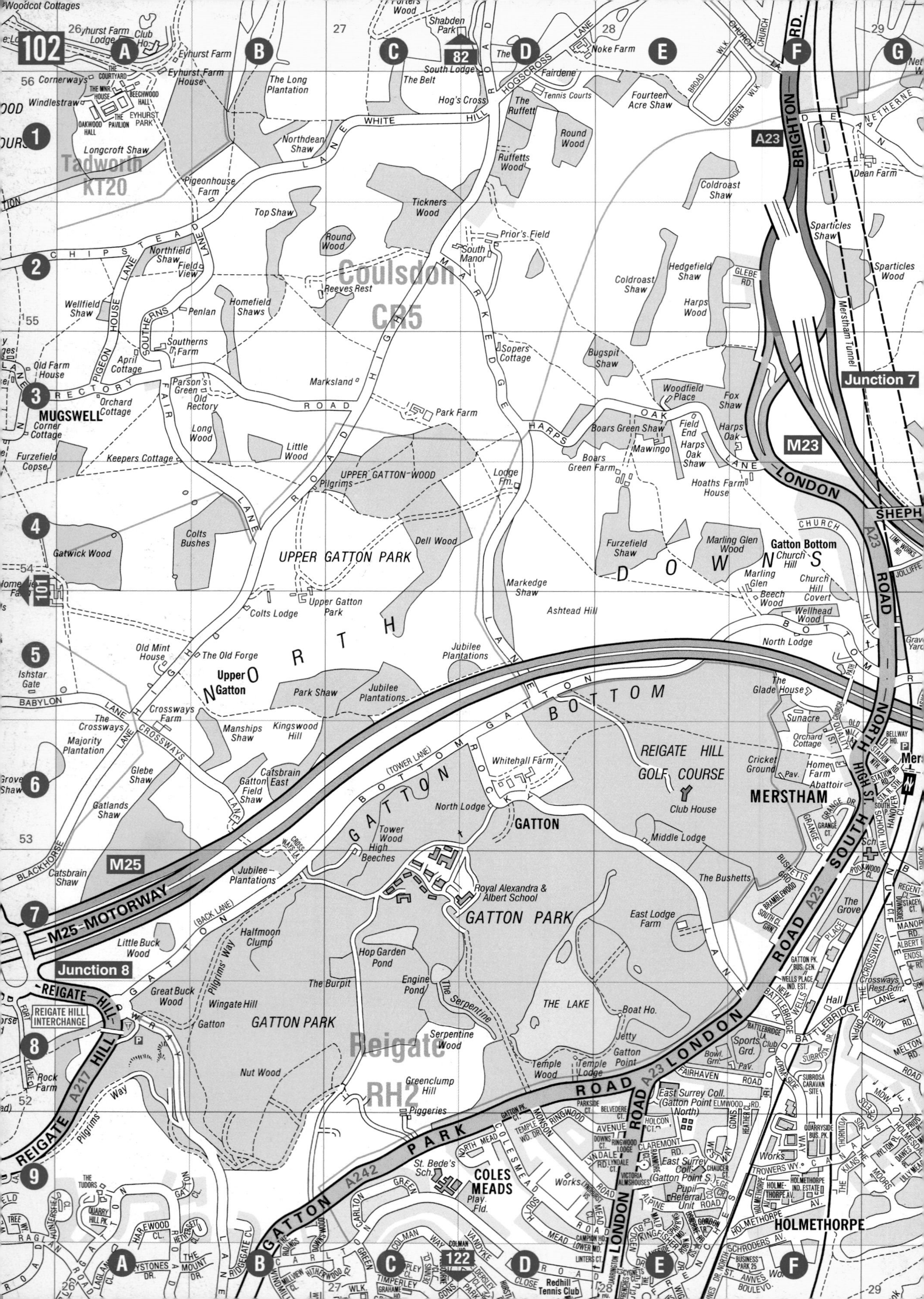

102
82
101
122
Coulsdon
CR5
Tadworth
KT20
Reigate
RH2
MUGSWELL
Upper Gatton
GATTON
MERSTHAM
COLES MEADS
HOLMETHORPE
Gatton Bottom
UPPER GATTON PARK
GATTON PARK
REIGATE HILL GOLF COURSE
NORTH DOWNS
UPPER GATTON WOOD
M25 MOTORWAY
M25
M23
A23
Junction 7
Junction 8
REIGATE HILL INTERCHANGE
Royal Alexandra & Albert School
East Surrey Coll. (Gatton Point North)
THE LAKE
Redhill Tennis Club

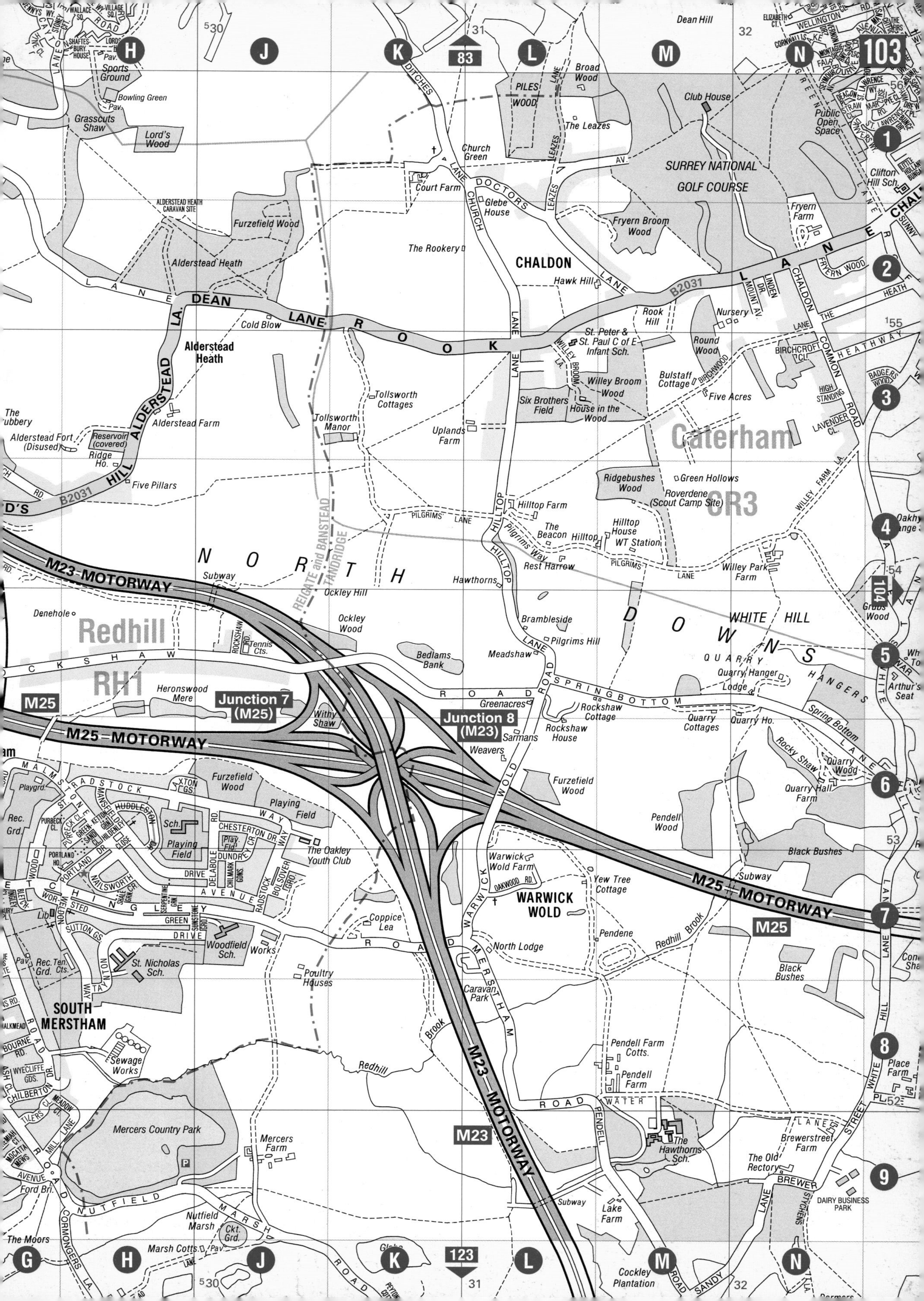

Sports Ground
Bowling Green
Grasscuts Shaw
Lord's Wood
Alderstead Heath Caravan Site
Furzefield Wood
Alderstead Heath
Dean Lane
Rook Lane
Cold Blow
Alderstead Hill
Alderstead Farm
Alderstead Fort (Disused)
Reservoir (covered)
Ridge Ho.
Five Pillars
B2031
Church Green
Court Farm
Glebe House
Doctors Lane
Church Lane
Ditches Lane
The Rookery
Piles Wood
Broad Wood
The Leazes
Chaldon
Hawk Hill
Rook Hill
St. Peter & St. Paul C of E Infant Sch.
Willey Broom Wood
Six Brothers Field
House in the Wood
Uplands Farm
Tollsworth Cottages
Tollsworth Manor
Dean Hill
Club House
Surrey National Golf Course
Fryern Broom Wood
Fryern Farm
Public Open Space
Clifton Hill Sch.
Nursery
Round Wood
Bulstaff Cottage
Five Acres
Caterham
CR3
Chaldon Common Road
Ridgebushes Wood
Green Hollows
Roverdene (Scout Camp Site)
Willey Farm La.
Hilltop Farm
The Beacon
Hilltop House
WT Station
Pilgrims' Lane
Pilgrims Way
Rest Harrow
Willey Park Farm
North Downs
Reigate and Banstead
Tandridge
White Hill
Quarry Hangers
Hawthorns
Ockley Hill
Ockley Wood
Brambleside
Pilgrims Hill
Meadshaw
Bedlams Bank
M23 Motorway
Subway
Denehole
Redhill
RH1
Rockshaw Road
Tennis Cts.
Heronswood Mere
Junction 7 (M25)
Junction 8 (M23)
Withy Shaw
M25
M25 Motorway
Springbottom Road
Greenacres
Rockshaw Cottage
Rockshaw House
Sarmans
Weavers
Quarry Hanger Lodge
Quarry Cottages
Quarry Ho.
Spring Bottom Lane
Rocky Shaw
Quarry Wood
Quarry Hall Farm
Furzefield Wood
Pendell Wood
Black Bushes
Arthur's Seat
Grubs Wood
104
83
Playing Field
Sch.
The Oakley Youth Club
Warwick Wold Farm
Warwick Wold
Yew Tree Cottage
Pendene
Redhill Brook
Coppice Lea
Poultry Houses
North Lodge
Caravan Park
Merstham Road
Woodfield Sch.
Works
St. Nicholas Sch.
South Merstham
Sewage Works
Redhill
Brook
Pendell Farm Cotts.
Pendell Farm
Water Road
Pendell Road
The Hawthorns Sch.
M23 Motorway
M23
Mercers Country Park
Mercers Farm
Ford Bri.
Nutfield Road
Nutfield Marsh
Ckt. Grd.
Marsh Cotts.
The Moors
Lake Farm
Cockley Plantation
Subway
Brewerstreet Farm
The Old Rectory
Brewer Street
Dairy Business Park
Place Farm
White Hill Lane
Black Bushes
Glebe
Sandy Lane
123
G H J K L M N
1 2 3 4 5 6 7 8 9
30 31 32
52 53 54 55 56

CATERHAM
Caterham-on-the-Hill
Caterham CR3
Godstone RH9
Redhill RH1
GODSTONE
NORTH DOWNS
CATERHAM BY-PASS
A22
M25 MOTORWAY
M25
Junction 6
GODSTONE INTERCHANGE
THE MARIE CURIE HOSPICE, CATERHAM
NORTH DOWNS CAPIO HOSP.
Caterham School
Caterham Preparatory School
Queens Park
Oldpark Wood
Gravelly Hill
The Roughets
The Orpheus Centre
Godstone Vineyards
Bay Pond Nature Reserve
Church Town
BLETCHINGLEY GOLF COURSE
DAIRY BUSINESS PARK
84
124
103

WOLDINGHAM
Marden Park
Woldingham School
Rookery
MARDEN PARK
NORTH DOWNS
Great Church Wood Nature Reserve
Oxted Tunnel
NORTH DOWNS GOLF COURSE
Woldingham Nature Reserve
Whistlers Wood
Greenhill Shaw
Warren Kennels
WT Station
Hell Shaw
Chalk Pit
Beech Plantation
Oxted Downs (East)
M25 MOTORWAY
M25
Chalkpit Wood
Armitage Wood
Hamfield Shaw
Lodge Wood
Five Acre Shaw
Rye Shaw
Rye Wood
Oxted Downs (West) & South Hawke
Tandridge Hill
Hanging Wood Nature Reserve
Robins Grove Wood
THE ABBEYS
Barrow Green Court
Barrow Green Farm
Oxted RH8
OXTED
OLD OXTED
Ridgeway Manor
Cemetery
The Bogs
Coney Hill Sand Pit
Tandridge Priory Farm
Oxted Sand Pit
GODSTONE GOLF CLUB
Rooks Nest
School Plantation
Furzefield Plantation
TANDRIDGE GOLF COURSE
Bushey Croft Rec. Grd.
Mill Barn
Oxted Mill
Broadham House
Windmillstadle Wood
The Birches
Nags Hall
Garden Centre
Moore's Shaw
Glebe Water
Palmers Wood Oilfield
Palmer's Wood
Flower Wood
Buttersgreen Shaw
Flint Hall Farm
Oak Pollard
Nixon's Pit
Whitefield Plantation
Hazel Shaw
Horse Shaw
Chaldon's Farm
Stubbs Copse
The Rumps
Templehill Plantation
Little Church Wood
Bundanoon
Club House
Hunters Hollow
Valleyfields
Riding Stables
Orchard Farm
Whistlers Wood Farm
Thorn Acres
Whistlers Hollow
Heathdown
Pilgrims Place
Wood Rising
South Hawke
Keepers Cott.
North Model Farm
The Firs
Greenacres
Priory Shaw
Duckpit Wood
Kennels
Barrow Green Farm Cotts.
OXTED ROAD
GODSTONE ROAD
A25
A22
GODSTONE BY-PASS
THE RIDGE
85
106
125

A
B
C
D
E
F
G
1
2
3
4
5
6
7
8
9
86
105
126
PITCHERS WOOD
NORTH DOWNS
Warlingham
CR6
Caterham
CR3
Oxted
RH8
LIMPSFIELD ROAD
B269
Paygate Cott.
BOTLEY HILL
Botley Hill Farm
WT Station
Park Lane Cotts.
Botley Hill Cotts.
RIDGE
Station
TITSEY PLANTATION
Hell Shaw
THE
Works
Beddlestead Lane
Beacon Shaw
PARK
Clarkslane Shaw
Church Farm
Club House
CHESTNUT
CLARKS LANE
B2024
Clarks Lane Farm
APPROACH RD.
WHITE LANE
RECTORY LANE
Coldharbour Beeches
High Trees
TITSEY ROAD
PILGRIMS LANE
Pilgrims' Farm
Pilgrims Cotts
EVELYN AVENUE
PILGRIMS
Rectory
Titsey Court
Titsey Place & Gardens
TITSEY
Lodge
The Rookery
TITSEY PARK
PITCHFONT LANE
Pitchfont Farm
Barton Shaw
Limpsfield Lodge Fm.
Park Farm
WATER LANE
River Eden
Roughfield Shaw
Church Wood
Square Wood
M25
Clacket Lane Service Area
TITSEY WOOD
BROOMLANDS
South Green
M25 MOTORWAY
Broomlands Farm
Ashen Coppice
Chalkpit Wood
Limpsfield Grange Sch.
SANDY
Playing Field
Downs Way Sch.
St. Mary's C of E Jun. Sch.
Tennis Courts
Games Ct.
Play. Fld.
Swimming Pool
Oxted Sch.
Laverock Sch.
Theatre
BLUEHOUSE LANE
Hookwood Park
HIGH STREET
Hookwood
Wymondley
Kentish Border
Hookwood Bungalows
Grubstreet Shaw
Grubstreet Copse
Grubbe Street Wood
Sunridge
Streatfield's Copse
Moorhouse Sand Pits
Halls
Pav.
Tennis Club
LIMPSFIELD
DETILLENS LA.
B2025
De Tillens
Scout Hall
Pebble Hill
Ckt. Gd.
Pebble Hill Ho.
Sch.
Club Ho.
The Gate House
Kennels
Cemetery
MASTER PARK
Oxted
Liby.
Tandridge DC Offs.
Leisure Cen.
Superstore
Mag.Cts.
OXTED
WESTERHAM HILL
A25
EAST HILL
WEST HILL
ROAD
KENT
Court Langley
ST. MICHAEL'S
Andrew's Wood
Oakshaw Cott
LIMPSFIELD COMMON
LIMPSFIELD CHART GOLF COURSE
Ballards Shaw
Ridlands Fm.
Briars Cross
RIDLANDS
LIMPSFIELD CHART
Woodhurst Bridge
Limpsfield Tunnel
Wildshaw
West Heath
West Heath
Pollards Wood
Broadway
Greenflags
The Red House
CHAPEL ROAD
Court Hayes
Hazelwood School
Oxted Mill
Viewlands
Stonehall Farm
Stone Hall
Playing Field
Pains Hill
Chartfield Ho.
Little Heath
Tenchleys Park
Tenchleys Wood
Reservoir (covered)
The Alders
Boulthurst Fm.
Hurst Green
Weir
Tanhouse
Broadham House

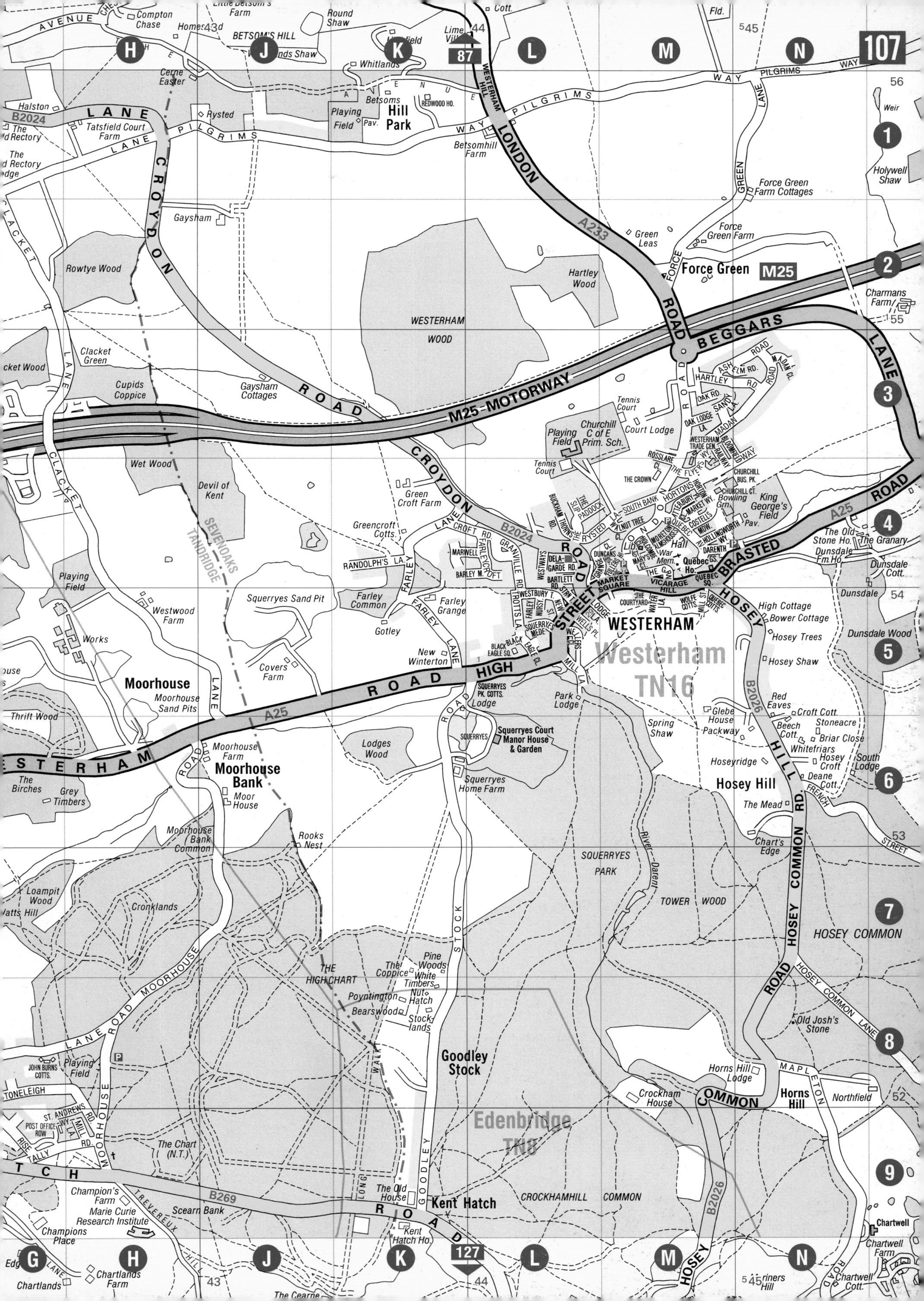

Westerham TN16
WESTERHAM
Edenbridge TN8
Force Green
Hill Park
Moorhouse
Moorhouse Bank
Hosey Hill
Goodley Stock
Kent Hatch
Horns Hill
M25-MOTORWAY
CROYDON ROAD
LONDON ROAD
HIGH STREET
WESTERHAM ROAD
BRASTED ROAD
PILGRIMS WAY
BEGGARS LANE
HOSEY COMMON ROAD
WESTERHAM WOOD
SQUERRYES PARK
TOWER WOOD
HOSEY COMMON
CROCKHAMHILL COMMON
THE HIGH CHART
Squerryes Court Manor House & Garden
Chartwell
87
127

A
B
C
D
E
F
G
88
Fleet
GU52
Queen Elizabeth Barracks
Soanes Copse
Wood Copse
Wakefords Copse
Parade Grd.
The Old Horns
Garden Cen.
Tennis Cts.
Redfields Racing Stables
Stillers Farm
Dachs Lodge
Blackmore Copse
Rifle Range
Playing Field
Leipzig Barracks
Greendane Copse
Bickley Copse
Chestnut Copse
Outridden Copse
Six Acre Copse
Chandler's Copse
Ewshot Camping Grd.
Bourley Camping Ground
Beacon Hill Cottages
Beaconhill Copse
Parkhurst Hill
Water Works
Firs Hill
Burn's Plain
Riddings Copse
Reservoir (covered)
Reservoir
Bourley Bottom
Bourley Hill
Beacon Hill Farm
Beacon Hill
DANGER
Seymour Farm
Pilridden Copse
Rec. Grd.
Hall
Abury Hill
Woodlands
Homecroft Farm
Hebrew Cottage
Midtrees
Caesar's Camp
Skains Copse
Turner's Copse
EWSHOT
Reservoir No.5
Combe Wood
Bushylease Farm
Bushylease Farm House
Ewshot Wood
Bricksbury Hill
DANGER AREA
Heath Ho.
Redlands
Orchard Farm
Redlands Farm
Warren Corner
Heath Corner
Comm. Cen.
Hale Sch.
FARNHAM ROAD
A287
BEACON HILL ROAD
B3013
ODIHAM ROAD
UPPER
FOLLY HILL
Club House
Ewshot Hall
Ewshot Farm
Lands Copse
The Warren
The Tileries
OAK PARK GOLF COURSE
Heath Hill
Farnham
Lawn Copse
Upper Old Park
UPPER OLD PARK LA.
Dora's Green Farm
Dora's Green
GU10
The Mount
CLARE PARK CLASSIC HOSPITAL
Clare Park
Knowle Farm
Claypit Wood
Middle Old Park
MIDDLE OLD PARK
Pond Copse
Lower Old Park
Old Park Farm
Lower Old Park Farm
Hilyour's Copse
Meads
Halls of Residence
University College for the Creative Arts (Farnham Campus)
Stocks Copse
Works
CRONDALL LA.
DORA'S GREEN LA.
BEAVERS HILL
128
CASTLE
47
48
49
50
51
81
82
83
1
2
3
4
5
6
7
8
9

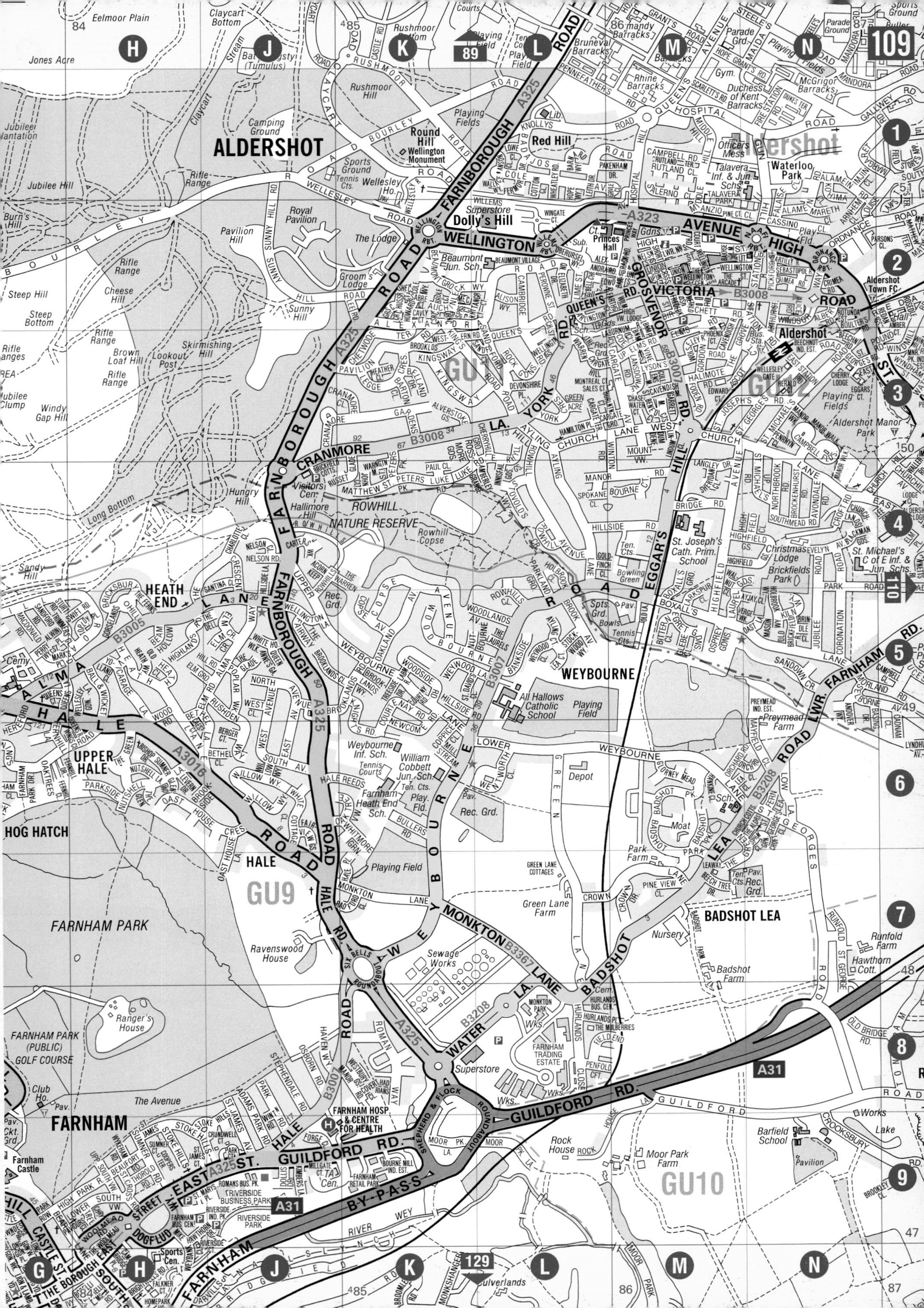
ALDERSHOT
FARNBOROUGH ROAD
WELLINGTON AVENUE
HIGH ST.
VICTORIA RD.
GROSVENOR RD.
EGGAR'S HILL
WEYBOURNE
HEATH END
UPPER HALE
HALE
HOG HATCH
FARNHAM PARK
FARNHAM
BADSHOT LEA
GUILDFORD RD.
FARNHAM BY-PASS
GU9
GU10
GU11
GU12
89
110
129

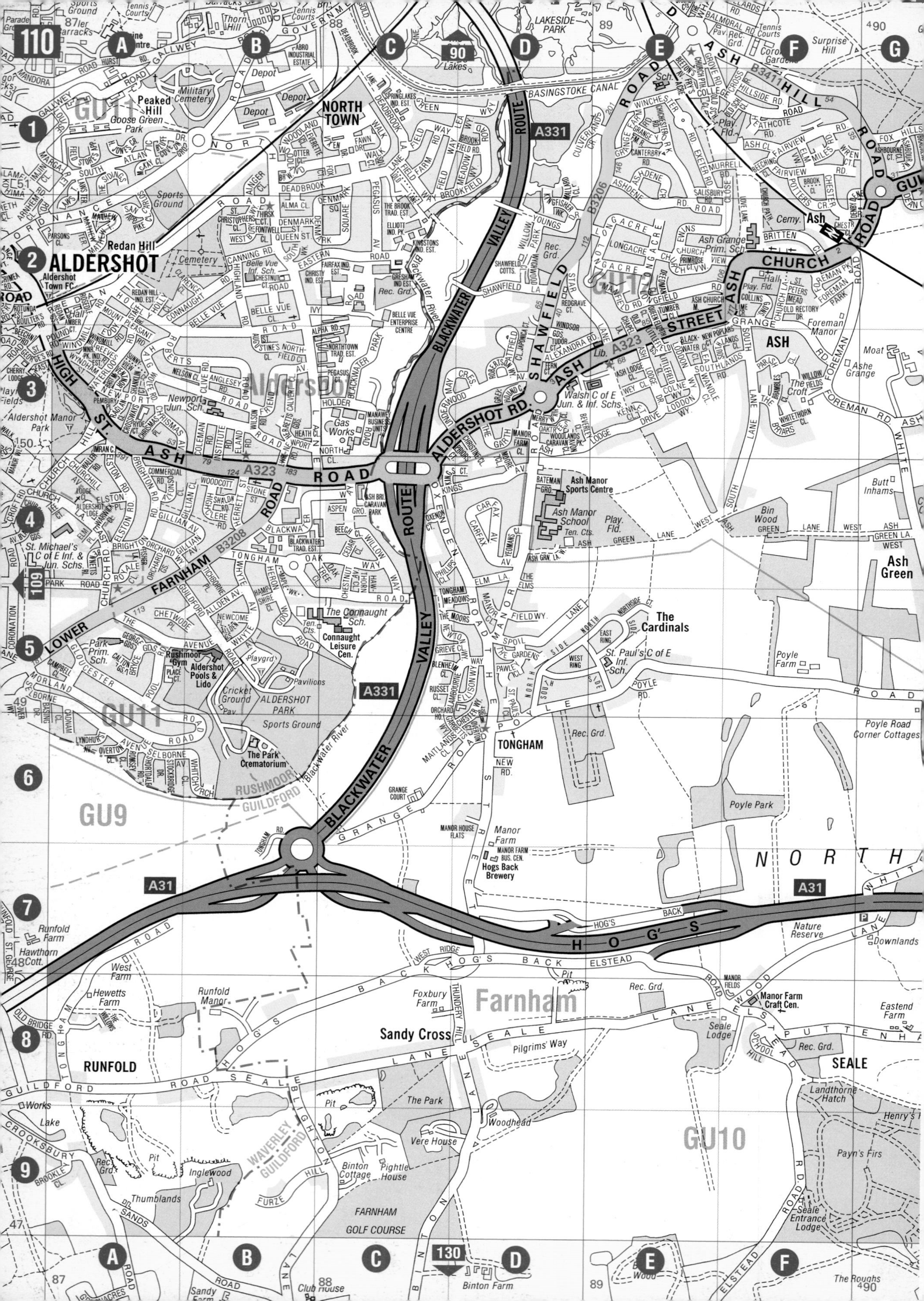

A
B
C
D
E
F
G
1
2
3
4
5
6
7
8
9
87
88
89
90
49
48
47
90
Lakes
LAKESIDE PARK
BASINGSTOKE CANAL
GU11
Peaked Hill
Goose Green Park
Military Cemetery
Depot
ABRO INDUSTRIAL ESTATE
NORTH TOWN
SPRINGLAKES IND. EST.
A331
ALDERSHOT
Aldershot Town FC
Redan Hill
Cemetery
Sports Ground
Belle Vue Inf. Sch.
Rec. Grd.
GRESHAM IND EST
BELLE VUE ENTERPRISE CENTRE
NORTHTOWN TRAD. EST.
PEGASUS CT. IND. EST.
MANAWEY BUSINESS UNITS
Gas Works
Aldershot
Newport Jun. Sch.
Aldershot Manor Park
Playing Fields
St. Michael's C of E Inf. & Jun. Schs.
109
BLACKWATER VALLEY ROUTE
Blackwater River
ASH ROAD
A323
FARNHAM ROAD
B3208
LOWER FARNHAM ROAD
HIGH ST.
ASH BRL CARAVAN PARK
BLACKWATER TRAD. EST.
The Connaught Sch.
Connaught Leisure Cen.
Park Prim. Sch.
Rushmoor Gym
Aldershot Pools & Lido
Cricket Ground
ALDERSHOT PARK
Sports Ground
Pavilions
The Park Crematorium
RUSHMOOR
GUILDFORD
GU9
A31
SHAWFIELD ROAD
B3206
Rec. Grd.
SHAWFIELD COTTS.
GU12
ASH STREET
ALDERSHOT RD.
Walsh C of E Jun. & Inf. Schs.
WOODLANDS CARAVAN PK.
Lib.
Ash Manor Sports Centre
Ash Manor School
Play. Fld.
Ten. Cts.
Ash Grange Prim. Sch.
Cemy.
Ash
CHURCH ROAD
ASH HILL ROAD
B3411
Surprise Hill
Tennis Courts
Foreman Manor
ASH
Moat
Ashe Grange
The Croft
FOREMAN RD.
Butt Inhams
Bin Wood
WEST ASH GREEN LA
Ash Green
The Cardinals
St. Paul's C of E Inf. Sch.
Poyle Farm
POYLE ROAD
Poyle Road Corner Cottages
TONGHAM
Rec. Grd.
Poyle Park
NORTH
GRANGE COURT
MANOR HOUSE FLATS
Manor Farm
MANOR FARM BUS. CEN.
Hogs Back Brewery
HOG'S BACK
HOGS BACK
Nature Reserve
Downlands
Runfold Farm
Hawthorn Cott.
West Farm
Hewetts Farm
Runfold Manor
Foxbury Farm
Farnham
Rec. Grd.
Pit
MANOR FIELDS
Manor Farm Craft Cen.
Eastend Farm
Seale Lodge
Sandy Cross
Pilgrims' Way
SEALE LANE
RUNFOLD
GUILDFORD ROAD
SEALE
Landthorne Hatch
Works
Lake
Rec. Grd.
Pit
The Park
Woodhead
Vere House
GU10
WAVERLEY
GUILDFORD
Inglewood
Thumblands
Binton Cottage
Pightle House
FARNHAM GOLF COURSE
Payn's Firs
Seale Entrance Lodge
130
Binton Farm
Club House
The Roughs

Normandy Common
Rand's Plantation
Orchard Dene
Hill Roughs Farm
Sandpit Farm
Normandy Pond
NORMANDY
Tickner's Bridge
PIRBRIGHT ROAD
GUILDFORD ROAD
A324
A323
ELM HILL
WYKE CROSS
WYKE
North Wyke Farm
Slade Cottage
Wyke Heath Farm
Fox Lodge
Elstowe
UPPER PINEWOOD RD.
NIGHTINGALE RD.
KIRRIEMUIR
Recreation Ground
Piggery
WYKE AV.
WYKE LANE
Wyke Lane Cottages
East Wyke Farm
Catherine Frith
Walden's Copse
Manor Fruit Farm
Elms Gardens (Nursery)
Oaklands (Nursery)
Great Westwood
Vogerfield Farm
Strawberry Farm
Buckhurst
Westwood Place
Pussey's Copse
Wanborough
STATION APPROACH
THE PADDOCKS
FLEXFORD ROAD
Whitegate Copse
Junction Cottages
Kiln Copse
Highfield Copse
Flexford
Beech Tree Farm
Christmaspie
Pound Cottages
Pound Farm House
Pound Farm
Old Cross Tree
Bushylees Copse
Rickwood Farm
Week Wood
WEST GREEN LANE
EAST GREEN LANE
Brickyard Copse
Tennis Court
Long Common
Broadmead Row
Grubground Copse
WANBOROUGH WOOD
WANBOROUGH
Wanborough Manor
Manor Place
Guildford
Whitegrass Copse
Inwood Copse
Inwood Farm
White Lane Farm
GU3
DOWNS
Reservoir (covered)
A31
HOG'S BACK
Pitfield Stables
Greys
Puttenham Hill
B3000
PUTTENHAM HILL
Newbarn Cottages
Stony Hill
Greys Home Farm
Crickets Hill
Williams Copse
DIANA COTTAGES
Play Fld.
Puttenham C of E Sch.
Bury Hill
War Mem.
PUTTENHAM
HOOK LA.
SEALE ROAD
Beggar's Corner
Shoelands House
Shoelands Farm
Little Lascombe
Little Common
Carpenters Field
Suffield Farm
Suffield Green
Old Warren
Totford Wood
Lodge
Totford Hatch
Lascombe House
Lower Lascombe House
HIGHFIELD LANE
Lascombe Farm
Robert's Moor
Long Bottom
Murtmoor Cottage
MURTMEAD LANE
Gore's Farm
SUFFIELD
Trout Pond

91
112
131

WILLEY GREEN
WOOD STREET VILLAGE
Pinks Hill
BROADSTREET
NORTH DOWNS
GU3
HOG'S BACK
WANBOROUGH
PUTTENHAM
COMPTON
GUILDFORD & GODALMING ROAD
A31
A3
B3000
92
111
132
Tickner's Bridge
Bales Farm
Ashfield Lodge Farm
Cleygate Farm
Cleygate Copse
Passenger's Farm
Russellplace Farm
Cricket Ground
Nursery
Hillplace Farm
Graylands Farm
Works
Wood Street Inf. Sch.
Hook Farm
Woodlands Farm
Backside Common
Chapelhouse Farm
Bushy Hill
Bushy Farm
Wildfields Farm
The Folly
Youth Hostel
West Flexford Farm
West Flexford Farm Cottages
Pond Hill
Wildfield Copse
Strawberry Grove
Blackwell Farm
Greencut Copse
Misley Copse
Manor Copse
Dean Bottom
Manor Farm Cotts.
Down Place
Wanborough Manor
Manor Place
East Flexford Holding
Rathfarnham Ho.
Lodge
Flexford House
Chalkpit Wood
THE SURREY RESEARCH PARK
Puttenham Hill
Upper Lodge
Greyfriars Farm
Gardeners Cott.
Monkshatch Cottage
Monkshatch Bungalow
Monkgrove Copse
Garden Cottage
The Watts Gallery
Club House
Cemy.
Frowsbury Hill
Monk Grove
Hurt Hills
Compton Heath
PUTTENHAM GOLF COURSE
Wanborough Common
Perton Rough
Perton Hill
Rowbury Hill
Coneycroft Farm
Sandy Knowe
The Manor House
Puttenham Heath
Summer Wood
Budburrow Hill
Watts Memorial Chapel
Polsted Manor
Hurlands
Rectory
Cypress Farm
Berthorpe
Berthorpe Farm
Westbury Copse
Bummoor Copse
Sewage Works
Pipkin Copse
Eastbury Manor
Compton St. Nicholas Church
Westbury Barn
Compton Wood
Pilgrims' Way
494
495
96
94
961
47
48
49
50
51

GUILDFORD
Guildford
STOUGHTON
Rydeshill
WOODBRIDGE HILL
Westborough
PARK BARN
Dennisville
GUILDFORD PARK
ONSLOW VILLAGE
ARTINGTON
LITTLETON
SHALFORD
GU1
GU2
GU4
UNIVERSITY OF SURREY
Guildford Cathedral
THE ROYAL SURREY COUNTY HOSPITAL
THE GUILDFORD NUFFIELD HOSP.
The Philip Henman Sports Grd.
Stoke New Cemetery
Stoke Mill Ho.
Guildford Lido
Guildford College (Stoke Park Campus)
Sunnydown Plantation
Reservoirs (Covered)
Henley Grove
Henley Fort School Camp
Piccard's Farm
Piccard's Rough
Conduit Farm
Sheepwalk
East Warren
West Warren
Pilgrim Gardens
Littleton Cross
College of Law (Braboeuf Manor)
Mount Browne (Police HQ)
Artington Manor Fm.
CHASE CHILDREN'S HOSPICE
St. Catherine's Lock
Shalford Junction
St. Catherine's Lockhouse
Shalford Park
Water Works
Rushy Platts Farm
Rush Croft
Orange Court Farm
LOSELEY PARK
Loseley House
Loseley Park
Moat Cottages
The Grove
Ashen Copse
Puddock Copse
Polsted Lodge
Rushcroft Farm House
Brickfields Farm
Grove Cottage
Manor Farm
Manor Farm Cotts.
ALDERSHOT ROAD
WORPLESTON RD.
WOODBRIDGE RD.
LADYMEAD
STOKE ROAD
WOKING ROAD
YORK ROAD
HIGH ST.
FARNHAM ROAD
PORTSMOUTH ROAD
SHALFORD ROAD
THE STREET
MILLBROOK
QUARRY ST.
BY PASS ROAD
A3
A31
A25
A246
A281
A320
A322
A323
A3100
93
133
202
114
G H J K L M N
1 2 3 4 5 6 7 8 9
97 98 99 500

114
94
202
113
134
ABBOTSWOOD
George Abbot School
Surrey County Cricket Centre
Sports Stadium
Guildford Spectrum Bowl
Spectrum Leisure Complex
Thorneycrofts
Burchatt's Farm Cotts.
Guildford Lido
Bowling Green
Guildford College (Stoke Park Campus)
STOKE PARK
Playing Field
Nursery
Home Farm
High Sch.
London Road
YORK ROAD
HIGH ST.
BUSHY HILL
Bushy Hill Jun. Sch.
St. Peter's Catholic Comp. Sch.
MERROW
Boxgrove Prim. Sch.
Tormead Sch.
Pit Farm Tennis Club
GU1
Offices
GUILDFORD GOLF
MERROW DOWNS
Merrow Downs
Harewarren
Tennis Courts
Urn Field
Playing Field
Warren Farm
Burwood Farm
The Warren
Holy Trinity School, Guildford
Pewley Down Inf. Sch.
Charlotteville
GUILDFORD
Pewley Hill
Pewley Down
NORTH
Guildford
Whiteways
The Shieling
Tyting Cotts.
GU4
Tyting Farm
Fairywood
South Warren Farm
Whinney Hill
Farthing Copse
Pilgrims' Way
ST. MARTHA'S HILL
St. Martha's Priory Lodge
Reservoir (covered)
Chantries
Halfpenny Copse
Great Halfpenny Farm
Old Great Halfpenny
Marigold Cottage
Chilworth Manor
Little Halfpenny Farm
Longmead
Tilehouse Farm
Shalford Mill
The Lodge
Manor Farm
Manor Cottage
East Shalford
SHALFORD
Kingfishers
Brickfield Cottage
Mud Wood
CHILWORTH
Old Manor Farm
Chilworth C of E Inf. Sch.
Chilworth
Fish Pond
Tangley Mere
Wood Cottage
Shalford
Old Croft
Playing Field
Tillingbourne Jun. Sch.
A3
A25
A3100
A246
A248
A281
B2234
PARKWAY
EPSOM ROAD
LONDON ROAD
BOXGROVE ROAD
WARREN ROAD
DOWNSIDE ROAD
ONE TREE HILL ROAD
WHITE LANE
HALFPENNY LANE
SHALFORD ROAD
THE STREET
NEW ROAD
DORKING ROAD
KINGS RD.
MERROW COMMON
Merrow Common

EAST CLANDON
CLANDON REGIS
NEW PARK
Ashley Park
The Queen's Royal Surrey Regiment Mus.
Clandon Park
The Rectory
Springfield Ho.
Temple Court
BULLARD COTTS.
PARKSIDE COTTS.
New Manor House
SNELGATE COTTS.
OLD EPSOM ROAD
BACK LANE
SCHOOL LA.
95
A246
A247
A25
THE STREET
EPSOM ROAD
BLAKES LANE
Blake's Lane Farm
STAPLE LANE
The Wilderness
Henchley Gate
Bampfylde Cotts.
Chalk Pit
GLEBE COTTS.
High Clandon
High Clandon Farm
Reservoir (covered)
Long Acre Farm
Sunray Farm
The Wild Wood
Chalk Pit
Dean Bottom
Sun Valley Farm
CLANDON DOWNS
Training Course
Netherlands
Old Scotland Farm
Harrowhill Copse
Amberwell
Harrowhill
NETHERLANDS
Tickners Copse
New Scotland Farm
TREE BOTTOM
Stables
Upper Lodge
Plovers Field
Harrow Hill Farm
Newlands Corner
DOWNS
116
Chantry Wood
The Roughs
SHERE ROAD
DROVE ROAD
Newlands Corner Countryside Centre
ALBURY DOWNS
The Boxwood
Mother Webb's Corner
White Lane Farm
WATER LANE
Newbarn
Pilgrims' Way
Silent Pool
Sherbourne Farm
Sherbourne Pond
GUILDFORD LANE
Timbercroft
Water Lane Cottages
SHERBOURNE COTTS.
Water Lane Farm
Weston Wood
Home Farm
Farm Hill Wood
SILVERWOOD COTTS.
Lidwell Copse
Colyers Hanger
Dalton Hill
Bourne
MILL REACH
POSTFORD MILL COTTAGES
Waterloo Pond
Postford Pond
CHILWORTH ROAD
THE STREET
Old Rectory
Hall
MILLENNIUM COTTS.
A248
SHERBOURNE
Cook's Place
Silver Wood
Tilling Bourne
Weston Farm
Waterloo
Albury Ho.
Rec. Grd.
WESTON YARD
Weston House
BOUNDARY COTTS.
WESTON FARM COTTAGES
ALBURY
OLD BAKERY
WESTONFIELDS
CHURCH LANE
WARREN LANE
NEW ROAD
ALBURY PARK
Oak Pollard
Cuckoo Copse
Belmount Copse
Rectory
GU5
Lockner Farm
ROSEACRE GARDENS
PINE VIEW CL.
Birmingham Farm
Res. (covered)
Lockner Lodge
Lockner Holt
DORKING RD.
Birget Hill
Albury Warren
BLACKHEATH LANE
PARK ROAD
135
LOCKNER HOLT
POSTFORD FARM COTTS.
SANDY LANE
Football & Cricket Ground
WARNERS LA.
LONDON ROAD
Kiln

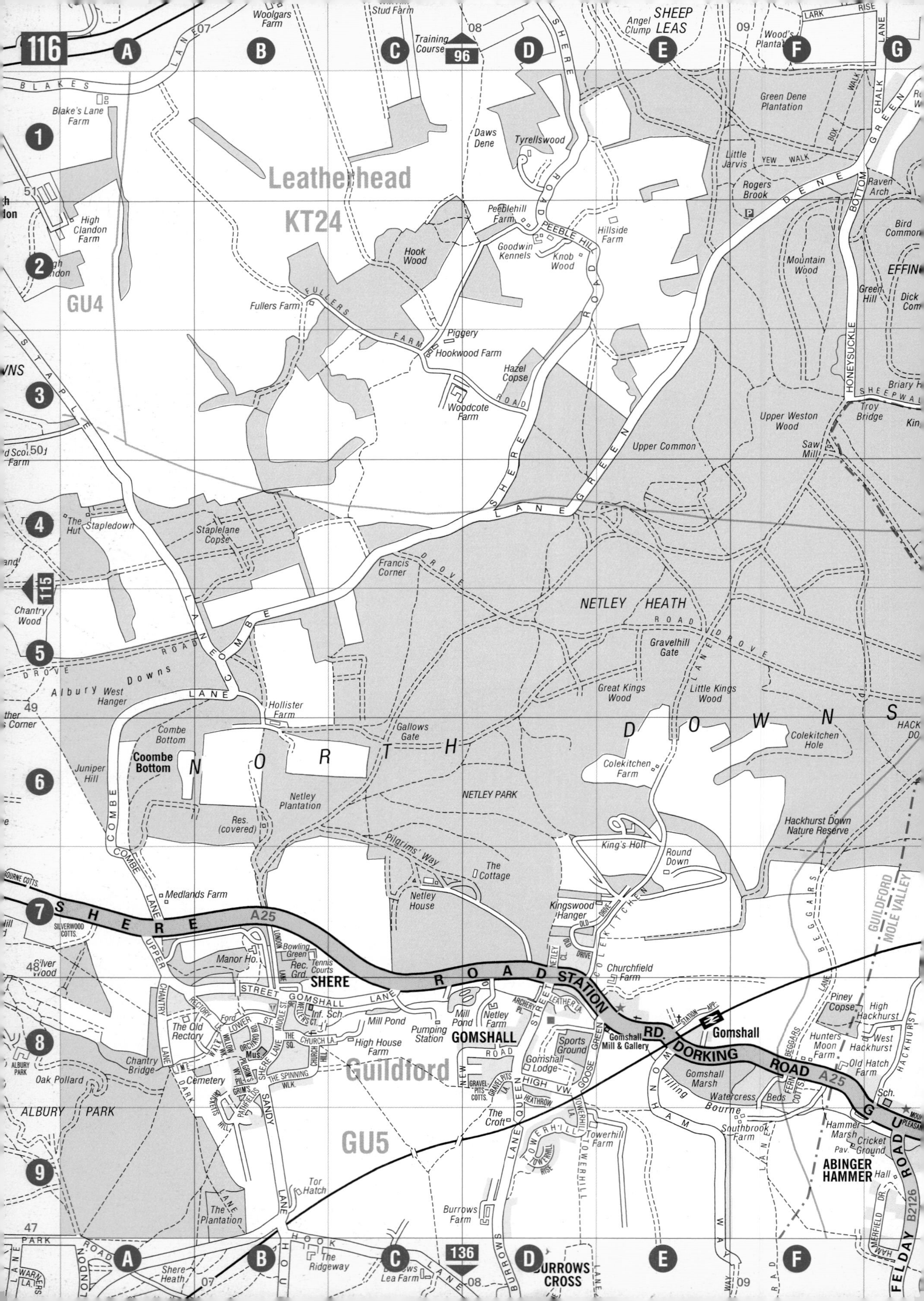

116
A
B
C
D
E
F
G
1
2
3
4
5
6
7
8
9
115
96
136
07
08
09
51
150
49
48
47
Woolgars Farm
Stud Farm
Training Course
Angel Clump
SHEEP LEAS
LARK RISE
Wood's Plantat.
BLAKES LANE
Blake's Lane Farm
High Clandon Farm
GU4
Leatherhead
KT24
Daws Dene
Tyrellswood
SHERE ROAD
Green Dene Plantation
Little Jarvis
YEW WALK
BOX WALK
CHALK LANE
GREEN DENE
Rogers Brook
Raven Arch
Bird Common
Peeblehill Farm
PEEBLE HILL ROAD
Hillside Farm
Goodwin Kennels
Knob Wood
Hook Wood
Mountain Wood
EFFIN
Green Hill
Dick Com
Fullers Farm
FULLERS FARM
Piggery
Hookwood Farm
Hazel Copse
ROAD
Woodcote Farm
HONEYSUCKLE BOTTOM
Briary H
SHEEPWAL
Troy Bridge
Upper Weston Wood
Saw Mill
Upper Common
STAPLE
Scot Farm
The Hut
Stapledown
Staplelane Copse
LANE
Francis Corner
DROVE
SHERE LANE
GREEN
Chantry Wood
COMBE LANE
NETLEY HEATH
ROAD
ROAD
DROVE
Gravelhill Gate
Albury Downs
West Hanger
Hollister Farm
Great Kings Wood
Little Kings Wood
D O W N S
Combe Bottom
Coombe Bottom
N O R T H
Gallows Gate
Colekitchen Hole
HACK DO
Juniper Hill
Colekitchen Farm
Netley Plantation
NETLEY PARK
Res. (covered)
Hackhurst Down Nature Reserve
Pilgrims' Way
King's Holt
Round Down
The Cottage
GUILDFORD MOLE VALLEY
Medlands Farm
Netley House
Kingswood Hanger
OLD DRIVE
COLEKITCHEN
BEGGARS LANE
SHERE ROAD A25
SILVERWOOD COTTS.
UPPER COMBE
Silver Wood
Manor Ho.
Bowling Green
Rec. Grd.
Tennis Courts
LONDON LANE
SHERE
ROAD
STATION
Churchfield Farm
NETLEY CL.
Piney Copse
High Hackhurst
CHANTRY LANE
STREET
GOMSHALL LANE
RECTORY LA.
Ford
LOWER ST.
MIDDLE ST.
Inf. Sch.
WELLERS CT.
Mill Pond
Netley Farm
ARCHERY PL.
LEATHER LA.
STATION APP.
Gomshall
RD.
The Old Rectory
WALNUT WK.
ORCHARD RD.
THE SQ.
CHURCH LA.
Mill Pond
Pumping Station
GOMSHALL
Gomshall Mill & Gallery
Sports Ground
Hunters Moon Farm
West Hackhurst
HACKHURST
Chantry Bridge
Mus.
CHURCH HILL
High House Farm
ROAD
Gomshall Lodge
DORKING ROAD A25
Old Hatch Farm
ALBURY PARK
Oak Pollard
Cemetery
THE SPINNING WLK.
Guildford
NEW ROAD
GRAVEL PITS CLOS.
GRAVEL PITS LA.
HIGH VW.
GOOSE GREEN
Gomshall Marsh
FERN COTTS.
Sch.
ALBURY PARK
SANDY LANE
DARK LANE
GRIM'S
PATHFIELDS
THE CROFT
HEATHROW
Tilling Bourne
Watercress Beds
HAM
Southbrook Farm
Hammer Marsh
Cricket Ground
Pav.
GU5
QUEEN LANE
TOWERHILL
TOWERHILL RISE
Towerhill Farm
ABINGER HAMMER
Hall
ROAD
Tor Hatch
Burrows Farm
The Plantation
LANE
HAM MERFIELD DR.
B2126
FELDAY ROAD
PARK ROAD
LONDON LANE
WARNERS LA.
Shere Heath
HOUND HOUSE ROAD
HOOK LANE
The Ridgeway
Burrows Lea Farm
BURROWS CROSS
BURROWS LANE
WAY
RAD

97
118
137
Effingham Hill
DOGKENNEL GREEN
RH5
RH4
Dorking
NORTH DOWNS
WHITE DOWNS
OAKEN GROVE
Wotton
RANMORE COMMON ROAD
WHITE DOWN LANE
CRITTEN LANE
HIGH BARN ROAD
HOGDEN LANE
GUILDFORD ROAD A25
COAST HILL A25
St. Teresa's School
Pilgrims' Way
Hazel Bucket
Robinsgrove Wood
Effingham Upper Common
Dunley Wood
Old Simm's Copse
Pickett's Hole
Abinger Roughs
Deerleap Wood
Park Farm
Wotton House
Damphurst Wood
Coombe Farmhouse
Crossways Farm
Paddington Farm
Abinger Mill
Birchin Copse
New Barn Farm
Hackhurst Farm

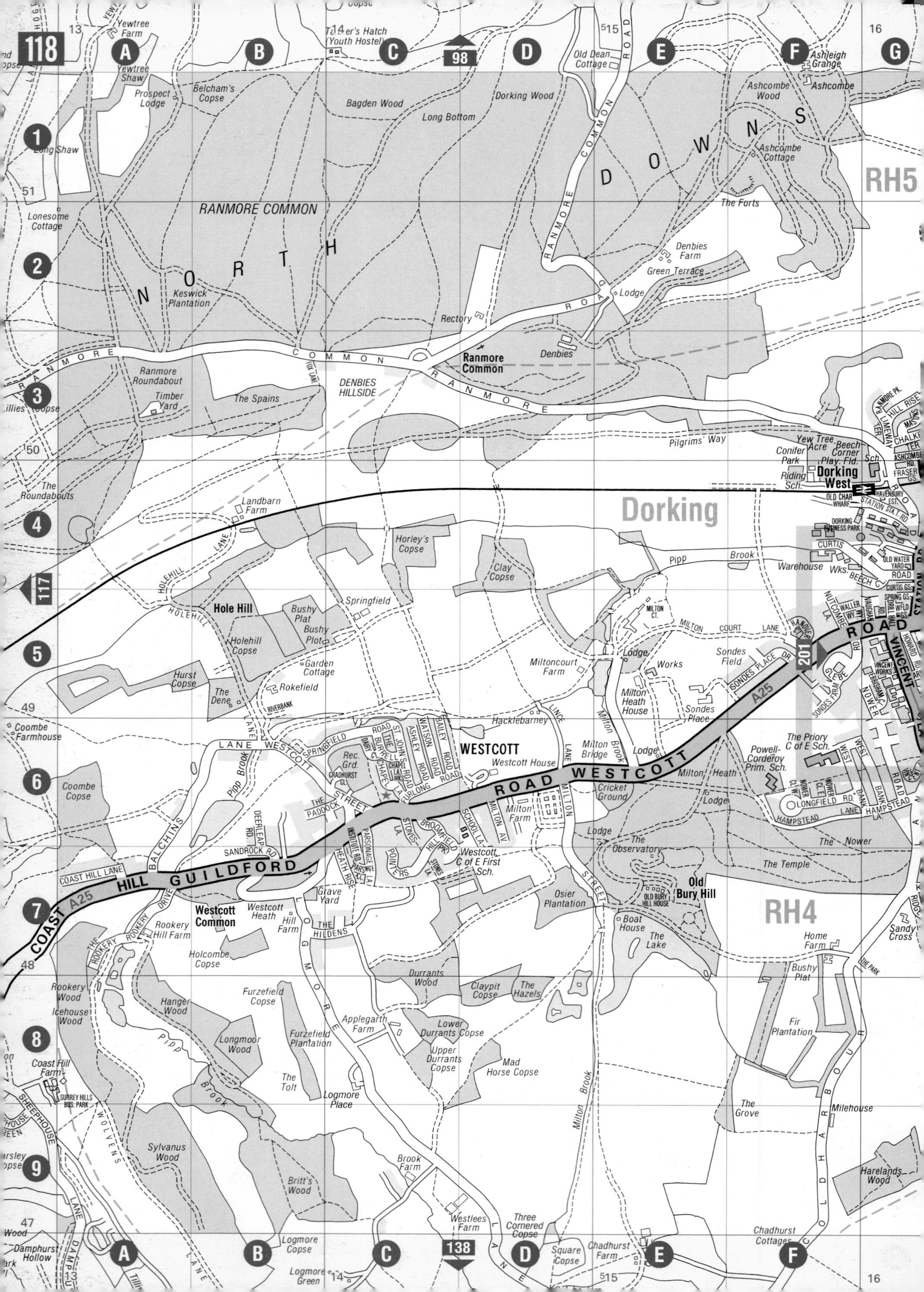

Yewtree Farm
Tanner's Hatch (Youth Hostel)
98
Old Dean Cottage
Ashleigh Grange
Yewtree Shaw
Prospect Lodge
Belcham's Copse
Bagden Wood
Dorking Wood
Long Bottom
Ashcombe Wood
Ashcombe
Long Shaw
NORTH DOWNS
Ashcombe Cottage
RH5
RANMORE COMMON
The Forts
Lonesome Cottage
RANMORE COMMON ROAD
Denbies Farm
Green Terrace
Lodge
Keswick Plantation
Rectory
Ranmore Roundabout
Ranmore Common
Denbies
DENBIES HILLSIDE
FOX LANE
Timber Yard
The Spains
Pilgrims' Way
Yew Tree Acre
Beech Corner Play. Fld.
Conifer Park
Riding Sch.
Dorking West
The Roundabouts
Landbarn Farm
Dorking
Horley's Copse
Clay Copse
Pipp Brook
Warehouse
Wks.
117
HOLEHILL LANE
Hole Hill
Bushy Plat
Bushy Plot
Springfield
MILTON COURT LANE
Holehill Copse
Garden Cottage
Miltoncourt Farm
Lodge
Works
Sondes Field
SONDES PLACE DR.
201
Hurst Copse
Rokefield
Milton Heath House
Sondes Place
The Dene
RIVERBANK
Coombe Farmhouse
Hacklebarney
LINCE LANE
WESTCOTT
Westcott House
Milton Bridge
Milton Brook
Lodge
The Priory C of E Sch.
Powell-Corderoy Prim. Sch.
Coombe Copse
Rec. Grd.
CRADHURST CL.
FURLONG
ROAD WESTCOTT
Milton Heath
Cricket Ground
Lodge
LONGFIELD RD.
HAMPSTEAD LANE
THE PADDOCK
STREET
Milton Farm
BALCHINS
DEERLEAP RD.
SANDROCK RD.
SCHOOL LA.
MILTON AV.
Lodge
The Observatory
The Nower
The Temple
COAST HILL LANE
GUILDFORD
Westcott C of E First Sch.
Old Bury Hill
OLD BURY HILL HOUSE
Osier Plantation
MILTON STREET
COAST HILL
A25
Grave Yard
Westcott Common
Westcott Heath
Hill Farm
THE HILDENS
RH4
Rookery Hill Farm
Boat House
The Lake
Home Farm
Sandy Cross
THE ROOKERY
POOKERY DRIVE
Holcombe Copse
LOGMORE
THE PARK
Rookery Wood
Durrants Wood
Claypit Copse
The Hazels
Bushy Plat
Icehouse Wood
Hanger Wood
Furzefield Copse
Applegarth Farm
Lower Durrants Copse
Fir Plantation
Longmoor Wood
Furzefield Plantation
Upper Durrants Copse
Mad Horse Copse
Coast Hill Farm
SURREY HILLS BUS. PARK
The Tolt
Logmore Place
Pipp Brook
Milton Brook
The Grove
Milehouse
SHEEPHOUSE
WOLVENS
Sylvanus Wood
COLDHARBOUR
Brook Farm
Britt's Wood
Harelands Wood
Westlees Farm
Three Cornered Copse
Chadhurst Farm
Chadhurst Cottages
Square Copse
Logmore Copse
138
Logmore Green
Damphurst Hollow

Boxhill & Westhumble
Mole Ford Cottages
Burford Lodge
The Whites
Flint Hill
The Birches
Gravel Pit Plantation
Playing Field
Keeper's Lodge
Woodman's Cottage
Village Hall
The Bungalow
Peter Labelliere's Grave
Short Box
Visitors Centre
BOX HILL COUNTRY PARK
Tadworth
Chestnut Lodge Farm
Denbies Lodge
Stepping Stones
Grove Lodge
The Lodge
Swiss Cottage
KT20
Oakwood House
Brockham Warren
Denbies Wine Estate, Winery & Visitors Centre
Boxlands
Salomon's Memorial
Oak Wood
Dukes Plantation
Brockham Hills
Riverdale
The Retreat
Boxhurst
BRADLEY LANE
Playing Field
Pilgrims' Way
Pixholme Court
Pavilion
Pixham Firs
PIXHAM LANE
RIVER MOLE
Purbrook Hall
Offs.
Sewage Works
Pixham
Dorking
Boxhill Farm
Foxbury
Deepdene Bridge
Boxhill Bridge
The Lodge
REIGATE ROAD
A25
ASHCOMBE ROAD
A2003
LONDON ROAD
Dorking (Deepdene)
CASTLE GARDENS
The Avenue
The Ashcombe Sch.
Ten. Cts.
Cemetery
Pixiewood House
Betchworth Castle (remains of)
COACH RD.
Play. Field
Meadowbank Recreation Ground
Pippbrook
Club House
BETCHWORTH PARK GOLF COURSE
Sewage Works
DORKING
Nursery
BETCHWORTH PARK
Dorking FC
Dorking Sports Cen.
Dorking Halls
DEEPDENE AVENUE
HIGH ST.
A25
Elmgrove Farm
Tanner's Bridge
Leigh Farm
Cotmandene
Deepdene Lodge
Park Farm
Betchworth
Kuoni House
Pondtail Farm
BROCKHAM
Rose Hill
RH3
St. Paul's C of E Prim. Sch.
Chartwood House
CHART PARK
Glory Farm Cottage
Field Plantation
Knight's Barn
DORKING COMM HOSP.
A24
Club House
Cedarwood Farm
DORKING GOLF COURSE
Felton's Farm
Minepits Shaw
TILEHURST LANE
Charlwood Copse
Goldenlands Farm
The Glory Wood
The Glory
Tower Hill
Reservoir (covered)
Wet Grove
Osierbed Copse
The Garth
Starhurst Sch.
Tanner's Brook
Bushbury Farm
Lawn Tennis & Squash Club
The Devils Den
TWEED LANE
Tweed Copse
Comm. Cen.
Bents Brook
Stonebridge
FLINT HILL
DEEPDENE
Sewage Works
Rough Rew
Play. Fld.
Scammells Copse
Prim. Sch.
Inholms Farm
Scammells Farm
BUSHBURY LANE
PARKPALE LANE
A24
Roothill Wood
Root Hill
Beldham's Farm
NORTH HOLMWOOD
Clay Pit
RH5
Holmwood Farm
Hall's Spring
Black Brook
Root Hill Farm
Stumbleholt
Orchard Copse
Cricket Ground
Roothill Wood
HORSHAM ROAD
Great Brockhamhurst
99
201
120
139

Box Hill
Tadworth
KT20
Brockham Hills
Boxhill Nurseries
Betchworth Clump
Dorking Lime Works
Fort (dismantled)
Roof of the World Caravan Park
Hillcrest Mobile Home Pk.
Village Hall
The Bungalow
Betchworth
The Quarry
Station Rd.
B2032
100
Depot
Wildecroft
Kemp's Farm Cottages
Glebe House
Rectory Lane
The Sloughs
Petty's Farm
Tranquil Dale
Slough La.
Buckland
The Green
Lawrence Lane
Reigate Road
A25
Pilgrims Way
Chalkpit La.
Bishop's Cotts.
Pilgrims Way Cotts.
Nursery
Crossways Farm
Hall
Buckland Court Gardens
Park Pit
Yewdells Cl.
Dungates La.
Broome Park
Betchworth
Cricket Ground
Cottage Farm
Old Reigate Road
Buckland Lodge
Betchworth
Dungate's Farm
Brockham Lane
The Cedars
Bramble Wood
Playing Field
Pavilion
Mill Hill La.
Old Kiln La.
Hartsfield Manor
Sandhills
Sandy Lane
The Acorns Infant School (Betchworth Base)
Wonham Hill
Wonham Hill Cottages
Wonham Wood Cottage
More Place
RH3
Wonham Manor
Wonham Lane
Little Borough
Kiln Lane
Nutwood Av.
Bowling Green
Borough Bridge
Brockham Court Farm
River Mole
Cemetery
The Walled Gdn.
Farm Cl.
Home Cl.
Cricket Ground
The Old House
Church St.
Mill Pond
Wonham Cottage
Wonham Mill
Mill Stream
Elmgrove
Tanners Ct.
Tanner's Hill
Tanner's Bridge
Green
Brockham Gn.
Anthony West Ho.
Brockham School
Play. Fld.
Betchworth House
Betchworth Bridge
The Street
Fryleigh
Fryleigh Shaw
119
Leighs Farm
Brockham
Wheelers La.
Middle Green
Wilderness Wood
Agland Copse
Little S... Farm
Playing Field
Warrenne Rd.
Oakdene Rd.
Oakdene Cl.
Tumbledown Farm
Oldpark Wood
Dendy's Wood
Keepers Cott.
Snowerhill Lane
Snowerhill Farm
Ricebridge Farm
Guzzle Copse
School Lane
The Mardle
Blind Lane
Moat House Farm
Knight's Ba...
Felton's Farm
Old Road
Nine Acres
Holly Cottage
Duffle's Plantation
Rice Bridge
Weir Mead Farm
Gadbrook Farm
Wellhouse Lane
Brook
Glenfield Rd.
Glenfield Cl.
Silverdale Cl.
Tanners Mdw.
Tanners Ct.
Kenward Ct.
Middle Street
Stroodgreen Farm
Strood Green
John's Copse
Riding's Copse
Knight's Gorse
Bushbury Road
Boxhill Way
The Close
Tynedale
Ridge
Jubilee Ter.
Tweed La.
Tweed Lane
The Rough
Gadbrook Copse
Tweed Copse
Gadbrook House
Elm Cottages
Abbots
Little Abbot's Farm
Great Oaks
Park Cl.
Gad Brook
Tapner's Bridge
Tapners Road
Mark Mead Plantation
Lodge
Rykens
Brockham Park Cottage
Hall Farm
Brockham Park
Brook Cottage
Coles Hill Farm
Coles Hill
Brockham Park Ho.
Lazell Gdns.
Oakley Gdns.
Playing Field
Highridge
Highridge Wood
Ashcroft Farm
Gadbrook Road
Hill View
Flanchford Road
Leigh Place
Moat
Dawesgreen
Abbots Pass Hall
Tapner's Road
Dawes Green House
Hook Farm
Rec. Grd.
Newdigate Rd.
Common Road
Bunce Common Road
The Acorns First School (Leigh Base)
Leigh Place Cotts.
Willow Cottage
Leigh
Brook Cottage
Root Hill Farm
Orchard Copse
Great Brockhamhurst
Brockhamhurst Road
Leigh Rd.
Bunts Place Farm
Bunts Place
140
Charman's Farm
Oakland

121
101
122
141
H
J
K
L
M
N
G
1
2
3
4
5
6
7
8
9
23
24
25
26
47
48
49
50
51
Northland Shaw
Bushy Shaw
Clifton's Shaw
Colleyland Shaw
Broadleas
Dowde's Farm
Bushfield Coppice
Claypit Shaw
Colley Copse
Colley Wood
Warehouses
Works
Sports Ground
Colley Pit
Tap Wood
Play. Fld.
Wks.
Offices
Fairhall
Nurseries
Round Alders
Shagbrook
Buckland Corner
BUCKLAND ROAD
ROAD WEST
A25
Cricket Ground
REIGATE HEATH GOLF COURSE
MOLE VALLEY
REIGATE and BANSTEAD
Reigate Heath
Reigate Heath Postmill
Club House
Ivy Cottage
Reigate
RH2
Playing Field
Pavilion
Rugby Club
Cricket Grd.
HIGH ST.
CHURCH STREET
LONDON RD.
Castle Grds.
Town Hall
Reigate Coll.
Superstore
Reigate
REIGATE
Priory Museum
Tennis Courts
Reigate Priory Playing Fields
Priory Pond
REIGATE PARK
Park Hill
Reservoir (covered)
Monument
LESBOURNE RD.
THE CLOSE
B2034
Bowling Grn.
Cemetery
Reigate Gram. Sch.
Fire Brigade East Division HQ
Brooklands Sch.
CROYDON RD.
A242
A217
BELL ST.
COCKSHOT HILL
Rosebank Cotts.
WOODHATCH
SOUTH PARK
King George's Field
Playing Field
Community Centre
Clayhall Farm
Littleton Manor Farm
Littleton
Wallace Brook
Heathfield
Heathfield Farm
Dungate Manor
Skimmington Cottages
The Lithe
Trumpet Hill
Trumpetshill Copse
June Farm
Stepstile Meadow
Gilbert's Farm
Santon House
FLANCHFORD ROAD
RIVER MOLE
CLAYHALL LANE
SLIPSHATCH ROAD
Greenlane Cottages
Flanchford Farm
Little Flanchford Farm
Flanchford Bridge
Mill Pond
The Lodge
Little Flanchford Cottages
Oakshade
Denshot Farm
Skeets Farm
Burys Court School
Butler's Shaw
Slipshatch Cotts.
Withy Wood
Slipshatch Wood
Hartswood Farm Cotts.
Hartswood Farm
Playing Fields
Park Plantation
Hilly Furze Field
Round Island
Pond Field Plantation
Old Sawpit Orchard
Upper Kiln Field Plantation
Kiln Field Plantation
Stable Plantation
Broad Ten Plantation
Gravelpit Plantation
Ninetythree Plantation
Twelve Acre Plantation
Birchett Copse
Firwood
Bures Manor
Magpie Shaw
River Field Plantation
Sidlow Bridge
Sidlow Bridge Centre
Church Meadow Farm
Riversid Meadow
DOVERS GREEN ROAD
DOVERSGREEN
Dovers Farm
Dovers Green Sch.
Woodhatch

A
B
C
D
E
F
G
1
2
3
4
5
6
7
8
9
26
27
28
29
51
50
49
48
47
102
142
121
COLES MEADS
HOLMETHORPE
REDHILL
Redhill
Wray Common
Wray Common Prim. Sch.
Brooklands Sch.
Fire Brigade East Division HQ
Redhill Tennis Club
Indoor Bowls Club
TA Centre
Johnston Ho.
Donyngs Rec. Cen.
Reffells Bri.
The Warwick Sch.
Kennedys Wood
Works
Redstone Hall
Hillsbrow
Byes Wood
Kingsfield Business Centre
Redstone Hill
Reigate Gram. Sch.
Reigate Parish Church Sch.
Cemetery
Reigate
RH2
REDHILL COMMON
Jubilee Plantation
Dunottar Day Sch. for Girls
St. John's
MEAD VALE
EARLSWOOD
Earlswood
Cemetery
RNIB Redhill College
Playing Field
Sports Ground
Redhill Brook
WOODHATCH
Reigate Sch.
Play. Fld.
REDHILL & REIGATE GOLF COURSE
EARLSWOOD COMMON
Cricket Ground
Club Ho.
Boat Houses
Boating Lake
New Pond
Earlswood Lakes
Sewage Works
Depot
Redhill Football Club
YMCA Sports Centre
Old Garston's House
Garston's Wood
REDHILL GOLF COURSE
Driving Range
EAST SURREY HOSPITAL
Redwood BUPA Diagnosis & Treatment Cen.
Robin Cook Farm
White Bushes
Hazelhurst Farm
Rushetts Farm
Dovers Green Sch.
New Pond Farm
Felland Copse
Recreation Ground
Earlswood Brook
DOVERS-GREEN
Turner's Shaw
Burnt Oak Farm
Cornfield Sch.
Petridge Wood Common
Maple Manor
Cricket Ground
Home Grove
Petridge Wood
Brookside Farm
Benting Wood
White Owl Farm
Church Meadow Farm
Sidlow
Sidlow Bridge
Riverside Meadows
Brick Field
The Plantation
Dean Farm
GATTON PARK ROAD
CROYDON ROAD
REIGATE ROAD
BLACKBOROUGH ROAD
STATION RD.
HATCHLANDS RD.
LONDON ROAD
BRIGHTON ROAD
THE CUTTING
HORLEY ROAD
WOODHATCH ROAD
REDSTONE HILL
NUTFIELD
A242
A25
B2034
A23
A2044
A217

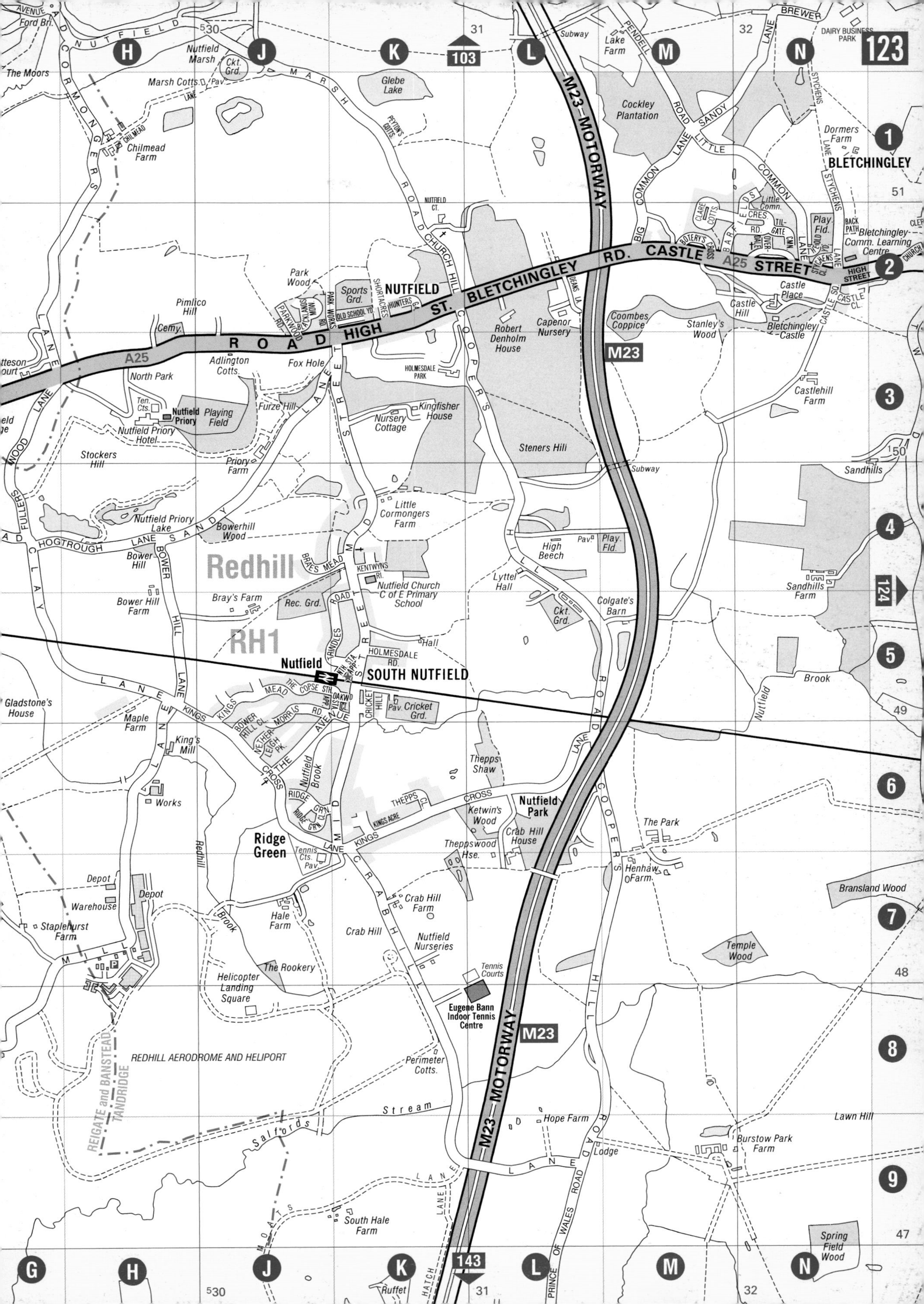

NUTFIELD
SOUTH NUTFIELD
BLETCHINGLEY
Redhill
RH1
Ridge Green
Nutfield Marsh
Nutfield Park
M23 MOTORWAY
A25
HIGH ST.
BLETCHINGLEY RD.
CASTLE STREET
Nutfield Priory
Nutfield Priory Hotel
Nutfield Priory Lake
Glebe Lake
Cockley Plantation
Chilmead Farm
Marsh Cotts.
The Moors
Ford Bri.
Park Wood
Pimlico Hill
Sports Grd.
North Park
Adlington Cotts.
Fox Hole
Playing Field
Furze Hill
Stockers Hill
Priory Farm
Bowerhill Wood
Bower Hill
Bower Hill Farm
Bray's Farm
Rec. Grd.
Nutfield Church C of E Primary School
Little Cormongers Farm
Kingfisher House
Nursery Cottage
Robert Denholm House
Capenor Nursery
Steners Hill
High Beech
Lyttel Hall
Play. Fld.
Colgate's Barn
Ckt. Grd.
Coombes Coppice
Stanley's Wood
Castle Hill
Castle Place
Bletchingley Castle
Castlehill Farm
Sandhills
Sandhills Farm
Dormers Farm
Bletchingley Comm. Learning Centre
Lake Farm
DAIRY BUSINESS PARK
Gladstone's House
Maple Farm
King's Mill
Works
Cricket Grd.
Thepps Shaw
Ketwin's Wood
Crab Hill House
Theppswood Hse.
The Park
Henhaw Farm
Bransland Wood
Depot
Warehouse
Staplehurst Farm
Hale Farm
Crab Hill Farm
Crab Hill
Nutfield Nurseries
The Rookery
Helicopter Landing Square
Eugene Bann Indoor Tennis Centre
Tennis Courts
Temple Wood
REDHILL AERODROME AND HELIPORT
Perimeter Cotts.
REIGATE and BANSTEAD
TANDRIDGE
Hope Farm
Lodge
Burstow Park Farm
Lawn Hill
South Hale Farm
Spring Field Wood
Ruffet
Salfords Stream
PRINCE OF WALES ROAD
COOPERS HILL ROAD
HOGTROUGH LANE
SANDY LANE
FULLERS WOOD LANE
CLAY LANE
KINGS CROSS LANE
KINGS LANE
MID STREET
CRAB HILL
THEPPS CL.
THE AVENUE
Subway
103
124
143
H J K L M N G
1 2 3 4 5 6 7 8 9

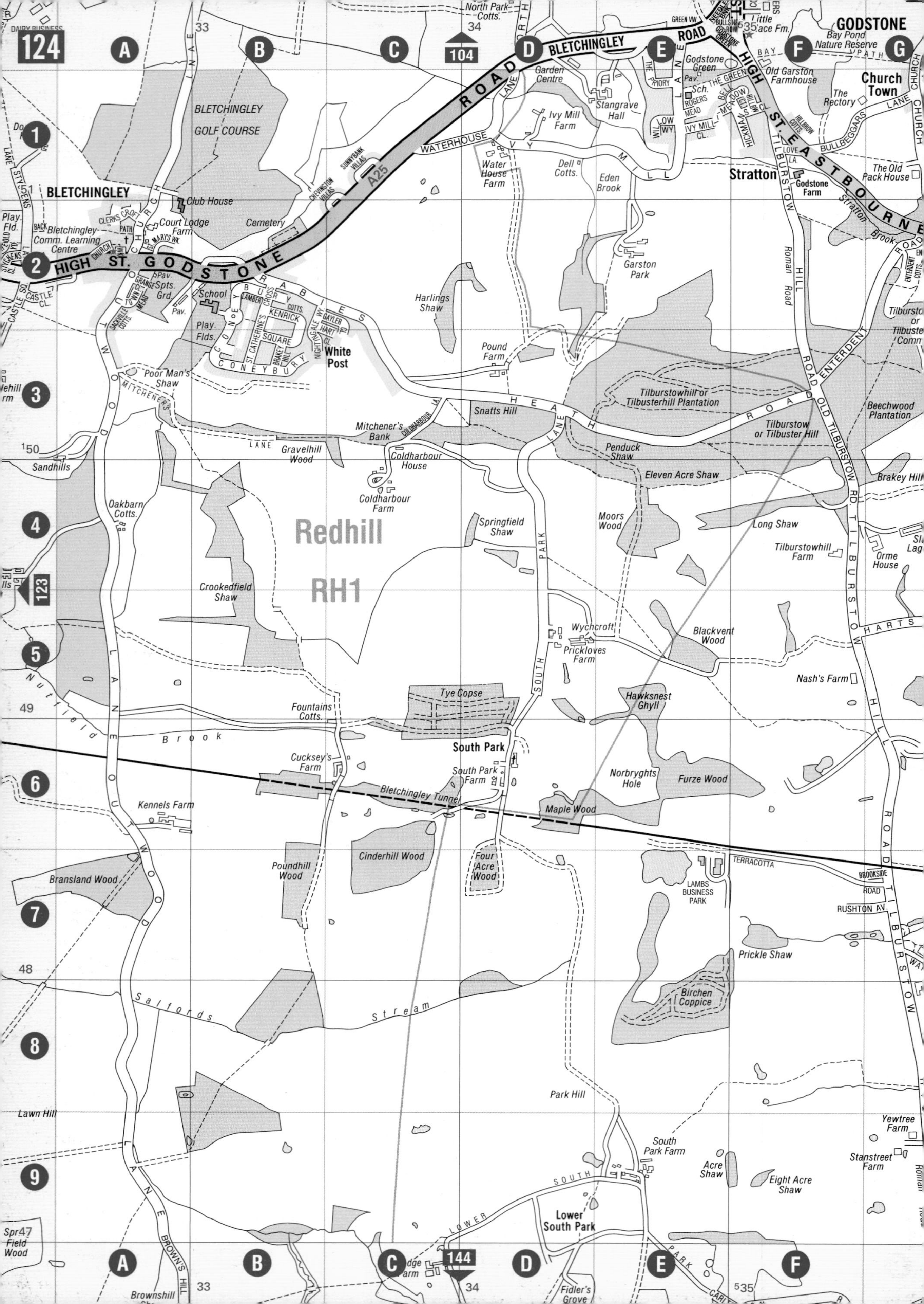

BLETCHINGLEY
BLETCHINGLEY GOLF COURSE
Club House
Court Lodge Farm
Cemetery
Bletchingley Comm. Learning Centre
HIGH ST.
GODSTONE ROAD
BLETCHINGLEY ROAD
A25
School
Play. Flds.
White Post
Poor Man's Shaw
Sandhills
Oakbarn Cotts.
Redhill
RH1
Crookedfield Shaw
Gravelhill Wood
Mitchener's Bank
Coldharbour House
Coldharbour Farm
Snatts Hill
Springfield Shaw
Harlings Shaw
Pound Farm
Garston Park
Water House Farm
Ivy Mill Farm
Dell Cotts.
Eden Brook
Stangrave Hall
Garden Centre
Godstone Green
GODSTONE
Bay Pond Nature Reserve
Church Town
Old Garston Farmhouse
The Rectory
The Old Pack House
Stratton
Godstone Farm
Tilburstowhill or Tilbusterhill Plantation
Beechwood Plantation
Tilburstow or Tilbuster Hill
Penduck Shaw
Eleven Acre Shaw
Brakey Hill
Moors Wood
Long Shaw
Tilburstowhill Farm
Orme House
Wychcroft
Prickloves Farm
Blackvent Wood
Nash's Farm
Hawksnest Ghyll
Tye Copse
Fountains Cotts.
South Park
Cucksey's Farm
South Park Farm
Norbryghts Hole
Furze Wood
Maple Wood
Bletchingley Tunnel
Kennels Farm
Bransland Wood
Poundhill Wood
Cinderhill Wood
Four Acre Wood
LAMBS BUSINESS PARK
Prickle Shaw
Birchen Coppice
Salfords Stream
Nutfield Brook
Park Hill
Lawn Hill
South Park Farm
Acre Shaw
Eight Acre Shaw
Yewtree Farm
Stanstreet Farm
Lower South Park
Brownshill
Fidler's Grove
OUTWOOD LANE
SOUTH PARK LANE
HEATH ROAD
TILBURSTOW HILL ROAD
104
123
144

125
TANDRIDGE GOLF COURSE
105
145
126
Garden Centre
Nags Hall
Moore's Shaw
Glebe Water
The Glebe House
Tennis Court
GODSTONE BY-PASS
A22
Castlehill Wood
Leigh Place
Leigh Place Pond
Castlehill Wood
B2236
Leigh Mill House
Refuse Tips
Smokey Hollow
Mereland Wood
Sewage Works
Gibbs Brook
Godstone
RH9
WONHAM PL.
EASTBOURNE ROAD
Oldpark Wood
JACKASS LANE
Little Court Farm
TANDRIDGE LANE
The Lodge
Tandridge Court
Tandridge Court Fm.
THE WALK
TANDRIDGE
Dean Shaw Cottages
Dean Shaw
St. Peter's C of E Inf. Sch.
Tandridge Hall
TANDRIDGE PARK
Windmillstadle Wood
The Birches
Flowergarden Plantation
Beechwood Hill
New Bustons Wood
Bustons Wood
Round Wood
Stonepit Shaw
Maizenhill Shaw
Southlands
Maizenhill Shaw
GROVE ROAD
Reddings Wood
Southlands Shaws
Southlands Lodge
SOUTHLANDS
Southlands Wood
Oxted Place
The Mount
Broadham Green
Broadham House
TANHOUSE RD.
BROADHAM HILL
BROADHAM GREEN ROAD
Perrysfield Fm.
Caperway Cottages
Rose Farm
HOPE LANE
Oxted
RH8
BROOK
Holly Bush Farm
Bushey Croft
GIBBS BROOK LANE
Stow Coppice
Newhouse Farm
NEW ROAD
MILES LANE
Brook Farm
Paygate Wood
Steadmanshill Wood
Barnfield Shaw
Park Pale
Postern Gate Farm
Piper's Wood
New Zealand Cottages
Gibbs Brook
Lagham Wood
LAGHAM PARK DR.
WOODLANDS
OAKLANDS
TREETOPS
STATION RD.
HUNTERS CHASE
EASTER WAY
LAGHAM GRANGE
ST. JOHNS CT.
St. Stephen's C of E Prim.Sch.
SOUTH GODSTONE
Playing Field
Pav.
Godstone
Wks.
Chathill
Chathill Park Farm
Old Hall Farm
Foyle Tolt
Pound Wood
Dodds Coppice
Depot
CROWHURST
Crowhurst Lane End
Drewsherne Farm
Brickmakers' Wood
Lagham Park Farm
Lagham Manor
Moat
RSPCA Animal Cen.
Works
Lagham Lodge Farm
Ashen Plantations
Playing Field
Hall
St. George's Cottages
Church Farm
Crowhurst
Lingfield
Bradford Wood
The Mount
FAYGATE LANE
Godstone Place
Hobbs Farm
Ashen Shaw
RH7
Stocks and Kingswood Farms
Gaysland Cottages
DANEMORE
Comforts Place Farm
36
37
38
39
51
50
49
48
47
G H J K L M N
1 2 3 4 5 6 7 8 9

Hurst Green
HURST GREEN
Holland
HOLLAND
Broadham Green
Pains Hill
Oxted
RH8
Merle Common
Lingfield
Crowhurst
RH7
Tanhouse Fm.
Stonehall Farm
Moor House Sch.
Mill Lane Playing Field
Hurst Green Inf. Sch.
Fairview Industrial Estate
King George's Field
Holland Junior Sch.
Sewage Treatment Works
Dunks Pond
Stockett's Manor
Stockett's Manor Farm
Coltsford House
Mill Pond
Boulthurst Fm.
Reservoir (covered)
Tenchleys
Tenchleys Wood
Loampit Wood
Whitegates Farm
Grants Cottage
Grants Paddock
Crabbett Wood
Crabbett Wood Farm
Doghurst
Redlane Cotts.
Itchingwood Common
Parishcroft Wood
Parishcroft Wood Farm
Red Lane Farm
Connerton Farm
Stockenden Fm.
Collesters Wood
Honesland Wood
Mollstones Wood
Gincox Farm
Finch's Cross
Gincox Tolt
Playing Fld.
Playing Field
Hall
Kitchengarden Shaw
Foyle Tolt
Foyle Fm.
Sunt Wood
Sunt Farm
Little Earls Wood
Great Earls Wood
High Ridge Farm
Comforts Cottage
Staffhurst Wood Nature Reserve
Five Acre Wood
Brills Farm
Couldens Farm
Monks Fm.
Caper's Farm
Kiln Coppice
White House Farm
Grubbs Farm
Butcherswood Bank
Black Robin's Farm
Partridge Fm.
Caterfield Bridge
Whitehouse Wood
Bombers Farm
Kennels
Galley's Wood
Wintersell Wood
Shingle Barn Farm
Wintersell Farm
Shinglebarn Wood
Oldhouse Farm
Mansionhouse Farm
Church Farm
Altar Cottages
Pound Farm
St. George's Cotts.
Hall
Broadham House
The Alders
Viewlands
Tanhouse Road
Church Way
Woodhurst Lane
Holland Road
Merle Common Road
Red Lane
Grants Lane
Staffhurst Wood Road
Wellhouse Lane
Monks Lane
Honeypot Lane
Caterfield Lane
Crowhurst Lane
Park Road
Popes Lane
Broadham Green Road
Gibbs Brook Lane
Pollards Wood Road
Itchingwood Common Road
Short Lane
Oak Road
Holland Lane
River Eden
Crooked River
106
125
146
A B C D E F G
1 2 3 4 5 6 7 8 9
39 40 41 42
51 50 49 48 47

KENT HATCH ROAD
KENT HATCH ROAD
107
CROCKHAMHILL COMMON
Champion's Farm
Champions Place
Scearn Bank
TREVEREUX
The Old House
Marie Curie Research Institute
Kent Hatch Ho.
Kent Hatch
Chartlands Farm
Chartlands
The Cearne
The Red House
B269
HOSEY COMMON ROAD
B2026
Froghole Farm
FROGHOLE
Froghole
Mariners Hill
Mariners
Chartwell Farm
Chartwell Cott.
MAPLETON ROAD
Eastfield
Little Mariners
Little Court
Crockham Hill Farm
Rusholme
Newlands
Roundmead Shaw
HILL
Trevereux
SMITHS LANE
Stubblefield
OAKDALE LA.
Crockham Hill C of E Prim. Sch.
CROCKHAM HILL
Chandlers
Chandler's Wood
Coachmans
The Moat Farm
DEANERY RD.
SPOUT
Kent Brook
West House
SWAYNESLAND ROAD
Swaynesland
Lewins
DAIRY LANE
Hurst Farm
Old Dairy Farm
Pav.
Ten. Ct.
Playing Field
DENNETTSLAND RD
TANDRIDGE
SEVENOAKS
POOTINGS LANE
Grange Farm
Crockham Grange
Longcroft Wood
Haftcroft Wood
Roman Road (course of)
Redland Farm
Edenbridge
GUILDABLES LANE
Guildables Park Farm
Guildables Wood
Sports Field
Model Fm.
Coakham Farm
Langhurst
TN8
Coakham Lodge Farm
Roselands
Oakfield Farm
Coakham Wood
Pootings
POOTINGS ROAD
Rushett
Birds Wood
HOLE LANE
Scamperdale Cottage
Appledore
Broxham Wood
MAIN ROAD
Batchelor's Farm
Gaywood Farm
Kent Brook
Broxham Manor
HOMESTEAD RD.
FAIRMEAD RD.
Troy Town
Swan Lane Farm
Yew Tree Farm
OAKFIELD RD.
HILDERS CL.
HIGHFIELDS RD.
CREST RD.
BROWNINGS
Hilders
Batchelor's Wood
Marlpit Hill
SWAN LANE
HILDERS LANE
TROY LANE
ASHCOMBE DR.
MARLHURST
Alfriston
MEADOW LA.
PIT
MARLPIT CL.
RIDGE LANE
SWAN RIDGE WAY
CROWN RD.
B2027
ELMS ROAD
Mowshurst
LITTLE BROWNS LANE
Little Browns Farm
Little Browns Wood
Crouch House Wood
Breezehurst Farm
Works
Edenbridge
SUNNYSIDE
Holdings Fm.
ST. BRELADE'S MOBILE HOME PARK
Hamsell Mead Fm.
STATION ROAD
FIRCROFT WAY
FIRCROFT BUSINESS CENTRE
MALLARD WAY
KESTREL CL.
WOODPECKER CL.
ROWFIELD
STACKFIELD
SMITHYFIELD
Sewage Works
Spitals Cross Estate
THE INDUSTRIAL ESTATE
EDENBRIDGE
EDENBRIDGE GOLF & COUNTRY CLUB
Moat
Spitals Cross
FOUR ELMS ROAD
SKINNERS LANE
CROUCH HOUSE ROAD
Ten. Cts.
Crouch House Farm
WESTWAYS
The Edenbridge Centre
Playing Fields
Works
147
CEDAR DR.
PARK AV.
43
44
545
51
150
49
48
47
G
H
J
K
L
M
N
1
2
3
4
5
6
7
8
9

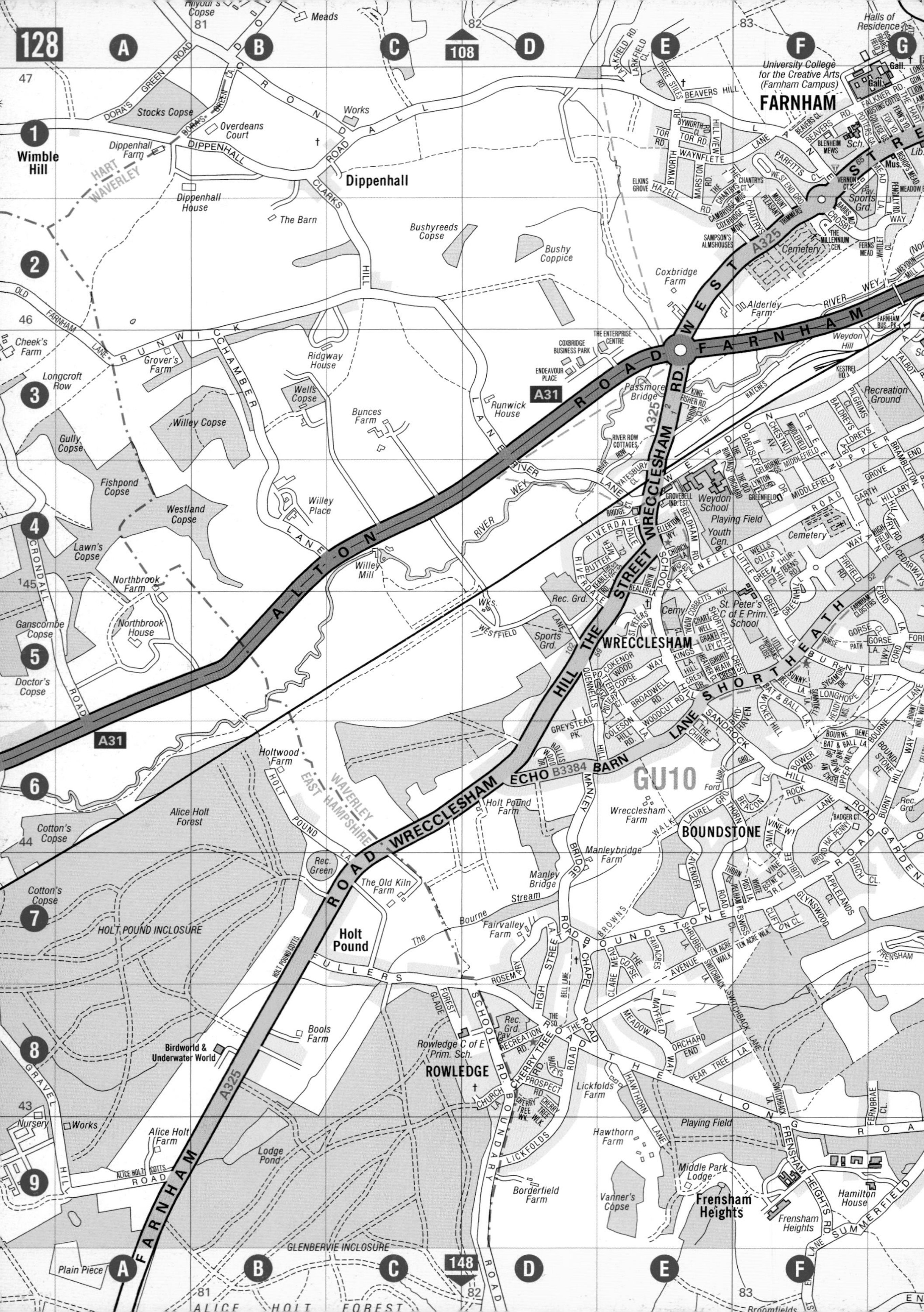
A
B
C
D
E
F
G
108
148
1
2
3
4
5
6
7
8
9
47
46
45
44
43
81
82
83
FARNHAM
Dippenhall
Wimble Hill
WRECCLESHAM
BOUNDSTONE
ROWLEDGE
Holt Pound
Frensham Heights
GU10
University College for the Creative Arts (Farnham Campus)
Halls of Residence
Stocks Copse
Overdeans Court
Dippenhall Farm
Dippenhall House
The Barn
Bushyreeds Copse
Bushy Coppice
Coxbridge Farm
Alderley Farm
Cheek's Farm
Grover's Farm
Ridgway House
Longcroft Row
Wells Copse
Bunces Farm
Runwick House
Willey Copse
Gully Copse
Fishpond Copse
Westland Copse
Willey Place
Willey Mill
Lawn's Copse
Northbrook Farm
Northbrook House
Ganscombe Copse
Doctor's Copse
Holtwood Farm
Alice Holt Forest
Cotton's Copse
HOLT POUND INCLOSURE
Holt Pound Farm
Wrecclesham Farm
Manleybridge Farm
Manley Bridge
The Old Kiln Farm
Rec. Green
Fairvalley Farm
Bools Farm
Birdworld & Underwater World
Rowledge C of E Prim. Sch.
Lickfolds Farm
Hawthorn Farm
Playing Field
Middle Park Lodge
Hamilton House
Alice Holt Farm
Lodge Pond
Borderfield Farm
Vanner's Copse
GLENBERVIE INCLOSURE
Plain Piece
ALICE HOLT FOREST
Nursery
Works
Weydon School
Playing Field
Youth Cen.
St. Peter's C of E Prim. School
Cemetery
Recreation Ground
Weydon Hill
Passmore Bridge
Sports Grd.
Rec. Grd.
THE ENTERPRISE CENTRE
COXBRIDGE BUSINESS PARK
ENDEAVOUR PLACE
A31
A325
B3384
ALTON ROAD
WEST STREET
FARNHAM RD.
WRECCLESHAM HILL
THE STREET
WRECCLESHAM ROAD
ECHO BARN LANE
SHORTHEATH ROAD
BOUNDSTONE ROAD
LONG ROAD
FRENSHAM HEIGHTS RD
SUMMERFIELD LANE
FARNHAM ROAD
FULLERS ROAD
ALICE HOLT COTTS
GRAVEL HILL
CRONDALL ROAD
DORA'S GREEN ROAD
CRONDALL LA.
DIPPENHALL
CLARKS HILL
RUNWICK LANE
CHAMBER LANE
RIVER LANE
WEYDON LANE
UPPER WEYBOURNE LANE
BEAVERS HILL
HAZELL RD.
BYWORTH RD.
WAYNFLETE LANE
SCHOOL HILL
BELDHAM RD.
MANLEY BRIDGE ROAD
HIGH STREET
CHAPEL ROAD
SCHOOL RD.
BOUNDARY ROAD
CHERRY TREE RD.
HART
WAVERLEY
EAST HAMPSHIRE
River Wey
The Bourne Stream
Frensham

129
109
149
130
Farnham
A31
BY PASS
CASTLE ST.
THE BOROUGH
EAST ST.
SOUTH ST.
UNION RD.
DOWNING ST.
Sports Cen.
Farnham Bus. Cen.
Riverside Business Park
Riverside Park
RIVER LANE
WEY
BRIDGEFIELD
BROOMLEAF RD.
WAVERLEY LANE
Farnham Maltings
New Ashgate Gall.
FIRGROVE HILL
St. Polycarp's Cath. Prim. Sch.
Hospice
South Farnham Sch.
The Abbey Sch.
Ten. Cts.
Play. Flds.
Farnham College
Rec. Grd.
COMPTON
Compton Hill
Culverlands
MOOR PARK LANE
Moor Park
Delarden House
The Thatched House
Compton Rec. Grd.
B3001
GU9
Abbey Business Park
Reservoir (Covered)
Priory Farm
Waverley Abbey House
Long Barn
Waverley Abbey (Remains)
Ancora Farm House
Redhill House
Red Hill
Monk's Walk Farm
Lodge Farm
MONKS WALK
TILFORD ROAD
Woodlarks Camp Site
A287
FRENSHAM ROAD
RIDGWAY ROAD
B3384
MIDDLE BOURNE
LOWER BOURNE
The Bourne School
Lodge Hill House
Lobswood Manor
Black Lake
Alice Holt Forest
Bourne Wood
Tilfordmill Bridge
Nightingale Farm
SHEEPHATCH LANE
Sheephatch Copse
Bournelands
HORTHEATH
THE BOURNE
Rec. Grd.
GONG HILL
Gong Hill
Birchen Hey
Edgeborough School
Play. Fld.
Games Ct.
Kennel Farm
More House School
MOONS HILL
FIFIELD LANE
Burtleys Copse
Keepers Field
MILLBRIDGE
REEDS ROAD
The Reeds
TANKERSFORD COMMON
Old Kiln Museum & Rural Life Centre
Tilford Reeds
Tilford House Farm
The Malt House
Meadow End Farm
Shortfield House
Hollow Dene
Saints of E In Sch.
G H J K L M N
1 2 3 4 5 6 7 8 9
84 485 86 87
43 44 45 46 47

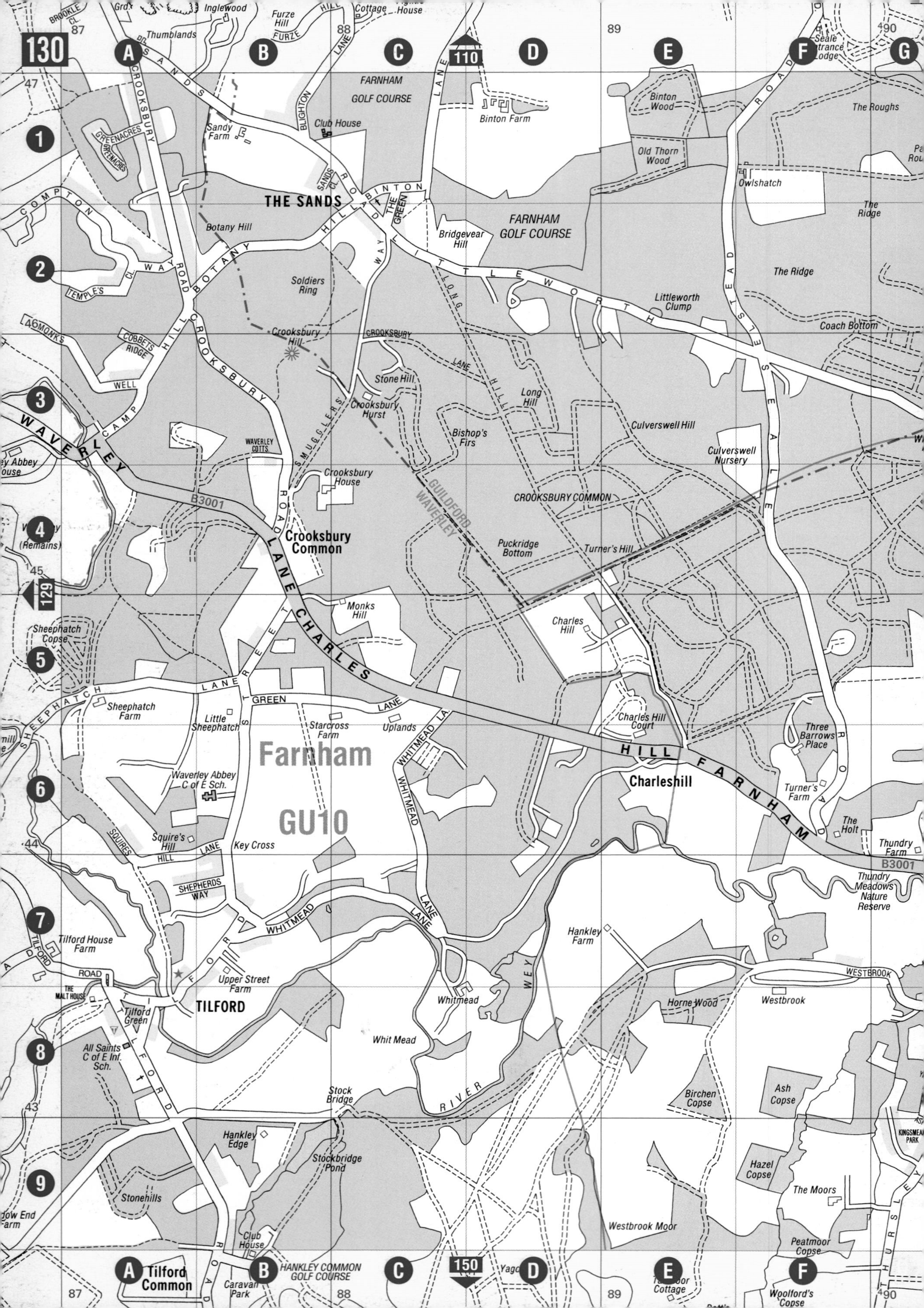
A
B
C
D
E
F
G
1
2
3
4
5
6
7
8
9
87
88
89
90
47
46
45
44
43
110
129
150
Inglewood
Thumblands
Furze Hill
FURZE HILL
Cottage
House
Seale Entrance Lodge
BROOKLE CL.
SANDS
CROOKSBURY ROAD
GREENACRES
FARNHAM GOLF COURSE
Club House
BLIGHTON LANE
LANE
Binton Farm
Binton Wood
The Roughs
Old Thorn Wood
Owlshatch
Sandy Farm
THE SANDS
SANDS CL
BINTON
THE GREEN
HILL ROAD
COMPTON WAY
Botany Hill
FARNHAM GOLF COURSE
Bridgevear Hill
The Ridge
TEMPLE'S CL
ROAD
BOTANY
Soldiers Ring
LITTLEWORTH
Littleworth Clump
The Ridge
MONKS WELL
COBBETS RIDGE
HILL
CROOKSBURY
Crooksbury Hill
CROOKSBURY LANE
LONG HILL
Coach Bottom
SEALE
STEAD
Stone Hill
Long Hill
CAMP
WAVERLEY
Crooksbury Hurst
SMUGGLERS
Bishop's Firs
Culverswell Hill
Culverswell Nursery
WAVERLEY COTTS
Crooksbury House
GUILDFORD WAVERLEY
CROOKSBURY COMMON
B3001
Crooksbury Common
(Remains)
Puckridge Bottom
Turner's Hill
Monks Hill
Charles Hill
Sheephatch Copse
LANE
STREET
CHARLES
Sheephatch Farm
SHEEPHATCH
GREEN
LANE
Little Sheephatch
Starcross Farm
Uplands
Charles Hill Court
Three Barrows Place
HILL
FARNHAM
Farnham
WHITMEAD LA
Charleshill
Turner's Farm
Waverley Abbey C of E Sch.
GU10
WHITMEAD LANE
The Holt
Thundry Farm
B3001
Squire's Hill
SQUIRES
HILL LANE
Key Cross
Thundry Meadows Nature Reserve
SHEPHERDS WAY
WHITMEAD
LANE
Tilford House Farm
TILFORD
ROAD
FORD
Hankley Farm
WEY
WESTBROOK
THE MALT HOUSE
Upper Street Farm
TILFORD
Whitmead
Horne Wood
Westbrook
Tilford Green
All Saints C of E Inf. Sch.
Whit Mead
Ash Copse
Stock Bridge
RIVER
Birchen Copse
KINGSMEAD PARK
Hankley Edge
Stockbridge Pond
Hazel Copse
The Moors
Stonehills
Westbrook Moor
Peatmoor Copse
Club House
Tilford Common
HANKLEY COMMON GOLF COURSE
Caravan Park
Cottage
Woolford's Copse

Guildford
GU3
Godalming
GU8
ELSTEAD
SHACKLEFORD
Peper Harow
Gatwick
PUTTENHAM COMMON
HAMPTON PARK
ROYAL COMMON
Bagmoor Common Nature Reserve
111
151
132

A
B
C
D
E
F
G
1
2
3
4
5
6
7
8
9
47
46
45
44
43
94
495
96
112
131
152
Berthorpe
Berthorpe Farm
COMPTON
Bummoor Copse
Sewage Works
Pipkin Copse
Eastbury Manor
Compton St. Nicholas Church
Nightingales
Westbury Barn
Round Hill
GU3
Playing Fld.
B3000
STREET
Compton Wood
Compton Common
The Common
Burl's R
Island Cottage
Kiln Copse
Lone Barn
New Barn
PUTTENHAM
A3
Two Stacks
Field Place
Eastbury Park
Eastbury Copse
Eastbury Barn
Prior's Wood
Prior's Field Sch.
Swim. Pool
Abbot's Wood
PRIORS HATCH LANE
BY-PASS
Fox Hanger
Meadow Barn
Fox Hanger Farm
BINSCOMBE
CHALK LANE
Home Farm
HURTMORE GOLF COURSE
SUMMERS ROAD
MARK WAY
HURTMORE ROAD
CORNER BUNGALOWS
Broom & Lees
SHACKLEFORD
Club House
HURTMORE
Charterhouse
NORTHWAY
North Lodge
Under Grn (Ckt. Grd.)
Charterhouse School
Games Court
Queens Sports Cen.
GODALMING
GRENVILLE ROAD
Hurtmore Holt
Granton Ho.
Dormy Lodge
Grenville
QUARRY RD.
Golf Course
Playing Fields
Play Fld.
Wildernesse
Glebe Farm
Mushroom Farm
Norney Grange
Lodge
Rec. Grd.
SHACKLEFORD ROAD
St. Mary's C of E Inf. Sch.
Rec. Grd.
By-Pass Cott.
Hurtmore Bottom
Ben Travers Theatre
FRITH HILL
Fir Walk
Running Track
Withy Bed
Fives Courts
Tennis Courts
Shackleford Heath
Norney Wood
NORNEY
SCHOOL LA.
RIVER WEY
Milton Wood
Racquets & Squash Cts.
Swimming Bath
PEPERHAROW ROAD
The Rough
ELSTEAD ROAD
Norney Farm
AND
Eashing Copse
Hell Ditch
GU7
Farnham Lodge
Twotree Hill
Mount Sion
GU8
Slowley Copse
Westbrook
Home Farm Cottages
Peper Harow
Godalming
GUILDFORD
WAVERLEY
WESTBROOK ROAD
Westhanger Cott.
Meath Home
WESTBROOK
The Bothy
EASHING
Eashing Farm
Halfway House
Westaway
Godalming
Upper Eashing
PEPER HAROW PARK
Abbey Mill Bus. Park
Lower Eashing
Nursery
HALFWAY LANE
Aaron's Hill
Ockford Wood
Eashing Lodge
THE DRIVE
THE HOLLOW
EASHING LANE
Oxenford Bridge
Eashing Bri.
Eashing Moor Copse
RIVER WEY
Brook Walk
Bonville Hanger
St. Mark's C of E Prim. Sch.
Eashing Cemetery
OCKFORD RIDGE
OCKFORD ROAD
St. Hilary's Sch.
SHACKSTEAD
MILFORD ROAD
B3001
A283
BY-PASS
Thurnets Copse
MILFORD
Garden Centre
Play-ground
Amberley Farm
GUILDFORD & GODALMING BY-PASS RD.
Active Workings
Ladywell Farm
A3100
PORTSMOUTH ROAD
LOWER MOUSHILL LA.
Weir

133
113
134
153
Guildford
GODALMING
FARNCOMBE
SHALFORD
BROADFORD
PEASMARSH
CATTESHALL
BUSBRIDGE
CROWNPITS
HOLLOWAY HILL
MUNSTEAD HEATH
GU4
GU5
GU8

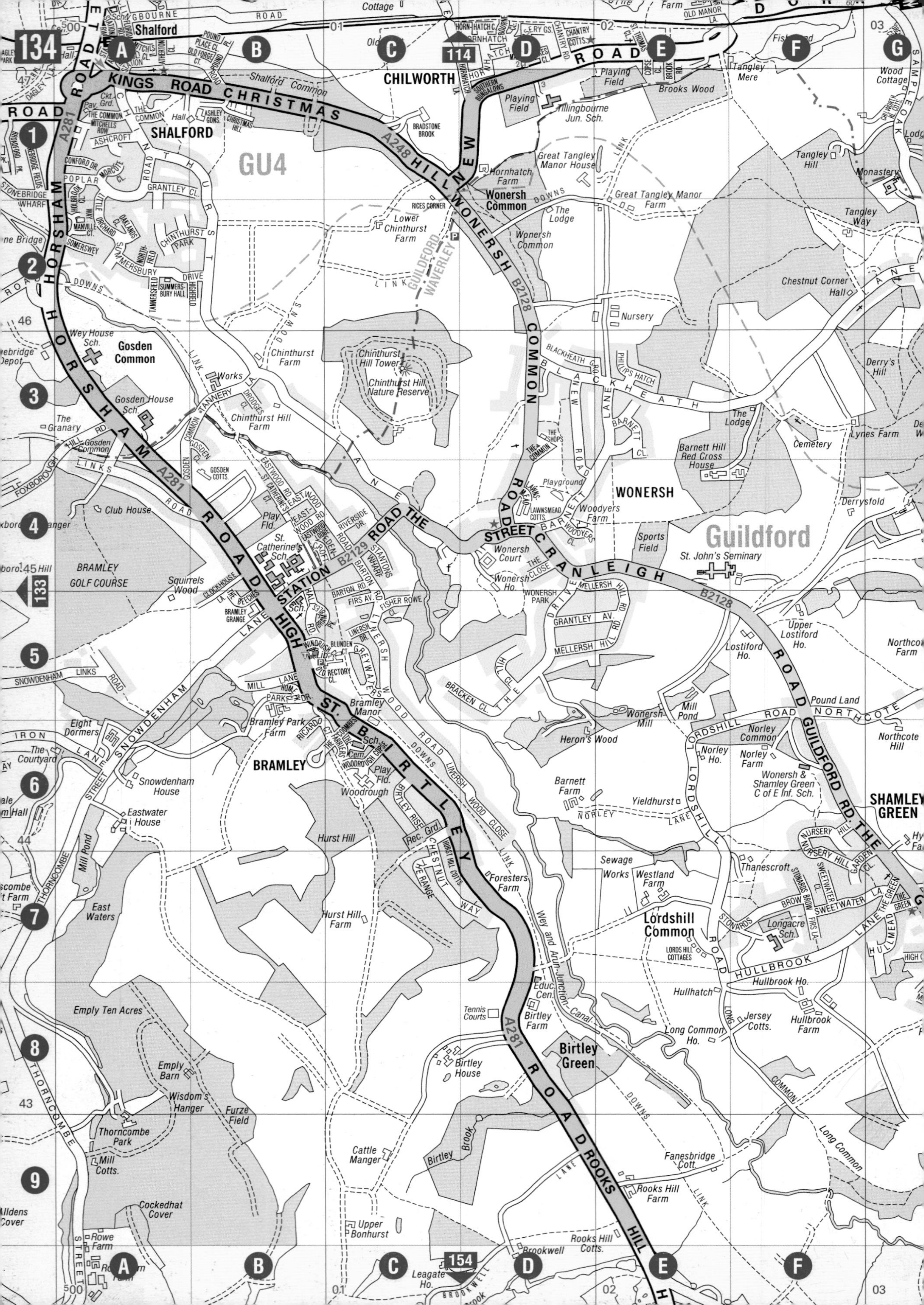
134
114
133
154
A
B
C
D
E
F
G
1
2
3
4
5
6
7
8
9
500
01
02
03
46
45
44
43
Shalford
SHALFORD
Chilworth
CHILWORTH
GU4
KINGS ROAD
CHRISTMAS HILL
A248
A281
HORSHAM ROAD
Shalford Common
Bradstone Brook
Playing Field
Tillingbourne Jun. Sch.
Brooks Wood
Tangley Mere
Wood Cottage
Great Tangley Manor House
Hornhatch Farm
Wonersh Common
Great Tangley Manor Farm
The Lodge
Rices Corner
Lower Chinthurst Farm
GUILDFORD - WAVERLEY
NEW ROAD
WONERSH COMMON
B2128
Tangley Hill
Monastery
Tangley Way
Chestnut Corner Hall
Nursery
Derry's Hill
Wey House Sch.
Gosden Common
Chinthurst Farm
Chinthurst Hill Tower
Chinthurst Hill Nature Reserve
Works
Gosden House Sch.
The Granary
Chinthurst Hill Farm
BLACKHEATH LANE
Barnett Hill Red Cross House
Cemetery
Lynes Farm
Club House
Play. Fld.
St. Catherine's Sch.
STATION ROAD
B2129
THE STREET
WONERSH
Woodyers Farm
Sports Field
Guildford
St. John's Seminary
Derrysfold
BRAMLEY GOLF COURSE
Squirrels Wood
Wonersh Court
Wonersh Ho.
Wonersh Park
CRANLEIGH ROAD
Upper Lostiford Ho.
Lostiford Ho.
Northcote Farm
HIGH STREET
Bramley Manor
Bramley Park Farm
BRAMLEY
Wonersh Mill
Mill Pond
Pound Land
NORTHCOTE ROAD
Eight Dormers
The Courtyard
SNOWDENHAM LANE
Heron's Wood
Norley Common
Norley Ho.
Norley Farm
Wonersh & Shamley Green C of E Inf. Sch.
Northcote Hill
Snowdenham House
Eastwater House
Woodrough
Barnett Farm
Yieldhurst
NORLEY LANE
LORDSHILL ROAD
GUILDFORD RD.
SHAMLEY GREEN
Mill Pond
Hurst Hill
ST. BIRTLEY ROAD
Sewage Works
Westland Farm
Thanescroft
Foresters Farm
East Waters
Hurst Hill Farm
Lordshill Common
Longacre Sch.
Wey and Arun Junction Canal
HULLBROOK LANE
Hullbrook Ho.
Hullhatch
Educ. Cen.
Tennis Courts
Birtley Farm
Jersey Cotts.
Hullbrook Farm
Long Common Ho.
Empty Ten Acres
Birtley House
Birtley Green
Empty Barn
Wisdom's Hanger
Furze Field
Thorncombe Park
Mill Cotts.
Cattle Manger
Birtley Brook
Fanesbridge Cott.
Long Common
Cockedhat Cover
Rooks Hill Farm
ROOKS HILL
Upper Bonhurst
Rowe Farm
Brookwell
Rooks Hill Cotts.
Leagate Ho.
THORNCOMBE STREET
IRON LANE

Blackheath
BLACKHEATH
LOCKNER HOLT
Aston House
Locknor Brake
War Memorial
Rosemary Hill
Ckt. Ground
Postford Farm Cotts.
Little Ford Farm
Ford Crossing
Watercress Beds
Lake
Kiln Rough
Albury Heath
Pav. Football & Cricket Ground
Woodside
Hare Dene
Brook Crossing
Fir Croft
Brook Lodge
Brook
Brook Farm
Broomfields
Mustard Copse
Foxholes Wood
Foxholes
Lipcombe Cotts
Home Villas
FARLEY GREEN
Edgeley Caravan Park
Club
Jugs Copse
Heathfields
Hallams Court
Pipers Landing
The Hallams
Northbrook Hill
Northbrook
Hallam's Farm
Jelley's Copse
Greenglade
Farley Green Hall Farm
Kingsfield
East Hills
Lockhurst Hatch La.
Darbyn's Brook
Rompin Downs
Farley Heath
FARLEY HEATH
Watercress Beds
Haldish Farm
Greenlane Farm
Nursery
Blackmoor Paddock
Holmcroft
Far Plantation
Skemp Pond
Mayorhouse Holt
New Field
Mardons
Blackmoor Lodge
Sheepwalk
Mayor House
Mayorhouse Farm
Sandhurst Copse
Reelhall Hill
Shamley Wood Ho.
Sandhurst Hill
Works
Kiln Hanger
Kilnhanger
Upper Woodhill Farm
Woodcock Hill
Tree Tops Caravan Park
GU5
The Burrows
Winterfold Cottages
Tumblers Court
Reelhall Farm
Woodhill Manor
Woodlands
Friars Oak
Reelhall
Plonks Farm
Pasturewood
Pithouse Copse
Helmet Copse
The Ball
Stroud Farm
Nail Copse
Madgehole Copse
Madgehole
Keepers Cottage
Franklin's Farm
Madgehole Farm
Grist Hill Farm
Winterfold Cottage
Winterfold Heath
Great Copse
Long Copse
Bisney Cott.
Stroud Common
Warren Cottage
Willinghurst Farm
Spring Wood
Rock Copse
Winterfold Hill
Willinghurst House
Spanish House
Barn Plaits
Garden Cottage
Lapscom Copse
Winterfold Heath
Stroud Lodge
Knob Copse
Kill Copse
Church Hill Stroud Common Guildford Rd.
B2128
Upper House Lane
Waverley Guildford
Birget Hill
Albury Warren
Lodge
Holt
Dorking Rd.
Lane Green
Madgehole Lane
Farley Heath Road
August La.
Brook Hill
Shophouse Lane
Ride Lane
Row Lane
Hurtwood Lane
Blackheath Lane
Sandy Lane
New Road
Park Road
Heath Lane
Warners La.
Little London
Brook Lane
Ponds Lane
Woodhill Lane
Dibdene La.
The Green
Stroud Lane
115
136
155

Little London
Parklands
Burrows Cross
Guildford
GU5
Hoe
Smoky Hole
Peaslake
Colman's Hill
Hurt Wood
Winterfold Forest
Cranleigh
GU6
The Warren

Dorking
RH5
SUTTON ABINGER
ABINGER COMMON
Friday Street
HOLMBURY ST. MARY
Feldemore
Felday
Pitland Street
Abinger Bottom
King George's Hill
Paddington Tolt
Raikes Farm
Sutton Abinger
Frolbury Manor
The Old Farm
Cony Copse
Woodhouse Farm
High Top Lawns
Fairhaven
Deers Hill
Woodhouse Copse
Woodhouse Pond
Felbury House
PASTURE WOOD
Tilling Bourne
Townhurst Wood
Ellix Wood
Ellix Plantation
Chandlers Wood
High Copse
Park Rew
Rectory Copse
Ellix Wood Cottages
Abinger Common School
The Rectory
Abinger Manor
Football Ground
Mark Ash
Whitings Wood
The Grove
Mundies Plantation
Mundies
Millpond Copse
Goddard's
Parkhurst Wood
Park House Farm
Park House
Feldemore Corner
Moon Hall Sch.
Belmont Sch.
The Old Barn
Beatrice Webb House
The Gables
Cottage Copse
Riding School
The Coppers
Pond Copse
Pasture Wood
Upper Foxmoor Wood
Pump House
High Ashes Farm
Furzefield Plantation
Highashes Wood
GREAT FOXMOOR WOOD
Stonymoor Wood
Burnthouse Copse
Rosiers Wood
Hopedene Farm
Smith's Wood
Buildings Copse
The Coach House
Upfolds Farm
Whitefield Wood
Bushy Copse
Tanhurst
Tanhurst Wood
Shiffolds
Pollard Corner
Ockham Farm House
Highfield Copse
Joldwynds
The Wilderness
Moseley Copse
The Aldermoor
Pipers Lea
Moxley
Holmbury Hill
Somerset Hill
Holmdale
Cricket Ground
Playing Field
Hall
Pitland Street House
Bulmer Farm
Hurtwood House
Holmbury House
Radnor House
Sherborne
Little Birketts
Great Aldermoor Copse
Pratsham Farm
Damphurst Wood
Damphurst Hollow
Oldpark Hill
The Wilderness
Bushy Wood
Kempslade Farm
Noons Copse
Mill Pond
Severells Copse
Lemon Farm
Sewer's Farm
Abinger Bottom
Leylands Farm
Sewer's Copse
High Toby
Foxholt
Deers Wood
Surrey Cottage
Highashes Hill
Reservoir (covered)
LEITH HILL PLACE (WEST)
MOLE VALLEY
GUILDFORD
B2126
HORSHAM ROAD
RAIKES HOLLOW
RAIKES LANE
WATER LANE
SUTTON LANE
ABINGER LANE
DONKEY LANE
FRIDAY STREET
NOONS CORNER RD
ABINGER COMMON ROAD
LEITH HILL LANE
SHEEPHOUSE LANE
HOLMBURY HILL
PASTURE WOOD ROAD
THREE MILE RD
RADNOR LA.
HOLMBURY LA.
COTTON ROW
TANHURST LA.
117
138
157

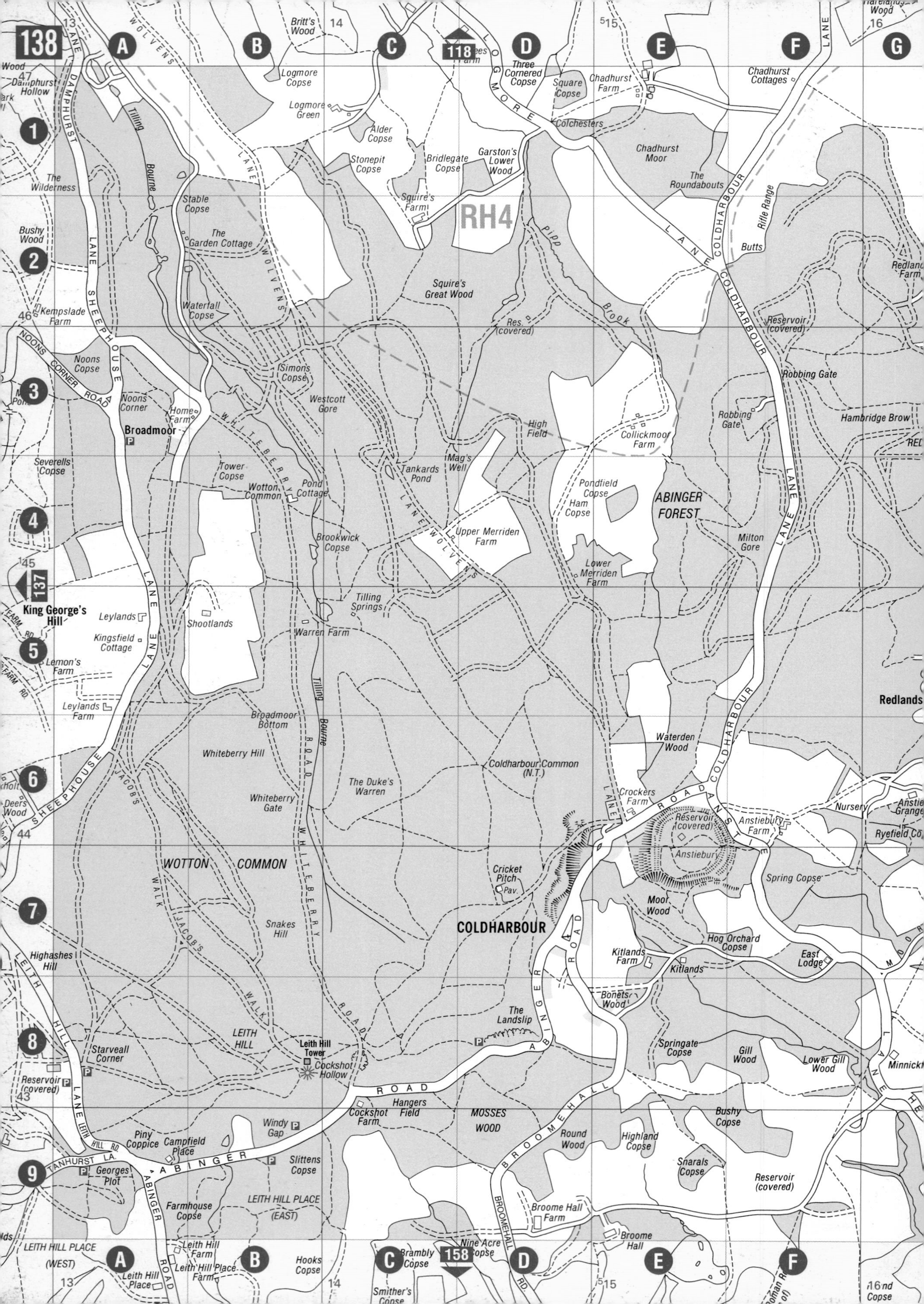

A
B
C
D
E
F
G
118
137
158
RH4
Logmore Copse
Logmore Green
Alder Copse
Stonepit Copse
Bridlegate Copse
Squire's Farm
Three Cornered Copse
Square Copse
Chadhurst Farm
Colchesters
Chadhurst Moor
The Roundabouts
Chadhurst Cottages
Garston's Lower Wood
Damphurst Hollow
The Wilderness
Bushy Wood
Kempslade Farm
Noons Copse
Noons Corner
Broadmoor
Home Farm
Severells Copse
Stable Copse
The Garden Cottage
Waterfall Copse
Simons Copse
Westcott Gore
Squire's Great Wood
Res. (covered)
Reservoir (covered)
Robbing Gate
Hambridge Brow
Redlands Farm
Redlands
Butts
Rifle Range
High Field
Collickmoor Farm
Mag's Well
Tankards Pond
Tower Copse
Wotton Common
Pond Cottage
Upper Merriden Farm
Pondfield Copse
Ham Copse
ABINGER FOREST
Milton Gore
Lower Merriden Farm
Brookwick Copse
King George's Hill
Leylands
Kingsfield Cottage
Lemon's Farm
Leylands Farm
Shootlands
Tilling Springs
Warren Farm
Broadmoor Bottom
Whiteberry Hill
Whiteberry Gate
The Duke's Warren
Coldharbour Common (N.T.)
Waterden Wood
Crockers Farm
Anstiebury
Anstiebury Farm
Nursery
Anstie Grange
Ryefield Co
Spring Copse
Deers Wood
WOTTON COMMON
Cricket Pitch
Pav.
COLDHARBOUR
Moor Wood
Hog Orchard Copse
Kitlands Farm
Kitlands
East Lodge
Snakes Hill
Highashes Hill
Bonets Wood
The Landslip
LEITH HILL
Leith Hill Tower
Cockshot Hollow
Starveall Corner
Reservoir (covered)
Springate Copse
Gill Wood
Lower Gill Wood
Minnick
Hangers Field
Cockshot Farm
MOSSES WOOD
Windy Gap
Piny Coppice
Campfield Place
Round Wood
Highland Copse
Bushy Copse
Snarals Copse
Slittens Copse
Georges Plot
Farmhouse Copse
LEITH HILL PLACE (EAST)
LEITH HILL PLACE (WEST)
Broome Hall Farm
Broome Hall
Leith Hill Farm
Leith Hill Place Farm
Leith Hill Place
Hooks Copse
Brambly Copse
Nine Acre Copse
Smither's Copse
Britt's Wood
WOLVENS LANE
LOGMORE LANE
DAMPHURST LANE
SHEEPHOUSE LANE
NOONS CORNER ROAD
WHITEBERRY LANE
WHITEBERRY ROAD
COLDHARBOUR LANE
ANSTIE LANE
COLDHARBOUR ROAD
ABINGER ROAD
BROOMEHALL ROAD
LEITH HILL LANE
LEITH HILL RD
TANHURST LA.
JACOB'S WALK
Tilling Bourne
Pipp Brook
13
14
515
16
47
46
45
44
43

NORTH HOLMWOOD
Holmwood Farm
Clay Pit
Stumblets
Black Brook
Root Hill Farm
Orchard Copse
Cricket Ground
Roothill Wood
Great Brockhamhurst
Inholms Farm
Blackbrook
Blackbrook Farm
Woodlands Park
Kiln Copse
Works
Gowan Lodge
Holmwood House
Oak-Lea
Brockhamhurst Cottage
Brook Meadow
Little Brook
Scammells Grove
Mid Holmwood
Ratsfield
Jessies Rough
RH3
Brook Lodge Farm
Betchworth
HOLMWOOD COMMON
Waterlands Farm
Gad Brook
Redlands Bank Farm
Hither Hawesrew
Lodge Farm
Railway Cottages
Football Ground
Bushy Croft
Eutrie House
Mill Bottom
Hawesrew Farm
Snelling Planted Field
Fourwents Pond
Oakdale
Mill House
Wymbletons Farm
Folly Farm
Brookfield Copse
Dorking
Cricket Ground
Biwater House
Holmwood Park Farm
Moor Lodge
Henfold Purification Plant
South Holmwood
South Lodge
Posterns Farm
Holmwood Cottage
Oakfield Farm
Redlands
The Vicarage
Betchets Green
Playing Field
HOLMWOOD COMMON
East Lodge
Swires Farm
Petersfield Farm
Betchetsgreen Copse
Holmwood Corner Common
Holmwood Corner
Pond Bay
Vigo Farm
Oakdene Cottages
Petersfield Copse
Lag Copse
Ewood Furze Field
Stockrydons
Anstie Grange Farm
A24
Brook Copse
Bregsell's Farm
Henfold Lake Fishery
Breakspear Farm
RH5
Moorhurst
Jersey Farm Cottages
Holmwood
Brickyard Copse
Cowless Field
Little Turners
Kiln Wood
REFFOLDS COPSE
Nobs Copse
Brook Wood
Brookwood Farm
Butlers Copse
Garston's Copse
Well Copse
Depot
Garston's Farm
Great Turners
Garston's Copse
Old St. John's
Playing Field
The Weald C of E Prim. School
Broadwood's Rough
BEARE GREEN
Henfold Farm
Newdigate Copse
The Slips
Trouts Farm
Rec. Grd.
Palmersbeare Farm
Ratfield Wood
Heath Wood
Sprots Copse
New Close Farm
Melville House
The Knowle
Wigmore Lodge
Front Wood
Crackerbarrel Farm
Brooklagg Farm
Beare Gill
Brick Works
Alder Copse
Recreation Ground
HORSHAM ROAD
HOCKLEY ROAD
CAPEL BY-PASS
A29
A24
HENFOLD LANE
LODGE ROAD
MILL ROAD
BROCKHAMHURST RD.
BRIMSTONE LANE
BLACKBROOK ROAD
HENFOLD DRIVE
NEWDIGATE ROAD
119
140
159
G H J K L M N
1 2 3 4 5 6 7 8 9
17 18 19
43 44 45 46 47

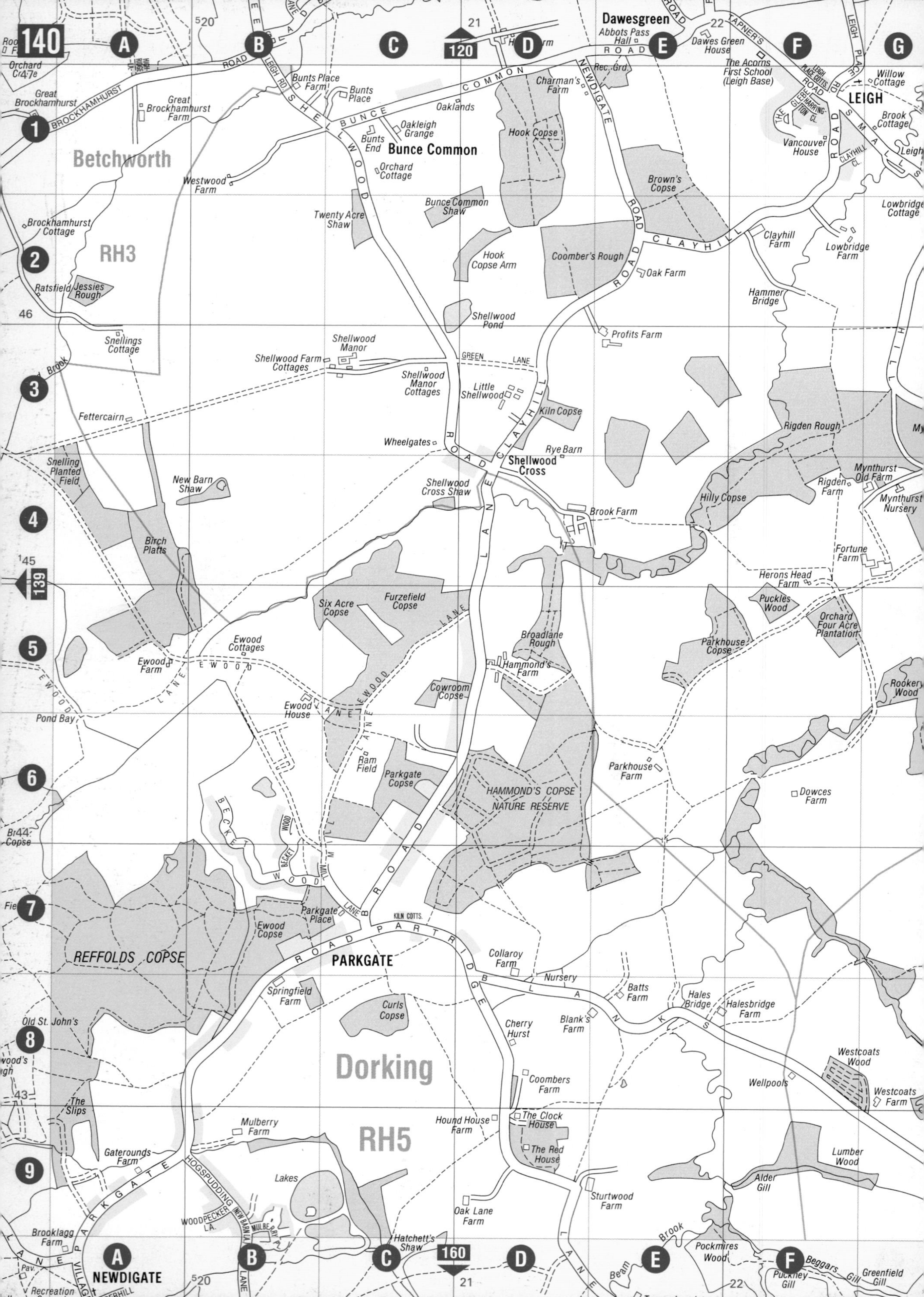

120
139
160
Dawesgreen
LEIGH
Bunce Common
Betchworth
RH3
Shellwood Cross
PARKGATE
Dorking
RH5
NEWDIGATE
REFFOLDS COPSE
HAMMOND'S COPSE NATURE RESERVE
Brockhamhurst Road
Bunce Common Road
Shellwood Road
Newdigate Road
Clayhill Road
Broad Lane
Partridge Road
Blanks Lane
Parkgate Road
Mill Lane
Ewood Lane
Green Lane
Hogspudding Lane
Great Brockhamhurst
Great Brockhamhurst Farm
Bunts Place Farm
Bunts Place
Bunts End
Oakleigh Grange
Oaklands
Orchard Cottage
Westwood Farm
Charman's Farm
Hook Copse
Brown's Copse
Abbots Pass Hall
Dawes Green House
The Acorns First School (Leigh Base)
Willow Cottage
Brook Cottage
Vancouver House
Lowbridge Cottage
Lowbridge Farm
Clayhill Farm
Brockhamhurst Cottage
Ratsfield
Jessies Rough
Twenty Acre Shaw
Bunce Common Shaw
Hook Copse Arm
Coomber's Rough
Oak Farm
Hammer Bridge
Shellwood Pond
Profits Farm
Snellings Cottage
Shellwood Manor
Shellwood Farm Cottages
Shellwood Manor Cottages
Little Shellwood
Kiln Copse
Fettercairn
Wheelgates
Rye Barn
Rigden Rough
Snelling Planted Field
New Barn Shaw
Shellwood Cross Shaw
Brook Farm
Hilly Copse
Rigden Farm
Mynthurst Old Farm
Mynthurst Nursery
Birch Platts
Fortune Farm
Herons Head Farm
Six Acre Copse
Furzefield Copse
Puckles Wood
Orchard Four Acre Plantation
Broadlane Rough
Ewood Cottages
Ewood Farm
Hammond's Farm
Parkhouse Copse
Cowroom Copse
Ewood House
Rookery Wood
Pond Bay
Ram Field
Parkgate Copse
Parkhouse Farm
Dowces Farm
Parkgate Place
Ewood Copse
Kiln Cotts.
Collaroy Farm
Nursery
Batts Farm
Hales Bridge
Halesbridge Farm
Springfield Farm
Curls Copse
Old St. John's
Cherry Hurst
Blank's Farm
Westcoats Wood
Wellpools
Coombers Farm
Westcoats Farm
The Slips
Mulberry Farm
Hound House Farm
The Clock House
The Red House
Lumber Wood
Gaterounds Farm
Lakes
Alder Gill
Sturtwood Farm
Oak Lane Farm
Woodpecker La.
Brooklagg Farm
Hatchett's Shaw
Pockmires Wood
Beggars Gill
Greenfield Gill
Puckney Gill
Recreation Ground
Village Lane

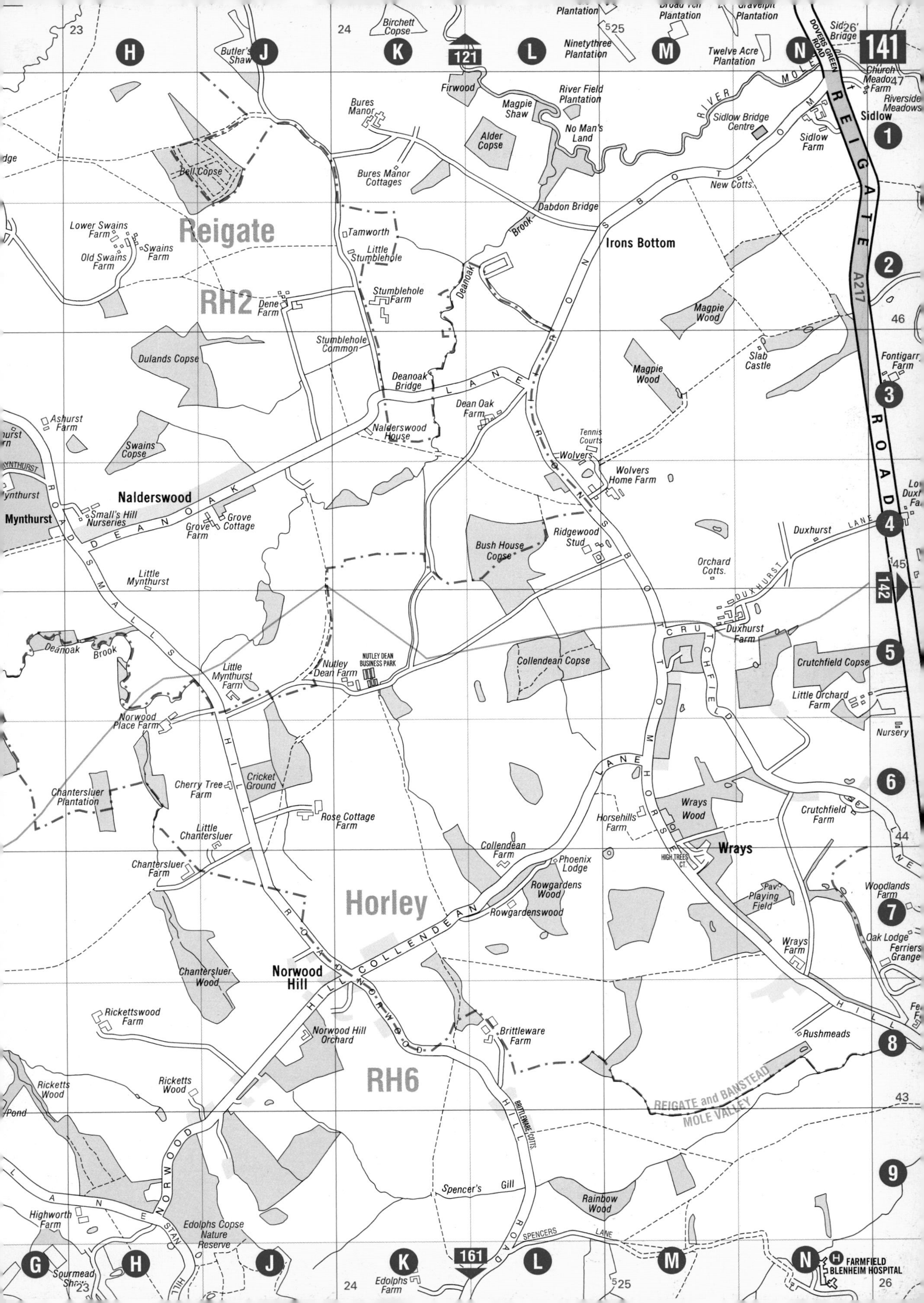
141
121
161
142
H
J
K
L
M
N
G
1
2
3
4
5
6
7
8
9
23
24
25
26
47
46
45
44
43
Reigate
RH2
Horley
RH6
Butler's Shaw
Birchett Copse
Plantation
Ninetythree Plantation
Broad Fen Plantation
Gravelpit Plantation
Twelve Acre Plantation
Sid Bridge
DOVERS GREEN ROAD
Church Meadow Farm
Riverside Meadows
Sidlow
Sidlow Farm
Sidlow Bridge Centre
RIVER MOLE
Firwood
Magpie Shaw
River Field Plantation
No Man's Land
Alder Copse
Bures Manor
Bures Manor Cottages
Bell Copse
Dabdon Bridge
Brook
New Cotts.
IRONS BOTTOM
Irons Bottom
REIGATE ROAD
A217
Lower Swains Farm
Swains Farm
Old Swains Farm
Tamworth
Little Stumblehole
Stumblehole Farm
Deanoak
Dene Farm
Magpie Wood
Slab Castle
Fontigarry Farm
Stumblehole Common
Dulands Copse
Deanoak Bridge
LANE
Dean Oak Farm
Nalderswood House
Ashurst Farm
Swains Copse
Tennis Courts
Wolvers
Wolvers Home Farm
MYNTHURST
Mynthurst
Nalderswood
DEANOAK
Small's Hill Nurseries
Grove Farm
Grove Cottage
Bush House Copse
Ridgewood Stud
Duxhurst
DUXHURST LANE
Orchard Cotts.
Little Mynthurst
SMALLS HILL ROAD
Deanoak Brook
Little Mynthurst Farm
Nutley Dean Farm
NUTLEY DEAN BUSINESS PARK
CRUTCHFIELD
Duxhurst Farm
Collendean Copse
Crutchfield Copse
Little Orchard Farm
Nursery
Norwood Place Farm
Cherry Tree Farm
Cricket Ground
Chantersluer Plantation
Rose Cottage Farm
HORSEHILLS LANE
Horsehills Farm
Wrays Wood
Crutchfield Farm
Little Chantersluer
Collendean Farm
Phoenix Lodge
HIGH TREES CT.
Wrays
Chantersluer Farm
Rowgardens Wood
Rowgardenswood
Pav
Playing Field
Woodlands Farm
Oak Lodge
Ferriers Grange
Wrays Farm
COLLENDEAN LANE
Chantersluer Wood
Norwood Hill
NORWOOD HILL ROAD
Rickettswood Farm
Norwood Hill Orchard
Brittleware Farm
Rushmeads
Ricketts Wood
Pond
BRITTLEWARE COTTS.
REIGATE and BANSTEAD
MOLE VALLEY
NORWOOD
Spencer's Gill
Rainbow Wood
LANE
Highworth Farm
Edolphs Copse Nature Reserve
SPENCERS LANE
Sourmead Shaw
Edolphs Farm
FARMFIELD
BLENHEIM HOSPITAL

142
122
141
162
A
B
C
D
E
F
G
Sidlow
Church Meadow Farm
Riverside Meadows
White Owl Farm
Benting Wood
Hollow Shaw
Home Grove
Petridge Wood
Lonesome Farm
Weir
Reigate
RH2
Kinnersley Manor
Kinnersley Manor Farm
New Rivernook Farm
Spinners Well
Layland's Cottages
Fontigarry Farm
Burfords Farm
Saxley Hill
Saxley Farm
Saxley Fruit Farm
Saxons Hill
Salfords Stream
Ladyland Farm
Lower Duxhurst Farm
DUXHURST LA.
Horseshoe Farm
Wick Farm
Meathgreen Bridge
SALFORDS
Salfords Bridge
Salfords
Dean Farm
Perry Wood
PERRYWOOD BUSINESS PARK
Rifle Range
Tennis Courts
Warehouses
Depot
Works
REDHILL DISTRIBUTION CENTRE
ORCHARD BUS. CEN.
FAIRLAWN BUS. PK.
SALFORDS IND. EST.
HEATH BUS. CEN.
ASTRA BUS. CEN.
Bonehurst Farm
Bonehurst Bridge
CAMBRIDGE LODGE MOBILE HOME PARK
Little Orchard Farm
Moat Farm
Nursery
Meath Green Farm
Cheswick Farm
Landens Farm
Meath Grn. Jun. Sch.
MEATH GREEN
Horley
RH6
Greatlake Farm
Hewitt's Farm
Burstow
REIGATE and BANSTEAD
MOLE VALLEY
Woodlands Farm
Oak Lodge
Ferriers Grange
Ferriers Forge
Sewage Works
Spencer's Gill
The New Defence
Horley Town FC
Play. Fld.
Sunnymead Farm
Hookwood House
Horley Anderson Sports Centre
Manorfield Prim. Sch.
Playing Field
Cemetery
Recreation Grd.
Yattendon Sch.
Gas Works
GATWICK METRO CENTRE
Oakwood Sports Cen.
Oakwood Sch. Playing Field
Westlands Farm
Hookwood Lodge
HOOKWOOD
SUNDIALS CARAVAN SITE
Ahed Depot
GATWICK PARK BUPA HOSP.
Superstore
Long Bri.
LONGBRIDGE RBT.
HORLEY
HAMPTON LODGE
Archway Thtre.
Horley
Care Hotel
FARMFIELD BLENHEIM HOSPITAL
BRIGHTON ROAD
A23
BONEHURST ROAD
REIGATE ROAD
A217
HONEYCROCK LANE
CROSSOAK
LODGE LANE
MEATH GREEN LANE
LONESOME LANE
RIVER MOLE
River Mole
BALCOMBE ROAD
B2036
HORSE HILL
MILL LANE
LANGSHOTT
MASON'S BRIDGE RD.
PICKETTS LANE
KINGSLEY ROAD
VICARAGE LANE
CHURCH ROAD
MASSETTS
SIDEWAYS
KENNEL LANE

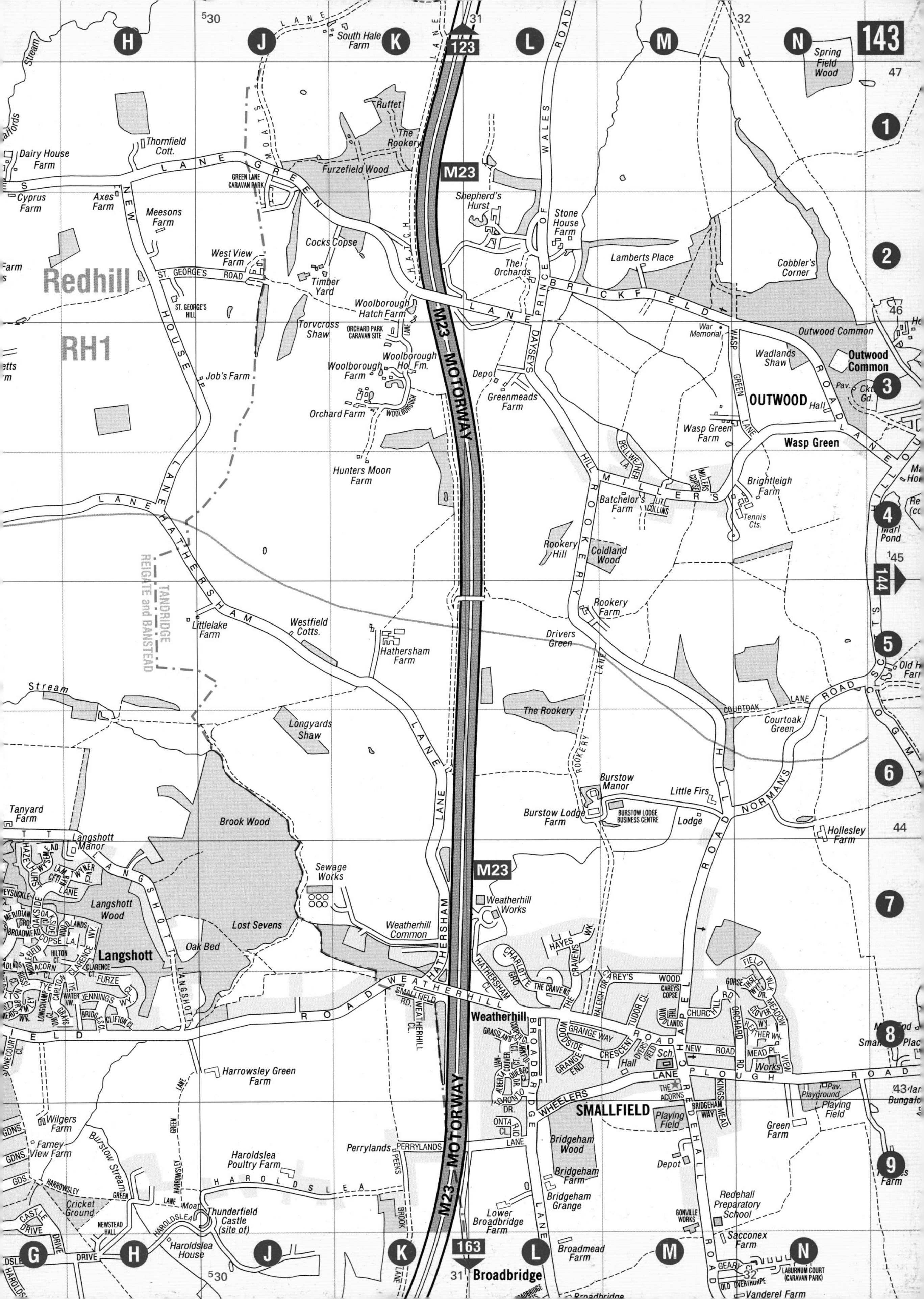
H
J
K
L
M
N
530
31
32
123
South Hale Farm
Spring Field Wood
47
1
2
3
4
5
6
7
8
9
Dairy House Farm
Thornfield Cott.
Cyprus Farm
Axes Farm
Meesons Farm
Ruffet
The Rookery
Furzefield Wood
GREEN LANE CARAVAN PARK
M23
Shepherd's Hurst
Stone House Farm
Cocks Copse
West View Farm
Lamberts Place
Cobbler's Corner
Redhill
ST. GEORGE'S ROAD
ST. GEORGE'S HILL
Timber Yard
The Orchards
Woolborough Hatch Farm
BRICKFIELD
46
RH1
Torvcross Shaw
ORCHARD PARK CARAVAN SITE
War Memorial
Outwood Common
Wadlands Shaw
Outwood Common
Job's Farm
Woolborough Farm
Woolborough Ho. Fm.
Depot
Greenmeads Farm
OUTWOOD
Hall
Pav.
Ckt. Gd.
Orchard Farm
WOOLBOROUGH
M23 MOTORWAY
Wasp Green Farm
Wasp Green
HILL
Hunters Moon Farm
BELLWETHER LA.
MILLERS
MILLERS COPSE
Brightleigh Farm
Batchelor's Farm
LIT. COLLINS
Tennis Cts.
Marl Pond
Rookery Hill
Coldland Wood
145
144
TANDRIDGE
REIGATE and BANSTEAD
Rookery Farm
Littlelake Farm
Westfield Cotts.
Hathersham Farm
Drivers Green
Old Farm
Stream
The Rookery
COURTOAK LANE ROAD
Courtoak Green
Longyards Shaw
ROOKERY
Burstow Manor
Little Firs
Tanyard Farm
Brook Wood
Burstow Lodge Farm
BURSTOW LODGE BUSINESS CENTRE
Lodge
Hollesley Farm
44
Langshott Manor
NORMAN'S
Sewage Works
M23
Langshott Wood
Weatherhill Works
Lost Sevens
Weatherhill Common
Oak Bed
Langshott
HATHERSHAM
HATHERSHAM CL.
CHARLOTTE GRO.
THE CRAVENS
HAYES WK.
CAREY'S WOOD
CAREYS COPSE
CHURCH HILL RD.
FIELD WK.
GORSE
WEATHERHILL
SMALLFIELD RD.
WEATHERHILL CL.
Weatherhill
GRANGE WAY
TUDOR CL.
ROAD
New Road
MEAD PL.
Works
RD.
VIEW
Harrowsley Green Farm
Hall
Sch.
LANE
PLOUGH
Pav.
Playground
ROAD
43
THE ACORNS
Playing Field
BROADBRIDGE
WHEELERS
SMALLFIELD
Playing Field
BRIDGEHAM WAY
Wilgers Farm
Green Farm
Farney View Farm
Burstow Stream
Perrylands
PERRYLANDS
Bridgeham Wood
Haroldslea Poultry Farm
HAROLDSLEA
Bridgeham Farm
Depot
Bridgeham Grange
Cricket Ground
Moat
Thunderfield Castle (site of)
Lower Broadbridge Farm
Redehall Preparatory School
GONVILLE WORKS
NEWSTEAD HALL
Haroldslea House
Sacconex Farm
G
163
Broadmead Farm
LABURNUM COURT (CARAVAN PARK)
Broadbridge
Vanderel Farm

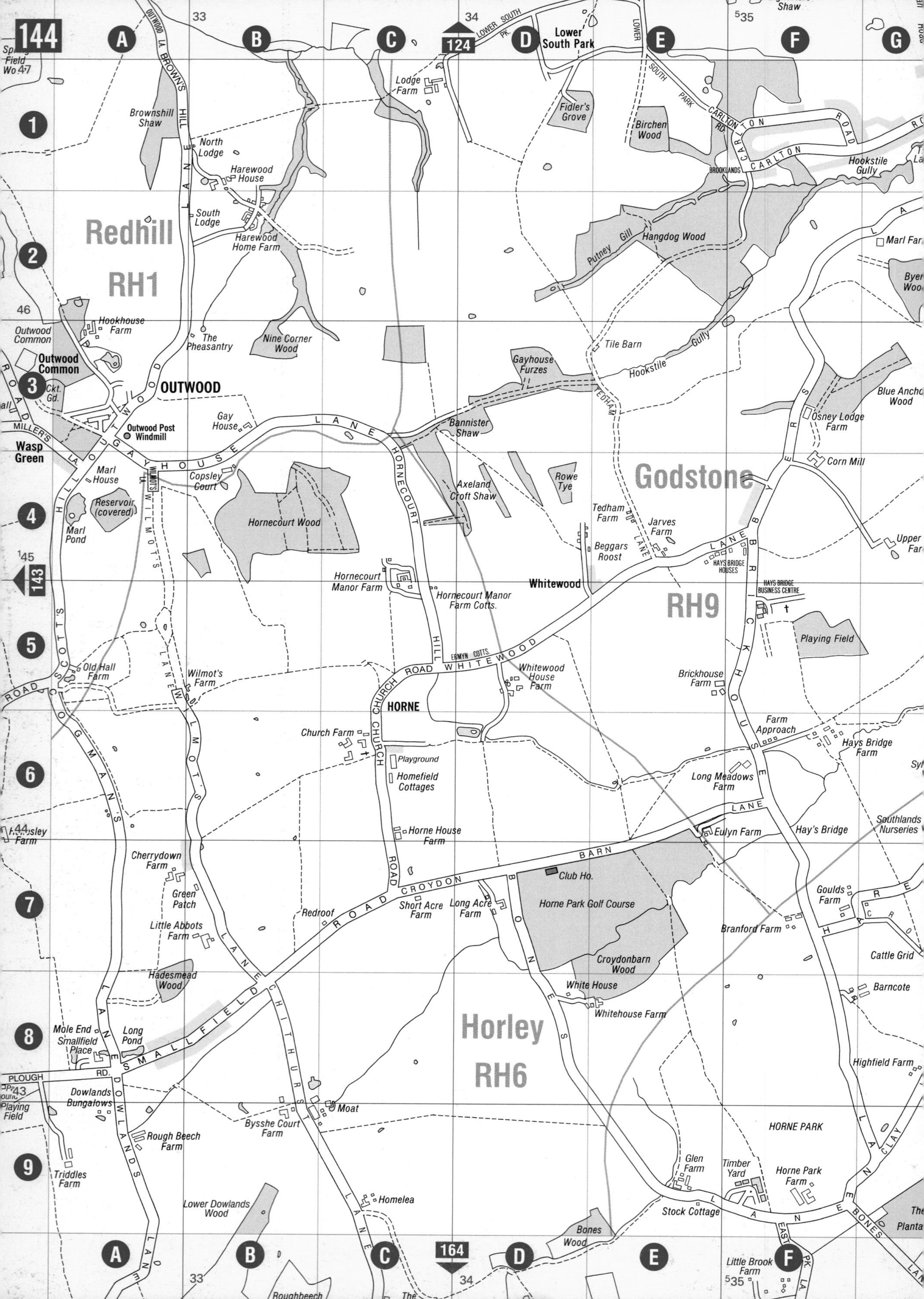

Redhill
RH1
Godstone
RH9
Horley
RH6
OUTWOOD
HORNE
Whitewood
Outwood Common
Wasp Green
Lower South Park
HORNE PARK
Brownshill Shaw
North Lodge
Harewood House
South Lodge
Harewood Home Farm
Lodge Farm
Fidler's Grove
Birchen Wood
Hookstile Gully
Putney Gill
Hangdog Wood
Marl Farm
Byers Wood
Hookhouse Farm
The Pheasantry
Nine Corner Wood
Tile Barn
Gayhouse Furzes
Blue Anchor Wood
Osney Lodge Farm
Corn Mill
Gay House
Outwood Post Windmill
Bannister Shaw
Marl House
Copsley Court
Axeland Croft Shaw
Rowe Tye
Reservoir (covered)
Marl Pond
Hornecourt Wood
Tedham Farm
Jarves Farm
Beggars Roost
Upper Farm
HAYS BRIDGE HOUSES
HAYS BRIDGE BUSINESS CENTRE
Hornecourt Manor Farm
Hornecourt Manor Farm Cotts.
Playing Field
Old Hall Farm
Wilmot's Farm
ERMYN COTTS.
Whitewood House Farm
Brickhouse Farm
Church Farm
Playground
Homefield Cottages
Farm Approach
Hays Bridge Farm
Long Meadows Farm
Horne House Farm
Eulyn Farm
Hay's Bridge
Southlands Nurseries
Cherrydown Farm
Green Patch
Club Ho.
Horne Park Golf Course
Redroof
Short Acre Farm
Long Acre Farm
Goulds Farm
Branford Farm
Little Abbots Farm
Croydonbarn Wood
Cattle Grid
Hadesmead Wood
White House
Whitehouse Farm
Barncote
Mole End
Smallfield Place
Long Pond
Highfield Farm
Dowlands Bungalows
Moat
Bysshe Court Farm
Rough Beech Farm
Triddles Farm
Glen Farm
Timber Yard
Horne Park Farm
Homelea
Lower Dowlands Wood
Stock Cottage
Bones Wood
Little Brook Farm
Roughbeech
Ckt. Gd.
BROOKLANDS
OUTWOOD LA.
BROWNS HILL LANE
LOWER SOUTH PK.
LOWER SOUTH PARK
CARLTON RD.
CARLTON ROAD
MILLERS LA.
OUTWOOD
GAYHOUSE LANE
HORNECOURT HILL
TEDHAM LANE
BRICKHOUSE LANE
WILMOTS LANE
SCOTTS HILL
COGMANS LANE
WHITEWOOD ROAD
CHURCH ROAD
CROYDON BARN LANE
ROAD
SMALLFIELD ROAD
CHITHURST LANE
BONES LANE
PLOUGH RD.
DOWLANDS LANE
CLAY LANE
EAST PK. LA.
HARE CROFT
Playing Field
33
34
535
46
145
44
43
A
B
C
D
E
F
G
1
2
3
4
5
6
7
8
9
124
143
164

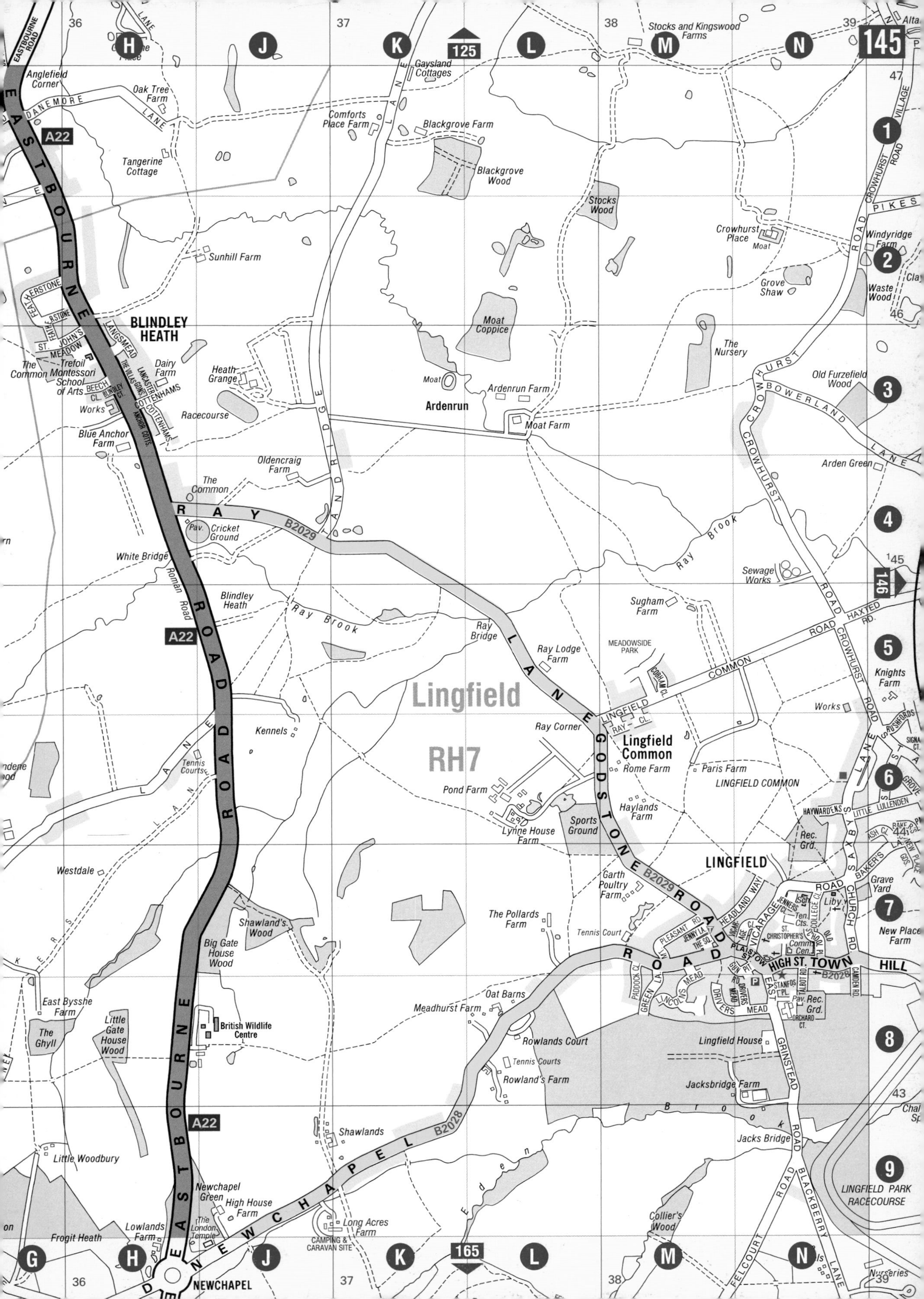

Anglefield Corner
Oak Tree Farm
DANEMORE
LANE
A22
Tangerine Cottage
Comforts Place Farm
Gaysland Cottages
Blackgrove Farm
Blackgrove Wood
Stocks and Kingswood Farms
Stocks Wood
Crowhurst Place
Moat
Windyridge Farm
Grove Shaw
Waste Wood
Sunhill Farm
BLINDLEY HEATH
Moat Coppice
The Nursery
Old Furzefield Wood
Dairy Farm
Heath Grange
The Common
Trefoil Montessori School of Arts
Works
Racecourse
Blue Anchor Farm
Ardenrun Farm
Ardenrun
Moat Farm
BOWERLAND LANE
Arden Green
Oldencraig Farm
The Common
RAY LANE
B2029
Cricket Ground
White Bridge
Ray Brook
Sewage Works
HAXTED RD.
Blindley Heath
Roman Road
EASTBOURNE ROAD
Sugham Farm
Ray Bridge
Ray Lodge Farm
MEADOWSIDE PARK
COMMON ROAD
CROWHURST ROAD
Knights Farm
Lingfield
Works
Kennels
Ray Corner
Lingfield Common
RH7
Rome Farm
Paris Farm
LINGFIELD COMMON
Tennis Courts
Pond Farm
Haylands Farm
Sports Ground
Lynne House Farm
GODSTONE ROAD
Rec. Grd.
Westdale
LINGFIELD
Garth Poultry Farm
Grave Yard
Shawland's Wood
The Pollards Farm
Tennis Court
HIGH ST.
TOWN HILL
Big Gate House Wood
East Bysshe Farm
Oat Barns
Meadhurst Farm
British Wildlife Centre
The Ghyll
Little Gate House Wood
Rowlands Court
Lingfield House
Tennis Courts
Rowland's Farm
Jacksbridge Farm
Brook
Shawlands
NEWCHAPEL ROAD
B2028
Jacks Bridge
Little Woodbury
Eden
Newchapel Green
High House Farm
Collier's Wood
Long Acres Farm
CAMPING & CARAVAN SITE
Lowlands Farm
Frogit Heath
The London Temple
NEWCHAPEL
LINGFIELD PARK RACECOURSE
FELCOURT ROAD
BLACKBERRY LANE
GRINSTEAD ROAD
Nurseries

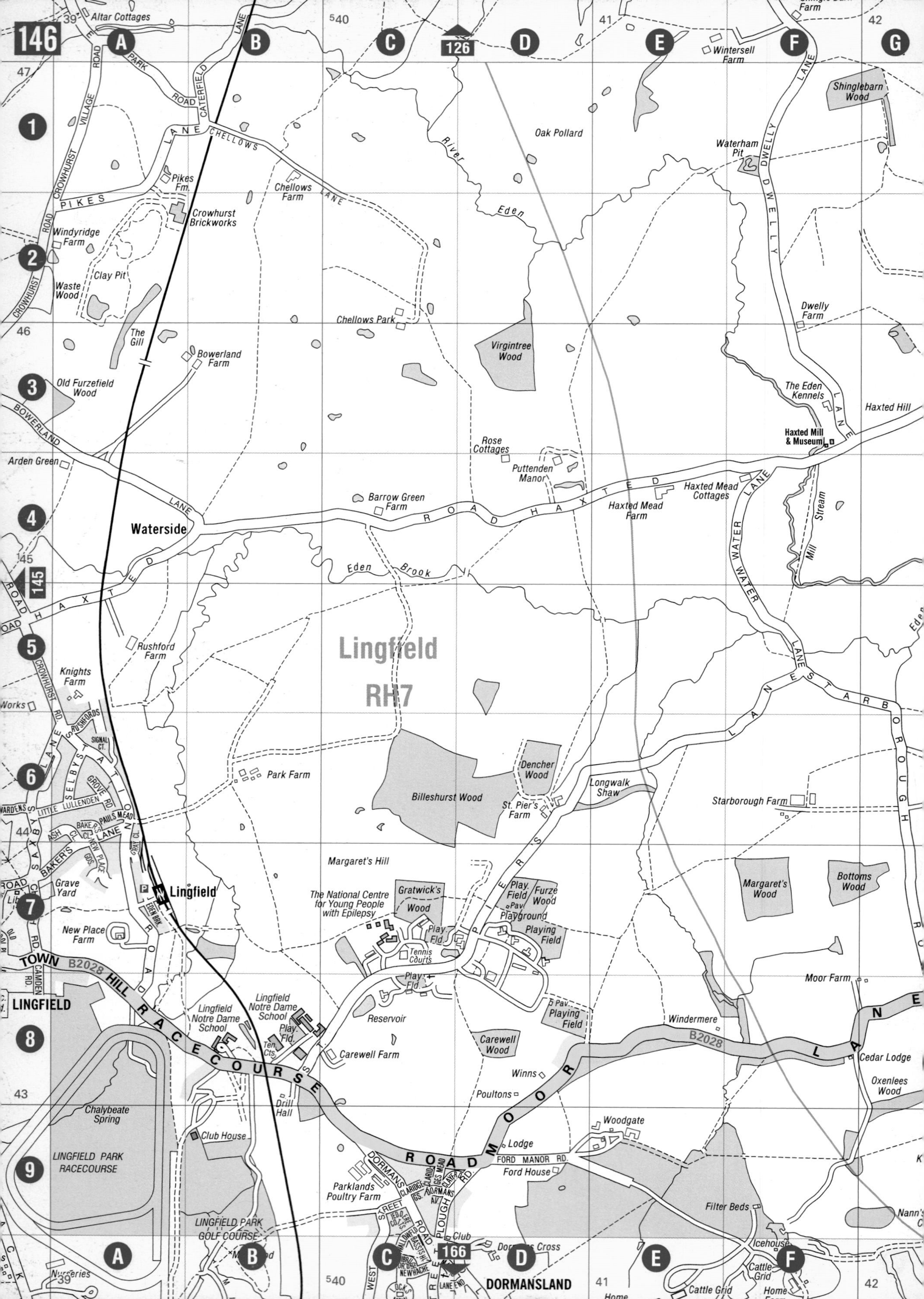

Altar Cottages
Wintersell Farm
Shinglebarn Wood
Oak Pollard
Waterham Pit
Pikes Fm.
Chellows Farm
Crowhurst Brickworks
Windyridge Farm
Clay Pit
Waste Wood
River Eden
Dwelly Farm
Chellows Park
The Gill
Bowerland Farm
Virgintree Wood
Old Furzefield Wood
The Eden Kennels
Haxted Hill
Haxted Mill & Museum
Rose Cottages
Puttenden Manor
Arden Green
Barrow Green Farm
Haxted Mead Cottages
Haxted Mead Farm
Waterside
Mill Stream
Eden Brook
Lingfield
RH7
Rushford Farm
Knights Farm
Dencher Wood
Park Farm
Billeshurst Wood
Longwalk Shaw
St. Pier's Farm
Starborough Farm
Margaret's Hill
Margaret's Wood
Bottoms Wood
Grave Yard
Lingfield
The National Centre for Young People with Epilepsy
Gratwick's Wood
Furze Wood
Playground
Playing Field
Tennis Courts
New Place Farm
Moor Farm
LINGFIELD
Lingfield Notre Dame School
Reservoir
Windermere
Carewell Wood
Carewell Farm
Cedar Lodge
Winns
Oxenlees Wood
Poultons
Drill Hall
Chalybeate Spring
Woodgate
Club House
Lodge
LINGFIELD PARK RACECOURSE
Ford House
Parklands Poultry Farm
Filter Beds
LINGFIELD PARK GOLF COURSE
Icehouse
Dormans Cross
Nurseries
Cattle Grid
DORMANSLAND
Home Farm
TOWN HILL
RACECOURSE ROAD
MOOR LANE
ROAD HAXTED
WATER LANE
DWELLY LANE
STARBOROUGH LANE
PIKES LANE
CHELLOWS LANE
BOWERLAND LANE
CROWHURST ROAD
B2028
126
145
166

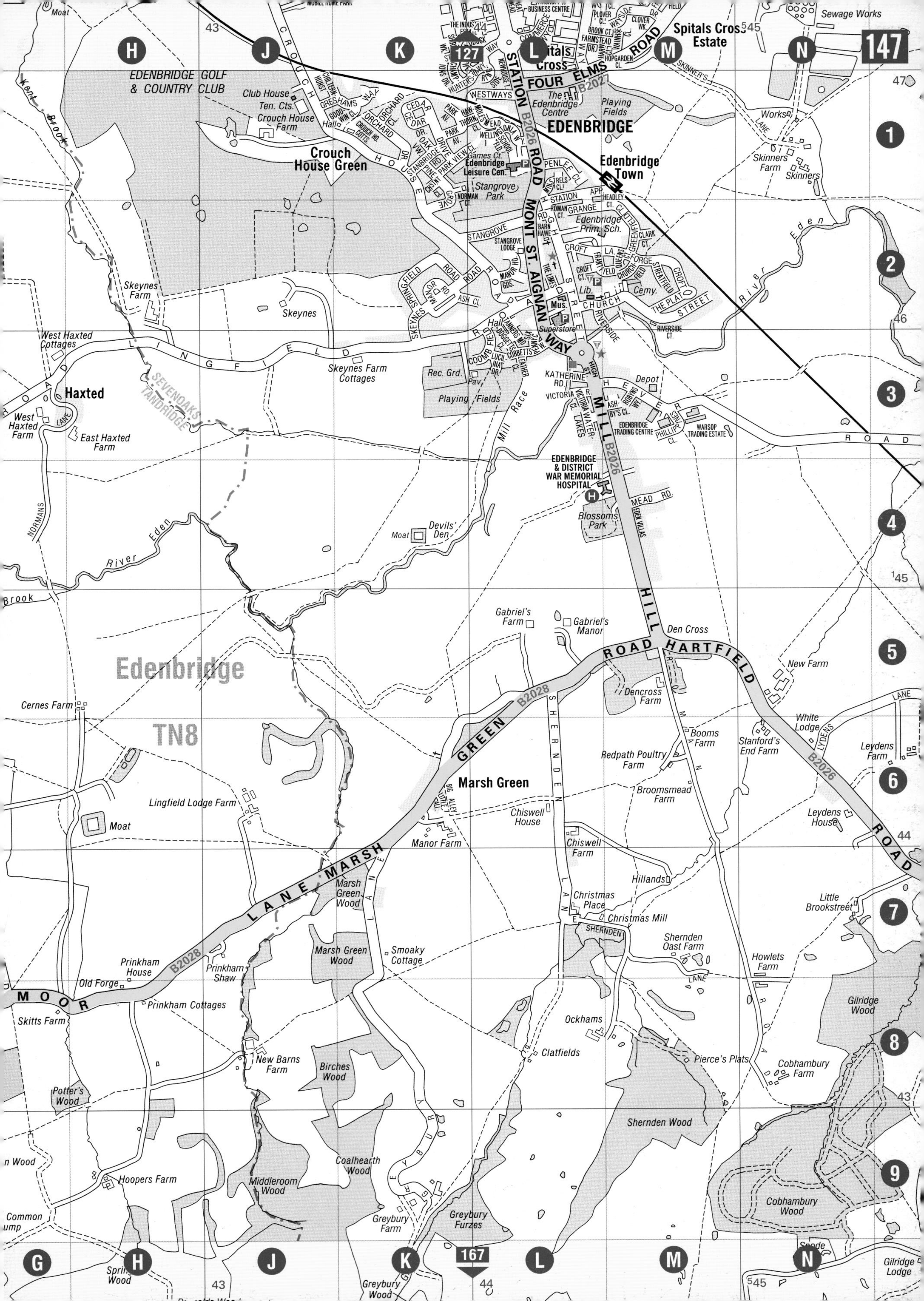
EDENBRIDGE GOLF & COUNTRY CLUB
Club House
Crouch House Farm
Crouch House Green
EDENBRIDGE
Edenbridge Town
Spitals Cross Estate
Sewage Works
FOUR ELMS ROAD
STATION ROAD
MONT ST. AIGNAN WAY
The Edenbridge Centre
Playing Fields
Edenbridge Leisure Cen.
Stangrove Park
Edenbridge Prim. Sch.
Skinners Farm
Skeynes Farm
Skeynes
West Haxted Cottages
Haxted
West Haxted Farm
East Haxted Farm
LINGFIELD ROAD
Skeynes Farm Cottages
Rec. Grd.
Playing Fields
River Eden
Mill Race
EDENBRIDGE & DISTRICT WAR MEMORIAL HOSPITAL
Blossoms Park
Devils' Den
Gabriel's Farm
Gabriel's Manor
Den Cross
HARTFIELD ROAD
Edenbridge
TN8
Cernes Farm
Dencross Farm
New Farm
Booms Farm
Redpath Poultry Farm
Stanford's End Farm
White Lodge
Leydens Farm
Marsh Green
Lingfield Lodge Farm
Moat
Chiswell House
Broomsmead Farm
Leydens House
Manor Farm
Chiswell Farm
MARSH GREEN ROAD
Marsh Green Wood
Hillands
Christmas Place
Christmas Mill
Little Brookstreet
Shernden Oast Farm
Smoaky Cottage
Prinkham House
Old Forge
Prinkham Shaw
Howlets Farm
Gilridge Wood
Prinkham Cottages
MOOR LANE
Skitts Farm
Ockhams
Clatfields
Pierce's Plats
Cobhambury Farm
New Barns Farm
Birches Wood
Potter's Wood
Shernden Wood
Coalhearth Wood
Middleroom Wood
Hoopers Farm
Cobhambury Wood
Greybury Farm
Greybury Furzes
Gilridge Lodge
Greybury Wood
127
167

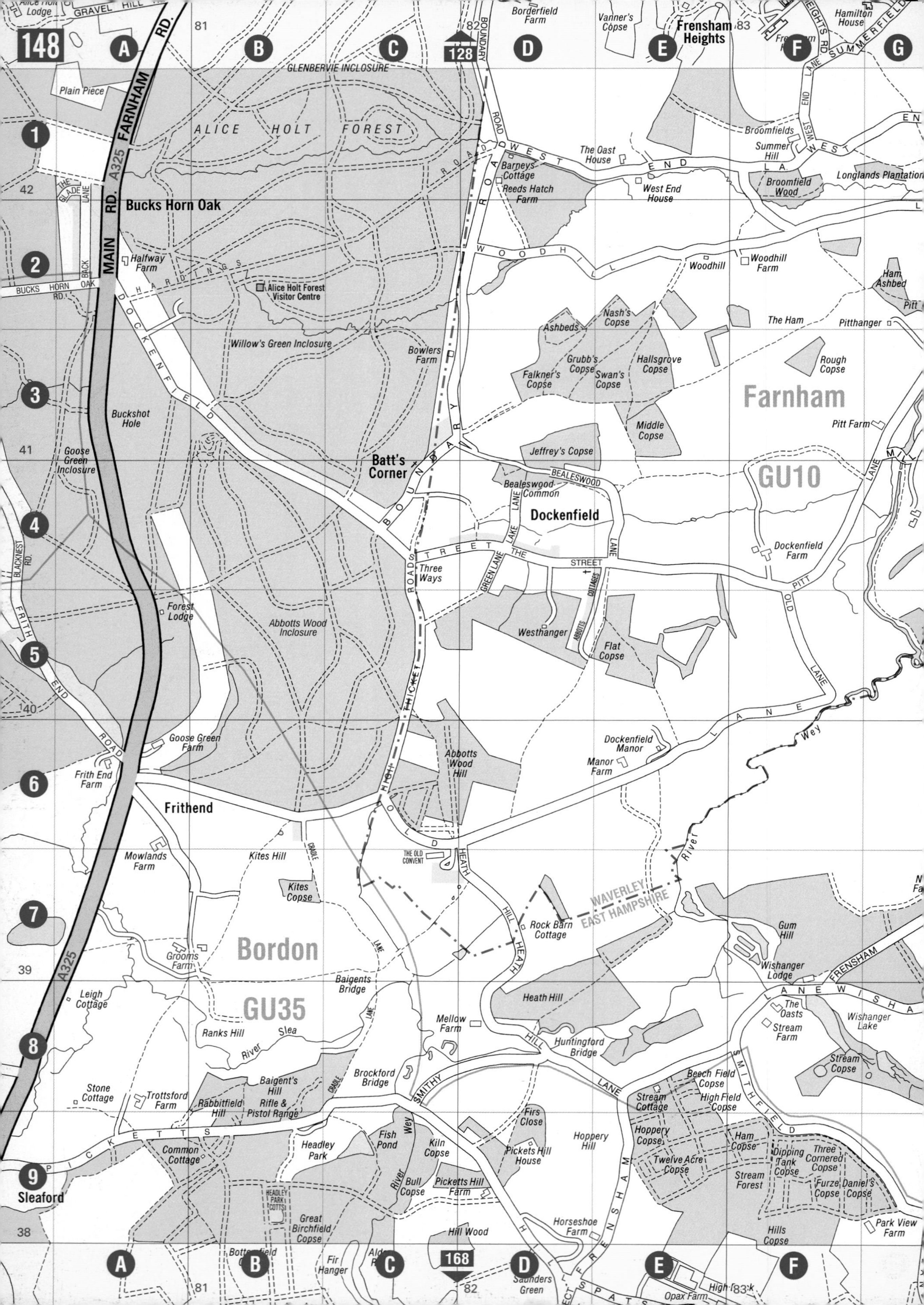
A
B
C
D
E
F
G
128
168
Alice Holt Forest
Glenbervie Inclosure
Plain Piece
Bucks Horn Oak
Halfway Farm
Alice Holt Forest Visitor Centre
Willow's Green Inclosure
Bowlers Farm
Buckshot Hole
Goose Green Inclosure
Batt's Corner
Forest Lodge
Abbotts Wood Inclosure
Goose Green Farm
Frith End Farm
Frithend
Mowlands Farm
Kites Hill
Kites Copse
Bordon
Grooms Farm
GU35
Leigh Cottage
Ranks Hill
River Slea
Baigents Bridge
Mellow Farm
Brockford Bridge
Stone Cottage
Trottsford Farm
Rabbitfield Hill
Baigent's Hill
Rifle & Pistol Range
Headley Park
Fish Pond
Kiln Copse
Common Cottage
Bull Copse
Picketts Hill Farm
Great Birchfield Copse
Hill Wood
Sleaford
Borderfield Farm
Vanner's Copse
Frensham Heights
Hamilton House
Broomfields
Summer Hill
The Oast House
Barneys Cottage
Reeds Hatch Farm
West End House
Broomfield Wood
Longlands Plantation
Woodhill
Woodhill Farm
Ham Ashbed
The Ham
Pitthanger
Ashbeds
Nash's Copse
Grubb's Copse
Swan's Copse
Hallsgrove Copse
Falkner's Copse
Rough Copse
Farnham
Middle Copse
Pitt Farm
Jeffrey's Copse
GU10
Bealeswood Common
Dockenfield
Dockenfield Farm
Three Ways
Westhanger
Flat Copse
Dockenfield Manor
Manor Farm
Abbotts Wood Hill
The Old Convent
Waverley
East Hampshire
Rock Barn Cottage
Gum Hill
Wishanger Lodge
Heath Hill
Huntingford Bridge
The Oasts
Stream Farm
Wishanger Lake
Stream Copse
Beech Field Copse
Stream Cottage
High Field Copse
Firs Close
Hoppery Hill
Hoppery Copse
Pickets Hill House
Ham Copse
Twelve Acre Copse
Dipping Tank Copse
Three Cornered Copse
Stream Forest
Furze Copse
Daniel's Copse
Horseshoe Farm
Hills Copse
Park View Farm
Saunders Green
Opax Farm
River Wey
A325
Main Rd.
Farnham Rd.
Bucks Horn Oak Rd.
Dockenfield
Boundary Road
West End
Woodhill
Bealeswood
The Street
Pitt Lane
Old Lane
Heath Hill
Smithy Lane
Frensham Lane
Wishanger Lane
Picketts
Frith End Road
Blacknest Rd.
High Thicket Road
Lake Lane
Green Lane
Abbotts Cottages
Cradle Lane
Smithfield
Headley Park Cotts
81
82
83
42
41
40
39
38
1
2
3
4
5
6
7
8
9

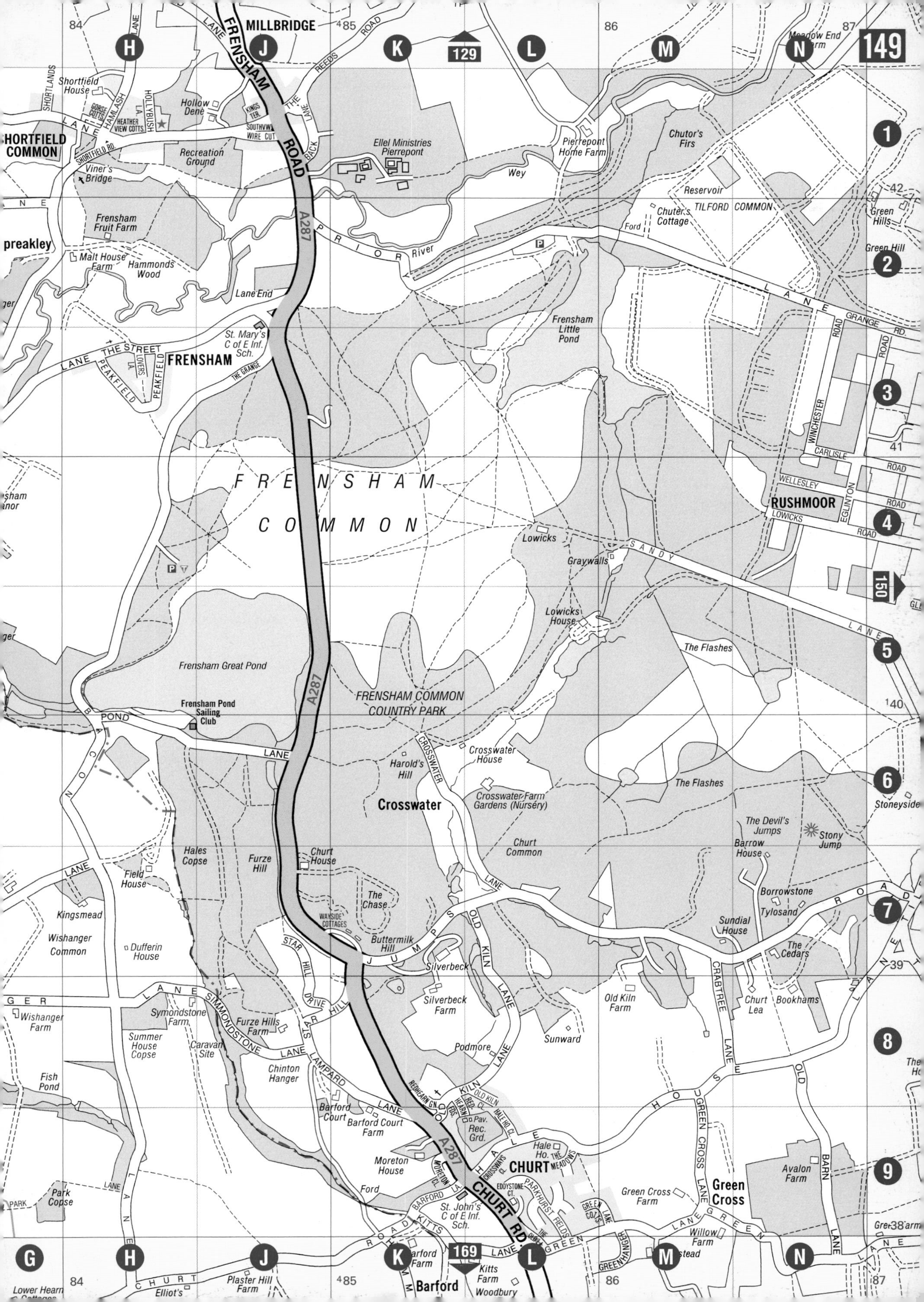
MILLBRIDGE
FRENSHAM ROAD
129
Shortfield House
Hollow Dene
SHORTFIELD COMMON
Recreation Ground
Ellel Ministries Pierrepont
Pierrepont Home Farm
Chutor's Firs
Viner's Bridge
Wey
Reservoir
Chuter's Cottage
TILFORD COMMON
Green Hills
Green Hill
Frensham Fruit Farm
Spreakley
Malt House Farm
Hammonds Wood
PRIORY LANE
River
Ford
Lane End
GRANGE RD.
St. Mary's C of E Inf. Sch.
FRENSHAM
THE STREET
Frensham Little Pond
WINCHESTER ROAD
CARLISLE ROAD
WELLESLEY ROAD
RUSHMOOR
LOWICKS ROAD
EGLINTON ROAD
FRENSHAM COMMON
Lowicks
Graywalls
SANDY LANE
150
Lowicks House
The Flashes
Frensham Great Pond
Frensham Pond Sailing Club
POND LANE
A287
FRENSHAM COMMON COUNTRY PARK
CROSSWATER LANE
Crosswater House
Harold's Hill
Crosswater
Crosswater Farm Gardens (Nursery)
The Flashes
Stoneyside
The Devil's Jumps
Barrow House
Stony Jump
Churt Common
Hales Copse
Furze Hill
Churt House
Field House
The Chase
Borrowstone
Tylosand
Kingsmead
Wishanger Common
Dufferin House
Buttermilk Hill
JUMPS ROAD
Silverbeck
Sundial House
The Cedars
STAR HILL
OLD KILN LANE
CRABTREE LANE
Silverbeck Farm
Old Kiln Farm
Churt Lea
Bookhams
Wishanger Farm
Symondstone Farm
SIMMONDSTONE LANE
Furze Hills Farm
Summer House Copse
Caravan Site
Podmore
Sunward
Fish Pond
Chinton Hanger
LAMPARD LANE
HALE HOUSE LANE
Barford Court
Barford Court Farm
Rec. Grd.
Pav.
Moreton House
Hale Ho.
CHURT
GREEN CROSS LANE
Green Cross
Avalon Farm
BARN LANE
Green Cross Farm
Park Copse
Ford
St. John's C of E Inf. Sch.
CHURT RD.
KITTS LANE
Willow Farm
169
Barford Farm
Kitts Farm
Barford
Woodbury
Plaster Hill Farm
Elliot's
Lower Hearn Cottages
84
485
86
87
42
41
140
39
38
G
H
J
K
L
M
N
1
2
3
4
5
6
7
8
9

Tilford Common
Caravan Park
HANKLEY COMMON GOLF COURSE
Yagden Hill
Westbrook
Tadmoor Cottage
Batt's Moor
Woolford's Copse
Woolford's Farm
Little Woolford's Copse
Green Hills
Green Hill
Lodge
Hillside Farm
Greenhills Farm
GRANGE ROAD
HANKLEY COMMON
Lion's Mouth
Heatherdown
Chailey Wood
Elmbeams Wood
The Timbers
Elstead Common
The Moat
RUSHMOOR
Melbreck Nursing Home
CARLISLE ROAD
WELLESLEY ROAD
LOWICKS ROAD
EGLINTON
WINCHESTER ROAD
Mackenzies
Truxford Wood
Truxford Riding Centre
WOOLFORDS LANE
THURSLEY ROAD
Kettlebury Hill
Farnham
GU10
GLEBE LA.
SANDY LANE
Gold Hill
Houndown Firs
Houndown
HOUNDOWN LANE
Beansides Wood
Nature Reserve
Cricket Ground
The Rookery
Dye House
DYE HOUSE
THE LANE
THE STREET
Stoneyside
Stony Jump
Lingwood
Holly Copse
Smallbrook Copse
Smallbrook
Wheeler's Farm
JUMPS ROAD
HALE HOUSE LANE
TILFORD ROAD
Churt Place Farm
Coombe Ridge
Wychmoor Copse
Pitch Place
Ronary
HOMEFIELD
Kettlebury Farm
Pitch Place Farm
Garden Cottage
Churt Place Nursery
Hill House
Hedge Farm
High Meadow
The Pack House
Hyde Copse
Hyde Farm
SAILORS LANE
Ridgeway Farm
HYDE LANE
Little Cowdray Farm
Lower Highfield Farm
Upper Highfield Farm
HIGHFIELD LANE
Upper Ridgeway Farm
Glenhead Farm
Punchbowl Farm
Cowdray Cross
BARN
High Barn Stock Farm
Marchants Farm
SILVER BIRCH COTTAGES
Fair View Farm
Vanhurst Copse
A3
PORTSMOUTH
Green Farm
GREEN LANE
Oak Grove
Hyde Hill
Heath
The Moors
Featmoor Copse
Stonehills
130
149
170
87
88
89
490
42
41
40
39
38

Guinea Copse
Ashen Copse
Thurnets Copse
Red House Farm
131
Bagmoor Wood
Bagmoor Cottage
Bagmoor Common Nature Reserve
Fir Plantation
Elstead Common
Kennel Moor
Burchetts Copse
Mistlebrooks Wood
Burchetts
Temple Hill
Borough Farm
Lower Level
Borough Copse
Mousehill Corner
Pudmore Pond
OCKLEY COMMON
Upper Level
Rodborough Hill
A3
RODBOROUGH HILL COTTAGES
Roundabouts
Forked Pond
WEBB ROAD
Home Pond
WITLEY COMMON
NATURE RESERVE
THURSLEY COMMON
Warren Mere
HAMMER POND COTTAGES
Silkmill Pond
Coldharbour Wood
Thursley Common National Nature Reserve
Birch Copse
Caravan Park
WARREN PARK
Witley Common Nature Centre
A286
152
Godalming
PORTSMOUTH ROAD
LEA
Hammer Pond
Penmead Copse
GU8
Tumuli
A3
Sewage Works
Tumulus
COACH ROAD
HASLEMERE
ROKE LANE
Heath House
Foldsdown
PORTSMOUTH ROAD
FRENCH
COSFORD RD
French Hill
Lake Cottages
Milford Lodge
The Shrubbery
Milhanger
Thursley Lake
Stable Lake
Thursley
OLD ROAD
The Grove
Witley Park
The Hanger
Upper Lake
West Firs
Reservoir (covered)
Parsonage House
Heath Hall
Witley Park House
Cosford House
Cosford Farm
Bedford Farm
Kiln Close
The Rocks
Rockwoods
Long Copse
Heath Hall Farm
HOUSE ROAD
Mount Pleasant
Bowlhead Green
Furzefield Wood
Longbeer Copse
Reservoir (covered)
Daws Copse
King's Firs
Chocolates
GREEN
Heath Hills
Blackhanger Farm
LANE
LOWER
BOWLHEAD
BEECH
Hanger Copse
Brook
Banacle Firs
Bedford and Hole Farm
HILL
Bowlhead Green Farm
Stables
Birch Copse
Recreation Ground Pav.
Emley Copse
Emley Farm
RUTTON
171
Smither's Hanger
Brook Farm
HASLEMERE
CHURCH LANE
Ox Heart Copse
BROOK
Beech Hanger
Rutton Hill
H J K L M N
G H J K L M N
1 2 3 4 5 6 7 8 9
91 92 93
42 41 140 39 38

152
Thurnets
A
B
C
D
E
F
G
94
495
96
132
Amberley Farm
MILFORD
MILFORD-BY-PASS RD.
A3
PORTSMOUTH ROAD
A3100
LOWER MOUSHILL LA.
Kennel Moor
Mousehill Down
42
GUILDFORD & GODALMING BY-PASS
ELMSIDE
Milford Sch.
CHERRY TREE RD.
CHURCH RD.
OAK TREE
Play. Fld.
Dower House
PORTSMOUTH
Garden Centre
Club Ho.
Lower Park
MILFORD GOLF COURSE
Weir
Wood Farm
Active Workings
Ladywell Convent
TUESLEY
Springwood Copse
MILFORD HOSPITAL
Tuesley Farm
Springwood Cottage
GU7
Upper Sattenham
Gall.
MOUSHILL
Pumping Station
Milford Heath
BUSDENS
Cemetery
A286
PETWORTH RD.
A283
Playing Field
Rodborough Technology College
The Copse
Milford
Tuesley Pond
Rake Manor
The Pleck
RAKE
GREEN
HEATHVIEW RD.
MERRYACRES
CRAMHURST
KHARTOUM RD.
41
HASLEMERE
WEBB RD.
Depot
Fowl House Farm
Shadwell Copse
Godalming
Poultry Farm
Cramhurst
GASDEN
YEW TREE
Nurseries
Wheelerstreet
WHEELERSTREET
PETWORTH
STATION
TUESLEY
Shad Well (spring)
Large Enton Lake
Lower Enton Lake
Small Enton Lake
Club House
Enton Green
Hydon Farm
WHEELER LANE
LITTLE LONDON
151
Depot
KESWICK
SUNNYHILL
LAKES
Upper Enton Lake
Foxall Wood
WEST SURREY GOLF COURSE
Playground
HYDESTILE COTTS.
ROKE LANE
MILL LANE
Mill Copse
Enton Mill Farm
MIDDLEMARCH
The Chandler C of E Jun. Sch.
NEWLANDS ESTATE
Play. Fld.
Playing Field
Barrow Hills School
Mare Hill
140
POTTER'S HILL
Fairacres
Great Enton
Potter's Barn
Linksmere
Sleepy Hollow
ROKE
Mare Hill Cottages
NORTHFIELD
Lake Cottage
WITLEY
Horsehatches
Hazel Copse
Old Enton
WEST SURREY GOLF COURSE
Hazel Copse
Chestnut Copse
Witley Ponds
Witley C of E Inf. Sch.
Hambledon Field
Boggy Lodge
Chapel Copse
Great House Cottages
Planted Piece
Bald Field
ROAD
Playing Field
Parson's Hanger
Culmer
Mill Lands Coppice
Enton Hall
GU8
Hooker's Ham
Hangerfield
Common Piece
The Close
39
Winkford Farm
CULMER
The Leg
SWEETWATER
Buss's Firs
Buss's Common
CULMER HILL
ROSE COTTAGES
Culmer Firs
Curtis's Piece
Parsonage House
Parsonage Farm
Culmer Common
Sweetwater Firs
Sweetwater Cottage
Busses Cottage
Hilltop Farm
Parsonage Farm Cottages
Pond Coppice
Playing Field
Sewage Works
Rough Acre
HAMBLEDON
Banacle Common
Culmer Hanger
Playing Field
Paddock Woods
Limekilns
Playing Field
King Edward's School
Wormley Hill Firs
Stonepit Hill
Moor Cottage
St. Dominic's Sch.
Malthouse Farm
Beech Hill
The Hill House
FRANKLIN CT.
BRIDEWELL CL.
Gorse Hill
Hambledon Common
PADDOCK CL.
GREEN
CHURCH
BANNACLE
BROOK
Banacle Firs
Sandhills
The Heights
WORMLEY
WORMLEY
HAMBLEDON PK.
MALTHOUSE
CRICKET
Fintry
Sandhills Common
Witley
Orchard Farm
Cricket Ground
38
STATION
COMBE LANE
A283
Ox Heart Copse
East Grove
Godalming East Grove
172
Oakhurst Cottage
Philpot's
BROOK
Kingwood
94
495
96
ROAD
Pond Field

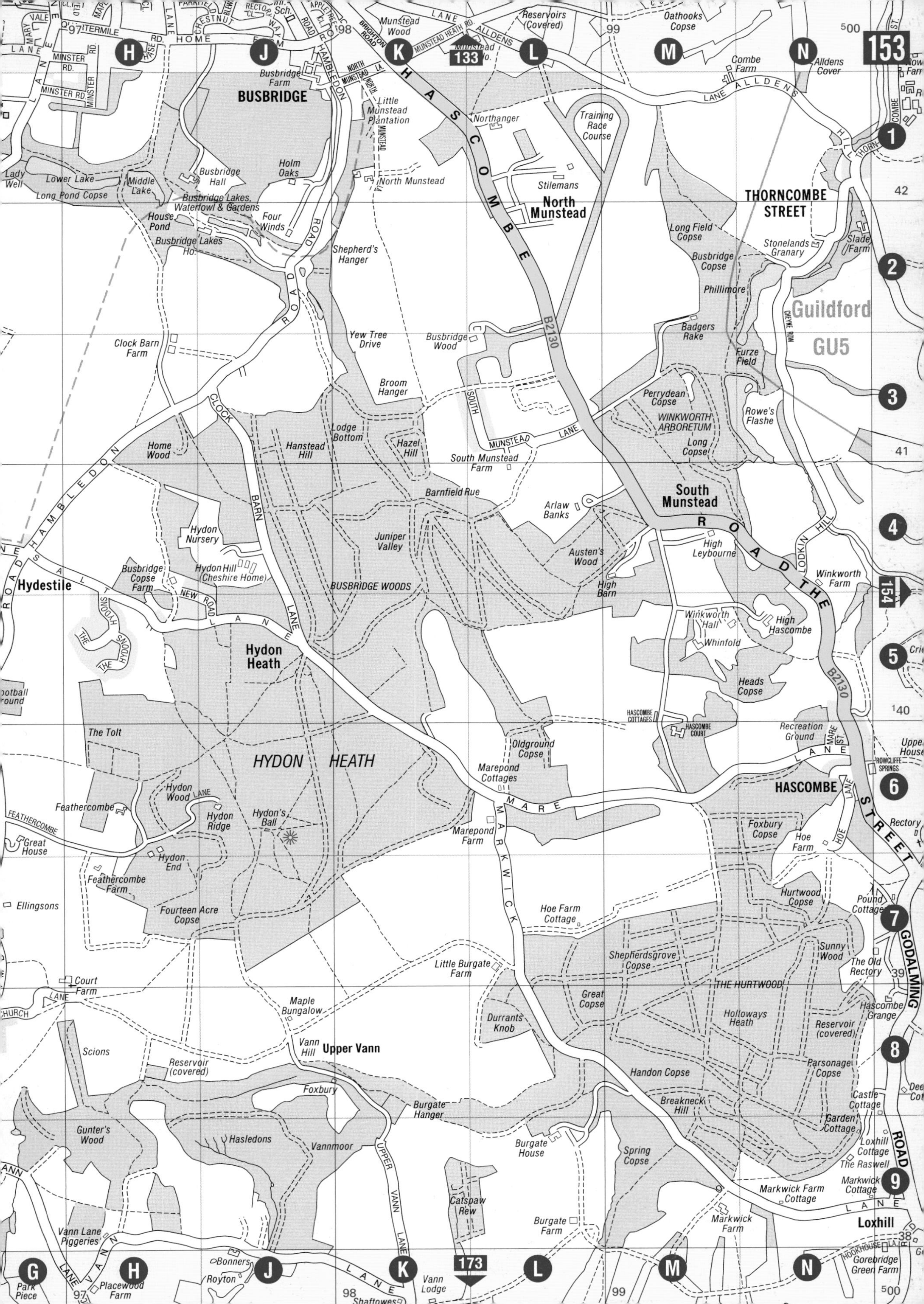

153
133
154
173
BUSBRIDGE
North Munstead
THORNCOMBE STREET
Guildford
GU5
South Munstead
Hydestile
Hydon Heath
HYDON HEATH
HASCOMBE
Upper Vann
Loxhill
BUSBRIDGE WOODS
THE HURTWOOD
WINKWORTH ARBORETUM
HASCOMBE ROAD
THE STREET
B2130
MARE LANE
MARKWICK LANE
HAMBLEDON ROAD
CLOCK BARN LANE
SALT LANE
NEW ROAD
UPPER VANN LANE
VANN LANE
ALLDENS LANE
MUNSTEAD HEATH RD.
SOUTH MUNSTEAD LANE
LODKIN HILL
GODALMING ROAD
HOOKHOUSE RD.
Busbridge Farm
Busbridge Hall
Busbridge Lakes, Waterfowl & Gardens
Busbridge Lakes Ho.
Lady Well
Lower Lake
Middle Lake
Long Pond Copse
House Pond
Holm Oaks
Four Winds
Little Munstead Plantation
North Munstead
Munstead Wood
Reservoirs (Covered)
Oathooks Copse
Combe Farm
Alldens Cover
Northanger
Training Race Course
Stilemans
Shepherd's Hanger
Long Field Copse
Busbridge Copse
Stonelands Granary
Slade Farm
Phillimore
Badgers Rake
Furze Field
Rowe's Flashe
Perrydean Copse
Long Copse
Clock Barn Farm
Yew Tree Drive
Busbridge Wood
Broom Hanger
Home Wood
Lodge Bottom
Hanstead Hill
Hazel Hill
South Munstead Farm
Barnfield Rue
Arlaw Banks
Juniper Valley
Hydon Nursery
Hydon Hill (Cheshire Home)
Busbridge Copse Farm
Austen's Wood
High Barn
High Leybourne
Winkworth Farm
Winkworth Hall
Whinfold
High Hascombe
Heads Copse
Hascombe Cottages
Hascombe Court
Recreation Ground
Oldground Copse
Marepond Cottages
Marepond Farm
The Tolt
Hydon Wood
Hydon Ridge
Hydon's Ball
Hydon End
Feathercombe
Feathercombe Farm
Great House
Ellingsons
Fourteen Acre Copse
Foxbury Copse
Hoe Farm
Rectory
Hurtwood Copse
Pound Cottage
Hoe Farm Cottage
Shepherdsgrove Copse
Sunny Wood
The Old Rectory
Little Burgate Farm
Court Farm
Maple Bungalow
Great Copse
Durrants Knob
Holloways Heath
Hascombe Grange
Reservoir (covered)
Scions
Vann Hill
Handon Copse
Parsonage Copse
Foxbury
Burgate Hanger
Breakneck Hill
Castle Cottage
Garden Cottage
Gunter's Wood
Hasledons
Vannmoor
Burgate House
Spring Copse
Loxhill Cottage
The Raswell
Markwick Cottage
Markwick Farm Cottage
Catspaw Rew
Burgate Farm
Markwick Farm
Vann Lane Piggeries
Bonners
Royton
Vann Lodge
Shaftowes
Park Piece
Placewood Farm
Gorebridge Green Farm
Rowcliffe Springs
H
J
K
L
M
N
G
1
2
3
4
5
6
7
8
9
42
41
140
39
38
97
98
99
500

154
A
B
C
D
E
F
G
500
01
02
03
134
Cockedhat Cover
Rowe Farm
Rowe Barn Farm
Upper Bonhurst
Rooks Hill Farm
Rooks Hill Cotts.
Brookwell
DOWNS LINK
Leagate Ho.
BROOKWELL
GATE
Ridings Brook
Rushett Common
Ckt. Grd.
Rushett Farm
THORNCOMBE
THORNCOMBE STREET
STREET
Lea Farm
Homing Copse
Grafham Farm
The Oast House
Slade Farm
Gatestreet Farm
Grafham House
Playing Fields
Guildford
Northbrook Copse
Honeymead Farm
Grafham Grange School
GRAFHAM
Wintershall Cottage
Yewtree Nob
Wintershall
Pinks Hill Farm
Selhurst Farm
A281
GU5
Scrubbins Pond
Fish Pond
Mallards Point
Milestone Cottage
Whipley Manor
41
Middle Copse
Selhurst Common
Tanyards
Goose Green Farm
Whipley Manor Farm
HILL
Kiln Copse
Great Brook
Goose Green
Palmers Cross
Palmers Cross House
Winkworth Farm
153
Langhurst Farm
Scotsland Farm
Juniper Hill
Scotsland Brook
Tilsey Great Copse
Cricket's Hill
Leg-of-Mutton Copse
Tilsey Farm
ROAD
PEPPERBOX LANE
Brooklands Farm
THE
40
Upper House
New Barn
Ham Barn
Roundabouts
ROWCLIFFE SPRINGS
HASCOMBE
Godalming
Coldbourne Copse
Carper's Pond
GU8
Battle Cottage
HOE
Rectory
Hascombe Place
CHURCH RD
SMITHBROOK GATE
Smithbrook Cottages
Olivers
Hascombe Place Farm
Nore Hanger
Nore Brook
Pound Cotts.
Smithbrook
Sunny Wood
The Old Rectory
Creek Copse
Smithbrook Manor
Tillings
Farm Cottage
SMITHBROOK KILNS
39
Pheasantry
Hascombe Grange
Reservoir (covered)
Telegraph Hill
Hascombe Hill
Coney Burroughs
Barrihurst Bungalow
Rydenwood
Barrihurst
HORSHAM
Hillcrest
Barrihurst
BARRIHURST LA
Castle Cottage
Deer Park Cottage
Hascombe Beech
Lodge Farm
Vineyard
Painshill Cottage
Garden Cottage
Loxhill Cottage
The Raswell
Markwick Cottage
B2130 ROAD
STREET GODALMING
Fir Field Copse
Lower Barrihurst Farm
Painshill Farm
HASCOMBE ROAD
B2130
Loxhill
MARKWICK LANE
Grubbins Farm
STOVOLDS ROAD
The Coach House
The Round House
Bayhurst Copse
38
GODALMING
Farlands
Rose Cottages
Sussex Lodges
HOOKHOUSE LA
Gorebridge Green Farm
Park Hatch
174
DUNSFOLD
STOVOLDS HILL
Sewage Works
HOOKHOUSE RD
ROAD
Majorland
The Lodge
1
2
3
4
5
6
7
8
9

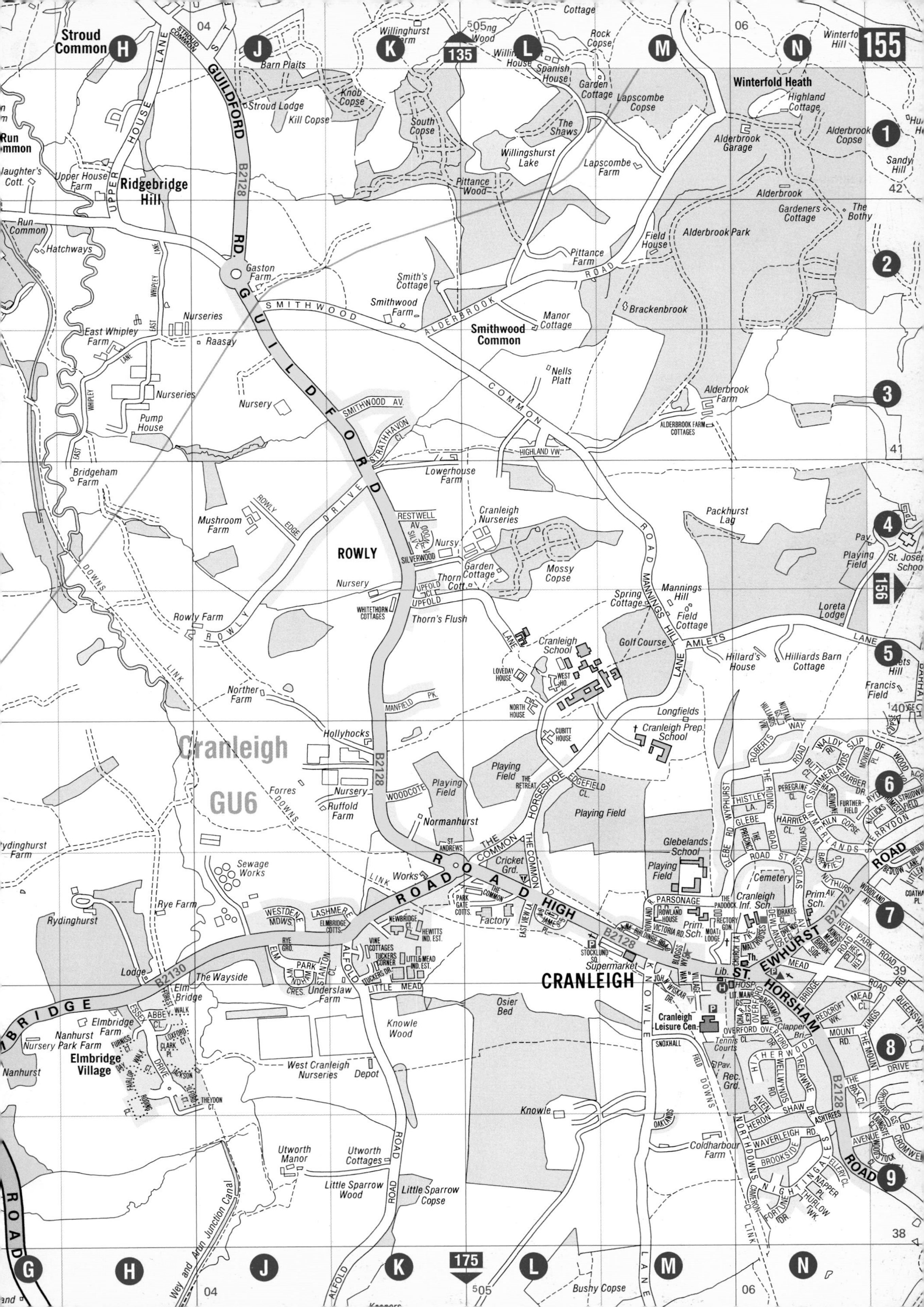
155
135
156
175
H
J
K
L
M
N
G
1
2
3
4
5
6
7
8
9
04
505
06
42
41
40
39
38
Stroud Common
Barn Plaits
Willinghurst Farm
Willinghurst House
Spanish House
Rock Copse
Garden Cottage
Cottage
Winterfold Hill
Winterfold Heath
Highland Cottage
Alderbrook Copse
Alderbrook Garage
Sandy Hill
Knob Copse
Stroud Lodge
Kill Copse
South Copse
The Shaws
Lapscombe Copse
Willingshurst Lake
Lapscombe Farm
Pittance Wood
Alderbrook
Gardeners Cottage
The Bothy
Alderbrook Park
Field House
Pittance Farm
Run Common
Slaughter's Cott.
Upper House Farm
Ridgebridge Hill
Hatchways
Gaston Farm
Smith's Cottage
Smithwood Farm
Smithwood Common
Manor Cottage
Brackenbrook
East Whipley Farm
Nurseries
Raasay
Nells Platt
Pump House
Nursery
Alderbrook Farm
ALDERBROOK FARM COTTAGES
HIGHLAND VW.
Bridgeham Farm
Lowerhouse Farm
Mushroom Farm
Cranleigh Nurseries
Packhurst Lag
ROWLY
Nursy.
Garden Cottage
Thorn Cott.
Mossy Copse
Playing Field
St. Joseph School
Rowly Farm
WHITETHORN COTTAGES
Thorn's Flush
Spring Cottage
Mannings Hill
Field Cottage
Loreta Lodge
Cranleigh School
Golf Course
Hillard's House
Hilliards Barn Cottage
Francis Field
LOVEDAY HOUSE
WEST HO.
Norther Farm
NORTH HOUSE
Longfields
Cranleigh Prep. School
Hollyhocks
CUBITT HOUSE
Cranleigh
GU6
Forres
Nursery
Ruffold Farm
Playing Field
THE RETREAT
Playing Field
Normanhurst
Rydinghurst Farm
Sewage Works
Works
Cricket Grd.
Glebelands School
Playing Field
Cemetery
Cranleigh Inf. Sch.
Prim. Sch.
Rye Farm
Rydinghurst
Factory
Prim. Sch.
Supermarket
CRANLEIGH
Lib.
HOSP.
Lodge
The Wayside
Elm Bridge
Elmbridge Farm
Nanhurst Farm
Nursery Park Farm
Elmbridge Village
Nanhurst
Underslaw Farm
Knowle Wood
Osier Bed
Cranleigh Leisure Cen.
Tennis Courts
Pav.
Rec. Grd.
West Cranleigh Nurseries
Depot
Knowle
Coldharbour Farm
Utworth Manor
Utworth Cottages
Little Sparrow Wood
Little Sparrow Copse
Wey and Arun Junction Canal
Bushy Copse
GUILDFORD RD.
B2128
UPPER HOUSE LANE
WHIPLEY LANE
EAST WHIPLEY LANE
SMITHWOOD
ALDERBROOK ROAD
COMMON
SMITHWOOD AV.
STRATHHAVON CL.
ROWLY EDGE
ROWLY DRIVE
RESTWELL AV.
SILVERWOOD
UPFOLD CL.
UPFOLD LANE
ROAD MANNINGS HILL LANE
AMLETS LANE
DOWNS LINK
MANFIELD PK.
WOODCOTE
HORSESHOE
EDGEFIELD CL.
THE COMMON
ST. ANDREWS
HIGH ROAD
B2130
ELMBRIDGE ROAD
WESTDENE MDWS.
LASHMERE
ELMBRIDGE COTTS.
RYE GRO.
PARK
STANTON CL.
ALFOLD RD.
VINE COTTAGES
TUCKERS CORNER
NEWBRIDGE CL.
HEWITTS IND. EST.
LITTLEMEAD IND. EST.
LITTLE MEAD
PARK GATE COTTS.
EAST VIEW LA.
ST. JAMES PL.
STOCKLUND SQ.
KNOWLE LANE
PARSONAGE
ROWLAND HOUSE
VICTORIA RD.
MOAT LODGE
RECTORY GDN.
ROWLAND RD.
EWHURST ROAD
B2127
HORSHAM ROAD
ABBEY WALK
LOXFORD CT.
CLARK PL.
FURNISS CT.
JACKSON CT.
THEYDON CT.
SNOXHALL
FIELD
DOWNS LINK
OVERFORD
Clapper Bri.
HITHERWOOD
WELLWYNDS RD.
TRELAWNE DR.
SHAW DR.
ASHTREES
HERON CL.
AVEN CL.
WAVERLEIGH RD.
BROOKSIDE
NORTHDOWNS
NIGHTINGALES
CAMERON CL.
FORTUNE DR.
THURLOW WK.
NAPPER PL.
ELLERY CL.
AVENUE
CROMWELL
MOUNT RD.
THE MOUNT
DRIVE
REDCROFT WK.
MEAD CL.
KINGS RD.
QUEENSWAY
NEW PARK ROAD
THE PADDOCK
GLEBE RD.
WYPHURST RD.
THISTLEY LA.
THE RIDING
ROBERTS WAY
WALDY RD.
SUMMERLANDS
BARBER DR.
HARRIER CL.
PEREGRINE CL.
KILN COPSE
SHERRYDON
NUTHURST AV.
WOODLAND AV.
BEDLOW LA.
COATHAM PL.
ST. NICOLAS AV.
DEWLANDS LA.
DRAKES CL.
CHURCH LA.
MALTHOUSES
BLOGGS WAY
WISKAR DR.
VILLAGE WAY
ST. HELENS

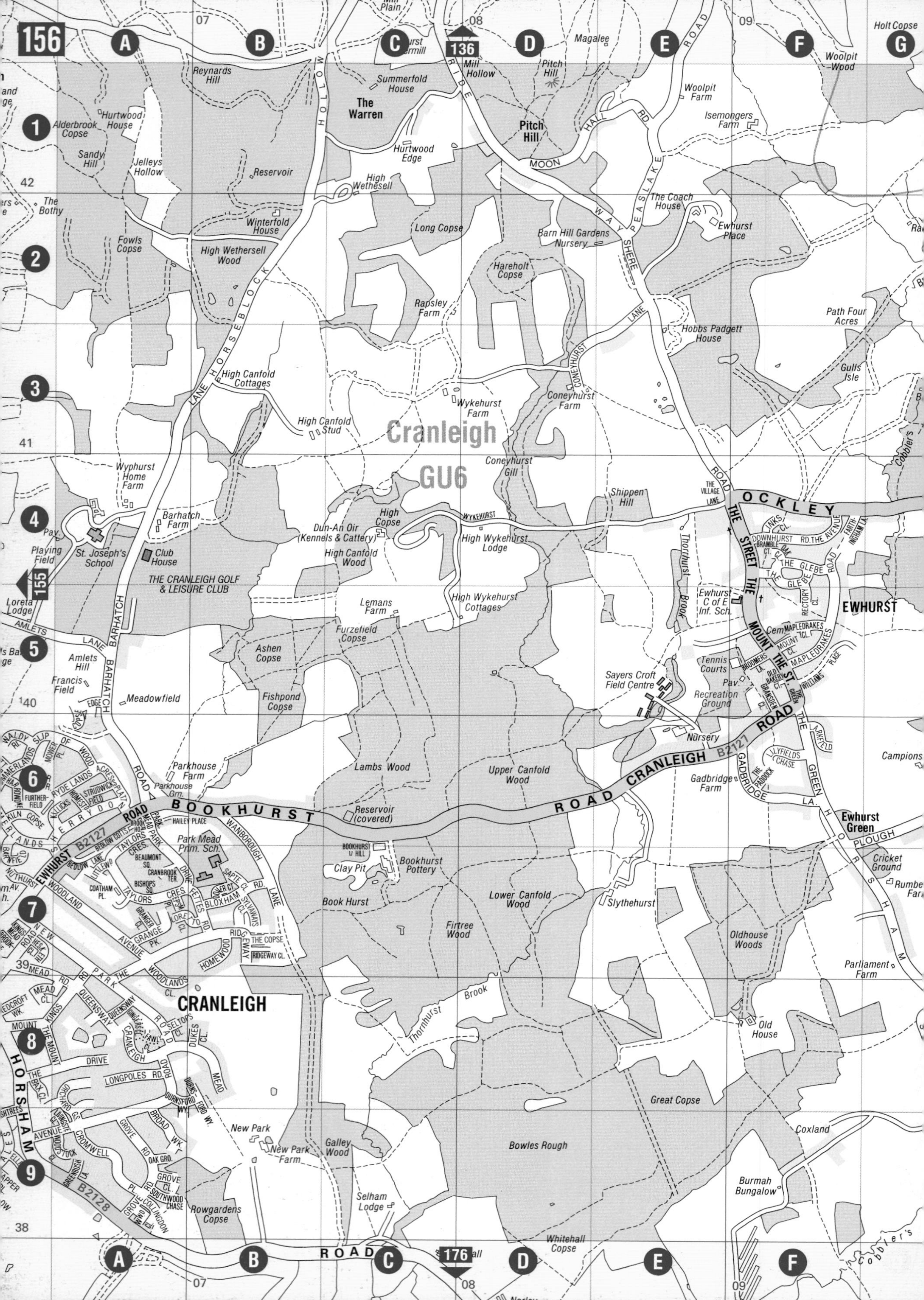

Cranleigh
GU6
CRANLEIGH
EWHURST
Ewhurst Green
The Warren
Pitch Hill
Reynards Hill
Summerfold House
Mill Hollow
Magalee
Holt Copse
Woolpit Wood
Woolpit Farm
Isemongers Farm
Alderbrook Copse
Hurtwood House
Sandy Hill
Jelleys Hollow
Reservoir
Hurtwood Edge
High Wethesell
Winterfold House
Fowls Copse
High Wethersell Wood
Long Copse
Barn Hill Gardens Nursery
The Coach House
Ewhurst Place
Hareholt Copse
Rapsley Farm
Hobbs Padgett House
Path Four Acres
Gulls Isle
High Canfold Cottages
High Canfold Stud
Wykehurst Farm
Coneyhurst Farm
Coneyhurst Gill
Shippen Hill
Wyphurst Home Farm
Barhatch Farm
St. Joseph's School
Club House
THE CRANLEIGH GOLF & LEISURE CLUB
Playing Field
Loreta Lodge
Dun-An Oir (Kennels & Cattery)
High Copse
High Canfold Wood
High Wykehurst Lodge
High Wykehurst Cottages
Lemans Farm
Furzefield Copse
Ashen Copse
Fishpond Copse
Amlets Hill
Francis Field
Meadowfield
Sayers Croft Field Centre
Tennis Courts
Recreation Ground
Nursery
Ewhurst C of E Inf. Sch.
Thorhurst Brook
Parkhouse Farm
Lambs Wood
Upper Canfold Wood
Gadbridge Farm
Campions
Reservoir (covered)
Park Mead Prim. Sch.
Bookhurst Pottery
Clay Pit
Book Hurst
Lower Canfold Wood
Slythehurst
Firtree Wood
Oldhouse Woods
Cricket Ground
Parliament Farm
Thornhurst Brook
Old House
Great Copse
Coxland
New Park
New Park Farm
Galley Wood
Bowles Rough
Burmah Bungalow
Selham Lodge
Rowgardens Copse
Whitehall Copse
OCKLEY ROAD
CRANLEIGH ROAD
BOOKHURST ROAD
HORSHAM ROAD
B2127
B2128
136
155
176

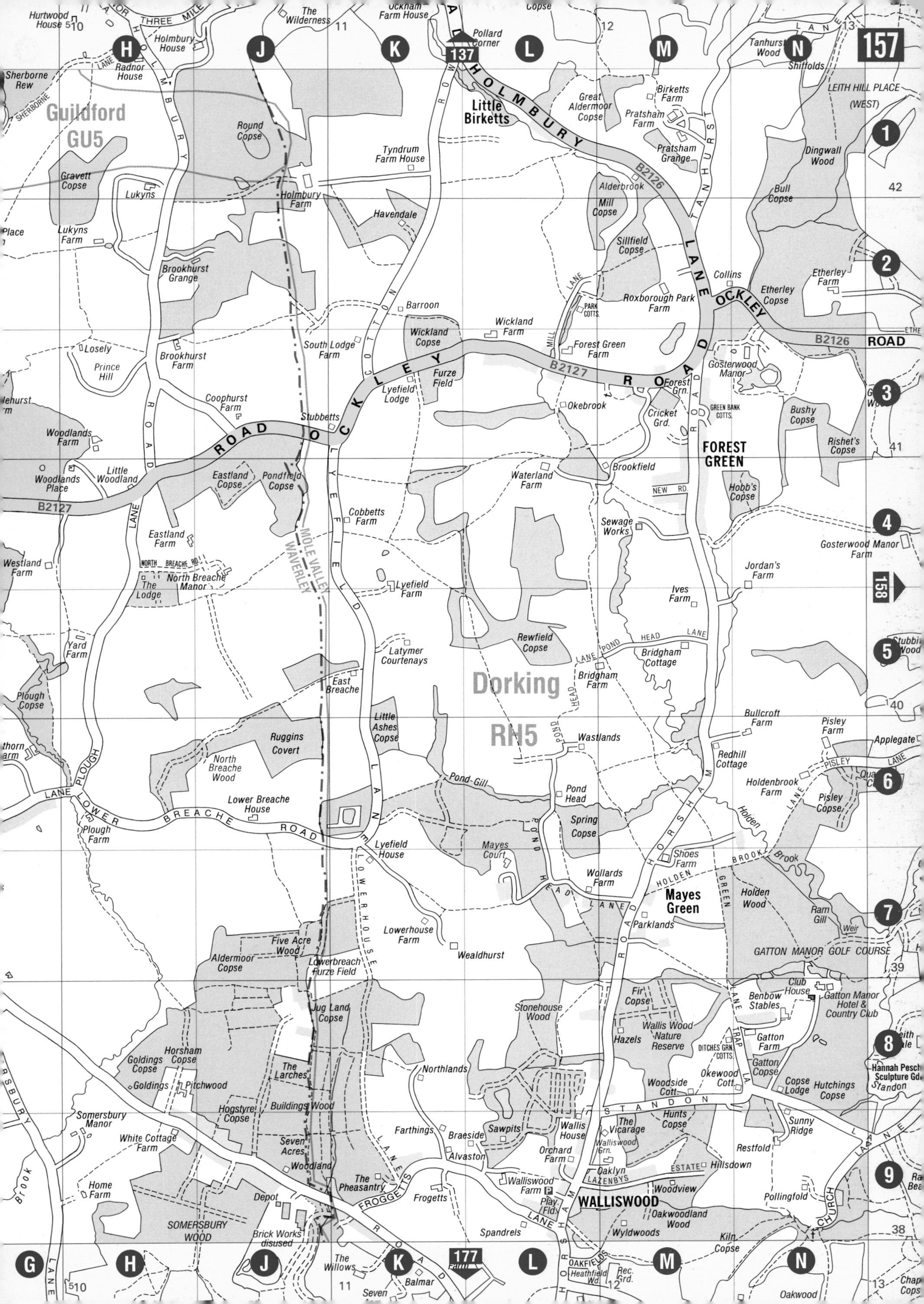

Guildford
GU5
Dorking
RH5
FOREST GREEN
Mayes Green
WALLISWOOD
Little Birketts
HOLMBURY LANE
OCKLEY ROAD
B2126
B2127
HORSHAM ROAD
LYEFIELD LANE
PLOUGH LANE
LOWER BREACHE ROAD
FROGGETTS ROAD
LOWERHOUSE LANE
POND HEAD LANE
HOLDEN BROOK
STANDON LANE
CHURCH LANE
PISLEY LANE
TANHURST LANE
MILL LANE
COTTON ROW
MOLE VALLEY
WAVERLEY
Sherborne Rew
Gravett Copse
Lukyns
Lukyns Farm
Round Copse
Holmbury Farm
Radnor House
Holmbury House
Hurtwood House
The Wilderness
Ockham Farm House
Pollard Corner
Tyndrum Farm House
Havendale
Brookhurst Grange
Brookhurst Farm
Losely
Prince Hill
Coophurst Farm
Woodlands Farm
Woodlands Place
Little Woodland
Eastland Copse
Pondfield Copse
Eastland Farm
Westland Farm
North Breache Manor
The Lodge
Yard Farm
Plough Copse
Plough Farm
Ruggins Covert
North Breache Wood
Lower Breache House
East Breache
Little Ashes Copse
Latymer Courtenays
Lyefield Farm
Cobbetts Farm
Stubbetts
Lyefield Lodge
South Lodge Farm
Barroon
Wickland Copse
Wickland Farm
Furze Field
Great Aldermoor Copse
Birketts Farm
Pratsham Farm
Pratsham Grange
Alderbrook
Mill Copse
Sillfield Copse
Roxborough Park Farm
Collins
Forest Green Farm
Park Cotts.
Okebrook
Cricket Grd.
Forest Grn.
Gosterwood Manor
Green Bank Cotts.
Waterland Farm
Brookfield
New Rd.
Hobb's Copse
Sewage Works
Ives Farm
Jordan's Farm
Gosterwood Manor Farm
Rewfield Copse
Bridgham Cottage
Bridgham Farm
Wastlands
Bullcroft Farm
Redhill Cottage
Pisley Farm
Applegate
Holdenbrook Farm
Pisley Copse
Pond-Gill
Pond Head
Spring Copse
Mayes Court
Lyefield House
Shoes Farm
Wollards Farm
Holden Wood
Ram Gill
Weir
Parklands
Lowerhouse Farm
Wealdhurst
GATTON MANOR GOLF COURSE
Club House
Gatton Manor Hotel & Country Club
Benbow Stables
Gatton Farm
Gatton Copse
Fir Copse
Stonehouse Wood
Hazels
Wallis Wood Nature Reserve
Ditches Grn Cotts.
Okewood Cott.
Woodside Cott.
Cope Lodge
Hutchings Copse
Sunny Ridge
Hunts Copse
The Vicarage
Walliswood Grn.
Wallis House
Sawpits
Orchard Farm
Oaklyn
LAZENBYS ESTATE
Hillsdown
Restfold
Woodview
Pollingfold
Oakwoodland Wood
Wyldwoods
Kiln Copse
Walliswood Farm
Play Fld.
Spandrels
Heathfield Wd.
Rec. Grd.
OAKFIELDS
Northlands
Farthings
Braeside
Alvaston
Frogetts
The Pheasantry
Five Acre Wood
Aldermoor Copse
Lowerbreach Furze Field
Jug Land Copse
Horsham Copse
Goldings Copse
Goldings
Pitchwood
The Larches
Buildings Wood
Hogstyre Copse
Seven Acres
Woodland
Somersbury Manor
White Cottage Farm
Home Farm
Depot
SOMERSBURY WOOD
Brick Works disused
The Willows
Balmar
Seven
Oakwood
Dingwall Wood
Bull Copse
Etherley Farm
Etherley Copse
Bushy Copse
Rishet's Copse
LEITH HILL PLACE (WEST)
Tanhurst Wood
Shiffolds
Hannah Peschar Sculpture Garden
Standon
Brook
H J K L M N G
137
158
177
10 11 12 13
42 41 40 39 38
1 2 3 4 5 6 7 8 9

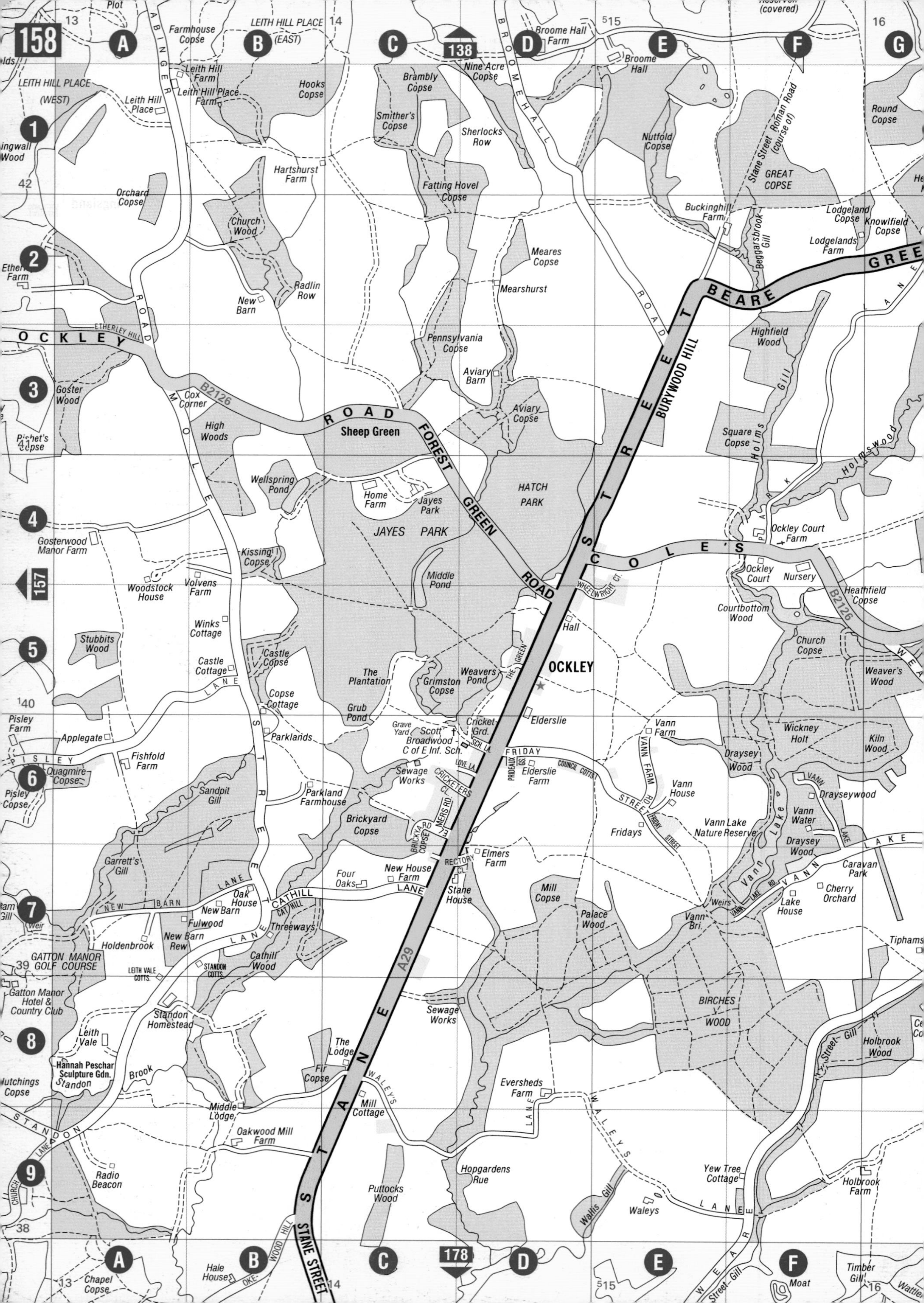

A
B
C
D
E
F
G
138
178
157
1
2
3
4
5
6
7
8
9
OCKLEY
Farmhouse Copse
LEITH HILL PLACE (EAST)
LEITH HILL PLACE (WEST)
Leith Hill Farm
Leith Hill Place Farm
Leith Hill Place
Hooks Copse
Brambly Copse
Smither's Copse
Nine Acre Copse
Broome Hall Farm
Broome Hall
Sherlocks Row
Nutfold Copse
Stane Street Roman Road (course of)
Round Copse
GREAT COPSE
Hartshurst Farm
Orchard Copse
Church Wood
Fatting Hovel Copse
Buckinghill Farm
Lodgeland Copse
Knowlfield Copse
Lodgelands Farm
Beggarsbrook Gill
Meares Copse
Mearshurst
Radlin Row
New Barn
BEARE GREEN
OCKLEY ROAD
ETHERLEY HILL
Highfield Wood
Pennsylvania Copse
Aviary Barn
Aviary Copse
Goster Wood
Cox Corner
B2126
High Woods
Sheep Green
FOREST GREEN ROAD
BURYWOOD HILL
STANE STREET
Square Copse
Holms Gill
Holmswood
Wellspring Pond
Home Farm
Jayes Park
JAYES PARK
HATCH PARK
Gosterwood Manor Farm
Kissing Copse
Ockley Court Farm
COLE'S LANE
Ockley Court
Nursery
Heathfield Copse
Woodstock House
Volvens Farm
Middle Pond
WHEELWRIGHT CT.
Hall
Courtbottom Wood
Winks Cottage
Stubbits Wood
Castle Copse
Castle Cottage
The Plantation
Grimston Copse
Weavers Pond
THE GREEN
OCKLEY
Church Copse
Weaver's Wood
Copse Cottage
Grub Pond
Cricket Grd.
Elderslie
Pisley Farm
Applegate
Parklands
Grave Yard
Scott Broadwood C of E Inf. Sch.
SCH. LA.
Vann Farm
Wickney Holt
Kiln Wood
Fishfold Farm
PISLEY
Quagmire Copse
Pisley Copse
FRIDAY STREET
COUNCIL COTTS.
PRIDEAUX GS.
Elderslie Farm
VANN FARM RD.
Draysey Wood
Vann House
Sandpit Gill
Sewage Works
LOVE LA.
CRICKETERS CL.
Parkland Farmhouse
Drayseywood
Vann Water
Brickyard Copse
BRICKYARD COPSE
MERS RD.
Fridays
Vann Lake Nature Reserve
Draysey Wood
VANN LAKE
Garrett's Gill
Elmers Farm
RECTORY CL.
Four Oaks
New House Farm
Caravan Park
Cherry Orchard
Lake House
Mill Copse
Stane House
Oak House
New Barn
NEW BARN LANE
CATHILL LANE
Fulwood
Threeways
Holdenbrook
New Barn Rew
Palace Wood
Weirs
Vann Bri.
Weir
A29
GATTON MANOR GOLF COURSE
LEITH VALE COTTS.
STANDON COTTS.
Cathill Wood
Tiphams
Gatton Manor Hotel & Country Club
Standon Homestead
Sewage Works
BIRCHES WOOD
Leith Vale
The Lodge
Fir Copse
Street Gill
Holbrook Wood
Hannah Peschar Sculpture Gdn.
Standon
Brook
Middle Lodge
Mill Cottage
WALEYS LANE
Eversheds Farm
Hutchings Copse
STANDON LANE
Oakwood Mill Farm
CHURCH LANE
Radio Beacon
Hopgardens Rue
Puttocks Wood
Yew Tree Cottage
Holbrook Farm
Wallis Gill
Waleys
WEARE STREET
OKE WOOD HILL
Hale House
Chapel Copse
Timber Gill
Moat
13
14
515
16
42
41
140
39
38

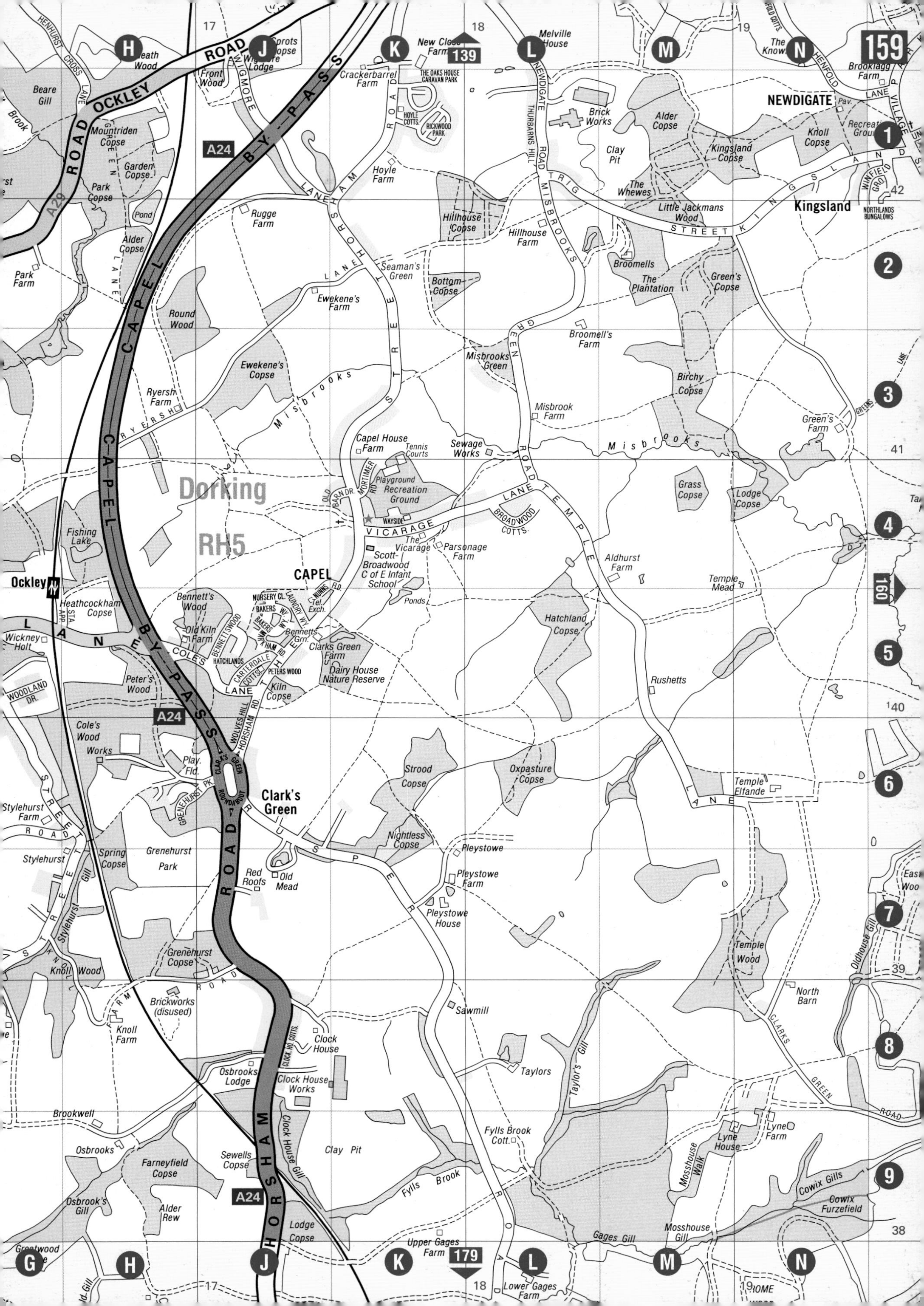
159
139
179
160
17
18
19
H
J
K
L
M
N
G
1
2
3
4
5
6
7
8
9
38
39
40
41
42
Dorking
RH5
CAPEL
NEWDIGATE
Kingsland
Ockley
Clark's Green
A24
A29
CAPEL BY-PASS
OCKLEY ROAD
HORSHAM ROAD
STREET KINGSLAND
TEMPLE LANE
VICARAGE LANE
RUSPER ROAD
MISBROOKS GREEN ROAD
TRIG STREET
NEWDIGATE ROAD
THURBARNS HILL
CLARKS GREEN ROAD
RYERSH LANE
COLES LANE
WIGMORE LANE
HENHURST CROSS LANE
GREEN LANE
STYLEHURST ROAD
KNOLL STREET
FARM ROAD
GRENEHURST PK.
WOLVES HILL
HORSHAM RD.
CLARK'S GREEN ROUNDABOUT
CLOCK HO. COTTS.
MORTIMER RD.
OLD BARN DR.
WAYSIDE
BROADWOOD COTTS.
NURSERY CL.
BAKERS WY.
LAUNDRY WY.
NUNNS FLD.
HATCHLANDS
CARTERDALE COTTS.
PETERS WOOD
BENNETTSWOOD
WOODLAND DR.
STA. APP.
VILLAGE
HENFOLD LANE
WINFIELD GRO.
NORTHLANDS BUNGALOWS
GREENS LANE
Heath Wood
Sprots Copse
Wigmore Lodge
Front Wood
Beare Gill
Mountriden Copse
Garden Copse
Park Copse
Pond
Alder Copse
Park Farm
Round Wood
Rugge Farm
Crackerbarrel Farm
New Close Farm
THE OAKS HOUSE CARAVAN PARK
HOYLE COTTS.
RICKWOOD PARK
Hoyle Farm
Melville House
Brick Works
Clay Pit
Alder Copse
Kingsland Copse
Knoll Copse
Recreation Ground
Pav.
Brooklagg Farm
The Knowe
The Whewes
Little Jackmans Wood
Hillhouse Copse
Hillhouse Farm
Broomells
The Plantation
Green's Copse
Seaman's Green
Bottom Copse
Ewekene's Farm
Ewekene's Copse
Broomell's Farm
Misbrooks Green
Birchy Copse
Misbrook Farm
Green's Farm
Misbrooks
Ryersh Farm
Capel House Farm
Tennis Courts
Sewage Works
Playground
Recreation Ground
Grass Copse
Lodge Copse
Fishing Lake
The Vicarage
Parsonage Farm
Scott-Broadwood C of E Infant School
Tel. Exch.
Ponds
Aldhurst Farm
Temple Mead
Heathcockham Copse
Bennett's Wood
Old Kiln Farm
Bennetts Grn.
Clarks Green Farm
Dairy House Nature Reserve
Hatchland Copse
Wickney Holt
Peter's Wood
Kiln Copse
Rushetts
Cole's Wood
Works
Play. Fld.
Strood Copse
Oxpasture Copse
Temple Elfande
Stylehurst Farm
Nightless Copse
Pleystowe
Pleystowe Farm
Pleystowe House
Stylehurst
Spring Copse
Grenehurst Park
Red Roofs
Old Mead
Stylehurst Gill
Temple Wood
Oldhouse Gill
North Barn
Knoll Wood
Grenehurst Copse
Brickworks (disused)
Sawmill
Knoll Farm
Clock House
Osbrooks Lodge
Clock House Works
Taylors
Taylor's Gill
Brookwell
Clock House Gill
Fylls Brook Cott.
Lyne Farm
Lyne House
Mosshouse Walk
Osbrooks
Sewells Copse
Clay Pit
Farneyfield Copse
Fylls Brook
Cowix Gills
Cowix Furzefield
Osbrook's Gill
Alder Rew
Lodge Copse
Upper Gages Farm
Gages Gill
Mosshouse Gill
Greatwood
Lower Gages Farm

160
A
B
C
D
E
F
G
140
159
180
NEWDIGATE
Kingsland
CUDWORTH
Dorking
RH5
Horsham
RH12
Langhurst
The Jordans
Brooklagg Farm
Rec. Ground
Newdigate C of E Infant Sch.
Horsielands Farm
Works
Hatchett's Shaw
Sturtwood Farm
Pockmires Wood
Puckney Gill
Greenfield Gill
Square Copse
Toogoolawah
Field Station
Cudworth Manor
Moat
Hillside Farm
Holly Farm
Gildings Farm
Floodhole Gill
Cudworth Manor Farm
Ash Farm
Burnt Oak Farm
The Gables
Greenings Farm
Green Lane Farm
Darragh House
Cudworth Copse
Copse View
Holmhush
Furzefield Farm
Roll's Furze
Acorn Wood
Cidermill Farm
Cidermill Gill
Tanhouse Farm
Home Farm
The Birches
Deer Park
Stable Cottage
Nursery
Newdigate Place
Fishponds
GLOVER'S PLANTATION
Mountnoddy Wood
Boothlands Farm
Newhouse Farm
Marelands Farm
Westlands
Westlands Farm
Alder Gill
Rose Cottage
Club House
RUSPER GOLF COURSE
Melton Hall Farm
Duke's Copse
Woodlands Farm
Jordan's Wood
Oaklands Park House
Ivyhouse Farm
Oaklands Park Farm
East Wood
Middlebarn Gill
Chaffolds Plantation
Chaffolds Copse
Scrag Copse
Jordans Farm
Medlands Farm
Orltons
Jordans
Oak House
Little Jordans
Orltons Copse
Chaffold's Farm
Gotwick Farm
Little Copse
Russley Acres
Peters
Keeper's Mount Kennels
Waffles Corner
Water Tank
Cophatch Corner
Dumbrels Copse
Peter's Farm
Cowix Farm
Ghyll Manor Farm
Nine Acre Rew
Langhurst Farm
Langhurst Hill
North Gate
Martins Farm
Venters Farm
Rusper House
MOLE VALLEY
HORSHAM

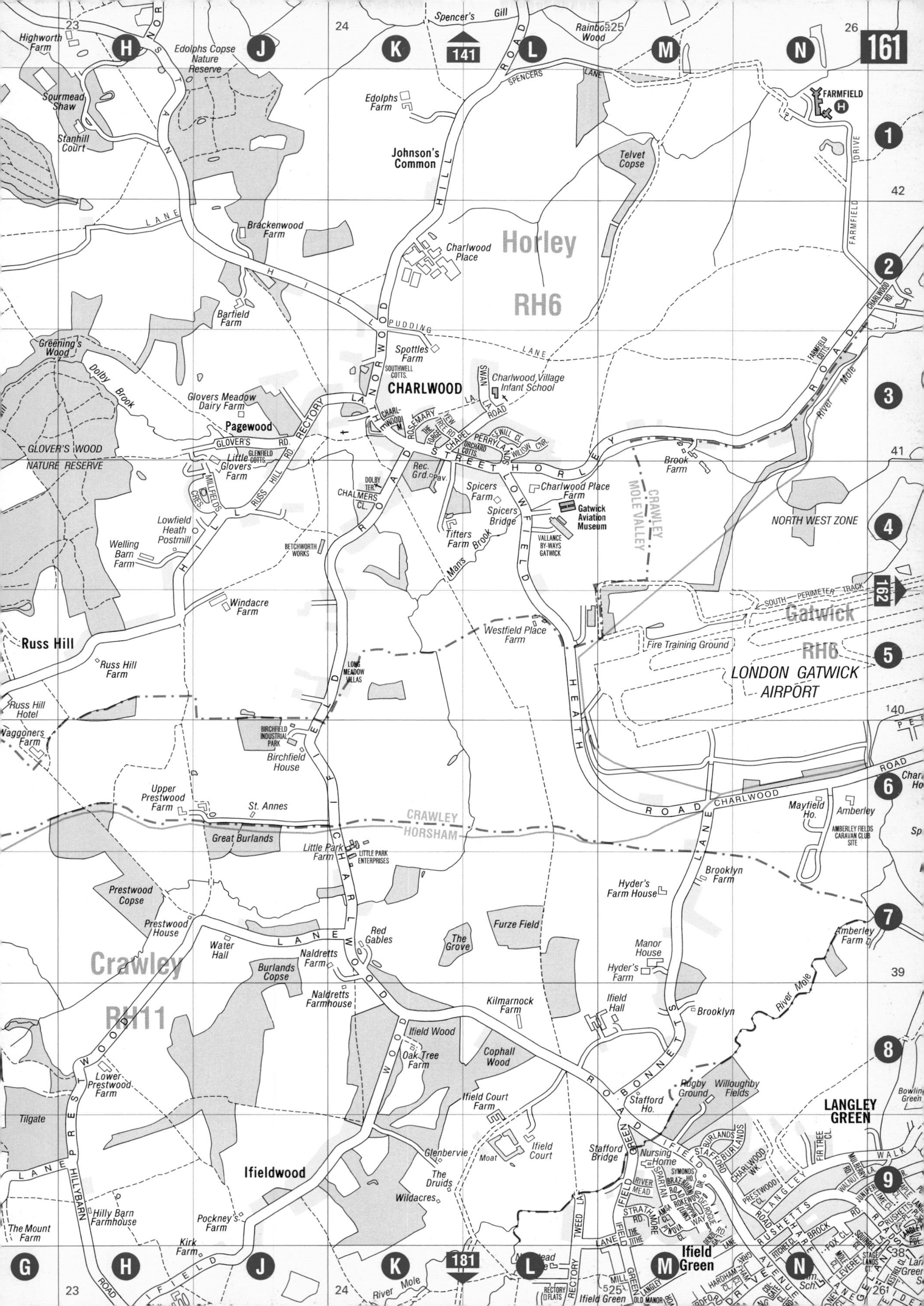

Highworth Farm
Edolphs Copse Nature Reserve
Spencer's Gill
141
Rainbow Wood
FARMFIELD
Sourmead Shaw
Stanhill Court
Edolphs Farm
Johnson's Common
Telvet Copse
Brackenwood Farm
Charlwood Place
Horley
RH6
Barfield Farm
Greening's Wood
Spottles Farm
Dolby Brook
Glovers Meadow Dairy Farm
CHARLWOOD
Charlwood Village Infant School
Pagewood
GLOVER'S WOOD NATURE RESERVE
Little Glovers Farm
Brook Farm
Spicers Farm
Charlwood Place Farm
Gatwick Aviation Museum
Spicers Bridge
Tifters Farm
CRAWLEY MOLE VALLEY
Lowfield Heath Postmill
Welling Barn Farm
NORTH WEST ZONE
162
Windacre Farm
Gatwick
Russ Hill
Westfield Place Farm
Fire Training Ground
RH6
Russ Hill Farm
LONDON GATWICK AIRPORT
Russ Hill Hotel
Waggoners Farm
Birchfield House
Upper Prestwood Farm
St. Annes
CRAWLEY HORSHAM
Mayfield Ho.
Amberley
AMBERLEY FIELDS CARAVAN CLUB SITE
Great Burlands
Little Park Farm
LITTLE PARK ENTERPRISES
Brooklyn Farm
Hyder's Farm House
Prestwood Copse
Prestwood House
Red Gables
Furze Field
Amberley Farm
Water Hall
The Grove
Manor House
Crawley
Naldretts Farm
Hyder's Farm
Burlands Copse
Naldretts Farmhouse
Kilmarnock Farm
Ifield Hall
RH11
Brooklyn
River Mole
Ifield Wood
Oak Tree Farm
Cophall Wood
Lower Prestwood Farm
Ifield Court Farm
Rugby Ground
Willoughby Fields
Stafford Ho.
LANGLEY GREEN
Tilgate
Glenbervie
Moat
Ifield Court
Stafford Bridge
Nursing Home
Ifieldwood
The Druids
Wildacres
Hilly Barn Farmhouse
Pockney's Farm
The Mount Farm
Kirk Farm
181
Ifield Green
River Mole

Ahed Depot
Superstore
Rec. Grd.
GATWICK PARK BUPA HOSP.
Hotel
FARMFIELD BLENHEIM HOSPITAL
Povey Cross Farm
Povey Cross
HORLEY
Horley
Archway Thtre.
Riverside Gdn. Pk.
Matbro House
Junction 9
A23
Depot
Fuel Farm
North Terminal Long Term Car Park
Timberham Crossroads
World Cargo Centre
Pier 5
NORTH TERMINAL
Pier 4
Pier 3
SATELLITE
Airbridge
SOUTH TERMINAL
Pier 6
Pier 2
Gatwick Airport Skyview
Gatwick Airport
Gatwick
RH6
Control Tower
Northern Ancillary Zone
Fire Station
NORTH WEST ZONE
LONDON GATWICK AIRPORT
Pier 1
South Terminal Long Term Car Park
Horleyland Wood
Sewage Works
Airport Maintenance
LOWFIELD HEATH
Huntsgreen Wood
Hawthorne Farm
The Beehive
GATWICK AIRPORT BEEHIVE AREA
Charlwood House
Amberley
AMBERLEY FIELDS CARAVAN CLUB SITE
Spikemead Farm
Ditsworthy Farm
Rowley Farm
Oldlands Bridge
Oldlands Farm
Tinsley Bridge
TINSLEY GREEN
Abattoir
PO Sorting Office
Crawley
Hotel
Hydehurst Furze
Rowley Wood
Gatwick Kennels
Amberley Farm
Windyridge Farm
County Oak
RH11
Works
Factory
Warehouse
Gasholder Station
The Larch
Playing Field
Bowling Green
LANGLEY GREEN
Football Ground
Summersvere Wood
The Birches
Sports Ground
Grattons Park
The Railway Field
Magpie Wood
Labs.
Sports Field
Ind. Est.
Hotel
Hazelwick Sch.
Milton Mount Prim. Sch.
LONDON ROAD
CRAWLEY AVENUE
A2011
BRIGHTON ROAD
AIRPORT WAY
PERIMETER ROAD
CHARLWOOD ROAD
FLEMING WAY
MANOR ROYAL
CRAWLEY
142
161
182

163
Horley
RH6
Broadbridge
Burstow
Fernhill
Shipley Bridge
Copthorne
Copthorne Common
Rickmans Green
RH10
Black Corner
Junction 9
Junction 10
M23 Motorway
A264
A2220
B2036
B2037
Reigate and Banstead
Tandridge
Crawley
Mid Sussex
143
164
183
Thunderfield Castle (site of)
Haroldslea House
The Plantation
The Roughs
Peeks Rough Farm
Bridgeham Farm
Bridgeham Grange
Lower Broadbridge Farm
Broadmead Farm
Broadbridge Farm
Broadbridge Stables
Poultry Houses
Collins Wood
Bellhatch Wood
Gunyah Farm
Redehall Preparatory School
Sacconex Farm
Vanderel Farm
Homestead Farm
Triddles Farm
Bridges Wood
Broadfield Farm
Fern Court Farm
Mushroom Farm
Gatwick House
Westlands Farm
Dalrana
Rede Hall
Redeham Hall
Redeham Hall Farm
Eastland Shaw
Keeper's Corner
Burstow Enterprise Park
Rivington Farm
Pullcotts Farm
Teizers Farm
Burstow Hall
Greenwood Flats
Park House
Brook Farm
Lodge
Kiln Heath Farm Bus. Cen.
Burstow Park Golf Course
Burstow Park Bus. Cen.
Club Ho.
Burstow Park Farm
Burstow Park
Newhouse Farm
Allingham Farm
Nyahlands Farm
The Hollies
Upper Pickett's
Allen's Wood
Courtlands
The Grange
Thornbridge Farm
The Rabbitry
Blackcorner Wood
Hollybush Business Centre
Playing Field
Stonelands Farm
Rec. Grd.
Wellfield Copse
Toovies Farm
Jun. Sch.
Club House
Copthorne Golf Course
Fairway Inf. Sch.
Heathy Ground
Surrey & Sussex Crematorium
Forge Wood
Heathyground Wood
Dragons Health Club
Hotel
Copthorne Common
Woodmans Farm
Coombers Wood Farm
Coombers Wood
Courthouse Farm
Pot Common
Copthorne Wood
Garden Centre
Driver's Wood
Rowfant Piggeries
King's Wood
Old Rowfant
Milton Mount Gdns.
Schlumberger House
Cricket Ground
Laburnum Court (Caravan Park)
Gonville Works
Borers Yard Ind. Est.
Effingham Road
Antlands Lane
Fernhill Road
Church Road
Copthorne Bank
Copthorne Road
Copthorne Way
Copthorne Common Road
Balcombe Road
Avenue
Hollow Old
Shipley Bridge Lane
Peeks Brook Lane
Redehall Road
Clay Hall Lane
Cross Lane
Borers Arms Road
Haroldslea Drive

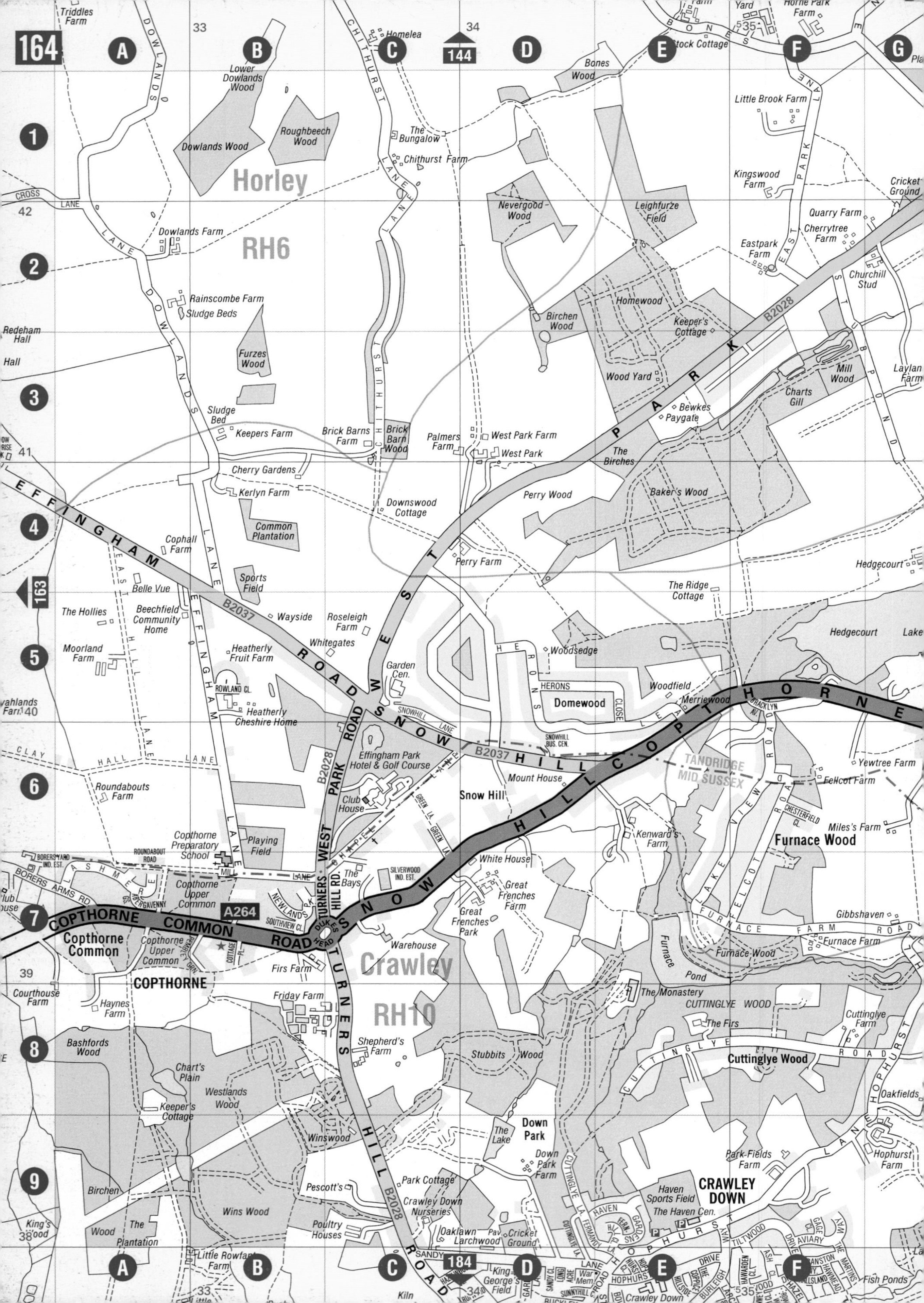
Horley
RH6
Crawley
RH10
COPTHORNE
CRAWLEY DOWN
Copthorne Common
Snow Hill
Domewood
Furnace Wood
Cuttinglye Wood
144
163
184
TANDRIDGE
MID SUSSEX

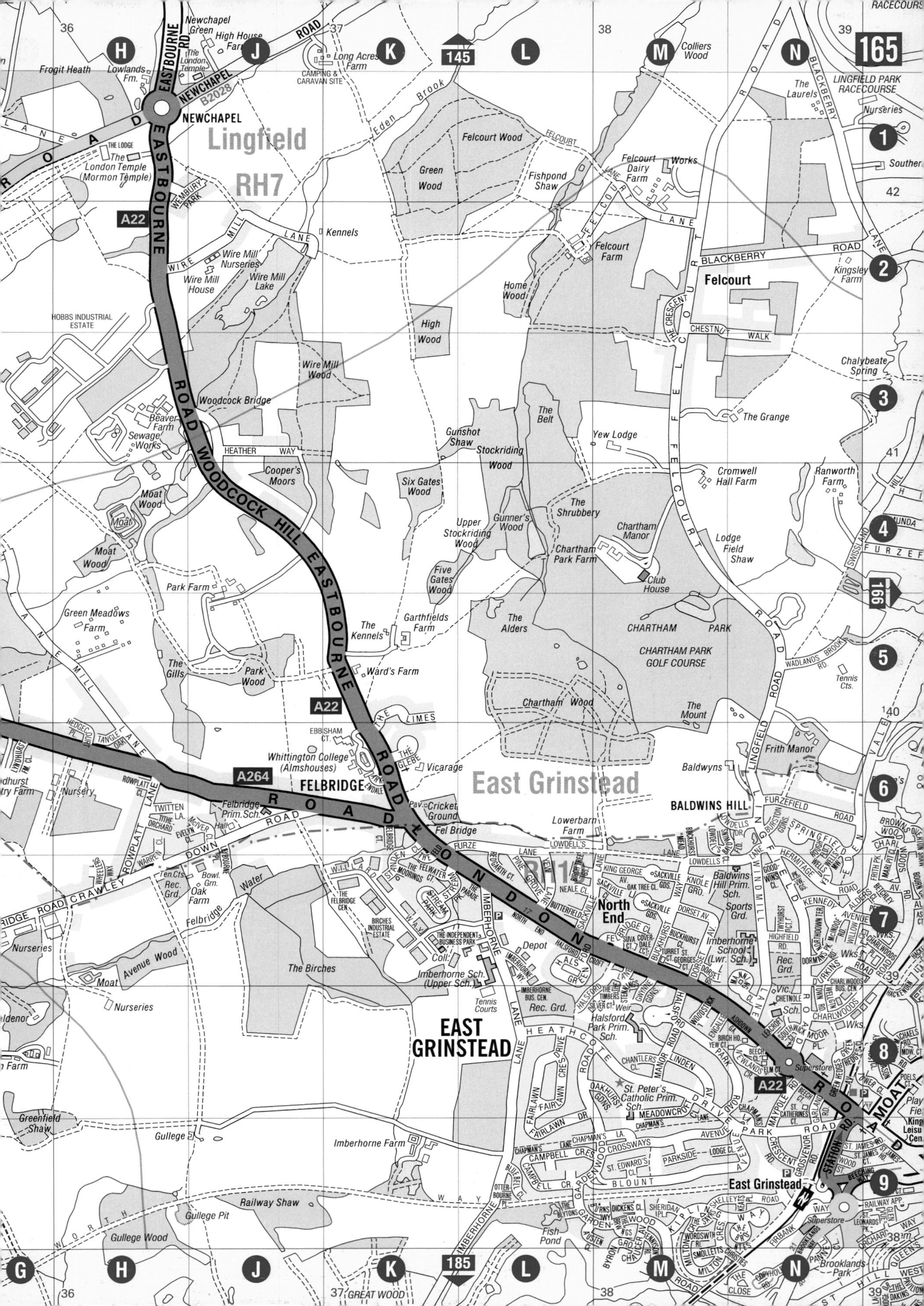
Lingfield
RH7
East Grinstead
EAST GRINSTEAD
RH19
NEWCHAPEL
FELBRIDGE
BALDWINS HILL
North End
Felcourt
145
166
185
A22
A264
B2028
EASTBOURNE ROAD
WOODCOCK HILL
LONDON ROAD
NEWCHAPEL ROAD
FELCOURT ROAD
LINGFIELD ROAD
BLACKBERRY ROAD
CRAWLEY DOWN ROAD
Newchapel Green
High House Farm
Long Acres Farm
CAMPING & CARAVAN SITE
Colliers Wood
LINGFIELD PARK RACECOURSE
The Laurels
Nurseries
Frogit Heath
Lowlands Fm.
The London Temple (Mormon Temple)
Felcourt Wood
Green Wood
Fishpond Shaw
Felcourt Dairy Farm
Works
Kennels
Wire Mill Nurseries
Wire Mill House
Wire Mill Lake
HOBBS INDUSTRIAL ESTATE
Felcourt Farm
Home Wood
High Wood
Kingsley Farm
Chalybeate Spring
The Grange
Wire Mill Wood
Woodcock Bridge
Beaver Farm
Sewage Works
Gunshot Shaw
The Belt
Yew Lodge
Stockriding Wood
Cooper's Moors
Six Gates Wood
Cromwell Hall Farm
Ranworth Farm
Moat Wood
The Shrubbery
Gunner's Wood
Upper Stockriding Wood
Chartham Manor
Chartham Park Farm
Lodge Field Shaw
Club House
Five Gates Wood
Park Farm
Green Meadows Farm
The Kennels
Garthfields Farm
The Alders
CHARTHAM PARK
CHARTHAM PARK GOLF COURSE
The Gills
Park Wood
Ward's Farm
Tennis Cts.
Chartham Wood
The Mount
Frith Manor
Whittington College (Almshouses)
Vicarage
Baldwyns
Felbridge Prim. Sch.
Cricket Ground
Fel Bridge
Lowerbarn Farm
Nursery
Oak Farm
Water
Baldwins Hill Prim. Sch.
Sports Grd.
Imberhorne School (Lwr. Sch.)
Rec. Grd.
Nurseries
Avenue Wood
Moat
The Birches
Depot
Imberhorne Sch. (Upper Sch.)
Tennis Courts
Halsford Park Prim. Sch.
Superstore
St. Peter's Catholic Prim. Sch.
Greenfield Shaw
Gullege
Imberhorne Farm
Railway Shaw
Gullege Pit
Gullege Wood
Fish Pond
East Grinstead
Brooklands Park
GREAT WOOD

166
A
B
C
D
E
F
G
1
2
3
4
5
6
7
8
9
39
540
41
42
140
146
165
186
Ford House
Parklands Poultry Farm
Filter Beds
LINGFIELD PARK RACECOURSE
Mill Wood
Club
Dormans Cross
Icehouse
Nurseries
Cattle Grid
Home Farm
Greathed Manor
Ford Manor
DORMANSLAND
Home Birches
Depots
Southernleigh
Waterfall
Dairy Wood
Moor Wood
LINGFIELD PARK GOLF COURSE
Rec. Grd.
Dormansland Prim. Sch.
Crosses Wood
Bog Wood
BLACKBERRY
BLACKBERRY RD.
Nine Acre Wood
Quaker's Platt
Lingfield
Matthews Wood
Noble's Green
St. John's Wood
Homes of St. Barnabas
Quaker's Platt Farm
Burnt Pit Farm
The Beacon
Farindons
Lodge
Dormans
LANE DORMANS STATION ROAD MUTTON HILL
Cricket Ground
Pav.
Ladycross Cottages
RH7
Chalybeate Spring
Playing Field
Burnpit Wood
Apsley Farm
Apsley Grange
Ladycross Farm
DORMANS PARK
Bulls Wood
Cowden Lodge
Cowden Birches
Bidbury Wood
Apsley
Ranworth Farm
Crabb Orchard Wood
Long Shaw
Bidbury
Luckens Shaw
Grid Sub Station
Two Houses
OSMUNDA BANK
FURZEFIELD
Blockfield Farm
CHASE THE
THE AVENUE
Walk Wood
PLAS NEWYDD
EDEN
LAKE VIEW
WILDERNESS RISE
Wilderwick Farm
Blockfield Wood
Tennis Courts
Cook's Pond Viaduct
The Wilderness Lake
Boxin Wood
Furze Field
Wilderwick House
Old Surrey Hall
Birchetts
The Barn
Moat
SWITE'S WOOD
Sewage Works
Moorhawes Wood
Moor Hawes Farm
Blackhatch Wood
Huntley's Shaw
Tennis Courts
Brown's Wood
The Alders
Stonequarry
Sandhawes Hill
Primrose Cottage
Wenlock Edge
Larches Farm
Gotwick Farm
Orchards Farm
Spring Copse
Stonequarry Wood
A264
Pumphouse Farm
Maynard Cottage
QUEEN VICTORIA HOSPITAL
MCINDOE CEN.
Ashplats House
East Grinstead
Fairlight Farm Bungalow
Fairlight Cottage
Minepit Wood
Blackwell Prim. Sch.
RH19
ASHPLATS WOOD
Fairlight Farm
Curz
Blackwell
Cemetery
Football Ground
Fairlight House
Kilnfield Wood
Mount Noddy
Stand
East Ct.
East Grinstead Town Mus.
Fairlight Wood
Playing Field
Kings Leisure Cen.
Gdns.
EAST GRINSTEAD
Playing Fields
A22
BEECHING WAY
The Atrium
Arts Cen.
Sackville Coll.
MID SUSSEX
WEALDEN
Pitlands Wood
Homestall Kennels
Superstore
Playing Field
Sackville Sch.
Dutton Homestall Poultry Farm
HOLTYE ROAD
LONDON ROAD
MOAT ROAD
LEWES ROAD
COLLEGE LA
B2110
Brooklands Park
Worsted Farm Cottages
Alder Shaw
Wood Cottage
The Bungalow
Shovelstrode Farm

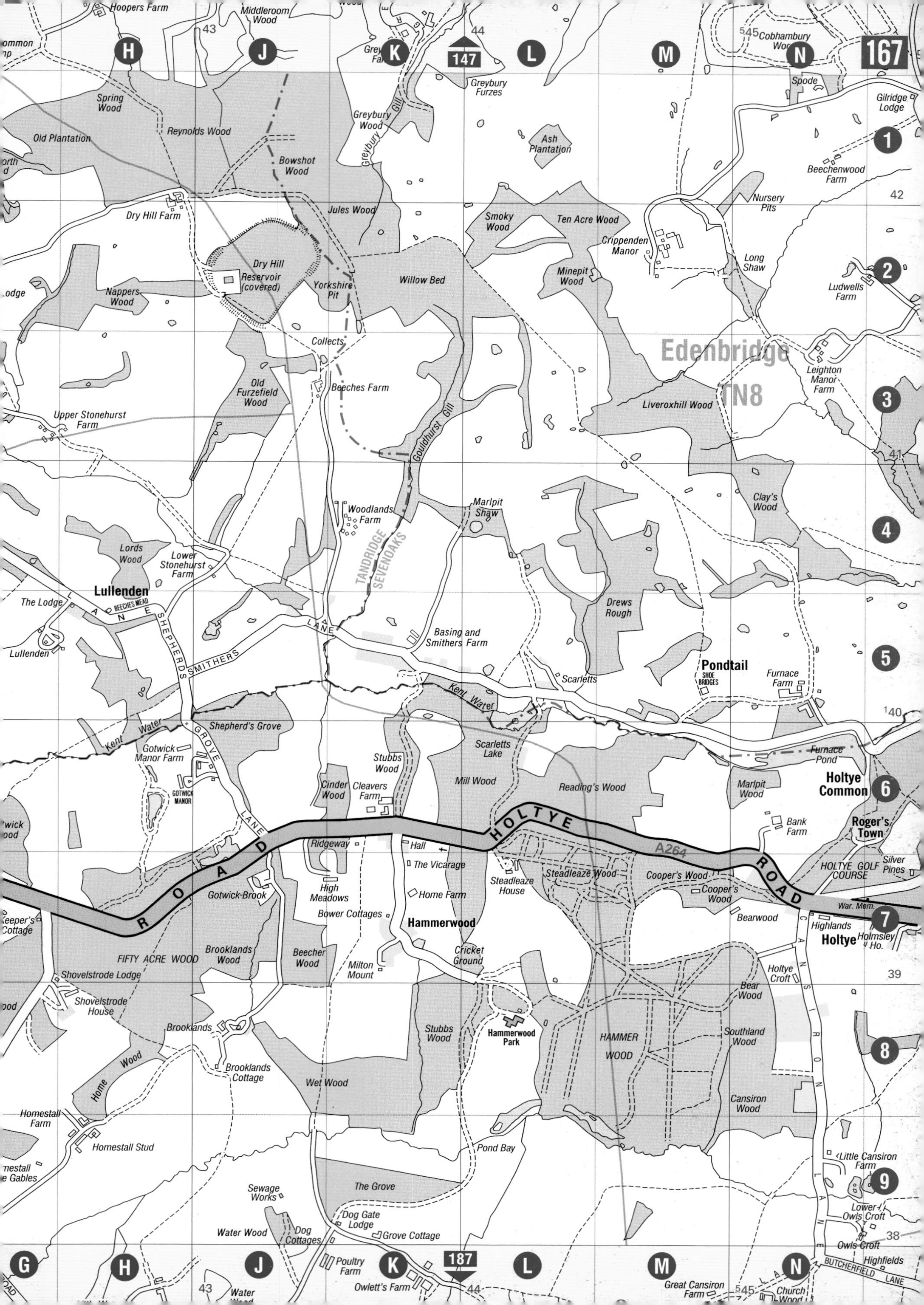

Hoopers Farm
Middleroom Wood
147
Greybury Furzes
Cobhambury Wood
Spode
Gilridge Lodge
Spring Wood
Old Plantation
Reynolds Wood
Greybury Wood
Greybury Gill
Ash Plantation
Bowshot Wood
Beechenwood Farm
Nursery Pits
Dry Hill Farm
Jules Wood
Smoky Wood
Ten Acre Wood
Crippenden Manor
Long Shaw
Dry Hill Reservoir (covered)
Nappers Wood
Yorkshire Pit
Willow Bed
Minepit Wood
Ludwells Farm
Collects
Edenbridge
TN8
Leighton Manor Farm
Old Furzefield Wood
Beeches Farm
Liveroxhill Wood
Upper Stonehurst Farm
Gouldhurst Gill
Woodlands Farm
Marlpit Shaw
Clay's Wood
TANDRIDGE
SEVENOAKS
Lords Wood
Lower Stonehurst Farm
Lullenden
Drews Rough
The Lodge
BEECHES MEAD
LANE
SHEPHERDS
SMITHERS
LANE
Basing and Smithers Farm
Lullenden
Pondtail
SHOE BRIDGES
Furnace Farm
Scarletts
Kent Water
Kent Water
Shepherd's Grove
GROVE
Gotwick Manor Farm
GOTWICK MANOR
Stubbs Wood
Scarletts Lake
Furnace Pond
Holtye Common
Cinder Wood
Cleavers Farm
Mill Wood
Reading's Wood
Marlpit Wood
LANE
Bank Farm
Roger's Town
HOLTYE
ROAD
A264
Ridgeway
Hall
The Vicarage
Steadleaze House
Steadleaze Wood
Cooper's Wood
Cooper's Wood
HOLTYE GOLF COURSE
Silver Pines
Keeper's Cottage
Gotwick-Brook
High Meadows
Home Farm
Bower Cottages
Hammerwood
Bearwood
War. Mem.
Highlands
Holtye
Holmsley Ho.
FIFTY ACRE WOOD
Brooklands Wood
Beecher Wood
Milton Mount
Cricket Ground
Holtye Croft
CANSIRON
Shovelstrode Lodge
Shovelstrode House
Bear Wood
Brooklands
Stubbs Wood
Hammerwood Park
HAMMER WOOD
Southland Wood
Home Wood
Brooklands Cottage
Wet Wood
Cansiron Wood
Homestall Farm
Homestall Stud
Pond Bay
Little Cansiron Farm
Sewage Works
The Grove
Lower Owls Croft
Dog Gate Lodge
Water Wood
Dog Cottages
Grove Cottage
Owls Croft
Highfields
Poultry Farm
187
BUTCHERFIELD LANE
Owlett's Farm
Great Cansiron Farm
Church Wood
Water Wood

Sleaford
148
Bordon
GU35
HEADLEY
LINDFORD
Deadwater
Standford
Hollywater
Passfield
Liphook
GU30
ARFORD
Beech Hill
Hearn
BROXHEAD COMMON (Nature Reserve)
Broxhead Farm
Lindford Farm
Lindford Bridge
Watermeadow Farm
Headley Mill Farm
Hatch House Farm
Midlands Farm
Huntingford Farm
Linstead Farm
Hartfield Farm
Curtis Farm
Headley Wood Farm
Headley Grange Farm
Headley Grange
Hilland Woods
Baldpate Cottage
Hurland Copse
High Hurlands
Reynolds House
Standford House
Standford Mill
Wey Valley Farm
Hatch Farm
Standford Grange
Sewage Works
Garthwaite
Passfield House Farm
Passfield Farm
Passfield Common
PASSFIELD COMMON
Hollywater Farm
Hollywater Green
Thornhill House
Thorn Hill
Hollywater Pond
Hollywater Clump
Lynchborough Wood
Conford Moor
Waterside Copse
Nursery
Passfield Manor
Coachroad Plantation
Whitehill Cemetery
Eveley Wood
The Meadow School
Mill Chase Community Sch.
Weyford Jun. & Inf. Schs
Fircones
Stream Farm
Bottomfield Copse
Great Birchfield Copse
Fir Hanger
Alder Red
Ten Acre Copse
Mountfield Wood
Great Wood
The Mount
Woodside
Taylor's Copse
Bull Copse
Picketts Hill Farm
Horseshoe Farm
Saunders Green
Prospect Hill Farm
Bayfields Farm
Hartfield House
Headley Meadows
Brambletye
High Breck
Opax Farm
Hearn House Farm
Hearn Copse
Hearn House
Little Hearn Copse
The Hanger
The Oaks
Curtis's Hill
Foxwood Lodge
Benifold
Windridge
Pentlow
Beech Hill Common
Beech Hill Ho.
The Holme C of E Prim. Sch.
Playing Field
Bowling Green
Tennis Cts.
Library
Hall
Rec. Grd.
Sheep Grove
The Frith
Coopers Bri.
Furze Daniel's Copse
LIPHOOK ROAD
HEADLEY ROAD
MILL LANE
CRABTREE LA.
FULLERS VALE
BEECH HILL ROAD
STANDFORD LANE
LINDFORD ROAD
BROXHEAD FARM RD.
B3004
B3002
BRAMSHOTT ROAD
TUNBRIDGE
GENTLES LANE
HURLAND LANE
WHITEHILL ROAD
HOLLYWATER ROAD
WALLDOWN RD
TULLS LANE
LONG CROSS HILL
FRENSHAM LANE
SPATS LANE
BARLEY MOW HILL
HEADLEY HILL ROAD
WOOLMER
A B C D E F G
1 2 3 4 5 6 7 8 9
81 82 83
38 37 36 35 34

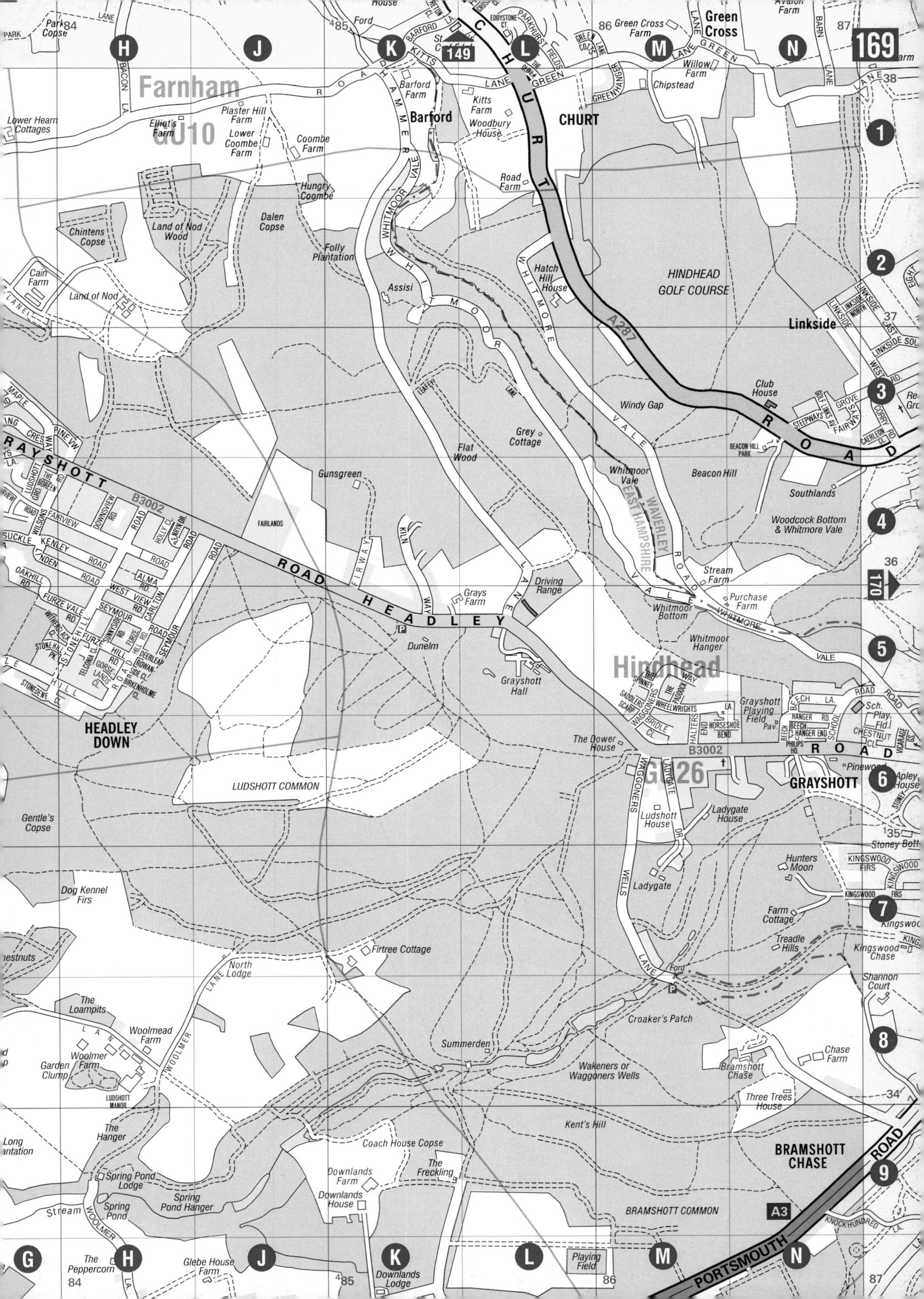

Farnham
GU10
Barford
CHURT
Green Cross
Chipstead
HINDHEAD GOLF COURSE
Linkside
Windy Gap
Beacon Hill
Southlands
Woodcock Bottom & Whitmore Vale
Stream Farm
Purchase Farm
Whitmoor Bottom
Whitmoor Hanger
Hindhead
Grayshott Playing Field
GRAYSHOTT
GU26
The Dower House
Ludshott House
Ladygate House
Ladygate
Hunters Moon
Farm Cottage
Treadle Hills
Kingswood Chase
Shannon Court
Croaker's Patch
Chase Farm
Bramshott Chase
Three Trees House
BRAMSHOTT CHASE
Wakeners or Waggoners Wells
Kent's Hill
Summerden
BRAMSHOTT COMMON
Coach House Copse
The Freckling
Downlands Farm
Downlands House
Downlands Lodge
Playing Field
A3
PORTSMOUTH ROAD
HEADLEY ROAD
B3002
GRAYSHOTT ROAD
HEADLEY DOWN
LUDSHOTT COMMON
Gentle's Copse
Dog Kennel Firs
Firtree Cottage
North Lodge
The Loampits
Woolmead Farm
Woolmer Farm
Garden Clump
LUDSHOTT MANOR
The Hanger
Spring Pond Lodge
Spring Pond
Spring Pond Hanger
Stream
The Peppercorn
Glebe House Farm
Dunelm
Grayshott Hall
Grays Farm
Driving Range
Gunsgreen
Flat Wood
Grey Cottage
FAIRLANDS
Assisi
Folly Plantation
Hatch Hill House
A287
Club House
Dalen Copse
Land of Nod Wood
Chintens Copse
Cain Farm
Land of Nod
Hungry Coombe
Coombe Farm
Lower Coombe Farm
Plaster Hill Farm
Elliot's Farm
Lower Hearn Cottages
Park Copse
Road Farm
Kitts Farm
Woodbury House
Barford Farm
Green Cross Farm
Willow Farm
Whitmoor Vale
Ford
149
170

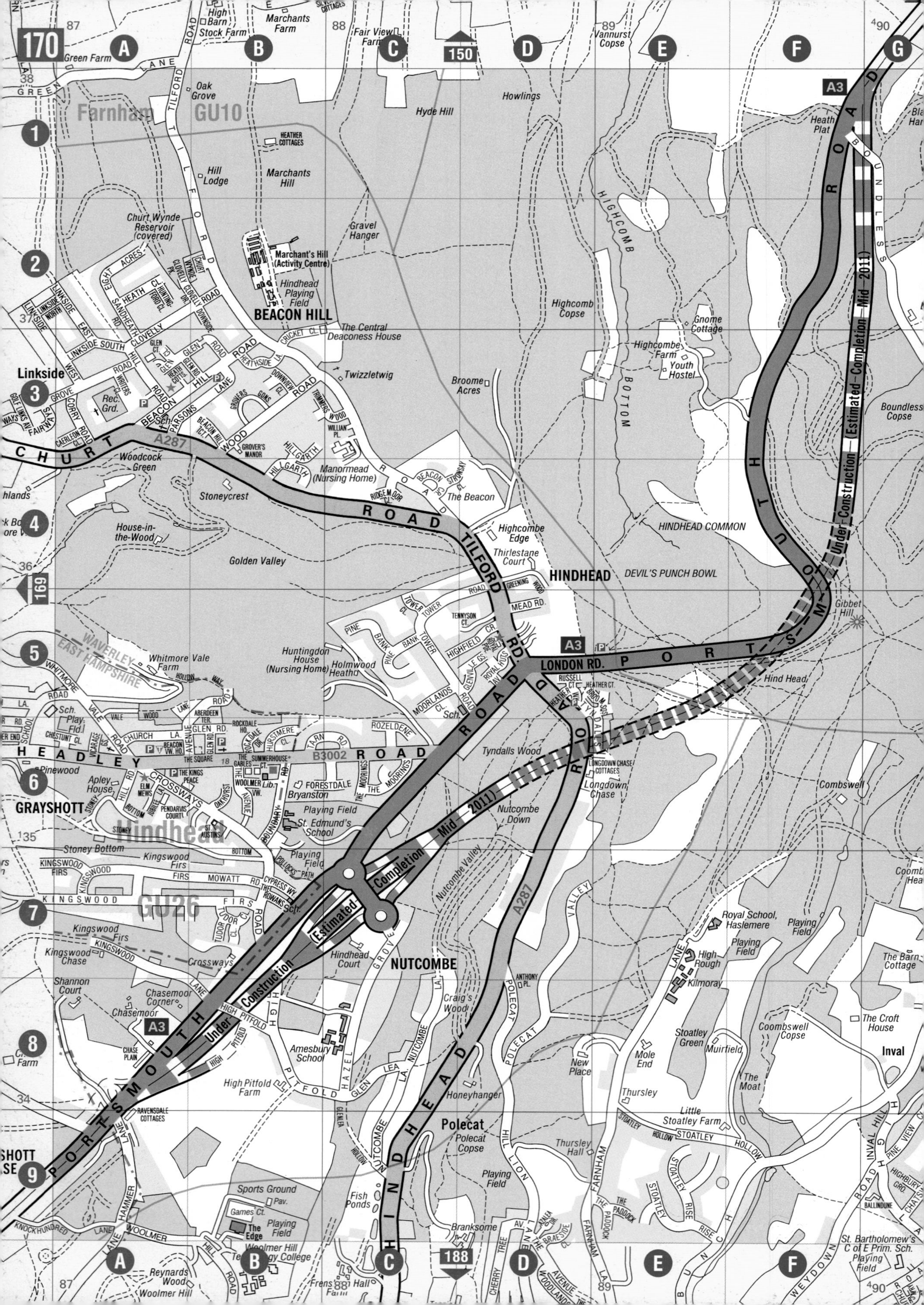

BEACON HILL
HINDHEAD
GRAYSHOTT
NUTCOMBE
Polecat
Linkside
HINDHEAD COMMON
DEVIL'S PUNCH BOWL
Farnham GU10
GU26
Hindhead
CHURT ROAD
TILFORD ROAD
HEADLEY ROAD
PORTSMOUTH ROAD
HINDHEAD ROAD
LONDON RD.
A3
A287
B3002
Under Construction (Estimated Completion Mid 2011)
150
169
188

171
151
172
189
91
92
93
H
J
K
L
M
N
G
1
2
3
4
5
6
7
8
9
38
37
36
35
34
Blackhanger Farm
Bedford and Hole Farm
Bowlhead Green Farm
Stables
Birch Copse
Hanger Copse
Brook
Recreation Ground Pav.
Banacle Firs
Ox Heart Copse
Brook Farm
Uplands Park
Smither's Hanger
Emley Copse
Emley Farm
Rutton Hill
Beech Hanger
CHURCH LANE
BROOK LANE
ROAD
Tylands Copse
Woodlands Cottages
Blackhanger Farm
Halnacker Copse
Hall's Cottage
The Soaks
Harry's Holt
Park Copse
Hopkiln Reeds
Park House
Hallnacker Cottage
RUTTON HILL
PARK ROAD
Sawpit Rew
Wareham House
Wareham Rew
A286
Sweet Marshes
Denyards Copse
Begley Copse
Godalming
The Roughs
Upper Birtley
Long Copse
High Button
Boundless Farm
Witley Farm
Deer Park
Old Birtley
Froglands
HASLEMERE ROAD
GU8
The Roundles
Creedhole Farm
Reeds Copse
Littlebrook Farm
Rices Farm
Holman's Grove
Marstrand Farm
Garson Copse
Hurthill Copse
Lower Birtley Farm
Pond Copse
Hundred Acre Copse
Shoelands
Hurt Hill
Hunters Croft
Halcyon House
Leith Copse
South Park Farm
Lower Park Farm
Invall
Stroud Wood
Prestwick
Little Prestwick Farm
Damson Cottage
Stroud
Tuder's Copse
Fowlshatch Copse
High Prestwick Cottages
High Prestwick Farm
PRESTWICK LANE
RED COTTS.
Grayswood Farm
The White House
Keffolds
Hall
Grayswood Copse
CHURCH CL.
Grayswood C of E Inf. School
Keffolds Farm
Primrose Hill Nursery
Haslemere
Ormiston Lodge
GRAYSWOOD MEWS
Grayswood House
LOWER RD
PADDOCK WY.
GRAYSWOOD COMMON
ASH TREE CL.
PARK CL.
Sewage Works
FRILLINGHURST WOOD
Frillinghurst Old Manor
Wispers Sch. for Girls
Rokers
KLONDYKE VILLAS
GU27
MOUNT HILL
CLAMMER HILL
GRAYSWOOD
UPPER MT.
Beech Farm
Grayswood Hill
Weydown Common
The Vicarage
Clammer Hill
WEYCOMBE ROAD
WHITFIELD CL.
SANDY LANE
Grayswood Common
PEPERHAM RD.
A287
GRAYSWOOD ROAD
HIGHERCOMBE RD.
Grayshurst
GRAYSWOOD PLACE
PARSONS GRN
PUCK'S HOLT
PLAYING FIELD CL.
BARTHOLOMEW CL.
GRAYS CL.
GATES LANE
CLAMMER HILL
HOLDFAST LANE
The Bungalows
Newhouse Great Copse
GERARDES LODGE
UPLANDS CL.
The Manor House
Imbhams Farm
THE SPINNEY
PEPERHAM HO.
HASLEMERE COMMUNITY HOSP.
St. Ives School
Great Carvers
THREE GATES LANE
CHURCH LA.
CUTHBERT ROW
AITKEN

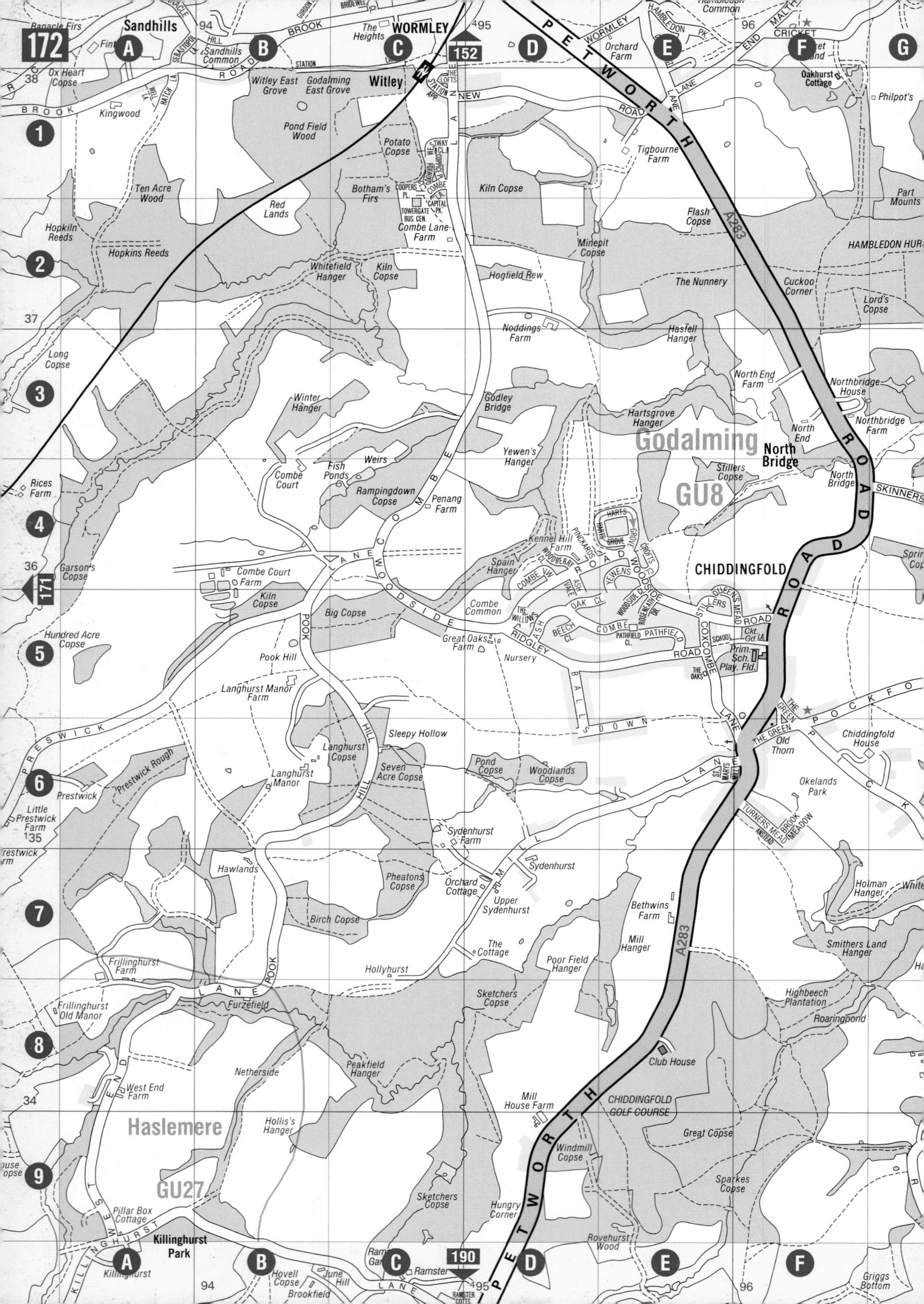

Sandhills
Wormley
Witley
Godalming
North Bridge
GU8
CHIDDINGFOLD
Haslemere
GU27
Killinghurst Park
Combe Court Farm
Sandhills Common
Witley East Grove
Godalming East Grove
Pond Field Wood
Kingwood
Ten Acre Wood
Red Lands
Hopkins Reeds
Whitefield Hanger
Kiln Copse
Tigbourne Farm
Flash Copse
Minepit Copse
Hogfield Rew
The Nunnery
Cuckoo Corner
Lord's Copse
Noddings Farm
Hasfell Hanger
North End Farm
Northbridge House
Northbridge Farm
Godley Bridge
Winter Hanger
Hartsgrove Hanger
Yewen's Hanger
Combe Court
Fish Ponds
Weirs
Rampingdown Copse
Penang Farm
Stillers Copse
Kennel Hill Farm
Spain Hanger
Big Copse
Combe Common
Great Oaks Farm
Nursery
Pook Hill
Langhurst Manor Farm
Sleepy Hollow
Langhurst Copse
Seven Acre Copse
Langhurst Manor
Pond Copse
Woodlands Copse
Sydenhurst Farm
Sydenhurst
Orchard Cottage
Upper Sydenhurst
Pheatons Copse
Birch Copse
Hawlands
Prestwick Rough
Prestwick
Little Prestwick Farm
Rices Farm
Garson's Copse
Hundred Acre Copse
Long Copse
Frillinghurst Farm
Frillinghurst Old Manor
Furzefield
Netherside
West End Farm
Hollis's Hanger
Pillar Box Cottage
Killinghurst
Hollyhurst
The Cottage
Bethwins Farm
Mill Hanger
Poor Field Hanger
Sketchers Copse
Peakfield Hanger
Club House
Mill House Farm
CHIDDINGFOLD GOLF COURSE
Windmill Copse
Great Copse
Sparkes Copse
Hungry Corner
Rovehurst Wood
Ramster
Hovell Copse
June Hill
Brookfield
Griggs Bottom
Highbeech Plantation
Roaringpond
Smithers Land Hanger
Holman Hanger
Okelands Park
Old Thorn
Chiddingfold House
Oakhurst Cottage
Philpot's
Part Mounts
HAMBLEDON HUR
Orchard Farm
Botham's Firs
Potato Copse
Combe Lane Farm
TOWERGATE BUS. CEN.
The Heights
Kiln Copse
A283
PETWORTH ROAD
WOODSIDE ROAD
RIDGLEY ROAD
COMBE LANE
POOK HILL
MILL LANE
PRESWICK LANE
BALLS DOWN
COXCOMBE LANE
PATHFIELD
STATION ROAD
BROOK ROAD
NEW ROAD
WEST END
KILLINGHURST LANE
Prim. Sch.
Play. Fld.
152
171
190

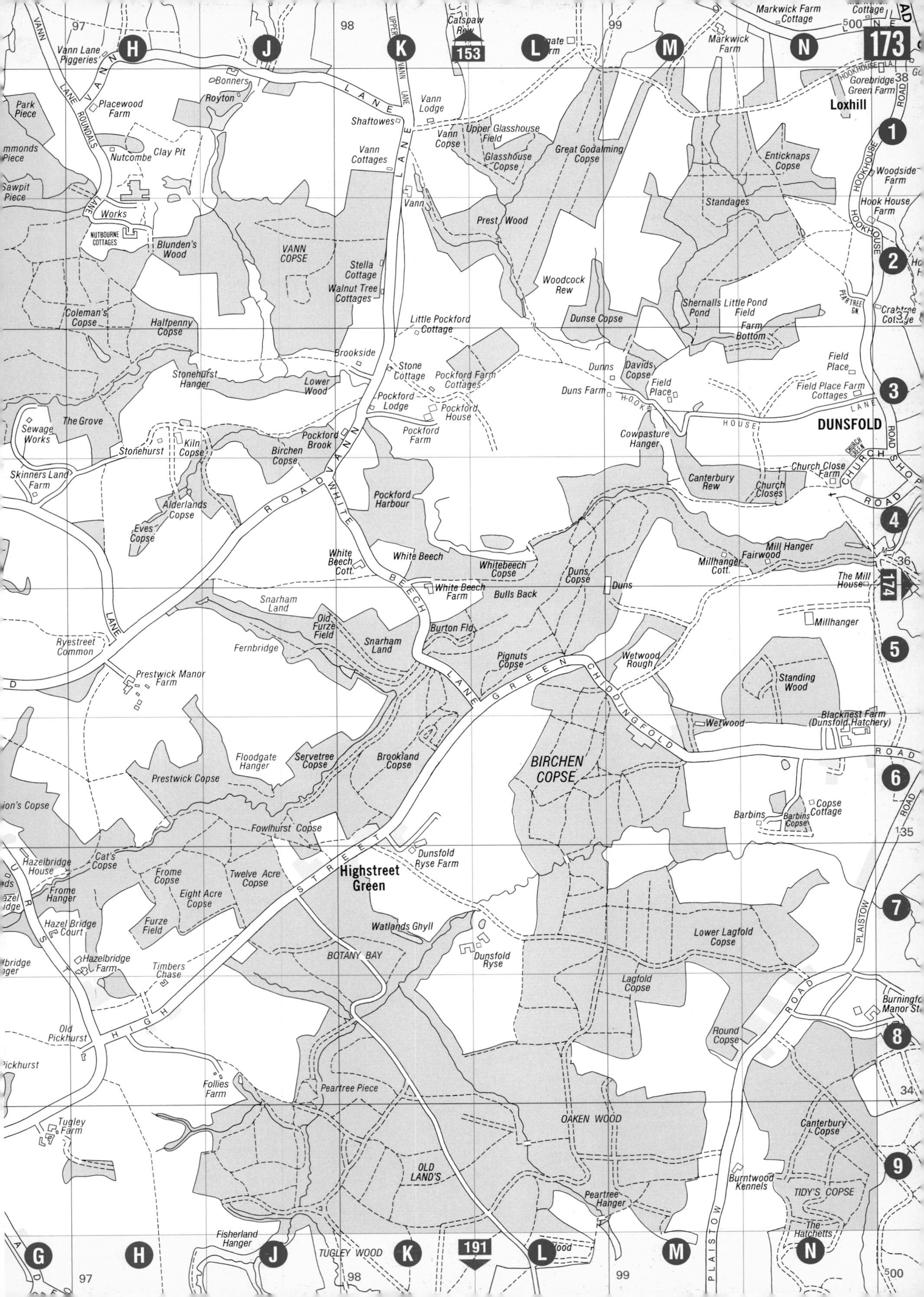

173
153
191
174
Loxhill
DUNSFOLD
Highstreet Green
Vann Lane Piggeries
Bonners
Royton
Placewood Farm
Park Piece
Nutcombe
Clay Pit
Works
NUTBOURNE COTTAGES
Blunden's Wood
VANN COPSE
Coleman's Copse
Halfpenny Copse
Stonehurst Hanger
Lower Wood
The Grove
Sewage Works
Stonehurst
Kiln Copse
Birchen Copse
Pockford Brook
Skinners Land Farm
Alderlands Copse
Eves Copse
Catspaw Rew
Vann Lodge
Shaftowes
Vann Copse
Upper Glasshouse Field
Glasshouse Copse
Vann Cottages
Vann
Great Godalming Copse
Prest Wood
Stella Cottage
Walnut Tree Cottages
Woodcock Rew
Little Pockford Cottage
Brookside
Stone Cottage
Pockford Farm Cottages
Pockford Lodge
Pockford House
Pockford Farm
Pockford Harbour
White Beech Cott.
White Beech
Whitebeech Copse
White Beech Farm
Bulls Back
Duns Copse
Duns
Snarham Land
Old Furze Field
Fernbridge
Ryestreet Common
Prestwick Manor Farm
Burton Fld
Pignuts Copse
Markwick Farm Cottage
Markwick Farm
Gorebridge Green Farm
Enticknaps Copse
Woodside Farm
Hook House Farm
Standages
Shernalls Pond
Little Pond Field
Farm Bottom
Dunse Copse
Crabtree Cottage
Dunns
Davids Copse
Field Place
Duns Farm
Field Place Farm Cottages
Cowpasture Hanger
Canterbury Rew
Church Closes
Church Close Farm
CHURCH GREEN
Millhanger Cott.
Fairwood
Mill Hanger
The Mill House
Millhanger
Wetwood Rough
Standing Wood
Wetwood
Blacknest Farm (Dunsfold Hatchery)
BIRCHEN COPSE
Barbins
Barbins Copse
Copse Cottage
Floodgate Hanger
Servetree Copse
Brookland Copse
Prestwick Copse
Fowlhurst Copse
Dunsfold Ryse Farm
Hazelbridge House
Cat's Copse
Frome Copse
Frome Hanger
Twelve Acre Copse
Eight Acre Copse
Furze Field
Hazel Bridge Court
Hazelbridge Farm
Timbers Chase
Watlands Ghyll
BOTANY BAY
Dunsfold Ryse
Lower Lagfold Copse
Lagfold Copse
Round Copse
Burningfold Manor
Old Pickhurst
Pickhurst
Follies Farm
Peartree Piece
OAKEN WOOD
Tugley Farm
OLD LAND'S
Peartree Hanger
Burntwood Kennels
Canterbury Copse
TIDY'S COPSE
The Hatchetts
Fisherland Hanger
TUGLEY WOOD
VANN LANE
UPPER VANN LANE
ROUNDALS LANE
VANN ROAD
WHITE BEECH LANE
CHIDDINGFOLD ROAD
HIGH STREET
HOOKHOUSE ROAD
HOOK HOUSE LANE
CHURCH ROAD
SHOP ROAD
PLAISTOW ROAD
PEARTREE GN.
G H J K L M N
1 2 3 4 5 6 7 8 9
97 98 99 500
34 35 36 37 38

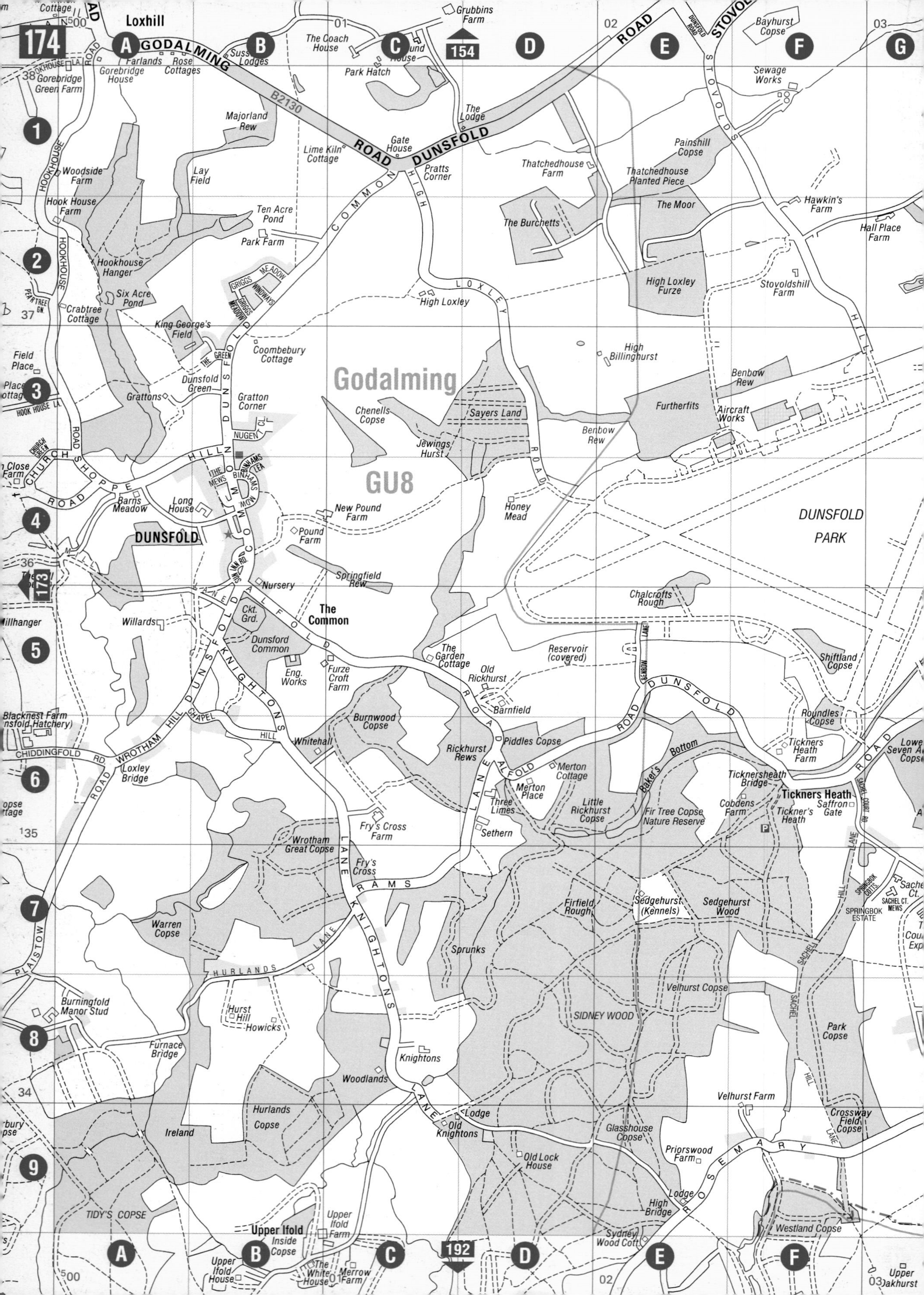
Loxhill
GODALMING ROAD DUNSFOLD ROAD
B2130
Grubbins Farm
154
173
192
Godalming
GU8
DUNSFOLD
DUNSFOLD PARK
The Common
Tickners Heath
Upper Ifold
SIDNEY WOOD
Farlands
Rose Cottages
Sussex Lodges
The Coach House
Park Hatch
Gorebridge House
Gorebridge Green Farm
Majorland Rew
Lime Kiln Cottage
Gate House
The Lodge
Pratts Corner
Lay Field
Woodside Farm
Hook House Farm
Ten Acre Pond
Park Farm
Hookhouse Hanger
Six Acre Pond
Crabtree Cottage
King George's Field
Coombebury Cottage
Dunsfold Green
Grattons
Gratton Corner
Field Place
Thatchedhouse Farm
Thatchedhouse Planted Piece
Painshill Copse
The Moor
The Burchetts
High Loxley
High Loxley Furze
Hawkin's Farm
Hall Place Farm
Stovoldshill Farm
Sewage Works
Bayhurst Copse
High Billinghurst
Benbow Rew
Furtherfits
Aircraft Works
Chenells Copse
Sayers Land
Jewings Hurst
Honey Mead
New Pound Farm
Pound Farm
Springfield Rew
Nursery
Barns Meadow
Long House
Willards
Ckt. Grd.
Dunsford Common
Eng. Works
Furze Croft Farm
The Garden Cottage
Old Rickhurst
Reservoir (covered)
Barnfield
Chalcrofts Rough
Shiftland Copse
Roundles Copse
Tickners Heath Farm
Blacknest Farm (Dunsfold Hatchery)
Loxley Bridge
Whitehall
Burnwood Copse
Rickhurst Rews
Piddles Copse
Merton Cottage
Merton Place
Three Limes
Sethern
Little Rickhurst Copse
Fir Tree Copse Nature Reserve
Ticknersheath Bridge
Cobdens Farm
Tickner's Heath
Saffron Gate
Baker's Bottom
Fry's Cross Farm
Fry's Cross
Wrotham Great Copse
Warren Copse
Firfield Rough
Sedgehurst (Kennels)
Sedgehurst Wood
Sprunks
Velhurst Copse
Park Copse
Springbok Estate
Hurst Hill
Howicks
Burningfold Manor Stud
Furnace Bridge
Knightons
Woodlands
Hurlands Copse
Ireland
Lodge
Old Knightons
Old Lock House
Glasshouse Copse
Velhurst Farm
Priorswood Farm
Crossway Field Copse
High Bridge
Lodge
Westland Copse
Sydney Wood Cott
Upper Ifold Farm
Inside Copse
Upper Ifold House
The White House
Merrow Farm
Tidy's Copse
Upper Oakhurst
HOOKHOUSE ROAD
CHURCH ROAD
SHOPPE HILL
DUNSFOLD COMMON
LOXLEY ROAD
HIGH
STOVOLDS HILL
DUNSFOLD ROAD
ALFOLD ROAD
KNIGHTONS LANE
WROTHAM HILL
CHIDDINGFOLD RD.
PLAISTOW ROAD
RAMS LANE
HURLANDS LANE
CHAPEL HILL
SACHEL HILL LANE
ROSEMARY LANE
BENBOW LANE
GRIGGS MEADOW
WINDWAYS
THE GREEN
NUGENT CL.
BINHAMS LEA
THE MEWS
SUN INN RD.
SACHEL COURT RD
SPRINGBOK COTTS
SACHEL CT. MEWS
A B C D E F G
1 2 3 4 5 6 7 8 9
500 01 02 03
38 37 36 135 34

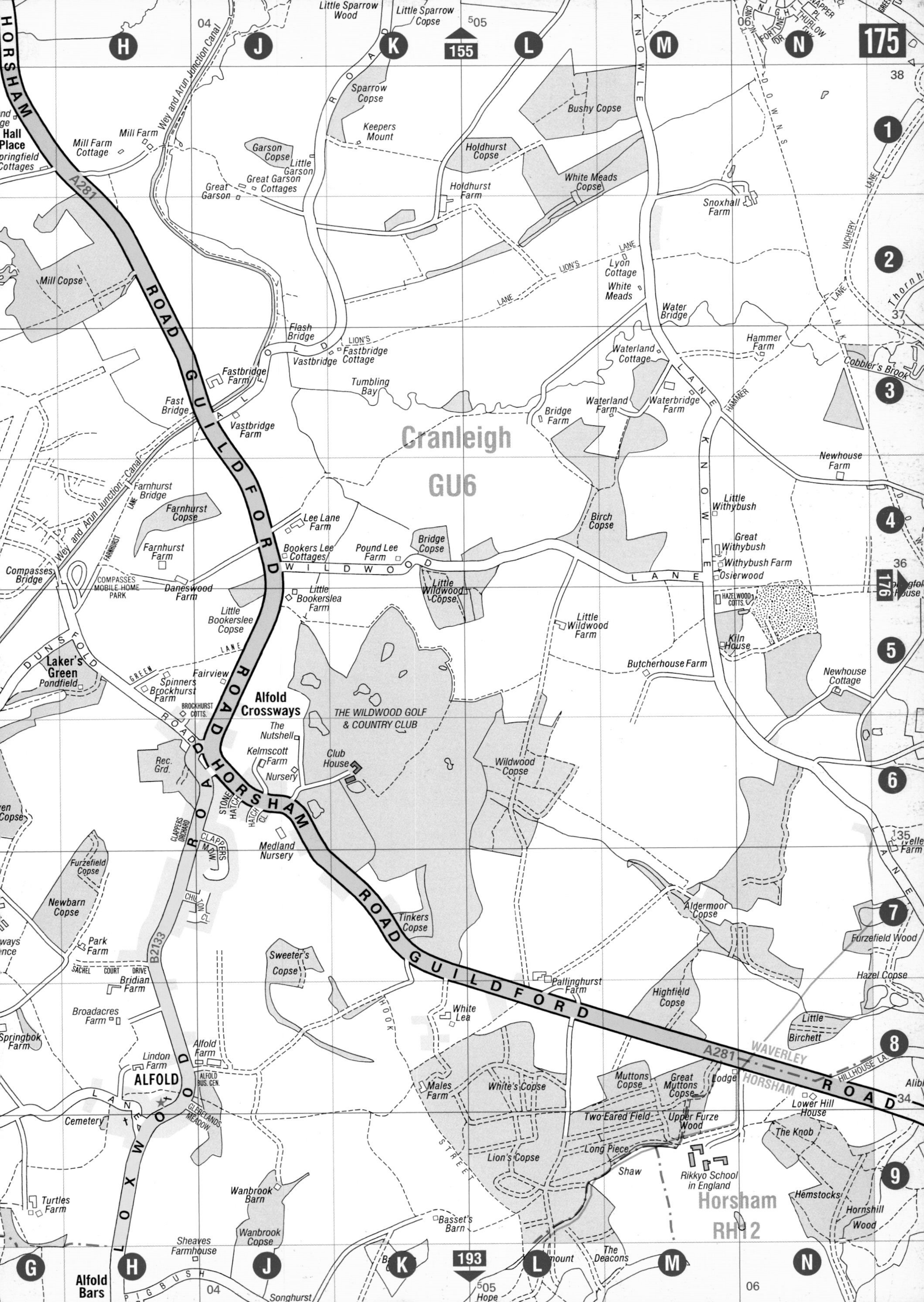

Cranleigh
GU6
Horsham
RH12
HORSHAM ROAD
GUILDFORD ROAD
A281
B2133
Alfold Crossways
ALFOLD
Alfold Bars
Laker's Green
THE WILDWOOD GOLF & COUNTRY CLUB
Club House
Wey and Arun Junction Canal
Little Sparrow Wood
Little Sparrow Copse
Sparrow Copse
Keepers Mount
Bushy Copse
Holdhurst Copse
Holdhurst Farm
White Meads Copse
Snoxhall Farm
Garson Copse
Little Garson
Great Garson
Great Garson Cottages
Mill Farm
Mill Farm Cottage
Hall Place
Mill Copse
Lyon Cottage
White Meads
LION'S LANE
Water Bridge
Flash Bridge
Vastbridge
Fastbridge Cottage
Tumbling Bay
Waterland Cottage
Hammer Farm
Cobbler's Brook
Fastbridge Farm
Fast Bridge
Vastbridge Farm
Bridge Farm
Waterland Farm
Waterbridge Farm
Newhouse Farm
Farnhurst Bridge
Farnhurst Copse
Farnhurst Farm
Lee Lane Farm
Birch Copse
Little Withybush
Great Withybush
Withybush Farm
Osierwood
Bookers Lee Cottages
Pound Lee Farm
Bridge Copse
WILDWOOD LANE
Little Wildwood Copse
Compasses Bridge
COMPASSES MOBILE HOME PARK
Daneswood Farm
Little Bookerslee Farm
Little Bookerslee Copse
Little Wildwood Farm
HAZELWOOD COTTS.
Kiln House
DUNSFOLD ROAD
GREEN LANE
Pondfield
Spinners Brockhurst Farm
Fairview
BROCKHURST COTTS.
Butcherhouse Farm
Newhouse Cottage
The Nutshell
Kelmscott Farm
Nursery
Rec. Grd.
Wildwood Copse
STONE HATCH
HATCH CL.
CLAPPERS ORCHARD
CLAPPERS MDW.
Medland Nursery
Furzefield Copse
Newbarn Copse
CHILTON CL.
Tinkers Copse
Aldermoor Copse
Furzefield Wood
Park Farm
SACHEL COURT DRIVE
Bridian Farm
Sweeter's Copse
Pallinghurst Farm
Highfield Copse
Hazel Copse
Broadacres Farm
White Lea
HOOK STREET
Little Birchett
Springbok Farm
Alfold Farm
Lindon Farm
ALFOLD BUS. CEN.
WAVERLEY
HORSHAM
HILLHOUSE LA.
Males Farm
White's Copse
Muttons Copse
Great Muttons Copse
Lodge
Lower Hill House
Cemetery
GLEBELANDS MEADOW
LOXWOOD ROAD
Two Eared Field
Upper Furze Wood
The Knob
Long Piece
Lion's Copse
Shaw
Rikkyo School in England
Hemstocks
Hornshill Wood
Turtles Farm
Wanbrook Barn
Wanbrook Copse
Basset's Barn
Sheaves Farmhouse
The Deacons
PIGBUSH LANE
Songhurst
Hope
KNOWLE LANE
DOWNS LINK
VACHERY LANE
HAMMER LANE

155
176
193

Cranleigh
GU6
HORSHAM ROAD
B2128
Whitehall
Whitehall Copse
Norley Farm
Owlbarn Copse
Longhurst Hill
Furzefield Copse
Rowgardens Copse
Selham Lodge
Burmah Bungalow
The Chalet
Windgate Cottage
Cobbler's Brook
The Wind Break
Tothill Wood
Thornhurst Brook
Vachery Pond
Vachery House
Home Wood
Eastgate Wood
Kiln Copse
Nightingales
Baynards
Brooklands Farm
Baynards Park
Song Hurst
Horsham Lodge
Baynard's Park
New Cottages
Home Farm
Vachery Farm
Moat
Newhouse Farm
Collins Copse
Collins Farm
White Cottage
BAYNARD'S PARK
Tillhouse Farm
Pollingfold House
Lodge Copse
Massers Wood
New Barn
Grub Copse
Newhouse Cottage
Works
Ruet
Nob Copse
North Wood
Maybanks Manor
Tolt Garth
Shrubs Copse
Baynards
Baynards Lodge
Ivelle Farm
Fair View
Broomhall Cottage
Tithe Cottage
Woodthorpe
Firtree Copse
Cox Green
HERMONGER
Withy Copse
Starveall Copse
Furzefield Wood
South Wood
Little Hawks Hill
Hazel Copse
Great Inholms
Inholms
Broomhall Copse
Hobbs Copse
Clay Pit
HAWKRIDGE
WAVERLEY
HORSHAM
Street C
HILLHOUSE LANE
Brick Works
HIGHCROFT DR.
Aliblastairs
Woodsomes Farm
GUILDFORD ROAD
A281
Four Winds
Lynwick
Greathouse Hanger
Greathouse Farm
SUMMERFOLD
CHURCH ST.
Dukes Farm
RUDGWICK
Lynwick Hanger
Canfields Farm
Hornshill Wood
Well Grove
Tip Pond
Gravatt's Farm
Gravatt's Hanger
Hornshill Farm
Old Cottage
Field Cottage
Swaynes
STATION RD.
THE SIDINGS
WOODFIELD
KILNFIELD RD
PONDFIELD RD.
DUBILEE
FRESHWOODS
KINGS
MARTLETTS CNR.
BROOKHURST
FURZE ROAD
THE RIDGE
COX GREEN ROAD
BAYNARDS ROAD
LINACRE DRIVE
STATION ROAD
LAWNS ROAD
COTTS
DOWNS LINK
KNOWLE LANE
COOKS HILL
LYNWICK
LYNWICK STREET
CHURCH STREET
VACHERY LANE
156
175
194
A B C D E F G
1 2 3 4 5 6 7 8 9
07 08 09
38 37 36 35 34

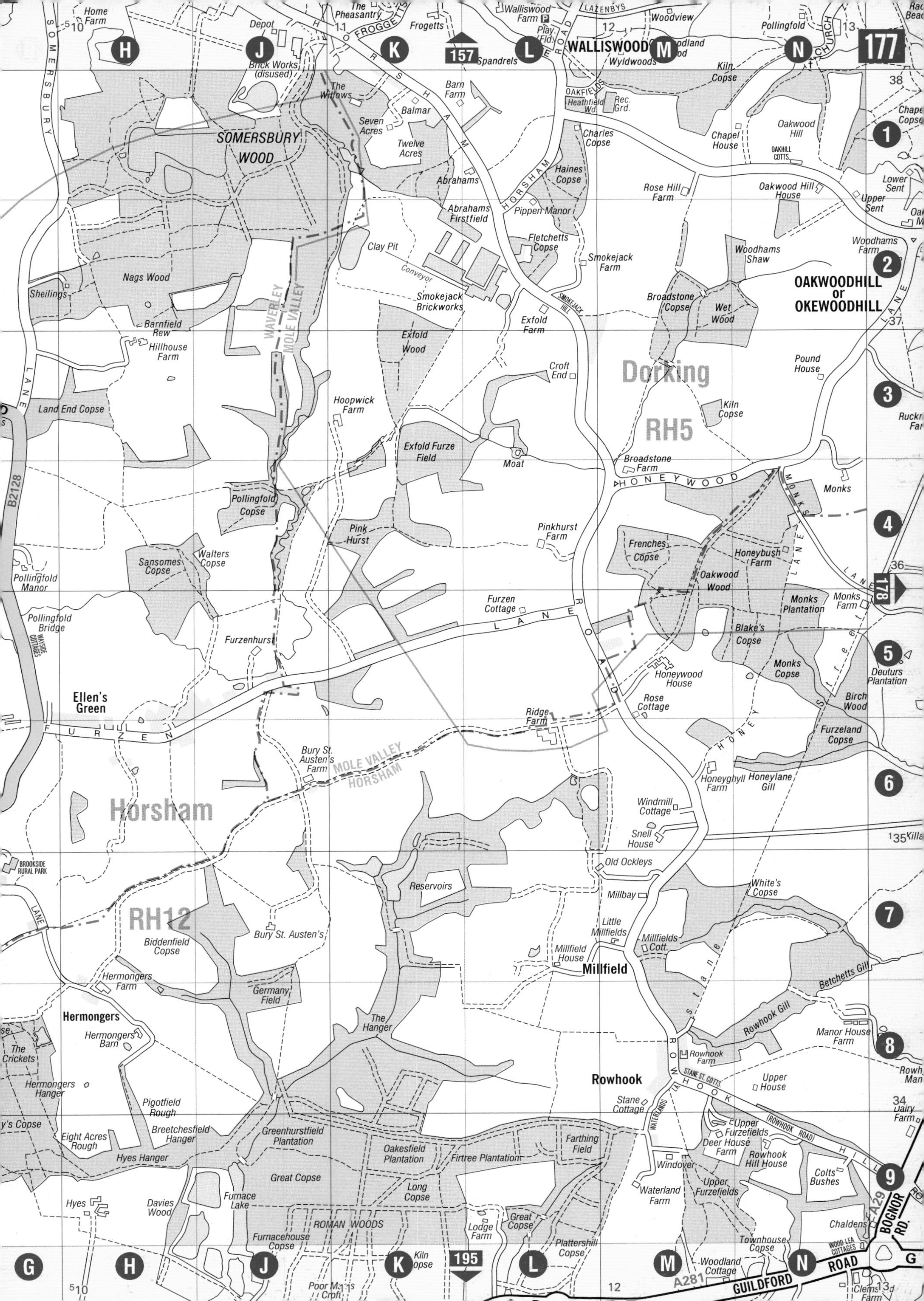
Home Farm
Depot
The Pheasantry
Frogetts
Walliswood Farm
Play. Fld.
Woodview
Pollingfold
157
Brick Works (disused)
Spandrels
WALLISWOOD
Woodland Wood
Wyldwoods
Kiln Copse
The Willows
Barn Farm
OAKFIELDS
Heathfield Wd.
Rec. Grd.
Chapel Copse
Balmar
Seven Acres
Twelve Acres
Charles Copse
Chapel House
Oakwood Hill
OAKHILL COTTS.
SOMERSBURY WOOD
Haines Copse
Rose Hill Farm
Oakwood Hill House
Lower Sent
Upper Sent
Abrahams
Abrahams Firstfield
Pippen Manor
Woodhams Farm
Fletchetts Copse
Clay Pit
Conveyor
Smokejack Farm
Woodhams Shaw
Nags Wood
Sheilings
Smokejack Brickworks
SMOKEJACK HILL
Broadstone Copse
Wet Wood
OAKWOODHILL or OKEWOODHILL
Barnfield Rew
WAVERLEY
MOLE VALLEY
Exfold Farm
Hillhouse Farm
Exfold Wood
Croft End
Dorking
Pound House
Land End Copse
Hoopwick Farm
Kiln Copse
RH5
Exfold Furze Field
Moat
Broadstone Farm
HONEYWOOD
Monks
B2128
Pollingfold Copse
Pink Hurst
Pinkhurst Farm
Frenches Copse
Honeybush Farm
Sansomes Copse
Walters Copse
Oakwood Wood
Pollingfold Manor
Furzen Cottage
Monks Plantation
Monks Farm
178
Pollingfold Bridge
WAYSIDE COTTAGES
Furzenhurst
LANE
ROAD
Blake's Copse
Monks Copse
Deuturs Plantation
Honeywood House
Ellen's Green
Rose Cottage
Birch Wood
FURZEN
Ridge Farm
Furzeland Copse
Bury St. Austen's Farm
MOLE VALLEY
HORSHAM
HONEY
Honeyghyll Farm
Honeylane Gill
Horsham
Windmill Cottage
Snell House
BROOKSIDE RURAL PARK
Old Ockleys
Reservoirs
White's Copse
Millbay
RH12
Little Millfields
Millfields Cott.
Bury St. Austen's
Biddenfield Copse
Millfield House
Millfield
Betchetts Gill
Hermongers Farm
Germany Field
Stane
Hermongers
Rowhook Gill
The Hanger
Manor House Farm
Hermongers Barn
The Crickets
Rowhook Farm
STANE ST. COTTS
Rowhook
Upper House
Hermongers Hanger
Pigotfield Rough
Stane Cottage
WATERLANDS LA.
Dairy Farm
Breetchesfield Hanger
Greenhurstfield Plantation
(ROWHOOK ROAD)
Upper Furzefields
Eight Acres Rough
Farthing Field
Deer House Farm
Rowhook Hill House
Hyes Hanger
Oakesfield Plantation
Firtree Plantation
Windover
Colts Bushes
Great Copse
Upper Furzefields
Waterland Farm
Hyes
Davies Wood
Furnace Lake
Long Copse
ROMAN WOODS
Lodge Farm
Great Copse
Chaldens
A29
BOGNOR RD.
Furnacehouse Copse
Plattershill Copse
Townhouse Copse
WOOD LEA COTTAGES
Kiln Copse
195
Woodland Cottage
ROAD
A281
GUILDFORD
Poor Mans Croft
Clems Farm
LANE
Upper Sent
Ruckmans Farm
Deuturs Plantation
Rowhook Manor

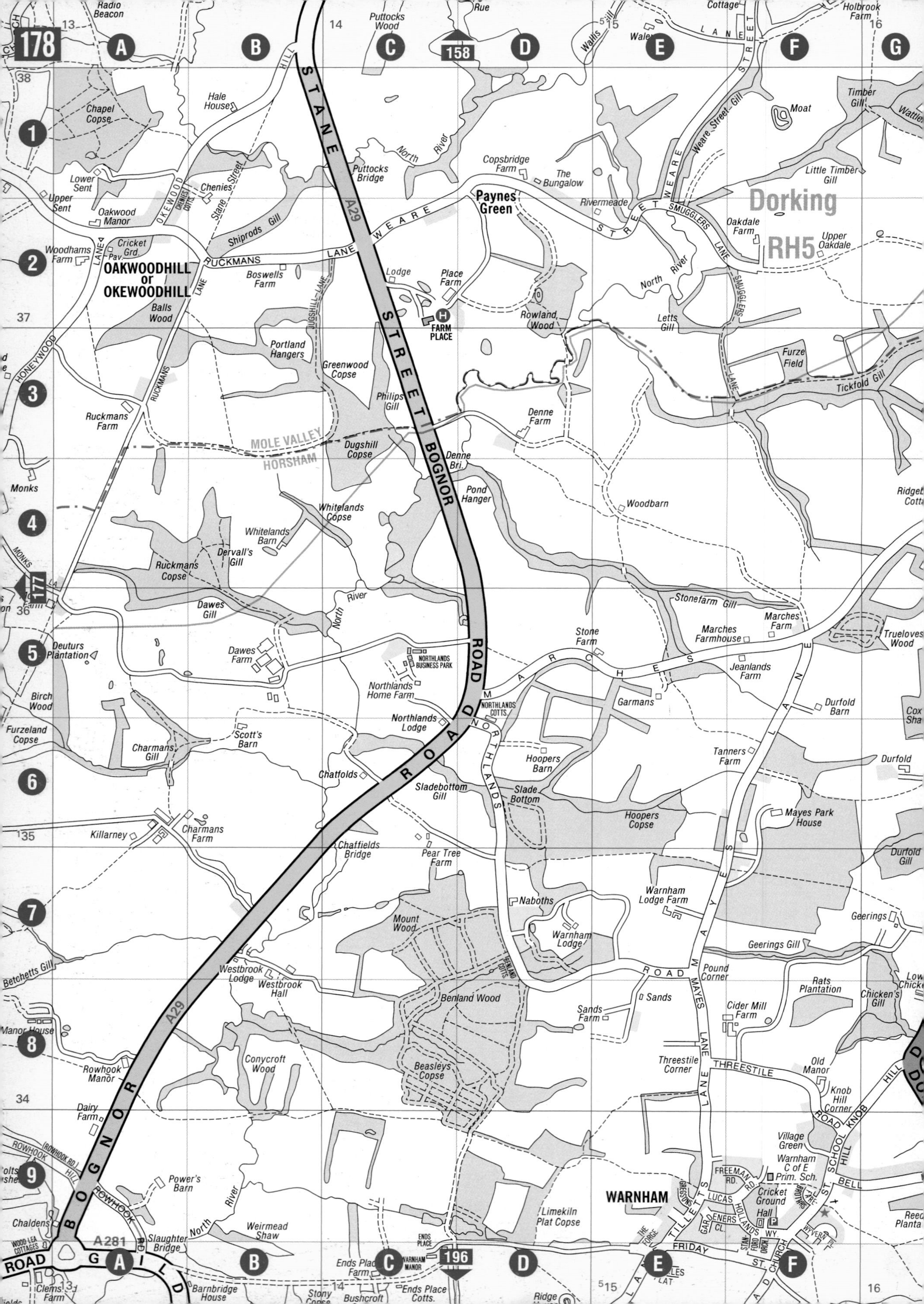
A
B
C
D
E
F
G
158
Radio Beacon
Puttocks Wood
Rue
Wallis Gill
Cottage
Holbrook Farm
Hale House
Chapel Copse
Lower Sent
Upper Sent
Oakwood Manor
Chenies
Stane Street
Shiprods Gill
Puttocks Bridge
North River
Copsbridge Farm
The Bungalow
Weare Street Gill
Moat
Timber Gill
Little Timber Gill
Dorking
RH5
Paynes Green
Rivermeade
Oakdale Farm
Upper Oakdale
Woodhams Farm
Cricket Grd.
OAKWOODHILL or OKEWOODHILL
RUCKMANS LANE
WEARE STREET
SMUGGLERS LANE
Boswells Farm
Lodge
Place Farm
FARM PLACE
Balls Wood
Rowland Wood
North River
Letts Gill
Portland Hangers
Greenwood Copse
Philips Gill
Furze Field
Tickfold Gill
HONEYWOOD
Ruckmans Farm
Denne Farm
MOLE VALLEY
HORSHAM
Dugshill Copse
Denne Bri.
STANE STREET
A29
BOGNOR ROAD
Pond Hanger
Woodbarn
Monks
Whitelands Copse
Whitelands Barn
Ruckmans Copse
Dervall's Gill
177
Dawes Gill
North River
Stonefarm Gill
Marches Farm
Trueloves Wood
Deuturs Plantation
Dawes Farm
NORTHLANDS BUSINESS PARK
Stone Farm
Marches Farmhouse
MARCHES ROAD
Jeanlands Farm
Northlands Home Farm
Garmans
Durfold Barn
Birch Wood
Northlands Lodge
NORTHLANDS COTTS.
Scott's Barn
Furzeland Copse
Charmans Gill
Hoopers Barn
Tanners Farm
Durfold
Chatfolds
Sladebottom Gill
Slade Bottom
Mayes Park House
Hoopers Copse
Killarney
Charmans Farm
Chaffields Bridge
Pear Tree Farm
Durfold Gill
Naboths
Warnham Lodge Farm
Mount Wood
Warnham Lodge
Geerings
Geerings Gill
MAYES LANE
Betchetts Gill
Westbrook Lodge
Westbrook Hall
BENLAND COTTS.
Pound Corner
Rats Plantation
Chicken's Gill
Benland Wood
Sands
Sands Farm
Cider Mill Farm
Manor House
Rowhook Manor
Conycroft Wood
Beasleys Copse
Threestile Corner
THREESTILE ROAD
Old Manor
Knob Hill Corner
34
Dairy Farm
SCHOOL HILL
Village Green
ROWHOOK HILL
Power's Barn
North River
FREEMAN RD.
Warnham C of E Prim. Sch.
Cricket Ground
Hall
LUCAS RD.
HOLLANDS WY.
WARNHAM
Chaldens
Weirmead Shaw
Limekiln Plat Copse
A281
Slaughter Bridge
ENDS PLACE
Ends Place Farm
WARNHAM MANOR
196
FRIDAY ST.
CHURCH ST.
Clems Farm
Barnbridge House
Stony Copse
Bushcroft
Ends Place Cotts.
Ridge

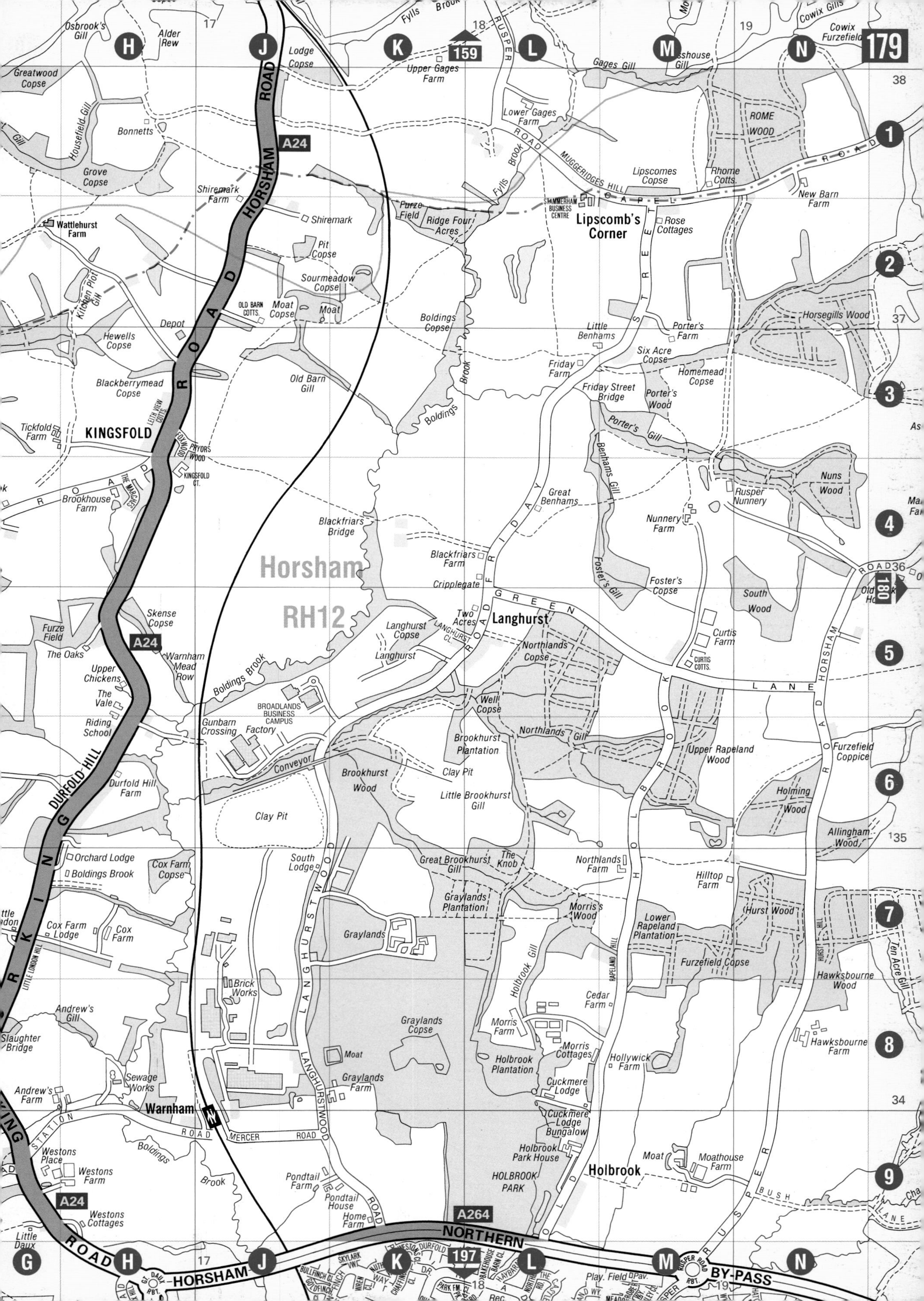

H
J
K
L
M
N
159
180
197
17
18
19
38
37
36
135
34
1
2
3
4
5
6
7
8
9
G
Osbrook's Gill
Alder Rew
Fylls Brook
Lodge Copse
Upper Gages Farm
RUSPER
Gages Gill
Cowix Gills
Cowix Furzefield
Greatwood Copse
HORSHAM ROAD
A24
Lower Gages Farm
ROME WOOD
Bonnetts
Housefield Gill
Grove Copse
MUGGERIDGES HILL
ROAD
Lipscomes Copse
Rhome Cotts.
New Barn Farm
Shiremark Farm
Shiremark
Fylls Brook
Furze Field
Ridge Four Acres
STAMMERHAM BUSINESS CENTRE
Lipscomb's Corner
Rose Cottages
CAPEL
Wattlehurst Farm
Pit Copse
Sourmeadow Copse
Kitchen Plot Gill
OLD BARN COTTS.
Moat Copse
Moat
Depot
Hewells Copse
Boldings Copse
Little Benhams
Porter's Farm
Horsegills Wood
Friday Farm
Six Acre Copse
Homemead Copse
Blackberrymead Copse
Old Barn Gill
Brook
Friday Street Bridge
Porter's Wood
Porter's Gill
Boldings
Tickfold Farm
KINGSFOLD
LEITH VIEW COTTS.
FOXWOOD
PRYORS WOOD
KINGSFOLD CT.
THE MARCHES
Brookhouse Farm
Benhams Gill
Great Benhams
Rusper Nunnery
Nuns Wood
Blackfriars Bridge
Nunnery Farm
FRIDAY STREET
Blackfriars Farm
Cripplegate
Foster's Gill
Foster's Copse
South Wood
Horsham
RH12
Skense Copse
Furze Field
The Oaks
Two Acres
Langhurst Copse
LANGHURST CL.
Langhurst
GREEN
Northlands Copse
Curtis Farm
CURTIS COTTS.
Upper Chickens
Warnham Mead Row
Boldings Brook
Langhurst
The Vale
BROADLANDS BUSINESS CAMPUS
Well Copse
LANE
Riding School
Gunbarn Crossing
Factory
Brookhurst Plantation
Northlands Gill
Upper Rapeland Wood
Furzefield Coppice
DURFOLD HILL
Conveyor
Brookhurst Wood
Clay Pit
Little Brookhurst Gill
Durfold Hill Farm
Holming Wood
HOLBROOK
Clay Pit
Allingham Wood
Orchard Lodge
Boldings Brook
Cox Farm Copse
South Lodge
Great Brookhurst Gill
The Knob
Northlands Farm
Hilltop Farm
Graylands Plantation
Morris's Wood
Hurst Wood
Lower Rapeland Plantation
Cox Farm Lodge
Cox Farm
Graylands
HURST HILL
Furzefield Copse
Ten Acre Gill
LITTLE LONDON HILL
Brick Works
LANGHURSTWOOD
Holbrook Gill
RAPELAND HILL
Hawksbourne Wood
Andrew's Gill
Cedar Farm
Graylands Copse
Morris Farm
Slaughter Bridge
Moat
Morris Cottages
Holbrook Plantation
Hollywick Farm
Hawksbourne Farm
Sewage Works
Graylands Farm
Cuckmere Lodge
Andrew's Farm
Warnham
Cuckmere Lodge Bungalow
STATION
ROAD
MERCER
ROAD
Boldings
Westons Place
Westons Farm
Holbrook Park House
Moat
Moathouse Farm
Holbrook
HOLBROOK PARK
Brook
Pondtail Farm
Pondtail House
BUSH
LANE
A24
Westons Cottages
Home Farm
A264
NORTHERN
Little Daux
ROAD
HORSHAM
BY-PASS
Play. Field
RUSPER ROAD RBT.

RUSPER
Horsham
RH12
FAYGATE
Lambs Green
Langhurst
Faygate
Higham
Rusper House
Furzefield Wood
Venters Farm
Venters
Rusperhouse Gill
Highams Gill
Yew Tree Cott.
Nurses Cottage
Ghyll Manor
Football Grd.
Rectory
Rusper Prim. Sch.
Hall
Quincefold
Longfield
Normans
Rosecroft
Fernbank
Petlers
Chowles Barn
Chowles Farm
Chowles Lodge
Lambs Green Bridge
Cobnor
Nursery
Horsegills Wood
Merrilees
Millfields Farm
Millfields House
Hand Copse
Kiln Copse
Baldhorns Copse
Dialpost Farm
Samcot
Sewage Farm
Ashfolds
Applegarth
Rusper Court Cotts.
Canonbury Cotts.
Yard
Slurry Pits
Rusper Court Farm
Mole Cottage
Court House Bridge
Rusper Court Manor
Saykers
Axmans Farm
Nuns Wood
Manns Farm
Baldhorns Park
Baldhorns Park Farm
Ashfold Cott.
Old Park Farm
Old Park House
The Lodge
Donnybrook
Seers Croft
Fay Cotts.
Fay Cottage Farm
South Wood
Reubens Gill
Sloughbrook Gill
Burnt Stubbs
Carylls Farm
Furze Field
Faygate Wood Farm
Carylls
Kilnwood Farm
Kilnwood Copse
Keeper's Cottage
Slurry Pits
Baldhorns Park Cottage
Coombers Farm
Rusper Copse
Furzefield Coppice
North Grange Farm
Carylls Lea
Allingham Wood
Wimland Corner
Culross
Faygate Place
Culross Grange
Faygate House
Caryll's Lea Farm
Fullers Shaw
Breakey Gill
Northland Copse
Wimland Farm
Orchard Copse
Durrants Copse
Bakehouse Copse
Horsehead Gill
Ten Acre Gill
Hawksbourne Wood
Warren Wood
Budd's Copse
Bush Copse
Timber Yard
Faygate Business Centre
Playing Field
Hall
Ash Copse
Greenbroom Copse
Budd's Farm
Durrants
The Castle
Seagraves Copse
Benson's Cottage
Benson's House
Sewage Works
Garden Cottage
Castle Copse
Benson's Farm
Little Clovers Farm
Hooks Copse
Benson's Farm Cottages
Dabsongill Pond
Holmbush
Owlcastle Farm
Channells Brook
Channells
Bush Copse
Beechwood
Rookfield Pond
Rookfield
Middle Hill
Holmbush Hill
Jenners Firs
Cricket Grd.
Old Forge
Langhurst Hill
Martins Farm
Peter's Farm
Dumbrels Copse
Nine Acre Rew
The Cottage
The Lodge
A264
CRAWLEY
160
179
198

181
161
199
182
Ifieldwood
Pockney's Farm
Kirk Farm
Druids
Wildacres
The Mount Farm
Hilly Barn Farm
Riding Stables
Bonwycks Place
The Court House
River Mole
The Grove
Broomhill House
Works
Granthams Bridge
Lower Barn
Crawley
RH11
Sandalwood
Furlong Farm
Stumbleholm Farm
IFIELD GOLF & COUNTRY CLUB
Club House
Hyde Hill
Newstead Lodge
Ifield Barn Theatre
Rectory Farm
Ifield Brook
Ruspers Keep
IFIELD
Playing Field
Ifield Green
Ifield
Manor Green Coll.
Manor Green Prim. Sch.
St. Margaret's C of E Prim. Sch.
Ifield Comm. Coll.
The Mill Prim. Sch.
Snell Hatch Cemetery
Ewhurst Place
Playing Field
Goffs Park
CRAWLEY
St. Wilfrid's Cath. Sch.
Ifield Watermill
Ifield Pond
GOSSOPS GREEN
Playing Field
Youth Cen.
Waterfield Prim. Sch.
Bewbush Water Garden
Bewbush Brook
Upper Bewbush
Copse
Capon Grove
Pondtail Shaw
Woldhurstlea Wood
The Holy Trinity C of E Sch.
Playing Field
BEWBUSH
Bewbush Leisure Centre
Playing Field
Landfill Site
BROADFIELD
Broadfield Brook
Playing Field
Mosque
Buchan Country Park
Countryside Centre
A264
ROAD HORSHAM
CRAWLEY SOUTH WEST BY-PASS
CRAWLEY AVENUE
A23
A2220
HORSHAM ROAD
BROADFIELD RBT.
BREWHURST RBT.
BEWBUSH RBT.
TOLLGATE RBT.
IFIELD RBT.
HOLMBUSH POTTERIES INDUSTRIAL ESTATE
Holmbush Farm World
Hopper Farm
Hopper's Brook
Spruce Hill Brook
Spruce Hill
Silver Hill
Island Pond
Middle Covert
Douster Pond
Target Hill
Creasey's Forest
Broadfield Kennels
Buchan Country Park
Island Pond
Buchan Hill Forest
Fish Pond
Buchan Hill
Creasy's Brook
Subway
Foxhole Pond
Shepherdsfield
COTTESMORE GOLF COURSE
Cottesmore School
PEASE POTTAGE FOREST
House Pond
Playing Field
Hotel
Club
Buchan House
PEASE POTTAGE GOLF COURSE
HOLMBUSH FOREST
HORSHAM
CRAWLEY
G H J K L M N
1 2 3 4 5 6 7 8 9
23 24 525 26
38 37 36 35 34

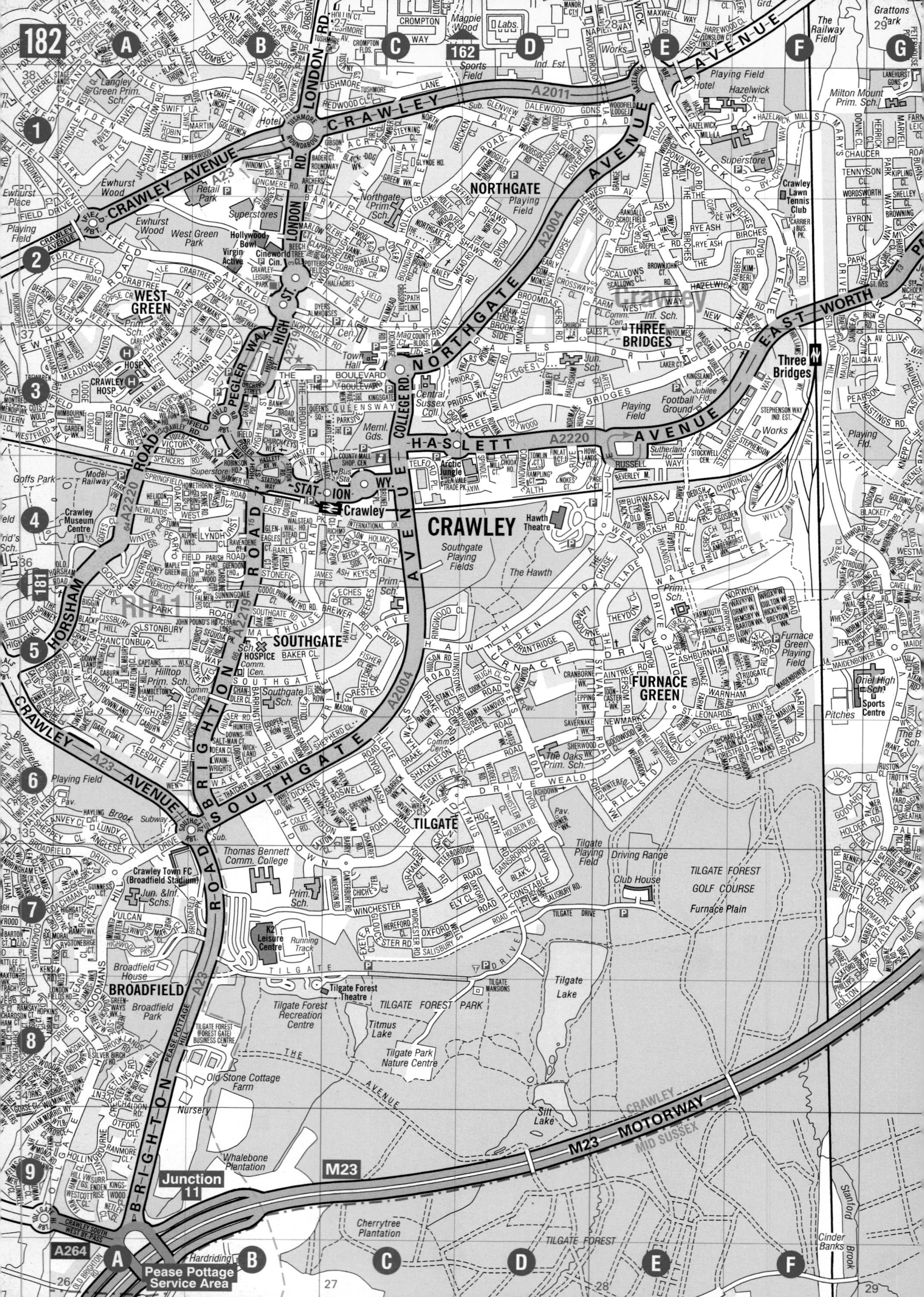
182
A
B
C
D
E
F
G
1
2
3
4
5
6
7
8
9
162
181
CRAWLEY
NORTHGATE
WEST GREEN
THREE BRIDGES
SOUTHGATE
FURNACE GREEN
TILGATE
BROADFIELD
RH11
CRAWLEY AVENUE
A2011
A23
A2004
A2220
A2219
A264
M23
LONDON RD.
HIGH ST.
PEGLER WAY
COLLEGE RD.
NORTHGATE AVENUE
HASLETT AVENUE
STATION WY.
EAST WORTH AVENUE
SOUTHGATE AVENUE
BRIGHTON ROAD
HORSHAM ROAD
CRAWLEY SOUTH WEST BY-PASS
M23 MOTORWAY
Junction 11
Pease Pottage Service Area
Crawley
Three Bridges
Ewhurst Wood
Ewhurst Place
West Green Park
Retail Park
Superstores
Hollywood Bowl
Virgin Active
Cineworld Cin.
Town Hall
Central Sussex Coll.
Meml. Gds.
Arctic Jungle
Hawth Theatre
The Hawth
Southgate Playing Fields
Crawley Museum Centre
Goffs Park
Model Railway
Crawley Hosp.
Hospice
Hilltop Prim. Sch.
Southgate Sch.
Thomas Bennett Comm. College
Crawley Town FC (Broadfield Stadium)
K2 Leisure Centre
Running Track
Broadfield House
Broadfield Park
Tilgate Forest Theatre
Tilgate Forest Recreation Centre
TILGATE FOREST PARK
Titmus Lake
Tilgate Park Nature Centre
Tilgate Lake
Silt Lake
Old Stone Cottage Farm
Nursery
Whalebone Plantation
Cherrytree Plantation
Hardriding
TILGATE FOREST
TILGATE FOREST GOLF COURSE
Furnace Plain
Driving Range
Club House
Tilgate Playing Field
The Oaks Prim. Sch.
Oriel High Sch.
Sports Centre
Pitches
Furnace Green Playing Field
Hazelwick Sch.
Milton Mount Prim. Sch.
Crawley Lawn Tennis Club
Football Ground
Jubilee Fld.
Playing Field
Northgate Prim. Sch.
Langley Green Prim. Sch.
Magpie Wood
Sports Field
The Railway Field
Grattons Park
Cinder Banks
Stanford Brook
CRAWLEY
MID SUSSEX

POUND HILL
MAIDENBOWER
WORTH
Crabbet Park
Rowfant
Worth Abbey
Whitely Hill
WORTHLODGE FOREST
WORTH FOREST
OLDHOUSE WARREN
COWDRAY FOREST
M23 MOTORWAY
Junction 10a
BALCOMBE ROAD
COPTHORNE ROAD
TURNERS HILL ROAD
PADDOCKHURST ROAD
Haywards Heath
RH17
RH10
163
184

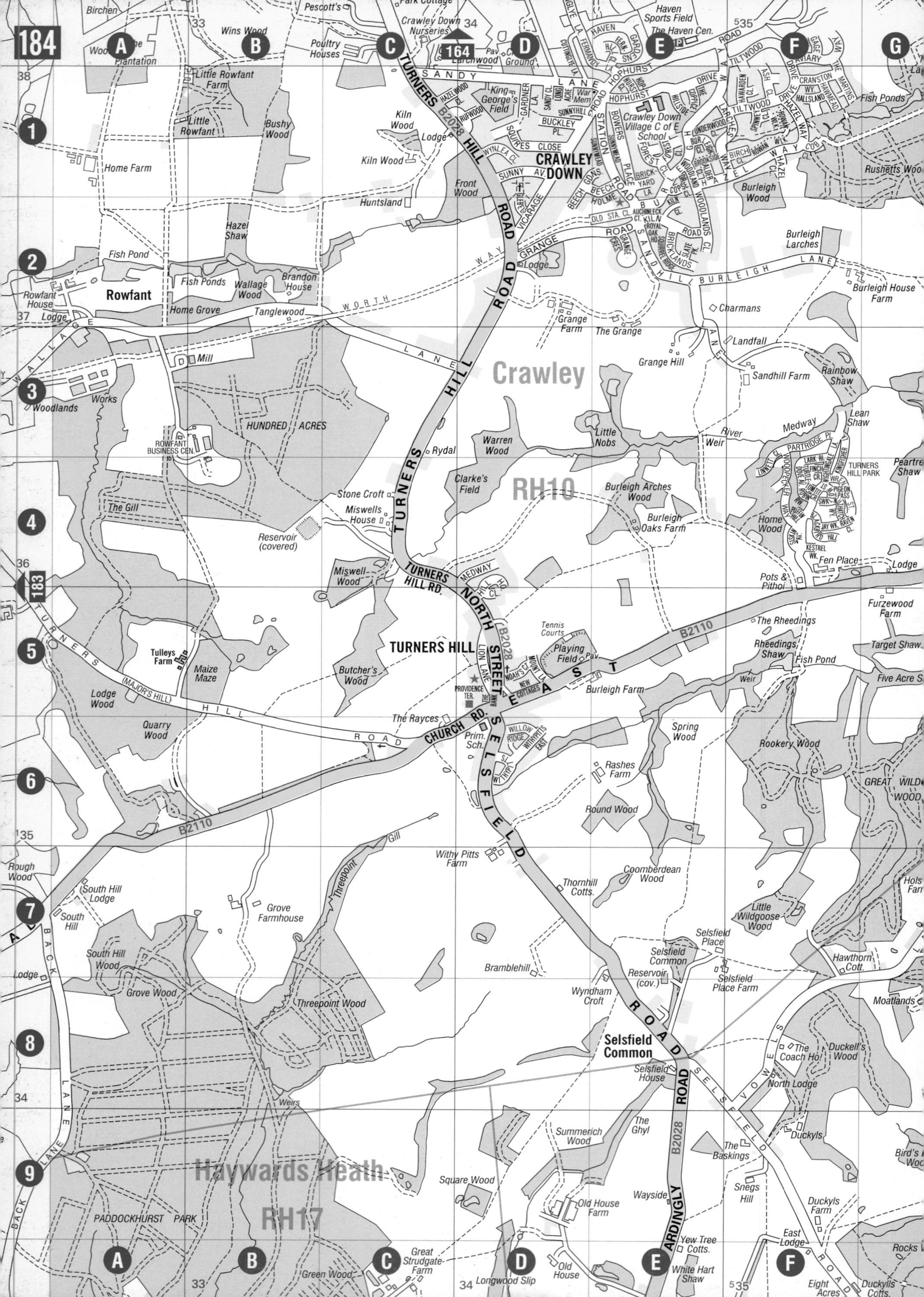

Birchen
Pescott's
Park Cottage
Crawley Down Nurseries
164
Haven Sports Field
The Haven Cen.
Wins Wood
Poultry Houses
Plantation
Little Rowfant Farm
Little Rowfant
Bushy Wood
Kiln Wood
Home Farm
King George's Field
Crawley Down Village C of E School
CRAWLEY DOWN
Front Wood
Huntsland
Hazel Shaw
Burleigh Wood
Rushetts Wood
Fish Ponds
Burleigh Larches
Fish Pond
Fish Ponds
Wallage Wood
Brandon House
Rowfant
Rowfant House
Lodge
Home Grove
Tanglewood
WORTH WAY
WORTH LANE
Grange Farm
The Grange
Charmans
Burleigh House Farm
Landfall
Grange Hill
Sandhill Farm
Rainbow Shaw
Mill
Works
Woodlands
Crawley
HUNDRED ACRES
ROWFANT BUSINESS CEN.
Warren Wood
Little Nobs
River Medway
Weir
Lean Shaw
Rydal
Clarke's Field
RH10
Burleigh Arches Wood
Burleigh Oaks Farm
TURNERS HILL PARK
Peartree Shaw
Home Wood
The Gill
Stone Croft
Miswells House
Reservoir (covered)
Fen Place
Lodge
Pots & Pithoi
Miswell Wood
TURNERS HILL RD.
NORTH STREET
B2028
Tennis Courts
Playing Field
Pav
Furzewood Farm
The Rheedings
B2110
Rheedings Shaw
Target Shaw
Fish Pond
Tulleys Farm
Maize Maze
TURNERS HILL
Butcher's Wood
PROVIDENCE TER.
Burleigh Farm
EAST
Weir
Five Acre Shaw
Lodge Wood
(MAJOR'S HILL)
TURNERS HILL ROAD
The Rayces
CHURCH RD.
SELSFIELD
Spring Wood
Rookery Wood
Quarry Wood
Prim. Sch.
Rashes Farm
GREAT WILDGOOSE WOOD
Round Wood
B2110
Withy Pitts Farm
Gill
Coomberdean Wood
Thornhill Cotts.
Rough Wood
South Hill Lodge
South Hill
Grove Farmhouse
Threepoint
Little Wildgoose Wood
South Hill Wood
Selsfield Place
Selsfield Common
Hawthorn Cott.
Reservoir (cov.)
Selsfield Place Farm
Bramblehill
Lodge
Wyndham Croft
Grove Wood
Threepoint Wood
Moatlands
Selsfield Common
The Coach Ho.
Duckell's Wood
Selsfield House
North Lodge
VOWELS
SELSFIELD ROAD
BACK LANE
Weirs
The Ghyl
Summerich Wood
The Baskings
Duckyls
Bird's Wood
Haywards Heath
Square Wood
Snegs Hill
Wayside
ARDINGLY ROAD
B2028
Old House Farm
Duckyls Farm
PADDOCKHURST PARK
RH17
East Lodge
Great Strudgate Farm
Yew Tree Cotts.
White Hart Shaw
Old House
Longwood Slip
Green Wood
Eight Acres
Duckyls Cotts.
Rocks
183

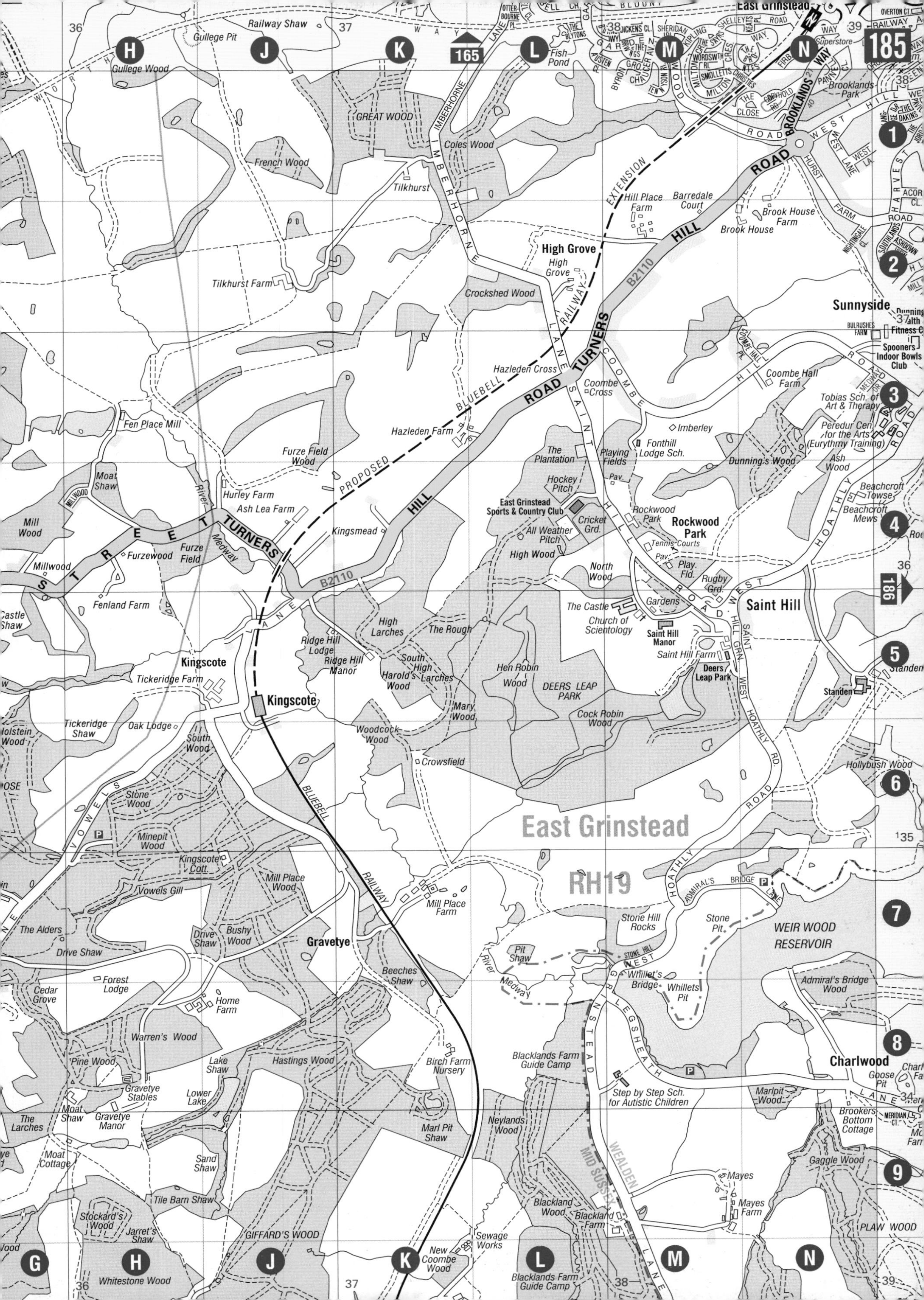
185
165
186
East Grinstead
RH19
Railway Shaw
Gullege Pit
Gullege Wood
Fish Pond
Great Wood
Coles Wood
French Wood
Tilkhurst
Tilkhurst Farm
Hill Place Farm
Barredale Court
Brook House Farm
Brook House
Brooklands Park
High Grove
Crockshed Wood
Sunnyside
Spooners Indoor Bowls Club
Hazleden Cross
Coombe Cross
Coombe Hall Farm
Tobias Sch. of Art & Therapy
Peredur Cen. for the Arts (Eurythmy Training)
Imberley
Fonthill Lodge Sch.
Hazleden Farm
Fen Place Mill
Furze Field Wood
The Plantation
Playing Fields
Dunning's Wood
Ash Wood
Beachcroft Towse
Beachcroft Mews
Moat Shaw
Hurley Farm
Ash Lea Farm
Hockey Pitch
East Grinstead Sports & Country Club
Cricket Grd.
Rockwood Park
All Weather Pitch
Mill Wood
Kingsmead
High Wood
Millwood
Furzewood
Furze Field
Tennis Courts
Play. Fld.
Rugby Grd.
North Wood
Fenland Farm
Gardens
The Castle
Church of Scientology
Saint Hill Manor
Saint Hill
Saint Hill Farm
Deers Leap Park
Castle Shaw
High Larches
The Rough
Ridge Hill Lodge
Ridge Hill Manor
Kingscote
Tickeridge Farm
South High Larches
Harold's Wood
Hen Robin Wood
DEERS LEAP PARK
Mary Wood
Standen
Holstein Wood
Tickeridge Shaw
Oak Lodge
South Wood
Woodcock Wood
Cock Robin Wood
Crowsfield
Hollybush Wood
Stone Wood
Minepit Wood
Kingscote Cott.
Mill Place Wood
Vowels Gill
Mill Place Farm
Admiral's Bridge
The Alders
Drive Shaw
Bushy Wood
Gravetye
Stone Hill Rocks
Stone Pit
WEIR WOOD RESERVOIR
Pit Shaw
Beeches Shaw
Whillet's Bridge
Whillets Pit
Admiral's Bridge Wood
Forest Lodge
Cedar Grove
Home Farm
Warren's Wood
Pine Wood
Lake Shaw
Hastings Wood
Birch Farm Nursery
Blacklands Farm Guide Camp
Charlwood
Goose Pit
Gravetye Stables
Lower Lake
Step by Step Sch. for Autistic Children
Marlpit Wood
Brookers Bottom Cottage
The Larches
Moat Shaw
Gravetye Manor
Neylands Wood
Marl Pit Shaw
Moat Cottage
Sand Shaw
Gaggle Wood
Mayes
Mayes Farm
Tile Barn Shaw
Blackland Wood
Blackland Farm
Stockard's Wood
Jarret's Shaw
GIFFARD'S WOOD
Sewage Works
PLAW WOOD
New Coombe Wood
Whitestone Wood
Blacklands Farm Guide Camp
TURNERS HILL ROAD
STREET
B2110
PROPOSED BLUEBELL RAILWAY EXTENSION
BLUEBELL RAILWAY
IMBERHORNE LANE
SAINT HILL ROAD
WEST HOATHLY RD.
HOATHLY ROAD
COOMBE HILL ROAD
MID SUSSEX
WEALDEN
GRINSTEAD LANE
LEGSHEATH LANE
VOWELS LANE
River Medway
WEST HILL
BROOKLANDS WAY
H J K L M N
G H J K L M N
1 2 3 4 5 6 7 8 9
36 37 38 39

EAST GRINSTEAD
East Grinstead
RH19
ASHURST WOOD
Sunnyside
Standen
Charlwood
Kidbrooke Park
Weir Wood
WEIR WOOD
RESERVOIR
Wall Hill
MID SUSSEX
WEALDEN
A22
LEWES ROAD
166
185
Sackville Sch.
Worsted Farm Cottages
Worsted Farm
Alder Shaw
Pitlands Wood
Dutton Homestall Poultry Farm
Wood Cottage
The Bungalow
Shovelstrode Farm
Fowl Wood
Berry Wood
Stoke Brunswick Sch.
High Lawns
Barton St. Mary
The Lodge
Brockhurst
Boat House
Greenacres
Home Farm
Foxbury
Luxford's
The Shaw
Luxford's Farm
Luxford's Wood
Blunds Hole
Wealden House
Beeches Farm
Playing Field
The Stables
Chance Coppice
Chance Cottage
Brambletye School
South Pond
Tennis Courts
Hounds Cottage
Leisure Pursuits
Brambletye Cottage
Sinderson House
Millwood Manor
High Wood
Minepit Wood
Meadowlands
Great Harwood's Farm
Toll Shaw
Kitchen Mead Shaw
Sewage Works
Millfield Farm
Minepits Wood
Horseshoe Farm
Rockingshill Wood
Rushett's Shaw
Jenkin's Wood
Standen Farm
Busses Farm
Botley Wood
Jenhurst Shaw
Jenhurst Wood
Busses Wood
Hollybush Wood
Horseshoe Wood
Water Works
Brambletye Barn Manor
Old Brambletye House
Brambletye Manor Farm
Moat
Weir Wood Cottages
Burnthouse Farm
Sailing Club House
Fishing Club House
Weir Wood Cotts.
South Park Farm
Monks Wood
Brakey Shaw
Alder Wood
Holme Rist
Court-in-Holmes
South Park Farm Cotts.
Kidbrooke Farm
Meadowbrook
Court Mead
Michael Hall School
Wychwood
Wretham Lodge
Springfield Lodge
Spring Hill Farm
Tylebrook Farm
Priors Field
Mudbrooks House
Newgale Farm
Priors Farm
Priors Hatch Farm
Greenfields School
Spring Hill Wildfowl Park
KIDBROOKE WOOD
KIDBROOKE PARK
Chalybeate Spring
Fernhill
Charlwood House
Charlwood Farm
Alder Moors
Goose Pit
Stoney Shaw
Hollow Shaw
Meridian Ct.
Brookers Bottom Cottage
Monkshill Farm Cotts.
Legsheath Cotts.
Round Wood
PLAW WOOD
Legsheath Farm
Tobias Sch. of Art & Therapy
Peredur Cen. for the Arts (Eurythmy Training)
Ash Wood
Beachcroft Towse
Dunnings Health & Fitness Club
Spooners Indoor Bowls Club
The Meads Prim. Sch.
Herontye House
The Hermitage
PRIORY
FOREST WAY

187
167
43
44
545
38
37
36
135
34
H
J
K
L
M
N
G
1
2
3
4
5
6
7
8
9
Edenbridge
TN8
Forest Row
RH18
Hartfield
TN7
FOREST ROW
Sewage Works
The Grove
Dog Gate Lodge
Water
Dog Cottages
Grove Cottage
Poultry Farm
Owlett's Farm
Water Wood
Little Water House
Great Water Farm
Little Water Farm
Owletts House
Harelands Kennels
Barton House
Playing Field
New Cottages
Salmon Wood
HOMESTALL RD.
Culver Farm
Songhurst Shaw
Goring Wood
Appletree Wood
Holden Wood
Great Cansiron Farm
Church Wood
Great Cansiron Farm
Acre Wood
Poultry Farm
CANSIRON LANE
BUTCHERFIELD LA.
Thornhill
Great Surries
Surries Wood
Leg of Mutton Shaw
Owletts Cottage
Bushy Shaw
Roughfield Wood
Thornhill Cottage
Box Farm
Great Surries Farm
Rest Harrow
Tanner's Hill Pett
Pollard Wood
Paupersdale Wood
Allens Cottages
Thornhill Farm
Homefield Cottages
Little Surries
Little Surries Wood
Woodcock Shaw
North Clays
Mount Pleasant Nursery
Little Surries Farm
Ashurstwood Abbey
Grove Farm
CANSIRON LANE
Shipyard Pett
Orchard Cotts.
Collingsbush Wood
Black Windmill Cottages
Wick Wood
Clay Wood
Home Wood
Hazel Wood
Highams Wood
Spanden Wood
The Jingle
Ashland Farm Cottages
Ashdown House School
Lower Parrock
Wallhill Farm
Minepits Wood
Pixton Hill Farm
Ashdown Farm
Beech House
Spanden
Gill Wood
Catland Shaw
Heasmans
Cedar Cotts.
Pixton Hill
Playing Field
Medway
Cobbers
River
Medway
Pumping Station
Emerson College
Tablehurst Farm
Tablehurst Manor
Sewage Works
FOREST WAY
Penfield Shaw
Playing Field
Blacklands Farm
Parrock Meadow
HARTFIELD ROAD
B2110
Brookside
Upper Parrock Farm
Parrock Lane Cotts.
Upper Parrock
Lines Bungalow
Lines Farm
Little Parrock
Parrock Place
Ashenplat Shaw
Play. Fld.
Prim. Sch.
Rystwood Lodge
Rystwood House
Wychcote
Andrews Bank
Paternoster Wood
Rystwood Farm
Little Parrock Farm
Little Parrock Cotts.
Shalesbrook
Highgate
Club House
Birlings Farm
Gorseycop Farm
Quabrook
Popular Farm
ROYAL ASHDOWN FOREST GOLF COURSE
Vale Cottage
Forest View
Yew Tree Hall Cott.
Holly Brook
Hollycroft
Upper Quabrook
Gatehouse Farm
SHEPHERD'S HILL
CAT ST.
Porch Cottage
Bank Cottage
Tompset's Bank
Old White's Farm
Yew Tree Hall
Little Shepherd's Farm
Forest View
Holly Hill
Wych Warren
Water Farm
Shepherd's Gate Cotts.
Bagerly
Foxbury Wood
Shepherd's Gate
Coleman's Hatch
Little Broadstone Farm
The Birches
Yew Tree Cottage
The Lodge

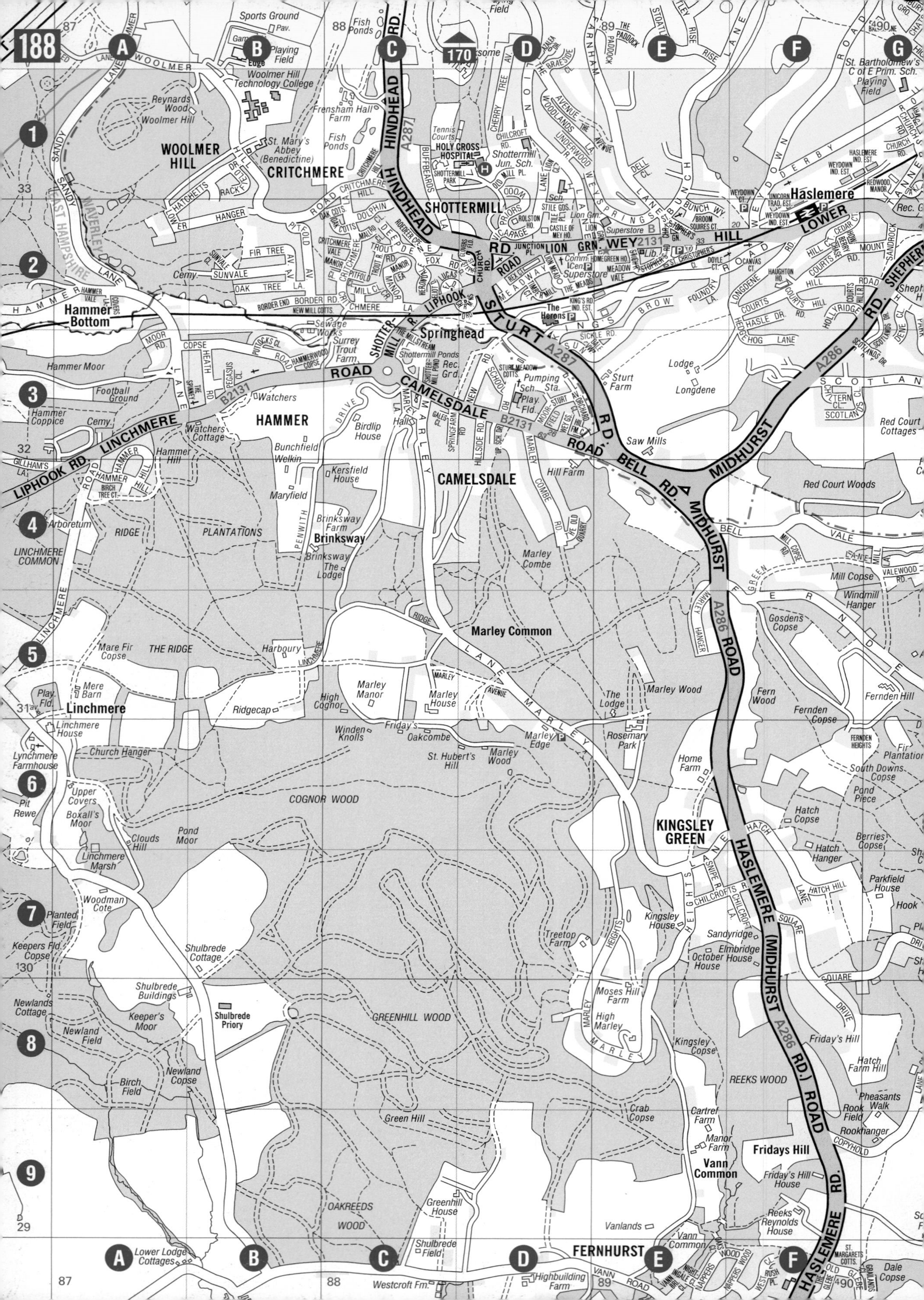
170
Sports Ground
Playing Field
Woolmer Hill Technology College
Reynards Wood
Woolmer Hill
WOOLMER HILL
St. Mary's Abbey (Benedictine)
CRITCHMERE
Frensham Hall Farm
Fish Ponds
HINDHEAD RD.
A287
Tennis Courts
HOLY CROSS HOSPITAL
Shottermill Jun. Sch.
SHOTTERMILL
Haslemere
LOWER
HILL
Superstore
Lion Grn.
Castle of Mey Ho.
Comm. Cen.
St. Bartholomew's C of E Prim. Sch.
Playing Field
WEYDOWN IND. EST.
HASLEMERE IND. EST.
UNICORN TRAD. EST.
Rec. Grd.
Hammer Bottom
Cemy.
WOOLMER LANE
SANDY LANE
HAMMER LANE
Springhead
Sewage Works
Surrey Trout Farm
Shottermill Ponds
SHOTTERMILL RD.
LIPHOOK RD.
STURT RD.
A287
The Herons
Sturt Farm
Lodge
Longdene
Hammer Moor
Football Ground
Hammer Coppice
HAMMER
Watchers
Watchers Cottage
B2131
LINCHMERE RD.
CAMELSDALE ROAD
Birdlip House
Bunchfield
Welkin
Kersfield House
Maryfield
Pumping Sta.
Play. Fld.
Saw Mills
Red Court Cottages
Red Court Woods
CAMELSDALE
Hill Farm
BELL RD.
MIDHURST RD.
A286
Hammer Hill
Arboretum
RIDGE
PLANTATIONS
LINCHMERE COMMON
Brinksway Farm
Brinksway
The Lodge
Marley Combe
BELL VALE LANE
Mill Copse
Windmill Hanger
Gosdens Copse
Marley Common
Mare Fir Copse
THE RIDGE
Harbury
Mere Barn
Play. Fld.
Linchmere
Linchmere House
Ridgecap
Marley Manor
High Cognor
Marley House
Winden Knolls
Friday's Oakcombe
St. Hubert's Hill
Marley Wood
Marley Edge
The Lodge
Marley Wood
Rosemary Park
Fern Wood
Fernden Hill
Fernden Copse
Church Hanger
Lynchmere Farmhouse
Upper Covers
Pit Rewe
Boxall's Moor
COGNOR WOOD
Pond Moor
Clouds Hill
Linchmere Marsh
Home Farm
South Downs Copse
Pond Piece
Hatch Copse
KINGSLEY GREEN
Hatch Hanger
Berries Copse
Parkfield House
Hook
Woodman Cote
Planted Field
Keepers Fld. Copse
Shulbrede Cottage
Treetop Farm
Kingsley House
Sandyridge
Elmbridge
October House
Shulbrede Buildings
Newlands Cottage
Keeper's Moor
Shulbrede Priory
GREENHILL WOOD
Moses Hill Farm
High Marley
Newland Field
Kingsley Copse
Friday's Hill
Hatch Farm Hill
Birch Field
Newland Copse
REEKS WOOD
Pheasants Walk
Crab Copse
Green Hill
Cartref Farm
Manor Farm
Rook Field
Rookhanger
Fridays Hill
Vann Common
Friday's Hill House
HASLEMERE (MIDHURST A286 RD.) ROAD
HASLEMERE RD.
OAKREEDS WOOD
Greenhill House
Vanlands
Reeks Reynolds House
Lower Lodge Cottages
Shulbrede Field
FERNHURST
Vann Common
Highbuilding Farm
Westcroft Fm.
Dale Copse
VANN ROAD
87
88
89
490
33
32
31
130
29

HASLEMERE
Haslemere Community Hospital
Haslemere Educational Museum
Town Hall
Haslemere Prep. Sch.
Lythe Hill
Lythe Hill Hotel
Ansteadbrook
Roundhurst
Haslemere
GU27
HOME WOOD
BLACK DOWN
ROUNDHURST COMMON
PETWORTH ROAD
B2131
A286
GRAYSWOOD RD.
HIGH ST.
HOLDFAST LANE
TENNYSON'S LANE
JAYS LANE
FERNDEN LANE
QUELL LANE
JOBSONS LANE
LONG REACH LANE
BULLOCKS LANE
KILLINGHURST LANE
HASTE HILL
CHASE LANE
The Manor House
Great Carvers
Beanfield Copse
The White House
Furnace Court
Furnace Moor
Verney Copse
Stream Cottage
New Cottages
Benham Stud
Knobby Copse
New Planted Piece
Almshouse Common
Mariners Rewe
Witley Copse
Meadfield
St. Ives School
Redcot
Imbhams Farm
Bungalows
Home Wood
High Barn Farm
Barford Copse
Barfold Wood
Hearne Copse
Anstead Brook Stud
Herne House
Hearne Farm
Little Stedlands
Chase Warren
Chase Wood
Chase Farm
Black Dog Copse
The Roughs
Owlden
Barfold Firs
Barfold Hole
Barfold
Jay's Farm
Silver Birches
Boarden Door Bottom
Waterworks Cottages
Ridden Corner
Ridden Corner Copse
The Lodge
Aldworth House
Hovel Copse
Moorland Copse
Fir Oval
Vale Wood
Planted Field
Alder Wood
Valewood Park
Wadesmarsh Farmhouse
Lye Wood
Upper Roundhurst Farm
Lower Roundhurst
Oakfield Cottages
Foxholes
Glasshouse Piece
Shalford Copse
Sheetlands
Flat Field
Garden Field Hanger
Ridge Hill
Fish Pond
Pudding Copse
Wades Marsh
Abesters Copse
Rickfield Copse
New Barn Copse
Beechy Hanger
Heathfield Hanger
Cotchet Farm
Black Down
Farall Nurseries
Paddock Copse
Pond Copse
Parkhurst House
Bullocks Copse
New Copse
Sheetland
Long Dene Row
Al Waha Arabian Stud
Abesters
Ramsfold Wood
Ramsfold House
Orchard Cottage
Hookhams Copse
Temple of the Winds
Castle Copse
Blackdown
Blackdown Hill Cotts.
Scouting Lane End
Homefield Hanger
Reeth Copse
Reeth
Sopers
Bridge Reeds
Hogs Hill Copse
Selham Copse
Pump Ho.
Cobblers
Upper Quell Copse
Quellhurst
Quellwood Common
Quell Wood
Becketts Farm
Shopp Hill Farm
WAVERLEY
CHICHESTER
PEN-Y-BOS TRACK
171
190

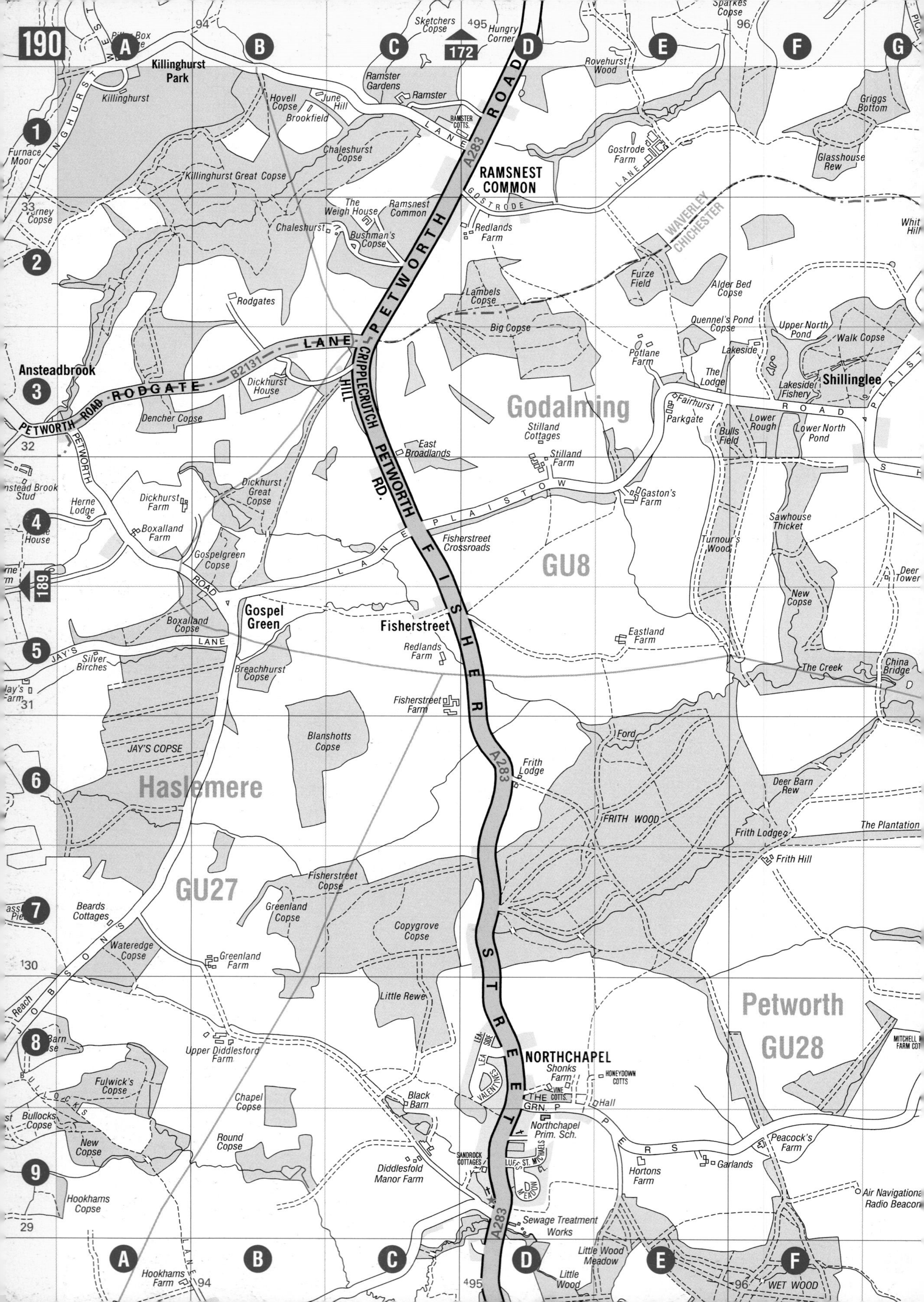

172
189
Killinghurst Park
Killinghurst
Furnace Moor
Hovell Copse
June Hill
Brookfield
Sketchers Copse
Hungry Corner
Ramster Gardens
Ramster
RAMSTER COTTS.
Rovehurst Wood
Sparkes Copse
Griggs Bottom
Glasshouse Rew
Gostrode Farm
Chaleshurst Copse
Killinghurst Great Copse
RAMSNEST COMMON
GOSTRODE
LANE
A283
PETWORTH ROAD
The Weigh House
Ramsnest Common
Chaleshurst
Bushman's Copse
Redlands Farm
WAVERLEY
CHICHESTER
Furze Field
Alder Bed Copse
Lambels Copse
Big Copse
Rodgates
Quennel's Pond Copse
Upper North Pond
Walk Copse
Lakeside
Potlane Farm
The Lodge
Lakeside Fishery
Shillinglee
Ansteadbrook
RODGATE LANE
B2131
Dickhurst House
CRIPPLECRUTCH HILL
Dencher Copse
PETWORTH ROAD
PETWORTH RD.
Godalming
Stilland Cottages
Stilland Farm
Fairhurst
Parkgate
Bulls Field
Lower Rough
Lower North Pond
ROAD
East Broadlands
Anstead Brook Stud
Herne Lodge
Dickhurst Farm
Dickhurst Great Copse
PLAISTOW LANE
Gaston's Farm
Sawhouse Thicket
Boxalland Farm
Fisherstreet Crossroads
Turnour's Wood
Gospelgreen Copse
GU8
Deer Tower
FISHER STREET
New Copse
ROAD
Gospel Green
Boxalland Copse
Fisherstreet
Eastland Farm
JAY'S LANE
Silver Birches
Redlands Farm
Breachhurst Copse
The Creek
China Bridge
Fisherstreet Farm
Blanshotts Copse
Ford
JAY'S COPSE
Frith Lodge
Deer Barn Rew
Haslemere
FRITH WOOD
The Plantation
Frith Lodge
Frith Hill
Fisherstreet Copse
GU27
Beards Cottages
Greenland Copse
Copygrove Copse
Wateredge Copse
Greenland Farm
JOBSON'S
Little Rewe
Petworth
GU28
Upper Diddlesford Farm
LEA SIDE
NORTHCHAPEL
Shonks Farm
HONEYDOWN COTTS
VALENTINES
LEA
THE COTTS.
VINE COTTS.
GRN.
Hall
Fulwick's Copse
Chapel Copse
Black Barn
Northchapel Prim. Sch.
Bullocks Copse
New Copse
Round Copse
Peacock's Farm
PERS
SANDROCK COTTAGES
ST. MICHAELS
Hortons Farm
Garlands
Diddlesfold Manor Farm
MEADOW
Hookhams Copse
Air Navigation Radio Beacon
Sewage Treatment Works
Little Wood Meadow
Hookhams Farm
LANE
Little Wood
WET WOOD
MITCHELL FARM COTT

Billingshurst
RH14
Fisherland Hanger
Tugley Wood
Oak Wood
Durfold Hatch Cott
Birch Copse
Peartree Hanger
Burntwood Kennels
The Hatchetts
Tidy's Copse
Robins Farm
Little Tugley
Durfold Hall Farm
Surrey Copse
The Holmes
Works
Oakhurst Farm
Dungate Farm
Club House
Surrey Belt
Surrey Cottage
Durfold Wood
Shillinglee Park Golf Course
Surrey Rough
Fisherlane Wood
Shillinglee Park
Icehouse Copse
Downlands
Downlands Wood
Shortland Copse
Newhouse Furze
Manorhill Copse
Pound Cottage
Paddock Copse
Old Furze Field
Manor Hill House Farm
Newhouse Farm
East End Farm
Winkins Wood Farm
Winkins Wood
Ashpark Wood
Weald Barn Farm
Cockhat Piece
Catfield Rew
Clay Pit
Brick Works
Short's Farm
Lyons Farm
Nine Acre Rew
Canada Farm
Beanfield Copse
Black Copse
Little Haymans Farm
Highbridge House
Landing Stage
Twenty Four Acres
Haymans Farm
Kingspark Wood
The Lake
Lake Cottage
Nell Ball
Park Mill Farm
Mill Copse
Ifold Copse
Birchfold Copse
Alder Platt
Hazel Tolt
Seven Acre Furze
Dale's Farm Hanger
Dale's Farm Copse
Sparrwood Hangar
Dale's Farm
Mitchell Park Farm
Chilsfold Farm
Sparrwood Farm
Red Copse
Hammer Cottages
Hammer Bridge
Piper's Cottages
Upper Frithfold Farm
Piper's Copse
Sixteen Acre Row
Roundwyck Copse
Roundwyck House
Freehold Copse
Kiln Copse
Frithfold Farm
Fisher Road
Plaistow Road
Durfold Wood
Dunsfold Road
Valentines
Shillinglee Road
Pipers Lane
Lane
Land's
173
192
H J K L M N G
97 98 99 500
1 2 3 4 5 6 7 8 9
33 32 31 130 29

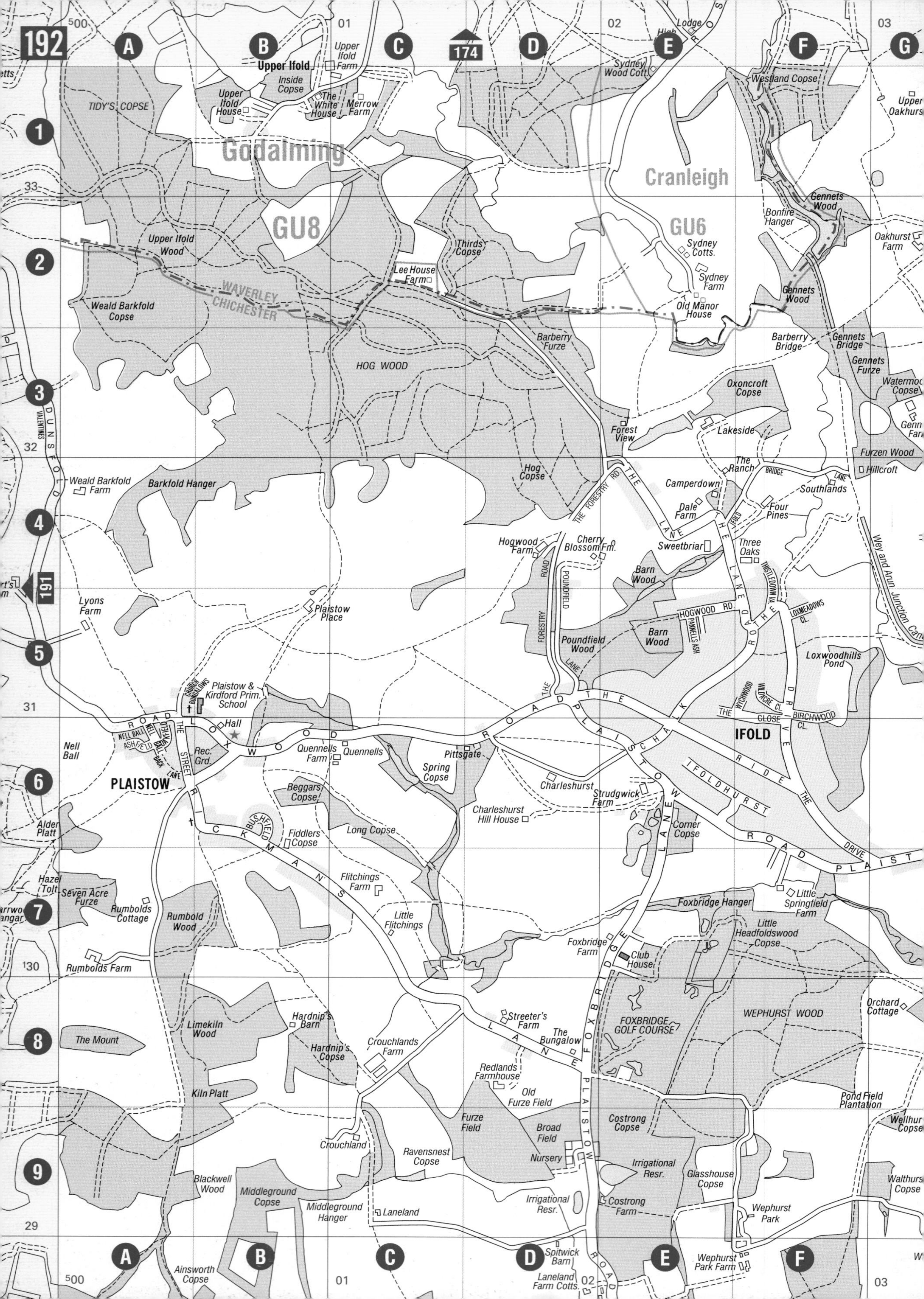
192
174
191
Upper Ifold
Inside Copse
Upper Ifold Farm
Upper Ifold House
The White House
Merrow Farm
TIDY'S COPSE
Godalming
GU8
Cranleigh
GU6
Sydney Wood Cott.
Westland Copse
Upper Oakhurst
Gennets Wood
Bonfire Hanger
Oakhurst Farm
Upper Ifold Wood
Thirds Copse
Sydney Cotts.
Sydney Farm
Old Manor House
Lee House Farm
WAVERLEY
CHICHESTER
Weald Barkfold Copse
Barberry Furze
Barberry Bridge
Gennets Bridge
Gennets Furze
HOG WOOD
Oxoncroft Copse
Forest View
Lakeside
Furzen Wood
Hillcroft
Weald Barkfold Farm
Barkfold Hanger
Hog Copse
The Ranch
Camperdown
Southlands
Dale Farm
Four Pines
Hogwood Farm
Cherry Blossom Fm.
Sweetbriar
Three Oaks
Barn Wood
Wey and Arun Junction Canal
Lyons Farm
Plaistow Place
HOGWOOD RD.
LOXMEADOWS CL.
Poundfield Wood
Loxwoodhills Pond
Plaistow & Kirdford Prim. School
Hall
Nell Ball
Rec. Grd.
Quennells Farm
Quennells
Pittsgate
Spring Copse
IFOLD
BIRCHWOOD CL.
PLAISTOW
Beggars Copse
Charleshurst
Strudgwick Farm
Charleshurst Hill House
Alder Platt
Fiddlers Copse
Long Copse
Corner Copse
Hazel Tolt
Seven Acre Furze
Rumbolds Cottage
Flitchings Farm
Foxbridge Hanger
Little Springfield Farm
Rumbold Wood
Little Flitchings
Little Headfoldswood Copse
Foxbridge Farm
Club House
Rumbolds Farm
Hardnip's Barn
Streeter's Farm
WEPHURST WOOD
Orchard Cottage
The Mount
Limekiln Wood
Hardnip's Copse
Crouchlands Farm
The Bungalow
FOXBRIDGE GOLF COURSE
Redlands Farmhouse
Old Furze Field
Kiln Platt
Pond Field Plantation
Furze Field
Broad Field
Costrong Copse
Crouchland
Ravensnest Copse
Nursery
Irrigational Resr.
Glasshouse Copse
Blackwell Wood
Middleground Copse
Middleground Hanger
Laneland
Costrong Farm
Wephurst Park
Spitwick Barn
Wephurst Park Farm
Ainsworth Copse
Laneland Farm Cotts.
DUNSFOLD
VALENTINES
PLAISTOW ROAD
LOXWOOD ROAD
KICKMANS LANE
FOXBRIDGE LANE
IFOLDHURST
THE RIDE
THE DRIVE
THE LANE
THE FORESTRY RD.
FORESTRY ROAD
POUNDFIELD LANE
PLAISTOW ROAD
CHALK ROAD
THE STREET
BRIDGE LANE

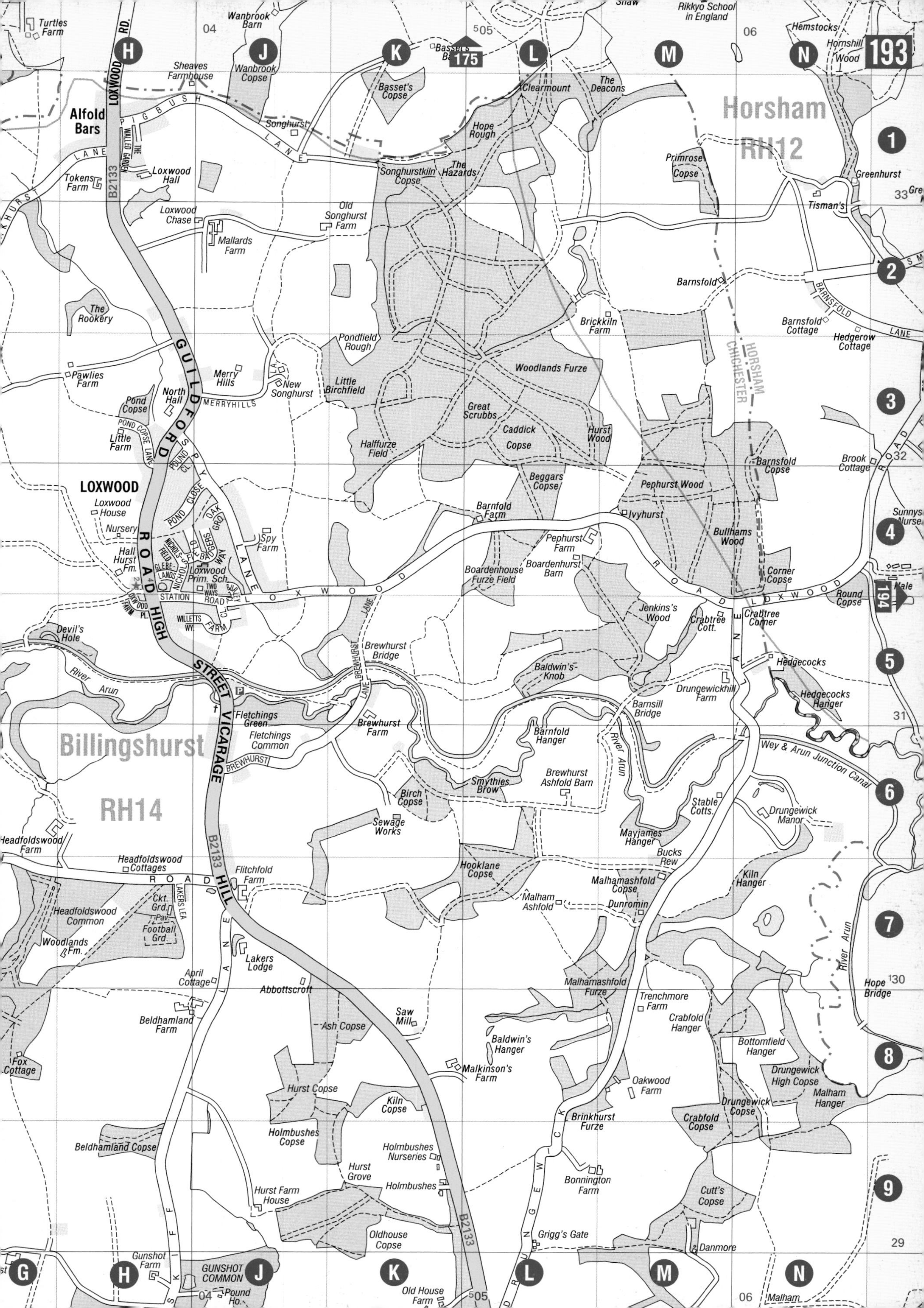

193
175
194
Horsham
RH12
RH14
Billingshurst
Alfold Bars
LOXWOOD
Turtles Farm
Wanbrook Barn
Wanbrook Copse
Sheaves Farmhouse
Songhurst
Basset's Copse
Clearmount
The Deacons
Rikkyo School in England
Hemstocks
Hornshill Wood
Hope Rough
The Hazards
Songhurstkiln Copse
Primrose Copse
Greenhurst
Tisman's
Tokens Farm
Loxwood Hall
Loxwood Chase
Mallards Farm
Old Songhurst Farm
Barnsfold
Barnsfold Cottage
Hedgerow Cottage
Brickkiln Farm
The Rookery
Pondfield Rough
Woodlands Furze
Pawlies Farm
Merry Hills
New Songhurst
Little Birchfield
North Hall
Pond Copse
Little Farm
Great Scrubbs
Caddick Copse
Hurst Wood
Halffurze Field
Barnsfold Copse
Brook Cottage
Beggars Copse
Pephurst Wood
Loxwood House
Nursery
Barnfold Farm
Ivyhurst
Sunnys Nurse
Spy Farm
Pephurst Farm
Bullhams Wood
Hall Hurst Fm.
Loxwood Prim. Sch.
Boardenhouse Furze Field
Boardenhurst Barn
Corner Copse
Round Copse
Hale
Devil's Hole
Jenkins's Wood
Crabtree Cott.
Crabtree Corner
Brewhurst Bridge
Baldwin's Knob
Hedgecocks
River Arun
Drungewickhill Farm
Hedgecocks Hanger
Fletchings Green
Fletchings Common
Brewhurst Farm
Barnsill Bridge
Barnfold Hanger
Wey & Arun Junction Canal
Smythies Brow
Brewhurst Ashfold Barn
Stable Cotts.
Drungewick Manor
Birch Copse
Sewage Works
Mayjames Hanger
Headfoldswood Farm
Headfoldswood Cottages
Bucks Rew
Flitchfold Farm
Hooklane Copse
Malhamashfold Copse
Kiln Hanger
Headfoldswood Common
Ckt. Grd.
Pav.
Football Grd.
Malham Ashfold
Dunromin
Woodlands Fm.
Lakers Lodge
April Cottage
Abbottscroft
Malhamashfold Furze
Trenchmore Farm
Hope Bridge
Beldhamland Farm
Saw Mill
Ash Copse
Crabfold Hanger
Baldwin's Hanger
Bottomfield Hanger
Fox Cottage
Malkinson's Farm
Drungewick High Copse
Hurst Copse
Oakwood Farm
Malham Hanger
Kiln Copse
Brinkhurst Furze
Drungewick Copse
Crabfold Copse
Holmbushes Copse
Beldhamland Copse
Holmbushes Nurseries
Hurst Grove
Bonnington Farm
Holmbushes
Cutt's Copse
Hurst Farm House
Oldhouse Copse
Grigg's Gate
Danmore
Gunshot Farm
GUNSHOT COMMON
Pound Ho.
Old House Farm
Malham
LOXWOOD RD.
B2133
PIGBUSH LANE
WALLED GARDEN
THE
GUILDFORD ROAD
HIGH STREET
VICARAGE HILL
MERRYHILLS
POND COPSE LANE
SPY LANE
POUND CL.
POND CLOSE
OAK GRO.
NICHOLSFIELD
GLEBE LANDS
BRIDGERS WAY
TWO WAYS
STATION ROAD
LOXWOOD ROAD
WILLETTS WY.
FARM CL.
BREWHURST LANE
BREWHURST
ROAD
LAKERS LEA
LANE
SKIFF LANE
DRUNGEWICK LANE
BARNSFOLD LANE
HORSHAM
CHICHESTER
G
H
J
K
L
M
N
1
2
3
4
5
6
7
8
9
04
05
06
33
32
31
130
29

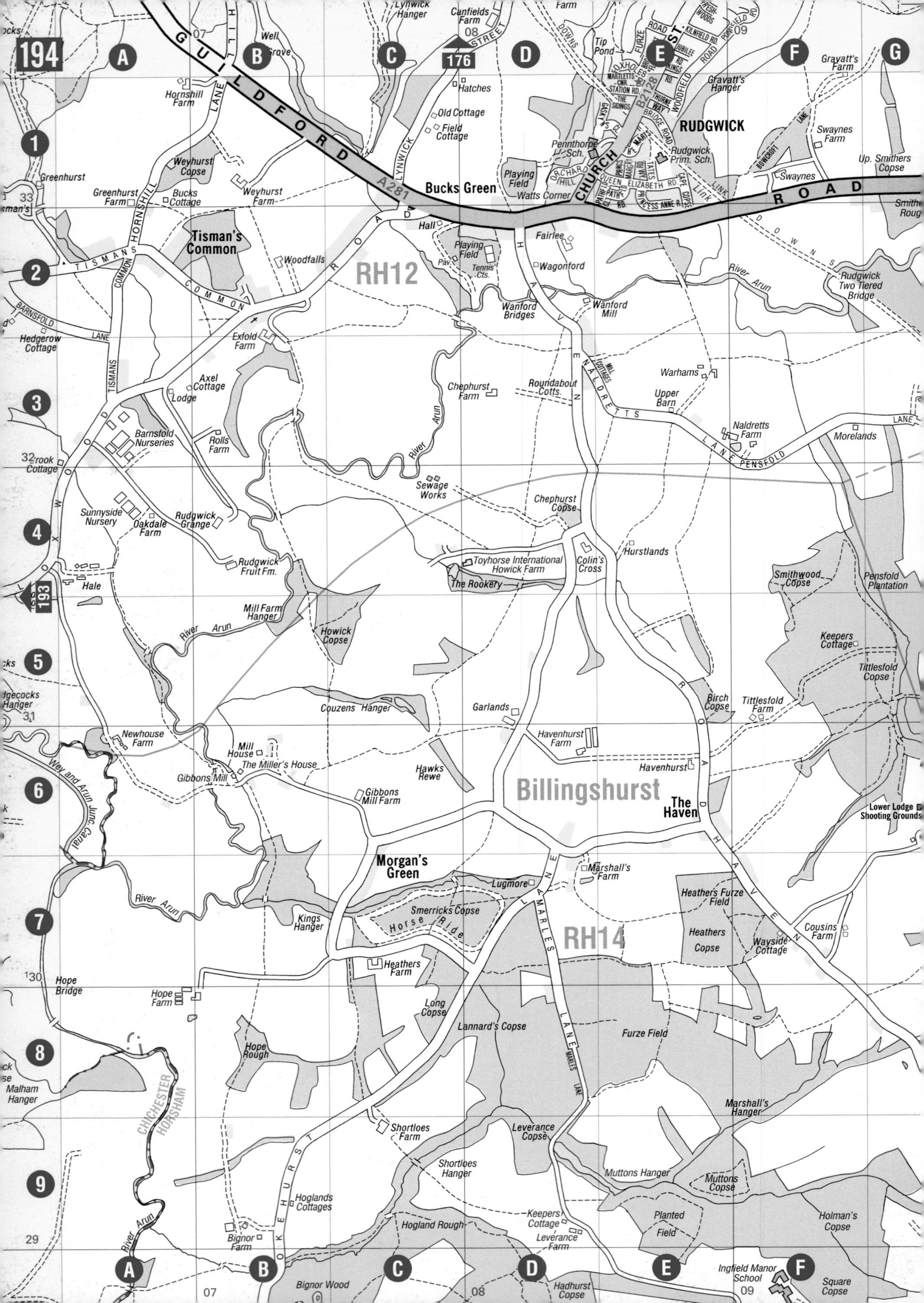

194
176
193
A
B
C
D
E
F
G
1
2
3
4
5
6
7
8
9
07
08
09
33
32
31
130
29
GUILDFORD ROAD
A281
RUDGWICK
Bucks Green
RH12
RH14
Billingshurst
Morgan's Green
The Haven
Tisman's Common
Lynwick Hanger
Canfields Farm
Well Grove
Hornshill Farm
Hatches
Old Cottage
Field Cottage
Tip Pond
B2128
Gravatt's Farm
Gravatt's Hanger
Swaynes Farm
Up. Smithers Copse
Swaynes
Pennthorpe Sch.
Rudgwick Prim. Sch.
Playing Field
Watts Corner
Weyhurst Copse
Greenhurst
Greenhurst Farm
Bucks Cottage
Weyhurst Farm
Hall
Fairlee
Wagonford
Woodfalls
Tennis Cts.
Pav.
River Arun
Rudgwick Two Tiered Bridge
Wanford Bridges
Wanford Mill
Hedgerow Cottage
Exfold Farm
Axel Cottage
Lodge
Chephurst Farm
Roundabout Cotts.
Warhams
Upper Barn
Naldretts Farm
Morelands
Barnsfold Nurseries
Rolls Farm
Sewage Works
Chephurst Copse
Sunnyside Nursery
Oakdale Farm
Rudgwick Grange
Rudgwick Fruit Fm.
Toyhorse International Howick Farm
The Rookery
Colin's Cross
Hurstlands
Smithwood Copse
Pensfold Plantation
Hale
Mill Farm Hanger
Howick Copse
Keepers Cottage
Tittlesfold Copse
Couzens Hanger
Garlands
Birch Copse
Tittlesfold Farm
Newhouse Farm
Mill House
The Miller's House
Gibbons Mill
Gibbons Mill Farm
Hawks Rewe
Havenhurst Farm
Havenhurst
Lower Lodge Shooting Grounds
Wey and Arun Junc. Canal
Marshall's Farm
Lugmore
Smerricks Copse
Horse Ride
Kings Hanger
Heathers Furze Field
Heathers Copse
Wayside Cottage
Cousins Farm
Heathers Farm
Hope Bridge
Hope Farm
Long Copse
Lannard's Copse
Furze Field
Hope Rough
Malham Hanger
CHICHESTER
HORSHAM
Marshall's Hanger
Shortloes Farm
Leverance Copse
Shortloes Hanger
Muttons Hanger
Muttons Copse
Hoglands Cottages
Hogland Rough
Keepers Cottage
Leverance Farm
Planted Field
Holman's Copse
Bignor Farm
Ingfield Manor School
Square Copse
Bignor Wood
Hadhurst Copse
OKEHURST
MARLES LANE
HAVEN ROAD
NALDRETTS LANE
PENSFOLD LANE
LOXWOOD ROAD
TISMANS COMMON
HORNSHILL LANE
BARNSFOLD LANE
LYNWICK STREET
CHURCH STREET

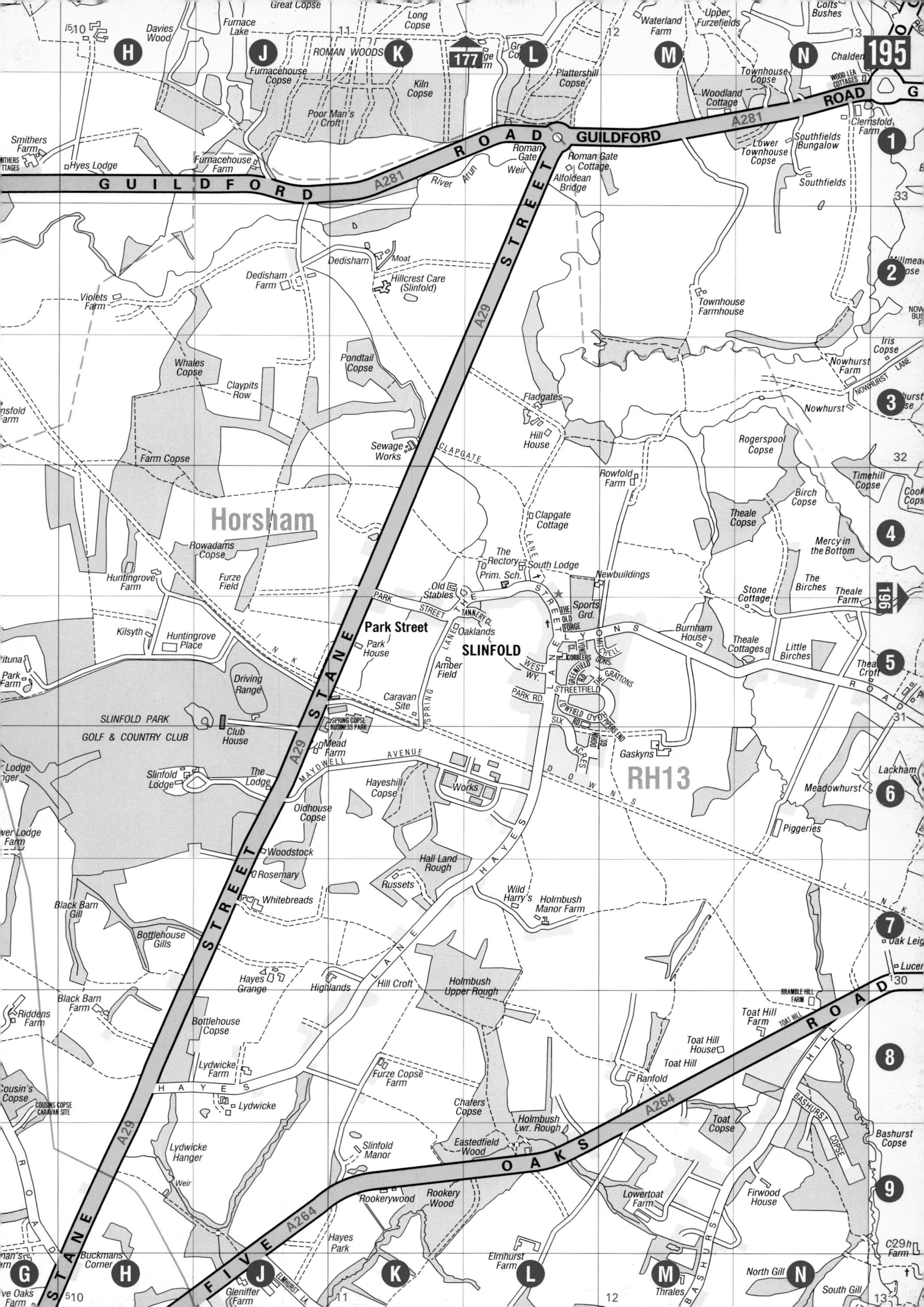

Great Copse
Davies Wood
Furnace Lake
Long Copse
Waterland Farm
Upper Furzefields
Colts Bushes
ROMAN WOODS
177
Chalden
Furnacehouse Copse
Kiln Copse
Plattershill Copse
Townhouse Copse
Woodland Cottage
WOOD LEA COTTAGES
Poor Man's Croft
GUILDFORD ROAD
A281
Clemsfold Farm
Smithers Farm
Hyes Lodge
Furnacehouse Farm
Roman Gate
Weir
Roman Gate Cottage
Alfoldean Bridge
Lower Townhouse Copse
Southfields Bungalow
Southfields
River Arun
Dedisham
Moat
Dedisham Farm
Hillcrest Care (Slinfold)
Violets Farm
Townhouse Farmhouse
STANE STREET
A29
Whales Copse
Pondtail Copse
Claypits Row
Iris Copse
Nowhurst Farm
NOWHURST LANE
Nowhurst
Fladgates
Hill House
Sewage Works
CLAPGATE LANE
Farm Copse
Rogerspool Copse
Rowfold Farm
Timehill Copse
Birch Copse
Horsham
Clapgate Cottage
Theale Copse
Mercy in the Bottom
Rowadams Copse
The Rectory
South Lodge
Prim. Sch.
Newbuildings
Huntingrove Farm
Furze Field
The Birches
Stone Cottage
Theale Farm
196
Old Stables
PARK STREET
TANNERY CL.
THE STREET
Sports Grd.
THE OLD FORGE
Kilsyth
Huntingrove Place
Park Street
Oaklands
SLINFOLD
LYONS ROAD
Burnham House
Theale Cottages
Little Birches
Park House
COBBLERS
MITCHELL GDNS.
LINK
Amber Field
WEST WY.
GREENFIELD RD.
THE GRATTONS
Theale Croft
Driving Range
PARK RD.
STREETFIELD
Caravan Site
SPRING LANE
SLINFOLD PARK GOLF & COUNTRY CLUB
Club House
SPRING COPSE BUSINESS PARK
LOWFIELD ROAD
PIPERS END
SIX ACRES
DORIN CT.
Gaskyns
Mead Farm
MAYDWELL AVENUE
DOWNS LINK
Lackham
Slinfold Lodge
The Lodge
Hayeshill Copse
Works
RH13
Meadowhurst
Oldhouse Copse
Piggeries
Woodstock
Hall Land Rough
Rosemary
Russets
Black Barn Gill
Whitebreads
Wild Harry's
Holmbush Manor Farm
HAYES LANE
Bottlehouse Gills
Oak Leigh
Lucer
Hayes Grange
Highlands
Hill Croft
Holmbush Upper Rough
BRAMBLE HILL FARM
Black Barn Farm
Riddens Farm
Toat Hill Farm
TOAT HILL
Bottlehouse Copse
Toat Hill House
Lydwicke Farm
Toat Hill
Ranfold
Cousin's Copse
COUSINS COPSE CARAVAN SITE
HAYES LANE
Lydwicke
Furze Copse Farm
FIVE OAKS ROAD
A264
BASHURST COPSE
Chafers Copse
Holmbush Lwr. Rough
Toat Copse
Bashurst Copse
Lydwicke Hanger
Slinfold Manor
Eastedfield Wood
Weir
Lowertoat Farm
Firwood House
Rookerywood
Rookery Wood
BASHURST HILL
Hayes Park
Elmhurst Farm
Buckmans Corner
North Gill
South Gill
Thrales
Gleniffer Farm
ELMHURST LA.
Farm

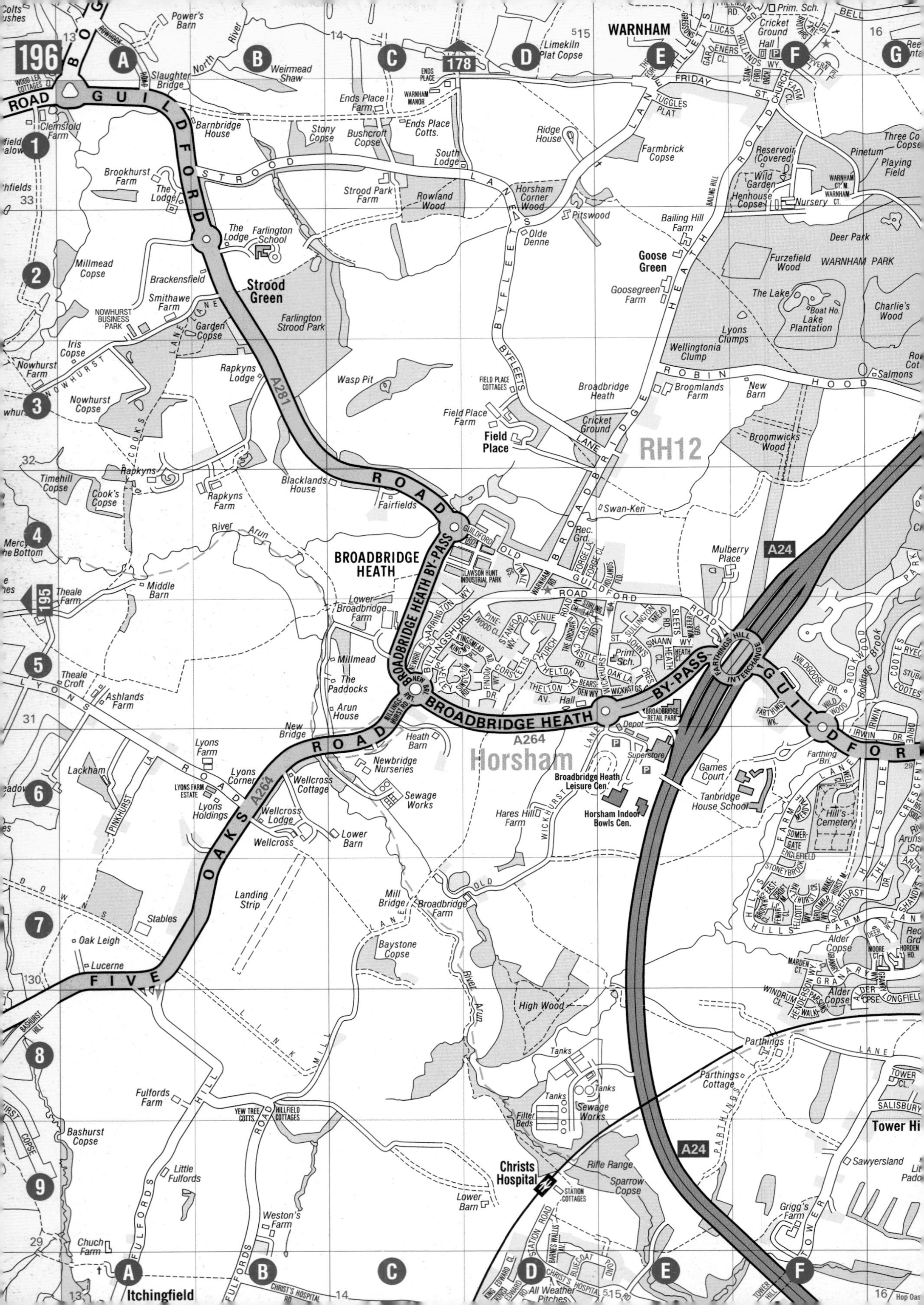
196
178
195
WARNHAM
BROADBRIDGE HEATH
Strood Green
Goose Green
Horsham
RH12
Field Place
Christs Hospital
Itchingfield
Tower Hill
GUILDFORD ROAD
A281
BROADBRIDGE HEATH BY-PASS
A264
FIVE OAKS ROAD
A24
WARNHAM PARK
Deer Park
Broadbridge Heath Leisure Cen.
Horsham Indoor Bowls Cen.
Tanbridge House School
Farlington School
Sewage Works
High Wood
Landing Strip

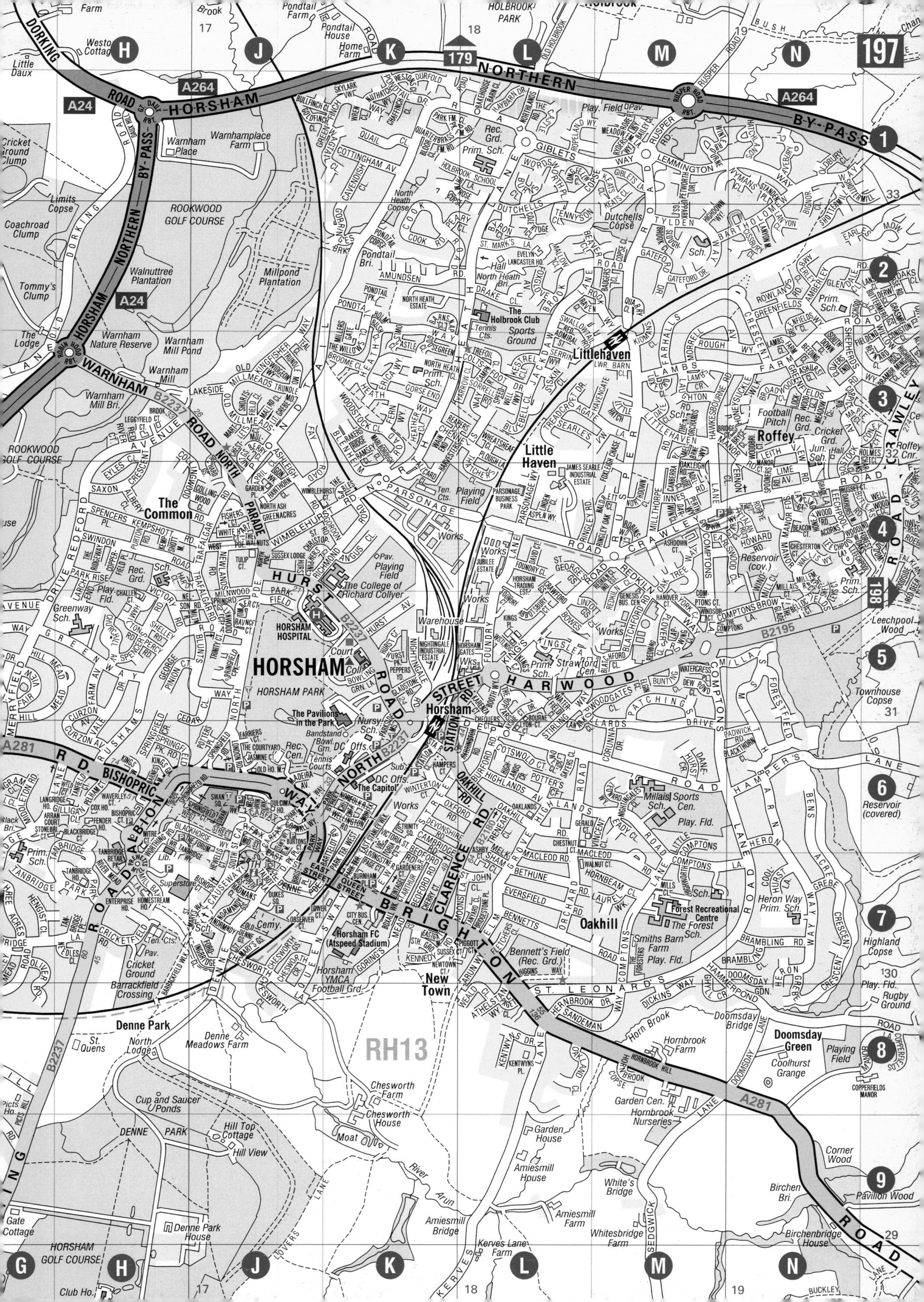
197
179
198
A264
A24
A281
B2237
B2195
B2180
NORTHERN BY-PASS
HORSHAM BY-PASS
NORTHERN
BY-PASS
DORKING ROAD
HORSHAM
Warnham Place
Warnhamplace Farm
ROOKWOOD GOLF COURSE
Limits Copse
Coachroad Clump
Cricket Ground Clump
Walnuttree Plantation
Millpond Plantation
Tommy's Clump
The Lodge
Warnham Nature Reserve
Warnham Mill Pond
Warnham Mill
Warnham Mill Bri.
WARNHAM ROAD
Little Daux
Weston Cottage
Pondtail Farm
Pondtail House
Home Farm
HOLBROOK PARK
Brook
Farm
Rec. Grd.
Prim. Sch.
North Heath Copse
Pondtail Bri.
North Heath Estate
The Holbrook Club Sports Ground
Tennis Cts.
Dutchells Copse
Littlehaven
Little Haven
James Searle Industrial Estate
Parsonage Business Park
Playing Field
The Common
Greenway Sch.
Rec. Grd.
Play. Fld.
The College of Richard Collyer
Playing Field
HORSHAM HOSPITAL
HORSHAM
HORSHAM PARK
The Pavilions in the Park
Court
Horsham
The Capitol
Superstore
Nightingale Industrial Estate
Warehouse
Works
Foundry
Horsham Trading Est.
Jubilee Estate
Genesis Bus. Cen.
Strawford Cen.
Roffey
Football Pitch
Cricket Grd.
Roffey Cnr.
Leechpool Wood
Townhouse Copse
Reservoir (covered)
Reservoir (cov.)
Millais Sch.
Sports Cen.
Play. Fld.
Oakhill
Forest Recreational Centre
The Forest Sch.
Smiths Barn Farm Play. Fld.
Heron Way Prim. Sch.
Highland Copse
Play. Fld.
Rugby Ground
Horsham FC (Atspeed Stadium)
Horsham YMCA Football Grd.
New Town
Bennett's Field (Rec. Grd.)
Cricket Ground
Barrackfield Crossing
Denne Park
St. Quens
North Lodge
Denne Meadows Farm
RH13
Chesworth Farm
Chesworth House
Cup and Saucer Ponds
Hill Top Cottage
Hill View
DENNE PARK
Moat
River Arun
Amiesmill Bridge
Amiesmill House
Amiesmill Farm
Garden House
Kerves Lane Farm
White's Bridge
Whitesbridge Farm
Garden Cen.
Hornbrook Nurseries
Hornbrook Farm
Horn Brook
Doomsday Bridge
Doomsday Green
Coolhurst Grange
Playing Field
Copperfields Manor
Corner Wood
Birchen Bri.
Pavilion Wood
Birchenbridge House
Gate Cottage
Denne Park House
HORSHAM GOLF COURSE
Club Ho.
Picts Ho.
BRIGHTON ROAD
HARWOOD ROAD
CRAWLEY ROAD
BISHOPRIC
ALBION WAY
NORTH PARADE
NORTH STREET
RUSPER ROAD
GREEN WAY
HURST ROAD
PARSONAGE ROAD
LEMMINGTON WAY
GIBLETS WAY
ST. LEONARDS WAY
HAMPERS LANE
COMPTONS LANE
SMITHS BARN
HIGHLANDS AV
CLARENCE RD.
OAKHILL RD.
STATION RD.
EAST STREET
QUEEN STREET
BUSH
G
H
J
K
L
M
N
1
2
3
4
5
6
7
8
9
17
18
19
29
30
31
32
33

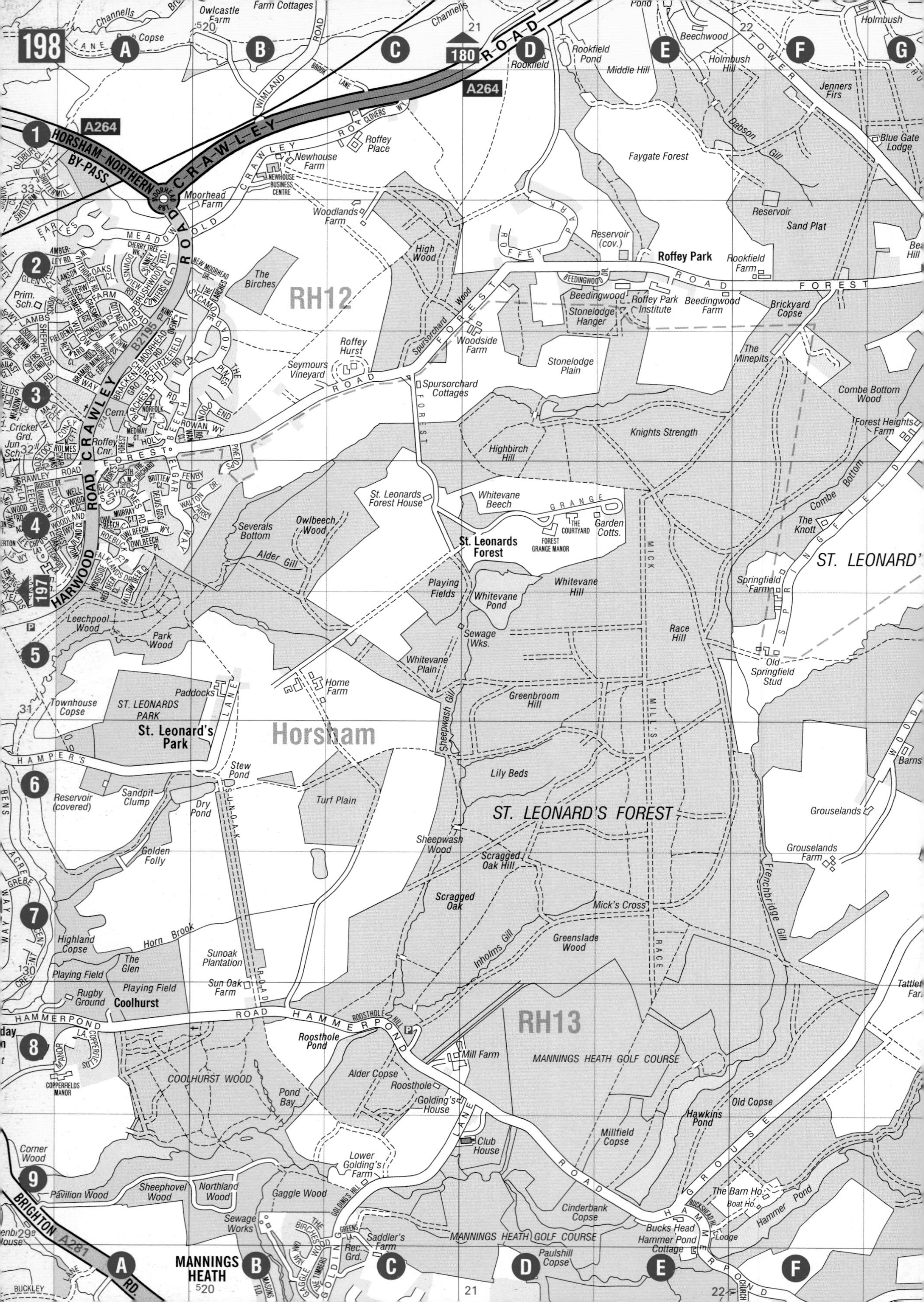

HORSHAM-NORTHERN BY-PASS
A264
CRAWLEY ROAD
Moorhead Farm
Newhouse Farm
Roffey Place
Woodlands Farm
High Wood
The Birches
RH12
Roffey Hurst
Seymours Vineyard
Spursorchard Wood
Woodside Farm
Spursorchard Cottages
FOREST ROAD
Roffey Park
Reservoir (cov.)
Beedingwood
Roffey Park Institute
Beedingwood Farm
Stonelodge Hanger
Stonelodge Plain
Brickyard Copse
The Minepits
Rookfield Farm
Rookfield Pond
Middle Hill
Faygate Forest
Beechwood
Holmbush Hill
Holmbush
Jenners Firs
Dabson Gill
Blue Gate Lodge
Reservoir
Sand Plat
Owlcastle Farm
Farm Cottages
Channells
Combe Bottom Wood
Forest Heights Farm
Knights Strength
Highbirch Hill
St. Leonards Forest House
Whitevane Beech
Forest Grange Manor
The Courtyard
Garden Cotts.
St. Leonards Forest
Severals Bottom
Owlbeech Wood
Alder Gill
Playing Fields
Whitevane Pond
Whitevane Hill
The Knott
Combe Bottom
ST. LEONARD'
Springfield Farm
Race Hill
Old Springfield Stud
Sewage Wks.
Whitevane Plain
Home Farm
Leechpool Wood
Park Wood
Paddocks
Townhouse Copse
ST. LEONARDS PARK
St. Leonard's Park
Horsham
Greenbroom Hill
Sheepwash Gill
Lily Beds
Turf Plain
ST. LEONARD'S FOREST
Stew Pond
Sandpit Clump
Reservoir (covered)
Dry Pond
Golden Folly
Sheepwash Wood
Scragged Oak Hill
Scragged Oak
Mick's Cross
Grouselands
Grouselands Farm
Frenchbridge Gill
Highland Copse
Horn Brook
Inholms Gill
Greenslade Wood
Sunoak Plantation
Sun Oak Farm
The Glen
Playing Field
Rugby Ground
Coolhurst
HAMMERPOND ROAD
Roosthole Pond
Mill Farm
RH13
MANNINGS HEATH GOLF COURSE
COOLHURST WOOD
Copperfields Manor
Alder Copse
Roosthole
Golding's House
Pond Bay
Old Copse
Hawkins Pond
Millfield Copse
Club House
Corner Wood
Lower Golding's Farm
Gaggle Wood
Pavilion Wood
Sheephovel Wood
Northland Wood
Sewage Works
Saddler's Farm
Rec. Grd.
Cinderbank Copse
The Barn Ho.
Boat Ho.
Hammer Pond
Bucks Head
Hammer Pond Cottage
Lodge
Paulshill Copse
MANNINGS HEATH
Tattle Far
Barns
BRIGHTON RD. A281
180
197

199
181
Foxhole Pond
Shephердsfield
Shepherdsfield Farm
COTTESMORE GOLF COURSE
Cottesmore School
House Pond
Playing Field
STABLE COTTAGES
PEASE POTTAGE FOREST
CRAWLEY STH. WEST BY-PASS
CRAWLEY
MID SUSSEX
PEASE POTTAGE GOLF COURSE
Hotel
Club House
Buchan House
HOLMBUSH FOREST
Black Hill Stud
Reservoir (covered)
Water Tower
Radar Station
Horsham Corner
Meteorological Station
Club Ho.
FOREST ROAD
HORSHAM ROAD
BLACK SWAN CL.
THE GREEN
HORSHAM RD.
BARN CL.
COLGATE
Colgate Prim. Sch.
THE WINCHES
Black Hill Wood
Crawley
Mast
PEASE POTTAGE
COTSFORD
Finches
BRIGHTON ROAD
BLACKHOUSE
Colgate Farm
Colgate Lodge
Shelley Cottages
Finches Shaw
A23
Hotel
Nursy.
BLACKHOUSE FARM IND. EST.
RH11
Southover Farm
Poultry House
Shelley Farm Cottages
Shelley Farm
OLD
TILGATE FOREST ROW
Tilgate Forest Row
Woodhurst Farm
Woodhurst
New Barn House
GROUSE ROAD
Furze Field
New Barn Farm
Shelley Middle Gill
Shelley Plain Farm
Hungry Down
Blindman's Wood
FOREST
Pyefall Gill
LANE
Greenbroom
Newstead Ghyll
Spring Farm
Woodhurst Plantation
Horse Bridge
BRIGHTON
B2114
NEW TREE COTTS.
The Pheasantry
The Larches
Desmond's Castle
Stone Edge Nursery
Cooper's Wood
Stedman's Wood
Woodlands House
Lythmere
Hyde Gill
Hydehill Wood
Peewit Ghyll
HORSHAM
MID SUSSEX
Nashland Wood
Elenge Plat Farm
Lower Grouse Farm
Newstead Farm
Nashlands Farm
Buttock Corner
Old Copse
Sandpits
Holkham's Corner
PIG POUND WALK
HOADLANDS COTTS.
Forest Lodge
Bunnyland
Hoggy Hole
Rough Park
Darkalley Gill
Hoadlands Farm
Mount Noddy
Wide Ride
Buckwheat Plantation
The Hyde
Home Beat
Haywards Heath
The Square
CEMETERY WK.
Duckhouse
Beechey Toll
Hoadlands Wood
Swiss Cott.
Hungry Bottom
Carter's Lodge
American Walk
Darkalley Pond
Upper Pond
Truckershatch Wood
Well Hill
TAYMANS TRACK
THE AVENUE
Fourteen Acre Wood
HANDCROSS
Carterslodge Pond
Chestnut Hill
RH17
WARREN COTTS.
Hall
CARTERSLODGE
Dropstone
Trucker's Hatch
WEST PARK ROAD
COVERT MEAD
Carter's Lodge
Truckers Ghyll
B2110
Badgers Plantation
Ashfold Cotts.
Hyde Gill
WARREN WOOD
Nostra Cottage
Hammerhill Wood
Ashfold Farm
Matcham's Grove
Scotchbank Wood
Homestead Wood
Marchant's Gill
High Beech Farm
Stoneraise
The Warren
Ashfold
West Park Farm
HORSHAM ROAD

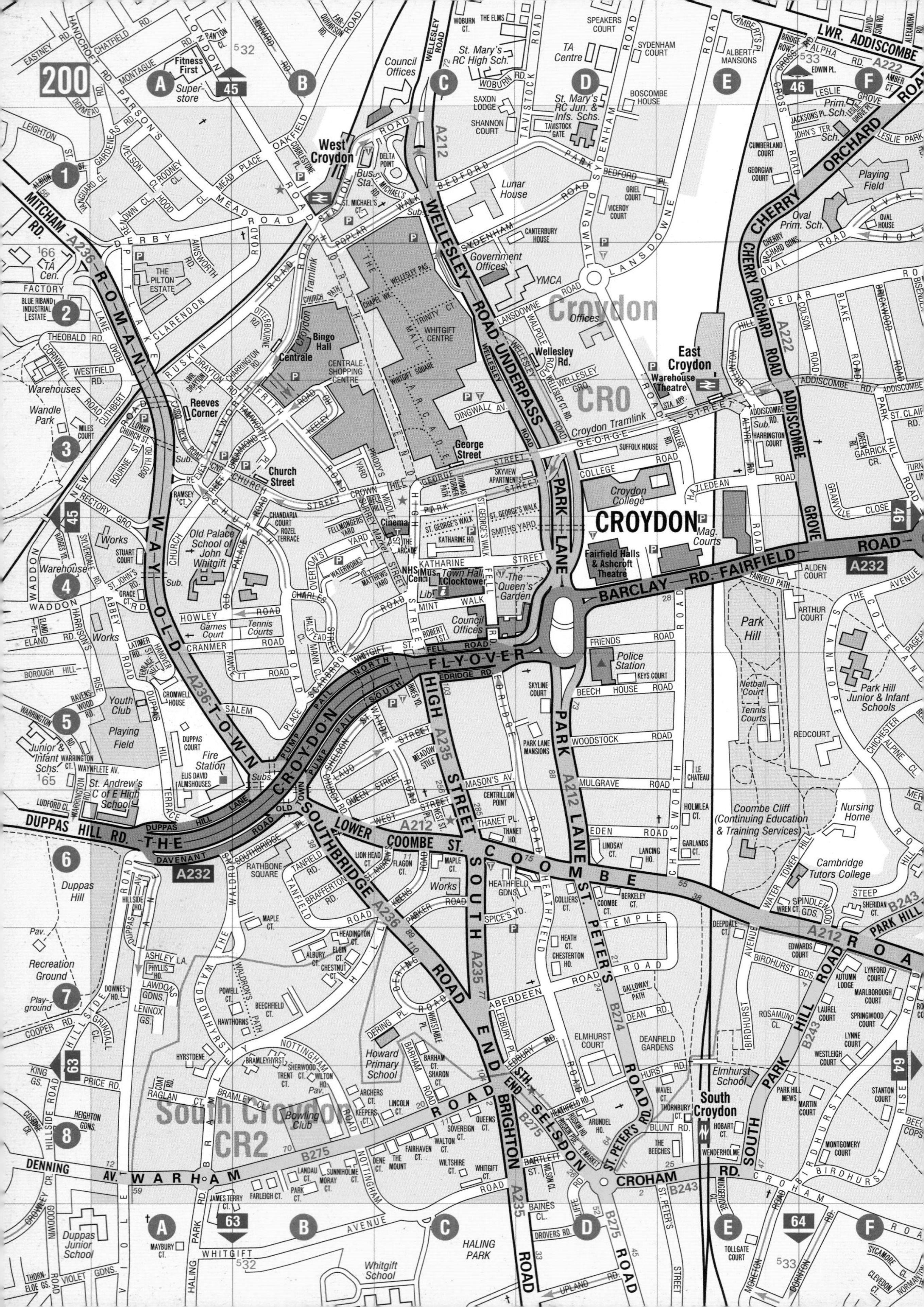

200
A
B
C
D
E
F
1
2
3
4
5
6
7
8
45
46
63
64
WEST CROYDON
West Croydon
East Croydon
CROYDON
Croydon
Offices
CR0
South Croydon
CR2
South Croydon
LWR. ADDISCOMBE
ADDISCOMBE RD.
ADDISCOMBE GROVE
CHERRY ORCHARD ROAD
CHERRY ORCHARD
A222
A232
A236
A212
A235
B274
B275
B243
MITCHAM RD.
ROMAN WAY
OLD TOWN
CROYDON FLYOVER
DUPPAS HILL RD.
THE DAVENANT
WELLESLEY ROAD UNDERPASS
WELLESLEY ROAD
PARK LANE
BARCLAY RD.
FAIRFIELD ROAD
GEORGE STREET
HIGH STREET
SOUTH END
BRIGHTON ROAD
SOUTHBRIDGE ROAD
LOWER COOMBE ST.
COOMBE ROAD
ST. PETER'S ROAD
SELSDON ROAD
CROHAM RD.
WARHAM AV.
DENNING AV.
SOUTH PARK HILL ROAD
PARK HILL ROAD
CHATSWORTH ROAD
LANSDOWNE ROAD
SYDENHAM ROAD
DINGWALL ROAD
TAVISTOCK ROAD
BEDFORD PARK
MEAD PLACE
DERBY ROAD
STATION ROAD
POPLAR WALK
CHURCH STREET
CROWN HILL
KATHARINE STREET
MINT WALK
FELL ROAD
CHARLES STREET
HOWLEY ROAD
CRANMER ROAD
WADDON NEW ROAD
WADDON
FRIENDS ROAD
BEECH HOUSE ROAD
WOODSTOCK ROAD
MULGRAVE ROAD
EDEN ROAD
TEMPLE ROAD
ABERDEEN ROAD
NOTTINGHAM ROAD
BRAMLEY HILL
HILLSIDE ROAD
COOPER RD.
PRICE RD.
WHITGIFT AVENUE
HALING PARK
Whitgift Centre
Centrale Shopping Centre
Bingo Hall
Lunar House
Government Offices
YMCA
Croydon Tramlink
Warehouse Theatre
Croydon College
Fairfield Halls & Ashcroft Theatre
Mag. Courts
Town Hall Clocktower
The Queen's Garden
Council Offices
Police Station
Park Hill
Park Hill Junior & Infant Schools
Coombe Cliff (Continuing Education & Training Services)
Nursing Home
Cambridge Tutors College
Oval Prim. Sch.
Playing Field
Old Palace School of John Whitgift
Reeves Corner
Church Street
George Street
Wellesley Rd.
Cinema
Fire Station
St. Andrew's C of E High School
Youth Club
Wandle Park
Duppas Hill
Recreation Ground
Howard Primary School
Bowling Club
Elmhurst School
Duppas Junior School
Whitgift School
St. Mary's RC High Sch.
St. Mary's RC Jun. & Infs. Schs.
TA Centre
Fitness First
Super-store
Works
Warehouses

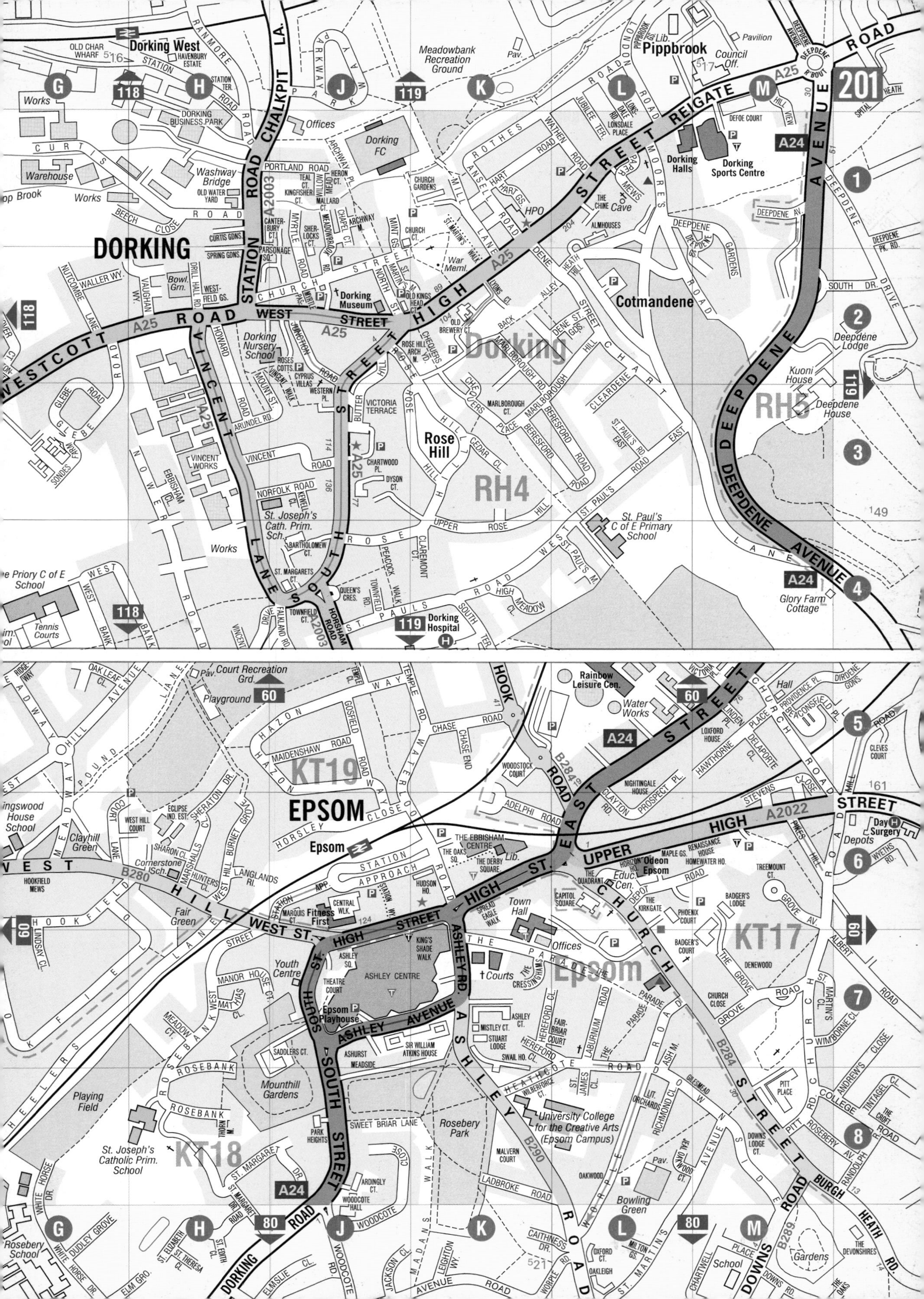
DORKING
Dorking West
Pippbrook
Meadowbank Recreation Ground
Dorking FC
Dorking Halls
Dorking Sports Centre
Council Off.
Cotmandene
Dorking Museum
Rose Hill
Deepdene Lodge
Kuoni House
Deepdene House
St. Joseph's Cath. Prim. Sch.
St. Paul's C of E Primary School
Dorking Hospital
Glory Farm Cottage
RH4
RH5
201
118
119
A25
A24
A2003
REIGATE ROAD
DEEPDENE AVENUE
HIGH STREET
WEST STREET
WESTCOTT ROAD
STATION ROAD
CHALKPIT LA.
VINCENT LANE
SOUTH STREET
EPSOM
Epsom
KT17
KT18
KT19
60
80
A2022
B280
B284
B289
B290
Court Recreation Grd.
Rainbow Leisure Cen.
Epsom Playhouse
ASHLEY CENTRE
Town Hall
Mounthill Gardens
Rosebery Park
University College for the Creative Arts (Epsom Campus)
St. Joseph's Catholic Prim. School
Rosebery School
Bowling Green
Playing Field
Fair Green
Clayhill Green
Kingswood House School
HIGH STREET
EAST STREET
UPPER HIGH ST
WEST HILL
ASHLEY AVENUE
ASHLEY ROAD
SOUTH STREET
DORKING ROAD
CHURCH STREET
WORPLE ROAD
DOWNS ROAD
BURGH HEATH RD.
Odeon Epsom
Day Surgery

LADYMEAD
STOKE PARK
WOODBRIDGE ROAD
STOKE ROAD
Guildford
GUILDFORD
GU1
GU2
YORK ROAD
HIGH STREET
EPSOM ROAD
LONDON ROAD
CHERTSEY ST.
FARNHAM ROAD
PORTSMOUTH ROAD
MILLBROOK
QUARRY ST.
SHALFORD ROAD
STOKE PARK
Recreation Ground
Sports Ground
Guildford College (Stoke Park Campus)
Guildford Lido
The Workshop Gym
Bowling Greens
Playing Field
Home Farm
Nursery
Guildford High School
London Road
University of Surrey
Crown Court
Odeon Cinema
Law Courts
The Friary
Bus Station
YMCA
The Electric Theatre
Guildhall & Guildford Ho. Gallery
Library
Allen Ho. Gardens
Royal Grammar School
Sandfield Primary School
Guildford Adult Learning Centre
Medieval Undercroft
Guildford Castle
Yvonne Arnaud Theatre
Guildford Boat Ho.
Guildford Borough Council Offices
Rack's Close
Pewley Hill
Pewley Down Infant School
Reservoir (covered)
MOUNT ALVERNIA BMI HOSP.
FARNHAM ROAD HOSPITAL
Guildford County School
St. Nicolas' C of E Infant Sch.
Cemetery
Guildford Sch. of Acting
RIVER WEY
Spectrum Leisure Centre & Guildford Spectrum Bowl
Superstore
Works
113
114

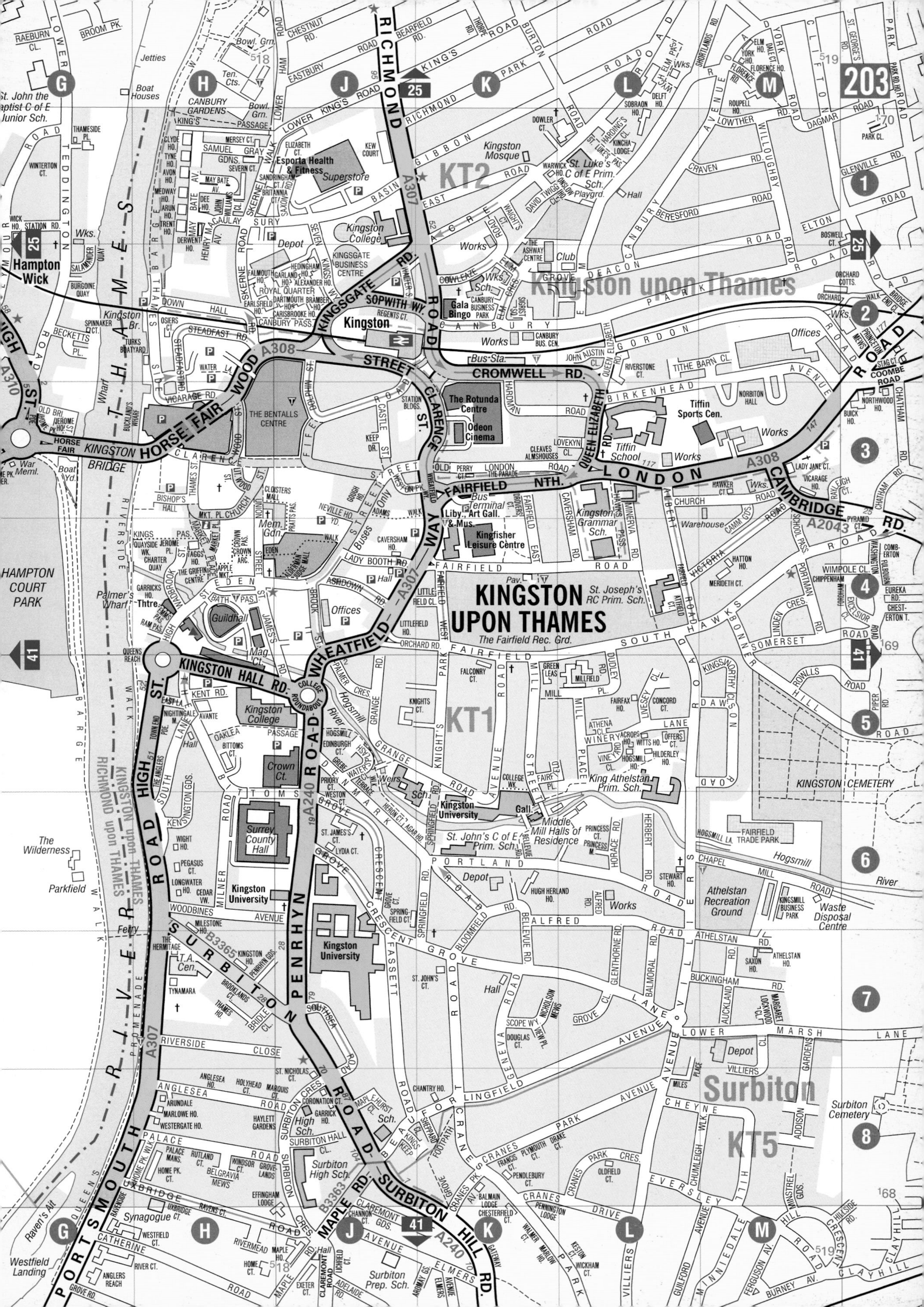

203
KINGSTON UPON THAMES
Kingston upon Thames
KT1
KT2
KT5
Surbiton
Kingston
HAMPTON COURT PARK
Hampton Wick
RIVER THAMES
KINGSTON upon THAMES
RICHMOND upon THAMES
KINGSTON CEMETERY
Surbiton Cemetery
The Wilderness
Parkfield
Raven's Ait
Westfield Landing
Palmer's Wharf
Kingston Br.
KINGSTON BRIDGE
CANBURY GARDENS
The Rotunda Centre
Odeon Cinema
THE BENTALLS CENTRE
Tiffin Sports Cen.
Tiffin School
Kingston Grammar Sch.
Kingfisher Leisure Centre
Liby., Art Gall. & Mus.
Bus Terminal
The Fairfield Rec. Grd.
St. Joseph's RC Prim. Sch.
King Athelstan Prim. Sch.
Middle Mill Halls of Residence
St. John's C of E Prim. Sch.
Kingston University
Kingston College
Surrey County Hall
Crown Ct.
Guildhall
Athelstan Recreation Ground
FAIRFIELD TRADE PARK
Waste Disposal Centre
KINGSMILL BUSINESS PARK
Surbiton High Sch.
Surbiton Prep. Sch.
Synagogue
Kingston Mosque
Esporta Health & Fitness
Superstore
Gala Bingo
KINGSGATE BUSINESS CENTRE
ROYAL QUARTER
St. Luke's C of E Prim. Sch.
Hogsmill River
RICHMOND ROAD
KINGSGATE RD.
CLARENCE ST.
WHEATFIELD WAY
HORSE FAIR
WOOD ST.
LONDON RD.
CAMBRIDGE RD.
PENRHYN ROAD
PORTSMOUTH ROAD
SURBITON ROAD
SURBITON HILL RD.
KINGSTON HALL RD.
HIGH ST.
CROMWELL RD.
FAIRFIELD NTH.
QUEEN ELIZABETH RD.
A307
A308
A240
A310
A2043
B3363
B3365
25
41
18
19
68
69
70
G
H
J
K
L
M
1
2
3
4
5
6
7
8

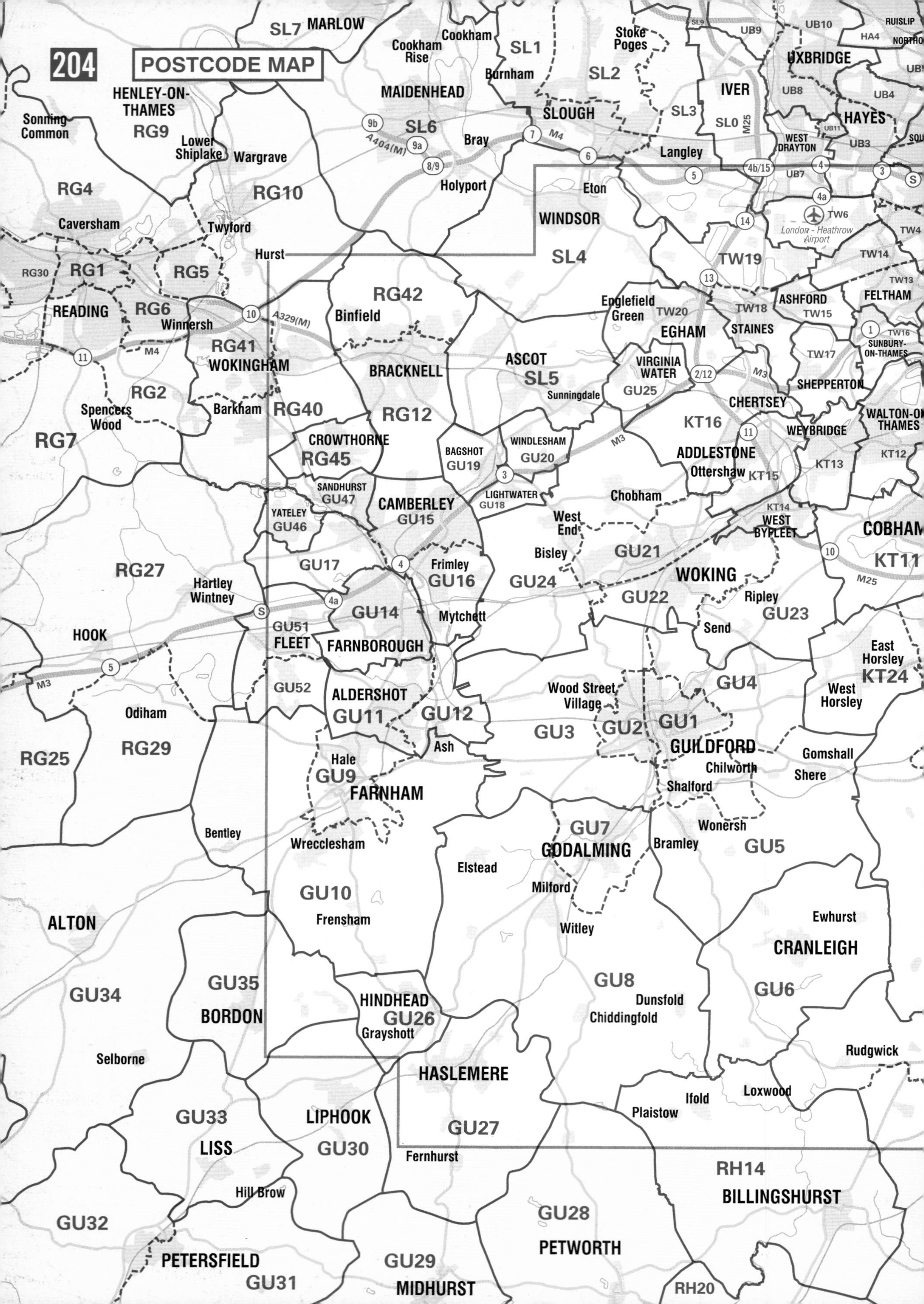

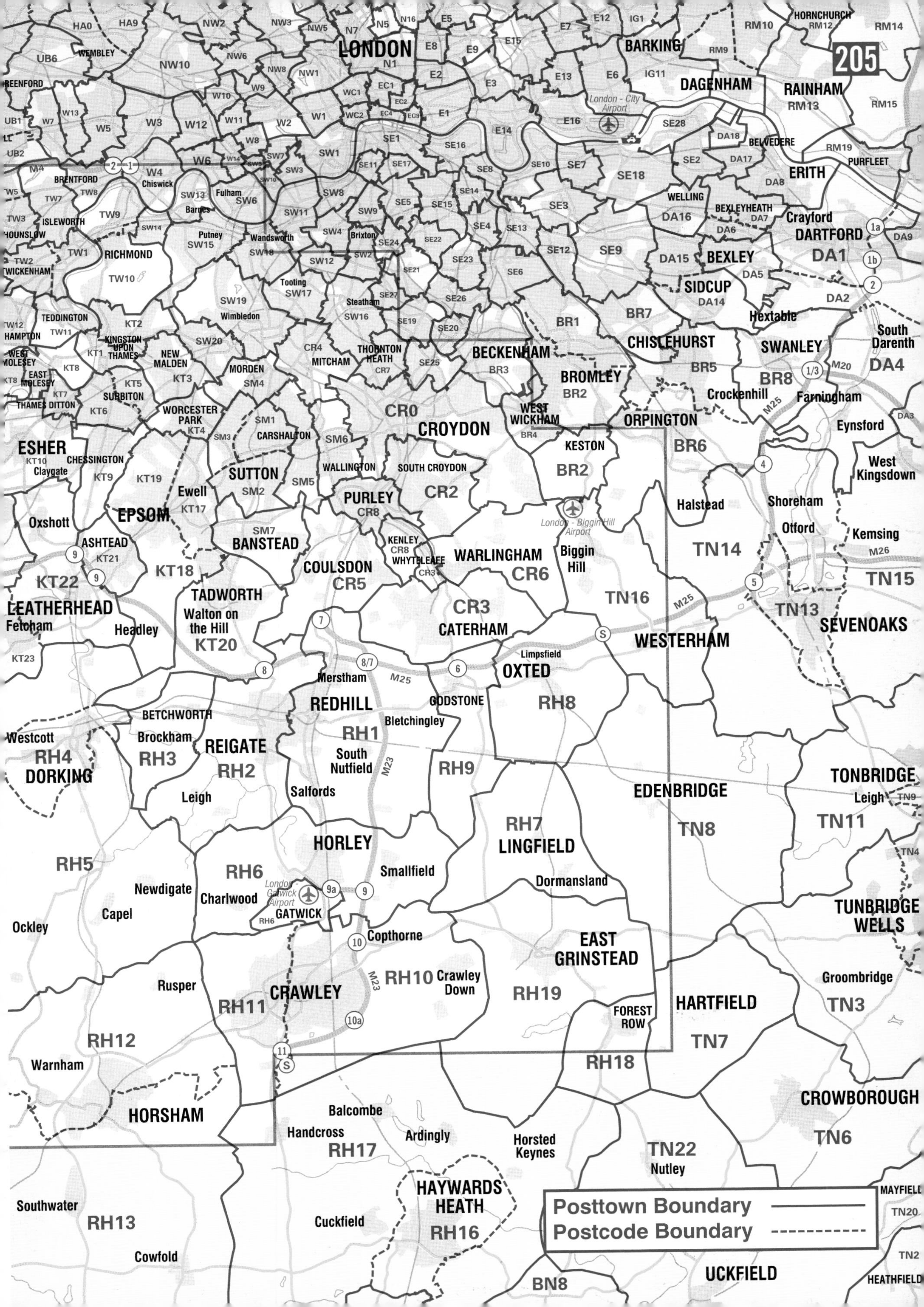
HA0
HA9
NW2
NW3
NW5
N7
N5
N16
E5
E7
E12
IG1
RM10
HORNCHURCH
RM12
RM14
LONDON
N1
E8
E9
E15
BARKING
RM9
WEMBLEY
NW10
NW6
UB6
NW8
NW1
E2
E13
E6
IG11
DAGENHAM
RAINHAM
RM13
RM15
REENFORD
W9
W10
WC1
EC1
E3
London - City Airport
EC2
W13
W7
W5
W3
W12
W11
W2
W1
WC2
EC4
EC3
E1
E16
SE28
UB1
W8
SE1
E14
DA18
BELVEDERE
RM19
PURFLEET
UB2
SE16
SW1
W6
W14
SW7
W4
M4
Chiswick
SW5
SW3
SW10
SE11
SE17
SE8
SE10
SE7
SE18
SE2
DA17
ERITH
BRENTFORD
TW8
DA8
TW5
TW7
SW13
Fulham
SW6
SW8
SE14
Barnes
SE5
SE15
SE3
WELLING
BEXLEYHEATH
Crayford
TW3
ISLEWORTH
TW9
SW11
SW9
DA16
DA7
HOUNSLOW
SW14
Putney
SW15
SW4
Brixton
SE4
SE13
DA6
DARTFORD
DA9
Wandsworth
SE22
SE24
TW2
TW1
RICHMOND
SW18
SW12
SW2
SE12
SE9
DA15
BEXLEY
DA1
TWICKENHAM
SE21
SE23
TW10
SE6
DA5
Tooting
SW17
SIDCUP
DA14
DA2
SE27
Steatham
SE26
SW19
Wimbledon
SW16
Hextable
TW12
TEDDINGTON
KT2
BR1
BR7
South Darenth
HAMPTON
TW11
SE19
SE20
CHISLEHURST
SWANLEY
KINGSTON UPON THAMES
SW20
CR4
THORNTON HEATH
KT1
NEW MALDEN
MITCHAM
BECKENHAM
BR5
M20
WEST MOLESEY
KT8
MORDEN
SE25
BR3
BROMLEY
BR8
DA4
KT3
CR7
EAST MOLESEY
KT5
SM4
BR2
Crockenhill
Farningham
KT7
SURBITON
THAMES DITTON
KT6
WORCESTER PARK
KT4
CR0
WEST WICKHAM
ORPINGTON
M25
DA3
SM1
CARSHALTON
CROYDON
Eynsford
ESHER
SM3
SM6
BR4
KT10
CHESSINGTON
KESTON
BR6
Claygate
KT9
KT19
SUTTON
WALLINGTON
SOUTH CROYDON
West Kingsdown
BR2
Ewell
SM2
SM5
CR2
EPSOM
PURLEY
CR8
Halstead
Shoreham
Oxshott
KT17
London - Biggin Hill Airport
SM7
Otford
ASHTEAD
BANSTEAD
KENLEY
Kemsing
KT21
CR8
Biggin Hill
TN14
WHYTELEAFE
WARLINGHAM
M26
KT18
COULSDON
CR3
CR6
KT22
CR5
TN15
TADWORTH
TN16
LEATHERHEAD
Walton on the Hill
CR3
TN13
Fetcham
Headley
CATERHAM
SEVENOAKS
KT20
WESTERHAM
KT23
Limpsfield
Merstham
OXTED
M25
RH8
BETCHWORTH
REDHILL
GODSTONE
Bletchingley
Westcott
Brockham
RH1
REIGATE
RH4
RH3
RH2
South Nutfield
RH9
TONBRIDGE
DORKING
M23
EDENBRIDGE
Leigh
Salfords
Leigh
TN9
TN11
RH7
LINGFIELD
TN8
HORLEY
TN4
RH5
RH6
Smallfield
Newdigate
Dormansland
Charlwood
London Gatwick Airport
TUNBRIDGE WELLS
Capel
GATWICK
RH6
Ockley
Copthorne
EAST GRINSTEAD
RH10
Crawley Down
Groombridge
Rusper
CRAWLEY
RH19
HARTFIELD
RH11
TN3
FOREST ROW
RH12
TN7
RH18
Warnham
CROWBOROUGH
HORSHAM
Balcombe
Handcross
Ardingly
Horsted Keynes
TN6
RH17
TN22
Nutley
HAYWARDS HEATH
MAYFIELD
Posttown Boundary
Postcode Boundary
Southwater
RH13
Cuckfield
RH16
TN20
Cowfold
TN2
UCKFIELD
BN8
HEATHFIELD

Nuffield
Nettlebed
Crocker End
Bix
Middle Assendon
Fawley
Hambleden
MARLOW
Bourne End
Hedgerley
Farnham Common
M40
Tatling End
Ickenham
Highmoor
Lower Assendon
Mill End
Abbey
Bisham
Cookham Dean
Cookham
Egypt
Stoke Poges
New Denham
UXBRIDGE
Hillingdon
Witheridge Hill
Maharajah's Well
Greys Court
Fawley Court
Aston
Remenham
Medmenham
Hurley
A404
Cookham Rise
East Burnham
Stoke Row
Satwell
Shepherd's Green
Checkendon
Wyfold Grange
Exlade Street
Rotherfield Greys
HENLEY -ON- THAMES
Remenham Hill
Pinkneys Green
Burnham
Farnham Royal
Wexham Street
Black Park
Iver Heath
Cowley
Gallowstree Common
Rotherfield Peppard
Harpsden
Cockpole Green
Burchett's Green
MAIDENHEAD
Taplow
SLOUGH
George Green
Shredding Green
Richings Park
West Drayton
Yiewsley
Sonning Common
Crazies Hill
Warren Row
Knowl Hill
Littlewick Green
Bray
Bray Wick
Cippenham
Langley
Cane End
Kidmore End
Binfield Heath
Lower Shiplake
Wargrave
Kiln Green
Woodlands Park
A404(M)
Dorney
Eton Wick
Upton
Sutton
Goring Heath
Tokers Green
Dunsden Green
Shiplake
Hare Hatch
White Waltham
Boveney
Eton
Harmondsworth
Sipson
Pangbourne
Mapledurham
Emmer Green
Charvil
Sonning
Waltham St. Lawrence
M4
Holyport
Moneyrow Green
Fifield
Oakley Green
Windsor
Datchet
Colnbrook
Poyle
Longford
Caversham Heights
Caversham
Play Hatch
Twyford
Ruscombe
West End
Touchen-end
Paley Street
WINDSOR
Horton
LONDON HEATHROW
Shurlock Row
Whistley Green
Hurst
Hawthorn Hill
Legoland
Frogmore House
Old Windsor
Wraysbury
M25
Stanwell Moor
Stanwell
Tilehurst
Woodley
Maiden's Green
Cranbourne
WINDSOR GREAT PARK
Hythe End
A30
East Bedfont
Calcot Row
READING
Earley
Winnersh
Binfield
Warfield
Newell Green
Winkfield
Winkfield Row
Woodside
Englefield Green
Egham Hythe
ASHFORD
A33
Popeswood
Priestwood
Burleigh
North Ascot
Savill
Obelisk
Runnymede
STAINES
A308
Trash Green
Sindlesham
Emmbrook
Bowlesgreen
Cheapside
Ascot
Virginia Water
EGHAM
Thorpe
Queen Mary Resr.
Burghfield
Three Mile Cross
Shinfield
WOKINGHAM
A329
BRACKNELL
South Ascot
Sunningdale
Laleham
Littleton
Burghfield Hill
Grazeley
Arborfield
Arborfield Cross
Eastheath
Easthampstead
Sunninghill
Trumps Green
Burghfield Common
Spencers Wood
Barkham
Gardeners Green
Broomhall
CHERTSEY
Shepperton
Lyne
Stratfield Mortimer
Beech Hill
Swallowfield
Arborfield Garrison
Look Out Discovery Centre
A322
Windlesham
Longcross
WEYBRIDGE
Farley Hill
Wick Hill
Crowthorne
Surrey Hill
Bagshot
Addlestone
Riseley
Finchampstead
Valley End
Burrowhill
Ottershaw
New Haw
Row Town
West End Green
Stratfield Saye
Eversley
Eversley Cross
Sandhurst
Little Sandhurst
CAMBERLEY
Lightwater
Chobham
Fairoaks
Woodham
Bramshill
Wellington
Fair Oak Green
Heckfield
Frogmore
Donkey Town
West End
Castle Green
Mimbridge
Bramley Green
Stratfield Turgis
Yateley
Cricket Hill
Blackwater
Frimley
Bisley
Horsell
Sheerwater
West Byfleet
Byfleet
Hazeley
Forest of Eversley
Hawley
Knaphill
Pyrford
Wisley
Sherfield on Loddon
Turgis Green
Hound Green
Mattingley
Dipley
Hartfordbridge
Fox Lane
Frimley Green
Deepcut
Brookwood
WOKING
Old Woking
Ripley
Martyr's Green
Hartley Wespall
Church End
Lyde Green
West Green
Hartley Wintney
FLEET
M3
West Heath
Mychett
Mayford
Send Marsh
Ockham
Rotherwick
Phoenix Green
Murrell Green
Elvetham Heath
Cove
A331
Pirbright
Cartbridge
Send
Burntcommon
A3
Chineham
Newnham
Hook
Winchfield
Pondtail
FARNBOROUGH
Basingstoke Canal Centre
Fox Corner
Worplesdon
Sutton Green
Nately Scures
Fleet
Ash Vale
Pitch Place
Jacobswell
Old Basing
Andwell
Dogmersfield
Church Crookham
Crookham Village
West Clandon
East Clandon
West Horsley
Up Nately
North Warnborough
Whitehall
ALDERSHOT
Willey Green
Fairlands
Stoughton
Burpham
Merrow
Mapledurwell
Greywell
Odiham
Hillside
Ewshot
Wyke
Normandy
Wood Street Village
Hatchlands
Mill Lane
Upper Hale
Weybourne
Ash
Flexford
Onslow Village
GUILDFORD
Tunworth
Winslade
Upton Grey
NORTH
Crondall
Warren Corner
Hale
Badshot Lea
Tongham
Wanborough
A31
Gomshall
Long Sutton
South Warnborough
Well
FARNHAM
Runfold
Seale
Puttenham
Compton
Littleton
Chilworth
Shalford
Albury
Shere
Abinger Hammer
Weston Patrick
Herriard
Dippenhall
The Sands
Crooksbury Hill
Shackleford
Peasmarsh
Farncombe
Blackheath
Brook
Sutton Abinger
Southrope
Jenkyn Place
Bentley
Wrecclesham
Waverley
Charleshill
Hurtmore
Bramley
Wonersh
Farley Green
Peaslake
Lower Froyle
The Bourne
Peper Harow
Eashing
Catteshall
GODALMING
Shamley Green
Golden Pot
Holt Pound
Rowledge
Tilford
Lasham
Upper Froyle
Bucks Horn Oak
Millbridge
Elstead
Milford
Busbridge
Thorncombe Street
Hurtwood Common
Shalden
Holybourne
Spreakley
Frensham
Little Pond
Frensham Common
Rushmoor
Thursley
Tuesley
Hydestile
Winkworth Arboretum
Grafham
Rowly
Ewhurst
Alton
Binsted
Blacknest
Batt's Corner
Wheatley
Crosswater Farm
Wheelerstreet
Witley
Hascombe
Cranleigh
Bentworth
Holt End
Wyck
Kingsley
Churt
Bowlhead Green
Wormley
Hambledon
Loxhill
Wivelrod
Beech
Jane Austen's House
B3004
East Worldham
Sleaford
Barford
Beacon Hill
Devil's Punch Bowl
Brook
Sandhills
Vachery Pond
Medstead
Chawton
Chawton Park Wood
West Worldham
Hartley Mauditt
Lindford
Arford
Gibbet Hill
Combe Common
Dunsfold
Alfold Crossways
South Town
Upper Farringdon
Oakhanger
Bordon
Hindhead
Chiddingfold
Old Thorn
Highstreet Green
Ellen's Green
Soldridge
Mid Hants Railway (Watercress Line)
Lower Farringdon
Gilbert White's
Whitehill
Headley
Headley Down
Grayshott
Grayswood
Four Marks
Standford
Passfield
Fir Tree Copse
Sidney Wood
Alfold
Alfold Bars
Newton Valence
Selborne
Blackmoor
Bramshott
Killinghurst
Haslemere
Bucks Green
Kitwood
Rotherfield Park
Conford
Shottermill
Ramsnest Common
East Tisted
Empshott
Greatham
DANGER AREAS
Hammer
Camelsdale
Haste Hill
Anstead Brook
Loxwood
Tisman's Common
Charlwood
Monkwood
Colemore
Griggs Green
Bohunt Manor
Linchmere
Fisherstreet
The Lake
Ifold
Plaistow
Longmoor Camp
Liphook
Shulbrede Priory
Kingsley Green
Black Down
Roundhurst Common
Hawkley
Liss Forest
Langley
Hollycombe Steam Collection
West Tisted
The Warren
Warren Corner
Liss
Fernhurst Ironworks
Lurgashall Winery
Northchapel
Ebernoe Brickworks
Roundstreet Common
Five Oaks
Oakshott
East Liss
Wardley
Newpound Common
High Cross
Rake
Milland
Woodmansgreen
Dial Green
Lurgashall
Ebernoe Common
Kirdford
Bailey Green
Privett
Stoner Hill
Hill Brow
Redford
Balls Cross
A272
Steep
Tullecombe
Froxfield Green
Church Common
Sheet
Borden
Henley
SCALE
1: 250,000
3 Miles
5 Kilometres
Wisborough Green
Ripling
Lower Bordean
Stroud
Fyning
Strood Green
Parbrook
Langrish
PETERSFIELD
B2199
Rogate
Chithurst
Iping
Woolbeding
Lodsworth
River
Upperton
Adversane
Habin

LONDON
RUISLIP
NORTHOLT
WEMBLEY
WILLESDEN
HAMPSTEAD
CAMDEN TOWN
ISLINGTON
HACKNEY
LEYTON
STRATFORD
ILFORD
BARKING
HORNCHURCH
DAGENHAM
Rainham
GREENFORD
EALING
ACTON
PADDINGTON
MARYLEBONE
FINSBURY
SHOREDITCH
BETHNAL GREEN
STEPNEY
POPLAR
WEST HAM
EAST HAM
CITY
WEST END
SOUTHALL
HESTON
Brentford
CHISWICK
KENSINGTON
WESTMINSTER
BERMONDSEY
CHELSEA
LAMBETH
HAMMERSMITH
BARNES
FULHAM
DEPTFORD
GREENWICH
WOOLWICH
ERITH
CAMBERWELL
BATTERSEA
BRIXTON
ISLEWORTH
HOUNSLOW
RICHMOND
PUTNEY
CLAPHAM
LEWISHAM
Bexleyheath
DARTFORD
ELTHAM
Bexley
WANDSWORTH
TWICKENHAM
CATFORD
SIDCUP
WIMBLEDON
STREATHAM
TEDDINGTON
Penge
CHISLEHURST
Swanley
KINGSTON UPON THAMES
MERTON
MITCHAM
BECKENHAM
BROMLEY
MORDEN
NEW MALDEN
SURBITON
WALTON-ON-THAMES
ORPINGTON
CARSHALTON
CROYDON
ESHER
SUTTON
WALLINGTON
Farnborough
EWELL
PURLEY
New Addington
EPSOM
Ashtead
BANSTEAD
COULSDON
Biggin Hill
Otford
LEATHERHEAD
WARLINGHAM
Fetcham
CATERHAM
Great Bookham
Westerham
SEVENOAKS
Oxted
REDHILL
REIGATE
DORKING
Edenbridge
HORLEY
Lingfield
Penshurst
LONDON GATWICK
CRAWLEY
EAST GRINSTEAD
Forest Row
Hartfield
CROWBOROUGH
HORSHAM
ASHDOWN FOREST
HAYWARDS HEATH
Cuckfield
Lindfield
Balcombe
Handcross
M25
M23
M26
M4
A23
A22
A24
A3
A264
A272
A21
A20
A2
A13
A26

INDEX

Including Streets, Places & Areas, Industrial Estates, Selected Flats & Walkways,
Junction Names, Service Areas, Stations and Selected Places of Interest.

HOW TO USE THIS INDEX

1. Each street name is followed by its Postcode District (or, if outside the London Postcodes, by its Locality abbreviation(s)) and then by its map reference;
e.g. **Aaron's Hill** GU7: Goda . . . .7E **132** is in the GU7 Postcode District and the Godalming Locality and is to be found in square 7E on page **132**. The page number is shown in bold type.

2. A strict alphabetical order is followed in which Av., Rd., St., etc. (though abbreviated) are read in full and as part of the street name;
e.g. **Apple Trees Pl.** appears after **Appletree Pl.** but before **Appletree Way**

3. Streets and a selection of flats and walkways too small to be shown on the maps, appear in the index with the thoroughfare to which it is connected shown in brackets;
e.g. **Abbeyfield** *GU1: Guil* . . . .4B **114** *(off Lwr. Edgeborough Rd.)*

4. Addresses that are in more than one part are referred to as not continuous.

5. Places and areas are shown in the index in BLUE TYPE and the map reference is to the actual map square in which the town centre or area is located and not to the place name shown on the map;
e.g. **ADDLESTONE** 1L **55**

6. An example of a selected place of interest is *Berkshire Yeomanry Mus.* 7G **4**

7. An example of a station is **Addlestone Station (Rail)** 1M **55**
Included are Rail **(Rail)**, Croydon Tramlink **(CT)**, Riverbus **(Riverbus)**, London Underground Stations **(Tube)** and Park and Ride **(Park & Ride)**

8. Junction names and Service Areas are shown in the index in **BOLD CAPITAL TYPE**; e.g. **APEX CORNER** 4N **23**

9. Map references for entries that appear on large scale pages **200-203** are shown first, with small scale map references shown in brackets; e.g. **Abbey Rd.** CR0: Croy 4A **200** (9M **45**)

GENERAL ABBREVIATIONS

All. : Alley	**Cl.** : Close	**Ga.** : Gate	**Mdws.** : Meadows	**Sth.** : South
App. : Approach	**Coll.** : College	**Gt.** : Great	**M.** : Mews	**Sq.** : Square
Arc. : Arcade	**Comn.** : Common	**Grn.** : Green	**Mt.** : Mount	**Sta.** : Station
Av. : Avenue	**Cnr.** : Corner	**Gro.** : Grove	**Mus.** : Museum	**St.** : Street
Blvd. : Boulevard	**Cott.** : Cottage	**Hgts.** : Heights	**Nth.** : North	**Ter.** : Terrace
Bri. : Bridge	**Cotts.** : Cottages	**Ho.** : House	**Pal.** : Palace	**Twr.** : Tower
B'way. : Broadway	**Ct.** : Court	**Ho's.** : Houses	**Pde.** : Parade	**Trad.** : Trading
Bldg. : Building	**Cres.** : Crescent	**Ind.** : Industrial	**Pk.** : Park	**Up.** : Upper
Bldgs. : Buildings	**Cft.** : Croft	**Info.** : Information	**Pas.** : Passage	**Va.** : Vale
Bungs. : Bungalows	**Dr.** : Drive	**Intl.** : International	**Pl.** : Place	**Vw.** : View
Bus. : Business	**E.** : East	**Junc.** : Junction	**Pct.** : Precinct	**Vs.** : Villas
Cvn. : Caravan	**Ent.** : Enterprise	**La.** : Lane	**Prom.** : Promenade	**Vis.** : Visitors
C'way. : Causeway	**Est.** : Estate	**Lit.** : Little	**Quad.** : Quadrant	**Wlk.** : Walk
Cen. : Centre	**Fld.** : Field	**Lwr.** : Lower	**Res.** : Residential	**W.** : West
Chu. : Church	**Flds.** : Fields	**Mnr.** : Manor	**Ri.** : Rise	**Yd.** : Yard
Chyd. : Churchyard	**Gdn.** : Garden	**Mans.** : Mansions	**Rd.** : Road	
Circ. : Circle	**Gdns.** : Gardens	**Mkt.** : Market	**Rdbt.** : Roundabout	
Cir. : Circus	**Gth.** : Garth	**Mdw.** : Meadow	**Shop.** : Shopping	

LOCALITY ABBREVIATIONS

A Com : **Abinger Common**	Char : **Charlwood**	Esh : **Esher**	Horl : **Horley**	North : **Northchapel**
A Ham : **Abinger Hammer**	Chea : **Cheam**	Eton : **Eton**	Horn : **Horne**	Nth H : **North Holmwood**
A'ton : **Addington**	Chels : **Chelsfield**	E Wic : **Eton Wick**	Hors : **Horsham**	N Hil : **Norwood Hill**
Addl : **Addlestone**	Chert : **Chertsey**	Ewe : **Ewell**	Hort : **Horton**	Nut : **Nutfield**
Alb : **Albury**	Ches : **Chessington**	Ewh : **Ewhurst**	Houn : **Hounslow**	Oak : **Oakwoodhill**
Alde : **Aldershot**	Chid : **Chiddingfold**	Ews : **Ewshot**	Hurst : **Hurst**	Ockh : **Ockham**
Alf : **Alfold**	Chil : **Chilworth**	Farnb : **Farnborough**	Hurt : **Hurtmore**	Ockl : **Ockley**
Art : **Artington**	Chip : **Chipstead**	Farnh : **Farnham**	Ifi : **Ifield**	O Win : **Old Windsor**
Asc : **Ascot**	Chob : **Chobham**	Fay : **Faygate**	Ifo : **Ifold**	Orp : **Orpington**
Ash : **Ash**	C Cro : **Church Crookham**	Fel : **Felbridge**	Isle : **Isleworth**	Otter : **Ottershaw**
A'ford : **Ashford**	Churt : **Churt**	Felc : **Felcourt**	Itch : **Itchingfield**	Out : **Outwood**
A Grn : **Ash Green**	Clay : **Claygate**	Felt : **Feltham**	J Wel : **Jacobs Well**	Owls : **Owlsmoor**
A'tead : **Ashtead**	Cob : **Cobham**	Fern : **Fernhurst**	Ken : **Kenley**	Oxs : **Oxshott**
Ash W : **Ashurst Wood**	Cold : **Coldharbour**	Fetc : **Fetcham**	Kes : **Keston**	Oxt : **Oxted**
B Lea : **Badshot Lea**	C Hat : **Coleman's Hatch**	Finch : **Finchampstead**	Kew : **Kew**	P St : **Paley Street**
Bag : **Bagshot**	Col : **Colgate**	Fleet : **Fleet**	K'fold : **Kingsfold**	Pass : **Passfield**
Bal : **Balcombe**	C Tow : **College Town**	Flex : **Flexford**	K Grn : **Kingsley Green**	P Pot : **Pease Pottage**
Ban : **Banstead**	Coln : **Colnbrook**	For G : **Forest Green**	K Tham : **Kingston upon Thames**	P'lake : **Peaslake**
B Grn : **Beare Green**	Comp : **Compton**	F Row : **Forest Row**	K'wood : **Kingswood**	P'marsh : **Peasmarsh**
Beck : **Beckenham**	Cop : **Copthorne**	Fren : **Frensham**	Kird : **Kirdford**	P Har : **Peper Harow**
Bedd : **Beddington**	Coul : **Coulsdon**	Frim : **Frimley**	Knap : **Knaphill**	Pirb : **Pirbright**
Bedf : **Bedfont**	Cove : **Cove**	Frim G : **Frimley Green**	Knoc : **Knockholt**	Plais : **Plaistow**
Betch : **Betchworth**	Cow : **Cowden**	Gat : **Gatwick**	Lale : **Laleham**	P Pla : **Plummers Plain**
B Hil : **Biggin Hill**	C'ford : **Cranford**	Goda : **Godalming**	Lang : **Langley**	Poy : **Poyle**
Bill : **Billingshurst**	Cranl : **Cranleigh**	Gods : **Godstone**	Leat : **Leatherhead**	P Bot : **Pratts Bottom**
Bin : **Binfield**	Craw : **Crawley**	Gorn : **Gomshall**	Leigh : **Leigh**	Pur : **Purley**
Bis : **Bisley**	Craw D : **Crawley Down**	G'hott : **Grayshott**	Ligh : **Lightwater**	Put : **Puttenham**
B'eath : **Blackheath**	C Hil : **Crockham Hill**	G'wood : **Grayswood**	Limp : **Limpsfield**	Pyr : **Pyrford**
B'nest : **Blacknest**	Cron : **Crondall**	Guil : **Guildford**	Linch : **Linchmere**	Ran C : **Ranmore Common**
B'water : **Blackwater**	Crow : **Crowthorne**	Hale : **Hale**	Lind : **Lindford**	Red : **Redhill**
Blet : **Bletchingley**	Croy : **Croydon**	Ham : **Ham**	Ling : **Lingfield**	Reig : **Reigate**
Blin H : **Blindley Heath**	Cud : **Cudham**	Hamb : **Hambledon**	Lip : **Liphook**	R Pk : **Richings Park**
Book : **Bookham**	Dat : **Datchet**	Hamm : **Hammerwood**	Lon A : **London Heathrow Airport**	Rich : **Richmond**
Bor : **Bordon**	Deep : **Deepcut**	Hamp : **Hampton**	L'cross : **Longcross**	Rip : **Ripley**
Bow G : **Bowlhead Green**	Dip : **Dippenhall**	H Hill : **Hampton Hill**	L'ford : **Longford**	Row : **Rowfant**
Box H : **Box Hill**	Dock : **Dockenfield**	H Wic : **Hampton Wick**	L Bou : **Lower Bourne**	Rowh : **Rowhook**
Brac : **Bracknell**	Dork : **Dorking**	Hand : **Handcross**	Lwr K : **Lower Kingswood**	Rowl : **Rowledge**
Braml : **Bramley**	Dorm : **Dormansland**	Hanw : **Hanworth**	L Hea : **Lowfield Heath**	Rudg : **Rudgwick**
Brams : **Bramshott**	D Pk : **Dormans Park**	Harl : **Harlington**	Loxh : **Loxhill**	Run : **Runfold**
Brast : **Brasted**	Dorn : **Dorney**	Harm : **Harmondsworth**	Loxw : **Loxwood**	Rush : **Rushmoor**
Brent : **Brentford**	Dow : **Downe**	Hart : **Hartfield**	Lyne : **Lyne**	Rusp : **Rusper**
Bro H : **Broadbridge Heath**	Down : **Downside**	Hasc : **Hascombe**	M Hea : **Mannings Heath**	Salf : **Salfords**
Brock : **Brockham**	Duns : **Dunsfold**	Hasl : **Haslemere**	M Grn : **Marsh Green**	Sande : **Sanderstead**
Brom : **Bromley**	E Cla : **East Clandon**	Haw : **Hawley**	Mers : **Merstham**	Sandh : **Sandhurst**
Brook : **Brook**	E Grin : **East Grinstead**	Hay : **Hayes**	Mick : **Mickleham**	Seal : **Seale**
B'wood : **Brookwood**	E Hor : **East Horsley**	Head : **Headley**	Mid H : **Mid Holmwood**	Sels : **Selsdon**
Buck : **Buckland**	E Mol : **East Molesey**	H Dwn : **Headley Down**	Mil : **Milford**	Send : **Send**
B Oak : **Bucks Horn Oak**	Eash : **Eashing**	H End : **Heath End**	Min : **Minley**	S'ford : **Shackleford**
B'ham : **Burpham**	Eden : **Edenbridge**	Hers : **Hersham**	Mit : **Mitcham**	Sha G : **Shamley Green**
Burs : **Burstow**	Eff : **Effingham**	Hest : **Heston**	Mord : **Morden**	Sharp : **Sharpthorne**
Bus : **Busbridge**	E Jun : **Effingham Junction**	Hev : **Hever**	Mytc : **Mytchett**	Shep : **Shepperton**
Byf : **Byfleet**	Egh : **Egham**	H Wood : **Hinchley Wood**	N Add : **New Addington**	Shere : **Shere**
Camb : **Camberley**	Els : **Elstead**	Hind : **Hindhead**	Newc : **Newchapel**	S Bri : **Shipley Bridge**
Cap : **Capel**	Eng G : **Englefield Green**	H Mary : **Holmbury St Mary**	Newd : **Newdigate**	S Row : **Shurlock Row**
Cars : **Carshalton**	Ent G : **Enton Green**	Holm : **Holmwood**	N Haw : **New Haw**	Sid : **Sidlow**
Cate : **Caterham**	Eps : **Epsom**	H Pou : **Holt Pound**	N Mal : **New Malden**	Sip : **Sipson**
	Eps D : **Epsom Downs**	Hook : **Hookwood**	Norm : **Normandy**	Slea : **Sleaford**

10 Pin—Albemarle

Slin : **Slinfold**
Slou : **Slough**
Smal : **Smallfield**
S'hall : **Southall**
S Croy : **South Croydon**
S Gods : **South Godstone**
Sth N : **South Nutfield**
Stain : **Staines**
Stand : **Standford**
Stan : **Stanwell**
Stan M : **Stanwell Moor**
Sto D : **Stoke D'Abernon**
Sunb : **Sunbury**
S'dale : **Sunningdale**
S'hill : **Sunninghill**
Surb : **Surbiton**
Sut : **Sutton**
Sut G : **Sutton Green**
Tad : **Tadworth**
Tand : **Tandridge**
Tats : **Tatsfield**
Tat C : **Tattenham Corner**
Tedd : **Teddington**
T Dit : **Thames Ditton**
Have : **The Haven**
T Hea : **Thornton Heath**
Thor : **Thorpe**
Thur : **Thursley**
Til : **Tilford**
T'sey : **Titsey**
Tong : **Tongham**
T Hil : **Turners Hill**
Twick : **Twickenham**
Twy : **Twyford**
U Hal : **Upper Hale**
U Har : **Upper Hartfield**
V Wat : **Virginia Water**
Wad : **Waddon**
W'ton : **Wallington**
W'wood : **Walliswood**
Wal T : **Walton-on-Thames**
Wal H : **Walton on the Hill**
Wan : **Wanborough**
Warf : **Warfield**
Warl : **Warlingham**
Warn : **Warnham**
W By : **West Byfleet**
W Cla : **West Clandon**
W Dray : **West Drayton**
W End : **West End**
W Hoa : **West Hoathly**
W Hors : **West Horsley**
W Mole : **West Molesey**
W Wick : **West Wickham**
Westc : **Westcott**
Weste : **Westerham**
Westh : **Westhumble**
Weybo : **Weybourne**
Weybr : **Weybridge**
White : **Whitehill**
Whit V : **Whiteley Village**
Whitt : **Whitton**
Whyte : **Whyteleafe**
Windl : **Windlesham**
W'sor : **Windsor**
Wink : **Winkfield**
Wink R : **Winkfield Row**
Win : **Winnersh**
W Grn : **Wisborough Green**
Wis : **Wisley**
Wit : **Witley**
Wok : **Woking**
W'ham : **Wokingham**
Wold : **Woldingham**
Wone : **Wonersh**
Wood : **Woodham**
Wood V : **Wood Street Village**
W Pk : **Worcester Park**
Worm : **Wormley**
Worp : **Worplesdon**
Wor : **Worth**
Wott : **Wotton**
Wray : **Wraysbury**
Wrec : **Wrecclesham**
W Cros : **Wych Cross**
Yate : **Yateley**

10 Pin *4B 74*
(in Big Apple)

A

AARON'S HILL 7E **132**
Aaron's Hill GU7: Goda 7E **132**
Abbess Cl. SW2 . . . . .2M **29**
Abbetts La. GU15: Camb 3N **69**
Abbey Bus. Pk.
GU9: Farnh 3M **129**
Abbey Chase KT16: Chert 6K **37**
Abbey Cl. GU6: Cranl 8H **155**
GU22: Pyr 3G **75**
RG12: Brac 4B **32**
RG40: W'ham 1B **30**
Abbey Ct. GU9: Farnh 1H **129**
GU15: Camb 1B **70**
KT16: Chert 6K **37**
TW12: Hamp 8A **24**
TW18: Lale 3L **37**
Abbeydore Cl.
GU35: Head 4D **168**
Abbey Dr. SW17 . . . . .6E **28**
TW18: Lale 2L **37**
Abbeyfield *GU1: Guil* *4B 114*
(off Lwr. Edgeborough Rd.)
Abbeyfield Cl. CR4: Mit 1C **44**
Abbey Fit Sports Cen. 1J **55**
Abbey Gdns. KT16: Chert 5J **37**
W6 . . . . .2K **13**
Abbey Grn. KT16: Chert 5J **37**
Abbey Ind. Est. CR4: Mit 4D **44**
Abbey Mdws. KT16: Chert 6L **37**
Abbey M. RH19: Ash W 3H **187**
TW7: Isle 4H **11**
TW18: Lale 3L **37**
Abbey Mill Bus. Pk.
GU7: Eash 7B **132**
Abbey Pde. *SW19* *8A 28*
(off Merton High St.)
Abbey Pl. KT16: Chert 2J **37**
RG42: Warf 6A **16**
Abbey Rd.
CR0: Croy 4A **200** (9M **45**)
CR2: Sels 6G **64**
GU21: Wok 4M **73**
GU25: V Wat 4N **35**
KT16: Chert 6K **37**
SW19 . . . . .8A **28**
TW17: Shep 7B **38**
Abbey St. GU9: Farnh 1H **129**
Abbey Wlk. KT8: W Mole 2B **40**
Abbey Way GU14: Farnb 1A **90**
Abbeywood GU12: A Va 9F **90**
SL5: S'dale 6D **34**
Abbot Cl. KT14: Byf 6M **55**
TW18: Stain 8M **21**
Abbot Rd.
GU1: Guil 7D **202** (5N **113**)
Abbots Av. KT19: Eps 7N **59**
Abbotsbury RG12: Brac 4L **31**
Abbotsbury Ct. RH13: Hors . . .5L **197**
Abbotsbury Rd. SM4: Mord . . .4N **43**
Abbots Cl. GU2: Guil 6H **113**
GU51: Fleet 4B **88**
Abbots Dr. GU25: V Wat 4L **35**
Abbotsfield Rd. RH11: Ifi 4J **181**
Abbotsford Cl. GU22: Wok 4C **74**
Abbots Grn. CR0: A'ton 3G **65**
Abbots Hospital GU1: Guil 5D **202**
Abbots La. CR8: Ken 3N **83**
Abbotsleigh Cl. SM2: Sut 4N **61**
Abbotsleigh Rd. SW16 . . . . . . .5G **28**
Abbots Mead TW10: Ham 5K **25**
Abbotsmede Cl. TW1: Twick . . .3F **24**
Abbots Pk. SW2 . . . . .2L **29**
Abbot's Ride GU9: Farnh 3K **129**
Abbots Ri. RH1: Red 1E **122**
Abbotstone Rd. SW15 . . . . .6H **13**
Abbots Wlk. SL4: W'sor 5B **4**
Abbots Way BR3: Beck 4H **47**
GU1: Guil 2F **114**
KT16: Chert 6H **37**
ABBOTSWOOD 1B **114**
Abbotswood GU1: Guil 1B **114**
KT13: Weybr 9G **38**
Abbotswood Cl. GU1: Guil 9B **94**
Abbotswood Dr.
KT13: Weybr 6E **56**
Abbotswood Rd.
SW16 . . . . .4H **29**
Abbott Av. SW20 . . . . .9J **27**
Abbott Cl. TW12: Hamp 7M **23**
Abbotts Cotts.
GU10: Dock 5D **148**
Abbotts Rd. CR4: Mit 3G **45**
(not continuous)
SM3: Chea 1K **61**
Abbott's Tilt KT12: Hers 9M **39**
Abbotts Wlk. CR3: Cate 9E **84**
Abelia Cl. GU24: W End 9B **52**
Abell Ct. KT15: Addl 2K **55**
Abercairn Rd. SW16 . . . . .8G **28**
Aberconway Rd.
SM4: Mord 3N **43**
Abercorn Cl. CR2: Sels 9G **64**
Abercorn Ho. GU17: Haw 5K **69**
Abercorn M. TW10: Rich 7M **11**
Abercorn Way GU21: Wok 5K **73**
Aberdare Cl. BR4: W Wick 8M **47**
Aberdeen Rd.
CR0: Croy 7C **200** (1N **63**)
Aberdeen Ter.
GU26: G'hott 5B **170**
Aberfoyle Rd. SW16 . . . . .7H **29**
(not continuous)
Abergavenny Gdns.
RH10: Cop 7A **164**
Abingdon *W14* *1L 13*
(off Kensington Village)
Abingdon Cl. GU21: Wok 5M **73**
KT4: W Pk 9G **43**
RG12: Brac 4C **32**
SW19 . . . . .7A **28**
Abingdon Ct. GU22: Wok 5B **74**
Abingdon Rd. GU47: Sandh 7H **49**
SW16 . . . . .1J **45**
Abinger Av. SM2: Chea 5H **61**
ABINGER BOTTOM 5N **137**
Abinger Cl. CR0: N Add 3M **65**
RH5: Nth H 9J **119**
SM6: W'ton 2J **63**
ABINGER COMMON 3L **137**
Abinger Comn. Rd.
RH5: A Com 4M **137**
Abinger Ct. *SM6: W'ton* *2J 63*
(off Abinger Cl.)
Abinger Dr. RH1: Red 5C **122**
Abinger Gdns. TW7: Isle 6E **10**
ABINGER HAMMER 9G **116**
Abinger Keep *RH6: Horl* *7G 142*
(off Langshott La.)
Abinger La.
RH5: A Com, A Ham 9J **117**
Abinger Rd.
RH5: Cold, H Mary, Ockl
. . . . .9A **138**
Abinger Way GU4: B'ham 7D **94**
Aboyne Dr. SW20 . . . . .1F **42**
Aboyne Rd. SW17 . . . . .4B **28**
Abrahams Rd.
RH11: Craw 8M **181**
Abro Ind. Est. GU11: Alde 9B **90**
Abury La. RG12: Brac 5E **32**
Acacia Av. GU22: Wok 7N **73**
GU47: Owls 6J **49**
TW8: Brent 3H **11**
TW17: Shep 4B **38**
TW19: Wray 7A **6**
Acacia Cl. KT15: Wood 6H **55**
SE20 . . . . .1D **46**
Acacia Ct. RG12: Brac 3N **31**
Acacia Dr. KT15: Wood 6H **55**
SM3: Sut 7L **43**
SM7: Ban 1J **81**
Acacia Gdns. BR4: W Wick 8M **47**
Acacia Gro. KT3: N Mal 2C **42**
Acacia M. UB7: Harm 2M **7**
Acacia Rd. BR3: Beck 2J **47**
CR4: Mit 1E **44**
GU1: Guil 2C **202** (3N **113**)
SW16 . . . . .9J **29**
TW12: Hamp 7A **24**
TW18: Stain 6K **21**
(not continuous)
Academy Cl. GU15: Camb 7C **50**
Academy Gdns. CR0: Croy 7C **46**
Academy Ga. GU15: Camb 9N **49**
Academy Pl. GU47: C Tow 8K **49**
Accommodation La.
UB7: Harm 2L **7**
UB7: L'ford 4J **7**
Accommodation Rd.
KT16: L'cross 9N **35**
KT17: Ewe 2F **60**
AC Court KT7: T Dit 5G **40**
Ace Pde. KT9: Ches 9L **41**
Acer Cl. RG42: Warf 9E **16**
Acer Dr. GU24: W End 9C **52**
Acer Rd. TN16: B Hil 3F **86**
Acfold Rd. SW6 . . . . .4N **13**
Acheulian Cl. GU9: Farnh 4H **129**
Achilles Pl. GU21: Wok 4M **73**
Ackmar Rd. SW6 . . . . .4M **13**
Ackrells Mead GU47: Sandh . . .6E **48**
Acorn Cl. RH6: Horl 7G **143**
RH19: E Grin 1A **186**
TW12: Hamp 7B **24**
Acorn Dr. RG40: W'ham 1B **30**
Acorn Gdns. SE19 . . . . .1C **46**
Acorn Gro. GU22: Wok 8A **74**
KT20: K'wood 2L **101**
UB3: Harl 3G **9**
Acorn Keep GU9: H End 4J **109**
Acorn M. GU14: Farnb 7M **69**
Acorn Rd. GU17: B'water 1G **69**
Acorns RH13: Hors 4N **197**
Acorns, The RH6: Smal 8M **143**
RH11: Craw 8N **181**
Acorns Way KT10: Esh 2C **58**
Acorn Way BR3: Beck 4M **47**
BR6: Farnb 1K **67**
Acqua Ho. TW9: Kew 3A **12**
Acre La. SM5: Cars 1E **62**
SM6: W'ton 1E **62**
Acre Pas. SL4: W'sor 4G **4**
Acre Rd.
KT2: K Tham 1K **203** (9L **25**)
SW19 . . . . .7B **28**
Acres Gdns. KT20: Tad 6J **81**
Acres Platt GU6: Cranl 6A **156**
Acropolis Ho.
KT1: K Tham 5L **203**
Acton La. W3 . . . . .1B **12**
Acuba Rd. SW18 . . . . .3N **27**
Adair Cl. SE25 . . . . .2E **46**
Adair Gdns. CR3: Cate 8N **83**
Adair Wlk. GU24: B'wood 8M **71**
Adams Cl. KT5: Surb 5M **41**
Adams Cft. GU24: B'wood 7N **71**
Adams Dr. GU51: Fleet 4C **88**
Adams M. SW17 . . . . .3D **28**
Adamson Ct. RH11: Craw 8N **181**
Adamson Way BR3: Beck 4M **47**
Adams Pk. Rd. GU9: Farnh . . .8J **109**
Adams Quarter TW8: Brent 2J **11**
Adams Rd. BR3: Beck 4H **47**
Adams Wlk.
KT1: K Tham 3J **203** (1L **41**)
Adams Way CR0: Croy 5C **46**
SE25 . . . . .4E **46**
Adam Wlk. SW6 . . . . .3H **13**
Adare Wlk. SW16 . . . . .4K **29**
ADDINGTON 2K **65**
Addington Bus. Cen.
CR0: N Add 6A **66**
Addington Cl. SL4: W'sor 6D **4**
Addington Ct. SW14 . . . . .6C **12**
Addington Hgts.
CR0: N Add 7M **65**
Addington Palace 3J **65**
Addington Rd.
BR4: W Wick 1M **65**
CR0: Croy 7L **45**
CR2: Sande, Sels 7D **64**
Addington Village Rd.
CR0: A'ton 3J **65**
(not continuous)
Addington Village Stop (CT)
. . . . .3K **65**
ADDISCOMBE 7D **46**
Addiscombe Av. CR0: Croy 7D **46**
Addiscombe Ct. Rd.
CR0: Croy 7B **46**
Addiscombe Gro.
CR0: Croy 3E **200** (8B **46**)
Addiscombe Rd.
CR0: Croy 3E **200** (8B **46**)
(not continuous)
RG45: Crow 3H **49**
Addiscombe Stop (CT) 7D **46**
Addison Av. TW3: Houn 4C **10**
Addison Cl. CR3: Cate 9A **84**
Addison Ct. GU1: Guil 5B **114**
Addison Gdns.
KT5: Surb 8M **203** (3M **41**)
Addison Pl. SE25 . . . . .3D **46**
Addison Rd. CR3: Cate 8A **84**
GU1: Guil 5F **202** (5A **114**)
GU16: Frim 6C **70**
GU21: Wok 4B **74**
SE25 . . . . .3D **46**
TW11: Tedd 7H **25**
Addisons Cl. CR0: Croy 8J **47**
ADDLESTONE 1L **55**
Addlestone Ho. KT15: Addl 9K **37**
ADDLESTONE MOOR 8J **37**
Addlestone Moor
KT15: Addl 8L **37**
Addlestone Pk. KT15: Addl 2K **55**
Addlestone Rd.
KT13: Weybr 1A **56**
KT15: Addl 1N **55**
Addlestone Station (Rail) 1M **55**
Adecroft Way KT8: W Mole 2C **40**
Adela Av. KT3: N Mal 4G **42**
Adela Ho. *W6* *1H 13*
(off Queen Caroline St.)
Adelaide Cl. RH11: Craw 9B **162**
RH12: Hors 4M **197**
Adelaide Pl. KT13: Weybr 1E **56**
Adelaide Rd.
KT6: Surb 8J **203** (4L **41**)
KT12: Wal T 9H **39**
SL4: W'sor 4J **5**
SW18 . . . . .8M **13**
TW5: Hest 4M **9**
TW9: Rich 7M **11**
TW11: Tedd 7F **24**
TW15: A'ford 6M **21**
Adelaide Sq. SL4: W'sor 5G **4**
Adelaide Ter. TW8: Brent 1K **11**
Adelina M. SW12 . . . . .2H **29**
Adeline Genee Theatre 5N **165**
Adelphi Cl. RH10: Craw 5H **183**
Adelphi Ct. W4 . . . . .2C **12**
Adelphi Rd.
KT17: Eps 6K **201** (9C **60**)
Adeney Cl. W6 . . . . .2J **13**
Adlers La. RH5: Westh 9G **99**
Adlington Pl. GU14: Farnb 3C **90**
Admark Ho. KT18: Eps 2A **80**
Admiral Ct. SM5: Cars 7C **44**
Admiral Ho. TW11: Tedd 5G **25**
Admiral Kepple Ct.
SL5: Asc 8J **17**
Admiral Rd. RH11: Craw 6M **181**
Admiral's Bri. La.
RH19: E Grin 7M **185**
Admirals Ct. GU1: Guil 2D **114**
Admirals Rd. GU24: Pirb 4K **91**
KT22: Fetc 4D **98**
KT23: Book 6C **98**
Admiral Stirling Ct.
KT13: Weybr 1A **56**
Admirals Wlk. CR5: Coul 7K **83**
RH5: Ran C 8B **98**
Admiralty Rd. TW11: Tedd 7F **24**
Admiralty Way GU15: Camb . . .2L **69**
TW11: Tedd 7F **24**
Admiral Way GU7: Goda 9G **132**
Adrian Ct. RH11: Craw 8N **181**
Adrian M. SW10 . . . . .2N **13**
Advance Rd. SE27 . . . . .5N **29**
Adversane Ct. *RH12: Hors* . . .*4K 197*
(off Blenheim Rd)
Aerodrome Way TW5: Hest 2K **9**
Aerospace Blvd.
GU14: Farnb 6L **89**
Agar Cl. KT6: Surb 8M **41**
Agar Cres. RG42: Brac 8N **15**
Agar Ho. KT1: K Tham 6J **203**
Agars Pl. SL3: Dat 2K **5**
Agate La. RH12: Hors 3L **197**
Agates La. KT21: A'tead 5K **79**
Agevin Ct. GU51: Fleet 2A **88**
Agincourt SL5: Asc 2N **33**
Agnes Scott Ct.
KT13: Weybr *9C 38*
(off Palace Dr.)
Agraria Rd. GU2: Guil 4L **113**
Agua Ho. KT16: Chert 6L **37**
Ailsa Av. TW1: Twick 8G **11**
Ailsa Cl. RH11: Craw 6N **181**
Ailsa Rd. TW1: Twick 8H **11**
Ainger Cl. GU12: Alde 1B **110**
Ainsdale Way GU21: Wok 5K **73**
Ainslie Wlk. SW12 . . . . .1F **28**
Ainsworth Rd.
CR0: Croy 2A **200** (7M **45**)
Aintree Cl. SL3: Poy 4G **6**
Aintree Est. *SW6* *3K 13*
(off Aintree St.)
Aintree Rd. RH10: Craw 5E **182**
Aintree St. SW6 . . . . .3K **13**
Airborne Forces Mus. 8M **89**
Airbourne Ho. *SM6: W'ton* *1G 62*
(off Maldon Rd.)
Aircraft Esplanade
GU14: Farnb 4A **90**
Airedale Av. W4 . . . . .1E **12**
Airedale Av. Sth. W4 . . . . .1E **12**
Airedale Rd. SW12 . . . . .1D **28**
Air Forces Memorial 5N **19**
Air Links Ind. Est.
TW13: Hanw 4M **23**
Airlinks Ind. Est. TW5: C'ford . . .1K **9**
Air Pk. Way TW13: Felt 3J **23**
Airport Bowl 4F **8**
Airport Ga. Bus. Cen.
UB7: Sip 3A **8**
Airport Ind. Est. TN16: B Hil 2F **86**
Airport Way RH6: Gat 2E **162**
TW19: Stan M 7H **7**
Aisgill Av. W14 . . . . .1L **13**
(not continuous)
Aisne Rd. GU16: Deep 5J **71**
Aiten Pl. W6 . . . . .1F **12**
Aitken Cl. CR4: Mit 6D **44**
Aitken Ho. GU27: Hasl 1G **189**
Aitman Dr. W4 . . . . .1N **11**
Aits Vw. KT8: W Mole 2B **40**
Akabusi Cl. CR0: Croy 5D **46**
Akehurst Cl. RH10: Cop 7L **163**
Akehurst St. SW15 . . . . .9F **12**
Akerman Rd. KT6: Surb 5J **41**
Alamein Rd. GU11: Alde 2N **109**
Alanbrooke Cl. GU21: Knap 5F **72**
Alanbrooke Rd. GU11: Alde 7B **90**
Alan Hilton Ct. *KT16: Otter* *3F 54*
(off Cheshire Cl.)
Alan Rd. SW19 . . . . .6K **27**
Alan Turing Rd. GU2: Guil 3G **113**
Albain Cres. TW15: A'ford 3N **21**
Alba M. SW18 . . . . .3M **27**
Albany Cl. GU51: Fleet 5C **88**
KT10: Esh 5A **58**
RH2: Reig 9M **101**
SW14 . . . . .7A **12**
Albany Ct. GU16: Camb 5A **70**
GU51: Fleet 4C **88**
KT13: Weybr 1C **56**
(Hillcrest)
KT13: Weybr 8F **38**
(Oatlands Dr.)
TW15: A'ford 8D **22**
TW20: Egh 5C **20**
Albany Cres. KT10: Clay 3E **58**
Albany M. KT2: K Tham 7K **25**
SM1: Sut 2N **61**
Albany Pde. TW8: Brent 2L **11**
Albany Pk. GU16: Camb 5N **69**
SL3: Coln 4F **6**
Albany Pk. Ind. Est.
GU16: Camb 5A **70**
Albany Pk. Rd.
KT2: K Tham 7K **25**
KT22: Leat 6G **78**
Albany Pas. TW10: Rich 8L **11**
Albany Pl. TW8: Brent 2K **11**
TW20: Egh 5D **20**
Albany Reach KT7: T Dit 4F **40**
Albany Rd. GU51: Fleet 5B **88**
KT3: N Mal 3C **42**
KT12: Hers 1L **57**
RH11: Craw 3N **181**
SL4: O Win 8K **5**
SL4: W'sor 5G **4**
SW19 . . . . .6N **27**
TW8: Brent 2K **11**
TW10: Rich 8M **11**
Albany Ter. *TW10: Rich* *8M 11*
(off Albany Pas.)
Albatross Gdns. CR2: Sels 7G **65**
Albemarle SW19 . . . . .3J **27**

Albemarle Av.—Ambleside Cl.

Albemarle Av. TW2: Whitt 2N 23
Albemarle Gdns.
KT3: N Mal 3C 42
Albemarle Pk. BR3: Beck 1L 47
Albemarle Rd. BR3: Beck 1M 47
Alben Rd. RG42: Bin 6H 15
Alberta Av. SM1: Sut 1K 61
Alberta Dr. RH6: Smal 8L 143
Albert Av. KT16: Chert 2J 37
Albert Carr Gdns.
SW16 6J 29
Albert Crane Ct.
RH11: Craw 1M 181
Albert Dr. GU21: Wok 2E 74
SW19 3K 27
TW18: Stain 6H 21
Albert Gro. SW20 9J 27
Albertine Cl. KT17: Eps D 3G 81
Albert Mans. CR0: Croy 1E 200
Albert M. RH1: Red 6E 122
Albert Pl. SL4: E Wic 1D 4
Albert Rd. CR4: Mit 2D 44
CR6: Warl 4J 85
GU11: Alde 2N 109
GU14: Farnb 3A 90
GU15: Camb 1A 70
GU19: Bag 6J 51
KT1: K Tham 3L 203 (1M 41)
KT3: N Mal 3E 42
KT15: Addl 1M 55
KT17: Eps 7M 201 (9E 60)
KT21: A'tead 5M 79
RG40: W'ham 3A 30
RG42: Brac 9N 15
RG45: Crow 2G 49
RH1: Mers 7G 102
RH6: Horl 7E 142
SE25 3D 46
SL4: O Win, W'sor 6G 5
SM1: Sut 2B 62
TW1: Twick 2F 24
TW3: Houn 7A 10
TW10: Rich 8L 11
TW11: Tedd 7F 24
TW12: H Hill 6C 24
TW15: A'ford 6A 22
TW20: Eng G 7N 19
Albert Rd. Nth. RH2: Reig 2L 121
Albert St. GU51: Fleet 5A 88
SL4: W'sor 4E 4
Albert Ter. W6 1F 12
(off Beavor La.)
Albert Wlk. RG45: Crow 2G 49
Albery Cl. RH12: Hors 4H 197
Albion SL3: Lang 1D 6
Albion Cl. RH10: Craw 4H 183
Albion Cotts. RH5: H Mary 5K 137
Albion Ct. SM2: Sut 4B 62
W6 1G 13
(off Albion Pl.)
Albion Ho. GU21: Wok 4B 74
Albion M. W6 1G 13
Albion Pl. SE25 2D 46
SL4: W'sor 5D 4
W6 1G 13
Albion Rd. GU47: Sandh 8G 49
KT2: K Tham 9B 26
RH2: Reig 4A 122
SM2: Sut 3B 62
TW2: Twick 2E 24
TW3: Houn 7A 10
Albion St.
CR0: Croy 1A 200 (7M 45)
Albion Way RH12: Hors 6H 197
TN8: Eden 8L 127
Albon Ho. SW18 9N 13
(off Neville Gill Cl.)
ALBURY 8K 115
Albury Av. SM2: Chea 5H 61
TW7: Isle 3F 10
Albury Cl. KT16: L'cross 9K 35
KT19: Eps 5A 60
TW12: Hamp 7B 24
Albury Cotts. GU12: Ash 2G 111
Albury Ct. CR2: S Croy 7B 200
CR4: Mit 1B 44
SM1: Sut 1A 62
ALBURY HEATH 1M 135
Albury Ho. GU1: Guil 5B 114
Albury Keep RH6: Horl 8F 142
(off Langshott La.)
Albury Pk. GU5: Alb 8N 115
Albury Pl. RH1: Mers 7G 103
Albury Rd. GU1: Guil 4B 114
KT9: Ches 2L 59
KT12: Hers 3F 56
RH1: Mers 7G 102
Alcester Ct. SM6: W'ton 1F 62
Alcester Rd. SM6: W'ton 1F 62
Alcock Cl. SM6: W'ton 4H 63
Alcock Rd. TW5: Hest 3L 9
Alcocks Cl. KT20: Tad 7K 81
Alcocks La.
KT20: K'wood, Tad 8K 81
Alcorn Cl. SM3: Sut 8M 43
Alcot Cl. RG45: Crow 3G 48
Alcott Cl. TW14: Felt 2G 22
Alden Ct.
CR0: Croy 4F 200 (9B 46)
Aldenham Ter. RG12: Brac 5A 32
Aldenholme KT13: Weybr 3F 56
Alden Vw. SL4: W'sor 4A 4
Alderbrook Cl. RG45: Crow 3D 48
Alderbrook Farm Cotts.
GU6: Cranl 3M 155
Alderbrook Rd.
GU6: Cranl 2K 155
SW12 1F 28
Alderbury Rd. SW13 2F 12
Alder Cl. GU12: A Va 6E 90
RH10: Craw D 1E 184
TW20: Eng G 6A 20
Aldercombe La.
CR3: Cate 5B 104
Alder Copse RH12: Hors 8F 196
Aldercroft CR5: Coul 3K 83
Alder Gro. GU46: Yate 1B 68
Aldergrove Gdns.
TW3: Houn 5M 9
Alder Lodge SW6 4H 13
Alderman Judge Mall
KT1: K Tham 4J 203
Alderman Willey Cl.
RG41: W'ham 2A 30
Alderney Av.
TW5: Hest, Isle 3B 10
Alder Rd. GU35: H Dwn 3G 168
SW14 6C 12
Alders, The BR4: W Wick 7L 47
GU9: B Lea 6N 109
KT14: W By 8L 55
SW16 5G 29
TW5: Hest 2N 9
TW13: Hanw 5M 23
Alders Av. RH19: E Grin 7N 165
Aldersbrook Dr.
KT2: K Tham 7M 25
Aldersey Rd. GU1: Guil 3B 114
Alders Gro. KT8: E Mol 4D 40
ALDERSHOT 2N 109
Aldershot Garrison Sports Cen.
7A 90
Aldershot Lodge
GU11: Alde 4A 110
Aldershot Military Mus. 7A 90
Aldershot Pools & Lido 5B 110
Aldershot Rd. GU2: Guil 7G 92
GU3: Guil, Norm, Worp 8B 92
GU12: Ash 3C 110
GU24: Pirb 5A 92
GU51: Fleet 5B 88
GU52: C Cro 9A 88
Aldershot Station (Rail) 3N 109
Aldershot Town FC 2N 109
Alderside Wlk.
TW20: Eng G 6A 20
Aldersmead Av. CR0: Croy 5G 47
Alders Rd. RH2: Reig 1N 121
ALDERSTEAD HEATH 3H 103
Alderstead Heath Cvn. Site
RH1: Mers 2H 103
Alderstead La. RH1: Mers 3H 103
Alders Vw. Dr.
RH19: E Grin 7A 166
Alderton Ct. KT8: W Mole 3N 39
(off Walton Rd.)
Alderton Rd. CR0: Croy 6C 46
Alderville Rd. SW6 5L 13
Alderwick Dr. TW3: Houn 6D 10
Alderwood Cl. CR3: Cate 3B 104
Aldingbourne Cl. RH11: Ifi 2L 181
Aldis M. SW17 6C 28
Aldis St. SW17 6C 28
Aldren Rd. SW17 4A 28
Aldrich Cres. CR0: N Add 5M 65
Aldrich Gdns. SM3: Chea 9L 43
Aldrich Ter. SW18 3A 28
Aldridge Pk. RG42: Wink R 7F 16
Aldridge Ri. KT3: N Mal 6D 42
Aldrington Rd. SW16 6G 29
Aldrin Pl. GU14: Cove 1J 89
Aldwick Cl. GU14: Farnb 8M 69
Aldwick Rd. CR0: Bedd 9K 45
Aldworth Cl. RG12: Brac 3M 31
Aldworth Gdns.
RG45: Crow 2F 48
Aldwych Cl. RH10: Craw 5H 183
Aldwyn Pl. TW20: Eng G 7L 19
Alexa Ct. SM2: Sut 3M 61
Alexander Cl. TW2: Twick 3E 24
Alexander Ct. BR3: Beck 1N 47
Alexander Cres. CR3: Cate 8N 83
Alexander Fleming Rd.
GU2: Guil 4G 113
Alexander Godley Cl.
KT21: A'tead 6M 79
Alexander Ho. GU11: Alde 2N 109
(off Station Rd.)
KT2: K Tham 2J 203
Alexander M. SW16 6G 29
Alexander Pl. RH8: Oxt 6A 106
Alexander Raby Mill
KT15: Addl 2N 55
(off Bourneside Rd.)
Alexander Rd. CR5: Coul 2F 82
GU11: Alde 2L 109
RH2: Reig 6M 121
TW20: Egh 6E 20
(not continuous)
Alexanders Wlk.
CR3: Cate 4C 104
Alexander Wlk. RG12: Brac 4N 31
Alexandra Av. CR6: Warl 4J 85
GU15: Camb 1M 69
SM1: Sut 9M 43
W4 3C 12
Alexandra Cl. GU47: C Tow 8K 49
KT12: Wal T 8H 39
TW15: A'ford 8E 22
TW18: Stain 7M 21
Alexandra Ct. GU14: Farnb 4A 90
RG40: W'ham 3B 30
RH10: Craw 4B 182
SL4: W'sor 5G 4
(off Alexandra Rd.)
TW3: Houn 5B 10
TW15: A'ford 7E 22
Alexandra Dr. KT5: Surb 6N 41
Alexandra Gdns.
GU21: Knap 5F 72
SM5: Cars 4E 62
TW3: Houn 5B 10
W4 3D 12
Alexandra Ho. W6 1H 13
(off Queen Caroline St.)
Alexandra Lodge
KT13: Weybr 1C 56
(off Monument Hill)
Alexandra Mans. KT17: Eps 9E 60
(off Alexandra Rd.)
Alexandra M. SW19 7L 27
Alexandra Pl. CR0: Croy 7B 46
GU1: Guil 5B 114
SE25 4A 46
Alexandra Rd.
CR0: Croy 1F 200 (7B 46)
CR4: Mit 8C 28
CR6: Warl 4J 85
GU11: Alde 2K 109
(not continuous)
GU12: Ash 3D 110
GU14: Farnb 3A 90
KT2: K Tham 8N 25
KT7: T Dit 4F 40
KT15: Addl 1M 55
(not continuous)
KT17: Eps 9E 60
SL4: W'sor 5G 4
SW14 6C 12
SW19 7L 27
TN16: B Hil 6D 86
TW1: Twick 9J 11
TW3: Houn 5B 10
TW8: Brent 2K 11
TW9: Kew 5M 11
TW15: A'ford 8E 22
TW20: Eng G 7M 19
Alexandra Sq. SM4: Mord 4M 43
Alexandra Ter.
GU1: Guil 4E 202 (4A 114)
GU11: Alde 2M 109
Alexandra Way KT19: Eps 7N 59
ALFOLD 8H 175
ALFOLD BARS 1H 193
Alfold Bus. Cen. GU6: Alf 8J 175
ALFOLD CROSSWAYS 5J 175
Alfold Rd. GU6: Alf, Cranl 7K 155
GU8: Duns 5B 174
Alfonso Cl. GU12: Alde 4A 110
Alford Cl. GU4: B'ham 9B 94
GU47: Sandh 8F 48
Alford Grn. CR0: N Add 3N 65
Alfred Cl. RH10: Wor 4J 183
W4 1C 12
Alfred Rd. GU9: Farnh 2H 129
KT1: K Tham 6K 203 (2L 41)
SE25 4D 46
SM1: Sut 2A 62
TW13: Felt 3K 23
Alfreton Cl. SW19 4J 27
Alfriston KT5: Surb 5M 41
Alfriston Av. CR0: Croy 6J 45
Alfriston Cl. KT5: Surb 4M 41
Alfriston Rd. GU16: Deep 7G 71
Algar Cl. TW7: Isle 6G 10
Algar Rd. TW7: Isle 6G 11
Algarve Rd. SW18 2N 27
Alice Crocker Ho.
RH19: E Grin 8A 166
Alice Gilliatt Ct. W14 2L 13
(off Star Rd.)
Alice Gough Memorial Homes
RG12: Brac 2N 31
Alice Holt Cotts.
GU10: H Pou 9A 128
Alice Holt Forest Vis. Cen.
2B 148
Alice M. TW11: Tedd 6F 24
Alice Rd. GU11: Alde 2N 109
Alice Ruston Pl.
GU22: Wok 6M 73
Alice Way TW3: Houn 7B 10
Alicia Av. RH10: Craw 3F 182
Alington Gro. SM6: W'ton 5G 63
Alison Cl. CR0: Croy 7G 46
GU14: Cove 2L 89
GU21: Wok 2A 74
Alison Dr. GU15: Camb 1D 70
Alison's Rd. GU11: Alde 8M 89
Alison Way GU11: Alde 2L 109
Alkerden Rd. W4 1D 12
Allan Cl. KT3: N Mal 4C 42
Allbrook Cl. TW11: Tedd 6E 24
Allcard Cl. RH12: Hors 4K 197
Allcot Cl. RH11: Craw 6K 181
Allden Av. GU12: Alde 5B 110
Allden Cotts. GU7: Goda 7E 132
(off Aaron's Hill)
Allden Gdns. GU12: Alde 5B 110
Alldens Hill GU5: Braml 1N 153
GU8: Bus 1N 153
Alldens La. GU8: Bus 9L 133
Allder Way CR2: S Croy 4M 63
Allenby Av. CR2: S Croy 5N 63
Allenby Rd. GU15: Camb 9M 49
TN16: B Hil 4G 86
Allen Cl. CR4: Mit 9F 28
TW16: Sunb 9J 23
Allendale Cl. GU47: Sandh 5F 48
Allenford Ho. SW15 9E 12
(off Tunworth Cres.)
Allen Ho. Pk. GU22: Wok 7M 73
Allen Rd. BR3: Beck 1G 46
CR0: Croy 7L 45
KT23: Book 4B 98
TW16: Sunb 9J 23
Allen's Cl. RH19: Ash W 3F 186
Allenswood SW19 2K 27
Allen Way SL3: Dat 4M 5
Allestree Rd. SW6 3K 13
Alleyn Pk. UB2: S'hall 1A 10
Allfarthing La. SW18 9N 13
Allgood Cl. SM4: Mord 5J 43
Alliance Cl. TW4: Houn 8N 9
Alliance Ct. TW15: A'ford 5D 22
Allingham Ct. GU7: Goda 4J 133
Allingham Gdns.
RH12: Hors 3A 198
Allingham Rd. RH2: Reig 6M 121
Allington Av. TW17: Shep 2F 38
Allington Cl. SW19 6J 27
Allington Ct. CR0: Croy 5F 46
(off Chart Cl.)
Allkins Ct. SL4: W'sor 5G 5
Alloway Cl. GU21: Wok 5L 73
All Saints Cl. RG40: W'ham 1B 30
All Saint's Ct. TW5: Hest 4L 9
(off Springwell Rd.)
All Saints Cres. GU14: Cove 6K 69
All Saints Dr. CR2: Sande 8C 64
All Saints Pas. SW18 8M 13
All Saints Ri. RG42: Warf 8B 16
All Saints Rd. GU18: Ligh 6N 51
SM1: Sut 9N 43
SW19 8A 28
(not continuous)
Allsmoor La. RG12: Brac 2D 32
All Souls Rd. SL5: Asc 3L 33
Allum Gro. KT20: Tad 8G 81
Allyington Way RH10: Wor 4H 183
Allyn Cl. TW18: Stain 7H 21
Alma Cl. GU12: Alde 2B 110
GU21: Knap 4H 73
Alma Cotts. GU14: Farnb 5A 90
Alma Ct. CR3: Cate 8N 83
(off Coulsdon Rd.)
Alma Cres. SM1: Sut 2K 61
Alma Gdns. GU16: Deep 6H 71
Alma Ho. TW8: Brent 2L 11
Alma La.
GU9: H End, U Hal 5G 109
Alma Pl. CR7: T Hea 4L 45
Alma Rd. GU35: H Dwn 4H 169
KT10: Esh 7E 40
RH2: Reig 2N 121
SL4: E Wic 1C 4
SL4: W'sor 5F 4
SM5: Cars 2C 62
SW18 7N 13
Alma Sq. GU14: Farnb 5A 90
Alma Ter. SW18 1B 28
Alma Way GU9: H End 5J 109
Almer Rd. SW20 8F 26
Almners Rd. KT16: Lyne 7C 36
(not continuous)
Almond Av. GU22: Wok 8N 73
SM5: Cars 8D 44
Almond Cl. GU1: Guil 9N 93
GU14: Farnb 7M 69
RH11: Craw 4M 181
SL4: W'sor 5E 4
TW13: Felt 2H 23
TW17: Shep 1D 38
TW20: Eng G 7L 19
Almond Ct. GU52: C Cro 7C 88
Almond Gro. TW8: Brent 3H 11
Almond Rd. KT19: Eps 7C 60
Almond Way CR4: Mit 4H 45
Almorah Rd. TW5: Hest 4L 9
Almsgate GU3: Comp 1F 132
Alms Heath GU23: Ockh 8C 76
Almshouse La. KT9: Ches 5J 59
Almshouses GU10: Wrec 4E 128
(off Riverdale)
KT16: Chert 6J 37
RH4: Dork 1L 201 (4H 119)
Alnwick Gro. SM4: Mord 3N 43
Aloes, The GU51: Fleet 5C 88
Alphabet Gdns. SM5: Cars 5B 44
Alpha Ct. CR3: Whyte 5D 84
Alpha Ho. RG45: Crow 2H 49
Alpha Pl. SM4: Mord 7J 43
Alpha Rd.
CR0: Croy 1F 200 (7B 46)
GU12: Alde 3B 110
GU22: Wok 3D 74
GU24: Chob 6J 53
KT5: Surb 5M 41
RH11: Craw 3A 182
TW11: Tedd 6D 24
Alpha Way TW20: Thor 9E 20
Alphea Cl. SW19 8C 28
Alphington Av. GU16: Frim 5C 70
Alphington Grn.
GU16: Frim 5C 70
Alpine Av. KT5: Surb 8B 42
Alpine Cl.
CR0: Croy 5F 200 (9B 46)
GU14: Cove 2J 89
SL5: S'hill 5A 34
Alpine Rd. KT12: Wal T 6H 39
RH1: Red 9E 102
Alpine Ski Cen. 9A 90
Alpine Vw. SM5: Cars 2C 62
Alpine Walks RH11: Craw 4A 182
Alresford Rd. GU2: Guil 4K 113
Alric Av. KT3: N Mal 2D 42
Alsace Wlk. GU15: Camb 5N 69
Alsford Cl. GU18: Ligh 8K 51
Alsom Av. KT4: W Pk 1F 60
Alston Cl. KT7: T Dit 6H 41
Alston Rd. SW17 5B 28
Altamont CR6: Warl 6E 84
Alterton Cl. GU21: Wok 4K 73
Alt Gro. SW19 8L 27
Althea St. SW6 5N 13
Althorne Rd. RH1: Red 5E 122
Althorp Rd. SW17 2D 28
Alton Cl. TW7: Isle 5F 10
Alton Ct. TW18: Stain 9G 21
Alton Gdns. TW2: Whitt 1D 24
Alton Ho. RH1: Red 1E 122
Alton Ride GU17: B'water 9H 49
Alton Rd. CR0: Wad 9L 45
GU10: Farnh 5B 128
GU51: Fleet 4D 88
SW15 2F 26
TW9: Rich 7L 11
Altyre Cl. BR3: Beck 4J 47
Altyre Rd.
CR0: Croy 3E 200 (8A 46)
Altyre Way BR3: Beck 4J 47
Alvernia Cl. GU7: Goda 9F 132
Alverstoke Gdns.
GU11: Alde 3K 109
Alverstone Av. SW19 3M 27
Alverstone Rd. KT3: N Mal 3E 42
Alverston Gdns. SE25 4B 46
Alvia Gdns. SM1: Sut 1A 62
Alway Av. KT19: Ewe 2C 60
Alwin Pl. GU9: U Hal 5G 109
Alwyn Av. W4 1C 12
Alwyn Cl. CR0: N Add 4L 65
Alwyne Ct. GU21: Wok 3A 74
Alwyne Rd. SW19 7L 27
Alwyns Cl. KT16: Chert 5J 37
Alwyns La. KT16: Chert 5H 37
Amalgamated Dr.
TW8: Brent 2H 11
Amanda Ct. TW15: A'ford 3A 22
(off Edward Way)
Ambarrow Cres.
GU47: Sandh 6E 48
Ambarrow Farm Courtyard
GU47: Sandh 5D 48
Ambarrow La. GU47: Sandh 5C 48
Ambassador RG12: Brac 4L 31
Ambassador, The
SL5: S'dale 6E 34
Ambassador Cl. TW3: Houn 5M 9
Ambassadors, The
Woking 4A 74
Amber Ct.
CR0: Croy 1F 200 (7B 46)
GU12: Alde 2A 110
KT5: Surb 6M 41
TW18: Stain 6H 21
(off Laleham Rd.)
Ambercroft Way CR5: Coul 6M 83
Amber Hill GU15: Camb 2F 70
Amberley Cl. GU23: Send 3H 95
RH10: Craw 3G 183
RH12: Hors 2N 197
Amberley Ct. RH11: Craw 7B 162
(off County Oak La.)
Amberley Dr. KT15: Wood 6H 55
Amberley Flds. Cvn. Club Site
RH11: L Hea 6N 161
Amberley Gdns. KT19: Ewe 1E 60
Amberley Grange
GU11: Alde 4L 109
Amberley Gro. CR0: Croy 6C 46
Amberley La. GU8: Mil 1B 152
Amberley Pl. SL4: W'sor 4G 4
(off Peascod St.)
Amberley Rd. GU8: Mil 9B 132
RH12: Hors 2N 197
Amberley Way SM4: Mord 6L 43
TW4: Houn 8K 9
Amberside Cl. TW7: Isle 9D 10
Amberwood Cl. SM6: W'ton 2J 63
Amberwood Dr.
GU15: Camb 8D 50
Amberwood Ri. KT3: N Mal 5D 42
Amblecote KT11: Cob 7M 57
Ambleside GU7: Goda 6K 133
RG45: Crow 3H 49
SW19 2K 27
Ambleside Av. BR3: Beck 4H 47
KT12: Wal T 7K 39
SW16 5H 29
Ambleside Cl. GU14: Cove 1K 89
GU16: Mytc 3E 90
RH1: Red 8F 122
RH11: Ifi 4J 181

Ambleside Cres.—Arundle Ho.

Ambleside Cres.
GU9: U Hal . . . 6F 108
Ambleside Dr. TW14: Felt . . . 2G 22
Ambleside Gdns. CR2: Sels . . . 5G 64
SM2: Sut . . . 3A 62
SW16 . . . 6H 29
Ambleside Rd. GU18: Ligh . . . 7K 51
Ambleside Way TW20: Egh . . . 8D 20
Ambrey Way SM6: W'ton . . . 5H 63
Ambrose Cl. BR6: Orp . . . 1N 67
Amelia Ho. TW9: Kew . . . 3A 12
W6 . . . 1H 13
(off Queen Caroline St.)
AMEN CORNER . . . 2J 31
Amen Cnr. SW17 . . . 7D 28
Amen Cnr. Bus. Pk.
RG12: Brac . . . 2J 31
Amenity Way SM4: Mord . . . 6H 43
American International
University of London, The
. . . 9L 11
(in Richmond University)
Amerland Rd. SW18 . . . 8L 13
Amersham Rd. CR0: Croy . . . 5N 45
Amesbury Av. SW2 . . . 3J 29
Amesbury Cl. KT4: W Pk . . . 7H 43
Amesbury Rd. TW13: Felt . . . 3L 23
Amethyst Ct. BR6: Chels . . . 2N 67
(off Farnborough Hill)
Amey Dr. KT23: Book . . . 2C 98
AMF Bowling
Purley . . . 9K 63
Amhurst Gdns. TW7: Isle . . . 5G 10
Amida Leisure Cen. . . . 4J 47
Amis Av. KT15: N Haw . . . 6J 55
KT19: Ewe . . . 3A 60
Amis Rd. GU21: Wok . . . 6H 73
Amity Gro. SW20 . . . 9G 27
Amity Way GU15: Camb . . . 1C 70
Amlets La. GU6: Cranl . . . 5M 155
Amorosa Cl. RH11: Ifi . . . 9M 161
Ampere Way CR0: Wad . . . 6J 45
Ampere Way Stop (CT) . . . 7K 45
Amstel Way GU21: Wok . . . 5J 73
Amundsen Rd.
RH12: Hors . . . 2K 197
Amyand Cotts. TW1: Twick . . . 9H 11
Amyand La. TW1: Twick . . . 1H 25
Amyand Pk. Gdns.
TW1: Twick . . . 1H 25
Amyand Pk. Rd.
TW1: Twick . . . 1G 25
Amy Cl. SM6: W'ton . . . 4J 63
Amy Rd. RH8: Oxt . . . 7A 106
Anarth Ct. KT13: Weybr . . . 7F 38
Ancaster Cres. KT3: N Mal . . . 5F 42
Ancaster Dr. SL5: Asc . . . 9J 17
Ancaster M. BR3: Beck . . . 2G 47
Ancaster Rd. BR3: Beck . . . 2G 46
Ancells Bus. Pk.
GU51: Fleet . . . 9D 68
Ancells Farm Nature Reserve
. . . 2C 88
Ancells Rd. GU51: Fleet . . . 9C 68
Anchor SW18 . . . 7N 13
Anchorage Cl. SW19 . . . 6M 27
Anchor Bus. Cen.
CR0: Bedd . . . 9J 45
Anchor Cl. GU3: Norm . . . 9N 91
Anchor Cotts. RH7: Blin H . . . 3H 145
Anchor Ct. RH12: Hors . . . 7J 197
Anchor Cres. GU21: Knap . . . 4G 72
Anchor Hill GU21: Knap . . . 4G 72
Anchor Mdw. GU14: Cove . . . 1L 89
Ancill Cl. W6 . . . 2K 13
Andermans SL4: W'sor . . . 4A 4
Anders Cnr. RG42: Brac . . . 9L 15
Anderson Cl. GU2: Guil . . . 8L 93
KT19: Eps . . . 8A 60
SM3: Sut . . . 7M 43
Anderson Ct. RH1: Red . . . 6E 122
Anderson Dr. TW15: A'ford . . . 5D 22
Anderson Hgts. SW16 . . . 1K 45
Anderson Ho. SW17 . . . 6B 28
Anderson Pl. GU19: Bag . . . 3J 51
TW3: Houn . . . 7B 10
Anderson Rd. KT13: Weybr . . . 9E 38
RH10: Craw . . . 7C 182
Andover Cl. KT19: Eps . . . 7C 60
TW14: Felt . . . 2G 23
Andover Ct. TW19: Stan . . . 1M 21
Andover Rd. GU17: B'water . . . 9H 49
TW2: Twick . . . 2D 24
Andover Way GU11: Alde . . . 5N 109
Andreck Ct. BR3: Beck . . . 1M 47
(off Crescent Rd.)
Andrewartha Rd.
GU14: Farnb . . . 3C 90
Andrew Cl. RG40: W'ham . . . 3D 30
Andrewes Ho. SM1: Sut . . . 1M 61
Andrew Reed Ho.
SW18 . . . 1K 27
(off Linstead Way)
Andrews Cl. GU52: C Cro . . . 7B 88
KT4: W Pk . . . 8H 43
KT17: Eps . . . 8M 201 (1E 80)
Andrew's Ho. CR2: S Croy . . . 3N 63
Andrews Rd. GU14: Cove . . . 9K 69
Andromeda Cl.
RH11: Craw . . . 5K 181
ANERLEY . . . 1E 46
Anerley Pk. SE20 . . . 1E 46
Anfield Cl. SW12 . . . 1G 28
Angas Ct. KT13: Weybr . . . 2D 56
Angel Cl. TW12: H Hill . . . 6C 24
Angel Ct. GU3: Comp . . . 9D 112
GU7: Goda . . . 7G 133
Angelfield TW3: Houn . . . 7B 10
Angel Ga.
GU1: Guil . . . 5C 202 (4N 113)
Angel Hill SM1: Sut . . . 9N 43
(not continuous)
Angel Hill Dr. SM1: Sut . . . 9N 43
Angelica Gdns. CR0: Croy . . . 7G 46
Angelica Rd. GU2: Guil . . . 8K 93
GU24: Bis . . . 2D 72
Angell Cl. RH10: Craw . . . 4G 182
Angel M. SW15 . . . 1F 26
Angelo M. SW16 . . . 2K 45
Angelo's SL4: Eton . . . 1G 4
(off Common La.)
Angel Pl. RG42: Bin . . . 7H 15
RH2: Reig . . . 6N 121
Angel Rd. KT7: T Dit . . . 6G 41
Angel Wlk. W6 . . . 1H 13
Angers Cl. GU15: Camb . . . 8G 50
Anglers, The KT1: K Tham . . . 5H 203
Anglers Cl. TW10: Ham . . . 5J 25
Anglers Reach
KT6: Surb . . . 8G 203 (4K 41)
Anglesea Ho.
KT1: K Tham . . . 8H 203
Anglesea Rd.
KT1: K Tham . . . 8H 203 (3K 41)
Anglesey Av. GU14: Cove . . . 7L 69
Anglesey Cl. RH11: Craw . . . 6A 182
TW15: A'ford . . . 4B 22
Anglesey Ct. Rd. SM5: Cars . . . 3E 62
Anglesey Gdns. SM5: Cars . . . 3E 62
Anglesey Rd. GU12: Alde . . . 3B 110
Angles Rd. SW16 . . . 5J 29
Anglo Way RH1: Red . . . 1F 122
Angora Way GU51: Fleet . . . 1C 88
Angus Cl. KT9: Ches . . . 2N 59
RH12: Hors . . . 4K 197
Angus Ho. SW2 . . . 1H 29
Ankerwycke Priory . . . 3A 20
Anlaby Rd. TW11: Tedd . . . 6E 24
Annadale Ct. RH1: Red . . . 2D 122
(off Warwick Rd.)
Annaleigh Pl. KT12: Hers . . . 1L 57
Annandale Dr.
GU10: L Bou . . . 5J 129
Annandale Rd. CR0: Croy . . . 8D 46
GU2: Guil . . . 5L 113
W4 . . . 1D 12
Annan Dr. SM5: Cars . . . 5E 62
Anne Armstrong Cl.
GU11: Alde . . . 8B 90
Anne Boleyn's Wlk.
KT2: K Tham . . . 6L 25
SM3: Chea . . . 4J 61
Anne Case M. KT3: N Mal . . . 2C 42
Anneforde Pl. RG42: Brac . . . 8M 15
Anners Cl. TW20: Thor . . . 2E 36
Annesley Dr. CR0: Croy . . . 9J 47
Anne's Wlk. CR3: Cate . . . 7B 84
Annes Way GU52: C Cro . . . 7C 88
Annett Cl. TW17: Shep . . . 3F 38
Annett Rd. KT12: Wal T . . . 6H 39
Anne Way KT8: W Mole . . . 3B 40
Ann Gream Ho.
RH19: E Grin . . . 8A 166
Annie Brookes Cl.
TW18: Stain . . . 4F 20
ANNINGSLEY PARK . . . 6E 54
Anningsley Pk. KT16: Otter . . . 6D 54
Annisdowne Cl.
RH5: A Ham . . . 2G 137
Annsworthy Av. CR7: T Hea . . . 2A 46
Annsworthy Cres.
SE25 . . . 1A 46
Ansell Gro. SM5: Cars . . . 7E 44
Ansell Rd. GU16: Frim . . . 6C 70
RH4: Dork . . . 1K 201 (4H 119)
SW17 . . . 4C 28
Anselm Cl. CR0: Croy . . . 9C 46
Anselm Rd. SW6 . . . 2M 13
Ansley Cl. CR2: Sande . . . 1E 84
Anson Cl. GU11: Alde . . . 1L 109
Anstead GU8: Chid . . . 6F 172
ANSTEADBROOK . . . 3N 189
Anstice Cl. W4 . . . 3D 12
Anstiebury Cl. RH5: B Grn . . . 8J 139
Anstie Grange Dr.
RH5: Holm . . . 6G 139
Anstie La. RH5: Cold . . . 6E 138
Anston Ct. GU2: Guil . . . 3H 113
Antelope Wlk. KT6: Surb . . . 4K 41
Anthony Ho. CR5: Coul . . . 9H 83
Anthony Pl. GU26: Hind . . . 7D 170
Anthony Rd. SE25 . . . 5D 46
ANTHONYS . . . 8C 54
Anthony Wall RG42: Warf . . . 9D 16
Anthony W. Ho.
RH3: Brock . . . 5A 120
Antlands La. RH6: S Bri . . . 4J 163
Antlands La. E. RH6: S Bri . . . 4K 163
Antlands La. W. RH6: S Bri . . . 4J 163
Anton Cres. SM1: Sut . . . 9M 43
Antrobus Cl. SM1: Sut . . . 2L 61
Anvil Cl. SW16 . . . 8G 28
Anvil La. KT11: Cob . . . 1H 77
Anvil Rd. TW16: Sunb . . . 2H 39
Anyards Rd. KT11: Cob . . . 9J 57
Anzio Cl. GU11: Alde . . . 2M 109
Anzio Gdns. CR3: Cate . . . 8N 83
Apeldoorn Dr. SM6: W'ton . . . 5J 63
Aperdele Rd. KT22: Leat . . . 5G 79
APERFIELD . . . 4G 87
Aperfield Rd. TN16: B Hil . . . 4G 87
Aperfields TN16: B Hil . . . 4G 86
Apers Av. GU22: Wok . . . 8B 74
APEX CORNER . . . 4N 23
Apex Ct. KT14: W By . . . 8K 55
Apex Dr. GU16: Frim . . . 5B 70
Apex Retail Pk.
TW13: Hanw . . . 4N 23
Apley Rd. RH2: Reig . . . 6M 121
Aplin Way GU18: Ligh . . . 7L 51
TW7: Isle . . . 4E 10
Apollo Dr. GU35: Bor . . . 7A 168
Apollo Pl. GU21: Wok . . . 6K 73
Apollo Ri. GU14: Cove . . . 1H 89
Apostle Way CR7: T Hea . . . 1M 45
Apperlie Dr. RH6: Horl . . . 1G 162
Appleby Cl. TW2: Twick . . . 3D 24
Appleby Gdns. TW14: Felt . . . 2G 22
Appleby Ho. KT19: Eps . . . 7C 60
Appledore RG12: Brac . . . 5L 31
Appledore Cl. SW17 . . . 3D 28
Appledore M. GU14: Farnb . . . 7M 69
Appledown Ri. CR5: Coul . . . 2G 83
Applefield RH10: Craw . . . 2C 182
Apple Gth. TW8: Brent . . . 1K 11
Applegarth CR0: N Add . . . 4L 65
(not continuous)
GU7: Goda . . . 4G 132
KT10: Clay . . . 2F 58
Applegarth Av. GU2: Guil . . . 3G 112
Apple Gro. KT9: Ches . . . 1L 59
Applelands Cl. GU10: Wrec . . . 7F 128
Apple Mkt. KT1: K Tham . . . 4H 203
Appleton Gdns. KT3: N Mal . . . 5F 42
Apple Tree Cl. KT22: Fetc . . . 2C 98
Appletree Cl. GU7: Bus . . . 9J 133
Appletree Ct. GU4: Guil . . . 9F 94
Appletree Pl. RG42: Brac . . . 9M 15
Apple Trees Pl. GU22: Wok . . . 6M 73
Appletree Way GU47: Owls . . . 6J 49
Appley Ct. GU15: Camb . . . 1N 69
Appley Dr. GU15: Camb . . . 9N 49
Approach, The KT23: Book . . . 1M 97
RH19: D Pk . . . 4B 166
Approach Rd. CR8: Pur . . . 8L 63
GU9: Farnh . . . 2H 129
KT8: W Mole . . . 4A 40
SW20 . . . 1H 43
TN16: Tats . . . 1D 106
TW15: A'ford . . . 7D 22
April Cl. BR6: Chels . . . 2N 67
GU15: Camb . . . 4A 70
KT21: A'tead . . . 5M 79
RH12: Hors . . . 4J 197
TW13: Felt . . . 4H 23
Aprilwood Cl. KT15: Wood . . . 7H 55
Apsey Ct. RG42: Bin . . . 8K 15
Apsley Ct. RH11: Craw . . . 5L 181
Apsley Ho. TW4: Houn . . . 7N 9
Apsley Rd. KT3: N Mal . . . 2B 42
SE25 . . . 3E 46
Aquarius TW1: Twick . . . 2H 25
Aquarius Ct. RH11: Craw . . . 5K 181
Aquila Cl. KT22: Leat . . . 8L 79
Arabella Dr. SW15 . . . 7D 12
Aragon Av. KT7: T Dit . . . 4F 40
KT17: Ewe . . . 6G 60
Aragon Cl. CR0: N Add . . . 6A 66
TW16: Sunb . . . 7G 22
Aragon Ct. GU21: Knap . . . 4G 72
KT8: E Mol . . . 3C 40
RG12: Brac . . . 3A 32
Aragon Pl. SM4: Mord . . . 6K 43
Aragon Rd. GU46: Yate . . . 2B 68
KT2: K Tham . . . 6L 25
SM4: Mord . . . 5J 43
Aragon Wlk. KT14: Byf . . . 9A 56
Aragorn Ct. GU2: Guil . . . 1L 113
Aram Ct. GU22: Wok . . . 2E 74
Aran Ct. KT13: Weybr . . . 8E 38
Arbor Cl. BR3: Beck . . . 1L 47
Arborfield Cl. SW2 . . . 2K 29
Arbour, The GU7: Hurt . . . 2C 132
Arbour Cl. KT22: Fetc . . . 1F 98
Arbrook Chase KT10: Esh . . . 3C 58
Arbrook Hall KT10: Clay . . . 3F 58
Arbrook La. KT10: Esh . . . 3C 58
Arbutus Cl. RH1: Red . . . 5A 122
Arbutus Rd. RH1: Red . . . 6A 122
Arcade CR0: Croy . . . 3C 200 (8N 45)
Arcade, The CR0: Croy . . . 4C 200
GU11: Alde . . . 2M 109
RG40: W'ham . . . 2B 30
Arcade Pde. KT9: Ches . . . 2K 59
Arcadia Cl. SM5: Cars . . . 1E 62
Arcadian Pl. SW18 . . . 1L 27
Archbishop Lanfranc School
Sports Cen. . . . 5J 45
Archbishop's Pl. SW2 . . . 1K 29
Archdale Pl. KT3: N Mal . . . 2A 42
Archel Rd. W14 . . . 2L 13
Archer Cl. KT2: K Tham . . . 8L 25
Archer M. TW12: H Hill . . . 7C 24
Archer Rd. SE25 . . . 3E 46
Archers Ct. CR2: S Croy . . . 8B 200
RH1: Red . . . 4D 122
(off Brighton Rd.)
RH10: Craw . . . 1B 182
Archery Pl. GU5: Gorn . . . 8D 116
Arches, The SL4: W'sor . . . 4F 4
(off Goswell Rd.)
Arch Rd. KT12: Hers . . . 9L 39
Archway Cl. SM6: Bedd . . . 9H 45
SW19 . . . 4N 27
Archway M.
RH4: Dork . . . 1J 201 (4G 119)
SW15 . . . 7K 13
(off Putney Bri. Rd.)
Archway Pl.
RH4: Dork . . . 1J 201 (4G 119)
Archway St. SW13 . . . 6D 12
Archway Theatre . . . 9F 142
Arctic Jungle Play Cen. . . . 4C 182
Arcturus Rd. RH11: Craw . . . 6K 181
Arden Cl. RG12: Brac . . . 1D 32
RH2: Reig . . . 7N 121
Arden Gro. BR6: Farnb . . . 1K 67
Arden Rd. RH10: Craw . . . 5D 182
ARDENRUN . . . 3K 145
Ardent Cl. SE25 . . . 2B 46
Ardesley Wood
KT13: Weybr . . . 1F 56
Ardfern Av. SW16 . . . 2L 45
Ardingly RG12: Brac . . . 5M 31
Ardingly Cl. CR0: Croy . . . 9G 47
RH11: Craw . . . 1N 181
Ardingly Ct.
KT18: Eps . . . 8J 201 (1C 80)
Ardingly Rd. RH19: W Hoa . . . 9E 184
Ardleigh Gdns. SM3: Sut . . . 6M 43
Ardlui Rd. SE27 . . . 3N 29
Ardmay Gdns.
KT6: Surb . . . 8K 203 (4L 41)
Ardmore Av. GU2: Guil . . . 1L 113
Ardmore Ho. GU2: Guil . . . 1L 113
Ardmore Way GU2: Guil . . . 1L 113
Ardrossan Av. GU15: Camb . . . 2E 70
Ardrossan Gdns. KT4: W Pk . . . 9F 42
Ardshiel Cl. SW15 . . . 6J 13
Ardshiel Dr. RH1: Red . . . 5C 122
Ardwell Cl. RG45: Crow . . . 2D 48
Ardwell Rd. SW2 . . . 3J 29
Ardwick Ct. GU14: Farnb . . . 3A 90
(off Sycamore Rd.)
Arena La. GU11: Alde . . . 9J 89
Arenal Dr. RG45: Crow . . . 4G 49
Arena Leisure Cen. . . . 9A 50
Arena Stop (CT) . . . 4F 46
Arethusa Way GU24: Bis . . . 3C 72
ARFORD . . . 3E 168
Arford Comn. GU35: Head . . . 3E 168
Arford Rd. GU35: Head . . . 4E 168
Argent Cl. TW20: Egh . . . 7E 20
Argent Ct. KT6: Ches . . . 9N 41
Argente Cl. GU51: Fleet . . . 1C 88
Argent Ter. GU47: C Tow . . . 7K 49
Argonaut Pk. SL3: Poy . . . 4H 7
Argon M. SW6 . . . 3M 13
Argosy Gdns. TW18: Stain . . . 7H 21
Argosy La. TW19: Stan . . . 1M 21
Argus Wlk. RH11: Craw . . . 6M 181
Argyle Av. TW3: Houn . . . 9A 10
(not continuous)
Argyle Pl. W6 . . . 1G 13
Argyle Rd. TW3: Houn . . . 8B 10
Argyle St. GU24: B'wood . . . 8L 71
Argyll Ct. GU51: Fleet . . . 4B 88
Ariel Way TW4: Houn . . . 6J 9
Arista Ct. TW20: Eng G . . . 6N 19
Ark, The W6 . . . 1J 13
(off Talgarth Rd.)
Arkell Gro. SE19 . . . 8M 29
Arkendale RH19: Fel . . . 6K 165
Arklow M. KT6: Surb . . . 8L 41
Arkwright Dr. RG42: Brac . . . 1J 31
Arkwright Ho. SW2 . . . 1J 29
(off Streatham Pl.)
Arkwright Rd. CR2: Sande . . . 6C 64
SL3: Poy . . . 5G 6
Arlesey Cl. SW15 . . . 8K 13
Arlington Bus. Pk.
RG12: Brac . . . 1M 31
Arlington Cl. RG42: Brac . . . 9M 15
SM1: Sut . . . 8M 43
TW1: Twick . . . 9J 11
Arlington Ct. RH2: Reig . . . 1N 121
UB3: Harl . . . 1F 8
Arlington Dr. SM5: Cars . . . 8D 44
Arlington Gdns. W4 . . . 1B 12
Arlington Ho. TW9: Kew . . . 3A 12
Arlington Lodge
KT13: Weybr . . . 1C 56
Arlington Pk. Mans.
W4 . . . 1B 12
(off Sutton La. Nth.)
Arlington Pas. TW11: Tedd . . . 5F 24
Arlington Rd. KT6: Surb . . . 5K 41
TW1: Twick . . . 9J 11
TW10: Ham . . . 3K 25
TW11: Tedd . . . 5F 24
TW15: A'ford . . . 6A 22
Arlington Sq. RG12: Brac . . . 1M 31
Arlington Ter. GU11: Alde . . . 2L 109
Armadale Rd. GU21: Wok . . . 4K 73
SW6 . . . 3M 13
TW14: Felt . . . 8H 9
Armfield Cl. KT8: W Mole . . . 4N 39
Armfield Cres. CR4: Mit . . . 1D 44
Armistice Gdns. SE25 . . . 2D 46
Armitage Ct. SL5: S'hill . . . 5N 33
Armitage Dr. GU16: Frim . . . 5D 70
Armoury La. RG45: Crow . . . 4F 48
Armoury Way SW18 . . . 8M 13
Armstrong Cl. KT12: Wal T . . . 5H 39
Armstrong Mall GU14: Cove . . . 1J 89
Armstrong Rd.
TW13: Hanw . . . 6M 23
TW20: Eng G . . . 7M 19
Armstrong Way
GU14: Farnb . . . 4G 88
Army Physical Training Corps Mus.
. . . 8N 89
Armytage Rd. TW5: Hest . . . 3L 9
Arnal Cres. SW18 . . . 1K 27
Arncliffe RG12: Brac . . . 4M 31
Arndale Wlk. SW18 . . . 8N 13
Arndale Way TW20: Egh . . . 6C 20
Arne Cl. RH11: Craw . . . 6L 181
Arne Gro. RH6: Horl . . . 6C 142
Arnewood Cl. KT22: Oxs . . . 1B 78
SW15 . . . 2F 26
Arneys La. CR4: Mit . . . 5E 44
Arnfield Cl. RH11: Ifi . . . 4K 181
Arnhem Cl. GU11: Alde . . . 2N 109
Arnhem Dr. CR0: N Add . . . 7N 65
Arnison Rd. KT8: E Mol . . . 3D 40
Arnold Cres. TW7: Isle . . . 8D 10
Arnold Dr. KT9: Ches . . . 3K 59
Arnold Mans. W14 . . . 2L 13
(off Queen's Club Gdns.)
Arnold Rd. GU21: Wok . . . 2D 74
SW17 . . . 8D 28
TW18: Stain . . . 8L 21
Arnott Cl. W4 . . . 1C 12
Arnulls Rd. SW16 . . . 7M 29
Arosa Rd. TW1: Twick . . . 9K 11
(not continuous)
Arragon Gdns. BR4: W Wick . . . 9L 47
SW16 . . . 8J 29
Arragon Rd. SW18 . . . 2M 27
TW1: Twick . . . 1G 24
Arran Cl. RH11: Craw . . . 6N 181
SM6: W'ton . . . 1F 62
Arrancourt RH12: Hors . . . 6G 197
Arran Way KT10: Esh . . . 8B 40
Arras Av. SM4: Mord . . . 4A 44
Arreton Mead GU21: Wok . . . 1B 74
Arrivals Rd. RH6: Gat . . . 2D 162
(not continuous)
Arrol Rd. BR3: Beck . . . 2F 46
Arrow Ind. Est. GU14: Farnb . . . 3L 89
Arrow Rd. GU14: Cove . . . 3L 89
Artel Cft. RH10: Craw . . . 3E 182
Artemis Pl. SW18 . . . 1L 27
Arterberry Rd. SW20 . . . 8H 27
Arthur Cl. GU9: Farnh . . . 2G 129
GU19: Bag . . . 6J 51
Arthur Ct. CR0: Croy . . . 4F 200
Arthur Henderson Ho.
SW6 . . . 5L 13
(off Fulham Rd.)
Arthur Rd. GU9: Farnh . . . 2G 129
(not continuous)
KT2: K Tham . . . 8N 25
KT3: N Mal . . . 4G 43
RH11: Ifi . . . 3K 181
RH13: Hors . . . 7K 197
SL4: W'sor . . . 4F 4
SW19 . . . 6L 27
TN16: B Hil . . . 2E 86
Arthur's Bri. Rd.
GU21: Wok . . . 4M 73
Arthur's Bri. Wharf
GU21: Wok . . . 4N 73
Arthurstone Birches
RG42: Bin . . . 6J 15
Arthur St. GU11: Alde . . . 2N 109
Artillery Rd.
GU1: Guil . . . 4C 202 (4N 113)
GU11: Alde . . . 2N 109
(High St.)
GU11: Alde . . . 6B 90
(North Rd.)
Artillery Ter.
GU1: Guil . . . 3C 202 (3N 113)
ARTINGTON . . . 8M 113
Artington Cl. BR6: Farnb . . . 1L 67
Artington Wlk.
GU2: Guil . . . 8B 202 (6M 113)
Arun Ct. SE25 . . . 4D 46
Arundale KT1: K Tham . . . 8H 203
Arundel Av. CR2: Sande . . . 6D 64
KT17: Ewe . . . 6G 60
SM4: Mord . . . 3L 43
Arundel Cl. CR0: Wad . . . 9M 45
GU30: Pass . . . 9C 168
GU51: Fleet . . . 5C 88
RH10: Craw . . . 3G 182
TW12: H Hill . . . 6B 24
Arundel Ct. BR2: Brom . . . 1N 47
SW13 . . . 2G 13
(off Arundel Ter.)
Arundel Ho. CR0: Croy . . . 8D 200
Arundel Mans. SW6 . . . 4L 13
(off Kelvedon Rd.)
Arundel Pl. GU9: Farnh . . . 1G 128
Arundel Rd. CR0: Croy . . . 5A 46
GU15: Camb . . . 2G 70
KT1: K Tham . . . 1A 42
RH4: Dork . . . 3H 201 (5G 118)
SM2: Chea, Sut . . . 4L 61
TW4: Houn . . . 6K 9
Arundel Ter. SW13 . . . 2G 13
Arundle Ho. GU1: Guil . . . 4D 202

Arun Ho.—Avenue, The

Arun Ho.
KT2: K Tham 1H 203 (9K 25)
Arunside RH12: Hors 7G 196
Arun Way RH13: Hors 7L 197
Ascent Ho. KT13: Weybr 2F 56
(off Ellesmere Rd.)
Aschurch Rd. CR0: Croy 6C 46
ASCOT 3L 33
Ascot Ct. GU11: Alde 3M 109
ASCOT HEATH 1K 33
Ascot M. SM6: W'ton 5G 63
Ascot Pk. SL5: Asc 2H 33
Ascot Racecourse 1K 33
Ascot Rd. RG42: Warf 1B 16
SW17 7E 28
TW14: Bedf 2B 22
Ascot Station (Rail) 3L 33
Ascot Towers SL5: Asc 1K 33
ASH 2E 110
Ashbourne RG12: Brac 5L 31
Ashbourne Cl. CR5: Coul 5G 83
GU12: Ash 1G 110
Ashbourne Ct. GU12: Ash 1G 110
Ashbourne Gro. W4 1D 12
Ashbourne Ri. BR6: Orp 1N 67
Ashbourne Rd. CR4: Mit 8E 28
Ashbourne Ter. SW19 8L 27
Ash Bri. Cvn. Pk.
GU12: Ash 4C 110
Ashbrook Rd. SL4: O Win 1L 19
Ashburnham Ct. BR3: Beck 1M 47
Ashburnham Pk. KT10: Esh 1C 58
Ashburnham Rd.
RH10: Craw 5E 182
TW10: Ham 4H 25
Ashburton Av. CR0: Croy 7E 46
Ashburton Cl. CR0: Croy 7D 46
Ashburton Ent. Cen.
SW15 9H 13
Ashburton Gdns. CR0: Croy 8D 46
Ashburton Memorial Homes
CR0: Croy 6E 46
Ashburton Rd. CR0: Croy 8D 46
Ashbury Cres. GU4: Guil 1E 114
Ashbury Dr. GU17: Haw 5M 69
Ashbury Pl. SW19 7A 28
Ashby Av. KT9: Ches 3N 59
Ashby Ct. RH13: Hors 6L 197
Ashby's Cl. TN8: Eden 3M 147
Ashby Wlk. CR0: Croy 5N 45
Ashby Way UB7: Sip 3B 8
Ash Church M. GU12: Ash 2E 110
Ash Church Rd. GU12: Ash 2F 110
Ash Cl. GU12: Ash 1F 110
GU17: B'water 1H 69
GU22: Pyr 2J 75
GU22: Wok 7A 74
KT3: N Mal 1C 42
KT20: Box H 9B 100
RH1: Mers 8G 103
RH7: Ling 6A 146
RH10: Craw D 1F 184
SE20 1F 46
SM5: Cars 8D 44
TN8: Eden 2K 147
Ash Combe GU8: Chid 5D 172
Ashcombe Av. KT6: Surb 6K 41
Ashcombe Cl. TW15: A'ford 4N 21
Ashcombe Dr. TN8: Eden 8K 127
Ashcombe Pde. GU22: Wok 7C 74
(off Kingfield Rd.)
Ashcombe Rd. RH1: Mers 5G 102
RH4: Dork 3G 118
SM5: Cars 3E 62
SW19 6M 27
Ashcombe Sq. KT3: N Mal 2B 42
Ashcombe St. SW6 5N 13
Ashcombe Ter. KT20: Tad 7G 80
Ash Ct. KT15: Addl 2K 55
KT19: Ewe 1B 60
KT22: Leat 7F 78
RG40: W'ham 2B 30
RH19: E Grin 7A 166
SW19 8K 27
Ashcroft GU4: Chil 1A 134
Ashcroft Pk. KT11: Cob 8M 57
Ashcroft Pl. KT22: Leat 8J 79
Ashcroft Ri. CR5: Coul 3J 83
Ashcroft Rd. KT9: Ches 9M 41
Ashcroft Sq. W6 1H 13
Ashcroft Theatre 4D 200
Ashdale KT23: Book 4C 98
Ashdale Cl. TW2: Whitt 1C 24
TW19: Stan 3N 21
Ashdale Pk. RG40: Finch 1B 48
Ashdale Way TW2: Whitt 1B 24
Ashdene Cl. TW15: A'ford 8D 22
Ashdene Cres. GU12: Ash 1E 110
Ashdene Ho. TW20: Eng G 7M 19
Ashdene Rd. GU12: Ash 1E 110
Ashdown Av. GU14: Farnb 2B 90
Ashdown Cl. BR3: Beck 1L 47
GU22: Wok 5A 74
RG12: Brac 1E 32
RH2: Reig 7N 121
RH18: F Row 7J 187
Ashdown Ct. RH10: Craw 6D 182
RH13: Hors 4M 197
SM2: Sut 3A 62
Ashdown Dr. RH10: Craw 6B 182
Ashdown Gdns. CR2: Sande 2E 84
Ashdown Ga.
RH19: E Grin 8N 165
Ashdown Ho. RH6: Gat 3E 162
Ashdown Pl. KT7: T Dit 6G 40
KT17: Ewe 4E 60
RH18: F Row 9G 186
Ashdown Rd.
KT1: K Tham 4J 203 (1L 41)
KT17: Eps 9E 60
RH2: Reig 7N 121
RH18: F Row 7H 187
Ashdown Vw.
RH19: E Grin 2A 186
Ashdown Way SW17 3E 28
Ash Dr. RH1: Red 5E 122
Ashe Ho. TW1: Twick 9K 11
Ashenden Rd. GU2: Guil 3J 113
Ashen Gro. SW19 4M 27
Ashen Va. CR2: Sels 5G 65
Asher Dr. SL5: Asc 9G 17
Ashfield RH14: Plais 6A 192
Ashfield Av. TW13: Felt 2J 23
Ashfield Cl. TW10: Ham 2L 25
Ashfield Grn. GU46: Yate 1E 68
Ashfield Ho. W14 1L 13
(off W. Cromwell Rd.)
Ashfields Ct. RH2: Reig 1N 121
ASHFORD 5A 22
Ashford Av. TW15: A'ford 7C 22
Ashford Bus. Complex
TW15: A'ford 6D 22
Ashford Cl. TW15: A'ford 5N 21
ASHFORD COMMON 8E 22
Ashford Cres.
TW15: A'ford 4N 21
Ashford Gdns. KT11: Cob 3L 77
Ashford Ind. Est.
TW15: A'ford 5D 22
ASHFORD PARK 5M 21
Ashford Rd. TW13: Felt 5E 22
TW15: A'ford 8D 22
TW18: Lale, Stain 1L 37
Ashford Sports Cen. 5M 21
Ashford Station (Rail) 5A 22
ASH GREEN 4G 111
Ash Grn. La. E.
GU12: A Grn 4G 111
Ash Grn. La. W.
GU12: Ash 4D 110
(not continuous)
Ash Grn. Rd. GU12: A Grn 3G 110
Ash Gro. BR4: W Wick 8M 47
GU2: Guil 3K 113
SE20 1F 46
TW5: Hest 4L 9
TW14: Felt 2F 22
TW18: Stain 7L 21
Ashgrove Rd.
TW15: A'ford 6D 22
Ash Hill Rd. GU12: A Va 9E 90
Ash Ho. TW15: A'ford 5A 22
(off Station Rd.)
Ashington Ct. RH12: Hors 3K 197
(off Woodstock Cl.)
Ashington Rd. SW6 5L 13
Ash Keys RH10: Craw 4C 182
Ashlake Rd. SW16 5J 29
Ash La. GU8: Els 9G 130
SL4: W'sor 5A 4
Ashlea Ct. CR6: Warl 5D 84
Ashleigh Av. TW20: Egh 8E 20
Ashleigh Cl. RH6: Horl 8D 142
Ashleigh Cotts.
RH5: Holm 4H 139
Ashleigh Gdns. SM1: Sut 8N 43
Ashleigh Rd. RH12: Hors 3J 197
SE20 2E 46
SW14 6D 12
Ashley Av.
KT18: Eps 7J 201 (9C 60)
SM4: Mord 4M 43
Ashley Cen.
KT18: Eps 7J 201 (9C 60)
Ashley Cl. GU16: Frim G 8E 70
KT12: Wal T 7G 38
KT23: Book 3N 97
Ashley Ct. GU21: Wok 5J 73
KT18: Eps 7K 201 (9C 60)
Ashley Dr. GU17: B'water 2H 69
KT12: Wal T 9H 39
SM7: Ban 1M 81
TW2: Whitt 1B 24
TW7: Isle 2E 10
Ashley Gdns. BR6: Orp 2N 67
GU4: Chil 1B 134
TW10: Ham 3K 25
Ashley Ho. GU7: Goda 3H 133
Ashley La.
CR0: Wad 7A 200 (1M 63)
ASHLEY PARK 9H 39
Ashley Pk. Av. KT12: Wal T 8G 39
Ashley Pk. Cres.
KT12: Wal T 7H 39
Ashley Pk. Rd. KT12: Wal T 8H 39
Ashley Pl. KT12: Wal T 8H 39
(off Ashley Rd.)
Ashley Ri. KT12: Wal T 1H 57
Ashley Rd. CR7: T Hea 3K 45
GU14: Farnb 1B 90
GU21: Wok 5J 73
KT7: T Dit 5F 40
KT12: Wal T 1G 57
KT18: Eps 1C 80
KT18: Eps, Eps D
7K 201 (9C 60)
Ashley Rd. RH4: Westc 6C 118
SW19 7N 27
TW9: Rich 6L 11
TW12: Hamp 9A 24
Ashley Sq. KT18: Eps 7J 201
Ashley Way GU24: W End 9A 52
Ashling Rd. CR0: Croy 7D 46
Ash Lodge TW16: Sunb 8G 22
(off Forest Dr.)
Ash Lodge Cl. GU12: Ash 3E 110
Ash Lodge Dr. GU12: Ash 3E 110
(not continuous)
Ashlone Rd. SW15 6H 13
Ashlyns Pk. KT11: Cob 9M 57
Ashlyns Way KT9: Ches 3K 59
Ash Manor Sports Cen. 4D 110
Ashmead Rd. TW14: Felt 2H 23
Ashmere Av. BR3: Beck 1N 47
Ashmere Cl. SM3: Chea 2J 61
Ash M.
KT18: Eps 7L 201 (9D 60)
Ashmore Ct. TW5: Hest 2A 10
Ashmore Ho. RH11: Craw 9B 162
Ashmore La. BR2: Kes 7E 66
RH12: Rusp 3B 180
SL4: Wink 1D 16
Ashridge GU14: Cove 7L 69
Ashridge Grn. RG42: Brac 9N 15
Ashridge Rd. RG40: W'ham 9C 14
Ashridge Way SM4: Mord 2L 43
TW16: Sunb 7H 23
Ash Rd. CR0: Croy 8K 47
GU12: Alde 3A 110
GU22: Wok 7N 73
GU24: Pirb 4C 92
RH10: Craw 2E 182
SM3: Sut 6K 43
TN16: Weste 3M 107
TW17: Shep 3B 38
Ash Station (Rail) 2F 110
Ashstead La. GU7: Goda 9F 132
Ash St. GU12: Ash 3D 110
ASHTEAD 5M 79
Ashtead Common National
Nature Reserve 2J 79
Ashtead Gap KT22: Leat 3H 79
ASHTEAD PARK 5N 79
Ashtead Station (Rail) 4L 79
Ashtead Woods Rd.
KT21: A'tead 4J 79
Ashton Cl. KT12: Hers 3J 57
SM1: Sut 1M 61
Ashton Gdns. TW4: Houn 7N 9
Ashton Rd. GU21: Wok 4J 73
Ashtree Av. CR4: Mit 1B 44
Ash Tree Cl. CR0: Croy 5H 47
GU14: Cove 2H 89
GU27: G'wood 8K 171
KT6: Surb 8L 41
Ashtree Cl. BR6: Farnb 1K 67
Ash Tree Cl. TW15: A'ford 6C 22
(off Feltham Hill Rd.)
Ashtrees GU6: Cranl 9N 155
Ash Tree Way CR0: Croy 4G 47
Ashurst KT18: Eps 7J 201 (1C 80)
Ashurst Cl. CR8: Ken 2A 84
KT22: Leat 8G 78
RH12: Hors 3N 197
Ashurst Dr. KT20: Box H 8A 100
RH10: Wor 3H 183
TW17: Shep 4N 37
Ashurst Gdns. SW2 2L 29
Ashurst Pk. SL5: S'hill 2B 34
Ashurst Pl. RH4: Dork 4J 119
Ashurst Rd. GU12: A Va 9D 90
KT20: Tad 8G 81
Ashurst Wlk. CR0: Croy 8E 46
ASHURSTWOOD 3F 186
ASH VALE 6E 90
Ash Va. GU8: Chid 4D 172
Ashvale Rd. SW17 6D 28
Ash Vale Station (Rail) 6E 90
Ash Vw. Cl. TW15: A'ford 7N 21
Ashview Gdns.
TW15: A'ford 6N 21
Ashville Way RG41: W'ham 3A 30
Ashway Cen., The
KT2: K Tham 2K 203 (9L 25)
Ashwell Av. GU15: Camb 9D 50
Ashwell Ct. TW15: A'ford 3N 21
Ashwick Cl. CR3: Cate 2D 104
Ashwindham Ct. GU21: Wok 5J 73
Ashwood CR6: Warl 7F 84
RH11: Craw 4B 182
Ashwood Ct. RH18: F Row 8H 187
Ashwood Gdns.
CR0: N Add 3M 65
Ashwood Pk. GU22: Wok 5C 74
KT22: Fetc 1C 98
Ashwood Pl. GU22: Wok 5C 74
SL5: S'dale 6B 34
Ashwood Rd. GU22: Wok 5B 74
TW20: Eng G 7L 19
Ashworth Est. CR0: Bedd 7J 45
Ashworth Pl. GU2: Guil 3J 113
Askill Dr. SW15 8K 13
Aslett St. SW18 1N 27
Asmar Cl. CR5: Coul 2J 83
Aspects SM1: Sut 2N 61
Aspen Cl. GU4: Guil 9F 94
KT11: Sto D 3M 77
TW18: Stain 4H 21
Aspen Ct. GU25: V Wat 3A 36
Aspen Gdns. CR4: Mit 4E 44
TW15: A'ford 6D 22
W6 1G 13
Aspen Gro. GU12: Alde 4C 110
Aspen Ho. CR6: Warl 2L 85
Aspenlea Rd. W6 2J 13
Aspen Sq. KT13: Weybr 9E 38
Aspen Va. CR3: Whyte 4C 84
Aspen Way RH12: Hors 4L 197
SM7: Ban 1J 81
TW13: Felt 4J 23
Aspin Way GU17: B'water 1G 68
Aspley Rd. SW18 8N 13
Asprey Gro. CR3: Cate 2D 104
Asprey M. BR3: Beck 4J 47
Asquith Ho. SM7: Ban 2L 81
(off Dunnymans Rd.)
Assembly Wlk. SM5: Cars 6C 44
Assher Rd. KT12: Hers 9M 39
Astede Pl. KT21: A'tead 5M 79
Astleham Rd. TW17: Shep 2N 37
Astley Ho. SW13 2G 13
(off Wyatt Dr.)
Astolat Bus. Pk., The
GU3: P'marsh 2M 133
Astolat Way
GU3: P'marsh 2M 133
Aston Cl. KT21: A'tead 5J 79
Aston Ct. RH11: Craw 8N 181
Aston Grange RG12: Brac 3C 32
Aston Grn. TW4: C'ford 5K 9
Aston Mead SL4: W'sor 4B 4
Aston Pl. SW16 7M 29
Aston Rd. KT10: Clay 2E 58
SW20 1H 43
Aston Ter. SW12 1F 28
Astonville St. SW18 2M 27
Aston Way KT18: Eps 2E 80
Astor Cl. KT2: K Tham 7A 26
KT15: Addl 1M 55
Astor Ct. SW6 3N 13
(off Maynard Cl.)
Astoria Ct. CR8: Pur 7M 63
(off High St.)
Astoria Mans. SW16 4J 29
Astra Bus. Cen. RH1: Salf 4F 142
Astral Towers RH10: Craw 8B 162
Astra Mead RG42: Wink R 7F 16
Astrid Ho. TW13: Felt 3K 23
Asylum Arch Rd.
RH1: Red 6D 122
Atalanta Cl. CR8: Pur 6L 63
Atalanta St. SW6 3J 13
Atbara Rd. GU52: C Cro 9B 88
TW11: Tedd 7H 25
Atcham Rd. TW3: Houn 7C 10
Atfield Gro. GU20: Windl 3A 52
Atheldene Rd. SW18 2N 27
Athelstan Cl. RH10: Wor 3J 183
Athelstan Ho.
KT1: K Tham 7M 203
Athelstan Rd.
KT1: K Tham 7M 203 (3M 41)
Athelstan Way RH13: Hors 8L 197
Athena Cl.
KT1: K Tham 5L 203 (2M 41)
Atherfield Ho. RH2: Reig 6A 122
(off Atherfield Rd.)
Atherfield Rd. RH2: Reig 6A 122
Atherley Way TW4: Houn 1N 23
Atherton Cl. GU4: Chil 9A 114
TW19: Stan 9M 7
Atherton Ct. SL4: Eton 3G 4
Atherton Dr. SW19 5J 27
Atherton Rd. SW13 3F 12
Athlone KT10: Clay 3E 58
Athlone Rd. SW2 1K 29
Athlone Sq. SL4: W'sor 4F 4
Atkins Cl. GU21: Wok 5K 73
TN16: B Hil 8E 66
Atkins Dr. BR4: W Wick 8N 47
Atkinson Ct. RH6: Horl 9F 142
Atkinson Rd. RH10: Craw 5G 182
Atkins Rd. SW12 1G 28
Atlanta Ct. CR7: T Hea 2N 45
Atlantic Ho. RH6: Gat 2E 162
Atney Rd. SW15 7K 13
Atrebatti Rd. GU47: Sandh 6H 49
Atrium, The 9A 166
Atrium, The GU7: Goda 7H 133
Atrium Ct. RG12: Brac 1A 32
Atspeed Stadium 7K 197
Attebrouche Ct. RG12: Brac 6B 32
Atte La. RG42: Warf 7A 16
Attenborough Cl.
GU51: Fleet 2C 88
Atterbury Cl. TN16: Weste 4M 107
Attfield Cl. GU12: Ash 3D 110
Attfield Ct. KT1: K Tham 4L 203
Attlee Cl. CR7: T Hea 4N 45
Attlee Gdns. GU52: C Cro 9A 88
Attlee Ho. RH11: Craw 7N 181
Attleford La. GU8: S'ford 5K 131
Attwood Cl. CR2: Sande 1E 84
Atwater Cl. SW2 2L 29
Atwell Pl. KT7: T Dit 7F 40
Atwood KT23: Book 2M 97
Atwood Av. TW9: Kew 5N 11
Atwoods All. TW9: Kew 4N 11
Aubyn Hill SE27 5N 29
Aubyn Sq. SW15 8F 12
Auchinleck Ct.
RH10: Craw D 2E 184
Auchinleck Way
GU11: Alde 2K 109
Auckland Cl. RH11: Craw 9B 162
Auckland Gdns. SE19 1B 46
Auckland Hill SE27 5N 29
Auckland Ho. KT12: Wal T 7H 39
Auckland Rd. CR3: Cate 9B 84
KT1: K Tham 7M 203 (3M 41)
SE19 1C 46
Auden Pl. SM3: Chea 1H 61
Audley Cl. KT15: Addl 2K 55
Audley Ct. TW2: Twick 4D 24
Audley Dr. CR6: Warl 2F 84
Audley Firs KT12: Hers 1K 57
Audley Ho. KT15: Addl 2K 55
Audley Pl. SM2: Sut 4N 61
Audley Rd. TW10: Rich 8M 11
Audley Way SL5: Asc 2H 33
Audrey Cl. BR3: Beck 5L 47
Audric Cl. KT2: K Tham 9N 25
Augur Cl. TW18: Stain 6H 21
Augusta Cl. KT8: W Mole 2N 39
Augusta Rd. TW2: Twick 3C 24
Augustine Cl. SL3: Poy 6G 7
Augustine Wlk. RG42: Warf 8C 16
August La. GU5: Alb 4M 135
Augustus Cl. TW8: Brent 3J 11
Augustus Ct. SW16 3H 29
TW13: Hanw 5N 23
Augustus Gdns.
GU15: Camb 1G 71
Augustus Rd. SW19 2J 27
Aultone Way SM1: Sut 8N 43
SM5: Cars 9D 44
Aultone Yd. Ind. Est.
SM5: Cars 9D 44
Aura Ho. TW9: Kew 4A 12
Aurelia Gdns. CR0: Croy 4K 45
Aurelia Rd. CR0: Croy 5J 45
Auriol Cl. KT4: W Pk 9D 42
Auriol Mans. W14 1K 13
(off Edith Rd.)
Auriol Pk. Rd. KT4: W Pk 9D 42
Auriol Rd. W14 1K 13
Aurum Cl. RH6: Horl 9F 142
Austen Apartments SE20 1E 46
Austen Cl. RH19: E Grin 9L 165
Austen Ct. KT22: Leat 8G 78
(off Highbury Dr.)
Austen Rd. GU1: Guil 4B 114
GU14: Farnb 8M 69
Austen Vw. SL3: Lang 2B 6
Austen Way SL3: Lang 2B 6
Austin Cl. CR5: Coul 5M 83
TW1: Twick 8J 11
Austins Cotts. GU9: Farnh 1G 128
Austin Way RG12: Brac 3A 32
Austyn Gdns. KT5: Surb 7A 42
Austyns Pl. KT17: Ewe 5F 60
Autumn Cl. RH11: Craw 4A 182
SW19 7A 28
Autumn Dr. SM2: Sut 5N 61
Autumn Lodge CR0: Croy 7F 200
Avalon Cl. SW20 1K 43
Avalon Rd. SW6 4N 13
Avante
KT1: K Tham 5H 203 (2K 41)
Avard Gdns. BR6: Farnb 1L 67
Avarn Rd. SW17 7D 28
Avebury RG12: Brac 5M 31
Avebury Cl. RH12: Hors 1N 197
Avebury Pk. KT6: Surb 6K 41
Avebury Rd. BR6: Orp 1M 67
SW19 9L 27
Aveley Cl. GU9: Farnh 4H 129
Aveley La. GU9: Farnh 5G 129
Aveling Cl. CR8: Pur 9K 63
RH10: Craw 5G 182
Aven Cl. GU6: Cranl 8N 155
Avening Rd. SW18 1M 27
Avening Ter. SW18 1M 27
Avenue, The BR2: Kes 1F 66
BR4: W Wick 6M 47
CR0: Croy 4F 200 (9B 46)
CR3: Whyte 6D 84
CR5: Coul 2H 83
GU3: Comp 1F 132
GU3: Worp 5H 93
GU6: Ewh 4F 156
GU7: Goda 1F 132
(New Pond Rd.)
GU7: Goda 9H 133
(The Drive)
GU10: Rowl 8D 128
(not continuous)
GU12: Alde 5A 110
GU15: Camb 2N 69
GU18: Ligh 6L 51
GU24: Chob 5K 53
GU26: G'hott 6B 170
GU27: Hasl 1D 188
KT4: W Pk 8E 42
KT5: Surb 5M 41
KT10: Clay 3E 58
KT15: N Haw 6J 55
KT17: Ewe 4G 60
KT20: Tad 9G 80
KT22: Oxs 7F 58
RG40: W'ham 7K 31
RG45: Crow 1F 48
RH1: Sth N 6J 123
RH3: Brock 3N 119
RH6: Horl 9D 142

Avenue, The—Barlow Rd.

Avenue, The RH10: Craw 8B 182
RH17: Hand 8L 199
RH19: E Grin 4C 166
SL3: Dat 4L 5
SL4: O Win 8L 5
SL5: Asc 8K 17
SM2: Chea 1K 61
SM3: Chea 4H 61
SM5: Cars 4E 62
SW18 . . . . .1C 28
TN16: Tats, Weste 9H 87
TW1: Twick 8H 11
TW3: Houn 8B 10
TW5: C'ford 3H 9
TW9: Kew 5M 11
TW12: Hamp 7N 23
TW16: Sunb 9J 23
TW18: Stain 9K 21
TW19: Wray 6N 5
TW20: Egh 5D 20
Avenue C KT15: Addl 9N 37
Avenue Cl. KT20: Tad 9G 81
TW5: C'ford 4J 9
Avenue Ct. KT20: Tad 1G 101
Avenue Cres. TW5: C'ford 4J 9
Avenue de Cagny
GU24: Pirb 9C 72
Avenue Elmers
KT6: Surb 8J 203 (4L 41)
Avenue Gdns. RH6: Horl 9G 142
SE25 . . . . .1D 46
SW14 . . . . .6D 12
TW5: C'ford 3J 9
TW11: Tedd 8F 24
Avenue One KT15: Addl 1N 55
Avenue Pde. TW16: Sunb 2J 39
Avenue Pk. Rd. SE27 . . . . .3M 29
Avenue Rd. BR3: Beck 1G 46
CR3: Cate 9A 84
GU6: Cranl 9N 155
GU14: Farnb 1B 90
GU26: G'hott 6A 170
GU51: Fleet 3A 88
KT1: K Tham 5K 203 (2L 41)
KT3: N Mal 3D 42
KT11: Cob 3L 77
KT18: Eps 8K 201 (1C 80)
SE20 . . . . .1G 46
SE25 . . . . .1C 46
SM2: Sut 6M 61
SM6: W'ton 4G 62
SM7: Ban 2N 81
SW16 . . . . .1H 45
SW20 . . . . .1G 42
TN16: Tats 7G 87
TW7: Isle 4F 10
TW8: Brent 1J 11
TW11: Tedd 8G 24
TW12: Hamp 9B 24
TW13: Felt 4G 23
TW18: Stain 6F 20
Avenue Road Stop (CT) 1G 47
Avenue Sth. KT5: Surb 6N 41
Avenue Sucy GU15: Camb 2M 69
(not continuous)
Avenue Ter. KT3: N Mal 2B 42
Avenue Three KT15: Addl 9N 37
Avenue Two KT15: Addl 1N 55
Avenue Vs. RH1: Mers 7G 103
Averil Gro. SW16 . . . . .7M 29
Averill St. W6 . . . . .2J 13
Avern Gdns. KT8: W Mole 3B 40
Avern Rd. KT8: W Mole 3B 40
Avery Ct. *GU11: Alde 2N 109*
(off Alice Rd.)
Aviary Rd. GU22: Pyr 3J 75
Aviary Way RH10: Craw D 9F 164
Aviator Pk. KT15: Addl 9M 37
Aviemore Cl. BR3: Beck 4J 47
Aviemore Way BR3: Beck 4H 47
Avington Cl.
GU1: Guil 2F 202 (3A 114)
Avoca Rd. SW17 . . . . .5E 28
Avocet Cres. GU47: C Tow 7J 49
Avon Cl. GU12: Ash 3D 110
GU14: Cove 7K 69
KT4: W Pk 8F 42
KT15: Addl 3J 55
SM1: Sut 1A 62
Avon Ct. GU9: Farnh 2H 129
RG42: Bin 7H 15
SW15 . . . . .8K 13
Avondale GU12: A Va 6D 90
Avondale Av. KT4: W Pk 7E 42
KT10: H Wood 9G 40
TW18: Stain 8H 21
Avondale Cl. KT12: Hers 2K 57
RH6: Horl 6D 142
Avondale Ct. *SM2: Sut 4A 62*
(off Brighton Rd.)
Avondale Gdns. TW4: Houn 8N 9
Avondale High CR3: Cate 8E 84
Avondale Rd. CR2: S Croy 3N 63
GU11: Alde 4N 109
GU51: Fleet 3B 88
SW14 . . . . .6D 12
SW19 . . . . .6N 27
TW15: A'ford 4M 21
Avon Gro. RG12: Brac 8A 16
Avon Ho.
KT2: K Tham 1H 203 (9K 25)
W14 . . . . .1L 13
(off Kensington Village)
Avonmead GU21: Wok 5M 73
Avonmore Av. GU1: Guil 2B 114
Avon Path CR2: S Croy 3N 63
Avon Rd. GU9: Farnh 2H 129
TW16: Sunb 8G 22
Avon Wlk. RH11: Craw 4L 181
Avonwick Rd. TW3: Houn 5B 10
Avro Way KT13: Weybr 6N 55
SM6: W'ton 4J 63
Award Rd. GU52: C Cro 8A 88
(not continuous)
Axbridge RG12: Brac 4C 32
Axes La. RH1: Salf 1G 142
Axis Pk. SL3: Lang 1D 6
Axwood KT18: Eps 2B 80
Ayebridges Av. TW20: Egh 8E 20
Ayesgarth GU52: C Cro 8C 88
Ayjay Cl. GU11: Alde 5N 109
Aylesbury Ct. SM1: Sut 9A 44
Aylesford Av. BR3: Beck 4H 47
Aylesham Way GU46: Yate 9A 48
Aylesworth Spur SL4: O Win . . .1L 19
Aylett Rd. SE25 . . . . .3E 46
TW7: Isle 5E 10
Ayliffe Cl. KT1: K Tham 1N 41
Ayling Ct. GU9: Weybo 5L 109
Ayling Hill GU11: Alde 3L 109
Ayling La. GU11: Alde 4L 109
Aylward Rd. SW20 . . . . .1L 43
Aymer Cl. TW18: Stain 9G 20
Aymer Dr. TW18: Stain 9G 21
Aynscombe Path
SW14 . . . . .5B 12
Ayrshire Gdns. GU51: Fleet 1C 88
Aysgarth RG12: Brac 5L 31
Aysgarth Ct. SM1: Sut 9N 43
Ayshe Ct. Dr. RH13: Hors 6L 197
Azalea Av. GU35: Lind 4B 168
Azalea Ct. GU22: Wok 6N 73
Azalea Dr. GU27: Hasl 9D 170
Azalea Gdns. GU52: C Cro 8C 88
Azalea Ho. TW13: Felt 2J 23
Azalea Way GU15: Camb 9F 50

B

Babbacombe Cl. KT9: Ches . . .2K 59
Babbage Way RG12: Brac 5M 31
Babbs Mead GU9: Farnh 2F 128
Baber Bri. Cvn. Site
TW14: Felt 8K 9
Baber Dr. TW14: Felt 9K 9
Babington Rd. SW16 . . . . .6H 29
Babylon La. KT20: Lwr K 5M 101
Bachelors Acre SL4: W'sor 4G 4
Bachelors La. GU23: Ockh 2A 96
Back All.
RH4: Dork 2K 201 (5H 119)
Back Dr. RG45: Crow 4G 48
Back Grn. KT12: Hers 3K 57
Back La. GU4: E Cla 9M 95
GU8: Els 7H 131
GU10: B Oak 2A 148
GU10: Fren 1J 149
RH2: Reig 7B 102
RH10: Bal, T Hil 7N 183
RH14: Plais 6A 192
RH17: T Hil 9N 183
TW8: Brent 2K 11
TW10: Ham 4J 25
Backley Gdns. SE25 . . . . .5D 46
Back of High St.
GU24: Chob 7H 53
Back Path RH1: Blet 2N 123
Back Rd. TW11: Tedd 8E 24
Bacon Cl. GU47: C Tow 8J 49
Bacon La. GU10: Churt 6H 149
Badajos Rd. GU11: Alde 1L 109
Baddeley Ho. *KT8: W Mole 4A 40*
(off Down St.)
Baden Cl. TW18: Stain 8K 21
Baden Dr. RH6: Horl 7C 142
Baden Powell Cl.
KT6: Surb 8M 41
Baden Powell Ct.
GU7: Goda 5G 132
Baden Rd. GU2: Guil 1K 113
Bader Cl. CR8: Ken 2A 84
Bader Ct. GU14: Cove 6L 69
RH10: Craw 1B 182
Badger Cl. GU2: Guil 9L 93
TW4: Houn 6K 9
TW13: Felt 4J 23
Badger Ct. GU10: Wrec 6F 128
Badger Dr. GU18: Ligh 6L 51
Badgersbridge Ride
SL4: Wink 1M 17
Badgers Cl. GU7: Goda 3G 133
GU21: Wok 5M 73
GU52: Fleet 5A 88
RH12: Hors 2M 197
TW15: A'ford 6A 22
Badgers Copse
GU15: Camb 3C 70
KT4: W Pk 8E 42
Badger's Ct.
KT17: Eps 7L 201 (9D 60)
Badgers Cross GU8: Mil 1C 152
Badgers Hill GU25: V Wat 4M 35
Badgers Hole CR0: Croy 1G 64
Badgers Hollow
GU7: Goda 5G 132
Badgers Holt GU46: Yate 1A 68
Badgers La. CR6: Warl 7F 84
Badger's Lodge
KT17: Eps 6M 201 (9D 60)
Badgers Sett RG45: Crow 2E 48
Badgers Wlk. CR3: Whyte 5C 84
CR8: Pur 7G 63
KT3: N Mal 1D 42
Badgers Way RG12: Brac 9D 16
RH14: Loxw 4J 193
RH19: E Grin 8B 166
Badgers Wood CR3: Cate 3A 104
Badger Wlk. GU3: Norm 6N 91
Badger Way GU10: Ews 4C 108
GU12: Alde 1B 110
Badgerwood Dr. GU16: Frim . . .4B 70
Badingham Dr. KT22: Fetc 1E 98
Badminton Rd. SW12 . . . . .1E 28
Badshot Farm La.
GU9: B Lea 7M 109
BADSHOT LEA 7M 109
Badshot Lea Rd.
GU9: B Lea 7L 109
Badshot Pk. GU9: B Lea 6M 109
Bagden Hill RH5: Westh 8D 98
Bagley's La. SW6 . . . . .4N 13
Bagot Cl. KT21: A'tead 3M 79
BAGSHOT 4J 51
Bagshot Grn. GU19: Bag 5J 51
Bagshot Rd. GU3: Worp 1F 92
GU19: Bag 2N 31
GU21: B'wood, Knap 5E 72
GU24: Chob, W End 8B 52
GU24: Wok 8E 72
RG12: Bag, Brac 2N 31
SL5: Asc 8M 33
TW20: Eng G 8M 19
Bagshot Station (Rail) 3J 51
Bahram Rd. KT19: Eps 6C 60
Baigents La. GU20: Windl 3A 52
Bailes La. GU3: Norm 9A 92
Bailey Cl. GU16: Frim 6B 70
RH12: Hors 1M 197
SL4: W'sor 5D 4
Bailey Cres. KT9: Ches 4K 59
Bailey Ho. *SW10 . . . . .3N 13*
(off Coleridge Gdns.)
Bailey M. *W4 . . . . .2A 12*
(off Hervert Gdns.)
Bailey Rd. RH4: Westc 6C 118
Baileys Cl. GU17: B'water 2H 69
Bailing Hill RH12: Warn 1E 196
Baillie Rd. GU1: Guil 4B 114
Bain Av. GU15: Camb 4N 69
Bainbridge Cl. TW10: Ham 6L 25
Baines Cl.
CR2: S Croy 8D 200 (2A 64)
Bainton Mead GU21: Wok 4K 73
Baird Cl. RH10: Craw 9E 162
Baird Dr. GU3: Wood V 2E 112
Baird Rd. GU14: Farnb 8A 70
Bakeham La. TW20: Eng G 8N 19
Bakehouse Barn Cl.
RH12: Hors 1L 197
Bakehouse Gdns.
GU52: C Cro 8C 88
Bakehouse M. GU11: Alde . . .2M 109
TW12: Hamp 8A 24
Bakehouse Rd. RH6: Horl 6D 142
Baker Boy La. CR0: Sels 9H 65
Baker Cl. RH10: Craw 5B 182
Baker La. CR4: Mit 1E 44
Bakers Cl. CR8: Ken 1N 83
RH7: Ling 6A 146
Bakers Ct. RH1: Red 4D 122
SE25 . . . . .2B 46
Bakers End SW20 . . . . .1K 43
Bakers Gdns. SM5: Cars 8C 44
Bakersgate Courtyard
GU24: Pirb 4D 92
Bakersgate Gdns.
GU24: Pirb 3D 92
Bakers La. RH7: Ling 7N 145
Bakers Mead RH9: Gods 8F 104
Baker St. KT13: Weybr 1B 56
Bakers Way RH5: Cap 5J 159
Baker's Yd.
GU1: Guil 5D 202 (4N 113)
Bakery M. KT6: Surb 7N 41
Bakewell Way KT3: N Mal 1D 42
Balaam Ho. SM1: Sut 1M 61
Balaclava Rd. KT6: Surb 6J 41
Balchins La. RH4: Westc 7A 118
Balcombe Ct. RH10: Craw 2H 183
Balcombe Gdns.
RH6: Horl 9G 142
Balcombe Rd. RH6: Horl 7F 142
RH10: Craw, Wor 2H 183
Baldreys GU9: Farnh 3F 128
Baldry Gdns. SW16 . . . . .7J 29
Baldwin Cl. RH10: Craw 6G 183
Baldwin Cres. GU4: Guil 1E 114
Baldwin Gdns. TW3: Houn 4C 10
Baldwin Ho. SW2 . . . . .2L 29
Baldwin's Bec *SL4: Eton 2G 4*
(off Baldwin's Shore)
Baldwins Fld.
RH19: E Grin 6N 165
BALDWINS HILL 7N 165
Baldwins Shore SL4: Eton 2G 4
Balfern Gro. W4 . . . . .1D 12
Balfont Cl. CR2: Sande 9D 64
Balfour Av. GU22: Wok 9A 74
Balfour Cres. RG12: Brac 4N 31
Balfour Gdns.
RH18: F Row 9G 187
Balfour Ho. KT13: Weybr 1B 56
Balfour Pl. SW15 . . . . .7G 12
Balfour Rd. KT13: Weybr 1B 56
SE25 . . . . .4D 46
SM5: Cars 4D 62
SW19 . . . . .8N 27
TW3: Houn 6B 10
Balgowan Cl. KT3: N Mal 4D 42
Balgowan Rd. BR3: Beck 2H 47
BALHAM 2E 28
Balham Continental Mkt.
SW12 . . . . .2F 28
(off Shipka Rd.)
Balham Gro. SW12 . . . . .1E 28
Balham High Rd.
SW12 . . . . .4E 28
SW17 . . . . .4E 28
Balham Hill SW12 . . . . .1F 28
Balham Leisure Cen. 3F 28
Balham New Rd.
SW12 . . . . .1F 28
Balham Pk. Rd. SW12 . . . . . . .2D 28
Balham Station (Rail & Tube)
. . . . .2F 28
Balham Sta. Rd. SW12 . . . . . . .2F 28
Balintore Ct. GU47: C Tow 7J 49
Ballands Nth., The
KT22: Fetc 9E 78
Ballands Sth., The
KT22: Fetc 1E 98
Ball & Wicket La.
GU9: U Hal 5H 109
Ballantine St. SW18 . . . . .7N 13
Ballantyne Dr.
KT20: K'wood 8L 81
Ballantyne Rd.
GU14: Farnb 8M 69
Ballard Cl. KT2: K Tham 8C 26
Ballard Ct. GU15: Camb 7E 50
Ballard Grn. SL4: W'sor 3B 4
Ballard Rd. GU15: Camb 7E 50
Ballards Farm Rd.
CR0: Croy 3E 64
CR2: Croy, S Croy 3D 64
Ballards Grn. KT20: Tad 6K 81
Ballards La. RH8: Limp 7E 106
Ballards Ri. CR2: Sels 3D 64
Ballards Way CR0: Croy 3D 64
CR2: Sels 3D 64
Ballater Rd. CR2: S Croy 2C 64
Ballencrieff Rd. SL5: S'dale . . .6C 34
Ballfield Rd. GU7: Goda 5G 133
Ballindune GU27: Hasl 9G 170
Balliol Cl. RH10: Craw 9G 163
Balliol Way GU47: Owls 6K 49
Ballsdown GU8: Chid 5D 172
Balmain Ct. TW3: Houn 4B 10
Balmain Lodge KT5: Surb 8K 203
Balmoral RH19: E Grin 1C 186
Balmoral Av. BR3: Beck 3H 47
Balmoral Cl. SW15 . . . . .9J 13
Balmoral Ct. KT4: W Pk 8G 42
RH11: Craw 7N 181
SE27 . . . . .5N 29
SM2: Sut 4M 61
Balmoral Cres.
GU9: U Hal 6G 108
KT8: W Mole 2A 40
Balmoral Dr. GU16: Frim 6C 70
GU22: Wok 3E 74
Balmoral Gdns. CR2: Sande 6A 64
SL4: W'sor 6G 4
Balmoral Ho. GU12: A Va 8D 90
Balmoral Rd. GU12: A Va 9E 90
KT1: K Tham . . .7L 203 (3M 41)
KT4: W Pk 9G 42
Balmoral Way SM2: Sut 6M 61
Balmuir Gdns. SW15 . . . . .7H 13
Balquhain Cl. KT21: A'tead 4K 79
Baltic Cen., The TW8: Brent . . .1K 11
Baltic Cl. SW19 . . . . .8B 28
Balvernie Gro. SW18 . . . . .1L 27
Balvernie M. SW18 . . . . .1M 27
Bampfylde Cl. SM6: W'ton 9G 44
Bampton Way GU21: Wok 5K 73
Banbury RG12: Brac 6C 32
Banbury Cl. GU16: Frim 7D 70
RG41: W'ham 2A 30
Banbury Ct. SM2: Sut 4M 61
Bancroft Cl. TW15: A'ford 6B 22
Bancroft Ct. RH2: Reig 3N 121
Bancroft Rd. RH2: Reig 3M 121
RH10: Craw 4H 183
Banders Ri. GU1: Guil 2E 114
Band La. TW20: Egh 6B 20
BANDONHILL 2H 63
Bandon Ri. SM6: W'ton 2H 63
Banfor Ct. SM6: W'ton 2G 62
Bangalore St. SW15 . . . . .6H 13
Bank, The RH10: T Hil 5D 184
Bank Av. CR4: Mit 1B 44
Bank Bldgs. Rd.
GU6: Cranl 7M 155
Bank Ho. KT15: Addl 1K 55
Bank La. KT2: K Tham 8L 25
RH10: Craw 3B 182
SW15 . . . . .8D 12
Bank M. SM1: Sut 3A 62
Bank Pct. RH10: Craw 9E 162
Bank Rd. GU11: Alde 8B 90
Banksian Wlk. TW7: Isle 4E 10
Bankside CR2: S Croy 3C 64
GU9: Weybo 5L 109
GU21: Wok 5L 73
(not continuous)
Bankside Cl. GU8: Els 8H 131
SM5: Cars 3C 62
TN16: B Hil 5E 86
TW7: Isle 7F 10
Bankside Dr. KT7: T Dit 7H 41
Bank's La. KT24: E Jun 1H 97
Banks Rd. RH10: Craw 3G 182
Banks Way GU4: B'ham 9B 94
Bank Ter. *GU5: Shere 8B 116*
(off Gomshall La.)
Bannacle Hill Rd.
GU8: Worm 9A 152
Bannister Cl. GU8: Wit 5C 152
SW2 . . . . .2L 29
Bannister Gdns. GU46: Yate . . .1E 68
Bannister's Rd. GU2: Guil 5J 113
Bannow Cl. KT19: Ewe 1D 60
BANSTEAD 2M 81
Banstead Rd. CR3: Cate 8A 84
CR8: Pur 7L 63
KT17: Ewe 6G 61
SM5: Cars 5B 62
SM7: Ban 6G 61
Banstead Rd. Sth.
SM2: Sut 7A 62
Banstead Sports Cen. 7H 81
Banstead Station (Rail) 1L 81
Banstead Way SM6: W'ton 2J 63
Banstead Wood SM7: Ban 5A 82
Barataria Pk. Cvn. Site
GU23: Rip 7H 75
Barbara Castle Cl.
SW6 . . . . .2L 13
Barbara Cl. GU52: C Cro 7C 88
TW17: Shep 4C 38
Barber Cl. RH10: Craw 7G 182
Barber Dr. GU6: Cranl 6N 155
Barberry Cl. GU52: Fleet 7B 88
Barberry Way GU17: Haw 4L 69
Barbon Cl. GU15: Camb 3H 71
Barchard St. SW18 . . . . .8N 13
Barclay Cl. KT22: Fetc 1B 98
SW6 . . . . .3M 13
Barclay Rd.
CR0: Croy 4D 200 (9A 46)
SW6 . . . . .3M 13
Barcombe Av. SW2 . . . . .3J 29
Bardeen Pl. RG12: Brac 2B 32
Bardney Rd. SM4: Mord 3N 43
Bardolph Av. CR0: Sels 5H 65
Bardolph Rd. TW9: Rich 6M 11
Bardon Wlk. GU21: Wok 4L 73
Bardsley Cl. CR0: Croy 9C 46
Bardsley Dr. GU9: Farnh 3F 128
Barfield Ct. RH1: Red 1E 122
Barfields RH1: Blet 2M 123
Barford Cl. GU51: Fleet 5E 88
Barford La. GU10: Churt 9K 149
Bargate Cl. KT3: N Mal 6F 42
Bargate Ct. GU2: Guil 3H 113
Bargate Ri. GU7: Goda 7F 132
Barge Cl. GU11: Alde 8C 90
Barge Wlk.
KT1: H Wic 5G 203 (2K 41)
KT8: E Mol 2D 40
(Hampton Ct. Cres.)
KT8: E Mol 5G 41
(The Island)
Barham Cl. KT13: Weybr 1D 56
Barham Ct. CR2: S Croy 7C 200
Barham Rd.
CR2: S Croy 7C 200 (1N 63)
SW20 . . . . .8F 26
Barhatch La. GU6: Cranl 5A 156
Barhatch Rd. GU6: Cranl 5A 156
Baring Rd. CR0: Croy 7D 46
Barker Cl. KT3: N Mal 3A 42
KT16: Chert 6G 37
TW9: Rich 5A 12
Barker Grn. RG12: Brac 4N 31
Barker Rd. KT16: Chert 6G 37
Barkers Mdw. SL5: Asc 9H 17
Barker Wlk. SW16 . . . . .4H 29
Barkham Rd. RG41: W'ham 3A 30
Barkhart Dr. RG40: W'ham 1B 30
Barkhart Gdns.
RG40: W'ham 1B 30
Barkis Mead GU47: Owls 5K 49
Barkston Gdns. SW5 . . . . .1N 13
Barkway Dr. BR6: Farnb 1J 67
Barley Cl. RH10: Craw 4B 182
Barley Mead RG42: Warf 8C 16
Barleymead RH6: Horl 7F 142
Barley Mow Cl.
GU21: Knap 4G 72
Barleymow Ct. RH3: Betch . . .3B 120
Barley Mow Hill
GU35: H Dwn 3E 168
Barley Mow La. GU21: Knap . . .3F 72
Barley Mow Pas. W4 . . . . .1C 12
Barley Mow Rd.
TW20: Eng G 6M 19
Barley Mow Way
TW17: Shep 3B 38
Barley Way GU51: Fleet 9C 68
Barlow Cl. SM6: W'ton 3J 63
Barlow Rd. RH11: Craw 6K 181
TW12: Hamp 8A 24

Barmouth Rd.—Beckett Cl.

Barmouth Rd. CR0: Croy 8G 47
SW18 .....1A 28
Barnard Cl. GU16: Frim 6D 70
SM6: W'ton 4H 63
TW16: Sunb 8J 23
Barnard Ct. GU21: Wok 5H 73
Barnard Gdns. KT3: N Mal 3F 42
Barnard Rd. CR4: Mit 2E 44
CR6: Warl 6L 85
Barnards Pl. CR2: S Croy 5M 63
Barnard Way GU11: Alde 1L 109
Barnato Cl. KT14: Byf 8N 55
Barnby Rd. GU21: Knap 4G 73
Barn Cl. GU15: Camb 9C 50
KT18: Eps 2B 80
KT20: Box H 1M 119
RG12: Brac 1B 32
RH11: P Pot 1N 199
SM7: Ban 2B 82
(not continuous)
TW15: A'ford 6C 22
Barn Cres. CR8: Pur 9A 64
Barncroft GU9: Farnh 2H 129
(not continuous)
Barneby Cl. TW2: Twick 2E 24
Barn Elms Athletic Track 4G 13
Barn Elms Pk. SW15 .....6H 13
BARNES 5E 12
Barnes All. TW12: Hamp 1C 40
Barnes Av. SW13 .....3F 12
UB2: S'hall 1N 9
Barnes Bridge Station (Rail) 5E 12
Barnes Cl. GU14: Farnb 1B 90
Barnes Common Nature Reserve 6F 12
Barnes Ct. CR7: T Hea 2N 45
Barnes End KT3: N Mal 4F 42
Barnes High St. SW13 .....5E 12
Barnes M. RH12: Hors 6H 197
Barnes Rd. GU7: Goda 3H 133
GU16: Frim 6C 70
Barnes Station (Rail) 6F 12
Barnes Wallis Av.
RH13: Hors 9D 196
Barnes Wallis Cl. KT24: Eff 5L 97
Barnes Wallis Dr.
KT13: Weybr 7N 55
Barnett Cl. GU5: Wone 3E 134
KT22: Leat 6H 79
Barnett Ct. RG12: Brac 1B 32
Barnett Grn. RG12: Brac 5N 31
Barnett La. GU5: Wone 4D 134
GU18: Ligh 8K 51
Barnett Row GU4: J Wel 7N 93
Barnett's Shaw RH8: Oxt 5N 105
Barnetts Way RH8: Oxt 5N 105
Barnett Wood La.
KT21: A'tead 5J 79
KT22: Leat 7H 79
Barn Fld. GU46: Yate 1C 68
Barnfield GU6: Cranl 7N 155
KT3: N Mal 5D 42
RH6: Horl 9E 142
SM7: Ban 1N 81
Barnfield Av. CR0: Croy 8F 46
CR4: Mit 3F 44
KT2: K Tham 5K 25
Barnfield Cl. CR5: Coul 6N 83
SW17 .....4B 28
Barnfield Cotts.
RH7: Dorm 1C 166
Barnfield Gdns.
KT2: K Tham 5L 25
Barnfield Rd. CR2: Sande 5B 64
RH10: Craw 2B 182
TN16: Tats 7F 86
Barnfield Way RH8: Oxt 2C 126
Barnfield Wood Cl.
BR3: Beck 5N 47
Barnfield Wood Rd.
BR3: Beck 5N 47
Barn Hawe TN8: Eden 2L 147
Barnlea Cl. TW13: Hanw 3M 23
Barnmead GU24: Chob 6J 53
Barn Mdw. Cl.
GU52: C Cro 1A 108
Barn Mdw. La. KT23: Book 2N 97
Barns, The GU8: S'ford 3N 131
Barnsbury Cl. KT3: N Mal 3B 42
Barnsbury Cres. KT5: Surb 7B 42
Barnsbury Farm Est.
GU22: Wok 7N 73
Barnsbury La. KT5: Surb 8A 42
Barnscroft SW20 .....2G 43
Barnsfold La. RH12: Rudg 2N 193
Barnsford Cres.
GU24: W End 9D 52
Barnsley Cl. GU12: A Va 3F 90
BARNSNAP 5G 199
Barnsnap Cl. RH12: Hors 2K 197
Barn Theatre, The
Oxted 6A 106
West Molesey 3A 40
Barnway TW20: Eng G 6M 19
Barnwood RH10: Craw 2G 183
Barnwood Cl. GU2: Guil 1H 113
Barnwood Ct. GU2: Guil 1H 113
Barnwood Rd. GU2: Guil 2H 113
Barnyard, The KT20: Wal H 2F 100
Baron Cl. SM2: Sut 6N 61
Baron Gro. CR4: Mit 3C 44
Baron Ho. SW19 .....9B 28
Barons, The TW1: Twick 9H 11
BARONS COURT 1K 13
Barons Ct. SM6: Bedd 9H 45
Baron's Ct. Rd. W14 .....1K 13
Barons Court Station (Tube) 1K 13
Barons Court Theatre *1K 13*
(off Comeragh Rd.)
Baronsfield Rd. TW1: Twick 9H 11
Baron's Hurst KT18: Eps 3B 80
Barons Keep W14 .....1K 13
Baronsmead Rd.
SW13 .....4F 12
Baron's Wlk. CR0: Croy 5H 47
Barons Way RH2: Reig 7M 121
TW20: Egh 7F 20
Baron Wlk. CR4: Mit 3C 44
Baroque Ct. TW3: Houn 6C 10
Barossa Rd. GU15: Camb 8B 50
Barracane Dr. RG45: Crow 2F 48
Barrackfield Wlk.
RH12: Hors 8H 197
Barrack La. SL4: W'sor 4G 5
Barrack Path GU21: Wok 5H 73
(not continuous)
Barrack Rd. GU2: Guil 1K 113
GU11: Alde 2M 109
TW4: Houn 7L 9
Barrens Brae GU22: Wok 5C 74
Barrens Cl. GU22: Wok 6C 74
Barrens Pk. GU22: Wok 5C 74
Barrett Cres. RG40: W'ham 2C 30
Barrett Rd. KT22: Fetc 2D 98
Barrhill Rd. SW2 .....3J 29
Barricane GU21: Wok 6L 73
Barrie Cl. CR5: Coul 3G 82
Barrie Ho. KT15: Addl 4J 55
Barrie Rd. GU9: U Hal 5F 108
BARRIHURST 8F 154
Barrihurst La. GU6: Cranl 8F 154
Barringer Sq. SW17 .....5E 28
Barrington Ct. RH1: Red 1E 122
RH4: Dork 6G 119
TW18: Stain 7H 21
(off Thameside)
Barrington Dr. KT22: Fetc 3D 98
Barrington Lodge
KT13: Weybr 2D 56
Barrington Rd. CR8: Pur 8G 62
RH4: Dork 6G 119
RH10: Craw 5B 182
RH13: Hors 6L 197
SM3: Sut 8M 43
Barrow Av. SM5: Cars 4D 62
Barrowgate Rd. W4 .....1B 12
Barrow Grn. Rd. RH8: Oxt 8K 105
Barrow Hedges Cl.
SM5: Cars 4C 62
Barrow Hedges Way
SM5: Cars 4C 62
Barrow Hill KT4: W Pk 8D 42
Barrow Hill Cl. KT4: W Pk 8D 42
Barrow Rd. CR0: Wad 2L 63
SW16 .....7H 29
Barrowsfield CR2: Sande 8C 64
Barrow Wlk. TW8: Brent 2J 11
Barrsbrook Farm Rd.
KT16: Chert 7G 37
Barrsbrook Hall
KT16: Chert 7G 37
Barr's La. GU21: Knap 3G 72
(not continuous)
Barry Av. SL4: W'sor 3F 4
Barry Cl. RH10: Craw 6C 182
Barry Sq. RG12: Brac 6B 32
Bars, The
GU1: Guil 4C 202 (4N 113)
Barston Rd. SE27 .....4N 29
Barstow Cres. SW2 .....2K 29
Bartholomew Cl.
GU27: Hasl 9H 171
Bartholomew Ct.
RH4: Dork 4J 201 (6G 119)
Bartholomew Pl.
RG42: Warf 8C 16
Bartholomew Way
RH12: Hors 2N 197
Bartlett Pl. GU16: Frim G 9D 70
Bartlett Rd. TN16: Weste 4L 107
Bartlett St.
CR2: S Croy 8D 200 (2A 64)
Barton, The KT11: Cob 8L 57
Barton Cl. GU11: Alde 3K 109
GU21: Knap 5F 72
KT15: Addl 3J 55
TW17: Shep 5C 38
Barton Ct. *W14 .....1K 13*
(off Baron's Ct. Rd.)
Barton Cres. RH19: E Grin 1C 186
Barton Grn. KT3: N Mal 1C 42
Barton Green Theatre 1C 42
Barton Ho. *SW6 .....6N 13*
(off Wandsworth Bri. Rd.)
Barton Pl. GU4: B'ham 9D 94
Barton Rd. GU5: Braml 4C 134
W14 .....1K 13
Bartons Dr. GU46: Yate 2C 68
Bartons Way GU14: Cove 7J 69
Barton Wlk. RH10: Craw 5F 182
Barts Cl. BR3: Beck 4K 47
Barttelot Rd. RH12: Hors 7K 197
Barwell Bus. Pk. KT9: Ches 4K 59
Barwell Cl. RG45: Crow 2E 48
Barwell Ct. KT9: Ches 4H 59
Barwell Cres. TN16: B Hil 8E 66
Barwell La. KT9: Ches 4J 59
Barwood Av. BR4: W Wick 7L 47
Basden Gro. TW13: Hanw 3A 24
Basden Ho. TW13: Hanw 3A 24
Basemoors RG12: Brac 1C 32
Basepoint Bus. Cen.
RH11: Craw 8B 162
Basford Way SL4: W'sor 6A 4
Bashford Way RH10: Craw 1H 183
Bashurst Copse
RH13: Itch 8N 195
Bashurst Hill RH13: Itch 9M 195
Basildene Rd. TW4: Houn 6L 9
Basildon Cl. SM2: Sut 5N 61
Basildon Way RH11: Craw 6K 181
Basil Gdns. CR0: Croy 7G 46
SE27 .....6N 29
Basingbourne Cl.
GU52: Fleet 7B 88
Basingbourne Rd.
GU52: Fleet 8A 88
Basing Cl. KT7: T Dit 6F 40
Basing Dr. GU11: Alde 5N 109
Basingfield Rd. KT7: T Dit 6F 40
Basinghall Gdns.
SM2: Sut 5N 61
Basing Rd. SM7: Ban 1L 81
Basingstoke Canal Cen. 2E 90
Basing Way KT7: T Dit 6F 40
Baskerville Rd. SW18 .....1C 28
Basset Cl. KT15: N Haw 6K 55
Bassett Cl. GU16: Frim 6C 70
SM2: Sut 5N 61
Bassett Dr. RH2: Reig 2M 121
Bassett Gdns. TW7: Isle 3C 10
Bassett Rd. GU22: Wok 3E 74
RH10: Craw 6H 183
Bassett's Cl. BR6: Farnb 1K 67
Bassetts Hill RH7: Dorm 1C 166
Bassett's Way BR6: Farnb 1K 67
Bassingham Rd.
SW18 .....1A 28
Baston Mnr. Rd.
BR2: Hay, Kes 1D 66
Baston Rd. BR2: Hay 1E 66
Basuto Rd. SW6 .....4M 13
Bat & Ball La. GU10: Wrec 5F 128
(not continuous)
Batavia Cl. TW16: Sunb 9J 23
Batavia Rd. TW16: Sunb 9J 23
Batcombe Mead
RG12: Brac 6C 32
Bateman Ct. RH10: Craw 6E 182
Bateman Gro. GU12: Ash 4D 110
Bates Cres. CR0: Wad 2L 63
SW16 .....8G 28
Bateson Way GU21: Wok 1E 74
Bates Wlk. KT15: Addl 3L 55
Bathgate Rd. SW19 .....4J 27
Bath Ho. Rd. CR0: Bedd 7J 45
Bath Pas.
KT1: K Tham 4H 203 (1K 41)
Bath Pl. *W6 .....1H 13*
(off Peabody Est.)
Bath Rd. GU15: Camb 9B 50
SL3: Coln 3E 6
SL3: Coln, Poy 4G 6
TW3: Houn 5L 9
TW4: Houn 5L 9
TW5: C'ford 4K 9
TW6: Lon A 4F 8
UB3: Harl 4F 8
UB7: Harm, Sip 4N 7
UB7: L'ford 4K 7
Baths App. SW6 .....3L 13
Bathurst Av. SW19 .....9N 27
Batley Cl. CR4: Mit 6D 44
Batsworth Rd. CR4: Mit 2B 44
Batten Av. GU21: Wok 6H 73
Battersea Ct. GU2: Guil 3L 113
Battlebridge La.
RH1: Mers, Red 8F 102
Battle Cl. SW19 .....7A 28
BATT'S CORNER 4C 148
Batts Hill RH1: Red 1C 122
RH2: Reig 1B 122
Batty's Barn Cl.
RG40: W'ham 3C 30
Baulk, The SW18 .....1M 27
Bavant Rd. SW16 .....1J 45
Bawtree Cl. SM2: Sut 6A 62
Bax Cl. GU6: Cranl 8N 155
Baxter Av. RH1: Red 3D 122
Baxter Cl. RH10: Craw 5F 182
Bayards CR6: Warl 5F 84
Bay Cl. RH6: Horl 5C 142
Bay Dr. RG12: Brac 1C 32
Bayeux KT20: Tad 9J 81
Bayfield Av. GU16: Frim 4B 70
Bayfield Rd. RH6: Horl 7C 142
Bayford Cl. GU17: Haw 5M 69
Baygrove M. KT1: H Wic 9J 25
Bayham Rd. SM4: Mord 3N 43
Bayhorne La. RH6: Horl 1G 162
Bay Ho. RG12: Brac 1C 32
Bayleaf Cl. TW12: H Hill 6D 24
Baylis M. TW1: Twick 1G 25
Bayliss Ct.
GU1: Guil 4B 202 (4M 113)
Baylis Wlk. RH11: Craw 8N 181
BAYNARDS 6B 176
BAYNARDS PARK 3D 176
Baynards Rd.
RH12: Rudg 7A 176
Baynton Rd. GU22: Wok 7D 74
Bayonne Rd. W6 .....2K 13
Bay Path RH9: Gods 9F 104
Bay Pond Nature Reserve 9F 104
Bay Rd. RG12: Brac 9C 16
Bays Farm Ct. UB7: L'ford 4L 7
Bay Tree Av. KT22: Leat 7G 79
Bay Trees RH8: Oxt 2D 126
Baywood Cl. GU14: Cove 9H 69
Bazalgette Cl. KT3: N Mal 4C 42
Bazalgette Gdns.
KT3: N Mal 4C 42
Beach Gro. TW13: Hanw 3A 24
Beach Ho. *SW5 .....1M 13*
(off Philbeach Gdns.)
TW13: Hanw 3A 24
Beachy Rd. RH11: Craw 8M 181
Beacon Cl. GU10: Wrec 6F 128
SM7: Ban 3J 81
Beacon Ct. RH13: Hors 4N 197
SL3: Coln 3E 6
Beacon Cres.
GU26: Hind 4C 170
Beacon Gro. SM5: Cars 1E 62
BEACON HILL 3A 170
Beacon Hill GU21: Wok 6M 73
RH7: Dorm 2D 166
Beacon Hill Ct.
GU26: Hind 3B 170
Beacon Hill Pk.
GU26: Hind 3N 169
Beacon Hill Rd.
GU10: Ews 5D 108
GU26: Hind 3A 170
GU52: C Cro 8C 88
Beacon Pl. CR0: Bedd 9J 45
Beacon Rd. TW6: Lon A 9B 8
Beaconsfield Cl. W4 .....1B 12
Beaconsfield Gdns.
KT10: Clay 4E 58
Beaconsfield Pl.
KT17: Eps 5M 201 (8D 60)
Beaconsfield Rd. CR0: Croy 5A 46
GU22: Wok 7B 74
KT3: N Mal 1C 42
KT5: Surb 6M 41
KT10: Clay 4E 58
KT18: Eps D 6C 80
TW1: Twick 9H 11
Beaconsfield Wlk.
SW6 .....4L 13
Beacon Vw. Ho.
GU26: G'hott 6A 170
Beacon Vw. Rd. GU8: Els 9G 130
Beacon Way SM7: Ban 3J 81
Beadles La. RH8: Oxt 8N 105
Beadlow Cl. SM5: Cars 5B 44
Beadman Pl. SE27 .....5M 29
Beadman St. SE27 .....5M 29
Beadon Rd. W6 .....1H 13
Beaford Gro. SW20 .....2K 43
Beagle Cl. TW13: Felt 5J 23
Beale Cl. RG40: W'ham 1A 30
Beale Ct. RH11: Craw 6M 181
Beales La. GU10: Wrec 4E 128
KT13: Weybr 9C 38
Beales Rd. KT23: Book 5B 98
Bealeswood La.
GU10: Dock 4D 148
Beam Hollow GU9: H End 5H 109
Bean Oak Rd.
RG40: W'ham 2D 30
Beard Rd. KT2: K Tham 6M 25
Beard's Hill TW12: Hamp 9A 24
Beard's Hill Cl.
TW12: Hamp 9A 24
Beard's Rd. TW15: A'ford 7F 22
BEARE GREEN 8K 139
Beare Grn. Ct. RH5: B Grn 7K 139
Beare Grn. Rd.
RH5: B Grn 2E 158
Beare Grn. Rdbt.
RH5: B Grn 9K 139
Bearfield Rd.
KT2: K Tham 1J 203 (8L 25)
Bear La. GU9: Farnh 9G 109
Bear Rd. TW13: Hanw 5L 23
Bears Den KT20: K'wood 9L 81
Bearsden Ct. SL5: S'dale 6C 34
Bearsden Way
RH12: Bro H 5D 196
Bears Rails Pk. SL4: O Win 1J 19
Bearwood Cl. KT15: Addl 3J 55
Bearwood Cotts.
GU10: Wrec 4E 128
(off The Street)
Bearwood Gdns.
GU51: Fleet 4B 88
Beasley's Ait La.
TW16: Sunb 5G 39
Beatrice Av. SW16 .....2K 45
Beatrice Ho. *W6 .....1H 13*
(off Queen Caroline St.)
Beatrice Rd. RH8: Oxt 7A 106
TW10: Rich 8M 11
Beatrix Ho. *SW5 .....1N 13*
(off Old Brompton Rd.)
Beattie Cl. KT23: Book 2N 97
TW14: Felt 1G 22
Beatty Av. GU1: Guil 2C 114
Beauchamp Rd.
KT8: W Mole, E Mol 4B 40
SE19 .....1A 46
SM1: Sut 1M 61
TW1: Twick 1G 25
Beauchamp Ter. SW15 .....6G 13
Beauclare Cl. KT22: Leat 7K 79
Beauclerc Ct. TW16: Sunb 1K 39
Beauclere Ho. SM2: Sut 3A 62
Beauclerk Cl. TW13: Felt 2J 23
Beauclerk Ho. SW16 .....4J 29
Beaufield Ga. GU27: Hasl 1H 189
Beaufort Cl. GU22: Wok 3E 74
RH2: Reig 2L 121
SW15 .....1G 27
Beaufort Ct. SW6 .....2M 13
TW10: Ham 5J 25
Beaufort Gdns. SL5: Asc 9J 17
SW16 .....8K 29
TW5: Hest 4M 9
Beaufort M. GU21: Wok 5N 73
SW6 .....2L 13
Beaufort Rd. GU9: Farnh 9H 109
GU12: A Va 8D 90
GU22: Wok 3E 74
GU52: C Cro 6C 88
KT1: K Tham 8J 203 (3L 41)
RH2: Reig 2L 121
TW1: Twick 1J 25
TW10: Ham 5J 25
Beauforts TW20: Eng G 6M 19
Beaufort Way KT17: Ewe 4F 60
Beaufoy Ho. SE27 .....4M 29
Beaufront Cl. GU15: Camb 8E 50
Beaufront Rd. GU15: Camb 8E 50
Beaulieu Cl. CR4: Mit 9E 28
RG12: Brac 2D 32
SL3: Dat 4L 5
TW1: Twick 9K 11
TW4: Houn 8N 9
Beaulieu Gdns.
GU17: B'water 1H 69
Beaumaris Pde.
GU16: Frim 6D 70
Beaumont *W14 .....1L 13*
(off Kensington Village)
Beaumont Av. TW9: Rich 6M 11
W14 .....1L 13
Beaumont Cl. KT2: K Tham 8N 25
RH11: Ifi 4K 181
Beaumont Ct. *GU51: Fleet 2A 88*
(off Harrow Rd.)
W4 .....1B 12
Beaumont Cres. W14 .....1L 13
Beaumont Dr. KT4: W Pk 6G 43
TW15: A'ford 6E 22
Beaumont Gdns.
RG12: Brac 4C 32
Beaumont Gro.
GU11: Alde 2K 109
Beaumont Pl. TW7: Isle 8F 10
Beaumont Rd. CR8: Pur 9L 63
SE19 .....7N 29
SL4: W'sor 5F 4
SW19 .....1K 27
Beaumonts RH1: Salf 2D 142
Beaumont Sq. GU6: Cranl 7A 156
Beaumont Village
GU11: Alde 2L 109
Beaverbrook Rdbt.
KT22: Leat 1K 99
Beaver Cl. RG41: W'ham 5A 30
RH12: Hors 2L 197
SM4: Mord 6H 43
TW12: Hamp 9B 24
Beaver La. GU46: Yate 1D 68
Beavers Cl. GU3: Guil 2H 113
GU9: Farnh 1F 128
Beavers Cres. TW4: Houn 7K 9
Beavers Hill GU9: Farnh 1E 128
Beavers La. TW4: Houn 5K 9
(not continuous)
Beavers La. Campsite
TW4: Houn 7L 9
Beavers M. GU35: Bor 5A 168
Beavers Rd. GU9: Farnh 1F 128
Beaver Water World 9D 86
Beavor Gro. *W6 .....1F 12*
(off Beavor La.)
Beavor La. W6 .....1F 12
Bechtel Ho. *W6 .....1J 13*
(off Hammersmith Rd.)
Beck Ct. BR3: Beck 2G 46
BECKENHAM 1M 47
Beckenham Crematorium
BR3: Beck 2F 46
Beckenham Gro.
BR2: Brom 1N 47
Beckenham Rd. BR3: Beck 1H 47
BR4: W Wick 6L 47
Beckenham Road Stop (CT) 1H 47
Beckenham Theatre Cen., The 1L 47
Beckenshaw Gdns.
SM7: Ban 2C 82
Becket Cl. SE25 .....5D 46
SW19 .....9N 27
(off High Path)
Beckett Av. CR8: Ken 2M 83
Beckett Chase SL3: Lang 1B 6
Beckett Cl. RG40: W'ham 2D 30
SW16 .....3H 29

Beckett La.—Bennings Cl.

Beckett La. RH11: Craw ... 9B 162
Beckett Rd. CR5: Coul ... 9H 83
Becketts Cl. TW14: Felt ... 9J 9
Becketts Pl.
KT1: H Wic ... 2G 203 (9K 25)
Beckett Way
RH19: E Grin ... 1B 186
Becket Wood RH5: Newd ... 6B 140
Beckford Av. RG12: Brac ... 5N 31
Beckford Rd. CR0: Croy ... 5C 46
Beckford Way RH10: Craw ... 7F 182
Beck Gdns. GU9: U Hal ... 6G 108
Beckingham Rd.
GU2: Guil ... 1K 113
Beck La. BR3: Beck ... 2G 46
Beck Rd. CR4: Mit ... 5D 44
Beck Way BR3: Beck ... 2J 47
Beckway Rd. SW16 ... 1H 45
Beclands Rd. SW17 ... 7E 28
Becmead Av. SW16 ... 5H 29
Bective Pl. SW15 ... 7L 13
Bective Rd. SW15 ... 7L 13
Bedale Cl. RH11: Craw ... 5A 182
BEDDINGTON ... 1J 63
BEDDINGTON CORNER ... 6E 44
Beddington Cross
CR0: Bedd ... 6H 45
Beddington Farm Rd.
CR0: Bedd ... 6J 45
Beddington Gdns.
SM5: Cars ... 3E 62
SM6: W'ton ... 3E 62
Beddington Gro.
SM6: W'ton ... 2H 63
Beddington La. CR0: Croy ... 4G 44
Beddington Lane Stop (CT) ... 5G 45
Beddington Pk. ... 8F 44
Beddington Pk. Cotts.
SM6: Bedd ... 9H 45
Beddington Ter. CR0: Croy ... 6K 45
Beddington Trad. Est.
CR0: Bedd ... 7J 45
Beddlestead La. CR6: Warl ... 4B 86
Bedfont Cl. CR4: Mit ... 1E 44
TW14: Bedf ... 9D 8
Bedfont Ct. TW19: Stan M ... 6J 7
Bedfont Ct. Est.
TW19: Stan M ... 7K 7
Bedfont Grn. Cl.
TW14: Bedf ... 2D 22
Bedfont Ind. Pk.
TW15: A'ford ... 4D 22
Bedfont Ind. Pk. Nth.
TW15: A'ford ... 4D 22
Bedfont Lakes Country Pk. ... 3D 22
Bedfont Lakes Country Pk. Vis. Cen.
... 4C 22
Bedfont La. TW13: Felt ... 1G 22
TW14: Felt ... 1G 22
Bedfont Rd. TW13: Felt ... 2D 22
TW14: Bedf ... 2D 22
TW19: Stan ... 9N 7
Bedfont Trad. Est.
TW14: Bedf ... 3E 22
Bedford Av. GU16: Frim G ... 9D 70
Bedford Cl. GU21: Wok ... 2M 73
W4 ... 2D 12
Bedford Ct. *CR0: Croy* ... *7N 45*
(off Tavistock Rd.)
Bedford Cres. GU16: Frim G ... 8C 70
Bedford Hill SW12 ... 2F 28
SW16 ... 2F 28
Bedford La. GU16: Frim G ... 8D 70
SL5: S'dale ... 4E 34
Bedford Pk.
CR0: Croy ... 1C 200 (7N 45)
Bedford Pas. *SW6* ... *3K 13*
(off Dawes Rd.)
Bedford Pl.
CR0: Croy ... 1D 200 (7A 46)
Bedford Rd.
GU1: Guil ... 4B 202 (4M 113)
KT4: W Pk ... 8H 43
RH13: Hors ... 7K 197
TW2: Twick ... 4D 24
Bedfordshire Down
RG42: Warf ... 7D 16
Bedford Ter. SM2: Sut ... 3A 62
Bedgebury Gdns.
SW19 ... 3K 27
Bedlow Cotts. GU6: Cranl ... 7A 156
Bedlow La. GU6: Cranl ... 7A 156
Bedlow Way CR0: Bedd ... 1K 63
Bedser Cl. CR7: T Hea ... 2N 45
GU21: Wok ... 3C 74
Bedster Gdns. KT8: W Mole ... 1B 40
Bedwell Gdns. UB3: Harl ... 1F 8
(not continuous)
Beech Av. CR2: Sande ... 7A 64
GU10: L Bou ... 6H 129
GU15: Camb ... 2B 70
KT24: Eff ... 6L 97
TN16: Tats ... 6F 86
TW8: Brent ... 3H 11
Beechbrook Av. GU46: Yate ... 1D 68
Beech Cl. GU8: Chid ... 5D 172
GU12: Alde ... 4C 110
KT11: Cob ... 8A 58
KT12: Hers ... 1K 57
KT14: Byf ... 8N 55
KT24: Eff ... 6L 97
RH4: Dork ... 1G 201 (4F 118)
RH7: Blin H ... 3H 145
Beech Cl. RH19: E Grin ... 8N 165
SM5: Cars ... 8D 44
SW15 ... 1F 26
SW19 ... 7H 27
TW15: A'ford ... 6E 22
TW16: Sunb ... 1L 39
TW19: Stan ... 1M 21
Beech Cl. Ct. KT11: Cob ... 7N 57
Beech Copse
CR2: S Croy ... 8F 200 (2B 64)
Beech Ct. *GU1: Guil* ... *4B 114*
(off Easington Pl.)
KT6: Surb ... 6K 41
RH19: E Grin ... 8N 165
Beech Cres. KT20: Box H ... 8B 100
Beechcroft KT21: A'tead ... 6M 79
Beechcroft Av. CR8: Ken ... 2A 84
KT3: N Mal ... 9B 26
Beechcroft Cl. BR6: Orp ... 1M 67
SL5: S'hill ... 3A 34
SW16 ... 6K 29
TW5: Hest ... 3M 9
Beechcroft Ct. RG12: Brac ... 2N 31
Beechcroft Dr. GU2: Guil ... 6G 113
Beechcroft Lodge SM2: Sut ... 4A 62
Beechcroft Mnr.
KT13: Weybr ... 9E 38
Beechcroft Rd. BR6: Orp ... 1M 67
KT9: Ches ... 9M 41
SW14 ... 6B 12
SW17 ... 3C 28
Beech Dell BR2: Kes ... 1H 67
Beechdene KT20: Tad ... 9G 80
Beech Dr. GU17: B'water ... 2J 69
GU23: Rip ... 2J 95
KT20: K'wood ... 9L 81
RH2: Reig ... 3B 122
Beechen Cliff Way TW7: Isle ... 5F 10
Beechen La. KT20: K'wood ... 3L 101
Beechers Cft. TN16: B Hil ... 4E 86
Beeches, The CR2: S Croy ... 8D 200
GU5: Braml ... 5B 134
GU12: A Va ... 4D 90
KT22: Fetc ... 2E 98
SM7: Ban ... 3M 81
TW3: Houn ... 4B 10
TW18: Stain ... 6J 21
Beeches Av. SM5: Cars ... 4C 62
Beeches Cl.
KT20: K'wood ... 1M 101
SE20 ... 1F 46
Beeches Cres.
RH10: Craw ... 5C 182
Beeches La. RH19: Ash W ... 3F 186
Beeches Mead
RH19: E Grin ... 5H 167
Beeches Rd. SM3: Sut ... 7K 43
SW17 ... 4C 28
Beeches Wlk. SM5: Cars ... 5B 62
Beeches Wood
KT20: K'wood ... 9M 81
Beechey Cl. RH10: Cop ... 7M 163
Beechey Way RH10: Cop ... 7M 163
Beech Farm La.
GU15: Camb ... 2D 70
Beech Farm Rd. CR6: Warl ... 7M 85
Beechfield SM7: Ban ... 9N 61
Beechfield Ct.
CR2: S Croy ... 7B 200
Beechfields RH19: E Grin ... 7B 166
Beech Gdns. GU21: Wok ... 2A 74
RH10: Craw D ... 2D 184
Beech Glen RG12: Brac ... 3N 31
Beech Gro. CR3: Cate ... 4B 104
CR4: Mit ... 4H 45
(not continuous)
GU2: Guil ... 3J 113
GU22: Wok ... 1N 93
GU24: B'wood ... 7N 71
(not continuous)
KT3: N Mal ... 2C 42
KT15: Addl ... 1K 55
KT18: Tat C ... 4G 80
KT23: Book ... 5A 98
Beech Hall KT16: Otter ... 4E 54
Beech Hanger End
GU26: G'hott ... 6N 169
Beech Hanger Rd.
GU26: G'hott ... 6N 169
BEECH HILL ... 3F 168
Beech Hill GU8: Bow G ... 9K 151
GU22: Wok ... 1N 93
GU35: H Dwn ... 5F 168
Beech Hill Rd.
GU35: Head ... 3E 168
SL5: S'dale ... 5C 34
Beech Holme
RH10: Craw D ... 1E 184
Beech Holt KT22: Leat ... 9J 79
Beech Ho. CR0: N Add ... 3L 65
RH10: Craw ... 8B 162
Beech Ho. Rd.
CR0: Croy ... 5D 200 (9A 46)
Beeching Cl. GU12: Ash ... 1F 110
Beeching Way
RH19: E Grin ... 9A 166
Beech La.
GU2: Guil ... 8A 202 (6M 113)
(not continuous)
GU3: Flex ... 4L 111
GU26: G'hott ... 5N 169
Beechlee SM6: W'ton ... 6G 62
Beech Lawn GU1: Guil ... 4B 114
Beech Lodge TW18: Stain ... 6G 21
Beechmeads KT11: Cob ... 9L 57
Beechmont Av.
GU25: V Wat ... 4N 35
Beechmore Gdns.
SM3: Chea ... 8J 43
Beechnut Dr.
GU17: B'water ... 9G 48
Beechnut Ind. Est.
GU12: Alde ... 3N 109
Beechnut Rd. GU12: Alde ... 3N 109
Beecholme SM7: Ban ... 1K 81
Beecholme Av. CR4: Mit ... 9F 28
Beech Ride GU47: Sandh ... 7G 49
GU52: Fleet ... 6A 88
Beech Rd. GU14: Farnb ... 7M 69
GU16: Frim G ... 8D 70
GU27: Hasl ... 1H 189
KT13: Weybr ... 1E 56
KT17: Eps ... 2E 80
RH1: Mers ... 4G 103
RH2: Reig ... 9M 101
RH12: Hors ... 3A 198
SW16 ... 1J 45
TN16: B Hil ... 6D 86
TW14: Bedf ... 1F 22
Beechrow TW10: Ham ... 5L 25
Beechside RH10: Craw ... 4C 182
Beechtree Av. TW20: Eng G ... 7L 19
Beech Tree Cl.
RH10: Craw ... 2B 182
Beech Tree Dr.
GU9: B Lea ... 7M 109
Beech Tree La. TW18: Lale ... 1K 37
Beech Tree Pl. SM1: Sut ... 2N 61
Beechvale *GU22: Wok* ... *5B 74*
(off Fairview Av.)
Beech Wlk. GU20: Windl ... 3A 52
KT17: Ewe ... 7F 60
Beech Way CR2: Sels ... 9G 65
GU7: Goda ... 8G 133
KT17: Eps ... 2E 80
TW2: Twick ... 4A 24
Beechway GU1: Guil ... 2D 114
Beechwood CR3: Cate ... 2D 104
Beechwood Av. BR6: Chels ... 2N 67
CR5: Coul ... 2F 82
CR7: T Hea ... 3M 45
KT13: Weybr ... 1F 56
KT20: K'wood ... 8M 81
TW9: Kew ... 4N 11
TW16: Sunb ... 7H 23
TW18: Stain ... 7K 21
Beechwood Cl. GU21: Knap ... 4H 73
KT6: Surb ... 6J 41
KT13: Weybr ... 1F 56
SL5: Asc ... 8J 17
Beechwood Ct. *KT12: Wal T* ... *9H 39*
(off Station Av.)
SM5: Cars ... 1D 62
TW16: Sunb ... 7H 23
W4 ... 2C 12
Beechwood Dr. BR2: Kes ... 1F 66
KT11: Cob ... 7A 58
Beechwood Gdns.
CR3: Cate ... 9D 84
Beechwood Gro. KT6: Surb ... 6J 41
Beechwood Hall
KT20: K'wood ... 1A 102
Beechwood La. CR6: Warl ... 6G 85
Beechwood Mnr.
KT13: Weybr ... 1F 56
Beechwood Pk.
KT20: Box H ... 9A 100
KT22: Leat ... 9J 79
Beechwood Rd. CR2: Sande ... 6B 64
CR3: Cate ... 9D 84
GU21: Knap ... 4H 73
GU25: V Wat ... 6K 35
Beechwood Vs. RH1: Salf ... 4E 142
Beecot La. KT12: Wal T ... 8K 39
Beeding Cl. RH12: Hors ... 3N 197
Beedingwood Dr.
RH12: Col ... 2D 198
Beedon Dr. RG12: Brac ... 5K 31
Beehive La. RG12: Bin ... 1H 31
Beehive Ring Rd.
RH6: Craw ... 5F 162
Beehive Rd. RG12: Bin ... 9J 15
TW18: Stain ... 6H 21
Beehive Way RH2: Reig ... 7N 121
Beeken Dene BR6: Farnb ... 1L 67
Beeleigh Rd. SM4: Mord ... 3N 43
Beemans Row SW18 ... 3A 28
Beeston Way TW14: Felt ... 9K 9
Beeton's Av. GU12: Ash ... 9E 90
Beggarhouse La.
RH5: Newd ... 2F 160
RH6: Char, Newd ... 2F 160
BEGGAR'S BUSH ... 3C 34
BEGGAR'S HILL ... 3E 60
Beggar's Hill KT17: Ewe ... 3E 60
Beggars La. GU24: Chob ... 7F 52
RH5: A Ham ... 8F 116
(not continuous)
TN16: Weste ... 3M 107
Beggars Roost La.
SM1: Sut ... 3M 61
Begonia Pl. TW12: Hamp ... 7A 24
Behenna Cl. RH11: Craw ... 4K 181
Beira St. SW12 ... 1F 28
Beldam Bri. Rd.
GU24: Chob, W End ... 9D 52
Beldham Gdns.
KT8: W Mole ... 1B 40
Beldham Rd. GU9: Farnh ... 4E 128
Belfast Rd. SE25 ... 3E 46
Belfield Rd. KT19: Ewe ... 5C 60
Belfry, The RH1: Red ... 2D 122
Belfry M. GU47: Sandh ... 7E 48
Belgrade Rd. TW12: Hamp ... 9B 24
Belgrave Cl. KT12: Hers ... 1J 57
Belgrave Ct. GU17: Haw ... 3J 69
W4 ... 1B 12
Belgrave Cres. TW16: Sunb ... 9J 23
Belgrave Mnr. GU22: Wok ... 6A 74
Belgrave Rd. CR4: Mit ... 2B 44
SE25 ... 3C 46
SW13 ... 3E 12
TW4: Houn ... 6N 9
TW16: Sunb ... 9J 23
Belgrave Wlk. CR4: Mit ... 2B 44
Belgrave Walk Stop (CT) ... 3B 44
Belgravia Ct. *RH6: Horl* ... *8F 142*
(off St Georges Cl.)
Belgravia M.
KT1: K Tham ... 8H 203 (3K 41)
Bellamy Cl. W14 ... 1L 13
Bellamy Ho. SW17 ... 5B 28
TW5: Hest ... 2A 10
Bellamy Rd. RH10: Craw ... 7G 182
Bellamy St. SW12 ... 1F 28
Belland Dr. GU11: Alde ... 3K 109
Bel La. TW13: Hanw ... 4M 23
Bellasis Av. SW2 ... 3J 29
Bell Bri. Rd. KT16: Chert ... 7H 37
Bell Cen., The
RH10: Craw ... 8D 162
Bell Chase GU11: Alde ... 2L 109
Bell Cl. GU14: Farnb ... 8A 70
Bell Cnr. KT16: Chert ... 6H 37
Bell Cres. CR5: Coul ... 8F 82
Bell Dr. SW18 ... 1K 27
Bellever Hill GU15: Camb ... 1C 70
Belle Vue Cl. GU12: Alde ... 2B 110
TW18: Stain ... 9J 21
Belle Vue Ent. Cen.
GU12: Alde ... 2C 110
Bellevue Pde. SW17 ... 2D 28
Belle Vue Pk. CR7: T Hea ... 2N 45
Belle Vue Rd. BR6: Dow ... 6J 67
GU12: Alde ... 2B 110
Bellevue Rd.
KT1: K Tham ... 6K 203 (2L 41)
(not continuous)
SW13 ... 5F 12
SW17 ... 2C 28
Bellew Rd. GU16: Deep ... 8F 70
Bellew St. SW17 ... 4A 28
Bellfield CR0: Sels ... 5H 65
BELLFIELDS ... 8M 93
Bellfields Ct. GU1: Guil ... 8M 93
Bellfields Rd. GU1: Guil ... 1N 113
Bell Foundry La.
RG40: W'ham ... 8A 14
Bell Hammer RH19: E Grin ... 1A 186
Bell Hill
CR0: Croy ... 3B 200 (8N 45)
Bell Ho. Gdns.
RG41: W'ham ... 2A 30
(not continuous)
Bellingham Cl.
GU15: Camb ... 2G 71
Bellingham Dr. RH2: Reig ... 3L 121
Bell Junc. TW3: Houn ... 6B 10
Bell La. GU10: Rowl ... 8D 128
GU17: B'water ... 1H 69
KT22: Fetc ... 1D 98
SL4: E Wic ... 1C 4
TW1: Twick ... 2G 25
Bell La. Cl. KT22: Fetc ... 1D 98
Bellmarsh Rd. KT15: Addl ... 1K 55
Bell Mdw. RH9: Gods ... 1E 124
Belloc Cl. RH10: Craw ... 2F 182
Belloc Ct. RH13: Hors ... 5N 197
Bello Cl. SE24 ... 1M 29
Bell Pde. SL4: W'sor ... 5C 4
Bell Pl. GU19: Bag ... 4K 51
Bell Rd. GU27: Hasl ... 4E 188
KT8: E Mol ... 4D 40
RH12: Warn ... 9F 178
TW3: Houn ... 6B 10
Bells All. SW6 ... 5M 13
Bellsfield Ct. *SL4: E Wic* ... *1C 4*
(off Bell La.)
Bells La. SL3: Hort ... 6D 6
Bell St. RH2: Reig ... 3M 121
Belltrees Gro.
SW16 ... 6K 29
Bell Va. La. GU27: Hasl ... 4F 188
Bell Vw. SL4: W'sor ... 6C 4
Bell Vw. Cl. SL4: W'sor ... 5C 4
Bellway Ho. RH1: Mers ... 6G 102
Bell Weir Cl. TW19: Stain ... 3D 20
Bellwether La. RH1: Out ... 3M 143
BELMONT ... 6M 61
Belmont KT13: Weybr ... 3D 56
Belmont Av. GU2: Guil ... 9J 93
KT3: N Mal ... 4F 42
Belmont Cl. GU14: Cove ... 7L 69
Belmont Cotts. *SL3: Coln* ... *3E 6*
(off High St.)
Belmont Gro. W4 ... 1C 12
Belmont M. GU15: Camb ... 3A 70
SW19 ... 3J 27
Belmont Ri. SM2: Sut ... 4L 61
Belmont Rd. BR3: Beck ... 1H 47
GU15: Camb ... 2A 70
KT22: Leat ... 9G 79
RG45: Crow ... 1G 49
RH2: Reig ... 4A 122
SE25 ... 4E 46
SM2: Sut ... 6M 61
SM6: W'ton ... 2F 62
TW2: Twick ... 3D 24
W4 ... 1C 12
Belmont Station (Rail) ... 6N 61
Belmont Ter. W4 ... 1C 12
Belmore Av. GU22: Pyr ... 3F 74
Beloe Cl. SW15 ... 7F 12
Belsize Gdns. SM1: Sut ... 1N 61
Belsize Grange KT16: Chert ... 6L 37
Belstone M. GU14: Farnb ... 7M 69
Beltane Dr. SW19 ... 4J 27
Belthorn Cres. SW12 ... 1G 29
Belton Rd. GU15: Camb ... 1C 70
Beltran Rd. SW6 ... 5N 13
Belvedere Av. SW19 ... 6K 27
Belvedere Cl. GU2: Guil ... 1L 113
KT10: Esh ... 2B 58
KT13: Weybr ... 2B 56
TW11: Tedd ... 6E 24
Belvedere Ct. GU17: Haw ... 3J 69
RH1: Red ... 8E 102
RH10: Craw ... 2F 182
SW15 ... 7H 13
Belvedere Dr. SW19 ... 6K 27
Belvedere Gdns.
KT8: W Mole ... 4N 39
Belvedere Gro. SW19 ... 6K 27
Belvedere Ho. KT13: Weybr ... 2C 56
Belvedere Rd. GU14: Farnb ... 3A 90
TN16: B Hil ... 5H 87
Belvedere Sq. SW19 ... 6K 27
Belvoir Cl. GU16: Frim ... 5D 70
Bembridge Ct. RG45: Crow ... 3D 48
Bembridge Ho.
KT2: K Tham ... *3M 203*
(off Coombe Rd.)
SW18 ... *9N 13*
(off Iron Mill Rd.)
Bemish Rd. SW15 ... 6J 13
Benbow La. GU8: Duns ... 5E 174
Benbricke Grn. RG42: Brac ... 8M 15
Benbrick Rd. GU2: Guil ... 4K 113
Bence, The TW20: Thor ... 2D 36
Bench, The TW10: Ham ... 4J 25
Bench Fld. CR2: S Croy ... 3C 64
Benchfield Cl.
RH19: E Grin ... 1D 186
Bencombe Rd. CR8: Pur ... 1L 83
Bencroft Rd. SW16 ... 8G 29
Bencurtis Pk. BR4: W Wick ... 9N 47
Bendemeer Rd. SW15 ... 6J 13
Bendon Valley SW18 ... 1N 27
Benedict Cl. BR6: Orp ... 1N 67
Benedict Dr. TW14: Bedf ... 1E 22
Benedict Grn. RG42: Warf ... 8C 16
Benedict Rd. CR4: Mit ... 2B 44
Benedict Wharf CR4: Mit ... 2C 44
Benen-Stock Rd.
TW19: Stan M ... 8J 7
Benetfeld Rd. RG42: Bin ... 7G 15
Benett Gdns. SW16 ... 1J 45
Benfleet Cl. KT11: Cob ... 8M 57
SM1: Sut ... 9A 44
Benham Cl. CR5: Coul ... 5M 83
KT9: Ches ... 3J 59
Benham Gdns. TW4: Houn ... 8N 9
Benham Ho. *SW10* ... *3N 13*
(off Coleridge Gdns.)
Benhams Cl. RH6: Horl ... 6E 142
Benhams Dr. RH6: Horl ... 6E 142
Benhill Av. SM1: Sut ... 1N 61
(not continuous)
Benhill Rd. SM1: Sut ... 9A 44
Benhill Wood Rd. SM1: Sut ... 9A 44
BENHILTON ... 8N 43
Benhilton Gdns. SM1: Sut ... 9N 43
Benhurst Cl. CR2: Sels ... 6G 64
Benhurst Ct. SW16 ... 6L 29
Benhurst Gdns. CR2: Sels ... 6F 64
Benhurst La. SW16 ... 6L 29
Benjamin Ct. TW15: A'ford ... 8D 22
Benjamin M. SW12 ... 1G 28
Benjamin Rd. RH10: Craw ... 5H 183
Benland Cotts.
RH12: Warn ... 7D 178
Benn Cl. RH8: Oxt ... 3C 126
Benner La. GU24: W End ... 8C 52
Bennets Courtyard
SW19 ... 9A 28
Bennett Cl. KT1: H Wic ... 9J 25
KT11: Cob ... 9H 57
RH10: Craw ... 7F 182
TW4: Houn ... 8M 9
Bennett Ct. GU15: Camb ... 1A 70
Bennetts Av. CR0: Croy ... 8H 47
Bennetts Cl. CR4: Mit ... 9F 28
Bennetts Farm Pl.
KT23: Book ... 3N 97
Bennetts Ri. GU11: Alde ... 4A 110
Bennetts Rd. RH13: Hors ... 7L 197
Bennett St. W4 ... 2D 12
Bennetts Way CR0: Croy ... 8H 47
Bennetts Wood RH5: Cap ... 5J 159
Benning Cl. SL4: W'sor ... 6A 4
Bennings Cl. RG42: Brac ... 8M 15

Benning Way—Bishop Sumner Dr.

Benning Way RG40: W'ham . . .9B 14
Benn's All. TW12: Hamp 1B 40
Benns Wlk. TW9: Rich 7L 11
(off Michelsdale Dr.)
Bens Acre RH13: Hors 6N 197
Bensbury Cl. SW15 . . . . .1G 27
Bensham Cl. CR7: T Hea 3N 45
Bensham Gro. CR7: T Hea 1N 45
Bensham La. CR0: Croy 6M 45
CR7: T Hea 4M 45
Bensham Mnr. Rd.
CR7: T Hea 3N 45
Bensham Mnr. Rd. Pas.
CR7: T Hea 3N 45
Benson Cl. TW3: Houn 7A 10
Benson Rd. CR0: Wad 9L 45
RG45: Crow 2E 48
Bensons La. RH12: Fay 8B 180
Bentalls Cen., The
KT1: K Tham . . .3H 203 (1K 41)
Benthall Gdns. CR8: Ken 4N 83
Bentham Av. GU21: Wok 2E 74
Bentley Cl. SW19 . . . . .4M 27
Bentley Copse GU15: Camb . . .2F 70
Bentley Dr. KT13: Weybr 5B 56
Bentley Pl. KT13: Weybr 1C 56
(off Baker St.)
Bentons La. SE27 . . . . .5N 29
Benton's Ri. SE27 . . . . .6N 29
Bentsbrook Cl. RH5: Nth H . . .9H 119
Bentsbrook Cotts.
RH5: Nth H 9H 119
Bentsbrook Pk.
RH5: Nth H 9H 119
Bentsbrook Rd.
RH5: Nth H 9H 119
Benwell Ct. TW16: Sunb 9H 23
Benwell Rd. GU24: B'wood 6C 72
Benwood Ct. SM1: Sut 9A 44
Beomonds KT16: Chert 6J 37
Beomonds Row KT16: Chert . . .6J 37
Berberis Cl. GU1: Guil 1M 113
(not continuous)
Berberis Ho. TW13: Felt 3H 23
Bere Rd. RG12: Brac 5C 32
Beresford Av. KT5: Surb 7A 42
TW1: Twick 9J 11
Beresford Cl. GU16: Frim G . . .8D 70
Beresford Gdns. TW4: Houn . . .8N 9
Beresford Rd.
KT2: K Tham . . .1L 203 (9M 25)
KT3: N Mal 3B 42
RH4: Dork 3L 201 (5H 119)
SM2: Sut 4L 61
Berestede Rd. W6 . . . . .1E 12
Bergenia Ct. GU24: W End 9B 52
Bergenia Ho. TW13: Felt 2J 23
Berisford M. SW18 . . . . .9N 13
Berkeley Av. TW4: C'ford 5H 9
Berkeley Cl. GU51: Fleet 4C 88
KT2: K Tham 8L 25
RH11: Craw 7J 181
TW19: Stain 3F 20
Berkeley Ct. CR0: Croy 6D 200
KT6: Surb 6K 41
KT13: Weybr 8E 38
KT21: A'tead 5M 79
SM6: W'ton 9G 44
Berkeley Cres. GU16: Frim 6E 70
Berkeley Dr. KT8: W Mole 2N 39
SL4: Wink 2M 17
Berkeley Gdns. KT10: Clay 3G 59
KT12: Wal T 6G 39
KT14: W By 1H 75
Berkeley Ho. TW8: Brent 2K 11
(off Albany Rd.)
Berkeley M. TW16: Sunb 2K 39
Berkeley Pl. KT18: Eps 2C 80
SW19 . . . . .7J 27
Berkeley Rd. SW13 . . . . .4F 12
Berkeleys, The KT22: Fetc 2E 98
SE25 . . . . .3D 46
Berkeley Waye TW5: Hest 2L 9
Berkley Cl. TW2: Twick 4E 24
(off Wellesley Rd.)
Berkley Ct.
GU1: Guil 2F 202 (3A 114)
Berkshire Cl. CR3: Cate 9A 84
Berkshire Ct. RG12: Brac 1L 31
Berkshire Rd. GU15: Camb 7D 50
Berkshire Sq. CR4: Mit 3J 45
Berkshire Way CR4: Mit 3J 45
RG12: Brac 2G 31
RG40: W'ham 2G 31
Berkshire Yeomanry Mus. 7G 4
Bernadine Cl. RG42: Warf 8C 16
Bernard Ct. GU15: Camb 2N 69
Bernard Gdns. SW19 . . . . .6L 27
Bernard Pl. KT17: Ewe 6H 61
Bernard Rd. SM6: W'ton 1F 62
Bernel Dr. CR0: Croy 9J 47
Berne Rd. CR7: T Hea 4N 45
Bernersh Cl. GU47: Sandh 6H 49
Berney Ho. BR3: Beck 4H 47
Berney Rd. CR0: Croy 6A 46
Berrington Dr. KT24: E Hor 2G 97
Berrybank GU47: C Tow 9K 49
Berry Ct. TW4: Houn 8N 9
Berrycroft RG12: Brac 9B 16
BERRYLANDS 5N 41
Berrylands KT5: Surb 5M 41
SW20 . . . . .2H 43
Berrylands Rd. KT5: Surb 5M 41
Berrylands Station (Rail) 3A 42
Berry La. GU3: Worp 3F 92
(not continuous)
GU22: Wok 3F 92
KT12: Hers 2L 57
(off The Green)
RG42: Warf 1D 16
Berry Meade
KT21: A'tead 4M 79
Berry Meade Cl.
KT21: A'tead 4M 79
Berrymeade Wlk.
RH11: Ifi 4K 181
Berrys Ct. KT14: Byf 7M 55
Berryscroft Ct. TW18: Stain . . .8L 21
Berryscroft Rd.
TW18: Stain 8L 21
BERRY'S GREEN 3K 87
Berry's Grn. Rd.
TN16: B Hil 3K 87
Berry's Hill TN16: B Hil 3K 87
Berry's La. KT14: Byf 7M 55
Berry Wlk. KT21: A'tead 6M 79
Berstead Wlk. RH11: Craw . . .6L 181
Bertal Rd. SW17 . . . . .5B 28
Bertram Cotts. SW19 . . . . .8M 27
Bertram Rd. KT2: K Tham 8N 25
Bertrand Ho. SW16 . . . . .4J 29
(off Leigham Av.)
Bert Rd. CR7: T Hea 4N 45
Berwick Cl. TW2: Whitt 2A 24
Berwick Gdns. SM1: Sut 9A 44
Berwyn Av. TW3: Houn 4B 10
Berwyn Rd. SE24 . . . . .2M 29
TW10: Rich 7A 12
Beryl Rd. W6 . . . . .1J 13
Berystede KT2: K Tham 8A 26
Besley St. SW16 . . . . .7G 29
Bessant Dr. TW9: Kew 4N 11
Bessborough Rd.
SW15 . . . . .2F 26
Bessemer Cl. SL3: Lang 1B 6
Beswick Gdns. RG12: Brac 9D 16
Beta Rd. GU14: Cove 9L 69
GU22: Wok 3D 74
GU24: Chob 6J 53
Beta Way TW20: Thor 9E 20
BETCHETS GREEN 5H 139
Betchets Grn. Rd.
RH5: Holm 5J 139
Betchley Cl. RH19: E Grin 7A 166
BETCHWORTH 3C 120
Betchworth Cl. SM1: Sut 2B 62
Betchworth Station (Rail) . . .1C 120
Betchworth Way
CR0: N Add 5M 65
Betchworth Works
RH6: Char 4J 161
Bethany Pl. GU21: Wok 5N 73
Bethany Waye TW14: Bedf 1F 22
Bethel Cl. GU9: U Hal 6J 109
Bethel La. GU9: U Hal 5H 109
Bethune Cl. RH10: Wor 4H 183
Bethune Rd. RH13: Hors 7L 197
Betjeman Cl. CR5: Coul 4K 83
Betjeman Wlk. GU46: Yate 2A 68
Betley Ct. KT12: Wal T 9J 39
Betony Cl. CR0: Croy 7G 47
Bettridge Rd. SW6 . . . . .5L 13
Betts Cl. BR3: Beck 1H 47
Betts Way KT6: Surb 7H 41
RH10: Craw 8B 162
SE20 . . . . .1E 46
Betula Cl. CR8: Ken 2A 84
Between Streets KT11: Cob . . .1H 77
Beulah Av. CR7: T Hea 1N 45
Beulah Ct. RH6: Horl 8E 142
Beulah Cres. CR7: T Hea 1N 45
Beulah Gro. CR0: Croy 5N 45
Beulah Hill SE19 . . . . .7M 29
Beulah Rd. CR7: T Hea 2N 45
SM1: Sut 1M 61
SW19 . . . . .8L 27
Beulah Wlk. CR3: Wold 7H 85
Bevan Ct. CR0: Wad 2L 63
RH11: Craw 8N 181
Bevan Ga. RG42: Brac 9M 15
Bevan Ho. TW1: Twick 9K 11
Bevan Pk. KT17: Ewe 6E 60
Beveree Stadium 9B 24
Beveren Cl. GU51: Fleet 1C 88
Beverley Av. SW20 . . . . .9E 26
TW4: Houn 7N 9
Beverley Cl. GU12: Ash 3D 110
GU15: Camb 9H 51
KT9: Ches 1J 59
KT13: Weybr 8F 38
KT15: Addl 2M 55
KT17: Ewe 7H 61
SW13 . . . . .5F 12
Beverley Cotts. SW15 . . . . . . .4D 26
Beverley Ct. TW4: Houn 7N 9
W4 . . . . .1B 12
Beverley Cres.
GU14: Cove 3L 89
Beverley Gdns. KT4: W Pk 7F 42
SW13 . . . . .6E 12
Beverley Hgts. RH2: Reig 1N 121
Beverley Hyrst CR0: Croy 8C 46
Beverley La. KT2: K Tham 8D 26
SW15 . . . . .4E 26
Beverley M. RH10: Craw 4E 182
Beverley Path SW13 . . . . .5E 12
Beverley Rd. CR3: Whyte 3B 84
CR4: Mit 3H 45
KT1: H Wic 9J 25
KT3: N Mal 3F 42
KT4: W Pk 8H 43
RG12: Brac 2B 32
SE20 . . . . .1E 46
SW13 . . . . .6E 12
TW16: Sunb 9G 22
W4 . . . . .1E 12
Beverley Trad. Est.
SM4: Mord 6J 43
Beverley Way SW20 . . . . .9E 26
Beverstone Rd. CR7: T Hea 3L 45
Bevill Allen Cl. SW17 . . . . . . .6D 28
Bevill Cl. SE25 . . . . .2D 46
Bevington Rd. BR3: Beck 1L 47
Bevin Sq. SW17 . . . . .4D 28
BEWBUSH 6L 181
Bewbush Dr. RH11: Craw 6K 181
Bewbush Leisure Cen. 7L 181
Bewbush Mnr. Rdbt.
RH11: Craw 7K 181
Bewbush Pl. RH11: Craw 6K 181
Bewbush Water Garden 5J 181
Bewley St. SW19 . . . . .7A 28
Bewlys Rd. SE27 . . . . .6M 29
Bexhill Cl. TW13: Felt 3M 23
Bexhill Rd. SW14 . . . . .6B 12
Bexley St. SL4: W'sor 4F 4
Beynon Rd. SM5: Cars 2D 62
Bicester Rd. TW9: Rich 6N 11
Bickersteth Rd. SW17 . . . . . . .7D 28
Bickley Ct. RH11: Craw 6M 181
Bickley St. SW17 . . . . .6C 28
Bicknell Cl.
GU1: Guil 1C 202 (2M 113)
Bicknell Rd. GU16: Frim 4C 70
Bickney Way KT22: Fetc 9C 78
Bicknoller Cl. SM2: Sut 6N 61
Bicton Cft. GU7: Goda 5H 133
Biddulph Rd. CR2: S Croy 6N 63
Bideford Cl. GU14: Farnb 7M 69
TW13: Hanw 4N 23
Bidhams Cres. KT20: Tad 8H 81
Bield, The RH2: Reig 5M 121
Bietigheim Way
GU15: Camb 9A 50
Big All. TN8: M Grn 6K 147
Big Apple 4B 74
Big Apple Leisure Cen. 3A 30
Big Barn Gro. RG42: Warf 8B 16
Big Comn. La. RH1: Blet 2M 123
Biggin Av. CR4: Mit 9D 28
Biggin Cl. RH11: Craw 5A 182
BIGGIN HILL 4F 86
Biggin Hill SE19 . . . . .9M 29
BIGGIN HILL AIRPORT 8F 66
Biggin Hill Bus. Pk.
TN16: B Hil 2F 86
Biggin Hill Cl. KT2: K Tham . . .6J 25
Biggin Way SE19 . . . . .8M 29
Bigginwood Rd. SW16 . . . . . . .8M 29
Biggs Row SW15 . . . . .6J 13
Bignor Cl. RH12: Hors 2N 197
Bilberry Cl. RH11: Craw 6N 181
Bilbets RH12: Hors 5J 197
(off Rushams Rd.)
Billet Rd. TW18: Stain 4J 21
BILL HILL 6A 14
BILLINGBEAR 4G 15
Billingbear Cvn. Pk.
RG40: W'ham 5E 14
Billingbear La.
RG40: W'ham 4D 14
RG42: Bin 4G 15
Billing Pl. SW10 . . . . .3N 13
Billing Rd. SW10 . . . . .3N 13
Billingshurst Rd.
RH12: Bro H 5C 196
Billing St. SW10 . . . . .3N 13
Billington Ct. RH19: E Grin . . .8A 166
Billinton Dr. RH10: Craw 3F 182
Billinton Hill
CR0: Croy 2E 200 (8A 46)
Billockby Cl. KT9: Ches 3M 59
Bilton Cen. KT22: Leat 6F 78
Bilton Cl. SL3: Poy 5G 7
Bilton Ind. Est. RG12: Brac . . .3K 31
Bindon Grn. SM4: Mord 3N 43
BINFIELD 7H 15
Binfield Rd. CR2: S Croy 2C 64
KT14: Byf 8N 55
RG10: S Row 1F 14
RG40: W'ham 2D 30
RG42: Bin, Brac 7L 15
Bingham Dr. GU21: Wok 5J 73
TW18: Stain 8M 21
Bingham Rd. CR0: Croy 7D 46
Bingley Rd. TW16: Sunb 8H 23
Binhams Lea GU8: Duns 4B 174
Binhams Mdw. GU8: Duns 4B 174
Binley Ho. SW15 . . . . .9E 12
Binney Ct. RH10: Craw 9J 163
Binns Rd. W4 . . . . .1D 12
Binns Ter. W4 . . . . .1D 12
BINSCOMBE 3G 133
Binscombe GU7: Goda 2G 132
Binscombe Cres.
GU7: Goda 4H 133
Binscombe La. GU7: Goda . . .3G 133
Binstead Cl. RH11: Craw 1N 181
Binstead Copse GU52: Fleet . . .6A 88
Binsted Dr. GU17: B'water 1J 69
Binton La. GU10: Seal 1C 130
Birchanger GU7: Goda 7H 133
Birchanger Rd. SE25 . . . . .4D 46
Birch Av. CR3: Cate 2A 104
GU51: Fleet 4A 88
KT22: Leat 7F 78
Birch Circ. GU7: Goda 3J 133
Birch Cl. GU10: Wrec 7F 128
GU15: Camb 7C 50
GU21: Wok 6M 73
GU23: Send 3H 95
KT15: N Haw 5M 55
RH10: Craw D 1F 184
SM7: Ban 1K 81
TW3: Houn 5D 10
TW8: Brent 3H 11
TW11: Tedd 6G 25
TW17: Shep 1F 38
Birch Ct. KT22: Leat 7F 78
RG45: Crow 2E 48
SM1: Sut 1A 62
SM6: W'ton 1F 62
Birchcroft Cl. CR3: Cate 3N 103
Birchdale Cl. KT14: W By 7L 55
Birch Dr. GU17: Haw 3J 69
Birchend Cl. CR2: S Croy 3A 64
Birches, The BR6: Farnb 1J 67
GU14: Cove 1J 89
GU17: B'water 1G 69
GU22: Wok 5B 74
KT24: E Hor 4F 96
RH10: Craw 1E 182
RH13: M Hea 9B 198
TW4: Houn 1N 23
Birches Cl. CR4: Mit 2D 44
KT18: Eps 2D 80
Birches Ind. Est.
RH19: E Grin 7K 165
Birches La. GU5: Gorn 1D 136
Birches Rd. RH12: Hors 3A 198
Birchett Rd. GU11: Alde 2M 109
GU14: Cove 9K 69
Birchetts Cl. RG42: Brac 9N 15
Birchfield Cl. CR5: Coul 3K 83
KT15: Addl 1K 55
Birchfield Ct. KT12: Wal T 6J 39
(off Grove Cres.)
Birchfield Gro. KT17: Ewe 6H 61
Birchfield Ind. Pk.
RH6: Char 6J 161
Birchfields GU15: Camb 2A 70
BIRCH GREEN 5J 21
Birch Grn. TW18: Stain 5H 21
Birch Gro. GU1: Guil 9M 93
GU22: Pyr 2F 74
KT11: Cob 1K 77
KT20: K'wood 2K 101
SL4: W'sor 4A 4
TW17: Shep 1F 38
Birchgrove Ho. TW9: Kew 3A 12
BIRCH HILL 6N 31
Birch Hill CR0: Croy 2G 65
Birch Hill Rd. RG12: Brac 6N 31
Birch Ho. RH19: E Grin 8M 165
SW2 . . . . .1L 29
(off Tulse Hill)
Birchington Rd. KT5: Surb 6M 41
SL4: W'sor 5D 4
Birchlands Av. SW12 . . . . .1D 28
Birchlands Ct.
GU47: Owls 5K 49
Birch La. CR8: Pur 7J 63
GU24: W End 8A 52
SL5: Asc 9E 16
Birch Lea RH10: Craw 9E 162
Birch Pde. GU51: Fleet 4A 88
Birch Platt GU24: W End 9A 52
Birch Rd. GU7: Goda 3J 133
GU20: Windl 3B 52
GU35: H Dwn 3F 168
TW13: Hanw 6L 23
Birch Side RG45: Crow 1E 48
Birch Tree Av. BR4: W Wick . . .2B 66
Birch Tree Ct. GU27: Hasl 4A 188
Birch Tree Gdns.
RH19: E Grin 7L 165
Birch Tree Vw. GU18: Ligh 6L 51
Birch Tree Way CR0: Croy 8E 46
Birch Va. KT11: Cob 8A 58
Birchview Cl. GU46: Yate 2B 68
Birch Wlk. CR4: Mit 9F 28
KT14: W By 8J 55
(not continuous)
Birch Way CR6: Warl 5H 85
GU12: A Va 6E 90
Birchway RH1: Red 5F 122
Birchwood Av. BR3: Beck 3J 47
SM6: W'ton 9E 44
Birchwood Cl. RH6: Horl 7F 142
RH10: Craw 6G 183
RH14: Ifo 5F 192
SM4: Mord 3N 43
Birchwood Ct. KT13: Weybr . . .2D 56
Birchwood Dr. GU18: Ligh 6N 51
KT14: W By 8J 55
Birchwood Gro.
TW12: Hamp 7A 24
Birchwood La. CR3: Cate 3M 103
KT10: Esh 5D 58
KT22: Oxs 5D 58
Birchwood Rd. KT14: W By 8J 55
SW17 . . . . .6F 28
Birdham Cl. RH11: Craw 1N 181
Birdhaven GU10: Wrec 5F 128
Birdhouse La. BR6: Dow 2J 87
Birdhurst Av.
CR2: S Croy 7E 200 (1A 64)
Birdhurst Ct. SM6: W'ton 4G 62
(off Woodcote Av.)
Birdhurst Gdns.
CR2: S Croy 7E 200 (1A 64)
Birdhurst Ri.
CR2: S Croy 8F 200 (2B 64)
Birdhurst Rd.
CR2: S Croy 8F 200 (2B 64)
SW19 . . . . .7C 28
Bird in Hand Path
CR0: Croy 6A 46
(off Sydenham Rd.)
Bird M. RG40: W'ham 2A 30
Birds Gro. GU21: Knap 5E 72
Birds Hill Dr. KT22: Oxs 9D 58
Birds Hill Ri. KT22: Oxs 9D 58
Birds Hill Rd. KT22: Oxs 8D 58
Birdswood Dr. GU21: Wok 6H 73
Bird Wlk. TW2: Whitt 2N 23
Birdwood Cl. CR2: Sels 7F 64
TW11: Tedd 5E 24
Birdwood Rd. GU15: Camb 9K 49
Birdworld & Underwater World
. . . . .8A 128
Birkbeck Hill SE21 . . . . .2M 29
Birkbeck Pl. GU47: Owls 6K 49
SE21 . . . . .3N 29
Birkbeck Rd. BR3: Beck 1F 46
SW19 . . . . .6N 27
Birkbeck Station (Rail & CT)
. . . . .2F 46
Birkdale RG12: Brac 6K 31
Birkdale Dr. RH11: Ifi 4J 181
Birkdale Gdns. CR0: Croy 1G 65
Birkenhead Av.
KT2: K Tham . . .3L 203 (1M 41)
Birkenholme Cl.
GU35: H Dwn 5H 169
Birkheads Rd. RH2: Reig 2M 121
Birkin Ct. KT14: Byf 7M 55
Birkwood Cl. SW12 . . . . .1H 29
Birnam Cl. GU23: Rip 2J 95
BIRTLEY GREEN 8D 134
Birtley Ri. GU5: Braml 6C 134
Birtley Rd. GU5: Braml 6C 134
Biscay Rd. W6 . . . . .1J 13
Biscoe Cl. TW5: Hest 2A 10
Bisenden Rd.
CR0: Croy 2F 200 (8B 46)
Bisham Cl. RH10: Craw 5H 183
SM5: Cars 7D 44
Bishams Ct. CR3: Cate 2C 104
Bishop Ct. TW9: Rich 6L 11
Bishopdale RG12: Brac 3M 31
Bishop Duppas Pk.
TW17: Shep 6F 38
Bishop Fox Way
KT8: W Mole 3N 39
Bishopric RH12: Hors 6H 197
Bishopric Ct. RH12: Hors 6H 197
Bishop's Av. SW6 . . . . .5J 13
Bishops Cl. CR5: Coul 5L 83
GU52: Fleet 7B 88
SM1: Sut 9M 43
TW10: Ham 4K 25
W4 . . . . .1B 12
Bishop's Cotts. RH3: Betch . . .2A 120
Bishops Ct. CR0: Croy 8C 46
GU2: Guil 6B 202
RH12: Hors 7J 197
SL5: Asc 7K 17
Bishop's Dr. RG40: W'ham 1B 30
TW14: Bedf 9E 8
Bishopsford Rd. SM4: Mord 6A 44
BISHOPS GATE 4K 19
Bishopsgate Rd.
TW20: Eng G 4J 19
Bishops Gro. GU20: Windl 3N 51
TW12: Hamp 5N 23
Bishops Gro. Cvn. Site
TW12: Hamp 5A 24
Bishop's Hall
KT1: K Tham 3H 203 (1K 41)
Bishops Hill KT12: Wal T 6H 39
Bishop's La. RG42: Warf 2E 16
Bishop's Mans. SW6 . . . . .5J 13
(not continuous)
Bishops Mead GU9: Farnh . . .1G 128
Bishopsmead Cl.
KT19: Ewe 6C 60
KT24: E Hor 6F 96
Bishopsmead Ct.
KT19: Ewe 6D 60
Bishopsmead Dr.
KT24: E Hor 7G 96
Bishopsmead Pde.
KT24: E Hor 7F 96
Bishops Pk. Rd. SW6 . . . . .5J 13
SW16 . . . . .9J 29
Bishops Pl. SM1: Sut 2A 62
Bishops Rd. CR0: Croy 6M 45
GU9: U Hal 6G 108
SW6 . . . . .4K 13
Bishops Sq. GU6: Cranl 7A 156
Bishopstone Wlk.
RH11: Craw 8A 182
Bishop Sumner Dr.
GU9: U Hal 6H 109

Bishops Wlk.—Borough Hill

Bishops Wlk. CR0: A'ton 2G 64
Bishops Way TW20: Egh 7F 20
Bishops Wharf GU1: Guil 5A 202
Bishops Wood GU21: Wok 4J 73
BISLEY 2C 72
BISLEY CAMP 6A 72
Bisley Cl. KT4: W Pk 7H 43
Bisley Grn. GU24: Bis 3C 72
Bison Ct. TW14: Felt 1J 23
Bissingen Way GU15: Camb 9B 50
Bitmead Cl. RH11: Ifi 4K 181
Bittams La. KT16: Chert 1F 54
Bittern Cl. GU11: Alde 5M 109
GU47: C Tow 7J 49
RH11: Ifi 4J 181
Bitterne Dr. GU21: Wok 4J 73
Bittoms, The
KT1: K Tham 5H 203 (2K 41)
(not continuous)
Bittoms Ct.
KT1: K Tham 5H 203 (2K 41)
Blackberry Cl. GU1: Guil 9L 93
TW17: Shep 3F 38
Blackberry Farm Cl.
TW5: Hest 3M 9
Blackberry La. RH7: Ling 9N 145
Blackberry Rd. RH7: Ling 2M 165
RH19: Felc, Ling 2M 165
Blackbird Cl. GU47: C Tow 7J 49
Blackbird Hill RH10: T Hil 4F 184
Blackborough Cl.
RH2: Reig 3A 122
Blackborough Rd.
RH2: Reig 4A 122
Blackbridge Ct.
RH12: Hors 6H 197
Blackbridge La.
RH12: Hors 7G 196
Blackbridge Rd. GU22: Wok 6N 73
BLACKBROOK 1L 139
Blackbrook Rd.
RH5: Holm, Nth H 9K 119
Blackburn, The KT23: Book 2N 97
Blackburn Trad. Est.
TW19: Stan 9A 8
Blackburn Way GU7: Goda 6J 133
TW4: Houn 8M 9
Blackbush Cl. SM2: Sut 4N 61
Blackbushe Bus. Pk.
GU46: Yate 2B 68
Blackbushe Pk. GU46: Yate 1B 68
Blackbushes Rd.
GU51: Fleet 8A 68
Blackcap Cl. RH11: Craw 5A 182
Blackcap Pl. GU47: C Tow 7K 49
BLACK CORNER 5H 163
Black Dog Wlk.
RH10: Craw 1C 182
Black Down 7K 189
Blackdown Av. GU22: Pyr 2G 74
Blackdown Cl. GU22: Pyr 3E 74
Blackdown Rd. GU16: Deep 7G 70
Black Eagle Cl.
TN16: Weste 5L 107
Black Eagle Sq.
TN16: Weste 5L 107
Blackett Cl. TW18: Stain 1G 37
Blackett Rd. RH10: Craw 4G 182
Blackett St. SW15 6J 13
Blackfold Rd. RH10: Craw 4E 182
Blackford Cl. CR2: S Croy 5M 63
Blackford's Path SW15 1F 26
BLACKHEATH 2G 135
Blackheath 2H 135
Blackheath RH10: Craw 1H 183
Blackheath Gro.
GU5: Wone 3D 134
Blackheath La.
GU4: B'eath 3D 134
GU5: Alb 2K 135
GU5: Wone 3D 134
Blackheath Rd. GU9: U Hal 5F 108
Blackhills KT10: Esh 5N 57
Black Horse Cl. SL4: W'sor 5A 4
Blackhorse La. CR0: Croy 6D 46
KT20: Lwr K 7N 101
Blackhorse Lane Stop (CT) 6D 46
Blackhorse Rd. GU22: Wok 7G 72
Blackhorse Way
RH12: Hors 6H 197
Black Horse Yd. SL4: W'sor 4G 5
Blackhouse Farm Ind. Est.
RH13: Col 3J 199
Blackhouse Rd. RH13: Col 2H 199
Black Lake Cl. TW20: Egh 9C 20
Blacklands Cres.
RH18: F Row 7H 187
Blacklands Mdw. RH1: Nut 2J 123
Black Lion La. W6 1F 12
Black Lion M. W6 1F 12
Blackman Gdns.
GU11: Alde 4N 109
Blackman's La. CR6: Warl 1A 86
Black Mdws. RG12: Brac 5A 32
Blackmoor Cl. SL5: Asc 1H 33
Blackmoor Wood SL5: Asc 1H 33
Blackmore Cres.
GU21: Wok 2E 74
Blackmore's Gro.
TW11: Tedd 7G 24
Blackness La. BR2: Kes 5F 66
GU22: Wok 6A 74
BLACKNEST 2E 34
Blacknest Ga. Rd.
SL5: S'hill 2E 34
Blacknest Rd.
GU25: V Wat 2G 35
GU34: B'nest 4A 148
SL5: S'hill 2G 35
Black Pond La.
GU10: L Bou 5H 129
Black Prince Cl. KT14: Byf 1A 76
Blackshaw Rd.
SW17 5A 28
Blacksmith Cl.
KT21: A'tead 6M 79
Blacksmith La. GU4: Guil 8E 114
Blacksmiths Hill
CR2: Sande 9D 64
Blacksmiths La.
KT16: Chert 6J 37
TW18: Lale 2K 37
Blacks Rd. W6 1H 13
Blackstone Cl. GU14: Cove 8J 69
RH1: Red 4C 122
Blackstone Hill RH1: Red 4B 122
Blackstroud La. E.
GU18: Ligh 7A 52
Blackstroud La. W.
GU18: Ligh 7A 52
Black Swan Cl.
RH11: P Pot 1N 199
Blackthorn Cl. RH2: Reig 5A 122
RH11: Craw 1A 182
RH13: Hors 6N 197
Blackthorn Ct. TW5: Hest 3M 9
Blackthorn Cres.
GU14: Cove 6L 69
Blackthorn Dr. GU18: Ligh 8M 51
Blackthorne Av. CR0: Croy 7F 46
Blackthorne Ct.
TW15: A'ford 8D 22
Blackthorne Cres. SL3: Poy 5G 7
Blackthorne Ind. Est.
SL3: Poy 6G 7
Blackthorne Rd.
KT23: Book 4C 98
SL3: Poy 6G 6
Blackthorn Pl. GU1: Guil 9M 93
Blackthorn Rd. RH2: Reig 5A 122
TN16: B Hil 3F 86
BLACKWATER 2J 69
Blackwater Cl. GU12: Ash 3E 110
Blackwater La.
RH10: Craw 4G 183
BLACKWATER PARK 2L 69
Blackwater Pk. GU12: Alde 3C 110
Blackwater Station (Rail) 2K 69
Blackwater Trad. Est.
GU12: Alde 4B 110
Blackwater Valley Relief Rd.
GU15: Camb 2L 69
Blackwater Valley Route
GU12: Alde 6C 110
GU14: Farnb 7B 70
Blackwater Vw.
RG40: Finch 5A 48
Blackwater Way
GU12: Alde 4B 110
BLACKWELL 8B 166
Blackwell Av. GU2: Guil 3G 112
Blackwell Farm Rd.
RH19: E Grin 7B 166
Blackwell Hollow
RH19: E Grin 8B 166
Blackwell Ho. SW4 1H 29
Blackwell Rd.
RH19: E Grin 8B 166
Blackwood Cl. KT14: W By 8L 55
Blade M. SW15 7L 13
Bladen Cl. KT13: Weybr 3E 56
Blades Cl. KT22: Leat 7K 79
Blades Ct. SW15 7L 13
W6 1G 13
(off Lower Mall)
Bladon Cl. GU1: Guil 2C 114
Bladon Ct. SW16 7J 29
Blagdon Rd. KT3: N Mal 3E 42
(not continuous)
Blagdon Wlk. TW11: Tedd 7J 25
Blair Av. KT10: Esh 8C 40
Blair Ct. BR3: Beck 1L 47
Blairderry Rd. SW2 3J 29
Blaire Pk. GU46: Yate 7A 48
Blaise Cl. GU14: Farnb 2B 90
Blake Cl. RG40: W'ham 9D 14
RG45: Crow 3H 49
RH10: Craw 7D 182
SM5: Cars 7C 44
Blakeden Dr. KT10: Clay 3F 58
Blakefield Gdns. CR5: Coul 5K 83
Blake Gdns. SW6 4N 13
Blakehall Rd. SM5: Cars 3D 62
Blake M. TW9: Kew 4N 11
Blakemore Gdns.
SW13 2G 12
Blakemore Rd. CR7: T Hea 4K 45
SW16 4J 29
Blakeney Cl. KT19: Eps 7C 60
Blakenham Rd. SW17 5D 28
Blake Rd.
CR0: Croy 2F 200 (8B 46)
CR4: Mit 2C 44
Blakes Av. KT3: N Mal 4E 42
Blakes Ct. KT16: Chert 7J 37
Blake's Grn. BR4: W Wick 7M 47
Blakes La. GU4: E Cla 1N 115
KT3: N Mal 4E 42
KT24: W Hors 9A 96
Blakesley Wlk. SW20 1L 43
Blakes Ride GU46: Yate 9A 48
Blakes Ter. KT3: N Mal 4F 42
Blakewood Cl. TW13: Hanw 5K 23
Blamire Dr. RG42: Bin 7L 15
Blanchard Ho. *TW1: Twick* 9K 11
(off Clevedon Rd.)
Blanchards Hill
GU4: J Wel, Sut G 6A 94
Blanchland Rd. SM4: Mord 4N 43
Blanchman's Rd. CR6: Warl 5H 85
Blandfield Rd. SW12 1E 28
Blandford Av. BR3: Beck 1H 47
TW2: Whitt 2B 24
Blandford Cl. CR0: Bedd 9J 45
GU22: Wok 4D 74
Blandford Rd. BR3: Beck 1F 46
TW11: Tedd 6D 24
Blane's La. RG12: Brac 7D 32
SL5: Asc 7D 32
Blanford M. RH2: Reig 3B 122
Blanford Rd. RH2: Reig 4A 122
Blanks La. RH5: Newd 8D 140
RH6: Char, Newd 8D 140
Blatchford Cl. RH13: Hors 5M 197
Blatchford Ct. KT12: Wal T 8H 39
Blatchford Rd.
RH13: Hors 5M 197
Blays Cl. TW20: Eng G 7M 19
Blay's La. TW20: Eng G 8L 19
Blegborough Rd. SW16 7G 29
Blencarn Cl. GU21: Wok 3J 73
Blendworth Point
SW15 2G 26
Blenheim Av. RG12: Brac 2A 32
Blenheim Bus. Cen.
CR4: Mit 1D 44
(off London Rd.)
Blenheim Cl. GU10: Tong 5C 110
KT14: W By 9H 55
RH10: Craw 9H 163
RH19: E Grin 7C 166
SM6: W'ton 4G 63
SW20 2H 43
Blenheim Ct. GU14: Farnb 3B 90
SM2: Sut 3A 62
TW18: Stain 5F 20
Blenheim Cres.
CR2: S Croy 4N 63
GU9: U Hal 7F 108
Blenheim Flds.
RH18: F Row 6G 187
Blenheim Gdns.
CR2: Sande 8D 64
GU22: Wok 6L 73
KT2: K Tham 8A 26
SM6: W'ton 3G 62
Blenheim Ho. TW3: Houn 6A 10
Blenheim M. GU9: Farnh 1F 128
Blenheim Pk. GU11: Alde 6A 90
Blenheim Pk. Rd.
CR2: S Croy 5N 63
Blenheim Pl. GU15: Camb 3A 70
TW11: Tedd 6F 24
Blenheim Rd. GU11: Alde 6N 89
KT19: Eps 7C 60
RH12: Hors 3K 197
SL3: Lang 1N 5
SM1: Sut 9M 43
SW20 2H 43
Blenheim Way TW7: Isle 4G 10
Blenkarne Rd. SW11 1D 28
Bleriot Rd. TW5: Hest 3K 9
BLETCHINGLEY 2A 124
Bletchingley Cl.
CR7: T Hea 3M 45
RH1: Mers 7G 103
Bletchingley Rd.
RH1: Mers 7G 102
RH1: Nut 2L 123
RH9: Gods 9D 104
Bletchmore Cl. UB3: Harl 1E 8
Blewburton Wlk.
RG12: Brac 3C 32
Blewfield GU7: Bus 9J 133
Bligh Cl. RH10: Craw 5D 182
Blighton La. GU10: Run 8B 110
Blincoe Cl. SW19 3J 27
Blind La. GU24: Chob 6C 52
RH3: Brock 6B 120
RH8: Oxt 8A 106
SM7: Ban 2C 82
Blindley Ct. RH7: Blin H 3H 145
BLINDLEY HEATH 3H 145
Blindley Rd. RH10: Craw 9H 163
Bloggs Way GU6: Cranl 7M 155
Blomfield Dale RG42: Brac 1J 31
Blondell Cl. UB7: Harm 2M 7
Bloomfield Cl. GU21: Knap 4H 73
Bloomfield Dr. RG12: Brac 8B 16
Bloomfield Rd.
KT1: K Tham 7K 203 (3L 41)
Bloomfield Ter.
TN16: Weste 3M 107
Bloom Gro. SE27 4M 29
Bloom Pk. Rd. SW6 3L 13
Bloomsbury Cl. KT19: Eps 6C 60
Bloomsbury Ct. *GU1: Guil* 5B 114
(off St Lukes Sq.)
TW5: C'ford 4J 9
Bloomsbury Pl. SW18 8N 13
Bloomsbury Way
GU17: Haw 3H 69
Bloor Cl. RH12: Hors 1K 197
Blore Ho. *SW10* 3N 13
(off Coleridge Gdns.)
Blossom Cl. CR2: S Croy 2C 64
Blossom Waye TW5: Hest 2M 9
Blount Av. RH19: E Grin 9M 165
Blount Cres. RG42: Bin 8K 15
Bloxham Cres.
TW12: Hamp 8N 23
Bloxham Rd. GU6: Cranl 7B 156
Bloxworth Cl. RG12: Brac 3D 32
SM6: W'ton 9G 45
Blue Anchor All. TW9: Rich 7L 11
Blue Ball La. TW20: Egh 6B 20
Blue Barn La.
KT13: Weybr 7B 56
Bluebell Cl. RH11: Craw 6N 181
RH12: Hors 3L 197
RH19: E Grin 9L 165
SM6: W'ton 7F 44
Bluebell Cott. GU3: Comp 2C 132
Bluebell Ct. GU22: Wok 6N 73
Bluebell Hill RG12: Brac 9C 16
Bluebell La. KT24: E Hor 7F 96
Bluebell M. GU15: Camb 8B 50
Bluebell Railway
Kingscote Station 6J 185
Bluebell Ri. GU18: Ligh 8M 51
Bluebell Rd. GU35: Lind 4B 168
Bluebell Wlk. GU51: Fleet 3A 88
Blueberry Gdns. CR5: Coul 3K 83
Blue Cedars SM7: Ban 1J 81
Blue Cedars Pl. KT11: Cob 8L 57
Bluecoat Pond RH13: Hors 9D 196
Bluecoat Wlk. RG12: Brac 4B 32
Bluefield Cl. TW12: Hamp 6A 24
Bluegates KT17: Ewe 4F 60
Bluehouse Gdns. RH8: Oxt 6C 106
Bluehouse La.
RH8: Limp, Oxt 6A 106
Blue Leaves Av. CR5: Coul 8H 83
Blueprint Apartments
SW12 1F 28
(off Balham Gro.)
Blue Pryor Ct.
GU52: C Cro 1A 108
Blue Riband Ind. Est.
CR0: Croy 2A 200 (8M 45)
Bluethroat Cl. GU47: C Tow 7K 49
Blue Water SW18 7N 13
Bluff Cove GU11: Alde 1A 110
Blundel La. KT11: Sto D 3N 77
Blundell Av. RH6: Horl 7D 142
Blunden Ct. GU5: Braml 5C 134
Blunden Rd. GU14: Cove 1L 89
Blunt Rd.
CR2: S Croy 8E 200 (2A 64)
Blunts Av. UB7: Sip 3B 8
Blunts Way RH12: Hors 5J 197
Blyth Cl. TW1: Twick 9F 10
Blytheswood Pl. SW16 5K 29
Blythewood La. SL5: Asc 2J 33
Blythwood Dr. GU16: Frim 4B 70
Blytons, The RH19: E Grin 9L 165
Board School Rd.
GU21: Wok 3B 74
Boars Head Yd. TW8: Brent 3K 11
Bocketts Farm Pk. 3F 98
Bocketts La. KT22: Fetc 2F 98
Bockhampton Rd.
KT2: K Tham 8M 25
Boddicott Cl. SW19 3K 27
Boddington Ho. *SW13* 2G 13
(off Wyatt Dr.)
Bodeites GU7: Goda 4E 132
Boden's Ride SL5: Asc 8H 33
(not continuous)
Bodiam Cl. RH10: Craw 3G 183
Bodiam Rd. SW16 8H 29
Bodicea M. TW4: Houn 9N 9
Bodley Cl. KT3: N Mal 4D 42
Bodley Mnr. Way SW2 1L 29
Bodley Rd. KT3: N Mal 5C 42
Bodmin Gro. SM4: Mord 4N 43
Bodmin St. SW18 2M 27
Bodnant Gdns. SW20 2F 42
Bogey La. BR6: Dow 4J 67
Bog La. RG12: Brac 4D 32
Bognor Rd.
RH12: Oak, Bro H, Warn, Rowh
4C 178
Boileau Rd. SW13 3F 12
Bois Hall Rd. KT15: Addl 2M 55
Bolderwood Way
BR4: W Wick 8L 47
Bolding Ho. La.
GU24: W End 9C 52
Boleyn Av. KT17: Ewe 6G 60
Boleyn Cl. RH10: Craw 6H 183
TW18: Stain 6G 20
Boleyn Ct. *GU21: Knap* 5F 72
(off Tudor Way)
KT8: E Mol 3D 40
(off Bridge Rd.)
RH1: Red 2E 122
(off St Anne's Ri.)
Boleyn Dr. KT8: W Mole 2N 39
Boleyn Gdns. BR4: W Wick 8L 47
Boleyn Gro. BR4: W Wick 8M 47
Boleyn Wlk. KT22: Leat 7F 78
Bolingbroke Gro.
SW11 1D 28
Bolney Ct. RH11: Craw 6L 181
Bolney Way TW13: Hanw 4M 23
Bolsover Gro. RH1: Mers 7J 103
Bolstead Rd. CR4: Mit 9F 28
Bolters La. SM7: Ban 1L 81
Bolters Rd. RH6: Horl 6E 142
Bolters Rd. Sth. RH6: Horl 6D 142
Bolton Av. SL4: W'sor 6G 4
Bolton Cl. KT9: Ches 3K 59
SE20 1D 46
Bolton Cres. SL4: W'sor 6F 4
Bolton Dr. SM5: Cars 6A 44
Bolton Gdns. SW5 1N 13
TW11: Tedd 7G 24
Bolton Gdns. M.
SW10 1N 13
Bolton Rd. KT9: Ches 3K 59
RH10: Craw 8F 182
SL4: W'sor 6F 4
W4 3B 12
Boltons, The SW10 1N 13
Boltons Cl. GU22: Pyr 3J 75
Boltons Ct. *SW5* 1N 13
(off Old Brompton Rd.)
Boltons La. GU22: Pyr 3J 75
RG42: Bin 7K 15
UB3: Harl 4D 8
(not continuous)
Boltons Pl. SW5 1N 13
Bombers La. TN16: Weste 6M 87
Bomer Cl. UB7: Sip 3B 8
Bonaly Ho. RH8: Oxt 9M 105
Bonchurch Cl. SM2: Sut 4N 61
Bond Gdns. SM6: W'ton 1G 63
Bond Rd. CR4: Mit 1C 44
CR6: Warl 5G 85
KT6: Surb 8M 41
Bond's La. RH5: Mid H 2H 139
Bond St. TW20: Eng G 6L 19
W4 1C 12
Bond Way RG12: Brac 9N 15
Bonehurst Rd. RH1: Salf 2E 142
RH6: Horl 2E 142
Bone Mill La. RH9: Gods 3H 125
Bones La. RH6: Horn 7D 144
RH7: Horn, Newc 9E 144
Bonner Hill Rd.
KT1: K Tham 4M 203 (1M 41)
(not continuous)
Bonners Cl. GU22: Wok 9B 74
Bonnetts La. RH11: Ifi 8M 161
Bonnys Rd. RH2: Reig 4J 121
Bonser Rd. TW1: Twick 3F 24
Bonsey Cl. GU22: Wok 8A 74
Bonsey La. GU22: Wok 8A 74
Bonseys La. GU24: Chob 5B 54
Bonsor Dr. KT20: K'wood 9K 81
Bonwicke Cotts.
RH10: Cop 4N 163
Bookham Comn. Rd.
KT23: Book 8M 77
Bookham Ct. CR4: Mit 2B 44
KT23: Book 1N 97
Bookham Gro. KT23: Book 4B 98
Bookham Ind. Est.
KT23: Book 1N 97
Bookham Rd. KT11: Down 6K 77
Bookham Station (Rail) 1N 97
Bookhurst Hill GU6: Cranl 7C 156
Bookhurst Rd.
GU6: Cranl, Ewh 6B 156
Boole Hgts. RG12: Brac 5M 31
Booth Dr. TW18: Stain 7M 21
Booth Ho. *TW8: Brent* 3J 11
(off High St.)
Booth Rd.
CR0: Croy 3A 200 (8M 45)
RH11: Craw 6K 181
Booth Way RH13: Hors 5L 197
Borage Cl. RH11: Craw 6M 181
Border Chase RH10: Cop 8L 163
Border Ct. RH19: E Grin 6B 166
Border End GU27: Hasl 2B 188
Border Gdns. CR0: Croy 1L 65
Bordergate CR4: Mit 9C 28
Border Rd. GU27: Hasl 2B 188
Borderside GU46: Yate 9A 48
Bordesley Rd. SM4: Mord 4N 43
Bordeston Ct. *TW8: Brent* 3J 11
(off The Ham)
Bordon Wlk. SW15 1F 26
Boreen, The GU35: H Dwn 4G 169
Borelli M. GU9: Farnh 1H 129
Borelli Yd. GU9: Farnh 1H 129
Borers Arms Rd.
RH10: Cop 6M 163
Borers Cl. RH10: Cop 6N 163
Borers Yd. Ind. Est.
RH10: Cop 7N 163
Borkwood Pk. BR6: Orp 1N 67
Borkwood Way BR6: Orp 1N 67
Borland Rd. TW11: Tedd 8H 25
Borley Ct. TW19: Stan 2N 21
Borneo St. SW15 6H 13
Borough, The GU9: Farnh 1G 129
RH3: Brock 4N 119
Borough Grange
CR2: Sande 8D 64
Borough Hall Complex 7H 133
Borough Hill
CR0: Wad 5A 200 (9M 45)

Borough Rd.—Bratten Ct.

Borough Rd. CR4: Mit 1C 44
GU7: Goda 6G 133
KT2: K Tham 9N 25
TN16: Tats 8F 86
TW7: Isle 4E 10
Borrodaile Rd. SW18 9N 13
Borrowdale Cl.
CR2: Sande 9C 64
RH11: Craw 5N 181
TW20: Egh 8D 20
Borrowdale Dr. CR2: Sande 8C 64
Borrowdale Gdns.
GU15: Camb 1H 71
Boscombe Cl. TW20: Egh 9E 20
Boscombe Gdns.
SW16 7J 29
Boscombe Ho. CR0: Croy 1D 200
Boscombe Rd. KT4: W Pk 7H 43
SW17 7E 28
SW19 9N 27
Bosham Rd. RH10: Craw 6G 183
Boshers Gdns. TW20: Egh 7B 20
Bosman Dr. GU20: Windl 9M 33
Bostock Av. RH12: Hors 4N 197
Bostock Ho. TW5: Hest 2A 10
Boston Ct. SE25 3C 46
SM2: Sut 4A 62
Boston Gdns. TW8: Brent 1G 11
W4 2D 12
Boston Ho. *SW5 1N 13*
(off Collingham Rd.)
BOSTON MANOR 1G 11
Boston Manor House 1H 11
Boston Mnr. Rd.
TW8: Brent 1H 11
Boston Manor Station (Tube) 1G 11
Boston Pk. Rd. TW8: Brent 1J 11
Boston Rd. CR0: Croy 5K 45
Boswell Ct. KT2: K Tham 1M 203
Boswell Path UB3: Harl 1G 8
Boswell Rd. CR7: T Hea 3N 45
RH10: Craw 6C 182
Boswell Row CR3: Cate 9D 84
Boswood Ct. TW3: Houn 6N 9
Botany Hill GU10: Seal 2B 130
Botery's Cross RH1: Blet 2M 123
Bothwell Rd. CR0: N Add 6M 65
Bothwell St. W6 2J 13
Bothy, The GU8: P Har 6A 132
GU22: Pyr 4H 75
SM7: Ban 5A 82
Botsford Rd. SW20 1K 43
Bottle La. RG42: Bin, Warf 1K 15
Boucher Cl. TW11: Tedd 6F 24
Boughton Hall Av.
GU23: Send 2H 95
Bouldish Farm Rd.
SL5: Asc 4K 33
Boulevard, The RG12: Brac 2J 31
RH10: Craw 3B 182
(not continuous)
SW17 3E 28
SW18 7N 13
Boulogne Rd. CR0: Croy 5N 45
Boulters Ho. RG12: Brac 3C 32
Boulter's Rd. GU11: Alde 2N 109
Boulthurst Way RH8: Oxt 1D 126
Boulton Ho. TW8: Brent 1L 11
Boundaries Rd. SW12 3D 28
TW13: Felt 2K 23
Boundary Bus. Cen.
GU21: Wok 2C 74
Boundary Bus. Ct. CR4: Mit 2B 44
Boundary Cl. KT1: K Tham 2A 42
RH10: Craw 2C 182
SE20 1D 46
UB2: S'hall 1A 10
Boundary Cotts. GU4: Guil 8J 115
Boundary Pk. KT13: Wal T 9F 38
Boundary Rd.
GU10: Dock, Rowl 4C 148
GU14: Farnb 3A 90
GU21: Wok 3C 74
GU26: G'hott 6B 170
RH10: Craw 2C 182
SM5: Cars 3F 62
SM6: W'ton 3F 62
SW19 7B 28
TW15: A'ford 6L 21
Boundary Way CR0: A'ton 2K 65
GU21: Wok 2C 74
Boundless Rd.
GU8: Brook 1G 170
BOUNDSTONE 6F 128
Boundstone Cl.
GU10: Wrec 6G 128
Boundstone Rd.
GU10: Fren, Rowl 7E 128
Bourdon Rd. SE20 1F 46
Bourg-de-Peage Av.
RH19: E Grin 9C 166
Bourke Cl. SW4 1J 29
Bourke Hill CR5: Chip 5D 82
Bourley La. GU10: Ews 2E 108
Bourley Rd. GU11: Alde 2G 108
GU52: C Cro 9D 88
BOURNE, THE 5J 129
Bourne, The GU52: Fleet 7B 88
Bourne Av. KT16: Chert 2J 37
SL4: W'sor 6F 4
Bourne Bus. Pk.
KT15: Addl 1M 55
Bourne Cl. GU4: Guil 9D 114
KT7: T Dit 8F 40
KT14: W By 9K 55
TW7: Isle 6E 10
Bourne Ct. CR3: Cate 1D 104
GU11: Alde 4M 109
RH13: Hors 5L 197
W4 2B 12
Bourne Dene GU10: Wrec 6F 128
Bourne Dr. CR4: Mit 1B 44
Bournefield Rd.
CR3: Whyte 5D 84
Bourne Firs GU10: L Bou 6J 129
Bourne Gro. GU10: L Bou 4K 129
KT21: A'tead 6K 79
Bourne Gro. Cl.
GU10: L Bou 4K 129
Bourne Gro. Dr.
GU10: L Bou 4K 129
Bourne Hall Mus. 5E 60
Bourne Hgts. GU9: Farnh 3H 129
Bourne Ho. TW15: A'ford 6B 22
Bourne La. CR3: Cate 8A 84
Bourne Mdw. TW20: Thor 3D 36
Bourne Mill Ind. Est.
GU9: Farnh 9K 109
Bournemouth Rd.
SW19 9M 27
Bourne Pk. Cl. CR8: Ken 3B 84
Bourne Pl. KT16: Chert 7J 37
W4 1C 12
Bourne Rd. GU7: Goda 3J 133
GU25: V Wat 4N 35
RH1: Mers 8G 103
Bourneside GU25: V Wat 6K 35
Bourneside Rd. KT15: Addl 1M 55
Bourne St.
CR0: Croy 3A 200 (8M 45)
Bournevale Rd. SW16 5J 29
Bourne Vw. CR8: Ken 2A 84
Bourne Way GU22: Wok 9N 73
KT15: Addl 2L 55
KT19: Ewe 1B 60
SM1: Sut 2L 61
Bousley Ri. KT16: Otter 3F 54
Bouverie Gdns. CR8: Pur 1K 83
Bouverie Rd. CR5: Chip 5E 82
Bouverie Way SL3: Lang 1A 6
BOVENEY 2A 4
Boveney Ho. *RG12: Brac 3C 32*
(off Segsbury Gro.)
Boveney New Rd. SL4: E Wic 1B 4
Boveney Rd. SL4: Dorn 1A 4
Bovingdon Rd. SW6 4N 13
Bovingdon Sq. CR4: Mit 3J 45
Bowater Gdns. TW16: Sunb 1K 39
Bowater Ridge KT13: Weybr 6E 56
Bowater Rd. RH10: Craw 6G 183
Bowcott Hill GU35: Head 4E 168
Bowcroft La. RH12: Rudg 1F 194
Bowden Cl. TW14: Bedf 2F 22
Bowden Rd. SL5: S'hill 4N 33
Bowenhurst Gdns.
GU52: C Cro 9B 88
Bowenhurst Rd.
GU52: C Cro 8B 88
Bowens Wood CR0: Sels 5J 65
Bowen Way CR5: Coul 9H 83
Bower, The RH10: Craw 4G 182
Bower Ct. GU22: Wok 3D 74
Bowerdean St. SW6 4N 13
Bower Hill Cl. RH1: Sth N 6J 123
Bower Hill La. RH1: Sth N 4H 123
Bowerland La. RH7: Ling 3N 145
Bower Rd. GU10: Wrec 6F 128
Bowers, The RG40: Finch 7A 30
Bowers Cl. GU4: B'ham 8C 94
Bowers Farm Dr.
GU4: B'ham 8C 94
Bowers La. GU4: B'ham 7C 94
Bowers Pl. RH10: Craw D 1E 184
Bowes Cl. RH13: Hors 5L 197
Bowes Lyon Cl. *SL4: W'sor 4F 4*
(off Alma Rd.)
Bowes Rd. KT12: Wal T 8J 39
TW18: Stain 6G 20
Bowfell Rd. W6 2H 13
Bowie Cl. SW4 1H 29
Bowland Dr. RG12: Brac 6C 32
Bow La. SM4: Mord 5K 43
BOWLHEAD GREEN 9K 151
Bowlhead Grn. Rd.
GU8: Bow G, Brook 9K 151
Bowling, The KT12: Wal T 6H 39
Bowling Grn. Cl.
SW15 1G 27
Bowling Grn. Ct.
GU16: Frim G 7C 70
Bowling Grn. La.
RH12: Hors 5K 197
Bowling Grn. Rd.
GU24: Chob 5H 53
Bowlings, The GU15: Camb 9A 50
Bowman Ct. RG45: Crow 3E 48
RH10: Craw 2B 182
(off London Rd.)
Bowman M. SW18 2L 27
Bowmans Mdw. SM6: W'ton 9F 44
Bowness Cl. RH11: Ifi 4J 181
Bowness Cres. SW15 6D 26
Bowness Dr. TW4: Houn 7M 9
Bowring Ho. *GU7: Goda 5J 133*
(off St Johns St.)
Bowry Dr. TW19: Wray 9B 6
Bowsley Ct. TW13: Felt 3H 23
Bowsprit, The KT11: Cob 2K 77
Bowyer Cres. RG40: W'ham 9B 14
Bowyers Cl. KT21: A'tead 5M 79
Bowyer's La. RG42: Warf 3N 15
Bowyer Wlk. SL5: Asc 9J 17
Boxall's Gro. GU11: Alde 5M 109
Boxall's La. GU11: Alde 5M 109
Boxall Wlk. RH13: Hors 7K 197
Box Cl. RH11: Craw 8A 182
Boxford Cl. CR2: Sels 8G 65
Boxford Ridge RG12: Brac 2N 31
Boxgrove Av. GU1: Guil 1C 114
Boxgrove La. GU1: Guil 2C 114
Boxgrove Rd. GU1: Guil 2C 114
BOX HILL 9B 100
Boxhill and Westhumble Station
(Rail) 9H 99
Box Hill Country Pk. 1K 119
Box Hill Country Pk. Vis. Cen.
1K 119
Boxhill Rd. KT20: Box H 1M 119
RH4: Dork 2L 119
Boxhill Way RH3: Brock 7A 120
Box La. RH19: Ash W 3G 186
Boxley Rd. SM4: Mord 3A 44
Box Ridge Av. CR8: Pur 8K 63
Box Tree Wlk. RH1: Red 6A 122
Box Wlk. KT24: E Hor 1F 116
Boxwood Way CR6: Warl 4G 85
Boyce Ho. SW16 6G 29
Boyd Cl. KT2: K Tham 8N 25
Boyd Ct. RG42: Brac 9M 15
Boyd Rd. SW19 7B 28
Boyle Farm Island
KT7: T Dit 5G 41
Boyle Farm Rd. KT7: T Dit 5G 40
Brabazon Av. SM6: W'ton 4J 63
Brabazon Rd. TW5: Hest 3K 9
Brabiner Gdns. CR0: N Add 6N 65
Brabon Rd. GU14: Cove 9L 69
Brabourne Ri. BR3: Beck 4M 47
Brabrook Ct. SM6: W'ton 1F 62
Bracebridge GU15: Camb 1M 69
Bracewood Gdns.
CR0: Croy 9C 46
Bracken Av. CR0: Croy 9K 47
SW12 1E 28
Bracken Bank SL5: Asc 9G 17
Bracken Cl. GU5: Wone 5C 134
GU22: Wok 5B 74
KT23: Book 2N 97
RH10: Cop 7M 163
RH10: Craw 1C 182
TW2: Whitt 1A 24
TW16: Sunb 7G 22
Brackendale Cl.
GU15: Camb 3C 70
TW3: Houn 4B 10
Brackendale Rd.
GU15: Camb 1B 70
Brackendene GU12: Ash 1G 110
Brackendene Cl.
GU21: Wok 2C 74
Bracken End TW7: Isle 8D 10
Bracken Gdns. SW13 5F 12
Bracken Gro. RH12: Hors 3A 198
Brackenhill KT11: Cob 8B 58
Bracken Hollow
GU15: Camb 7F 50
Bracken La. GU46: Yate 9A 48
Brackenlea GU7: Goda 4G 132
Bracken Path KT18: Eps 9A 60
Brackens, The RG45: Crow 9F 30
SL5: Asc 2F 32
Brackenside RH6: Horl 7F 142
Bracken Way GU3: Guil 1H 113
GU24: Chob 6J 53
Brackenwood GU15: Camb 1H 71
TW16: Sunb 9H 23
Brackenwood Rd.
GU21: Wok 6G 73
Bracklesham Cl.
GU14: Farnb 7M 69
Brackley KT13: Weybr 2E 56
Brackley Cl. SM6: W'ton 4J 63
Brackley Rd. W4 1D 12
Brackley Ter. W4 1D 12
Bracklyn Av. RH19: D Pk 5B 166
RH19: Fel 5F 164
BRACKNELL 1N 31
Bracknell Beeches
RG12: Brac 2N 31
Bracknell Cl. GU15: Camb 6D 50
Bracknell Ent. Cen.
RG12: Brac 1M 31
Bracknell Rd. GU15: Camb 5D 50
GU19: Bag 1H 51
RG12: Brac 7D 32
RG42: Warf 6C 16
RG45: Crow 2H 49
Bracknell Sports & Leisure Cen.
4A 32
Bracknell Station (Rail) 2N 31
Bracknell Wlk.
RH11: Craw 7K 181
Bracondale KT10: Esh 2C 58
Bradbourne St. SW6 5M 13
Bradbury Rd. RH10: Craw 6G 182
Braddock Cl. TW7: Isle 5F 10
Braddon Rd. TW9: Rich 6M 11
Bradenhurst Cl. CR3: Cate 4C 104
Bradfield Cl. GU4: B'ham 9C 94
GU22: Wok 5A 74
Bradfields RG12: Brac 4B 32
Bradford Dr. KT19: Ewe 3E 60
Brading Rd. CR0: Croy 5K 45
SW2 1K 29
Bradley Cl. SM2: Sut 6M 61
Bradley Hall *TW20: Eng G 4M 19*
(off Coopers Hill La.)
Bradley La. RH4: Dork 1H 119
RH5: Dork 1G 119
Bradley M. SW17 2D 28
Bradley Rd. SE19 7N 29
Bradmore Way CR5: Coul 4J 83
Bradshaw Cl. SL4: W'sor 4B 4
SW19 7M 27
Bradshaws Cl. SE25 2D 46
Bradstock Rd. KT17: Ewe 2F 60
Bradstone Brook
GU4: Chil 1C 134
Braeburn Rd. RH11: Ifi 9M 161
Brae Ct. KT2: K Tham 9N 25
Braemar SW15 9J 13
Braemar Av. CR2: S Croy 6N 63
CR7: T Hea 2L 45
SW19 3M 27
Braemar Cl. GU7: Goda 8G 132
GU16: Frim 6D 70
Braemar Gdns.
BR4: W Wick 7M 47
Braemar Rd. KT4: W Pk 9G 42
TW8: Brent 2K 11
Braeside KT15: N Haw 7K 55
RG12: Bin 1H 31
Braeside Av. SW19 9K 27
Braeside Cl. GU27: Hasl 9D 170
Braeside Rd. SW16 8G 29
Braes Mead RH1: Sth N 4J 123
Brafferton Rd.
CR0: Croy 6B 200 (1N 63)
Braganza Ct. *GU1: Guil 2C 114*
(off London Rd.)
Bragg Rd. TW11: Tedd 7E 24
Braid Cl. TW13: Hanw 3N 23
Brailsford Cl. CR4: Mit 8C 28
Brain Flowers Hall
SL5: S'hill 2C 34
(off Buckhurst Rd.)
Brainton Av. TW14: Felt 1J 23
Brakes Ri. GU47: C Tow 7K 49
Brakey Hill RH1: Blet 3B 124
Bramber Cl. RH10: Craw 1C 182
RH12: Hors 3A 198
Bramber Ct. *W14 2L 13*
(off North End Rd.)
Bramber Ho. KT2: K Tham 2J 203
Bramber Rd. W14 2L 13
Bramber Way CR6: Warl 3J 85
Brambleacres Cl. SM2: Sut 4M 61
Bramble Bank GU16: Frim G 8E 70
Bramble Banks SM5: Cars 5E 62
Bramble Cl. BR3: Beck 4M 47
CR0: Croy 1K 65
GU3: Guil 1H 113
RH1: Red 5E 122
RH8: Oxt 2D 126
RH10: Cop 7M 163
TW17: Shep 2E 38
Bramble Ct. GU6: Ewh 4F 156
Brambledene Cl.
GU21: Wok 5M 73
Brambledown TW18: Stain 9K 21
Brambledown Rd.
CR2: Sande 4B 64
SM5: Cars 4E 62
SM6: W'ton 4E 62
Bramblegate RG45: Crow 1F 48
Bramblehall La.
KT20: Box H 1M 119
Bramble Hill Farm
RH13: Slin 8N 195
Bramble La. TW12: Hamp 7N 23
Bramble Ri. KT11: Cob 2K 77
Brambles, The GU7: Goda 4G 133
RG45: Crow 1C 48
SW19 6L 27
(off Woodside)
UB7: W Dray 1M 7
Brambles Cl. CR3: Cate 9B 84
GU12: Ash 3F 110
TW7: Isle 3H 11
Brambles Pk. GU5: Braml 5B 134
Brambleton Av.
GU9: Farnh 3G 128
Bramble Twitten
RH19: E Grin 9C 166
Brambletye La.
RH18: F Row 5F 186
Brambletye Pk. Rd.
RH1: Red 5D 122
Brambletye Rd.
RH10: Craw 4E 182
Bramble Wlk. KT18: Eps 1A 80
RH1: Red 5E 122
Bramble Way GU23: Rip 2H 95
Bramblewood RH1: Mers 7F 102
Bramblewood Cl.
SM5: Cars 7C 44
Brambling Cl. RH13: Hors 7N 197
Brambling Rd.
RH13: Hors 7N 197
Bramcote GU15: Camb 1G 71
Bramcote Av. CR4: Mit 3D 44
Bramcote Ct. *CR4: Mit 3D 44*
(off Bramcote Av.)
Bramcote Ho. KT13: Weybr 1D 56
Bramcote Rd. SW15 7G 13
Bramerton Rd. BR3: Beck 2J 47
Bramham Gdns. KT9: Ches 1K 59
SW5 1N 13
BRAMLEY 5B 134
Bramley Av. CR5: Coul 2G 82
TW17: Shep 2F 38
Bramley Bank Nature Reserve
3F 64
Bramley Bus. Cen.
GU5: Braml 4B 134
(off Station Rd.)
Bramley Cl.
CR2: S Croy 8A 200 (2N 63)
KT16: Chert 7K 37
RH1: Red 5C 122
RH10: Craw 3D 182
TW2: Whitt 9C 10
TW18: Stain 7L 21
Bramley Ct. CR4: Mit 1B 44
RG45: Crow 2C 48
RH1: Red 1C 122
Bramley Grange
GU5: Braml 5B 134
Bramley Gro. KT21: A'tead 6L 79
RG45: Crow 2C 48
Bramley Hill
CR2: S Croy 8A 200 (2M 63)
Bramley Ho. RH1: Red 4E 122
SW15 9E 12
(off Tunworth Cres.)
TW4: Houn 7N 9
Bramleyhyrst CR2: S Croy 7B 200
Bramley La. GU17: B'water 1G 69
Bramley Rd. GU15: Camb 4N 69
SM1: Sut 2B 62
SM2: Chea 5J 61
Bramley Wlk. RH6: Horl 8G 143
Bramley Way BR4: W Wick 8L 47
KT21: A'tead 4M 79
TW4: Houn 8N 9
Bramling Av. GU46: Yate 9A 48
Brampton Gdns. KT12: Hers 2K 57
Brampton Rd. CR0: Croy 6C 46
Bramshaw Ri. KT3: N Mal 5D 42
Bramshot Dr. GU51: Fleet 3B 88
Bramshot La. GU14: Cove 8H 69
GU51: Fleet 1F 88
Bramshot Rd. GU14: Farnb 3F 88
BRAMSHOTT CHASE 9N 169
Bramshott Ct.
GU30: Brams 9F 168
Bramshott Rd. GU30: Pass 8E 168
Bramston Rd. SW17 4A 28
Bramswell Rd. GU7: Goda 5J 133
Bramwell Cl. TW16: Sunb 1L 39
Brancaster La. CR8: Pur 6N 63
Brancaster Rd. SW16 4J 29
Brandlehow Rd. SW15 7L 13
Brandon Cl. GU15: Camb 2H 71
RH10: Craw 5H 183
Brandon Mans. *W14 2K 13*
(off Queen's Club Gdns.)
Brandon Rd. GU52: C Cro 1A 108
SM1: Sut 1N 61
UB2: S'hall 1N 9
Brandreth Rd. SW17 3F 28
Brandries, The SM6: Bedd 9H 45
BRANDS HILL 2D 6
Brandsland RH2: Reig 7N 121
Brands Rd. SL3: Lang 2D 6
Brandy Way SM2: Sut 4M 61
Brangwyn Cres. SW19 9A 28
Branksea St. SW6 3K 13
Branksome *KT13: Weybr 3E 56*
(off Gower Rd.)
Branksome Cl. GU15: Camb 9C 50
KT12: Wal T 8L 39
TW11: Tedd 5D 24
Branksome Hill Rd.
GU47: C Tow 8K 49
Branksome Pk. Rd.
GU15: Camb 9C 50
Branksome Rd. SW19 9M 27
Branksome Way KT3: N Mal 9B 26
Branksomewood Rd.
GU51: Fleet 3A 88
Bransby Rd. KT9: Ches 3L 59
Branstone Rd. TW9: Kew 4M 11
Brantridge Rd.
RH10: Craw 5D 182
Brants Bri. RG12: Brac 1C 32
Brantwood Av. TW7: Isle 7G 10
Brantwood Cl. KT14: W By 9J 55
Brantwood Ct. *KT14: W By 9H 55*
(off Brantwood Dr.)
Brantwood Dr. KT14: W By 9H 55
Brantwood Gdns.
KT14: W By 9H 55
Brantwood Rd. CR2: S Croy 5N 63
Brasenose Dr. SW13 2H 13
Brassey Cl. RH8: Oxt 7C 106
TW14: Felt 2H 23
Brassey Hill RH8: Oxt 8C 106
Brassey Rd. RH8: Oxt 8B 106
Brasted Cl. SM2: Sut 6M 61
Brasted Rd. TN16: Weste 4N 107
Brathway Rd. SW18 1M 27
Brattain Ct. RG12: Brac 2B 32
Bratten Ct. CR0: Croy 5A 46

Bravington Cl.—Broadway Cen., The

Bravington Cl.
TW17: Shep . . . 4A 38
Braxted Pk. SW16 . . . 7K 29
Braybourne Dr. TW7: Isle . . . 3F 10
Braybrooke Rd.
RG42: Brac . . . 8N 15
Bray Cl. RH10: Craw . . . 5H 183
Bray Ct. SW16 . . . 6J 29
Braycourt Av. KT12: Wal T . . . 6J 39
Braye Cl. GU47: Sandh . . . 6H 49
Bray Gdns. GU22: Pyr . . . 3G 74
Bray Rd. GU2: Guil . . . 4L 113
KT11: Sto D . . . 3M 77
Braywood Av. TW20: Egh . . . 7B 20
Braziers La. RG42: Wink R . . . 6H 17
Brazil Cl. CR0: Bedd . . . 6J 45
Breakfield CR5: Coul . . . 3J 83
Breamore Cl. SW15 . . . 2F 26
Breamwater Gdns.
TW10: Ham . . . 4H 25
Breasley Cl. SW15 . . . 7G 13
Brecon Cl. CR4: Mit . . . 2J 45
GU14: Cove . . . 7J 69
KT4: W Pk . . . 8H 43
Brecon Rd. W6 . . . 2K 13
Brecons, The KT13: Weybr . . . 1E 56
Bredin Ho. *SW10* . . . *3N 13*
(off Coleridge Gdns.)
Bredon Rd. CR0: Croy . . . 6C 46
Bredune CR8: Ken . . . 2A 84
Breech, The GU47: C Tow . . . 8K 49
Breech La. KT20: Wal H . . . 2F 100
Breer St. SW6 . . . 6N 13
Breezehurst Dr.
RH11: Craw . . . 6K 181
Breezehurst Rdbt.
RH11: Craw . . . 7M 181
Bregsells La. RH5: B Grn . . . 7K 139
Bremer Rd. TW18: Stain . . . 4J 21
Bremner Av. RH6: Horl . . . 7D 142
Brenda Rd. SW17 . . . 3D 28
Brende Gdns. KT8: W Mole . . . 3B 40
Brendon Cl. KT10: Esh . . . 3C 58
UB3: Harl . . . 3D 8
Brendon Dr. KT10: Esh . . . 3C 58
Brendon Rd. GU14: Cove . . . 7J 69
Brenley Cl. CR4: Mit . . . 2E 44
BRENTFORD . . . 2K 11
Brentford Bus. Cen.
TW8: Brent . . . 3J 11
BRENTFORD END . . . 3H 11
Brentford FC . . . 2K 11
Brentford Fountain Leisure Cen.
. . . 1N 11
Brentford Ho. TW1: Twick . . . 1H 25
Brentford Musical Mus. . . . 2M 11
Brentford Station (Rail) . . . 2J 11
Brent Lea TW8: Brent . . . 3J 11
Brentmoor Rd.
GU24: W End . . . 9N 51
Brent Rd. CR2: Sels . . . 5E 64
TW8: Brent . . . 2H 11
Brent Side TW8: Brent . . . 2J 11
Brentside Executive Cen.
TW8: Brent . . . 2H 11
Brentwaters Bus. Pk.
TW8: Brent . . . 3J 11
Brent Way TW8: Brent . . . 3K 11
Brentwick Gdns. TW8: Brent . . . 1L 11
Brentwood Ct. KT15: Addl . . . 1K 55
Bret Hart Rd. GU16: Frim . . . 5C 70
Bretlands Rd. KT16: Chert . . . 8G 36
Brettgrave KT19: Eps . . . 6B 60
Brett Ho. Cl. SW15 . . . 1J 27
Brettingham Cl.
RH11: Craw . . . 6K 181
Brewer Rd. RH10: Craw . . . 5C 182
Brewers Cl. GU14: Cove . . . 9M 69
Brewers La. TW9: Rich . . . 8K 11
Brewer St. RH1: Blet . . . 9N 103
Brewery La. KT14: Byf . . . 9N 55
TW1: Twick . . . 1F 24
Brewery M. Cen. TW7: Isle . . . 6G 10
Brewery Rd. GU21: Wok . . . 4N 73
Brewhouse Gallery & Myers Mus.
. . . 2G 5
Brewhouse La. SW15 . . . 6K 13
Brew Ho. Rd. RH3: Brock . . . 7B 120
Brewhurst La. RH14: Loxw . . . 6J 193
Breydon Wlk. RH10: Craw . . . 5F 182
Brian Av. CR2: Sande . . . 8B 64
Briane Rd. KT19: Eps . . . 6B 60
Briar Av. GU18: Ligh . . . 8K 51
SW16 . . . 8K 29
Briar Banks SM5: Cars . . . 5E 62
Briar Cl. CR6: Warl . . . 3K 85
KT14: W By . . . 7K 55
RH11: Craw . . . 9A 162
TN8: Eden . . . 9M 127
TW7: Isle . . . 8F 10
TW12: Hamp . . . 6N 23
Briar Ct. SM3: Chea . . . 1H 61
SW15 . . . 7G 13
Briar Gro. CR2: Sande . . . 9D 64
Briar Hill CR8: Pur . . . 7J 63
Briar La. CR0: A'ton . . . 1L 65
SM5: Cars . . . 5E 62
Briarleas Ct. GU14: Farnb . . . 5B 90
Briar Patch GU7: Goda . . . 5G 133
Briar Rd. GU23: Send . . . 2D 94
SW16 . . . 2J 45
TW2: Twick . . . 2E 24
TW17: Shep . . . 4A 38
Briars, The GU12: Ash . . . 3F 110
GU52: C Cro . . . 7B 88
SL3: Lang . . . 1B 6
TW19: Stan M . . . 8J 7
Briars Cl. GU14: Cove . . . 2J 89
Briars Ct. KT22: Oxs . . . 1D 78
Briars Wood RH6: Horl . . . 7G 142
Briarswood Cl.
RH10: Craw . . . 1H 183
Briarswood Way
BR6: Chels . . . 2N 67
Briar Wlk. KT14: W By . . . 8J 55
SW15 . . . 7G 13
Briar Way GU4: B'ham . . . 8D 94
Briarwood Cl. TW13: Felt . . . 5F 22
Briarwood Ct. *KT4: W Pk* . . . *7F 42*
(off The Avenue)
Briarwood Rd. GU21: Wok . . . 6G 73
KT17: Ewe . . . 3F 60
Briavels Ct. KT18: Eps . . . 2D 80
Brickbat All. KT22: Leat . . . 8H 79
Brick Farm Cl. TW9: Kew . . . 4A 12
Brickfield Cl. TW8: Brent . . . 3J 11
Brickfield Cotts.
GU3: Flex . . . 3A 112
GU11: Alde . . . 4J 109
RG45: Crow . . . 4E 48
Brickfield Farm Gdns.
BR6: Farnb . . . 1L 67
Brickfield La. UB3: Harl . . . 2E 8
Brickfield Rd. CR7: T Hea . . . 9M 29
RH1: Out . . . 2L 143
SW19 . . . 5N 27
Brickfields Ind. Pk.
RG12: Brac . . . 1L 31
BRICK HILL . . . 1F 52
Brickhouse La. RH7: Newc . . . 7F 144
RH9: S Gods . . . 4F 144
Brick Kiln La. RH8: Limp . . . 8E 106
Bricklands RH10: Craw D . . . 2E 184
Brick La. GU51: Fleet . . . 3A 88
Bricksbury Hill GU9: U Hal . . . 5H 109
Brickwood Rd.
CR0: Croy . . . 2F 200 (8B 46)
Brickyard Copse RH5: Ockl . . . 6C 158
Brickyard La. RH5: Wott . . . 1L 137
RH10: Craw D . . . 1E 184
Brideake Cl. RH11: Craw . . . 6M 181
Bridewell Cl. GU8: Worm . . . 9C 152
Bridge Av. W6 . . . 1H 13
Bridge Av. Mans. *W6* . . . *1H 13*
(off Bridge Av.)
Bridge Barn La. GU21: Wok . . . 5N 73
Bridge Cl. GU21: Wok . . . 4M 73
KT12: Wal T . . . 6G 38
KT14: Byf . . . 8A 56
TW11: Tedd . . . 5F 24
TW18: Stain . . . 5G 20
Bridge Ct. GU10: Wrec . . . 4E 128
GU21: Wok . . . 4N 73
KT12: Wal T . . . *7G 39*
(off Bridge St.)
KT13: Weybr . . . 1C 56
KT22: Leat . . . 9G 79
BRIDGE END . . . 7C 76
Bridge End GU15: Camb . . . 2N 69
Bridge End Cl.
KT2: K Tham . . . 2M 203 (9N 25)
Bridgefield GU9: Farnh . . . 1J 129
Bridgefield Cl. SM7: Ban . . . 2H 81
Bridgefield Rd. SM1: Sut . . . 3M 61
Bridgefoot TW16: Sunb . . . 9G 23
Bridge Gdns. KT8: E Mol . . . 3D 40
TW15: A'ford . . . 8D 22
Bridgeham Cl. KT13: Weybr . . . 2B 56
Bridgeham Way
RH6: Smal . . . 9M 143
Bridgehill Cl. GU2: Guil . . . 1K 113
Bridge Ho. KT16: Chert . . . 6L 37
SM2: Sut . . . *3N 61*
(off Bridge Rd.)
Bridge Ind. Est. RH6: Horl . . . 8F 142
Bridgelands RH10: Cop . . . 7L 163
Bridge La. GU25: V Wat . . . 4A 36
Bridgeman Ct. SL4: W'sor . . . 5D 4
Bridgeman Dr. SL4: W'sor . . . 5D 4
Bridgeman Rd. TW11: Tedd . . . 7G 24
Bridge Mead GU24: Pirb . . . 4C 92
Bridgemead *GU16: Frim* . . . *6A 70*
(off Frimley High St.)
Bridge M. GU7: Goda . . . 7H 133
GU10: Tong . . . 5D 110
GU21: Wok . . . 4N 73
Bridgend Rd. SW18 . . . 7N 13
Bridge Pk. GU4: Guil . . . 9E 94
Bridgepark SW18 . . . 8M 13
Bridge Pl. CR0: Croy . . . 7A 46
Bridge Retail Pk.
RG40: W'ham . . . 3A 30
Bridge Rd. GU6: Cranl . . . 8N 155
GU7: Goda . . . 6H 133
GU11: Alde . . . 4M 109
GU14: Cove . . . 1L 89
GU15: Camb . . . 3N 69
GU19: Bag . . . 4J 51
GU27: Hasl . . . 1G 189
KT8: E Mol . . . 3D 40
KT9: Ches . . . 2L 59
KT13: Weybr . . . 1A 56
KT16: Chert . . . 6K 37
KT17: Eps . . . 8E 60
RH12: Rudg . . . 1E 194
SL5: S'hill . . . 4A 34
Bridge Rd. SM2: Sut . . . 3N 61
SM6: W'ton . . . 2F 62
TW1: Twick . . . 9H 11
TW3: Houn, Isle . . . 6D 10
TW7: Isle . . . 6D 10
Bridge Row
CR0: Croy . . . 1E 200 (7A 46)
Bridges Cl. RH6: Horl . . . 8H 143
Bridges Ct. RH12: Hors . . . 3M 197
Bridges La. CR0: Bedd . . . 1J 63
Bridges Pl. RH12: Hors . . . 7J 197
SW6 . . . 4L 13
Bridge Sq. GU9: Farnh . . . 1H 129
Bridges Rd. SW19 . . . 7N 27
Bridges Rd. M. SW19 . . . 7N 27
Bridgestone Pl.
RH13: Hors . . . 7L 197
Bridge St.
GU1: Guil . . . 5B 202 (4M 113)
GU7: Goda . . . 7H 133
KT12: Wal T . . . 7F 38
KT22: Leat . . . 9G 79
SL3: Coln . . . 3F 6
TW9: Rich . . . 8K 11
TW18: Stain . . . 5G 21
W4 . . . 1C 12
Bridge St. Pas. GU1: Guil . . . 5B 202
Bridge Vw. SL5: S'dale . . . 6E 34
W6 . . . 1H 13
Bridge Wlk. GU46: Yate . . . 8C 48
Bridgewater GU21: Wok . . . 3B 74
Bridgewater Ct. SL3: Lang . . . 1C 6
Bridgewater Rd.
KT13: Weybr . . . 3E 56
Bridgewater Ter. SL4: W'sor . . . 4G 4
Bridgewater Way SL4: W'sor . . . 4G 4
Bridge Way CR5: Chip . . . 6C 82
KT11: Cob . . . 9G 57
TW2: Whitt . . . 1C 24
Bridge Wharf KT16: Chert . . . 6L 37
Bridge Wharf Rd. TW7: Isle . . . 6H 11
Bridgewood Rd. KT4: W Pk . . . 1F 60
SW16 . . . 8H 29
Bridgford St. SW18 . . . 4A 28
Bridle Cl. GU26: G'hott . . . 6M 169
KT1: K Tham . . . 7H 203 (3K 41)
KT19: Ewe . . . 2C 60
TW16: Sunb . . . 2H 39
Bridle Ct. GU11: Alde . . . 2K 109
Bridle End KT17: Eps . . . 9E 60
Bridle La. KT11: Sto D . . . 2B 78
KT22: Oxs . . . 2B 78
TW1: Twick . . . 9H 11
Bridle Path CR0: Bedd . . . 9J 45
(not continuous)
GU10: Ews . . . 4C 108
Bridle Path, The KT17: Ewe . . . 6H 61
Bridlepath Way TW14: Bedf . . . 1F 22
Bridle Rd. CR0: Croy . . . 9K 47
(not continuous)
CR2: Sande . . . 5D 64
KT10: Clay . . . 3H 59
KT17: Eps . . . 9E 60
Bridle Rd., The CR8: Pur . . . 6J 63
Bridle Way BR6: Farnb . . . 1L 67
CR0: Croy . . . 2K 65
RH10: Craw . . . 2H 183
Bridle Way, The CR0: Sels . . . 6H 65
Bridleway, The CR5: Coul . . . 1F 82
SM6: W'ton . . . 2G 63
Bridleway Cl. KT17: Ewe . . . 6H 61
Bridlington Cl. TN16: B Hil . . . 6D 86
Bridport Rd. CR7: T Hea . . . 2L 45
Brier Lea KT20: Lwr K . . . 4L 101
Brierley CR0: N Add . . . 3L 65
(not continuous)
Brierley Cl. SE25 . . . 3D 46
Brierley Rd. SW12 . . . 3G 28
Brierly Cl. GU2: Guil . . . 1K 113
Brier Rd. KT20: Tad . . . 6G 81
Brigade Pl. CR3: Cate . . . 9N 83
Briggs Cl. CR4: Mit . . . 9F 28
Bright Hill
GU1: Guil . . . 6D 202 (5A 114)
Brightlands Rd. RH2: Reig . . . 1A 122
Brightman Rd. SW18 . . . 2B 28
Brighton Cl. KT15: Addl . . . 2L 55
Brighton Rd.
CR2: S Croy . . . 8C 200 (2N 63)
CR5: Coul . . . 4H 83
(not continuous)
CR8: Pur . . . 7L 63
GU7: Bus, Goda . . . 7H 133
GU12: Alde . . . 4A 110
KT6: Surb . . . 5J 41
KT15: Addl . . . 2L 55
KT20: K'wood, Tad, Lwr K
. . . 8K 81
RH1: Mers . . . 1F 102
RH1: Red . . . 4D 122
RH1: Salf . . . 1E 142
RH6: Craw, Gat . . . 1D 162
RH6: Gat . . . 1D 162
RH6: Horl . . . 9D 142
RH10: Craw . . . 1D 182
RH11: Craw . . . 9A 182
RH11: Hand, P Pot . . . 4N 199
RH13: Hors, M Hea . . . 7K 197
RH17: Hand . . . 4N 199
SM2: Ban, Sut . . . 7M 61
SM7: Ban . . . 3L 81
Brighton Ter. RH1: Red . . . 4D 122
Brightside Av. TW18: Stain . . . 8L 21
Brightwell Cl. CR0: Croy . . . 7L 45
Brightwell Cres. SW17 . . . 6D 28
Brightwells Rd.
GU9: Farnh . . . 1H 129
Brigstock Rd. CR5: Coul . . . 2F 82
CR7: T Hea . . . 4L 45
Brimshot La. GU24: Chob . . . 5H 53
Brimstone La. RH5: Holm . . . 3M 139
Brind Cotts. GU24: Chob . . . 6J 53
Brindle Cl. GU11: Alde . . . 5N 109
Brindles, The SM7: Ban . . . 4L 81
Brinkley KT1: K Tham . . . 1N 41
Brinkley Rd. KT4: W Pk . . . 8G 42
BRINKSWAY . . . 4B 188
Brinksway GU51: Fleet . . . 4A 88
Brinkworth Pl. SL4: O Win . . . 1L 19
Brinn's La. GU17: B'water . . . 1H 69
Brinsworth Cl. TW2: Twick . . . 2D 24
Brinsworth Ho. TW2: Twick . . . 3D 24
Brisbane Av. SW19 . . . 9N 27
Brisbane Cl. RH11: Craw . . . 9B 162
Briscoe Rd. SW19 . . . 7B 28
Brisson Cl. KT10: Esh . . . 3N 57
Bristol Cl. RH10: Craw . . . 9H 163
SM6: W'ton . . . 4J 63
TW4: Houn . . . 1A 24
TW19: Stan . . . 9N 7
Bristol Ct. TW19: Stan . . . 9N 7
Bristol Gdns. SW15 . . . 1H 27
Bristol Rd. SM4: Mord . . . 4A 44
Bristow Rd. CR0: Bedd . . . 1J 63
GU15: Camb . . . 3N 69
TW3: Houn . . . 6C 10
Britannia Cl. GU35: Bor . . . 6A 168
Britannia Ct. *KT2: K Tham* . . . *1H 203*
(off Skerne Wlk.)
Britannia Ind. Est. SL3: Poy . . . 5G 6
Britannia La. TW2: Whitt . . . 1C 24
Britannia Rd. KT5: Surb . . . 6M 41
SW6 . . . 3N 13
(not continuous)
Britannia Way *SW6* . . . *3N 13*
(off Britannia Rd.)
TW19: Stan . . . 1M 21
British Disabled
Water-Ski Association . . . 2E 20
British Gro. W4 . . . 1E 12
British Gro. Pas. W4 . . . 1E 12
British Gro. Sth. *W4* . . . *1E 12*
(off British Gro. Pas.)
British Rail New Yd.
RH10: Craw . . . 8F 162
British Wildlife Cen. . . . 8J 145
Briton Cl. CR2: Sande . . . 7B 64
Briton Cres. CR2: Sande . . . 7B 64
Briton Hill Rd. CR2: Sande . . . 6B 64
Brittain Ct. GU47: Sandh . . . 8H 49
Brittain Rd. KT12: Hers . . . 2L 57
Britten Cl. GU12: Ash . . . 2F 110
RH11: Craw . . . 6L 181
RH13: Hors . . . 4A 198
Brittenden Cl. BR6: Chels . . . 3N 67
Brittens Cl. GU2: Guil . . . 7K 93
Brittleware Cotts.
RH6: Char . . . 8L 141
Brixton Hill SW2 . . . 1J 29
Brixton Hill Pl. SW2 . . . 1J 29
Broadacre TW18: Stain . . . 6J 21
Broad Acres GU7: Goda . . . 3H 133
Broadacres GU3: Guil . . . 1H 113
BROADBRIDGE . . . 1L 163
Broadbridge Cotts.
RH6: Smal . . . 1L 163
BROADBRIDGE HEATH . . . 5D 196
Broadbridge Heath By-Pass
RH12: Bro H . . . 5C 196
Broadbridge Heath Leisure Cen.
. . . 6D 196
Broadbridge Heath Rd.
RH12: Bro H, Warn . . . 4D 196
Broadbridge La. RH6: Smal . . . 8L 143
Broadbridge Retail Pk.
RH12: Bro H . . . 5E 196
Broad Cl. KT12: Hers . . . 9L 39
Broadcommon Rd.
RG10: Hurst . . . 2A 14
Broadcoombe CR2: Sels . . . 4F 64
Broadeaves Cl. CR2: S Croy . . . 2B 64
BROADFIELD . . . 7N 181
Broadfield Barton
RH11: Craw . . . 7N 181
Broadfield Cl. CR0: Wad . . . 8K 45
KT20: Tad . . . 7H 81
Broadfield Dr. RH11: Craw . . . 6N 181
Broadfield Pk. . . . 8A 182
Broadfield Pk. RH11: Craw . . . 7B 182
Broadfield Pl. RH11: Craw . . . 7N 181
Broadfield Rd. GU5: P'lake . . . 2E 136
Broadfield Rdbt.
RH11: Craw . . . 6N 181
Broadfields KT8: E Mol . . . 5E 40
Broadfield Stadium . . . 7A 182
BROADFORD . . . 1N 133
Broadford La. GU24: Chob . . . 8H 53
Broadford Pk. GU4: Chil . . . 1N 133
Broadford Pk. Bus. Cen.
GU4: Chil . . . 1N 133
Broadford Rd.
GU3: P'marsh . . . 2M 133
GU4: Chil . . . 2M 133
Broadgates Rd. SW18 . . . 2B 28
BROAD GREEN . . . 6M 45
Broad Grn. Av. CR0: Croy . . . 6M 45
BROADHAM GREEN . . . 1N 125
Broadham Grn. Rd.
RH8: Oxt . . . 1N 125
Broadham Pl. RH8: Oxt . . . 9N 105
Broad Ha'penny
GU10: Wrec . . . 7F 128
Broad Highway KT11: Cob . . . 1L 77
Broadhurst GU14: Cove . . . 1H 89
KT21: A'tead . . . 3L 79
Broadhurst Cl. TW10: Rich . . . 8M 11
Broadhurst Gdns.
RH2: Reig . . . 6N 121
Broadhurst M. GU12: Alde . . . 3A 110
Broadlands GU14: Farnb . . . 3C 90
GU16: Frim . . . 6D 70
RH6: Horl . . . 7G 142
TW13: Hanw . . . 4A 24
Broadlands Av. SW16 . . . 3J 29
TW17: Shep . . . 5D 38
Broadlands Bus. Campus
RH12: Hors . . . 5J 179
Broadlands Cl. SW16 . . . 3J 29
Broadlands Ct. RG42: Brac . . . 9K 15
TW9: Kew . . . *3N 11*
(off Kew Gdns. Rd.)
Broadlands Dr. CR6: Warl . . . 6F 84
SL5: Asc, S'hill . . . 6N 33
Broadlands Way KT3: N Mal . . . 5E 42
Broad La. RG12: Brac . . . 2A 32
RH5: Leigh, Newd . . . 7C 140
TW12: Hamp . . . 8N 23
Broadley Grn. GU20: Windl . . . 4A 52
Broadleys SL4: W'sor . . . 3C 4
Broadmead GU14: Cove . . . 2J 89
KT21: A'tead . . . 4M 79
RH1: Mers . . . *6G 102*
(off Station Rd.)
RH6: Horl . . . 7G 143
W14 . . . 1K 13
Broadmead Av. KT4: W Pk . . . 6F 42
Broadmead Cl.
TW12: Hamp . . . 7A 24
Broadmead Rd.
GU23: Send . . . 9D 74
Broadmeads GU23: Send . . . 9D 74
BROADMOOR . . . 3A 138
Broadmoor Est. RG45: Crow . . . 3J 49
Broad Oak TW16: Sunb . . . 7G 23
Broadoaks KT6: Surb . . . 8A 42
Broadoaks Cres.
KT14: W By . . . 9K 55
Broadpool Cotts. SL5: Asc . . . 8L 17
Broadrick Heath
RG42: Warf . . . 8B 16
Broadstone RH18: F Row . . . 7J 187
Broad St.
GU3: Guil, Wood V . . . 1F 112
GU24: W End . . . 9A 52
RG40: W'ham . . . 2B 30
TW11: Tedd . . . 7F 24
BROAD STREET COMMON . . . 9G 92
Broad St. Wlk.
RG40: W'ham . . . *2B 30*
(off Broad St.)
Broadview Rd. SW16 . . . 8H 29
Broad Wlk. CR3: Cate . . . 9C 84
CR5: Coul . . . 1E 102
GU6: Cranl . . . 9A 156
GU16: Frim . . . 4C 70
KT18: Tat C . . . 6J 81
RH10: Craw . . . 3B 182
TW5: Hest . . . 4L 9
TW9: Kew . . . 3M 11
Broad Wlk., The
KT8: E Mol . . . 3F 40
Broadwater Cl. GU21: Wok . . . 8F 54
KT12: Hers . . . 2H 57
TW19: Wray . . . 1B 20
Broadwater Gdns.
BR6: Farnb . . . 1K 67
Broadwater La. GU7: Goda . . . 5J 133
Broad Water Pl.
KT13: Weybr . . . 9C 38
Broadwater Pl.
KT13: Weybr . . . 8F 38
Broadwater Ri. GU1: Guil . . . 4C 114
Broadwater Rd.
SW17 . . . 5C 28
Broadwater Rd. Nth.
KT12: Hers . . . 2G 57
Broadwater Rd. Sth.
KT12: Hers . . . 2G 57
Broadway GU21: Knap . . . 5E 72
RG12: Brac . . . 1N 31
SL4: Wink . . . 2M 17
TW18: Stain . . . 6K 21
Broadway, The CR0: Bedd . . . 1J 63
GU21: Wok . . . 4B 74
GU47: Sandh . . . 8G 49
KT7: T Dit . . . 7E 40
KT15: N Haw . . . 6J 55
RH10: Craw . . . 3B 182
SM1: Sut . . . 2A 62
SM3: Chea . . . 3K 61
SW13 . . . 5D 12
SW19 . . . 7L 27
TW18: Lale . . . 2L 37
Broadway Arc. *W6* . . . *1H 13*
(off Hammersmith B'way.)
Broadway Av. CR0: Croy . . . 4A 46
TW1: Twick . . . 9H 11
Broadway Cen., The
W6 . . . 1H 13

Broadway Chambers—Bucklands Rd.

Broadway Chambers *W6 . . . 1H 13* (off Hammersmith B'way.)
Broadway Cl. CR2: Sande . . . 1E 84
Broadway Ct. BR3: Beck . . . 2M 47
GU21: Knap . . . 4F 72
SW19 . . . 7M 27
Broadway Gdns. CR4: Mit . . . 3C 44
Broadway Ho. GU21: Knap . . . 5F 72
Broadway Mans. *SW6 . . . 3M 13* (off Fulham Rd.)
Broadway Mkt. SW17 . . . 5D 28
Broadway Pl. SW19 . . . 7L 27
Broadway Rd. GU18: Ligh . . . 6N 51
GU20: Windl . . . 6N 51
Broadwell Ct. *TW5: Hest . . . 4L 9* (off Springwell Rd.)
Broadwell Rd. GU10: Wrec . . . 5E 128
Broadwood Cl. RH12: Hors . . . 3N 197
Broadwood Cotts. RH5: Cap . . . 4L 159
Broadwood Ri. RH11: Craw . . . 8M 181
Broadwood Rd. CR5: Coul . . . 8H 83
Brocas St. SL4: Eton . . . 3G 4
Brocas Ter. SL4: Eton . . . 3G 4
Brockbridge Ho. SW15 . . . 9E 12
Brock Cl. GU16: Deep . . . 6H 71
Brockdene Dr. BR2: Kes . . . 1F 66
Brockenhurst KT8: W Mole . . . 4N 39
Brockenhurst Av. KT4: W Pk . . . 7D 42
Brockenhurst Cl. GU21: Wok . . . 1B 74
Brockenhurst Dr. GU46: Yate . . . 2C 68
Brockenhurst Rd. CR0: Croy . . . 6E 46
GU11: Alde . . . 4N 109
RG12: Brac . . . 2D 32
SL5: Asc . . . 3L 33
Brockenhurst Way SW16 . . . 1H 45
BROCKHAM . . . 5A 120
Brockham Cl. SW19 . . . 6L 27
Brockham Cres. CR0: N Add . . . 4N 65
Brockham Dr. SW2 . . . 1K 29
Brockham Grn. RH3: Brock . . . 4A 120
Brockham Hill *KT20: Box H . . . 9B 100* (off Boxhill Rd.)
Brockham Hill Pk. KT20: Box H . . . 9B 100
Brockham Ho. *SW2 . . . 1K 29* (off Brockham Dr.)
Brockhamhurst Rd. RH3: Betch . . . 1N 139
Brockham Keep *RH6: Horl . . . 7G 142* (off Langshott La.)
Brockham La. RH3: Brock . . . 3N 119
Brockham Pk. . . . 8B 120
Brockham Pk. Ho. RH3: Betch . . . 9B 120
BROCK HILL . . . 5E 16
Brockhill GU21: Wok . . . 4K 73
Brockhurst Cl. RH12: Hors . . . 7F 196
Brockhurst Cotts. GU6: Alf . . . 5H 175
Brocklands GU46: Yate . . . 2A 68
Brocklebank Ct. CR3: Whyte . . . 5D 84
Brocklebank Rd. SW18 . . . 1A 28
Brocklesby Rd. SE25 . . . 3E 46
Brockley Combe KT13: Weybr . . . 1E 56
Brock Rd. RH11: Craw . . . 9N 161
Brocks Cl. GU7: Goda . . . 6K 133
Brocks Dr. GU3: Worp . . . 8F 92
SM3: Chea . . . 9K 43
Brockshot Cl. TW8: Brent . . . 1K 11
Brock Way GU25: V Wat . . . 4M 35
Brockway SL3: Lang . . . 1D 6
Brockway Cl. GU1: Guil . . . 2D 114
Brockwell Av. BR3: Beck . . . 4L 47
Brockwell Pk. . . . 1M 29
Brockwell Pk. Gdns. SE24 . . . 1L 29
Brockwell Pk. Row SW2 . . . 1L 29
Broderick Gro. KT23: Book . . . 4A 98
Brodie Rd. GU1: Guil . . . 5E 202 (4A 114)
Brodrick Rd. SW17 . . . 3C 28
Brograve Gdns. BR3: Beck . . . 1L 47
Broke Ct. GU4: Guil . . . 9E 94
Broken Furlong SL4: Eton . . . 1E 4
Brokes Cres. RH2: Reig . . . 1M 121
Brokes Rd. RH2: Reig . . . 1M 121
Bromford Cl. RH8: Oxt . . . 2C 126
Bromley Gro. BR2: Brom . . . 1N 47
Bromley Rd. BR2: Brom . . . 1L 47
BR3: Beck . . . 1L 47
Brompton Cl. SE20 . . . 1D 46
TW4: Houn . . . 8N 9
Brompton Pk. Cres. SW6 . . . 2N 13
Brompton Vs. *SW6 . . . 2M 13* (off Ongar Rd.)
Bronsart Rd. SW6 . . . 3K 13
Bronson Rd. SW20 . . . 1J 43
Bronte Ct. *RH1: Red . . . 2E 122* (off St Anne's Ri.)
Bronte Ho. SW4 . . . 1G 29
Brontes, The RH19: E Grin . . . 9N 165
BROOK
GU5 . . . 2N 135
GU8 . . . 9N 151
Brook, The RH10: Craw . . . 2B 182
Brook Av. GU9: Weybo . . . 5L 109
Brook Cl. GU12: Ash . . . 1F 110
GU47: Owls . . . 6K 49
GU51: Fleet . . . 5B 88
KT19: Ewe . . . 5D 60
RH4: Dork . . . 3J 119
RH19: E Grin . . . 9D 166
SW17 . . . 3E 28
SW20 . . . 2G 43
TW19: Stan . . . 1A 22
Brook Cotts. GU46: Yate . . . 9B 48
Brook Ct. *GU14: Cove . . . 9H 69* (off Melrose Av.)
RH12: Hors . . . 3H 197
TN8: Eden . . . 9L 127
Brook Dr. RG12: Brac . . . 3C 32
Brooke Ct. GU16: Frim G . . . 8D 70
Brooke Forest GU3: Worp . . . 8F 92
Brooke Pl. RG42: Bin . . . 6J 15
Brookers Cl. KT21: A'tead . . . 4J 79
Brookers Cnr. RG45: Crow . . . 2H 49
Brookers Row RG45: Crow . . . 1H 49
Brook Farm Rd. KT11: Cob . . . 2L 77
Brookfield GU7: Goda . . . 3K 133
GU21: Wok . . . 3L 73
Brookfield Av. SM1: Sut . . . 1B 62
Brookfield Cl. KT16: Otter . . . 3F 54
KT21: A'tead . . . 7L 79
RH1: Red . . . 9E 122
Brookfield Gdns. KT10: Clay . . . 3F 58
Brookfield Pl. KT11: Cob . . . 2M 77
Brookfield Rd. GU12: Alde . . . 1C 110
Brookfields Av. CR4: Mit . . . 4C 44
Brook Gdns. GU14: Cove . . . 3L 89
KT2: K Tham . . . 9B 26
SW13 . . . 6E 12
Brook Grn. *GU24: Chob . . . 6J 53* (off Chertsey Rd.)
RG42: Brac . . . 9L 15 (not continuous)
Brook Hill GU5: Alb . . . 3M 135
RH8: Oxt . . . 8M 105
Brookhill Cl. RH10: Cop . . . 7L 163
Brookhill Rd. RH10: Cop . . . 8L 163
Brook Ho. *GU6: Cranl . . . 6A 156* (off Park Dr.)
GU9: Hale . . . 6J 109 (off Fairview Gdns.)
Brookhouse Rd. GU14: Cove . . . 2L 89
Brookhurst Fld. RH12: Rudg . . . 9E 176
Brookhurst Rd. KT15: Addl . . . 3K 55
Brookland Ct. RH2: Reig . . . 1N 121
BROOKLANDS . . . 6A 56
Brooklands GU11: Alde . . . 3K 109
RH9: S Gods . . . 1E 144
Brooklands, The TW7: Isle . . . 4D 10
Brooklands Av. SW19 . . . 3N 27
Brooklands Bus. Pk. KT13: Weybr . . . 7N 55
Brooklands Cl. GU9: H End . . . 5J 109
KT11: Cob . . . 2M 77
TW16: Sunb . . . 9F 22
Brooklands Ct. CR4: Mit . . . 1B 44
KT1: K Tham . . . 7H 203
KT15: N Haw . . . 6M 55
Brooklands Dr. KT13: Weybr . . . 6A 56
Brooklands Ind. Est. KT13: Weybr . . . 6N 55
Brooklands La. KT13: Weybr . . . 3A 56
Brooklands Mus. . . . 5A 56
Brooklands Pl. TW12: H Hill . . . 6B 24
Brooklands Rd.
GU9: H End . . . 5K 109
KT7: T Dit . . . 7F 40
KT13: Weybr . . . 7B 56
RH11: Craw . . . 8A 182
Brooklands Way
GU9: H End . . . 5K 109
RH1: Red . . . 1C 122
RH19: E Grin . . . 1N 185
Brook La. GU5: Alb . . . 2N 135
GU23: Send . . . 9G 74
GU24: Chob . . . 7G 53
RH12: Fay . . . 9B 180
Brook La. Bus. Cen. TW8: Brent . . . 1K 11
Brook La. Nth. TW8: Brent . . . 1K 11 (not continuous)
Brookley Cl. GU10: Run . . . 9A 110
Brookleys GU24: Chob . . . 6J 53
Brookly Gdns. GU51: Fleet . . . 3C 88
Brooklyn Av. SE25 . . . 3E 46
Brooklyn Cl. GU22: Wok . . . 6A 74
SM5: Cars . . . 8C 44
Brooklyn Ct. GU22: Wok . . . 6A 74
Brooklyn Gro. SE25 . . . 3E 46
Brooklyn Rd. GU22: Wok . . . 5A 74
SE25 . . . 3E 46
Brook Mead GU8: Mil . . . 2C 152
KT19: Ewe . . . 3D 60
Brookmead CR0: Bedd . . . 5G 45
Brookmead Ct. GU6: Cranl . . . 8N 155
GU9: Farnh . . . 2G 128
Brookmead Ind. Est. CR0: Bedd . . . 5G 45
Brook Mdw. GU8: Chid . . . 6F 172
Brookmead Rd. CR0: Croy . . . 5G 45
Brook Rd. CR7: T Hea . . . 3N 45
GU4: Guil . . . 1E 134
GU8: Brook, Worm . . . 1N 171
GU15: Camb . . . 2N 69
GU19: Bag . . . 5J 51
KT6: Surb . . . 8L 41
RH1: Mers . . . 7G 102
RH1: Red . . . 4D 122
RH12: Hors . . . 2L 197
TW1: Twick . . . 9G 11
Brook Rd. Sth. TW8: Brent . . . 2K 11
Brooksby Cl. GU17: B'water . . . 1G 68
Brooks Cl. KT13: Weybr . . . 6B 56
Brookscroft CR0: Sels . . . 6J 65
BROOKSIDE . . . 7K 17
Brookside GU4: J Wel . . . 7N 93
GU6: Cranl . . . 7N 155 (Ewhurst Rd.)
GU6: Cranl . . . 9N 155 (Northdowns)
GU9: Hale . . . 6H 109
GU47: Sandh . . . 8H 49
KT16: Chert . . . 6G 37
RH5: B Grn . . . 5M 139
RH9: S Gods . . . 7G 124
RH10: Cop . . . 7L 163
RH10: Craw . . . 2D 182
RH10: Craw D . . . 1E 184
SL3: Coln . . . 3E 6
SM5: Cars . . . 2E 62
Brookside Av. TW15: A'ford . . . 6L 21
TW19: Wray . . . 6A 6
Brookside Cl. TW13: Felt . . . 4H 23
Brookside Cres. KT4: W Pk . . . 7F 42
Brookside Res. Pk. Homes GU14: Farnb . . . 5M 69
Brookside Rural Pk. RH12: Rudg . . . 7G 177
Brookside Way CR0: Croy . . . 5G 46
Brooks La. W4 . . . 2N 11
Brooks Rd. W4 . . . 1N 11
Brook St. KT1: K Tham . . . 4J 203 (1L 41)
SL4: W'sor . . . 5G 5
Brook Trad. Est., The GU12: Alde . . . 2C 110
Brook Valley RH5: Mid H . . . 2H 139
Brookview RH10: Cop . . . 7L 163
Brookview Rd. SW16 . . . 6G 28
Brookville Rd. SW6 . . . 3L 13
Brook Way KT22: Leat . . . 5G 78
Brookwell La. GU5: Braml . . . 1C 154
BROOKWOOD . . . 7D 72
Brookwood RH6: Horl . . . 7F 142
Brookwood Av. SW13 . . . 5E 12
Brookwood Ho. *RH6: Horl . . . 5F 142* (off Skipton Way)
Brookwood Lye Rd. GU24: B'wood . . . 7E 72
Brookwood Pk. RH6: Horl . . . 9F 142
Brookwood Rd. GU14: Farnb . . . 1B 90
SW18 . . . 2L 27
TW3: Houn . . . 5B 10
Brookwood Station (Rail) . . . 8D 72
Broom Acres GU47: Sandh . . . 7G 49
GU52: Fleet . . . 7A 88
Broom Cl. KT10: Esh . . . 2B 58
TW11: Tedd . . . 8K 25
Broomcroft Cl. GU22: Pyr . . . 3F 74
Broomcroft Dr. GU22: Pyr . . . 2F 74
Broomdashers Rd. RH10: Craw . . . 2D 182
Broome Cl. GU46: Yate . . . 8B 48
KT18: Head . . . 4B 100
RH12: Hors . . . 3K 197
Broome Cotts. RH4: Dork . . . 4J 119
Broome Ct. KT20: Tad . . . 6K 81
RG12: Brac . . . 2N 31
Broomehall Rd. RH5: Cold, Ockl . . . 9D 138
Broome Lodge *TW18: Stain . . . 6K 21* (off Kingston Rd.)
Broome Rd. TW12: Hamp . . . 8N 23
Broomers La. GU6: Ewh . . . 5F 156
Broom Fld. GU18: Ligh . . . 8L 51
Broomfield GU2: Guil . . . 2H 113
GU8: Els . . . 7J 131
TW16: Sunb . . . 9H 23
TW18: Stain . . . 7J 21
Broomfield Cl. GU3: Guil . . . 1H 113
SL5: S'dale . . . 6E 34
Broomfield Ct. KT13: Weybr . . . 3C 56
Broomfield Pk. RH4: Westc . . . 6C 118
SL5: S'dale . . . 5E 34
Broomfield Ride KT22: Oxs . . . 8D 58
Broomfield Rd. BR3: Beck . . . 2H 47
KT5: Surb . . . 7M 41
KT15: N Haw . . . 7K 55
TW9: Kew . . . 4M 11
TW11: Tedd . . . 7J 25
Broomfields KT10: Esh . . . 2C 58
Broom Gdns. CR0: Croy . . . 9K 47
BROOMHALL . . . 5D 34
Broom Hall KT22: Oxs . . . 1D 78
Broomhall End *GU21: Wok . . . 3A 74* (off Broomhall La.)
Broomhall La. GU21: Wok . . . 3A 74
SL5: S'dale . . . 5D 34
Broomhall Rd. CR2: Sande . . . 5A 64
GU21: Wok . . . 3A 74
Broomhill GU10: Ews . . . 4C 108
Broomhill Rd. GU14: Cove . . . 9J 69
SW18 . . . 8M 13
Broomhouse La. SW6 . . . 5M 13 (not continuous)
Broomhouse Rd. SW6 . . . 5M 13
Broomhurst Ct. RH4: Dork . . . 7H 119
Broomlands La. RH8: Limp, T'sey . . . 4F 106
Broom La. GU24: Chob . . . 5H 53
Broomleaf Cnr. GU9: Farnh . . . 1J 129
Broomleaf Rd. GU9: Farnh . . . 1J 129
Broomloan La. SM1: Sut . . . 8M 43
Broom Lock TW11: Tedd . . . 7J 25
Broom Pk. TW11: Tedd . . . 1G 203 (8K 25)
Broom Rd. CR0: Croy . . . 9K 47
TW11: Tedd . . . 6H 25
Broom Squires GU26: Hind . . . 5E 170
Broom Squires Ct. GU27: Hasl . . . 2E 188
Broomsquires Rd. GU19: Bag . . . 5K 51
Broom Water TW11: Tedd . . . 7J 25
Broom Water W. TW11: Tedd . . . 6J 25
Broom Way GU17: Haw . . . 2K 69
KT13: Weybr . . . 1F 56
Broomwicks Pl. *RH12: Bro H . . . 5E 196* (off Sullington Mead)
Broomwood Cl. CR0: Croy . . . 4G 47
Broomwood Way GU10: L Bou . . . 5H 129
Broster Gdns. SE25 . . . 2C 46
Brougham Pl. GU9: U Hal . . . 5G 108
Brough Cl. KT2: K Tham . . . 6K 25
Broughton Av. TW10: Ham . . . 4H 25
Broughton M. GU16: Frim . . . 5D 70
Broughton Rd. CR7: T Hea . . . 5L 45
SW6 . . . 5N 13
Brow, The RH1: Red . . . 8E 122
Browell Ho. *GU1: Guil . . . 2F 114* (off Merrow St.)
Browells La. TW13: Felt . . . 3J 23 (not continuous)
Brown Bear Ct. TW13: Hanw . . . 5L 23
Brown Cl. SM6: W'ton . . . 4J 63
Browne Cl. GU22: Wok . . . 7D 74
Browngraves Rd. UB3: Harl . . . 3D 8
Browning Av. KT4: W Pk . . . 7G 42
SM1: Sut . . . 1C 62
Browning Cl. GU15: Camb . . . 2G 70
RH10: Craw . . . 2G 182
TW12: Hamp . . . 5N 23
Browning Ct. *W14 . . . 2L 13* (off Turneville Rd.)
Browning Rd. KT22: Fetc . . . 3D 98
Brownings TN8: Eden . . . 8L 127
Brownings, The RH19: E Grin . . . 9M 165
Browning Way TW5: Hest . . . 4L 9
Brownjohn Ct. RH10: Craw . . . 2E 182
Brownlow Dr. RG42: Brac . . . 8A 16
Brownlow Rd. CR0: Croy . . . 1B 64
RH1: Red . . . 3C 122
Brownrigg Cres. RG12: Brac . . . 9C 16
Brownrigg Rd. TW15: A'ford . . . 5B 22
Brown's Hill RH1: Out . . . 1A 144
Browns La. KT24: Eff . . . 5L 97
Brownsover Rd. GU14: Cove . . . 1H 89
Brown's Rd. KT5: Surb . . . 6M 41
Browns Wlk. GU10: Rowl . . . 7E 128
Browns Wood RH19: E Grin . . . 6A 166
BROX . . . 4E 54
Broxhead Common (Nature Reserve) . . . 2A 168
Broxhead Farm Rd. GU35: Lind . . . 2A 168
Broxhead Trad. Est. GU35: Lind . . . 3A 168
Broxholme Cl. SE25 . . . 3A 46
Broxholme Ho. *SW6 . . . 4N 13* (off Harwood Rd.)
Broxholm Rd. SE27 . . . 4L 29
Brox La. KT15: Addl . . . 4E 54
KT16: Otter . . . 4E 54
Brox M. KT16: Otter . . . 3E 54
Brox Rd. KT16: Otter . . . 3E 54
Bruce Av. TW17: Shep . . . 5D 38
Bruce Cl. KT14: Byf . . . 9M 55
Bruce Dr. CR2: Sels . . . 5G 64
Bruce Hall M. SW17 . . . 5E 28
Bruce Rd. CR4: Mit . . . 8E 28
SE25 . . . 3A 46
Bruce Wlk. SL4: W'sor . . . 5A 4
Brudenell SL4: W'sor . . . 6C 4
Brudenell Rd. SW17 . . . 4D 28
Brumana Cl. KT13: Weybr . . . 3C 56
Brumfield Rd. KT19: Ewe . . . 2B 60
Brunel Cen., The RH10: Craw . . . 8D 162
Brunel Cl. TW5: C'ford . . . 3J 9
Brunel Dr. RG45: Crow . . . 8H 31
Brunel Pl. RH10: Craw . . . 4C 182
Brunel University Runnymede Campus . . . 4N 19
Brunel Wlk. TW2: Whitt . . . 1A 24
Brunner Ct. KT16: Otter . . . 2E 54
Brunswick RG12: Brac . . . 6M 31
Brunswick Cl. KT7: T Dit . . . 7F 40
KT12: Wal T . . . 8K 39
RH10: Craw . . . 5E 182
TW2: Twick . . . 4D 24
Brunswick Ct. *RH10: Craw . . . 5E 182* (off Brunswick Cl.)
SM1: Sut . . . 1N 61
Brunswick Dr. GU24: B'wood . . . 7A 72
Brunswick Gro. KT11: Cob . . . 9K 57
Brunswick M. SW16 . . . 7H 29
Brunswick Rd. GU16: Deep . . . 8G 71
GU24: B'wood . . . 8L 71 (not continuous)
KT2: K Tham . . . 9N 25
SM1: Sut . . . 1N 61
Brunswick Ter. BR3: Beck . . . 1L 47
Bruntile Cl. GU14: Farnb . . . 4B 90
Brushfield Way GU21: Knap . . . 6F 72
Brushwood Rd. RH12: Hors . . . 2A 198
Bruton Rd. SM4: Mord . . . 3A 44
Bruton Way RG12: Brac . . . 6C 32
Bryan Cl. TW16: Sunb . . . 8H 23
Bryan's All. SW6 . . . 5N 13
Bryanston Av. TW2: Whitt . . . 2B 24
Bryanstone Av. GU2: Guil . . . 8J 93
Bryanstone Cl. GU2: Guil . . . 9J 93
GU52: C Cro . . . 7B 88
Bryanstone Ct. SM1: Sut . . . 9A 44
Bryanstone Gro. GU2: Guil . . . 8J 93
Bryce Cl. RH12: Hors . . . 3N 197
Bryce Gdns. GU11: Alde . . . 5A 110
Bryer Pl. SL4: W'sor . . . 6A 4
Brympton Cl. RH4: Dork . . . 7G 119
Brynford Cl. GU21: Wok . . . 2A 74
Bryn Rd. GU10: Wrec . . . 4E 128
Bryony Ho. RG42: Brac . . . 9K 15
Bryony Rd. GU1: Guil . . . 9D 94
Bryony Way TW16: Sunb . . . 7H 23
Buccaneer Way GU14: Farnb . . . 5G 89
Buccleuch Rd. SL3: Dat . . . 3K 5
Buchan, The GU15: Camb . . . 7E 50
Buchan Country Pk. . . . 7K 181
BUCHAN HILL . . . 9M 181
Buchan Pk. RH11: Craw . . . 7L 181
Buchans Lawn RH11: Craw . . . 7N 181
Bucharest Rd. SW18 . . . 1A 28
Buckfast Rd. SM4: Mord . . . 3N 43
Buckham Thorns Rd. TN16: Weste . . . 4L 107
Buckhold Rd. SW18 . . . 9M 13
Buckhurst Av. SM5: Cars . . . 7C 44
Buckhurst Cl. RH1: Red . . . 1C 122
RH19: E Grin . . . 7M 165
Buckhurst Gro. RG40: W'ham . . . 3E 30
BUCKHURST HILL . . . 9C 18
Buckhurst Hill RG12: Brac . . . 3D 32
Buckhurst La. SL5: S'hill . . . 2C 34
Buckhurst Mead RH19: E Grin . . . 6M 165
Buckhurst Rd.
GU16: Frim G . . . 8D 70
SL5: Asc, S'hill . . . 9C 18
TN16: Weste . . . 8J 87
Buckhurst Way RH19: E Grin . . . 7M 165
Buckingham Av. CR7: T Hea . . . 9L 29
KT8: W Mole . . . 1B 40
TW14: Felt . . . 9J 9
Buckingham Cl. GU1: Guil . . . 2B 114
TW12: Hamp . . . 6N 23
Buckingham Ct.
RH11: Craw . . . 7N 181
SM2: Sut . . . 5M 61
TW18: Stain . . . 5J 21 (off Kingston Rd.)
Buckingham Dr. RH19: E Grin . . . 1C 186
Buckingham Gdns.
CR7: T Hea . . . 1L 45
KT8: W Mole . . . 1B 40
Buckingham Ga. RH6: Gat . . . 3G 162
Buckingham Rd. CR4: Mit . . . 3J 45
KT1: K Tham . . . 7L 203 (3M 41)
RH5: Holm . . . 5J 139
TW10: Ham . . . 3K 25
TW12: Hamp . . . 5N 23
Buckingham Way
GU16: Frim . . . 5D 70
SM6: W'ton . . . 5G 63
BUCKLAND . . . 2F 120
Buckland Cl. GU14: Farnb . . . 7A 70
Buckland Ct. Gdns. RH3: Buck . . . 2F 120
Buckland Cres. SL4: W'sor . . . 4C 4
Buckland La. KT20: Wal H . . . 6F 100
RH3: Buck . . . 8F 100
Buckland Rd. BR6: Orp . . . 1N 67
KT9: Ches . . . 2M 59
KT20: Lwr K . . . 7L 101
RH2: Reig . . . 2J 121
SM2: Chea . . . 6H 61
Bucklands Rd. TW11: Tedd . . . 7J 25

Buckland's Wharf—Byron Gro.

Buckland's Wharf
KT1: K Tham ... 3G 203 (1K 41)
Buckland Wlk.
SM4: Mord ... 3A 44
Buckland Way KT4: W Pk ... 7H 43
Bucklebury RG12: Brac ... 6M 31
Buckleigh Av. SW20 ... 2K 43
Buckleigh Rd. SW16 ... 7H 29
Buckle La. RG42: Warf ... 3M 15
Bucklers All. SW6 ... 2L 13
(not continuous)
Buckler's Way SM5: Cars ... 9D 44
Buckles Way SM7: Ban ... 3K 81
Buckley La.
RH13: Hors, M Hea ... 9N 197
Buckley Pl. RH10: Craw D ... 1D 184
Buckmans Rd.
RH11: Craw ... 2B 182
Bucknall Way BR3: Beck ... 3L 47
Bucknills Cl. KT18: Eps ... 1B 80
Bucks Cl. KT14: W By ... 1K 75
Bucks Copse RG41: W'ham ... 3A 30
BUCKS GREEN ... 1E 194
Buckshead Hill
RH13: P Pla ... 9E 198
BUCKS HORN OAK ... 2A 148
Bucks Horn Oak Rd.
GU34: B'nest ... 2A 148
Buckswood Dr.
RH11: Craw ... 5M 181
Buckthorn Cl. RG40: W'ham ... 1D 30
Buckthorns RG42: Brac ... 8K 15
Buddleia Ho. TW13: Felt ... 2H 23
Budd's All. TW1: Twick ... 8J 11
Budebury Rd. TW18: Stain ... 6J 21
Budge La. CR4: Mit ... 6D 44
Budgen Cl. RH10: Craw ... 9H 163
Budgen Dr. RH1: Red ... 9E 102
Budge's Gdns.
RG40: W'ham ... 1C 30
Budge's Rd. RG40: W'ham ... 1C 30
Budham Way RG12: Brac ... 5N 31
Buer Rd. SW6 ... 5K 13
Buff Av. SM7: Ban ... 1N 81
Buffbeards La. GU27: Hasl ... 1C 188
Buffers La. KT22: Leat ... 6G 79
Bug Hill CR3: Wold ... 7G 84
CR6: Wold ... 7G 84
Buick Ho.
KT2: K Tham ... 3M 203 (1N 41)
Bulbeggars La. RH9: Gods ... 1F 124
Bulganak Rd. CR7: T Hea ... 3N 45
Bulkeley Av. SL4: W'sor ... 6E 4
Bulkeley Cl. TW20: Eng G ... 6M 19
Bullard Cotts. GU4: W Cla ... 1H 115
Bullard Rd. TW11: Tedd ... 7E 24
Bullbeggars La. GU21: Wok ... 3L 73
BULLBROOK ... 1C 32
Bullbrook Dr. RG12: Brac ... 9C 16
Bullbrook Row RG12: Brac ... 1C 32
Buller Ct. GU14: Farnb ... 4A 90
Buller Rd. CR7: T Hea ... 1A 46
Bullers Rd. GU9: Weybo ... 6K 109
Bullfinch Cl. GU47: C Tow ... 7K 49
RH6: Horl ... 7C 142
RH12: Hors ... 1J 197
Bullfinch Rd. CR2: Sels ... 6G 64
Bull Hill KT22: Leat ... 8G 79
Bull La. RG42: Brac ... 9N 15
Bullocks La. GU27: Hasl ... 8N 189
GU28: Hasl ... 8N 189
Bullrush Cl. CR0: Croy ... 5B 46
SM5: Cars ... 8C 44
Bull's All. SW14 ... 5C 12
Bulls Head Row
RH9: Gods ... 9E 104
BULLSWATER COMMON ... 3D 92
Bullswater Comn. Rd.
GU24: Pirb ... 4D 92
Bullswater La. GU24: Pirb ... 3D 92
Bulmer Cotts.
RH5: H Mary ... 6K 137
Bulow Est. *SW6* ... *4N 13*
(off Pearscroft Rd.)
Bulrushes Farm
RH19: E Grin ... 2N 185
Bulstrode Av. TW3: Houn ... 5N 9
Bulstrode Gdns. TW3: Houn ... 6A 10
Bulstrode Rd. TW3: Houn ... 6A 10
Bunbury Way KT17: Eps D ... 3G 80
BUNCE COMMON ... 1C 140
Bunce Comn. Rd.
RH2: Leigh ... 1C 140
Bunce Dr. CR3: Cate ... 1A 104
Bunce's Cl. SL4: E Wic ... 1E 4
Bunch La. GU27: Hasl ... 1E 188
Bunch Way GU27: Hasl ... 2E 188
Bundy's Way TW18: Stain ... 7H 21
Bungalow Rd. SE25 ... 3B 46
Bungalows, The GU2: Guil ... 7J 93
SM6: W'ton ... 2F 62
SW16 ... 8F 28
Bunting Cl. CR4: Mit ... 4D 44
RH13: Hors ... 5M 197
Buntings, The GU9: Farnh ... 3E 128
Bunyan Cl. RH11: Craw ... 6K 181
Bunyan's La. GU24: Chob ... 1F 72
Bunyard Dr. GU21: Wok ... 1E 74
Burbage Grn. RG12: Brac ... 4D 32
Burbage Rd. SE24 ... 1N 29
Burbeach Cl. RH11: Craw ... 6N 181
Burberry Cl. KT3: N Mal ... 1D 42
Burbidge Rd. TW17: Shep ... 3B 38
Burbury Woods
GU15: Camb ... 9C 50
Burchets Hollow
GU5: P'lake ... 4E 136
Burchetts Way
TW17: Shep ... 5C 38
Burcote KT13: Weybr ... 3E 56
Burcote Rd. SW18 ... 1B 28
Burcott Gdns. KT15: Addl ... 3L 55
Burcott Rd. CR8: Pur ... 1L 83
Burden Cl. TW8: Brent ... 1J 11
Burdenshott Hill GU3: Worp ... 3K 93
Burdenshott Av.
TW10: Rich ... 7A 12
Burdenshott Rd.
GU3: Worp ... 3K 93
Burden Way GU2: Guil ... 7L 93
Burdett Av. SW20 ... 9F 26
Burdett Cl. RH10: Wor ... 4H 183
Burdett Rd. CR0: Croy ... 5A 46
TW9: Rich ... 5M 11
Burdock Cl. CR0: Croy ... 7G 47
GU18: Ligh ... 7M 51
RH11: Craw ... 7M 181
Burdon La. SM2: Chea ... 4K 61
Burdon Pk. SM2: Chea ... 5L 61
Burfield Cl. SW17 ... 5B 28
Burfield Dr. CR6: Warl ... 6F 84
Burfield Rd. SL4: O Win ... 9K 5
Burford Bri. Rdbt.
RH5: Mick ... 9J 99
Burford Ct. RG40: W'ham ... 3D 30
Burford Ho. KT17: Ewe ... 7H 61
TW8: Brent ... 1K 11
Burford La. KT17: Ewe ... 7H 61
Burford Lea GU8: Els ... 7J 131
Burford Rd. GU15: Camb ... 2N 69
KT4: W Pk ... 6E 42
RH13: Hors ... 6L 197
SM1: Sut ... 8M 43
TW8: Brent ... 1L 11
Burford Wlk. SW6 ... 3N 13
Burford Way CR0: N Add ... 3M 65
Burge Cl. GU14: Cove ... 1H 89
Burges Gro. SW13 ... 3G 13
Burgess Cl. TW13: Hanw ... 5M 23
Burgess M. SW19 ... 7N 27
Burgess Rd. SM1: Sut ... 1N 61
Burges Way TW18: Stain ... 6J 21
Burgh Cl. RH10: Craw ... 9H 163
Burgh Cft. KT17: Eps ... 2E 80
Burghead Cl. GU47: C Tow ... 8J 49
Burghfield KT17: Eps ... 2E 80
BURGH HEATH ... 6K 81
Burgh Heath Rd.
KT17: Eps, Eps D
... 8M 201 (1E 80)
Burghley Av. KT3: N Mal ... 9C 26
Burghley Hall Cl.
SW19 ... 2K 27
Burghley Ho. SW19 ... 4K 27
Burghley Pl. CR4: Mit ... 4D 44
Burghley Rd. SW19 ... 5J 27
Burgh Mt. SM7: Ban ... 2L 81
Burgh Wood SM7: Ban ... 2K 81
Burgoine Quay
KT1: H Wic ... 2G 203 (9K 25)
Burgos Cl. CR0: Wad ... 3L 63
Burgoyne Rd. GU15: Camb ... 9E 50
SE25 ... 3C 46
TW16: Sunb ... 7G 22
BURHILL ... 5J 57
Burhill Rd. KT12: Hers ... 5J 57
Burke Cl. SW15 ... 7D 12
Burket Cl. UB2: S'hall ... 1M 9
Burlands RH11: Craw ... 9M 161
Burlea Cl. KT12: Hers ... 2J 57
BURLEIGH ... 9K 17
Burleigh Av. SM6: W'ton ... 9E 44
Burleigh Cl. KT15: Addl ... 2K 55
RH10: Craw D ... 1E 184
Burleigh Gdns. GU21: Wok ... 4B 74
TW15: A'ford ... 6D 22
Burleigh La.
RH10: Craw D ... 2E 184
SL5: Asc ... 9J 17
Burleigh Pk. KT11: Cob ... 8M 57
Burleigh Pl. SW15 ... 8J 13
Burleigh Rd. GU16: Frim ... 6B 70
KT15: Addl ... 2K 55
SL5: Asc ... 1J 33
SM3: Sut ... 7K 43
Burleigh Way
RH10: Craw D ... 1E 184
Burley Cl. RH14: Loxw ... 4J 193
SW16 ... 1H 45
Burley Orchard KT16: Chert ... 5J 37
Burleys Rd. RH10: Craw ... 3G 183
Burley Way GU17: B'water ... 9H 49
Burlingham Cl. GU4: Guil ... 1F 114
Burlings, The SL5: Asc ... 1J 33
Burlington Av. TW9: Kew ... 4N 11
Burlington Cl. TW14: Bedf ... 1E 22
Burlington Ct. GU11: Alde ... 3M 109
GU17: Haw ... 3J 69
RH1: Red ... *2D 122*
(off Station Rd.)
Burlington Gdns. SW6 ... 5K 13
W4 ... 1B 12
Burlington La. W4 ... 3B 12
Burlington M. SW15 ... 8L 13
Burlington Pl. RH2: Reig ... 2M 121
SW6 ... 5K 13
Burlington Rd. CR7: T Hea ... 1N 45
KT3: N Mal ... 3E 42
SW6 ... 5K 13
TW7: Isle ... 4D 10
W4 ... 1B 12
Burlsdon Way RG12: Brac ... 9C 16
Burma Rd. GU24: Chob ... 9J 35
Burmarsh Ct. SE20 ... 1F 46
Burmester Rd. SW17 ... 4A 28
Burnaby Cres. W4 ... 2B 12
Burnaby Gdns. W4 ... 2A 12
Burnbury Rd. SW12 ... 2G 29
Burn Cl. KT15: Addl ... 1M 55
KT22: Oxs ... 2D 78
Burne-Jones Dr.
GU47: C Tow ... 9J 49
Burnell Av. TW10: Ham ... 6J 25
Burnell Rd. SM1: Sut ... 1N 61
Burnet Av. GU1: Guil ... 9D 94
Burnet Cl. GU24: W End ... 9B 52
Burnet Gro.
KT19: Eps ... 6H 201 (9B 60)
Burnetts Rd. SL4: W'sor ... 4B 4
Burney Av.
KT5: Surb ... 8M 203 (4M 41)
Burney Cl. KT22: Fetc ... 3C 98
Burney Ct. RH11: Craw ... 6M 181
Burney Ho. *KT22: Leat* ... *8G 78*
(off Highbury Dr.)
Burney Rd. RH5: Westh ... 9G 99
Burnfoot Av. SW6 ... 4K 13
Burnham Cl. GU21: Knap ... 5G 73
SL4: W'sor ... 5A 4
Burnham Dr. KT4: W Pk ... 8J 43
RH2: Reig ... 2M 121
Burnham Gdns. CR0: Croy ... 6C 46
TW4: C'ford ... 4J 9
Burnham Ga.
GU1: Guil ... 2C 202 (3N 113)
Burnham Gro. RG42: Brac ... 8A 16
Burnham Mnr. GU15: Camb ... 7E 50
Burnham Pl. RH13: Hors ... 7K 197
Burnham Rd. GU21: Knap ... 5G 73
SM4: Mord ... 3N 43
Burnhams Gro. KT19: Eps ... 7A 60
Burnhams Rd. KT23: Book ... 2M 97
Burnham St. KT2: K Tham ... 9N 25
Burnhill Rd. BR3: Beck ... 1K 47
Burn Moor Chase
RG12: Brac ... 6C 32
Burnsall Cl. GU14: Farnb ... 8N 69
Burns Av. GU52: C Cro ... 7C 88
TW14: Felt ... 9H 9
Burns Cl. GU14: Farnb ... 8L 69
RH12: Hors ... 1L 197
SM5: Cars ... 5E 62
SW19 ... 7B 28
Burns Dr. SM7: Ban ... 1K 81
Burnside GU51: Fleet ... 4B 88
KT21: A'tead ... 5M 79
Burnside Cl. TW1: Twick ... 9G 10
Burnside Ct. SM5: Cars ... 9E 44
Burns Rd. RH10: Craw ... 1G 182
Burns Way RH12: Fay ... 8H 181
RH19: E Grin ... 9M 165
TW5: Hest ... 5L 9
BURNTCOMMON ... 3H 95
Burnt Comn. Cl. GU23: Rip ... 3H 95
Burnt Comn. La. GU23: Rip ... 3J 95
Burnt Hill Rd.
GU10: L Bou, Wrec ... 5F 128
Burnt Hill Way
GU10: Wrec ... 6G 128
(not continuous)
Burnt Ho. Gdns.
RG42: Warf ... 8C 16
Burnt Ho. La. RH12: Rusp ... 2E 180
Burnthouse Ride
RG12: Brac ... 3J 31
Burnthwaite Rd. SW6 ... 3L 13
Burntoak La. RH5: Newd ... 2D 160
Burnt Pollard La.
GU18: Ligh ... 6B 52
Burntwood Cl. CR3: Cate ... 8D 84
SW18 ... 2C 28
Burntwood Grange Rd.
SW18 ... 2B 28
Burntwood La. CR3: Cate ... 9B 84
SW17 ... 4A 28
BURPHAM ... 9D 94
Burpham Court Farm Pk. ... 7B 94
Burpham La. GU4: B'ham ... 7C 94
Burrell, The RH4: Westc ... 6C 118
Burrell Cl. CR0: Croy ... 5H 47
Burrell Ct. RH11: Craw ... 5L 181
Burrell Rd. GU16: Frim ... 6A 70
Burrell Row BR3: Beck ... 1K 47
Burrells, The KT16: Chert ... 7K 37
Burr Hill La. GU24: Chob ... 5J 53
Burritt Rd. KT1: K Tham ... 1N 41
BURROW HILL ... 9B 72
BURROWHILL ... 5H 53
Burrow Hill Grn.
GU24: Chob ... 5G 53
Burrows Cl. GU2: Guil ... 2J 113
KT23: Book ... 2N 97
BURROWS CROSS ... 1D 136
Burrows Cross
GU5: Gorn, P'lake ... 1D 136
Burrows La. GU5: Gorn ... 1D 136
Burrow Wlk. SE21 ... 1N 29
Burr Rd. SW18 ... 2M 27
Burrwood Gdns. GU12: A Va ... 9E 90
Burstead Cl. KT11: Cob ... 8L 57
Burstock Rd. SW15 ... 7K 13
Burston Gdns.
RH19: E Grin ... 6N 165
Burston Rd. SW15 ... 8J 13
Burston Vs. *SW15* ... *8J 13*
(off St John's Av.)
BURSTOW ... 3L 163
Burstow Ent. Pk.
RH6: Smal ... 3N 163
Burstow Lodge Bus. Cen.
RH6: Smal ... 6M 143
Burstow Pk. Bus. Cen.
RH6: S Bri ... 5L 163
Burstow Rd. SW20 ... 9K 27
Burtenshaw Rd.
KT7: T Dit ... 6G 41
Burton Cl. CR7: T Hea ... 2A 46
GU20: Windl ... 3A 52
KT9: Ches ... 4K 59
RH6: Horl ... 9E 142
Burton Ct. KT7: T Dit ... 5G 40
SE20 ... 1F 46
Burton Dr. GU3: Worp ... 7D 92
Burton Gdns. TW5: Houn ... 4N 9
Burton Rd.
KT2: K Tham ... 1K 203 (8L 25)
Burtons Ct. RH12: Hors ... 6J 197
Burton's Rd. TW12: H Hill ... 5B 24
Burton Way SL4: W'sor ... 6B 4
Burtop Rd. Est. SW17 ... 4A 28
Burwash Rd. RH10: Craw ... 4E 182
Burway Cres. KT16: Chert ... 3J 37
Burwell KT1: K Tham ... 4M 203
Burwood Av. CR8: Ken ... 1M 83
Burwood Cl. GU1: Guil ... 2F 114
KT6: Surb ... 7N 41
KT12: Hers ... 3K 57
RH2: Reig ... 3B 122
Burwood Pde. *KT16: Chert* ... *6J 37*
(off Guildford St.)
BURWOOD PARK
KT11 ... 8H 57
KT12 ... 2G 57
Burwood Pk. Rd.
KT12: Hers ... 1J 57
Burwood Rd. KT12: Hers ... 4F 56
Bury Cl. GU21: Wok ... 3N 73
Bury Flds.
GU2: Guil ... 7B 202 (5M 113)
Bury Gro. SM4: Mord ... 4N 43
Bury La. GU21: Wok ... 3M 73
Bury M. GU2: Guil ... 7B 202
Burys, The GU7: Goda ... 6H 133
Bury St.
GU2: Guil ... 7B 202 (5M 113)
Burywood Hill RH5: Ockl ... 3E 158
BUSBRIDGE ... 9J 133
Busbridge Lakes, Waterfowl &
Gardens ... 1H 153
Busbridge La. GU7: Goda ... 8G 133
Busby Ho. SW16 ... 5G 29
Busch Cl. TW7: Isle ... 4H 11
Busdens Cl. GU8: Mil ... 2C 152
Busdens La. GU8: Mil ... 2C 152
Busdens Way GU8: Mil ... 2C 152
Bushbury Rd.
RH3: Betch, Brock ... 8N 119
Bush Cl. KT15: Addl ... 2L 55
Bush Cotts. SW18 ... 8M 13
Bushell Cl. SW2 ... 3K 29
Bushetts Gro. RH1: Mers ... 7F 102
Bushey Cl. CR8: Ken ... 3C 84
Bushey Ct. SW20 ... 2G 43
Bushey Cft. RH8: Oxt ... 8M 105
Bushey Down SW12 ... 3F 28
Bushey La. SM1: Sut ... 1M 61
BUSHEY MEAD ... 1J 43
Bushey Rd. CR0: Croy ... 8K 47
SM1: Sut ... 1M 61
SW20 ... 2G 42
Bushey Shaw KT21: A'tead ... 4H 79
Bushey Way BR3: Beck ... 5N 47
Bushfield RH14: Plais ... 6B 192
Bushfield Dr. RH1: Red ... 8E 122
Bush La. GU23: Send ... 2F 94
RH12: Hors ... 9N 179
Bushnell Rd. SW17 ... 3F 28
Bush Rd. TW9: Kew ... 2M 11
TW17: Shep ... 4A 38
Bush Wlk. RG40: W'ham ... 2B 30
Bushwood Rd. TW9: Kew ... 2N 11
Bushy Ct. *KT1: H Wic* ... *9J 25*
(off Up. Teddington Rd.)
BUSHY HILL ... 2F 114
Bushy Hill Dr. GU1: Guil ... 1D 114
Bushy Pk. Gdns.
TW11: Tedd ... 6D 24
Bushy Pk. Rd. TW11: Tedd ... 8H 25
(not continuous)
Bushy Rd. KT22: Fetc ... 9B 78
TW11: Tedd ... 7F 24
Business Cen., The
RG41: W'ham ... 4A 30
Business Pk. 5 KT22: Leat ... 7F 78
Business Pk. 8 KT22: Leat ... 6H 79
Business Pk. 25 RH1: Red ... 1F 122
Busk Cres. GU14: Cove ... 2L 89
Butcherfield La. TN7: Hart ... 1N 187
Butchers Yd. *BR6: Dow* ... *7J 67*
(off High St.)
Bute Av. TW10: Ham ... 3L 25
Bute Ct. SM6: W'ton ... 2G 62
Bute Gdns. SM6: W'ton ... 2G 63
TW10: Ham ... 2L 25
Bute Gdns. W. SM6: W'ton ... 2G 62
Bute Rd. CR0: Croy ... 7L 45
SM6: W'ton ... 1G 62
Butler Rd. GU19: Bag ... 5K 51
RG45: Crow ... 1G 48
Butlers Cl. SL4: W'sor ... 4A 4
TW3: Houn ... 6N 9
Butlers Dene Rd.
CR3: Wold ... 7J 85
Butlers Hill KT24: W Hors ... 8C 96
Butler's Pl. GU8: Mil ... 1D 152
Butlers Rd. RH13: Hors ... 4N 197
Butt Cl. GU6: Cranl ... 6N 155
Buttercup Cl. GU35: Lind ... 4B 168
RG40: W'ham ... 2E 30
Buttercup Sq. TW19: Stan ... 2M 21
Butterfield RH19: E Grin ... 7L 165
Butterfield Cl. TW1: Twick ... 9F 10
Butterfields GU15: Camb ... 2N 69
Butterfly Wlk.
CR6: Warl, Wold ... 7F 84
Butter Hill
RH4: Dork ... 3J 201 (5G 119)
SM5: Cars ... 9E 44
SM6: W'ton ... 9E 44
Buttermer Cl. GU10: Wrec ... 4D 128
Buttermere Cl. GU14: Cove ... 1K 89
RH12: Hors ... 2A 198
SM4: Mord ... 5J 43
TW14: Felt ... 2G 22
Buttermere Ct. *GU12: A Va* ... *9D 90*
(off Lakeside Cl.)
Buttermere Dr.
GU15: Camb ... 1H 71
SW15 ... 8K 13
Buttermere Gdns. CR8: Pur ... 9A 64
RG12: Brac ... 2A 32
Buttermere Way TW20: Egh ... 8D 20
Buttersteep Ri. SL5: Asc ... 7G 33
Butterwick W6 ... 1J 13
Butt La. GU3: Put ... 7L 111
Butts, The TW8: Brent ... 2J 11
TW16: Sunb ... 2K 39
Butts Cl. RH11: Craw ... 2N 181
Butts Cres. TW13: Hanw ... 4A 24
Butts La. GU7: Goda ... 7G 133
(not continuous)
Butts Rd. GU21: Wok ... 4A 74
Buxton Av. CR3: Cate ... 8B 84
Buxton Cl. KT19: Eps ... 7A 60
Buxton Cres. SM3: Chea ... 1K 61
Buxton Dr. KT3: N Mal ... 1C 42
Buxton La. CR3: Cate ... 7A 84
Buxton Pl. CR3: Cate ... 7A 84
Buxton Rd. CR7: T Hea ... 4M 45
SW14 ... 6D 12
TW15: A'ford ... 6M 21
Byam St. SW6 ... 5N 13
Byards Cft. SW16 ... 9H 29
Byatt Wlk. TW12: Hamp ... 7M 23
Bychurch End TW11: Tedd ... 6F 24
Bycroft Way RH10: Craw ... 1F 182
Byegrove Rd. SW19 ... 7B 28
Byerley Way RH10: Craw ... 2H 183
Byers La. RH9: S Gods ... 4F 144
Byeway, The SW14 ... 6B 12
Byeways TW2: Twick ... 4B 24
Byeways, The KT5: Surb ... 4N 41
Byfeld Gdns. SW13 ... 4F 12
Byfield Rd. TW7: Isle ... 6G 10
BYFLEET ... 8N 55
Byfleet Ind. Est. KT14: Byf ... 6M 55
Byfleet Lawn Tennis Club ... 1J 75
Byfleet & New Haw Station (Rail)
... 6M 55
Byfleet Rd. KT11: Cob ... 8B 56
KT14: Byf ... 8B 56
KT15: N Haw ... 4M 55
Byfleets La.
RH12: Bro H, Warn ... 2D 196
Byfleet Technical Cen.
KT14: Byf ... 7M 55
Bygrove CR0: N Add ... 3L 65
Byland Cl. SM5: Cars ... 6A 44
Bylands GU22: Wok ... 6C 74
Byne Rd. SM5: Cars ... 8C 44
Bynes Rd. CR2: S Croy ... 4A 64
By-Pass Rd. KT22: Leat ... 7H 79
Byrd Rd. RH11: Craw ... 6L 181
Byrefield Rd. GU2: Guil ... 9J 93
Byrne Rd. SW12 ... 2F 28
Byron SL3: Lang ... 1D 6
Byron Av. CR5: Coul ... 2J 83
GU15: Camb ... 3F 70
KT3: N Mal ... 4F 42
SM1: Sut ... 1B 62
TW4: C'ford ... 5H 9
Byron Av. E. SM1: Sut ... 1B 62
Byron Cl. GU21: Knap ... 4H 73
GU46: Yate ... 2A 68
GU51: Fleet ... 5B 88
KT12: Wal T ... 7M 39
RH10: Craw ... 2F 182
RH12: Hors ... 2L 197
SE20 ... 2E 46
SW16 ... 7J 29
TW12: Hamp ... 5N 23
Byron Ct. SL4: W'sor ... 6D 4
Byron Dr. RG45: Crow ... 4G 48
Byron Gdns. SM1: Sut ... 1B 62
Byron Gro. RH19: E Grin ... 1M 185

Byron Pl.—Carlson Ct.

Byron Pl. KT22: Leat 9H 79
Byron Rd. CR2: Sels 6E 64
KT15: Addl 1N 55
Byton Rd. SW17 7D 28
Byttom Hill RH5: Mick 4J 99
Byward Av. TW14: Felt 9K 9
Byway, The KT19: Ewe 1E 60
SM2: Sut 5B 62
Byways GU46: Yate 1A 68
Byways, The KT21: A'tead 5K 79
Bywood RG12: Brac 6M 31
Bywood Av. CR0: Croy 5F 46
Bywood Cl. CR8: Ken 2M 83
SM7: Ban 4L 81
Byworth Cl. GU9: Farnh 1E 128
Byworth Rd. GU9: Farnh 1E 128

C

Cabbage Hill RG42: Warf 6L 15
Cabbage Hill La. RG42: Bin 5K 15
Cabbel Pl. KT15: Addl 1L 55
Cabell Rd. GU2: Guil 2G 113
Caberfeigh Cl. RH1: Red 3B 122
Cabin Moss RG12: Brac 6C 32
Cable Ho. Ct. GU21: Wok 2A 74
Cabrera Av. GU25: V Wat 5M 35
Cabrera Cl. GU25: V Wat 5N 35
Cabrol Rd. GU14: Farnb 9M 69
Caburn Ct. RH11: Craw 5A 182
Caburn Hgts. RH11: Craw 5A 182
Caci Ho. *W14* *1L 13*
(off Kensington Village)
Cacket's La. TN14: Cud 2M 87
Cackstones, The
RH10: Craw 1H 183
Cadbury Cl. TW7: Isle 4G 11
TW16: Sunb 8F 22
Cadbury Rd. TW16: Sunb 8F 22
Caddy Cl. TW20: Egh 6C 20
Cader Rd. SW18 1A 28
Cadet Way GU52: C Cro 9C 88
Cadman Ct. *W4* *1A 12*
(off Chaseley Dr.)
Cadmer Cl. KT3: N Mal 3D 42
Cadnam Cl. GU11: Alde 6A 110
Cadnam Point SW15 2G 26
Cadogan Cl. BR3: Beck 1N 47
TW11: Tedd 6E 24
Cadogan Ct. GU15: Camb 3C 70
GU51: Fleet 4A 88
SM2: Sut 3N 61
Cadogan Ho. *GU1: Guil* *4B 114*
(off St Lukes Sq.)
Cadogan Pl. CR8: Ken 4N 83
Cadogan Rd. GU11: Alde 6B 90
KT6: Surb 4K 41
Caenshill Ho. KT13: Weybr 4B 56
Caenshill Pl. KT13: Weybr 4B 56
Caenshill Rd. KT13: Weybr 4B 56
Caenswood Hill
KT13: Weybr 6B 56
Caenwood Cl. KT13: Weybr 3B 56
Caen Wood Rd.
KT21: A'tead 5J 79
Caerleon Cl. GU26: Hind 3A 170
KT10: Clay 4H 59
Caernarvon GU16: Frim 6D 70
Caernarvon Cl. CR4: Mit 2J 45
Caesar Ct. GU11: Alde 2K 109
Caesars Camp Rd.
GU15: Camb 7D 50
Caesar's Cl. GU15: Camb 7D 50
Caesars Ct. GU9: U Hal 6H 109
Caesars Ga. RG42: Warf 8C 16
Caesars Wlk. CR4: Mit 4D 44
Caesars Way TW17: Shep 5E 38
Caffins Cl. RH10: Craw 1C 182
Cage Yd. RH2: Reig 3M 121
Caillard Rd. KT14: Byf 7N 55
Cain Rd. RG12: Brac 1J 31
Cain's La. TW14: Felt 8F 8
Cairn Cl. GU15: Camb 3F 70
Cairn Ct. KT17: Ewe 6E 60
Cairngorm Cl. TW11: Tedd 6G 24
Cairngorm Pl. GU14: Cove 7K 69
Cairo New Rd.
CR0: Croy 3A **200** (8M 45)
Caistor M. SW12 1F 28
Caistor Rd. SW12 1F 28
Caithness Dr.
KT18: Eps 8K **201** (1C 80)
Caithness Rd. CR4: Mit 8F 28
Calbourne Rd. SW12 1D 28
Calcott Pk. GU46: Yate 9B 48
Caldbeck Av. KT4: W Pk 8F 42
Caldbeck Ho. *RH11: Craw* *6L 181*
(off Salvington Rd.)
Caldecote KT1: K Tham 4M 203
Calder Ct. SL3: Lang 1B 6
Calderdale Cl.
RH11: Craw 5N 181
Calder Rd. SM4: Mord 4A 44
Calder Way SL3: Poy 6G 7
Caldwell Ho. *SW13* *3H 13*
(off Trinity Chu. Rd.)
Caldwell Rd. GU20: Windl 2A 52
Caledonian Ho.
RH10: Craw *1B 182*
(off Barnfield Rd.)
Caledonian Way RH6: Gat 3F 162
Caledonia Rd. TW19: Stan 2N 21
Caledon Pl. GU4: B'ham 9C 94
Caledon Rd. SM6: W'ton 1E 62
Calfridus Way RG12: Brac 2C 32
California Cl. SM2: Sut 6M 61
California Rd.
KT3: N Mal 3A 42
Callender Ct. *CR0: Croy* *5N 45*
(off Harry Cl.)
Calley Down Cres.
CR0: N Add 6N 65
Callis Farm Cl. TW19: Stan 9N 7
Callisto Cl. RH11: Craw 6K 181
Callow Fld. CR8: Pur 9L 63
Callow Hill GU25: V Wat 2M 35
Calluna Ct. GU22: Wok 5B 74
Calluna Dr. RH10: Cop 8L 163
Calonne Rd. SW19 5J 27
Calshot Rd. TW6: Lon A 5B 8
(not continuous)
Calshot Way GU16: Frim 7E 70
TW6: Lon A 5B 8
(not continuous)
Calthorpe Gdns. SM1: Sut 9A 44
Calton Gdns. GU11: Alde 5A 110
Calverley Ct. KT19: Ewe 1C 60
Calverley Rd. KT17: Ewe 3F 60
Calvert Cl. GU12: Alde 3B 110
KT19: Eps 6A 60
Calvert Ct. TW9: Rich 7M 11
Calvert Cres. RH4: Dork 3H 119
Calvert Rd. KT24: Eff 6J 97
RH4: Dork 3H 119
Calvin Cl. GU15: Camb 2F 70
Calvin Wlk. RH11: Craw 6K 181
Camac Rd. TW2: Twick 2D 24
Camargue Pl. GU7: Goda 7J 133
Cambalt Rd. SW15 8J 13
Camber Cl. RH10: Craw 3G 183
CAMBERLEY 9B 50
Camberley Av. SW20 1G 42
Camberley Bus. Cen.
GU15: Camb 1M 69
Camberley Cl. SM3: Chea 9J 43
Camberley Indoor Bowling Club 3N 69
Camberley Rd. TW6: Lon A 6B 8
Camberley Station (Rail) 1B 70
Camberley Theatre, The 9B 50
Camberley Towers
GU15: Camb *1B 70*
(off Up. Gordon Rd.)
Camborne Cl. TW6: Lon A 6B 8
Camborne Cres. TW6: Lon A 6B 8
Camborne M. SW18 1M 27
Camborne Rd. CR0: Croy 6D 46
SM2: Sut 4M 61
SM4: Mord 4J 43
SW18 1M 27
TW6: Lon A 6B 8
Camborne Way TW5: Hest 4A 10
TW6: Lon A 6B 8
Cambourne Wlk.
TW10: Rich 9K 11
Cambray Rd. SW12 2G 29
Cambria Cl. TW3: Houn 7A 10
Cambria Ct. TW14: Felt 1J 23
TW18: Stain 5G 20
Cambria Gdns. TW19: Stan 1N 21
(not continuous)
Cambrian Cl. GU15: Camb 1N 69
SE27 4M 29
Cambrian Rd. GU14: Cove 7J 69
TW10: Rich 9M 11
Cambrian Way RG40: Finch 8A 30
Cambria St. SW6 3N 13
Cambridge Av. KT3: N Mal 2D 42
(not continuous)
Cambridge Cl. GU21: Wok 5J 73
SW20 9G 26
TW4: Houn 7M 9
UB7: Harm 2M 7
Cambridge Cotts.
TW9: Kew 2N 11
Cambridge Cres.
TW11: Tedd 6G 24
Cambridge Gdns.
KT1: K Tham 1N 41
Cambridge Gro. W6 1G 13
Cambridge Gro. Rd.
KT1: K Tham 2N 41
(not continuous)
Cambridge Ho. SL4: W'sor 4F 4
Cambridge Lodge Mobile Home Pk.
RH6: Horl 5E 142
Cambridge Mdws.
GU9: Farnh 2E 128
Cambridge Pk. TW1: Twick 9J 11
Cambridge Pk. Ct.
TW1: Twick 1K 25
Cambridge Pl. GU9: Farnh 1H 129
Cambridge Rd. CR4: Mit 2G 44
GU11: Alde 2L 109
GU47: Owls 6K 49
KT1: K Tham 3M **203** (1M 41)
KT3: N Mal 3C 42
KT8: W Mole 3N 39
KT12: Wal T 5J 39
RG45: Crow 3H 49
RH13: Hors 6K 197
SE20 2E 46
SM5: Cars 3C 62
SW13 5E 12
SW20 9F 26
Cambridge Rd. TW1: Twick 9K 11
TW4: Houn 7M 9
TW9: Kew 3N 11
TW11: Tedd 5F 24
TW12: Hamp 8N 23
TW15: A'ford 8D 22
Cambridge Rd. E.
GU14: Farnb 4A 90
(not continuous)
Cambridge Rd. Nth.
W4 1A 12
Cambridge Rd. Sth.
W4 1A 12
Cambridge Rd. W.
GU14: Farnb 4A 90
(not continuous)
Cambridgeshire Cl.
RG42: Warf 8D 16
Cambridge Sq.
GU15: Camb *9A 50*
(off Cambridge Wlk.)
RH1: Red 6E 122
Cambridge Wlk.
GU15: Camb 9A 50
Camden Av. TW13: Felt 2K 23
Camden Cotts.
KT13: Weybr 9B 38
Camden Gdns. CR7: T Hea 2M 45
SM1: Sut 2N 61
Camden Rd. RH7: Ling 8N 145
SM1: Sut 2N 61
SM5: Cars 1D 62
Camden Wlk. GU51: Fleet 4D 88
Camden Way CR7: T Hea 2M 45
Cameford Ct. SW2 1J 29
Camel Gro. KT2: K Tham 6K 25
Camellia Ct. GU24: W End 9C 52
Camellia Ho. *TW13: Felt* *2H 23*
(off Tilley Rd.)
Camellia Pl. TW2: Whitt 1B 24
Camelot Cl. SW19 5L 27
TN16: B Hil 3E 86
Camelot Ct. RH11: Ifi 3K 181
CAMELSDALE 3D 188
Camelsdale Rd.
GU27: Hasl 3C 188
Cameron Cl. GU6: Cranl 9N 155
Cameron Pl. SW16 3L 29
Cameron Rd. CR0: Croy 5M 45
GU11: Alde 6B 90
Cameron Sq. CR4: Mit 9C 28
Camgate Cen., The
TW19: Stan 9A 8
Camilla Cl. KT23: Book 3B 98
TW16: Sunb 7G 22
Camilla Dr. RH5: Westh 8G 98
Camille Cl. SE25 2D 46
Camm Av. SL4: W'sor 6B 4
Camm Gdns.
KT1: K Tham 4M **203** (1M 41)
KT7: T Dit 6F 40
Camomile Av. CR4: Mit 9D 28
Campana Rd. SW6 4M 13
Campaspe Bus. Pk.
TW16: Sunb 4G 38
Campbell Av. GU22: Wok 8B 74
Campbell Cir. KT13: Weybr 6A 56
Campbell Cl. GU11: Alde 5A 110
GU46: Yate 9E 48
GU51: Fleet 4A 88
KT14: Byf 8M 55
SW16 5H 29
TW2: Twick 2D 24
Campbell Cres.
RH19: E Grin 9L 165
Campbell Flds.
GU11: Alde 3N 109
Campbell Pl. GU16: Frim 3D 70
Campbell Rd. CR0: Croy 6M 45
CR3: Cate 8A 84
GU11: Alde 1M 109
KT8: E Mol 2E 40
KT13: Weybr 4B 56
RH10: Craw 5G 182
TW2: Twick 3D 24
Campden Rd. CR2: S Croy 2B 64
Campen Cl. SW19 3K 27
Camp End Rd. KT13: Weybr 8D 56
Camperdown Ho. SL4: W'sor 5F 4
Camp Farm Rd. GU11: Alde 8B 90
Camp Hill GU10: Farnh 3A 130
Camphill Ct. KT14: W By 8J 55
Camphill Ind. Est.
KT14: W By 7K 55
Camphill Rd. KT14: W By 8J 55
Camping & Cvn. Site
RH7: Ling 1J 165
Campion Cl. CR0: Croy 1B 64
GU17: Haw 3L 69
GU35: Lind 5B 168
Campion Dr. KT20: Tad 7G 81
Campion Ho. RG42: Brac 9K 15
RH1: Red 9D 102
Campion Rd. RH12: Hors 3L 197
SW15 7H 13
TW7: Isle 4F 10
Campion Way
RG40: W'ham 1D 30
Camp Rd. CR3: Wold 7H 85
GU14: Farnb 5A 90
SW19 6G 26
(not continuous)
Camp Vw. SW19 6G 27
Camrose Av. TW13: Felt 5K 23
Camrose Cl. CR0: Croy 6H 47
SM4: Mord 3M 43
Canada Av. RH1: Red 7E 122
Canada Copse GU8: Mil 9B 132
Canada Dr. RH1: Red 7E 122
Canada Rd. GU16: Deep 6H 71
KT11: Cob 9K 57
KT14: Byf 7M 55
Canadian Memorial Av.
TW20: Eng G 1J 35
Canal Bank GU12: A Va 9E 90
KT15: Addl 3M 55
Canal Bank M. GU21: Wok 4A 74
Canal Bri. KT15: Addl 4M 55
Canal Cl. GU11: Alde 8B 90
Canal Cotts. GU12: A Va 9E 90
Canalside RH1: Mers, Red 9F 102
Canal Wlk. CR0 5B 46
Canberra Cl. GU46: Yate 7A 48
RH11: Craw 9B 162
Canberra Pl. RH12: Hors 4M 197
Canberra Rd. TW6: Lon A 6B 8
Canbury Av.
KT2: K Tham 1L **203** (9M 25)
Canbury Bus. Cen.
KT2: K Tham 2K **203** (9L 25)
Canbury Bus. Pk.
KT2: K Tham 2K 203
Canbury Ct. KT2: K Tham 8K 25
Canbury Pk. Rd.
KT2: K Tham 2K **203** (9L 25)
Canbury Pas.
KT2: K Tham 2H **203** (9K 25)
Candleford Cl. RG12: Brac 8A 16
Candler M. TW1: Twick 1G 25
Candlerush Cl. GU22: Wok 4D 74
Candover Cl. UB7: Harm 3M 7
Candy Cft. KT23: Book 4B 98
Canes La. GU35: Lind 4A 168
Canewdon Cl. GU22: Wok 6A 74
Canford Dr. KT15: Addl 8K 37
Canford Gdns. KT3: N Mal 5D 42
Canford Pl. TW11: Tedd 7J 25
Canham Rd. SE25 2B 46
Can Hatch KT20: Tad 5K 81
Canmore Gdns. SW16 8G 29
Canning Rd. CR0: Croy 8C 46
GU12: Alde 2B 110
Cannizaro Rd. SW19 7H 27
Cannon Cl. GU47: C Tow 7L 49
SW20 2H 43
TW12: Hamp 7B 24
Cannon Cres. GU24: Chob 7H 53
Cannon Gro. KT22: Fetc 9E 78
Cannon Hill RG12: Brac 5A 32
Cannon Hill La. SW20 4J 43
Cannon M. SL5: Asc 9F 16
Cannons Health Club
Crabbet Park 2K 183
Fulham 4J 13
Norbury 1K 45
Sutton 3M 61
Twickenham 1E 24
West Byfleet 1K 75
Cannonside KT22: Fetc 9E 78
Cannon Way KT8: W Mole 3A 40
KT22: Fetc 8E 78
Canonbury Cotts.
RH12: Rusp 3E 180
Canons Cl. RH2: Reig 2L 121
Canon's Hill CR5: Coul, Pur 4M 83
Canons La. KT20: Tad 5K 81
Canons Leisure Cen., The 3D 44
Canon's Wlk. CR0: Croy 9G 46
Canons Yd. RH2: Reig 6N 121
Canopus Way TW19: Stan 1N 21
Cansiron La.
RH19: Ash W 3H 187
TN8: Ash W, Cow, Hart 7N 167
Cantelupe M.
RH19: E Grin *9B 166*
(off Cantelupe Rd.)
Cantelupe Rd.
RH19: E Grin 9B 166
Canter, The RH10: Craw 2J 183
Canterbury Cl. KT4: W Pk 8J 43
Canterbury Ct. *CR2: S Croy* *4N 63*
(off St Augustines Av.)
GU14: Farnb *3B 90*
(off Canterbury Gdns.)
RH4: Dork 1J 201
TW15: A'ford 5A 22
Canterbury Gdns.
GU14: Farnb 3B 90
Canterbury Gro. SE27 5L 29
Canterbury Hall KT4: W Pk 6G 43
Canterbury Ho. CR0: Croy 1D 200
KT19: Eps *7N 59*
(off Queen Alexandra's Way)
Canterbury M. KT22: Oxs 9C 58
SL4: W'sor 5D 4
Canterbury Rd. CR0: Croy 6K 45
GU2: Guil 1J 113
GU12: Ash 1E 110
GU14: Farnb 3B 90
RH10: Craw 7C 182
SM4: Mord 6N 43
TW13: Hanw 3M 23
Canterbury Wlk.
GU14: Farnb 3B 90
CANTLEY 9B 14
Cantley Cres.
RG41: W'ham 9A 14
Cantley Gdns. SE19 1C 46
Canvas Ct. GU27: Hasl 2F 188
Canvey Cl. RH11: Craw 6A 182
Cape Copse RH12: Rudg 1E 194
CAPEL 4K 159
Capel Av. SM6: W'ton 2K 63
Capel By-Pass
RH5: B Grn, Cap, Ockl 3H 159
Capel La. RH11: Craw 4L 181
Capel Rd. RH12: Rusp 2M 179
Capercaillie Cl. RG12 Brac 3J 31
Capern Rd. SW18 2A 28
Capital Bus. Cen.
CR2: S Croy 4A 64
Capital Ind. Est. CR4: Mit 4D 44
Capital Interchange Way
TW8: Brent 1N 11
Capital Pk. GU8: Worm 2C 172
GU22: Wok 8D 74
Capitol, The 6K 197
Capitol Sq.
KT18: Eps 6L **201** (9D 60)
Capricorn Cl. RH11: Craw 5K 181
Capri Rd. CR0: Croy 7C 46
Capsey Rd. RH11: Ifi 3K 181
Capstans Wharf GU21: Wok 5J 73
Captains Wlk. RH11: Craw 5A 182
Capua Ct. RH10: Craw 8G 163
Caradon Cl. GU21: Wok 5L 73
Caraway Cl. RH11: Craw 7N 181
Caraway Pl. GU2: Guil 7K 93
SM6: W'ton 9F 44
Carbery La. SL5: Asc 2M 33
Cardamom Cl. GU2: Guil 8K 93
Card Hill RH18: F Row 8H 187
Cardigan Cl. GU21: Wok 5H 73
Cardigan Rd. SW13 5F 12
SW19 7A 28
TW10: Rich 9L 11
Cardinal Av. KT2: K Tham 6L 25
SM4: Mord 5K 43
Cardinal Cl. CR2: Sande 9D 64
KT4: W Pk 1F 60
SM4: Mord 5K 43
Cardinal Cres. KT3: N Mal 1B 42
Cardinal Dr. KT12: Wal T 7L 39
Cardinal Ho. *GU14: Farnb* *1A 90*
(off Jubilee Hall Rd.)
Cardinal Pl. SW15 7J 13
Cardinal Rd. TW13: Felt 2J 23
CARDINALS, THE 5E 110
Cardinals, The
GU10: Tong *5D 110*
(off South Side)
RG12: Brac 3N 31
Cardinals Wlk.
TW12: Hamp 8C 24
TW16: Sunb 7F 22
Cardingham GU21: Wok 4K 73
Cardington Sq. TW4: Houn 7L 9
Cardwell Cres. SL5: S'hill 4N 33
Cardwells Keep GU2: Guil 9K 93
Carew Cl. CR5: Coul 6M 83
Carew Ct. SM2: Sut 5N 61
Carew Manor & Dovecote 9G 45
Carew Mnr. Cotts.
SM6: Bedd 9H 45
Carew Rd. CR4: Mit 1E 44
CR7: T Hea 3M 45
SM6: W'ton 3G 63
TW15: A'ford 7D 22
Carey Cl. SL4: W'sor 6E 4
Carey Ho. RH11: Craw 3A 182
Carey Rd. RG40: W'ham 3B 30
Careys Copse RH6: Smal 8M 143
Carey's Wood RH6: Smal 8M 143
Carfax RH12: Hors 6J 197
Carfax Av. GU10: Tong 4D 110
Carfax Rd. UB3: Harl 1G 9
Cargate Av. GU11: Alde 3M 109
Cargate Gro. GU11: Alde 3M 109
Cargate Hill GU11: Alde 3L 109
Cargate Ter. GU11: Alde 3L 109
Cargill Rd. SW18 2N 27
Cargo Forecourt Rd.
RH6: Gat 3B 162
Cargo Point TW19: Stan 9A 8
Cargo Rd. RH6: Gat 2B 162
Cargreen Pl. SE25 3C 46
Cargreen Rd. SE25 3C 46
Carisbrooke GU16: Frim 6D 70
Carisbrooke Cl. TW4: Houn 1M 23
Carisbrooke Ct. SM2: Chea 4L 61
Carisbrooke Ho.
KT2: K Tham 2J 203
TW10: Rich 8N 11
Carisbrooke Rd. CR4: Mit 3H 45
Carleton Av. SM6: W'ton 5H 63
Carleton Cl. KT10: Esh 7D 40
Carlingford Gdns. CR4: Mit 8D 28
Carlingford Rd. SM4: Mord 5J 43
Carlin Pl. GU15: Camb 2A 70
Carlinwark Dr. GU15: Camb 8D 50
Carlisle Cl. KT2: K Tham 9N 25
Carlisle M. KT2: K Tham 9N 25
Carlisle Rd. GU10: Rush 3N 149
SM1: Sut 3L 61
TW12: Hamp 8B 24
Carlisle Way SW17 6E 28
Carlos St. GU7: Goda 7H 133
Carlson Ct. SW15 7L 13

Carlton Av.—Central Wlk.

Carlton Av. CR2: S Croy 4B **64**
TW14: Felt 9K **9**
UB3: Harl 1F **8**
Carlton Cl. GU15: Camb 3F **70**
GU21: Wok 1B **74**
KT9: Ches 3K **59**
RH10: Craw 4C **182**
Carlton Ct. RH6: Horl 6E **142**
TW18: Stain 6J **21**
Carlton Cres. GU52: C Cro 7C **88**
SM3: Chea 1K **61**
Carlton Dr. SW15 8J **13**
Carlton Grn. RH1: Red 9C **102**
Carlton Ho. TW3: Houn 9A **10**
TW14: Felt 9G **8**
Carlton Pk. Av.
SW20 1J **43**
Carlton Pl. *KT13: Weybr* *1C 56*
(off Castle Vw. Rd.)
Carlton Rd. CR2: S Croy 3A **64**
GU21: Wok 1C **74**
GU35: H Dwn 5H **169**
KT3: N Mal 1D **42**
KT12: Wal T 6J **39**
RH1: Red 1B **122**
RH2: Reig 1B **122**
RH9: S Gods 1F **144**
SW14 6B **12**
TW16: Sunb 8G **22**
Carlton Towers
SM5: Cars 9D **44**
Carlton Tye RH6: Horl 8G **142**
Carlton Vs. SW15 8K **13**
Carlwell St. SW17 6C **28**
Carlyle Cl. KT8: W Mole 1B **40**
Carlyle Ct. RG45: Crow 3H **49**
SW6 *4N 13*
(off Imperial Rd.)
Carlyle Ho. *KT8: W Mole* *4A 40*
(off Down St.)
Carlyle Pl. SW15 7J **13**
Carlyle Rd. CR0: Croy 8D **46**
TW18: Stain 8J **21**
W5 1J **11**
Carlyon Cl. GU14: Farnb 1A **90**
GU16: Mytc 1D **90**
Carlys Cl. BR3: Beck 1G **47**
Carmalt Gdns. KT12: Hers 2K **57**
SW15 7H **13**
Carman Wlk. RH11: Craw 8N **181**
Carmarthen Cl.
GU14: Farnb 7L **69**
Carmel Cl. GU22: Wok 5A **74**
TW9: Rich 5A **12**
Carmel Lodge *SW6* *2M 13*
(off Lillie Rd.)
Carmichael Ct. *SW13* *5E 12*
(off Grove Rd.)
Carmichael M. SW18 1B **28**
Carmichael Rd. SE25 4C **46**
Carminia Rd. SW17 3F **28**
Carnation Cl. RG45: Crow 8G **30**
Carnation Dr. RG42: Wink R 7E **16**
Carnegie Cl. KT6: Surb 8M **41**
Carnegie Pl. SW19 4J **27**
Carnforth Cl. KT19: Ewe 3A **60**
Carnforth Rd. SW16 8H **29**
(not continuous)
Carnie Lodge SW17 4F **28**
Carnival Pool 3A **30**
Carnival Sq. GU51: Fleet 4A **88**
Carnoustie RG12: Brac 6K **31**
Carnwath Rd. SW6 6M **13**
Carolina Rd. CR7: T Hea 1M **45**
Caroline Cl. CR0: Croy 1B **64**
SW16 4K **29**
TW7: Isle 3D **10**
Caroline Ct. RH11: Craw 4B **182**
TW15: A'ford 7C **22**
Caroline Ho. *W6* *1H 13*
(off Queen Caroline St.)
Caroline Pl. UB3: Harl 3F **8**
Caroline Rd. SW19 8L **27**
Caroline Wlk. *W6* *2K 13*
(off Lillie Rd.)
Caroline Way GU16: Frim 5D **70**
Carolyn Cl. GU21: Wok 6J **73**
Carpenter Cl. KT17: Ewe 5E **60**
Carpenters Ct. TW2: Twick 3E **24**
Carrara Wharf SW6 6K **13**
Carriage Pl. SW16 6G **29**
Carrick Cl. TW7: Isle 6G **10**
Carrick Ga. KT10: Esh 9C **40**
Carrick La. GU46: Yate 9D **48**
Carrier Bus. Pk.
RH10: Craw 2F **182**
Carrigshaun KT13: Weybr 2E **56**
Carrington Av. TW3: Houn 8B **10**
Carrington Cl. CR0: Croy 6H **47**
KT2: K Tham 6B **26**
RH1: Red 2D **122**
Carrington La. GU12: A Va 5E **90**
Carrington Pl. KT10: Esh 1B **58**
Carrington Rd. TW10: Rich 7N **11**
Carroll Av. GU1: Guil 3D **114**
Carroll Cres. SL5: Asc 4K **33**
Carrow Rd. KT12: Wal T 9L **39**
CARSHALTON 1E **62**
Carshalton Athletic FC 9C **44**
CARSHALTON BEECHES 5C **62**
Carshalton Beeches Station (Rail)
3D **62**
Carshalton Gro. SM1: Sut 1B **62**
Carshalton Lodge
KT13: Weybr *9E 38*
(off Oatlands Dr.)
CARSHALTON ON THE HILL 4E **62**
Carshalton Pk. Rd.
SM5: Cars 2D **62**
Carshalton Pl. SM5: Cars 2E **62**
Carshalton Rd. CR4: Mit 3E **44**
GU15: Camb 6E **50**
SM1: Sut 2A **62**
SM5: Cars 2A **62**
SM7: Ban 1D **82**
Carshalton Station (Rail) 1D **62**
Carslake Rd. SW15 9H **13**
Carson Rd. SE21 3N **29**
CARTBRIDGE 9D **74**
Cartbridge Cl. GU23: Send 1D **94**
Carter Cl. SL4: W'sor 5D **4**
SM6: W'ton 4H **63**
Carterdale Cotts.
RH5: Cap 5J **159**
Carter Rd. RH10: Craw 6H **183**
SW19 7B **28**
Carters Cl. GU1: Guil 8A **94**
KT4: W Pk 8J **43**
Carter's Cotts. RH1: Red 5C **122**
Carter's Hill RG40: W'ham 5F **14**
RG42: Bin 5F **14**
Carters Hill Pk.
RG40: W'ham 5E **14**
Carters La. GU22: Wok 7E **74**
Carterslodge La.
RH17: Hand 9J **199**
Cartersmead Cl. RH6: Horl 7F **142**
Carters Rd. KT17: Eps 2E **80**
Carters Wlk. GU9: H End 4J **109**
Carter's Yd. SW18 8M **13**
Carthona Dr. GU52: Fleet 6A **88**
Carthouse Cotts. GU4: Guil 9E **94**
Carthouse La. GU21: Wok 1H **73**
Cartmel Cl. RH2: Reig 1C **122**
Cartmel Gdns. SM4: Mord 4A **44**
Cartwright Way SW13 3G **13**
Carville Cres. TW8: Brent 1L **11**
Carylls Cotts. RH12: Fay 8E **180**
Cascades CR0: Sels 6J **65**
Cascades Ct. SW19 8L **27**
Caselden Cl. KT15: Addl 2L **55**
Casewick Rd. SE27 6L **29**
Casher Rd. RH10: Craw 6G **183**
Cassidy Rd. SW6 3M **13**
(not continuous)
Cassilis Rd. TW1: Twick 8H **11**
Cassino Cl. GU11: Alde 2N **109**
Cassiobury Av. TW14: Felt 1G **22**
Cassland Rd. CR7: T Hea 3A **46**
Cassocks Sq. TW17: Shep 6E **38**
Castello Av. SW15 8H **13**
CASTELNAU 2G **12**
Castelnau SW13 4F **12**
Castelnau Gdns.
SW13 2G **13**
Castelnau Mans.
SW13 *2G 13*
(off Castelnau, not continuous)
Castelnau Row SW13 2G **12**
Castle, The RH12: Hors 1L **197**
Castle Av. KT17: Ewe 5F **60**
SL3: Dat 2K **5**
Castle Bus. Cen.
TW12: Hamp *9B 24*
(off Castle M.)
Castle Cl. BR2: Brom 2N **47**
GU14: Farnb 3C **90**
GU15: Camb 2D **70**
RH1: Blet 2N **123**
RH2: Reig 7N **121**
SW19 4J **27**
TW16: Sunb 8F **22**
Castlecombe Dr. SW19 1J **27**
Castle Ct. GU9: Farnh 9G **108**
Castlecraig Ct. GU47: C Tow 8J **49**
Castle Dr. RH2: Reig 7M **121**
RH6: Horl 1G **162**
Castle Farm Cvn. Site
SL4: W'sor 5A **4**
Castle Fld. GU9: Farnh 9G **108**
Castlefield Ct. RH2: Reig 3N **121**
Castlefield Rd. RH2: Reig 3M **121**
Castle Gdns. RH4: Dork 3M **119**
Castlegate TW9: Rich 6M **11**
CASTLE GREEN 9G **53**
Castle Grn. KT13: Weybr 9F **38**
Castle Gro. Rd.
GU24: Chob 9G **53**
Castle Hill
GU1: Guil 7C **202** (5N **113**)
GU9: Farnh 9G **108**
SL4: W'sor 4G **5**
Castle Hill Av. CR0: N Add 5L **65**
Castle Hill Rd.
TW20: Eng G 5L **19**
Castle Ho. SM2: Sut 3M **61**
Castlemaine Av.
CR2: S Croy 2C **64**
KT17: Ewe 5G **61**
Castle M. KT13: Weybr 9F **38**
SW17 5C **28**
TW12: Hamp 9B **24**
(not continuous)
Castle of Mey Ho.
GU27: Hasl 2D **188**
Castle Pde. KT17: Ewe 4F **60**
Castle Rd. CR5: Chip 7C **82**
GU11: Alde 9K **89**
GU15: Camb 2C **70**
GU21: Wok 1B **74**
KT13: Weybr 9E **38**
KT18: Eps 2A **80**
RH12: Bro H 5D **196**
TW7: Isle 5F **10**
Castle Row W4 1C **12**
Castle Sq.
GU1: Guil 6D **202** (5N **113**)
RH1: Blet 2N **123**
Castle St.
GU1: Guil 6C **202** (5N **113**)
GU9: Farnh 9G **109**
GU52: Fleet 6A **88**
KT1: K Tham 3J **203** (1L **41**)
RH1: Blet 2M **123**
Castleton Cl. CR0: Croy 5H **47**
SM7: Ban 2M **81**
Castleton Dr. SM7: Ban 2M **81**
Castleton Rd. CR4: Mit 3H **45**
(not continuous)
Castletown Rd. W14 1K **13**
Castle Vw. KT18: Eps 1A **80**
Castle Vw. Rd.
KT13: Weybr 1C **56**
Castleview Rd. SL3: Lang 1M **5**
Castle Wlk. RH2: Reig 3M **121**
TW16: Sunb 2K **39**
Castle Way KT17: Ewe 6F **60**
SW19 4J **27**
TW13: Hanw 5K **23**
Castle Yd. TW10: Rich 8K **11**
Castor Ct. GU46: Yate 8A **48**
GU52: C Cro 8C **88**
Caswall Cl. RG42: Bin 7H **15**
Caswall Ride GU46: Yate 1D **68**
Caswell Cl. GU14: Farnb 8L **69**
Catalina Rd. TW6: Lon A 5C **8**
Catalpa Cl. GU1: Guil 1M **113**
Catena Ri. GU18: Ligh 6L **51**
Caterfield La. RH7: Ling 1B **146**
RH8: Ling, Oxt 8C **126**
Cater Gdns. GU2: Guil 1J **113**
CATERHAM 2D **104**
Caterham By-Pass
CR3: Cate 8E **84**
Caterham Cl. CR3: Cate 7B **84**
(not continuous)
GU24: Pirb 8B **72**
Caterham Dr. CR5: Coul 5M **83**
CATERHAM-ON-THE-HILL 9B **84**
Caterham Station (Rail) 2D **104**
Caterways RH12: Hors 5G **197**
Cathcart Rd. SW10 2N **13**
Cathedral Cl. GU2: Guil 4L **113**
Cathedral Ct. GU2: Guil 3K **113**
Cathedral Hill GU2: Guil 2K **113**
Cathedral Hill Ind. Est.
GU2: Guil 2K **113**
Cathedral Pl. *GU1: Guil* *2C 202*
(off Old School Cl.)
Cathedral Vw. GU2: Guil 3J **113**
Catherine Cl. KT14: Byf 1N **75**
Catherine Ct. SW19 6L **27**
Catherine Dr. TW9: Rich 7L **11**
TW16: Sunb 7G **22**
Catherine Gdns.
TW3: Houn 7D **10**
Catherine Howard Ct.
KT13: Weybr *9C 38*
(off Old Palace Rd.)
Catherine Rd.
KT6: Surb 8G **203** (4K **41**)
Catherine Wheel Rd.
TW8: Brent 3K **11**
Cat Hill RH5: Ockl 7B **158**
Cathill La. RH5: Ockl 7B **158**
Cathles Rd. SW12 1F **28**
Catlin Cres. TW17: Shep 4E **38**
Catlin Gdns. RH9: Gods 8E **104**
Cator Cl. CR0: N Add 7A **66**
Cator Cres. CR0: N Add 7A **66**
Cator La. BR3: Beck 1J **47**
Cator Rd. SM5: Cars 2D **62**
Cato's Hill KT10: Esh 1B **58**
Cat St. TN7: C Hat, U Har 9N **187**
CATTESHALL 6K **133**
Catteshall Hatch
GU7: Goda 5K **133**
Catteshall La. GU7: Goda 7H **133**
Catteshall Rd. GU7: Goda 5K **133**
(not continuous)
Catteshall Ter. *GU7: Goda* *6K 133*
(off Catteshall Rd.)
Causeway RH12: Hors 7J **197**
Causeway, The KT9: Ches 1L **59**
KT10: Clay 4F **58**
SM2: Sut 5A **62**
SM5: Cars 9E **44**
SW18 8N **13**
(not continuous)
SW19 6H **27**
TW4: Houn 7H **9**
TW11: Tedd 7F **24**
TW14: Felt, Houn 7H **9**
TW18: Stain 5E **20**
Causeway Corporate Cen.
TW18: Stain 5E **20**
Causeway Ct. GU21: Wok 5J **73**
Causewayside *GU27: Hasl* *1H 189*
(off High St.)
Cavalier Ct. KT5: Surb 5M **41**
Cavalier Way
RH19: E Grin 2B **186**
Cavalry Ct. GU11: Alde 2K **109**
Cavalry Cres. SL4: W'sor 6F **4**
TW4: Houn 7L **9**
Cavalry Gdns. SW15 8L **13**
Cavan's Rd. GU11: Alde 7A **90**
Cavell Way GU21: Knap 6F **72**
KT19: Eps 7N **59**
RH10: Craw 4G **182**
Cavendish Av. KT3: N Mal 4F **42**
Cavendish Cl. RH12: Hors 1K **197**
TW16: Sunb 7G **22**
Cavendish Ct. GU17: Haw 3J **69**
KT13: Weybr 3D **56**
KT16: Chert *7J 37*
(off Victory Rd.)
SL3: Poy 4G **6**
SM6: W'ton 3F **62**
TW16: Sunb 7G **22**
Cavendish Dr. KT10: Clay 2E **58**
Cavendish Gdns.
GU52: C Cro 8A **88**
RH1: Red 2E **122**
Cavendish Meads
SL5: S'hill 5N **33**
Cavendish M. GU11: Alde 3M **109**
Cavendish Pde. TW4: Houn 5M **9**
Cavendish Pk. Cvn. Site
GU47: C Tow 9K **49**
Cavendish Rd. CR0: Croy 7M **45**
GU11: Alde 3M **109**
GU22: Wok 6N **73**
GU52: C Cro 9A **88**
KT3: N Mal 3E **42**
KT13: Weybr 5C **56**
RH1: Red 3E **122**
SM2: Sut 4A **62**
SW12 1G **28**
SW19 8B **28**
TW16: Sunb 7G **22**
W4 4B **12**
Cavendish Ter. TW13: Felt 3H **23**
Cavendish Wlk. KT19: Eps 7A **60**
Cavendish Way
BR4: W Wick 7L **47**
Cavenham Cl. GU22: Wok 6A **74**
Caverleigh Way KT4: W Pk 7F **42**
Cave Rd. TW10: Ham 5J **25**
Caversham Av. SM3: Chea 8K **43**
Caversham Ho.
KT1: K Tham 4J **203**
Caversham Rd.
KT1: K Tham 3L **203** (1M **41**)
Caves Farm Cl.
GU47: Sandh 7F **48**
Cawcott Dr. SL4: W'sor 4B **4**
Cawsey Way GU21: Wok 4A **74**
Caxton Av. KT15: Addl 3J **55**
Caxton Cl. RH10: Craw 6B **182**
Caxton Gdns. GU2: Guil 2L **113**
Caxton La. RH8: Limp 9G **106**
Caxton M. TW8: Brent 2K **11**
Caxton Ri. RH1: Red 2E **122**
Caxton Rd. SW19 6A **28**
Cayton Rd. CR5: Coul 9G **83**
Cearn Way CR5: Coul 2K **83**
Cecil Cl. KT9: Ches 1K **59**
TW15: A'ford 8D **22**
Cecil Ct. CR0: Croy 8C **46**
SW10 *2N 13*
(off Fawcett St.)
Cecil Pl. CR4: Mit 4D **44**
Cecil Rd. CR0: Croy 5J **45**
SM1: Sut 3L **61**
SW19 8N **27**
TW3: Houn 5C **10**
TW15: A'ford 8D **22**
Cedar Av. GU17: B'water 1J **69**
KT11: Cob 2K **77**
TW2: Whitt 9B **10**
Cedar Cl. CR6: Warl 6H **85**
GU12: Alde 4C **110**
GU19: Bag 4J **51**
KT8: E Mol 3E **40**
KT10: Esh 3N **57**
KT17: Eps 1E **80**
RG40: W'ham 2B **30**
RH2: Reig 5A **122**
RH4: Dork 3K **201** (5H **119**)
RH11: Craw 9A **162**
RH12: Hors 5H **197**
SE21 2N **29**
SM5: Cars 3D **62**
SW15 5C **26**
TW18: Lale 2L **37**
Cedar Ct. GU27: Hasl 2F **188**
KT15: Addl 1L **55**
KT16: Otter 2E **54**
KT22: Fetc 9G **78**
SL4: W'sor 5D **4**
SM2: Sut 3A **62**
SW19 4J **27**
TW8: Brent 2J **11**
TW20: Egh 5C **20**
Cedarcroft Rd. KT9: Ches 1M **59**
Cedar Dr. GU51: Fleet 4D **88**
KT22: Fetc 1E **98**
RG42: Brac 8A **16**
SL5: S'dale 6D **34**
SL5: S'hill 3G **35**
TN8: Eden 1K **147**
Cedar Gdns. GU21: Wok 5L **73**
GU24: Chob 6J **53**
SM2: Sut 3A **62**
Cedar Gro. GU24: Bis 2D **72**
KT13: Weybr 1D **56**
Cedar Hgts. TW10: Ham 2L **25**
Cedar Hill KT18: Eps 3B **80**
Cedar Ho. GU4: Guil 1E **114**
KT22: Leat 6F **78**
TW9: Kew 4A **12**
TW16: Sunb *8G 22*
(off Spelthorne Gro.)
Cedarland Ter. SW20 8G **27**
Cedar La. GU16: Frim 6B **70**
Cedar Lodge GU27: Hasl 3J **189**
RH10: Craw 5B **182**
Cedarne Rd. SW6 3N **13**
Cedar Pk. CR3: Cate 8B **84**
Cedar Rd.
CR0: Croy 2E **200** (8A **46**)
GU14: Farnb 2A **90**
GU22: Wok 7L **73**
KT8: E Mol 3E **40**
KT11: Cob 1J **77**
KT13: Weybr 1B **56**
SM2: Sut 3A **62**
TW4: C'ford 5K **9**
TW11: Tedd 6G **24**
TW14: Bedf 2E **22**
Cedars RG12: Brac 3D **32**
SM7: Ban 1D **82**
Cedars, The GU1: B'ham 9C **94**
GU8: Mil 2B **152**
GU24: Pirb 9A **72**
GU51: Fleet 5C **88**
KT14: Byf 8A **56**
KT22: Leat 8K **79**
KT23: Book 4C **98**
RH2: Reig 3B **122**
RH3: Brock 3N **119**
SM6: W'ton 1G **63**
TW11: Tedd 7F **24**
Cedars Av. CR4: Mit 3E **44**
Cedars Cl. GU47: Sandh 7E **48**
Cedars Ct. GU1: B'ham 9C **94**
Cedars Rd. BR3: Beck 1H **47**
CR0: Bedd 9J **45**
KT1: H Wic 9J **25**
SM4: Mord 3M **43**
SW13 5F **12**
W4 1B **12**
Cedar Ter. TW9: Rich 7L **11**
Cedar Tree Gro. SE27 6M **29**
Cedar Vw. GU52: C Cro 7C **88**
KT1: K Tham 6H **203**
Cedarville Gdns.
SW16 7K **29**
Cedar Wlk. CR8: Ken 3N **83**
KT10: Clay 3F **58**
KT20: Tad 7K **81**
Cedar Way GU1: Guil 1M **113**
SL3: Lang 1A **6**
TW16: Sunb 8F **22**
Cedarways GU9: Farnh 4G **128**
Celandine Cl. RG45: Crow 1H **49**
RH11: Craw 6N **181**
Celandine Ct. GU46: Yate 8A **48**
Celandine Rd. KT12: Hers 1M **57**
Celery La. GU10: Wrec 6G **128**
Celia Cres. TW15: A'ford 7M **21**
Cell Farm Av. SL4: O Win 8L **5**
Celtic Rd. KT14: Byf 1N **75**
Cemetery La. TW17: Shep 6C **38**
Cemetery Pales
GU24: B'wood 9C **72**
Cemetery Wlk.
RH17: Hand 7K **199**
Centaur Ct. TW8: Brent 1L **11**
Centaurs Bus. Pk.
TW7: Isle 2G **10**
Centenary Ct. *RH1: Red* *2D 122*
(off Warwick Rd.)
Centennial Ct. RG12: Brac 1M **31**
Central Av. KT8: W Mole 3N **39**
SM6: W'ton 2J **63**
TW3: Houn 7C **10**
Central Ct. KT15: Addl 1L **55**
Centrale Shop. Cen.
CR0: Croy 2B **200** (8N **45**)
Centrale Stop (CT)
2B **200** (8N **45**)
Central Gdns. SM4: Mord 4N **43**
Central Hill SE19 6N **29**
Central La. SL4: Wink 2M **17**
Central Mall *SW18* *9N 13*
(off South Mall)
Central Pde. CR0: N Add 6M **65**
KT6: Surb 5L **41**
KT8: W Mole 3N **39**
RH1: Red 2D **122**
RH6: Horl 9E **142**
TW5: Hest 3N **9**
TW14: Felt 1K **23**
Central Pk. Est. TW4: Houn 8L **9**
Central Pl. SE25 4D **46**
Central Rd. KT4: W Pk 7F **42**
SM4: Mord 5M **43**
Central School Path
SW14 6B **12**
Central Ter. BR3: Beck 2G **46**
Central Wlk.
KT19: Eps 6J **201** (9C **60**)
RG40: W'ham 2B **30**

Central Way—Chaucer Cl.

Central Way RH8: Oxt ... 5N 105
SL4: Wink ... 2M 17
SM5: Cars ... 4C 62
TW14: Felt ... 8H 9
Centre, The KT12: Wal T ... 7H 39
TW3: Houn ... 6B 10
TW13: Felt ... 2H 23
Centre Ct. Shop. Cen.
SW19 ... 7L 27
Centre Rd. SL4: W'sor ... 3A 4
Centre Sq. *SW18* ... *8M 13*
(off Buckhold Rd.)
Centrillion Point
CR0: Croy ... 6C 200
Centrium GU22: Wok ... 4B 74
Centurion Cl. GU47: C Tow ... 7J 49
Centurion Ct. SM6: W'ton ... 8F 44
Century Ct. GU21: Wok ... 3B 74
Century Ho. SM7: Ban ... 2N 81
SW15 ... 7J 13
Century Rd. TW18: Stain ... 6E 20
Century Way GU24: B'wood ... 6A 72
Cerne Rd. SM4: Mord ... 5A 44
Cerotus Pl. KT16: Chert ... 6H 37
Chadacre Rd. KT17: Ewe ... 3G 60
Chadhurst Cl. RH5: Nth H ... 8K 119
Chadwick Av. SW19 ... 7M 27
Chadwick Cl. RH11: Craw ... 8N 181
SW15 ... 1E 26
TW11: Tedd ... 7G 25
Chadwick M. W4 ... 2A 12
Chadwick Pl. KT6: Surb ... 6J 41
Chadworth Way KT10: Clay ... 2D 58
Chaffers Mead
KT21: A'tead ... 3M 79
Chaffinch Av. CR0: Croy ... 5G 46
Chaffinch Bus. Pk.
BR3: Beck ... 3G 47
Chaffinch Cl. CR0: Croy ... 4G 46
GU47: C Tow ... 7J 49
KT6: Surb ... 9N 41
RH11: Craw ... 1B 182
RH12: Hors ... 1K 197
Chaffinch Rd. BR3: Beck ... 1H 47
Chaffinch Way RH6: Horl ... 7C 142
Chailey Cl. RH11: Craw ... 6M 181
TW5: Hest ... 4L 9
Chailey Pl. KT12: Hers ... 1M 57
Chalcot Cl. SM2: Sut ... 4M 61
Chalcot M. SW16 ... 4J 29
Chalcott Gdns. KT6: Surb ... 7J 41
CHALDON ... 2L 103
Chaldon Cl. RH1: Red ... 5C 122
Chaldon Comn. Rd.
CR3: Cate ... 2N 103
Chaldon Ct. SE19 ... 1A 46
Chaldon Path CR7: T Hea ... 3M 45
Chaldon Rd. CR3: Cate ... 2A 104
RH11: Craw ... 8A 182
SW6 ... 3K 13
Chaldon Way CR5: Coul ... 4J 83
Chale Rd. SW2 ... 1J 29
Chalet Ct. CR7: T Hea ... 4N 45
Chale Wlk. SM2: Sut ... 5N 61
Chalfont Dr. GU14: Farnb ... 3A 90
Chalfont Rd. SE25 ... 2C 46
Chalford Cl. KT8: W Mole ... 3A 40
Chalgrove Av. SM4: Mord ... 4M 43
Chalgrove Rd. SM2: Sut ... 4B 62
Chalice Cl. SM6: W'ton ... 3H 63
CHALKER'S CORNER ... 6A 12
Chalk Hill Rd. W6 ... 1J 13
Chalk La. GU8: S'ford ... 3A 132
KT18: Eps, Eps D ... 2C 80
(not continuous)
KT21: A'tead ... 6M 79
KT24: E Hor ... 1G 116
Chalkley Cl. CR4: Mit ... 1D 44
Chalkmead RH1: Mers ... 8G 103
Chalk Paddock KT18: Eps ... 2C 80
Chalk Pit Cotts.
KT24: W Hors ... 8C 96
Chalkpit La. KT23: Book ... 5N 97
RH3: Betch ... 2A 120
RH4: Dork ... 1J 201 (4G 119)
RH8: Oxt ... 3M 105
Chalk Pit Rd. KT18: Eps D ... 6B 80
SM7: Ban ... 4M 81
Chalkpit Ter. RH4: Dork ... 3G 118
Chalk Pit Way SM1: Sut ... 2A 62
Chalkpit Wood RH8: Oxt ... 5N 105
Chalk Rd. GU7: Goda ... 6G 133
RH14: Ifo ... 6E 192
Chalky La. KT9: Ches ... 6K 59
Challen Ct. RH12: Hors ... 5H 197
Challenge Ct. KT22: Leat ... 6H 79
TW2: Twick ... 1E 24
Challenge Rd. TW15: A'ford ... 4E 22
Challice Way SW2 ... 2K 29
Challis Pl. RG42: Brac ... 9K 15
Challis Rd. TW8: Brent ... 1K 11
Challock Cl. TN16: B Hil ... 3E 86
Challoner Ct. BR2: Brom ... 1N 47
W14 ... *1L 13*
(off Challoner St.)
Challoner Cres. W14 ... 1L 13
Challoner Mans. *W14* ... *1L 13*
(off Challoner St.)
Challoners Cl. KT8: E Mol ... 3D 40
Challoner St. W14 ... 1L 13
Chalmers Cl. RH6: Char ... 4K 161
Chalmers Rd. SM7: Ban ... 2B 82
TW15: A'ford ... 6C 22
Chalmers Rd. E.
TW15: A'ford ... 5C 22
Chalmers Way TW14: Felt ... 8J 9
Chamberlain Cres.
BR4: W Wick ... 7L 47
Chamberlain Gdns.
TW3: Houn ... 4C 10
Chamberlain Wlk.
TW13: Hanw ... *5M 23*
(off Swift Rd.)
Chamberlain Way
KT6: Surb ... 6L 41
Chamber La.
GU10: Farnh ... 3B 128
Chamberlens Garages
W6 ... *1G 12*
(off Dalling Rd.)
Chambers Bus. Pk.
UB7: Sip ... 2B 8
Chambers Pl. CR2: S Croy ... 4A 64
Chambers Rd. GU12: A Va ... 8F 90
Chambon Pl. W6 ... 1F 12
Chamomile Gdns.
GU14: Cove ... 9H 69
Champion Down KT24: Eff ... 6M 97
Champions Dr. TN8: Eden ... 9K 127
Champion Way
GU52: C Cro ... 8B 88
Champney Cl. SL3: Hort ... 6C 6
Champneys Cl. SM2: Chea ... 4L 61
Chancellor Ct. GU2: Guil ... 4G 113
(not continuous)
Chancellor Gdns.
CR2: S Croy ... 5M 63
Chancellor Gro. SE21 ... 3N 29
Chancellor's Rd. W6 ... 1H 13
Chancellor's St. W6 ... 1H 13
Chancellors Wharf W6 ... 1H 13
Chancel Mans. RG42: Warf ... 7A 16
Chancery La. BR3: Beck ... 1L 47
Chancery M. SW17 ... 3C 28
Chanctonbury Chase
RH1: Red ... 3E 122
Chanctonbury Dr.
SL5: S'dale ... 6B 34
Chanctonbury Gdns.
SM2: Sut ... 4N 61
Chanctonbury Way
RH11: Craw ... 5A 182
Chandaria Ct. *CR0: Croy* ... *3B 200*
(off Church Rd.)
Chandler Cl. RH10: Craw ... 5B 182
TW12: Hamp ... 9A 24
Chandler Ct. RH6: Horl ... 8F 142
TW14: Felt ... 9H 9
Chandlers Cl.
KT8: W Mole ... 4B 40
TW14: Felt ... 1G 22
Chandlers La. GU46: Yate ... 8B 48
Chandlers Rd. GU12: A Va ... 9F 90
Chandlers Way SW2 ... 1L 29
Chandler Way RH5: Dork ... 7J 119
Chandon Lodge SM2: Sut ... 4A 62
Chandos Gdns. CR5: Coul ... 6M 83
Chandos Rd. TW18: Stain ... 6F 20
Channel Cl. TW5: Hest ... 4A 10
Channings GU21: Wok ... 2A 74
Channon Ct. KT6: Surb ... 8J 203
Chantilly Way KT19: Eps ... 6A 60
Chantlers Cl.
RH19: E Grin ... 8M 165
Chanton Dr. KT17: Chea ... 6H 61
Chantrey Rd. RH10: Craw ... 6C 182
Chantry Cl. KT21: A'tead ... 6J 79
RH6: Horl ... 7D 142
SL4: W'sor ... 4D 4
TW16: Sunb ... 8H 23
Chantry Cotts. GU4: Guil ... 9D 114
Chantry Ct. *GU16: Frim* ... *5B 70*
(off Church Rd.)
SM5: Cars ... 9C 44
Chantry Ho.
KT1: K Tham ... 8K 203 (3L 41)
Chantry Hurst KT18: Eps ... 2C 80
Chantry La. GU5: Shere ... 8A 116
Chantry Rd. GU4: Guil ... 9D 114
GU19: Bag ... 5H 51
KT9: Ches ... 2M 59
KT16: Chert ... 6L 37
Chantrys, The GU9: Farnh ... 1E 128
Chantrys Ct. *GU9: Farnh* ... *1F 128*
(off The Chantrys)
Chantry Vw. Rd. GU1: Guil
... 8D 202 & 8F 202 (6N 113)
Chantry Way CR4: Mit ... 2B 44
Chapel Av. KT15: Addl ... 1K 55
Chapel Cl. GU8: Mil ... 9C 132
Chapel Ct. GU8: Mil ... 1C 152
RH4: Dork ... 1J 201 (4G 119)
Chapel Farm Animal Trail ... 8G 98
Chapel Farm Mobile Home Pk.
GU3: Norm ... 9B 92
Chapel Flds. GU7: Goda ... 4G 132
Chapel Gdns. GU35: Lind ... 4A 168
CHAPEL GREEN ... 4A 30
Chapel Grn. CR8: Pur ... 9L 63
Chapel Gro. KT15: Addl ... 1K 55
KT18: Tat C ... 6H 81
Chapel Hill GU8: Duns ... 6B 174
KT24: Eff ... 5L 97
Chapelhouse Cl.
GU2: Guil ... 3H 113
Chapelier Ho. SW18 ... 7M 13
Chapel La. GU8: Mil ... 9C 132
GU14: Cove ... 6L 69
GU19: Bag ... 5H 51
GU24: Pirb ... 9D 72
KT23: Book, Westh ... 6C 98
RG42: Bin ... 8H 15
RH4: Westc ... 6C 118
RH5: Westh ... 8E 98
RH10: Craw D ... 7C 164
RH18: F Row ... 8H 187
RH19: Ash W ... 3F 186
Chapel La. Works
RH4: Westc ... *6C 118*
(off Chapel La.)
Chapel Mill Rd.
KT1: K Tham ... 6M 203 (2M 41)
Chapel Pk. Rd. KT15: Addl ... 1K 55
Chapel Rd. CR6: Warl ... 5G 84
GU10: Rowl ... 7D 128
GU15: Camb ... 1N 69
KT20: Tad ... 1H 101
RH1: Red ... 3D 122
RH6: Char ... 3K 161
RH6: Smal ... 8M 143
RH8: Limp ... 8E 106
SE27 ... 5M 29
TW1: Twick ... 1H 25
TW3: Houn ... 6B 10
Chapel Sq. GU15: Camb ... 9L 49
GU25: V Wat ... 3A 36
Chapel St.
GU1: Guil ... 6C 202 (5N 113)
GU14: Farnb ... 8B 70
GU21: Wok ... 4B 74
Chapel Ter. RG42: Bin ... 8H 15
Chapel Vw. CR2: Sels ... 3F 64
Chapel Wlk.
CR0: Croy ... 2B 200 (8N 45)
CR5: Coul ... 9H 83
Chapel Way KT18: Tat C ... 6H 81
Chapel Yd. *SW18* ... *8N 13*
(off Wandsworth High St.)
Chaplain's Hill RG45: Crow ... 3J 49
Chaplin Cres. TW16: Sunb ... 7F 22
Chaplin M. SL3: Lang ... 1B 6
Chapman Rd. CR0: Croy ... 7L 45
RH10: Craw ... 7G 182
Chapman's La.
RH19: E Grin ... 9L 165
(not continuous)
Chapman Sq. SW19 ... 3J 27
Chapter Ho. *GU14: Farnb* ... *1A 90*
(off Jubilee Hall Rd.)
Chapter M. SL4: W'sor ... 3G 5
Chapter Way SW19 ... 9B 28
TW12: Hamp ... 5A 24
Chara Pl. W4 ... 2C 12
Charcot Ho. SW15 ... 9E 12
Chardin Rd. W4 ... 1D 12
Chard Rd. TW6: Lon A ... 5C 8
Chargate Cl. KT12: Hers ... 3G 57
Charing Cl. BR6: Orp ... 1N 67
Charing Ct. BR2: Brom ... 1N 47
Charing Cross Sports Club ... 2J 13
Chariotts Pl. SL4: W'sor ... 4G 4
Charlbury Cl. RG12: Brac ... 3D 32
Charlecombe Ct.
TW18: Stain ... 6K 21
Charlecote Cl. GU14: Farnb ... 2B 90
Charles Babbage Cl.
KT9: Ches ... 4J 59
Charles Cobb Gdns.
CR0: Wad ... 2L 63
Charlesfield Rd.
RH6: Horl ... 7D 142
Charles Haller St.
SW2 ... 1L 29
Charles Harrod Ct.
SW13 ... *2H 13*
(off Somerville Av.)
CHARLESHILL ... 6E 130
Charles Hill GU10: Til ... 5B 130
Charles Ho. *KT16: Chert* ... *7H 37*
(off Sth. Guildford St.)
SL4: W'sor ... 4F 4
Charles Lesser Ho.
KT9: Ches ... 2K 59
Charles Nex M. SE21 ... 3N 29
Charles Rd. SW19 ... 9M 27
TW18: Stain ... 7M 21
Charles Sq. RG12: Brac ... 1M 32
Charles St.
CR0: Croy ... 4B 200 (9N 45)
KT16: Chert ... 7H 37
SL4: W'sor ... 4F 4
SW13 ... 5D 12
TW3: Houn ... 5N 9
Charleston Cl. TW13: Felt ... 4H 23
Charleston Ct. RH10: Craw ... 6F 182
Charlesworth Pl.
SW13 ... 6D 12
Charleville Ct. *W14* ... *1L 13*
(off Charleville Rd.)
Charleville Mans.
W14 ... *1K 13*
(off Charleville Rd.)
Charleville M. TW7: Isle ... 7H 11
Charleville Rd. W14 ... 1K 13
Charlmont Rd. SW17 ... 7C 28
Charlock Cl. RH11: Craw ... 7M 181
Charlock Way GU1: Guil ... 9D 94
Charlotte Cl. GU9: H End ... 4J 109
KT21: A'tead ... 5L 79
Charlotte Ct. GU1: Guil ... 5B 114
KT10: Esh ... 2C 58
RH11: Craw ... *3A 182*
(off Leopold Rd.)
Charlotte Gro. RH6: Smal ... 7L 143
Charlotte Ho. *W6* ... *1H 13*
(off Queen Caroline St.)
Charlotte M. GU14: Farnb ... 9B 70
KT10: Esh ... *1B 58*
(off Heather Pl.)
Charlotte Rd. SM6: W'ton ... 3G 63
SW13 ... 4E 12
Charlotte Sq. TW10: Rich ... 9M 11
CHARLOTTEVILLE ... 5B 114
CHARLTON ... 2D 38
Charlton Av. KT12: Hers ... 1J 57
Charlton Ct. GU47: Owls ... 6J 49
Charlton Dr. TN16: B Hil ... 4F 86
Charlton Gdns. CR5: Coul ... 5G 83
Charlton Ho. TW8: Brent ... 2L 11
Charlton Kings
KT13: Weybr ... 9F 38
Charlton La. TW17: Shep ... 2D 38
(not continuous)
Charlton Rd. TW17: Shep ... 2D 38
Charlton Sq. *SL4: W'sor* ... *5A 4*
(off Guards Rd.)
CHARLWOOD
RH6 ... 3K 161
RH19 ... 8A 186
Charlwood CR0: Sels ... 5J 65
Charlwood Cl. KT23: Book ... 2B 98
RH10: Cop ... 6L 163
Charlwood Dr. KT22: Oxs ... 2D 78
Charlwood Ho. TW9: Kew ... 3A 12
Charlwood La.
RH5: Newd ... 5F 160
Charlwood M. RH6: Char ... 3K 161
Charlwood Pl. RH2: Reig ... 3L 121
Charlwood Rd. RH6: Gat ... 2A 162
RH11: Ifi ... 7K 161
RH11: L Hea ... 6N 161
SW15 ... 7J 13
Charlwoods Bus. Cen.
RH19: E Grin ... 7N 165
Charlwoods Pl.
RH19: E Grin ... 7A 166
Charlwoods Rd.
RH19: E Grin ... 8N 165
Charlwood Ter. SW15 ... 7J 13
Charlwood Wlk.
RH11: Craw ... 9N 161
Charman Rd. RH1: Red ... 3C 122
Charmans Cl. RH12: Hors ... 3A 198
Charm Cl. RH6: Horl ... 7C 142
Charminster Av.
SW19 ... 1M 43
Charminster Ct. KT6: Surb ... 6K 41
Charminster Rd. KT4: W Pk ... 7J 43
Charmouth Ct. TW10: Rich ... 8M 11
Charnwood SL5: S'dale ... 5C 34
Charnwood Av. SW19 ... 1M 43
Charnwood Cl. KT3: N Mal ... 3D 42
Charnwood Rd. SE25 ... 4A 46
Charrington Bowl ... 8A 42
Charrington Rd.
CR0: Croy ... 2B 200 (8N 45)
Charrington Way
RH12: Bro H ... 5C 196
Charta Rd. TW20: Egh ... 6E 20
Chart Cl. CR0: Croy ... 5F 46
CR4: Mit ... 3D 44
RH5: Dork ... 7K 119
Chart Downs RH5: Dork ... 7J 119
Charter Ct. KT3: N Mal ... 2D 42
Charter Cres. TW4: Houn ... 7M 9
CHARTERHOUSE ... 4F 132
Charter Ho. *SM2: Sut* ... *3N 61*
(off Mulgrave Rd.)
Charterhouse GU7: Goda ... 5E 132
Charterhouse Cl.
RG12: Brac ... 4C 32
Charterhouse Rd.
GU7: Goda ... 4G 132
Charter Pl. TW18: Stain ... 7J 21
Charter Quay KT1: K Tham ... 4H 203
Charter Rd. KT1: K Tham ... 2A 42
Charters Cl. SL5: S'hill ... 4A 34
Charters La. SL5: S'hill ... 4A 34
Charters Leisure Cen. ... 6A 34
Charter Sq. KT1: K Tham ... 1A 42
Charters Rd. SL5: S'dale ... 6A 34
Charters Way SL5: S'dale ... 6C 34
Charter Wlk. *GU27: Hasl* ... *2G 189*
(off West St.)
Chartfield Av. SW15 ... 8G 13
Chartfield Pl. KT13: Weybr ... 2C 56
Chartfield Rd. RH2: Reig ... 4A 122
Chartfield Sq. SW15 ... 8J 13
Chart Gdns. RH5: Dork ... 8J 119
Chartham Gro. SE27 ... 4M 29
Chartham Rd. SE25 ... 2E 46
Chart Ho. CR4: Mit ... 1D 44
Chart Ho. Rd. GU12: A Va ... 6E 90
Chart La. RH2: Reig ... 3N 121
RH4: Dork ... 2L 201 (5H 119)
Chart La. Sth.
RH5: Dork, Nth H ... 7J 119
Chart, The (NT) ... 9H 107
Charts Cl. GU6: Cranl ... 8N 155
Chart Way RH12: Hors ... 6J 197
Chartway RH2: Reig ... 2N 121
Chartwell ... 9N 107
Chartwell GU9: Farnh ... 5E 128
GU16: Frim G ... 9C 70
GU22: Wok ... *5A 74*
(off Mt. Hermon Rd.)
Chartwell Cl. CR0: Croy ... 7A 46
Chartwell Ct. Grange
RH4: Dork ... 8H 119
Chartwell Dr. BR6: Farnb ... 2M 67
Chartwell Gdns. GU11: Alde ... 6A 90
SM3: Chea ... 1K 61
Chartwell Lodge
RH5: Nth H ... 9H 119
Chartwell Pl.
KT18: Eps ... 8M 201 (1D 80)
SM3: Chea ... 1K 61
Chartwood Pl. RH4: Dork ... 3J 201
Charwood SW16 ... 5L 29
Charwood Rd.
RG40: W'ham ... 2D 30
Chase, The CR5: Coul ... 1G 83
GU2: Guil ... 4K 113
GU14: Farnb ... 8B 70
KT20: K'wood ... 9M 81
KT21: A'tead ... 5J 79
KT22: Oxs ... 2C 78
KT24: E Hor ... 4G 96
RG45: Crow ... 1F 48
RH2: Reig ... 4B 122
RH10: Craw ... 4E 182
SL5: Asc ... 8L 17
SM6: W'ton ... 2J 63
SW16 ... 8K 29
SW20 ... 9K 27
TW16: Sunb ... 9J 23
Chase Ct. SW20 ... 1K 43
TW7: Isle ... 5G 10
Chase End
KT19: Eps ... 5K 201 (8C 60)
Chasefield Cl. GU4: B'ham ... 9C 94
Chasefield Rd. SW17 ... 5D 28
Chase Gdns. RG42: Bin ... 6H 15
TW2: Whitt ... 1D 24
Chase La. GU27: Hasl ... 4H 189
Chaseley Ct. KT13: Weybr ... 7F 38
Chaseley Dr. CR2: Sande ... 6A 64
W4 ... 1A 12
Chasemore Cl. CR4: Mit ... 6D 44
Chasemore Gdns.
CR0: Wad ... 2L 63
Chasemore Ho. *SW6* ... *3K 13*
(off Williams Cl.)
Chase Plain GU26: Hind ... 8A 170
Chase Rd. GU35: Lind ... 5A 168
KT19: Eps ... 5K 201 (8C 60)
Chaseside Av. SW20 ... 9K 27
Chaseside Gdns.
KT16: Chert ... 6K 37
Chasewater Ct.
GU11: Alde ... 3M 109
Chatelet Cl. RH6: Horl ... 7F 142
Chatfield Cl. GU14: Farnb ... 3A 90
Chatfield Ct. CR3: Cate ... 9A 84
Chatfield Dr. GU4: Guil ... 1E 114
Chatfield Rd.
CR0: Croy ... 1A 200 (7M 45)
Chatfields RH11: Craw ... 5N 181
Chatham Cl. SM3: Sut ... 6L 43
Chatham Ho. *SM6: W'ton* ... *2F 62*
(off Melbourne Rd.)
Chatham M. GU2: Guil ... 9K 93
Chatham Rd.
KT1: K Tham ... 3M 203 (1N 41)
CHATHILL ... 6L 125
Chatley Heath Semaphore Tower
... 4E 76
Chatsfield KT17: Ewe ... 6F 60
Chatsworth Av.
GU27: Hasl ... 9G 170
SW20 ... 9K 27
Chatsworth Cl. W4 ... 2B 12
Chatsworth Ct. SW16 ... 2K 45
Chatsworth Cres.
TW3: Houn ... 7D 10
Chatsworth Gdns.
KT3: N Mal ... 4E 42
Chatsworth Gro.
GU9: U Hal ... 6G 108
Chatsworth Hgts.
GU15: Camb ... 8E 50
Chatsworth Lodge *W4* ... *1C 12*
(off Bourne Pl.)
Chatsworth Pk. SM7: Ban ... 4N 81
Chatsworth Pl. CR4: Mit ... 2D 44
KT22: Oxs ... 9D 58
TW11: Tedd ... 5G 24
Chatsworth Rd.
CR0: Croy ... 6E 200 (1A 64)
GU14: Farnb ... 2C 90
SM3: Chea ... 2J 61
W4 ... 2B 12
Chatsworth Way SE27 ... 4M 29
CHATTERN HILL ... 5C 22
Chattern Hill TW15: A'ford ... 5C 22
Chattern Rd. TW15: A'ford ... 5D 22
Chatterton Ct. TW9: Kew ... 5M 11
Chatton Row GU24: Bis ... 4D 72
Chaucer Av. KT13: Weybr ... 4B 56
RH19: E Grin ... 1M 185
TW4: C'ford ... 5J 9
TW9: Rich ... 6N 11
Chaucer Cl. RG40: W'ham ... 2E 30
SL4: W'sor ... 6G 4
SM7: Ban ... 1K 81

Chaucer Ct.—Chilton Ct.

Chaucer Ct.
GU2: Guil ... 7B 202 (5M 113)
RH1: Red ... 9E 102
Chaucer Gdns. SM1: Sut ... 9M 43
(not continuous)
Chaucer Grn. CR0: Croy ... 6E 46
Chaucer Gro. GU15: Camb ... 1B 70
Chaucer Ho. SM1: Sut ... 9M 43
(off Chaucer Gdns.)
Chaucer Mans. W14 ... 2K 13
(off Queen's Club Gdns.)
Chaucer Rd. GU14: Farnb ... 8L 69
RG45: Crow ... 4G 48
RH10: Craw ... 1F 182
SM1: Sut ... 1M 61
TW15: A'ford ... 5N 21
Chaucer Way KT15: Addl ... 3J 55
SW19 ... 6B 28
Chavasse Way GU14: Cove ... 9J 69
Chave Cft. KT18: Tat C ... 6H 81
Chavecroft Ter. KT18: Tat C ... 6H 81
CHAVEY DOWN ... 9F 16
Chavey Down Rd.
RG42: Wink R ... 6F 16
Chaworth Cl. KT16: Otter ... 3E 54
Chaworth Rd. KT16: Otter ... 3E 54
Chawridge La. SL4: Wink ... 2G 16
Cheals Rdbt. RH11: Craw ... 5N 181
CHEAM ... 3K 61
Cheam Cl. KT20: Tad ... 8G 81
RG12: Brac ... 4B 32
Cheam Comn. Rd.
KT4: W Pk ... 8G 43
Cheam Leisure Cen. ... 1J 61
Cheam Mans. SM3: Chea ... 4K 61
Cheam Pk. Way SM3: Chea ... 3K 61
Cheam Rd. KT17: Ewe ... 6F 60
SM1: Sut ... 3L 61
SM2: Chea ... 6F 60
Cheam Sports Club ... 4J 61
Cheam Station (Rail) ... 4K 61
CHEAM VILLAGE ... 3K 61
CHEAPSIDE ... 9B 18
Cheapside GU21: Wok ... 1N 73
Cheapside Rd. SL5: Asc ... 2N 33
Cheeseman Cl.
RG40: W'ham ... 1C 30
TW12: Hamp ... 7M 23
Cheesemans Ter. W14 ... 1L 13
(not continuous)
Cheffery Ct. TW15: A'ford ... 7C 22
Chellows La. RH7: Ling ... 1B 146
Chelmsford Cl. SM2: Sut ... 5M 61
W6 ... 2J 13
Chelsea Cl. KT4: W Pk ... 6F 42
TW12: H Hill ... 6C 24
Chelsea FC ... 3N 13
Chelsea Flds. SW19 ... 9B 28
Chelsea Gdns. SM3: Chea ... 1K 61
Chelsea Studios SW6 ... 3N 13
(off Fulham Rd.)
Chelsea Village SW6 ... 3N 13
(off Fulham Rd.)
CHELSHAM ... 4K 85
Chelsham Cl. CR6: Warl ... 5H 85
CHELSHAM COMMON ... 3L 85
Chelsham Comn. Rd.
CR6: Warl ... 4K 85
Chelsham Ct. Rd.
CR6: Warl ... 5N 85
Chelsham Rd. CR2: S Croy ... 4A 64
CR6: Warl ... 5J 85
Cheltenham Av. TW1: Twick ... 1G 25
Cheltenham Cl. KT3: N Mal ... 2B 42
Cheltenham Vs.
TW19: Stan M ... 9H 7
Chelverton Rd. SW15 ... 7J 13
Chelwood Cl. CR5: Coul ... 6G 82
KT17: Eps ... 8E 60
RH10: Craw ... 5D 182
Chelwood Dr. GU47: Sandh ... 6E 48
Chelwood Gdns. TW9: Kew ... 5N 11
Chelwood Gdns. Pas.
TW9: Kew ... 5N 11
Cheney Cl. RG42: Bin ... 7J 15
Cheney Ct. RG45: Crow ... 2H 49
(off Pinewood Av.)
Chenies Cotts. RH5: Oak ... 2A 178
Chenies Ho. W4 ... 3E 12
(off Corney Reach Way)
Cheniston Cl. KT14: W By ... 9J 55
Cheniston Ct. SL5: S'dale ... 6D 34
Chennells Brook Cotts.
RH12: Hors ... 1M 197
(off Giblets La.)
Chennells Way
RH12: Hors ... 3K 197
Chepstow Cl. RH10: Craw ... 3J 183
SW15 ... 8K 13
Chepstow Ri. CR0: Croy ... 9B 46
Chepstow Rd. CR0: Croy ... 9B 46
Chequer Grange
RH18: F Row ... 8G 187
Chequer Mead Theatre & Arts Cen.
... 9B 166
Chequer Rd. RH19: E Grin ... 9B 166
Chequers Cl. KT20: Wal H ... 3F 100
RH6: Horl ... 7E 142
Chequers Ct. RH13: Hors ... 5L 197
Chequers Dr. RH6: Horl ... 7E 142
Chequers La. KT20: Wal H ... 3F 100
Chequers Pl.
RH4: Dork ... 3K 201 (5H 119)
Chequers Yd.
RH4: Dork ... 2K 201 (5H 119)
Chequer Tree Cl.
GU21: Knap ... 3H 73
Cherberry Cl. GU51: Fleet ... 1C 88
Cherbury Cl. RG12: Brac ... 2C 32
Cherimoya Gdns.
KT8: W Mole ... 2B 40
Cherington Way SL5: Asc ... 1J 33
Cheriton Ct. KT12: Wal T ... 7K 39
Cheriton Sq. SW17 ... 3E 28
Cheriton Way
GU17: B'water ... 1J 69
Cherkley Hill KT22: Leat ... 4J 99
Cherrimans Orchard
GU27: Hasl ... 2D 188
Cherry Bank Cotts.
RH5: H Mary ... 6K 137
Cherry Cl. SM4: Mord ... 3K 43
SM5: Cars ... 8D 44
SM7: Ban ... 1J 81
SW2 ... 1L 29
Cherrycot Hill BR6: Farnb ... 1L 67
Cherrycot Ri. BR6: Farnb ... 1L 67
Cherry Cotts. KT20: Wal H ... 2G 100
Cherry Ct. RH13: Hors ... 7K 197
Cherry Cres. TW8: Brent ... 3H 11
Cherrydale Rd.
GU15: Camb ... 1H 71
Cherry Gth. TW8: Brent ... 1K 11
Cherry Grn. Cl. RH1: Red ... 5F 122
Cherry Hill Gdns.
CR0: Wad ... 1K 63
Cherryhill Gro. GU11: Alde ... 3L 109
Cherryhurst GU8: Worm ... 9E 152
Cherry La. RH11: Craw ... 9A 162
Cherry Laurel Wlk.
SW2 ... 1K 29
Cherry Lodge GU12: Alde ... 3N 109
Cherry Orchard
KT21: A'tead ... 5A 80
TW18: Stain ... 6J 21
Cherry Orchard Gdns.
CR0: Croy ... 2E 200 (7A 46)
KT8: W Mole ... 2N 39
Cherry Orchard Rd.
CR0: Croy ... 1E 200 (8A 46)
KT8: W Mole ... 2A 40
Cherry St. GU21: Wok ... 5A 74
Cherry Tree Av. GU2: Guil ... 3J 113
GU27: Hasl ... 1D 188
TW18: Stain ... 7K 21
Cherry Tree Cl.
GU9: Farnh ... 9H 109
GU14: Cove ... 9H 69
GU47: Owls ... 6J 49
RH10: Craw ... 1H 183
Cherry Tree Ct. CR5: Coul ... 5K 83
KT22: Leat ... 7F 78
(off Park Vw. Rd.)
Cherry Tree Dr. RG12: Brac ... 2B 32
SW16 ... 4J 29
Cherry Tree Grn.
CR2: Sande ... 1E 84
Cherry Tree La.
GU7: Goda ... 3G 133
Cherry Tree Rd. GU8: Mil ... 1B 152
GU10: Rowl ... 8D 128
Cherrytrees CR5: Coul ... 8H 83
Cherry Tree Wlk.
BR3: Beck ... 3J 47
BR4: W Wick ... 1B 66
GU10: Rowl ... 8D 128
(not continuous)
RH12: Hors ... 2A 198
Cherry Way KT19: Ewe ... 3C 60
SL3: Hort ... 6E 6
TW17: Shep ... 3E 38
Cherrywood Av.
TW20: Eng G ... 8L 19
Cherrywood Cl.
KT2: K Tham ... 8N 25
Cherrywood Ct. TW11: Tedd ... 6G 24
Cherrywood Dr. SW15 ... 8J 13
Cherrywood La. SM4: Mord ... 3K 43
Cherrywood Rd.
GU14: Farnb ... 7M 69
CHERTSEY ... 6J 37
Chertsey Abbey (Remains of)
... 5J 37
Chertsey Bri. Rd.
KT16: Chert ... 6M 37
Chertsey Cl. CR8: Ken ... 2M 83
Chertsey Ct. SW14 ... 6A 12
Chertsey Cres. CR0: N Add ... 6M 65
Chertsey Dr. SM3: Chea ... 8K 43
Chertsey Ho. KT16: Chert ... 7L 37
Chertsey La. KT19: Eps ... 8N 59
TW18: Stain ... 6G 20
CHERTSEY LOCK ... 6L 37
CHERTSEY MEADS ... 7N 37
Chertsey Meads
KT16: Chert ... 7M 37
Chertsey Mus. ... 5J 37
Chertsey Rd. GU20: Windl ... 3A 52
GU21: Wok ... 4B 74
GU24: Chob ... 6J 53
(Alpha Rd.)
GU24: Chob ... 3A 52
(Windsor Rd.)
KT14: Byf ... 7M 55
KT15: Addl ... 8K 37
TW1: Twick ... 9F 10
Chertsey Rd. TW2: Twick ... 3B 24
TW13: Felt ... 4F 22
TW15: A'ford ... 8E 22
TW16: Sunb ... 8E 22
TW17: Shep ... 6N 37
CHERTSEY SOUTH ... 9G 36
Chertsey Station (Rail) ... 7H 37
Chertsey St.
GU1: Guil ... 5D 202 (4N 113)
SW17 ... 6E 28
Chertsey Wlk. KT16: Chert ... 6J 37
Chervil Cl. TW13: Felt ... 4H 23
Cherwell Cl. SL3: Lang ... 2D 6
Cherwell Ct. KT19: Ewe ... 1B 60
Cherwell Wlk. RH11: Craw ... 4L 181
Cheryls Cl. SW6 ... 4N 13
Cheselden Rd.
GU1: Guil ... 5E 202 (4A 114)
Chesfield Rd. KT2: K Tham ... 8L 25
Chesham Cl. SM2: Chea ... 6K 61
Chesham Cres. SE20 ... 1F 46
Chesham M.
GU1: Guil ... 5F 202 (4A 114)
Chesham Rd. GU1: Guil ... 4B 114
KT1: K Tham ... 1N 41
SE20 ... 1F 46
SW19 ... 6B 28
Cheshire Cl. CR4: Mit ... 2J 45
KT16: Otter ... 3E 54
Cheshire Gdns. KT9: Ches ... 3K 59
Cheshire Ho. KT16: Otter ... 3F 54
(off Cheshire Cl.)
SM4: Mord ... 6N 43
Cheshire Pk. RG42: Warf ... 7C 16
Chesilton Cres.
GU52: C Cro ... 8B 88
Chesilton Rd. SW6 ... 4L 13
Chesney Cres. CR0: N Add ... 4M 65
Chessell Cl. CR7: T Hea ... 3M 45
Chessholme Ct.
TW16: Sunb ... 8F 22
(off Scotts Av.)
Chessholme Rd.
TW15: A'ford ... 7D 22
CHESSINGTON ... 2M 59
Chessington Cl. KT19: Ewe ... 3B 60
Chessington Hall Gdns.
KT9: Ches ... 4K 59
Chessington Hill Pk.
KT9: Ches ... 2N 59
Chessington Ho. KT17: Ewe ... 5E 60
(off Spring St.)
Chessington North Station (Rail)
... 2L 59
Chessington Pde.
KT9: Ches ... 3K 59
Chessington Pk. KT9: Ches ... 1N 59
Chessington Rd. KT17: Ewe ... 5C 60
KT19: Ewe ... 3N 59
Chessington South Station (Rail)
... 4K 59
Chessington Sports Cen. ... 4K 59
Chessington Trade Pk.
KT9: Ches ... 1N 59
Chessington Way
BR4: W Wick ... 8L 47
Chessington World of Adventures
... 6J 59
Chesson Rd. W14 ... 2L 13
Chester Av. TW2: Whitt ... 2N 23
TW10: Rich ... 9M 11
Chesterblade La.
RG12: Brac ... 6B 32
Chester Cl. GU2: Guil ... 1J 113
GU12: Ash ... 2F 110
RH4: Dork ... 3J 119
SM1: Sut ... 8M 43
SW13 ... 6G 13
TW10: Rich ... 9M 11
TW15: A'ford ... 6E 22
Chesterfield Cl. RH19: Fel ... 6F 164
Chesterfield Ct.
KT5: Surb ... 8K 203
Chesterfield Dr.
KT10: H Wood ... 8G 40
Chesterfield M.
TW15: A'ford ... 5N 21
Chesterfield Rd. KT19: Ewe ... 4C 60
TW15: A'ford ... 5N 21
W4 ... 2B 12
Chester Gdns. SM4: Mord ... 5A 44
Chesterman Ct. W4 ... 3D 12
(off Corney Reach Way)
Chester Rd. GU12: Ash ... 1F 110
KT24: Eff ... 6J 97
SW19 ... 7H 27
TW4: Houn ... 6J 9
TW6: Lon A ... 6B 8
Chesters RH6: Horl ... 6C 142
Chesters, The KT3: N Mal ... 9D 26
Chesters Rd. GU15: Camb ... 1F 70
Chesterton Cl.
RH19: E Grin ... 2B 186
SW18 ... 8M 13
Chesterton Ct.
RH13: Hors ... 4N 197
Chesterton Dr. RH1: Mers ... 6J 103
TW19: Stan ... 2A 22
Chesterton Ho. CR0: Croy ... 7D 200
Chesterton Ter.
KT1: K Tham ... 4M 203 (1N 41)
Chester Way GU10: Tong ... 6D 110
Chestnut All. SW6 ... 2L 13
Chestnut Av. BR4: W Wick ... 2A 66
GU2: Guil ... 6M 113
GU9: Farnh ... 3F 128
GU12: Alde ... 5C 110
GU15: Camb ... 9E 50
GU25: V Wat ... 3J 35
GU27: Hasl ... 1G 189
KT8: E Mol ... 2F 40
KT10: Esh ... 6D 40
KT12: Whit V ... 5F 56
KT13: Weybr ... 4D 56
KT19: Ewe ... 1D 60
SW14 ... 6C 12
TN16: Tats, Weste ... 9F 86
TW8: Brent ... 1K 11
TW11: Tedd ... 1F 40
TW12: Hamp ... 8A 24
Chestnut Chase
RG42: Warf ... 8E 16
Chestnut Cl. GU17: B'water ... 2K 69
GU23: Rip ... 3H 95
GU26: G'hott ... 6A 170
GU51: Fleet ... 1D 88
KT15: Addl ... 2M 55
KT20: K'wood ... 1M 101
RH1: Red ... 5F 122
RH19: E Grin ... 9C 166
SM5: Cars ... 7D 44
SW16 ... 5L 29
TN8: Eden ... 1K 147
TW15: A'ford ... 5C 22
TW16: Sunb ... 7G 22
TW20: Eng G ... 7L 19
UB7: Harl, Sip ... 3C 8
Chestnut Copse RH8: Oxt ... 1D 126
Chestnut Ct. CR2: S Croy ... 7B 200
GU12: Alde ... 2B 110
KT22: Leat ... 7F 78
RH1: Red ... 5D 122
RH13: Hors ... 6L 197
SW6 ... 2L 13
TW13: Hanw ... 6L 23
Chestnut Cres.
KT12: Whit V ... 5F 56
(not continuous)
Chestnut Dr. SL4: W'sor ... 7B 4
TW20: Egh ... 7N 19
Chestnut End
GU35: Head ... 5F 168
Chestnut Gdns.
RH12: Hors ... 3J 197
Chestnut Gro. CR2: Sels ... 4E 64
CR4: Mit ... 4H 45
GU22: Wok ... 7A 74
GU51: Fleet ... 3C 88
KT3: N Mal ... 2C 42
SW12 ... 1E 28
TW7: Isle ... 7G 10
TW18: Stain ... 7L 21
Chestnut La. GU24: Chob ... 2F 52
KT13: Weybr ... 2C 56
Chestnut Mnr. Cl.
TW18: Stain ... 6K 21
Chestnut Mead RH1: Red ... 2C 122
Chestnut Pl. KT13: Weybr ... 2C 56
(off Pine Gro.)
KT17: Ewe ... 7F 60
KT21: A'tead ... 6L 79
Chestnut Rd.
GU1: Guil ... 2C 202 (3N 113)
GU14: Farnb ... 9M 69
KT2: K Tham ... 1J 203 (8L 25)
RH6: Horl ... 6F 142
SE27 ... 4M 29
SW20 ... 1J 43
TW2: Twick ... 3E 24
TW15: A'ford ... 5C 22
Chestnuts, The KT12: Wal T ... 8J 39
RH6: Horl ... 6F 142
Chestnut Ter. SM1: Sut ... 1N 61
Chestnut Tree Gro.
GU14: Cove ... 9H 69
Chestnut Vw. GU14: Farnb ... 4A 90
(off Alexandra Rd.)
Chestnut Wlk. KT12: Whit V ... 5F 56
KT14: Byf ... 8N 55
RH11: Craw ... 9A 162
RH19: Felc ... 2M 165
TW17: Shep ... 3F 38
Chestnut Way GU5: Braml ... 6C 134
GU7: Bus ... 9J 133
TW13: Felt ... 4J 23
Cheston Av. CR0: Croy ... 8H 47
Chesworth Cl. RH13: Hors ... 8J 197
Chesworth Cres.
RH13: Hors ... 7J 197
Chesworth Gdns.
RH13: Hors ... 7J 197
Chesworth La. RH13: Hors ... 7J 197
Chetnole RH19: E Grin ... 8N 165
Chetwode Cl.
RG40: W'ham ... 2D 30
Chetwode Dr. KT18: Tat C ... 5J 81
Chetwode Pl. GU12: Alde ... 5A 110
Chetwode Rd. KT20: Tad ... 6H 81
SW17 ... 4D 28
Chetwode Ter. GU11: Alde ... 3K 109
Chetwoode Rd.
RH11: Craw ... 7J 181
Chevening Cl. RH11: Craw ... 8A 182
Chevening Rd. SE19 ... 7N 29
CHEVERELLS ... 9A 86
Chevington Vs. RH1: Blet ... 1B 124
Cheviot Cl. GU14: Cove ... 7K 69
GU15: Camb ... 2G 71
SM2: Sut ... 5B 62
SM7: Ban ... 2N 81
UB3: Harl ... 3E 8
Cheviot Dr. GU51: Fleet ... 1C 88
Cheviot Gdns. SE27 ... 5M 29
Cheviot Rd. GU47: Sandh ... 5E 48
SE27 ... 6L 29
SL3: Lang ... 1C 6
Cheviot Wlk. RH11: Craw ... 3N 181
Chevremont
GU1: Guil ... 5F 202 (4A 114)
Chewter Cl. GU19: Bag ... 4K 51
Chewter La. GU20: Windl ... 1M 51
Cheyham Gdns.
SM2: Chea ... 6J 61
Cheyham Way SM2: Chea ... 6K 61
Cheylesmore Dr.
GU16: Frim ... 3H 71
Cheyne Av. TW2: Whitt ... 2N 23
Cheyne Ct. SM7: Ban ... 2N 81
Cheyne Hill
KT5: Surb ... 8L 203 (3M 41)
Cheynell Wlk. RH11: Craw ... 5L 181
Cheyne Pk. Dr.
BR4: W Wick ... 9M 47
Cheyne Rd. TW15: A'ford ... 8E 22
Cheyne Row GU5: Braml ... 2N 153
Cheyne Wlk. CR0: Croy ... 8D 46
RH6: Horl ... 1D 162
Cheyne Way GU14: Cove ... 7L 69
Chichele Gdns. CR0: Croy ... 1B 64
Chichele Rd. RH8: Oxt ... 6A 106
Chicheley Ct. GU14: Farnb ... 8M 69
Chichester Cl. GU8: Wit ... 5B 152
RH4: Dork ... 3H 119
RH10: Craw ... 7C 182
TW12: Hamp ... 7N 23
Chichester Ct. KT17: Ewe ... 5E 60
TW19: Stan ... 2N 21
Chichester Dr. CR8: Pur ... 8K 63
Chichester Ho. KT19: Eps ... 8N 59
Chichester M. SE27 ... 5L 29
Chichester Rd.
CR0: Croy ... 5F 200 (9B 46)
GU12: Ash ... 1E 110
RH4: Dork ... 2H 119
Chichester Ter.
RH12: Hors ... 6K 197
Chichester Way TW14: Felt ... 1K 23
CHIDDINGFOLD ... 5F 172
Chiddingfold Rd.
GU8: Duns ... 5L 173
Chiddingly Cl. RH10: Craw ... 4E 182
Chiddingstone Cl.
SM2: Sut ... 6M 61
Chiddingstone St.
SW6 ... 5M 13
Chilberton Dr. RH1: Mers ... 8G 103
Chilbolton TW20: Egh ... 6A 20
Chilbrook Rd. KT11: Down ... 5H 77
Chilcombe Ho. SW15 ... 1F 26
(off Fontley Way)
Chilcroft La. GU27: K Grn ... 7F 188
Chilcroft Rd. GU27: Hasl ... 1D 188
Chilcrofts Rd. GU27: K Grn ... 7E 188
Child Cl. RG40: W'ham ... 9C 14
Childebert Rd. SW17 ... 3F 28
Childerley KT1: K Tham ... 2N 41
(off Burritt Rd.)
Childerley St. SW6 ... 4K 13
Childs Hall Cl. KT23: Book ... 3N 97
Childs Hall Dr. KT23: Book ... 3N 97
Childs Hall Rd. KT23: Book ... 3N 97
Chilham Cl. GU16: Frim ... 6D 70
Chillerton Rd. SW17 ... 6E 28
Chillingford Ho. SW17 ... 5A 28
Chillingham Way
GU15: Camb ... 2A 70
Chillingworth Gdns.
TW1: Twick ... 4F 24
Chilmans Dr. KT23: Book ... 3B 98
Chilmark Gdns. KT3: N Mal ... 5F 42
RH1: Mers ... 7J 103
Chilmark Rd. SW16 ... 1H 45
Chilmead RH1: Red ... 2D 122
Chilmead La. RH1: Nut ... 1H 123
Chilsey Grn. Rd.
KT16: Chert ... 5G 37
Chiltern Av. GU14: Cove ... 1J 89
TW2: Whitt ... 2A 24
Chiltern Cl. CR0: Croy ... 9B 46
GU14: Cove ... 1H 89
GU22: Wok ... 9M 73
GU27: Hasl ... 3F 188
GU52: C Cro ... 7C 88
KT4: W Pk ... 7H 43
RH11: Craw ... 3N 181
TW18: Stain ... 6J 21
Chiltern Ct. SL4: W'sor ... 4E 4
(off Fawcett Rd.)
Chiltern Ct. M. SL4: W'sor ... 4E 4
(off Fawcett Rd.)
Chiltern Dr. KT5: Surb ... 5N 41
Chiltern Hurst TN8: Eden ... 1J 147
Chiltern Rd. GU47: Sandh ... 6E 48
SM2: Sut ... 5N 61
Chilterns, The SM2: Sut ... 5N 61
Chiltington Ct. RH12: Hors ... 4K 197
(off Blenheim Rd.)
Chilton Cl. GU6: Alf ... 7H 175
Chilton Ct. KT12: Wal T ... 1H 57

Chilton Farm Pk.—Church Wlk.

Chilton Farm Pk.
GU14: Cove 1H 89
Chilton Rd. TW9: Rich 6N 11
Chiltons Cl. SM7: Ban 2N 81
Chilvers Cl. TW2: Twick 3E 24
CHILWORTH 9E 114
Chilworth Ct. SW19 2J 27
Chilworth Gdns. SM1: Sut 9A 44
Chilworth Hill Cotts.
GU4: Guil 1G 134
Chilworth Manor 8F 114
Chilworth Rd. GU5: Alb 8J 115
Chilworth Station (Rail) 9G 114
China M. SW2 1K 29
Chinchilla Dr. TW4: Houn 5K 9
Chine, The GU10: Wrec 6E 128
RH4: Dork 1L 201 (4H 119)
Chingford Av. GU14: Farnb 9A 70
Chinnock Cl. GU52: Fleet 6A 88
Chinthurst Hill Nature Reserve 3C 134
Chinthurst Hill Tower 3C 134
Chinthurst La. GU4: Chil 1A 134
GU5: Braml, Wone 1A 134
Chinthurst M. CR5: Coul 3E 82
Chinthurst Pk. GU4: Chil 2A 134
Chiphouse Wood Nature Reserve 7A 82
Chippendale Cl.
GU17: Haw 2K 69
Chippendale Rd.
RH11: Craw 8N 181
Chippenham KT1: K Tham 4M 203
CHIPSTEAD 5D 82
Chipstead Av. CR7: T Hea 3M 45
CHIPSTEAD BOTTOM 8B 82
Chipstead Cl. CR5: Coul 3E 82
RH1: Red 4D 122
SM2: Sut 5N 61
Chipstead Ct. GU21: Knap 4H 73
Chipstead La.
CR5: Chip, Coul 2A 102
KT20: K'wood 3L 101
Chipstead Rd. SM7: Ban 4L 81
(not continuous)
Chipstead Station (Rail) 5D 82
Chipstead Sta. Pde.
CR5: Chip 5D 82
Chipstead St. SW6 4M 13
Chipstead Valley Rd.
CR5: Coul 3E 82
Chipstead Way SM7: Ban 3D 82
Chirton Wlk. GU21: Wok 5K 73
Chisbury Cl. RG12: Brac 5C 32
Chisholm Ct. W6 1F 12
Chisholm Rd. CR0: Croy 8B 46
TW10: Rich 9M 11
Chislehurst Rd. TW10: Rich 8L 11
Chislett Gdns. GU47: Sandh 7E 48
CHISWICK 1C 12
Chiswick Bri. W4 5B 12
Chiswick Cl. CR0: Bedd 9K 45
Chiswick Comn. Rd.
W4 1C 12
Chiswick Community Sports Hall 3C 12
Chiswick Ct. W4 1A 12
Chiswick High Rd.
TW8: Brent 1N 11
(not continuous)
Chiswick House 2D 12
Chiswick La. W4 1D 12
Chiswick La. Sth. W4 2E 12
Chiswick Mall W4 2E 12
W6 1F 12
Chiswick Plaza W4 2B 12
Chiswick Quay W4 4B 12
CHISWICK RDBT. 1N 11
Chiswick Sq. W4 2D 12
Chiswick Staithe W4 4B 12
Chiswick Station (Rail) 3B 12
Chiswick Ter. *W4 1B 12*
(off Chiswick Rd.)
Chiswick Village W4 2N 11
Chiswick Wharf W4 2E 12
Chithurst La. RH6: Horn 8B 144
Chittenden Cotts.
GU23: Wis 3N 75
Chitterfield Ga. UB7: Sip 3B 8
CHITTYS COMMON 8J 93
Chittys Wlk. GU3: Guil 8J 93
Chive Ct. GU14: Cove 1H 89
Chivelston SW19 2J 27
Chivenor Gro. KT2: K Tham 6K 25
Chives Pl. RG42: Warf 8B 16
CHOBHAM 7H 53
Chobham Bus. Cen.
GU24: Chob 6N 53
Chobham Cl. KT16: Otter 3D 54
Chobham Common Memorial Cross 8G 34
Chobham Common Nature Reserve 9G 34
Chobham Gdns. SW19 3J 27
Chobham La. GU24: Chob 9J 35
GU25: V Wat 9J 35
Chobham Mus. 7H 53
Chobham Pk. Dr.
GU24: Chob 6K 53
Chobham Rd. GU16: Frim 5C 70
GU21: Knap, Wok 5E 72
GU21: Wok 3A 74
(Brewery Rd., not continuous)
Chobham Rd. GU21: Wok 9M 53
(Horsell Comn. Rd.)
GU21: Wok 4B 74
(The Broadway)
GU24: Chob 6E 34
KT16: Otter 4C 54
SL5: S'dale 6E 34
Choda Ct. RH10: Craw 4D 182
Choir Grn. GU21: Knap 4H 73
Cholmley Rd. KT7: T Dit 5H 41
Cholmley Ter. *KT7: T Dit 6H 41*
(off Portsmouth Rd.)
Cholmley Vs. *KT7: T Dit 5H 41*
(off Portsmouth Rd.)
Cholmondeley Wlk.
TW9: Rich 8J 11
(not continuous)
Chrislaine Cl. TW19: Stan 9M 7
Chrismas Av. GU12: Alde 3A 110
Chrismas Pl. GU12: Alde 3A 110
Christabel Cl. TW7: Isle 6E 10
Christchurch Av.
TW11: Tedd 6G 24
Christchurch Cl.
GU52: C Cro 9A 88
SW19 8B 28
Christchurch Dr.
GU17: B'water 9H 49
Christchurch Flats
TW9: Rich 6L 11
Christchurch Gdns.
KT19: Eps 7A 60
Christchurch Ho. *SW2 2K 29*
(off Christchurch Rd.)
Christ Church Mt.
KT19: Eps 8A 60
(not continuous)
Christchurch Pk. SM2: Sut 4A 62
Christchurch Pl. KT19: Eps 7A 60
Christ Chu. Rd. BR3: Beck 1K 47
KT19: Eps 8L 59
SW14 8A 12
Christchurch Rd. CR8: Pur 7M 63
GU25: V Wat 2K 35
KT5: Surb 5M 41
SW2 2K 29
SW19 8B 28
Christchurch Way
GU21: Wok 4B 74
Christian Flds. SW16 8L 29
Christian Sq. SL4: W'sor 4F 4
Christie Cl. GU1: Guil 9N 93
GU18: Ligh 6N 51
KT23: Book 3N 97
Christie Dr. CR0: Croy 4D 46
Christies RH19: E Grin 1N 185
Christie Wlk. CR3: Cate 9A 84
GU46: Yate 2B 68
Christine Cl. GU12: Ash 3D 110
Christmas Hill GU4: Chil 1B 134
(not continuous)
Christmas Pie Av.
GU3: Flex 3M 111
Christmas Tree Farm 8J 67
Christopher Ct. KT20: Tad 1H 101
TW15: A'ford 6N 21
Christopher Rd.
RH19: E Grin 9A 166
Christ's College Ski Cen. 9L 93
Christ's Hospital Rd.
RH13: Hors 9D 196
RH13: Itch 9B 196
(not continuous)
Christs Hospital Station (Rail) 9D 196
Christy Ind. Est.
GU12: Alde 2B 110
Christy Rd. TN16: B Hil 2E 86
Chrystie La. KT23: Book 4B 98
Chuchlands Way KT4: W Pk 8J 43
Chucks La. KT20: Wal H 2G 101
Chudleigh Ct. GU14: Farnb 1N 89
Chudleigh Gdns. SM1: Sut 9A 44
Chudleigh Rd. TW2: Twick 9E 10
(not continuous)
Chuff Cnr. RG42: Warf 7B 16
Chumleigh Wlk.
KT5: Surb 8L 203 (3M 41)
Church All. CR0: Croy 7L 45
Church App. TN14: Cud 2L 87
TW19: Stan 9M 7
TW20: Thor 2E 36
Church Av. BR3: Beck 1K 47
GU14: Farnb 1A 90
SW14 6C 12
Church Bungs. RH14: Plais 5A 192
Church Circ. GU14: Farnb 3A 90
Church Cl. GU4: Chil 8N 113
GU8: Mil 1C 152
GU21: Wok 3N 73
GU24: B'wood 8C 72
GU27: G'wood 7K 171
KT15: Addl 1K 55
KT17: Eps 7M 201 (9D 60)
KT20: Lwr K 5L 101
KT22: Fetc 2D 98
SL4: Eton 2G 4
TW3: Houn 5M 9
TW18: Lale 2L 37
Church Cotts. GU9: B Lea 6M 109
KT15: Addl 9N 37
RH11: Ifi 1L 181
(off Ifield St.)
Church Ct. *GU51: Fleet 4A 88*
(Branksomewood Rd.)
GU51: Fleet 4A 88
(Church Rd.)
RH2: Reig 3N 121
RH4: Dork 1K 201
TW9: Rich 8K 11
Churchcroft Cl. SW12 1E 28
CHURCH CROOKHAM 8B 88
Church Dr. BR4: W Wick 1A 66
CHURCH END 8A 76
Church Est. Almshouses
TW9: Rich 7M 11
(off Sheen Rd.)
Church Farm La.
SM3: Chea 3K 61
Churchfield TN8: Eden 2M 147
Churchfield Ct. RH2: Reig 3N 121
Churchfield Ho. *KT11: Cob 1J 77*
(off Lushington Dr.)
Churchfield Mans.
SW6 5L 13
(off New Kings Rd.)
Churchfield Pl. KT13: Weybr 1B 56
TW17: Shep 6C 38
Churchfield Rd.
KT12: Wal T 7H 39
KT13: Weybr 1B 56
RH2: Reig 2L 121
Church Flds. GU35: Head 4C 168
Churchfields GU4: B'ham 7C 94
GU8: Wit 6B 152
GU21: Wok 3A 74
KT8: W Mole 2A 40
Churchfields Av.
KT13: Weybr 1C 56
TW13: Hanw 4N 23
Churchfields Rd. BR3: Beck 1G 47
Church Gdns. KT22: Leat 7H 79
RH4: Dork 1K 201 (4H 119)
Church Ga. SW6 6K 13
Church Grn. GU8: Duns 3N 173
GU27: Hasl 1G 189
KT12: Hers 3K 57
KT20: Wal H 2F 100
Church Gro. GU51: Fleet 4A 88
KT1: H Wic 9J 25
Church Hill CR3: Cate 2C 104
CR8: Pur 6J 63
GU5: Sha G 7G 135
GU5: Shere 8B 116
GU12: Alde 4N 109
GU15: Camb 1C 70
GU21: Wok 3N 73
GU22: Pyr 4H 75
GU27: Hasl 1G 189
RG42: Bin 4H 15
RH1: Mers 4F 102
RH1: Nut 2K 123
RH7: Dorm 2C 166
SM5: Cars 2D 62
SW19 6L 27
TN14: B Hil 2L 87
TN16: Tats 9F 86
Church Hill Rd. KT6: Surb 4L 41
SM3: Chea 9J 43
Churchill Av. GU12: Alde 4A 110
RH12: Hors 5H 197
Churchill Bus. Pk.
TN16: Weste 4N 107
Churchill Cl. CR6: Warl 4F 84
GU14: Farnb 6N 69
KT22: Fetc 1E 98
TW14: Felt 2G 23
Churchill Ct. BR6: Farnb 2L 67
RH10: Craw 9E 162
TN16: Weste 4M 107
TW18: Stain 7K 21
Churchill Cres.
GU14: Farnb 6N 69
GU35: Head 5E 168
GU46: Yate 1C 68
Churchill Dr. KT13: Weybr 1D 56
Churchill Ho. *SM7: Ban 1L 81*
(off Dunnymans Rd.)
Churchill Rd. CR2: S Croy 5N 63
GU1: Guil 4F 202 (4A 114)
KT19: Eps 7N 59
RH6: Smal 8M 143
SL3: Lang 1B 6
SL5: Asc 1K 33
Churchill Way TN16: B Hil 2F 86
TW16: Sunb 6H 23
CHURCH LAMMAS 5G 20
Churchlands GU11: Alde 4N 109
Church La. CR3: Cate 2L 103
CR5: Coul 9E 82
CR6: Warl 4G 84
(Church Rd.)
CR6: Warl 3L 85
(Ledgers Rd.)
GU3: Worp 5H 93
GU5: Alb 8K 115
GU5: Shere 8B 116
GU6: Cranl 7N 155
GU8: Brook, Wit 1N 171
GU8: Hamb 8G 153
GU10: Ews 3C 108
GU10: Rowl 8D 128
GU10: Wrec 4E 128
GU12: Ash 2F 110
GU14: Cove 1K 89
GU23: Send 4D 94
Church La. GU24: Bis 2D 72
GU24: Pirb 9A 72
GU26: G'hott 6A 170
GU27: Hasl 1G 189
GU35: Head 3C 168
KT7: T Dit 5F 40
KT9: Ches 3M 59
KT13: Weybr 1B 56
KT18: Head 2B 100
KT18: Tad 4J 81
RG42: Bin 4J 15
RG42: Warf 4B 16
RH1: Blet 2A 124
RH5: Newd 1A 160
RH5: Oak 9N 157
RH6: Burs 3K 163
RH6: Horl 4J 163
RH8: Oxt 8N 105
RH9: Gods 1G 124
RH10: Cop 8L 163
RH10: Craw 2D 182
RH12: Bro H 5D 196
RH13: P Pla 9F 198
RH19: E Grin 9B 166
SL4: W'sor 4G 5
SL5: S'dale 4E 34
SL5: S'hill 3A 34
SM6: Bedd 9H 45
(not continuous)
SW17 6D 28
SW19 9L 27
TW1: Twick 2G 25
TW10: Ham 2L 25
TW11: Tedd 6F 24
Church La. Av. CR5: Coul 9F 82
Church La. Dr. CR5: Coul 9F 82
Church La. E. GU11: Alde 3M 109
Church La. W. GU11: Alde 3L 109
Church Mdw. KT6: Surb 8J 41
Church M. GU46: Yate 8C 48
KT15: Addl 1L 55
Churchmore Rd.
SW16 9G 29
Church Paddock Ct.
SM6: Bedd 9H 45
Church Pde. TW15: A'ford 5A 22
Church Pk. RH11: L Hea 5C 162
Church Pas. GU9: Farnh 1G 129
KT6: Surb 4L 41
TW1: Twick 2H 25
Church Path
CR0: Croy 2B 200 (8N 45)
CR4: Mit 2C 44
(not continuous)
CR5: Coul 5L 83
GU12: A Va 9E 90
GU12: Ash 1F 110
GU14: Cove 1K 89
GU14: Farnb 5A 90
(Queen's Rd.)
GU14: Farnb 1A 90
(Rectory Rd.)
GU21: Wok 4B 74
KT11: Cob 1J 77
RH1: Mers 5F 102
RH12: Rusp 4B 180
SL5: Asc, S'hill 2B 34
SW14 6C 12
(not continuous)
SW19 1L 43
(not continuous)
Church Pl. CR4: Mit 2C 44
Church Ri. KT9: Ches 3M 59
Church Rd. BR2: Brom 2N 47
BR2: Kes 4F 66
BR6: Farnb 2L 67
CR0: Croy 3A 200 (9N 45)
(not continuous)
CR3: Cate 1C 104
CR3: Whyte 5C 84
CR3: Wold 9G 85
CR4: Mit 1B 44
CR6: Warl 4G 84
CR8: Ken 2A 84
CR8: Pur 6J 63
GU1: Guil 4C 202 (4N 113)
GU8: Duns 4N 173
GU8: Hasc 7A 154
GU8: Mil 2C 152
GU11: Alde 5A 110
GU16: Frim 5B 70
GU19: Bag 4H 51
GU20: Windl 3M 51
GU21: Wok 2A 74
(Beech Gdns.)
GU21: Wok 6K 73
(St John's Hill Rd.)
GU24: W End 8C 52
GU27: Hasl 1G 188
(Derby Rd.)
GU27: Hasl 2D 188
(Liphook Rd.)
GU47: Owls 6K 49
GU47: Sandh 6E 48
GU51: Fleet 3A 88
KT1: K Tham 3L 203 (1M 41)
KT4: W Pk 7D 42
KT6: Surb 7J 41
KT8: E Mol 3D 40
KT10: Clay 3F 58
KT14: Byf 1N 75
KT15: Addl 2J 55
KT17: Eps 5M 201 (8D 60)
Church Rd. KT19: Ewe 4C 60
KT21: A'tead 5K 79
KT22: Leat 9H 79
KT23: Book 1N 97
RG12: Brac 1A 32
RH1: Red 5C 122
RH2: Reig 5M 121
RH6: Burs, Smal, S Bri 3L 163
RH6: Horl 9D 142
(not continuous)
RH6: Horn 5C 144
RH7: Ling 7N 145
RH10: Cop 7M 163
RH10: T Hil 6C 184
RH10: Wor 3J 183
RH11: L Hea 5C 162
RH12: Bro H 5D 196
RH12: Hors 3A 198
SL4: O Win 8L 5
SL4: Wink 4G 16
SL5: Asc 3L 33
(Lyndhurst Rd.)
SL5: Asc 9F 16
(Priory Rd.)
SL5: S'dale 5D 34
SM3: Chea 3K 61
SM6: Bedd 9H 45
SW13 5E 12
SW19 6K 27
(High St. Wimbledon)
SW19 9B 28
(Western Rd.)
TN16: B Hil 4F 86
TW5: C'ford 1J 9
TW5: Hest 3A 10
TW7: Isle 4D 10
TW9: Rich 7L 11
TW10: Ham 5K 25
TW10: Rich 8L 11
TW11: Tedd 5E 24
TW13: Hanw 6L 23
TW15: A'ford 4A 22
TW17: Shep 6C 38
TW20: Egh 6B 20
Church Rd. E. GU14: Farnb 4B 90
RG45: Crow 2G 49
Church Rd. Ind. Est.
RH11: L Hea 5D 162
Church Rd. W. GU14: Farnb 4A 90
RG45: Crow 3G 48
Church Row *SW6 3N 13*
(off Park Rd.)
Church Side KT18: Eps 9A 60
Churchside Cl. TN16: B Hil 4E 86
Church Sq. TW17: Shep 6C 38
Church St.
CR0: Croy 4A 200 (9M 45)
GU7: Goda 7G 132
GU11: Alde 2L 109
GU22: Wok 8E 74
KT1: K Tham 3H 203 (1K 41)
KT10: Esh 1B 58
KT11: Cob 2J 77
KT12: Wal T 7H 39
KT13: Weybr 1B 56
KT17: Eps 6L 201 (9D 60)
KT17: Ewe 5F 60
KT22: Leat 9H 79
(not continuous)
KT24: Eff 5L 97
RG45: Crow 2G 48
RH2: Reig 3M 121
RH3: Betch 4D 120
RH4: Dork 2J 201 (5G 119)
RH11: Craw 3A 182
RH12: Rudg 1D 194
RH12: Warn 1F 196
SL4: W'sor 4G 5
SM1: Sut 2N 61
TN8: Eden 2L 147
TW1: Twick 2G 25
TW7: Isle 6H 11
TW12: Hamp 9C 24
TW16: Sunb 2J 39
TW18: Stain 5F 20
W4 2E 12
Church St. E. GU21: Wok 4B 74
Church Street Stop (CT) 3B 200 (8N 45)
Church St. W. GU21: Wok 4A 74
Church Stretton Rd.
TW3: Houn 8C 10
Church Ter. RH5: Holm 5J 139
SL4: W'sor 5B 4
TW10: Rich 8K 11
CHURCH TOWN 1G 124
Church Vw. GU12: Ash 2E 110
(not continuous)
GU46: Yate 8C 48
TW10: Rich 8L 11
Church Vw. Cl. RH6: Horl 9D 142
Churchview Rd. TW2: Twick 2D 24
Church Villa TW16: Sunb 2J 39
Church Wlk. CR3: Cate 2D 104
GU7: Goda 5J 133
(not continuous)
KT7: T Dit 5F 40
KT12: Wal T 7H 39
(not continuous)
KT13: Weybr 9B 38
KT16: Chert 5J 37
KT22: Leat 9H 79

Church Wlk. RH1: Blet ... 2A 124
RH2: Reig ... 3N 121
(not continuous)
RH6: Horl ... 9D 142
RH10: Craw ... 3B 182
RH12: Col ... 9G 180
SW13 ... 4F 12
SW15 ... 8G 13
SW16 ... 1G 45
SW20 ... 2H 43
TW8: Brent ... 2J 11
(not continuous)
TW9: Rich ... 8K 11
Churchward Ho. W14 ... 1L 13
(off Ivatt Pl.)
Church Way CR2: Sande ... 6C 64
RH8: Oxt ... 1B 126
Churston Cl. SW2 ... 2L 29
Churston Dr. SM4: Mord ... 4J 43
CHURT ... 9L 149
Churt Rd. GU10: Churt ... 9L 149
GU26: Hind ... 9L 149
GU35: H Dwn ... 3F 168
Churt Wynde GU26: Hind ... 2B 170
Chuter Ede Ho. SW6 ... 2L 13
(off North End Rd.)
Chuters Cl. KT14: Byf ... 8N 55
Chuters Gro. KT17: Eps ... 8E 60
Cinder Path GU22: Wok ... 6M 73
Cinema, The ... 7A 106
Cineworld Cinema
Crawley ... 2B 182
Feltham ... 3J 23
Hammersmith ... 1G 12
Wandsworth ... 8N 13
Cinnamon Cl. CR0: Croy ... 6J 45
SL4: W'sor ... 4C 4
Cinnamon Gdns. GU2: Guil ... 7K 93
Circle, The GU7: Goda ... 5J 133
Circle Gdns. KT14: Byf ... 9A 56
SW19 ... 1M 43
Circle Hill Rd. RG45: Crow ... 2H 49
Circle Rd. KT12: Whit V ... 5F 56
Circuit Cen. KT13: Weybr ... 7N 55
Circus, The KT22: Leat ... 7H 79
(off Kingston Rd.)
Cirrus Cl. SM6: W'ton ... 4J 63
Cissbury Cl. RH12: Hors ... 2N 197
Cissbury Hill RH11: Craw ... 5A 182
City Bus. Cen. RH13: Hors ... 7K 197
City Bus. Cen., The
RH11: Craw ... 8B 162
City Limits
Croydon ... 3L 63
(off Purley Way)
City Pl. RH6: Craw ... 5F 162
City Wharf Ho. KT7: T Dit ... 5H 41
Civic Cen. ... 4A 74
Clacket La. TN16: Weste ... 2G 107
CLACKET LANE SERVICE AREA
... 3G 106
Clacy Grn. RG42: Brac ... 8M 15
Claireville Ct. RH2: Reig ... 3B 122
Clairvale Rd. TW5: Hest ... 4L 9
Clairview Rd. SW16 ... 6F 28
Clammer Hill
GU27: G'wood ... 8K 171
Clammer Hill Rd.
GU27: G'wood ... 9K 171
Clancarty Rd. SW6 ... 5M 13
Clandon Av. TW20: Egh ... 8E 20
Clandon Cl. KT17: Ewe ... 3E 60
Clandon Ct. GU14: Farnb ... 2B 90
Clandon Ho. GU1: Guil ... 5C 114
Clandon M. RH4: Dork ... 8H 119
CLANDON PARK ... 1J 115
Clandon Pk. ... 1J 115
Clandon Pk. House ... 1J 115
Clandon Rd.
GU1: Guil ... 4F 202 (4A 114)
GU4: W Cla ... 3H 95
GU23: Send ... 3H 95
Clandon Station (Rail) ... 7K 95
Clandon Ter. SW20 ... 1J 43
Clanfield Ride GU17: B'water ... 1J 69
Clapgate La. RH13: Slin ... 3K 195
CLAPHAM PARK ... 1H 29
Clapham Pk. Est. SW4 ... 1H 29
Clappers Ga. RH10: Craw ... 2B 182
Clappers La. GU24: Chob ... 7E 54
Clappers Mdw. GU6: Alf ... 6J 175
Clappers Orchard GU6: Alf ... 6H 175
Clare Av. RG40: W'ham ... 1B 30
Clare Cl. KT14: W By ... 9J 55
RH10: Craw ... 9G 162
Clare Cotts. RH1: Blet ... 2M 123
Clare Ct. CR3: Wold ... 1K 105
GU51: Fleet ... 4B 88
Clare Cres. KT22: Leat ... 5G 79
Claredale GU22: Wok ... 6A 74
Clarefield Ct. SL5: S'dale ... 6D 34
Clare Gdns. TW20: Egh ... 6C 20
Clare Hill KT10: Esh ... 2B 58
Clare Lawn Av. SW14 ... 8B 12
Clare Mead GU10: Rowl ... 8E 128
Clare M. SW6 ... 3N 13
Claremont TW17: Shep ... 5C 38
(off Laleham Rd.)
Claremont Av. GU15: Camb ... 1D 70
GU22: Wok ... 6A 74
KT3: N Mal ... 4F 42
KT10: Esh ... 3N 57
KT12: Hers ... 1L 57
Claremont Av. TW16: Sunb ... 9J 23
Claremont Cl. BR6: Farnb ... 1J 67
CR2: Sande ... 2E 84
KT12: Hers ... 2K 57
SW2 ... 2J 29
Claremont Ct.
RH4: Dork ... 4K 201 (6H 119)
Claremont Dr. GU22: Wok ... 6A 74
KT10: Esh ... 5A 58
TW17: Shep ... 5C 38
Claremont End KT10: Esh ... 3B 58
Claremont Gdns.
KT6: Surb ... 8J 203 (4L 41)
Claremont Gro. W4 ... 3D 12
Claremont Ho. SM2: Sut ... 4N 61
Claremont Landscape Gdns.
... 4N 57
Claremont La. KT10: Esh ... 2B 58
CLAREMONT PARK ... 4A 58
Claremont Pk. Rd.
KT10: Esh ... 3B 58
Claremont Pl. GU17: Haw ... 3L 69
KT10: Clay ... 3F 58
Claremont Rd. CR0: Croy ... 7D 46
KT6: Surb ... 8J 203 (4L 41)
KT10: Clay ... 4E 58
KT14: W By ... 8J 55
RH1: Red ... 9E 102
SL4: W'sor ... 5F 4
TW1: Twick ... 1H 25
TW11: Tedd ... 6F 24
TW18: Stain ... 6F 20
Claremont Ter. KT7: T Dit ... 6H 41
Claremount Cl. KT18: Tat C ... 4H 81
Claremount Gdns.
KT18: Tat C ... 4H 81
Clarence Av. KT3: N Mal ... 1B 42
SW4 ... 1H 29
Clarence Cl. GU12: Alde ... 2A 110
KT12: Hers ... 1J 57
Clarence Ct. GU51: Fleet ... 4B 88
RH6: Horl ... 7H 143
SL4: W'sor ... 4E 4
TW20: Egh ... 6B 20
(off Clarence St.)
W6 ... 1G 13
(off Cambridge Gro.)
Clarence Cres. SL4: W'sor ... 4F 4
SW4 ... 1H 29
Clarence Dr. GU15: Camb ... 8F 50
RH19: E Grin ... 2B 186
TW20: Eng G ... 5M 19
Clarence Ho. KT12: Hers ... 2J 57
(off Queens Rd.)
Clarence La. SW15 ... 9D 12
Clarence M. SW12 ... 1F 28
Clarence Rd. CR0: Croy ... 6A 46
GU51: Fleet ... 5A 88
KT12: Hers ... 1J 57
RH1: Red ... 6B 122
RH13: Hors ... 7K 197
SL4: W'sor ... 5D 4
SM1: Sut ... 2N 61
SM6: W'ton ... 2F 62
SW19 ... 7N 27
TN16: B Hil ... 5H 87
TW9: Kew ... 4M 11
TW11: Tedd ... 7F 24
W4 ... 1N 11
Clarence St.
KT1: K Tham ... 3H 203 (1K 41)
(not continuous)
TW9: Rich ... 7L 11
TW18: Stain ... 5G 21
TW20: Egh ... 7B 20
Clarence Ter. TW3: Houn ... 7B 10
Clarence Wlk. RH1: Red ... 6B 122
Clarence Way RH6: Horl ... 7H 143
Clarendon Ct. GU17: Haw ... 3J 69
GU51: Fleet ... 4A 88
SL4: W'sor ... 4E 4
TW5: C'ford ... 4H 9
TW9: Kew ... 4M 11
Clarendon Cres.
TW2: Twick ... 4D 24
Clarendon Dr. SW15 ... 7H 13
Clarendon Ga. KT16: Otter ... 3F 54
Clarendon Gro. CR4: Mit ... 2D 44
Clarendon M. KT21: A'tead ... 6M 79
(off Parker's La.)
Clarendon Rd.
CR0: Croy ... 2A 200 (8M 45)
RH1: Red ... 2D 122
SM6: W'ton ... 3G 62
SW19 ... 8C 28
TW15: A'ford ... 5A 22
Clare Pl. SW15 ... 1E 26
Clare Rd. TW4: Houn ... 6N 9
TW19: Stan ... 2M 21
Clares, The CR3: Cate ... 2D 104
Claret Gdns. SE25 ... 2B 46
Clareville Rd. CR3: Cate ... 2D 104
Clare Wood KT22: Leat ... 5H 79
Clarewood Dr. GU15: Camb ... 9C 50
Clarice Way SM6: W'ton ... 5J 63
Claridge Ct. SW6 ... 5L 13
Claridge Gdns. RH7: Dorm ... 9C 146
Claridges Mead RH7: Dorm ... 9C 146
Clarke Cl. CR0: Croy ... 5N 45
Clarke Cres. GU15: Camb ... 8K 49
Clarkes Av. KT4: W Pk ... 7J 43
Clark Ho. SW10 ... 3N 13
(off Coleridge Gdns.)
Clark Pl. GU6: Cranl ... 8H 155
Clark Rd. RH11: Craw ... 8M 181
CLARK'S GREEN ... 6J 159
Clarks Grn. Rd.
RH5: Cap, Newd, Rusp
... 8N 159
Clark's Grn. Rdbt.
RH5: Cap ... 6J 159
Clarks Hill GU10: Dip ... 1B 128
Clarks La. RH8: Warl ... 1C 106
TN16: Tats ... 1F 106
Clark Way TW5: Hest ... 3L 9
Claudia Pl. SW19 ... 2K 27
Claverdale Rd. SW2 ... 1K 29
Claverdon RG12: Brac ... 6M 31
Claver Dr. SL5: S'hill ... 3A 34
Clavering Av. SW13 ... 2G 13
Clavering Cl. TW1: Twick ... 5G 24
Claverton KT21: A'tead ... 4L 79
Claxton Gro. W6 ... 1J 13
Clay Av. CR4: Mit ... 1F 44
Claybrook Rd. W6 ... 2J 13
Claycart Rd. GU11: Alde ... 9J 89
(not continuous)
Clay Cl. KT15: Addl ... 2K 55
(off Monks Cres.)
Clay Cnr. KT16: Chert ... 7K 37
Claydon Ct. TW18: Stain ... 5J 21
(off Kingston Rd.)
Claydon Dr. CR0: Bedd ... 1J 63
Claydon Gdns. GU17: Haw ... 5M 69
Claydon Rd. GU21: Wok ... 3K 73
Clayford RH7: Dorm ... 9C 146
CLAYGATE ... 3F 58
Claygate Cres. CR0: N Add ... 3M 65
Claygate La. KT7: T Dit ... 7G 40
KT10: Clay, H Wood ... 8G 40
Claygate Lodge Cl.
KT10: Clay ... 4E 58
Claygate Rd. RH4: Dork ... 7H 119
Claygate Station (Rail) ... 3E 58
Clayhall Ho. RH2: Reig ... 2M 121
(off Somers Cl.)
Clay Hall La. RH10: Cop ... 6N 163
Clayhall La. RH2: Reig ... 7J 121
SL4: O Win ... 8J 5
(not continuous)
Clayhanger GU4: Guil ... 1E 114
Clayhill
KT5: Surb ... 8M 203 (4N 41)
Clayhill Cl. RG12: Brac ... 2D 32
RH2: Leigh ... 1F 140
Clayhill Rd. RH2: Leigh ... 3D 140
Clay La. GU4: B'ham, J Wel ... 6N 93
KT18: Head ... 2A 100
RG40: W'ham ... 2E 30
RH1: Sth N ... 4G 123
RH7: Newc ... 9G 144
TW19: Stan ... 1A 22
Claymore Cl. SM4: Mord ... 6M 43
Claypole Dr. TW5: Hest ... 4M 9
Clayponds Av. TW8 ... 1L 11
Clayponds Gdns. W5 ... 1K 11
(not continuous)
Clayponds La. TW8: Brent ... 1L 11
(not continuous)
Clays Cl. RH19: E Grin ... 1A 186
Clayton Cres. TW8: Brent ... 1K 11
Clayton Dr. GU2: Guil ... 9J 93
Clayton Gro. RG12: Brac ... 9C 16
Clayton Hill RH11: Craw ... 5A 182
Clayton Ho. KT7: T Dit ... 7H 41
SW13 ... 3H 13
(off Trinity Church Rd.)
Clayton Mead RH9: Gods ... 8E 104
Clayton Rd. GU14: Cove ... 5L 69
KT9: Ches ... 1J 59
KT17: Eps ... 6L 201 (8D 60)
TW7: Isle ... 6E 10
Cleardene
RH4: Dork ... 3L 201 (5H 119)
Cleardown GU22: Wok ... 5D 74
Clears, The RH2: Reig ... 1K 121
Clears Cotts. RH2: Reig ... 1K 121
Clearsprings GU18: Ligh ... 6L 51
Clearwater Pl. KT6: Surb ... 5J 41
Clearway Ct. CR3: Cate ... 9D 84
Cleave Av. BR6: Chels ... 3N 67
UB3: Harl ... 1F 8
Cleaveland Rd. KT6: Surb ... 4K 41
Cleave Prior CR5: Chip ... 6C 82
Cleaverholme Cl.
SE25 ... 5E 46
Cleaves Almshouses
KT2: K Tham ... 3K 203
Cleeve, The GU1: Guil ... 3C 114
Cleeve Ct. TW14: Bedf ... 2F 22
Cleeve Rd. KT22: Leat ... 7F 78
Cleeves Ct. RH1: Red ... 2E 122
(off St Anne's Mt.)
Cleeve Way SM1: Sut ... 7N 43
SW15 ... 1E 26
Clem Attlee Ct. SW6 ... 2L 13
Clem Attlee Pde. SW6 ... 2L 13
(off North End Rd.)
Clement Cl. CR8: Pur ... 3M 83
Clement Gdns. UB3: Harl ... 1F 8
Clement Rd. BR3: Beck ... 1G 47
SW19 ... 6K 27
Clements Ct. TW4: Houn ... 7L 9
Clements Ho. KT22: Leat ... 6G 78
Clements Mead KT22: Leat ... 6G 79
Clements Pl. TW8: Brent ... 1K 11
Clements Rd. KT12: Wal T ... 8J 39
Clensham Ct. SM1: Sut ... 8M 43
Clensham La. SM1: Sut ... 8M 43
Cleopatra Pl. RG42: Warf ... 8C 16
Clerics Wlk. TW17: Shep ... 6E 38
Clerks Cft. RH1: Blet ... 2A 124
Clevedon KT13: Weybr ... 2E 56
Clevedon Ct.
CR2: S Croy ... 8F 200 (2B 64)
GU14: Farnb ... 2B 90
GU16: Frim ... 6E 70
Clevedon Gdns. TW5: C'ford ... 4J 9
Clevedon Ho. SM1: Sut ... 1A 62
Clevedon Rd. KT1: K Tham ... 1N 41
TW1: Twick ... 9K 11
(not continuous)
Cleve Ho. RG12: Brac ... 3C 32
Cleveland Av. SW20 ... 1L 43
TW12: Hamp ... 8N 23
W4 ... 1E 12
Cleveland Cl. KT12: Wal T ... 9J 39
Cleveland Dr. TW18: Stain ... 1K 37
Cleveland Gdns. KT4: W Pk ... 8D 42
SW13 ... 5E 12
Cleveland Pk. TW19: Stan ... 9N 7
Cleveland Ri. SM4: Mord ... 6J 43
Cleveland Rd. KT3: N Mal ... 3D 42
KT4: W Pk ... 8D 42
SW13 ... 5E 12
TW7: Isle ... 7G 10
Cleve Pl. KT13: Weybr ... 2E 56
Cleves Av. KT17: Ewe ... 5G 61
Cleves Cl. KT11: Cob ... 1J 77
Cleves Ct.
KT17: Eps ... 5M 201 (8E 60)
SL4: W'sor ... 6C 4
Cleves Cres. CR0: N Add ... 7M 65
Cleves Rd. TW10: Ham ... 4J 25
Cleves Way TW12: Hamp ... 8N 23
TW16: Sunb ... 7G 22
Cleves Wood KT13: Weybr ... 1F 56
Clewborough Dr.
GU15: Camb ... 9F 50
Clewer Av. SL4: W'sor ... 5D 4
Clewer Ct. Rd. SL4: W'sor ... 3E 4
Clewer Flds. SL4: W'sor ... 4F 4
CLEWER GREEN ... 5C 4
CLEWER HILL ... 6B 4
Clewer Hill Rd. SL4: W'sor ... 5B 4
CLEWER NEW TOWN ... 5E 4
Clewer New Town
SL4: W'sor ... 5D 4
Clewer Pk. SL4: W'sor ... 3D 4
CLEWER ST ANDREW ... 3D 4
CLEWER ST STEPHEN ... 3E 4
CLEWER VILLAGE ... 4D 4
CLEWER WITHIN ... 4F 4
Clew's La. GU24: Bis ... 3D 72
Clifden Rd. TW1: Twick ... 2F 24
TW8: Brent ... 2K 11
Cliff End CR8: Pur ... 8M 63
Cliffe Ri. GU7: Goda ... 8F 132
Cliffe Rd.
CR2: S Croy ... 8D 200 (2A 64)
GU7: Goda ... 9E 132
Cliffe Wlk. SM1: Sut ... 2A 62
(off Greyhound Rd.)
Clifford Av. SM6: W'ton ... 1G 62
SW14 ... 6A 12
(not continuous)
Clifford Gro. TW15: A'ford ... 5B 22
Clifford Haigh Ho.
SW6 ... 3J 13
Clifford Ho. W14 ... 1L 13
(off Edith Vs.)
Clifford Mnr. Rd.
GU4: Guil ... 7A 114
Clifford Rd. SE25 ... 3D 46
TW4: Houn ... 6L 9
TW10: Ham ... 3K 25
Clifton Av. SM2: Sut ... 7N 61
TW13: Felt ... 4K 23
Clifton Cl. BR6: Farnb ... 2L 67
CR3: Cate ... 1A 104
GU10: Wrec ... 7F 128
KT15: Addl ... 8K 37
RH6: Horl ... 8H 143
Clifton Ct. KT5: Surb ... 6M 41
TW19: Stan ... 9N 7
Clifton Gdns. GU16: Frim G ... 8D 70
W4 ... 1C 12
(not continuous)
Clifton Lodge SL4: E Wic ... 1D 4
Clifton M. SE25 ... 3B 46
Clifton Pde. TW13: Felt ... 4K 23
Clifton Pk. Av. SW20 ... 1H 43
Clifton Pl. SM7: Ban ... 2M 81
Clifton Ri. SL4: W'sor ... 4A 4
Clifton Rd. CR5: Coul ... 2F 82
KT2: K Tham ... 1M 203 (8M 25)
RG41: W'ham ... 1A 30
RH10: Craw ... 4G 183
SE25 ... 3B 46
SM6: W'ton ... 2F 62
SW19 ... 7J 27
TW7: Isle ... 5E 10
TW11: Tedd ... 5E 24
Clifton's La. RH2: Reig ... 1J 121
Clifton Ter. RH4: Dork ... 6H 119
(off Cliftonville)
Cliftonville RH4: Dork ... 6H 119
Clifton Wlk. W6 ... 1G 13
(off King St.)
Clifton Way GU21: Wok ... 4J 73
TW6: Lon A ... 6B 8
Climping Rd. RH11: Craw ... 1N 181
Cline Rd. GU1: Guil ... 5B 114
Clinton Av. KT8: E Mol ... 3C 40
Clinton Cl. GU21: Knap ... 5G 73
KT13: Weybr ... 8C 38
Clinton Hill RH7: Dorm ... 1C 166
Clinton Ho. KT6: Surb ... 6K 41
(off Lovelace Gdns)
Clinton Rd. KT22: Leat ... 1J 99
Clintons Grn. RG42: Brac ... 9M 15
Clippesby Cl. KT9: Ches ... 3M 59
Clipstone Rd. TW3: Houn ... 6A 10
Clitheroe Rd. GU17: Min ... 5E 68
Clitherow Ct. TW8: Brent ... 1J 11
Clitherow Gdns.
RH10: Craw ... 4C 182
Clitherow Pas. TW8: Brent ... 1J 11
Clitherow Rd. TW8: Brent ... 1H 11
Cliveden Pl. TW17: Shep ... 5D 38
Cliveden Rd. SW19 ... 9L 27
Clive Grn. RG12: Brac ... 4N 31
(not continuous)
Clive Rd. GU12: Alde ... 3B 110
KT10: Esh ... 1B 58
SW19 ... 7C 28
TW1: Twick ... 5F 24
TW14: Felt ... 9H 9
Clive Way RH10: Craw ... 3G 182
Clock Barn La. GU8: Bus ... 3J 153
CLOCK HOUSE ... 1F 82
Clockhouse, The
SW19 ... 4H 27
Clock Ho. Cl. KT14: Byf ... 8A 56
Clockhouse Cl. SW19 ... 3H 27
Clock Ho. Cotts. RH5: Cap ... 8J 159
Clockhouse Ct. BR3: Beck ... 1H 47
GU1: Guil ... 8M 93
GU27: Hasl ... 2G 189
Clockhouse La.
GU5: Braml ... 5B 134
TW14: Bedf ... 5B 22
TW15: A'ford ... 5B 22
Clockhouse La. E.
TW20: Egh ... 8D 20
Clockhouse La. W.
TW20: Egh ... 8C 20
Clock Ho. Mead KT22: Oxs ... 1B 78
Clockhouse Pl. SW15 ... 9K 13
Clock Ho. Rd. BR3: Beck ... 2H 47
Clockhouse Rd.
GU14: Farnb ... 1N 89
CLOCKHOUSE RDBT. ... 2C 22
Clockhouse Rdbt.
GU14: Farnb ... 1N 89
Clock House Station (Rail) ... 1H 47
Clock Twr. Ind. Est.
TW7: Isle ... 6F 10
Clock Twr. Rd. TW7: Isle ... 6F 10
Clodhouse Hill
GU22: Wok ... 9G 73
Cloister Cl. TW11: Tedd ... 6H 25
Cloister Gdns. SE25 ... 5E 46
Cloisters, The GU4: B'ham ... 9C 94
GU16: Frim ... 5B 70
GU22: Wok ... 8D 74
TW7: Isle ... 6G 10
(off Pulteney Cl.)
Cloisters Mall
KT1: K Tham ... 3H 203 (1L 41)
Cloncurry St. SW6 ... 5J 13
Clonmel Rd. SW6 ... 3L 13
TW11: Tedd ... 5D 24
Clonmore St. SW18 ... 2L 27
Close, The BR3: Beck ... 3H 47
CR4: Mit ... 3D 44
CR8: Pur ... 6M 63
(Pampisford Rd.)
CR8: Pur ... 6K 63
(Russell Hill)
GU5: Wone ... 4D 134
GU7: Goda ... 8J 133
GU9: Farnh ... 2J 129
GU16: Frim ... 6A 70
GU18: Ligh ... 6L 51
GU25: V Wat ... 4N 35
GU47: C Tow ... 7K 49
KT3: N Mal ... 1B 42
KT6: Surb ... 5L 41
KT10: Esh ... 3B 58
KT12: Hers ... 2H 57
KT14: W By ... 9J 55
RH2: Reig ... 4N 121
RH3: Brock ... 7B 120
RH6: Horl ... 1G 163
RH14: Ifo ... 5E 192
RH19: E Grin ... 1N 185
SE25 ... 2D 46
SL5: Asc ... 1H 33
SM3: Sut ... 6L 43
SM5: Cars ... 5C 62
TN16: B Hil ... 3K 87
TW7: Isle ... 5D 10
TW9: Rich ... 6A 12
Closeworth Rd.
GU14: Farnb ... 5C 90
Cloudesdale Rd. SW17 ... 3F 28
Clouston Cl. SM6: W'ton ... 2J 63
Clouston Rd. GU14: Cove ... 9L 69
Clovelly Av. CR6: Warl ... 6E 84
Clovelly Ct. KT17: Eps ... 9E 60
(off Alexandra Rd.)

Clovelly Dr. GU26: Hind 2A 170
Clovelly Pk. GU26: Hind 2A 170
Clovelly Rd. GU26: Hind 3A 170
TW3: Houn 5A 10
Clover Cl. GU35: Lind 4B 168
RG40: W'ham 1D 30
Clover Ct. GU22: Wok 5N 73
Cloverdale Ct. SM6: W'ton 3F 62
Cloverfields RH6: Horl 7F 142
Clover Hill CR5: Coul 8F 82
Cloverlands RH10: Craw 1D 182
Clover La. GU46: Yate 9A 48
Clover Lea GU7: Goda 3H 133
Clover Rd. GU2: Guil 2H 113
Clovers Cotts. RH12: Fay 8E 180
Clovers End RH12: Hors 3N 197
Clovers Way RH12: Fay 1C 198
Clover Wlk. TN8: Eden 9M 127
Clover Way RH6: Smal 8N 143
SM6: W'ton 7E 44
Clowser Cl. SM1: Sut 2A 62
Clubhouse Rd. GU11: Alde 8L 89
Club La. RG45: Crow 2J 49
Club Row GU24: B'wood 6A 72
Clump Av. KT20: Box H 9B 100
Clumps, The TW15: A'ford 5E 22
Clumps Rd. GU10: L Bou 7K 129
Clunbury Av. UB2: S'hall 1N 9
Cluny M. SW5 1M 13
Clyde Av. CR2: Sande 2E 84
Clyde Cl. RH1: Red 2E 122
Clyde Flats SW6 3L 13
(off Rhylston Rd.)
Clyde Ho.
KT2: K Tham 1H 203 (9K 25)
Clyde Rd. CR0: Croy 8C 46
SM1: Sut 2M 61
SM6: W'ton 3G 63
TW19: Stan 2M 21
Clydesdale Cl. TW7: Isle 6F 10
Clydesdale Gdns.
TW10: Rich 7A 12
Clymping Dene TW14: Felt 1J 23
Clyve Way TW18: Stain 9G 21
Coach Ho. Cl. GU16: Frim 3C 70
Coach Ho. Gdns.
GU51: Fleet 2B 88
Coach Ho. La. SW19 5J 27
Coach Ho. M. RH1: Red 4D 122
SM2: Sut 3N 61
Coach Ho. Yd. SW18 7N 13
Coachlads Av. GU2: Guil 3J 113
Coachman's Dr.
RH11: Craw 7N 181
Coachmans Gro.
GU47: Sandh 8G 49
Coachmans Lodge
SL4: W'sor 5G 5
(off Frances Rd.)
Coach Rd. KT16: Otter 3E 54
RH3: Brock 3L 119
RH6: Gat 2D 162
SL5: Asc 8J 17
(not continuous)
Coaldale Wlk. SE21 1N 29
Coalecroft Rd. SW15 7H 13
Coal Port Cl. BR6: Chels 3N 67
Coast Hill RH4: Westc 8N 117
Coast Hill La. RH4: Westc 7A 118
Coates Cl. CR7: T Hea 2N 45
Coates Wlk. TW8: Brent 2L 11
Coatham Pl. GU6: Cranl 7A 156
Cobb Cl. SL3: Dat 4N 5
Cobbets Ridge
GU10: Farnh 3A 130
Cobbett Cl. RH10: Craw 1G 183
Cobbett Hill Rd. GU3: Norm 6B 92
Cobbett Rd. GU2: Guil 2J 113
TW2: Whitt 2A 24
Cobbetts Cl. GU3: Norm 7C 92
GU21: Wok 4L 73
Cobbetts Hill KT13: Weybr 3C 56
Cobbett's La. GU17: B'water 1E 68
GU46: Yate 1E 68
Cobbetts M. GU9: Farnh 1G 128
Cobbetts Wlk. GU24: Bis 2D 72
Cobbetts Way GU9: Farnh 5E 128
TN8: Eden 3L 147
Cobblers RH13: Slin 5L 195
Cobblers Wlk. TW1: H Wic 9H 25
KT8: E Mol 9H 25
TW11: Tedd 9G 24
TW12: Hamp, Tedd 9C 24
(not continuous)
Cobbles Cres. RH10: Craw 2C 182
Cobblestone Pl.
CR0: Croy 1B 200 (7N 45)
Cobb's Hall SW6 2J 13
(off Fulham Pal. Rd.)
Cobb's Rd. TW4: Houn 7N 9
Cob Cl. RH10: Craw D 1F 184
Cobden La. GU27: Hasl 1H 189
Cobden Rd. BR6: Farnb 1M 67
SE25 4D 46
COBHAM 1J 77
Cobham Av. KT3: N Mal 4F 42
Cobham Bus Mus. 8D 56
Cobham Cl. RH7: Ling 5M 145
SM6: W'ton 3J 63
m Ct. CR4: Mit 1B 44
m Ga. KT11: Cob 1J 77
m Grange KT11: Cob 1J 77
(off Between Streets)
Cobham Mill 2K 77
Cobham Pk. KT11: Down 3J 77
Cobham Pk. Rd.
KT11: Down 4J 77
Cobham Rd. KT1: K Tham 1N 41
KT11: Sto D 5A 78
KT22: Fetc 8A 78
TW5: Hest 3K 9
Cobham & Stoke D'Abernon Station (Rail) 4M 77
Cobham Way KT24: E Hor 4F 96
RH10: Craw 6F 162
Cobnor Cl. RH11: Craw 5L 181
Cobs Way KT15: N Haw 6L 55
Coburg Cres. SW2 2K 29
Coburn Ho. RH10: Craw 2F 182
(off Trafalgar Gdns.)
Cob Wlk. RH11: Craw 3M 181
Coby Technology Pk.
GU14: Farnb 4F 88
Cochrane Pl. GU20: Windl 2A 52
Cochrane Rd. SW19 8K 27
Cock-A-Dobby GU47: Sandh 6F 48
COCKCROW HILL 7K 41
Cock La. KT22: Fetc 9C 78
Cockpit Path RG40: W'ham 3B 30
Cocks Cres. KT3: N Mal 3E 42
Cocksett Av. BR6: Chels 3N 67
Cockshot Hill RH2: Reig 4N 121
Cockshot Rd. RH2: Reig 4N 121
Cock's La. RG42: Warf 3E 16
Coda Cen., The SW6 3K 13
Codrington Ct. GU21: Wok 5J 73
Cody Cl. GU12: A Va 8D 90
SM6: W'ton 4H 63
Cody Ct. GU14: Farnb 7A 70
Cody Rd. GU14: Cove 2L 89
Cody Technology Pk.
GU14: Farnb 5H 89
Coe Av. SE25 5D 46
Coe Cl. GU11: Alde 3M 109
Cogman's La
RH6: Out, Smal 6A 144
Cogman's La. RH1: Out 6A 144
Cokenor Wood
GU10: Wrec 5E 128
Cokers La. SE21 2N 29
Colbalt Cl. BR3: Beck 3G 47
Colbeck GU52: C Cro 9C 88
Colbeck M. SW7 1N 13
Colborne Way KT4: W Pk 9H 43
Colbred Cnr. GU51: Fleet 1D 88
Colburn Av. CR3: Cate 2C 104
Colburn Cres. GU4: B'ham 9C 94
Colburn Way SM1: Sut 9B 44
Colby Rd. KT12: Wal T 7H 39
Colchester Va.
RH18: F Row 7G 186
Colcokes Rd. SM7: Ban 3M 81
Cold Blows CR4: Mit 2D 44
COLDHARBOUR 7D 138
Coldharbour Cl. TW20: Thor 2E 36
Coldharbour Common (NT) 6D 138
Cold Harbour La.
GU14: Cove 6K 69
(not continuous)
Coldharbour La. CR8: Pur 7L 63
GU22: Pyr 2H 75
GU24: W End 7C 52
RH1: Blet 3C 124
RH4: Dork 2E 138
RH5: Cold, Dork 2E 138
TW20: Thor 2E 36
Coldharbour Rd. CR0: Wad 2L 63
GU22: Pyr 2H 75
KT14: W By 1H 75
Coldharbour Way CR0: Wad 2L 63
Coldshott RH8: Oxt 2C 126
Coldstream Gdns.
SW18 9L 13
Coldstream Rd. CR3: Cate 8N 83
Cole Av. GU11: Alde 1L 109
Colebrook KT16: Otter 3F 54
Colebrook Cl. SW15 1J 27
Colebrooke Rd. RH1: Red 1C 122
Colebrook Pl. KT16: Otter 4D 54
Colebrook Rd. SW16 9J 29
Cole Cl. RH11: Craw 8N 181
Cole Ct. TW1: Twick 1G 24
Coleford Bri. Rd.
GU16: Mytc 1B 90
Coleford Cl. GU16: Mytc 2D 90
Coleford Paddocks
GU16: Mytc 1D 90
Coleford Rd. SW18 8N 13
Cole Gdns. TW5: C'ford 3H 9
Coleherne Ct. SW5 1N 13
Coleherne Mans. SW5 1N 13
(off Old Brompton Rd.)
Coleherne M. SW10 1N 13
Coleherne Rd. SW10 1N 13
Colehill Gdns. SW6 5K 13
Colehill La. SW6 4K 13
Colekitchen La. GU5: Gorn 7E 116
Coleman Cl. SE25 1D 46
Coleman Ct. SW18 1M 27
Coleman Rd. GU12: Alde 3B 110
COLEMAN'S HATCH 9N 187
COLE PARK 9G 11
Cole Pk. Gdns. TW1: Twick 8G 10
Cole Pk. Rd. TW1: Twick 9G 10
Cole Pk. Vw. TW1: Twick 9G 11
Coleridge Av. GU46: Yate 1D 68
SM1: Sut 1C 62
Coleridge Cl. RG45: Crow 3H 49
RH12: Hors 2L 197
Coleridge Cres. SL3: Poy 4G 6
Coleridge Gdns. SW10 3N 13
Coleridge Rd. CR0: Croy 6F 46
TW15: A'ford 5N 21
Coleridge Sq. SW10 3N 13
(off Coleridge Gdns.)
Coleridge Way UB7: W Dray 1A 8
Cole Rd. TW1: Twick 9G 10
Colesburg Rd. BR3: Beck 2J 47
Colescroft Hill CR8: Pur 2L 83
Coleshill Rd. TW11: Tedd 7E 24
Cole's La. RH5: Cap, Ockl 4E 158
Colesmead Rd. RH1: Red 9D 102
COLES MEADS 9D 102
Coleson Hill Rd.
GU10: Wrec 6E 128
Colet Gdns. W14 1J 13
Colet Rd. RH10: Craw 6B 182
Coleville Rd. GU14: Cove 9L 69
Coley Av. GU22: Wok 5C 74
COLGATE 2H 199
Colgate Cl. RH11: Craw 1N 181
Colin Cl. BR4: W Wick 1B 66
CR0: Croy 9J 47
Colinette Rd. SW15 7H 13
Colin Rd. CR3: Cate 1D 104
Coliseum Bus. Cen.
GU15: Camb 3M 69
Coliston Pas. SW18 1M 27
(off Coliston Rd.)
Coliston Rd. SW18 1M 27
Collamore Av. SW18 2C 28
Collard Cl. CR3: Cate 7A 84
Collards Ga. GU27: Hasl 2H 189
Collards La. GU27: Hasl 2H 189
College Av. KT17: Eps 1E 80
TW20: Egh 7D 20
College Cl. GU15: Camb 7B 50
RH7: Ling 7N 145
RH19: E Grin 9B 166
TW2: Twick 2D 24
College Ct. W6 1H 13
(off Queen Caroline St.)
College Cres. GU47: C Tow 7K 49
RH1: Red 9E 102
SL4: W'sor 5E 4
College Dr. KT7: T Dit 6E 40
College Flds. Bus. Cen.
SW19: Mit 9C 28
College Gdns.
GU9: Farnh 1G 128
KT3: N Mal 4E 42
SW17 3C 28
(not continuous)
College Hill GU7: Goda 9F 132
GU27: Hasl 2G 189
College Hill Ter.
GU27: Hasl 2G 189
College La. GU22: Wok 6M 73
RH19: E Grin 9B 166
College M. SW18 8N 13
College Ride GU15: Camb 8B 50
GU19: Bag 6E 50
College Rd.
CR0: Croy 3D 200 (8A 46)
GU1: Guil 4C 202 (4N 113)
GU12: A Va 1E 110
GU22: Wok 3D 74
GU47: C Tow 8K 49
KT17: Eps 8M 201 (1E 80)
RH10: Craw 3C 182
SW19 7B 28
TW7: Isle 4F 10
College Rdbt.
KT1: K Tham 5J 203 (2L 41)
COLLEGE TOWN 9K 49
College Wlk.
KT1: K Tham 5K 203 (2L 41)
College Way TW15: A'ford 5A 22
Collendean La. RH6: N Hil 7K 141
Collens Fld. GU24: Pirb 2C 92
Colletts All. RH12: Hors 6J 197
(off Middle St.)
Colley La. RH2: Reig 2K 121
Colley Mnr. Dr. RH2: Reig 2J 121
Colley Way RH2: Reig 9K 101
Collier Cl. GU14: Cove 9J 69
KT19: Ewe 3N 59
Collier Row RH10: Craw 5B 182
Colliers CR3: Cate 3D 104
Colliers Cl. GU21: Wok 4L 73
Colliers Ct. CR0: Croy 6D 200
Colliers Shaw BR2: Kes 2F 66
Colliers Water La.
CR7: T Hea 4L 45
COLLIERS WOOD 8B 28
COLLIERS WOOD 8B 28
Colliers Wood Station (Tube) 8B 28
Collier Way GU4: Guil 1F 114
Collignwood Mt.
GU15: Camb 9E 50
Collingdon GU6: Cranl 9A 156
Collingham Gdns.
SW5 1N 13
Collingham Rd. SW5 1N 13
Collingsbourne KT15: Addl 1L 55
Collingwood GU14: Farnb 3C 90
Collingwood Av. KT5: Surb 7B 42
Collingwood Cl. RH6: Horl 7F 142
RH12: Hors 4J 197
RH19: E Grin 2B 186
TW2: Whitt 1A 24
Collingwood Cres.
GU1: Guil 2C 114
Collingwood Grange Cl.
GU15: Camb 7F 50
Collingwood Pl.
KT12: Wal T 9H 39
Collingwood Ri.
GU15: Camb 8E 50
Collingwood Rd. CR4: Mit 2C 44
RH10: Craw 4H 183
RH12: Hors 3H 197
SM1: Sut 9M 43
Collingwoof Pl.
GU15: Camb 7F 50
Collins Gdns. GU12: Ash 2F 110
Collins Path TW12: Hamp 7N 23
Collins Rd. RH11: Craw 5K 181
Collis All. TW2: Twick 2E 24
Collyer Av. CR0: Bedd 1J 63
Collyer Rd. CR0: Bedd 1J 63
Colman Cl. KT18: Tat C 4H 81
Colman Ho. RH1: Red 1D 122
COLMAN'S HILL 4F 136
Colman's Hill GU5: P'lake 4F 136
Colman Way RH1: Red 1C 122
Colmer Rd. SW16 9J 29
COLNBROOK 3F 6
Colnbrook By-Pass
SL3: Coln, Lang 2E 6
UB7: Harm 3K 7
Colnbrook Ct. SL3: Poy 4H 7
Colndale Rd. SL3: Poy 5G 6
Colne Bank SL3: Hort 6E 6
Colnebridge Cl.
TW18: Stain 5G 21
Colne Ct. KT19: Ewe 1B 60
Colne Dr. KT12: Wal T 9L 39
Colne Reach TW19: Stan M 8H 7
Colne Rd. TW1: Twick 2E 24
TW2: Twick 2E 24
Colne Wlk. RH11: Craw 5L 181
Colne Way GU12: Ash 3E 110
TW19: Stain 3D 20
Coln Trad. Est. SL3: Poy 4H 7
Colonel's La. KT16: Chert 5J 37
Colonial Av. TW2: Whitt 9C 10
Colonial Rd. TW14: Felt 1F 22
Colonnades, The CR0: Wad 3L 63
Colonsay Rd. RH11: Craw 6N 181
Colour House Theatre 9A 28
Colson Rd.
CR0: Croy 2F 200 (8B 46)
Colson Way SW16 5G 29
Colston Av. SM5: Cars 1C 62
Colston Ct. SM5: Cars 1D 62
Colston Rd. SW14 7B 12
Coltash Rd. RH10: Craw 4E 182
Coltsfoot Dr. GU1: Guil 9C 94
RH12: Hors 3L 197
Coltsfoot La. RH8: Oxt 2B 126
Coltsfoot Rd. GU35: Lind 4B 168
Columbia Av. KT4: W Pk 6E 42
Columbia Cen., The
RG12: Brac 1N 31
Columbia Sq. SW14 7B 12
Columbine Av. CR2: S Croy 4M 63
Columbus Dr. GU14: Cove 1H 89
Colville Gdns. GU18: Ligh 7N 51
Colvin Rd. CR7: T Hea 4L 45
Colwith Rd. W6 2H 13
Colwood Gdns. SW19 8B 28
Colworth Rd. CR0: Croy 7D 46
Colwyn Cl. GU46: Yate 9B 48
RH11: Craw 5L 181
SW16 6G 28
Colwyn Cres. TW3: Houn 4C 10
Colyton Cl. GU21: Wok 5M 73
Colyton La. SW16 6L 29
Combe La. GU5: Shere 6A 116
GU8: Bus 9M 133
GU8: Chid, Worm 4C 172
GU8: Worm 1C 172
GU14: Farnb 8M 69
Combemartin Rd.
SW18 1K 27
Combe Ri. GU10: L Bou 6J 129
Combermere Cl. SL4: W'sor 5E 4
Combermere Rd.
SM4: Mord 5N 43
Combe Rd. GU7: Goda 3H 133
Comberton KT1: K Tham 4M 203
Comeragh Cl. GU22: Wok 7K 73
Comeragh M. W14 1K 13
Comeragh Rd. W14 1K 13
Comet Cl. GU12: A Va 8D 90
Comet Rd. GU14: Farnb 5G 89
TW19: Stan 1M 21
Comforts Farm Av.
RH8: Oxt 2B 126
Comfrey Cl. GU14: Cove 9H 69
RG40: W'ham 9D 14
Commerce Pk. CR0: Wad 8K 45
Commerce Rd. TW8: Brent 2J 11
Commerce Way CR0: Wad 8K 45
TN8: Eden 9L 127
Commercial Rd.
GU1: Guil 5C 202 (4N 113)
GU12: Alde 4A 110
TW18: Stain 7J 21
Commercial Way
GU21: Wok 4A 74
Commodore Ct.
GU14: Farnb 5A 90
COMMON, THE
GU3 1F 132
GU8 5C 174
KT23 9N 77
RH12 4J 197
Common, The GU4: Chil 1A 134
(not continuous)
GU5: Wone 3D 134
GU6: Cranl 7L 155
KT21: A'tead 3K 79
UB2: S'hall 1L 9
UB7: W Dray 1L 7
Common Cl. GU21: Wok 1N 73
Commondale SW15 6H 13
Commonfield La.
SW17 6C 28
Commonfield Rd.
SM7: Ban 1M 81
Commonfields
GU24: W End 8D 52
Common La. KT10: Clay 4G 58
KT15: N Haw 5L 55
SL4: Eton 1G 4
Common La. Ho. SL4: Eton 1G 4
(off Common La.)
Common Rd. KT10: Clay 3G 58
RH1: Red 5D 122
SL3: Lang 1C 6
SL4: Dorn, E Wic 1B 4
SL4: E Wic 1C 4
SW13 6G 12
Common Side KT18: Eps 2N 79
Commonside BR2: Kes 1E 66
KT23: Book 9A 78
(not continuous)
Commonside Cl. CR5: Coul 7M 83
SM2: Sut 7N 61
Commonside E. CR4: Mit 2E 44
(not continuous)
Commonside W. CR4: Mit 2D 44
Commonwealth Dr.
RH10: Craw 3D 182
Commonwealth Rd.
CR3: Cate 1D 104
Community Cl. TW5: C'ford 4J 9
Community Wlk. KT10: Esh 1C 58
Compass Cl. TW15: A'ford 8D 22
Compasses Mobile Home Pk.
GU6: Alf 4H 175
Compass Hill TW10: Rich 9K 11
Compass Ho. SW18 7N 13
Compassion Cl.
RH11: Craw 4K 181
Comper Cl. RH11: Craw 5K 181
Comport Grn. CR0: N Add 8A 66
COMPTON
GU3 9D 112
GU9 1K 129
Compton Cl. GU47: Sandh 6H 49
GU52: C Cro 8C 88
KT10: Esh 3D 58
RG12: Brac 5K 31
Compton Ct. GU1: Guil 4B 114
SM1: Sut 1A 62
Compton Cres. KT9: Ches 2L 59
W4 2B 12
Compton Gdns. KT15: Addl 2K 55
(off Monks Cres.)
Compton Hgts. GU2: Guil 6G 113
Compton Pl. Bus. Cen.
GU15: Camb 2M 69
(off Surrey Av.)
Compton Rd. CR0: Croy 7E 46
GU52: C Cro 8C 88
SW19 7L 27
Comptons, The
RH13: Hors 5M 197
Comptons Brow La.
RH13: Hors 5N 197
Comptons Ct. RH13: Hors 5M 197
Comptons La. RH13: Hors 4M 197
Compton Way
GU10: Farnh 1M 129
Comsaye Wlk. RG12: Brac 4A 32
Conaways Cl. KT17: Ewe 6F 60
Concord Ct. KT1: K Tham 5L 203
Concorde Bus. Pk.
TN16: B Hil 2F 86
Concorde Cl. TW3: Houn 5B 10
Concorde Ct. SL4: W'sor 5D 4
Concorde Rd. GU14: Farnb 4H 89
Concord Ho. KT3: N Mal 2D 42
Conde Way GU35: Bor 7A 168
Condor Ct.
GU2: Guil 7B 202 (5M 113)
Condor Rd. TW18: Lale 2L 37
Conduit, The RH1: Blet 7A 104
Conduit La. CR0: Croy 2D 64
CR2: S Croy 2D 64
SL3: Lang 2A 6
Coney Acre SE21 2N 29
Coneyberry RH2: Reig 7A 122
Coneybury RH1: Blet 3B 124
Coneybury Cl. CR6: Warl 6E 84
Coney Cl. RH11: Craw 1N 181
Coney Cft. RH12: Hors 3A 198
Coney Grange RG42: Warf 7N 15
CONEY HALL 1A 66
Coneyhurst La. GU6: Ewh 3D 156

Conford Dr.—Cotts Wood Dr.

Conford Dr. GU4: Chil 1A 134
Coniers Way GU4: B'ham 9D 94
Conifer Cl. BR6: Orp 1M 67
GU52: C Cro 8A 88
RH2: Reig 1M 121
Conifer Ct. *TW15: A'ford* *6A 22*
(off The Crescent)
Conifer Dr. GU15: Camb 9E 50
Conifer Gdns. SM1: Sut 8N 43
SW16 4J 29
Conifer La. TW20: Egh 6E 20
Conifer Pk. KT17: Eps 7D 60
Conifers KT13: Weybr 1F 56
Conifers, The RG45: Crow 9F 30
Conifers Cl. RH12: Hors 2A 198
TW11: Tedd 8H 25
Coniger Rd. SW6 5M 13
Coningsby RG12: Brac 3A 32
Coningsby Ct. CR4: Mit 1E 44
Coningsby Rd.
CR2: S Croy 5N 63
Conista Ct. GU21: Wok 3J 73
Coniston Cl. GU14: Cove 2K 89
GU15: Camb 3G 71
RH11: Ifi 5J 181
RH12: Hors 3A 198
SW13 3E 12
SW20 5J 43
W4 3B 12
Coniston Ct. *GU12: A Va* *9D 90*
(off Lakeside Cl.)
GU18: Ligh 6M 51
KT13: Weybr 3C 56
SM6: W'ton 1F 62
TW15: A'ford 4M 21
Coniston Dr. GU9: U Hal 6F 108
Coniston Gdns. SM2: Sut 3B 62
Coniston Rd. CR0: Croy 6D 46
CR5: Coul 3G 82
GU22: Wok 7D 74
TW2: Whitt 9B 10
Coniston Way KT9: Ches 9L 41
RH2: Reig 2C 122
TW20: Egh 8D 20
Connaught Av. SW14 6B 12
TW4: Houn 7M 9
TW15: A'ford 5N 21
Connaught Barracks
GU11: Alde 7B 90
Connaught Bus. Cen.
CR0: Wad 3K 63
CR4: Mit 4D 44
Connaught Cl. GU46: Yate 9A 48
RG45: Crow 4E 48
SM1: Sut 8B 44
Connaught Cres.
GU24: B'wood 7C 72
Connaught Dr. KT13: Weybr 7B 56
Connaught Gdns.
RH10: Craw 1B 182
SM4: Mord 3A 44
Connaught Leisure Cen. 5C 110
Connaught M. SW6 4K 13
Connaught Rd. GU12: Alde 2A 110
GU15: Camb 1D 70
GU19: Bag 4G 51
GU24: B'wood 8B 72
GU51: Fleet 5A 88
KT3: N Mal 3D 42
SM1: Sut 8B 44
TW10: Rich 8M 11
TW11: Tedd 6D 24
Connicut La. KT23: Book 6B 98
Connolly Ct. GU25: V Wat 3A 36
Connop Way GU16: Frim 3D 70
Conquest Rd. KT15: Addl 2J 55
Conrad Dr. KT4: W Pk 7H 43
Consfield Av. KT3: N Mal 3F 42
Consort Ct. *GU22: Wok* *5A 74*
(off York Rd.)
Consort Dr. GU15: Camb 8G 50
Consort Ho. RH6: Horl 8E 142
Consort M. TW7: Isle 8D 10
Consort Way RH6: Horl 8E 142
Consort Way E. RH6: Horl 9F 142
Constable Ct. *W4* *1A 12*
(off Chaseley Dr.)
Constable Gdns. TW7: Isle 8D 10
Constable Rd. RH10: Craw 7D 182
Constable Way
GU47: C Tow 9K 49
Constance Cl. SW15 5C 26
Constance Rd. CR0: Croy 6M 45
SM1: Sut 1A 62
TW2: Whitt 1B 24
Constantius Ct.
GU52: C Cro *9A 88*
(off Brandon Rd.)
Constant Rd. GU14: Farnb 3F 88
Constitution Hill
GU22: Wok 6A 74
Contessa Cl. BR6: Farnb 2N 67
Control Twr. Rd. RH6: Gat 4B 162
(not continuous)
TW6: Lon A 6B 8
Convent Hill SE19 7N 29
Convent La. KT11: Cob 7F 56
Convent Lodge
TW15: A'ford 6C 22
Convent Rd. SL4: W'sor 5C 4
TW15: A'ford 6B 22
Convent Way UB2: S'hall 1K 9
Conway Cl. GU16: Frim 5D 70
Conway Dr. GU14: Cove 1J 89
SM2: Sut 3N 61
TW15: A'ford 7D 22
Conway Gdns. CR4: Mit 3J 45
Conway Rd. SW20 9H 27
TW4: Houn 1N 23
TW6: Lon A 6C 8
TW13: Hanw 6L 23
Conway Wlk. TW12: Hamp 7N 23
Conyers Cl. KT12: Hers 2L 57
Conyer's Rd. SW16 6H 29
Cooke Ri. RG42: Warf 7A 16
Cookes La. SM3: Chea 3K 61
Cookham Cl. GU47: Sandh 6H 49
Cookham Rd. RG12: Brac 1K 31
Cook Rd. RH10: Craw 5C 182
RH12: Hors 2K 197
Cooks Hill RH12: Rudg 8A 176
Cook's La. RH12: Bro H 3A 196
Cooks Mead RH12: Rusp 2C 180
Cooks Mdw. RH12: Rusp 2C 180
Cook Way GU2: Guil 2G 113
Coolarne Ri. GU15: Camb 9E 50
Coolgardie Rd.
TW15: A'ford 6D 22
Coolham Ct. RH11: Ifi 3L 181
COOLHURST 8A 198
Coolhurst La. RH13: Hors 7N 197
COOMBE 8C 26
Coombe, The RH3: Betch 9C 100
Coombe Av. CR0: Croy 1B 64
Coombe Bank
KT2: K Tham 9D 26
COOMBE BOTTOM 6A 116
Coombe Cl. GU16: Frim 6B 70
RH11: Craw 9B 162
TW3: Houn 7A 10
Coombe Ct. CR0: Croy 6D 200
Coombe Cres. TW12: Hamp 8N 23
Coombe Dr. GU51: Fleet 4D 88
KT15: Addl 3H 55
Coombe End KT2: K Tham 8C 26
Coombefield Cl. KT3: N Mal 4D 42
Coombe Gdns. KT3: N Mal 3E 42
SW20 1F 42
Coombe Hall Pk.
RH19: E Grin 3N 185
Coombe Hill Ct. SL4: W'sor 6A 4
Coombe Hill Glade
KT2: K Tham 8D 26
Coombe Hill Rd.
KT2: K Tham 8D 26
RH19: E Grin 3M 185
Coombe Ho. Chase
KT3: N Mal 9C 26
Coombelands La.
KT15: Addl 3J 55
COOMBE LANE 9E 26
Coombe La. CR0: Croy 2E 64
GU3: Worp 7F 92
(not continuous)
KT12: Whit V 5G 56
SL5: S'hill 3N 33
SW20 9E 26
Coombe La. Flyover
SW20 9E 26
Coombe Lane Stop (CT) 2F 64
Coombe La. W.
KT2: K Tham 9A 26
Coombe Mnr. GU24: Bis 2D 72
Coombe Neville
KT2: K Tham 8C 26
Coombe Pk. KT2: K Tham 6B 26
Coombe Pine RG12: Brac 5B 32
Coombe Pl. KT2: K Tham 6B 26
Coomber Ho. *SW6* *6N 13*
(off Wandsworth Bri. Rd.)
Coombe Ridings
KT2: K Tham 6B 26
Coombe Ri. KT2: K Tham 9B 26
Coombe Rd.
CR0: Croy 6C 200 (1A 64)
GU46: Yate 8A 48
KT2: K Tham 2M 203 (9N 25)
KT3: N Mal 1D 42
TW12: Hamp 7N 23
W4 1D 12
Coomber Way CR0: Bedd 6H 45
Coombes, The GU5: Braml 6C 134
Coombe Vw. GU8: Chid 4D 172
Coombe Wlk. SM1: Sut 9N 43
Coombe Way KT14: Byf 8A 56
Coombe Wood Hill
CR8: Pur 9N 63
Coombe Wood Rd.
KT2: K Tham 6B 26
Coomb Fld. TN8: Eden 3L 147
Coomer M. SW6 2L 13
Coomer Pl. SW6 2L 13
Coomer Rd. SW6 2L 13
Cooper Cl. RH6: Smal 8L 143
Cooper Cres. SM5: Cars 9D 44
Cooper Ho. TW4: Houn 6N 9
Cooper Rd.
CR0: Wad 7A 200 (1M 63)
GU1: Guil 5B 114
GU20: Windl 3A 52
Cooper Row RH10: Craw 6B 182
Coopers Cl. TW18: Stain 6G 21
Coopers Ct. *TW7: Isle* *5F 10*
(off Woodlands Rd.)
Coopers Hill Dr.
GU24: B'wood 7N 71
Coopers Hill La.
TW20: Egh, Eng G 4M 19
(not continuous)
Cooper's Hill Rd.
RH1: Nut, Sth N 3L 123
Coopers La. TW18: Stain 5J 21
Coopers M. BR3: Beck 1K 47
Coopers Pl. GU8: Worm 1C 172
Coopers Ri. GU7: Goda 8E 132
Coopers Ter. GU9: Farnh 9H 109
Coopers Wood RH17: Hand 5N 199
Coos La. RH17: Hand 9M 199
Coote Cl. RG42: Bin 6H 15
Cootes Av. RH12: Hors 5G 196
Copeland Ho. SW17 5B 28
Copelands Cl. GU15: Camb 2H 71
Copenhagen Wlk.
RG45: Crow 3G 49
Copenhagen Way
KT12: Wal T 9J 39
Copgate Path SW16 7K 29
Copleigh Dr. KT20: Tad 7K 81
Copley Cl. GU21: Wok 6H 73
RH1: Red 1C 122
Copley Pk. SW16 7K 29
Copley Way KT20: Tad 7J 81
Copnall Way RH12: Hors 6J 197
Coppard Gdns. KT9: Ches 3J 59
Copped Hall Dr.
GU15: Camb 9G 50
Copped Hall Way
GU15: Camb 9G 50
Copper Beech RG42: Warf 9E 16
Copper Beech Cl.
GU22: Wok 8L 73
SL4: W'sor 4A 4
Copper Beeches Ct.
TW7: Isle 4D 10
Copper Beech Ho.
GU22: Wok 4B 74
Copperfield Av.
GU47: Owls 5K 49
Copperfield Cl. CR2: Sande 7N 63
Copperfield Ct. KT22: Leat 8G 79
Copperfield Pl.
RH12: Hors 4H 197
Copperfield Ri. KT15: Addl 2H 55
Copperfields KT22: Fetc 9C 78
RH13: Hors 8A 198
Copperfields Mnr.
RH13: Hors 8A 198
Copper Mill Dr. TW7: Isle 5F 10
Copper Mill La. SW17 5A 28
Coppermill Rd. TW19: Wray 9C 6
Coppice, The GU52: C Cro 7B 88
RH10: Craw D 1E 184
TW15: A'ford 7C 22
Coppice Cl. BR3: Beck 3L 47
GU2: Guil 2G 113
GU9: Weybo 6K 109
SW20 2H 43
Coppice Dr. SW15 9G 12
TW19: Wray 1N 19
Coppice End GU22: Pyr 3G 74
Coppice Gdns. GU46: Yate 1B 68
RG45: Crow 2E 48
Coppice Grn. RG42: Brac 8L 15
(not continuous)
Coppice La. RH2: Reig 1L 121
Coppice Pl. GU8: Worm 1C 172
Coppice Rd. RH2: Reig 2K 121
RH12: Hors 3N 197
Coppice Wlk. RH10: Craw 2E 182
Coppid Beech La.
RG40: W'ham 2F 30
Copping Cl. CR0: Croy 1B 64
Coppins, The CR0: N Add 3L 65
Coppsfield KT8: W Mole 2A 40
Copse, The CR3: Cate 4D 104
GU6: Cranl 7B 156
GU10: Rowl 7E 128
GU14: Cove 2J 89
KT22: Fetc 1B 98
RG12: Brac 2B 32
RH1: Sth N 5J 123
RH10: Craw *3E 182*
(off Gales Dr.)
SL4: Wink 2L 17
Copse Av. BR4: W Wick 8L 47
GU9: Weybo 5K 109
Copse Cl. GU4: Guil 1E 134
GU15: Camb 9E 50
RH10: Craw D 1E 184
RH12: Hors 2M 197
RH19: E Grin 7C 166
Copse Cres. RH11: Craw 2A 182
Copse Dr. RG41: W'ham 1A 30
Copse Edge GU6: Cranl 6A 156
GU8: Els 8G 131
Copse Edge Av. KT17: Eps 9E 60
Copse End GU15: Camb 9D 50
Copse Glade KT6: Surb 6K 41
COPSE HILL 8G 26
Copse Hill CR8: Pur 9J 63
SM2: Sut 4N 61
SW20 9F 26
Copse La. GU46: Yate 7A 48
RH6: Horl 7G 143
Copsem Dr. KT10: Esh 3B 58
Copsem La. KT10: Esh, Oxs 3C 58
KT22: Oxs 3C 58
Copsem Way KT10: Esh 3C 58
Copsem Wood KT22: Oxs 7C 58
Copse Rd. GU21: Wok 5J 73
GU27: Hasl 3B 188
KT11: Cob 9J 57
RH1: Red 5A 122
Copse Side GU7: Goda 3G 133
Copse Vw. CR2: Sels 5G 65
Copse Way GU10: Wrec 5E 128
Copse Wood Ct. RH2: Reig 1C 122
Copsleigh Av. RH1: Red 1E 142
Copsleigh Cl. RH1: Red 9E 122
Copsleigh Way RH1: Red 9E 122
Coptain Ho. SW18 7M 13
Copthall Gdns. TW1: Twick 2F 24
Copthall Way KT15: N Haw 6H 55
Copt Hill La. KT20: Tad 7K 81
COPTHORNE 7L 163
Copthorne Av. SW12 1H 29
Copthorne Bank
RH10: Cop 4N 163
Copthorne Chase
TW15: A'ford 5A 22
Copthorne Cl. TW17: Shep 5D 38
COPTHORNE COMMON 7A 164
Copthorne Comn. Rd.
RH10: Cop 8L 163
Copthorne Ct. KT22: Leat 9G 79
Copthorne Dr. GU18: Ligh 6M 51
Copthorne Ri. CR2: Sande 9A 64
Copthorne Rd. KT22: Leat 7H 79
RH10: Cop 6E 164
RH10: Craw 1H 183
RH19: Cop, Fel 6E 164
Copthorne Way
RH10: Craw 8J 163
Copyhold Hill GU27: Fern 8G 188
Copyhold La. GU27: Fern 9F 188
Copyhold Rd.
RH19: E Grin 1N 185
Coral Reef Leisure Pool 6B 32
Coram Ho. *W4* *1D 12*
(off Wood St.)
Corban Rd. TW3: Houn 6A 10
Corbet Cl. SM6: W'ton 7E 44
Corbet Rd. KT17: Ewe 6D 60
Corbett Cl. CR0: N Add 8N 65
Corbett Dr. GU18: Ligh 8K 51
Corbiere Ct. SW19 7J 27
Corby Cl. RH11: Craw 6K 181
TW20: Eng G 7M 19
Corby Dr. TW20: Eng G 7L 19
Cordelia Cft. RG42: Warf 9C 16
Cordelia Gdns.
GU12: A Va 4D 90
TW19: Stan 1N 21
Cordelia Rd. TW19: Stan 1N 21
Corderoy Pl. KT16: Chert 5G 37
Cordrey Gdns. CR5: Coul 2J 83
(not continuous)
Cordrey Ho. KT15: Addl 8J 37
Cordwalles Cres.
GU15: Camb 7D 50
Coresbrook Way
GU21: Knap 5D 72
Corfe Cl. KT21: A'tead 5J 79
TW4: Houn 2M 23
Corfe Gdns. GU16: Frim 5D 70
Corfe Way GU14: Farnb 4C 90
Coriander Cl. GU14: Cove 9H 69
Coriander Cres. GU2: Guil 7K 93
Corinthian Way
TW19: Stan 1M 21
Corkran Rd. KT6: Surb 6K 41
Corkscrew Hill
BR4: W Wick 8M 47
Cork Tree Ho. *SE27* *6M 29*
(off Lakeview Rd.)
Cormongers La. RH1: Nut 9H 103
Cormorant Pl. GU47: C Tow 8J 49
SM1: Sut 2L 61
Cornbunting Cl.
GU47: C Tow 7J 49
Corn Cft. RG42: Warf 8B 16
Cornel Ho. SL4: W'sor 6G 4
Cornelia Cl. GU14: Cove 2J 89
Cornelia Ho. *TW1: Twick* *9K 11*
(off Denton Rd.)
Corner, The KT14: W By 9J 55
Corner Bungs. GU7: Hurt 3E 132
Cornercroft *SM3: Chea* *2J 61*
(off Wickham Av.)
Corner Farm Cl. KT20: Tad 9H 81
Corner Fielde SW2 2K 29
Cornerside TW15: A'ford 8D 22
Cornerstone Ho. CR0: Croy 6N 45
Corney Reach Way W4 3D 12
Corney Rd. W4 2D 12
Cornfield Rd. RH2: Reig 4A 122
Cornfields GU7: Goda 3J 133
GU46: Yate 2A 68
Cornflower La. CR0: Croy 7G 47
Cornford Gro. SW12 3F 28
Cornhill Cl. KT15: Addl 8K 37
Cornish Ho. TW8: Brent 1M 11
Cornwall Av. KT10: Clay 4F 58
KT14: Byf 1A 76
Cornwall Cl. GU15: Camb 8D 50
RG42: Warf 7D 16
SL4: E Wic 1B 4
Cornwall Gdns.
RH19: E Grin 1B 186
SE25 3C 46
Cornwall Gro. W4 1D 12
Cornwallis Cl. CR3: Cate 9N 83
Cornwall Rd.
CR0: Croy 2A 200 (8M 45)
SM2: Sut 4L 61
TW1: Twick 1G 25
Cornwall Way TW18: Stain 7G 20
Cornwell Rd. SL4: O Win 9K 5
Coronation Av. SL4: W'sor 5K 5
Coronation Ct.
KT1: K Tham *8J 203*
(off Surbiton Rd.)
Coronation Rd.
GU11: Alde 5N 109
GU46: Yate 8D 48
RH19: E Grin 2A 186
SL5: Asc 7L 33
UB3: Harl 1G 9
Coronation Sq.
RG40: W'ham 1C 30
Coronation Wlk. TW2: Whitt 2A 24
Coronet, The RH6: Horl 1G 162
Coronet Cl. RH10: Craw 2J 183
Corporate Dr. TW13: Felt 4J 23
Corporation Av. TW4: Houn 7M 9
Corrib Dr. SM1: Sut 2C 62
Corrie Gdns. GU25: V Wat 6M 35
Corrie Rd. GU22: Wok 7D 74
KT15: Addl 1M 55
Corrigan Av. CR5: Coul 2E 82
Corringway GU52: C Cro 7C 88
Corry Rd. GU26: Hind 3A 170
Corsair Cl. TW19: Stan 1M 21
Corsair Rd. TW19: Stan 1N 21
Corscombe Cl.
KT2: K Tham 6B 26
Corsehill St. SW16 7G 28
Corsham Way RG45: Crow 2G 48
Corsletts Av. RH12: Bro H 5D 196
Corston Hollow *RH1: Red* *4D 122*
(off Woodlands Rd.)
Cortayne Ct. TW2: Twick 3E 24
Cortayne Rd. SW6 5L 13
Cortis Rd. SW15 9G 13
Cortis Ter. SW15 9G 13
Corunna Dr. RH13: Hors 6M 197
Cosdach Av. SM6: W'ton 4H 63
Cosedge Cres.
CR0: Wad 8A 200 (2L 63)
Cosford Rd. GU8: Thur 6J 151
Costells Mdw.
TN16: Weste 4M 107
Coteford St. SW17 5D 28
Cotelands
CR0: Croy 4F 200 (9B 46)
Cotford Rd. CR7: T Hea 3N 45
Cotherstone KT19: Ewe 6C 60
Cotherstone Rd. SW2 2K 29
Cotland Acres RH1: Red 5B 122
Cotman Cl. SW15 9J 13
COTMANDENE 2L 201 (5H 119)
Cotsford RH11: P Pot 2N 199
Cotsford Av. KT3: N Mal 4B 42
Cotswold Cl. GU14: Cove 7K 69
KT2: K Tham 7B 26
KT10: H Wood 8F 40
RH11: Craw 3N 181
TW18: Stain 6J 21
Cotswold Ct. GU51: Fleet 4A 88
RH13: Hors 6L 197
Cotswold Rd. GU47: Sandh 6E 48
SM2: Sut 6N 61
TW12: Hamp 6A 24
Cotswold St. SE27 5M 29
Cotswold Way KT4: W Pk 8H 43
Cottage Cl. KT16: Otter 3E 54
RH12: Hors 2A 198
Cottage Farm Way
TW20: Thor 2E 36
Cottage Gdns. GU14: Cove 1L 89
Cottage Gro. KT6: Surb 5K 41
Cottage Pl. RH10: Cop 7B 164
Cottage Rd. KT19: Ewe 4C 60
Cottenham Dr. SW20 8G 27
Cottenham Pde. SW20 1G 43
COTTENHAM PARK 9G 27
Cottenham Pk. Rd.
SW20 9F 26
(not continuous)
Cottenham Pl. SW20 8G 27
Cottenhams RH7: Blin H 3H 145
Cotterell Cl. RG42: Brac 8N 15
Cotterell Ct. GU52: C Cro 9A 88
Cotterill Rd. KT6: Surb 8L 41
Cottesbrooke Cl. SL3: Coln 4F 6
Cottesloe Cl. GU24: Bis 3C 72
Cottesmore RG12: Brac 6M 31
Cottimore Av. KT12: Wal T 7J 39
Cottimore Cres.
KT12: Wal T 6J 39
Cottimore La. KT12: Wal T 6J 39
(not continuous)
Cottimore Ter. KT12: Wal T 6J 39
Cottingham Av.
RH12: Hors 1K 197
Cottington Rd. TW13: Hanw 5L 23
Cotton Cl. GU11: Alde 1L 109
Cottongrass Cl. CR0: Croy 7G 46
Cotton Hall Ho. *SL4: Eton* *2F 4*
(off Eton Wick Rd.)
Cotton Ho. SW2 1J 29
Cotton Row RH5: H Mary 3K 157
Cotton Wlk. RH11: Craw 8M 181
Cottrell Flats GU14: Farnb 5B 90
Cotts Wood Dr. GU4: B'ham 7C 94

Couchmore Av.—Cricket Cl.

Couchmore Av.
KT10: H Wood 8E 40
COULSDON 3H 83
Coulsdon Common 8N 83
Coulsdon Ct. Rd. CR5: Coul ...3K 83
Coulsdon La. CR5: Chip 6D 82
Coulsdon Nth. Ind. Est.
CR5: Coul 3H 83
Coulsdon Pl. CR3: Cate 9A 84
Coulsdon Ri. CR5: Coul 4J 83
Coulsdon Rd.
CR3: Cate, Coul 9A 84
CR5: Coul 2K 83
Coulsdon South Station (Rail)
......................3H 83
Coulthurst Ct. *SW16* *8J 29*
(off Heybridge Av.)
Council Cotts. GU23: Wis 2M 75
GU24: W End 8C 52
RH5: Ockl 6D 158
Countisbury Gdns.
KT15: Addl 2K 55
Country Way TW13: Hanw 7J 23
County Bldgs. RH10: Craw ...3C 182
County La. RG42: Warf 7B 16
County Mall Shop. Cen.
RH10: Craw 3C 182
COUNTY OAK 8B 162
County Oak La.
RH11: Craw 8B 162
County Oak Retail Pk.
RH11: Craw 8B 162
County Oak Way
RH11: Craw 8B 162
County Pde. TW8: Brent 3K 11
County Rd. CR7: T Hea 1M 45
Courland Rd. KT15: Addl 9K 37
Course Rd. SL5: Asc 2L 33
Court, The CR6: Warl 5H 85
GU2: Guil 7B 202 (5M 113)
Court Av. CR5: Coul 5L 83
Court Bushes Rd.
CR3: Warl 6D 84
Court Cl. RH19: E Grin 9B 166
SM6: W'ton 4H 63
TW2: Twick 4B 24
Court Cl. Av. TW2: Twick 4B 24
Court Cres. KT9: Ches 2K 59
RH19: E Grin 9B 166
Court Downs Rd. BR3: Beck ...1L 47
Court Dr. CR0: Wad 1K 63
GU52: Fleet 7B 88
SM1: Sut 1C 62
Courtenay Av. SM2: Sut 5M 61
Courtenay Dr. BR3: Beck 1N 47
Courtenay M. GU21: Wok 3C 74
Courtenay Pl. RH4: Dork 3K 119
Courtenay Rd.
GU9: Weybo 5K 109
(not continuous)
GU21: Wok 3C 74
KT4: W Pk 9H 43
Court Farm Av. KT19: Ewe 2C 60
Court Farm Gdns.
KT19: Eps 7B 60
Court Farm Ind. Est.
TW19: Stan 9A 8
Court Farm Pk. CR6: Warl 3D 84
Court Farm Rd. CR6: Warl 5D 84
Courtfield Gdns. SW5 ....1N 13
Courtfield M. SW5 ....1N 13
Courtfield Ri. BR4: W Wick ...9N 47
Courtfield Rd. TW15: A'ford ...7C 22
Court Gdns. GU15: Camb 1A 70
Court Grn. Hgts.
GU22: Wok 7M 73
Court Haw SM7: Ban 2C 82
Court Hill CR2: Sande 8B 64
CR5: Chip 5C 82
Courthope Rd. SW19 ....6K 27
Courthope Vs. SW19 ....8K 27
Court Ho. Mans. KT19: Eps ...8C 60
Courtland Av. SW16 ....8K 29
Courtlands KT12: Wal T 6H 39
TW10: Rich 8N 11
Courtlands Av. KT10: Esh 3N 57
SL3: Lang 1N 5
TW9: Kew 5A 12
TW12: Hamp 7N 23
Courtlands Cl. CR2: Sande 6C 64
Courtlands Cres. SM7: Ban ...2M 81
Courtlands Dr. KT19: Ewe 3D 60
Courtlands Rd. KT5: Surb 6N 41
Court La.
KT19: Eps 6G 201 (9B 60)
Courtleas KT11: Cob 9A 58
Court Lodge Rd. RH6: Horl ...7C 142
Courtmoor Av. GU52: Fleet 6B 88
Courtney Cres. SM5: Cars 4D 62
Courtney Pl. CR0: Wad 9L 45
KT11: Cob 8N 57
RG42: Bin 7H 15
Courtney Rd. CR0: Wad 9L 45
SW19 ....8C 28
TW6: Lon A 6B 8
Courtney Way TW6: Lon A 5B 8
Courtoak La. RH1: Out 6M 143
Court Rd. CR3: Cate 1A 104
GU11: Alde 2M 109
RH9: Gods 9F 104
SE25 ....1C 46
SM7: Ban 3M 81
UB2: S'hall 1N 9
Court Royal SW15 ....8K 13
Courts Hill Rd. GU27: Hasl ...2F 188
Courts Mt. Rd.
GU27: Hasl 2F 188
Court Way TW2: Twick 1F 24
Court Wood La. CR0: Sels 7J 65
Court Yd., The KT14: W By 8J 55
Courtyard, The BR2: Kes 3G 66
CR3: Whyte 5C 84
KT20: K'wood 1A 102
RG12: Brac 1B 32
RG40: W'ham 3B 30
RH10: Craw 4B 182
RH12: Hors 6J 197
RH13: Col 4D 198
RH19: E Grin 9D 166
TN16: Weste 5M 107
Courtyard Theatre, The
Chipstead Bottom 7D 82
Cousins Copse Cvn. Site
RH14: Slin 8G 195
Coutts Av. KT9: Ches 2L 59
Coval Gdns. SW14 ....7A 12
Coval La. SW14 ....7A 12
Coval Pas. SW14 ....7B 12
Coval Rd. SW14 ....7A 12
COVE 9H 69
Cove Ct. GU14: Cove 9H 69
Coveham Cres. KT11: Cob 9H 57
Coventry Hall SW16 ....6J 29
Coventry Rd. SE25 ....3D 46
Coverack Cl. CR0: Croy 6H 47
Coverdale Ct.
RH19: E Grin 7M 165
Coverdale Gdns.
CR0: Croy 9C 46
Cove Rd. GU14: Cove 1L 89
GU51: Fleet 1C 88
Covers La. GU27: Lip 2A 188
Covert, The GU14: Cove 6K 69
SL5: Asc 6M 33
Covert Cl. RH10: Craw 2C 182
Covert Mead RH17: Hand 9N 199
Coverton Rd. SW17 ....6C 28
Coverts Cl. GU9: Farnh 8K 109
Coverts Rd. KT10: Clay 4F 58
Coves Farm Wood
RG42: Brac 1J 31
Covey, The RH10: Craw 1H 183
Covey Cl. GU14: Farnb 6M 69
SW19 ....1N 43
Covington Gdns.
SW16 ....8M 29
Covington Way SW16 ....7K 29
(not continuous)
Cowbridge Mdw.
GU24: Pirb 1C 92
Cowdray Cl. RH10: Craw 4G 183
Cowdrey Rd. SW19 ....6N 27
Cowfold Cl. RH11: Craw 6L 181
Cowick Rd. SW17 ....5D 28
Cow La. GU7: Goda 7G 133
Cowleaze Rd.
KT2: K Tham 2K 203 (9L 25)
Cowley Av. KT16: Chert 6H 37
Cowley Cl. CR2: Sels 5F 64
Cowley Cres. KT12: Hers 1K 57
Cowley La. KT16: Chert 6H 37
Cowley Lodge KT16: Chert 6H 37
Cowley Rd. SW14 ....6D 12
Coworth Cl. SL5: S'dale 4E 34
Coworth Rd. SL5: S'dale 4D 34
Cowper Av. SM1: Sut 1B 62
Cowper Cl. KT16: Chert 5H 37
Cowper Gdns. SM6: W'ton 3G 63
Cowper Rd. KT2: K Tham 6M 25
SW19 ....7A 28
COWSHOT COMMON 7B 72
Cowshot Cres.
GU24: B'wood 7A 72
Cowslip Cl. GU35: Lind 5B 168
Cowslip La. GU21: Wok 2L 73
RH5: Mick 6G 99
Coxbridge Bus. Pk.
GU10: Farnh 3D 128
Coxbridge Mdw.
GU9: Farnh 2E 128
Coxcombe La. GU8: Chid 5E 172
Coxcomb Wlk. RH11: Craw ...5L 181
Coxdean KT18: Tat C 6H 81
COX GREEN 7F 176
Cox Grn. GU47: C Tow 9J 49
Cox Grn. Rd. RH12: Rudg 7C 176
Cox Ho. RH12: Hors 6H 197
W6 ....*2K 13*
(off Field Rd.)
Cox La. KT9: Ches 1M 59
KT19: Ewe 2A 60
(not continuous)
Coxley Ri. CR8: Pur 9N 63
Coxmoor Cl. GU52: C Cro 8D 88
Coxs Av. TW17: Shep 2F 38
Coxwold Path KT9: Ches 4L 59
CRABBET PARK 2J 183
Crabbet Pk. RH10: Wor 2K 183
Crabbet Rd. RH10: Craw 2F 182
Crabbs Cft. Cl.
BR6: Farnb 2L 67
Crabhill La. RH1: Sth N 7K 123
Crabtree Cl. KT23: Book 4C 98
Crabtree Dr. KT22: Leat 2J 99
Crabtree Gdns.
GU35: Head 4D 168
Crabtree La. GU10: Churt ...8M 149
GU35: Head 4D 168
KT18: Head 4B 100
KT23: Book 4C 98
RH5: Westh 8F 98
SW6 ....3H 13
(not continuous)
Crabtree Office Village
TW20: Thor 1E 36
Crabtree Rd. GU15: Camb 4N 69
RH11: Craw 2A 182
TW20: Thor 1E 36
Crabtree Wlk. CR0: Croy 7D 46
Crabwood RH8: Oxt 6A 106
Craddocks Av.
KT21: A'tead 4L 79
Craddocks Cl. KT21: A'tead ...3N 79
Craddocks Pde.
KT21: A'tead 4L 79
(not continuous)
Cradhurst Cl. RH4: Westc 6C 118
Cradle La.
GU35: Head, Slea 6B 148
Crafts Study Cen. (Gallery)
......................1G 128
Craigans RH11: Craw 3M 181
Craigen Av. CR0: Croy 7E 46
Craigmore Twr.
GU22: Wok *6A 74*
(off Guildford Rd.)
Craignair Rd. SW2 ....1L 29
Craignish Av. SW16 ....1K 45
Craig Rd. TW10: Ham 5J 25
Craigwell Av. TW13: Felt 4H 23
Craigwell Cl. TW18: Stain 9G 21
Crail Cl. RG41: W'ham 5A 30
Crakell Rd. RH2: Reig 4A 122
Crake Pl. GU47: C Tow 7J 49
CRAMHURST 4B 152
Cramhurst La. GU8: Wit 4B 152
Crammond Cl. W6 ....2K 13
Cramond Ct. TW14: Bedf 2F 22
Crampshaw La.
KT21: A'tead 6M 79
Cranberry Wlk. GU17: Haw 3L 69
Cranborne Av. KT6: Surb 9N 41
Cranborne Wlk.
RH10: Craw 5D 182
CRANBOURNE 2M 17
Cranbourne Av. SL4: W'sor 5C 4
Cranbourne Cl. KT12: Hers ...3K 57
RH6: Horl 6F 142
SW16 ....2J 45
Cranbourne Cotts.
SL4: Wink 4M 17
Cranbourne Hall Cvn. Site
SL4: Wink 2L 17
Cranbourne Hall Cotts.
SL4: Wink 2M 17
Cranbourne Towers
SL5: Asc 9H 17
Cranbrook Ct. GU51: Fleet 2B 88
TW8: Brent 2J 11
Cranbrook Dr. KT10: Esh 7C 40
TW2: Whitt 2B 24
Cranbrook Rd. CR7: T Hea 1N 45
SW19 ....8K 27
TW4: Houn 7N 9
W4 ....1D 12
Cranbrook Ter. GU6: Cranl 7A 156
Cranbury Rd. SW6 ....5N 13
Crane Av. TW7: Isle 8G 10
Cranebank M. TW1: Twick 7G 11
Cranebrook TW2: Twick 3C 24
Crane Ct. GU47: C Tow 7J 49
KT19: Ewe 1B 60
Craneford Cl. TW2: Twick 1F 24
Craneford Way TW2: Twick 1E 24
Crane Ho. TW13: Hanw 4A 24
Crane Lodge Rd.
TW5: C'ford 2J 9
Crane Mead Ct. TW1: Twick ...1F 24
Crane Pk. Island Nature Reserve
......................3N 23
Crane Pk. Rd. TW2: Whitt 3B 24
Crane Rd. TW2: Twick 2E 24
TW19: Stan 9B 8
Cranes Dr.
KT5: Surb 8K 203 (3L 41)
Cranes Pk.
KT5: Surb 8K 203 (3L 41)
Cranes Pk. Av.
KT5: Surb 8K 203 (3L 41)
Cranes Pk. Cres.
KT5: Surb 8L 203 (3M 41)
Craneswater UB3: Harl 3G 9
Craneswater Pk.
UB2: S'hall 1N 9
Crane Way TW2: Whitt 1C 24
Cranfield Cl. SE27 ....4N 29
Cranfield Ct. GU21: Wok 5K 73
Cranfield Rd. E. SM5: Cars ...5E 62
Cranfield Rd. W.
SM5: Cars 5D 62
CRANFORD 4H 9
Cranford Av. GU52: C Cro 8A 88
TW19: Stan 1N 21
Cranford Cl. CR8: Pur 9N 63
SW20 ....8G 26
TW19: Stan 1N 21
Cranford Community College
Sports Cen. 2J 9
Cranford Dr. UB3: Harl 1G 8
Cranford La.
TW5: C'ford, Hest 3J 9
TW6: Lon A 4G 8
(Bath Rd.)
TW6: Lon A 6G 8
(Elmdon Rd.)
UB3: C'ford, Harl 2E 8
Cranford Pk. Dr. GU46: Yate ...9C 48
Cranford Ri. KT10: Esh 2C 58
CRANLEIGH 7M 155
Cranleigh Arts Cen. 7N 155
Cranleigh Cl. CR2: Sande 8D 64
SE20 ....1E 46
Cranleigh Ct. CR4: Mit 2B 44
GU14: Cove 1L 89
TW9: Rich 6N 11
Cranleigh Gdns.
CR2: Sande 8D 64
KT2: K Tham 7M 25
SE25 ....2B 46
SM1: Sut 8N 43
Cranleigh Leisure Cen. 8M 155
Cranleigh Mead
GU6: Cranl 8A 156
Cranleigh Rd. GU5: Wone 4D 134
GU6: Ewh 6E 156
KT10: Esh 7C 40
SW19 ....2M 43
TW13: Felt 5G 22
Cranley Cl. GU1: Guil 3C 114
Cranley Dene GU1: Guil 3C 114
Cranley Gdns. SM6: W'ton 4G 62
Cranley Pl. GU21: Knap 5G 72
Cranley Rd. GU1: Guil 3B 114
KT12: Hers 2G 56
Cranmer Cl. CR6: Warl 4H 85
KT13: Weybr 4B 56
SM4: Mord 5J 43
Cranmer Ct. *GU21: Knap* *5F 72*
(off Hampton Cl.)
TW12: H Hill 6B 24
Cranmer Farm Cl. CR4: Mit ...3D 44
Cranmer Gdns. CR6: Warl 4H 85
Cranmer Rd.
CR0: Croy 4A 200 (9M 45)
CR4: Mit 3D 44
KT2: K Tham 6L 25
TW12: H Hill 6B 24
Cranmer Ter. SW17 ....6B 28
Cranmer Wlk. RH10: Craw 4G 183
Cranmore Av. TW7: Isle 3C 10
Cranmore Cl. GU11: Alde 3K 109
Cranmore Cotts.
KT24: W Hors 7C 96
Cranmore Ct. GU16: Mytc 1D 90
Cranmore Gdns.
GU11: Alde 3J 109
Cranmore La. GU11: Alde 3J 109
KT24: W Hors 7C 96
(not continuous)
Cranmore Rd. GU16: Mytc 1D 90
Cranston Cl. RH2: Reig 4N 121
TW3: Houn 5M 9
Cranston Rd. RH19: E Grin ...8A 166
Cranston Way
RH10: Craw D 1F 184
Cranstoun Cl. GU3: Guil 8J 93
Cranwell Gro. GU18: Ligh 7K 51
TW17: Shep 3A 38
Cranwell Rd. TW6: Lon A 5C 8
Craster Rd. SW2 ....1K 29
Cravan Av. TW13: Felt 3H 23
Craven Cl. GU10: L Bou 5H 129
Craven Cottage 5J 13
Craven Ct. *RH19: E Grin* *8B 166*
(off Badger's Way)
Craven Gdns. SW19 ....6M 27
Craven Rd. CR0: Croy 7E 46
KT2: K Tham ...1M 203 (9M 25)
RH10: Craw 4F 182
Cravens, The RH6: Smal 8L 143
Crawford Cl. TW7: Isle 5E 10
Crawford Gdns.
GU15: Camb 1N 69
RH13: Hors 4L 197
Crawfurd Way
RH19: E Grin 8A 166
CRAWLEY 3B 182
Crawley Av. RH10: Craw 1C 182
RH11: Craw 3M 181
Crawley Bus. Quarter
RH10: Craw 8C 162
Crawley Chase
RG42: Wink R 7F 16
CRAWLEY DOWN 2E 184
Crawley Down Rd.
RH19: Fel 7H 165
Crawley Dr. GU15: Camb 9D 50
Crawley Foyer RH11: Craw ...3A 182
Crawley Goods Yd.
RH10: Craw 7F 162
CRAWLEY HILL 1B 70
Crawley Hill GU15: Camb 1D 70
Crawley La. RH10: Craw 2G 182
Crawley Lawn Tennis Club
......................1F 182
Crawley Leisure Pk.
RH10: Craw 2B 182
Crawley Mus. Cen. 4A 182
Crawley Ridge GU15: Camb ...9D 50
Crawley Ri. GU15: Camb 8E 50
Crawley Rd. RH11: Fay 1B 198
RH12: Hors, Fay 4M 197
Crawley Sth. W. By-Pass
RH11: P Pot 7K 181
Crawley Station (Rail) 4C 182
Crawley Town FC 7A 182
Crawley Wood Cl.
GU15: Camb 1D 70
Crawshaw Rd. KT16: Otter 3F 54
Crawters Cl. RH10: Craw 2D 182
Cray Av. KT21: A'tead 3L 79
Crayke Hill KT9: Ches 4L 59
Crayonne Cl. TW16: Sunb 9F 22
Crealock St. SW18 ....9N 13
Creasys Dr. RH11: Craw 8M 181
Credenhill St. SW16 ....7G 28
Crediton Way KT10: Clay 2G 58
Credon Cl. GU14: Cove 9L 69
Creek, The TW16: Sunb 4H 39
Creek Cotts. *KT8: E Mol* *3E 40*
(off Creek Rd.)
Creek Rd. KT8: E Mol 3E 40
Cree's Mdw. GU20: Windl 3N 51
Crefeld Cl. W6 ....2K 13
Cremorne Gdns.
KT19: Ewe 6C 60
Crerar Cl. GU14: Cove 2J 89
Crescent, The BR3: Beck 1K 47
BR4: W Wick 5N 47
CR0: Croy 4A 46
CR3: Wold 1K 105
GU2: Guil 2K 113
GU9: H End 4J 109
GU14: Farnb 2A 90
GU17: Haw 2J 69
GU46: Yate 8C 48
KT3: N Mal 2B 42
KT6: Surb 4L 41
KT8: W Mole 3A 40
KT13: Weybr 9B 38
KT16: Chert 3J 37
KT18: Eps 1N 79
(not continuous)
KT22: Leat 9H 79
RH1: Red 6B 122
RH2: Reig 3N 121
RH6: Horl 1E 162
(not continuous)
RH12: Hors 7G 196
RH19: Felc 2M 165
SM1: Sut 2B 62
SM2: Sut 7M 61
SW13 ....5E 12
SW19 ....4M 27
TW15: A'ford 6A 22
TW17: Shep 6G 38
TW20: Egh 7A 20
UB3: Harl 3D 8
Crescent Ct. KT6: Surb 4K 41
RH6: Horl 1E 162
Crescent Gdns. SW19 ....4M 27
Crescent Gro. CR4: Mit 3C 44
Crescent Hill RH19: D Pk 4A 166
Crescent La. GU12: A Va 8F 90
Crescent Rd. BR3: Beck 1L 47
CR3: Cate 2D 104
KT2: K Tham 8N 25
RG40: W'ham 3B 30
RH1: Blet 2N 123
RH2: Reig 5M 121
RH19: E Grin 9N 165
SW20 ....9J 27
TW17: Shep 4D 38
Crescent Stables
SW15 ....8K 13
Crescent Way BR6: Orp 2N 67
RH6: Horl 1E 162
SW16 ....7K 29
Cresford Rd. SW6 ....4N 13
Cressage Ho. *TW8: Brent* *2L 11*
(off Ealing Rd.)
Cressall Cl. KT22: Leat 7H 79
Cressall Mead KT22: Leat 7H 79
Cressex Cl. RG42: Bin 7H 15
Cressida Chase RG42: Warf ...8C 16
Cressingham Gro. SM1: Sut ...1A 62
Cressinghams, The
KT18: Eps 7K 201 (9C 60)
Cresswell Ho. *TW19: Stan* *9N 7*
(off Douglas Rd.)
Cresswell Rd. SE25 ....3D 46
TW1: Twick 9K 11
TW13: Hanw 4M 23
Cressy Ho. SW15 ....6G 12
Crest, The KT5: Surb 4N 41
Cresta Dr. KT15: Wood 6H 55
Crest Hill GU5: P'lake 2E 136
Creston Av. GU21: Knap 4H 73
Creston Way KT4: W Pk 7J 43
Crest Rd. CR2: Sels 4E 64
Crestway SW15 ....9F 12
Crestwood Way TW4: Houn 8M 9
Creswell GU21: Knap 4G 73
Creswell Cnr. GU21: Knap 4G 73
Creswell Dr. BR3: Beck 4L 47
Crewdson Rd. RH6: Horl 8F 142
Crewe Ct. KT20: Tad 9H 81
Crewe's Av. CR6: Warl 3F 84
Crewe's Cl. CR6: Warl 4F 84
Crewe's Farm La.
CR6: Warl 3G 85
Crewe's La. CR6: Warl 3F 84
Crichton Av. SM6: Bedd 2H 63
Crichton Rd. SM5: Cars 3D 62
Cricket Cl. GU26: Hind 3B 170

Cricket Ct. RH19: E Grin 7A 166
Cricketers Cl. KT9: Ches 1K 59
RH5: Ockl 6C 158
Cricketers La.
GU20: Windl 2A 52
RG42: Warf 6E 16
Cricketers M. SW18 ....8N 13
Cricketers Ter. SM5: Cars 9C 44
Cricket Fld. Gro.
RG45: Crow 3J 49
Cricketfield Rd.
RH12: Hors 7H 197
Cricket Grn. CR4: Mit 2D 44
GU8: Hamb 9F 152
CRICKET HILL 1C 68
Cricket Hill GU46: Yate 3D 68
RH1: Sth N 5K 123
Cricket Hill La. GU46: Yate 3C 68
Cricket La. GU10: L Bou 5J 129
Cricket Lea GU35: Lind 4A 168
CRICKETS HILL 3D 94
Cricketts Hill GU5: Shere 8B 116
Cricket Vw. KT13: Weybr 2C 56
Cricket Way KT13: Weybr 8F 38
Cricklade Av. SW2 ....3J 29
Crieff Ct. TW11: Tedd 8J 25
Crieff Rd. SW18 ....1A 28
Criffel Av. SW2 ....3H 29
Crimea Rd. GU11: Alde 2N 109
(not continuous)
Crimp Hill
SL4: Eng G, O Win 1J 19
TW20: Eng G 4K 19
Cripley Rd. GU14: Cove 8J 69
Cripplecrutch Hill
GU8: Chid 3C 190
Cripps Ho. RH11: Craw 7N 181
Crispen Rd. TW13: Hanw 5M 23
Crisp Gdns. RG42: Bin 8K 15
Crispin Cl. CR0: Bedd 8J 45
KT21: A'tead 5M 79
Crispin Cres. CR0: Bedd 9H 45
Crisp Rd. W6 ....1H 13
Cristowe Rd. SW6 ....5L 13
CRITCHMERE 1C 188
Critchmere Hill
GU27: Hasl 1C 188
Critchmere La. GU27: Hasl ...2C 188
Critchmere Va.
GU27: Hasl 2C 188
Criterion Bldgs. KT7: T Dit 6H 41
(off Portsmouth Rd.)
Critten La. RH5: Ran C 3L 117
Crocker Cl. SL5: Asc 9K 17
Crockers La. RH7: Ling 7G 144
Crockerton Rd. SW17 ....3D 28
Crockery La. GU4: E Cla 7M 95
Crockford Cl. KT15: Addl 1L 55
Crockford Pk. Rd.
KT15: Addl 2L 55
Crockford Pl. RG42: Bin 8L 15
Crockham Cl. RH11: Craw ...5A 182
CROCKHAM HILL 2L 127
Crocknorth Rd.
KT24: E Hor 1G 117
(not continuous)
RH5: Ran C 1G 117
Crocus Cl. CR0: Croy 7G 47
Croffets KT20: Tad 8J 81
Croft, The CR0: Croy 9C 46
GU8: Els 8J 131
GU46: Yate 8C 48
KT17: Eps 8M 201 (1E 80)
KT22: Fetc 1E 98
RG40: W'ham 3C 30
RG42: Brac 8N 15
RH11: Craw 3M 181
TW5: Hest 2M 9
Croft Av. BR4: W Wick 7M 47
RH4: Dork 3H 119
Croft Cl. UB3: Harl 3D 8
Croft Cnr. SL4: O Win 8L 5
Croft Ct. TN8: Eden 2L 147
Croft End Cl. KT9: Ches 9M 41
Crofters SL4: O Win 9K 5
Crofters Cl. GU16: Deep 5H 71
GU47: Sandh 7F 48
RH1: Red 5F 122
TW7: Isle 8D 10
TW19: Stan 9L 7
Crofters Mead CR0: Sels 5J 65
Croft La. GU46: Yate 8B 48
TN8: Eden 2L 147
Croftleigh Av. CR8: Pur 3L 83
Crofton KT21: A'tead 5L 79
Crofton Av. KT12: Wal T 9K 39
W4 ....3B 12
Crofton Cl. KT16: Otter 4E 54
RG12: Brac 4C 32
Crofton M. GU1: Guil 4B 114
Crofton Rd. BR6: Farnb, Orp ...1J 67
Crofton Ter. TW9: Rich 7M 11
Croft Rd. CR3: Wold 9K 85
GU7: Goda 7G 133
GU8: Wit 5B 152
GU11: Alde 4N 109
SM1: Sut 2C 62
SW16 ....9L 29
SW19 ....8A 28
TN16: Weste 4K 107
Crofts, The TW17: Shep 3F 38
Crofts Cl. GU8: Chid 4E 172
Croftside, The SE25 ....2D 46

Croft Way GU16: Frim 4D 70
RH12: Hors 5G 196
Croftway TW10: Ham 4H 25
Croham Cl. CR2: S Croy 4B 64
Croham Mnr. Rd.
CR2: S Croy 4B 64
Croham Mt. CR2: S Croy 4B 64
Croham Pk. Av.
CR2: S Croy 2B 64
Croham Rd.
CR2: S Croy 8D 200 (2B 64)
Croham Valley Rd.
CR2: Sels 3D 64
Croindene Rd. SW16 ....9J 29
Cromar Ct. GU21: Wok 3M 73
Cromerhyde SM4: Mord 4N 43
Cromer Rd. SE25 ....2E 46
SW17 ....7E 28
TW6: Lon A 5B 8
Cromer Vs. Rd.
SW18 ....9L 13
Cromford Cl. BR6: Orp 1N 67
Cromford Rd. SW18 ....8M 13
Cromford Way KT3: N Mal 9C 26
Crompton Flds.
RH10: Craw 9C 162
Crompton Way
RH10: Craw 1C 182
Cromwell Av. KT3: N Mal 4E 42
W6 ....1G 12
Cromwell Cl. KT12: Wal T 7J 39
Cromwell Ct. GU21: Knap 6F 72
(off Tudor Way)
Cromwell Gro. CR3: Cate 8N 83
Cromwell Ho.
CR0: Croy 5A 200 (9M 45)
Cromwell Pl. GU6: Cranl 9A 156
RH19: E Grin 2B 186
SW14 ....6B 12
Cromwell Rd. BR3: Beck 1H 47
CR0: Croy 6A 46
CR3: Cate 8N 83
GU15: Camb 8B 50
KT2: K Tham 2K 203 (9L 25)
KT4: W Pk 9C 42
KT12: Wal T 7J 39
RH1: Red 3D 122
SL5: Asc 3M 33
SW19 ....6M 27
TW3: Houn 7A 10
TW11: Tedd 7G 24
TW13: Felt 2J 23
Cromwell St. TW3: Houn 7A 10
Cromwell Wlk. RH1: Red 3D 122
Cromwell Way GU14: Farnb 7N 69
Crondace Rd. SW6 ....4M 13
Crondall Ct. GU15: Camb 2N 69
Crondall End GU46: Yate 8B 48
Crondall Ho. SW15 ....1F 26
Crondall La. GU9: Farnh 1B 128
GU10: Dip 1B 128
Crondall Rd. GU10: Farnh 4A 128
Cronks Hill RH1: Red 5B 122
RH2: Reig 5A 122
Cronks Hill Cl. RH1: Red 5B 122
Cronks Hill Rd. RH1: Red 5B 122
Crooked Billet SW19 ....7H 27
CROOKED BILLET RDBT. 5J 21
Crookham Rd. GU51: C Cro 5A 88
SW6 ....4L 13
CROOKSBURY COMMON 4B 130
Crooksbury La. GU10: Seal 2C 130
Crooksbury Rd.
GU10: Farnh, Run, Til ...9N 109
Crosby Cl. TW13: Hanw 4M 23
Crosby Gdns. GU46: Yate 8A 48
Crosby Hill Dr. GU15: Camb ...8D 50
Crosby Wlk. SW2 ....1L 29
Crosby Way GU9: Farnh 2F 128
SW2 ....1L 29
Crossacres GU22: Pyr 3G 75
Cross Deep TW1: Twick 3F 24
Cross Deep Gdns.
TW1: Twick 3F 24
Crossfell RG12: Brac 3M 31
Crossfield Pl. KT13: Weybr 4C 56
Cross Gdns. GU16: Frim G 8D 70
Cross Gates Cl. RG12: Brac ...2D 32
Cross Keys RH10: Craw 3B 182
Cross Lances Rd.
TW3: Houn 7B 10
Crossland Ho. GU25: V Wat ...3A 36
(off Holloway Dr.)
Crossland Rd. CR7: T Hea 5M 45
RH1: Red 3E 122
Crosslands KT16: Chert 1G 55
Crosslands Av. UB2: S'hall 1N 9
Crosslands Rd. KT19: Ewe 3C 60
Cross La. GU16: Frim G 8D 70
KT16: Otter 3D 54
RH6: Smal 2N 163
Cross Lanes
GU1: Guil 3F 202 (3B 114)
Crossley Cl. TN16: B Hil 2F 86
Crossman Ct. RH11: Craw ...8M 181
Cross Oak SL4: W'sor 5D 4
Crossoak La. RH1: Salf 4F 142
Crosspath RH10: Craw 2C 182
Cross Rd.
CR0: Croy 1E 200 (7A 46)
CR8: Pur 9M 63
GU12: A Va 1F 110
KT2: K Tham 8M 25

Cross Rd. KT13: Weybr 9E 38
KT20: Tad 9H 81
SL5: S'dale 7C 34
SM1: Sut 2B 62
SM2: Sut 6M 61
SW19 ....8M 27
TW13: Hanw 5M 23
Crossroads, The KT24: Eff 6L 97
Cross St. GU11: Alde 2M 109
GU14: Farnb 5A 90
RG40: W'ham 2B 30
SW13 ....5D 12
TW12: H Hill 6C 24
CROSSWATER 6K 149
Crosswater Farm Gdns. 6L 149
Crosswater La.
GU10: Churt 6K 149
Crossway KT12: Wal T 8J 39
RG12: Brac 1A 32
RH6: Gat 2D 162
SW20 ....3H 43
Crossways CR2: Sels 4H 65
GU12: Alde 3A 110
KT24: Eff 2M 97
RH10: Craw 2D 182
SM2: Sut 5B 62
TN16: Tats 8E 86
TW16: Sunb 8G 23
TW20: Egh 7F 20
Crossways, The CR5: Coul 6K 83
GU2: Guil 5J 113
KT5: Surb 7A 42
RH1: Mers 7G 102
TW5: Hest 3N 9
Crossways Av.
RH19: E Grin 9M 165
Crossways Cl.
GU10: Churt 9L 149
RH10: Craw 2D 182
Crossways Ct. SL4: W'sor 5F 4
(off Osbourne Rd.)
Crossways La. RH2: Reig 6A 102
(not continuous)
Crossways Rd. BR3: Beck 3K 47
CR4: Mit 2F 44
GU26: G'hott 6A 170
Crosswell Cl. TW17: Shep 1D 38
Crouchfield RH4: Dork 8J 119
Crouch Ho. Cotts.
TN8: Eden 1K 147
CROUCH HOUSE GREEN 1K 147
Crouch Ho. Rd. TN8: Eden ...9J 127
Crouch La. SL4: Wink 1J 17
Crouch Oak La. KT15: Addl 1L 55
Crowberry Cl. RH11: Craw ...7M 181
Crowborough Cl. CR6: Warl ...5H 85
Crowborough Dr. CR6: Warl ...5H 85
Crowborough Rd.
SW17 ....7E 28
Crowcroft Cl. GU2: Guil 8L 93
Crowhill BR6: Dow 6J 67
Crowholt GU10: Wrec 6E 128
(off Echo Barn La.)
CROWHURST 9A 126
Crowhurst Cl. RH10: Wor 3J 183
Crowhurst Keep
RH10: Wor 3J 183
Crowhurst La. RH7: Ling 7L 125
RH8: Ling 7L 125
CROWHURST LANE END 7L 125
Crowhurst Mead
RH9: Gods 8F 104
Crowhurst Rd. RH7: Ling 3N 145
Crowhurst Village Rd.
RH7: Ling 1A 146
Crowland Rd. CR7: T Hea 3A 46
Crowland Wlk. SM4: Mord 5N 43
Crowley Cres.
CR0: Wad 8A 200 (2L 63)
Crown, The TN16: Weste 4M 107
Crown All. RH12: Hors 6J 197
(off Carfax)
Crown Arc.
KT1: K Tham 4H 203 (1K 41)
Crown Ash Hill TN16: B Hil 1D 86
Crown Ash La. CR6: Warl 3C 86
TN16: B Hil, Warl 3C 86
Crownbourne Ct. SM1: Sut 1N 61
(off St Nicholas Way)
Crown Cl. KT12: Wal T 6K 39
SL3: Coln 3E 6
Crown Cotts. SL4: W'sor 7G 4
Crown Ct. GU7: Goda 7H 133
Crown Dale SE19 ....7M 29
Crown Dr. GU9: B Lea 7M 109
Crown Gdns. GU51: Fleet 5C 88
Crown Hgts.
GU1: Guil 8E 202 (6A 114)
Crown Hill
CR0: Croy 3B 200 (8N 45)
Crown Hill Ct. SL5: Asc 4M 33
Crown Ho. KT3: N Mal 2B 42
Crown La. GU9: B Lea 7L 109
GU25: V Wat 5N 35
SM4: Mord 3M 43
SW16 ....6L 29
Crown La. Gdns.
SW16 ....6L 29
Crown Mdw. SL3: Coln 3D 6
Crown Pde. SM4: Mord 2M 43
Crown Pas. KT1: K Tham 4H 203
(off Church St.)
CROWNPITS 8J 133

Crownpits La. GU7: Goda ...8H 133
Crown Pl. GU47: Owls 6K 49
Crown Point SE19 ....7M 29
Crown Ri. KT16: Chert 7H 37
Crown Rd. GU25: V Wat 5M 35
KT3: N Mal 9B 26
SM1: Sut 1N 61
SM4: Mord 3N 43
TN8: Eden 9M 127
TW1: Twick 9H 11
Crown Row RG12: Brac 5B 32
Crown Sq. GU21: Wok 4B 74
Crown St. TW20: Egh 5C 20
Crown Ter. TW9: Rich 7M 11
Crowntree Cl. TW7: Isle 2F 10
Crown Wlk. GU7: Goda 7H 133
CROWN WOOD 5B 32
Crown Yd. TW3: Houn 6C 10
Crowther Av. TW8: Brent 1L 11
Crowther Cl. SW6 ....2L 13
(off Bucklers All.)
Crowther Rd. SE25 ....4D 46
CROWTHORNE 2H 49
Crowthorne Bus. Est.
RG45: Crow 9H 31
Crowthorne Cl. SW18 ....1L 27
Crowthorne Lodge
RG12: Brac 3N 31
(off Crowthorne Rd.)
Crowthorne Rd.
GU47: Sandh 7F 48
RG12: Brac 8K 31
(Nine Mile Ride)
RG12: Brac 4M 31
(Threshfield)
RG45: Crow 1J 49
Crowthorne Rd. Nth.
RG12: Brac 2N 31
Crowthorne Station (Rail) 3D 48
Croxall Ho. KT12: Wal T 5K 39
Croxden Wlk. SM4: Mord 5A 44
Croxted Cl. SE21 ....1N 29
Croxted M. SE24 ....1N 29
Croxted Rd. SE21 ....1N 29
SE24 ....1N 29
Croyde Av. UB3: Harl 1F 8
Croyde Cl. GU14: Farnb 8M 69
CROYDON 4C 200 (9N 45)
Croydon Airport Ind. Est.
CR0: Wad 3K 63
Croydon Airport Vis. Cen. 3L 63
Croydon Barn La.
RH6: Horn 7C 144
RH9: S Gods 7C 144
Croydon Clocktower 4C 200
(off Katherine St.)
Croydon Crematorium
CR0: Croy 4K 45
Croydon Flyover, The
CR0: Croy 6A 200 (1M 63)
Croydon Gro. CR0: Croy 7M 45
Croydon La. SM7: Ban 1A 82
Croydon La. Sth. SM7: Ban ...1A 82
Croydon Rd. BR2: Hay, Kes 1E 66
BR2: Kes 1E 66
BR3: Beck 3G 46
BR4: Hay, W Wick 1C 66
CR0: Bedd, Wad 1F 62
CR0: Croy 3E 44
CR3: Cate 1D 104
CR4: Mit 3E 44
RH2: Reig 3N 121
SE20 ....1E 46
SM6: Bedd, W'ton 1F 62
TN16: Weste 1H 107
TW6: Lon A 5C 8
Croydon Rd. Ind. Est.
BR3: Beck 3G 46
Croydon Sports Arena 4F 46
Croydon Sports Club 7F 64
Croylands Dr. KT6: Surb 6L 41
Croysdale Av. TW16: Sunb 2H 39
Crozier Dr. CR2: Sels 6E 64
Cruch La. SL6: P St 1B 16
Cruikshank Lea
GU47: C Tow 9K 49
Crunden Rd. CR2: S Croy 4A 64
Crundwell Ct. GU9: Farnh 9J 109
Crusader Gdns. CR0: Croy 9B 46
Crusoe Rd. CR4: Mit 8D 28
Crutchfield La. KT12: Wal T ...8J 39
RH6: Sid 5M 141
Crutchley Rd. RG40: W'ham ...1C 30
Crystal Palace FC 3B 46
Cubitt Ho. GU6: Cranl 6L 155
SW4 ....1G 28
Cubitt Way GU21: Knap 5G 72
Cuckfield Cl. RH11: Craw 6L 181
Cuckmere Cres.
RH11: Craw 4L 181
Cuckoo La. GU24: W End 9A 52
Cuckoo Pound TW17: Shep 4F 38
Cuckoo Va. GU24: W End 9A 52
Cudas Cl. KT19: Ewe 1E 60
Cuddington Av. KT4: W Pk 9E 42
Cuddington Cl. KT20: Tad 7H 81
Cuddington Ct. SM2: Chea 5J 61
Cuddington Glade
KT19: Eps 8N 59
Cuddington Pk. Cl.
SM7: Ban 9L 61
Cuddington Way SM2: Chea ...8J 61
CUDHAM 2M 87

Cudham Cl. SM2: Sut 6M 61
Cudham Dr. CR0: N Add 6M 65
Cudham La. Nth. BR6: Dow 6N 67
TN14: Cud 1L 87
Cudham La. Sth.
TN14: Cud, Knoc 2L 87
Cudham Pk. Rd. TN14: Cud ...6N 67
Cudham Rd. BR6: Dow 7J 67
TN16: Tats 6G 86
CUDWORTH 2D 160
Cudworth La. RH5: Newd 1B 160
Cudworth Pk. RH5: Newd 2E 160
Culdrose Ho. GU11: Alde 2M 109
(off Frederick St.)
Culham Ho. RG12: Brac 3C 32
Cullen Cl. GU46: Yate 1B 68
Cullens M. GU11: Alde 3M 109
Cullerne Cl. KT17: Ewe 6E 60
Cullesden Rd. CR8: Ken 2M 83
Cull's Rd. GU3: Flex 3M 111
CULMER 8C 152
Culmer Hill GU8: Worm 8C 152
Culmer La. GU8: Worm 7C 152
Culmington Rd.
CR2: S Croy 5N 63
Culsac Rd. KT6: Surb 8L 41
Culvercroft RG42: Bin 8K 15
Culverden Ct. KT13: Weybr 9E 38
(off Oatlands Dr.))
Culverden Rd. SW12 ....3G 28
Culverden Ter. KT13: Weybr ...9E 38
Culver Dr. RH8: Oxt 8A 106
Culverhay KT21: A'tead 3L 79
Culverhouse Gdns.
SW16 ....4K 29
Culverlands Cres.
GU12: Ash 1D 110
Culver Rd. GU47: Owls 6J 49
Culvers Av. SM5: Cars 8D 44
Culvers Retreat SM5: Cars 7D 44
Culvers Way SM5: Cars 8D 44
Culworth Ho.
GU1: Guil 5F 202 (4A 114)
Culzean Cl. SE27 ....4M 29
Cumberland Av. GU2: Guil 7K 93
Cumberland Cl. KT19: Ewe 6D 60
SW20 ....8J 27
TW1: Twick 9H 11
Cumberland Ct.
CR0: Croy 1E 200 (7A 46)
Cumberland Dr. KT9: Ches 9L 41
KT10: H Wood 8G 40
RG12: Brac 9B 16
Cumberland Ho.
KT2: K Tham 8A 26
Cumberland Obelisk 8J 19
Cumberland Pl.
TW16: Sunb 3H 39
Cumberland Rd.
GU15: Camb 1G 70
SE25 ....5E 46
SW13 ....4E 12
TW9: Kew 3N 11
TW15: A'ford 4M 21
Cumberlands CR8: Ken 2A 84
Cumberland St.
TW18: Stain 6F 20
Cumberlow Av. SE25 ....2C 46
Cumbernauld Gdns.
TW16: Sunb 6G 22
Cumbernauld Wlk.
RH11: Craw 7K 181
Cumbrae Gdns. KT6: Surb 8K 41
Cumbria Ct. GU14: Farnb 4C 90
RH2: Reig 2B 122
Cumnor Gdns. KT17: Ewe 3F 60
Cumnor Ri. CR8: Ken 4N 83
Cumnor Rd. SM2: Sut 3A 62
Cumnor Way RG12: Brac 3C 32
Cunliffe Cl. KT18: Head 2A 100
Cunliffe Pde. KT19: Ewe 1E 60
Cunliffe Rd. KT19: Ewe 1E 60
Cunliffe St. SW16 ....7G 29
Cunningham Av. GU1: Guil ...2C 114
Cunningham Cl.
BR4: W Wick 8L 47
Cunningham Rd. SM7: Ban ...2B 82
Cunnington Rd.
GU14: Farnb 3C 90
Cunworth Ct. RG12: Brac 5L 31
Curchin Cl. TN16: B Hil 8E 66
Curfew Bell Rd.
KT16: Chert 6H 37
Curfew Yd. SL4: W'sor 3G 4
Curlew Cl. CR2: Sels 7G 64
Curlew Ct. GU11: Alde 5M 109
(off Boxhalls La.)
KT6: Surb 9N 41
Curlew Gdns. GU4: Guil 1F 114
Curley Hill Rd. GU18: Ligh 8J 51
Curling Cl. CR5: Coul 7K 83
Curling Va. GU2: Guil 5K 113
Curly Bri. Cl. GU14: Cove 6L 69
Curnick's La. SE27 ....5N 29
Curran Av. SM6: W'ton 9E 44
Currie Hill Cl. SW19 ....5L 27
Curteys Wlk. RH11: Craw 6L 181
Curtis Cl. GU15: Camb 8G 50
GU35: Head 3D 168
Curtis Ct. GU52: C Cro 8B 88
Curtis Fld. Rd. SW16 ....5K 29
Curtis Gdns.
RH4: Dork 1H 201 (4G 118)

Curtis La.—Delft Ho.

Curtis La. GU35: Head 3C 168
Curtis Rd. KT19: Ewe 1B 60
RH4: Dork 1G 201 (4F 118)
TW4: Houn 1N 23
Curtis's Cotts. RH12: Hors ...5M 179
Curvan Cl. KT17: Ewe 6E 60
Curzon Av. RH12: Hors 5H 197
Curzon Cl. BR6: Orp 1M 67
KT13: Weybr 1B 56
Curzon Ct. *SW6 .....4N 13*
(off Imperial Rd.)
Curzon Dr. GU52: C Cro 8C 88
Curzon Rd. CR7: T Hea 5L 45
KT13: Weybr 2B 56
Cusack Cl. TW1: Twick 5F 24
Cuthbert Gdns. SE25 .....2B 46
Cuthbert Rd.
CR0: Croy 3A 200 (8M 45)
GU12: A Va 7F 90
Cuthbert Row GU27: Hasl ...1G 189
Cutthroat All. TW10: Ham 3J 25
Cutting, The RH1: Red 5D 122
Cuttinglye La.
RH10: Craw D 9D 164
Cuttinglye Rd.
RH10: Craw D 8E 164
CUTTINGLYE WOOD 8F 164
Cutts Rd. GU11: Alde 6B 90
Cyclamen Cl. TW12: Hamp 7A 24
Cyclamen Way KT19: Ewe ...2B 60
Cygmus Ct. *CR8: Pur 7M 63*
(off Brighton Rd.)
Cygnet Av. TW14: Felt 1K 23
Cygnet Cl. GU21: Wok 3L 73
Cygnet Ct. GU51: Fleet 2C 88
Cygnets, The
TW13: Hanw 5M 23
TW18: Stain 6H 21
Cygnets Cl. RH1: Red 1E 122
Cypress Av. TW2: Whitt 1C 24
Cypress Cl. RG40: Finch 8A 30
Cypress Ct. GU25: V Wat 3A 36
SM1: Sut 2M 61
Cypress Dr. GU51: Fleet 4E 88
Cypress Gro. GU12: A Va 6D 90
Cypress Hill Ct.
GU14: Cove 5L 69
Cypress Ho. SL3: Lang 1D 6
Cypress Rd. GU1: Guil 1M 113
SE25 .....1B 46
Cypress Wlk. TW20: Eng G 7L 19
Cypress Way GU17: B'water 1G 68
GU26: Hind 7B 170
SM7: Ban 1J 81
Cyprus Rd. GU16: Deep 6H 71
Cyprus Vs. RH4: Dork 2J 201

D

D'Abernon Chase
KT22: Oxs 1G 79
D'Abernon Cl. KT10: Esh 1A 58
D'Abernon Dr. KT11: Sto D 3M 77
Dacre Rd. CR0: Croy 6J 45
Dade Way UB2: S'hall 1N 9
Daffodil Cl. CR0: Croy 7G 47
Daffodil Dr. GU24: Bis 3D 72
Daffodil Pl. TW12: Hamp 7A 24
Dafforne Rd. SW17 .....4E 28
Dagden Rd. GU4: Chil 9A 114
Dagley Farm Pk. Homes
GU4: Chil 9N 113
Dagley La. GU4: Chil 8N 113
Dagmar Rd.
KT2: K Tham ...1M 203 (9M 25)
SE25 .....4B 46
SL4: W'sor 5G 4
Dagnall Pk. SE25 .....5B 46
Dagnall Rd. SE25 .....4B 46
Dagnan Rd. SW12 .....1F 28
Dahlia Gdns. CR4: Mit 3H 45
Dahomey Rd. SW16 .....7G 28
Daimler Way SM6: W'ton 4J 63
Dairy Bus. Pk. RH1: Blet 9N 103
Dairy Cl. CR7: T Hea 1N 45
RH4: Westc 6C 118
Dairyfields RH11: Craw 4M 181
Dairy House Nature Reserve
.....5K 159
Dairy La. TN8: C Hil 3J 127
Dairyman's Wlk.
GU4: B'ham 7D 94
Dairy Wlk. SW19 .....5K 27
Daisy Cl. CR0: Croy 7G 47
Daisy La. SW6 .....6M 13
Daisy Mdw. TW20: Egh 6C 20
Dakin Cl. RH10: Craw 7G 183
Dakins, The RH19: E Grin ...1A 186
Dakota Cl. SM6: W'ton 4K 63
Dalby Rd. SW18 .....7N 13
Dalcross RG12: Brac 5C 32
Dalcross Rd. TW4: Houn 5M 9
Dale, The BR2: Kes 1F 66
Dale Av. TW4: Houn 6M 9
Dalebury Rd. SW17 .....3D 28
Dale Cl. GU10: Wrec 4E 128
KT15: Addl 2K 55
RH12: Hors 3M 197
SL5: S'dale 4D 34
Dale Copse *GU27: Fern 9F 188*
(off Old Glebe)
Dale Ct. KT2: K Tham 1M 203
Daledene *RH19: E Grin 1B 186*
(off Lewes Rd.)
Dale Gdns. GU47: Sandh 7F 48
Dalegarth Gdns. CR8: Pur 9A 64
Daleham Av. TW20: Egh 7C 20
Dale Lodge Rd.
SL5: S'dale 4D 34
Dale Pk. Av. SM5: Cars 8D 44
Dale Pk. Rd. SE19 .....9N 29
Dale Rd. CR8: Pur 8L 63
KT12: Wal T 6G 39
RH18: F Row 8H 187
SM1: Sut 1L 61
TW16: Sunb 8G 22
Daleside Rd. KT19: Ewe 3C 60
SW16 .....6F 28
Dale St. W4 .....1D 12
Dale Vw. GU21: Wok 5L 73
GU27: Hasl 3E 188
KT18: Head 1A 100
Dalewood Gdns. KT4: W Pk ...8G 43
RH10: Craw 1D 182
Dalkeith Rd. SE21 .....2N 29
Dallas Rd. SM3: Chea 3K 61
Dallaway Gdns.
RH19: E Grin 9A 166
Dalley Ct. GU47: C Tow 8J 49
Dalling Rd. W6 .....1G 12
Dallington Cl. KT12: Hers 3K 57
Dalmally Rd. CR0: Croy 6C 46
Dalmany Pas. CR0: Croy 6C 46
Dalmeny Av. SW16 .....1L 45
Dalmeny Cres. TW3: Houn 7D 10
Dalmeny Rd. KT4: W Pk 9G 42
SM5: Cars 4E 62
Dalmore Av. KT10: Clay 3F 58
Dalmore Rd. SE21 .....3N 29
Dalston Cl. GU15: Camb 3H 71
Dalton Av. CR4: Mit 1C 44
Dalton Cl. CR8: Pur 8N 63
RH11: Craw 8M 181
Dalton Grn. SL3: Lang 2B 6
Dalton St. SE27 .....3M 29
Damascene Wlk. SE21 .....2N 29
Damask Cl. GU24: W End 9B 52
Damasks Ct. SM1: Sut 7N 43
Damphurst La.
RH5: A Com, Wott 1A 138
Dampier Wlk. RH11: Craw ...8N 181
Damson Way SM5: Cars 5D 62
Danbrook Rd. SW16 .....9J 29
Danbury M. SM6: W'ton 1F 62
Danby Ct. RH6: Horl 6E 142
Dancer Rd. SW6 .....4L 13
TW9: Rich 6N 11
Danebury CR0: N Add 3M 65
Danebury Av. SW15 .....9D 12
(not continuous)
Danebury Wlk. GU16: Frim 6D 70
Dane Cl. BR6: Farnb 2M 67
Dane Ct. GU22: Pyr 2H 75
Danecourt Gdns. CR0: Croy ...9C 46
Danehurst TW8: Brent 3J 11
Danehurst Cl. TW20: Egh 7A 20
Danehurst Ct. KT17: Eps 9E 60
Danehurst Cres.
RH13: Hors 6M 197
Danehurst St. SW6 .....4K 13
Danemere St. SW15 .....6H 13
Danemore La.
RH9: S Gods 1G 145
Dane Rd. CR6: Warl 4G 84
SW19 .....9A 28
TW15: A'ford 7D 22
Danesbury Rd. TW13: Felt 2J 23
Danes Cl. KT22: Oxs 1C 78
Danescourt Cres. SM1: Sut 8A 44
Danesfield GU23: Rip, Send 1H 95
Danesfield Cl. KT12: Wal T ...9J 39
Danes Hill GU22: Wok 5C 74
Daneshill RH1: Red 2C 122
Daneshill Cl. RH1: Red 2C 122
Daneshill School Dr.
KT22: Oxs 1D 78
Danesmead KT11: Cob 7A 58
Danesrood GU1: Guil 4B 114
Danes Way KT22: Oxs 1D 78
Daneswood Cl.
KT13: Weybr 2C 56
Danetree Cl. KT19: Ewe 4B 60
Danetree Rd. KT19: Ewe 4B 60
Daniel Cl. SW17 .....7C 28
TW4: Houn 1N 23
Daniel Lambert Mill
KT15: Addl 2N 55
(off Bourneside Rd.)
Daniell Way CR0: Wad 7J 45
Daniels Ho. *RH10: Craw 2F 182*
(off Trafalgar Gdns.)
Daniels La. CR6: Warl 3J 85
Daniel Way SM7: Ban 1N 81
Dan Leno Wlk. SW6 .....3N 13
Dan Mason Dr. W4 .....5B 12
Danone Ct. *GU1: Guil 3C 202*
(off Park Rd.)
Danses Cl. GU4: Guil 1F 114
Danvers Way CR3: Cate 1N 103
Da Palma Ct. *SW6 .....2M 13*
(off Anselm Rd.)
Dapdune Ct.
GU1: Guil 3B 202 (3M 113)
Dapdune Rd.
GU1: Guil 3C 202 (3N 113)
Dapdune Wharf ...2A 202 (3M 113)
Dapdune Wharf Vis. Cen.
.....3B 202 (3M 113)
Daphne Ct. KT4: W Pk 8D 42
Daphne Jackson Rd.
GU2: Guil 4H 113
Daphne St. SW18 .....9N 13
Darby Cl. CR3: Cate 9N 83
Darby Cres. TW16: Sunb 1K 39
Darby Gdns. TW16: Sunb 1K 39
DARBY GREEN 9F 48
Darby Grn. La.
GU17: B'water 1F 68
Darby Grn. Rd.
GU17: B'water 1F 68
Darby Va. RG42: Warf 7N 15
Darcy Av. SM6: W'ton 1G 63
Darcy Cl. CR5: Coul 6M 83
D'Arcy Pl. KT21: A'tead 4M 79
Darcy Rd. KT21: A'tead 4M 79
SM3: Chea 1J 61
SW16 .....1J 45
TW7: Isle 4G 11
Darell Rd. TW9: Rich 6N 11
Darenth Gdns.
TN16: Weste 4M 107
Darenth Way RH6: Horl 6D 142
Dare's La. GU10: Ews 3A 108
Darfield Rd. GU4: B'ham 9C 94
Darfur St. SW15 .....6J 13
Dark Dale SL5: Asc 4E 32
Dark La. GU3: Put 8M 111
GU5: Shere 8A 116
GU20: Windl 3M 51
Darlan Rd. SW6 .....3L 13
Darlaston Rd. SW19 .....8J 27
Darley Cl. CR0: Croy 5H 47
KT15: Addl 2L 55
Darleydale RH11: Craw 6A 182
Darleydale Cl. GU47: Owls 5J 49
Darley Dene Ct.
KT15: Addl 1L 55
Darley Dr. KT3: N Mal 1C 42
Darley Gdns. SM4: Mord 5A 44
Darling Ho. TW1: Twick 9K 11
Darlington Rd. SE27 .....6M 29
Darmaine Cl. CR2: S Croy 4N 63
Darnley Pk. KT13: Weybr 9C 38
Darracott Cl. GU15: Camb 7F 50
Darrick Wood School Sports Cen.
.....1L 67
Darset Av. GU51: Fleet 3B 88
Dart Cl. SL3: Lang 1D 6
Dart Ct. RH19: E Grin 7C 166
Dartmouth Av. GU21: Wok 1E 74
Dartmouth Cl. RG12: Brac 2C 32
Dartmouth Grn. GU21: Wok ...1F 74
Dartmouth Ho.
KT2: K Tham 2J 203
Dartmouth Path
GU21: Wok 1F 74
Dartmouth Pl. W4 .....2D 12
Dartnell Av. KT14: W By 8K 55
Dartnell Cl. KT14: W By 8K 55
Dartnell Ct. KT14: W By 8L 55
Dartnell Cres. KT14: W By 8K 55
DARTNELL PARK 8L 55
Dartnell Pk. Rd.
KT14: W By 8K 55
Dartnell Pl. KT14: W By 8K 55
Dartnell Rd. CR0: Croy 6C 46
Dart Rd. GU14: Cove 8J 69
Darvel Cl. GU21: Wok 3K 73
Darvills La. GU9: Farnh 1H 129
RG10: S Row 1E 14
Darwall Dr. SL5: Asc 1H 33
Darwin Cl. BR6: Farnb 2M 67
RH12: Hors 4M 197
Darwin Ct. *GU15: Camb 3N 69*
(off Watchetts Rd.)
Darwin Gro. GU11: Alde 1A 110
Darwin Leisure Cen. 2H 87
Darwin Pl. RG12: Brac 3A 32
Darwin Rd. W5 .....1J 11
Daryngton Dr. GU1: Guil 3D 114
Dashwood Cl.
KT14: W By 8L 55
RG12: Brac 9B 16
Dashwood Lang Rd.
KT15: Addl 1M 55
Dassett Rd. SE27 .....6M 29
DATCHET 3L 5
DATCHET COMMON 4N 5
Datchet Pl. SL3: Dat 4L 5
Datchet Rd. SL3: Hort 6B 6
SL3: Slou 1J 5
SL4: O Win 7K 5
SL4: W'sor 3G 5
Datchet Station (Rail) 4L 5
Daubeney Pl. *TW12: Hamp 9C 24*
(off High St.)
Daux Hill RH12: Warn 1H 197
Davenant Rd.
CR0: Croy 6A 200 (1M 63)
Davenport Cl. TW11: Tedd 7G 24
Davenport Lodge
TW5: Hest 3M 9
Davenport Rd. RG12: Brac 9C 16
Daventry Cl. SL3: Poy 4H 7
Daventry Ct. RG42: Brac 9N 15
David Cl. RH6: Horl 7F 142
UB3: Harl 3F 8
David Lean Cinema 4C 200
David Lloyd Leisure
Brooklands 6B 56
Cheam 4J 61
Epsom 6N 59
Fulham Broadway 3M 13
(within Fulham Broadway Shop. Cen.)
Hounslow 1K 9
Kingfield Green 7B 74
Kingston upon Thames
.....3K 203
(in The Rotunda Cen.)
Merton 2J 43
David Rd. SL3: Poy 5H 7
Davidson Rd.
CR0: Croy 1F 200 (7B 46)
David Twigg Cl.
KT2: K Tham 1K 203 (9L 25)
Davies Cl. CR0: Croy 5D 46
GU7: Goda 4G 133
Daviesites GU7: Goda 4E 132
Davies Wlk. TW7: Isle 4D 10
Davis Cl. RH11: Craw 8M 181
Davis Gdns. GU47: C Tow 8K 49
Davison Cl. KT19: Eps 7A 60
Davison Rd. SL3: Lang 1B 6
Davis Rd. KT9: Ches 1N 59
KT13: Weybr 6A 56
Davmor Ct. TW8: Brent 1J 11
Davos Cl. GU22: Wok 6A 74
Davy Cl. RG40: W'ham 3B 30
Dawell Dr. TN16: B Hil 4E 86
Dawes Av. TW7: Isle 8G 10
Dawes Ct. KT10: Esh 1B 58
DAWESGREEN 9E 120
Dawes Pl. RH1: Mers 9G 102
Dawes Rd. SW6 .....3K 13
Dawley Ride SL3: Poy 4G 6
Dawlish Av. SW18 .....3N 27
Dawnay Cl. SL5: Asc 9K 17
Dawnay Gdns. SW18 .....3B 28
Dawnay Rd. GU15: Camb 7N 49
(not continuous)
KT23: Book 4B 98
SW18 .....3A 28
Dawn Cl. TW4: Houn 6M 9
Dawney Hill GU24: Pirb 8B 72
Dawneys Rd. GU24: Pirb 9B 72
Dawn Redwood Cl.
SL3: Hort 6C 6
Dawn Ri. RH10: Cop 7L 163
Dawsmere Cl. GU15: Camb 1G 71
Dawson Cl. SL4: W'sor 5D 4
Dawson Rd.
KT1: K Tham ..5M 203 (2M 41)
KT14: Byf 7M 55
Dax Ct. TW16: Sunb 2K 39
Daybrook Rd. SW19 .....1N 43
Day Ct. GU6: Cranl 8H 155
Daylesford Av. SW15 .....7F 12
Daymerslea Ridge
KT22: Leat 8J 79
Days Acre CR2: Sande 6C 64
Daysbrook Rd. SW2 .....2K 29
Dayseys Hill RH1: Out 3L 143
Dayspring GU2: Guil 8L 93
Deacon Cl. CR8: Pur 5J 63
KT11: Down 6J 77
RG40: W'ham 9B 14
Deacon Ct. SL4: W'sor 5A 4
Deacon Fld. GU2: Guil 2K 113
Deacon Pl. CR3: Cate 1N 103
Deacon Rd.
KT2: K Tham ..2L 203 (9M 25)
Deacons Ct. TW1: Twick 3F 24
Deacons Leas BR6: Orp 1M 67
Deacons Wlk. TW12: Hamp ...5A 24
Deadbrook La. GU12: Alde ...1B 110
DEADWATER 5A 168
Deal M. W5 .....1K 11
Deal Rd. SW17 .....7E 28
Dealtry Rd. SW15 .....7H 13
Dean Cl. GU12: Ash 2G 110
GU22: Pyr 2G 74
SL4: W'sor 6A 4
Deanery Pl. *GU7: Goda 7G 133*
(off Church St.)
Deanery Rd. GU7: Goda 6G 133
TN8: C Hil 2L 127
Deanfield Gdns.
CR0: Croy 7D 200 (1A 64)
Dean Gro. RG40: W'ham 1B 30
Deanhill Ct. SW14 .....7A 12
Deanhill Rd. SW14 .....7A 12
Dean La. RH1: Mers 1F 102
Deanoak La. RH2: Leigh 4H 141
Dean Pde. GU15: Camb 7D 50
Dean Rd.
CR0: Croy 7D 200 (1A 64)
GU7: Goda 5G 132
TW3: Houn 8B 10
TW12: Hamp 6A 24
Deans Cl. CR0: Croy 9C 46
KT20: Wal H 2G 100
W4 .....2A 12
Deans Ct. GU20: Windl 4A 52
Deansfield CR3: Cate 3C 104
Deansgate RG12: Brac 6N 31
Deanside GU15: Camb 7D 50
Deans La. KT20: Wal H 2G 101
RH1: Nut 2L 123
W4 .....2A 12
(off Deans Cl.)
Deans Rd. RH1: Mers 8G 102
SM1: Sut 9N 43
Dean's Wlk. CR5: Coul 5L 83
Dean Wlk. KT23: Book 4B 98
Dearn Gdns. CR4: Mit 2C 44
Debden Cl. KT2: K Tham 6K 25
Deborah Cl. TW7: Isle 4E 10
De Brome Rd. TW13: Felt 2K 23
De Burgh Gdns. KT20: Tad 6J 81
De Burgh Pk. SM7: Ban 2N 81
Deburgh Rd. SW19 .....8A 28
Decimus Cl. CR7: T Hea 3A 46
Dedisham Cl. RH10: Craw 4E 182
Dedswell Dr. GU4: W Cla 7J 95
DEDWORTH 5B 4
Dedworth Dr. SL4: W'sor 4C 4
DEDWORTH GREEN 6A 4
Dedworth Mnr. SL4: W'sor 4C 4
Dedworth Rd. SL4: W'sor 5A 4
Deedman Cl. GU12: Ash 2E 110
Dee Ho. KT2: K Tham 1H 203
Deen City Farm 1A 44
DEEPCUT 7G 71
Deepcut Bri. Rd.
GU16: Deep 8G 70
Deepdale RG12: Brac 3M 31
SW19 .....5J 27
Deepdale Ct. CR0: Croy 6E 200
Deepdene GU10: L Bou 5J 129
GU27: Hasl 2C 188
Deepdene Av. CR0: Croy 9C 46
RH4: Dork 1M 201 (3J 119)
RH5: Dork 3M 201 (8J 119)
Deepdene Av. Rd.
RH4: Dork 3J 119
Deepdene Dr.
RH5: Dork 1M 201 (4J 119)
Deepdene Gdns.
RH4: Dork 1L 201 (4H 119)
SW2 .....1K 29
Deepdene Pk. Rd.
RH5: Dork 1M 201 (4J 119)
Deepdene Rdbt.
RH4: Dork 1M 201 (4J 119)
Deepdene Va. RH4: Dork 4J 119
Deepdene Wood
RH5: Dork 5J 119
Deep Fld. SL3: Dat 3L 5
Deepfield Rd. RG12: Brac 1B 32
Deepfields RH6: Horl 6D 142
Deepfield Way CR5: Coul 3J 83
Deep Pool La. GU24: Wok 1L 73
Deeprose Cl. GU2: Guil 8L 93
Deepwell Cl. TW7: Isle 4G 10
Deep Well Dr. GU15: Camb 1C 70
Deerbarn Rd. GU2: Guil 2L 113
Deerbrook Rd. SE24 .....2M 29
Deerhurst Cl. TW13: Felt 5J 23
Deerhurst Cres. TW12: H Hill ..6C 24
Deerhurst Pk. RH18: F Row 7J 187
Deerhurst Rd. SW16 .....6K 29
Deerings Rd. RH2: Reig 3N 121
Deer Leap GU18: Ligh 7L 51
Deerleap GU35: H Dwn 5H 169
Deerleap Rd. RH4: Westc 6B 118
Dee Rd. SL4: W'sor 3A 4
TW9: Rich 7M 11
Deer Pk. Cl. KT2: K Tham 8A 26
Deer Pk. Gdns. CR4: Mit 3B 44
Deer Pk. Rd. SW19 .....1N 43
Deer Rock Hill RG12: Brac 5A 32
Deer Rock Rd. GU15: Camb 8D 50
Deers Farm Cl. GU23: Wis 3N 75
Deers Leap Pk. 5M 185
Deerswood Cl. CR3: Cate 2D 104
RH11: Craw 2N 181
Deerswood Ct.
RH11: Craw 2M 181
Deerswood Rd.
RH11: Craw 3N 181
Deer Way RH12: Hors 7G 196
Deeside Rd. SW17 .....4B 28
Dee Way KT19: Ewe 6D 60
Defiant Way SM6: W'ton 4J 63
Defoe Av. TW9: Kew 3N 11
Defoe Cl. SW17 .....7C 28
Defoe Ct.
RH4: Dork 1M 201 (4J 119)
Defoe Pl. SW17 .....5D 28
De Havilland Dr.
KT13: Weybr 7N 55
De Havilland Rd. TW5: Hest ...3K 9
De Havilland Way
TW19: Stan 9M 7
Delabole Rd. RH1: Mers 7J 103
Delacy Ct. SM2: Sut 7M 61
Delaford St. SW6 .....3K 13
Delagarde Rd.
TN16: Weste 4L 107
Delamare Cres. CR0: Croy 5F 46
Delamere Rd. RH2: Reig 7N 121
SW20 .....9J 27
Delancey Ct. *RH12: Hors 4J 197*
(off Wimblehurst Rd.)
Delaporte Cl.
KT17: Eps 5M 201 (8D 60)
De Lara Way GU21: Wok 5N 73
De La Warr Rd.
RH19: E Grin 9B 166
Delcombe Av. KT4: W Pk 7H 43
Delderfield KT22: Leat 7K 79
Delfont Cl. RH10: Craw 5H 183
Delft Ho. KT2: K Tham 1L 203

Delia St. SW18 1N **27**
Delius Gdns. RH13: Hors 4A **198**
Dell, The GU9: H End 5J **109**
GU21: Wok 6M **73**
GU46: Yate 1B **68**
KT20: Tad 8H **81**
RH2: Reig 2M **121**
RH6: Horl 7F **142**
RH19: E Grin 9D **166**
TW8: Brent 2J **11**
TW14: Felt 1J **23**
TW20: Eng G 4K **19**
Dellbow Rd. TW14: Felt 8J **9**
Dell Cl. GU27: Hasl 1E **188**
KT22: Fetc 1D **98**
RH5: Mick 5J **99**
SM6: W'ton 1G **63**
Dell Cnr. RG12: Brac 1K **31**
Deller St. RG42: Bin 8L **15**
Dell Gro. GU16: Frim 4D **70**
Dell La. KT17: Ewe 2F **60**
Dell Rd. KT17: Ewe 3F **60**
RG40: Finch 5A **48**
Dells Cl. TW11: Tedd 7F **24**
Dell Wlk. KT3: N Mal 1D **42**
Delmey Cl. CR0: Croy 9C **46**
Delorme St. W6 2J **13**
Delrogue Rd. RH11: Ifi 9M **161**
Delta Bungs. *RH6: Horl 1E 162*
(off Delta Dr.)
Delta Cl. GU24: Chob 6J **53**
KT4: W Pk 9E **42**
Delta Dr. RH6: Horl 1E **162**
Delta Ho. KT16: Chert 6L **37**
RH6: Horl 1E 162
(off Delta Dr.)
Delta Pk. SW18 7N **13**
Delta Point CR0: Croy 1C **200**
Delta Rd. GU21: Wok 3C **74**
GU24: Chob 6J **53**
KT4: W Pk 9D **42**
Delta Way TW20: Thor 9E **20**
Delves KT20: Tad 8J **81**
Delville Cl. GU14: Cove 2J **89**
Delvino Rd. SW6 4M **13**
De Mel Cl. KT19: Eps 8A **60**
Demesne Rd. SM6: W'ton 1H **63**
De Montfort Pde.
SW16 4J **29**
De Montfort Rd. SW16 4J **29**
De Morgan Cen., The 8M **13**
De Morgan Rd. SW6 6N **13**
Dempsey Wlk. RH11: Craw 1M **181**
Dempster Cl. KT6: Surb 7J **41**
Denbies Dr. RH5: Dork 1H **119**
Denbies Wine Estate, Winery & Vis. Cen. 1H **119**
Denbigh Cl. SM1: Sut 2L **61**
Denbigh Gdns. TW10: Rich 8M **11**
Denbigh Rd. GU27: Hasl 3H **189**
TW3: Houn 5B **10**
Denby Dene GU12: Ash 2F **110**
Denby Rd. KT11: Cob 8K **57**
Denchers Plat RH11: Craw 9B **162**
Dencliffe TW15: A'ford 6B **22**
Den Cl. BR3: Beck 2N **47**
Dene, The CR0: Croy 1G **64**
KT8: W Mole 4N **39**
RH5: A Ham 9J **117**
SM2: Chea 7L **61**
Dene Av. TW3: Houn 6N **9**
Dene Cl. CR5: Chip 6C **82**
GU10: L Bou 5K **129**
GU15: Camb 7E **50**
GU27: Hasl 3G **188**
KT4: W Pk 8E **42**
RG12: Brac 8A **16**
RH6: Horl 6C **142**
Dene Ct. CR2: S Croy 8C **200**
GU4: Guil 9D **94**
Denefield Dr. CR8: Ken 2A **84**
Dene Gdns. KT7: T Dit 8G **40**
Denehurst Gdns.
TW2: Twick 1D **24**
TW10: Rich 7N **11**
Denehyrst Ct. GU1: Guil 4F **202**
Dene La. GU10: L Bou 5J **129**
Dene La. W. GU10: L Bou 6K **129**
Dene Pl. GU21: Wok 5M **73**
Dene Rd.
GU1: Guil 4E **202** (4A **114**)
GU14: Cove 2L **89**
KT21: A'tead 6M **79**
Dene St.
RH4: Dork 2K **201** (5H **119**)
Dene St. Gdns.
RH4: Dork 2L **201** (5H **119**)
Dene Tye RH10: Craw 2H **183**
Dene Wlk. GU10: L Bou 5J **129**
Denewood
KT17: Eps 7M **201** (9D **60**)
Denfield RH4: Dork 7H **119**
Denham Cres. CR4: Mit 3D **44**
Denham Dr. GU46: Yate 1C **68**
Denham Gro. RG12: Brac 5A **32**
Denham Pl. *RH5: B Grn 7K 139*
(off Old Horsham Rd.)
Denham Rd. KT17: Eps 8E **60**
TW14: Felt 1K **23**
TW20: Egh 5C **20**
Denholm Gdns. GU4: B'ham 9C **94**
Denison Rd. SW19 7B **28**
TW13: Felt 5G **23**
Denleigh Gdns. KT7: T Dit 5E **40**
Denly Way GU18: Ligh 6N **51**
Denman Cl. GU51: Fleet 4D **88**
Denman Dr. KT10: Clay 2G **58**
TW15: A'ford 7C **22**
Denmans RH10: Craw 2H **183**
Denmark Av. SW19 8K **27**
Denmark Ct. *KT13: Weybr 9C 38*
(off Grotto Rd.)
SM4: Mord 5M **43**
Denmark Gdns.
SM5: Cars 9D **44**
Denmark Path SE25 4E **46**
Denmark Rd.
GU1: Guil 4E **202** (4A **114**)
KT1: K Tham 5J **203** (2L **41**)
SE25 4D **46**
SM5: Cars 9D **44**
SW19 7J **27**
TW2: Twick 4D **24**
Denmark Sq. GU12: Alde 2B **110**
Denmark St. GU12: Alde 2B **110**
RG40: W'ham 3B **30**
Denmark Wlk. SE27 5N **29**
Denmead Ct. RG12: Brac 5C **32**
Denmead Ho. *SW15 9E 12*
(off Highcliffe Dr.)
Denmead Rd.
CR0: Croy 1A **200** (7M **45**)
Denmore Ct. SM6: W'ton 2F **62**
Dennan Rd. KT6: Surb 7M **41**
Dennard Way BR6: Farnb 1K **67**
Denne Pde. RH12: Hors 7J **197**
DENNE PARK 7J **197**
Denne Rd. RH11: Craw 4B **182**
RH12: Hors 7J **197**
Dennett Rd. CR0: Croy 7L **45**
Dennettsland Rd.
TN8: C Hil 3L **127**
Denning Av.
CR0: Wad 8A **200** (1L **63**)
Denning Cl. TW12: Hamp 6N **23**
Denningtons, The
KT4: W Pk 8D **42**
Dennis Cl. RH1: Red 1C **122**
TW15: A'ford 8E **22**
Dennis Ho. SM1: Sut 1N **61**
Dennis Pk. Cres.
SW20 9K **27**
Dennis Reeve Cl. CR4: Mit 9D **28**
Dennis Rd. KT8: E Mol 3C **40**
Dennistoun Cl. GU15: Camb 1B **70**
DENNISVILLE 4K **113**
Dennis Way GU1: Guil 7A **94**
Den Rd. BR2: Brom 2N **47**
Densham Dr. CR8: Pur 1L **83**
Denton Cl. RH1: Red 8E **122**
Denton Gro. KT12: Wal T 8M **39**
Denton Rd. RG40: W'ham 2B **30**
TW1: Twick 9K **11**
Denton St. SW18 9N **13**
Denton Way GU16: Frim 4B **70**
GU21: Wok 4J **73**
Dents Gro. KT20: Lwr K 6L **101**
Dents Rd. SW11 1D **28**
Den Vale Trad. Pk.
RH10: Craw 4C **182**
Denvale Wlk. GU21: Wok 5K **73**
Denzil Rd.
GU2: Guil 5A **202** (4L **113**)
Deodar Rd. SW15 7K **13**
Departures Rd. RH6: Gat 2D **162**
Depot Rd.
KT17: Eps 6L **201** (9D **60**)
RH11: Craw 9B **162**
RH13: Hors 6L **197**
TW3: Houn 6D **10**
Derby Arms Rd. KT18: Eps D 4E **80**
Derby Cl. KT18: Tat C 6G **81**
Derby Rd.
CR0: Croy 1A **200** (7M **45**)
GU2: Guil 3J **113**
GU27: Hasl 1F **188**
KT5: Surb 7N **41**
SM1: Sut 3L **61**
SW14 7A **12**
SW19 8M **27**
TW3: Houn 7B **10**
Derby Rd. Ind. Est.
TW3: Houn 7B **10**
Derbyshire Grn. RG42: Warf 8D **16**
Derby Sq., The KT19: Eps 6K **201**
Derby Stables Rd.
KT18: Eps D 4E **80**
Derek Av. KT19: Ewe 3N **59**
SM6: W'ton 1F **62**
Derek Cl. KT19: Ewe 2A **60**
Derek Horn Ct. GU15: Camb 9N **49**
Deri Dene Cl. TW19: Stan 9N **7**
Dering Pl.
CR0: Croy 7C **200** (1N **63**)
Dering Rd.
CR0: Croy 7C **200** (1N **63**)
Derinton Rd. SW17 5D **28**
Deronda Rd. SE24 2M **29**
De Ros Pl. TW20: Egh 7C **20**
Deroy Cl. SM5: Cars 3D **62**
Derrick Av. CR2: Sande 6N **63**
Derrick Rd. BR3: Beck 2J **47**
Derry Cl. GU12: A Va 8D **90**
Derrydown GU22: Wok 8M **73**
Derry Rd. CR0: Bedd 9J **45**
GU14: Cove 6L **69**
Derwent Av. GU12: A Va 9D **90**
SW15 5D **26**
Derwent Cl. GU9: U Hal 6F **108**
GU14: Cove 1K **89**
KT10: Clay 3E **58**
KT15: Addl 2M **55**
RH11: Craw 4L **181**
RH12: Hors 2A **198**
TW14: Felt 2G **22**
Derwent Dr. CR8: Pur 9A **64**
Derwent Ho. KT2: K Tham 1H **203**
SE20 1E 46
(off Derwent Rd.)
Derwent Lodge KT4: W Pk 8G **42**
TW7: Isle 5D **10**
Derwent Rd. GU18: Ligh 7M **51**
SE20 1D **46**
SW20 5J **43**
TW2: Whitt 9B **10**
TW20: Egh 8D **20**
Derwent Wlk. SM6: W'ton 4F **62**
Desborough Cl. TW17: Shep 6B **38**
Desborough Ho. *W14 2L 13*
(off North End Rd.)
Desborough Sailing Club 6C **38**
Desford Ct. TW15: A'ford 3B **22**
Desford Way TW15: A'ford 3A **22**
De Stafford Sports Cen. 8C **84**
Detillens La. RH8: Limp 7C **106**
Detling Rd. RH11: Craw 8A **182**
Dettingen Cres. GU16: Deep 6H **71**
Dettingen Rd. GU16: Deep 6J **71**
Devana End SM5: Cars 9D **44**
Devas Rd. SW20 9H **27**
Devenish Cl. SL5: S'hill 5A **34**
Devenish La. SL5: S'dale 7A **34**
Devenish Rd.
SL5: S'dale, S'hill 5N **33**
Deveraux Cl. BR3: Beck 4M **47**
De Vere Cl. SM6: W'ton 4J **63**
Devereux La. SW13 3G **12**
Devereux Rd. SL4: W'sor 5G **4**
SW11 1D **28**
Devey Cl. KT2: K Tham 8E **26**
Devil's Highway, The
RG45: Crow 2D **48**
Devil's Jumps, The 6N **149**
Devil's La. TW18: Stain 8F **20**
TW20: Egh 7E **20**
Devil's Punch Bowl 4E **170**
De Vitre Grn. RG40: W'ham 1E **30**
Devitt Cl. KT21: A'tead 3N **79**
Devoil Cl. GU4: B'ham 8D **94**
Devoke Way KT12: Wal T 8L **39**
Devon Av. TW2: Twick 2C **24**
Devon Bank
GU2: Guil 8B **202** (6M **113**)
Devon Chase RG42: Warf 7C **16**
Devon Cl. CR8: Ken 3C **84**
GU47: C Tow 8J **49**
GU51: Fleet 1C **88**
Devon Ct. TW12: Hamp 8A **24**
Devon Cres. RH1: Red 3B **122**
Devoncroft Gdns.
TW1: Twick 1G **25**
Devon Ho. CR3: Cate 2C **104**
Devonhurst Pl. W4 1C **12**
Devon Rd. KT12: Hers 1K **57**
RH1: Mers 8G **102**
SM2: Chea 5K **61**
Devonshire Av. GU21: Wok 1E **74**
KT20: Box H 9B **100**
SM2: Sut 4A **62**
Devonshire Dr.
GU15: Camb 8D **50**
KT6: Surb 7K **41**
Devonshire Gdns. W4 3B **12**
Devonshire Ho. SM2: Sut 4A **62**
Devonshire M. W4 1D **12**
Devonshire Pas. W4 1D **12**
Devonshire Pl. GU11: Alde 3L **109**
Devonshire Point
TW15: A'ford 4D **22**
Devonshire Rd. CR0: Croy 6A **46**
KT13: Weybr 1B **56**
RH13: Hors 6K **197**
SM2: Sut 4A **62**
SM5: Cars 1E **62**
SW19 8C **28**
TW13: Hanw 4M **23**
W4 1D **12**
Devonshires, The
KT18: Eps 8M **201** (1E **80**)
Devonshire St. W4 1D **12**
Devonshire Way CR0: Croy 8H **47**
Devon Way KT9: Ches 2J **59**
KT19: Ewe 2A **60**
Devon Waye TW5: Hest 3N **9**
Dewar Cl. RH11: Ifi 4K **181**
Dewar Spur SL3: Lang 2B **6**
Dewey St. SW17 6D **28**
Dewlands RH9: Gods 9F **104**
(not continuous)
Dewlands Cl. GU6: Cranl 7N **155**
Dewlands La. GU6: Cranl 7N **155**
Dewlands Rd. RH9: Gods 9F **104**
Dew Pond Cl. RH13: Hors 5M **197**
Dewsbury Gdns. KT4: W Pk 9F **42**
Dexter Dr. RH19: E Grin 1A **186**
Dexter Way GU51: Fleet 1C **88**
Diamedes Av. TW19: Stan 1M **21**
Diamond Ct. *RH1: Red 2E 122*
(off St Anne's Mt.)
Diamond Est. SW17 4C **28**
Diamond Hill GU15: Camb 8C **50**
Diamond Pl. RH2: Reig 2N **121**
Diamond Ridge
GU15: Camb 8B **50**
Diana Cotts. GU10: Seal 8J **111**
Diana Gdns. KT6: Surb 8M **41**
Diana Ho. SW13 4E **12**
Diana Wlk. *RH6: Horl 8F 142*
(off High St.)
Dianthus Cl. KT16: Chert 6G **37**
Dianthus Ct. GU22: Wok 5N **73**
Dianthus Pl. RG42: Wink R 7F **16**
Dibdene La. GU5: Sha G 7H **135**
Dibdin Cl. SM1: Sut 9M **43**
Dibdin Rd. SM1: Sut 9M **43**
Diceland Rd. SM7: Ban 3L **81**
Dickens Cl. RH19: E Grin 9M **165**
TW10: Ham 3L **25**
UB3: Harl 1F **8**
Dickens Ct. RG41: W'ham 2A **30**
Dickens Dr. KT15: Addl 3H **55**
Dickenson Rd. TW13: Hanw 6K **23**
Dickensons La. SE25 4D **46**
(not continuous)
Dickensons Pl. SE25 5D **46**
Dickens Pl. SL3: Poy 4G **7**
Dickens Rd. RH10: Craw 6B **182**
Dickens Way GU46: Yate 1B **68**
Dickenswood Cl.
SE19 8M **29**
Dickerage La. KT3: N Mal 2B **42**
Dickerage Rd. KT1: K Tham 9B **26**
KT3: N Mal 1B **42**
Dickins Way RH13: Hors 8M **197**
Dick Turpin Way TW14: Felt 7G **9**
Dieppe Cl. W14 1L **13**
Digby Mans. *W6 1G 13*
(off Hammersmith Bri. Rd.)
Digby Pl. CR0: Croy 9C **46**
Digby Way KT14: Byf 8A **56**
Digdens Ri. KT18: Eps 2B **80**
Dighton Rd. SW18 8N **13**
Dillon Cotts. GU4: B'ham 7E **94**
Dilston Rd. KT22: Leat 6G **79**
Dilton Gdns. SW15 2F **26**
Dimes Pl. W6 1G **13**
Dingle, The RH11: Craw 3N **181**
Dingle Cl. RH11: Craw 2N **181**
Dingle Rd. TW15: A'ford 6C **22**
Dingley La. SW16 3H **29**
Dingwall Av.
CR0: Croy 3C **200** (8N **45**)
Dingwall Rd.
CR0: Croy 1D **200** (7A **46**)
SM5: Cars 5D **62**
SW18 1A **28**
Dinorben Av. GU52: Fleet 6A **88**
Dinorben Beeches
GU52: Fleet 6A **88**
Dinorben Cl. GU52: Fleet 6A **88**
Dinsdale Cl. GU22: Wok 5C **74**
Dinsdale Gdns. SE25 4B **46**
Dinsmore Rd. SW12 1F **28**
Dinton Rd. KT2: K Tham 8M **25**
SW19 7B **28**
Dione Wlk. RH11: Craw 6K **181**
DIPPENHALL 1B **128**
Dippenhall Rd. GU10: Dip 1B **128**
Diprose Lodge SW17 5B **28**
Dirdene Cl. KT17: Eps 8E **60**
Dirdene Gdns.
KT17: Eps 5M **201** (8E **60**)
Dirdene Gro. KT17: Eps 8D **60**
Dirtham La. KT24: Eff 6J **97**
(not continuous)
Dirty La. RH19: Ash W 3G **187**
Disbrowe Rd. W6 2K **13**
Discovery Pk. RH10: Craw 7E **162**
Disraeli Ct. SL3: Lang 2D **6**
Disraeli Gdns. SW15 7L **13**
Disraeli Rd. SW15 7K **13**
Distillery La. W6 1H **13**
Distillery Rd. W6 1H **13**
Distillery Wlk. TW8: Brent 2L **11**
Ditches Grn. Cotts.
RH5: Ockl 8M **157**
Ditches La. CR3: Cate, Coul 7J **83**
CR5: Coul 7J **83**
Ditchling RG12: Brac 6M **31**
Ditchling Hill RH11: Craw 6A **182**
Ditton Cl. KT7: T Dit 6G **40**
Dittoncroft Cl. CR0: Croy 1B **64**
Ditton Grange Cl. KT6: Surb 7K **41**
Ditton Grange Dr. KT6: Surb 7K **41**
Ditton Hill KT6: Surb 7J **41**
Ditton Hill Rd. KT6: Surb 7J **41**
Ditton Lawn KT7: T Dit 7G **40**
Ditton Pk. Rd. SL3: Lang 2A **6**
Ditton Reach KT7: T Dit 5H **41**
Ditton Rd. KT6: Surb 8K **41**
SL3: Dat 4N **5**
SL3: Lang 1B **6**
UB2: S'hall 1N **9**
Divis Way *SW15 9G 13*
(off Dover Pk. Dr.)
Dixon Dr. KT13: Weybr 6A **56**
Dixon Pl. BR4: W Wick 7L **47**
Dixon Rd. SE25 2B **46**
Dobbins Pl. RH11: Ifi 4J **181**
Doble Ct. CR2: Sande 8D **64**
Dobson Rd. RH11: Craw 9B **162**
DOCKENFIELD 4D **148**
Dockenfield St.
GU10: Dock 2A **148**
Dockett Eddy KT16: Chert 7N **37**
Dockett Eddy La.
TW17: Shep 7A **38**
Dockett Moorings
KT16: Chert 7N **37**
Dock Rd. TW8: Brent 3K **11**
Dockwell Cl. TW14: Felt 7H **9**
Dockwell's Ind. Est.
TW14: Felt 8J **9**
Doctor Johnson Av.
SW17 4F **28**
Doctors La. CR3: Cate 1L **103**
Dodbrooke Rd. SE27 4L **29**
Dodds Cres. KT14: W By 1K **75**
Dodd's La. GU22: Pyr 1J **75**
Dodds Pk. RH3: Brock 5A **120**
Doel Cl. SW19 8A **28**
Dogflud Way GU9: Farnh 9H **109**
Doggetts Cl. TN8: Eden 3L **147**
Doghurst Av. UB3: Harl 3C **8**
Doghurst Dr. UB7: Sip 3C **8**
Doghurst La. CR5: Chip 7D **82**
DOGKENNEL GREEN 3L **117**
Dogkennel Grn.
RH5: Ran C 3L **117**
Dolby Rd. SW6 5L **13**
Dolby Ter. RH6: Char 4K **161**
Dollary Pde. *KT1: K Tham 2A 42*
(off Kingston Rd.)
Dolleyshill Cvn. Pk.
GU3: Norm 8K **91**
Dolliffe Cl. CR4: Mit 1C **44**
Dollis Cl. RH10: Craw 4G **182**
Dollis Dr. GU9: Farnh 9J **109**
DOLLY'S HILL 2K **109**
Dolphin Cl. GU27: Hasl 2C **188**
KT6: Surb 4K **41**
Dolphin Ct. RG12: Brac 3A **32**
TW18: Stain 4J **21**
Dolphin Ct. Nth.
TW18: Stain 4J **21**
Dolphin Est. TW16: Sunb 9F **22**
Dolphin Ho. SW18 7N **13**
Dolphin Rd. TW16: Sunb 9F **22**
Dolphin Rd. Nth.
TW16: Sunb 9F **22**
Dolphin Rd. Sth.
TW16: Sunb 9E **22**
Dolphin Rd. W. TW16: Sunb 9F **22**
Dolphin Sq. W4 3D **12**
Dolphin St.
KT1: K Tham 3J **203** (1L **41**)
Doman Rd. GU15: Camb 2L **69**
Dome, The RH1: Red 2D **122**
Dome Hill CR3: Cate 5B **104**
Dome Hill Peak CR3: Cate 4B **104**
Domelton Ho. *SW18 9N 13*
(off Iron Mill Rd.)
Dome Way RH1: Red 2D **122**
DOMEWOOD 5D **164**
Dominion Cl. TW3: Houn 5D **10**
Dominion Rd. CR0: Croy 6C **46**
Donald Rd. CR0: Croy 6L **45**
Donald Woods Gdns.
KT5: Surb 8A **42**
Doncaster Wlk.
RH10: Craw 5E **182**
Doncastle Rd. RG12: Brac 2K **31**
Doneraile St. SW6 5J **13**
Donkey La. RH5: A Com 3L **137**
RH6: Horl 3H **163**
UB7: W Dray 1L **7**
DONKEY TOWN 9A **52**
Donnafields GU24: Bis 3D **72**
Donne Cl. RH10: Craw 1F **182**
Donne Gdns. GU22: Pyr 2G **74**
Donnelly Ct. *SW6 3K 13*
(off Dawes Rd.)
Donne Pl. CR4: Mit 3F **44**
Donnington Cl.
GU15: Camb 2N **69**
Donnington Ct.
RH11: Craw 6L **181**
Donnington Rd. KT4: W Pk 8F **42**
Donnybrook RG12: Brac 6M **31**
Donnybrook Rd. SW16 8G **29**
Donovan Cl. KT19: Eps 6C **60**
Donyngs Recreation Cen. 2C **122**
Doods Pk. Rd. RH2: Reig 2A **122**
Doods Pl. RH2: Reig 2B **122**
Doods Rd. RH2: Reig 2A **122**
Doods Way RH2: Reig 2B **122**
Doomsday Gdn.
RH13: Hors 7N **197**
DOOMSDAY GREEN 8N **197**
Doomsday La. RH13: Hors 8N **197**
Doone Cl. TW11: Tedd 7G **24**
Doral Way SM5: Cars 2D **62**
Doran Ct. RH1: Red 3B **122**
Doran Dr. RH1: Red 3B **122**
Doran Gdns. RH1: Red 3B **122**
Dora Rd. SW19 6M **27**
DORA'S GREEN 7B **108**
Dora's Grn. La.
GU10: Ews 5C **108**
Dora's Grn. Rd. GU10: Dip 1A **128**
Dorcas Ct. GU15: Camb 3N **69**
Dorchester Ct. GU15: Camb 9N **49**
GU22: Wok 3C **74**
RH2: Reig 2B **122**
TW18: Stain 5J **21**

Dorchester Dr.—Dukes Rd.

Dorchester Dr. TW14: Bedf 9F 8
Dorchester Gro. W4 . . . . .1D 12
Dorchester Ho. TW9: Kew 3A 12
Dorchester M. KT3: N Mal 3C 42
TW1: Twick 9J 11
Dorchester Rd. KT4: W Pk 7H 43
KT13: Weybr 9C 38
SM4: Mord 6N 43
Doreen Cl. GU14: Cove 7K 69
Dore Gdns. SM4: Mord 6N 43
Dorey Ho. TW8: Brent 3J 11
(off High St.)
Dorian Dr. SL5: Asc 9B 18
Doria Rd. SW6 . . . . .5L 13
Doric Dr. KT20: Tad 7L 81
Dorien Rd. SW20 . . . . .1J 43
Dorin Ct. CR6: Warl 7E 84
GU22: Pyr 2G 74
Doris Rd. TW15: A'ford 7E 22
DORKING 2J 201 (5G 119)
Dorking Bus. Pk.
RH4: Dork 1H 201 (4F 118)
Dorking Cl. KT4: W Pk 8J 43
Dorking (Deepdene) Station (Rail)
. . . . .3J 119
Dorking Halls 1L 201 (4H 119)
Dorking Lawn Tennis & Squash Club
. . . . .7G 119
Dorking Mus. 2J 201 (5G 119)
Dorking Rd. GU4: Guil 9F 114
(not continuous)
GU5: Gorn 8E 116
KT18: Eps 8H 201 (3N 79)
KT20: Tad, Wal H 7D 100
KT22: Leat 9H 79
KT23: Book 4B 98
RH5: A Ham 8E 116
RH12: K'fold, Warn 8G 178
Dorking Sports Cen.
. . . . .1M 201 (4J 119)
Dorking Station (Rail) 3J 119
Dorking Vs. GU21: Knap 4G 72
Dorking West Station (Rail)
. . . . .1H 201 (4F 118)
Dorlcote GU8: Wit 5B 152
Dorlcote Rd. SW18 . . . . .1C 28
Dorling Dr. KT17: Eps 8E 60
Dorly Cl. TW17: Shep 4F 38
Dormans RH11: Craw 4M 181
Dormans Av.
RH7: Dorm 9C 146
Dormans Cl. RH7: Dorm 2C 166
Dormans Gdns.
RH19: D Pk 4A 166
Dormans High St.
RH7: Dorm 2C 166
DORMANSLAND 1C 166
DORMANS PARK 4A 166
Dormans Pk. Rd.
RH19: D Pk 3A 166
RH19: E Grin 7N 165
Dormans Rd. RH7: Dorm 9C 146
Dormans Station (Rail) 2B 166
Dormans Sta. Rd.
RH7: Dorm 3B 166
Dormay St. SW18 . . . . .8N 13
Dormer Cl. RG45: Crow 2F 48
Dormers Cl. GU7: Goda 4G 133
Dorncliffe Rd. SW6 . . . . .5K 13
Dorney Gro. KT13: Weybr 8C 38
Dorney Lake Rowing Cen. 3A 4
Dorney Way TW4: Houn 8M 9
Dornford Gdns. CR5: Coul 6N 83
Dornton Rd.
CR2: S Croy 8E 200 (3A 64)
SW12 . . . . .3F 28
Dorothy Pettingell Ho.
SM1: Sut 9N 43
(off Angel Hill)
Dorrien Wlk. SW16 . . . . .3H 29
Dorrington Ct. SE25 . . . . .1B 46
Dorrington Way
BR3: Beck 4M 47
Dorrit Cres. GU3: Guil 1H 113
Dorset Av. RH19: E Grin 7M 165
Dorset Ct. GU15: Camb 7D 50
KT17: Eps 8E 60
Dorset Dr. GU22: Wok 4D 74
Dorset Gdns. CR4: Mit 3K 45
RH19: E Grin 7M 165
Dorset Rd. BR3: Beck 2G 46
CR4: Mit 1C 44
GU12: A Va 8F 90
SL4: W'sor 5F 4
SM2: Sut 6M 61
SW19 . . . . .9M 27
TW15: A'ford 4M 21
Dorset Sq. KT19: Ewe 6C 60
Dorset Va. RG42: Warf 7C 16
Dorset Way KT14: Byf 6M 55
TW2: Twick 2D 24
Dorset Waye TW5: Hest 3N 9
Dorset Wharf W6 . . . . .3H 13
(off Rainville Rd.)
Dorsten Pl. RH11: Craw 6K 181
Dorsten Sq. RH11: Craw 6L 181
Dorton Vs. UB7: Sip 3B 8
Dorton Way GU23: Rip 8K 75
Douai Cl. GU14: Farnb 1A 90
Douai Gro. TW12: Hamp 9C 24
Douglas Av. KT3: N Mal 3G 42
Douglas Cl. GU4: J Wel 6N 93
SM6: W'ton 3J 63
Douglas Ct. CR3: Cate 9N 83
GU51: Fleet 2B 88
(off Fleet Rd.)
KT1: K Tham 7K 203
TN16: B Hil 4G 86
Douglas Dr. CR0: Croy 9K 47
GU7: Goda 6J 133
Douglas Gro. GU10: L Bou . . .6H 129
Douglas Ho. KT6: Surb 7M 41
RH2: Reig 2M 121
Douglas Ho's. KT23: Book 2A 98
Douglas Johnstone Ho.
SW6 . . . . .2L 13
(off Clem Attlee Ct.)
Douglas La. TW19: Wray 8B 6
Douglas Mans. TW3: Houn 6B 10
Douglas M. SM7: Ban 3L 81
Douglas Pl. GU14: Cove 9M 69
Douglas Rd. KT1: K Tham 1A 42
KT6: Surb 8M 41
KT10: Esh 8B 40
KT15: Addl 9K 37
RH2: Reig 2M 121
TW3: Houn 6B 10
TW19: Stan 9M 7
Douglas Robinson Ct.
SW16 . . . . .8J 29
(off Streatham High Rd.)
Douglas Sq. SM4: Mord 5M 43
Doultons, The TW18: Stain 8J 21
Dounesforth Gdns.
SW18 . . . . .2N 27
Dove Cl. CR2: Sels 7G 64
RH11: Craw 1B 182
SM6: W'ton 4K 63
Dovecote Cl. KT13: Weybr 9C 38
Dovecote Gdns. SW14 . . . . . . .6C 12
Dovedale Cl. GU4: B'ham 9C 94
GU47: Owls 5J 49
Dovedale Cres.
RH11: Craw 5N 181
Dovedale Ri. CR4: Mit 8D 28
Dovehouse Grn.
KT13: Weybr 9E 38
Dover Ct. GU6: Cranl 7B 156
Dovercourt Av. CR7: T Hea 4L 45
Dovercourt La. SM1: Sut 9A 44
Doverfield Rd. GU4: B'ham 9C 94
SW2 . . . . .1J 29
Dover Gdns. SM5: Cars 9D 44
Dover Ho. Rd. SW15 . . . . .7F 12
Dover Pk. Dr. SW15 . . . . .9G 12
DOVERSGREEN 7N 121
Dovers Grn. Rd.
RH2: Reig 6N 121
Doversmead GU21: Knap 3H 73
Dover Ter. TW9: Rich 5M 11
(off Sandycombe Rd.)
Doveton Rd. CR2: S Croy 2A 64
Dowdeswell Cl. SW15 . . . . . . .7D 12
Dowding Ct. RG45: Crow 1H 49
Dowding Rd. TN16: B Hil 2F 86
Dower Av. SM6: W'ton 5F 62
Dower Pk. SL4: W'sor 7B 4
Dower Wlk. RH11: Craw 4M 181
Dowes Ho. SW16 . . . . .4J 29
Dowgate Ho. KT13: Weybr 9B 38
Dowlands La. RH6: Smal 8A 144
RH10: Cop 8A 144
Dowlans Cl. KT23: Book 5A 98
Dowlans Rd. KT23: Book 5B 98
Dowler Ct.
KT2: K Tham 1K 203 (9L 25)
DOWLESGREEN 1D 30
Dowles Grn. RG40: W'ham 9D 14
Dowman Cl. SW19 . . . . .8N 27
Downbury M. SW18 . . . . .8M 13
DOWNE 7J 67
Downe Av. TN14: Cud 8M 67
Downe Bank Nature Reserve
. . . . .9K 67
Downe Cl. RH6: Horl 6C 142
Downer Mdw. GU7: Goda 3H 133
Downe Rd. BR2: Kes 5F 66
CR4: Mit 1D 44
TN14: Cud 9L 67
Downes Cl. TW1: Twick 9H 11
Downes Ho. CR0: Wad 7A 200
Downe Ter. TW10: Rich 9L 11
Downfield KT4: W Pk 7E 42
Down Hall Rd.
KT2: K Tham 2H 203 (9K 25)
Downham Ct. KT12: Wal T 9K 39
(off Long Lodge Dr.)
Down House and Darwin Mus.
. . . . .8J 67
Downhurst Rd. GU6: Ewh 4F 156
Downing Av. GU2: Guil 4J 113
Downing St. GU9: Farnh 1G 129
Downland Cl. KT18: Tat C 5G 81
Downland Ct. RH11: Craw 5A 182
Downland Dr. RH11: Craw 5A 182
Downland Gdns.
KT18: Tat C 5G 81
Downland Pl. RH11: Craw 5A 182
Downlands Cl. CR5: Coul 1F 82
Downlands Rd. CR8: Pur 9J 63
Downland Way KT18: Tat C 5G 81
Down La. GU2: Guil 6G 112
GU3: Comp 9E 112
Downmill Rd. RG12: Brac 1L 31
DOWN PARK 9D 164
Down Pl. W6 . . . . .1G 13
Down Rd. GU1: Guil 3D 114
TW11: Tedd 7H 25
Downs, The KT22: Leat 3J 99
SW20 . . . . .8J 27
Downs Av. KT18: Eps 1D 80
Downsbridge Rd.
BR3: Beck 1N 47
Downs Cl. GU14: Cove 7K 69
Downs Ct. RH1: Red 9E 102
Downs Ct. Rd. CR8: Pur 8M 63
Downsend Lodge
KT22: Leat 8J 79
(off Epsom Rd.)
Downs Hill Rd. KT18: Eps 1D 80
Downshire Way
RG12: Brac 1M 31
RG42: Brac 9M 15
Downs Ho. Rd.
KT18: Eps D 5D 80
DOWNSIDE 5J 77
Downside GU26: Hind 2B 170
KT16: Chert 7H 37
KT18: Eps 8L 201 (1D 80)
RG12: Brac 2N 31
TW1: Twick 4F 24
TW16: Sunb 9H 23
Downside Bri. Rd.
KT11: Cob 1J 77
Downside Cl. SW19 . . . . .7A 28
Downside Comn.
KT11: Down 5J 77
Downside Comn. Rd.
KT11: Down 5J 77
Downside Ct. RH1: Mers 7G 102
Downside Orchard
GU22: Wok 4C 74
Downside Rd. GU4: Guil 4D 114
KT11: Down 3J 77
SM2: Sut 3B 62
Downside Wlk. TW8: Brent 2K 11
(off Windmill Rd.)
Downs La. KT22: Leat 1H 99
Downs Link GU4: Guil 8F 114
GU5: Braml 2A 134
GU5: Braml, Chil, Wone
. . . . .3B 134
GU5: Wone 2D 134
GU6: Cranl 4H 155
RH12: Cranl 8M 155
RH12: Rudg, Slin 8D 176
RH13: Slin, Itch 2F 194
Downs Lodge Ct.
KT17: Eps 8M 201 (1D 80)
Downsman Ct.
RH10: Craw 6B 182
Downs Res. Site, The
CR3: Cate 5E 104
Downs Rd. BR3: Beck 1L 47
(not continuous)
CR5: Coul 5H 83
CR7: T Hea 9N 29
CR8: Pur 7M 63
KT18: Eps D 7B 80
KT18: Eps, Eps D
. . . . .8M 201 (2D 80)
RH5: Mick 6J 99
SM2: Sut 6N 61
Downs Side SM2: Chea 7L 61
Down St. KT8: W Mole 4A 40
Downs Vw. KT20: Tad 8G 80
RH4: Dork 3K 119
TW7: Isle 4F 10
Downsview Av. GU22: Wok 8B 74
Downsview Cl. KT11: Down 6J 77
Downsview Ct. GU1: Guil 8M 93
Downsview Gdns.
RH4: Dork 6H 119
SE19 . . . . .8M 29
Downs Vw. Rd.
KT23: Book 5C 98
Downsview Rd.
GU35: H Dwn 4H 169
RH12: Hors 2A 198
SE19 . . . . .8N 29
Downs Way KT18: Eps 3E 80
KT20: Tad 8G 80
KT23: Book 4C 98
RH8: Oxt 5A 106
Downsway BR6: Orp 2N 67
CR2: Sande 7B 64
CR3: Whyte 3C 84
GU1: Guil 3G 114
Downsway, The SM2: Sut 5A 62
Downsway Cl. KT20: Tad 8F 80
Downs Wood KT18: Tat C 4G 80
Downswood RH2: Reig 9B 102
Downton Av. SW2 . . . . .3J 29
Downview Cl. GU26: Hind 3B 170
Down Yhonda GU8: Els 8G 131
Doyle Ct. GU27: Hasl 2E 188
Doyle Gdns. GU46: Yate 2B 68
Doyle Ho. SW13 . . . . .3H 13
(off Trinity Chu. Rd.)
Doyle Rd. SE25 . . . . .3D 46
D'Oyly Carte Island
KT13: Weybr 7C 38
Draco Ga. SW15 . . . . .6H 13
Dragon La. KT13: Weybr 7B 56
Dragons Health Club
Copthorne 8L 163
Epsom 1C 60
Purley 4L 63
Dragoon Ct. GU11: Alde 2K 109
Drake Av. CR3: Cate 9N 83
GU16: Mytc 4E 90
TW18: Stain 6H 21
Drake Cl. RG12: Brac 4N 31
RH12: Hors 2L 197
Drake Ct. KT5: Surb 8K 203
Drakefield Rd. SW17 . . . . .4E 28
Drake Rd. CR0: Croy 6K 45
CR4: Mit 5E 44
KT9: Ches 2N 59
RH6: Horl 8C 142
RH10: Craw 5C 182
Drakes Cl. GU6: Cranl 7N 155
KT10: Esh 1A 58
Drakes Way GU22: Wok 9N 73
Drakewood Rd. SW16 . . . . . . .8H 29
Draper Cl. TW7: Isle 5D 10
Drapers Cres. KT12: Whit V . . .6G 56
Drax Av. SW20 . . . . .8F 26
Draxmont SW19 . . . . .7K 27
Draycot Rd. KT6: Surb 7N 41
Draycott RG12: Brac 4C 32
Draycott M. SW6 . . . . .5L 13
(off Laurel Bank Gdns.)
Dray Ct. GU2: Guil 4L 113
Drayhorse Dr. GU19: Bag 5J 51
Draymans Way TW7: Isle 6F 10
Drayton Cl. KT22: Fetc 2E 98
RG12: Brac 1B 32
TW4: Houn 8N 9
Drayton Rd.
CR0: Croy 2A 200 (8M 45)
Dreadnought Cl. SW19 . . . . . . .9A 28
(off Nelson Gro. Rd.)
SW19 . . . . .1B 44
(Brangwyn Cres.)
Dresden Way KT13: Weybr 2D 56
Drew Ho. SW16 . . . . .4J 29
Drewitts Ct. KT12: Wal T 7G 39
Drew Pl. CR3: Cate 1A 104
Drewstead La. SW16 . . . . .3H 29
Drewstead Rd. SW16 . . . . .3H 29
Drey Ct. KT4: W Pk 7E 42
Drift, The BR2: Brom 1F 66
DRIFT BRIDGE 1H 81
Drifters Dr. GU16: Deep 5H 71
Drift La. KT11: Sto D 3N 77
Drift Rd. KT24: E Jun 2E 96
SL4: Wink 1L 17
Drift Way SL3: Coln 4E 6
Driftway, The CR4: Mit 9E 28
KT22: Leat 1H 99
(not continuous)
RH11: Craw 2B 182
SM7: Ban 2H 81
Driftways GU46: Yate 8C 48
(off White Lion Way)
Driftwood Dr. CR8: Ken 4M 83
Drill Hall Rd. KT16: Chert 6J 37
RH4: Dork 2H 201 (5G 118)
Drive, The BR3: Beck 1K 47
BR4: W Wick 6N 47
CR5: Coul 1J 83
CR7: T Hea 3A 46
GU2: Guil 3J 113
(Beech Gro.)
GU2: Guil 5J 113
(Crossways, The)
GU3: Art 7L 113
GU5: Wone 5D 134
GU6: Cranl 8N 155
GU7: Eash 7B 132
GU7: Goda 9H 133
GU8: P Har 7B 132
(not continuous)
GU9: Farnh 4G 129
GU22: Wok 7L 73
GU25: V Wat 4B 36
KT2: K Tham 8B 26
KT6: Surb 6L 41
KT10: Esh 7C 40
KT11: Cob 1M 77
KT18: Head 1L 99
KT19: Ewe 3E 60
KT20: Lwr K 4L 101
KT22: Fetc 9E 78
KT22: Leat 1L 99
RH6: Horl 9F 142
RH10: Cop 7N 163
RH12: Rusp 2D 180
RH14: Ifo 5F 192
SL3: Dat 4L 5
SM2: Chea 8L 61
SM4: Mord 4A 44
SM5: Cars 5D 62
SM6: W'ton 6G 62
SM7: Ban 4K 81
SW6 . . . . .5K 13
SW20 . . . . .8H 27
TW3: Houn 5D 10
TW7: Isle 5D 10
TW14: Felt 1K 23
TW15: A'ford 8E 22
TW19: Wray 8N 5
Drive Mans. SW6 . . . . .5K 13
(off Fulham Rd.)
Drive Mead CR5: Coul 1J 83
Drive Rd. CR5: Coul 7H 83
(not continuous)
Drivers Mead RH7: Ling 8M 145
Drive Spur KT20: K'wood 8N 81
Drodges Cl. GU5: Braml 3B 134
Droitwich Cl. RG12: Brac 2B 32
Dromore Rd. SW15 . . . . .9K 13
Drove Rd. GU4: Guil 5H 115
(not continuous)
GU5: Gorn, Shere 4C 116
GU5: Shere 5N 115
RH5: Ran C 5J 117
Drovers Ct. KT1: K Tham 3K 203
Drovers End GU51: Fleet 1D 88
Drovers Rd.
CR2: S Croy 8D 200 (2A 64)
Drovers Way GU9: U Hal 6F 108
GU12: A Grn 3G 111
(not continuous)
RG12: Brac 2D 32
Druce Wood SL5: Asc 9J 17
Druids Cl. KT21: A'tead 7M 79
Druids Way BR2: Brom 3N 47
Drumaline Ridge
KT4: W Pk 8D 42
Drummond Cl. RG12: Brac 9D 16
Drummond Ct.
GU1: Guil 3C 202 (3N 113)
Drummond Gdns.
KT19: Eps 7B 60
Drummond Ho. SL4: W'sor 6G 4
(off Balmoral Gdns.)
Drummond Pl. TW1: Twick 1H 25
Drummond Rd.
CR0: Croy 3B 200 (8N 45)
(not continuous)
GU1: Guil 3C 202 (3N 113)
RH11: Ifi 4K 181
Drummonds Pl. TW9: Rich 7L 11
Drungewick La.
RH14: W Grn 9L 193
Drury Cl. RH10: Craw 5H 183
Drury Cres. CR0: Wad 8L 45
Dryad St. SW15 . . . . .6J 13
Dry Arch Rd. SL5: S'dale 5C 34
Dryburgh Rd. SW15 . . . . .6G 13
Dryden RG12: Brac 6M 31
Dryden Mans. W14 . . . . .2K 13
(off Queen's Club Gdns.)
Dryden Rd. GU14: Farnb 8L 69
SW19 . . . . .7A 28
Drynham Pk. KT13: Weybr 9F 38
Du Cane Ct. SW17 . . . . .2E 28
Ducavel Ho. SW2 . . . . .2K 29
Duchess Cl. RG45: Crow 9G 30
SM1: Sut 1A 62
Duchess Ct. KT13: Weybr 9E 38
Duchess of Kent Cl.
GU2: Guil 8L 93
Ducks Wlk. TW1: Twick 8J 11
Dudley Cl. KT15: Addl 9L 37
Dudley Ct. GU52: C Cro 7B 88
Dudley Dr. SM4: Mord 7K 43
Dudley Gro.
KT18: Eps 8G 201 (1B 80)
Dudley Pl. TW19: Stan 9A 8
Dudley Rd.
KT1: K Tham . . .5L 203 (2M 41)
KT12: Wal T 5H 39
SW19 . . . . .7M 27
TW9: Rich 5M 11
TW14: Bedf 2D 22
TW15: A'ford 6A 22
Dudset La. TW5: C'ford 4H 9
Duett Ct. TW5: Hest 3M 9
Duffield Rd. KT20: Wal H 2G 100
Duffins Orchard KT16: Otter . . .4E 54
Duffins Orchard Mobile Homes
KT16: Otter 4E 54
Dugdale Ho. TW20: Egh 6E 20
(off Pooley Grn. Rd.)
Duke Cl. RH10: Craw 7G 182
Duke of Cambridge Cl.
TW2: Whitt 9D 10
Duke of Cornwall Av.
GU15: Camb 6B 50
Duke of Edinburgh Rd.
SM1: Sut 8B 44
Duke Rd. W4 . . . . .1C 12
Dukes Av. KT2: K Tham 5J 25
KT3: N Mal 2D 42
TW4: Houn 7M 9
TW10: Ham 5J 25
W4 . . . . .1C 12
Dukes Cl. GU6: Cranl 8B 156
GU9: U Hal 6F 108
TW12: Hamp 6N 23
TW15: A'ford 5D 22
Dukes Ct. GU21: Wok 4B 74
KT15: Addl 1L 55
KT19: Ewe 5D 60
SW14 . . . . .5C 12
Dukes Covert GU19: Bag 1J 51
Duke's Dr. GU7: Goda 4E 132
Dukes Ga. W4 . . . . .1B 12
Dukes Grn. Av. TW14: Felt 8H 9
Dukes Head RH10: Craw D . . .7B 164
Dukes Head Pas.
TW12: Hamp 8C 24
Dukes Hill CR3: Wold 7H 85
GU19: Bag 1J 51
Dukeshill Rd. RG42: Brac 9N 15
Dukes La. SL4: W'sor 8D 18
SL5: Asc 8D 18
Dukes Pk. GU11: Alde 7B 90
Dukes Ride RG45: Crow 3D 48
RH5: Nth H 8K 119
Dukes Rd. KT12: Hers 2L 57
RH5: Newd 4A 160

Dukes Sq.—Edgehill Ct.

Dukes Sq. RH12: Hors ... 7J 197
Dukes Ter. GU11: Alde ... 1N 109
Duke St. GU21: Wok ... 4B 74
SL4: W'sor ... 3F 4
SM1: Sut ... 1B 62
TW9: Rich ... 7K 11
Dukes Wlk. GU9: U Hal ... 6F 108
Dukes Wood RG45: Crow ... 1G 49
(not continuous)
Dulverton Rd. CR2: Sels ... 6F 64
Dumas Cl. GU46: Yate ... 1B 68
Dumbarton Ct. SW2 ... 1J 29
Dumbarton Rd. SW2 ... 1J 29
Dumbleton Cl. KT1: K Tham ... 9A 26
Dump Rd. GU14: Farnb ... 4K 89
Dumsey Eyot KT16: Chert ... 6N 37
Dumville Dr. RH9: Gods ... 9E 104
Dunally Pk. TW17: Shep ... 6E 38
Dunbar Av. BR3: Beck ... 3H 47
SW16 ... 1L 45
Dunbar Ct. KT12: Wal T ... 7K 39
SM1: Sut ... 2B 62
Dunbar Rd. GU16: Frim ... 7D 70
KT3: N Mal ... 3B 42
Dunbar St. SE27 ... 4N 29
Dunboe Pl. TW17: Shep ... 6D 38
Dunboyne Pl. SL4: O Win ... 7K 5
Dunbridge Ho. *SW15* ... *9E 12*
(off Highcliffe Dr.)
Duncan Dr. GU1: Guil ... 2C 114
RG40: W'ham ... 3C 30
Duncan Gdns. TW18: Stain ... 7J 21
Duncannon Cres. SL4: W'sor ... 6A 4
Duncan Rd. KT20: Tad ... 6K 81
TW9: Rich ... 7L 11
Duncans Yd. TN16: Weste ... 4M 107
Duncombe Ct. TW18: Stain ... 8H 21
Duncombe Rd. GU7: Goda ... 9G 133
Duncroft SL4: W'sor ... 6C 4
Duncroft Cl. RH2: Reig ... 3L 121
Duncroft Mnr. TW18: Stain ... 5G 20
Duncton Cl. RH11: Craw ... 1N 181
Dundaff Cl. GU15: Camb ... 1E 70
Dundas Cl. RG12: Brac ... 3N 31
Dundas Gdns. KT8: W Mole ... 2B 40
Dundee Rd. SE25 ... 4E 46
Dundela Gdns. KT4: W Pk ... 1G 61
Dundonald Rd. SW19 ... 8K 27
(not continuous)
Dundonald Road Stop (CT) ... 8L 27
Dundrey Cres. RH1: Mers ... 7J 103
Dunedin Dr. CR3: Cate ... 3B 104
Dunelm Gro. SE27 ... 4N 29
Dunfee Way KT14: Byf ... 8N 55
Dunford Pl. RG42: Bin ... 8K 15
Dungarvan Av. SW15 ... 7F 12
Dungates La. RH3: Buck ... 2F 120
Dungells Farm Cl.
GU46: Yate ... 2C 68
Dungells La. GU46: Yate ... 2B 68
Dunheved Cl. CR7: T Hea ... 5L 45
Dunheved Rd. Nth.
CR7: T Hea ... 5L 45
Dunheved Rd. Sth.
CR7: T Hea ... 5L 45
Dunheved Rd. W.
CR7: T Hea ... 5L 45
Dunhill Point SW15 ... 2F 26
Dunkeld Rd. SE25 ... 3A 46
Dunkirk St. SE27 ... 5N 29
Dunleary Cl. TW4: Houn ... 1N 23
Dunley Dr. CR0: N Add ... 4L 65
Dunlin Cl. RH1: Red ... 8C 122
Dunlin Ri. GU4: Guil ... 1F 114
Dunmail Dr. CR8: Pur ... 1B 84
Dunmore GU2: Guil ... 2G 113
Dunmore Rd. SW20 ... 9H 27
Dunmow Cl. TW13: Hanw ... 4M 23
Dunmow Hill GU51: Fleet ... 3B 88
Dunmow Ho. KT14: Byf ... 9N 55
Dunnets GU21: Knap ... 4H 73
Dunnings Health & Fitness Club
... 2A 186
Dunning's Rd. RH19: E Grin ... 3A 186
Dunnymans Rd. SM7: Ban ... 2L 81
Dunottar Cl. RH1: Red ... 5B 122
Dunraven Av. RH1: Salf ... 1F 142
DUNSBOROUGH PARK ... 7L 75
Dunsbury Cl. SM2: Sut ... 5N 61
Dunsdon Av. GU2: Guil ... 4L 113
DUNSFOLD ... 4B 174
Dunsfold Cl. RH11: Craw ... 4M 181
SM2: Sut ... *4N 61*
(off Blackbush Cl.)
Dunsfold Comn.
GU8: Duns, Loxh ... 5B 174
Dunsfold Ri. CR5: Coul ... 9H 63
Dunsfold Rd.
GU6: Alf, Duns ... 5E 174
GU6: Cranl ... 1C 174
GU8: Loxh ... 1C 174
RH14: Plais ... 2N 191
Dunsfold Way CR0: N Add ... 5L 65
Dunsford Way SW15 ... 9G 13
Dunsmore Rd. KT12: Wal T ... 5J 39
Dunstable Rd. KT8: W Mole ... 3N 39
TW9: Rich ... 7L 11
Dunstall Pk. GU14: Farnb ... 7M 69
Dunstall Rd. SW20 ... 7G 27
Dunstall Way KT8: W Mole ... 2B 40
Dunstan Rd. CR5: Coul ... 4H 83
Dunster Av. SM4: Mord ... 7J 43
Dunster Way SM6: W'ton ... 7E 44
Dunston Ct. TW18: Stain ... 5J 21
Dunton Cl. KT6: Surb ... 7L 41
Duntshill Rd. SW18 ... 2N 27
Dunvegan Cl. KT8: W Mole ... 3B 40
Dunvegan Ho. RH1: Red ... 3D 122
Dupont Rd. SW20 ... 1J 43
Duppas Av.
CR0: Wad ... 7A 200 (1M 63)
Duppas Cl. TW17: Shep ... 4E 38
Duppas Ct. CR0: Croy ... 5A 200
Duppas Hill La.
CR0: Croy ... 6A 200 (1M 63)
Duppas Hill Rd.
CR0: Wad ... 6A 200 (1L 63)
Duppas Hill Ter.
CR0: Croy ... 5A 200 (9M 45)
Duppas Rd. CR0: Wad ... 9L 45
Durand Cl. SM5: Cars ... 7D 44
Durban Rd. BR3: Beck ... 1J 47
SE27 ... 5N 29
Durbin Rd. KT9: Ches ... 1L 59
Durfold Dr. RH2: Reig ... 3A 122
Durfold Hill RH12: Warn ... 6H 179
Durfold Rd. RH12: Hors ... 1K 197
Durfold Wood RH14: Plais ... 2M 191
Durford Cres. SW15 ... 2G 26
Durham Av. TW5: Hest ... 1N 9
Durham Cl. GU2: Guil ... 1J 113
RH10: Craw ... 7C 182
(not continuous)
SW20 ... 1G 43
Durham Ct. TW11: Tedd ... 5E 24
Durham Dr. GU16: Deep ... 5H 71
Durham Rd. GU47: Owls ... 5K 49
SW20 ... 9G 27
TW14: Felt ... 1K 23
Durham Wharf Dr.
TW8: Brent ... 3J 11
Durkins Rd. RH19: E Grin ... 7N 165
(not continuous)
Durleston Pk. Dr.
KT23: Book ... 3C 98
Durley Mead RG12: Brac ... 4D 32
Durlston Rd. KT2: K Tham ... 7L 25
Durnford Ho. *SL4: Eton* ... *2G 4*
(off Slough Rd.)
Durning Pl. SL5: Asc ... 2M 33
Durnsford Av. GU52: Fleet ... 6B 88
SW19 ... 3M 27
Durnsford Rd. SW19 ... 3M 27
Durnsford Way GU6: Cranl ... 8A 156
Durrant Way BR6: Farnb ... 2M 67
Durrell Rd. SW6 ... 4L 13
Durrell Way TW17: Shep ... 5E 38
Durrington Av. SW20 ... 8H 27
Durrington Pk. Rd.
SW20 ... 9H 27
Dutch Barn Cl. TW19: Stan ... 9M 7
Dutchells Copse
RH12: Hors ... 2L 197
Dutch Elm Av. SL4: W'sor ... 3J 5
Dutch Gdns. KT2: K Tham ... 7A 26
Dutch Yd. SW18 ... 8M 13
Duval Pl. GU19: Bag ... 4J 51
Duxberry Av. TW13: Felt ... 4K 23
Duxhurst La. RH2: Sid ... 5N 141
Dwelly La. TN8: Eden ... 6D 126
Dye Ho. Rd. GU8: Thur ... 6E 150
Dyer Ho. TW12: Hamp ... 9B 24
Dyer Rd. RG40: W'ham ... 1D 30
Dyers Almhouses
RH10: Craw ... 2B 182
Dyers Fld. RH6: Smal ... 8M 143
Dyers La. SW15 ... 7G 13
Dykes Path GU21: Wok ... 2E 74
Dymchurch Cl. BR6: Orp ... 1N 67
Dymes Path SW19 ... 3J 27
Dymock St. SW6 ... 6N 13
Dynevor Pl. GU3: Worp ... 8F 92
Dynevor Rd. TW10: Rich ... 8L 11
Dysart Av. KT2: K Tham ... 6J 25
Dyson Cl. SL4: W'sor ... 6E 4
Dyson Ct.
RH4: Dork ... 3J 201 (5G 119)
Dyson Wlk. RH11: Craw ... 8N 181

E

Eady Cl. RH13: Hors ... 6M 197
Eagle Cl. RG45: Crow ... 1F 48
SM6: W'ton ... 3J 63
Eaglehurst Cotts. RG42: Bin ... 6H 15
Eagle Rd.
GU1: Guil ... 3D 202 (3N 113)
TW6: Lon A ... 6G 8
Eagles Dr. TN16: Tats ... 5F 86
Eagles Nest GU47: Sandh ... 6F 48
Eagle Trad. Est. CR4: Mit ... 5D 44
Ealing Pk. Gdns. W5 ... 1J 11
Ealing Rd. TW8: Brent ... 1K 11
Ealing Rd. Trad. Est.
TW8: Brent ... 1K 11
Eardley Cres. SW5 ... 1M 13
Eardley Rd. SW16 ... 6G 29
Earhart Way
TW6: C'ford, Lon A ... 6H 9
Earldom Rd. SW15 ... 7H 13
Earle Cft. RG42: Warf ... 8A 16
Earle Gdns. KT2: K Tham ... 8L 25
Earle Ho. *RH19: E Grin* ... *8B 166*
(off Badger's Way)
Earles Mdw. RH12: Hors ... 2N 197
Earleswood KT11: Cob ... 8M 57
Earleydene SL5: Asc ... 7M 33
Earl of Chester Dr.
GU16: Deep ... 6H 71
Earl Rd. SW14 ... 7B 12
Earlsbourne GU52: C Cro ... 9C 88
Earlsbrook Rd. RH1: Red ... 5D 122
(not continuous)
EARL'S COURT ... 1N 13
Earls Court Exhibition Building
... 1M 13
Earl's Ct. Gdns. SW5 ... 1N 13
Earls Ct. Rd. SW5 ... 1M 13
Earl's Ct. Sq. SW5 ... 1N 13
Earl's Court Station (Tube) ... 1N 13
EARLSFIELD ... 2A 28
Earlsfield Ho.
KT2: K Tham ... 2H 203
Earlsfield Rd. SW18 ... 2A 28
Earlsfield Station (Rail) ... 2A 28
Earls Gro. GU15: Camb ... 9C 50
Earls Ho. TW9: Kew ... 3A 12
Earlsthorpe M. SW12 ... 1E 28
EARLSWOOD ... 5D 122
Earlswood RG12: Brac ... 6N 31
Earlswood Av. CR7: T Hea ... 4L 45
Earlswood Cl. RH13: Hors ... 4M 197
Earlswood Ct. RH1: Red ... 5D 122
Earlswood Rd. RH1: Red ... 4D 122
Earlswood Station (Rail) ... 5D 122
Early Commons
RH10: Craw ... 2D 182
(not continuous)
Easby Cres. SM4: Mord ... 5N 43
Easedale Ho. TW7: Isle ... 8F 10
EASHING ... 7C 132
Eashing La. GU7: Eash ... 7C 132
GU8: Mil ... 9C 132
Eashing Point *SW15* ... *2G 26*
(off Wanborough Dr.)
Easington Pl. GU1: Guil ... 4B 114
East Av. GU9: H End ... 6J 109
KT12: Whit V ... 6G 56
SM6: W'ton ... 2K 63
Eastbank Rd. TW12: H Hill ... 6C 24
EAST BEDFONT ... 1F 22
Eastbourne Gdns.
SW14 ... 6B 12
Eastbourne Rd.
RH7: Blin H, Newc, Ling
... 1H 165
RH9: Gods, S Gods ... 1F 124
RH19: Fel ... 4J 165
SW17 ... 7E 28
TW8: Brent ... 1J 11
TW13: Felt ... 3L 23
W4 ... 2B 12
Eastbrook Cl. GU21: Wok ... 3C 74
Eastbury Ct. RG42: Brac ... 8L 15
Eastbury Gro. W4 ... 1D 12
Eastbury La. GU3: Comp ... 9D 112
Eastbury Rd.
KT2: K Tham ... 1J 203 (8L 25)
Eastchurch Rd.
TW6: Lon A ... 5F 8
EAST CLANDON ... 9M 95
Eastcote Av. KT8: W Mole ... 4N 39
Eastcote Ho. KT17: Eps ... 8D 60
Eastcote Pl. SL5: Asc ... 9H 17
East Court ... 8B 166
East Cres. SL4: W'sor ... 4C 4
Eastcroft Ct. GU1: Guil ... 4C 114
Eastcroft M. RH12: Hors ... 7F 196
Eastcroft Rd. KT19: Ewe ... 4D 60
East Croydon Station (Rail & CT)
... 3E 200 (8A 46)
Eastdean Av. KT18: Eps ... 9A 60
East Dr. GU25: V Wat ... 6K 35
SM5: Cars ... 5C 62
Eastern Av. KT16: Chert ... 2J 37
Eastern Bus. Pk.
TW6: Lon A ... 5F 8
EASTERN INDUSTRIAL AREA
... 1B 32
Eastern La. RG45: Crow ... 3L 49
Eastern Perimeter Rd.
TW6: Lon A ... 5G 8
Eastern Rd. GU12: Alde ... 2B 110
RG12: Brac ... 1B 32
Eastern Vw. TN16: B Hil ... 4E 86
Easter Way RH9: S Gods ... 6H 125
EAST EWELL ... 6H 61
Eastfield Rd. RH1: Red ... 4G 122
Eastfields GU8: Wit ... 5C 152
Eastfields Av. SW18 ... 7M 13
Eastfields Rd. CR4: Mit ... 1E 44
E. Flexford La. GU3: Wan ... 5C 112
East Gdns. GU22: Wok ... 4E 74
SW17 ... 7C 28
Eastgate SM7: Ban ... 1L 81
Eastgate Gdns.
GU1: Guil ... 4E 202 (4A 114)
Eastgate M. RH13: Hors ... 7K 197
East Grn. GU17: B'water ... 2H 69
EAST GRINSTEAD ... 9A 166
E. Grinstead Rd.
RH7: Ling ... 8N 145
East Grinstead Sports & Country Club
... 4L 185
East Grinstead Station (Rail)
... 9N 165
East Grinstead Town Mus. ... 8B 166
EASTHAMPSTEAD ... 4N 31
Easthampstead Mobile Home Pk.
RG40: W'ham ... 8H 31
Easthampstead Pk.
Crematorium & Cemetery
RG40: W'ham ... 7J 31
Easthampstead Rd.
RG12: Brac ... 1M 31
RG40: W'ham ... 3C 30
Eastheath Av. RG41: W'ham ... 4A 30
Eastheath Gdns.
RG41: W'ham ... 5A 30
East Hill CR2: Sande ... 6B 64
GU22: Wok ... 3E 74
RH8: Oxt ... 7A 106
RH19: D Pk ... 4A 166
SW18 ... 8N 13
TN16: B Hil ... 5D 86
E. Hill Ct. RH8: Oxt ... 8A 106
E. Hill La. RH10: Cop ... 4A 164
E. Hill Rd. RH8: Oxt ... 7A 106
EAST HORSLEY ... 7G 96
E. India Way CR0: Croy ... 7C 46
Eastlands Cl. RH8: Oxt ... 5N 105
Eastlands Way RH8: Oxt ... 5N 105
East La.
KT1: K Tham ... 5H 203 (2K 41)
KT24: W Hors ... 4D 96
Eastleigh Cl. SM2: Sut ... 4N 61
Eastleigh Wlk. SW15 ... 1F 26
Eastleigh Way TW14: Felt ... 2H 23
EASTLY END ... 2G 36
East Mall *TW18: Stain* ... *5H 21*
(in Elmsleigh Shop. Cen.)
Eastman Ho. SW4 ... 1G 29
Eastman Way KT19: Eps ... 6A 60
Eastmead GU14: Farnb ... 1N 89
GU21: Wok ... 4L 73
East Meads GU2: Guil ... 4J 113
Eastmearn Rd. SE21 ... 3N 29
East M. RH12: Hors ... 6J 197
EAST MOLESEY ... 3D 40
Eastmont Rd.
KT10: H Wood ... 8E 40
Eastney Rd.
CR0: Croy ... 1A 200 (7M 45)
Eastnor Cl. RH2: Reig ... 5L 121
Eastnor Pl. RH2: Reig ... 5M 121
Eastnor Rd. RH2: Reig ... 6M 121
East Pk. RH10: Craw ... 4B 182
East Pk. La. RH7: Newc ... 2F 164
East Parkside CR6: Warl ... 3K 85
East Pl. SE27 ... 5N 29
East Putney Station (Tube) ... 8K 13
East Ramp TW6: Lon A ... 4C 8
East Ring GU10: Tong ... 5E 110
East Rd.
KT2: K Tham ... 1K 203 (9L 25)
KT13: Weybr ... 4E 56
RH2: Reig ... 2L 121
SW19 ... 7A 28
TW14: Bedf ... 1E 22
EAST SHALFORD ... 9C 114
E. Shalford La. GU4: Guil ... 8A 114
EAST SHEEN ... 7B 12
E. Sheen Av. SW14 ... 8C 12
E. Station Cl. GU12: Alde ... 3N 109
E. Stratton Cl. RG12: Brac ... 4D 32
East St. GU9: Farnh ... 9H 109
KT17: Eps ... 6L 201 (9D 60)
KT23: Book ... 3B 98
RH10: T Hil ... 5D 184
RH12: Hors ... 7J 197
RH12: Rusp ... 2C 180
TW8: Brent ... 3J 11
East Surrey Mus. ... 2C 104
East Ter. SL4: W'sor ... 4H 5
East Vw. Cotts.
GU6: Cranl ... 7L 155
East Vw. La. GU6: Cranl ... 7L 155
East Wlk. RH2: Reig ... 3N 121
East Way CR0: Croy ... 8H 47
GU2: Guil ... 3J 113
Eastway KT19: Eps ... 7C 60
RH6: Gat ... 3F 162
SM4: Mord ... 4J 43
SM6: W'ton ... 1G 62
E. Whipley La.
GU5: Sha G ... 3H 155
Eastwick Dr. KT23: Book ... 1A 98
Eastwick Pk. Av.
KT23: Book ... 2B 98
Eastwick Rd. KT12: Hers ... 3J 57
KT23: Book ... 3B 98
Eastwood KT13: Weybr ... 3E 56
RH10: Craw ... 3D 182
Eastwood Lodge
GU5: Braml ... 4B 134
Eastwood Rd. GU5: Braml ... 4B 134
Eastwood St. SW16 ... 7G 28
EASTWORTH ... 7K 37
Eastworth Rd. KT16: Chert ... 7J 37
Eaton Ct. GU1: Guil ... 1C 114
Eaton Dr. KT2: K Tham ... 8N 25
Eaton Ho. *GU1: Guil* ... *5B 114*
(off St Lukes Sq.)
Eaton Pk. KT11: Cob ... 1M 77
Eaton Pk. Rd. KT11: Cob ... 1M 77
Eaton Rd. GU15: Camb ... 2N 69
SM2: Sut ... 3B 62
TW3: Houn ... 7D 10
Eatonville Rd. SW17 ... 3D 28
Eatonville Vs. SW17 ... 3D 28
Eaves Cl. KT15: Addl ... 3L 55
Ebbage Ct. GU22: Wok ... 5A 74
Ebbas Way KT18: Eps ... 2A 80
Ebbisham Cen., The
KT19: Eps ... 6K 201 (9C 60)
Ebbisham Cl.
RH4: Dork ... 3H 201 (5G 118)
Ebbisham Ct. RH19: Fel ... 6J 165
Ebbisham La.
KT20: Eps D, Wal H, Tad
... 8E 80
Ebbisham Rd. KT4: W Pk ... 8H 43
KT18: Eps ... 1A 80
Ebbisham Sports Club ... 7B 60
Ebenezer Wlk. SW16 ... 9G 28
Ebner St. SW18 ... 8N 13
Ebor Cotts. SW15 ... 4D 26
Ebury Cl. BR2: Kes ... 1G 67
Ebury M. SE27 ... 4M 29
Ecclesbourne Rd.
CR7: T Hea ... 4N 45
Eccleshill RH5: Nth H ... 9J 119
Echelforde Dr.
TW15: A'ford ... 5B 22
Echo Barn La. GU10: Wrec ... 6D 128
Echo Pit Rd.
GU1: Guil ... 8F 202 (7A 114)
Eclipse, The KT10: Esh ... 8B 40
Eclipse Ind. Est.
KT19: Eps ... 6H 201 (9B 60)
Ecob Cl. GU3: Guil ... 8J 93
Ecton Rd. KT15: Addl ... 1K 55
Edar Ho. CR0: N Add ... 3L 65
Eddeys Cl. GU35: H Dwn ... 3G 169
Eddeys La. GU35: H Dwn ... 3G 168
Eddington Cl. CR0: N Add ... 3M 65
Eddington Hill
RH11: Craw ... 8M 181
Eddington Rd. RG12: Brac ... 5K 31
Eddiscombe Rd. SW6 ... 5L 13
Eddy Rd. GU12: Alde ... 3A 110
Eddystone Ct. GU10: Churt ... 9L 149
Eddystone Wlk. TW19: Stan ... 1N 21
Ede Cl. TW3: Houn ... 6N 9
Ede Ct. KT17: Eps ... 8E 60
EDENBRIDGE ... 2L 147
Edenbridge Leisure Cen. ... 1L 147
Edenbridge Station (Rail) ... 9K 127
Edenbridge Town Station (Rail)
... 1M 147
Edenbridge Trad. Cen.
TN8: Eden ... 3M 147
Eden Brook RH7: Ling ... 7A 146
Edenbrook GU17: Haw ... 4L 69
Eden Cl. KT15: N Haw ... 6K 55
SL3: Lang ... 1C 6
Edencourt Rd. SW16 ... 7F 28
Edencroft GU5: Braml ... 4B 134
Edenfield Gdns. KT4: W Pk ... 9E 42
Eden Gro. Rd. KT14: Byf ... 9N 55
Edenhurst Av. SW6 ... 6L 13
Eden M. SW17 ... 4A 28
EDEN PARK ... 4K 47
Eden Pk. Av. BR3: Beck ... 3H 47
(not continuous)
Eden Park Station (Rail) ... 4K 47
Eden Pl. SL5: S'dale ... 6D 34
Eden Rd. BR3: Beck ... 3H 47
CR0: Croy ... 6D 200 (1A 64)
RH11: Craw ... 5L 181
SE27 ... 5M 29
Edenside Rd. KT23: Book ... 2N 97
Edensor Gdns. W4 ... 3D 12
Edensor Rd. W4 ... 3D 12
Eden St.
KT1: K Tham ... 4H 203 (1K 41)
Eden Va. RH19: E Grin ... 7N 165
(not continuous)
Edenvale Cl. CR4: Mit ... 8E 28
Edenvale Rd. CR4: Mit ... 8E 28
Edenvale St. SW6 ... 5N 13
Eden Valley Mus., The ... 2L 147
Eden Vs. TN8: Eden ... 4M 147
Eden Wlk.
KT1: K Tham ... 4H 203 (1L 41)
Eden Way BR3: Beck ... 4J 47
CR6: Warl ... 5H 85
Ederline Av. SW16 ... 2K 45
Edes Fld. RH2: Reig ... 5K 121
Edgar Cl. RH10: Wor ... 4J 183
Edgar Ct. KT3: N Mal ... 1D 42
Edgarley Ter. SW6 ... 4K 13
Edgar Rd. CR2: Sande ... 5A 64
TN16: Tats ... 8F 86
TW4: Houn ... 1N 23
Edgbarrow Ct. RG45: Crow ... 4F 48
Edgbarrow Ri. GU47: Sandh ... 5F 48
Edgbarrow Sports Cen. ... 4H 49
Edgcumbe Pk. Dr.
RG45: Crow ... 2F 48
Edge, The ... 9B 170
Edgeborough Ct. GU1: Guil ... 4B 114
Edge Cl. KT13: Weybr ... 4B 56
Edgecombe Ho. SW19 ... 2K 27
Edgecoombe CR2: Sels ... 4F 64
Edgecoombe Cl.
KT2: K Tham ... 8C 26
Edgedale Cl. RG45: Crow ... 3G 49
Edgefield Cl. GU6: Cranl ... 6L 155
RH1: Red ... 8E 122
Edge Hill SW19 ... 8J 27
Edgehill GU1: Guil ... 4B 114
Edge Hill Ct. SW19 ... 8J 27
Edgehill Ct. KT12: Wal T ... 7K 39

A-Z Surrey 235

Edgehill Rd.—Elm Vw. Ho.

Edgehill Rd. CR4: Mit 9F 28
CR8: Pur 6L 63
Edgeley KT23: Book 2M 97
Edgeley Cvn. Pk. GU5: Alb . . .3N 135
Edgell Cl. GU25: V Wat 2B 36
Edgell Rd. TW18: Stain 6H 21
Edgel St. SW18 . . . . .7N 13
Edgemoor Rd. GU16: Frim 3G 70
Edge Point Cl. SE27 . . . . .6M 29
Edgewood Cl. RG45: Crow 9F 30
Edgewood Grn. CR0: Croy 7G 47
Edgeworth Cl. CR3: Whyte 5D 84
Edgington Rd. SW16 . . . . .7H 29
Edinburgh Cl. GU12: A Va 8E 90
Edinburgh Ct. *GU11: Alde 2L 109*
(off Queen Elizabeth Dr.)
KT1: K Tham 5J 203
SW20 . . . . .4J 43
Edinburgh Dr. TW18: Stain 7M 21
Edinburgh Gdns. SL4: W'sor 6G 5
Edinburgh Ho.
RH11: Craw 7N 181
Edinburgh Rd. SM1: Sut 8A 44
Edinburgh Way
RH19: E Grin 2B 186
Edith Gdns. KT5: Surb 6A 42
Edith Ho. *W6 . . . . .1H 13*
(off Queen Caroline St.)
Edith Rd. SE25 . . . . .4A 46
SW19 . . . . .7N 27
W14 . . . . .1K 13
Edith Row SW6 . . . . .4N 13
Edith Summerskill Ho.
SW6 . . . . .3L 13
(off Clem Attlee Est.)
Edith Vs. W14 . . . . .1L 13
Edmonds Ct. RG12: Brac 9A 16
Edmund Gro. TW13: Hanw 3N 23
Edmund Rd. CR4: Mit 2C 44
Edna Rd. SW20 . . . . .1J 43
Edney Cl. GU52: C Cro 7C 88
Edolphs Copse Nature Reserve
. . . . .9H 141
Edrich Rd. RH11: Craw 8M 181
Edridge Rd.
CR0: Croy 5C 200 (9N 45)
Edward II Av. KT14: Byf 1A 76
Edward Av. GU15: Camb 1M 69
SM4: Mord 4B 44
Edward Cl. TW12: H Hill 6C 24
Edward Ct. GU11: Alde 3M 109
RG40: W'ham 3A 30
TW18: Stain 7L 21
Edward Ho.
GU1: Guil 3D 202 (3N 113)
RH1: Red 6E 122
Edward Rd. CR0: Croy 6B 46
CR5: Coul 2H 83
GU9: Farnh 4H 129
GU20: Windl 3A 52
TN16: B Hil 5G 87
TW12: H Hill 6C 24
TW14: Felt 8E 8
Edwards Cl. KT4: W Pk 8J 43
Edwards Ct. *CR0: Croy 7E 200*
(off South Pk. Hill Rd.)
Edward St. GU11: Alde 2L 109
Edward Way TW15: A'ford 3A 22
Edwin Cl. KT24: W Hors 3E 96
Edwin Pl. CR0: Croy 1F 200
Edwin Rd. KT24: W Hors 3D 96
TW1: Twick 2F 24
TW2: Twick 2E 24
Edwin Stray Ho.
TW13: Hanw 3A 24
Edwyn Ho. *SW18 . . . . .9N 13*
(off Neville Gill Cl.)
Eel Brook Cl. SW6 . . . . .4N 13
Eelmoor Plain Rd.
GU11: Alde 9J 89
Eelmoor Rd. GU11: Alde 8J 89
GU14: Farnb 3L 89
Eel Pie Island TW1: Twick 2G 25
Effie Pl. SW6 . . . . .3M 13
Effie Rd. SW6 . . . . .3M 13
EFFINGHAM 5L 97
Effingham Cl. SM2: Sut 4N 61
EFFINGHAM COMMON 2G 97
Effingham Comn. Rd.
KT24: Eff, E Jun 1H 97
Effingham Community Sports Cen.
. . . . .5M 97
Effingham Ct. *GU22: Wok 6A 74*
(off Constitution Hill)
EFFINGHAM HILL 1L 117
EFFINGHAM JUNCTION 1H 97
Effingham Junction Station (Rail)
. . . . .1H 97
Effingham La. RH10: Cop 5B 164
Effingham Lodge
KT1: K Tham 8H 203 (3K 41)
Effingham Pl. KT24: Eff 5L 97
Effingham Rd. CR0: Croy 6K 45
KT6: Surb 6H 41
RH2: Reig 4N 121
RH6: Cop 4N 163
RH10: Cop 4A 164
Effort St. SW17 . . . . .6C 28
Effra Cl. SW19 . . . . .7N 27
Effra Rd. SW19 . . . . .7N 27
Egan Cl. CR8: Ken 7A 84
Egbury Ho. *SW15 . . . . .9E 12*
(off Tangley Gro.)
Egerton Ct. GU2: Guil 3H 113
Egerton Pl. KT13: Weybr 3D 56
Egerton Rd. GU2: Guil 3H 113
GU15: Camb 9K 49
KT3: N Mal 3E 42
KT13: Weybr 3D 56
SE25 . . . . .2B 46
TW2: Twick 1E 24
Egerton Way UB3: Harl 3C 8
Eggars Ct. GU12: Alde 3N 109
Eggar's Hill GU11: Alde 4M 109
EGHAM 6C 20
Egham Bus. Village
TW20: Thor 1E 36
Egham By-Pass TW20: Egh 6B 20
Egham Cl. SM3: Chea 8K 43
SW19 . . . . .3K 27
Egham Cres. SM3: Chea 9K 43
Egham Hill
TW20: Egh, Eng G 7N 19
EGHAM HYTHE 6G 21
Egham Mus. 6C 20
Egham Rdbt. TW18: Stain 6G 20
Egham Sports Cen. 7D 20
Egham Station (Rail) 6C 20
EGHAM WICK 8K 19
Eglantine Rd. SW18 . . . . .8N 13
Egleston Rd. SM4: Mord 5N 43
Egley Dr. GU22: Wok 9N 73
Egley Rd. GU22: Wok 9N 73
Eglinton Rd. GU10: Rush 4N 149
Eglise Rd. CR6: Warl 4H 85
Egliston M. SW15 . . . . .6H 13
Egliston Rd. SW15 . . . . .6H 13
Egmont Av. KT6: Surb 7M 41
Egmont Ct. KT12: Wal T 6J 39
Egmont Pk. Rd.
KT20: Wal H 3F 100
Egmont Rd. KT3: N Mal 3E 42
KT6: Surb 7M 41
KT12: Wal T 6J 39
SM2: Sut 4A 62
Egmont Way KT20: Tad 6K 81
Egremont Rd. SE27 . . . . .4L 29
Egret Gdns. GU11: Alde 5M 109
Eight Acres GU26: Hind 2A 170
Eighteenth Rd. CR4: Mit 3J 45
Eighth Av. KT20: Lwr K 4K 101
Eileen Rd. SE25 . . . . .4A 46
Eindhoven Cl. SM5: Cars 7E 44
Eland Pl.
CR0: Wad 4A 200 (9M 45)
Eland Rd.
CR0: Wad 4A 200 (9M 45)
GU12: Alde 3B 110
Elberon Av. CR0: Bedd 5G 45
Elbe St. SW6 . . . . .5N 13
Elborough Rd. SE25 . . . . .4D 46
Elborough St. SW18 . . . . .2M 27
Elbourne Ho. *RH6: Horl 8F 142*
(off Lumley Rd.)
Elbow Mdw. SL3: Poy 4H 7
Elcho Rd. GU24: B'wood 6N 71
Elderberry Gro. SE27 . . . . .5N 29
Elderberry Rd. GU35: Lind 5B 168
Elder Cl. GU4: B'ham 9C 94
Elderfield Pl. SW17 . . . . .5F 28
Elder Gdns. SE27 . . . . .6N 29
Eldergrove GU14: Farnb 4C 90
Elder Rd. GU24: Bis 2D 72
SE27 . . . . .5N 29
Eldersley Cl. RH1: Red 1D 122
Eldersley Gdns. RH1: Red 1D 122
Elderslie Cl. BR3: Beck 4K 47
Eldertree Pl. CR4: Mit 9G 28
Eldertree Way CR4: Mit 9G 28
Elder Way RH5: Nth H 9J 119
Elderwood Pl. SE27 . . . . .6N 29
Eldon Av. CR0: Croy 8F 46
TW5: Hest 3A 10
Eldon Ct. KT13: Weybr 2D 56
Eldon Dr. GU10: L Bou 6J 129
Eldon Pk. SE25 . . . . .3E 46
Eldon Rd. CR3: Cate 8A 84
Eldrick Ct. TW14: Bedf 2E 22
Eldridge Cl. TW14: Felt 2H 23
Eleanor Av. KT19: Ewe 6C 60
Eleanor Cl. GU30: Pass 9C 168
Eleanor Ct.
GU1: Guil 6D 202 (5N 113)
Eleanor Gro. SW13 . . . . .6D 12
Eleanor Ho. *W6 . . . . .1H 13*
(off Queen Caroline St.)
Electra Av. TW6: Lon A 6G 8
Electric Pde. KT6: Surb 5K 41
Electric Theatre, The
. . . . .6B 202 (4M 113)
Eleventh Av. KT20: Lwr K 4L 101
Elfin Gro. TW11: Tedd 6F 24
Elford Ct. RG42: Bin 6J 15
Elgal Cl. BR6: Farnb 2K 67
Elgar Av. KT5: Surb 7N 41
RG45: Crow 9G 30
SW16 . . . . .2J 45
Elgar Way RH13: Hors 4A 198
Elger Way RH10: Cop 6L 163
Elgin Av. TW15: A'ford 7D 22
Elgin Cl. RH13: Hors 5M 197
Elgin Ct. CR2: S Croy 7B 200
Elgin Cres. CR3: Cate 9D 84
TW6: Lon A 5F 8
Elgin Gdns. GU1: Guil 2C 114
Elgin Pl. KT13: Weybr 3D 56
Elgin Rd. CR0: Croy 8C 46
GU17: Min 5D 68
KT13: Weybr 2B 56
SM1: Sut 9A 44
SM6: W'ton 3G 62
Elgin Way GU16: Frim 6D 70
Eliot Cl. GU15: Camb 8F 50
Eliot Ct. SW18 . . . . .9N 13
Eliot Dr. GU27: Hasl 2C 188
Eliot Gdns. SW15 . . . . .7F 12
Elis David Almshouses
CR0: Croy 5A 200 (9M 45)
Elizabethan Cl. TW19: Stan . . .1M 21
Elizabethan Way
RH10: Craw 4G 183
TW19: Stan 1M 21
Elizabeth Av. GU19: Bag 5K 51
TW18: Stain 7L 21
Elizabeth Barnes Ct.
SW6 . . . . .5N 13
(off Marinefield Rd.)
Elizabeth Cl. RG12: Brac 3A 32
SM1: Sut 1L 61
Elizabeth Cotts. TW9: Kew 4M 11
Elizabeth Ct. *CR0: Croy 9B 46*
(off The Avenue)
CR3: Cate 9N 83
CR3: Whyte 5C 84
GU7: Goda 4H 133
GU11: Alde 2L 109
(off Queen Elizabeth Dr.)
KT2: K Tham 1J 203 (9L 25)
KT13: Weybr 1E 56
RG41: W'ham 2A 30
RH6: Horl 8E 142
SL4: W'sor 5F 4
(off St Leonard's Rd.)
TW11: Tedd 6E 24
TW16: Sunb 2K 39
(off Elizabeth Gdns.)
Elizabeth Cres.
RH19: E Grin 7B 166
Elizabeth Dr. GU52: C Cro 8B 88
SM7: Ban 5A 82
Elizabeth Fry Ho. UB3: Harl 1G 8
Elizabeth Gdns. SL5: Asc 4M 33
TW7: Isle 7G 11
TW16: Sunb 2K 39
Elizabeth Hart Ct.
KT13: Weybr 2A 56
Elizabeth Ho. CR3: Cate 2D 104
SM3: Chea 3K 61
(off Park La.)
SM7: Ban 5A 82
W6 . . . . .1H 13
(off Queen Caroline St.)
Elizabeth Rd. GU7: Goda 4H 133
RG40: W'ham 2C 30
Elizabeth Way TW13: Hanw 5K 23
Elkins Gdns. GU4: B'ham 9C 94
Elkins Gro. GU9: Farnh 1E 128
Ella Cl. BR3: Beck 1K 47
Ellaline Rd. W6 . . . . .2J 13
Elland Rd. KT12: Wal T 8L 39
Ellenborough Cl.
RG12: Brac 9B 16
Ellenborough Pl.
SW15 . . . . .7F 12
Ellenbridge Way
CR2: Sande 5B 64
Ellen Dr. GU51: Fleet 1D 88
ELLEN'S GREEN 5H 177
Ellen Wilkinson Ho.
SW6 . . . . .2L 13
(off Clem Attlee Ct.)
Elleray Ct. GU12: A Va 8E 90
Elleray Rd. TW11: Tedd 7F 24
Ellerby St. SW6 . . . . .4J 13
Ellerdine Rd. TW3: Houn 7C 10
Ellerker Gdns. TW10: Rich 9L 11
Ellerman Av. TW2: Whitt 2N 23
Ellerton Rd. KT6: Surb 8M 41
SW13 . . . . .4F 12
SW18 . . . . .2B 28
SW20 . . . . .8F 26
Ellerton Way GU10: Wrec 4E 128
Ellery Cl. GU6: Cranl 9N 155
Elles Av. GU1: Guil 3E 114
Elles Cl. GU14: Farnb 2N 89
Ellesfield Av. RG12: Brac 3K 31
Ellesmere Av. BR3: Beck 1L 47
Ellesmere Cl. SL3: Dat 2K 5
Ellesmere Ct. KT13: Weybr 3F 56
W4 . . . . .1C 12
Ellesmere Dr. CR2: Sande 1E 84
Ellesmere Pl. KT12: Hers 2F 56
Ellesmere Rd. KT13: Weybr 4F 56
TW1: Twick 9J 11
W4 . . . . .2B 12
Elles Rd. GU14: Farnb 3K 89
Ellice Rd. RH8: Oxt 7B 106
Ellies M. TW15: A'ford 3N 21
Ellingham GU22: Wok 6A 74
Ellingham Rd. KT9: Ches 3K 59
Ellington Rd. TW3: Houn 5B 10
TW13: Felt 5G 22
Ellington Way KT18: Tat C 4G 81
Elliot Cl. RH10: Craw 4G 182
Elliott Ct. RG42: Bin 7H 15
Elliott Gdns. TW17: Shep 3B 38
Elliott Ind. Est.
GU12: Alde 2C 110
Elliott Ri. SL5: Asc 1H 33
Elliott Rd. CR7: T Hea 3M 45
W4 . . . . .1D 12
Ellis Av. GU2: Guil 5J 113
Ellis Cl. CR5: Coul 7K 83
Ellis Farm Cl. GU22: Wok 9N 73
Ellisfield Dr. SW15 . . . . .1F 26
Ellison Cl. SL4: W'sor 6C 4
Ellison Ho. *SL4: W'sor 4G 4*
(off Victoria St.)
Ellison Rd. SW13 . . . . .5E 12
SW16 . . . . .8H 29
Ellison Way GU10: Tong 5D 110
RG40: W'ham 2A 30
Ellis Rd. CR4: Mit 5D 44
CR5: Coul 7K 83
RG45: Crow 1F 48
Ellman Rd. RH11: Craw 5L 181
Ellora Rd. SW16 . . . . .6H 29
Ellson Cl. RH10: Craw 5G 182
Ellswood Ct. KT6: Surb 6K 41
Ellwood Pl. RH11: Craw 3L 181
Elm Av. SM5: Cars 6D 62
TW19: Stan 3N 21
Elm Bank GU46: Yate 8B 48
Elmbank Av. GU2: Guil 4K 113
TW20: Eng G 7L 19
Elm Bank Gdns. SW13 . . . . . . .5D 12
Elmbourne Rd. SW17 . . . . .4F 28
Elmbridge Av. KT5: Surb 4A 42
Elmbridge Cotts.
GU6: Cranl 7J 155
Elmbridge Est. GU22: Wok 6B 74
Elmbridge La. GU22: Wok 6B 74
Elmbridge Mus. 1B 56
Elmbridge Rd. GU6: Cranl 8G 154
ELMBRIDGE VILLAGE 8H 155
Elmbridge Village
GU6: Cranl 8H 155
(off Essex Dr.)
Elmbridge Xcel Leisure Complex
. . . . .4J 39
Elmbrook Cl. TW16: Sunb 9J 23
Elmbrook Rd. SM1: Sut 1L 61
Elm Cl. CR2: S Croy 3B 64
CR6: Warl 4G 84
GU21: Wok 2N 73
GU23: Rip 2J 95
KT5: Surb 6B 42
KT20: Box H 8B 100
KT22: Leat 9H 79
SM5: Cars 7D 44
SW20 . . . . .3H 43
TW2: Twick 3B 24
TW19: Stan 2M 21
ELM CORNER 6B 76
Elm Cotts. CR4: Mit 1D 44
TN8: Eden 8K 127
Elm Ct. CR4: Mit 1D 44
GU21: Knap 4G 73
GU47: Owls 5K 49
KT8: W Mole 3B 40
RH19: E Grin 8N 165
(Newlands Cres.)
RH19: E Grin 1A 186
(The Jordans)
TW16: Sunb 8G 23
(off Grangewood Dr.)
Elmcourt Rd. SE27 . . . . .3M 29
Elm Cres. GU9: H End 5J 109
KT2: K Tham 2K 203 (9L 25)
Elm Cft. SL3: Dat 4M 5
Elmcroft *GU22: Wok 5B 74*
(off Fairview Av.)
KT23: Book 2A 98
Elmcroft Cl. GU16: Frim G 7D 70
KT9: Ches 9L 41
TW14: Felt 9G 9
Elmcroft Ct. RH10: Craw 3C 182
Elmcroft Dr. KT9: Ches 9L 41
TW15: A'ford 6B 22
Elmdene KT5: Surb 7B 42
Elmdene Cl. BR3: Beck 5J 47
Elmdon Pl. GU1: Guil 2B 114
Elmdon Rd. TW4: Houn 5L 9
TW6: Lon A 6G 8
Elm Dr. GU24: Chob 6J 53
KT22: Leat 1H 99
RH19: E Grin 9C 166
SL4: Wink 3M 17
TW16: Sunb 1K 39
Elmer Cotts. KT22: Fetc 1G 98
Elmer Gdns. TW7: Isle 6D 10
Elmer M. KT22: Fetc 9G 78
Elmers Dr. TW11: Tedd 7H 25
ELMERS END 3G 47
Elmers End Rd. BR3: Beck 1F 46
SE20 . . . . .1F 46
Elmers End Station (Rail & CT)
. . . . .3G 47
Elmerside Rd. BR3: Beck 3H 47
Elmers Lodge BR3: Beck 3G 47
Elmers Rd. RH5: Ockl 6C 158
SE25 . . . . .6D 46
Elm Farm Cvn. Pk.
KT16: Lyne 6D 36
Elmfield KT23: Book 1A 98
Elmfield Av. CR4: Mit 9E 28
TW11: Tedd 6F 24
Elm Fld. Cotts.
GU3: Wood V 2D 112
Elmfield Ct. *GU35: Lind 4A 168*
(off Liphook Rd.)
Elmfield Ho. GU4: Guil 1E 114
Elmfield Rd. SW17 . . . . .3E 28
Elmfield Way CR2: Sande 5C 64
Elm Gdns. CR4: Mit 3H 45
KT10: Clay 3F 58
KT18: Tat C 6H 81
Elmgate Av. TW13: Felt 4J 23
Elm Gro. CR3: Cate 9B 84
GU9: H End 5H 109
GU24: Bis 3D 72
KT2: K Tham 2K 203 (9L 25)
KT12: Wal T 7H 39
KT18: Eps 8H 201 (1B 80)
RH13: Hors 7L 197
SM1: Sut 1N 61
SW19 . . . . .8K 27
Elmgrove Cl. GU21: Wok 6G 73
Elmgrove M. KT13: Weybr 9C 38
Elm Gro. Pde. SM6: W'ton 9E 44
Elm Gro. Rd. KT11: Cob 3L 77
SW13 . . . . .4F 12
Elmgrove Rd. CR0: Croy 6E 46
GU14: Farnb 1N 89
KT13: Weybr 1B 56
ELM HILL 9K 91
Elm Hill GU3: Norm 1J 111
Elm Ho. KT2: K Tham 1M 203
Elmhurst Av. CR4: Mit 8F 28
Elmhurst Ct.
CR0: Croy 7D 200 (1A 64)
GU1: Guil 4B 114
GU15: Camb 1B 70
Elmhurst Dr. RH4: Dork 7H 119
Elmhurst La. RH13: Slin 9J 195
Elmhurst Lodge SM2: Sut 4A 62
Elm La. GU10: Tong 4D 110
GU23: Ockh 6B 76
KT11: Ockh 6B 76
Elm Lodge SW6 . . . . .4H 13
Elm M. GU26: G'hott 6A 170
Elmore Rd. CR5: Chip, Coul . . .8D 82
Elm Pk. GU6: Cranl 7J 155
SL5: S'dale 7B 34
SW2 . . . . .1K 29
Elm Pk. Gdns. CR2: Sels 6F 64
Elm Pk. Rd. SE25 . . . . .2C 46
Elm Pl. GU11: Alde 4A 110
TW15: A'ford 6B 22
Elm Rd. BR3: Beck 1J 47
CR6: Warl 4G 84
CR7: T Hea 3A 46
CR8: Pur 9M 63
GU7: Goda 3J 133
GU9: H End 5J 109
GU21: Wok 5N 73
(Kingsway)
GU21: Wok 2B 74
(Woodham Ri.)
KT2: K Tham . . .2L 203 (9M 25)
KT3: N Mal 1C 42
KT9: Ches 1L 59
KT10: Clay 3F 58
KT17: Ewe 3E 60
KT22: Leat 9H 79
RH1: Red 3C 122
SL4: W'sor 6E 4
SM6: W'ton 7E 44
SW14 . . . . .6B 12
TN16: Weste 3N 107
TW14: Bedf 2E 22
Elm Rd. W. SM3: Sut 6L 43
Elms, The CR0: Croy 1C 200
CR6: Warl 2F 84
GU10: Tong 4D 110
GU17: Haw 2K 69
KT10: Clay 4F 58
RG42: Warf 7E 16
SW13 . . . . .6E 12
TW15: A'ford 6B 22
Elms Cres. SW4 . . . . .1G 29
Elmshaw Rd. SW15 . . . . .8F 12
Elmshorn KT17: Eps D 3H 81
Elmside CR0: N Add 3L 65
GU2: Guil 4K 113
GU8: Mil 1C 152
Elmsleigh Cen., The
TW18: Stain 5H 21
Elmsleigh Ct. SM1: Sut 9N 43
Elmsleigh Ho. *TW2: Twick 3D 24*
(off Staines Rd.)
Elmsleigh Rd. GU14: Cove 1L 89
TW2: Twick 3D 24
TW18: Stain 6H 21
Elmslie Cl.
KT18: Eps 8J 201 (1B 80)
Elms Rd. GU11: Alde 3M 109
GU51: Fleet 4D 88
RG40: W'ham 3A 30
Elmstead Cl. KT19: Ewe 2D 60
Elmstead Gdns. KT4: W Pk 9F 42
Elmstead Rd. KT14: W By 9J 55
Elmstone Rd. SW6 . . . . .4M 13
Elmsway TW15: A'ford 6B 22
Elmswood KT23: Book 2N 97
Elmsworth Av. TW3: Houn 5B 10
Elm Tree Av. KT10: Esh 6D 40
Elm Tree Cl. KT16: Chert 8G 37
RH6: Horl 7E 142
TW15: A'ford 6C 22
Elmtree Cl. KT14: Byf 9N 55
Elmtree Rd. TW11: Tedd 5E 24
Elm Tree Wlk. GU14: Cove 6L 69
Elm Vw. GU12: Ash 1F 110
Elm Vw. Ho. UB3: Harl 1E 8

Fairchildes Rd. CR6: Warl 1N 85
Faircroft Ct. TW11: Tedd 7G 25
Faircross RG12: Brac 2N 31
Fairdale Gdns. SW15 ....7G 13
Fairdene Rd. CR5: Coul 5H 83
Fairfax RG42: Brac 9M 15
Fairfax Av. KT17: Ewe 5G 60
RH1: Red 2C 122
Fairfax Cl. KT12: Wal T 7J 39
RH8: Oxt 8N 105
Fairfax Ho. KT1: K Tham 5L 203
Fairfax Ind. Est.
GU12: Alde 2C 110
Fairfax M. GU14: Farnb 3B 90
SW15 ....7H 13
Fairfax Rd. GU14: Farnb 7N 69
GU22: Wok 7D 74
TW11: Tedd 7G 25
FAIRFIELD 8H 79
Fairfield
KT1: K Tham ...4L 203 (1M 41)
Fairfield, The GU9: Farnh 1H 129
(not continuous)
Fairfield App. TW19: Wray 9N 5
Fairfield Av. RH6: Horl 9E 142
SL3: Dat 3M 5
TW2: Whitt 2B 24
TW18: Stain 5H 21
Fairfield Cl. CR4: Mit 8C 28
GU2: Guil 2K 113
KT19: Ewe 2D 60
RH4: Dork 3H 119
SL3: Dat 3N 5
Fairfield Cotts. KT23: Book 3B 98
Fairfield Ct. *KT22: Leat 8H 79*
(off Linden Rd.)
Fairfield Dr. GU16: Frim 3C 70
RH4: Dork 3H 119
SW18 ....8N 13
Fairfield E.
KT1: K Tham 3K 203 (1L 41)
Fairfield Halls
Ashcroft Theatre
...............4D 200 (9A 46)
Fairfield La. GU24: W End 8D 52
Fairfield Lodge *GU2: Guil 2K 113*
(off Fairfield Ri.)
Fairfield Nth.
KT1: K Tham 3K 203 (1L 41)
Fairfield Pk. KT11: Cob 1L 77
Fairfield Path
CR0: Croy 4E 200 (9A 46)
Fairfield Pl.
KT1: K Tham 5K 203 (2L 41)
Fairfield Ri. GU2: Guil 2J 113
Fairfield Rd. BR3: Beck 1K 47
CR0: Croy 4E 200 (9A 46)
KT1: K Tham 4K 203 (1L 41)
(not continuous)
KT22: Leat 8H 79
RH19: E Grin 1B 186
TW19: Wray 9N 5
Fairfields KT16: Chert 7J 37
Fairfield Sth.
KT1: K Tham 4K 203 (1L 41)
Fairfields Rd. TW3: Houn 6C 10
Fairfield St. SW18 ....8N 13
Fairfield Trade Pk.
KT1: K Tham ...6M 203 (2M 41)
Fairfield Wlk. *KT22: Leat 8H 79*
(off Fairfield Rd.)
Fairfield Way CR5: Coul 1H 83
KT19: Ewe 2D 60
Fairfield W.
KT1: K Tham 4K 203 (1L 41)
Fairford Av. CR0: Croy 4G 47
Fairford Cl. CR0: Croy 4H 47
KT14: W By 1H 75
RH2: Reig 1A 122
Fairford Ct. SM2: Sut 4N 61
Fairford Gdns. KT4: W Pk 8E 42
Fairgreen Rd. CR7: T Hea 4M 45
Fairhall Ct. KT5: Surb 6M 41
Fairhaven TW20: Egh 6B 20
Fairhaven Av. CR0: Croy 5G 46
Fairhaven Ct. CR2: S Croy ...8C 200
TW20: Egh 6B 20
Fairhaven Rd. RH1: Red 8E 102
Fairholme TW14: Bedf 1E 22
Fairholme Cres.
KT21: A'tead 4J 79
Fairholme Gdns.
GU9: Farnh 2H 129
Fairholme Rd. CR0: Croy 6L 45
SM1: Sut 3L 61
TW15: A'ford 6N 21
W14 ....1K 13
Fairland Cl. GU52: Fleet 5C 88
FAIRLANDS 8F 92
Fairlands GU35: H Dwn 4J 169
Fairlands Av. CR7: T Hea 3K 45
GU3: Worp 8F 92
SM1: Sut 8M 43
Fairlands Ct. GU3: Worp 8F 92
Fairlands Rd. GU3: Worp 7F 92
Fair La. CR5: Coul 3A 102
Fairlawn KT13: Weybr 2F 56
KT23: Book 2N 97
Fairlawn Bus. Pk.
RH1: Salf 3F 142
Fair Lawn Cl. KT10: Clay 3F 58
Fairlawn Cl. KT2: K Tham 7B 26
TW13: Hanw 5N 23
Fairlawn Cres.
RH19: E Grin 8L 165
Fairlawn Dr. RH1: Red 5C 122
RH19: E Grin 8L 165
Fairlawnes SM6: W'ton 2F 62
Fairlawn Gro. SM7: Ban 9B 62
Fairlawn Pk. GU21: Wok 1A 74
SL4: W'sor 7B 4
Fairlawn Rd. SM5: Ban, Sut ...7A 62
(not continuous)
SW19 ....8L 27
Fairlawns GU1: Guil 3E 114
KT15: Addl 2K 55
KT15: Wood 7H 55
RH6: Horl 9F 142
TW1: Twick 9J 11
TW16: Sunb 2H 39
Fairlawns Cl. TW18: Stain 7K 21
Fairlight TW12: H Hill 6B 24
Fairlight Av. SL4: W'sor 5G 4
Fairlight Cl. KT4: W Pk 1H 61
Fairlight Rd. SW17 ....5B 28
Fairline Ct. BR3: Beck 1M 47
Fairlop Wlk. GU6: Cranl 8H 155
Fairmead GU21: Wok 5M 73
KT5: Surb 7A 42
Fairmead Cl. GU47: C Tow 8K 49
KT3: N Mal 2C 42
TW5: Hest 3L 9
Fairmead Ct. TW9: Rich 5A 12
Fairmead Rd. CR0: Croy 6K 45
TN8: Eden 7L 127
Fairmeads KT11: Cob 9N 57
FAIRMILE 8M 57
Fairmile GU52: Fleet 7A 88
Fairmile Av. KT11: Cob 1M 77
SW16 ....6H 29
Fairmile Ct. KT11: Cob 8M 57
Fairmile Ho. TW11: Tedd 5G 25
Fairmile La. KT11: Cob 8L 57
Fairmile Pk. Copse
KT11: Cob 9N 57
Fairmile Pk. Rd. KT11: Cob 9N 57
Fairoak Cl. CR8: Ken 2M 83
KT22: Oxs 8D 58
Fairoak La. KT9: Ches 8C 58
KT22: Oxs 8C 58
Fairoaks Airport 6A 54
Fairoaks Cvn. Pk.
GU3: Worp 7D 92
Fairoaks Ct. *KT15: Addl 2K 55*
(off Lane Cl.)
Fairs Rd. KT22: Leat 6G 79
Fairstone Ct. RH6: Horl 7F 142
Fair St. TW3: Houn 6C 10
Fair Vw. RH12: Hors 5G 197
Fairview KT17: Ewe 7H 61
Fairview Av. GU22: Wok 5A 74
Fairview Cl. GU22: Wok 5B 74
Fairview Ct. *RH19: E Grin 1B 186*
(off Fairfield Rd.)
TW15: A'ford 6B 22
Fairview Dr. BR6: Orp 1M 67
TW17: Shep 4A 38
Fairview Gdns. GU9: Hale 6J 109
Fairview Ho. SW2 ....1K 29
Fairview Ind. Est.
RH8: Oxt 2C 126
Fairview Pl. SW2 ....1K 29
Fairview Rd. GU12: Ash 1F 110
GU35: H Dwn 4G 169
KT17: Ewe 7E 60
RG40: W'ham 3B 30
SM1: Sut 2B 62
SW16 ....9K 29
Fairview Ter. GU35: Head 3F 168
Fairwater Dr. KT15: N Haw 5M 55
Fairwater Ho. TW11: Tedd 5G 25
Fairway GU1: Guil 2F 114
GU25: V Wat 5M 35
KT16: Chert 7K 37
RH10: Cop 8M 163
RH11: Ifi 4J 181
SM5: Cars 7A 62
SW20 ....2H 43
Fairway, The GU3: Worp 2F 92
GU7: Goda 9J 133
GU9: H End 5J 109
GU14: Farnb 4F 88
(not continuous)
GU15: Camb 3E 70
KT3: N Mal 9C 26
KT8: W Mole 2B 40
KT13: Weybr 7B 56
KT22: Leat 5G 79
Fairway Cl. CR0: Croy 4H 47
GU22: Wok 6L 73
KT19: Ewe 1B 60
RH10: Cop 8L 163
TW4: Houn 8K 9
(Green La.)
TW4: Houn 8L 9
(Staines Rd.)
Fairway Gdns. BR3: Beck 5N 47
Fairway Hgts. GU15: Camb 9F 50
Fairways CR8: Ken 4N 83
GU26: Hind 3N 169
TW7: Isle 4D 10
TW11: Tedd 8K 25
TW15: A'ford 7C 22
Fairways, The RH1: Red 6B 122
Fairway Trad. Est.
TW4: Houn 8K 9
Fairwell La. KT24: W Hors 6C 96
Faithfull Cl. RG42: Warf 7N 15
Fakenham Way
GU47: Owls 6J 49
Falaise TW20: Egh 6A 20
Falaise Cl. GU11: Alde 2N 109
Falcon Cl. GU18: Ligh 7K 51
RH11: Craw 1B 182
W4 ....2B 12
Falcon Ct. GU16: Frim 5B 70
GU21: Wok 9E 54
Falcon Dr. TW19: Stan 9M 7
Falconer Rd. GU51: Fleet 2A 88
Falcon Ho. *SW5 ....1N 13*
(off Old Brompton Rd.)
Falconhurst KT22: Oxs 2D 78
Falcon Rd.
GU1: Guil 4D 202 (4N 113)
(not continuous)
TW12: Hamp 8N 23
Falconry Ct. KT1: K Tham 5K 203
Falcons Cl. TN16: B Hil 4F 86
Falcon Way GU46: Yate 9A 48
TW14: Felt 8J 9
TW16: Sunb 1F 38
Falcon Wood KT22: Leat 7F 78
Falconwood KT24: E Hor 2G 96
TW20: Egh 6A 20
Falconwood Rd. CR0: Sels 5J 65
Falcourt Cl. SM1: Sut 2N 61
Falkland Ct. GU14: Farnb 5C 90
Falkland Gdns. RH4: Dork ...6G 119
Falkland Gro. RH4: Dork 6G 118
Falkland Ho. *W14 ....1L 13*
(off Edith Vs.)
Falkland Pk. Av. SE25 ....2B 46
Falkland Rd.
RH4: Dork 4J 201 (6G 119)
Falklands Dr. RH13: Hors 4A 198
Falkner Ct. GU9: Farnh 1H 129
Falkner Ho. GU51: Fleet 1D 88
Falkner Rd. GU9: Farnh 1G 128
Falkners Cl. GU51: Fleet 1D 88
Fallow Deer Cl.
RH13: Hors 5A 198
Fallowfield GU46: Yate 8A 48
GU51: Fleet 1D 88
Fallowfield Way RH6: Horl ...7F 142
Fallsbrook Rd. SW16 ....7F 28
Falmer Cl. RH11: Craw 5B 182
Falmouth Cl. GU15: Camb 2E 70
Falmouth Ho.
KT2: K Tham 2H 203
Falmouth Rd. KT12: Hers 1K 57
Falstaff M. *TW12: H Hill 6D 24*
(off Parkside)
Falstone GU21: Wok 5L 73
Famet Av. CR8: Pur 9N 63
Famet Cl. CR8: Pur 9N 63
Famet Gdns. CR8: Ken 9N 63
Famet Wlk. CR8: Pur 9N 63
Fanes Cl. RG42: Brac 9L 15
Fane St. W14 ....2L 13
Fangrove Pk. KT16: Lyne 7C 36
Fanshawe Rd. TW10: Ham 5J 25
FANTAIL, THE 1H 67
Fanthorpe St. SW15 ....6H 13
Faraday Av. RH19: E Grin 3B 186
Faraday Cen., The
RH10: Craw 9D 162
Faraday Ct. RH10: Craw 8C 162
Faraday Mans. *W14 ....2K 13*
(off Queen's Club Gdns.)
Faraday Pl. KT8: W Mole 3A 40
Faraday Rd.
GU1: Guil 1B 202 (2M 113)
GU14: Farnb 8A 70
KT8: W Mole 3A 40
RH10: Craw 8D 162
SW19 ....7M 27
Faraday Way CR0: Wad 7K 45
Farcrosse Cl. GU47: Sandh 7H 49
Farebrothers RH12: Warn 9F 178
Fareham Dr. GU46: Yate 8A 48
Fareham Rd. TW14: Felt 1K 23
Farewell Pl. CR4: Mit 9C 28
Farhalls Cres.
RH12: Hors 3M 197
Faringdon Cl. GU47: Sandh ...6H 49
Faringdon Dr. RG12: Brac 4B 32
Farington Acres
KT13: Weybr 9E 38
Faris Barn Dr. KT15: Wood 8H 55
Faris La. KT15: Wood 7H 55
FARLEIGH 1J 85
FARLEIGH COMMON 1H 85
Farleigh Ct.
CR2: S Croy ...8B 200 (2N 63)
GU2: Guil 3H 113
Farleigh Ct. Rd. CR6: Warl 1J 85
Farleigh Dean Cres.
CR0: Sels 7L 65
Farleigh Rd. CR6: Warl 5G 85
KT15: N Haw 7J 55
Farleton Cl. KT13: Weybr 3E 56
Farley Copse RG42: Brac 9K 15
Farley Ct. GU14: Farnb 3B 90
Farleycroft TN16: Weste 4L 107
FARLEY GREEN 3M 135
FARLEY HEATH 4L 135
Farley Heath Rd.
GU5: Sha G 7J 135
Farley La. TN16: Weste 4K 107
Farley Nursery
TN16: Weste 5L 107
Farley Pk. RH8: Oxt 8N 105
Farley Pl. SE25 ....3D 46
Farley Rd. CR2: Sels 4E 64
Farleys Cl. KT24: W Hors 4D 96
FARLEY WOOD 1J 31
Farlington Pl. SW15 ....1G 26
Farlow Rd. SW15 ....6J 13
Farlton Rd. SW18 ....2N 27
Farm Av. RH12: Hors 5H 197
SW16 ....5J 29
Farm Cl. CR5: Chip 7D 82
GU1: Guil 9N 93
GU3: Worp 7F 92
GU46: Yate 1C 68
KT14: Byf 8A 56
KT16: Lyne 5C 36
KT22: Fetc 2D 98
KT24: E Hor 6G 96
RG42: Brac 9L 15
RG45: Crow 9H 31
RH10: Craw 2E 182
RH12: Warn 1F 196
RH14: Loxw 5J 193
RH19: E Grin 1D 186
SL5: S'hill 4N 33
SM2: Sut 4B 62
SM6: W'ton 6G 63
SW6 ....3M 13
TW17: Shep 6B 38
TW18: Stain 6G 20
Farm Cotts. RG40: W'ham 9A 14
Farm Ct. GU16: Frim 4D 70
Farmdale Rd. SM5: Cars 4C 62
Farm Dr. CR0: Croy 8J 47
CR8: Pur 8H 63
GU51: Fleet 1C 88
SL4: O Win 9L 5
Farmers Rd. TW18: Stain 6G 20
Farmet Ct. *RH19: E Grin 7M 165*
(off Halsford La.)
Farmfield Cotts.
RH6: Char 3N 161
Farmfield Dr. RH6: Char 2N 161
Farm Flds. CR2: Sande 7B 64
Farmhouse Cl. GU22: Pyr 2F 74
Farmhouse Rd. SW16 ....8G 29
Farmington Av. SM1: Sut 9B 44
Farm La. CR0: Croy 8J 47
CR8: Pur 6G 63
GU23: Send 2E 94
KT15: Addl 4J 55
KT18: Eps D 4N 79
KT21: A'tead 4N 79
KT24: E Hor 6G 96
RG45: Crow 5D 48
SM5: Cars 6D 62
SW6 ....2M 13
(not continuous)
Farm La. Trad. Est.
SW6 ....2M 13
Farmleigh Cl. RH10: Craw ...1G 182
Farmleigh Gro. KT12: Hers 2G 56
Farm M. CR4: Mit 1F 44
Farm Rd. CR6: Warl 6H 85
GU12: Alde 1C 110
GU16: Frim 4C 70
GU22: Wok 7D 74
KT10: Esh 7B 40
SM2: Sut 4B 62
SM4: Mord 4N 43
TW4: Houn 2M 23
TW18: Stain 7K 21
Farmstead KT19: Eps 5N 59
Farmstead Ct. *SM6: W'ton 2F 62*
(off Melbourne Rd.)
Farmstead Dr. TN8: Eden ...9L 127
Farm Vw. GU46: Yate 1C 68
KT20: Lwr K 5L 101
Farmview KT11: Cob 3L 77
Farm Wlk. GU2: Guil 5J 113
GU12: A Grn 4G 111
RH6: Horl 8D 142
Farm Way KT4: W Pk 9H 43
TW19: Stan M 9H 7
Farm Yd. SL4: W'sor 3G 5
Farnan Rd. SW16 ....6J 29
FARNBOROUGH
BR6 ....2L 67
GU14 ....1L 89
Farnborough Aerospace Cen.
GU14: Farnb 5L 89
Farnborough Airport 5K 89
Farnborough Av. CR2: Sels 5G 65
Farnborough Bus. Cen.
GU14: Farnb 3L 89
Farnborough Bus. Pk.
GU14: Farnb 3M 89
Farnborough Comn.
BR6: Farnb 1H 67
Farnborough Cres.
CR2: Sels 5H 65
Farnborough Ga. Retail Pk.
GU14: Farnb 7A 70
FARNBOROUGH GREEN 8A 70
Farnborough Hill
BR6: Chels, Farnb 2M 67
Farnborough Ho.
SW15 ....2F 26
Farnborough Leisure Cen. 2N 89
Farnborough Main Station (Rail)
........................9N 69
Farnborough North Station (Rail)
........................8B 70
FARNBOROUGH PARK 2A 90
Farnborough Rd.
GU9: H End 4J 109
GU11: Alde 1K 109
GU14: Farnb 5N 89
FARNBOROUGH STREET 1A 90
Farnborough St.
GU14: Farnb 8B 70
Farnborough Town FC 6M 69
Farnborough Way
BR6: Chels, Farnb 2L 67
FARNCOMBE 4H 133
Farncombe Boat House 5K 133
Farncombe Hill
GU7: Goda 4G 132
(not continuous)
Farncombe Station (Rail) 4J 133
Farncombe St. GU7: Goda ...4H 133
Farnell M. KT13: Weybr 9C 38
SW5 ....1N 13
Farnell Rd. TW7: Isle 6D 10
TW18: Stain 4J 21
Farney Fld. GU5: P'lake 2E 136
FARNHAM 1H 129
Farnham Bus. Cen.
GU9: Farnh 9H 109
Farnham Bus. Pk.
GU9: Farnh 2G 128
Farnham By-Pass
GU9: Farnh 3E 128
Farnham Castle 9G 109
Farnham Cloisters
GU10: Wrec 5F 128
Farnham Cl. RG12: Brac 1B 32
RH11: Craw 9A 182
Farnham Ct. SM3: Chea 3K 61
Farnham Gdns. SW20 ....1G 42
Farnham La. GU27: Hasl 9D 170
Farnham Maltings 1G 129
Farnham Mus. 1G 128
Farnham Pk. Cl.
GU9: U Hal 6G 108
Farnham Pk. Dr.
GU9: U Hal 6G 109
Farnham Retail Pk.
GU9: Farnh 9K 109
Farnham Rd. GU1: Guil 6G 112
GU2: Guil 6A 202 (6G 112)
GU8: Els 6E 130
GU10: B Oak, H Pou 1A 148
GU10: Ews 3A 108
GU51: Fleet 4E 88
Farnham Sports Cen. 1H 129
Farnham Station (Rail) 2H 129
Farnham Trad. Est.
GU9: Farnh 8L 109
Farnhurst La. GU6: Alf 4H 175
Farningham RG12: Brac 5C 32
Farningham Ct. SW16 ....8H 29
Farningham Cres.
CR3: Cate 1D 104
Farningham Ho. RG12: Brac ...5C 32
Farningham Rd. CR3: Cate ...1D 104
Farnley GU21: Wok 4J 73
Farnley Rd. SE25 ....3A 46
Farquhar Rd. SW19 ....4M 27
Farquharson Rd.
CR0: Croy 1B 200 (7N 45)
Farrell Cl. GU15: Camb 3A 70
Farren Av. GU14: Farnb 3N 89
(not continuous)
Farrer Ct. TW1: Twick 1K 25
Farrer Ho. *SL4: Eton 1F 4*
(off Common La.)
Farrer's Pl. CR0: Croy 1G 64
Farrier Cl. TW16: Sunb 3H 39
Farrier Pl. SM1: Sut 9N 43
Farriers, The GU5: Braml 6C 134
TN8: Eden 9K 127
Farriers Cl. KT17: Eps 8D 60
Farriers Ct. RH12: Hors 6J 197
Farriers Rd. KT17: Eps 7D 60
Farriery Way GU11: Alde 8L 89
Farringdon Ho. TW9: Kew 3A 12
Farthing Barn La. BR6: Dow ...5J 67
Farthing Flds. GU35: Head ...4D 168
Farthingham La. GU6: Ewh ...4F 156
Farthings GU21: Knap 3H 73
Farthings, The
KT2: K Tham 9N 25
Farthings Hill *RH12: Hors 5F 196*
(off Guildford Rd.)
Farthings Hill Interchange
RH12: Bro H, Hors 5E 196
FARTHING STREET 5H 67
Farthing St. BR6: Dow 4H 67
Farthings Wlk. RH12: Hors ...5F 196
Farthing Way CR5: Coul 4H 83
Fassett Rd.
KT1: K Tham 7J 203 (3L 41)
Fauconberg Ct. *W4 ....2B 12*
(off Fauconberg Rd.)
Fauconberg Rd. W4 ....2B 12
Faulkner Cl. RH11: Craw 9N 181
Faulkner Pl. GU19: Bag 3J 51
Faulkners Rd. KT12: Hers 2K 57
Favart Rd. SW6 ....4M 13
Faversham Rd. BR3: Beck 1J 47
GU47: Owls 6J 49
SM4: Mord 5N 43
Fawcett Cl. SW16 ....6L 29

Fawcett Ct.—Fiske Ct.

Fawcett Ct. *SW10* 2N 13
(off Fawcett St.)
Fawcett Rd.
CR0: Croy 5A 200 (9N 45)
SL4: W'sor 4E 4
Fawcett St. SW10 . . . . .2N 13
Fawcus Cl. KT10: Clay 3E 58
Fawe Pk. M. SW15 . . . . .7L 13
Fawe Pk. Rd. SW15 . . . . .7L 13
Fawler Mead RG12: Brac 3D 32
Fawley Cl. GU6: Cranl 8A 156
Fawn Dr. GU12: Alde 1C 110
Fawns Mnr. Cl. TW14: Bedf . . .2D 22
Fawns Mnr. Rd. TW14: Bedf . . .2E 22
Fawsley Cl. SL3: Poy 3G 6
Fay Cotts. RH12: Fay 5D 180
FAYGATE 8E 180
Faygate Bus. Cen.
RH12: Fay 8E 180
Faygate La. RH9: S Gods 9H 125
RH12: Rusp, Fay 2D 180
Faygate Rd. SW2 . . . . .3K 29
Faygate Station (Rail) 8E 180
Fayland Av. SW16 . . . . .6G 28
Fay Rd. RH12: Hors 3J 197
Fays Pas.
GU1: Guil 5B 202 (4M 113)
Fearn Cl. KT24: E Hor 7F 96
Fearnley Cres.
TW12: Hamp 6M 23
Featherbed La. CR0: Sels 4J 65
CR6: Warl 4J 65
Feathercombe La.
GU8: Hamb 6G 153
Feathers La. TW19: Wray 3C 20
Featherstone RH7: Blin H 3G 145
Fee Farm Rd. KT10: Clay 4F 58
FELBRIDGE 6K 165
Felbridge Av. RH10: Craw . . .2H 183
Felbridge Cen., The
RH19: E Grin 7K 165
Felbridge Cl. GU16: Frim 4D 70
RH19: E Grin 7M 165
SM2: Sut 5N 61
SW16 . . . . .5L 29
Felbridge Ct. RH19: E Grin . . .6K 165
TW13: Felt *2J 23*
(off High St.)
UB3: Harl 2E 8
Felbridge Rd. RH19: Fel 7G 164
Felcot Rd. RH19: Fel 7F 164
Felcott Cl. KT12: Hers 9K 39
Felcott Rd. KT12: Hers 9K 39
FELCOURT 2M 165
Felcourt La. RH7: Felc 1L 165
RH19: Felc 2L 165
Felcourt Rd.
RH7: Felc, Ling 3M 165
RH19: D Pk, Felc, E Grin
. . . . .3M 165
Feld, The RH19: E Grin 7K 165
FELDAY 6J 137
Felday Glade RH5: H Mary . . .6J 137
Felday Ho's. RH5: H Mary . . .4J 137
Felday Rd. RH5: A Ham 9G 116
FELDEMORE 5K 137
Feldemore Cotts.
RH5: H Mary 5K 137
Felden St. SW6 . . . . .4L 13
Felgate M. W6 . . . . .1G 12
Felix Dr. GU4: W Cla 6J 95
Felix La. TW17: Shep 5F 38
Felix Rd. KT12: Wal T 5H 39
Felland Way RH2: Reig 7B 122
Fellbrook TW10: Ham 4H 25
Fellcott Way RH12: Hors 7F 196
Fellmongers Yd.
CR0: Croy 4B 200
Fellowes Rd. SM5: Cars 9C 44
Fellow Grn. GU24: W End 9C 52
Fellow Grn. Rd.
GU24: W End 9C 52
Fellows Rd. GU14: Farnb 4B 90
Fell Rd.
CR0: Croy 4C 200 (9N 45)
(not continuous)
Felmingham Rd. SE20 . . . . . . .1F 46
Felnex Trad. Est.
SM6: W'ton 8E 44
Felsberg Rd. SW2 . . . . .1J 29
Felsham M. *SW15* *6J 13*
(off Felsham Rd.)
Felsham Rd. SW15 . . . . .6H 13
Felstead Rd. KT19: Eps 7C 60
FELTHAM 3H 23
Feltham Airparcs Leisure Cen.
. . . . .3L 23
Feltham Arenas 1H 23
Feltham Av. KT8: E Mol 3E 40
Felthambrook Ind. Est.
TW13: Felt 4J 23
Felthambrook Way
TW13: Felt 4J 23
Feltham Bus. Complex
TW13: Felt 3J 23
Feltham Corporate Cen.
TW13: Felt 4J 23
FELTHAMHILL 6G 23
Feltham Hill Rd.
TW15: A'ford 6B 22
Feltham Rd. CR4: Mit 1D 44
RH1: Red 8D 122
TW15: A'ford 5B 22
Feltham Station (Rail) 2J 23
Feltham Wlk. RH1: Red 8D 122
Felwater Ct. RH19: E Grin 7K 165
Fenby Cl. RH13: Hors 4A 198
Fenchurch Rd. RH10: Craw . . .5F 182
Fencote RG12: Brac 5B 32
Fendall Rd. KT19: Ewe 2B 60
Fender Ho. RH12: Hors 6H 197
Fenelon Pl. W14 . . . . .1L 13
Fengates Rd. RH1: Red 3C 122
Fenhurst Cl. RH12: Hors 7F 196
Fen La. SW13 . . . . .4G 12
Fenmore Rd. CR8: Ken 7A 84
Fennel Cl. CR0: Croy 7G 47
GU1: Guil 9D 94
GU14: Cove 1G 89
SL5: Asc 4L 33
Fennel Cres. RH11: Craw 7N 181
Fennells Mead KT17: Ewe 5E 60
Fenner Ho. KT12: Hers 1H 57
Fenn Ho. TW7: Isle 4H 11
Fennscombe Ct.
GU24: W End 9B 52
Fenns La. GU24: W End 9B 52
Fenns Way GU21: Wok 2A 74
Fenn's Yd. GU9: Farnh 1G 128
Fenton Av. TW18: Stain 7L 21
Fenton Cl. RH1: Red 3E 122
Fenton Ho. TW5: Hest 2A 10
Fenton Rd. RH1: Red 3E 122
Fentum Rd. GU2: Guil 1K 113
Fenwick Cl. GU21: Wok 5L 73
Fenwick Pl. CR2: S Croy 4M 63
Ferbies GU52: Fleet 7B 88
Ferguson Av.
KT5: Surb 8M 203 (4M 41)
Ferguson Cl. BR2: Brom 2N 47
Fermandy La.
RH10: Craw D 9D 164
Fermor Dr. GU11: Alde 1L 109
Fern Av. CR4: Mit 3H 45
Fernbank Av. KT12: Wal T 6M 39
Fernbank Cres. SL5: Asc 9H 17
Fernbank Pl. SL5: Asc 9G 17
Fernbank Rd. KT15: Addl 2J 55
SL5: Asc 2G 33
Fernbrae Cl. GU10: Rowl 8G 128
Fern Cl. CR6: Warl 5H 85
GU16: Frim 3F 70
RG45: Crow 9G 30
Fern Cotts. RH5: A Ham 8F 116
Fern Ct. GU12: Ash 3D 110
Ferndale GU3: Guil 1H 113
Ferndale Av. KT16: Chert 9G 36
TW4: Houn 6M 9
Ferndale Rd. GU21: Wok 3B 74
GU52: C Cro 9A 88
SE25 . . . . .4E 46
SM7: Ban 3L 81
TW15: A'ford 6M 21
Ferndale Way BR6: Farnb 2M 67
Fernden Hgts. GU27: Hasl 6F 188
Fernden La.
GU27: Hasl, Fern, K Grn
. . . . .5F 188
Fernden Ri. GU7: Goda 4H 133
Ferndown RH6: Horl 6E 142
RH10: Craw 8H 163
Ferndown Cl. GU1: Guil 4C 114
SM2: Sut 3B 62
Ferndown Ct.
GU1: Guil 1B 202 (2M 113)
Ferndown Gdns.
GU14: Cove 1K 89
KT11: Cob 9K 57
Fern Dr. GU51: C Cro 7A 88
Fernery, The TW18: Stain 6G 21
Ferney Ct. KT14: Byf 7M 55
Ferney Meade Way
TW7: Isle 5G 11
Ferney Rd. KT14: Byf 8M 55
Fern Gro. TW14: Felt 1J 23
Ferngrove Cl. KT22: Fetc 1E 98
Fernham Rd. CR7: T Hea 2N 45
FERNHILL 3J 163
Fernhill KT22: Oxs 1D 78
Fernhill Cl. GU9: U Hal 6G 109
GU17: Haw 5L 69
GU22: Wok 7M 73
RG42: Brac 8L 15
RH10: Craw D 9E 164
Fernhill Dr. GU9: U Hal 6G 109
Fernhill Gdns. KT2: K Tham . . .6K 25
Fernhill La. GU9: U Hal 6G 109
GU17: Haw 5K 69
GU22: Wok 7M 73
(not continuous)
Fernhill Pk. GU22: Wok 7M 73
Fern Hill Pl. BR6: Farnb 2L 67
Fernhill Rd. GU14: Cove 9K 69
GU17: Haw 4K 69
RH6: Horl 3H 163
Fernhill Wlk. GU17: Haw 5L 69
Fernhurst Cl. RH11: Craw 1N 181
Fernhurst Rd. CR0: Croy 6E 46
SW6 . . . . .4K 13
TW15: A'ford 5D 22
Ferniehurst GU15: Camb 2D 70
Fernihough Cl.
KT13: Weybr 6B 56
Fernlands Cl. KT16: Chert 9G 37
Fern La. TW5: Hest 1N 9
Fernlea KT23: Book 2B 98
Fernlea Pl. KT11: Cob 7L 57
Fernlea Rd. CR4: Mit 1E 44
SW12 . . . . .2F 28
Fernleigh Cl. CR0: Wad 1L 63
KT12: Wal T 9J 39
Fernleigh Ri. GU16: Deep 7G 71
Fernley Ho. GU7: Goda 3H 133
Fern Rd. GU7: Goda 5J 133
Ferns, The GU9: U Hal 5H 109
GU14: Farnb 5B 90
Ferns Cl. CR2: Sande 6E 64
Fernshaw Rd. SW10 . . . . .2N 13
Fernside Av. TW13: Felt 5J 23
Fernside Rd. SW12 . . . . .2D 28
Ferns Mead GU9: Farnh 2F 128
Fernthorpe Rd. SW16 . . . . . . .7G 29
Fern Towers CR3: Cate 3D 104
Fern Wlk. TW15: A'ford 6M 21
Fern Way RH12: Hors 3K 197
Fernwood CR0: Sels 5H 65
SW19 . . . . .2L 27
Fernwood Av. SW16 . . . . .5H 29
Feroners Cl. RH10: Craw 5E 182
Feroners Ct. *RH10: Craw* *5E 182*
(off Feroners Cl.)
Ferrard Cl. SL5: Asc 9H 17
Ferraro Cl. TW5: Hest 2A 10
Ferrers Av. SM6: Bedd 1H 63
Ferrers Rd. SW16 . . . . .6H 29
Ferrier Ind. Est. *SW18* *7N 13*
(off Ferrier St.)
Ferrier St. SW18 . . . . .7N 13
Ferriers Way KT18: Tat C 5H 81
Ferring Cl. RH11: Craw 2N 181
Ferris Av. CR0: Croy 9J 47
Ferry Av. TW18: Stain 8G 21
Ferry La. GU2: Guil 7M 113
KT16: Chert 5J 37
SW13 . . . . .2E 12
TW8: Brent 2L 11
TW9: Kew 2M 11
TW17: Shep 7B 38
TW18: Lale 2L 37
TW19: Wray 3D 20
Ferrymoor TW10: Ham 4H 25
Ferry Quays *TW8: Brent* *3K 11*
(off Point Wharf La.)
TW8: Brent 2L 11
(Ferry La.)
Ferry Rd. KT7: T Dit 5H 41
KT8: W Mole 2A 40
SW13 . . . . .3F 12
TW1: Twick 2H 25
TW11: Tedd 6H 25
Ferry Sq. TW8: Brent 3L 11
Ferry Wharf TW8: Brent 3L 11
Festing Rd. SW15 . . . . .6J 13
Festival Ct. RH10: Craw 5G 183
SM1: Sut 6N 43
Festival Wlk. SM5: Cars 1D 62
FETCHAM 1D 98
Fetcham Comn. La.
KT22: Fetc 8B 78
FETCHAM DOWNS 4D 98
Fetcham Pk. Dr. KT22: Fetc . . .1E 98
Fettes Rd. GU6: Cranl 7B 156
FICKLESHOLE 1N 85
Fiddicroft Av. SM7: Ban 1N 81
Field Cl. CR2: Sande 1E 84
GU4: Guil 1F 114
KT8: W Mole 4B 40
KT9: Ches 2J 59
TW4: C'ford 4J 9
UB3: Harl 3D 8
FIELDCOMMON 6N 39
Fieldcommon La.
KT12: Wal T 7M 39
Field Ct. RH8: Oxt 5A 106
SW19 . . . . .4M 27
Field Dr. TN8: Eden 9M 127
Field End CR5: Coul 1H 83
GU9: Farnh 8L 109
GU24: W End 9C 52
Fieldend RH12: Hors 3N 197
TW1: Twick 5F 24
Fieldend Rd. SW16 . . . . .9G 29
Fielden Pl. RG12: Brac 1D 32
Fielders Grn. GU1: Guil 3C 114
Fieldfare Av. GU46: Yate 9A 48
Fieldfare Dr. RG12: Brac 3J 31
Fieldgate Ct. KT11: Cob 1H 77
Fieldgate La. CR4: Mit 1C 44
Field Ho. Cl. SL5: Asc 7L 33
Fieldhouse Rd. SW12 . . . . .2G 29
Fieldhouse Vs. SM7: Ban 2C 82
Fieldhurst SL3: Lang 1B 6
Fieldhurst Cl. KT15: Addl 2K 55
Fielding Av. TW2: Twick 4C 24
Fielding Gdns. RG45: Crow 3G 48
Fielding Ho. *W4* *2D 12*
(off Devonshire Rd.)
Fielding M. *SW13* *2G 12*
(off Jenner Pl.)
Fielding Rd. GU47: C Tow 9K 49
Fieldings, The GU21: Wok 3J 73
RH6: Horl 7F 142
SM7: Ban 4L 81
Field La. GU7: Goda 4J 133
GU16: Frim 5B 70
(not continuous)
TW8: Brent 3J 11
TW11: Tedd 6G 24
Field Pk. RG12: Brac 9B 16
Fieldpark Gdns. CR0: Croy 7H 47
Field Path GU14: Cove 5L 69
FIELD PLACE 3D 196
Field Pl. GU7: Goda 4H 133
KT3: N Mal 5E 42
Field Pl. Cotts.
RH12: Bro H 3D 196
Field Rd. GU14: Cove 5L 69
TW14: Felt 9J 9
W6 . . . . .1K 13
Fieldsend Rd. SM3: Chea 2K 61
Fieldside Cl. BR6: Farnb 1L 67
Field Stores App.
GU11: Alde 1A 110
Field Vw. TW13: Felt 5E 22
TW20: Egh 6E 20
Fieldview RH6: Horl 7F 142
SW18 . . . . .2B 28
Field Vw. Cotts.
GU7: Goda 7E 132
Fieldview Ct. TW18: Stain 6J 21
Field Wlk. *RH6: Horl* *8D 142*
(off Ct. Lodge Rd.)
RH6: Smal 7N 143
Field Way GU10: Tong 5D 110
GU12: Alde 1C 110
GU23: Rip 3H 95
Fieldway CR0: N Add 4L 65
GU27: Hasl 1G 189
Fieldway Stop (CT) 4L 65
Fifehead Cl. TW15: A'ford 7N 21
Fife Rd.
KT1: K Tham 3J 203 (1L 41)
(not continuous)
SW14 . . . . .8B 12
Fife Way KT23: Book 3A 98
Fifield La. GU10: Fren 9H 129
Fifteenth Av. KT20: Lwr K 4L 101
Fifth Av. KT20: K'wood 3K 101
Fifth Cross Rd. TW2: Twick . . .3D 24
Figges Rd. CR4: Mit 8E 28
Figgswood CR5: Coul 9G 83
Filbert Cres. RH11: Craw 3M 181
Filby Rd. KT9: Ches 3M 59
Filey Cl. RH11: Craw 5L 181
SM2: Sut 4A 62
TN16: B Hil 6D 86
Filmer Chambers *SW6* *4K 13*
(off Filmer Rd.)
Filmer Gro. GU7: Goda 6H 133
Filmer Rd. SL4: W'sor 5A 4
SW6 . . . . .4K 13
Finborough Ho. *SW10* *2N 13*
(off Finborough Rd.)
Finborough Rd. SW10 . . . . . . .1N 13
SW17 . . . . .7D 28
Finborough Theatre, The *2N 13*
(off Finborough Rd.)
Fincham End Dr.
RG45: Crow 3E 48
Finchampstead Rd.
RG41: W'ham 6A 30
Finch Av. SE27 . . . . .5N 29
Finch Cl. GU21: Knap 4F 72
Finch Cres. RH10: T Hil 4F 184
Finchdean Ho. SW15 . . . . .1E 26
Finch Dr. TW14: Felt 1L 23
Finches Ri. GU1: Guil 1D 114
Finch Rd.
GU1: Guil 3D 202 (3N 113)
Findhorn Cl. GU47: C Tow 8J 49
Findings, The GU14: Cove 6K 69
Findlay Dr. GU3: Guil 8J 93
Findon Cl. SW18 . . . . .9M 13
Findon Ct. KT15: Addl 2H 55
Findon Rd. RH11: Craw 1N 181
Findon Way RH12: Bro H 5D 196
Finlat Ct. RH10: Craw 3D 182
Finlay Gdns. KT15: Addl 1L 55
Finlays Cl. KT9: Ches 2N 59
Finlay St. SW6 . . . . .4J 13
Finmere RG12: Brac 6A 32
Finnart Cl. KT13: Weybr 1D 56
Finnart Ho. Dr. KT13: Weybr . . .1D 56
Finney Dr. GU20: Windl 3A 52
Finney La. TW7: Isle 4G 11
Finsbury Cl. RH11: Craw 7A 182
Finstock Grn. RG12: Brac 3D 32
Fintry Pl. GU14: Cove 7K 69
Fintry Wlk. *GU14: Cove* *7K 69*
(off Pennine Way)
Finucane Ct. *TW9: Rich* *6M 11*
(off Lwr. Mortlake Rd.)
Fiona Cl. KT23: Book 2A 98
Fir Acre Rd. GU12: A Va 7D 90
Firbank Dr. GU21: Wok 6L 73
Firbank La. GU21: Wok 6L 73
Firbank Pl. TW20: Eng G 7L 19
Firbank Way RH19: E Grin 9N 165
Fir Cl. GU51: Fleet 5A 88
KT12: Wal T 6H 39
Fircroft Cl. GU51: Fleet 4A 88
Fircroft Bus. Cen.
TN8: Eden 9L 127
Fircroft Cl. GU22: Wok 5B 74
Fircroft Ct. GU22: Wok 5B 74
Fircroft Rd. KT9: Ches 1M 59
SW17 . . . . .3D 28
TW20: Eng G 8M 19
Fircroft Way TN8: Eden 9L 127
Fir Dene BR6: Farnb 1H 67
Firdene KT5: Surb 7B 42
Fir Dr. GU17: Haw 3J 69
Fireball Hill SL5: S'dale 6A 34
Fire Bell All. KT6: Surb 5L 41
Fire Sta. M. BR3: Beck 1K 47
Fire Sta. Rd. GU11: Alde 1N 109
Fire Thorn Cl. GU52: Fleet 6B 88
Firfield Rd. GU9: Farnh 4F 128
KT15: Addl 1J 55
Firfields KT13: Weybr 3C 56
Firglen Dr. GU46: Yate 8C 48
Fir Grange Av. KT13: Weybr . . .2C 56
Fir Gro. KT3: N Mal 5E 42
Firgrove GU21: Wok 6L 73
Firgrove Ct. GU9: Farnh 2G 129
GU14: Farnb 1N 89
Firgrove Hill GU9: Farnh 2H 129
Firgrove Pde. GU14: Farnb 1N 89
Firgrove Rd. GU14: Farnb 1N 89
GU46: Yate 9A 48
Firlands KT13: Weybr 3F 56
RG12: Brac 4A 32
RH6: Horl 7F 142
Firlands Av. GU15: Camb 1B 70
Firle Cl. RH10: Craw 1C 182
Firle Ct. KT17: Eps 8E 60
Fir Rd. SM3: Sut 7L 43
TW13: Hanw 6L 23
Firs, The CR3: Cate 9A 84
GU3: Art 7L 113
GU24: Bis 3D 72
KT14: Byf 8M 55
KT23: Book 2C 98
RG12: Brac 4D 32
Firs Av. GU5: Braml 5C 134
SL4: W'sor 6C 4
SW14 . . . . .7B 12
Firsby Av. CR0: Croy 7G 47
Firs Cl. CR4: Mit 9F 28
GU14: Farnb 3A 90
KT10: Clay 3E 58
RH4: Dork 7G 119
Firsdene Cl. KT16: Otter 3F 54
Firs Dr. TW5: C'ford 3J 9
Firs La. GU5: Sha G 7F 134
Firs Rd. CR8: Ken 2M 83
First Av. KT8: W Mole 3N 39
KT12: Wal T 5J 39
KT19: Ewe 5D 60
KT20: K'wood 3K 101
SW14 . . . . .6D 12
First Cl. KT8: W Mole 2C 40
First Cross Rd. TW2: Twick 3E 24
First Quarter KT19: Eps 7D 60
First Slip KT22: Leat 5G 79
Firstway SW20 . . . . .1H 43
Firsway GU2: Guil 2J 113
Firswood Av. KT19: Ewe 2D 60
Firth Gdns. SW6 . . . . .4K 13
Fir Tree All. *GU11: Alde* *2M 109*
(off Heathland St.)
Fir Tree Av. GU27: Hasl 2B 188
Firtree Av. CR4: Mit 1E 44
Fir Tree Cl. KT10: Esh 2C 58
KT17: Eps D 2H 81
KT19: Ewe 1E 60
KT22: Leat 1J 99
RH11: Craw 9N 161
SL5: Asc 6L 33
Firtree Cl. GU47: Sandh 6E 48
SW16 . . . . .6G 29
Fir Tree Gdns. CR0: Croy 1K 65
Fir Tree Gro. SM5: Cars 4D 62
Fir Tree Pl. TW15: A'ford 6B 22
Fir Tree Rd. GU1: Guil 9M 93
KT17: Eps D 3G 80
KT22: Leat 1J 99
SM7: Ban 1H 81
TW4: Houn 7M 9
Fir Tree Wlk. RH2: Reig 3B 122
Fir Tree Way GU52: Fleet 5C 88
Fir Wlk. SM3: Chea 3J 61
Firway GU26: G'hott 4K 169
Firwood Cl. GU21: Wok 6H 73
Firwood Dr. GU15: Camb 1A 70
Firwood Rd. GU25: V Wat 5H 35
Fisher Cl. CR0: Croy 7C 46
KT12: Hers 1J 57
RH10: Craw 5C 182
Fisher Grn. RG42: Bin 7G 15
Fisher La.
GU8: Chid, Duns 1G 191
GU12: Alde 4A 110
Fisherman KT16: Chert 7L 37
Fisherman Cl. TW10: Ham 5H 25
Fisherman's Pl. W4 . . . . .2E 12
Fishermen's Cl. GU11: Alde . . .8C 90
Fisher Rowe Cl.
GU5: Braml 5C 134
Fishers RH6: Horl 7G 142
Fisher's Cl. SW16 . . . . .4H 29
Fishers Ct. RH12: Hors 4J 197
Fishersdene KT10: Clay 4G 58
Fisher's La. W4 . . . . .1C 12
FISHERSTREET 5C 190
Fisher St. GU8: Chid 4C 190
GU28: Chid, North 4C 190
Fishers Wood SL5: S'dale 7F 34
Fishing Temple Pk. Homes
TW18: Stain 9H 21
Fishponds Rd. BR2: Kes 2F 66
SW17 . . . . .5C 28
Fisk Cl. TW16: Sunb 7G 23
Fiske Ct. GU46: Yate 9D 48
SM2: Sut 4A 62

Fitchet Cl.—Francis Ho.

Fitchet Cl. RH11: Craw 1N 181
Fitness First Health Club
Croydon 1A 200 (7M 45)
Epsom 6J 201 (9C 60)
Fleet 4A 88
Godalming 7H 133
(off High St.)
Mitcham 1D 44
Purley 8K 63
Tooting Bec 4E 28
Fitrooms 2L 13
Fitzalan Ho. KT17: Ewe 6E 60
Fitzalan Rd. KT10: Clay 4E 58
RH13: Hors 4N 197
Fitzgeorge Av. KT3: N Mal 9C 26
W14 ......1K 13
Fitzgerald Av. SW14 ......6D 12
Fitzgerald Rd. KT7: T Dit 5G 40
SW14 ......6C 12
Fitzhugh Dr. GU51: Fleet 2A 88
Fitzhugh Gro. SW18 ......1B 28
Fitzjames Av. CR0: Croy 8D 46
W14 ......1K 13
Fitzjohn Cl. GU4: Guil 9E 94
Fitzrobert Pl. TW20: Egh 7C 20
Fitzroy Cl. RG12: Brac 5M 31
Fitzroy Ct. CR0: Croy 6A 46
Fitzroy Cres. W4 ......3C 12
Fitzwilliam Av. TW9: Rich 5M 11
Fitzwilliam Ho. TW9: Rich 7K 11
Fitzwygram Cl.
TW12: H Hill 6C 24
Fiveacre Cl. CR7: T Hea 5L 45
Five Acres RH10: Craw 1C 182
Five Acres Cl. GU35: Lind 4A 168
Five Oaks Cl. GU21: Wok 6G 73
Five Oaks Rd.
RH13: Slin, Bro H, Itch 9J 195
Five Ways Bus. Cen.
TW13: Felt 4J 23
FIVEWAYS CORNER 1L 63
Flag Cl. CR0: Croy 7G 47
Flagon Ct. CR0: Croy 6C 200
(off St Andrew's Rd.)
Flambard Way GU7: Goda 7G 133
Flamborough Cl.
TN16: B Hil 6D 86
Flamsteed Hgts.
RH11: Craw 8M 181
Flanchford Ho.
RH2: Reig 2M 121
(off Somers Cl.)
Flanchford Rd. RH2: Leigh 9E 120
RH2: Reig 5H 121
Flanders Ct. TW20: Egh 6E 20
Flanders Cres. SW17 ......8D 28
Flather Cl. SW16 ......6G 29
Flats, The GU17: B'water 2G 69
Flaxley Rd. SM4: Mord 6N 43
Flaxman Ho. W4 ......1D 12
(off Devonshire St.)
Fleece Rd. KT6: Surb 7J 41
FLEET 4B 88
Fleetbrook Ho. SL3: Dat 4N 5
Fleet Bus. Pk. GU52: C Cro 9C 88
Fleet Cl. KT8: W Mole 4N 39
Fleet La. KT8: W Mole 5N 39
Fleet Mill GU51: Fleet 1C 88
Fleet Pond (Nature Reserve)
......2C 88
Fleet Rd. GU11: Alde 6F 88
GU14: Cove 1G 89
GU51: Cove 1G 88
GU51: Fleet 2E 88
(Cove Rd.)
GU51: Fleet 5A 88
(Reading Rd. Nth.)
KT11: Cob 8B 56
Fleetside KT8: W Mole 4N 39
Fleet Station (Rail) 2C 88
Fleetway TW20: Thor 2E 36
Fleetwood Cl. CR0: Croy 9C 46
KT9: Ches 4K 59
KT20: Tad 7J 81
Fleetwood Ct. KT14: W By 9J 55
TW19: Stan 9M 7
Fleetwood Rd. KT1: K Tham 2A 42
Fleetwood Sq. KT1: K Tham 2A 42
Fleming Cen., The
RH10: Craw 8C 162
Fleming Cl. GU14: Farnb 8B 70
Fleming Ct. CR0: Wad 2L 63
Fleming Mead CR4: Mit 8C 28
Fleming Wlk.
RH19: E Grin 3B 186
Fleming Way RH10: Craw 8C 162
TW7: Isle 7F 10
Fleming Way Ind. Cen.
RH10: Craw 7D 162
Fleming Way Rdbt.
RH10: Craw 8B 162
Flemish Flds. KT16: Chert 6J 37
Flemish Pl. RG42: Warf 8B 16
Fletcher Cl. KT16: Otter 3G 54
RH10: Craw 5C 182
Fletcher Gdns. RG42: Brac 9J 15
Fletcher Rd. KT16: Otter 3F 54
Fletchers Cl. RH13: Hors 7L 197
Fleur Gates SW19 ......1J 27
FLEXFORD 3M 111
Flexford Grn. RG12: Brac 5K 31
Flexford Rd. GU3: Flex 4M 111
(not continuous)
Flexlands La. GU24: Chob 6E 52
Flint Cl. BR6: Chels 3N 67
CR0: Croy 5K 45
KT23: Book 4C 98
RH1: Red 2D 122
RH10: Craw 6F 182
SM7: Ban 1N 81
Flint Cotts. KT22: Leat 8H 79
(off Gravel Hill)
Flintgrove RG12: Brac 9B 16
Flint Hill RH4: Dork 7H 119
Flint Hill Cl. RH4: Dork 8H 119
Flintlock Cl. TW19: Stan M 7J 7
Flitwick Grange GU8: Mil 1C 152
Flock Mill Pl. SW18 ......2N 27
Flockton Ho. KT13: Weybr 8B 38
Flood La. TW1: Twick 2G 25
Flora Gdns. CR0: N Add 7M 65
Floral Ct. KT21: A'tead 5J 79
Floral Ho. KT16: Chert 7H 37
(off Fox La. Sth.)
Florence Av. KT15: N Haw 7J 55
SM4: Mord 4A 44
Florence Cl. GU46: Yate 9B 48
KT12: Wal T 6J 39
Florence Ct. GU21: Knap 5F 72
SW19 ......7K 27
Florence Gdns.
TW18: Stain 8K 21
W4 ......2B 12
Florence Ho. KT2: K Tham 1M 203
Florence Rd. BR3: Beck 1H 47
CR2: Sande 5A 64
GU47: C Tow 8J 49
GU52: Fleet 7B 88
KT2: K Tham 1M 203 (8M 25)
KT12: Wal T 6J 39
SW19 ......7N 27
TW13: Felt 2J 23
Florence Ter. SW15 ......4D 26
Florence Way GU21: Knap 5F 72
SW12 ......2D 28
Florian Av. SM1: Sut 1B 62
Florian Rd. SW15 ......7K 13
Florida Ct. TW18: Stain 5J 21
Florida Rd. CR7: T Hea 9M 29
GU4: Chil 9A 114
Florys Ct. SW19 ......2K 27
Floss St. SW15 ......5H 13
Flower Cres. KT16: Otter 3D 54
Flower La. RH9: Gods 8G 105
Flowersmead SW17 ......3E 28
Flower Wlk.
GU2: Guil 8B 202 (6M 113)
Floyd's La. GU22: Pyr 3J 75
Floyer Cl. TW10: Rich 8M 11
Flyers Way, The
TN16: Weste 4M 107
Foden Rd. GU11: Alde 3M 109
Folder's La. RG42: Brac 8A 16
Foley M. KT10: Clay 3E 58
Foley Rd. KT10: Clay 4E 58
TN16: B Hil 5F 86
Foley Wood KT10: Clay 4F 58
Folkestone Ct. SL3: Lang 1C 6
Follett Cl. SL4: O Win 9L 5
Folly, The GU18: Ligh 8M 51
Folly Cl. GU52: Fleet 6B 88
Follyfield Rd. SM7: Ban 1M 81
Follyhatch La. GU12: Ash 1J 111
Folly Hill
GU9: Farnh, U Hal 6F 108
Folly La. RH5: Holm 4H 139
Folly La. Nth. GU9: U Hal 5G 108
Folly La. Sth. GU9: U Hal 6F 108
Fontaine Rd. SW16 ......8K 29
Fontana Cl. RH10: Wor 4H 183
Fontenoy Rd. SW12 ......3F 28
Fonthill Cl. SE20 ......1D 46
Fontley Way SW15 ......1F 26
Fontmell Cl. TW15: A'ford 6B 22
Fontmell Pk. TW15: A'ford 6A 22
(not continuous)
Fontwell Cl. GU12: Alde 2B 110
Fontwell Rd. RH10: Craw 6E 182
Footpath, The SW15 ......9F 12
Forbench Cl. GU23: Rip 9K 75
Forbes Chase
GU47: C Tow 8J 49
Forbes Ct. RH10: Craw 7F 182
Forbes Ho. W4 ......1N 11
(off Stonehill Rd.)
Forbe's Ride SL4: Wink 1L 17
FORCE GREEN 2M 107
Force Grn. La.
TN16: Weste 2M 107
Fordbridge Cl. KT16: Chert 7K 37
Fordbridge Ct.
TW15: A'ford 7N 21
Fordbridge Pk. TW16: Sunb 5G 38
Fordbridge Rd.
TW15: A'ford 7N 21
TW16: Sunb 5F 38
TW17: Shep 5F 38
FORDBRIDGE RDBT. 7N 21
Ford Cl. CR7: T Hea 4M 45
TW15: A'ford 7N 21
TW17: Shep 3B 38
Fordham KT1: K Tham 4M 203
Fordham Cl. KT4: W Pk 7G 42
Fordingbridge Cl.
RH12: Hors 7J 197
Ford La. GU10: Wrec 5G 128
Ford Mnr. Cotts.
RH7: Dorm 1D 166
Ford Mnr. Rd.
RH7: Dorm 9D 146
Ford Rd. GU22: Wok 7D 74
GU24: Bis, W End 1B 72
GU24: Chob 6F 52
KT16: Chert 7K 37
TW15: A'ford 5A 22
Fordwater Rd. KT16: Chert 7K 37
Fordwater Trad. Est.
KT16: Chert 7L 37
Fordwells Dr. RG12: Brac 3D 32
Foreman Ct. TW1: Twick 2F 24
Foreman Pk. GU12: Ash 2F 110
Foreman Rd. GU12: A Grn 3F 110
Forest Cl. GU22: Pyr 2F 74
KT24: E Hor 3G 96
RH10: Craw D 1E 184
RH12: Hors 4A 198
SL5: Asc 2G 33
Forest Cres. KT21: A'tead 3N 79
FORESTDALE 5J 65
Forestdale GU26: Hind 6B 170
Forestdale Cen., The
CR0: Sels 4J 65
Forest Dean GU51: Fleet 1D 88
Forest Dene Ct. SM2: Sut 3A 62
Forest Dr. BR2: Kes 1G 66
GU10: L Bou 7H 129
KT20: K'wood 8L 81
TW16: Sunb 8G 22
Forest End GU47: Sandh 6E 48
GU52: Fleet 7A 88
Forest End Rd.
GU47: Sandh 6E 48
Forester Rd. RH10: Craw 5C 182
Foresters, The
RH13: Hors 7M 197
Foresters Cl. GU21: Wok 5J 73
SM6: W'ton 4H 63
Foresters Dr. SM6: W'ton 4H 63
Foresters Sq. RG12: Brac 2C 32
Foresters Way RG45: Crow 9K 31
Forestfield RH10: Craw 6E 182
RH13: Hors 5N 197
Forest Glade GU10: Rowl 8C 128
Forest Grange
RH13: Hors, Col 3C 198
Forest Grange Mnr.
RH13: Col 4D 198
FOREST GREEN 3M 157
Forest Grn. RG12: Brac 9B 16
Forest Grn. Rd. RH5: Ockl 3C 158
Forest Hills GU15: Camb 2N 69
Forest La. GU35: Lind 3B 168
KT24: E Hor 2G 97
Forest Lodge RH19: E Grin 1B 186
Forest M. RH12: Hors 3A 198
Forest Oaks RH13: Hors 4A 198
FOREST PARK 5D 32
Forest Recreational Cen. 7M 197
Forest Ridge BR2: Kes 1G 67
BR3: Beck 2K 47
Forest Rd. GU22: Pyr 2F 74
KT24: E Hor, E Jun 5G 96
RG40: W'ham 7A 14
RG42: Bin 7A 14
RG42: Warf, Wink R 6C 16
RG45: Crow 2H 49
RH11: P Pot 2K 199
RH12: Hors, Col 4A 198
RH12: P Pot 2K 199
RH18: F Row 8K 187
SL4: W'sor 5A 4
(Ash La.)
SL4: W'sor 2A 18
(Plain Ride)
SL5: Asc 6C 16
SM3: Sut 7M 43
TW9: Kew 3N 11
TW13: Felt 3K 23
FOREST ROW 6H 187
Forest Row Bus. Pk.
RH18: F Row 6H 187
Forestry Rd., The
RH14: Plais 5D 192
(not continuous)
Forest Side KT4: W Pk 7E 42
Forest Vw. RH10: Craw 6E 182
Forest Vw. Rd.
RH19: E Grin 3A 186
Forest Wlk. GU6: Cranl 8H 155
Forest Way KT21: A'tead 4M 79
RG42: Warf 8E 16
RH19: E Grin 1C 186
Forge, The RH6: Char 3K 161
RH12: Warn 9E 178
UB3: Harl 2E 8
Forge Av. CR5: Coul 7L 83
Forge Bri. La. CR5: Coul 9F 82
Forge Cl. GU9: Farnh 9J 109
RH12: Bro H 4D 196
Forge Cotts. RH12: Bro H 4D 196
(off Forge Cl.)
Forge Cft. TN8: Eden 2M 147
Forge Dr. KT10: Clay 4G 58
Forge End GU21: Wok 4A 74
Forgefield TN16: B Hil 3F 86
Forge La. GU11: Alde 7L 89
RH10: Craw 2E 182
RH12: Bro H 4D 196
SM3: Chea 4K 61
Forge La. TW10: Ham 2L 25
TW13: Hanw 6M 23
TW16: Sunb 2H 39
Forge M. CR0: A'ton 2K 65
Forge Pl. RH6: Hook 1C 162
Forge Rd. RH10: Craw 2E 182
Forge Steading SM7: Ban 2N 81
Forge Wood RH10: Craw 7H 163
Forge Wood Ind. Est.
RH10: Craw 8F 162
Forrest Gdns. SW16 ......2K 45
Forster Rd. BR3: Beck 2H 47
GU2: Guil 8K 93
SW2 ......1J 29
Forsythia Pl. GU1: Guil 1M 113
Forsyth Path GU21: Wok 9F 54
Forsyth Rd. GU21: Wok 2E 74
Fortescue Av. TW2: Twick 4C 24
Fortescue Rd.
KT13: Weybr 1A 56
SW19 ......8B 28
Forth Cl. GU14: Cove 8J 69
Fort La. RH2: Reig 8N 101
Fort Narrien GU15: Camb 9K 49
Fort Rd.
GU1: Guil 8E 202 (6A 114)
KT20: Box H 9A 100
Fortrose Cl. GU47: C Tow 8J 49
Fortrose Gdns. SW2 ......2J 29
Fortune Dr. GU6: Cranl 9N 155
Forty Footpath SW14 ......6B 12
Forty Foot Rd. KT22: Leat 8J 79
(not continuous)
Forum, The KT8: W Mole 3B 40
RH12: Hors 6J 197
Forval Cl. CR4: Mit 4D 44
Foskett Rd. SW6 ......5L 13
Foss Av. CR0: Wad 2L 63
Fosse Way KT14: W By 9H 55
Fosseway RG45: Crow 2E 48
Fossewood Dr. GU15: Camb 7B 50
Foss Rd. SW17 ......5B 28
Foster Av. SL4: W'sor 6B 4
Fosterdown RH9: Gods 7E 104
Foster Rd. W4 ......1C 12
Fosters Gro. GU20: Windl 1M 51
Fosters La. GU21: Knap 4F 72
Foster's Way SW18 ......2N 27
Foulser Rd. SW17 ......4D 28
Foulsham Rd. CR7: T Hea 2N 45
Foundation Units GU1: Guil 8A 94
Founders Gdns. SE19 ......8N 29
Foundry Cl. RH13: Hors 4L 197
Foundry Ct. KT16: Chert 6J 37
RH13: Hors 5L 197
Foundry La. GU27: Hasl 2E 188
RH13: Hors 5L 197
SL3: Hort 6D 6
Foundry M. KT16: Chert 6J 37
(off Gogmore La.)
TW3: Houn 7B 10
Foundry Pl. SW18 ......1N 27
Fountain Dr. SM5: Cars 4D 62
Fountain Gdns. SL4: W'sor 6G 4
Fountain Ho. CR4: Mit 1D 44
Fountain Rd. CR7: T Hea 2N 45
RH1: Red 5C 122
SW17 ......6B 28
Fountain Rdbt. KT3: N Mal 3D 42
Fountains Av. TW13: Hanw 4N 23
Fountains Cl. RH11: Craw 5M 181
TW13: Hanw 3N 23
(not continuous)
Fountains Gth. RG12: Brac 2M 31
Four Acres GU1: Guil 1E 114
KT11: Cob 9M 57
Four Elms Rd. TN8: Eden 1L 147
Fourfield Cl. KT18: Head 9B 80
Four Oaks RH18: F Row 7H 187
Four Seasons Cres.
SM3: Sut 8L 43
Four Sq. Ct. TW3: Houn 9A 10
Fourteenth Av.
KT20: Lwr K 4K 101
Fourth Av. KT20: Lwr K 3K 101
Fourth Cross Rd.
TW2: Twick 3D 24
Fourth Dr. CR5: Coul 3G 83
Four Wents KT11: Cob 1K 77
Fowler Av. GU14: Farnb 3N 89
Fowler Cl. RH10: Craw 5G 182
Fowler Rd. CR4: Mit 1E 44
GU14: Cove 2L 89
Fowlerscroft GU3: Comp 1E 132
Fowlers La. RG42: Brac 9N 15
Fowlers Mead GU24: Chob 5H 53
Fowler's Rd. GU11: Alde 7A 90
Foxacre CR3: Cate 9B 84
Foxborough Cl. SL3: Lang 1C 6
Foxborough Hill
GU5: Braml 4N 133
Foxborough Hill Rd.
GU5: Braml 4N 133
(not continuous)
Foxbourne Rd. SW17 ......3E 28
Foxbridge La.
RH14: Kird, Loxw 8D 192
Foxburrows Av. GU2: Guil 3J 113
Foxburrows Ct. GU2: Guil 2J 113
Fox Cl. GU12: Alde 1C 110
GU22: Pyr 2F 74
KT13: Weybr 2E 56
RH11: Craw 9N 161
Foxcombe CR0: N Add 3L 65
(not continuous)
Foxcombe Rd. SW15 ......2F 26
FOX CORNER 3F 92
Fox Covert GU18: Ligh 7L 51
KT22: Fetc 2D 98
Fox Covert Cl. SL5: S'hill 4N 33
Foxcroft GU52: C Cro 8B 88
Fox Dene GU7: Goda 9F 132
Foxdown Cl. GU15: Camb 1A 70
Fox Dr. GU46: Yate 8C 48
Foxearth Cl. TN16: B Hil 5G 87
Foxearth Rd. CR2: Sels 6F 64
Foxearth Spur CR2: Sels 5F 64
Foxenden Rd.
GU1: Guil 4E 202 (4A 114)
Foxes Dale BR2: Brom 2N 47
Foxes Path GU4: Sut G 4B 94
Foxglove Av. RH12: Hors 2L 197
Foxglove Cl. RG42: Wink R 7E 16
TN8: Eden 9M 127
(off Wayside Dr.)
TW19: Stan 2M 21
Foxglove Gdns. CR8: Pur 7J 63
GU4: Guil 1E 114
Foxglove La. KT9: Ches 1N 59
Foxglove Wlk.
RH11: Craw 6N 181
Foxglove Way SM6: W'ton 7F 44
Fox Gro. KT12: Wal T 6J 39
Foxgrove Dr. GU21: Wok 2C 74
Foxhanger Gdns.
GU22: Wok 3C 74
Fox Heath GU14: Cove 2H 89
Foxheath RG12: Brac 4C 32
Fox Hill BR2: Kes 2E 66
Foxhill Cres. GU15: Camb 7F 50
Foxhills GU21: Wok 4M 73
Foxhills Cl. KT16: Otter 3D 54
Fox Hills La. GU12: Ash 1G 110
Foxhills M. KT16: L'cross 9D 36
Foxhills Rd. KT16: Otter 1C 54
Foxholes KT13: Weybr 2E 56
RH12: Rudg 9E 176
Foxhurst Rd. GU12: A Va 8E 90
Foxlake Rd. KT14: Byf 8A 56
FOX LANE 6K 69
Fox La. BR2: Kes 2D 66
CR3: Cate 8M 83
KT23: Book 2M 97
RH2: Reig 9N 101
RH5: Ran C 3B 118
Fox La. Nth. KT16: Chert 7H 37
Fox La. Sth. KT16: Chert 7H 37
Foxleigh Chase
RH12: Hors 4M 197
Foxley Cl. GU17: B'water 1H 69
RH1: Red 8E 122
Foxley Ct. SM2: Sut 4A 62
Foxley Gdns. CR8: Pur 9M 63
Foxley Hall CR8: Pur 9L 63
Foxley Hill Rd. CR8: Pur 8L 63
Foxley La. CR8: Pur 7G 63
RG42: Bin 7G 14
Foxley Rd. CR7: T Hea 3M 45
CR8: Ken 1M 83
Foxon Cl. CR3: Cate 8B 84
Foxon La. CR3: Cate 8A 84
Foxon La. Gdns.
CR3: Cate 8B 84
Fox Rd. GU10: L Bou 4H 129
GU27: Hasl 2C 188
Fox's Path CR4: Mit 1C 44
Foxton Gro. CR4: Mit 1B 44
Foxwarren KT10: Clay 5F 58
Fox Way GU10: Ews 5C 108
Fox Wood KT12: Whit V 4G 56
Foxwood GU51: Fleet 2D 88
RH12: K'fold 3H 179
Foxwood Cl. GU8: Worm 1C 172
TW13: Felt 4J 23
Fox Yd. GU9: Farnh 1G 128
Foye La. GU52: C Cro 8C 88
Frailey Cl. GU22: Wok 3D 74
Frailey Hill GU22: Wok 3D 74
Framfield Cl. RH11: Craw 1M 181
Framfield Rd. CR4: Mit 8E 28
Frampton Cl. SM2: Sut 4M 61
Frampton Rd. TW4: Houn 8M 9
France Hill Dr. GU15: Camb 1A 70
Frances Ct. SE25 ......2D 46
Frances Rd. SL4: W'sor 6F 4
Franche Ct. Rd. SW17 ......4A 28
Francis Av. TW13: Felt 4H 23
Francis Barber Cl.
SW16 ......6K 29
Franciscan Rd.
SW17 ......6D 28
Francis Chichester Cl.
SL5: Asc 4M 33
Francis Cl. KT19: Ewe 1C 60
TW17: Shep 3B 38
Francis Ct. GU2: Guil 1L 113
KT5: Surb 8K 203
Francis Crick Rd.
GU2: Guil 4G 113
Francis Edwards Way
RH11: Craw 7K 181
Francis Gdns. RG42: Warf 8B 16
Francis Gro. SW19 ......7L 27
(not continuous)
Francis Ho. SW10 ......3N 13
(off Coleridge Gdns.)

Francis Rd. CR0: Croy 6M 45
CR3: Cate 9A 84
SM6: W'ton 3G 63
TW4: Houn 5L 9
Francis Way GU15: Camb 2G 70
Frank Beswick Ho.
SW6 . . . .*2L 13*
(off Clem Attlee Ct.)
Franklands Dr. KT15: Addl 4H 55
Franklin Cl. KT1: K Tham 2N 41
SE27 . . . . .4M 29
Franklin Ct. *GU2: Guil* *3J 113*
(off Derby Rd.)
GU8: Worm 9C 152
GU14: Cove *1H 89*
(off Whetstone Rd.)
Franklin Cres. CR4: Mit 3G 45
Franklin Rd. RH10: Craw 4G 183
Franklin Sq. W14 . . . . .1L 13
Franklin Way CR0: Wad 6J 45
Franklyn Cres. SL4: W'sor 6A 4
Franklyn Rd. GU7: Goda 8E 132
KT12: Wal T 5H 39
Franks Av. KT3: N Mal 3B 42
Franksfield GU5: P'lake 4F 136
(not continuous)
Frank Soskice Ho.
SW6 . . . .*2L 13*
(off Clem Attlee Ct.)
Franks Rd. GU2: Guil 9K 93
Frank Towell Ct. TW14: Felt . . .1H 23
Frant Fld. TN8: Eden 2L 147
Frant Rd. CR7: T Hea 4M 45
Fraser Gdns. RH4: Dork 4G 118
Fraser Ho. TW8: Brent 1M 11
Fraser Mead GU47: C Tow 9K 49
Fraser Rd. RG42: Brac 9N 15
Fraser St. W4 . . . . .1D 12
Fraynes Cft. GU51: Fleet 5A 88
Frederick Cl. SM1: Sut 1L 61
Frederick Gdns. CR0: Croy . . .5M 45
SM1: Sut 2L 61
Frederick Rd. SM1: Sut 2L 61
Frederick Sanger Rd.
GU2: Guil 4G 113
Frederick St. GU11: Alde 2M 109
Fredley Pk. RH5: Mick 7J 99
Freeborn Way RG12: Brac 9C 16
Freedown La. SM2: Sut 9N 61
Freelands Av. CR2: Sels 5G 64
Freelands Rd. KT11: Cob 1J 77
Freeman Cl. TW17: Shep 3F 38
Freeman Ct. SW16 . . . . .1J 45
Freeman Dr. KT8: W Mole 2N 39
Freeman Rd. RH12: Warn 9F 178
SM4: Mord 4B 44
Freemantle Rd. GU19: Bag 3J 51
Freemasons Pl. *CR0: Croy* *7B 46*
(off Freemasons Rd.)
Freemasons Rd. CR0: Croy . . .7B 46
Free Prae Rd. KT16: Chert 7J 37
Freesia Dr. GU24: Bis 3D 72
Freestone Yd. *SL3: Coln* *3F 6*
(off Park St.)
French Apartments, The
CR8: Pur 8L 63
Frenchaye KT15: Addl 2L 55
Frenches, The RH1: Red 1E 122
Frenches Ct. RH1: Red 1E 122
Frenches Rd. RH1: Red 1E 122
French Gdns. GU17: Haw 2J 69
KT11: Cob 1K 77
Frenchlands Hatch
KT24: E Hor 5F 96
French La.
GU8: Bow G, Thur 6K 151
French St. TN16: Weste 6N 107
TW16: Sunb 1K 39
French's Wells GU21: Wok 4L 73
FRENSHAM 3H 149
Frensham RG12: Brac 5B 32
Frensham Av. GU51: Fleet 4D 88
Frensham Cl. GU46: Yate 9A 48
Frensham Common Country Pk.
. . . . .5K 149
Frensham Ct. SW19 . . . . .2B 44
Frensham Dr. CR0: N Add 4M 65
SW15 . . . . .4E 26
(not continuous)
FRENSHAM HEIGHTS 9F 128
Frensham Hgts. Rd.
GU10: Rowl 9F 128
Frensham La. GU10: Churt . . .7F 148
GU35: Head 1D 168
GU35: Head, Lind 3B 168
Frensham Pond Sailing Club
. . . . .5H 149
Frensham Rd. CR8: Ken 1M 83
GU9: Farnh 3H 129
GU10: Fren, L Bou 3H 129
RG45: Crow 1G 49
Frensham Va.
GU10: L Bou 7G 129
Frensham Way KT17: Eps D . . .3H 81
Freshborough Ct.
GU1: Guil 4B 114
Freshfield Bank
RH18: F Row 7G 186
Freshfield Cl. RH10: Craw . . .4E 182
Freshfield Flats
KT20: Lwr K 5L 101
Freshfields CR0: Croy 7J 47
Freshford St. SW18 . . . . .4A 28
Freshmount Gdns.
KT19: Eps 7A 60
Freshwater Cl. SW17 . . . . .7E 28
Freshwater Pde.
RH12: Hors *6H 197*
(off Bishopric)
Freshwater Rd. SW17 . . . . .7E 28
Freshwood Cl. BR3: Beck 1L 47
Freshwood Dr. GU46: Yate 2C 68
Freshwoods RH12: Rudg 9E 176
Freshwood Way
SM6: W'ton 5F 62
Frewin Rd. SW18 . . . . .2B 28
Friar M. SE27 . . . . .4M 29
Friars Av. SW15 . . . . .4E 26
Friars Ct. SM6: W'ton 1F 62
Friars Fld. GU9: Farnh 9G 108
Friar's Ga. GU2: Guil 5K 113
Friars Keep RG12: Brac 3N 31
Friars La. TW9: Rich 8K 11
Friars Orchard KT22: Fetc 8D 78
Friars Ri. GU22: Wok 5C 74
Friars Rd. GU25: V Wat 3N 35
Friars Rookery
RH10: Craw 3D 182
Friars Stile Pl. TW10: Rich 9L 11
Friars Stile Rd. TW10: Rich . . .9L 11
Friars Way KT16: Chert 5J 37
Friars Wood CR0: Sels 5H 65
Friary, The
GU1: Guil 5B 202 (4M 113)
SL4: O Win 9M 5
Friary Bri.
GU1: Guil 6B 202 (5M 113)
Friary Ct. GU21: Wok 5J 73
FRIARY ISLAND 9M 5
Friary Island TW19: Wray 9M 5
Friary Pas.
GU1: Guil 6B 202 (5M 113)
Friary Rd. SL5: Asc 5L 33
TW19: Wray 1M 19
(not continuous)
Friary St.
GU1: Guil 6B 202 (5N 113)
Friary Way RH10: Craw 4B 182
Friday Rd. CR4: Mit 8D 28
FRIDAYS HILL 9F 188
FRIDAY STREET 3N 137
Friday St. RH5: Ockl 6D 158
RH12: Rusp 4L 179
RH12: Warn 1E 196
Friday St. Rd.
RH5: A Com 3M 137
Friend Av. GU12: Alde 3B 110
Friends Cl. RH11: Craw 9B 162
Friendship Way RG12: Brac . . .2N 31
Friends Rd.
CR0: Croy 4D 200 (9A 46)
CR8: Pur 8M 63
Friends Wlk. TW18: Stain 6H 21
Friesian Cl. GU51: Fleet 1C 88
FRIMLEY 6A 70
Frimley Aqueduct 9E 70
Frimley Av. SM6: W'ton 2J 63
Frimley Bus. Pk.
GU16: Frim 6A 70
Frimley By-Pass
GU16: Frim 6A 70
Frimley Cl. CR0: N Add 4M 65
SW19 . . . . .3K 27
Frimley Cres. CR0: N Add 4M 65
Frimley Gdns. CR4: Mit 2C 44
FRIMLEY GREEN 8D 70
Frimley Grn. Rd.
GU16: Frim, Frim G 5B 70
Frimley Gro. Gdns.
GU16: Frim 5B 70
Frimley Hall Dr.
GU15: Camb 9D 50
Frimley High St.
GU16: Frim 6A 70
Frimley Lodge Pk.
GU16: Frim G 9D 70
FRIMLEY RIDGE 3F 70
Frimley Rd. GU12: A Va 4E 90
GU15: Camb 1M 69
GU16: Camb, Frim 5A 70
KT9: Ches 2K 59
Frimley Station (Rail) 6A 70
Frinton Rd. SW17 . . . . .7E 28
Friston St. SW6 . . . . .5N 13
Friston Wlk. RH11: Craw 1M 181
Fritham Cl. KT3: N Mal 5D 42
FRITHEND 6A 148
Frith End Rd. GU35: Slea 5A 148
FRITH HILL 5G 132
Frith Hill Rd. GU7: Goda 4G 133
GU16: Deep, Frim 5E 70
Frith Knowle KT12: Hers 2J 57
Frith Pk. RH19: E Grin 7A 166
Frith Rd.
CR0: Croy 3B 200 (8N 45)
Friths Dr. RH2: Reig 9N 101
Frithwald Rd. KT16: Chert 6H 37
Frobisher RG12: Brac 6A 32
Frobisher Cl. CR8: Ken 4N 83
Frobisher Ct. SM3: Chea 4K 61
Frobisher Cres. TW19: Stan . . .1N 21
Frobisher Gdns. GU1: Guil . . .2C 114
TW19: Stan 1N 21
Frodsham Way GU47: Owls 5K 49
Froggetts La.
RH5: W'wood 9K 157
Frog Gro. La.
GU3: Wood V 1C 112
Froghall Dr. RG40: W'ham 2D 30
FROGHOLE 1M 127
Froghole La. TN8: Weste 1M 127
TN16: Weste 1M 127
Frog La. GU4: Sut G 3A 94
RG12: Brac 2M 31
FROGMORE
GU17 . . . . .1H 69
SL4 . . . . .6J 5
Frogmore SW18 . . . . .8M 13
Frogmore Border SL4: W'sor . . .6H 5
Frogmore Cl. SM3: Chea 9J 43
Frogmore Ct.
GU17: B'water 2H 69
UB2: S'hall 1N 9
Frogmore Dr. SL4: W'sor 4H 5
Frogmore Gdns. SM3: Chea . . .1K 61
Frogmore Gro.
GU17: B'water 2H 69
Frogmore House 5J 5
Frogmore Leisure Cen. *1E 68*
(off Potley Hill Rd.)
Frogmore Pk. Dr.
GU17: B'water 2H 69
Frogmore Rd.
GU17: B'water 1G 69
Frome Cl. GU14: Cove 8J 69
Fromondes Rd. SM3: Chea 2K 61
Fromow Gdns. GU20: Windl . . .3A 52
Froxfield Down RG12: Brac . . .4D 32
Fruen Rd. TW14: Felt 1G 23
Fry Cl. RH11: Craw 8N 181
Fryday Gro. M. *SW12* *1G 29*
(off Weir Rd.)
Fryern Wood CR3: Cate 2N 103
Frylands Ct. CR0: N Add 7M 65
Fry La. GU19: Bag 5H 51
Frymley Vw. SL4: W'sor 4A 4
Fry's Acre GU12: A Va 1E 110
Fry's La. GU46: Yate 8D 48
Fryston Av. CR0: Croy 8D 46
CR5: Coul 1F 82
Fuchsia Way GU24: W End 9B 52
Fuel Farm Rd. RH6: Gat 1C 162
Fugelmere Rd. GU51: Fleet 3D 88
Fugelmere Wlk.
GU51: Fleet 3D 88
Fulbourn KT1: K Tham 4M 203
Fulbourne Cl. RH1: Red 1C 122
Fulbrook Av. KT15: N Haw 7J 55
Fulford Ho. KT19: Ewe 4C 60
Fulford Rd. CR3: Cate 8A 84
KT19: Ewe 4C 60
Fulfords Hill RH13: Itch 9A 196
Fulfords Rd. RH13: Itch 9B 196
FULHAM 5K 13
FULHAM BROADWAY 3M 13
Fulham B'way. SW6 . . . . .3M 13
Fulham B'way. Shop. Cen.
SW6 . . . .*3M 13*
(off Fulham B'way.)
Fulham Broadway Station (Tube)
. . . . .3M 13
Fulham Cl. RH11: Craw 7N 181
Fulham Ct. SW6 . . . . .4M 13
Fulham FC 4J 13
Fulham High St. SW6 . . . . .5K 13
Fulham Palace 5K 13
Fulham Pal. Rd. SW6 . . . . .1H 13
W6 . . . . .1H 13
Fulham Pk. Gdns.
SW6 . . . . .5L 13
Fulham Pk. Rd. SW6 . . . . .5L 13
Fulham Pools 2K 13
Fulham Rd. SW6 . . . . .5K 13
(Fulham High St.)
SW6 . . . . .3N 13
(King's Rd.)
SW10 . . . . .3N 13
Fullbrook La. GU8: Els 6G 130
Fullbrooks Av. KT4: W Pk 7E 42
Fullbrook School Sports Cen.
. . . . .8J 55
Fullers Av. KT6: Surb 8M 41
Fullers Farm Rd.
KT24: W Hors 2B 116
Fuller's Griffin Brewery & Vis. Cen.
. . . . .2E 12
Fullers Hill TN16: Weste 4M 107
Fullers Rd. GU10: Rowl 7B 128
Fullers Va. GU35: Head 4E 168
Fullers Way Nth. KT6: Surb . . .9M 41
Fullers Way Sth. KT9: Ches . . .1L 59
Fuller's Wood CR0: Croy 2K 65
Fullers Wood La.
RH1: Sth N 4G 123
Fullerton Cl. KT14: Byf 1A 76
Fullerton Ct. TW11: Tedd 7G 25
Fullerton Dr. KT14: Byf 1N 75
Fullerton Rd. CR0: Croy 6C 46
KT14: Byf 1N 75
SM5: Cars 5C 62
SW18 . . . . .8N 13
Fullerton Way KT14: Byf 1N 75
Fuller Way UB3: Harl 1G 8
Fullmer Way KT15: Wood 6H 55
Fulmar Cl. KT5: Surb 5M 41
RH11: Ifi 4J 181
Fulmar Dr. RH19: E Grin 7C 166
Fulmead St. SW6 . . . . .4N 13
Fulmer Cl. TW12: Hamp 6M 23
Fulstone Cl. TW4: Houn 7N 9
Fulvens GU5: P'lake 2F 136
FULWELL 5D 24
Fulwell Pk. Av. TW2: Twick 3B 24
Fulwell Rd. TW11: Tedd 5D 24
Fulwell Station (Rail) 5D 24
Fulwood Gdns. TW1: Twick 9F 10
Fulwood Wlk. SW19 . . . . .2K 27
Furlong Cl. SM6: W'ton 7F 44
Furlong Rd. RH4: Westc 6C 118
Furlongs, The KT10: Esh 9B 40
Furlong Way RH6: Gat 2D 162
Furlough, The GU22: Wok 3C 74
Furmage St. SW18 . . . . .1N 27
Furnace Dr. RH10: Craw 5D 182
Furnace Farm Rd.
RH10: Craw 5E 182
RH19: Fel 7E 164
FURNACE GREEN 5E 182
Furnace Pde. RH10: Craw 5E 182
Furnace Pl. RH10: Craw 5E 182
FURNACE WOOD 6F 164
Furneaux Av. SE27 . . . . .6M 29
Furness SL4: W'sor 5A 4
Furness Rd. SM4: Mord 5N 43
SW6 . . . . .5N 13
Furness Row SL4: W'sor 5A 4
Furniss Ct. GU6: Cranl 8H 155
Furnival Cl. GU25: V Wat 5N 35
Furrows, The KT12: Wal T 8K 39
Furrows Pl. CR3: Cate 1C 104
Furse Cl. GU15: Camb 2G 70
Furtherfield GU6: Cranl 6N 155
Furtherfield Cl. CR0: Croy 5L 45
Further Vell-Mead
GU52: C Cro 9A 88
Furzebank SL5: S'hill 3A 34
Furze Cl. GU12: A Va 5E 90
RH1: Red 2D 122
RH6: Horl 8H 143
FURZEDOWN 6F 28
Furzedown Cl. TW20: Egh 7A 20
Furzedown Dr. SW17 . . . . .6F 28
Furzedown Rd. SM2: Sut 7A 62
SW17 . . . . .6F 28
Furze Fld. KT22: Oxs 9D 58
Furzefield RH11: Craw 2N 181
Furzefield Chase
RH19: D Pk 4A 166
Furzefield Cres. RH2: Reig . . .5A 122
Furzefield Rd. RH2: Reig 5A 122
RH12: Hors 3A 198
RH19: E Grin 6N 165
Furze Gro. KT20: K'wood 8L 81
Furze Hall KT20: K'wood 8L 81
FURZE HILL 8L 81
Furze Hill CR8: Pur 7J 63
GU10: Run 9B 110
KT20: K'wood 7L 81
RH1: Red 2C 122
Furzehill Cotts. GU24: Pirb 9N 71
Furze Hill Cres.
RG45: Crow 3H 49
Furze Hill Rd.
GU35: H Dwn 5G 168
Furze La. CR8: Pur 7J 63
GU7: Goda 3J 133
RH19: E Grin 6L 165
Furzemoors RG12: Brac 4N 31
Furzen La. RH5: W'wood 6H 177
RH12: Rudg, W'wood 6H 177
Furze Pl. RH1: Red 2D 122
Furze Rd. CR7: T Hea 2N 45
KT15: Addl 3H 55
RH12: Rudg 9E 176
Furze Va. Rd.
GU35: H Dwn 5G 169
Furzewood TW16: Sunb 9H 23
Fuzzens Wlk. SL4: W'sor 5B 4
Fydler's Cl. SL4: Wink 7M 17
Fyfield Cl. BR2: Brom 3N 47
GU17: B'water 1J 69

G

Gable Ct. *RH1: Red* *2E 122*
(off St Anne's Mt.)
Gable End GU14: Farnb 1N 89
Gables, The GU2: Guil 9L 93
GU26: G'hott 6B 170
KT13: Weybr 2D 56
KT22: Oxs 8C 58
RH6: Horl 9E 142
RH10: Cop 7M 163
RH12: Hors 4K 197
SM7: Ban 4L 81
Gables Av. TW15: A'ford 6A 22
Gables Cl. GU12: A Va 8E 90
GU14: Cove 1M 89
GU22: Wok 7B 74
SL3: Dat 2K 5
Gables Ct. GU22: Wok 7B 74
Gables Rd. GU52: C Cro 9A 88
Gables Way SM7: Ban 4L 81
Gabriel Cl. TW13: Hanw 5M 23
Gabriel Dr. GU15: Camb 2F 70
Gabriel Rd. RH10: Craw 7G 183
Gadbridge La. GU6: Ewh 6F 156
Gadbrook Rd. RH3: Betch 9B 120
Gadd Cl. RG40: W'ham 1E 30
Gadesden Rd. KT19: Ewe 3B 60
(not continuous)
Gaffney Cl. GU11: Alde 6B 90
Gafton Bank SM7: Ban 4M 81
Gage Cl. RH10: Craw D 9F 164
Gage Ridge RH18: F Row 7G 187
Gaggle Wood
RH13: M Hea 9B 198
Gainsborough RG12: Brac 5A 32
Gainsborough Cl.
GU14: Farnb 3B 90
GU15: Camb 8D 50
KT10: Esh 7E 40
Gainsborough Ct.
GU51: Fleet 4B 88
KT12: Wal T 1H 57
KT19: Ewe 3E 60
W4 . . . .*1A 12*
(off Chaseley Dr.)
Gainsborough Dr.
CR2: Sande 9D 64
SL5: Asc 2H 33
Gainsborough Gdns.
TW7: Isle 8D 10
Gainsborough Mans.
W14 . . . .*2K 13*
(off Queen's Club Gdns.)
Gainsborough Pl.
KT11: Cob 2M 77
Gainsborough Rd.
KT3: N Mal 5C 42
KT19: Eps 6B 60
RH10: Craw 7D 182
TW9: Rich 5M 11
Gainsborough Ter. *SM2: Sut* *4L 61*
(off Belmont Ri.)
Gaist Av. CR3: Cate 9E 84
Gala Bingo
Feltham 3J 23
Hounslow 7A 10
Kingston upon Thames
. . . . .2K 203 (9L 25)
Thornton Heath 4L 45
Tooting 6C 28
Woking *4B 74*
(in Big Apple)
Wokingham 2B 30
Galahad Rd. RH11: Ifi 3K 181
Galata Rd. SW13 . . . . .3F 12
Galba Ct. TW8: Brent 3K 11
Gale Cl. CR4: Mit 2B 44
TW12: Hamp 7M 23
Gale Cres. SM7: Ban 4M 81
Gale Dr. GU18: Ligh 6L 51
Galena Arches *W6* *1G 13*
(off Galena Rd.)
Galena Rd. W6 . . . . .1G 13
Galen Cl. KT19: Eps 7N 59
Galesbury Rd. SW18 . . . . .1A 28
Gales Cl. GU4: Guil 9F 94
GU27: Hasl 3C 188
Gales Dr. RH10: Craw 3D 182
Gales Pl. RH10: Craw 3D 182
Galgate Cl. SW19 . . . . .2J 27
Galileo Ct. RG12: Brac 1C 32
Galleries, The *GU11: Alde* . . .*2M 109*
(off High St.)
Gallery Ct. *SW10* *2N 13*
(off Gunter Gro.)
Gallery Rd. GU24: B'wood 6A 72
Galleymead Rd. SL3: Poy 4H 7
Gallica Ct. SM1: Sut 7N 43
Gallop, The CR2: Sels 4E 64
GU46: Yate 8C 48
SL4: W'sor 1F 18
SM2: Sut 5B 62
Gallops, The KT10: Esh 9B 40
Galloway Cl. GU51: Fleet 1D 88
Galloway Path
CR0: Croy 7D 200 (1A 64)
Gallwey Rd. GU11: Alde 1N 109
Gally Hill Rd. GU52: C Cro 8A 88
Gallys Rd. SL4: W'sor 5A 4
Galpins Rd. CR7: T Hea 4J 45
Galsworthy Rd.
KT2: K Tham 8A 26
KT16: Chert 6J 37
Galton Rd. SL5: S'dale 5C 34
Galvani Way CR0: Wad 7K 45
Galveston Rd. SW15 . . . . .8L 13
Galvins Cl. GU2: Guil 9K 93
Galway Rd. GU46: Yate 2B 68
Gambles La. GU23: Rip 2L 95
Gambole Rd. SW17 . . . . .5C 28
Gamlen Rd. SW15 . . . . .7J 13
Gander Grn. Cres.
TW12: Hamp 9A 24
Gander Grn. La. SM1: Sut 9L 43
SM3: Chea 8K 43
Gangers Hill CR3: Wold 6H 105
RH9: Gods 6H 105
Ganghill GU1: Guil 1C 114
Ganymede Ct. RH11: Craw 6K 181
Gapemouth Rd. GU24: Pirb 9H 71
Gap Rd. SW19 . . . . .6M 27
Garbetts Way GU10: Tong 6C 110
Garbrand Wlk. KT17: Ewe 5E 60
Garden Av. CR4: Mit 8F 28
Garden Cl. GU5: Sha G 7F 134
GU14: Cove 2K 89
KT15: Addl 1M 55
KT22: Leat 2J 99
RH19: E Grin 2B 186
SM6: W'ton 2J 63
SM7: Ban 2M 81

Garden Cl.—Glen Ct.

Garden Cl. SW15 1H **27**
TW12: Hamp 6N **23**
TW15: A'ford 7D **22**
Garden Ct. CR0: Croy 8C **46**
TW9: Kew 4M **11**
TW12: Hamp 6N **23**
Gardener Gro. TW13: Hanw 3N **23**
Gardeners Cl. RH12: Warn 9E **178**
Gardeners Ct. RH13: Hors 7K **197**
GARDENERS GREEN 6D **30**
Gardeners Grn.
RH12: Rusp 3B **180**
Gardener's Hill Rd.
GU10: Fren, Wrec 6G **128**
Gardeners Rd.
CR0: Croy 1A **200** (7M **45**)
RG42: Wink R 7F **16**
Gardener's Wlk.
KT23: Book 4B **98**
Gardenfields KT20: Tad 6K **81**
Garden Ho., The *W6 2J 13*
(off Bothwell St.)
Garden Ho. La.
RH19: E Grin 2B **186**
Gardenia Dr. GU24: W End 9C **52**
Garden La. SW2 2K **29**
Garden Pl. RH12: Hors 4J **197**
Garden Rd. KT12: Wal T 5J **39**
SE20 1F **46**
TW9: Rich 6N **11**
Garden Royal SW15 9J **13**
Gardens, The BR3: Beck 1M **47**
GU10: Tong 5D **110**
GU24: Pirb 9C **72**
KT10: Esh 1A **58**
KT11: Cob 6D **76**
TW14: Felt 8E **8**
Garden Wlk. BR3: Beck 1J **47**
CR5: Coul 1F **102**
RH11: Craw 3A **182**
RH12: Hors 4J **197**
Gardenwood Rd.
RH19: E Grin 9L **165**
Gardiner Ct. CR2: S Croy 3N **63**
Gardner Ho. TW13: Hanw 3N **23**
Gardner La. RH10: Craw D 1D **184**
Gardner Pl. TW14: Felt 9J **9**
Gardner Rd.
GU1: Guil 2C **202** (3N **113**)
Garendon Gdns.
SM4: Mord 6N **43**
Garendon Rd. SM4: Mord 6N **43**
Gareth Cl. KT4: W Pk 8J **43**
Gareth Ct. SW16 4H **29**
Garfield Pl. SL4: W'sor 5G **4**
Garfield Rd. GU15: Camb 1A **70**
KT15: Addl 2L **55**
SW19 6A **28**
TW1: Twick 2G **25**
Garibaldi Rd. RH1: Red 4D **122**
Garland Ct. *RH19: E Grin 9N 165*
(off Garland Rd.)
Garland Dr. TW3: Houn 5C **10**
Garland Ho. KT2: K Tham 2J **203**
Garland Rd. RH19: E Grin 8N **165**
Garlands Ct. CR0: Croy 6E **200**
TN8: Eden 1L 147
(off Minstrels Cl.)
Garlands Rd. KT22: Leat 8H **79**
RH1: Red 4D **122**
Garland Way CR3: Cate 9A **84**
Garlichill Rd. KT18: Tat C 4G **81**
Garner Ct. *TW19: Stan 9M 7*
(off Jeppesen Ct.)
Garnet Rd. CR7: T Hea 3N **45**
Garrad's Rd. SW16 4H **29**
Garrard Rd. SM7: Ban 3M **81**
Garratt Cl. CR0: Bedd 1J **63**
Garratt Ct. SW18 1N **27**
Garratt La. SW17 4A **28**
SW18 9N **13**
Garratts La. SM7: Ban 3L **81**
Garratt Ter. SW17 5C **28**
Garraway Ct. *SW13 3H 13*
(off Wyatt Dr.)
Garrett Cl. RH10: Craw 5G **183**
Garrett M. GU11: Alde 3M **109**
Garrick Cl. KT12: Hers 1J **57**
TW9: Rich 8K **11**
TW18: Stain 8J **21**
Garrick Cres.
CR0: Croy 3F **200** (8B **46**)
Garrick Gdns. KT8: W Mole 2A **40**
Garrick Ho. KT1: K Tham 8J **203**
W4 2D **12**
Garrick Rd. TW9: Rich 5N **11**
Garricks Ho. KT1: K Tham 4H **203**
Garrick Wlk. RH10: Craw 6C **182**
Garrick Way GU16: Frim G 7C **70**
Garrison Cl. TW4: Houn 8N **9**
Garrison La. KT9: Ches 4K **59**
Garrones, The
RH10: Craw 2H **183**
Garsdale Ter. *W14 1L 13*
(off Aisgill Av.)
Garside Cl. TW12: Hamp 7B **24**
Garson Cl. KT10: Esh 2N **57**
Garson La. TW19: Wray 1N **19**
Garson Rd. KT10: Esh 3N **57**
Garson's La. RG42: Warf 2E **16**
Garston Gdns. CR8: Ken 2A **84**
Garston La. CR8: Ken 1A **84**
Garstons, The KT23: Book 3A **98**
Garswood RG12: Brac 5B **32**
Garth, The GU12: Ash 3D **110**
GU14: Farnb 1B **90**
KT11: Cob 9M **57**
TW12: H Hill 7B **24**
Garth Cl. GU9: Farnh 4F **128**
KT2: K Tham 6M **25**
SM4: Mord 6J **43**
Garth Ct. RH4: Dork 7H **119**
W4 1C **12**
Garth Hunt Cotts.
RG42: Brac 7N **15**
Garth Rd. KT2: K Tham 6M **25**
SM4: Mord 5H **43**
W4 1C **12**
Garth Rd. Ind. Est.
SM4: Mord 7J **43**
Garthside TW10: Ham 6L **25**
Garth Sq. RG42: Brac 8N **15**
Gartmoor Gdns. SW19 2L **27**
Garton Cl. RH11: Ifi 4K **181**
Garton Pl. SW18 9N **13**
Gascoigne Rd. CR0: N Add 6M **65**
KT13: Weybr 9C **38**
Gasden Copse GU8: Wit 5A **152**
Gasden Dr. GU8: Wit 4A **152**
Gasden La. GU8: Wit 4A **152**
Gaskarth Rd. SW12 1F **28**
Gaskyns Cl. RH12: Rudg 1E **194**
Gassiot Rd. SW17 5D **28**
Gassiot Way SM1: Sut 9B **44**
Gasson Wood Rd.
RH11: Craw 5K **181**
Gastein Rd. W6 2J **13**
Gaston Bell Cl. TW9: Rich 6M **11**
Gaston Bri. Rd.
TW17: Shep 5E **38**
Gaston Rd. CR4: Mit 2E **44**
Gaston Way TW17: Shep 4E **38**
Gatcombe Cres. SL5: Asc 9K **17**
Gate Cen., The TW8: Brent 3G **11**
Gateford Dr. RH12: Hors 2M **197**
Gatehouse Cl. KT2: K Tham 8B **26**
SL4: W'sor 7E **4**
Gates, The GU51: Fleet 1D **88**
Gates Cl. RH10: Craw 7G **182**
Gatesden Cl. KT22: Fetc 1C **98**
Gatesden Rd. KT22: Fetc 9C **78**
Gates Grn. Rd. BR2: Kes 1B **66**
BR4: W Wick 1B **66**
Gateside Rd. SW17 4D **28**
Gate St. GU5: Braml 1C **154**
(not continuous)
Gateway KT13: Weybr 9C **38**
Gateway, The GU21: Wok 1D **74**
Gateways GU1: Guil 3C **114**
KT6: Surb 8K **203**
Gateways, The *TW9: Rich 7K 11*
(off Park La.)
Gateways Ct. SM6: W'ton 2F **62**
Gatfield Gro. TW13: Hanw 3A **24**
Gatfield Ho. TW13: Hanw 3N **23**
Gatley Av. KT19: Ewe 2A **60**
Gatley Dr. GU4: B'ham 9B **94**
GATTON 6D **102**
GATTON BOTTOM 4F **102**
Gatton Bottom RH1: Mers 5D **102**
RH2: Reig 7A **102**
Gatton Cl. RH2: Reig 9A **102**
SM2: Sut 5N **61**
Gatton Pk. Bus. Cen.
RH1: Mers 7F **102**
Gatton Pk. Ct. RH1: Red 8D **102**
Gatton Pk. Rd. RH1: Red 1B **122**
RH2: Reig 1B **122**
Gatton Rd. RH2: Reig 1A **122**
SW17 5C **28**
GATWICK 5K **131**
GATWICK AIRPORT 3E **162**
Gatwick Airport Beehive Area
RH6: Craw 5E **162**
Gatwick Airport Skyview 3E **162**
Gatwick Airport Station (Rail)
3F **162**
Gatwick Aviation Mus. 4L **161**
Gatwick Bus. Pk.
RH6: Craw 6F **162**
Gatwick Ga. RH11: L Hea 5C **162**
Gatwick Ga. Ind. Est.
RH11: L Hea 5C **162**
Gatwick Intl. Distribution Cen.
RH10: Craw 6F **162**
Gatwick Metro Cen.
RH6: Horl 8F **142**
Gatwick Rd. RH6: Craw 5E **162**
RH10: Craw 9E **162**
SW18 1L **27**
Gatwick Rd. Rdbt.
RH6: Craw 5E **162**
Gatwick Way RH6: Gat 2D **162**
Gauntlett Rd. SM1: Sut 2B **62**
Gavell Rd. KT11: Cob 9H **57**
Gaveston Cl. KT14: Byf 9A **56**
Gaveston Rd. KT22: Leat 7G **78**
Gavina Cl. SM4: Mord 4C **44**
Gawton Cres. CR5: Coul 9G **83**
Gayfere Rd. KT17: Ewe 2F **60**
Gayhouse La. RH1: Out 3A **144**
Gayler Cl. RH1: Blet 2C **124**
Gaynesford Rd. SM5: Cars 4D **62**
Gay St. SW15 6J **13**
Gayton Cl. KT21: A'tead 5L **79**
Gayton Ct. RH2: Reig 2M **121**
Gayville Rd. SW11 1D **28**
Gaywood Cl. SW2 2K **29**
Gaywood Rd. KT21: A'tead 5M **79**
Gearing Cl. SW17 5E **28**
Geary Cl. RH6: Smal 1M **163**
Geffers Ride SL5: Asc 2J **33**
Gemini Cl. RH11: Craw 5K **181**
Gemmell Cl. CR8: Pur 1K **83**
Genesis Bus. Cen.
RH13: Hors 5M **197**
Genesis Bus. Pk.
GU21: Wok 2E **74**
Genesis Cl. TW19: Stan 2A **22**
Geneva Cl. TW17: Shep 1F **38**
Geneva Rd. CR7: T Hea 4N **45**
KT1: K Tham 8K **203** (3L **41**)
Genoa Av. SW15 8H **13**
Genoa Rd. SE20 1F **46**
Gentles La. GU30: Pass 8F **168**
GU35: Head 6F **168**
Genyn Rd.
GU2: Guil 5A **202** (4L **113**)
George Denyer Cl.
GU27: Hasl 1G **189**
George Eliot Cl. GU8: Wit 5C **152**
George Gdns. GU11: Alde 5A **110**
GU51: Fleet 4C **88**
George Gro. Rd. SE20 1D **46**
Georgeham Rd. GU47: Owls 5J **49**
George Horley Pl.
RH5: Newd 1A **160**
Georgelands GU23: Rip 8K **75**
George Lindgren Ho.
SW6 3L 13
(off Clem Attlee Ct.)
George Pinion Ct.
RH12: Hors 5H **197**
George Rd.
GU1: Guil 3C **202** (3N **113**)
GU7: Goda 4H **133**
GU8: Mil 9C **132**
GU51: Fleet 4C **88**
KT2: K Tham 8A **26**
(not continuous)
KT3: N Mal 3E **42**
George Sq. SW19 2M **43**
George's Rd. TN16: Tats 7F **86**
George's Sq. *SW6 2L 13*
(off North End Rd.)
Georges Ter. CR3: Cate 9A **84**
George St.
CR0: Croy 3C **200** (8N **45**)
GU24: B'wood 8L **71**
TW3: Houn 5N **9**
TW9: Rich 8K **11**
TW18: Stain 5H **21**
George Street Stop (CT)
3C **200** (8N **45**)
George Wyver Cl. SW19 1K **27**
Georgian Cl. GU15: Camb 8C **50**
RH10: Craw 4H **183**
TW18: Stain 5K **21**
Georgian Ct. CR0: Croy 1E **200**
SW16 5J **29**
Georgia Rd. CR7: T Hea 9M **29**
KT3: N Mal 3B **42**
Georgina Ct. GU51: Fleet 4B **88**
Gerald Ct. RH13: Hors 6L **197**
Geraldine Rd. W4 2N **11**
Gerald's Gro. SM7: Ban 1J **81**
Geranium Cl. RG45: Crow 8G **30**
Gerard Av. TW4: Houn 1A **24**
Gerardes Lodge
GU27: Hasl 9H **171**
Gerard Rd. SW13 4E **12**
Germander Dr. GU24: Bis 2D **72**
Gernigan Ho. SW18 1B **28**
Gerrards Mead SM7: Ban 3L **81**
Gervis Ct. TW7: Isle 3C **10**
Ghyll Cres. RH13: Hors 8M **197**
Giant Arches Rd. SE24 1N **29**
Gibbet La. GU15: Camb 7E **50**
Gibbins La. RG42: Warf 6B **16**
Gibbon Rd.
KT2: K Tham 1K **203** (9L **25**)
Gibbons Cl. GU47: Sandh 7H **49**
RH10: Craw 6G **183**
Gibbon Wlk. SW15 7F **12**
Gibb's Acre GU24: Pirb 1C **92**
Gibbs Brook La. RH8: Oxt 5N **125**
Gibbs Grn. W14 1L **13**
(not continuous)
Gibbs Grn. Cl. W14 1L **13**
Gibbs Way GU46: Yate 2A **68**
Giblets La. RH12: Hors 1M **197**
Giblets Way RH12: Hors 1L **197**
Gibraltar Cres. KT19: Ewe 6D **60**
Gibson Cl. KT9: Ches 2J **59**
TW7: Isle 6E **10**
Gibson Ct. KT10: H Wood 8F **40**
SL3: Lang 1B **6**
Gibson Dr. RG12: Brac 2B **32**
Gibson Ho. SM1: Sut 1M **61**
Gibson M. TW1: Twick 9J **11**
Gibson Pl. RH10: Craw 1C **182**
TW19: Stan 9L **7**
Gibson Rd. SM1: Sut 2N **61**
Gibsons Hill SW16 8L **29**
(not continuous)
Gidd Hill CR5: Coul 3E **82**
Giffard Dr. GU14: Cove 9L **69**
Giffards Cl. RH19: E Grin 9B **166**
Giffards Mdw. GU9: Farnh 2K **129**
Giffard Way GU2: Guil 9K **93**
GIGGSHILL 6G **40**
Giggs Hill Gdns. KT7: T Dit 7G **40**
Giggs Hill Rd. KT7: T Dit 6G **40**
Gilbert Cl. *SW19 9N 27*
(off High Path)
Gilbert Ho. *SW13 3G 13*
(off Trinity Chu. Rd.)
Gilbert Rd. GU16: Camb 5A **70**
SW19 8A **28**
Gilbert Scott SW18 9K **13**
Gilberts Lodge KT17: Eps 8D **60**
Gilbert St. TW3: Houn 6C **10**
Gilbert Way CR0: Wad 8K **45**
SL3: Lang 1B **6**
Gilbey Rd. SW17 5C **28**
Gilders Rd. KT9: Ches 4M **59**
Gilesmead KT18: Eps 8L **201**
Giles Travers Cl.
TW20: Thor 2E **36**
Gilham La. RH18: F Row 7G **187**
Gilhams Av. SM7: Ban 8J **61**
Gill Av. GU2: Guil 4H **113**
Gillespie Ho. *GU25: V Wat 3A 36*
(off Holloway Dr.)
Gillett Ct. RH13: Hors 4A **198**
GILLETTE CORNER 3G **11**
Gillett Rd. CR7: T Hea 3A **46**
Gillham's La. GU27: Hasl 4A **188**
Gilliam Gro. CR8: Pur 6L **63**
Gillian Av. GU12: Alde 4A **110**
Gillian Cl. GU12: Alde 4B **110**
Gillian Pk. Rd. SM3: Sut 7L **43**
Gilliat Dr. GU4: Guil 1F **114**
Gilligan Cl. RH12: Hors 6H **197**
Gill Ri. RG42: Warf 7A **16**
Gilmais KT23: Book 3C **98**
Gilman Cres. SL4: W'sor 6A **4**
Gilmore Cres. TW15: A'ford 6B **22**
Gilpin Av. SW14 7C **12**
Gilpin Cl. CR4: Mit 1C **44**
Gilpin Cres. TW2: Whitt 1B **24**
Gilpin Way UB3: Harl 3E **8**
Gilsland Rd. CR7: T Hea 3A **46**
Gilstead Rd. SW6 5N **13**
Gingers Cl. GU6: Cranl 8A **156**
Ginhams Rd. RH11: Craw 3N **181**
Gipsy La. RG12: Brac 1B **32**
RG40: W'ham 3B **30**
SW15 6G **12**
Gipsy Rd. SE27 5N **29**
Gipsy Rd. Gdns. SE27 5N **29**
Girdlestoneites GU7: Goda 4F **132**
Girdwood Rd. SW18 1K **27**
Girling Way TW14: Felt 6H **9**
Gironde Rd. SW6 3L **13**
Girton Cl. GU47: Owls 6K **49**
Girton Gdns. CR0: Croy 9K **47**
Gisbourne Cl. SM6: Bedd 9H **45**
GIVONS GROVE 4J **99**
Givons Gro. KT22: Leat 3H **99**
Givons Gro. Rdbt.
KT22: Leat 2H **99**
Glade, The BR4: W Wick 9L **47**
CR0: Croy 4G **46**
CR5: Coul 6L **83**
GU9: H End 5J **109**
GU10: B Oak 1A **148**
GU16: Mytc 3E **90**
KT14: W By 9G **54**
KT17: Ewe 3F **60**
KT20: K'wood 8M **81**
KT22: Fetc 9A **78**
RH10: Craw 5E **182**
RH13: Hors 5N **197**
SL5: S'hill 4N **33**
SM2: Chea 5K **61**
TW18: Stain 7K **21**
Glade Cl. KT6: Surb 8K **41**
Glade Gdns. CR0: Croy 6H **47**
Glade M. GU1: Guil 4B **114**
Glades, The KT6: Surb 6L **41**
RH19: E Grin 9D **166**
Gladeside CR0: Croy 5G **46**
Gladeside Cl. KT9: Ches 4K **59**
Gladeside Ct. CR6: Warl 7E **84**
Glade Spur KT20: K'wood 8N **81**
Gladiator Way
GU14: Farnb 5M **89**
Gladioli Cl. TW12: Hamp 7A **24**
Gladsmuir Cl. KT12: Wal T 8K **39**
Gladstone Av. TW2: Twick 2D **24**
TW14: Felt 9H **9**
Gladstone Gdns.
TW3: Houn 4C **10**
Gladstone Ho. CR4: Mit 1D **44**
Gladstone Pl. KT8: E Mol 4E **40**
Gladstone Rd. BR6: Farnb 2L **67**
CR0: Croy 6A **46**
KT1: K Tham 2N **41**
KT6: Surb 8K **41**
KT21: A'tead 5K **79**
RH12: Hors 5K **197**
SW19 8M **27**
Gladstone Ter. *SE27 6N 29*
(off Bentons La.)
Gladwyn Rd. SW15 6J **13**
Glamis Cl. GU16: Frim 7D **70**
Glamorgan Cl. CR4: Mit 2J **45**
Glamorgan Rd. KT1: H Wic 8J **25**
Glanfield Rd. BR3: Beck 3J **47**
GLANTY 5E **20**
Glanty, The TW20: Egh 5D **20**
Glanville Wlk.
RH11: Craw 6M **181**
Glasbrook Av. TW2: Whitt 2N **23**
Glasford St. SW17 7D **28**
Glassonby Wlk.
GU15: Camb 1G **70**
(not continuous)
Glastonbury Rd.
SM4: Mord 6M **43**
Glayshers Hill
GU35: H Dwn 3F **168**
Glazbury Rd. W14 1K **13**
Glazebrook Rd.
TW11: Tedd 8F **24**
Glaziers La. GU3: Norm 1M **111**
Gleave Cl. RH19: E Grin 8C **166**
Glebe, The GU6: Ewh 4F **156**
GU17: Haw 2K **69**
KT4: W Pk 7E **42**
RH2: Leigh 1F **140**
RH6: Horl 8D **142**
RH10: Cop 7M **163**
RH19: Fel 6K **165**
SW16 5H **29**
Glebe Av. CR4: Mit 1C **44**
Glebe Cl. CR2: Sande 7C **64**
GU11: Alde 5M **109**
GU18: Ligh 6N **51**
KT23: Book 4A **98**
RH10: Craw 2C **182**
W4 1D **12**
Glebe Cotts. GU4: W Cla 1K **115**
TW13: Hanw 4A 24
(off Twickenham Rd.)
Glebe Ct. CR4: Mit 2D **44**
GU1: Guil 3B **114**
GU51: Fleet 4A **88**
Glebe Gdns. KT3: N Mal 6D **42**
KT14: Byf 1M **75**
Glebe Hyrst CR2: Sande 8C **64**
Glebeland Gdns.
TW17: Shep 5D **38**
Glebeland Rd. GU15: Camb 2L **69**
Glebelands KT8: W Mole 4B **40**
KT10: Clay 5F **58**
RH10: Craw D 2D **184**
RH14: Loxw 4H **193**
Glebelands Mdw. GU6: Alf 8H **175**
Glebelands Rd.
RG40: W'ham 1B **30**
TW14: Felt 2H **23**
Glebe La. GU10: Rush 5A **150**
RH5: A Com 3L **137**
Glebe Path CR4: Mit 2D **44**
Glebe Rd. CR6: Warl 4G **84**
GU6: Cranl 7M **155**
GU14: Cove 9L **69**
GU35: Head 4D **168**
KT21: A'tead 5K **79**
RH1: Mers 2F **102**
RH4: Dork 3G **201** (5F **118**)
SL4: O Win 8L **5**
SM2: Chea 5K **61**
SM5: Cars 3D **62**
SW13 5F **12**
TW18: Stain 6K **21**
TW20: Egh 6E **20**
Glebe Side TW1: Twick 9F **10**
Glebe Sq. CR4: Mit 2D **44**
Glebe St. W4 1D **12**
Glebe Ter. W4 1D **12**
Glebe Way BR4: W Wick 8M **47**
CR2: Sande 7C **64**
TW13: Hanw 4A **24**
Glebewood RG12: Brac 4A **32**
Gledhow Gdns. SW5 1N **13**
Gledhow Wood
KT20: K'wood 8N **81**
Gledstanes Rd. W14 1K **13**
Gleeson Dr. BR6: Chels 2N **67**
Gleeson M. KT15: Addl 1L **55**
Glegg Pl. SW15 7J **13**
Glen, The CR0: Croy 9G **47**
GU9: U Hal 6H **109**
KT15: Addl 2H **55**
RH1: Red 5D **122**
SL5: S'hill 3A **34**
UB2: S'hall 1N **9**
Glen Albyn Rd. SW19 3J **27**
Glenallan Ho. *W14 1L 13*
(off North End Cres.)
Glenalmond Ho.
TW15: A'ford 4N **21**
Glena Mt. SM1: Sut 1A **62**
Glen Av. TW15: A'ford 5B **22**
Glenavon Cl. KT10: Clay 3G **58**
Glenavon Ct. KT4: W Pk 8G **43**
Glenavon Gdns. GU46: Yate 2C **68**
Glenbuck Ct. KT6: Surb 5L **41**
Glenbuck Rd. KT6: Surb 5K **41**
Glenburnie Rd. SW17 4D **28**
Glencairn Rd. SW16 9J **29**
Glencar Ct. SE19 7M **29**
Glen Cl. GU26: Hind 3A **170**
KT20: K'wood 1K **101**
TW17: Shep 3B **38**
Glencoe Cl. GU16: Frim 6E **70**
Glencoe Rd. KT13: Weybr 9B **38**
Glen Ct. GU21: Wok 6K **73**
GU26: Hind 3A **170**
KT14: Byf 7M **55**
KT15: Addl 2H **55**
TW18: Stain 8H **21**

Glendale Cl. GU21: Wok 5M **73**	Gloucester Gdns.
RH12: Hors 2N **197**	GU19: Bag 4J **51**
Glendale Dr. GU4: B'ham ...9E **94**	SM1: Sut 8N **43**
SW19 ....6L **27**	Gloucester Rd. TW10: Rich ..8N **11**
Glendale M. BR3: Beck 1L **47**	GU2: Guil 1J **113**
Glendale Ri. CR8: Ken 2M **83**	GU11: Alde 5A **109**
Glendarvon St. SW15 .....6J **13**	GU19: Bag 4J **51**
Glendene Av. KT24: E Hor ..4F **96**	KT1: K Tham 1N **41**
Glendon Ho. RH10: Craw ...4B **182**	RH1: Red 2D **122**
Glendower Gdns.	RH10: Craw 7C **182**
SW14 ....6C **12**	TW2: Twick 2C **24**
Glendower Rd. SW14 ......6C **12**	TW4: Houn 7M **9**
Glendyne Cl. RH19: E Grin ..1C **186**	TW9: Kew 3N **11**

(Index page — columns continue. Full detailed transcription of every entry not reproduced here.)

Grange, The—Green Mead

Grange, The RH6: Horl ... 5F 142
SL4: O Win ... 8L 5
SW19 ... 7J 27
W4 ... 1A 12
Grange Av. RG45: Crow ... 1G 48
SE25 ... 1B 46
TW2: Twick ... 3E 24
Grangecliffe Gdns.
SE25 ... 1B 46
Grange Cl. GU2: Guil ... 8L 93
GU7: Goda ... 6K 133
GU15: Camb ... 7F 50
KT8: W Mole ... 3B 40
KT22: Leat ... 7K 79
RH1: Blet ... 2A 124
RH1: Mers ... 6F 102
RH10: Craw ... 1E 182
TN8: Eden ... 2L 147
TN16: Weste ... 4L 107
TW5: Hest ... 2N 9
TW19: Wray ... 9A 6
Grange Ct. GU10: Tong ... 6C 110
KT12: Wal T ... 8H 39
RH1: Mers ... 6F 102
RH9: S Gods ... 7H 125
SM2: Sut ... 4N 61
SM6: W'ton ... 9F 44
TW17: Shep ... 3B 38
TW18: Stain ... 6J 21
TW20: Egh ... 6B 20
Grange Cres.
RH10: Craw D ... 2E 184
Grange Dr. GU21: Wok ... 2A 74
RH1: Mers ... 6F 102
Grange End RH6: Smal ... 8L 143
Grange Est. GU52: C Cro ... 8A 88
Grange Farm Rd.
GU12: Ash ... 1E 110
Grangefields Rd.
GU4: J Wel ... 6N 93
Grange Gdns. SE25 ... 1B 46
SM7: Ban ... 9N 61
Grange Hill SE25 ... 1B 46
Grange Lodge SW19 ... 7J 27
Grange Mans. KT17: Ewe ... 4E 60
Grange Mdw. SM7: Ban ... 9N 61
Grange M. TW13: Felt ... 5H 23
Grangemount KT22: Leat ... 7K 79
Grange Pk. GU6: Cranl ... 7A 156
GU21: Wok ... 2A 74
Grange Pk. Pl. SW20 ... 8G 26
Grange Pk. Rd.
CR7: T Hea ... 3A 46
Grange Pl. KT12: Wal T ... 8H 39
TW18: Lale ... 1L 37
Grange Rd. CR2: S Croy ... 6N 63
CR3: Cate ... 3D 104
CR7: T Hea ... 3A 46
GU2: Guil ... 7L 93
GU10: Til ... 2N 149
GU10: Tong ... 6C 110
GU12: Ash ... 2F 110
GU14: Farnb ... 7N 69
GU15: Camb ... 1C 70
GU21: Wok ... 1A 74
GU24: Pirb ... 9N 71
GU52: C Cro ... 8A 88
KT1: K Tham ... 5J 203 (2L 41)
KT8: W Mole ... 3B 40
KT9: Ches ... 1L 59
KT12: Hers ... 1M 57
KT15: N Haw ... 6J 55
KT22: Leat ... 7K 79
RG42: Brac ... 9A 16
RH10: Craw D ... 2D 184
SE19 ... 3A 46
SE25 ... 3A 46
SM2: Sut ... 4M 61
SW13 ... 4F 12
TW20: Egh ... 6B 20
(not continuous)
W4 ... 1A 12
Grange Va. SM2: Sut ... 4N 61
Grange Way RH6: Smal ... 8L 143
Grangewood Dr.
TW16: Sunb ... 8G 22
Grangewood Ter. SE25 ... 1A 46
Gransden Cl. GU6: Ewh ... 5F 156
Grantchester *KT1: K Tham ... 1N 41*
(off St Peters Rd.)
Grant Cl. TW17: Shep ... 5C 38
Grantham Cl. GU47: Owls ... 6K 49
Grantham Ct. KT2: K Tham ... 6K 25
Grantham Dr. GU14: Cove ... 9J 69
Grantham Ho. TW16: Sunb ... 8F 22
Grantham Rd. W4 ... 3D 12
Grantley Av. GU5: Wone ... 5D 134
Grantley Cl. GU4: Chil ... 1A 134
Grantley Ct. GU9: Farnh ... 5E 128
Grantley Dr. GU52: Fleet ... 6A 88
Grantley Gdns. GU2: Guil ... 2K 113
Grantley Pl. KT10: Esh ... 2B 58
Grantley Rd. GU2: Guil ... 2K 113
TW4: C'ford ... 5K 9
Granton Rd. SW16 ... 9G 29
Grant Pl. CR0: Croy ... 7C 46
Grant Rd. CR0: Croy ... 7C 46
RG45: Crow ... 4H 49
Grants La. RH8: Limp ... 1E 126
TN8: Eden, Limp ... 1E 126
Grant Wlk. SL5: S'dale ... 7B 34
Grant Way TW7: Isle ... 2G 10
Grantwood Cl. RH1: Red ... 8E 122
Granville Av. TW3: Houn ... 8A 10
TW13: Felt ... 3H 23
Granville Cl.
CR0: Croy ... 3F 200 (8B 46)
KT13: Weybr ... 3D 56
KT14: Byf ... 9A 56
Granville Gdns. SW16 ... 9K 29
Granville Pl. SW6 ... 3N 13
Granville Rd. GU22: Wok ... 7B 74
KT13: Weybr ... 4D 56
RH8: Oxt ... 7B 106
SW18 ... 1L 27
SW19 ... 8M 27
TN16: Weste ... 4L 107
Granwood Ct. TW7: Isle ... 4E 10
Grapsome Cl. KT9: Ches ... 4J 59
Grasholm Way SL3: Lang ... 1E 6
Grasmere SL4: W'sor ... 3B 4
Grasmere Av. SW15 ... 5C 26
SW19 ... 2M 43
TW3: Houn ... 9B 10
Grasmere Cl. GU1: Guil ... 2D 114
TW14: Felt ... 2G 22
TW20: Egh ... 8D 20
Grasmere Ct. SM2: Sut ... 3A 62
SW13 ... 2F 12
(off Verdun Rd.)
Grasmere Gdns.
RH12: Hors ... 2A 198
Grasmere Rd. CR8: Pur ... 7M 63
GU9: U Hal ... 6F 108
GU14: Cove ... 2K 89
GU18: Ligh ... 6M 51
SE25 ... 5E 46
SW16 ... 6K 29
Grasmere Way KT14: Byf ... 8A 56
Grassfield Cl. CR5: Coul ... 6F 82
Grasslands RH6: Smal ... 8L 143
Grassmere RH6: Horl ... 7G 142
Grassmount CR8: Pur ... 6G 63
Grass Way SM6: W'ton ... 1G 62
Gratton Dr. SL4: W'sor ... 7B 4
Grattons, The RH13: Slin ... 5M 195
Grattons Dr. RH10: Craw ... 9G 162
Gravel Hill CR0: A'ton ... 3G 64
KT22: Leat ... 8H 79
Gravel Hill Rd.
GU10: H Pou ... 8A 128
Gravel Hill Stop (CT) ... 3H 65
Gravelly Hill CR3: Cate ... 6B 104
Gravelpits Cotts.
GU5: Gorn ... 8D 116
Gravelpits La. GU5: Gorn ... 8D 116
Gravel Rd. GU9: U Hal ... 5G 108
GU14: Farnb ... 5B 90
GU52: C Cro ... 7C 88
TW2: Twick ... 2E 24
Gravenel Gdns. *SW17 ... 6C 28*
(off Nutwell St.)
Graveney Rd. RH10: Craw ... 4G 182
SW17 ... 5C 28
Gravetts La. GU3: Guil ... 8H 93
GRAVETYE ... 7J 185
Gravetye Cl. RH10: Craw ... 5E 182
Gray Cl. KT15: Addl ... 2K 55
RH7: Ling ... 7A 146
Grayham Cres. KT3: N Mal ... 3C 42
Grayham Rd. KT3: N Mal ... 3C 42
Graylands GU21: Wok ... 3A 74
Graylands Cl. GU21: Wok ... 3A 74
Graylands Ct. GU1: Guil ... 4B 114
Grayling KT16: Chert ... 7L 37
Gray Pl. KT16: Otter ... 3F 54
RG42: Brac ... 9K 15
Grays Cl. GU27: Hasl ... 9J 171
Grayscroft Rd. SW16 ... 8H 29
Grayshot Dr. GU17: B'water ... 1H 69
GRAYSHOTT ... 6A 170
Grayshott Laurels
GU35: Lind ... 4B 168
Grayshott Rd.
GU35: H Dwn ... 3G 169
Grays La. KT18: Eps D ... 6M 79
KT21: A'tead ... 6M 79
TW15: A'ford ... 5C 22
Grays Rd. GU7: Goda ... 4J 133
TN14: Weste ... 7M 87
TN16: Weste ... 8K 87
GRAYSWOOD ... 7K 171
Grays Wood RH6: Horl ... 8G 143
Grayswood Comn.
GU27: G'wood ... 8K 171
Grayswood Dr. GU16: Mytc ... 4E 90
Grayswood Gdns.
SW20 ... 1G 42
Grayswood M.
GU27: G'wood ... 7K 171
Grayswood Pl. GU27: Hasl ... 9J 171
Grayswood Point
SW15 ... 2F 26
Grayswood Rd.
GU27: Hasl, G'wood ... 1H 189
Great Austins GU9: Farnh ... 3J 129
Gt. Austins Ho. GU9: Farnh ... 3J 129
Great Benty UB7: W Dray ... 1N 7
GREAT BOOKHAM ... 4B 98
Great Bookham Common ... 8N 77
GREAT BURGH ... 4H 81
Gt. Chertsey Rd.
TW2: Twick ... 4N 23
TW13: Hanw, Twick ... 4N 23
W4 ... 5B 12
Gt. Church La. W6 ... 1J 13
Great Church Wood Nature Reserve ... 3J 105
Great Cockcrow Railway ... 7F 36
Gt. Daux Rdbt.
RH12: Warn ... 1H 197
Great Ellshams SM7: Ban ... 3M 81
GREAT ENTON ... 6D 152
Greatfield Cl. GU14: Farnb ... 6N 69
Great Fld. Pl.
RH19: E Grin ... 7D 166
Greatfield Rd.
GU14: Farnb ... 6M 69
Greatford Dr. GU1: Guil ... 3F 114
Gt. Gatton Cl. CR0: Croy ... 6H 47
Gt. George St. GU7: Goda ... 7H 133
Gt. Goodwin Dr. GU1: Guil ... 1D 114
Greatham Rd. RH10: Craw ... 6G 182
Greatham Wlk. SW15 ... 2F 26
Greathead Manor ... 1E 166
GREAT HOLLANDS ... 5L 31
Gt. Hollands Rd.
RG12: Brac ... 5K 31
Gt. Hollands Sq.
RG12: Brac ... 5L 31
Great Ho. Ct. RH19: E Grin ... 1B 186
Greathurst End KT23: Book ... 2N 97
Greatlake Ct. *RH6: Horl ... 7F 142*
(off Tanyard Way)
Great Mead TN8: Eden ... 9L 127
Gt. Oaks Pk. GU4: B'ham ... 7D 94
Great Quarry
GU1: Guil ... 8D 202 (6N 113)
Great Sth. W. Rd.
TW4: Houn ... 1D 22
TW14: Bedf, Felt ... 1D 22
Great Tattenhams
KT18: Tat C ... 5G 81
Great W. Rd. TW5: Hest ... 5L 9
TW7: Brent, Isle ... 3E 10
TW8: Brent ... 3G 11
W4 ... 1E 12
(Cedars Rd.)
W4 ... 1A 12
(Harvard Rd.)
W6 ... 1E 12
Great W. Trad. Est.
TW8: Brent ... 2H 11
Greatwood Cl. KT16: Otter ... 5E 54
Gt. Woodcote Dr. CR8: Pur ... 6H 63
Gt. Woodcote Pk. CR8: Pur ... 6H 63
Greaves Pl. SW17 ... 5C 28
Grebe Ct. SM1: Sut ... 2L 61
Grebe Cres. RH13: Hors ... 7N 197
Grebe Ter.
KT1: K Tham ... 5J 203 (2L 41)
Grecian Cres. SE19 ... 7M 29
GREEN, THE ... 9C 72
Green, The CR0: Sels ... 5J 65
CR3: Wold ... 1K 105
CR6: Warl ... 4G 84
GU5: Sha G ... 6F 134
GU6: Ewh ... 5F 156
GU8: Chid ... 5F 172
GU8: Duns ... 3B 174
GU8: Els ... 7H 131
GU9: B Lea ... 7M 109
GU9: U Hal ... 6H 109
GU10: Seal ... 2C 130
GU16: Frim G ... 8D 70
GU17: B'water ... 2H 69
GU23: Rip ... 8L 75
GU28: North ... 8D 190
GU46: Yate ... 9A 48
KT3: N Mal ... 2C 42
KT10: Clay ... 3F 58
KT12: Hers ... 2L 57
KT12: Whit V ... 6F 56
KT17: Ewe ... 7F 60
KT20: Tad ... 1J 101
(Dorking Rd.)
KT20: Tad ... 6K 81
(Reigate Rd.)
KT22: Fetc ... 2D 98
RG12: Brac ... 3N 31
RH3: Buck ... 2F 120
RH5: Ockl ... 5D 158
RH9: Gods ... 1E 124
RH10: Cop ... 7M 163
RH11: Craw ... 2A 182
SL3: Dat ... 3M 5
SM1: Sut ... 9N 43
SM4: Mord ... 3K 43
SM5: Cars ... 1E 62
SW19 ... 6J 27
TN16: Weste ... 4M 107
TW2: Twick ... 2E 24
TW5: Hest ... 2A 10
TW9: Rich ... 8K 11
TW13: Felt ... 3J 23
TW15: A'ford ... 6M 21
TW17: Shep ... 3F 38
TW19: Wray ... 9A 6
TW20: Eng G ... 5M 19
Green Acre GU11: Alde ... 3L 109
GU21: Knap ... 3H 73
Greenacre SL4: W'sor ... 5B 4
Greenacre Ct.
TW20: Eng G ... 7M 19
Greenacre Pl. SM6: W'ton ... 8F 44
Green Acres CR0: Croy ... 9C 46
Greenacres GU10: Run ... 1A 130
GU35: Bor ... 5A 168
KT20: Lwr K ... 6L 101
Greenacres KT23: Book ... 2B 98
RH8: Oxt ... 5A 106
RH10: Craw ... 4E 182
RH12: Hors ... 4J 197
Greenacres Cl. BR6: Farnb ... 1L 67
Greenaway Ter. *TW19: Stan ... 2N 21*
(off Victory Cl.)
Green Bank Cotts.
RH5: For G ... 3M 157
Greenbank Way
GU15: Camb ... 4B 70
Greenbush La. GU6: Cranl ... 9A 156
Green Bus. Cen., The
TW18: Stain ... 5E 20
Green Cl. SM5: Cars ... 8D 44
TW13: Hanw ... 6M 23
Green Ct. TW16: Sunb ... 7G 23
Greencourt Av. CR0: Croy ... 8E 46
Greencourt Gdns.
CR0: Croy ... 7E 46
Green Cft. GU9: B Lea ... 6N 109
RG40: W'ham ... 9D 14
Greencroft GU1: Guil ... 3D 114
GU14: Farnb ... 1N 89
Greencroft Rd. TW5: Hest ... 4N 9
GREEN CROSS ... 9M 149
Green Cross La.
GU10: Churt ... 9M 149
Green Curve SM7: Ban ... 1L 81
Green Dene KT24: E Hor ... 4D 116
Green Dragon La.
TW8: Brent ... 1L 11
Green Dragons Airsports ... 7L 85
Green Dr. GU23: Rip ... 1H 95
RG40: W'ham ... 4D 30
SL3: Lang ... 1A 6
(not continuous)
Greene Fielde End
TW18: Stain ... 8M 21
Green End GU46: Yate ... 8C 48
KT9: Ches ... 1L 59
Greener Ct. *CR0: Croy ... 5M 45*
(off Goodman Ct.)
Green Farm Rd. GU19: Bag ... 4K 51
Greenfield GU9: Farnh ... 4F 128
TN8: Eden ... 2M 147
Greenfield Av. KT5: Surb ... 6A 42
Greenfield Ho. SW19 ... 2J 27
TW20: Eng G ... 7L 19
(off Kings La.)
Greenfield Link CR5: Coul ... 2J 83
Greenfield Rd. GU9: Farnh ... 4E 128
RH13: Slin ... 5L 195
Greenfields Cl. RH6: Horl ... 6C 142
RH12: Hors ... 2N 197
Greenfields Pl.
RH5: B Grn ... 7K 139
Greenfields Rd. RH6: Horl ... 6D 142
RH12: Hors ... 3N 197
Greenfields Way
RH12: Hors ... 2N 197
Greenfield Way RG45: Crow ... 9F 30
Green Finch Cl.
RG45: Crow ... 1E 48
Greenfinch Cl. GU47: Owls ... 7J 49
Greenfinch Way
RH12: Hors ... 1J 197
Greenford Rd. SM1: Sut ... 1N 61
(not continuous)
Green Gables GU14: Cove ... 6L 69
Green Gdns. BR6: Farnb ... 2L 67
Green Glades GU52: C Cro ... 8A 88
Greenham Ho. TW7: Isle ... 6D 10
Greenham Wlk. GU21: Wok ... 5M 73
Greenham Wood
RG12: Brac ... 5A 32
Greenhanger GU10: Churt ... 1M 169
Greenhaven GU46: Yate ... 1A 68
Greenhayes Av. SM7: Ban ... 1M 81
Greenhayes Cl. RH2: Reig ... 3A 122
Greenhayes Gdns.
SM7: Ban ... 2M 81
Green Hedges TW1: Twick ... 8J 11
Green Hedges Av.
RH19: E Grin ... 8N 165
Green Hedges Cl.
RH19: E Grin ... 8N 165
Greenheys Pl. GU22: Wok ... 5B 74
Green Hill BR6: Dow ... 8H 67
Greenhill SM1: Sut ... 8A 44
Greenhill Av. CR3: Cate ... 8E 84
Green Hill Cl. GU15: Camb ... 9G 51
Greenhill Cl. GU7: Goda ... 8G 133
GU9: Farnh ... 4F 128
Greenhill Gdns. GU4: Guil ... 1E 114
Green Hill La. CR6: Warl ... 4H 85
Green Hill Rd. GU15: Camb ... 9G 51
Greenhill Rd. GU9: Farnh ... 4J 129
Greenhills GU9: Farnh ... 3K 129
Greenhill Way GU9: Farnh ... 5F 128
Greenholme GU15: Camb ... 1H 71
Greenhow RG12: Brac ... 2M 31
Greenhurst La. RH8: Oxt ... 1B 126
Greenhurst Rd. SE27 ... 6L 29
Greening Wood
GU26: Hind ... 4D 170
Greenlake Ter. TW18: Stain ... 8J 21
Greenlands KT16: Chert ... 9E 36
KT19: Ewe ... 2A 60
Greenlands Rd.
GU15: Camb ... 5N 69
KT13: Weybr ... 9C 38
TW18: Stain ... 5J 21
Greenland Way CR0: Bedd ... 6H 45
Green La. CR3: Cate ... 9N 83
CR5: Coul ... 4L 101
CR6: Warl ... 3H 85
CR7: T Hea ... 8K 29
CR8: Pur ... 7G 63
GU1: Guil ... 3D 114
GU3: Wood V ... 1D 112
GU4: W Cla ... 5J 95
GU5: Sha G ... 5H 135
GU6: Alf ... 5H 175
GU7: Goda ... 2G 133
GU8: Mil ... 2B 152
GU9: B Lea, Weybo ... 6L 109
GU9: Farnh ... 3F 128
GU10: Churt ... 1L 169
GU10: Dock ... 4D 148
GU10: Til ... 5B 130
GU17: B'water ... 2G 69
GU17: Haw ... 2K 69
GU19: Bag ... 9F 32
(Bagshot Rd.)
GU19: Bag ... 5K 51
(Whitmoor Rd.)
GU22: Wok ... 8L 73
GU23: Ockh ... 2C 96
GU24: Chob ... 6J 53
GU27: Hasl ... 4F 188
GU46: Yate ... 9A 48
GU47: Sandh ... 8H 49
KT3: N Mal ... 4B 42
KT4: W Pk ... 7F 42
KT8: W Mole ... 4B 40
KT9: Ches ... 5K 59
KT11: Cob ... 8M 57
KT12: Hers ... 3J 57
KT14: Byf ... 8A 56
KT15: Addl ... 8G 36
KT16: Chert ... 8G 36
KT20: Lwr K ... 4L 101
KT21: A'tead ... 4J 79
KT22: Leat ... 8K 79
(not continuous)
RG40: W'ham ... 6F 14
RH1: Blet ... 9B 104
RH1: Out ... 1J 143
RH1: Red ... 1C 122
(Carlton Rd.)
RH1: Red ... 8E 122
(Spencer's Way)
RH2: Leigh ... 3D 140
RH2: Reig ... 3L 121
RH5: B Grn ... 1H 159
RH5: Newd ... 2C 160
RH5: Ockl ... 7M 157
RH6: S Bri ... 3K 163
RH7: Ling ... 8M 145
RH10: Craw ... 1C 182
RH10: Craw D ... 6C 164
RH10: Wor ... 3H 183
RH12: Hors ... 5L 179
SL3: Dat ... 4L 5
SL4: W'sor ... 5D 4
SL5: Asc ... 9B 18
SM4: Mord ... 5M 43
(Central Rd.)
SM4: Mord ... 6H 43
(Lwr. Morden La.)
SW16 ... 8K 29
TW4: Houn ... 6J 9
TW13: Hanw ... 6M 23
TW16: Sunb ... 8G 22
TW17: Shep ... 5D 38
TW18: Stain ... 9G 20
TW20: Egh ... 5D 20
(Avenue, The)
TW20: Egh ... 6D 20
(Vicarage Dr.)
TW20: Thor ... 1E 36
Green La. Av. KT12: Hers ... 2K 57
Green La. Cvn. Pk.
RH1: Salf ... 1J 143
Green La. Cl. GU15: Camb ... 8A 50
KT14: Byf ... 8A 56
KT16: Chert ... 8G 36
Green La. Cotts.
GU9: B Lea ... 7L 109
GU10: Churt ... 9L 149
Green La. E. GU3: Flex ... 4K 111
(not continuous)
Green La. Gdns.
CR7: T Hea ... 1N 45
Green Lanes KT19: Ewe ... 5D 60
(not continuous)
Green La. W. GU12: A Grn ... 4J 111
KT24: W Hors ... 3B 96
Greenlaw Gdns. KT3: N Mal ... 6E 42
Green Lawn La. TW8 ... 1K 11
Green Leaf Av. SM6: Bedd ... 1H 63
Greenleaf Cl. SW2 ... 1L 29
Greenlea Pk. SW19 ... 8B 28
Green Leas KT1: K Tham ... 5K 203
TW16: Sunb ... 7G 23
Greenleas GU16: Frim ... 4C 70
Green Leas Cl. TW16: Sunb ... 7G 23
Greenleas Cl. GU46: Yate ... 8B 48
Greenleaves Ct.
TW15: A'ford ... 7C 22
Green Leys GU52: C Cro ... 9A 88
Green Line Wlk. TW9: Kew ... 4A 12
Green Man La. TW14: Felt ... 7H 9
(not continuous)
Green Mead KT10: Esh ... 3N 57

Greenmead Cl.—Gunton Rd.

Greenmead Cl. SE25 . . . . .4D 46
Greenmeads GU22: Wok 9A 74
Greenoak Ri. TN16: B Hil 5E 86
Green Oaks UB2: S'hall 1L 9
Greenoak Way SW19 . . . . .5J 27
Greenock Rd. SW16 . . . . .9H 29
Greeno Cres. TW17: Shep 4B 38
Green Pde. TW3: Houn 8B 10
Green Pk. TW18: Stain 4G 20
Green Ride RG12: Brac 6D 32
Green Rd. GU23: Ockh 2D 96
TW20: Thor 3C 36
Greensand Cl. RH1: Mers 6H 103
Green Sand Rd. RH1: Red . . .2E 122
Greens Health & Fitness
Purley 3L 63
Greenside RG45: Crow 2E 48
Greenside Cl. GU4: Guil 1E 114
Greenside Cotts. GU23: Rip . . .8L 75
Greenside Dr. KT21: A'tead 5H 79
Greenside Rd. CR0: Croy 6L 45
Greenside Wlk. TN16: B Hil . . .5D 86
Greenslade Av.
KT21: A'tead 6A 80
Greens La. RH5: Newd 3N 159
RH13: M Hea 9C 198
Green's School La.
GU14: Farnb 1M 89
(not continuous)
Greenstead Gdns.
SW15 . . . . .8G 12
Greenstede Av.
RH19: E Grin 7B 166
Green St. TW16: Sunb 9H 23
GREEN STREET GREEN 3N 67
Greenvale Rd. GU21: Knap 5G 73
Green Vw. KT9: Ches 4M 59
RH9: Gods 9E 104
Green Vw., The
RH11: P Pot 1N 199
Greenview Av. BR3: Beck 5H 47
CR0: Croy 5H 47
Greenview Ct. TW15: A'ford . . .5A 22
Green Wlk. RH10: Craw 1C 182
TW12: Hamp 7N 23
UB2: S'hall 1A 10
Green Wlk., The
GU51: Fleet 1A 88
Green Way GU12: Alde 1C 110
RH1: Red 1C 122
SM6: W'ton 1G 62
TW16: Sunb 3H 39
Greenway KT23: Book 1B 98
RH12: Hors 5H 197
SW20 . . . . .3H 43
TN16: Tats 7E 86
Greenway, The KT18: Eps 1N 79
RH8: Oxt 2D 126
TW4: Houn 7N 9
Greenway Cl. KT14: W By 9J 55
Greenway Dr. TW18: Stain 9M 21
Greenway Gdns. CR0: Croy 9J 47
Greenways BR3: Beck 2K 47
GU47: Sandh 6G 49
GU52: Fleet 7A 88
KT10: H Wood 1E 58
KT20: Wal H 3G 100
TW20: Egh 6A 20
Greenways, The
TW1: Twick 9G 11
Greenways Dr. SL5: S'dale 7B 34
Greenways Wlk.
RH11: Craw 8A 182
Greenwell Cl. RH9: Gods 8E 104
Greenwich Cl. RH11: Craw . . .7A 182
Greenwood SL5: Asc 9G 17
Greenwood, The GU1: Guil . . .2C 114
Greenwood Bus. Cen.
CR0: Croy 6C 46
Greenwood Cl. KT7: T Dit 7G 41
KT15: Wood 7H 55
SM4: Mord 3K 43
Greenwood Cotts.
SL5: S'dale 5F 34
Greenwood Ct.
RH11: Craw 8N 181
Greenwood Dr. RH1: Red 8E 122
Greenwood Gdns.
CR3: Cate 3D 104
RH8: Oxt 3C 126
Greenwood La.
TW12: H Hill 6B 24
Greenwood Pk.
KT2: K Tham 8D 26
Greenwood Rd. CR0: Croy 6M 45
CR4: Mit 2H 45
GU21: Wok 7H 73
GU24: B'wood 8M 71
KT7: T Dit 7G 41
RG45: Crow 1F 48
TW7: Isle 6F 10
Green Wrythe Cres.
SM5: Cars 7C 44
Green Wrythe La.
SM5: Cars 5B 44
Gregory Cl. GU21: Wok 4M 73
RH10: Craw 7G 182
Gregory Dr. SL4: O Win 9L 5
Gregsons RH12: Warn 9E 178
Grenaby Av. CR0: Croy 6A 46
Grenaby Rd. CR0: Croy 6A 46
Grenadier Pl. CR3: Cate 9N 83
Grenadier Rd. GU12: A Va 9F 90
Grenadiers Way
GU14: Cove 2H 89
Grena Gdns. TW9: Rich 7M 11
Grena Rd. TW9: Rich 7M 11
Grendon Cl. RH6: Horl 6D 142
Grenehurst Pk. RH5: Cap 6H 159
Grenfell Rd. CR4: Mit 7D 28
Grennell Cl. SM1: Sut 8B 44
Grennell Rd. SM1: Sut 8A 44
Grenside Rd. KT13: Weybr 9C 38
Grenville Cl. KT5: Surb 7B 42
KT11: Cob 9L 57
Grenville Gdns.
GU16: Frim G 8C 70
Grenville M. TW12: H Hill 6B 24
Grenville Pl. RG12: Brac 1A 32
(off The Ring)
Grenville Rd. CR0: N Add 5M 65
GU8: S'ford 4A 132
Gresham Av. CR6: Warl 5H 85
Gresham Ct. RH8: Oxt 7B 106
Gresham Ct. CR8: Pur 7L 63
GU15: Camb 2D 70
TW18: Stain 6J 21
Gresham Ind. Est.
GU12: Alde 2C 110
Gresham Pl. RH8: Oxt 7B 106
Gresham Rd. BR3: Beck 1H 47
RH8: Oxt 6B 106
SE25 . . . . .3D 46
TW3: Houn 4C 10
TW12: Hamp 7A 24
TW18: Stain 6H 21
Greshams Way TN8: Eden 1J 147
Gresham Wlk. RH10: Craw . . .6C 182
(not continuous)
Gresham Way GU16: Frim G . . .8C 70
SW19 . . . . .4N 27
Gresham Way Ind. Est.
SW19 . . . . .4N 27
(off Gresham Way)
Gressenhall Rd. SW18 . . . . . . .9L 13
Greswell St. SW6 . . . . .4J 13
Greta Bank KT24: W Hors 4D 96
Greville Av. CR2: Sels 6G 64
Greville Cl. GU2: Guil 3H 113
GU11: Alde 1M 109
KT21: A'tead 6L 79
TW1: Twick 1H 25
Greville Ct. KT21: A'tead 5L 79
(off Park Rd.)
KT21: A'tead 5L 79
(Greville Pk. Rd.)
KT23: Book 3B 98
Greville Pk. Av.
KT21: A'tead 5L 79
Greville Pk. Rd.
KT21: A'tead 5L 79
Greville Rd. TW10: Rich 9M 11
Grey Alders SM7: Ban 1H 81
Greybury La. TN8: M Grn 9K 147
Greyfields Cl. CR8: Pur 9M 63
Greyfriars Dr. GU24: Bis 2D 72
SL5: Asc 4M 33
Greyfriars Rd. GU23: Rip 2J 95
Greyhound Cl. GU12: Ash 3D 110
Greyhound La. SW16 . . . . .7H 29
Greyhound Mans. W6 . . . . .2K 13
(off Greyhound Rd.)
Greyhound Rd. SM1: Sut 2A 62
W6 . . . . .2J 13
W14 . . . . .2K 13
Greyhound Slip
RH10: Craw 2H 183
Greyhound Ter. SW16 . . . . .9G 29
Greylees GU7: Goda 6H 133
Greys Ct. GU11: Alde 2K 109
Greys Pk. Cl. BR2: Kes 2F 66
Greystead Pk. GU10: Wrec . . .6D 128
Greystock Rd. RG42: Warf 7B 16
Greystoke Ct. RG45: Crow 3F 48
Greystone Cl. CR2: Sels 7F 64
Greystones Cl. RH1: Red 5B 122
Greystones Dr. RH2: Reig 1A 122
Greyswood St. SW16 . . . . .7F 28
Greythorne Rd. GU21: Wok 5K 73
Greywaters GU5: Braml 5C 134
Grice Av. TN16: B Hil 9D 66
Grier Cl. RH11: Ifi 4K 181
Grierson Ho. SW16 . . . . .5G 29
Grieve Cl. GU10: Tong 5C 110
Griffin Cen. TW14: Felt 8J 9
Griffin Cen., The
KT1: K Tham 4H 203
Griffin Ct. KT21: A'tead 6M 79
KT23: Book 4B 98
TW8: Brent 2L 11
W4 . . . . .1E 12
Griffin Ho. W6 . . . . .1J 13
(off Hammersmith Rd.)
Griffin Pk. 2K 11
Griffin Way KT23: Book 4A 98
TW16: Sunb 1H 39
Griffiths Cl. KT4: W Pk 8G 43
Griffiths Rd. SW19 . . . . .8M 27
Griffits Path RH18: F Row 7G 187
Griffon Cl. GU14: Cove 2J 89
Griggs Mdw. GU8: Duns 2B 174
Grimston Rd. SW6 . . . . .5L 13
Grimwade Av. CR0: Croy 9D 46
Grimwood Rd. TW1: Twick 1F 24
Grindall Cl.
CR0: Wad 7A 200 (1M 63)
Grindley Gdns. CR0: Croy 5C 46
Grindstone Cres.
GU21: Knap 5E 72
GRINDSTONE HANDLE CORNER
. . . . .5E 72
Grinstead La.
RH19: F Row 8L 185
Grisedale Cl. CR8: Pur 1B 84
RH11: Craw 5A 182
Grisedale Gdns. CR8: Pur 1B 84
Grobars Av. GU21: Wok 2M 73
Grogan Cl. TW12: Hamp 7N 23
Groombridge Cl. KT12: Hers . . .2J 57
Groombridge Way
RH12: Hors 7F 196
Groom Cres. SW18 . . . . .1B 28
Groomfield Cl. SW17 . . . . .5E 28
Grooms, The RH10: Craw 1H 183
Groom Wlk. GU1: Guil 9A 94
Grosse Way SW15 . . . . .9G 13
Grosvenor Av. SM5: Cars 3D 62
SW14 . . . . .6D 12
TW10: Rich 8L 11
Grosvenor Cl. RH6: Horl 1E 162
Grosvenor Ct. GU4: B'ham 9D 94
GU17: Haw 3J 69
RH19: E Grin 9N 165
(off Grosvenor Rd.)
SM2: Sut 3N 61
SM4: Mord 3M 43
TW11: Tedd 7G 25
Grosvenor Gdns.
KT2: K Tham 7K 25
SM6: W'ton 4G 62
SW14 . . . . .6D 12
Grosvenor Hill SW19 . . . . .7K 27
Grosvenor Ho. GU1: Guil 4B 114
SM1: Sut 2N 61
Grosvenor M. RH2: Reig 6N 121
Grosvenor Pl. GU21: Wok 4B 74
(off Burleigh Gdns.)
KT13: Weybr 9E 38
Grosvenor Rd. BR4: W Wick . . .7L 47
GU7: Goda 8H 133
GU11: Alde 2M 109
GU24: Chob 9G 52
KT18: Eps D 6C 80
RH19: E Grin 9N 165
SE25 . . . . .3C 46
SM6: W'ton 3F 62
TW1: Twick 2G 24
TW3: Houn 6N 9
TW8: Brent 2K 11
TW10: Rich 8L 11
TW18: Stain 8J 21
W4 . . . . .1A 12
Groton Rd. SW18 . . . . .3N 27
Grotto Rd. KT13: Weybr 9C 38
TW1: Twick 3F 24
Grouse Mdws. RG12: Brac 3J 31
Grouse Rd.
RH11: Col, P Pot 3K 199
RH13: P Pla, Col 9E 198
Grove, The BR4: W Wick 9L 47
CR3: Cate 8N 83
CR5: Coul 2H 83
GU11: Alde 3M 109
GU14: Farnb 4B 90
GU16: Frim 5B 70
GU21: Wok 3B 74
KT12: Wal T 6J 39
KT15: Addl 2K 55
KT17: Eps 7M 201 (9D 60)
KT17: Ewe 6E 60
RH6: Horl 9F 142
RH11: Craw 3A 182
SL5: Asc 9G 17
TN16: B Hil 5F 86
TW1: Twick 9H 11
TW7: Isle 4E 10
TW11: Tedd 5G 24
TW20: Egh 6C 20
Grove Av.
KT17: Eps 6M 201 (9D 60)
SM1: Sut 3M 61
TW1: Twick 2F 24
Grovebarns TW18: Stain 7J 21
Grovebell Ind. Est.
GU10: Wrec 4E 128
Grove Cl. GU6: Cranl 9A 156
KT1: K Tham 7L 203 (3M 41)
KT19: Eps 6N 59
RG40: W'ham 9D 30
SL4: O Win 1L 19
TW13: Hanw 5M 23
Grove Cnr. KT23: Book 4B 98
Grove Cotts. W4 . . . . .2D 12
Grove Ct. KT1: K Tham 6J 203
KT8: E Mol 3D 40
TW3: Houn 7A 10
TW20: Egh 6C 20
Grove Cres.
KT1: K Tham 6J 203 (2L 41)
KT12: Wal T 6J 39
TW13: Hanw 5M 23
Grove Cross Rd. GU16: Frim . . .5B 70
Grove End GU19: Bag 3K 51
Grove End La. KT10: Esh 7D 40
Grove End Rd. GU9: Farnh 4G 128
Grove Farm Pk. GU16: Mytc . . .4D 90
Grovefields Av. GU16: Frim 5B 70
Grove Footpath
KT5: Surb 8K 203 (3L 41)
Grove Gdns. TW10: Rich 9M 11
TW11: Tedd 5G 24
GROVE HEATH 1K 95
Grove Heath Ct. GU23: Rip 2L 95
Grove Heath Nth.
GU23: Rip 9K 75
Grove Heath Rd.
GU23: Rip 1K 95
Grovehill Rd. RH1: Red 3D 122
Grove Ho. RH1: Red 3D 122
(off Huntingdon Rd.)
Groveland Av. SW16 . . . . .8K 29
Groveland Rd. BR3: Beck 2J 47
Grovelands GU10: L Bou 4K 129
KT1: K Tham 8H 203
KT8: W Mole 3A 40
RH6: Horl 9F 142
Grovelands Rd. CR8: Pur 8J 63
Groveland Way KT3: N Mal 4B 42
Grove La. CR5: Ban, Coul 8D 62
(not continuous)
KT1: K Tham 7K 203 (3L 41)
RG42: Wink R 6F 16
Groveley Rd. TW13: Felt 6G 22
TW16: Sunb 6G 22
Grove Mill Pl. SM5: Cars 9E 44
GROVE PARK 4B 12
Grove Pk. Bri. W4 . . . . .3B 12
Grove Pk. Gdns. W4 . . . . .3A 12
Grove Pk. M. W4 . . . . .3B 12
Grove Pk. Rd. W4 . . . . .3A 12
Grove Pk. Ter. W4 . . . . .3A 12
(not continuous)
Grove Pl. KT13: Weybr 2D 56
SW12 . . . . .1F 28
Grove Rd. CR4: Mit 2E 44
(not continuous)
CR7: T Hea 3L 45
GU1: Guil 3E 114
GU6: Cranl 9A 156
GU7: Goda 8F 132
GU12: A Va 9E 90
GU15: Camb 1D 70
GU21: Wok 3B 74
GU26: Hind 3N 169
GU52: C Cro 8C 88
KT6: Surb 8G 203 (4K 41)
KT8: E Mol 3D 40
KT16: Chert 5H 37
KT17: Eps 7M 201 (9D 60)
KT21: A'tead 5M 79
RH1: Red 3D 122
RH6: Horl 7C 142
RH7: Ling 6A 146
RH8: Tand 2M 125
SL4: W'sor 5F 4
SM1: Sut 3M 61
SW13 . . . . .5E 12
SW19 . . . . .8A 28
TN16: Tats 7E 86
TW2: Twick 4D 24
TW3: Houn 7A 10
TW7: Isle 4E 10
TW8: Brent 1J 11
TW10: Rich 9M 11
TW17: Shep 5D 38
Grovers Farm Cotts.
KT15: Wood 7G 55
Grovers Gdns. GU26: Hind . . .3B 170
Grover's Mnr. GU26: Hind . . .3B 170
Grove Shaw KT20: K'wood . . .2K 101
Groveside KT23: Book 4A 98
Groveside Cl. KT23: Book 5A 98
SM5: Cars 8C 44
Grovestile Waye
TW14: Bedf 1E 22
Grove Ter. TW11: Tedd 5G 24
Grove Way KT10: Esh 6C 40
Grovewood TW9: Kew 4N 11
Grove Wood Hill CR5: Coul . . .1G 83
Grub St. RH8: Limp 6E 106
Guardian Ct. GU8: Els 8G 131
Guards Av. CR3: Cate 9N 83
Guards Ct. SL5: S'dale 6E 34
Guards Rd. SL4: W'sor 5A 4
Guards Wlk. SL4: W'sor 5A 4
Guards Way CR3: Cate 9N 83
Guerdon Pl. RG12: Brac 6B 32
Guernsey Cl. GU4: B'ham 7C 94
RH11: Craw 7M 181
TW5: Hest 3A 10
Guernsey Dr. GU51: Fleet 1C 88
Guernsey Farm Dr.
GU21: Wok 2N 73
Guernsey Gro. SE24 . . . . .1N 29
Guildables La. TN8: Eden 4G 127
Guildcroft GU1: Guil 3C 114
Guildersfield Rd. SW16 . . . . . . .8J 29
GUILDFORD 6C 202 (3K 113)
Guildford & Godalming By-Pass Rd.
GU2: Guil 9D 112
GU3: Comp 9D 112
GU8: Mil 1B 152
GU8: P Har 7B 132
Guildford Av. TW13: Felt 3G 23
Guildford Boat House
. . . . .7C 202 (5N 113)
Guildford Bus. Pk. GU2: Guil . .2L 113
Guildford Bus. Pk. Rd.
GU2: Guil 2L 113
Guildford Castle . . .6C 202 (5N 113)
Guildford Cathedral 3K 113
Guildford Ct. GU2: Guil 3K 113
Guildford Crematorium
GU7: Goda 3L 133
Guildford Ind. Est.
GU2: Guil 3K 113
Guildford La. GU5: Alb 6G 115
GU22: Wok 6N 73
Guildford Lido 1D 202 (2N 113)
Guildford Lodge Dr.
KT24: E Hor 7G 96
Guildford Mus. . . .6C 202 (5N 113)
GUILDFORD PARK 4L 113
Guildford Pk. Av.
GU2: Guil 4A 202 (4L 113)
Guildford Pk. Rd.
GU2: Guil 5A 202 (4L 113)
Guildford Rd. CR0: Croy 5A 46
GU3: Norm 1K 111
GU3: Worp 1C 92
GU4: Sut G 5N 93
GU5: Sha G 6F 134
(Northcote La.)
GU5: Sha G 1J 155
(Up. House La.)
GU6: Alf 3J 175
GU6: Alf, Rudg 7K 175
GU6: Cranl 1J 155
GU7: Goda 4K 133
GU9: Farnh 9J 109
GU10: Farnh, Run 8L 109
GU12: Alde 5B 110
GU12: Ash 1G 110
GU16: Deep, Frim G 8D 70
GU18: Ligh 6L 51
GU19: Bag, Ligh 4J 51
(not continuous)
GU21: Knap 8B 52
GU21: Wok 7D 54
GU22: Wok 9N 73
(Westfield Rd.)
GU22: Wok 6A 74
(Wych Hill La.)
GU24: Bis, W End 8B 52
GU24: Chob 1G 73
GU24: Pirb 1C 92
GU51: Fleet 5D 88
KT16: Otter, Chert 2E 54
KT22: Fetc 3D 98
KT23: Book 5M 97
KT24: E Hor, Eff 7G 96
RH4: Westc 7A 118
RH5: A Ham, Wott 9G 116
RH12: Hors 5F 196
RH12: Rudg 7K 175
RH12: Slin, Bro H 1L 195
RH13: Rudg, Slin 1H 195
RH14: Loxw 3H 193
Guildford Rd. E.
GU14: Farnb 4A 90
Guildford Rd. W.
GU14: Farnb 4A 90
Guildford Spectrum Bowl
. . . . .1F 202 (1A 114)
Guildford Station (Rail)
. . . . .5A 202 (4M 113)
Guildford St. KT16: Chert 6H 37
TW18: Stain 7J 21
Guildford Way SM6: W'ton 2J 63
Guildhall & Guildford House Gallery
. . . . .5D 202 (4N 113)
Guildown Av.
GU2: Guil 8A 202 (6L 113)
Guildown Rd.
GU2: Guil 8A 202 (6L 113)
Guildway, The GU3: Art 9M 113
Guileshill La. GU23: Ockh 1N 95
Guilford Av.
KT5: Surb 8L 203 (4M 41)
Guillemont Flds.
GU14: Cove 9J 69
Guillemont Pk. GU17: Min 8H 69
Guillemot Path RH11: Ifi 4J 181
Guinea Wlk. RG12: Brac 3J 31
Guinevere Rd. RH11: Ifi 3K 181
Guinness Ct. CR0: Croy 8C 46
GU21: Wok 5J 73
RH11: Craw 7A 182
Guinness Trust Bldgs. W6 . . . . .1J 13
(off Fulham Pal. Rd.)
Guion Rd. SW6 . . . . .5L 13
Gumbrells Cl. GU3: Worp 8F 92
Gumley Gdns. TW7: Isle 6G 10
Gun Hill GU11: Alde 1N 109
Gunnell Cl. CR0: Croy 5C 46
SE25 . . . . .5D 46
(off Backley Gdns.)
GUNNERSBURY 1A 12
Gunnersbury Av. W4 . . . . .1N 11
Gunnersbury Cl. W4 . . . . .1A 12
Gunnersbury M. W4 . . . . .1A 12
Gunnersbury Station (Rail & Tube)
. . . . .1A 12
Gunnersbury Triangle
Nature Reserve 1B 12
Gunners Rd. SW18 . . . . .3B 28
Gunning Cl. RH11: Craw 6M 181
Gun Pit Rd. RH7: Ling 7N 145
Gunter Gro. SW10 . . . . .2N 13
Gunter Hall Studios SW10 . . . . .2N 13
(off Gunter Gro.)
Gunters Mead KT10: Oxs 7C 58
(not continuous)
Gunterstone Rd. W14 . . . . .1K 13
Gunton Rd. SW17 . . . . .7E 28

Gurdon's La. GU8: Worm ... 9B 152
(not continuous)
Gurney Cres. CR0: Croy ... 7K 45
Gurney Ho. UB3: Harl ... 1F 8
Gurney Rd. SM5: Cars ... 1E 62
Gurney's Cl. RH1: Red ... 4D 122
Guyatt Gdns. CR4: Mit ... 1E 44
Guy Rd. SM6: Bedd ... 9H 45
Gwalior Rd. SW15 ... 7J 13
Gwendolen Av. SW15 ... 7J 13
Gwendolen Cl. SW15 ... 8J 13
Gwendolen Ho. *TW19: Stan* ... *2N 21*
(off Yeoman Dr.)
Gwendwr Rd. W14 ... 1K 13
Gwydor Rd. BR3: Beck ... 2G 47
Gwyn Cl. SW6 ... 3N 13
Gwynne Av. CR0: Croy ... 6G 46
Gwynne Cl. SL4: W'sor ... 4B 4
W4 ... 2E 12
Gwynne Ct. *GU2: Guil* ... *8L 93*
(off Grange Rd.)
Gwynne Gdns.
RH19: E Grin ... 8M 165
Gwynne Rd. CR3: Cate ... 1A 104

H

Habershon Dr. GU16: Frim ... 4H 71
Haccombe Rd. SW19 ... 7A 28
HACKBRIDGE ... 7E 44
Hackbridge Grn.
SM6: W'ton ... 8E 44
Hackbridge Pk. Gdns.
SM5: Cars ... 8D 44
Hackbridge Rd. SM6: W'ton ... 8E 44
Hackbridge Station (Rail) ... 8F 44
Hackenden Cl.
RH19: E Grin ... 7A 166
Hackenden Cotts.
RH19: E Grin ... 7A 166
Hackenden La.
RH19: E Grin ... 8A 166
Hacketts La. GU22: Pyr ... 1H 75
Hackhurst Down Nature Reserve
... 6F 116
Hackhurst La.
RH5: A Ham ... 8G 116
Haddenhurst Ct. RG42: Bin ... 7H 15
Haddon Cl. KT3: N Mal ... 4E 42
KT13: Weybr ... 9F 38
Haddon Rd. SM1: Sut ... 1N 61
(not continuous)
Hadfield Rd. TW19: Stan ... 9M 7
Hadleigh Cl. SW20 ... 1L 43
Hadleigh Dr. SM2: Sut ... 5M 61
Hadleigh Gdns.
GU16: Frim G ... 8C 70
Hadley Ct. *SL3: Poy* ... *4G 7*
(off Coleridge Cres.)
Hadley Gdns. UB2: S'hall ... 1N 9
W4 ... 1C 12
Hadley Pl. KT13: Weybr ... 4B 56
Hadley Rd. CR4: Mit ... 3H 45
Hadleys GU10: Rowl ... 8D 128
Hadley Wood Ri. CR8: Ken ... 1M 83
Hadmans Cl. RH12: Hors ... 7J 197
Hadrian Cl. TW19: Stan ... 1N 21
Hadrian Ct. SM2: Sut ... 4N 61
Hadrians GU9: Farnh ... 8K 109
Hadrian Way TW19: Stan ... 1M 21
(not continuous)
Haggard Rd. TW1: Twick ... 1H 25
Haigh Cres. RH1: Red ... 5F 122
Haig La. GU52: C Cro ... 8C 88
Haig Pl. SM4: Mord ... 5M 43
Haig Rd. GU12: Alde ... 3A 110
GU15: Camb ... 9L 49
TN16: B Hil ... 4G 86
Hailes Cl. SW19 ... 7A 28
Hailey Pl. GU6: Cranl ... 6A 156
Hailsham Av. SW2 ... 3K 29
Hailsham Cl. GU47: Owls ... 6J 49
KT6: Surb ... 6K 41
Hailsham Rd. SW17 ... 7E 28
Haines Ct. KT13: Weybr ... 2E 56
Haines Wlk. SM4: Mord ... 6N 43
Haining Cl. W4 ... 1N 11
Haining Gdns. GU16: Mytc ... 2E 90
Hainthorpe Rd. SE27 ... 4M 29
Halcyon *GU9: U Hal* ... *5F 108*
(off Lawday Link)
Haldane Pl. SW18 ... 2N 27
Haldane Rd. SW6 ... 3L 13
Haldon Rd. SW18 ... 9L 13
HALE ... 7J 109
Halebourne La.
GU24: Chob, W End ... 4D 52
Hale Cl. BR6: Farnb ... 1L 67
Hale End RG12: Brac ... 3D 32
Hale Ends GU22: Wok ... 8L 73
Hale Ho. Cl. GU10: Churt ... 9L 149
Hale Ho. La. GU10: Churt ... 9L 149
Hale Path SE27 ... 5M 29
Hale Pit Rd. KT23: Book ... 4C 98
Hale Pl. GU9: Hale ... 7K 109
Hale Reeds GU9: H End ... 6J 109
Hale Rd. GU9: Farnh, Hale ... 7J 109
Hales Fld. GU27: Hasl ... 2G 189
Hales Oak KT23: Book ... 4C 98
Halesowen Rd. SM4: Mord ... 6N 43
Hale St. TW18: Stain ... 5G 21
Haleswood KT11: Cob ... 1J 77
Hale Way GU16: Frim ... 6B 70
Halewood RG12: Brac ... 5L 31
Half Acre TW8: Brent ... 2K 11
Halfacres RH10: Craw ... 2C 182
Half Moon Cotts.
GU23: Rip ... 8L 75
Half Moon Hill GU27: Hasl ... 2G 189
Half Moon St. GU19: Bag ... 4J 51
Halford Rd. SW6 ... 2M 13
TW10: Rich ... 8L 11
Halfpenny Cl. GU4: Guil ... 9F 114
Halfpenny La. GU4: Guil ... 6E 114
SL5: S'dale ... 6D 34
Halfway Grn. KT12: Wal T ... 9J 39
Halfway La. GU7: Eash ... 7D 132
Haliburton Rd. TW1: Twick ... 8G 11
Halifax Cl. GU14: Cove ... 2L 89
RH10: Craw ... 9J 163
TW11: Tedd ... 7E 24
Halifax Rd. RG12: Brac ... 2A 32
Halimote Rd. GU11: Alde ... 3M 109
Haling Down Pas. CR8: Pur ... 6M 63
(not continuous)
Haling Gro. CR2: S Croy ... 4N 63
Haling Pk. Gdns.
CR2: S Croy ... 3M 63
Haling Pk. Rd.
CR2: S Croy ... 8A 200 (2M 63)
Haling Rd. CR2: S Croy ... 3A 64
Hallam Rd. GU7: Goda ... 5J 133
SW13 ... 6G 13
Halland Cl. RH10: Craw ... 2E 182
Halland Ct. *TN8: Eden* ... *2L 147*
(off Stangrove Rd.)
Hallane Ho. SE27 ... 6N 29
Hallbrooke Gdns.
RG42: Bin ... 8K 15
Hall Cl. GU7: Goda ... 4H 133
GU15: Camb ... 9C 50
Hall Ct. SL3: Dat ... 3L 5
TW11: Tedd ... 6F 24
Hall Dene Cl. GU1: Guil ... 2E 114
Hall Dr. GU52: Fleet ... 7C 88
Halley Cl. RH11: Craw ... 8N 181
Halley Dr. SL5: Asc ... 1H 33
Halley's App. GU21: Wok ... 4K 73
Halley's Ct. GU21: Wok ... 5K 73
Halley's Wlk. KT15: Addl ... 4L 55
Hall Farm Cres. GU46: Yate ... 1C 68
Hall Farm Dr. TW2: Whitt ... 1D 24
Hallgrove Bottom
GU19: Bag ... 2K 51
Hall Gro. Farm Ind. Est.
GU19: Bag ... 2K 51
Hall Hill RH8: Oxt ... 9N 105
Halliards, The KT12: Wal T ... 5H 39
Halliford Cl. TW17: Shep ... 3E 38
Halliford Rd. TW16: Sunb ... 4F 38
TW17: Shep ... 4F 38
Halliloo Valley Rd.
CR3: Wold ... 7G 85
Hallington Cl. GU21: Wok ... 4L 73
Hall La. GU46: Yate ... 1B 68
UB3: Harl ... 3E 8
Hallmark Cl. GU47: C Tow ... 7K 49
Hallmead Rd. SM1: Sut ... 9N 43
Hallowell Av. CR0: Bedd ... 1J 63
Hallowell Cl. CR4: Mit ... 2E 44
Hallowes Cl. GU2: Guil ... 7L 93
Hallowfield Way CR4: Mit ... 2B 44
Hallows Gro. TW16: Sunb ... 6G 23
HALL PLACE ... 1G 175
Hall Pl. GU21: Wok ... 3C 74
Hall Pl. Dr. KT13: Weybr ... 2F 56
Hall Rd. GU5: Braml ... 5B 134
SM6: W'ton ... 5F 62
TW7: Isle ... 8D 10
Halls Dr. RH12: Fay ... 8E 180
Halls Farm Cl. GU21: Knap ... 4G 73
Hallsland RH10: Craw D ... 1F 184
Hallsland Way RH8: Oxt ... 2B 126
Hall Way CR8: Pur ... 9M 63
Halnaker Wlk. RH11: Craw ... 6L 181
Halsford Cft. RH19: E Grin ... 7L 165
Halsford Grn.
RH19: E Grin ... 7L 165
Halsford La. RH19: E Grin ... 8L 165
Halsford Pk. Rd.
RH19: E Grin ... 8M 165
Halstead Cl.
CR0: Croy ... 4B 200 (9N 45)
Halters End GU26: G'hott ... 6M 169
Halton Rd. CR3: Cate ... 7B 84
HAM ... 4J 25
Ham, The TW8: Brent ... 3J 11
Hamble Av. GU17: B'water ... 1J 69
Hamble Cl. GU21: Wok ... 4K 73
Hambleden Ct. RG12: Brac ... 3C 32
HAMBLEDON ... 9F 152
Hambledon Gdns.
SE25 ... 2C 46
Hambledon Hill KT18: Eps ... 3B 80
Hambledon Pk.
GU8: Hamb ... 9E 152
Hambledon Pl. KT23: Book ... 1A 98
Hambledon Rd. CR3: Cate ... 1A 104
GU7: Bus ... 9J 133
(not continuous)
GU8: Bus, Hamb ... 7G 153
SW18 ... 1L 27
Hambledon Va. KT18: Eps ... 3B 80
Hamblehyrst BR3: Beck ... 1L 47
Hamble St. SW6 ... 6N 13
Hambleton Cl. GU16: Frim ... 3F 70
KT4: W Pk ... 8H 43
Hambleton Ct. RH11: Craw ... 5A 182
Hambleton Hill
RH11: Craw ... 5A 182
Hamble Wlk. GU21: Wok ... 5K 73
Hambridge Way SW2 ... 1L 29
Hambrook Rd. SE25 ... 2E 46
Hambro Rd. SW16 ... 7H 29
Ham Cl. TW10: Ham ... 4J 25
(not continuous)
Ham Comn. TW10: Ham ... 4K 25
Ham Cft. Cl. TW13: Felt ... 4H 23
Hamesmoor Rd.
GU16: Mytc ... 1C 90
Hamesmoor Way
GU16: Mytc ... 1D 90
Ham Farm Rd.
TW10: Ham ... 5K 25
Hamfield Cl. RH8: Oxt ... 5M 105
Ham Ga. Av. TW10: Ham ... 4K 25
Hamhaugh Island
TW17: Shep ... 8B 38
Ham House ... 2J 25
Hamilton Av. GU22: Pyr ... 2G 75
KT6: Surb ... 8N 41
KT11: Cob ... 9H 57
SM3: Chea ... 8K 43
Hamilton Cl. CR8: Pur ... 8M 63
GU2: Guil ... 7K 93
GU19: Bag ... 4J 51
GU35: Bor ... 5A 168
KT16: Chert ... 7H 37
KT19: Eps ... 8B 60
TW11: Tedd ... 7H 25
TW13: Felt ... 6G 22
Hamilton Ct. CR0: Croy ... 7D 46
KT11: Cob ... 9H 57
KT23: Book ... 3B 98
SW15 ... 6K 13
Hamilton Cres. TW3: Houn ... 8B 10
Hamilton Dr. GU2: Guil ... 7K 93
SL5: S'dale ... 6B 34
Hamilton Gdns.
GU14: Cove ... 9H 69
Hamilton Gordon Ct.
GU1: Guil ... 1B 202 (2M 113)
Hamilton Ho. W4 ... 2D 12
Hamilton M. *KT13: Weybr* ... *1B 56*
(off Holstein Av.)
SW18 ... 2M 27
SW19 ... 8M 27
Hamilton Pde. TW13: Felt ... 5G 23
Hamilton Pl. GU2: Guil ... 7K 93
GU11: Alde ... 3L 109
KT14: W By ... 9H 55
KT20: K'wood ... 9L 81
TW16: Sunb ... 8J 23
Hamilton Rd. CR7: T Hea ... 2A 46
GU52: C Cro ... 7C 88
RH12: Hors ... 5H 197
SW19 ... 8N 27
TW2: Twick ... 2E 24
TW8: Brent ... 2K 11
TW13: Felt ... 5G 22
Hamilton Rd. M.
SW19 ... 8N 27
Hamilton Way SM6: W'ton ... 5H 63
HAM ISLAND ... 7N 5
Ham Lands Nature Reserve
... 3G 25
Ham La. GU8: Els ... 7H 131
SL4: O Win ... 8M 5
TW20: Eng G ... 5L 19
Hamlash La. GU10: Fren ... 1H 149
Hamlet M. SE21 ... 2N 29
Hamlet St. RG42: Warf ... 9C 16
Hamlyn Ho. TW13: Felt ... 2H 23
Hamm Ct. KT13: Weybr ... 8N 37
HAMMER ... 3B 188
HAMMER BOTTOM ... 2A 188
Hammerfield Dr.
RH5: A Ham ... 1G 136
Hammer Hill GU27: Hasl ... 4A 188
Hammer La. GU6: Cranl ... 3M 175
GU10: Churt ... 1K 169
GU26: G'hott ... 1K 169
GU26: Hasl ... 9A 170
GU27: Lip ... 2A 188
Hammer Pond Cotts.
GU8: Thur ... 4K 151
Hammerpond Rd.
RH13: Hors, M Hea, Col
... 7M 197
RH13: P Pla ... 9E 198
Hammersley Rd.
GU11: Alde ... 6N 89
HAMMERSMITH ... 1H 13
Hammersmith Bri. W6 ... 1G 13
Hammersmith Bri. Rd.
W6 ... 1H 13
HAMMERSMITH BROADWAY
... 1H 13
Hammersmith B'way.
W6 ... 1H 13
Hammersmith Fitness &
Squash Cen. ... *1J 13*
(off Chalk Hill Rd.)
HAMMERSMITH FLYOVER ... 1H 13
Hammersmith Flyover
W6 ... 1H 13
Hammersmith Ind. Est.
W6 ... 2H 13
Hammersmith Rd. W6 ... 1J 13
W14 ... 1J 13
Hammersmith Station (Tube)
... 1H 13
Hammersmith Ter. W6 ... 1F 12
Hammer Va. GU27: Lip ... 2A 188
HAMMERWOOD ... 7K 167
Hammerwood Copse
GU27: Hasl ... 3B 188
Hammerwood Pk. ... 8L 167
Hammerwood Rd.
RH19: Ash W ... 3F 186
Hammer Yd. RH10: Craw ... 4B 182
Hamm Moor La. KT15: Addl ... 2N 55
Hammond Av. CR4: Mit ... 1F 44
Hammond Cl. GU21: Wok ... 2M 73
TW12: Hamp ... 9A 24
Hammond Ct. *RG42: Brac* ... *9M 15*
(off Crescent Rd.)
Hammond Rd. GU21: Wok ... 2M 73
RH11: Craw ... 9N 181
Hammond's Copse Nature Reserve
... 6D 140
Hammond Way GU18: Ligh ... 6M 51
HAM MOOR ... 1N 55
Hamond Cl. CR2: S Croy ... 5M 63
Hampden Av. BR3: Beck ... 1H 47
Hampden Cl. RH10: Craw ... 9J 163
Hampden Cres. RG12: Brac ... 2A 32
Hampden Rd. BR3: Beck ... 1H 47
KT1: K Tham ... 2N 41
Hampers Ct. RH13: Hors ... 6K 197
Hamper's La. RH13: Hors ... 6N 197
Hampshire Cl. GU12: Alde ... 5B 110
Hampshire Ct. KT15: Addl ... 2L 55
Hampshire Hog La.
W6 ... 1G 12
Hampshire Ri. RG42: Warf ... 7D 16
Hampshire Rd.
GU15: Camb ... 7D 50
Hampstead La. RH4: Dork ... 6F 118
Hampstead Rd.
RG40: W'ham ... 6F 30
RH4: Dork ... 6G 118
Hampstead Wlk.
RH11: Craw ... 7A 182
HAMPTON ... 9B 24
Hampton & Richmond Borough FC
... 9B 24
Hampton Cl. GU21: Knap ... 6F 72
GU52: C Cro ... 9B 88
SW20 ... 8H 27
HAMPTON COURT ... 3E 40
Hampton Court ... 1E 40
HAMPTON COURT ... 2E 40
Hampton Ct. Av. KT8: E Mol ... 5D 40
Hampton Ct. Bri.
KT8: E Mol ... 3E 40
Hampton Ct. Cres.
KT8: E Mol ... 2D 40
Hampton Ct. Est.
KT7: E Mol ... 3E 40
Hampton Ct. M. *KT8: E Mol* ... *3E 40*
(off Feltham Av.)
Hampton Court Palace ... 3F 40
Hampton Ct. Pde.
KT8: E Mol ... 3E 40
Hampton Ct. Rd. KT1: H Wic ... 2F 40
KT8: E Mol ... 2F 40
TW12: Hamp ... 1C 40
Hampton Court Station (Rail)
... 3E 40
Hampton Ct. Way KT7: T Dit ... 8E 40
KT8: E Mol ... 8E 40
Hampton Farm Ind. Est.
TW13: Hanw ... 4M 23
Hampton Gro. KT17: Ewe ... 7E 60
HAMPTON HILL ... 6C 24
Hampton Hill Bus. Pk.
TW12: H Hill ... *6C 24*
(off High St.)
Hampton Hill Playhouse Theatre
... 6C 24
Hampton La. TW13: Hanw ... 5M 23
Hampton Lodge RH6: Horl ... 9E 142
Hampton Open Air Pool ... 8C 24
Hampton Rd. CR0: Croy ... 5N 45
GU9: U Hal ... 6F 108
KT4: W Pk ... 8F 42
RH1: Red ... 8D 122
TW2: Twick ... 4D 24
TW11: Tedd ... 6D 24
TW12: Tedd ... 6D 24
Hampton Rd. E.
TW13: H Hill ... 5N 23
Hampton Rd. Ind. Pk.
CR0: Croy ... 5N 45
Hampton Rd. W.
TW13: Hanw ... 4M 23
Hampton Sport, Arts & Fitness Cen.
... 6A 24
Hampton Station (Rail) ... 9A 24
Hampton Way
RH19: E Grin ... 2B 186
HAMPTON WICK ... 2G 203 (9J 25)
Hampton Wick Station (Rail)
... 2G 203 (9J 25)
Hampton Youth Project (Sports Hall)
... 7N 23
Ham Ridings TW10: Ham ... 6M 25
HAMSEY GREEN ... 3E 84
Hamsey Grn. Gdns.
CR6: Warl ... 3E 84
Hamsey Way CR2: Sande ... 2E 84
Ham St. TW10: Ham ... 2H 25
Ham Vw. CR0: Croy ... 5H 47
Hanah Ct. SW19 ... 8J 27
Hanbury Dr. TN16: B Hil ... 9D 66
Hanbury Path GU21: Wok ... 1F 74
Hanbury Rd. RH11: Ifi ... 4K 181
Hanbury Way
GU15: Camb ... 3A 70
Hancocks Mt. SL5: S'hill ... 5A 34
Hancombe Rd.
GU47: Sandh ... 6F 48
Handcroft Rd.
CR0: Croy ... 1A 200 (6M 45)
HANDCROSS ... 8N 199
Handel Mans. SW13 ... 3H 13
Handford La. GU46: Yate ... 1C 68
Handinhand La.
KT20: Box H ... 8B 100
Handley Page Rd.
SM6: W'ton ... 4K 63
Handside Cl. KT4: W Pk ... 7J 43
Hanford Cl. SW18 ... 2M 27
Hanford Row SW19 ... 7H 27
Hanger, The GU35: Head ... 2D 168
Hanger Ct. GU21: Knap ... 4H 73
Hangerfield Cl. GU46: Yate ... 1B 68
Hanger Hill KT13: Weybr ... 3C 56
Hanging Wood Nature Reserve
... 6J 105
Hangrove Hill BR6: Dow ... 9K 67
Hankins Ct. GU52: Fleet ... 6B 88
Hanley Cl. SL4: W'sor ... 4A 4
Hannah Cl. BR3: Beck ... 2M 47
Hannah M. SM6: W'ton ... 4G 63
Hannah Peschar Sculpture Garden
... 8A 158
Hannay Wlk. SW16 ... 3H 29
Hannell Rd. SW6 ... 3K 13
Hannen Rd. SE27 ... 4M 29
Hannibal Rd. TW19: Stan ... 1M 21
Hannibal Way CR0: Wad ... 2K 63
Hanover Av. TW13: Felt ... 2H 23
Hanover Cl. GU16: Frim ... 5C 70
GU46: Yate ... 8C 48
RH1: Mers ... 6G 102
RH10: Craw ... 5D 182
(not continuous)
SL4: W'sor ... 4C 4
SM3: Chea ... 1K 61
TW9: Kew ... 3N 11
TW20: Eng G ... 7L 19
Hanover Ct. GU1: Guil ... 1N 113
GU22: Wok ... 6A 74
RH4: Dork ... 2G 201 (5F 118)
RH13: Hors ... 5M 197
SW15 ... 7E 12
Hanover Dr. GU51: Fleet ... 1D 88
Hanover Gdns. GU14: Cove ... 8K 69
RG12: Brac ... 6L 31
Hanover Pk. SL5: Asc ... 9K 17
Hanover Rd. SW19 ... 8A 28
Hanover St.
CR0: Croy ... 4A 200 (9M 45)
Hanover Ter. TW7: Isle ... 4G 11
Hanover Wlk. KT13: Weybr ... 9E 38
Hanover Way SL4: W'sor ... 5C 4
Hansler Ct. *SW19* ... *2K 27*
(off Princes Way)
Hansler Gro. KT8: E Mol ... 3D 40
Hanson Cl. GU4: B'ham ... 9B 94
GU15: Camb ... 8F 50
SW12 ... 1F 28
SW14 ... 6B 12
Hansworth Ho.
RH10: Craw ... *4B 182*
(off Brighton Rd.)
HANWORTH
RG12 ... 6M 31
TW13 ... 5L 23
Hanworth Cl. RG12: Brac ... 5A 32
Hanworth La. KT16: Chert ... 7H 37
Hanworth Rd. RG12: Brac ... 7M 31
RH1: Red ... 8D 122
TW3: Houn ... 9A 10
TW4: Houn ... 2M 23
TW12: Hamp ... 5N 23
TW13: Felt ... 2J 23
TW16: Sunb ... 8H 23
(not continuous)
Hanworth Ter. TW3: Houn ... 7B 10
Hanworth Trad. Est.
KT16: Chert ... 7H 37
TW13: Hanw ... 4M 23
Harberson Rd. SW12 ... 2F 28
Harbledown Rd.
CR2: Sande ... 7D 64
SW6 ... 4M 13
Harbord St. SW6 ... 4J 13
Harborough Rd.
SW16 ... 5K 29
Harbour Cl. GU14: Farnb ... 6M 69
Harbourfield Rd. SM7: Ban ... 2N 81
Harbridge Av. SW15 ... 1E 26
Harbury Rd. SM5: Cars ... 5C 62
Harcourt TW19: Wray ... 9A 6
Harcourt Av. SM6: W'ton ... 1F 62
Harcourt Cl. TW7: Isle ... 6G 11
TW20: Egh ... 7E 20
Harcourt Cotts. GU3: Put ... 8N 111
Harcourt Fld. SM6: W'ton ... 1F 62
Harcourt Lodge
SM6: W'ton ... 1F 62

Harcourt Rd.—Hawthorn Av.

Harcourt Rd. CR7: T Hea 5K **45**
GU15: Camb 1M **69**
RG12: Brac 5N **31**
SL4: W'sor 4B **4**
SM6: W'ton 1F **62**
SW19 8M **27**
Harcourt Ter. SW10 1N **13**
Harcourt Way RH9: S Gods 6H **125**
Hardcastle Cl. CR0: Croy 5D **46**
Hardcourts Cl. BR4: W Wick 9L **47**
Hardell Cl. TW20: Egh 6C **20**
Hardel Ri. SW2 2M **29**
Hardel Wlk. SW2 1L **29**
Harden Farm Cl. CR5: Coul 8G **83**
Hardham Cl. RH11: Craw 1M **181**
Harding Cl. CR0: Croy 9C **46**
Harding Ho. *SW13 2G 13*
(off Wyatt Dr.)
Harding Rd. KT18: Eps D 6D **80**
Harding's Cl.
KT2: K Tham 1L **203** (9M **25**)
Harding Spur SL3: Lang 2B **6**
Hardings Rd. GU10: B Oak 2A **148**
Hardman Rd.
KT2: K Tham 3K **203** (1L **41**)
Hardwell Way RG12: Brac 3C **32**
Hardwick Cl. KT22: Oxs 2C **78**
Hardwicke Av. TW5: Hest 4A **10**
Hardwicke Rd. RH2: Reig 2M **121**
TW10: Ham 5J **25**
Hardwick La. KT16: Lyne 6E **36**
Hardwick Pl. SW16 8G **29**
Hardwick Rd. RH1: Red 5B **122**
Hardwicks Way SW18 8M **13**
Hardy Av. GU46: Yate 2B **68**
Hardy Cl. RH5: Nth H 9H **119**
RH6: Horl 8C **142**
RH10: Craw 2G **182**
RH12: Hors 4H **197**
Hardy Grn. RG45: Crow 3G **49**
Hardy Ho. SW4 1G **29**
SW18 1N **27**
Hardy Rd. SW19 8N **27**
Hardy's M. KT8: E Mol 3E **40**
Harebell Hill KT11: Cob 1L **77**
Harecroft KT22: Fetc 2B **98**
RH4: Dork 8J **119**
Harefield KT10: H Wood 9E **40**
Harefield Av. SM2: Chea 5K **61**
Harefield Rd. SW16 8K **29**
Hare Hill KT15: Addl 3G **55**
Hare Hill Cl. GU22: Pyr 2J **75**
Harelands Cl. GU21: Wok 4M **73**
Harelands La. GU21: Wok 5M **73**
(not continuous)
Hare La. GU7: Goda 5J **133**
KT10: Clay 2D **58**
RH7: Ling 7F **144**
RH11: Craw 9N **161**
Harendon KT20: Tad 8H **81**
Hares Bank CR0: N Add 6N **65**
Harestone Dr. CR3: Cate 2C **104**
Harestone Hill CR3: Cate 4C **104**
Harestone La. CR3: Cate 3B **104**
(not continuous)
Harestone Valley Rd.
CR3: Cate 4B **104**
Hareward Rd. GU4: Guil 1E **114**
Harewood Cl. RH2: Reig 9A **102**
RH10: Craw 9E **162**
Harewood Gdns.
CR2: Sande 2E **84**
Harewood Rd. CR2: S Croy 3B **64**
SW19 7C **28**
TW7: Isle 3F **10**
Harfield Rd. TW16: Sunb 1L **39**
Harkness Cl. KT17: Eps D 3H **81**
Harkness Ct. *SM1: Sut 7N 43*
(off Cleeve Way)
Harland Av. CR0: Croy 9C **46**
Harland Cl. SW19 2N **43**
Harlands Gro. BR6: Farnb 1K **67**
Harlech Gdns. TW5: Hest 2K **9**
Harlech Rd. GU17: Haw 2J **69**
Harlequin Av. TW8: Brent 2G **11**
Harlequin Cl. TW7: Isle 8E **10**
Harlequin Rd. TW11: Tedd 8H **25**
Harlequins RLFC 1E **24**
Harlequins RUFC 1E **24**
Harlequin Theatre & Cinema 2D **122**
Harley Gdns. BR6: Orp 1N **67**
HARLINGTON 2E **8**
Harlington Cen., The 4A **88**
Harlington Cl. UB3: Harl 3D **8**
HARLINGTON CORNER 4E **8**
Harlington Rd. E.
TW13: Felt 1J **23**
TW13: Hanw 5N **23**
TW14: Felt 1J **23**
Harlington Rd. W. TW14: Felt 9J **9**
Harlington Way GU51: Fleet 4A **88**
Harlow Ct. *RH2: Reig 3B 122*
(off Wray Comn. Rd.)
Harman Pl. CR8: Pur 7M **63**
Harmans Dr. RH19: E Grin 9D **166**
Harmans Mead
RH19: E Grin 9D **166**
HARMANS WATER 3C **32**
Harman's Water Rd.
RG12: Brac 4A **32**
Harmar Cl. RG40: W'ham 2D **30**
Harmes Way GU11: Alde 6B **90**
HARMONDSWORTH 2M **7**
Harmondsworth La.
UB7: Harm, Sip 2N **7**
Harmondsworth Moor Waterside 2K **7**
Harmondsworth Moor Waterside Vis. Cen. 2K **7**
Harmondsworth Rd.
UB7: W Dray 1N **7**
Harmony Cl. RH11: Craw 5K **181**
SM6: W'ton 5J **63**
Harms Gro. GU4: Guil 9E **94**
Harold Rd. RH10: Wor 4J **183**
SM1: Sut 1B **62**
Haroldslea RH6: Horl 1H **163**
Haroldslea Cl. RH6: Horl 1G **163**
Haroldslea Dr. RH6: Horl 1G **162**
Harold Wilson Ho.
SW6 2L 13
(off Clem Attlee Ct.)
Harpenden Rd. SE27 4M **29**
Harper Dr. RH10: Craw 7G **182**
Harper M. SW17 4A **28**
Harper's Rd. GU12: Ash 1G **111**
Harpers Yd. *TW7: Isle 5E 10*
(off Rennels Way)
Harpesford Av. GU25: V Wat 4L **35**
Harps Oak La. RH1: Mers 3D **102**
Harpswood Cl. CR5: Coul 9G **83**
Harpton Cl. GU46: Yate 8C **48**
Harpton Pde. GU46: Yate 8C **48**
Harpurs KT20: Tad 9J **81**
Harrier Cen., The 3C **60**
Harrier Cl. GU6: Cranl 6N **155**
Harrier Ct. *RH10: Craw 9H 163*
(off Bristol Cl.)
TW4: Houn 6M **9**
Harrier Rd. GU14: Farnb 4H **89**
Harrier Way RG12: Brac 3J **31**
Harriet Gdns. CR0: Croy 8D **46**
Harriet Ho. *SW6 3N 13*
(off Wandon Rd.)
Harriet Tubman Cl. SW2 1K **29**
Harrington Cl. CR0: Bedd 8J **45**
RH2: Leigh 1F **140**
SL4: W'sor 7C **4**
Harrington Ct.
CR0: Croy 3E **200** (8A **46**)
Harrington Gdns. SW7 1N **13**
Harrington Rd. SE25 3D **46**
Harrington Road Stop (CT) 2F **46**
Harriott's Cl. KT21: A'tead 7J **79**
Harriott's La. KT21: A'tead 6J **79**
Harris Cl. RH11: Craw 6N **181**
TW3: Houn 4A **10**
Harrison Cl. RH2: Reig 4N **121**
Harrison's Ri.
CR0: Wad 4A **200** (9M **45**)
Harrison Way TW17: Shep 4C **38**
Harris Path RH11: Craw 6N **181**
Harris Way TW16: Sunb 9F **22**
Harrogate Ct. SL3: Lang 1C **6**
Harroway Mnr. KT22: Fetc 9F **78**
Harrow Bottom Rd.
GU25: V Wat 5B **36**
Harrow Cl. KT9: Ches 4K **59**
KT15: Addl 8K **37**
RH4: Dork 6G **119**
TN8: Eden 9M **127**
Harrowdene GU6: Cranl 6N **155**
Harrowdene Gdns.
TW11: Tedd 7G **25**
Harrow Gdns. CR6: Warl 3J **85**
Harrowgate Gdns.
RH4: Dork 7H **119**
Harrowlands Pk.
RH4: Dork 6H **119**
Harrow La. GU7: Goda 4H **133**
Harrow Rd. CR6: Warl 2J **85**
GU51: Fleet 2A **88**
SM5: Cars 3C **62**
TW14: Bedf 3B **22**
Harrow Rd. E. RH4: Dork 7H **119**
Harrow Rd. W. RH4: Dork 7G **118**
Harrowsley Ct. RH6: Horl 7F **142**
Harrowsley Grn. La.
RH6: Horl 9G **143**
Harrow Way TW17: Shep 1D **38**
Harry Cl. CR0: Croy 5N **45**
Hart, The GU9: Farnh 1G **128**
Hart Cen., The GU51: Fleet 4A **88**
Hart Cl. GU14: Cove 6K **69**
RG42: Brac 8N **15**
RH1: Blet 2B **124**
Hart Dene Ct. GU19: Bag 4J **51**
Hart Dyke Cl. RG41: W'ham 6A **30**
Harte Rd. TW3: Houn 5N **9**
Hartfield Cres.
BR4: W Wick 1C **66**
SW19 8L **27**
Hartfield Rd. BR4: W Wick 1C **66**
KT9: Ches 2K **59**
RH18: F Row 6H **187**
SW19 8L **27**
TN8: Hev, M Grn 5M **147**
Hartford Ri. GU15: Camb 9B **50**
Hartford Rd. GU51: Fleet 2A **88**
KT19: Ewe 3A **60**
Hart Gdns.
RH4: Dork 1K **201** (4H **119**)
Hartham Cl. TW7: Isle 4G **10**
Hartham Rd. TW7: Isle 4F **10**
Harting Ct. RH11: Craw 6L **181**
Hartington Cl. BR6: Farnb 2L **67**
RH2: Reig 1M **121**
Hartington Ct. W4 3A **12**
Hartington Rd. TW1: Twick 1H **25**
W4 3A **12**
Hartismere Rd. SW6 3L **13**
Hartland Cl. KT15: N Haw 6L **55**
Hartland Pl. GU14: Farnb 8M **69**
Hartland Rd. KT15: Addl 4J **55**
SM4: Mord 6M **43**
TW7: Isle 6G **11**
TW12: H Hill 5B **24**
Hartlands, The
TW5: C'ford 2J **9**
Hartland Way CR0: Croy 9H **47**
SM4: Mord 6L **43**
Hartley Cl. GU17: B'water 1G **69**
Hartley Copse SL4: O Win 9K **5**
Hartley Down CR8: Pur 2K **83**
Hartley Farm CR8: Pur 2K **83**
Hartley Hill CR8: Pur 2K **83**
Hartley Old Rd. CR8: Pur 2K **83**
Hartley Rd. CR0: Croy 6N **45**
TN16: Weste 3M **107**
Hartley Way CR8: Pur 2K **83**
Hart M. GU46: Yate 9A **48**
Hartop Point *SW6 3K 13*
(off Pellant Rd.)
Hart Rd. KT14: Byf 9N **55**
RH4: Dork 1K **201** (4H **119**)
Hartscroft CR0: Sels 5H **65**
Harts Gdns. GU2: Guil 9L **93**
Harts Gro. GU8: Chid 4E **172**
Hartshill GU2: Guil 2G **113**
Hartshill Wlk. GU21: Wok 3L **73**
Harts La. RH9: S Gods 5G **124**
Hartsleaf Cl. GU51: Fleet 5A **88**
Harts Leap Cl.
GU47: Sandh 6G **48**
Harts Leap Rd.
GU47: Sandh 7F **48**
Hartspiece Rd. RH1: Red 5E **122**
Hartswood RH5: Nth H 8J **119**
Hartswood Av. RH2: Reig 7M **121**
Harts Yd. GU7: Goda 7H **133**
GU9: Farnh 1G **129**
Harvard Hill W4 2A **12**
Harvard La. W4 1B **12**
Harvard Rd. GU47: Owls 6K **49**
TW7: Isle 4E **10**
W4 1A **12**
Harvest Bank Rd.
BR4: W Wick 1B **66**
Harvest Cl. GU46: Yate 2A **68**
Harvest Ct. KT10: Esh 8A **40**
TW17: Shep 3B **38**
Harvest Cres. GU51: Fleet 9C **68**
Harvester Rd. KT19: Eps 6C **60**
Harvesters RH12: Hors 4K **197**
Harvesters Cl. TW7: Isle 8D **10**
Harvest Hill GU7: Goda 7G **132**
RH19: E Grin 1A **186**
Harvest La. KT7: T Dit 5G **40**
Harvest Lea RG42: Warf 9E **16**
Harvest Ride RG42: Warf 7M **15**
Harvest Rd. RH10: Craw 5G **183**
TW13: Felt 5H **23**
TW20: Eng G 6N **19**
Harvestside RH6: Horl 7G **142**
Harvey Cl. RH11: Craw 8M **181**
Harvey Ct. KT19: Eps 5A **60**
Harvey Dr. TW12: Hamp 9B **24**
Harvey Gdns. GU1: Guil 6F **202**
Harvey Ho. TW8: Brent 1L **11**
Harvey Lodge GU1: Guil 5F **202**
Harvey Rd.
GU1: Guil 6E **202** (5A **114**)
GU14: Cove 9H **69**
KT12: Wal T 6G **39**
TW4: Houn 1N **23**
Harwood Av. CR4: Mit 2C **44**
Harwood Ct. SW15 7H **13**
Harwood Gdns. SL4: O Win 1L **19**
Harwood M. SW6 3M **13**
Harwood Pk. RH1: Salf 3E **142**
Harwood Rd. RH13: Hors 5L **197**
SW6 3M **13**
Harwoods Cl.
RH19: E Grin 2B **186**
Harwoods La.
RH19: E Grin 2B **186**
Harwood Ter. SW6 4N **13**
HASCOMBE 6N **153**
Hascombe Cotts.
GU8: Bus 5M **153**
Hascombe Ct. GU8: Hasc 6M **153**
RH11: Craw 4M **181**
Hascombe Rd. GU6: Cranl 9E **154**
GU8: Bus 1K **153**
Haslam Av. SM3: Sut 7K **43**
Hasle Dr. GU27: Hasl 2F **188**
HASLEMERE 2G **189**
Haslemere and Heathrow Est., The
TW4: C'ford 5J **9**
Haslemere Av. CR4: Mit 1B **44**
SW18 3N **27**
TW5: C'ford 5K **9**
Haslemere Cl. GU16: Frim 3G **70**
SM6: W'ton 2J **63**
TW12: Hamp 6N **23**
Haslemere Educational Mus. 1H **189**
Haslemere Hall 1G **189**
Haslemere Ind. Est.
GU27: Hasl 1F **188**
SW18 3N **27**
Haslemere Rd. CR7: T Hea 4M **45**
GU8: Brook, Wit 4M **171**
GU8: Mil, Wit 6N **151**
GU27: K Grn, Fern 7F **188**
SL4: W'sor 4D **4**
Haslemere Station (Rail) 2F **188**
Haslett Av. E. RH10: Craw 3C **182**
Haslett Av. W. RH10: Craw 4B **182**
Haslett Rd. TW17: Shep 1F **38**
Hassall Ct. GU22: Wok 8C **74**
Hassocks Ct. RH11: Craw 6L **181**
Hassocks Rd. SW16 9H **29**
Hassock Wood BR2: Kes 1F **66**
Haste Hill GU27: Hasl 3H **189**
Hastings Cl. GU16: Frim 7E **70**
Hastings Ct. TW11: Tedd 6D **24**
Hastings Dr. KT6: Surb 5J **41**
Hastings Rd. CR0: Croy 7C **46**
RH10: Craw 3G **182**
Hastings Vw. RG12: Brac 3A **32**
Hasty Cl. CR4: Mit 9F **28**
Hatch Cl. GU6: Alf 6J **175**
KT15: Addl 9K **37**
Hatch End GU20: Windl 3A **52**
RH18: F Row 7H **187**
Hatches, The GU9: Farnh 3E **128**
GU16: Frim G 8B **70**
(not continuous)
Hatchet La. SL4: Wink 5L **17**
SL5: Asc 6L **17**
Hatchett Rd. TW14: Bedf 2D **22**
Hatchetts Dr. GU27: Hasl 2A **188**
Hatch Farm M. KT15: Addl 9L **37**
HATCHFORD 6F **76**
HATCHFORD END 6D **76**
Hatchford Mnr. KT11: Cob 5F **76**
Hatch Gdns. KT20: Tad 7J **81**
Hatchgate RH6: Horl 9D **142**
Hatchgate Copse
RG12: Brac 5K **31**
Hatch Hill GU27: K Grn 7F **188**
Hatchingtan, The
GU3: Worp 4M **93**
HATCHLANDS 9A **96**
Hatchlands RH5: Cap 5J **159**
RH12: Hors 1N **197**
Hatchlands Pk. 8A **96**
Hatchlands Rd. RH1: Red 3C **122**
Hatch La. CR5: Ban 2D **82**
GU8: Worm 1A **172**
GU23: Ockh 7C **76**
GU27: K Grn 6F **188**
KT11: Ockh 5C **76**
RH1: Out, Sth N 2K **143**
SL4: W'sor 6D **4**
UB7: Harm 3M **7**
Hatch Pl. KT2: K Tham 6M **25**
Hatch Ride RG40: W'ham 8E **30**
RG45: Crow 8F **30**
Hatch Rd. SW16 1J **45**
Hatfeild Mead SM4: Mord 4M **43**
Hatfield Cl. CR4: Mit 3B **44**
KT14: W By 8K **55**
SM2: Sut 5N **61**
Hatfield Gdns. GU14: Farnb 2C **90**
Hatfield Ho. GU12: A Va 8D **90**
Hatfield Rd. KT21: A'tead 6M **79**
Hatfield Wlk. RH11: Craw 6K **181**
Hathaway Ct. *RH1: Red 2E 122*
(off St Anne's Ri.)
Hathaway Rd. CR0: Croy 6M **45**
Hatherleigh Cl. KT9: Ches 2K **59**
SM4: Mord 3M **43**
Hatherley Rd. TW9: Kew 4M **11**
Hatherop Rd. TW12: Hamp 8N **23**
Hathersham Cl. RH6: Smal 7L **143**
Hathersham La.
RH6: Smal 4H **143**
Hatherwood GU46: Yate 1E **68**
KT22: Leat 8K **79**
HATTON 7G **9**
Hatton Ct. SL4: W'sor 5F **4**
HATTON CROSS 7G **8**
Hatton Cross Cen.
TW6: Lon A 6G **8**
Hatton Cross Station (Tube) 7G **8**
Hatton Gdns. CR4: Mit 4D **44**
Hatton Grn. TW14: Felt 7H **9**
HATTON HILL 2N **51**
Hatton Hill GU20: Windl 1M **51**
Hatton Ho. KT1: K Tham 4M **203**
Hatton Rd. CR0: Croy 7L **45**
TW14: Bedf, Felt 1D **22**
Hatton Rd. Sth. TW14: Felt 7G **8**
Haughton Ho. GU27: Hasl 2F **188**
Havana Rd. SW19 3M **27**
Havelock Rd. CR0: Croy 8C **46**
RG41: W'ham 2A **30**
SW19 6A **28**
Havelock St. RG41: W'ham 2A **30**
HAVEN, THE 6E **194**
Haven, The TW9: Rich 6N **11**
TW16: Sunb 8H **23**
Havenbury Est.
RH4: Dork 1H **201** (4G **118**)
Haven Cl. KT10: H Wood 8E **40**
SW19 4J **27**
Haven Ct. BR3: Beck 1M **47**
KT5: Surb 5M **41**
KT10: H Wood 8E **40**
Haven Dr. KT19: Ewe 7A **60**
Haven Gdns.
RH10: Craw D 9E **164**
Havengate RH12: Hors 3M **197**
Haven Pl. KT10: H Wood 8E **40**
Haven Rd. RH12: Rudg 2D **194**
RH14: Slin, Have 7F **194**
TW15: A'ford 5C **22**
Haven Way GU9: Farnh 8J **109**
KT19: Eps 7A **60**
Haverfield Gdns. TW9: Kew 3N **11**
Haverhill Rd. SW12 2G **28**
Havers Av. KT12: Hers 2L **57**
Haversham Cl.
RH10: Craw 3D **182**
TW1: Twick 9K **11**
Haversham Dr. RG12: Brac 5N **31**
Haversham Ho. RH6: Horl 6F **142**
Havisham Pl. SE19 8M **29**
Hawarden Cl.
RH10: Craw D 1F **184**
Hawarden Gro. SE24 1N **29**
Hawarden Rd. CR3: Cate 8N **83**
Hawes La. BR4: W Wick 7M **47**
Hawes Rd. KT20: Tad 7J **81**
Haweswater Ct. *GU12: A Va 8D 90*
(off Lakeside Cl.)
Haweswater Ho. TW7: Isle 8F **10**
Hawker Ct. KT1: K Tham 3M **203**
Hawker Rd. CR0: Wad 3L **63**
GU12: A Va 8D **90**
Hawkesbourne Rd.
RH12: Hors 3M **197**
Hawkesbury Rd. SW15 8G **12**
Hawkes Leap GU20: Windl 1M **51**
Hawkesley Cl. TW1: Twick 5G **24**
Hawkesmoor Rd.
RH11: Craw 5K **181**
Hawkes Rd. CR4: Mit 9D **28**
TW14: Felt 1H **23**
Hawkesworth Dr.
GU19: Bag 6H **51**
Hawkewood Rd.
TW16: Sunb 2H **39**
Hawkfield Ct. TW7: Isle 5E **10**
Hawkhirst Rd. CR3: Ken 4B **84**
CR8: Ken 2A **84**
Hawkhurst KT11: Cob 1A **78**
Hawkhurst Gdns. KT9: Ches 1L **59**
Hawkhurst Rd. SW16 9H **29**
Hawkhurst Wlk.
RH10: Craw 5F **182**
Hawkhurst Way
BR4: W Wick 8L **47**
KT3: N Mal 4C **42**
Hawkins Cl. GU46: Yate 1A **68**
RG12: Brac 1E **32**
Hawkins Rd. RH10: Craw 6C **182**
TW11: Tedd 7H **25**
Hawkins Way GU52: Fleet 5D **88**
RG40: W'ham 2D **30**
Hawk La. RG12: Brac 3A **32**
Hawkley Gdns. SE27 3M **29**
Hawkridge RH12: Rudg 8F **176**
Hawkridge Ct. RG12: Brac 3C **32**
Hawksbrook La. BR3: Beck 5L **47**
(not continuous)
Hawkshaw Cl. SW2 1J **29**
Hawk's Hill KT22: Fetc 1F **98**
Hawks Hill Cl. KT22: Fetc 1F **98**
Hawkshill Cl. KT10: Esh 3A **58**
Hawk's Hill Ct. KT22: Fetc 1F **98**
Hawk's Hill Ho. KT22: Fetc 2F **98**
Hawkshill Pl. KT10: Esh 3A **58**
Hawkshill Way KT10: Esh 3N **57**
Hawksmoore Dr.
RH5: B Grn 7J **139**
Hawksmoor St. W6 2J **13**
Hawks Pas. KT1: K Tham 3L **203**
Hawks Rd.
KT1: K Tham 4M **203** (1M **41**)
Hawksview KT11: Cob 9N **57**
Hawksway TW18: Stain 4H **21**
Hawkswell Cl. GU21: Wok 4J **73**
Hawkswell Wlk. GU21: Wok 4J **73**
Hawkswood Av.
GU16: Frim 4D **70**
Hawkswood Ho. *RG42: Brac 9K 15*
(off Moordale Av.)
Hawkwell GU52: C Cro 9C **88**
Hawkwood Dell KT23: Book 4A **98**
Hawkwood Ri. KT23: Book 4A **98**
HAWLEY 3L **69**
Hawley Cl. TW12: Hamp 7N **23**
Hawley Ct. GU14: Cove 6K **69**
Hawley Grn. GU17: Haw 3K **69**
Hawley Gro. GU17: Haw 4K **69**
HAWLEY LANE 7M **69**
Hawley La. GU14: Farnb 5M **69**
(not continuous)
Hawley La. Ind. Est.
GU14: Farnb 6N **69**
Hawley Lodge GU17: Haw 4L **69**
Hawley Rd. GU17: Haw 2J **69**
HAWLEY'S CORNER 8K **87**
Hawley Way
TW15: A'ford 6B **22**
Hawmead RH10: Craw D 1F **184**
Haworth Rd. RH10: Craw 4F **182**
Haws La. TW19: Stan M 9J **7**
Hawth Av. RH10: Craw 5C **182**
Hawth Cl. RH10: Craw 5C **182**
Hawthorn Av. CR7: T Hea 9M **29**

Hawthorn Cl.—Heights Cl.

Hawthorn Cl. GU12: Alde 4C 110
GU22: Wok 7A 74
RG42: Brac 9M 15
RH1: Red 8E 122
RH11: Craw 9A 162
RH12: Hors 4J 197
SM7: Ban 1K 81
TN8: Eden 1L 147
TW5: C'ford 3J 9
TW12: Hamp 6A 24
Hawthorn Ct. GU14: Farnb 5A 90
TW9: Kew 4A 12
TW15: A'ford 8D 22
Hawthorn Cres. CR2: Sels 7F 64
SW17 6E 28
Hawthorn Dr. BR4: W Wick 1A 66
Hawthorne Av. CR4: Mit 1B 44
SL4: Wink 3M 17
SM5: Cars 4E 62
TN16: B Hil 2F 86
Hawthorne Cl. SM1: Sut 8A 44
Hawthorne Ct. KT12: Wal T 7L 39
TW19: Stan 1M 21
(off Hawthorne Way)
Hawthorne Cres.
GU17: Haw 2K 69
Hawthorne Dr. SL4: Wink 3M 17
Hawthorne Pl.
KT17: Eps 5M 201 (8D 60)
Hawthorne Rd. TW18: Stain 6E 20
Hawthorne Way
GU4: B'ham 8D 94
SL4: Wink 2M 17
TW19: Stan 1M 21
Hawthorn Hatch TW8: Brent 3H 11
HAWTHORN HILL 1B 16
Hawthorn La. GU10: Rowl 8E 128
RG42: Warf 1C 16
Hawthorn Pl. GU4: Guil 1F 114
Hawthorn Rd. GU7: Goda 9E 132
GU16: Frim 4D 70
GU22: Wok 7N 73
GU23: Rip 2J 95
SM1: Sut 3C 62
SM6: W'ton 4F 62
TW8: Brent 3H 11
TW13: Felt 2H 23
Hawthorns CR2: S Croy 7A 200
Hawthorns, The KT17: Ewe 4E 60
RH8: Oxt 2C 126
SL3: Poy 4H 7
Hawthorn Way GU24: Bis 3D 72
KT15: N Haw 6L 55
RH1: Red 5F 122
TW17: Shep 3E 38
Hawth Theatre 4D 182
Hawtrey Ho. *SL4: Eton 2G 4*
(off Slough Rd.)
Hawtrey Rd. SL4: W'sor 5F 4
HAXTED 3G 147
Haxted Mill & Mus. 3F 146
Haxted Rd. RH7: Ling 5A 146
TN8: Eden 5A 146
Haybarn Dr. RH12: Hors 1L 197
Haycroft Cl. CR5: Coul 5M 83
Haycroft Rd. KT6: Surb 8K 41
Hayden Ct. KT15: N Haw 7K 55
TW13: Felt 5F 22
Haydn Av. CR8: Pur 1L 83
Haydon Pk. Rd. SW19 6M 27
Haydon Pl.
GU1: Guil 4C 202 (4N 113)
GU14: Cove 6M 69
GU46: Yate 9D 48
Haydons Rd. SW19 6N 27
Haydons Road Station (Rail)
6A 28
Hayes, The KT18: Eps D 6D 80
Hayes Barton GU22: Pyr 3F 74
Hayes Chase BR4: W Wick 5N 47
Hayes Ct. SW2 2J 29
Hayes Cres. SM3: Chea 1J 61
Hayesens Ho. SW17 5A 28
Hayes La. BR3: Beck 2M 47
CR8: Ken 3M 83
RH13: Slin 8H 195
Hayes Wlk. RH6: Smal 7L 143
Hayes Way BR3: Beck 3M 47
Hayfields RH6: Horl 7F 142
Haygarth Pl. SW19 6J 27
Haygreen Cl. KT2: K Tham 7A 26
Haylett Gdns.
KT1: K Tham 8H 203 (3K 41)
Hayley Grn. RG42: Warf 6D 16
Hayling Av. TW13: Felt 4H 23
Hayling Ct. RH11: Craw 6A 182
SM3: Chea 1H 61
Haymeads Dr. KT10: Esh 3C 58
Haymer Gdns. KT4: W Pk 9F 42
Hayne Rd. BR3: Beck 1J 47
Haynes Cl. GU23: Rip 9K 75
SL3: Lang 1B 6
Haynt Wlk. SW20 2K 43
Hays Bri. Bus. Cen.
RH9: S Gods 5F 144
Hays Bri. Ho's.
RH9: S Gods 4E 144
Hayse Hill SL4: W'sor 4A 4
Haysleigh Gdns. SE20 1D 46
Hays Wlk. SM2: Chea 6J 61
Haywain RH8: Oxt 8N 105
Hayward Cl. SW19 8N 27
Haywardens RH7: Ling 6N 145
Hayward Gdns. SW15 9H 13
Hayward Rd. KT7: T Dit 7F 40
Haywards RH10: Craw 9H 163
Haywards Mead SL4: E Wic 1C 4
Haywood RG12: Brac 6A 32
Haywood Dr. GU52: Fleet 6B 88
Haywood Ri. BR6: Orp 2N 67
Hazel Av. GU1: Guil 8M 93
GU14: Cove 2L 89
(not continuous)
Hazel Bank SE25 1B 46
Hazelbank KT5: Surb 7B 42
Hazelbank Ct. KT16: Chert 7L 37
Hazelbank Rd. KT16: Chert 7L 37
Hazelbourne Rd.
SW12 1F 28
Hazelbury Cl. SW19 1M 43
Hazel Cl. CR0: Croy 6G 46
CR4: Mit 3H 45
RH2: Reig 5A 122
RH10: Craw D 1F 184
RH11: Craw 9A 162
TW2: Whitt 1C 24
TW8: Brent 3H 11
TW20: Eng G 7L 19
Hazel Ct. CR6: Warl 4H 85
GU1: Guil 8N 93
Hazeldene KT15: Addl 2L 55
Hazeldene Ct. CR8: Ken 2A 84
Hazel Dr. GU23: Rip 3H 95
Hazel Gro. GU26: Hind 8C 170
TW13: Felt 2H 23
TW18: Stain 7K 21
Hazelhurst BR3: Beck 1N 47
RH6: Horl 7G 143
Hazelhurst Cl. GU4: B'ham 7D 94
Hazelhurst Cres.
RH12: Hors 7F 196
Hazelhurst Dr. RH10: Wor 3J 183
Hazelhurst Rd. SW17 5A 28
Hazel La. TW10: Ham 3L 25
Hazell Hill RG12: Brac 2A 32
Hazell Rd. GU9: Farnh 1E 128
Hazel Mead KT17: Ewe 6F 60
Hazelmere Cl. KT22: Leat 6H 79
TW14: Felt 9F 8
Hazelmere Ct. SW2 2K 29
Hazel Pde. KT22: Fetc 9C 78
Hazel Rd. GU12: A Grn 5G 111
GU16: Mytc 3E 90
KT14: W By 1J 75
RH2: Reig 5A 122
Hazel Wlk. RH5: Nth H 8J 119
Hazel Way CR5: Chip 6D 82
KT22: Fetc 9C 78
RH10: Craw D 1F 184
Hazelway Cl. KT22: Fetc 1C 98
Hazelwick Av. RH10: Craw 1E 182
Hazelwick Ct. RH10: Craw 1E 182
Hazelwick Mill La.
RH10: Craw 1E 182
(not continuous)
Hazelwick Rd. RH10: Craw 2E 182
Hazelwick Rdbt.
RH10: Craw 1E 182
HAZELWOOD 7M 67
Hazelwood GU8: Els 7J 131
RH4: Dork 6H 119
RH11: Craw 3M 181
Hazelwood Av. SM4: Mord 3N 43
Hazelwood Cl.
RH10: Craw D 1C 184
Hazelwood Cotts.
GU6: Cranl 5M 175
GU7: Goda 7G 132
Hazelwood Ct. GU14: Cove 6K 69
KT6: Surb 5L 41
Hazelwood Gro. CR2: Sande 9E 64
Hazelwood Hgts. RH8: Oxt 9C 106
Hazelwood Ho's.
BR2: Brom 2N 47
Hazelwood La. CR5: Chip 5C 82
RG42: Bin, Warf 1M 15
Hazelwood Rd. GU21: Knap 5H 73
RH8: Oxt 1D 126
TN14: Cud 8M 67
Hazlebury Rd. SW6 5N 13
Hazledean Rd.
CR0: Croy 3E 200 (8A 46)
Hazledene Rd. W4 2B 12
Hazlemere Gdns.
KT4: W Pk 7F 42
Hazlewell Rd. SW15 8H 13
Hazlitt Cl. TW13: Hanw 5M 23
Hazon Way
KT19: Eps 5H 201 (8B 60)
Headcorn Pl. CR7: T Hea 3K 45
Headcorn Rd. CR7: T Hea 3K 45
Headington Cl.
RG40: W'ham 9C 14
Headington Ct. CR0: Croy 7B 200
Headington Dr.
RG40: W'ham 9C 14
Headington Rd. SW18 3A 28
Headlam Rd. SW4 1H 29
(not continuous)
Headland Way RH7: Ling 7M 145
HEADLEY
GU35 3C 168
KT18 4C 100
Headley Av. SM6: W'ton 2K 63
Headley Cl. KT19: Ewe 3N 59
RH10: Craw 9H 163
Headley Comn. Rd.
KT18: Head, Wal H 5C 100
Headley Ct. KT18: Head 1A 100
TN8: Eden 1M 147
HEADLEY DOWN 4G 169
Headley Dr. CR0: N Add 4L 65
KT18: Tat C 6G 81
Headley Flds. GU35: Head 4D 168
Headley Gro. KT20: Tad 7H 81
Headley Heath 6A 100
Headley Heath App.
KT20: Box H 8A 100
RH5: Mick 7N 99
Headley Hill Rd.
GU35: Head 4E 168
Headley La. GU30: Pass 8D 168
RH5: Mick 7J 99
Headley Mill 5B 168
Headley Pk. Cotts.
GU35: Head 9B 148
Headley Rd. GU26: G'hott 5K 169
GU35: Lind 4B 168
KT18: Eps D 7B 80
KT18: Eps D, Head 9N 79
KT18: Eps, Eps D 5A 80
KT22: Leat 9J 79
Headon Ct. GU9: Farnh 2J 129
Headway, The KT17: Ewe 5E 60
Headway Cl. TW10: Ham 5J 25
Hearmon Cl. GU46: Yate 9D 48
HEARN 2G 168
Hearne Rd. W4 2N 11
Hearn Va. GU35: H Dwn 2F 168
Hearnville Rd. SW12 2E 28
Hearn Wlk. RG12: Brac 9C 16
Hearsey Gdns.
GU17: B'water 9G 49
(not continuous)
Heart, The KT12: Wal T 7H 39
HEATH, THE 3C 56
Heath, The CR3: Cate 2N 103
GU3: Put 8A 112
Heathacre SL3: Coln 4G 6
Heatham Pk. TW2: Twick 1F 24
Heathbridge KT13: Weybr 4B 56
Heathbridge App.
KT13: Weybr 3B 56
Heath Bus. Cen. RH1: Salf 4F 142
TW3: Houn 7C 10
Heath Cl. CR2: S Croy 3M 63
GU9: U Hal 5H 109
GU12: Alde 3B 110
GU25: V Wat 3N 35
GU26: Hind 2A 170
RG41: W'ham 4A 30
RH12: Bro H 5E 196
SM7: Ban 1N 81
TW19: Stan 9L 7
UB3: Harl 3E 8
Heath Cnr. GU15: Camb 3E 70
Heathcote KT20: Tad 8J 81
Heathcote Cl. *GU12: A Va 1E 110*
(off Church Path)
Heathcote Ct. *SL4: W'sor 6G 4*
(off Osbourne Rd.)
Heathcote Dr.
RH19: E Grin 8L 165
Heathcote Rd. GU12: Ash 1F 110
GU15: Camb 1B 70
KT18: Eps 8K 201 (1C 80)
TW1: Twick 9H 11
Heathcotes RH10: Craw 5H 183
Heath Cotts. GU10: Fren 8J 129
GU26: Hind 3A 170
Heath Ct. CR0: Croy 7D 200
GU19: Bag 4J 51
RH12: Bro H 5E 196
TW4: Houn 7N 9
Heathcroft Av. TW16: Sunb 8G 22
Heathdale Av. TW4: Houn 6M 9
Heathdene KT20: Tad 5K 81
Heathdene Rd. SM6: W'ton 4F 62
SW16 8K 29
Heathdown Rd. GU22: Pyr 2F 74
Heath Dr. GU23: Send 9D 74
GU24: B'wood 7D 72
KT20: Wal H 3F 100
SM2: Sut 5A 62
SW20 3H 43
HEATH END 5H 109
Heatherbank Cl. KT11: Cob 7L 57
Heather Cl. GU2: Guil 2L 113
GU9: Farnh 5E 128
GU11: Alde 3K 109
GU12: A Va 8F 90
GU21: Wok 2M 73
KT15: N Haw 6K 55
KT20: K'wood 9K 81
RH1: Red 9F 102
RH10: Cop 8M 163
RH12: Hors 3K 197
TW7: Isle 8D 10
TW12: Hamp 9N 23
Heather Cotts. GU26: Hind 1B 170
Heather Ct. GU26: Hind 5E 170
Heatherdale Cl.
KT2: K Tham 7N 25
Heatherdale Rd.
GU15: Camb 2A 70
Heatherdene KT24: W Hors 3E 96
Heatherdene Av.
RG45: Crow 3D 48
Heatherdene Cl. CR4: Mit 3B 44
Heather Dr. GU35: Lind 4A 168
GU52: C Cro 8A 88
SL5: S'dale 6E 34
Heatherfield La.
KT13: Weybr 2F 56
Heatherfields KT15: N Haw 6K 55
Heather Gdns. GU14: Cove 3J 89
SM2: Sut 3M 61
Heatherlands RH6: Horl 7F 142
(not continuous)
TW16: Sunb 7H 23
Heatherlea Gro. KT4: W Pk 7G 43
Heatherleigh Ct.
RH12: Hors 4J 197
(off North Pde.)
Heatherley Cl. GU15: Camb 1N 69
Heatherley Rd. GU15: Camb 1N 69
Heather Mead GU16: Frim 4D 70
Heather Mead Ct.
GU16: Frim 4D 70
Heathermount RG12: Brac 3C 32
Heathermount Dr.
RG45: Crow 1E 48
Heathermount Gdns.
RG45: Crow 1E 48
Heather Pl. KT10: Esh 1B 58
Heather Ridge Arc.
GU15: Camb 2G 71
Heathers, The TW19: Stan 1A 22
Heatherset Cl. KT10: Esh 2C 58
Heatherset Gdns.
SW16 8K 29
HEATHERSIDE 2G 71
Heatherside Cl. KT23: Book 3N 97
Heatherside Dr.
GU25: V Wat 5K 35
Heatherside Rd. KT19: Ewe 4C 60
Heathersland RH4: Dork 8J 119
Heathervale Cvn. Pk.
KT15: N Haw 6L 55
Heathervale Rd.
KT15: N Haw 6K 55
Heathervale Way
KT15: N Haw 6L 55
Heather Vw. Cotts.
GU10: Fren 1H 149
Heather Wlk. GU24: B'wood 8A 72
KT12: Whit V 6F 56
RH6: Smal 8N 143
RH11: Craw 6N 181
TW2: Whitt 1A 24
(off Stephenson Rd.)
Heather Way CR2: Sels 5G 65
GU24: Chob 4H 53
GU26: Hind 5D 170
RH19: Fel 3J 165
Heatherway RG45: Crow 2F 48
Heathfield KT11: Cob 1A 78
RH10: Craw 9H 163
(not continuous)
Heathfield Av. SL5: S'dale 4B 34
SW18 1B 28
Heathfield Cl. BR2: Kes 2E 66
GU7: Goda 9H 133
GU22: Wok 5C 74
Heathfield Ct. W4 1C 12
Heathfield Dr. CR4: Mit 9C 28
RH1: Red 8C 122
Heathfield Gdns.
CR0: Croy 6C 200 (1A 64)
W4 1B 12
Heathfield Nth. TW2: Twick 1E 24
Heathfield Rd. BR2: Kes 2E 66
CR0: Croy 6D 200 (1A 64)
GU22: Wok 5C 74
KT12: Hers 1M 57
SW18 1B 28
Heathfields Cl. KT21: A'tead 5J 79
Heathfields Ct. TW4: Houn 8M 9
Heathfield Sth. TW2: Twick 1F 24
Heathfield Sq. SW18 1B 28
Heathfield Ter. W4 1B 12
Heathfield Va. CR2: Sels 5G 65
Heath Gdns. TW1: Twick 2F 24
Heath Gro. TW16: Sunb 8G 23
Heath Hill GU10: Dock 7D 148
RH4: Dork 2L 201 (5H 119)
Heath Hill Rd. Nth.
RG45: Crow 2G 48
Heath Hill Rd. Sth.
RG45: Crow 2G 49
Heath Ho. Rd. GU22: Wok 9F 72
Heathlands KT20: Tad 9J 81
RG12: Brac 3M 31
Heathlands Cl. GU21: Wok 1A 74
TW1: Twick 3F 24
TW16: Sunb 1H 39
Heathlands Ct. GU46: Yate 2D 68
RG40: W'ham 8E 30
Heathlands Rd.
RG40: W'ham 5E 30
Heathland St. GU11: Alde 2M 109
Heathlands Way TW4: Houn 8M 9
Heathland Vis. Cen. 6K 51
Heath La. GU5: Alb 1N 135
GU7: Bus 9K 133
GU9: U Hal 5H 109
GU10: Ews 6A 108
Heathmans Rd. SW6 4L 13
Heath Mead SW19 4J 27
Heath M. GU23: Rip 1K 95
Heath Mill La. GU3: Worp 3E 92
(not continuous)
Heathmoors RG12: Brac 4A 32
Heathpark Dr. GU20: Windl 3B 52
Heath Pl. GU19: Bag 4J 51
Heath Ride RG40: Finch 1A 48
RG45: Crow 2B 48
Heath Ridge Grn.
KT11: Cob 9A 58
Heath Ri. GU15: Camb 1B 70
GU23: Rip 1K 95
GU25: V Wat 3N 35
RH4: Westc 7C 118
SW15 9J 13
Heath Rd. CR3: Cate 1A 104
CR7: T Hea 2N 45
GU19: Bag 4J 51
GU21: Wok 2B 74
GU27: Hasl 3B 188
KT13: Weybr 1B 56
KT22: Oxs 8C 58
TW1: Twick 2F 24
TW2: Twick 2F 24
TW3: Houn, Isle 7B 10
Heathrow GU5: Gorn 8D 116
HEATHROW AIRPORT 6B 8
Heathrow Blvd. UB7: Sip 3A 8
(not continuous)
Heathrow C'way. Cen.
TW4: Houn 6J 9
Heathrow Central Station (Rail)
6B 8
Heathrow Cl. UB7: L'ford 4K 7
Heathrow Gateway
TW4: Houn 1M 23
Heathrow Intl. Trad. Est.
TW4: Houn 6J 9
Heathrow Terminals 1, 2 & 3 Station (Tube) 6C 8
Heathrow Terminal 4 Station (Rail)
9D 8
Heathrow Terminal 4 Station (Tube)
8D 8
Heathrow Terminal 5 Station (Rail & Tube, Open 2008)
6L 7
Heathrow Vis. Cen. 4D 8
Heath Royal SW15 9J 13
Heathside KT10: H Wood 9E 40
KT13: Weybr 2C 56
TW4: Houn 1N 23
Heathside Cl.
KT10: H Wood 9E 40
Heathside Ct. KT20: Tad 1G 101
Heathside Cres. GU22: Wok 4B 74
Heathside Gdns.
GU22: Wok 4C 74
Heathside La. GU26: Hind 3B 170
Heathside Pk. GU15: Camb 8G 50
Heathside Pk. Rd.
GU22: Wok 5B 74
Heathside Pl. KT18: Tat C 5J 81
Heathside Rd. GU22: Wok 5B 74
Heathurst Rd. CR2: Sande 5A 64
Heath Va. Bri. Rd.
GU12: A Va 7E 90
Heath Vw. KT24: E Hor 3G 97
Heathview Gdns. SW15 1H 27
Heathview Rd. CR7: T Hea 3L 45
GU8: Mil 3B 152
Heath Way RH12: Hors 3K 197
Heathway CR0: Croy 9J 47
CR3: Cate 3N 103
GU15: Camb 1B 70
KT24: E Hor 2G 97
SL5: Asc 9J 17
Heathway Cl. GU15: Camb 1B 70
Heathwood Cl. GU46: Yate 8C 48
Heathyfields Rd.
GU9: U Hal 6E 108
Heaton Rd. CR4: Mit 8E 28
Hebbecastle Down
RG42: Warf 7N 15
Hebdon Rd. SW17 4C 28
Heber Mans. *W14 2K 13*
(off Queen's Club Gdns.)
Heckets Ct. KT10: Esh 6C 58
Heckfield Pl. SW6 3M 13
Hectors La. RH19: E Grin 2E 186
Heddon Cl. TW7: Isle 7G 10
Heddon Wlk. GU14: Farnb 7M 69
Hedgecourt Pl. RH19: Fel 6H 165
Hedge Cft. GU46: Yate 9A 48
Hedgecroft Cotts. GU23: Rip 8K 75
Hedgehog La. GU27: Hasl 2F 188
Hedge La. RG42: Warf 7B 16
Hedgerley Ct. GU21: Wok 4M 73
Hedgers Almshouses
GU1: Guil 2F 114
(off Wykeham Rd.)
GU4: Guil 2F 114
(off Wykeham Rd.)
Hedgeside RH11: Craw 8A 182
Hedgeway GU2: Guil 5K 113
Hedingham Cl. RH6: Horl 7G 142
Hedingham Ho.
KT2: K Tham 2J 203
Hedley Rd. TW2: Whitt 1A 24
Heenan Cl. GU16: Frim G 7C 70
Heidegger Cres. SW13 3G 13
Heighton Gdns.
CR0: Wad 8A 200 (2M 63)
Heights, The KT13: Weybr 6B 56
Heights Cl. SM7: Ban 3K 81
SW20 8G 27

Helby Rd.—High St.

Helby Rd. SW4 ....1H 29
Helder St. CR2: S Croy 3A 64
Heldmann Cl. TW3: Isle 7D 10
Helena Rd. SL4: W'sor 5G 4
Helen Av. TW14: Felt 1J 23
Helen Cl. KT8: W Mole 3B 40
Helen Ct. GU14: Farnb 1N 89
Helford Wlk. GU21: Wok 5K 73
Helgiford Gdns.
TW16: Sunb 8F 22
Helicon Ho. RH11: Craw 4A 182
Helios Rd. SM6: W'ton 7E 44
Helix Bus. Pk. GU15: Camb 3N 69
Helix Rd. SW2 ....1K 29
Helm Cl. KT19: Eps 8N 59
Helme Cl. SW19 ....6L 27
Helmsdale GU21: Wok 5L 73
RG12: Brac 4B 32
Helmsdale Rd. SW16 ....9H 29
Helston Cl. GU16: Frim 7E 70
Helston La. SL4: W'sor 4E 4
Helvellyn Cl. TW20: Egh 8D 20
Hemingford Rd. SM3: Chea 1H 61
Hemlock Cl. KT20: K'wood 1K 101
Hemming Cl. TW12: Hamp 9A 24
Hemmings Mead
KT19: Ewe 3B 60
Hemmyng Cnr. RG42: Warf 7A 16
Hempshaw Av. SM7: Ban 3D 82
Hemsby Rd. KT9: Ches 3M 59
Hemsby Wlk. RH10: Craw 5F 182
Hemsley Ct. GU2: Guil 9K 93
Hemwood Rd. SL4: W'sor 6A 4
Henage La. GU22: Wok 7E 74
Henbane Ct. RH11: Craw 7M 181
Henbit Cl. KT20: Tad 6G 81
Henchley Dene GU4: Guil 9F 94
Henderson Av. GU2: Guil 8L 93
Henderson Rd. CR0: Croy 5A 46
RH11: Craw 8N 181
SW18 ....1C 28
TN16: B Hil 8E 66
Henderson Way
RH12: Hors 8F 196
Hendfield Ct. SM6: W'ton 3F 62
Hendham Rd. SW17 ....3C 28
Hendon Gro. KT19: Eps 5N 59
Hendon Way TW19: Stan 9M 7
Hendrick Av. SW12 ....1D 28
Heneage Cres. CR0: N Add 6M 65
Henfield Rd. SW19 ....9L 27
Henfold Cotts. RH5: Newd 9N 139
Henfold Dr. RH5: B Grn 8K 139
Henfold La.
RH5: B Grn, Holm 4L 139
RH5: B Grn, Newd 8M 139
Hengelo Gdns. CR4: Mit 3B 44
Hengist Cl. RH12: Hors 7G 197
Hengist Way BR2: Brom 3N 47
Hengrove Cres.
TW15: A'ford 4M 21
Henhurst Cross La.
RH5: B Grn 8G 138
Henley Av. SM3: Chea 9K 43
Henley Bank GU2: Guil 5K 113
Henley Cl. GU14: Cove 6K 69
RH10: Craw 6H 183
TW7: Isle 4F 10
Henley Ct. GU22: Wok 7D 74
TW20: Egh 5C 20
Henley Dr. GU16: Frim G 7C 70
KT2: K Tham 8E 26
Henley Fort Bungs.
GU2: Guil 6K 113
Henley Gdns. GU46: Yate 1C 68
Henley Ga. GU3: Norm 5N 91
GU24: Pirb 5N 91
Henley Pk. GU3: Norm 7N 91
Henley Way TW13: Hanw 6L 23
Henlow Pl. TW10: Ham 3K 25
HENLYS RDBT. 5K 9
Hennessy Ct. GU21: Wok 9E 54
Henrietta Ct. TW1: Twick 1J 25
(off Richmond Rd.)
Henrietta Ho. W6 ....1H 13
(off Queen Caroline St.)
Henry Ct. GU12: A Va 4E 90
(off Frimley Rd.)
Henry Doulton Dr.
SW17 ....5E 28
Henry Hatch Ct. SM2: Sut 4A 62
Henry Jackson Rd.
SW15 ....6J 13
Henry Lodge KT12: Hers 3K 57
Henry Macaulay Av.
KT2: K Tham 2H 203 (9K 25)
Henry Peters Dr.
TW11: Tedd 6E 24
(off Somerset Gdns.)
Henry Tate M. SW16 ....6K 29
Henshaw Cl. RH11: Craw 5L 181
Henslow Way GU21: Wok 1F 74
Henson Rd. RH10: Craw 2F 182
Hensworth Rd.
TW15: A'ford 6M 21
Henty Cl. RH11: Craw 6K 181
Henty Wlk. SW15 ....8G 12
Hepple Cl. TW7: Isle 5H 11
Hepplestone Cl. SW15 ....9G 13
Hepplewhite Cl.
RH11: Craw 8N 181
Hepworth Ct. SM3: Sut 7M 43
Hepworth Cft. GU47: C Tow 9K 49
Hepworth Rd. SW16 ....8J 29
Hepworth Way KT12: Wal T 7G 39
Herald Ct. GU12: Alde 3N 109
Herald Gdns. SM6: W'ton 8F 44
Herbert Cl. RG12: Brac 4N 31
Herbert Cres. GU21: Knap 5H 73
Herbert Gdns. W4 ....2A 12
Herbert M. SW2 ....1L 29
Herbert Morrison Ho. SW6 ....2L 13
(off Clem Attlee Ct.)
Herbert Rd.
KT1: K Tham 6L 203 (2M 41)
SW19 ....8L 27
(not continuous)
Herbs End GU14: Cove 9H 69
Hercules Way GU14: Farnb 6L 89
Hereford Cl. GU2: Guil 1J 113
KT18: Eps 7K 201 (9C 60)
RH10: Craw 7C 182
TW18: Stain 9K 21
Hereford Copse GU22: Wok 6L 73
Hereford Ct. SM2: Sut 4M 61
Hereford Gdns. TW2: Twick 2C 24
Hereford Ho. SW10 ....3N 13
(off Fulham Rd.)
Hereford La. GU9: U Hal 6G 109
Hereford Mead GU51: Fleet 1C 88
Hereford Rd. TW13: Felt 2K 23
Hereford Way KT9: Ches 2J 59
Hereward Av. CR8: Pur 7L 63
Hereward Rd. SW17 ....5D 28
Heriot Cl. KT16: Chert 6H 37
Heriot Rd. KT16: Chert 6J 37
Heritage Cl. TW16: Sunb 9H 23
Heritage Ct. TW20: Egh 6C 20
(off Station Rd.)
Heritage Hill BR2: Kes 2E 66
Heritage Lawn RH6: Horl 7G 142
Heritage Pl. SW18 ....2A 28
Herlwyn Gdns. SW17 ....5D 28
Herm Cl. RH11: Craw 7M 181
TW7: Isle 3C 10
Hermes Cl. GU51: Fleet 4D 88
Hermes Pl. RG12: Brac 3B 32
Hermes Way SM6: W'ton 4H 63
Hermitage, The
KT1: K Tham 7H 203 (3K 41)
RG42: Warf 6B 16
SW13 ....4E 12
TW10: Rich 8L 11
TW13: Felt 4G 23
Hermitage Bri. Cotts.
GU21: Wok 6F 72
Hermitage Cl. GU14: Farnb 4B 90
GU16: Frim 5D 70
KT10: Clay 3G 58
TW17: Shep 3B 38
Hermitage Ct. TW18: Stain 6H 21
Hermitage Dr. SL5: Asc 1J 33
Hermitage Gdns. SE19 ....8N 29
Hermitage Grn. SW16 ....9J 29
Hermitage La. CR0: Croy 6D 46
RH19: E Grin 1B 186
SE25 ....5D 46
(not continuous)
SL4: W'sor 6D 4
SW16 ....8K 29
Hermitage Pde. SL5: Asc 2L 33
Hermitage Path SW16 ....9J 29
Hermitage Rd. CR8: Ken 2N 83
GU21: Wok 6G 72
RH19: E Grin 7N 165
SE19 ....8N 29
Hermitage Vs. SW6 ....2M 13
(off Lillie Rd.)
Hermitage Woods Cres.
GU21: Wok 6H 73
Hermitage Woods Est.
GU21: Wok 6H 73
Hermits Rd. RH10: Craw 2D 182
HERMONGERS 8H 177
Hermonger's La.
RH12: Rudg 7G 176
Hernbrook Dr. RH13: Hors 8L 197
Herndon Cl. TW20: Egh 5C 20
Herndon Rd. SW18 ....8N 13
Herne Rd. KT6: Surb 8K 41
Hernes Cl. TW18: Stain 9K 21
Heron Cl. GU2: Guil 9L 93
GU9: Farnh 3E 128
GU16: Mytc 1D 90
GU52: C Cro 7D 88
RH11: Craw 1A 182
SL5: Asc 9H 17
SM1: Sut 2L 61
TN8: Eden 9L 127
Heron Ct. GU47: Sandh 8H 49
KT1: K Tham 6J 203 (2L 41)
KT17: Eps 1F 80
RH4: Dork 1J 201
TW19: Stan 2N 21
Heron Dale KT15: Addl 2M 55
Herondale CR2: Sels 5G 65
GU27: Hasl 2C 188
RG12: Brac 6A 32
Herondale Av. SW18 ....2B 28
Heronfield TW20: Eng G 7M 19
Heron Pl. RH19: E Grin 1B 186
Heron Rd. CR0: Croy 8B 46
TW1: Twick 7G 11
Heronry, The KT12: Hers 3H 57
Heronsbrook SL5: Asc 1B 34
Herons Cl. RH10: Cop 5D 164
Heronscourt GU18: Ligh 7N 51
Herons Cft. KT13: Weybr 3D 56
Heron Shaw GU6: Cranl 9N 155
Herons Lea RH10: Cop 5D 164
Heron's Pl. TW7: Isle 6H 11
Heron Sq. TW9: Rich 8K 11
Herons Swimming &
Fitness Cen., The 2D 188
Herons Way GU24: B'wood 8A 72
RG40: W'ham 1D 30
Herons Wood Ct.
RH6: Horl 7F 142
Herontye Dr. RH19: E Grin 1B 186
Herontye Ho. RH19: E Grin 2B 186
Heron Vw. TW8: Brent 3J 11
(off Commerce Rd.)
Heron Wlk. GU21: Wok 1E 74
Heron Way RH13: Hors 6N 197
TW14: Felt 7H 9
Heron Wood Rd.
GU12: Alde 4B 110
Herretts Gdns. GU12: Alde 3B 110
Herrett St. GU12: Alde 4B 110
Herrick Cl. GU16: Frim 3G 70
RH10: Craw 1G 182
Herrings La. GU20: Windl 2A 52
KT16: Chert 5J 37
Herriot Ct. GU46: Yate 2B 68
Herschel Grange
RG42: Warf 6B 16
Herschel Wlk. RH11: Craw 8N 181
HERSHAM 2K 57
Hersham By-Pass
KT12: Hers 2J 57
Hersham Cl. SW15 ....1F 26
Hersham Gdns. KT12: Hers 1J 57
HERSHAM GREEN 2L 57
Hersham Grn. Shop. Cen.
KT12: Hers 2L 57
Hersham Pl. KT12: Hers 2L 57
Hersham Rd.
KT12: Hers, Wal T 7H 39
Hersham Station (Rail) 9M 39
Hersham Trad. Est.
KT12: Wal T 8M 39
Hershell Ct. SW14 ....7A 12
Hertford Av. SW14 ....8C 12
Hertford Way CR4: Mit 3J 45
Hesiers Hill CR6: Warl 4A 86
Hesiers Rd. CR6: Warl 3A 86
Hesketh Cl. GU6: Cranl 7N 155
Heslop Rd. SW12 ....2D 28
Hesper M. SW5 ....1N 13
Hessle Gro. KT17: Ewe 7E 60
Hestercombe Av. SW6 ....5K 13
Hesterman Way CR0: Wad 7K 45
Hester Ter. TW9: Rich 6N 11
HESTON 3A 10
Heston Av. TW5: Hest 2M 9
Heston Cen., The
TW5: C'ford 1K 9
Heston Community Sports Hall
....3A 10
Heston Grange TW5: Hest 2N 9
Heston Grange La.
TW5: Hest 2N 9
Heston Ind. Mall TW5: Hest 3N 9
Heston Phoenix Distribution Pk.
TW5: Hest 2K 9
Heston Pool 2N 9
Heston Rd. RH1: Red 7D 122
TW5: Hest 2A 10
HESTON SERVICE AREA 2L 9
Heston Wlk. RH1: Red 7D 122
Hetherington Rd.
TW17: Shep 1D 38
Hethersett Cl. RH2: Reig 9A 102
Hever Rd. TN8: Eden, Hev 3M 147
Hevers Av. RH6: Horl 7D 142
Hevers Cnr. RH6: Horl 7D 142
Hewers Way KT20: Tad 7G 81
Hewitt Cl. CR0: Croy 9K 47
Hewitts Ind. Est.
GU6: Cranl 7K 155
Hewlett Pl. GU19: Bag 4K 51
Hexham Cl. GU47: Owls 5J 49
RH10: Craw 3J 183
Hexham Gdns. TW7: Isle 3G 11
Hexham Rd. SE27 ....3N 29
SM4: Mord 7N 43
Hextalls La. CR3: Blet 6A 104
RH1: Blet 6A 104
Heybridge Av. SW16 ....8J 29
Heyford Av. SW20 ....2L 43
Heyford Rd. CR4: Mit 1C 44
Heymede KT22: Leat 1J 99
Heythorpe Cl. GU21: Wok 4J 73
Heythorp St. SW18 ....2L 27
Heywood Ct. GU7: Goda 4F 132
Heywood Dr. GU19: Bag 5G 51
Hibbert's All. SL4: W'sor 4G 4
Hibernia Gdns. TW3: Houn 7A 10
Hibernia Rd. TW3: Houn 7A 10
Hickey's Almshouses
TW9: Rich 7M 11
Hickling Wlk. RH10: Craw 5F 182
Hickmans Cl. RH9: Gods 1F 124
Hicks La. GU17: B'water 1G 69
Hidcote Cl. GU22: Wok 3D 74
Hidcote Gdns. SW20 ....2G 42
Higgins Wlk. TW12: Hamp 7M 23
(off Abbott Cl.)
Higgins Way RH13: Hors 7L 197
Higgs La. GU19: Bag 4H 51
(not continuous)
Highacre RH4: Dork 8H 119
Highams Hill CR6: B Hil 8C 66
RH11: Craw 4L 181
Highams La. GU24: Chob 3D 52
High Ashton KT2: K Tham 8A 26
High Barn La. RH5: Ran C 3L 117
High Barn Rd.
KT24: Eff, Ran C 7L 97
Highbarrow Cl. CR8: Pur 6K 63
Highbarrow Rd. CR0: Croy 7D 46
High Beech CR2: S Croy 4B 64
RG12: Brac 3D 32
High Beeches GU16: Frim 4B 70
KT13: Weybr 3F 56
SM7: Ban 1H 81
High Beeches Cl.
CR8: Pur 6H 63
Highbirch Cl. RH12: Hors 3A 198
High Broom Cres.
BR4: W Wick 6L 47
Highbury Av. CR7: T Hea 1L 45
Highbury Cl. BR4: W Wick 8L 47
KT3: N Mal 3B 42
Highbury Cres.
GU15: Camb 8E 50
Highbury Dr. KT22: Leat 8G 78
Highbury Gro. GU27: Hasl 9G 170
Highbury Rd. SW19 ....6K 27
HIGH BUTTON 3H 171
High Cedar Dr. SW20 ....8H 27
HIGH CLANDON 2N 115
Highclere GU1: Guil 1C 114
SL5: S'hill 4A 34
Highclere Cl. CR8: Ken 2N 83
RG12: Brac 1C 32
Highclere Ct. GU21: Knap 4F 72
Highclere Dr. GU15: Camb 8E 50
Highclere Gdns.
GU21: Knap 4F 72
Highclere Rd. GU12: Alde 4B 110
GU21: Knap 4F 72
KT3: N Mal 2C 42
Highcliffe Dr. SW15 ....9E 12
High Cl. RG40: W'ham 1B 30
(off Wiltshire Rd.)
High Coombe Pl.
KT2: K Tham 7C 26
High Copse GU9: U Hal 6F 108
Highcotts La. GU4: W Cla 4H 95
High Cft. GU5: Sha G 7G 134
Highcroft GU8: Mil 2B 152
Highcroft Ct. KT23: Book 1A 98
Highcroft Dr. RH12: Rudg 8F 176
Highcross Way SW15 ....2F 26
HIGH CURLEY 8J 51
Highdaun Dr. SW16 ....3K 45
Highdene GU22: Wok 5B 74
(off Fairview Av.)
Highdown GU51: Fleet 3B 88
KT4: W Pk 8D 42
Highdown Cl. SM7: Ban 3L 81
Highdown Ct. RH10: Craw 6F 182
Highdown La. SM2: Sut 7N 61
Highdown Rd. SW15 ....9G 12
Highdown Way
RH12: Hors 2M 197
High Dr. CR3: Wold 9J 85
KT3: N Mal 9B 26
KT22: Oxs 1D 78
High Elms Country Pk. 4M 67
High Elms Nature Cen. 4M 67
High Elms Rd. BR6: Dow 7J 67
Higher Alham RG12: Brac 6C 32
Highercombe Rd.
GU27: Hasl 9J 171
Higher Dr. CR8: Pur 9L 63
KT24: E Hor 5F 96
SM7: Ban 8J 61
Higher Grn. KT17: Eps 9F 60
Highfield GU4: Chil 2B 134
RG12: Brac 5L 31
SM7: Ban 4C 82
Highfield Av. GU11: Alde 5M 109
Highfield Cl. GU9: Farnh 4G 128
GU11: Alde 4N 109
GU14: Cove 1L 89
KT6: Surb 7J 41
KT14: W By 9J 55
KT22: Oxs 7D 58
RG40: W'ham 2A 30
TW20: Eng G 7M 19
Highfield Ct. TW20: Eng G 7N 19
(off Highfield Rd.)
Highfield Cres. GU26: Hind 5C 170
Highfield Dr. BR4: W Wick 8L 47
CR3: Cate 9D 84
KT19: Ewe 3E 60
Highfield Gdns.
GU11: Alde 4M 109
Highfield Ho. RH11: Craw 2B 182
(off Town Mead)
Highfield La. GU3: Put 9L 111
GU8: Thur 8F 150
Highfield Path
GU14: Cove 1L 89
Highfield Rd. CR3: Cate 9D 84
CR8: Pur 6K 63
GU14: Cove 1L 89
KT5: Surb 6B 42
KT12: Wal T 7H 39
KT14: W By 9J 55
Highfield Rd. KT16: Chert 7J 37
RH19: E Grin 7N 165
SL4: W'sor 6C 4
SM1: Sut 2C 62
TN16: B Hil 4E 86
TW7: Isle 4F 10
TW13: Felt 2H 23
(off Railway Ter.)
TW13: Felt 3H 23
(Tiley Rd.)
TW16: Sunb 4G 38
TW20: Eng G 7M 19
High Flds. SL5: S'dale 4C 34
Highfields KT21: A'tead 6K 79
KT22: Fetc 2D 98
KT24: E Hor 6G 96
RH18: F Row 7H 187
SM1: Sut 8M 43
Highfields Rd. TN8: Eden 7L 127
High Foleys KT10: Clay 4H 59
High Gables BR2: Brom 1N 47
High Gdns. GU22: Wok 6L 73
High Gth. KT10: Esh 3C 58
HIGHGATE 8H 187
Highgate Ct. RH11: Craw 7A 182
Highgate La. GU14: Farnb 9A 70
Highgate Rd.
RH18: F Row 8G 187
Highgate Works
RH18: F Row 8G 187
HIGH GROVE 2L 185
Highgrove GU14: Farnb 7N 69
Highgrove Av. SL5: Asc 9K 17
Highgrove Ct. SM1: Sut 3M 61
Highgrove Ho. GU4: Guil 1E 114
Highgrove M. SM5: Cars 9D 44
High Hill Rd. CR6: Warl 2M 85
Highland Cotts. SM6: W'ton 1G 62
Highland Dr. GU51: Fleet 1C 88
Highland Pk. TW13: Felt 5G 23
Highland Rd. CR8: Pur 1L 83
GU12: Alde 2B 110
GU15: Camb 7C 50
RH5: B Grn 8J 139
Highlands KT21: A'tead 6J 79
Highlands, The KT24: E Hor 3F 96
Highlands Av. KT22: Leat 9J 79
RH13: Hors 6L 197
Highlands Cl. GU9: Farnh 4G 128
KT22: Leat 9H 79
TW3: Houn 4B 10
Highlands Cres.
RH13: Hors 6L 197
Highlands Heath
SW15 ....1H 27
Highlands La. GU22: Wok 8A 74
Highlands Pk. KT22: Leat 1K 99
Highlands Rd. GU9: H End 5H 109
KT22: Leat 9H 79
RH2: Reig 2B 122
RH13: Hors 6L 197
Highland Vw. GU6: Cranl 3L 155
Highland Vw. Pk. Homes
UB7: W Dray 1L 7
High La. CR3: Wold 6J 85
CR6: Warl, Wold 5J 85
GU27: Hasl 9G 170
High Loxley Rd.
GU8: Loxh 1C 174
High Mead BR4: W Wick 8N 47
High Mdw. Cl.
RH4: Dork 4K 201 (6H 119)
High Mdw. Pl. KT16: Chert 5H 37
High Oaks RH11: Craw 5N 181
High Pde., The SW16 ....4J 29
High Pk. Av. KT24: E Hor 4G 96
(not continuous)
TW9: Kew 4N 11
High Pk. Rd. GU9: Farnh 9G 109
TW9: Kew 4N 11
High Path SW19 ....9N 27
High Path Rd. GU1: Guil 3E 114
High Pewley
GU1: Guil 7E 202 (5A 114)
High Pine Cl. KT13: Weybr 2D 56
High Pines CR6: Warl 6F 84
High Pines Cvn. Site, The
RG42: Wink R 4F 16
High Pitfold GU26: Hind 8B 170
Highpoint KT13: Weybr 2B 56
High Ridge GU7: Goda 9F 132
Highridge Cl. KT18: Eps 1D 80
Highridge La. RH3: Betch 9A 120
High Rd. CR5: Chip, Coul 3C 102
KT14: Byf 8M 55
RH2: Reig 5A 102
High Standing CR3: Cate 3N 103
High St. BR3: Beck 1K 47
BR4: W Wick 7L 47
BR6: Chels 4N 67
BR6: Dow 7J 67
BR6: Farnb 2K 67
CR0: Croy 3C 200 (8N 45)
(not continuous)
CR3: Cate 1B 104
CR8: Pur 7L 63
GU1: Guil 6C 202 (5N 113)
(not continuous)
GU2: Guil 6B 202 (5M 113)
(not continuous)
GU5: Braml 5B 134
GU6: Cranl 7L 155
GU7: Goda 7G 133

Holland Av.—Horewood Rd.

Holland Av. SM2: Sut 5M 61
SW20 . . . . .9E 26
Holland Cl. GU9: Farnh 3K 129
KT19: Eps 7B 60
RH1: Red 3D 122
Holland Ct. KT6: Surb 6K 41
Holland Cres. RH8: Oxt 2C 126
Holland Gdns. GU51: Fleet 5B 88
TW8: Brent 2M 11
TW20: Thor 1H 37
Holland Ho. SL4: Eton 2F 4
(off Common La.)
Holland La. RH8: Oxt 2C 126
Holland Pines RG12: Brac 6L 31
Holland Rd. RH8: Oxt 2C 126
SE25 . . . . .4D 46
Hollands, The GU22: Wok 5A 74
KT4: W Pk 7E 42
TW13: Hanw 5L 23
Hollands Ct. RH19: E Grin . . .6C 166
Hollands Fld. RH12: Bro H . . .4E 196
Hollands Way RH12: Warn . . .9F 178
RH19: E Grin 6C 166
Hollerith Ri. RG12: Brac 5N 31
Holles Cl. TW12: Hamp 7A 24
Hollies, The GU17: Haw 5M 69
KT15: Addl 2L 55
(off Crockford Pk. Rd.)
RH8: Oxt 2D 126
Hollies Av. KT14: W By 9H 55
Hollies Cl. SW16 . . . . .7L 29
TW1: Twick 3F 24
Hollies Ct. KT15: Addl 2L 55
Hollies Way SW12 . . . . .1E 28
Hollin Ct. RH10: Craw 9C 162
Hollingbourne Cres.
RH11: Craw 9A 182
Hollingsworth Ct. KT6: Surb . . .6K 41
Hollingsworth Rd. CR0: Croy . . .3E 64
Hollington Cres. KT3: N Mal . . .5E 42
Hollingworth Cl.
KT8: W Mole 3N 39
Hollingworth Way
TN16: Weste 4M 107
Hollis Row RH1: Red 5D 122
Hollis Wood Dr.
GU10: Wrec 6D 128
Hollman Gdns. SW16 . . . . . . .7M 29
Hollow, The GU7: Eash 7C 132
GU10: Ews 5A 108
RH11: Craw 4L 181
Holloway Cl. UB7: Harm 1N 7
Holloway Dr. GU25: V Wat 3A 36
HOLLOWAY HILL 9H 133
Holloway Hill GU7: Goda 7G 133
KT16: Chert 9E 36
Holloway Ho. TW20: Egh 6B 20
Holloway La.
UB7: Harm, W Dray 2M 7
Holloway St. TW3: Houn 6B 10
Hollow Cl. GU2: Guil 4L 113
Hollow La. GU25: V Wat 2M 35
GU35: Head 3D 168
RH5: A Com, Wott 9L 117
RH7: Dorm 1D 166
RH19: E Grin 4F 166
Hollows, The TW8: Brent 2M 11
Hollow Way GU26: G'hott 5A 170
Holly Acre GU46: Yate 1C 68
Holly Av. GU16: Frim 3F 70
KT12: Wal T 7L 39
KT15: N Haw 6J 55
Hollybank GU24: W End 9C 52
Hollybank Cl. TW12: Hamp 6A 24
Holly Bank Rd. GU22: Wok 8L 73
Hollybank Rd. KT14: W By 1J 75
Hollybrook Pk. GU35: Bor 6A 168
Hollybush Bus. Cen.
RH10: S Bri 6K 163
Hollybush Cl. RH10: Craw . . .2C 182
Hollybush Ind. Est.
GU11: Alde 8C 90
Holly Bush La.
TW12: Hamp 8N 23
Hollybush La. GU10: Fren 1H 149
GU11: Alde 8C 90
GU23: Rip 6M 75
Hollybush Ride
GU20: Windl 9K 33
RG40: Finch 2B 48
RG45: Crow 3B 48
Hollybush Rd. KT2: K Tham . . .6L 25
RH10: Craw 2C 182
Holly Cl. BR3: Beck 3M 47
GU12: Alde 2A 110
GU14: Cove 1M 89
GU21: Wok 6L 73
GU35: H Dwn 4H 169
KT16: L'cross 9K 35
RH10: Craw 1E 182
RH12: Hors 3A 198
SM6: W'ton 4F 62
TW13: Hanw 6M 23
TW20: Eng G 7L 19
Hollycombe TW20: Eng G 5M 19
Holly Ct. KT16: Chert 7H 37
(off King St.)
KT22: Leat 9G 79
(off Belmont Rd.)
RG45: Crow 3D 48
SM2: Sut 4M 61
Holly Cres. BR3: Beck 4J 47
SL4: W'sor 5A 4
Hollycroft Cl.
CR2: S Croy 8F 200 (2B 64)
UB7: Sip 2B 8
Hollycroft Gdns. UB7: Sip 2B 8
Hollydale Dr. BR2: Brom 1H 67
Holly Dr. SL4: O Win 8H 5
Holly Farm Rd. UB2: S'hall 1M 9
Hollyfield Rd. KT5: Surb 6M 41
Hollyfields Cl. GU15: Camb . . .1N 69
Holly Ga. KT15: Addl 1K 55
Holly Grn. KT13: Weybr 1E 56
Hollygrove Cl. TW3: Houn 7N 9
Holly Hedge Cl. GU16: Frim . . .4C 70
Holly Hedge Rd. GU16: Frim . . .4C 70
Hollyhedge Rd. KT11: Cob 1J 77
HOLLY HILL 9N 187
Holly Hill Dr. SM7: Ban 3M 81
Holly Hill Pk. SM7: Ban 4M 81
Hollyhock Dr. GU24: Bis 2D 72
Hollyhook Cl. RG45: Crow 1F 48
Holly Ho. RG12: Brac 5N 31
TW8: Brent 2J 11
Holly La. GU3: Worp 7F 92
GU7: Goda 7F 132
SM7: Ban 3M 81
Holly La. E. SM7: Ban 3M 81
Holly La. W. SM7: Ban 4M 81
Holly Lea GU4: J Wel 6N 93
Holly Lodge GU22: Wok 4B 74
(off Heathside Cres.)
Holly Lodge Mobile Home Pk.
KT20: Lwr K 4K 101
Hollymead SM5: Cars 9D 44
Hollymead Rd. CR5: Chip 5E 82
Hollymeoak Rd. CR5: Coul 6F 82
Hollymoor La. KT19: Ewe 6C 60
Holly Pde. KT11: Cob 1J 77
(off High St.)
Hollyridge GU27: Hasl 2F 188
Holly Rd. GU12: Alde 2A 110
GU14: Cove 1L 89
RH2: Reig 5N 121
TW1: Twick 2F 24
TW3: Houn 7B 10
TW12: H Hill 7C 24
W4 . . . . .1C 12
Holly Spring Cotts.
RG12: Brac 8B 16
Holly Spring La. RG12: Brac . . .9A 16
Hollytree Cl. SW19 . . . . .2J 27
Hollytree Gdns. GU16: Frim . . .6B 70
Holly Tree Rd. CR3: Cate 9B 84
Holly Wlk. SL4: W'sor 5B 18
HOLLYWATER 8A 168
Hollywater Rd. GU30: Pass . . .9A 168
GU35: Bor, White 8A 168
Holly Way CR4: Mit 3H 45
GU17: B'water 2J 69
Hollywood Bowl
Bracknell 1N 31
Crawley 2B 182
Hollywood Rd. SW10 . . . . .2N 13
Hollywoods CR0: Sels 5J 65
Holman Cl. RH11: Craw 9N 181
Holman Ct. KT17: Ewe 5F 60
Holman Hunt Ho. W6 . . . . .1K 13
(off Field Rd.)
Holman Rd. KT19: Ewe 2B 60
Holmbank Dr. TW17: Shep 3F 38
Holmbrook Cl. GU14: Cove 1H 89
Holmbrook Gdns.
GU14: Cove 1H 89
Holmbury Av. RG45: Crow 9F 30
Holmbury Cl. RH11: Craw 5A 182
Holmbury Ct. CR2: S Croy 2B 64
SW17 . . . . .4D 28
SW19 . . . . .8C 28
Holmbury Dr. RH5: Nth H 8J 119
Holmbury Gro. CR0: Sels 4J 65
Holmbury Hill Rd.
RH5: H Mary 9J 137
Holmbury Keep RH6: Horl . . .7G 142
(off Maize Cft.)
Holmbury La.
RH5: For G, H Mary 1L 157
Holmbury Rd.
GU5: H Mary 9H 137
GU6: Ewh 9H 137
RH5: H Mary 9H 137
HOLMBURY ST MARY 6K 137
Holmbush Cl. RH12: Hors 2K 197
Holmbush Ct. RH12: Fay 8G 181
Holmbush Farm World
RH12: Fay 8G 181
Holmbush Potteries Ind. Est.
RH12: Fay 8H 181
Holmbush Rd. SW15 . . . . .9K 13
Holm Cl. KT15: Wood 8G 55
Holm Ct. GU7: Goda 4G 132
Holmcroft KT20: Wal H 3G 101
RH10: Craw 4C 182
Holmdene Cl. BR3: Beck 1M 47
Holmead Rd. SW6 . . . . .3N 13
Holme Chase KT13: Weybr 3D 56
Holme Cl. RG45: Crow 9F 30
Holme Ct. TW7: Isle 6G 10
Holmefield Pl. KT15: N Haw . . .6K 55
HOLME GREEN 5E 30
Holmes Cl. CR8: Pur 9K 63
GU22: Wok 8B 74
SL5: S'hill 5N 33
Holmes Ct. GU26: G'hott 6B 170
(off Boundary Rd.)
Holmesdale KT13: Weybr 3E 56
(off Bridgewater Rd.)
Holmesdale Av.
RH1: Mers 9G 102
SW14 . . . . .6A 12
Holmesdale Cl. GU1: Guil 2D 114
SE25 . . . . .2C 46
Holmesdale Mnr.
RH1: Red 1E 122
Holmesdale Natural History Mus.
. . . . .3N 121
Holmesdale Pk. RH1: Nut 3K 123
Holmesdale Rd. CR0: Croy 4A 46
RH1: Sth N 5K 123
RH2: Reig 2M 121
RH5: Nth H 9H 119
SE25 . . . . .4A 46
TW9: Kew 4M 11
TW11: Tedd 8J 25
Holmesdale Ter.
RH5: Nth H 9H 119
Holmesdale Vs.
RH5: Mid H 2H 139
Holmes Place Health Club
Croydon 4C 200 (9N 45)
Hammersmith 1J 13
(off Hammersmith Rd.)
Merton 7A 28
Holmes Rd. SW19 . . . . .8A 28
TW1: Twick 3F 24
Holmeswood SM2: Sut 3N 61
HOLMETHORPE 9F 102
Holmethorpe Av. RH1: Red . . .9F 102
Holmethorpe Ind. Est.
RH1: Red 9F 102
Holmewood Gdns.
SW2 . . . . .1K 29
Holmewood Rd. SE25 . . . . .2B 46
SW2 . . . . .1J 29
Holmgrove Ho. CR8: Pur 8L 63
Holming End RH12: Hors 3A 198
Holmlea Ct. CR0: Croy 6E 200
Holmlea Rd. SL3: Dat 4N 5
Holmlea Wlk. SL3: Dat 4M 5
Holm Oak Cl. SW15 . . . . .9L 13
Holmoaks Ho. BR3: Beck 1M 47
Holmside Rd. SW12 . . . . .1E 28
Holmsley Cl. KT3: N Mal 5E 42
Holmsley Ho. SW15 . . . . .1E 26
(off Tangley Gro.)
Holm Ter. RH4: Dork 8H 119
Holmwood Av. CR2: Sande 9C 64
Holmwood Cl. KT15: Addl 2J 55
KT24: E Hor 6F 96
SM2: Chea 5J 61
HOLMWOOD CORNER 6K 139
Holmwood Gdns.
SM6: W'ton 3F 62
Holmwood Rd. KT9: Ches 2K 59
SM2: Chea 5H 61
Holmwood Station (Rail) 7J 139
Holmwood Vw. Rd.
RH5: Mid H 2H 139
Holne Chase SM4: Mord 5L 43
Holroyd Cl. KT10: Clay 5F 58
Holroyd Rd. KT10: Clay 5F 58
SW15 . . . . .7H 13
Holsart Cl. KT20: Tad 9G 81
Holstein Av. KT13: Weybr 1B 56
Holst Mans. SW13 . . . . .2H 13
Holsworthy Way KT9: Ches 2J 59
Holt, The SM4: Mord 3M 43
SM6: W'ton 1G 62
Holt Cl. GU14: Farnb 7A 70
Holt La. RG41: W'ham 1A 30
Holton Heath RG12: Brac 3D 32
HOLT POUND 7C 128
Holt Pound Cotts.
GU10: H Pou 7B 128
Holt Pound La.
GU10: H Pou 6B 128
Holtwood Rd. KT22: Oxs 9C 58
HOLTYE 7N 167
Holtye Av. RH19: E Grin 7B 166
HOLTYE COMMON 6N 167
Holtye Pl. RH19: E Grin 7C 166
Holtye Rd. RH19: E Grin 8B 166
RH19: Hamm 6L 167
TN8: Cow, Hamm 6L 167
Holtye Wlk. RH10: Craw 5E 182
Holwood Cl. KT12: Wal T 8K 39
Holwood Pk. Av.
BR6: Farnb 1H 67
Holybourne Av. SW15 . . . . .1F 26
Holyhead Ct. KT1: K Tham 8H 203
Holyoake Av. GU21: Wok 4M 73
Holyoake Cres. GU21: Wok . . .4M 73
Holyport Rd. SW6 . . . . .3J 13
Holyrood RH19: E Grin 2C 186
Holyrood Pl. RH11: Craw 7N 181
Holywell Cl. GU14: Farnb 7M 69
TW19: Stan 2N 21
Holywell Way TW19: Stan 2N 21
Hombrook Dr. RG42: Brac 9K 15
Hombrook Ho. RG42: Brac 9K 15
Homebeech Ho. GU22: Wok . . .5A 74
(off Mt. Hermon Rd.)
Home Cl. GU25: V Wat 5N 35
KT22: Fetc 8D 78
RH10: Craw 1G 183
SM5: Cars 8D 44
Home Ct.
KT6: K Tham 8H 203 (4K 41)
Home Farm Cl.
GU14: Farnb 8B 70
KT7: T Dit 6F 40
KT10: Esh 3B 58
KT16: Otter 4C 54
KT20: Tad 4J 81
RH3: Betch 4D 120
TW17: Shep 3F 38
Home Farm Cotts.
GU8: P Har 6N 131
Home Farm Gdns.
KT12: Wal T 8K 39
Home Farm Ho.
RH12: Hors 6J 197
(off Springfield Rd.)
Home Farm Rd. GU7: Bus 9H 133
Homefield GU8: Thur 7G 150
SM4: Mord 3M 43
Homefield Av. KT12: Hers 1L 57
Homefield Cl. KT15: Wood 8G 55
KT22: Leat 8J 79
RH6: Horl 7F 142
Homefield Gdns. CR4: Mit 1A 44
KT20: Tad 7H 81
Homefield Pk. SM1: Sut 3N 61
Homefield Rd. CR5: Coul 6M 83
CR6: Warl 6F 84
KT12: Wal T 6M 39
SW19 . . . . .7J 27
W4 . . . . .1E 12
Homegreen Ho.
GU27: Hasl 2E 188
Homeland Dr. SM2: Sut 5N 61
Homelands KT22: Leat 8J 79
Homelea Cl. GU14: Farnb 6N 69
Homeleigh Ct. SW16 . . . . .4J 29
Homeleigh Cres.
GU12: A Va 5E 90
Home Mdw. SM7: Ban 3M 81
Homemead Rd. CR0: Croy 5G 45
Home Pk. KT8: E Mol 4J 41
RH8: Oxt 9C 106
Home Pk. Cl. GU5: Braml 5B 134
Home Pk. Ct.
KT1: K Tham 8H 203
Homepark Ho. GU9: Farnh . . .1H 129
Home Pk. Pde.
KT1: H Wic 3G 203
Home Pk. Rd. GU46: Yate 9C 48
SW19 . . . . .5L 27
Home Pk. Ter. KT1: H Wic . . .3G 203
Home Pk. Wlk.
KT1: K Tham 8H 203 (3K 41)
Homer Rd. CR0: Croy 5G 47
Homersham Rd.
KT1: K Tham 1N 41
Homers Rd. SL4: W'sor 4A 4
Homesdale Rd. CR3: Cate . . .1A 104
Homestall GU2: Guil 3G 113
Homestall Rd.
RH19: Ash W 9G 166
Homestead GU6: Cranl 6A 156
Homestead & Middle Vw.
Mobile Home Pk.
GU3: Norm 9B 92
Homestead Dr. GU3: Norm 9A 92
Homestead Gdns.
KT10: Clay 2E 58
Homestead Rd. CR3: Cate . . .1A 104
SW6 . . . . .3L 13
TN8: Eden 7K 127
TW18: Stain 7K 21
Homestead Way
CR0: N Add 7M 65
Homestream Ho.
RH12: Hors 7H 197
Homethorne Ho.
RH11: Craw 4A 182
Home Vs. GU5: Alb 3L 135
Homewater Ho.
KT17: Eps 6M 201 (9D 60)
Homewaters Av.
TW16: Sunb 9G 23
Homewood GU6: Cranl 7B 156
Homewood Cl.
TW12: Hamp 7N 23
Homewoods SW12 . . . . .1G 28
Homeworth Ho. GU22: Wok . . .5A 74
(off Mt. Hermon Rd.)
Hone Hill GU47: Sandh 7G 48
Hones Yd. Bus. Pk.
GU9: Farnh 1J 129
Honeybrook Rd. SW12 . . . . . . .1G 28
Honeycrock Ct. RH1: Salf 1E 142
Honeycrock La. RH1: Salf 1E 142
Honeydown Cotts.
GU28: North 8E 190
HONEYHILL 7E 30
Honey Hill RG40: W'ham 6E 30
Honeyhill Rd. RG42: Brac 9M 15
Honey La.
RH12: Oak, Rowh 6M 177
Honey La. Ho. SW10 . . . . .2N 13
(off Finborough Rd.)
Honeypot La. TN8: Eden 8F 126
Honeypots Rd. GU22: Wok 9N 73
Honeysuckle Bottom
KT24: E Hor 3F 116
Honeysuckle Cl.
RG45: Crow 9F 30
RH6: Horl 7G 143
Honeysuckle Gdns.
CR0: Croy 6G 47
Honeysuckle La.
GU35: H Dwn 4G 168
RH5: Nth H 8J 119
RH11: Craw 9A 162
Honeysuckle Wlk.
RH12: Hors 3N 197
Honeywood Heritage Cen. 2D 62
Honeywood La. RH5: Oak . . .4M 177
Honeywood Rd.
RH13: Hors 4N 197
TW7: Isle 7G 10
Honeywood Wlk. SM5: Cars . . .1D 62
Honister Gdns. GU51: Fleet . . .3D 88
Honister Hgts. CR8: Pur 1A 84
Honister Wlk. GU15: Camb 2H 71
Honnor Gdns. TW7: Isle 5D 10
Honnor Rd. TW18: Stain 8M 21
Hood Av. SW14 . . . . .8B 12
Hood Cl.
CR0: Croy 1A 200 (7M 45)
Hood Rd. SW20 . . . . .8E 26
HOOK 2L 59
Hooke Rd. KT24: E Hor 3G 97
Hookfield
KT19: Eps 6G 201 (9B 60)
Hookfield M.
KT19: Eps 6G 201 (9B 60)
HOOK HEATH 7L 73
Hook Heath Av. GU22: Wok 6L 73
Hook Heath Gdns.
GU22: Wok 8J 73
Hook Heath Rd. GU22: Wok . . .8H 73
Hook Hill CR2: Sande 6B 64
Hook Hill La. GU22: Wok 8L 73
Hook Hill Pk. GU22: Wok 8L 73
Hook Ho. La. GU8: Duns 3M 173
Hookhouse La. GU8: Loxh . . .1N 173
Hookhouse Rd.
GU8: Duns, Loxh 1N 173
HOOK JUNC. 9L 41
Hook La. GU3: Put 8N 111
GU5: Shere 1B 136
GU24: W End 9N 51
Hookley Cl. GU8: Els 8J 131
Hookley La. GU8: Els 8J 131
Hook Mill La. GU18: Ligh 5A 52
Hook Ri. Nth. KT6: Surb 9L 41
Hook Ri. Sth. KT6: Surb 9L 41
Hook Ri. Sth. Ind. Pk.
KT6: Ches 9M 41
Hook Rd. KT6: Surb 8L 41
KT9: Ches 2K 59
KT19: Eps, Ewe
. . . . .5K 201 (4B 60)
Hookstile La. GU9: Farnh 2H 129
Hookstone La.
GU24: W End 7C 52
Hook St. GU6: Alf 8K 175
HOOKWOOD 9B 142
Hookwood Cnr. RH8: Limp . . .6D 106
Hookwood Cotts.
KT18: Head 2B 100
HOOKWOOD PARK 6D 106
Hookwood Pk. RH8: Limp 7D 106
HOOLEY 8F 82
Hooley La. RH1: Red 4D 122
Hope Av. RG12: Brac 6C 32
Hope Cl. SM1: Sut 2A 62
TW8: Brent 1L 11
Hope Cotts. RG12: Brac 2A 32
Hope Ct. RH11: Craw 8N 181
Hope Fountain GU15: Camb . . .2E 70
Hope Grant's Rd.
GU11: Alde 9M 89
(not continuous)
Hope Ho. CR0: Croy 6F 200
Hope La. GU9: U Hal 6G 108
Hopeman Cl. GU47: C Tow 7J 49
Hopes Cl. TW5: Hest 2A 10
Hope St. GU8: Els 7H 131
Hope Way GU11: Alde 1L 109
Hopfield GU21: Wok 3A 74
Hopfield Av. KT14: Byf 8N 55
Hopgarden Cl. TN8: Eden 9M 127
Hophurst Cl.
RH10: Craw D 1E 184
Hophurst Dr.
RH10: Craw D 1E 184
Hophurst Hill
RH10: Craw D 8G 164
Hophurst La.
RH10: Craw D 1E 184
Hopkin Cl. GU2: Guil 8L 93
Hopkins Ct. RH11: Craw 8N 181
Hopper Va. RG12: Brac 5M 31
Hoppety, The KT20: Tad 9J 81
Hoppingwood Av.
KT3: N Mal 2D 42
Hopton Ct. GU2: Guil 3H 113
(off Park Barn Dr.)
Hopton Gdns. KT3: N Mal 5F 42
Hopton Rd. SW16 . . . . .6J 29
Hopwood Cl. SW17 . . . . .4A 28
Horace Rd.
KT1: K Tham . . .6L 203 (2M 41)
Horatio Av. RG42: Warf 9C 16
Horatio Ho. W6 . . . . .1J 13
(off Fulham Pal. Rd.)
Horatio Pl. SW19 . . . . .9M 27
Horatius Way CR0: Wad 2K 63
Hordern Ho. RH12: Hors 7G 196
Horder Rd. SW6 . . . . .4K 13
Horewood Rd. RG12: Brac 5N 31

Horizon Bus. Village
KT13: Weybr 8B 56
Horizon Ct. SM2: Chea 4K 61
(off Up. Mulgrave Rd.)
Horizon Ho.
KT17: Eps 6L 201 (9D 60)
HORLEY 8F 142
Horley Anderson Sports Cen.
. . . . .8C 142
Horley Lodge La.
RH1: Salf 3D 142
Horley Rd. RH1: Red 5D 122
RH6: Char 4L 161
Horley Row RH6: Horl 7D 142
Horley Station (Rail) 9F 142
Hormer Cl. GU47: Owls 6J 49
Hornbeam Cl. GU14: Cove 9H 69
GU47: Owls 6J 49
RH13: Hors 7M 197
Hornbeam Copse
RG42: Warf 9E 16
Hornbeam Cres.
TW8: Brent 3H 11
Hornbeam Gdns.
KT3: N Mal 5F 42
Hornbeam Rd. GU1: Guil 9M 93
RH2: Reig 6N 121
Hornbeam Ter. SM5: Cars 7C 44
Hornbeam Wlk.
KT12: Whit V 5G 56
TW10: Rich 3M 25
Hornbrook Copse
RH13: Hors 8M 197
Hornbrook Hill
RH13: Hors 8M 197
Hornby Av. RG12: Brac 6B 32
Hornchurch Cl.
KT2: K Tham 5K 25
Hornchurch Hill
CR3: Whyte 5C 84
Horndean Cl.
RH10: Craw 8H 163
SW15 . . . . .2F 26
Horndean Rd. RG12: Brac 5D 32
HORNE 5C 144
Hornecourt Hill RH6: Horn . . .4C 144
Horner La. CR4: Mit 1B 44
Horne Rd. TW17: Shep 3B 38
Horne Way SW15 . . . . .5H 13
Hornhatch GU4: Guil 9D 114
Hornhatch Cl. GU4: Guil 9D 114
(not continuous)
Hornhatch La. GU4: Guil 9C 114
Horn Rd. GU14: Cove 9K 69
HORNS GREEN 4N 87
HORNS HILL 8N 107
Hornshill La. RH12: Rudg 2A 194
Horseblock Hollow
GU6: Cranl 3B 156
Horsebrass Dr. GU19: Bag 5J 51
Horsecroft SM7: Ban 4L 81
Horsecroft Mdws. SM7: Ban . . .3L 81
Horse Fair
KT1: K Tham 3G 203 (1K 41)
Horsegate Ride SL5: Asc 5L 33
(Coronation Rd.)
SL5: Asc 4F 32
(Swinley Rd.)
Horse Hill RH6: Sid 6M 141
HORSELL 3M 73
Horsell Birch GU21: Wok 2K 73
(not continuous)
Horsell Comn. Rd.
GU21: Wok 1M 73
Horsell Ct. KT16: Chert 6K 37
Horsell Moor GU21: Wok 4N 73
Horsell Pk. GU21: Wok 3N 73
Horsell Pk. Cl. GU21: Wok 3N 73
Horsell Ri. GU21: Wok 2N 73
Horsell Ri. Cl. GU21: Wok 2N 73
Horsell Va. GU21: Wok 3A 74
Horsell Way GU21: Wok 3M 73
Horse Ride SM5: Cars 6C 62
Horseshoe, The CR5: Coul 9H 63
GU7: Goda 8F 132
SM7: Ban 2L 81
Horseshoe Bend
GU26: G'hott 6M 169
Horseshoe Cl.
GU15: Camb 7D 50
RH10: Craw 2H 183
Horseshoe Cres.
GU15: Camb 7D 50
GU35: Bor 6A 168
Horse Shoe Grn. SM1: Sut 8N 43
Horseshoe Lake Watersports Cen.
. . . . .6C 48
Horseshoe La. GU6: Cranl 6L 155
GU12: A Va 6E 90
Horseshoe La. E.
GU1: Guil 2D 114
Horseshoe La. W.
GU1: Guil 2D 114
HORSHAM 6J 197
Horsham FC 7K 197
Horsham Gates
RH13: Hors 5L 197
Horsham Indoor Bowls Cen.
. . . . .6D 196
Horsham Mus. 7J 197
(off Causeway)
Horsham Northern By-Pass
RH12: Warn, Hors 2H 197

Horsham Rd. GU4: Chil 2A 134
GU5: Braml 1E 154
(Rooks Hill)
GU5: Braml 2N 133
(Trunley Heath Rd.)
GU6: Alf 6J 175
GU6: Cranl 8F 154
(Barrihurst La.)
GU6: Cranl 8N 155
(Bridge Rd.)
GU6: Ewh 6F 156
GU47: Owls 6J 49
RH4: Dork 4J 201 (6G 119)
RH5: A Ham, H Mary 2G 136
RH5: B Grn 2K 159
RH5: Cap 2J 179
RH5: For G, Ockl, W'wood
. . . . .1L 177
RH5: Holm 4J 139
RH5: Holm, Mid H, Nth H
. . . . .9H 119
RH5: W'wood 6F 156
RH11: Craw 7K 181
RH11: P Pot 2M 199
RH12: Rudg 8N 155
RH12: Rusp 5N 179
RH17: P Pla, Hand 9K 199
TW14: Bedf 9D 8
Horsham Station (Rail) 5K 197
Horsham Trad. Est.
RH13: Hors 4L 197
Horsley Cl.
KT19: Eps 6J 201 (9C 60)
Horsley Dr. CR0: N Add 4M 65
KT2: K Tham 6K 25
Horsley Rd. KT11: Down 9H 77
Horsley Station (Rail) 3F 96
Horsnape Gdns.
RG42: Bin 7G 15
Horsneile La. RG42: Brac 8N 15
Hortensia Ho. SW10 . . . . .3N 13
(off Gunter Gro.)
Hortensia Rd. SW10 . . . . .3N 13
Horticultural Pl. W4 . . . . .1C 12
HORTON
KT19 . . . . .7B 60
SL3 . . . . .6C 6
Horton Country Pk. 6M 59
Horton Cres. KT19: Eps 7N 59
Horton Footpath KT19: Eps 7B 60
Horton Gdns. KT19: Eps 7B 60
SL3: Hort 6B 6
Horton Hill KT19: Eps 7B 60
Horton Ho. W6 . . . . .1K 13
(off Field Rd.)
Horton La. KT19: Eps 8N 59
Horton Pk. Children's Farm
. . . . .6N 59
Horton Pl. TN16: Weste 4M 107
Horton Rd. SL3: Coln, Hort 5C 6
SL3: Dat, Hort 3L 5
SL3: Poy 6G 6
TW19: Stan M 7H 7
Hortons Way TN16: Weste . . .4M 107
Horton Trad. Est. SL3: Hort 6E 6
Horton Way CR0: Croy 4G 46
Horvath Cl. KT13: Weybr 1E 56
Hosack Rd. SW17 . . . . .3E 28
Hosey Comn. La.
TN16: Weste 8N 107
Hosey Comn. Rd.
TN8: C Hil, Weste 2L 127
TN16: Weste 7N 107
HOSEY HILL 6N 107
Hosey Hill TN16: Weste 5N 107
Hoskins, The RH8: Oxt 7A 106
(off Station Rd. W.)
Hoskins Cl. UB3: Harl 1G 8
Hoskins Pl. RH19: E Grin 6C 166
Hoskins Pl. Ind. Est.
GU15: Camb 3N 69
Hoskins Rd. RH8: Oxt 7A 106
(not continuous)
Hoskins Wlk. RH8: Oxt 7A 106
(off Station Rd. W.)
Hospital Bri. Rd.
TW2: Twick, Whitt 1B 24
HOSPITAL BRIDGE RDBT. 3B 24
Hospital Hill GU11: Alde 1M 109
Hospital Rd. GU11: Alde 1M 109
TW3: Houn 6A 10
Hostel Rd. GU14: Farnb 5N 89
Hotham Cl. KT8: W Mole 2A 40
Hotham Rd. SW15 . . . . .6H 13
SW19 . . . . .8A 28
Hotham Rd. M. SW19 . . . . .8A 28
Houblon Rd. TW10: Rich 8L 11
Houghton Cl. TW12: Hamp 7M 23
Houghton Rd. RH10: Craw . . .6G 182
Houlder Cres. CR0: Wad 3M 63
Houlton Ct. GU19: Bag 5J 51
Hound Ho. Rd. GU5: Shere . . .1B 136
Houndown La. GU8: Thur 6E 150
HOUNSLOW 6B 10
Hounslow and District Indoor
Bowls Club 5N 9
(off Sutton La.)
Hounslow Av. TW3: Houn 8B 10
Hounslow Bus. Pk.
TW3: Houn 7A 10
Hounslow Central Station (Tube)
. . . . .6B 10
Hounslow Cen. TW3: Houn 6B 10

Hounslow East Station (Tube)
. . . . .5C 10
Hounslow Gdns.
TW3: Houn 8B 10
Hounslow Heath Nature Reserve
. . . . .9L 9
Hounslow Manor Sports Hall
. . . . .5C 10
Hounslow Rd. TW2: Whitt 9B 10
TW13: Hanw 5L 23
TW14: Felt 2J 23
Hounslow Station (Rail) 8B 10
Hounslow Urban Farm 8H 9
HOUNSLOW WEST 5M 9
Hounslow West Station (Tube)
. . . . .5M 9
Household Cavalry Mus. 6E 4
Houseman Rd. GU14: Farnb 8L 69
Houston Pl. KT10: Esh 7D 40
Houston Rd. KT6: Surb 5H 41
Houston Way RG45: Crow 2C 48
Houstoun Ct. TW5: Hest 3N 9
Hove Gdns. SM1: Sut 7N 43
Howard Av. KT17: Ewe 6F 60
Howard Cl. GU51: Fleet 4D 88
KT20: Wal H 3E 100
KT21: A'tead 5M 79
KT22: Leat 1J 99
KT24: W Hors 3E 96
RG12: Brac 4M 31
TW12: Hamp 8C 24
TW16: Sunb 7G 22
Howard Cole Way
GU11: Alde 2K 109
Howard Ct. GU21: Knap 6F 72
(off Tudor Way)
RH2: Reig 2A 122
Howard Dr. GU14: Cove 1G 89
Howard Gdns. GU1: Guil 2C 114
Howard Pl. RH2: Reig 1M 121
Howard Ridge GU4: B'ham 8C 94
Howard Rd. CR5: Coul 2G 83
KT3: N Mal 2D 42
KT5: Surb 5M 41
KT23: Book 5B 98
KT24: E Jun 1H 97
RG40: W'ham 3B 30
RH2: Reig 4N 121
RH4: Dork 2H 201 (5G 118)
RH5: Nth H 9J 119
RH11: Craw 7K 181
RH13: Hors 4N 197
SE25 . . . . .4D 46
TW7: Isle 6F 10
Howards Cl. GU22: Wok 7C 74
Howards Crest Cl.
BR3: Beck 1M 47
Howards Ho. RH2: Reig 2N 121
Howards La. KT15: Addl 3H 55
SW15 . . . . .7G 13
Howards Rd. GU22: Wok 7B 74
Howard St. KT7: T Dit 6H 41
Howberry Chase
GU27: Hasl 2F 188
Howberry Rd. CR7: T Hea 9N 29
Howden Rd. SE25 . . . . .1C 46
Howe, The GU14: Farnb 4F 88
Howe Dr. CR3: Cate 9A 84
Howe La. RG42: Bin 2J 15
Howell Cl. RG42: Warf 7A 16
Howell Hill SM2: Chea 6H 61
Howell Hill Cl. KT17: Ewe 7H 61
Howell Hill Gro. KT17: Ewe 6H 61
Howgate Rd. SW14 . . . . .6C 12
Howitts Cl. KT10: Esh 3A 58
Howland Ho. SW16 . . . . .4J 29
Howlands Ct. RH10: Craw 4D 182
How La. CR5: Chip 4E 82
Howley Rd.
CR0: Croy 4A 200 (9M 45)
Howorth Ct. RG12: Brac 3D 32
Howsman Rd. SW13 . . . . .2F 12
Howson Ter. TW10: Rich 9L 11
Hoylake Cl. RH11: Ifi 4J 181
Hoylake Gdns. CR4: Mit 2G 44
Hoyland Ho. RH11: Craw 3L 181
Hoyle Cotts. RH5: B Grn 1K 159
Hoyle Rd. SW17 . . . . .6C 28
Hubbard Dr. KT9: Ches 3K 59
Hubbard Rd. SE27 . . . . .5N 29
Hubberholme RG12: Brac 2M 31
Hubert Cl. SW19 . . . . .9A 28
(off Nelson Gro. Rd.)
Huddleston Cres.
RH1: Mers 6H 103
Hudson Ct. GU2: Guil 3J 113
Hudson Gdns. BR6: Chels 3N 67
Hudson Ho.
KT19: Eps 6K 201 (9C 60)
SW10 . . . . .3N 13
(off Hortensia Rd.)
Hudson Pl. SL3: Lang 1B 6
Hudson Rd. RH10: Craw 5C 182
UB3: Harl 2E 8
Hudsons KT20: Tad 8J 81
Huggins Pl. SW2 . . . . .2K 29
Hugh Dalton Av. SW6 . . . . .2L 13
Hugh De Port La.
GU51: Fleet 2A 88
Hughenden Rd. KT4: W Pk 6F 42
Hughes Rd. RG40: W'ham 1C 30
TW15: A'ford 7D 22
Hughes Wlk. CR0: Croy 6N 45

Hugh Gaitskell Cl.
SW6 . . . . .2L 13
Hugh Herland Ho.
KT1: K Tham . . .6K 203 (2L 41)
Hugon Rd. SW6 . . . . .6N 13
Hullbrook La. GU5: Sha G 7F 134
Hullmead GU5: Sha G 7G 134
Hulton Cl. KT22: Leat 1J 99
Hulverston Cl. SM2: Sut 6N 61
Humber Cl. GU47: Sandh 7J 49
Humber Way GU47: Sandh 7J 49
SL3: Lang 1C 6
Humbolt Cl. GU2: Guil 3J 113
Humbolt Rd. W6 . . . . .2K 13
Hummer Rd. TW20: Egh 5C 20
Humphrey Cl. KT22: Fetc 9C 78
Humphrey Pk.
GU52: C Cro 1A 108
(not continuous)
Humphries Yd. RG12: Brac 3A 32
Hungerford Cl.
GU47: Sandh 7H 49
Hungerford Sq.
KT13: Weybr 1E 56
Hungry Hill La.
GU23: Rip, Send 4L 95
Hunstanton Cl. RH11: Ifi 4J 181
SL3: Coln 3E 6
Hunston Rd. SM4: Mord 7N 43
Hunter Cl. SM6: W'ton 4J 63
Hunter Ct. KT19: Eps 6N 59
Hunter Ho. RH10: Craw 6B 182
SW5 . . . . .1M 13
(off Old Brompton Rd.)
TW13: Felt 2H 23
(off Lemon Gro.)
Hunter Rd. CR7: T Hea 2A 46
GU1: Guil 5F 202 (4A 114)
GU14: Cove 2L 89
RH10: Craw 6B 182
SW20 . . . . .9H 27
Hunters Chase
RH9: S Gods 6J 125
Hunters Cl.
KT19: Eps 6H 201 (9B 60)
SW12 . . . . .2E 28
Hunters Ct. TW9: Rich 8K 11
Huntersfield Cl. RH2: Reig . . .9N 101
Hunters Ga. RH1: Nut 2K 123
Hunters Gro. BR6: Farnb 1L 67
Hunters M. SL4: W'sor 4F 4
Hunter's Rd. KT9: Ches 9L 41
Hunters Way CR0: Croy 1B 64
TN8: Eden 1K 147
Hunting Cl. KT10: Esh 1A 58
Huntingdon Cl. CR4: Mit 2J 45
Huntingdon Gdns.
KT4: W Pk 9H 43
W4 . . . . .3B 12
Huntingdon Rd. GU21: Wok 4J 73
RH1: Red 3D 122
Huntingfield CR0: Sels 4J 65
Huntingfield Rd. SW15 . . . . . . .7F 12
Huntingfield Way
TW20: Egh 8F 20
Huntingford Cl.
GU26: Hind 2A 170
Hunting Ga. Dr. KT9: Ches 4L 59
Hunting Ga. M. SM1: Sut 9N 43
TW2: Twick 2E 24
Huntley Cl. TW19: Stan 1N 21
Huntley Ho. KT12: Whit V 5G 56
Huntley Way SW20 . . . . .1F 42
Huntly Rd. SE25 . . . . .3B 46
Hunts Cl. GU2: Guil 2G 112
Huntsgreen Ct. RG12: Brac 1A 32
HUNTS HILL 9M 91
Hunts Hill Rd. GU3: Norm 8L 91
Huntsmans Cl. CR6: Warl 6F 84
KT22: Fetc 2D 98
TW13: Felt 5J 23
Huntsmans Ct. CR3: Cate 8N 83
(off Coulsdon Rd.)
Huntsmans Mdw. SL5: Asc 9K 17
Huntsman's M. GU16: Mytc . . .2D 90
Huntsmoor Rd. KT19: Ewe 2C 60
Huntspill St. SW17 . . . . .4A 28
Hurland La. GU35: Head 5E 168
Hurlands Bus. Cen.
GU9: Farnh 8L 109
Hurlands Cl. GU9: Farnh 8L 109
Hurlands La. GU8: Duns 7B 174
Hurlands Pl. GU9: Farnh 8L 109
Hurley Cl. KT12: Wal T 8J 39
Hurley Ct. RG12: Brac 3C 32
Hurley Gdns. GU4: B'ham 9C 94
Hurlford GU21: Wok 4K 73
HURLINGHAM 6N 13
Hurlingham Bus. Pk.
SW6 . . . . .6M 13
Hurlingham Club, The 6M 13
Hurlingham Ct. SW6 . . . . .6L 13
Hurlingham Gdns.
SW6 . . . . .6L 13
Hurlingham Retail Pk.
SW6 . . . . .6N 13
Hurlingham Rd. SW6 . . . . .5L 13
Hurlingham Sq. SW6 . . . . . . .6M 13
Hurlingham Stadium 6L 13
Hurlstone Rd. SE25 . . . . .4B 46
Hurn Ct. TW4: Houn 5L 9
Hurn Ct. Rd. TW4: Houn 5L 9
Hurnford Cl. CR2: Sande 6B 64

Huron Cl. BR6: Chels 3N 67
Huron Rd. SW17 . . . . .3E 28
Hurricane Rd. SM6: W'ton 4J 63
Hurricane Way SL3: Lang 1D 6
Hurst-An-Clays
RH19: E Grin 1A 186
Hurst Av. RH12: Hors 5K 197
Hurstbourne KT10: Clay 3F 58
Hurstbourne Ho. SW15 . . . . . . .9E 12
(off Tangley Gro.)
Hurst Cl. GU22: Wok 7M 73
KT9: Ches 2N 59
KT18: Head 2B 100
RG12: Brac 4M 31
RH11: Craw 5L 181
Hurst Ct. RH12: Hors 5K 197
Hurstcourt Rd. SM1: Sut 8N 43
Hurst Cft.
GU1: Guil 8F 202 (6A 114)
Hurstdene Av. TW18: Stain 7K 21
Hurst Dr. KT20: Wal H 4F 100
Hurst Farm Cl. GU8: Mil 9C 132
Hurst Farm Rd.
RH19: E Grin 1N 185
Hurstfield Rd. KT8: W Mole . . .2A 40
HURST GREEN 1C 126
Hurst Grn. Cl. RH8: Oxt 1C 126
Hurst Grn. Rd. RH8: Oxt 1B 126
Hurst Green Station (Rail) . . .1B 126
Hurst Gro. KT12: Wal T 7G 38
Hurst Hill RH12: Hors 7N 179
Hurst Hill Cotts.
GU5: Braml 6C 134
Hurstlands RH8: Oxt 1C 126
Hurst La. KT8: E Mol 3C 40
KT18: Head 2B 100
TW20: Egh 1C 36
Hurstleigh Cl. RH1: Red 1D 122
Hurstleigh Dr. RH1: Red 1D 122
Hurst Lodge KT13: Weybr 3E 56
(off Gower Rd.)
Hurstmere Cl.
GU26: G'hott 6B 170
HURST PARK 1C 40
Hurst Pk. RH12: Hors 5K 197
Hurst Pool 2B 40
Hurst Rd.
CR0: Croy 8D 200 (2A 64)
GU11: Alde 9A 90
GU14: Farnb 6N 69
KT8: W Mole, E Mol 2B 40
KT12: Wal T 4K 39
KT18: Head 1C 100
KT19: Eps 7C 60
KT20: Wal H 1C 100
RH6: Horl 7C 142
RH12: Hors 4J 197
Hurstview Grange
CR2: S Croy 4M 63
Hurst Vw. Rd. CR2: S Croy 4B 64
Hurst Way CR2: S Croy 3B 64
GU22: Pyr 1G 75
Hurstwood SL5: Asc 5L 33
Hurtbank Cotts.
RH5: H Mary 5K 137
HURTMORE 4C 132
HURTMORE BOTTOM 5C 132
Hurtmore Chase GU7: Hurt . . .4E 132
Hurtmore Rd. GU7: Hurt 4C 132
Hurtwood La. GU5: Alb 5N 135
Hurtwood Rd. KT12: Wal T 6N 39
Huson Rd. RG42: Warf 7A 16
Hussar Ct. GU11: Alde 2K 109
Hussars Cl. TW4: Houn 6M 9
Hutchingsons Rd.
CR0: N Add 7M 65
Hutchinson's Bank Nature Reserve
. . . . .8M 65
Hutchins Way RH6: Horl 6D 142
Hutsons Cl. RG40: W'ham 9C 14
Hutton Cl. GU20: Windl 4A 52
KT12: Hers 2J 57
Hutton M. SW15 . . . . .8G 12
Hutton Rd. GU12: A Va 7E 90
Huxley Cl. GU7: Goda 4G 132
Huxley Rd. GU2: Guil 4G 113
Hyacinth Cl. TW12: Hamp 7A 24
Hyacinth Rd. SW15 . . . . .2F 26
Hyde Cl. TW15: A'ford 7F 22
Hyde Dr. RH11: Ifi 4K 181
Hyde Farm M. SW12 . . . . .2H 29
Hyde Heath Ct.
RH10: Craw 1H 183
Hyde Ho. TW3: Houn 6C 10
Hyde La. GU8: Thur 8E 150
GU10: Churt 9B 150
GU23: Ockh 7C 76
Hyde Rd. CR2: Sande 9B 64
TW10: Rich 8M 11
HYDESTILE 4G 153
Hydestile Cotts.
GU8: Hamb 5G 152
Hyde Ter. TW15: A'ford 7F 22
Hydethorpe Rd. SW12 . . . . . . .2G 28
Hyde Wlk. SM4: Mord 6M 43
HYDON HEATH 5J 153
Hydon Heath 6J 153
Hydons, The GU8: Hamb 5H 153
Hydro Ho. KT16: Chert 7L 37
Hylands Cl. KT18: Eps 2B 80
RH10: Craw 4E 182
Hylands M. KT18: Eps 2B 80
Hylands Rd. KT18: Eps 2B 80

Hylle Cl.—Jubilee Av.

Hylle Cl. SL4: W'sor 4B 4
Hylton Pl. RH1: Mers 9G 102
Hyndman Cl. RH11: Craw 9N 181
Hyperion Ct. RH11: Craw 5K 181
Hyperion Ho. SW2 ....1K 29
Hyperion Pl. KT19: Ewe 5C 60
Hyperion Wlk. RH6: Horl 1F 162
Hyrstdene
CR2: S Croy 7A 200 (1M 63)
Hythe, The TW18: Stain 6G 20
Hythe Cl. RG12: Brac 4C 32
HYTHE END 3D 20
Hythe End Rd. TW19: Wray 3B 20
Hythe Fld. Av. TW20: Egh 7F 20
Hythe Pk. Rd. TW20: Egh 6E 20
Hythe Rd. CR7: T Hea 1A 46
TW18: Stain 6F 20

I

Ibbotson Ct. SL3: Poy 4G 7
Iberian Av. SM6: Bedd 1H 63
Iberian Way GU15: Camb 9E 50
Ibis La. W4 ....4B 12
Ibsley Gdns. SW15 ....2F 26
Icehouse Wood RH8: Oxt 9A 106
Icklesham Ho. *RH11: Craw* *6L 181*
(off Salvington Rd.)
Icklingham Ga. KT11: Cob 8K 57
Icklingham Rd. KT11: Cob 8K 57
Idlecombe Rd. SW17 ....7E 28
Idmiston Rd. KT4: W Pk 6E 42
SE27 ....4N 29
Idmiston Sq. KT4: W Pk 6E 42
Iffley Ct. TW18: Stain 6H 21
IFIELD 2M 181
Ifield Av. RH11: Craw 9M 161
Ifield Barn Theatre 1L 181
Ifield Cl. RH1: Red 5C 122
Ifield Dr. RH11: Ifi 2L 181
IFIELD GREEN 1M 181
Ifield Grn. RH11: Ifi 9M 161
Ifield Pk. RH11: Craw 3L 181
Ifield Pond 4K 181
Ifield Rd. RH6: Char 6K 161
RH10: Craw 3B 182
RH11: Craw 2N 181
SW10 ....2N 13
Ifield Rd. Rdbt.
RH11: Craw 3B 182
Ifield Rdbt. RH11: Craw 2A 182
Ifield Station (Rail) 3M 181
Ifield St. RH11: Ifi 1L 181
Ifield Watermill 4K 181
IFIELDWOOD 9J 161
Ifield Wood RH11: Ifi 2H 181
IFOLD 5F 192
Ifold Bri. La. RH14: Ifo 4E 192
Ifoldhurst RH14: Ifo 6E 192
Ifold Rd. RH1: Red 5E 122
Ikea Ampere Way Stop (CT) 7K 45
Ikona Ct. KT13: Weybr 2D 56
Ilex Cl. GU46: Yate 9A 48
TW16: Sunb 1K 39
TW20: Eng G 8L 19
Ilex Ho. KT15: N Haw 6J 55
Ilex Way SW16 ....6L 29
Ilford Ct. GU6: Cranl 8H 155
Illingworth SL4: W'sor 6B 4
Illingworth Cl. CR4: Mit 2B 44
Illingworth Gro. RG12: Brac 9D 16
Imadene Cl. GU35: Lind 5A 168
Imadene Cres. GU35: Lind 5A 168
Imber Cl. KT10: Esh 1B 58
Imber Ct. Trad. Est.
KT8: E Mol 5D 40
Imber Cross KT7: T Dit 5F 40
Imber Gro. KT10: Esh 6D 40
Imberhorne Bus. Cen.
RH19: E Grin 8L 165
Imberhorne La.
RH19: E Grin 7L 165
Imberhorne Way
RH19: E Grin 7L 165
Imber Pk. Rd. KT10: Esh 7D 40
Imjin Cl. GU11: Alde 1N 109
Impact Ct. SE20 ....1E 46
Imperial College London
Silwood Pk. Campus 2B 34
Imperial Ct. SL4: W'sor 6D 4
Imperial Gdns. CR4: Mit 2F 44
Imperial Pk. KT22: Leat 7G 79
Imperial Rd. SL4: W'sor 6D 4
SW6 ....4N 13
TW14: Felt 1F 22
Imperial Sq. SW6 ....4N 13
Imperial Way CR0: Wad 3K 63
Imran Ct. GU12: Alde 3A 110
Ince Rd. KT12: Hers 3F 56
Inchwood CR0: A'ton 1L 65
RG12: Brac 7A 32
Independence Ho. *SW19* *9B 28*
(off Chapter Way)
Independent Bus. Pk., The
RH19: E Grin 7K 165
Industrial Est., The
TN8: Eden 9K 127
Ingatestone Rd. SE25 ....3E 46
Ingham Cl. CR2: Sels 5G 64
Ingham Rd. CR2: Sels 5F 64
Ingleboro Dr. CR8: Pur 9A 64
Ingleby Way SM6: W'ton 5H 63
Ingle Dell GU15: Camb 2B 70
Inglehurst KT15: N Haw 6K 55
Inglemere Rd. CR4: Mit 8D 28
Ingleside SL3: Poy 4G 7
Inglethorpe St. SW6 ....4J 13
Ingleton RG12: Brac 2M 31
Ingleton Rd. SM5: Cars 5C 62
Inglewood CR0: Sels 5H 65
GU21: Wok 5L 73
KT16: Chert 9H 37
Inglewood Av. GU15: Camb 2G 71
Inglewood M. KT6: Surb 7N 41
Inglis Rd. CR0: Croy 7C 46
Ingram Cl. RH12: Hors 6G 197
Ingram Rd. CR7: T Hea 9N 29
Ingrams Cl. KT12: Hers 2K 57
Ingress St. W4 ....1D 12
Inholmes RH10: Craw 3E 182
Inholmes Dr. GU51: Fleet 2A 88
Inholms La. RH5: Nth H 9H 119
Ink, The GU46: Yate 8B 48
Inkerman Rd. GU21: Knap 5H 73
SL4: E Wic 1C 4
Inkerman Way GU21: Wok 5H 73
Inkpen La. RH18: F Row 8H 187
Inman Rd. SW18 ....1A 28
Innered Ct. *CR0: Croy* *5N 45*
(off Harry Cl.)
Inner Pk. Rd. SW19 ....2J 27
Inner Ring E. TW6: Lon A 6C 8
Inner Ring W. TW6: Lon A 6B 8
Innes Cl. SW20 ....1K 43
Innes Gdns. SW15 ....9G 13
Innes Rd. RH12: Hors 4M 197
Innes Yd.
CR0: Croy 5C 200 (9N 45)
Innings La. RG42: Warf 9B 16
Innisfail Gdns. GU11: Alde 4L 109
Innova Ct. CR0: Croy 7B 46
Institute Rd. GU11: Alde 6A 90
GU12: Alde 3B 110
RH4: Westc 6C 118
Institute Wlk. RH19: E Grin 9A 166
Instow Gdns. GU14: Farnb 7M 69
Interface Ho. *TW3: Houn* *6A 10*
(off Staines Rd.)
International Av. TW5: C'ford 1K 9
International Dr.
RH10: Craw 4C 182
International Way
TW16: Sunb 9F 22
INVAL 8G 170
Inval Hill GU27: Hasl 9G 170
Inveresk Gdns. KT4: W Pk 9F 42
Inverness Rd. KT4: W Pk 7J 43
TW3: Houn 7N 9
Inverness Way GU47: C Tow 8J 49
Invicta Cl. TW14: Felt 2G 22
Invincible Rd. GU14: Farnb 3M 89
Invincible Rd. Ind. Est.
GU14: Farnb 2M 89
Inwood Av. CR5: Coul 7L 83
TW3: Houn 6C 10
Inwood Bus. Pk.
TW3: Houn 7B 10
Inwood Cl. CR0: Croy 8H 47
Inwood Ct. KT12: Wal T 8K 39
Inwood Rd. TW3: Houn 7B 10
Iona Cl. RH11: Craw 6N 181
SM4: Mord 6N 43
Iona Ho. *GU11: Alde* *2M 109*
(off Nelson St.)
Ipswich Rd. SW17 ....7E 28
Ira Ct. SE27 ....3M 29
Irene Rd. KT11: Sto D 1B 78
SW6 ....4M 13
Ireton Av. KT12: Wal T 8F 38
Iris Cl. CR0: Croy 7G 46
KT6: Surb 6M 41
Iris Dr. GU24: Bis 2D 72
Iris Rd. GU24: Bis 2D 72
KT19: Ewe 2A 60
Iron La. GU5: Braml 6N 133
Iron Mill Pl. SW18 ....9N 13
Iron Mill Rd. SW18 ....9N 13
IRONS BOTTOM 2M 141
Ironsbottom RH2: Sid 3L 141
RH6: Sid 3L 141
Irvine Dr. GU14: Cove 6K 69
Irvine Pl. GU25: V Wat 4A 36
Irving Mans. *W14* *2K 13*
(off Queen's Club Gdns.)
Irving Wlk. RH10: Craw 6C 182
Irwin Dr. RH12: Hors 5G 196
Irwin Rd. GU2: Guil 4K 113
Isabel Hill Cl. TW12: Hamp 1B 40
Isabella Dr. BR6: Farnb 1L 67
Isabella Ho. *W6* *1H 13*
(off Queen Caroline St.)
Isabella Pl. KT2: K Tham 6M 25
Isbells Dr. RH2: Reig 4N 121
Isham Rd. SW16 ....1J 45
Isis Cl. SW15 ....7H 13
Isis Ct. W4 ....3A 12
Isis Ho. KT16: Chert 6L 37
Isis St. SW18 ....3A 28
Isis Way GU47: Sandh 7J 49
Island, The KT7: T Dit 5G 40
KT11: Down 5J 77
KT13: Addl 3N 55
TW19: Wray 4C 20
UB7: L'ford 3L 7
Island Cl. TW18: Stain 5G 20
Island Farm Av.
KT8: W Mole 4N 39
Island Farm Rd.
KT8: W Mole 4N 39
Island Rd. CR4: Mit 8D 28
Islandstone La.
RG10: Hurst 3A 14
Islay Gdns. TW4: Houn 8L 9
ISLEWORTH 6G 11
Isleworth Ait Nature Reserve
....6H 11
Isleworth Bus. Complex
TW7: Isle 5F 10
Isleworth Prom.
TW1: Twick 7H 11
Isleworth Recreation Cen. 7F 10
Isleworth Station (Rail) 5F 10
Itchell Dr. GU51: Fleet 2A 88
ITCHINGFIELD 9A 196
ITCHINGWOOD COMMON 1F 126
Itchingwood Comn. Rd.
RH8: Limp 2E 126
Ivanhoe Cl. RH11: Craw 9B 162
Ivanhoe Rd. TW4: Houn 6L 9
Ivatt Pl. W14 ....1L 13
Iveagh Cl. RH11: Craw 8A 182
Iveagh Ct. BR3: Beck 2M 47
RG12: Brac 4B 32
Iveagh Rd. GU2: Guil 4L 113
Ively Rd. GU14: Cove 2K 89
(not continuous)
GU14: Farnb 5F 88
Iverna Gdns. TW14: Felt 8E 8
Ivers Way CR0: N Add 4L 65
Ives Cl. GU46: Yate 8A 48
Ivor Cl. GU1: Guil 4B 114
Ivory Ct. TW13: Felt 2H 23
Ivory Wlk. RH11: Craw 5K 181
Ivybank GU7: Goda 5H 133
Ivybridge Cl. TW1: Twick 1G 24
Ivy Bri. Retail Pk. TW7: Isle 9G 10
Ivy Cl. TW16: Sunb 1K 39
Ivydale Rd. SM5: Cars 8D 44
Ivyday Gro. SW16 ....4K 29
Ivydene GU21: Knap 5E 72
KT8: W Mole 4N 39
Ivydene Cl. RH1: Red 8F 122
SM1: Sut 1A 62
Ivydene Ind. Est.
RH19: Ash W 2F 186
Ivy Dene La. RH19: Ash W 3F 186
Ivy Dr. GU18: Ligh 8L 51
Ivy Gdns. CR4: Mit 2H 45
Ivyhouse Cotts.
RH5: Newd 6F 160
Ivy La. GU9: Farnh 1G 129
GU22: Wok 4D 74
TW4: Houn 7N 9
Ivy Mill Cl. RH9: Gods 1E 124
Ivy Mill La. RH9: Gods 1D 124
Ivymount Rd. SE27 ....4L 29
Ivy Rd. GU12: Alde 2B 110
KT6: Surb 7N 41
SW17 ....6C 28
TW3: Houn 7B 10

J

Jacaranda Cl. KT3: N Mal 2D 42
Jacaranda Ho. KT15: Addl 8M 37
Jackass La. BR2: Kes 2D 66
RH8: Gods, Tand 9J 105
Jackdaw Cl. RH11: Craw 1A 182
Jackdaw La. RH12: Hors 3L 197
Jack Goodchild Way
KT1: K Tham 2A 42
Jackmans La. GU21: Wok 6K 73
Jackson Cl. GU6: Cranl 8H 155
KT18: Eps 8J 201 (1C 80)
RG12: Brac 4N 31
Jackson Rd. RH11: Craw 9N 181
Jacksons Pl.
CR0: Croy 1E 200 (7A 46)
Jackson's Way CR0: Croy 9K 47
Jackson Way KT19: Eps 5N 59
Jacob Cl. RG42: Brac 1J 31
SL4: W'sor 4B 4
Jacobean Cl. RH10: Craw 4G 183
Jacob Rd. GU15: Camb 8M 49
Jacobs Ct. RH10: Craw 2G 182
Jacob's Ladder CR6: Warl 6D 84
Jacob's Wlk. RH5: A Com 6A 138
JACOBS WELL 6N 93
Jacob's Well Rd.
GU4: J Wel 7N 93
Jaffray Pl. SE27 ....5M 29
Jaggard Way SW12 ....1D 28
Jail La. TN16: B Hil 2F 86
Jamaica Rd. CR7: T Hea 5M 45
James Black Rd.
GU2: Guil 4G 113
James Boswell Cl.
SW16 ....5K 29
James Est. CR4: Mit 1D 44
James Hockey Gallery 1G 128
James Mdw. SL3: Lang 2B 6
James Pl. RH10: Craw 4B 182
James Rd. GU3: P'marsh 2M 133
GU15: Camb 4N 69
James's Cotts. TW9: Kew 3N 11
James Searle Ind. Est.
RH12: Hors 4L 197
James St. SL4: W'sor 4G 4
TW3: Houn 6D 10
James Ter. *SW14* *6C 12*
(off Church Path)
James Terry Ct.
CR2: S Croy 8B 200
Jameston RG12: Brac 7A 32
James Watt Way
RH10: Craw 7E 162
James Way GU15: Camb 4N 69
Jamieson Ho. TW4: Houn 9N 9
Jamnagar Cl. TW18: Stain 7H 21
Janoway Hill La.
GU21: Wok 6M 73
Japonica Cl. GU21: Wok 5M 73
Japonica Ct. GU12: Ash 3D 110
Japonica Ho. KT15: Addl 8M 37
Jarratt Ho. *SL4: W'sor* *6E 4*
(off St Leonard's Rd.)
Jarrett Cl. SW2 ....2M 29
Jarrow Cl. SM4: Mord 4N 43
Jarvis Cl. RH11: Craw 9N 181
Jarvis Rd. CR2: S Croy 3A 64
Jasmine Cl. GU21: Wok 3J 73
RH1: Red 8E 122
Jasmine Ct. RH12: Hors 6J 197
SW19 ....6M 27
Jasmine Gdns. CR0: Croy 9L 47
Jasmine Way KT8: E Mol 3E 40
Jasmin Ho. KT15: Addl 8M 37
Jasmin Rd. KT19: Ewe 2A 60
Jason Cl. KT13: Weybr 2D 56
RH1: Red 8C 122
Jasons Dr. GU4: Guil 9E 94
Java Ho. GU17: Min 8H 69
Javelin Ct. RH10: Craw 9H 163
Jay Av. KT15: Addl 9N 37
Jay's La. GU27: Hasl 6M 189
Jays Nest Cl. GU17: B'water 2J 69
Jay Wlk. RH10: T Hil 4F 184
Jeal Oakwood Ct.
KT18: Eps 8L 201 (1D 80)
JEALOTT'S HILL 2N 15
Jean Batten Cl. SM6: W'ton 4K 63
Jean Ho. SW17 ....6C 28
Jean Orr Ct. GU52: C Cro 8B 88
Jeans Ct. RH11: Craw 8N 181
Jebb Av. SW2 ....1J 29
(not continuous)
Jeddere Cotts. RH7: Dorm 9C 146
Jefferson Rd.
GU24: B'wood 7N 71
Jeffries Pas.
GU1: Guil 5D 202 (4N 113)
Jeffries Rd. KT24: W Hors 9C 96
Jeffs Cl. TW12: Hamp 7B 24
Jeffs Rd. SM1: Sut 1L 61
Jemmett Cl. KT2: K Tham 9A 26
Jengar Cl. SM1: Sut 1N 61
Jenkins Ct. GU19: Bag 5H 51
Jenkins Hill GU19: Bag 5H 51
Jenkins Pl. GU14: Farnb 5B 90
Jenner Dr. GU24: W End 9D 52
Jenner Pl. SW13 ....2G 12
Jenner Rd.
GU1: Guil 5E 202 (4A 114)
RH10: Craw 7D 162
Jenners Cl. RH7: Ling 7N 145
Jenner Way KT19: Eps 5N 59
Jennett Rd. CR0: Wad 9L 45
Jennings Cl. KT6: Surb 6J 41
KT15: N Haw 5L 55
Jennings Way RH6: Horl 8H 143
Jenny La. RH7: Ling 7M 145
Jennys Wlk. GU46: Yate 9D 48
Jennys Way CR5: Coul 9G 83
Jephtha Rd. SW18 ....9M 13
Jeppos La. CR4: Mit 3D 44
Jepson Ho. *SW6* *4N 13*
(off Pearscroft Rd.)
Jerdan Pl. SW6 ....3M 13
Jeremiah Ct. RH1: Mers 9G 103
Jerome Cnr. RG45: Crow 4H 49
Jerome Ho. KT1: H Wic 3G 203
Jerome Pl. *KT1: K Tham* *4H 203*
(off Wadbrook St.)
Jersey Cl. GU4: B'ham 7D 94
GU51: Fleet 1C 88
KT16: Chert 9H 37
Jersey Pl. SL5: S'hill 5A 34
Jersey Rd. RH11: Craw 7M 181
SW17 ....7F 28
TW3: Houn 4B 10
TW5: Hest 4B 10
TW7: Isle 3D 10
Jervis Rd. SW6 ....2L 13
Jerviston Gdns. SW16 ....7L 29
Jesmond Cl. CR4: Mit 2F 44
Jesmond Rd. CR0: Croy 6C 46
Jessamy Rd. KT13: Weybr 8B 38
Jesse Cl. GU46: Yate 1E 68
Jessel Mans. *W14* *2K 13*
(off Queen's Club Gdns.)
Jesses La. GU5: P'lake 4D 136
Jessett Dr. GU52: C Cro 9A 88
Jessiman Ter. TW17: Shep 4B 38
Jessop Av. UB2: S'hall 1N 9
Jessops Way
CR0: Bedd, Mit 5G 44
Jetty Ho. KT16: Chert 6L 37
Jevington RG12: Brac 7A 32
Jewels Hill TN16: B Hil 8C 66
Jewel Wlk. RH11: Craw 6M 181
Jew's Row SW18 ....7N 13
Jeypore Pas. SW18 ....1A 28
Jeypore Rd. SW18 ....1A 28
Jig's La. Nth. RG42: Warf 7C 16
Jig's La. Sth. RG42: Warf 9C 16
Jillian Cl. TW12: Hamp 8A 24
Jim Griffiths Ho. *SW6* *2L 13*
(off Clem Attlee Ct.)
Joan Bicknell Cen., The 3B 28
Joanna Ho. *W6* *1H 13*
(off Queen Caroline St.)
Jobson's La. GU8: Hasl 9N 189
GU27: Hasl 9N 189
Jocelyn Rd. TW9: Rich 6L 11
Jockey Mead RH12: Hors 7G 197
Jock's La. RG42: Brac 9K 15
Jodrell Cl. TW7: Isle 4G 10
Joe Hunte Ct. SE27 ....6M 29
John Austin Cl.
KT2: K Tham 2L 203 (9M 25)
John Bunn Mill *KT15: Addl* *2N 55*
(off Bourneside Rd.)
John Burns Cotts.
RH8: Limp 8G 107
John Cl. GU11: Alde 4K 109
John Cobb Rd. KT13: Weybr 4B 56
John F Kennedy Memorial 3M 19
John Gale Ct. *KT17: Ewe* *5E 60*
(off West St.)
John Goddard Way
TW13: Felt 3J 23
John Kaye Ct. TW17: Shep 4B 38
John Knight Lodge
SW6 ....3M 13
John Nike Leisuresport Complex
....1H 31
John Nike Way RG12: Brac 1H 31
John Pl. RG42: Warf 8C 16
John Pound's Ho.
RH11: Craw 5A 182
John Russell Cl. GU2: Guil 9K 93
John's Cl. TW15: A'ford 5D 22
Johnsdale RH8: Oxt 7B 106
John's La. SM4: Mord 4A 44
John Smith Av. SW6 ....3L 13
John Smith Hall *SL5: S'hill* *2C 34*
(off Buckhurst Rd.)
Johnson Dr. RG40: Finch 9A 30
Johnson Mans. *W14* *2K 13*
(off Queen's Club Gdns.)
Johnson Rd. CR0: Croy 6A 46
TW5: Hest 3K 9
Johnsons Cl. SM5: Cars 8D 44
JOHNSON'S COMMON 1K 161
Johnsons Dr. TW12: Hamp 9C 24
Johnson Wlk. RH10: Craw 6C 182
Johnson Way GU52: C Cro 8B 88
John's Rd. TN16: Tats 7F 86
John's Ter.
CR0: Croy 1F 200 (7B 46)
Johnston Grn. GU2: Guil 8K 93
Johnston Wlk. GU2: Guil 8K 93
John Strachey Ho.
SW6 ....*2L 13*
(off Clem Attlee Ct.)
John St. SE25 ....3D 46
TW3: Houn 5M 9
Johns Wlk. CR3: Warl 6D 84
John Watkin Cl. KT19: Eps 5A 60
John Wesley Ct.
TW1: Twick 2G 24
John Wheatley Ho.
SW6 ....*2L 13*
(off Clem Attlee Ct.)
John Williams Cl.
KT2: K Tham 1H 203 (9K 25)
John Wiskar Dr.
GU6: Cranl 7M 155
Joinville Pl. KT15: Addl 1M 55
Jolesfield Ct. RH11: Craw 6L 181
Jolive Ct. GU1: Guil 4C 114
Jolliffe Rd. RH1: Mers 4G 102
Jones Cnr. SL5: Asc 9J 17
Jones M. SW15 ....7K 13
Jones Wlk. TW10: Rich 9M 11
Jonquil Gdns. TW12: Hamp 7A 24
Jonson Cl. CR4: Mit 3F 44
Jordan Cl. CR2: Sande 7C 64
Jordan Ct. SW15 ....7J 13
JORDANS, THE 7C 160
Jordans, The RH19: E Grin 1A 186
Jordans Cl. GU1: Guil 2C 114
RH1: Red 8E 122
RH11: Craw 1B 182
TW7: Isle 4E 10
TW19: Stan 1L 21
Jordans Cres. RH11: Craw 9B 162
Jordans M. TW2: Twick 3E 24
Joseph Ct. RG42: Warf 7C 16
Josephine Av. KT20: Lwr K 4L 101
Josephine Cl. KT20: Lwr K 5L 101
Joseph Locke Way
KT10: Esh 8A 40
Joseph's Rd.
GU1: Guil 1C 202 (2N 113)
Joshua Cl. CR2: S Croy 4M 63
Jourdelay's *SL4: Eton* *2G 4*
(off Jourdelay's Pas.)
Jourdelay's Pas. SL4: Eton 2G 4
Jubilee Arch SL4: W'sor 4G 4
Jubilee Av. RG41: W'ham 1A 30
SL5: Asc 9J 17
TW2: Whitt 2C 24

Jubilee Cl.—Kiln M.

Jubilee Cl. GU14: Cove 1J 89
KT1: H Wic 9J 25
SL5: Asc 9J 17
TW19: Stan 1L 21
Jubilee Cotts. SL3: Lang 1D 6
Jubilee Ct. BR4: W Wick 7M 47
RG12: Brac 2A 32
SL5: Asc 8J 17
TW3: Houn 6B 10
(off Bristow Rd.)
TW18: Stain 6J 21
Jubilee Cres. KT15: Addl 2M 55
Jubilee Dr. GU12: A Va 7E 90
Jubilee Est. RH13: Hors 4L 197
Jubilee Hall Rd.
GU14: Farnb 1A 90
Jubilee La. GU10: Wrec 7F 128
GU26: G'hott 6A 170
Jubilee Rd. GU11: Alde 5N 109
GU16: Mytc 3E 90
RH12: Rudg 9E 176
SM3: Chea 4J 61
Jubilee Ter. RH3: Brock 7B 120
RH4: Dork 1L 201 (4H 119)
Jubilee Vs. KT10: Esh 7D 40
Jubilee Wlk. RH10: Craw 3E 182
RH12: Hors 6J 197
(off Albion Way)
Jubilee Way KT9: Ches 1N 59
SL3: Dat 3M 5
SW19 9N 27
TW14: Felt 2H 23
Judge's Ter. RH19: E Grin 1A 186
Judge Wlk. KT10: Clay 3E 58
Judy's Pas. SL4: Eton 1F 4
Jug Hill TN16: B Hil 3F 86
Jugshill La. RH5: Oak 2B 178
Julian Cl. GU21: Wok 5M 73
Julian Hill KT13: Weybr 4B 56
Julien Rd. CR5: Coul 2H 83
Juliet Gdns. RG42: Warf 9D 16
Julius Hill RG42: Warf 9D 16
Jumps Rd. GU10: Churt 7K 149
Junction Pl. GU27: Hasl 2D 188
Junction Rd. CR2: S Croy 2A 64
GU18: Ligh 6M 51
RH4: Dork 2J 201 (5G 119)
TW8: Brent 1K 11
TW15: A'ford 6D 22
W5 1K 11
June Cl. CR5: Coul 1F 82
June La. RH1: Salf 1F 142
Junewood Cl. KT15: Wood 7H 55
Juniper RG12: Brac 7A 32
Juniper Cl. GU1: Guil 7L 93
KT9: Ches 2M 59
RH2: Reig 5A 122
RH8: Oxt 2D 126
TN16: B Hil 4G 87
Juniper Ct. KT8: W Mole 3B 40
TW3: Houn 7B 10
(off Grove Rd.)
Juniper Dr. GU24: Bis 2D 72
Juniper Gdns. SW16 9G 28
TW16: Sunb 7G 23
Juniper Ho. TW9: Kew 4A 12
Juniper Pl. GU4: Chil 1N 133
Juniper Rd. GU14: Cove 9H 69
RH2: Reig 5A 122
RH11: Craw 9A 162
Juniper Wlk. RH3: Brock 5B 120
Jura Cl. RH11: Craw 6N 181
Justin Cl. TW8: Brent 3K 11
Justin Plaza CR4: Mit 3C 44
Jutland Gdns. CR5: Coul 7K 83
Jutland Ho. SL4: W'sor 5C 4
Jutland Pl. TW20: Egh 6E 20
Juxon Cl. RH11: Craw 5L 181

K

K2 Leisure Cen. 7B 182
Kalima Cvn. Site
GU24: Chob 6L 53
Kamran Ct. GU11: Alde 5M 109
(off Boxhalls La.)
Karenza Ct. RH13: Hors 5L 197
Kashmir Cl. KT15: N Haw 5M 55
Kashmir Ct. GU14: Farnb 4A 90
Katana GU22: Wok 6A 74
(off Brooklyn Rd.)
Katharine Ho. CR0: Croy 4C 200
Katharine St.
CR0: Croy 4C 200 (9N 45)
Katherine Cl. KT15: Addl 3J 55
Katherine Ct. GU15: Camb 1B 70
(off Up. Gordon Rd.)
GU21: Knap 6F 72
(off Tudor Way)
Katherine M. CR3: Whyte 4C 84
Katherine Rd. TN8: Eden 3L 147
TW1: Twick 2G 24
Kathleen Godfree Ct.
SW19 7M 27
Kay Av. KT15: Addl 9N 37
Kay Cres. GU35: H Dwn 3F 168
Kaye Ct. GU1: Guil 9M 93
Kaye Don Way
KT13: Weybr 6B 56
Kayemoor Rd. SM2: Sut 3B 62
Kaynes Pk. SL5: Asc 9J 17
Keable Rd. GU10: Wrec 4E 128
Kean Ho. TW1: Twick 9K 11
(off Arosa Rd.)
Kearton Cl. CR8: Ken 4N 83
Kearton Pl. CR3: Cate 9D 84
Keate Ho. SL4: Eton 2G 4
(off Keates La.)
Keates Grn. RG42: Brac 9N 15
Keates La. SL4: Eton 2F 4
Keats Av. RH1: Red 1E 122
Keats Cl. RH12: Hors 1M 197
SW19 7B 28
Keats Gdns. GU51: Fleet 4C 88
Keats Pl. RH19: E Grin 9N 165
Keats Way CR0: Croy 5F 46
GU46: Yate 2A 68
RG45: Crow 9G 30
UB7: W Dray 1A 8
Keble Cl. KT4: W Pk 7E 42
RH10: Craw 9H 163
Keble Pl. SW13 2G 13
Keble St. SW17 5A 28
Keble Way GU47: Owls 5K 49
Kedeston Ct. SM1: Sut 7N 43
Keel KT16: Chert 7L 37
Keeler Cl. SL4: W'sor 6B 4
Keeley Rd.
CR0: Croy 3B 200 (8N 45)
Keens Cl. SW16 6H 29
Keens La. GU3: Guil 8J 93
Keens Pk. Rd. GU3: Guil 8J 93
Keens Rd.
CR0: Croy 6C 200 (1N 63)
Keep, The KT2: K Tham 7M 25
Keepers Cl. GU4: Guil 9F 94
Keepers Coombe
RG12: Brac 5B 32
KEEPER'S CORNER 4N 163
Keepers Ct. CR2: S Croy 8B 200
Keepers Farm Cl. SL4: W'sor 5B 4
(not continuous)
Keepers M. TW11: Tedd 7J 25
Keepers Wlk. GU25: V Wat 4N 35
Keephatch Rd.
RG40: W'ham 9D 14
Keevil Dr. SW19 1J 27
Keir, The SW19 6H 27
Keir Hardie Ho.
RH11: Craw 8N 181
W6 2J 13
(off Fulham Pal. Rd.)
Keith Lucas Rd.
GU14: Cove 3L 89
Keith Pk. Cres. TN16: B Hil 9D 66
Keldholme RG12: Brac 2M 31
Kelling Gdns. CR0: Croy 6M 45
Kellino St. SW17 5D 28
Kelly Cl. TW17: Shep 1F 38
Kelmscott Ri. RH11: Craw 9N 181
Kelsall Pl. SL5: Asc 6M 33
Kelsey Cl. RH6: Horl 8D 142
Kelsey Ga. BR3: Beck 1L 47
Kelsey Gro. GU46: Yate 1D 68
Kelsey La. BR3: Beck 1K 47
Kelsey Pk. Av. BR3: Beck 1L 47
(not continuous)
Kelsey Pk. Rd. BR3: Beck 1K 47
Kelsey Sq. BR3: Beck 1K 47
Kelsey Way BR3: Beck 2K 47
Kelso Cl. RH10: Craw 2J 183
Kelso Rd. SM5: Cars 6A 44
Kelvedon Av. KT12: Hers 4F 56
Kelvedon Cl. KT2: K Tham 7N 25
Kelvedon Rd. SW6 3L 13
Kelvin Av. KT22: Leat 6F 78
TW11: Tedd 7E 24
Kelvinbrook KT8: W Mole 2B 40
Kelvin Bus. Cen.
RH10: Craw 9D 162
Kelvin Cl. KT19: Ewe 3N 59
Kelvin Ct. TW7: Isle 5E 10
Kelvin Dr. TW1: Twick 9H 11
Kelvin Gdns. CR0: Wad 6J 45
Kelvin Ga. RG12: Brac 1B 32
Kelvin Gro. KT9: Ches 9K 41
Kelvington Cl. CR0: Croy 6H 47
Kelvin La. RH10: Craw 8D 162
Kelvin Way RH10: Craw 8D 162
Kemble Cl. KT13: Weybr 1E 56
Kemble Cotts. KT15: Addl 1J 55
Kemble Rd. CR0: Wad 9M 45
Kembleside Rd. TN16: B Hil 5E 86
Kemerton Rd. BR3: Beck 1L 47
CR0: Croy 6C 46
Kemishford GU22: Wok 1K 93
Kemnal Pk. GU27: Hasl 1H 189
Kemp Ct. GU19: Bag 5K 51
Kemp Gdns. CR0: Croy 5N 45
Kempsford Gdns. SW5 1M 13
Kempshott M. RH12: Hors 4H 197
Kempshott Rd.
RH12: Hors 4H 197
SW16 8H 29
Kempson Rd. SW6 4M 13
Kempton Av. TW16: Sunb 9J 23
Kempton Ct. GU14: Cove 3L 89
TW16: Sunb 9J 23
Kempton Pk. TW12: Hamp 9N 23
Kempton Pk. Racecourse 8K 23
Kempton Park Station (Rail)
8J 23
Kempton Rd. TW12: Hamp 1N 39
(not continuous)
Kempton Wlk. CR0: Croy 5H 47
Kemsing Cl. CR7: T Hea 3N 45
Kemsley Rd. TN16: Tats 6F 86
Kendal Cl. GU14: Cove 1K 89
RH2: Reig 2B 122
TW14: Felt 2G 22
Kendale Cl. RH10: Craw 7G 183
Kendal Gdns. SM1: Sut 8A 44
Kendal Gro. GU15: Camb 2H 71
Kendal Ho. SE20 1D 46
(off Derwent Rd.)
Kendall Av. BR3: Beck 1H 47
CR2: Sande 5A 64
Kendall Av. Sth.
CR2: Sande 6N 63
Kendall Ct. SW19 7B 28
Kendall Rd. BR3: Beck 1H 47
TW7: Isle 5G 10
Kendal Pl. SW15 8L 13
Kendor Av. KT19: Eps 7B 60
Kendra Hall Rd.
CR2: S Croy 4M 63
Kendrey Gdns. TW2: Whitt 1E 24
Kendrick Cl. RG40: W'ham 3B 30
Kenilford Rd. SW12 1F 28
Kenilworth Av. KT11: Sto D 1B 78
RG12: Brac 9A 16
SW19 6M 27
Kenilworth Cl.
RH11: Craw 7N 181
SM7: Ban 3N 81
Kenilworth Cres.
GU51: Fleet 3D 88
Kenilworth Dr. KT12: Wal T 9L 39
Kenilworth Gdns.
TW18: Stain 6L 21
Kenilworth Rd. GU14: Cove 9H 69
GU51: Fleet 4C 88
(not continuous)
KT17: Ewe 2F 60
TW15: A'ford 4M 21
KENLEY 1N 83
KENLEY AERODROME 6A 84
Kenley Gdns. CR7: T Hea 3M 45
Kenley La. CR8: Ken 1N 83
Kenley Rd. GU35: H Dwn 4G 169
KT1: K Tham 1A 42
SW19 1M 43
TW1: Twick 9H 11
Kenley Station (Rail) 1N 83
Kenley Wlk. SM3: Chea 1J 61
Kenlor Rd. SW17 6B 28
Kenmara Cl. RH10: Craw 9E 162
Kenmara Ct. RH10: Craw 8E 162
Kenmare Dr. CR4: Mit 8D 28
Kenmare Rd. CR7: T Hea 5L 45
Kenmore Cl. GU16: Frim 6B 70
GU52: C Cro 8C 88
TW9: Kew 3N 11
Kenmore Rd. CR8: Ken 1M 83
Kennard Ct. RH18: F Row 6G 187
Kenneally SL4: W'sor 5A 4
Kenneally Cl. SL4: W'sor 5A 4
Kenneally Row SL4: W'sor 5A 4
(off Liddell Sq.)
Kenneally Wlk. SL4: W'sor 5A 4
(off Guards Rd.)
Kennedy Av. RH19: E Grin 7N 165
Kennedy Cl. CR4: Mit 9E 28
Kennedy Ct. TW15: A'ford 6D 22
Kennedy Rd. RH13: Hors 7K 197
Kennel Av. SL5: Asc 9K 17
Kennel Cl. KT22: Fetc 2C 98
SL5: Asc 7K 17
Kennel Grn. SL5: Asc 9J 17
Kennel La. GU10: Fren 9H 129
GU20: Windl 2N 51
KT22: Fetc 9B 78
(not continuous)
RG42: Brac 8N 15
RH6: Hook 9B 142
Kennel Ride SL5: Asc 9K 17
Kennels La. GU14: Cove 2G 88
(not continuous)
Kennel Wood SL5: Asc 9K 17
Kennelwood Cres.
CR0: N Add 7N 65
Kennet Cl. GU12: Ash 3E 110
GU14: Cove 8K 69
RH11: Craw 4L 181
Kenneth Rd. SM7: Ban 2B 82
Kenneth Younger Ho.
SW6 2L 13
(off Clem Attlee Ct.)
Kennet Rd. TW7: Isle 6F 10
Kennet Sq. CR4: Mit 9C 28
Kennett Ct. W4 3A 12
Kenny Dr. SM5: Cars 5E 62
Kenrick Sq. RH1: Blet 2B 124
Kensington Av. CR7: T Hea 9L 29
Kensington Gdns.
KT1: K Tham 6H 203 (2K 41)
(not continuous)
Kensington Hall Gdns.
W14 1L 13
Kensington Mans.
SW5 1M 13
(off Trebovir Rd., not continuous)
Kensington Rd.
RH11: Craw 7N 181
Kensington Ter.
CR2: S Croy 4A 64
Kensington Village
W14 1L 13
Kent Cl. BR6: Chels 3N 67
CR4: Mit 3J 45
TW18: Stain 7M 21
Kent Dr. TW11: Tedd 6E 24
Kent Folly RG42: Warf 7D 16
Kent Ga. Way CR0: A'ton 3J 65
KENT HATCH 9K 107
Kent Hatch Rd.
RH8: C Hil, Limp 7E 106
TN8: C Hil 7E 106
Kent Ho. W4 1D 12
(off Devonshire St.)
Kentigern Dr. RG45: Crow 2J 49
Kenton Av. TW16: Sunb 1L 39
Kenton Cl. GU16: Frim 4D 70
RG12: Brac 1B 32
Kenton Ct. TW1: Twick 9K 11
Kentone Ct. SE25 3E 46
Kentons La. SL4: W'sor 5B 4
Kenton Way GU21: Wok 4J 73
Kent Rd. BR4: W Wick 7L 47
GU20: Windl 2A 52
GU22: Wok 3D 74
GU51: Fleet 4C 88
KT1: K Tham 5H 203 (2K 41)
KT8: E Mol 3C 40
TW9: Kew 3N 11
Kent's Pas. TW12: Hamp 9N 23
Kent Way KT6: Surb 9L 41
Kentwode Grn. SW13 3F 12
Kentwyns Dr. RH13: Hors 8L 197
Kentwyns Pl. RH13: Hors 8L 197
Kentwyns Ri. RH1: Sth N 4K 123
Kenward Ct. RH3: Brock 7B 120
Kenway Rd. SW5 1N 13
Kenwith Av. GU51: Fleet 4D 88
Kenwood Cl. UB7: Sip 2B 8
Kenwood Dr. BR3: Beck 2M 47
KT12: Hers 3J 57
Kenwood Pk. KT13: Weybr 3E 56
Kenwood Ridge CR8: Ken 4M 83
Kenworth Gro. GU18: Ligh 6L 51
Kenwyn Rd. SW20 9H 27
Kenya Ct. RH6: Horl 7D 142
Kenyngton Ct. TW16: Sunb 6H 23
Kenyngton Dr. TW16: Sunb 6H 23
Kenyon Mans. W14 2K 13
(off Queen's Club Gdns.)
Kenyons KT24: W Hors 6C 96
Kenyon St. SW6 4J 13
Keogh Cl. GU12: A Va 3F 90
Keppel Rd. RH4: Dork 3H 119
Keppel Spur SL4: O Win 1L 19
Kepple Pl. GU19: Bag 4J 51
Kepple St. SL4: W'sor 5G 5
Kerria Way GU24: W End 9B 52
Kerrill Av. CR5: Coul 6L 83
Kerry Cl. GU51: Fleet 9C 68
Kerry Ter. GU21: Wok 3D 74
Kersey Dr. CR2: Sels 8F 64
Kersfield Ho. SW15 9J 13
Kersfield Rd. SW15 9J 13
Kersland Cotts.
GU7: Hurt 4C 132
Kerves La. RH13: Hors 9K 197
KESTON 2E 66
Keston Av. BR2: Kes 2E 66
CR5: Coul 6L 83
KT15: N Haw 7J 55
Keston Ct. KT5: Surb 8L 203
Keston Gdns. BR2: Kes 1E 66
KESTON MARK 1G 67
KESTON MARK 1G 66
Keston Pk. Cl. BR2: Kes 1H 67
Keston Rd. CR7: T Hea 5L 45
Kestrel Av. TW18: Stain 4H 21
Kestrel Cl. GU4: Guil 1F 114
GU10: Ews 5C 108
GU12: A Va 6E 90
KT2: K Tham 5K 25
KT19: Eps 8N 59
RH11: Craw 1A 182
RH12: Hors 3L 197
TN8: Eden 9M 127
Kestrel Ct. CR2: S Croy 3N 63
SM6: W'ton 2G 63
Kestrel Ho. GU9: Farnh 3F 128
Kestrel Wlk. RH10: T Hil 4F 184
Kestrel Way CR0: N Add 5N 65
GU21: Wok 2L 73
Keswick Av. SW15 6D 26
SW19 1M 43
TW17: Shep 2F 38
Keswick B'way. SW15 8L 13
(off Up. Richmond Rd.)
Keswick Cl. GU15: Camb 2H 71
RH11: Ifi 5J 181
SM1: Sut 1A 62
Keswick Dr. GU18: Ligh 7M 51
Keswick Rd. GU8: Wit 4A 152
KT22: Fetc 2C 98
KT23: Book 3B 98
SW15 8K 13
TW2: Whitt 9C 10
TW20: Egh 8D 20
Ketcher Grn. RG42: Bin 5H 15
Kettering Ct. CR7: T Hea 3N 45
Kettering St. SW16 7G 28
Kettlewell Cl. GU21: Wok 1N 73
Kettlewell Dr. GU21: Wok 1A 74
Kettlewell Hill GU21: Wok 1A 74
Ketton Grn. RH1: Mers 6H 103
Kevan Dr. GU23: Send 3G 95
Kevin Cl. TW4: Houn 5L 9
Kevins Dr. GU46: Yate 8D 48
Kevins Gro. GU51: Fleet 4C 88
KEW 3N 11
KEW BRIDGE 1M 11
Kew Bri. TW8: Brent 2N 11
TW9: Kew 2N 11
Kew Bri. Arches TW9: Kew 2N 11
Kew Bri. Ct. W4 1N 11
Kew Bri. Distribution Cen.
TW8: Brent 1M 11
Kew Bri. Rd. TW8: Brent 2M 11
Kew Bridge Station (Rail) 1M 11
Kew Bridge Steam Mus. 1M 11
Kew Ct.
KT2: K Tham 1J 203 (9L 25)
Kew Cres. SM3: Chea 9K 43
Kew Foot Rd. TW9: Rich 7L 11
Kew Gdns. 3L 11
Kew Gdns. Plants & People Exhibition 3M 11
Kew Gdns. Rd. TW9: Kew 3M 11
Kew Gardens Station (Rail & Tube) 4N 11
Kew Gdns. Vis. Cen. 4M 11
KEW GREEN 3N 11
Kew Grn. TW9: Kew 2M 11
Kew Mdw. Path TW9: Kew 4A 12
TW9: Rich 5B 12
Kew Palace 2M 11
Kew Retail Pk. TW9: Kew 4A 12
Kew Riverside Pk.
TW9: Kew 3A 12
Kew Rd. TW9: Kew 2N 11
TW9: Rich 7L 11
Keymer Cl. TN16: B Hil 3E 86
Keymer Rd. RH11: Craw 4A 182
SW2 3K 29
Keynes Cl. GU52: C Cro 9C 88
Keynsham Rd. SM4: Mord 7N 43
Keynsham Wlk. SM4: Mord 7N 43
Keynsham Way GU47: Owls 5J 49
Keys Ct. CR0: Croy 5D 200
Keysham Av. TW5: C'ford 4H 9
Keywood Dr. TW16: Sunb 7H 23
Khama Rd. SW17 5C 28
Khartoum Rd. GU8: Wit 4B 152
SW17 5B 28
Kibble Grn. RG12: Brac 5A 32
Kidborough Down
KT23: Book 5A 98
Kidborough Rd.
RH11: Craw 4L 181
KIDBROOKE PARK 8F 186
Kidbrooke Ri.
RH18: F Row 7G 187
Kidderminster Pl.
CR0: Croy 7M 45
Kidderminster Rd.
CR0: Croy 7M 45
Kidmans Cl. RH12: Hors 3M 197
Kidworth Cl. RH6: Horl 6D 142
Kielder Wlk. GU15: Camb 2G 71
Kier Pk. SL5: Asc 2N 33
Kilberry Cl. TW7: Isle 4D 10
Kilburns Mill Cl.
SM6: W'ton 8F 44
Kilcorral Cl. KT17: Eps 1F 80
Kilkie St. SW6 5N 13
Killasser Ct. KT20: Tad 1H 101
Killester Gdns. KT4: W Pk 1G 61
Killick Ho. SM1: Sut 1N 61
Killick M. SM3: Chea 3K 61
Killicks GU6: Cranl 6A 156
Killieser Av. SW2 3J 29
Killigrew Ho. TW16: Sunb 8F 22
Killinghurst La. GU8: Chid 2N 189
GU27: Hasl 2N 189
KILLINGHURST PARK 9A 172
Killy Hill GU24: Chob 4H 53
Kilmaine Rd. SW6 3K 13
Kilmarnock Pk. RH2: Reig 2N 121
Kilmartin Av. SW16 2L 45
Kilmartin Gdns. GU16: Frim 5D 70
Kilmington Cl. RG12: Brac 6C 32
Kilmington Rd. SW13 2F 12
Kilmiston Av. TW17: Shep 5D 38
Kilmiston Ho. TW17: Shep 5D 38
Kilmore Dr. GU15: Camb 2F 70
Kilmorey Gdns. TW1: Twick 8H 11
Kilmorey Rd. TW1: Twick 7H 11
Kilmuir Cl. GU47: C Tow 8J 49
Kiln Av. GU27: Hasl 9G 171
Kiln Cl. RH10: Craw D 2E 184
UB3: Harl 2E 8
Kiln Copse GU6: Cranl 6N 155
Kiln Cotts. RH5: Newd 7C 140
Kilnfield Rd. RH12: Rudg 9E 176
Kiln Heath Farm Bus. Cen.
RH6: S Bri 5L 163
Kiln La. GU10: L Bou 5G 129
GU23: Rip 2J 95
GU24: Bis 4E 72
KT17: Eps 7D 60
RG12: Brac 1M 31
RH3: Betch, Brock 4A 120
RH6: Horl 2E 142
SL4: Wink 7M 17
SL5: S'dale 4D 34
Kilnmead RH10: Craw 2B 182
Kilnmead Cl. RH10: Craw 2C 182
Kiln Mdws. GU3: Worp 8F 92
Kiln M. SW17 6B 28

Kiln Ride RG40: Finch … 8A 30
Kiln Ride Extension
RG40: Finch … 1A 48
Kiln Rd. RH10: Craw D … 2E 184
Kilns, The RH1: Mers, Red … 9F 102
Kilnside KT10: Clay … 4G 58
Kiln Wlk. RH1: Red … 8E 122
Kiln Way GU11: Alde … 5N 109
GU26: G'hott … 4K 169
Kilnwood La. RH11: Fay … 6E 180
RH12: Fay … 6E 180
Kilometre, The RG45: Crow … 3E 48
Kilross Rd. TW14: Bedf … 2E 22
Kilrue La. KT12: Hers … 1G 57
Kilrush Ter. GU21: Wok … 3C 74
Kilsha Rd. KT12: Wal T … 5K 39
Kimbell Gdns. SW6 … 4K 13
Kimber Cl. SL4: W'sor … 6D 4
Kimber Ct. GU4: Guil … 1F 114
Kimberley GU52: C Cro … 9C 88
RG12: Brac … 7A 32
Kimberley Cl. RH6: Horl … 8C 142
SL3: Lang … 1B 6
Kimberley Pl. CR8: Pur … 7L 63
Kimberley Ride KT11: Cob … 9B 58
Kimberley Rd. BR3: Beck … 1G 47
CR0: Croy … 5M 45
RH10: Craw … 2F 182
Kimberley Wlk. KT12: Wal T … 6J 39
Kimber Rd. SW18 … 1M 27
Kimbers La. GU9: Farnh … 9J 109
Kimble Rd. SW19 … 7B 28
Kimmeridge RG12: Brac … 5C 32
Kimpton Ho. SW15 … 1F 26
Kimpton Ind. Est. SM3: Sut … 8L 43
Kimpton Link Bus. Cen.
SM3: Sut … 8L 43
Kimpton Pk. Way SM1: Sut … 8L 43
SM3: Sut … 8K 43
Kimpton Rd. SM3: Sut … 8L 43
Kimpton Trade & Bus. Cen.
SM3: Sut … 8L 43
Kinburn Dr. TW20: Egh … 6A 20
Kincha Lodge
KT2: K Tham … 1L 203
Kindersley Cl.
RH19: E Grin … 7D 166
Kinfauns Rd. SW2 … 3L 29
King Acre Ct. TW18: Stain … 4G 20
King Charles Cres.
KT5: Surb … 6M 41
King Charles Ho. *SW6* … *3N 13*
(off Wandon Rd.)
King Charles Rd.
KT5: Surb … 4M 41
King Charles Wlk.
SW19 … 2K 27
Kingcup Cl. CR0: Croy … 6G 46
Kingcup Dr. GU24: Bis … 2D 72
King Edward VII Av.
SL4: W'sor … 3H 5
King Edward Cl.
RH13: Hors … 9D 196
King Edward Ct. SL4: W'sor … 4G 4
King Edward Ct. Shop. Cen.
SL4: W'sor … 4F 4
King Edward Dr. KT9: Ches … 9L 41
King Edward M. SW13 … 4F 12
King Edward Rd.
RH13: Hors … 9D 196
King Edward's Cl. SL5: Asc … 9J 17
King Edwards Gro.
TW11: Tedd … 7H 25
King Edwards Mans.
SW6 … *3M 13*
(off Fulham Rd.)
King Edward's Ri. SL5: Asc … 8J 17
King Edward's Rd. SL5: Asc … 9J 17
KINGFIELD … 7C 74
Kingfield Cl. GU22: Wok … 7B 74
Kingfield Dr. GU22: Wok … 7B 74
Kingfield Gdns. GU22: Wok … 7B 74
KINGFIELD GREEN … 7B 74
Kingfield Rd. GU22: Wok … 7A 74
Kingfield Stadium … 7B 74
Kingfisher Cl. GU14: Cove … 8H 69
GU52: C Cro … 8B 88
KT12: Hers … 2M 57
RH10: Craw … 8E 162
Kingfisher Ct. *GU21: Wok* … *4A 74*
(off Vale Rd.)
GU21: Wok … 1E 74
(Blackmore Cres.)
GU51: Fleet … *5A 88*
(off Connaught Rd.)
KT8: E Mol … 3E 40
RH4: Dork … 1J 201
SM1: Sut … 2L 61
SW19 … 3J 27
TW3: Houn … 8B 10
TW7: Isle … 5D 10
Kingfisher Dr. GU4: Guil … 1E 114
GU46: Yate … 9A 48
RH1: Red … 9E 102
TW10: Ham … 5H 25
TW18: Stain … 5H 21
Kingfisher Gdns. CR2: Sels … 7G 65
Kingfisher La. RH10: T Hil … 4F 184
Kingfisher Leisure Cen.
… 4K 203 (1L 41)
Kingfisher Ri.
RH19: E Grin … 1B 186
Kingfisher Rd. GU9: Farnh … 3E 128
Kingfisher Wlk.
GU12: Ash … 2D 110
Kingfisher Way BR3: Beck … 4G 46
RH12: Hors … 3J 197
King Gdns.
CR0: Wad … 8A 200 (2M 63)
King George VI Av.
CR4: Mit … 3D 44
TN16: B Hil … 3F 86
King George Av.
KT12: Wal T … 7L 39
RH19: E Grin … 7M 165
King George Cl.
GU14: Farnb … 3B 90
TW16: Sunb … 6F 22
King George's Dr.
KT15: N Haw … 6J 55
KING GEORGE'S HILL … 5N 137
King George's Ind. Est.
KT9: Ches … 1N 59
King George Sq.
TW10: Rich … 9M 11
Kingham Cl. SW18 … 1A 28
Kingham Pl. *GU9: Farnh* … *1G 129*
(off West St.)
King Henry Rd. GU51: Fleet … 2A 88
King Henry's Dr.
CR0: N Add … 5L 65
King Henry's Drive Stop (CT)
… 5L 65
King Henry's Reach
W6 … 2H 13
King Henry's Rd.
KT1: K Tham … 2A 42
King John La. TW19: Wray … 8N 5
King John's Cl. TW19: Wray … 8N 5
King John St. GU51: Fleet … 2A 88
Kinglake Ct. GU21: Wok … 5H 73
Kingpost Pde. GU4: B'ham … 9D 94
Kings Acre RH1: Sth N … 6K 123
Kings Apartments
GU15: Camb … 2A 70
Kings Arbour UB2: S'hall … 1M 9
King's Arms All. TW8: Brent … 2K 11
Kings Arms Way
KT16: Chert … 7H 37
Kings Av. GU10: Tong … 4C 110
GU24: B'wood … 6A 72
KT3: N Mal … 3D 42
KT14: Byf … 8M 55
RH1: Red … 5C 122
SM5: Cars … 4C 62
SW4 … 2H 29
SW12 … 2H 29
TW3: Houn … 4B 10
TW16: Sunb … 6G 23
Kingsbridge Cotts.
RG40: W'ham … 9C 30
Kingsbridge Rd.
KT12: Wal T … 6J 39
SM4: Mord … 5J 43
UB2: S'hall … 1N 9
Kingsbrook KT22: Leat … 5G 79
Kingsbury Cres.
TW18: Stain … 5F 20
Kingsbury Dr. SL4: O Win … 1K 19
Kings Chase KT8: E Mol … 2C 40
Kingsclear Pk. GU15: Camb … 2B 70
Kingsclere Cl. SW15 … 1F 26
Kingscliffe Gdns.
SW19 … 2L 27
Kings Cl. KT7: T Dit … 5G 41
KT12: Wal T … 7J 39
TW18: Stain … 8M 21
King's Club, The (Sports Cen.)
… 7H 27
Kings Copse RH19: E Grin … 1B 186
KINGSCOTE … 5H 185
Kingscote Hill RH11: Craw … 5N 181
Kingscote Rd. CR0: Croy … 6E 46
KT3: N Mal … 2C 42
Kingscote Station
Bluebell Railway … 5J 185
Kings Ct. GU10: Tong … 4C 110
KT12: Wal T … 9J 39
KT14: Byf … 7M 55
KT20: Tad … 9G 81
RH13: Hors … 5L 197
W6 … 1F 12
Kings Ct. M. KT8: E Mol … 4D 40
Kingscourt Rd. SW16 … 4H 29
King's Cres. GU15: Camb … 7A 50
Kingscroft GU51: Fleet … 5B 88
Kingscroft La. RG42: Warf … 3D 16
Kingscroft Rd. KT22: Leat … 7H 79
SM7: Ban … 2B 82
Kings Cross La.
RH1: Sth N … 5H 123
Kingsdene KT20: Tad … 8G 80
Kingsdown Av. CR2: S Croy … 6M 63
Kingsdowne Rd. KT6: Surb … 6L 41
Kingsdown Rd. KT17: Eps … 9F 60
SM3: Chea … 2K 61
Kings Dr. KT5: Surb … 6N 41
KT7: T Dit … 6H 41
KT12: Whit V … 5G 57
TW11: Tedd … 6D 24
Kings Farm Av. TW10: Rich … 7N 11
Kingsfield GU5: Alb … 4N 135
SL4: W'sor … 4A 4
Kingsfield Bus. Cen.
RH1: Red … 4E 122
Kingsfield Way RH1: Red … 4E 122
KINGSFOLD … 3H 179
Kingsfold Ct. RH12: K'fold … 4H 179
Kings Ga. *GU7: Goda* … *5J 133*
(off King's Rd.)
KT15: Addl … 1K 55
RH12: Hors … 6H 197
Kingsgate RH10: Craw … 3C 182
Kingsgate Bus. Cen.
KT2: K Tham … 2J 203
Kingsgate Rd.
KT1: K Tham … 2J 203 (9L 25)
KT2: K Tham … 2J 203 (9L 25)
Kings Glade GU46: Yate … 9E 48
Kingsgrove Ind. Est.
GU14: Cove … 2M 89
Kingshead La. KT14: Byf … 7M 55
Kingshill Av. KT4: W Pk … 6F 42
Kings Keep GU47: Sandh … 6G 49
GU52: Fleet … 7B 88
KT1: K Tham … 8J 203 (3L 41)
SW15 … 8J 13
KINGSLAND … 2N 159
Kingsland RH5: Newd … 2N 159
Kingsland Ct. RH10: Craw … 3E 182
Kings La. GU10: Wrec … 5E 128
GU20: Windl … 2B 52
SM1: Sut … 3B 62
TW20: Eng G … 6K 19
Kingslawn Cl. SW15 … 8G 13
Kingslea KT22: Leat … 7G 79
RH13: Hors … 5L 197
Kingslee Ct. SM2: Sut … 4N 61
Kingsleigh Cl. TW8: Brent … 2K 11
Kingsleigh Pl. CR4: Mit … 2D 44
Kings Leisure Cen. … 9A 166
Kingsley Av. GU15: Camb … 2A 70
SM1: Sut … 1B 62
SM7: Ban … 2M 81
TW3: Houn … 5C 10
TW20: Eng G … 7L 19
Kingsley Cl. RG45: Crow … 4G 49
RH6: Horl … 6D 142
Kingsley Ct. *GU11: Alde* … *2N 109*
(off Windsor Way)
KT4: W Pk … *8E 42*
(off The Avenue)
KT12: Wal T … *9H 39*
(off Ashley Pk. Rd.)
Kingsley Dr. KT4: W Pk … 8E 42
Kingsley Gdns. KT16: Otter … 3F 54
KINGSLEY GREEN … 7F 188
Kingsley Gro. RH2: Reig … 6M 121
Kingsley Mans. *W14* … *2K 13*
(off Greyhound Rd.)
Kingsley Rd. CR0: Croy … 7L 45
GU14: Farnb … 8L 69
RH6: Horl … 6D 142
RH11: Craw … 6M 181
SW19 … 6N 27
TW3: Houn … 4B 10
Kingslyn Cres. SE19 … 1B 46
Kings Mall W6 … 1H 13
Kings Mead GU6: Cranl … 7N 155
RH1: Sth N … 5J 123
RH6: Smal … 8M 143
Kingsmead GU14: Farnb … 1N 89
GU16: Frim G … 7C 70
GU21: Wok … 3C 74
KT13: Weybr … 3E 56
TN16: B Hil … 3F 86
TW10: Rich … 9M 11
Kingsmead Av. CR4: Mit … 2G 45
KT4: W Pk … 8G 42
KT6: Surb … 8N 41
TW16: Sunb … 1K 39
Kingsmead Cl. KT19: Ewe … 4C 60
RH12: Hors … 2A 198
TW11: Tedd … 7H 25
Kingsmead Lodge SM2: Sut … 3B 62
Kingsmeadow … 2N 41
Kingsmeadow Athletics Cen.
… 2N 41
Kings Mead Pk. KT10: Clay … 4E 58
Kingsmead Pk. GU8: Els … 9G 130
Kingsmead Pl.
RH12: Bro H … 5C 196
Kingsmead Rd.
RH12: Bro H … 5D 196
SW2 … 3L 29
Kingsmead Shop. Cen.
GU14: Farnb … 1N 89
Kingsmere Cl. SW15 … 6J 13
Kingsmere Rd. RG42: Brac … 9L 15
SW19 … 3J 27
Kings M. GU16: Frim G … 8D 70
RH12: Hors … 6H 197
Kingsmill Bus. Pk.
KT1: K Tham … 6M 203 (2M 41)
Kings Mill La.
RH1: Red, Sth N … 8F 122
Kingsnympton Pk.
KT2: K Tham … 8A 26
Kingsoak Ho. GU21: Wok … 3C 74
King's Paddock
TW12: Hamp … 9C 24
Kings Pde. GU51: Fleet … 3B 88
SM5: Cars … *9D 44*
(off Wrythe La.)
Kingspark Bus. Cen.
KT3: N Mal … 3B 42
Kings Pas.
KT1: K Tham … 4H 203 (1K 41)
KT2: K Tham … 1H 203 (9K 25)
Kings Peace, The
GU26: G'hott … 6A 170
King's Pl. W4 … 1B 12
King's Ride GU15: Camb … 6B 50
(not continuous)
SL5: Asc … 4G 32
Kings Ride Ga.
TW10: Rich … 7N 11
Kings Ride Pk.
SL5: Asc … 4G 33
Kingsridge SW19 … 3K 27
Kings Rd. CR4: Mit … 2E 44
GU1: Guil … 3D 202 (3N 113)
GU4: Chil … 1A 134
GU6: Cranl … 8N 155
GU7: Goda … 5J 133
GU11: Alde … 3K 109
GU21: Wok … 3C 74
GU24: W End … 1D 72
GU27: Hasl … 2D 188
GU51: Fleet … 3B 88
KT2: K Tham … 1K 203 (8L 25)
KT6: Surb … 7J 41
KT12: Wal T … 8J 39
KT15: N Haw … 6K 55
RG45: Crow … 3G 49
RH6: Horl … 8E 142
RH12: Rudg … 9E 176
RH13: Hors … 5L 197
SE25 … 2D 46
SL4: W'sor … 7G 4
SL5: S'dale, S'hill … 4A 34
SM2: Sut … 6M 61
SW6 … 3N 13
SW10 … 3N 13
SW14 … 6C 12
SW19 … 7M 27
TN16: B Hil … 3E 86
TW1: Twick … 9H 11
TW10: Rich … 9M 11
TW11: Tedd … 6D 24
TW13: Felt … 2K 23
TW20: Egh … 5C 20
King's Rd. Ind. Est.
GU27: Hasl … 2D 188
King's Shade Wlk.
KT19: Eps … 7K 201 (9C 60)
King Stable St. SL4: Eton … 3G 4
Kings Ter. GU10: Fren … 1J 149
SL3: Lang … 2D 6
TW7: Isle … 7G 11
Kingston Av. KT22: Leat … 8H 79
KT24: E Hor … 4F 96
SM3: Chea … 9K 43
TW14: Felt … 9F 8
Kingston Bri.
KT1: K Tham … 3G 203 (1K 41)
Kingston Bus. Cen.
KT9: Ches … 9L 41
Kingston By-Pass
KT3: N Mal … 4D 42
KT6: Surb … 9K 41
SW15 … 5D 26
SW20 … 1F 42
Kingston By-Pass Rd.
KT6: Surb … 8E 40
KT10: Esh, H Wood … 8E 40
Kingston Cl. TW11: Tedd … 7H 25
Kingston Cres.
TW15: A'ford … 6L 21
Kingston Gdns. CR0: Bedd … 9J 45
Kingston Hall Rd.
KT1: K Tham … 5H 203 (2K 41)
Kingston Hill KT2: K Tham … 9N 25
Kingston Hill Pl.
KT2: K Tham … 5B 26
Kingston Ho.
KT1: K Tham … 7H 203
Kingston Ho. Est.
KT6: Surb … 5H 41
Kingston Ho. Gdns.
KT22: Leat … 8H 79
Kingstonian FC … 2N 41
Kingston La.
KT24: W Hors … 5B 96
TW11: Tedd … 6G 25
Kingston Lodge KT3: N Mal … 3D 42
Kingston Ri. KT15: N Haw … 6J 55
Kingston Rd. GU15: Camb … 7D 50
KT1: K Tham … 2A 42
KT3: N Mal … 2A 42
KT4: W Pk … 8A 42
KT5: Surb … 8A 42
KT17: Ewe … 5E 60
KT19: Ewe … 8A 42
KT22: Leat … 5G 78
(not continuous)
SW15 … 3F 26
SW19 … 3F 26
(Norstead Pl.)
SW19 … 1K 43
(Watery La.)
SW20 … 1J 43
TW11: Tedd … 6H 25
TW15: A'ford … 7N 21
TW18: Stain … 5H 21
Kingstons Ind. Est.
GU12: Alde … 2C 110
Kingston Sq. *KT22: Leat* … *6G 79*
(off Buffers La.)
Kingston Station (Rail)
… 2J 203 (9L 25)
Kingston Theatre … 4H 203 (1K 41)
Kingston University
Grange Rd. … 6K 203 (2L 41)
Kingston Hill … 6C 26
Penrhyn Rd. … 7J 203 (3L 41)
Roehampton Vale Cen.
… 4E 26
Kingston upon Thames Crematorium
KT1: K Tham … 2N 41
Kingston upon Thames Library,
Art Gallery and Mus.
… 3K 203 (1L 41)
KINGSTON VALE … 5D 26
Kingston Va. SW15 … 5C 26
King St. KT16: Chert … 7J 37
RH19: E Grin … 9A 166
TW1: Twick … 2G 24
TW9: Rich … 8K 11
W6 … 1F 12
King St. Cloisters *W6* … *1G 13*
(off Clifton Wlk.)
King St. Pde. *TW1: Twick* … *2G 24*
(off King St.)
Kings Wlk. CR2: Sande … 1E 84
GU15: Camb … 9L 49
Kings Warren KT22: Oxs … 7C 58
King's Way CR0: Wad … 2K 63
Kingsway BR4: W Wick … 1B 66
GU11: Alde … 3K 109
GU17: B'water … 1J 69
GU21: Wok … 5N 73
KT3: N Mal … 3H 43
SW14 … 6A 12
TW19: Stan … 2M 21
Kingsway, The KT17: Ewe … 7D 60
Kingsway Av. CR2: Sels … 5F 64
GU21: Wok … 5N 73
Kingsway Bus. Pk.
TW12: Hamp … 9N 23
Kingsway Rd. SM3: Chea … 4K 61
Kingsway Ter. KT13: Weybr … 5B 56
Kingswey Bus. Pk.
GU21: Wok … 1E 74
Kingswick Cl. SL5: S'hill … 3B 34
Kingswick Dr. SL5: S'hill … 3A 34
KINGSWOOD … 2K 101
Kingswood SL5: Asc … 3G 33
Kingswood Av. BR2: Brom … 2N 47
CR2: Sande … 2E 84
CR7: T Hea … 4L 45
TW3: Houn … 4N 9
TW12: Hamp … 7B 24
Kingswood Cl. GU1: Guil … 2E 114
GU15: Camb … 7E 50
KT3: N Mal … 5E 42
KT6: Surb … 6L 41
KT13: Weybr … 4C 56
RH11: Craw … 9A 182
TW15: A'ford … 6D 22
TW20: Eng G … 5N 19
Kingswood Ct. GU21: Wok … 3A 74
GU51: Fleet … 4B 88
KT20: K'wood … 2K 101
Kingswood Creek
TW19: Wray … 8N 5
Kingswood Dr. SM2: Sut … 5N 61
SM5: Cars … 7D 44
Kingswood Flds. Bus. Pk.
KT20: K'wood … 3M 101
Kingswood Firs
GU26: G'hott … 7N 169
Kingswood Grange
KT20: Lwr K … 6M 101
Kingswood Ho.
KT20: K'wood … 7L 81
Kingswood La. CR2: Sande … 1G 84
CR6: Warl … 2F 84
(not continuous)
GU26: G'hott … 7A 170
Kingswood Pk.
KT20: K'wood … 8K 81
Kingswood Pl. CR3: Cate … 1C 104
TN8: Eden … 9L 127
Kingswood Ri.
TW20: Eng G … 6N 19
Kingswood Rd. BR2: Brom … 3N 47
KT20: Tad … 8G 80
SW2 … 1J 29
SW19 … 8L 27
Kingswood Station (Rail) … 8L 81
Kingswood Way CR2: Sels … 9F 64
(not continuous)
SM6: W'ton … 2J 63
Kingsworth Cl. BR3: Beck … 4H 47
Kingsworthy Cl.
KT1: K Tham … 5M 203 (2M 41)
Kings Yd. SL5: Asc … 3J 33
SW15 … *6H 13*
(off Lwr. Richmond Rd.)
Kingwood Rd. SW6 … 4K 13
Kinloss Rd. SM5: Cars … 6A 44
Kinnaird Av. W4 … 3B 12
Kinnersley Wlk.
RH2: Reig … 8M 121
Kinnibrugh Dr. RH7: Dorm … 1C 166
Kinnoul Rd. W6 … 2K 13
Kinross Av. KT4: W Pk … 8F 42
SL5: Asc … 4K 33
Kinross Cl. TW16: Sunb … 6G 23
Kinross Ct. SL5: Asc … 4K 33
Kinross Dr. TW16: Sunb … 6G 22
Kinsella Gdns. SW19 … 6G 26
Kintyre Cl. SW16 … 1K 45
Kintyre Ct. SW2 … 1J 29

Kipings—Langhurst

Kipings KT20: Tad 8J **81**
Kipling Cl. GU46: Yate 2B **68**
RH10: Craw 1G **182**
Kipling Ct. RH13: Hors 4N **197**
SL4: W'sor 5E **4**
Kipling Dr. SW19 . . . . .7B **28**
Kipling Hall RG45: Crow 2G **48**
Kipling Way RH19: E Grin . . .9M **165**
Kirby Cl. KT19: Ewe 2E **60**
Kirby Rd. GU21: Wok 4M **73**
Kirby Way KT12: Wal T 5K **39**
Kirdford Cl. RH11: Craw 1M **181**
Kirkby Ct. GU16: Frim 5C **70**
Kirkefields GU2: Guil 9K **93**
Kirkgate, The
KT17: Eps 6L **201** (9D **60**)
Kirkham Cl. GU47: Owls 5J **49**
Kirk Knoll GU35: Head 4E **168**
Kirkland Av. GU21: Wok 3H **73**
Kirkleas Rd. KT6: Surb 7L **41**
Kirklees Rd. CR7: T Hea 4L **45**
Kirkley Rd. SW19 . . . . .9M **27**
Kirkly Cl. CR2: Sande 5B **64**
Kirk Ri. SM1: Sut 9N **43**
Kirkstall Gdns. SW2 . . . . .2J **29**
Kirkstall Rd. SW2 . . . . .2H **29**
Kirksted Rd. SM4: Mord 7N **43**
Kirkstone Cl. GU15: Camb 2H **71**
Kirrane Cl. KT3: N Mal 4E **42**
Kirriemuir Gdns.
GU12: Ash 1H **111**
Kirsty Cl. RH5: Dork 7J **119**
Kirton Lodge SW18 . . . . .9N **13**
Kitchener Rd. CR7: T Hea 2A **46**
GU11: Alde 7B **90**
Kites Cl. RH11: Craw 3A **182**
Kithurst Cl. RH11: Craw 5B **182**
Kitsmead RH10: Cop 8L **163**
Kitsmead La. KT16: L'cross . . .7M **35**
Kitson Rd. SW13 . . . . .4F **12**
Kittiwake Cl. CR2: Sels 6H **65**
RH11: Ifi 5J **181**
Kittiwake Pl. SM1: Sut 2L **61**
Kitts La. GU10: Churt 9K **149**
Klondyke Vs.
GU27: G'wood 8L **171**
KNAPHILL 4G **72**
Knapp Rd. TW15: A'ford 5A **22**
Knapton M. SW17 . . . . .7E **28**
Knaresborough Dr.
SW18 . . . . .2N **27**
Kneller Gdns. TW7: Isle 9D **10**
Kneller Rd. KT3: N Mal 6D **42**
TW2: Whitt 9C **10**
Knepp Cl. RH10: Craw 3G **182**
Knevett Ter. TW3: Houn 7A **10**
Knighton Cl. CR2: S Croy 5M **63**
RH10: Craw 8H **163**
Knighton Rd. RH1: Red 5E **122**
Knightons La. GU8: Duns 5B **174**
Knightsbridge Ct. *SL3: Lang 1C 6*
(off High St.)
Knightsbridge Cres.
TW18: Stain 7K **21**
Knightsbridge Gro.
GU15: Camb 8C **50**
Knightsbridge Ho.
GU1: Guil 4B 114
(off St Lukes Sq.)
Knightsbridge Rd.
GU15: Camb 8C **50**
Knights Cl. KT8: W Mole 4N **39**
SL4: W'sor 4A **4**
TW20: Egh 7F **20**
Knights Ct.
KT1: K Tham 5J **203** (2L **41**)
Knights Hill SE27 . . . . .6M **29**
Knight's Hill Sq. SE27 . . . . . . .5M **29**
Knight's Pk.
KT1: K Tham 5K **203** (2L **41**)
Knights Pl. RH1: Red 2E **122**
SL4: W'sor 6F **4**
TW2: Twick 2E **24**
Knights Rd. GU9: H End 5K **109**
Knights Way GU15: Camb 2G **70**
Knightswood GU21: Wok 5J **73**
RG12: Brac 7N **31**
Knightwood Cl.
GU14: Farnb 3C **90**
RH2: Reig 5M **121**
Knightwood Cres.
KT3: N Mal 5D **42**
Knipp Hill KT11: Cob 9N **57**
Knivet Rd. SW6 . . . . .2M **13**
Knobfield RH5: A Ham 3G **136**
Knob Hill RH12: Warn 9F **178**
Knockholt Cl. SM2: Sut 6N **61**
Knockholt Main Rd.
TN14: Knoc 6N **87**
Knockhundred La.
GU26: Lip 9N **169**
Knole Cl. CR0: Croy 5F **46**
RH10: Craw 2H **183**
Knole Gro. RH19: E Grin 7M **165**
Knole Wood SL5: S'dale 7B **34**
Knoll, The BR3: Beck 1L **47**
KT11: Cob 9A **58**
KT16: Chert 7H **37**
KT22: Leat 8J **79**
Knoll Cl. GU51: Fleet 3B **88**
Knoll Ct. GU51: Fleet 2B **88**
Knoll Farm Rd. RH5: Cap 7G **159**
Knollmead KT5: Surb 7B **42**
Knoll Pk. Rd. KT16: Chert 7H **37**
Knoll Quarry GU7: Goda 5H **133**
Knoll Rd. GU7: Goda 5G **133**
GU15: Camb 9B **50**
GU51: Fleet 3B **88**
RH4: Dork 7G **118**
SW18 . . . . .8N **13**
KNOLL RDBT. 8J **79**
Knoll Rdbt. KT22: Leat 8J **79**
Knolls, The KT17: Eps D 3H **81**
Knolls Cl. KT4: W Pk 9G **42**
Knoll Wlk. GU15: Camb 9B **50**
Knoll Wood GU7: Goda 5G **133**
Knollys Cl. SW16 . . . . .4L **29**
Knollys Rd. GU11: Alde 1L **109**
SW16 . . . . .4K **29**
Knook, The GU47: C Tow 8J **49**
Knowle, The GU35: Head 3G **168**
KT20: Tad 8H **81**
Knowle Cl. RH10: Cop 7N **163**
Knowledge Ct. SW16 . . . . . . .2K **45**
Knowle Dr. RH10: Cop 7M **163**
Knowle Gdns. KT14: W By 9H **55**
KNOWLE GREEN 6K **21**
Knowle Grn. TW18: Stain 6J **21**
Knowle Gro. GU25: V Wat 6M **35**
Knowle Gro. Cl.
GU25: V Wat 6M **35**
KNOWLE HILL 6M **35**
Knowle Hill GU25: V Wat 6L **35**
Knowle La.
GU6: Cranl, Rudg 8M **155**
RH12: Rudg 4M **175**
Knowle Lodge CR3: Cate 1D **104**
Knowle Pk. KT11: Cob 3M **77**
Knowle Pk. Av. TW18: Stain . . .7K **21**
Knowle Rd. TW2: Twick 2E **24**
Knowles Av. RG45: Crow 2E **48**
Knowles Ho. *SW18 . . . . .9N 13*
(off Neville Gill Cl.)
Knowl Hill GU22: Wok 6D **74**
Knox Grn. RG42: Bin 6H **15**
Knox Rd. GU2: Guil 7K **93**
Kohat Ct. GU11: Alde 2L **109**
Kohat Rd. SW19 . . . . .6N **27**
Kohima Cl. GU11: Alde 1N **109**
Koonowla Cl. TN16: B Hil 2F **86**
Kooringa CR6: Warl 6E **84**
Korda Cl. TW17: Shep 2A **38**
Korea Cotts. KT11: Cob 3L **77**
Kotan Dr. TW18: Stain 5E **20**
Kramer M. SW5 . . . . .1M **13**
Kreisel Wlk. TW9: Kew 2M **11**
Kristina Ct. *SM2: Sut 3M 61*
(off Overton Rd.)
Krooner Rd. GU15: Camb 3N **69**
Kuala Gdns. SW16 . . . . .9K **29**
Kyle Cl. RG12: Brac 2N **31**
Kynaston Av. CR7: T Hea 4N **45**
Kynaston Ct. CR3: Cate 3B **104**
Kynaston Cres. CR7: T Hea 4N **45**
Kynaston Rd. CR7: T Hea 4N **45**
Kyngeshene Gdns.
GU1: Guil 4D **114**
Kynnersley Cl. SM5: Cars 9D **44**

L

Laburnhum Rd. GU22: Wok . . .7N **73**
Laburnum Av. SM1: Sut 9C **44**
Laburnum Cl. GU1: Guil 9M **93**
GU11: Alde 3M **109**
Laburnum Ct. (Cvn. Pk.)
RH6: Smal 1N **163**
Laburnum Cres.
TW16: Sunb 9J **23**
Laburnum Gdns. CR0: Croy . . .6G **46**
GU52: C Cro 8C **88**
Laburnum Gro. KT3: N Mal 1C **42**
SL3: Lang 2D **6**
TW3: Houn 7N **9**
Laburnum Ho. BR2: Brom 1N **47**
Laburnum Pas.
GU11: Alde 2M **109**
Laburnum Pl. TW20: Eng G 7L **19**
Laburnum Rd. CR4: Mit 1E **44**
GU9: Weybo 5K **109**
GU11: Alde 3M **109**
KT16: Chert 7J **37**
KT18: Eps 7L **201** (9D **60**)
SW19 . . . . .8A **28**
UB3: Harl 1H **9**
Laburnums, The
GU17: B'water 1G **68**
Laburnum Way TW19: Stan . . .2A **22**
Lacey Av. CR5: Coul 7L **83**
Lacey Cl. TW20: Egh 8F **20**
Lacey Dr. CR5: Coul 7M **83**
TW12: Hamp 9N **23**
Lacey Grn. CR5: Coul 7L **83**
Lackford Rd. CR5: Chip 5D **82**
Lackland Ct. *GU51: Fleet 2A 88*
(off King John St.)
Lacock Cl. SW19 . . . . .7A **28**
Lacrosse Way SW16 . . . . .9H **29**
Lacy Rd. SW15 . . . . .7J **13**
(not continuous)
Ladas Rd. SE27 . . . . .5N **29**
Ladbroke Cotts. *RH1: Red 2E 122*
(off Ladbroke Rd.)
Ladbroke Ct. RH1: Red 1E **122**
Ladbroke Gro. RH1: Red 2E **122**
Ladbroke Hurst RH7: Dorm . . .1C **166**
Ladbroke Rd.
KT18: Eps 8K **201** (1C **80**)
RH1: Red 2E **122**
RH6: Horl 6F **142**
Ladbrook Rd. SE25 . . . . .3A **46**
Ladderstile Ride
TW10: Rich 6A **26**
Ladybank RG12: Brac 7N **31**
Lady Booth Rd.
KT1: K Tham 4J **203** (1L **41**)
Ladycroft Gdns. BR6: Farnb . . .2L **67**
Ladycroft Way BR6: Farnb 2L **67**
Ladycross GU8: Mil 2B **152**
Ladyegate Cl. RH5: Dork 4K **119**
Ladyegate Rd. RH5: Dork 5J **119**
Lady Elizabeth Ho.
SW14 . . . . .6B **12**
Lady Forsdyke Way
KT19: Eps 5N **59**
Ladygate Dr. GU26: G'hott . . .6M **169**
Ladygrove CR0: Sels 5H **65**
Ladygrove Dr. GU4: B'ham 7C **94**
Lady Harewood Way
KT19: Eps 5N **59**
Lady Hay KT4: W Pk 8E **42**
Lady Jane Ct.
KT2: K Tham 3M **203**
Lady Margaret Rd.
RH11: Craw 2M **181**
SL5: S'dale 7C **34**
Lady Margaret Wlk.
RH11: Craw 2M **181**
Ladymead
GU1: Guil 1B **202** (2M **113**)
Ladymead Cl. RH10: Craw 6G **183**
Ladymead Retail Cen.
GU1: Guil 1B **202** (2M **113**)
Ladythorpe Cl. KT15: Addl 1K **55**
Ladywood Av. GU14: Cove 1H **89**
Ladywood Rd. KT6: Surb 8N **41**
Laffan's Rd. GU11: Alde 7H **89**
LA Fitness
Ewell 8H **61**
Goldsworth 4N **73**
Old Isleworth 6H 11
(off Swan St.)
Purley 6N **63**
Lafone Av. TW13: Felt 3K **23**
Lagham Pk. RH9: S Gods 6H **125**
Lagham Rd. RH9: S Gods 7H **125**
Laglands Cl. RH2: Reig 1A **122**
Laings Av. CR4: Mit 1D **44**
Lainlock Pl. TW3: Houn 4B **10**
Lainson St. SW18 . . . . .1M **27**
Lairdale Cl. SE21 . . . . .2N **29**
Laird Ct. GU19: Bag 6J **51**
Laitwood Rd. SW12 . . . . .2F **28**
Lake Cl. KT14: Byf 8M **55**
SW19 . . . . .6L **27**
Lake End Way RG45: Crow 3F **48**
Lake Gdns. SM6: W'ton 9F **44**
TW10: Ham 3H **25**
Lakehall Gdns. CR7: T Hea . . .4M **45**
Lakehall Rd. CR7: T Hea 4M **45**
Lakehurst Rd. KT19: Ewe 2D **60**
Lakeland Dr. GU16: Frim 5C **70**
Lake La. GU10: Dock 4D **148**
RH6: Horl 6G **142**
Laker Ct. RH10: Craw 3E **182**
Lake Rd. CR0: Croy 8J **47**
GU16: Deep 8E **70**
GU25: V Wat 4L **35**
SW19 . . . . .6L **27**
Laker Pl. SW15 . . . . .9K **13**
LAKER'S GREEN 5H **175**
Lakers Lea RH14: Loxw 7H **193**
Lakers Ri. SM7: Ban 3C **82**
Lakes Cl. GU4: Guil 9D **114**
Lakeside BR3: Beck 2L **47**
GU21: Wok 6H **73**
KT2: K Tham 8A **26**
KT13: Weybr 8F **38**
KT19: Ewe 3D **60**
RG42: Brac 8A **16**
RH1: Red 1E **122**
RH12: Hors 3J **197**
SM6: W'ton 1F **62**
Lakeside, The
GU17: B'water 2J **69**
Lakeside Bus. Pk.
GU47: Sandh 8F **48**
Lakeside Cl. GU12: A Va 9D **90**
GU21: Wok 6H **73**
SE25 . . . . .1D **46**
Lakeside Ct. GU51: Fleet 2C **88**
Lakeside Dr. KT10: Esh 3C **58**
Lakeside Gdns. GU14: Cove . . .7J **69**
Lakeside Grange
KT13: Weybr 9D **38**
Lakeside Ind. Est. SL3: Coln . . .2H **7**
Lakeside Pk. KT16: Chert 7L **37**
Lakeside Rd. GU11: Alde 9C **90**
GU14: Farnb 6M **89**
SL0: R Pk 3H **7**
SL3: Coln, R Pk 3H **7**
Lakes La. GU8: Wit 5C **152**
Lakes Rd. BR2: Kes 2E **66**
Lakestreet Grn. RH8: Limp . . .7F **106**
Lake Vw. RH5: Nth H 8J **119**
RH19: D Pk 5B **166**
Lakeview Pk. Cvn. Site
SL4: Wink 2J **17**
Lake Vw. Rd. RH19: Fel 7E **164**
Lakeview Rd. SE27 . . . . .6L **29**
LALEHAM 2L **37**
Laleham Abbey TW18: Lale . . .3L **37**
Laleham Cl. TW18: Stain 9K **21**
Laleham Ct. GU21: Wok 3A **74**
SM1: Sut 2A **62**
LALEHAM REACH 2J **37**
Laleham Reach KT16: Chert . . .2J **37**
Laleham Rd. TW17: Shep 3A **38**
TW18: Stain 6H **21**
Lalor St. SW6 . . . . .5K **13**
Lamberhurst Rd.
SE27 . . . . .5L **29**
Lamberhurst Wlk.
RH10: Craw 4E **182**
Lambert Av. TW9: Rich 6N **11**
Lambert Cl. TN16: B Hil 3F **86**
Lambert Cotts. RH1: Blet 2B **124**
Lambert Cres.
GU17: B'water 2H **69**
Lambert Lodge *TW8: Brent 1K 11*
(off Layton Rd.)
Lambert Rd. SM7: Ban 1M **81**
Lambert's Pl.
CR0: Croy 1E **200** (7A **46**)
Lamberts Rd. KT5: Surb 4L **41**
Lambeth Cl. RH11: Craw 7N **181**
Lambeth Crematorium
SW17 . . . . .5A **28**
Lambeth Rd. CR0: Croy 6L **45**
Lambeth Wlk. RH11: Craw 7N **181**
Lambly Hill GU25: V Wat 2A **36**
Lamborne Cl. GU47: Sandh 6F **48**
Lambourn Cl.
CR2: S Croy 5M **63**
RH19: E Grin 7A **166**
Lambourne Av. SW19 . . . . .5L **27**
Lambourne Cl.
RH10: Craw 5D **182**
Lambourne Cres.
GU21: Wok 9F **54**
Lambourne Dr. GU19: Bag 5H **51**
KT11: Cob 2L **77**
Lambourne Gro.
RG12: Brac 1C **32**
Lambourne Way
GU10: Tong 5C **110**
Lambourn Gro.
KT1: K Tham 1A **42**
Lambrook Ter. SW6 . . . . .4K **13**
Lambs Bus. Pk.
RH9: S Gods 7E **124**
Lambs Cres. RH12: Hors 3M **197**
Lambs Farm Cl.
RH12: Hors 3N **197**
Lambs Farm Rd.
RH12: Hors 3M **197**
LAMBS GREEN 3E **180**
Lambs Grn. RH12: Rusp 4E **180**
Lambton Ho. SL4: W'sor 6D **4**
Lambton Rd. SW20 . . . . .9H **27**
Lambyn Cft. RH6: Horl 7G **143**
LAMDA 1J 13
(off Talgarth Rd.)
Lammas Av. CR4: Mit 1E **44**
SL4: W'sor 5F **4**
Lammas Cl. GU7: Goda 5K **133**
TW18: Stain 4G **20**
Lammas Ct. *GU7: Goda 6H 133*
(off Old Station Way)
SL4: W'sor 5F **4**
TW19: Stain 3F **20**
Lammas Dr. TW18: Stain 5F **20**
Lammas Hill KT10: Esh 1B **58**
Lammas La.
KT10: Esh, Hers 1N **57**
Lammas Mead RG42: Bin 8K **15**
Lammas Rd. GU7: Goda 6K **133**
TW10: Ham 5J **25**
Lammermoor Rd.
SW12 . . . . .1F **28**
Lampard La. GU10: Churt 8J **149**
Lampeter Cl. GU22: Wok 5A **74**
Lampeter Sq. W6 . . . . .2K **13**
Lamports Ct. *GU9: Farnh 2H 129*
(off Firgrove Hill)
Lampson Ct. RH10: Cop 7N **163**
LAMPTON 4B **10**
Lampton Av. TW3: Houn 4B **10**
Lampton Ct. TW3: Houn 4B **10**
Lampton Ho. Cl.
SW19 . . . . .5J **27**
Lampton Pk. Rd.
TW3: Houn 5B **10**
Lampton Rd. TW3: Houn 5B **10**
Lanark Cl. GU16: Frim 4C **70**
RH13: Hors 6L **197**
Lancashire Hill RG42: Warf . . .7D **16**
Lancaster Av. CR4: Mit 4J **45**
GU1: Guil 5C **114**
GU9: Farnh 3H **129**
SE27 . . . . .3M **29**
SW19 . . . . .6J **27**
Lancaster Cl. GU12: A Va 8D **90**
GU21: Wok 3C **74**
KT2: K Tham 6K **25**
RH10: Craw 9H **163**
TW15: A'ford 5N **21**
TW19: Stan 9N **7**
TW20: Eng G 6N **19**
Lancaster Cotts.
TW10: Rich 9L **11**
Lancaster Ct. KT12: Wal T 6H **39**
KT19: Ewe 6C **60**
SE27 . . . . .3M **29**
SM2: Sut 4M 61
(off Mulgrave Rd.)
SM7: Ban 1L **81**
SW6 . . . . .3L **13**
TW19: Stan 2N **21**
Lancaster Dr. GU15: Camb 9B **50**
RH19: E Grin 7C **166**
Lancaster Gdns.
KT2: K Tham 6K **25**
RH7: Blin H 3H **145**
SW19 . . . . .6K **27**
Lancaster Ho. RG12: Brac 4N **31**
RH1: Red 6C **122**
Lancaster M. SW18 . . . . .8N **13**
TW10: Rich 9L **11**
Lancaster Pk. TW10: Rich 8L **11**
Lancaster Pl. SW19 . . . . .6J **27**
TW1: Twick 9G **11**
TW4: Houn 5K **9**
Lancaster Rd. SE25 . . . . .1C **46**
SW19 . . . . .6J **27**
Lancaster Way GU14: Farnb . . .7A **70**
KT4: W Pk 6G **43**
Lancastrian Rd. SM6: W'ton . . .4J **63**
Lancelot Cl. RH11: Ifi 3K **181**
Lancer Ct. GU11: Alde 2K **109**
Lanchester Dr. RG45: Crow 9H **31**
Lancing Cl. RH11: Craw 1M **181**
Lancing Ct. RH12: Hors 4N **197**
Lancing Ho. CR0: Croy 6D **200**
Lancing Rd. CR0: Croy 6K **45**
TW13: Felt 3G **22**
Landau Ct. CR2: S Croy 8B **200**
Landen Ct. RG40: W'ham 4A **30**
Landen Pk. RH6: Horl 6C **142**
Landford Rd. SW15 . . . . .6H **13**
Landgrove Rd. SW19 . . . . . . .6M **27**
Landmark Arts Cen. 6H **25**
Landmark Ho. *W6 . . . . .1H 13*
(off Hammersmith Bri. Rd.)
Landon Way TW15: A'ford 7C **22**
Landridge Rd. SW6 . . . . .5L **13**
Landscape Rd. CR6: Warl 6E **84**
Landseer Cl. GU47: C Tow 9K **49**
SW19 . . . . .9A **28**
Landseer Rd. KT3: N Mal 6C **42**
SM1: Sut 3M **61**
Lands End La. GU35: Lind 4A **168**
Lane, The GU8: Thur 6G **150**
GU25: V Wat 2A **36**
KT16: Chert 2J **37**
RH14: Ifo 4E **192**
Lane Cl. KT15: Addl 2K **55**
Lane End GU8: Hamb 1E **172**
KT18: Eps 1A **80**
RH7: Dorm 1C **166**
SW15 . . . . .9J **13**
Lane End Dr. GU21: Knap 4F **72**
Lane Gdns. KT10: Clay 4F **58**
Lanehurst Gdns.
RH10: Craw 1G **182**
Lanercost Cl. SW2 . . . . .3L **29**
Lanercost Rd. RH11: Craw 4A **182**
SW2 . . . . .3L **29**
Laneway SW15 . . . . .8G **12**
Lanfrey Pl. W14 . . . . .1L **13**
Langaller La. KT22: Fetc 9B **78**
Langborough Rd.
RG40: W'ham 3B **30**
Langbourne Way
KT10: Clay 3G **58**
Lang Cl. KT22: Fetc 1B **98**
Langcroft Cl. SM5: Cars 9D **44**
Langdale Av. CR4: Mit 2D **44**
Langdale Cl. GU14: Cove 1K **89**
GU21: Wok 3M **73**
SW14 . . . . .7A **12**
Langdale Ct. *GU12: A Va 8D 90*
(off Lakeside Cl.)
Langdale Dr. SL5: Asc 1J **33**
Langdale Pde. CR4: Mit 2D **44**
Langdale Rd. CR7: T Hea 3L **45**
RH11: Ifi 5J **181**
Langdon Cl. GU15: Camb 2G **70**
Langdon Pk. TW11: Tedd 8J **25**
Langdon Pl. SW14 . . . . .6B **12**
Langdon Rd. SM4: Mord 4A **44**
Langdon Wlk. SM4: Mord 4A **44**
Langford Rd. SW6 . . . . .5N **13**
Langham Cl. GU7: Goda 6J **133**
Langham Ct. GU9: Farnh 4H **129**
SW20 . . . . .1H **43**
Langham Dene CR8: Ken 2M **83**
Langham Gdns. TW10: Ham 5J **25**
Langham Ho. Cl.
TW10: Ham 5K **25**
Langham Mans. *SW5 . . . . .1N 13*
(off Earl's Ct. Sq.)
Langham Pk. GU7: Goda 6J **133**
Langham Pl. TW20: Egh 6B **20**
W4 . . . . .2D **12**
Langham Rd. SW20 . . . . .9H **27**
TW11: Tedd 6H **25**
Langholm Cl. SW12 . . . . .1H **29**
Langhorn Dr. TW2: Twick 1E **24**
Lang Ho. TW19: Stan 2N **21**
LANGHURST
RH12, Horsham 5L **179**
RH12, Rusper 9F **160**
TN8 . . . . .5G **127**

Leigh Ct. Cl.—Linnet Cl.

Leigh Ct. Cl. KT11: Cob 1K 77
Leigh Cres. CR0: N Add 4L 65
Leigh Hill Rd. KT11: Cob 2K 77
Leighlands RH10: Craw 1G 183
Leigh La. GU9: Farnh 3K 129
Leigh Orchard Cl.
SW16 ......4K 29
Leigh Pk. SL3: Dat 3L 5
Leigh Pl. KT11: Cob 2K 77
TW13: Felt 2K 23
Leigh Pl. Cotts.
RH2: Leigh 9F 120
Leigh Pl. La. RH9: Gods 1G 125
Leigh Pl. Rd. RH2: Leigh 9F 120
Leigh Rd. KT11: Cob 1J 77
RH3: Betch 9B 120
TW3: Houn 7D 10
Leigh Sq. SL4: W'sor 5A 4
Leighton Gdns. CR0: Croy 7M 45
CR2: Sande 9E 64
Leighton Mans. *W14* *2K 13*
(off Greyhound Rd.)
Leighton St.
CR0: Croy 1A 200 (7M 45)
Leighton Way
KT18: Eps 8K 201 (1C 80)
Leinster Av. SW14 ......6B 12
Leipzig Rd. GU52: C Cro 1C 108
Leisure La. KT14: W By 8K 55
Leisure Pursuits 3G 186
Leisure W. TW13: Felt 3J 23
Leith Cl. RG45: Crow 9F 30
Leithcote Gdns.
SW16 ......5K 29
Leithcote Path SW16 ......4K 29
Leith Dr. GU11: Alde 1L 109
Leith Gro. RH5: B Grn 7K 139
Leith Hill La.
RH5: A Com, H Mary 4M 137
Leith Hill Place (East) 9B 138
Leith Hill Place (West) 1N 157
Leith Hill Rd.
RH5: H Mary 9A 138
Leith Hill Tower 8B 138
Leith Lea RH5: B Grn 7K 139
Leith Rd. KT17: Eps 8D 60
RH5: B Grn 8J 139
Leith Towers SM2: Sut 4N 61
Leith Va. Cotts. RH5: Ockl 7A 158
Leith Vw. RH5: Nth H 9J 119
Leith Vw. Cotts.
RH12: K'fold 3H 179
Leith Vw. Rd. RH12: Hors 3N 197
Lela Av. TW4: Houn 5K 9
Le Marchant Rd.
GU15: Camb 3D 70
GU16: Frim 3D 70
Le May Cl. RH6: Horl 7E 142
Lemington Gro. RG12: Brac 5N 31
Lemmington Way
RH12: Hors 1M 197
Lemon Gro. TW13: Felt 2H 23
Lemon's Farm Rd.
RH5: A Com 5N 137
Lemuel St. SW18 ......9N 13
Lendore Rd. GU16: Frim 6B 70
Lenelby Rd. KT6: Surb 7N 41
Leney Cl. RG40: W'ham 9C 14
Len Freeman Pl. SW6 ......2L 13
Lenham Rd. CR7: T Hea 1A 46
SM1: Sut 1N 61
Lennard Rd.
CR0: Croy 1B 200 (7N 45)
Lennel Gdns. GU52: C Cro 7D 88
Lennox Ct. *RH1: Red* *2E 122*
(off St Anne's Ri.)
Lennox Gdns.
CR0: Wad 7A 200 (1M 63)
Lennox Ho. *TW1: Twick* *9K 11*
(off Clevedon Rd.)
Lenten Cl. GU5: P'lake 2E 136
Lenton Ri. TW9: Rich 6L 11
Leo Ct. TW8: Brent 3K 11
Leominster Rd. SM4: Mord 5A 44
Leominster Wlk.
SM4: Mord 5A 44
Leonard Av. SM4: Mord 4A 44
Leonard Cl. GU16: Frim 6B 70
Leonard Rd. SW16 ......9G 28
Leonardslee Ct.
RH10: Craw 5F 182
Leonard Way RH13: Hors 6M 197
Leopold Av. GU14: Farnb 9N 69
SW19 ......6L 27
Leopold Rd. RH11: Craw 3A 182
SW19 ......5L 27
Leopold Ter. SW19 ......6L 27
Le Personne Homes
CR3: Cate *9A 84*
(off Banstead Rd.)
Le Personne Rd. CR3: Cate 9A 84
Leppington RG12: Brac 7N 31
Leret Way KT22: Leat 8H 79
Lerry Cl. W14 ......2L 13
Lesbourne Rd. RH2: Reig 4N 121
Leslie Dunne Ho. SL4: W'sor 5B 4
Leslie Gdns. SM2: Sut 3M 61
Leslie Gro.
CR0: Croy 1F 200 (7B 46)
Leslie Gro. Pl.
CR0: Croy 1F 200 (7B 46)
Leslie Pk. Rd.
CR0: Croy 1F 200 (7B 46)
Leslie Rd. GU24: Chob 6H 53
RH4: Dork 3K 119
Lessingham Av. SW17 ......5D 28
Lessness Rd. SM4: Mord 5A 44
Lestock Cl. *SE25* *2D 46*
(off Manor Rd.)
Lestock Way GU51: Fleet 4D 88
Letchworth Av. TW14: Felt 1G 22
Letchworth Ct. RH11: Craw 6K 181
Letchworth St. SW17 ......5D 28
Letcombe Sq. RG12: Brac 3C 32
Letterstone Rd. SW6 ......3L 13
Lettice St. SW6 ......4L 13
Levana Cl. SW19 ......2K 27
Levehurst Ho. SE27 ......6N 29
Leveret Cl. CR0: N Add 7N 65
Leveret La. RH11: Craw 1N 181
Leverette Cl. GU12: Alde 1B 110
Leverkusen Rd.
RG12: Brac 2N 31
Levern Dr. GU9: U Hal 6H 109
Leverson St. SW16 ......7G 28
Levett Rd. KT22: Leat 7H 79
Levylsdene GU1: Guil 3E 114
Levylsdene Ct. GU1: Guil 3F 114
Lewes Cl. RH10: Craw 3G 183
Lewes Ct. *CR4: Mit* *2D 44*
(off Chatsworth Pl.)
Lewesdon Cl. SW19 ......2J 27
Lewes Rd.
RH18: F Row, W Cros 9F 186
RH19: Ash W, F Row, E Grin
......1B 186
Lewin Rd. SW14 ......6C 12
SW16 ......7H 29
Lewins Rd. KT18: Eps 1A 80
Lewin Ter. TW14: Bedf 1E 22
Lewis Cl. KT15: Addl 1L 55
Lewis Ct. *KT22: Leat* *8G 78*
(off Highbury Dr.)
Lewisham Cl. RH11: Craw 7A 182
Lewisham Way GU47: Owls 6J 49
Lewis Ho. RG12: Brac 5N 31
Lewis Rd. CR4: Mit 1B 44
(not continuous)
SM1: Sut 1N 61
TW10: Rich 8K 11
Lewiston Cl. KT4: W Pk 6G 43
Leworth Pl. SL4: W'sor 4G 4
Lexden Rd. CR4: Mit 3H 45
Lexington Ct. CR8: Pur 6N 63
Lexton Gdns. SW12 ......2H 29
Leyborne Pk. TW9: Kew 4N 11
Leybourne Av. KT14: Byf 9A 56
Leybourne Cl. KT14: Byf 9A 56
RH11: Craw 8A 182
Leybourne Pl. RH19: Fel 7J 165
Leyburn Gdns. CR0: Croy 8B 46
Leycester Cl. GU20: Windl 1M 51
Leyfield KT4: W Pk 7D 42
Leylands SW18 ......9L 13
Leylands La. TW19: Stan M 7H 7
(not continuous)
Ley Rd. GU14: Farnb 6M 69
Leys, The KT12: Hers 1N 57
Leyside RG45: Crow 2F 48
Leys Rd. KT22: Oxs 8D 58
Leyton Rd. SW19 ......8A 28
Liberty Av. SW19 ......9B 28
Liberty Hall Rd. KT15: Addl 2J 55
Liberty La. KT15: Addl 2J 55
Liberty M. SW12 ......1F 28
Liberty Point *CR0: Croy* *6D 46*
(off Blackhorse La.)
Liberty Ri. KT15: Addl 3J 55
Library and Lifetime Mus.
......4C 200
Library Way TW2: Whitt 1C 24
Lichfield Ct. KT6: Surb 8J 203
TW9: Rich 8L 11
Lichfield Gdns. TW9: Rich 7L 11
Lichfield Rd. TW4: Houn 6K 9
TW9: Kew 4M 11
Lichfields RG12: Brac 1C 32
Lichfield Ter. *TW9: Rich* *8L 11*
(off Sheen Rd.)
Lichfield Way CR2: Sels 6G 65
Lickey Ho. *W14* *2L 13*
(off North End Rd.)
Lickfolds Rd. GU10: Rowl 9D 128
Liddell SL4: W'sor 6A 4
Liddell Pl. SL4: W'sor 5A 4
Liddell Sq. SL4: W'sor 5A 4
Liddell Way SL4: W'sor 6A 4
SL5: Asc 4K 33
Liddington Hall Dr.
GU3: Guil 9H 93
Liddington New Rd.
GU3: Guil 9H 93
Lidiard Rd. SW18 ......3A 28
Lido Rd.
GU1: Guil 1D 202 (2N 113)
Lidsey Cl. RH10: Craw 5G 183
Lidstone Cl. GU21: Wok 4L 73
Liffords Pl. SW13 ......5E 12
Lifford St. SW15 ......7J 13
Lightermans Wlk.
SW18 ......7M 13
LIGHTWATER 6L 51
Lightwater By-Pass
GU18: Ligh 5L 51
Lightwater Country Pk. 7J 51
Lightwater Leisure Cen. 6K 51
Lightwater Mdw.
GU18: Ligh 7M 51
Lightwater Rd. GU18: Ligh 7M 51
Lightwood RG12: Brac 5B 32
Lilac Av. GU22: Wok 7N 73
Lilac Cl. GU1: Guil 8M 93
Lilac Ct. TW11: Tedd 5F 24
Lilac Gdns. CR0: Croy 9K 47
Lilian Rd. SW16 ......9G 28
Lilleshall Rd. SM4: Mord 5B 44
Lilley Ct. RG45: Crow 3G 49
Lilley Dr. KT20: K'wood 9N 81
Lillian Rd. SW13 ......2F 12
Lillie Mans. *SW6* *2K 13*
(off Lillie Rd.)
Lillie Rd. SW6 ......2K 13
TN16: B Hil 5F 86
Lillie Road Fitness Cen. 3J 13
Lillie Yd. SW6 ......2M 13
Lilliot's La. KT22: Leat 6G 79
Lillymead RH1: Mers 9G 102
Lily Cl. W14 ......1J 13
(not continuous)
Lily Ct. RG41: W'ham 2A 30
Lilyfields Chase GU6: Ewh 6F 156
Lily Hill Dr. RG12: Brac 1C 32
Lily Hill Rd. RG12: Brac 1C 32
Lilyville Rd. SW6 ......4L 13
Lime Av. GU15: Camb 9E 50
RH12: Hors 4N 197
SL4: W'sor 4J 5
(Adelaide Rd.)
SL4: W'sor 4C 18
(Sheet St. Rd.)
SL5: Asc 5F 32
Limebush Cl. KT15: N Haw 5L 55
Lime Cl. GU4: W Cla 6K 95
RH2: Reig 6N 121
RH10: Cop 7M 163
RH11: Craw 9A 162
SM5: Cars 8D 44
Lime Ct. CR4: Mit 1B 44
Lime Cres. GU12: Ash 2F 110
TW16: Sunb 1K 39
Limecroft GU46: Yate 1B 68
Limecroft Cl. KT19: Ewe 4C 60
Limecroft Rd. GU21: Knap 4E 72
Lime Dr. GU51: Fleet 1C 88
Lime Gro. CR6: Warl 5H 85
GU1: Guil 8L 93
GU4: W Cla 6J 95
GU22: Wok 8A 74
KT3: N Mal 2C 42
KT15: Addl 1J 55
TW1: Twick 9F 10
Lime Ho. TW9: Kew 4A 12
Lime Lodge *TW16: Sunb* *8G 22*
(off Forest Dr.)
Lime Mdw. Av. CR2: Sande 9D 64
Lime Quarry M. GU4: Guil 2F 114
Limerick Cl. RG42: Brac 9M 15
SW12 ......1G 28
Lime Rd. TW9: Rich 7M 11
Limes, The *GU21: Wok* *3C 74*
(off Maybury Rd.)
GU21: Wok 2N 73
(Ridgeway)
KT8: W Mole 3B 40
KT19: Eps 6A 60
KT22: Leat 1H 99
RG42: Warf 6D 16
RH12: Hors *4J 197*
(off Trafalgar Rd.)
RH19: Fel 5K 165
SL4: W'sor 4A 4
SW18 ......9M 13
TN8: Eden 2L 147
Limes Av. CR0: Wad 9L 45
RH6: Horl 9F 142
SM5: Cars 7D 44
SW13 ......5E 12
Limes Cl. TW15: A'ford 6B 22
Limes Fld. Rd. SW14 ......6D 12
Limes Gdns. SW18 ......9M 13
Limes M. TW20: Egh 6B 20
Limes Pl. CR0: Croy 6A 46
Limes Rd. BR3: Beck 1L 47
CR0: Croy 6A 46
GU14: Cove 9H 69
KT13: Weybr 1B 56
TW20: Egh 6B 20
Limes Row BR6: Farnb 2K 67
Lime St. GU11: Alde 2L 109
Lime Tree Av. KT7: T Dit 7E 40
KT10: Esh, T Dit 7D 40
Lime Tree Cl. KT23: Book 2A 98
Limetree Cl. SW2 ......2K 29
Lime Tree Copse
RG42: Warf 8E 16
Lime Tree Ct. CR2: S Croy 3N 63
KT21: A'tead 5L 79
Lime Tree Gro. CR0: Croy 9J 47
Lime Tree Pl. CR4: Mit 9F 28
Lime Tree Rd. TW5: Hest 4B 10
Lime Tree Wlk.
BR4: W Wick 1B 66
GU14: Farnb 5C 90
GU21: Wok 3N 73
GU25: V Wat 3A 36
Limetree Wlk. SW17 ......6E 28
Lime Wlk. GU5: Shere 8A 116
KT8: E Mol 3F 40
RG12: Brac 3A 32
Limeway Ter. RH4: Dork 3G 118
Limewood Cl. BR3: Beck 4M 47
GU21: Wok 7G 73
Lime Works Rd.
RH1: Mers 4G 102
LIMPSFIELD 7D 106
Limpsfield Av. CR7: T Hea 4K 45
SW19 ......3J 27
LIMPSFIELD CHART 8G 107
Limpsfield Rd. CR2: Sande 8D 64
CR6: Warl 3F 84
Linacre Ct. W6 ......1J 13
Linacre Dr. GU6: Cranl 7D 176
RH12: Cranl, Rudg 7D 176
Lince La. RH4: Westc 5D 118
Linchfield Rd. SL3: Dat 4M 5
LINCHMERE 6A 188
Linchmere Pl.
RH11: Craw 2M 181
Linchmere Ridge
GU27: Hasl 5B 188
Linchmere Rd.
GU27: Linch, Hasl 5A 188
Lincoln Av. SW19 ......4J 27
TW2: Twick 3C 24
Lincoln Cl. GU12: A Va 8D 90
GU15: Camb 2F 70
RH6: Horl 9E 142
RH10: Craw 6C 182
SE25 ......5D 46
Lincoln Ct. CR2: S Croy 8C 200
KT13: Weybr *3E 56*
(off Old Av.)
Lincoln Dr. GU22: Pyr 2G 74
Lincoln M. SE21 ......3N 29
Lincoln Rd. CR4: Mit 4J 45
GU2: Guil 1J 113
KT3: N Mal 2B 42
KT4: W Pk 7G 42
RH4: Dork 3J 119
SE25 ......2E 46
TW13: Hanw 4N 23
Lincolnshire Gdns.
RG42: Warf 8C 16
Lincolns Mead RH7: Ling 8M 145
Lincoln Wlk. KT19: Ewe 6C 60
(not continuous)
Lincoln Way TW16: Sunb 9F 22
Lincombe Ct. KT15: Addl 2K 55
Lindale Cl. GU25: V Wat 3J 35
Lindbergh Rd. SM6: W'ton 4J 63
Linden RG12: Brac 4D 32
SL3: Lang 1D 6
Linden Av. CR5: Coul 3F 82
CR7: T Hea 3M 45
RH19: E Grin 8M 165
TW3: Houn 8B 10
Linden Cl. KT7: T Dit 6F 40
KT15: N Haw 7J 55
KT20: Tad 7J 81
RH10: Craw 6E 182
RH12: Hors 4L 197
Linden Ct. GU15: Camb 8D 50
KT22: Leat 8H 79
TW20: Eng G 7L 19
Linden Cres.
KT1: K Tham 4M 203 (1M 41)
Linden Dr. CR3: Cate 2N 103
Linden Gdns. KT22: Leat 8J 79
W4 ......1D 12
Linden Gro. CR6: Warl 5H 85
KT3: N Mal 2D 42
KT12: Wal T 8G 39
TW11: Tedd 6F 24
Lindenhill Rd. RG42: Brac 9L 15
Linden Ho. TW12: Hamp 7A 24
Linden Lea RH4: Dork 7J 119
Linden Leas BR4: W Wick 8N 47
Linden Pit Path KT22: Leat 8H 79
(not continuous)
Linden Pl. CR4: Mit 3C 44
KT17: Eps 5M 201 (8D 60)
KT24: E Hor 4F 96
TW18: Stain 5J 21
Linden Rd.
GU1: Guil 2C 202 (3N 113)
GU35: H Dwn 4G 169
KT13: Weybr 5D 56
KT22: Leat 8H 79
TW12: Hamp 8A 24
Lindens, The CR0: N Add 3M 65
GU9: Farnh 2J 129
GU16: Mytc 2D 90
GU35: Lind 3B 168
RH10: Cop 7M 163
W4 ......4B 12
Lindens Cl. KT24: Eff 6M 97
Linden Way CR8: Pur 6G 63
GU22: Wok 8B 74
GU23: Rip 3H 95
TW17: Shep 4D 38
Lindfield Gdns. GU1: Guil 2B 114
Lindfield Rd. CR0: Croy 5C 46
LINDFORD 4A 168
Lindford Chase
GU35: Lind 4A 168
Lindford Rd.
GU35: Bor, Lind 3A 168
Lindford Wey GU35: Lind 4A 168
Lindgren Wlk. RH11: Craw 8N 181
Lindisfarne Rd. SW20 ......8F 26
Lindley Ct. KT1: H Wic 9J 25
Lindley Pl. TW9: Kew 4N 11
Lindley Rd. KT12: Wal T 9L 39
RH9: Gods 8F 104
Lindores Rd. SM5: Cars 6A 44
Lind Rd. SM1: Sut 2A 62
Lindrop St. SW6 ......5N 13
Lindsay Cl. KT9: Ches 4L 59
KT19: Eps 7G 201 (9B 60)
TW19: Stan 8M 7
Lindsay Ct. CR0: Croy 6D 200
Lindsay Dr. TW17: Shep 5E 38
Lindsay Rd. KT4: W Pk 8G 43
KT15: N Haw 6J 55
TW12: H Hill 5B 24
Lindsey Cl. CR4: Mit 3J 45
Lindsey Gdns. TW14: Bedf 1E 22
Lindum Cl. GU11: Alde 3M 109
Lindum Dene GU11: Alde 3M 109
Lindum Rd. TW11: Tedd 8J 25
Lindvale GU21: Wok 2A 74
Lindway SE27 ......6M 29
Linersh Dr. GU5: Braml 5C 134
Linersh Wood Cl.
GU5: Braml 6C 134
Linersh Wood Rd.
GU5: Braml 5C 134
Lines Rd. GU11: Alde 6B 90
Linfield Cl. KT12: Hers 2J 57
Ling Cres. GU35: H Dwn 3G 169
Ling Dr. GU18: Ligh 8K 51
LINGFIELD 7N 145
Lingfield Av.
KT1: K Tham 8K 203 (3L 41)
LINGFIELD COMMON 6M 145
Lingfield Comn. Rd.
RH7: Ling 6M 145
Lingfield Dr. RH10: Craw 2J 183
Lingfield Gdns. CR5: Coul 6M 83
Lingfield Pk. Racecourse 9A 146
Lingfield Rd. KT4: W Pk 9H 43
RH19: E Grin 6N 165
SW19 ......6J 27
TN8: Eden 3H 147
Lingfield Station (Rail) 7A 146
Lingmala Gro. GU52: C Cro 8C 88
Lings Coppice SE21 ......3N 29
Lingwell Rd. SW17 ......4C 28
Lingwood RG12: Brac 5A 32
Lingwood Gdns. TW7: Isle 3E 10
Link, The RH11: Craw 3B 182
(not continuous)
TW11: Tedd 7F 24
Link 10 RH10: Craw 9D 162
Link Av. GU22: Pyr 2F 74
Linkfield KT8: W Mole 2B 40
Linkfield Cnr. RH1: Red 3B 122
(Hatchlands Rd.)
RH1: Red 3C 122
(Linkfield St.)
Linkfield Gdns. RH1: Red 3C 122
Linkfield La. RH1: Red 2C 122
Linkfield Lodge RH1: Red 2C 122
Linkfield Rd. TW7: Isle 5F 10
Linkfield St. RH1: Red 3C 122
Link La. SM6: W'ton 3H 63
Link Rd. KT15: Addl 1N 55
SL3: Dat 4M 5
SM6: W'ton 7E 44
TW14: Felt 1G 23
Links, The KT12: Wal T 8H 39
SL5: Asc 1J 33
Links Av. SM4: Mord 3M 43
(not continuous)
Links Brow KT22: Fetc 2E 98
Links Bus. Cen. GU22: Wok 6E 74
Links Cl. GU6: Ewh 4F 156
KT21: A'tead 4J 79
Linkscroft Av. TW15: A'ford 7C 22
Links Gdns. SW16 ......8L 29
Links Grn. Way KT11: Cob 1A 78
LINKSIDE 2N 169
Linkside KT3: N Mal 1D 42
Linkside E. GU26: Hind 2A 170
Linkside Nth. GU26: Hind 2N 169
Linkside Sth. GU26: Hind 3A 170
Linkside W. GU26: Hind 2N 169
Links Pl. KT21: A'tead 4K 79
Links Rd. BR4: W Wick 7M 47
GU5: Braml 4A 134
KT17: Eps 9F 60
KT21: A'tead 5J 79
SW17 ......7E 28
TW15: A'ford 6N 21
Links Vw. Av. RH3: Brock 3N 119
Links Vw. Ct. TW12: H Hill 5D 24
Links Vw. Rd. CR0: Croy 9K 47
TW12: H Hill 6C 24
Links Way BR3: Beck 5K 47
GU14: Cove 2H 89
KT23: Book 6M 97
Link Way TW18: Stain 7K 21
Linkway GU2: Guil 2J 113
GU15: Camb 2A 70
GU22: Wok 4E 74
GU52: Fleet 7A 88
RG45: Crow 2E 48
SW20 ......2G 43
TW10: Ham 3H 25
Linkway, The SM2: Sut 5A 62
Linkway Pde. GU52: Fleet 7A 88
Linley Ct. SM1: Sut 1A 62
Linnell Cl. RH11: Craw 9N 181
Linnell Rd. RH1: Red 4E 122
Linnet Cl. CR2: Sels 6G 65

Linnet Gro.—Long Gdn. Wlk. W.

Linnet Gro. GU4: Guil ...1F 114
Linnet M. SW12 ...1E 28
Linnett Cl. RH10: T Hil ...4F 184
Linsford Bus. Pk.
GU16: Mytc ...2C 90
Linsford La. GU16: Mytc ...2D 90
Linslade Cl. TW4: Houn ...8M 9
Linstead Rd. GU14: Cove ...6K 69
Linstead Way SW18 ...1K 27
Linsted La. GU35: Head ...2C 168
Lintaine Cl. W6 ...2K 13
Linters Ct. RH1: Red ...1D 122
Linton Cl. CR4: Mit ...6D 44
Linton Glade CR0: Sels ...5H 65
(not continuous)
Linton Gro. SE27 ...6M 29
Lintons La. KT17: Eps ...8D 60
Lintott Ct. TW19: Stan ...9M 7
Lintott Gdns. RH13: Hors ...5L 197
Linver Rd. SW6 ...5M 13
Lion & Lamb Way
GU9: Farnh ...1G 128
Lion & Lamb Yd.
GU9: Farnh ...1G 129
Lion Av. TW1: Twick ...2F 24
Lion Cl. GU27: Hasl ...1D 188
TW17: Shep ...2N 37
Lionel Rd. Nth. TW8: Brent ...1L 11
Lionel Rd. Sth. TW8: Brent ...1M 11
Liongate Ent. Pk. CR4: Mit ...3B 44
Lion Ga. Gdns. TW9: Rich ...6M 11
Lion Ga. M. SW18 ...1M 27
Liongate M. KT8: E Mol ...2F 40
Lion Grn. GU27: Hasl ...2D 188
Lion Grn. Rd. CR5: Coul ...3H 83
Lion Head Ct. CR0: Croy ...6B 200
Lion La. GU27: Hasl ...9D 170
RH1: Red ...2D 122
RH10: T Hil ...5D 184
Lion Mead GU27: Hasl ...2D 188
Lion Pk. Av. KT9: Ches ...1N 59
Lion Retail Pk. GU22: Wok ...3D 74
Lion Rd. CR0: Croy ...4N 45
TW1: Twick ...2F 24
Lion's La. GU6: Cranl ...3K 175
(not continuous)
Lion Way GU52: C Cro ...8C 88
TW8: Brent ...3K 11
Lion Wharf Rd. TW7: Isle ...6H 11
Lipcombe Cotts. GU5: Alb ...3L 135
Liphook Rd. GU27: Hasl ...2C 188
GU27: Hasl, Linch, Lip
...4A 188
GU30: Pass ...6D 168
GU35: Head ...6D 168
GU35: Lind ...4A 168
GU35: White ...9A 168
LIPSCOMB'S CORNER ...2M 179
Lipsham Cl. SM7: Ban ...9B 62
Lisbon Av. TW2: Twick ...3C 24
Liscombe RG12: Brac ...6N 31
Liscombe Ho. RG12: Brac ...6N 31
Liskeard Dr. GU14: Farnb ...8M 69
Liskeard Lodge CR3: Cate ...4D 104
Lisle Cl. SW17 ...5F 28
Lismore *SW19* ...*6L 27*
(off Woodside)
Lismore Cl. TW7: Isle ...5G 10
Lismore Cres. RH11: Craw ...6N 181
Lismore Rd. CR2: S Croy ...3B 64
Lismoyne Cl. GU51: Fleet ...3A 88
Lissant Cl. KT6: Surb ...6K 41
Lissoms Rd. CR5: Chip ...5E 82
Lister Av. RH19: E Grin ...3A 186
Lister Cl. CR4: Mit ...9C 28
Listergate Ct. SW15 ...7H 13
Lister Ho. UB3: Harl ...1F 8
Litchfield Av. SM4: Mord ...6L 43
Litchfield Gdns. KT11: Cob ...1J 77
Litchfield Rd. SM1: Sut ...1A 62
Litchfield Way GU2: Guil ...5J 113
Lithgow's Rd. TW6: Lon A ...7F 8
Little Acre BR3: Beck ...2K 47
Little All. TN8: M Grn ...6K 147
Lit. Austins Rd.
GU9: Farnh ...3J 129
Little Benty UB7: W Dray ...1M 7
Lit. Birch Cl. KT15: N Haw ...5M 55
LITTLE BIRKETTS ...1L 157
Lit. Boltons, The SW5 ...1N 13
SW10 ...1N 13
LITTLE BOOKHAM ...2N 97
LITTLE BOOKHAM COMMON
...9M 77
Lit. Bookham St.
KT23: Book ...1N 97
Little Borough RH3: Brock ...4N 119
Littlebrook Cl. CR0: Croy ...5G 47
Lit. Browns La. TN8: Eden ...8H 127
Little Buntings SL4: W'sor ...6C 4
Little Chesters
KT20: Wal H ...3F 100
Little Collins RH1: Out ...4M 143
Littlecombe Cl. SW15 ...9J 13
Little Comn. La.
RH1: Blet ...1M 123
Little Comptons
RH13: Hors ...6M 197
Little Copse GU46: Yate ...8C 48
GU52: Fleet ...6A 88
Littlecote Cl. SW19 ...1K 27
Little Crabtree
RH11: Craw ...2A 182
Lit. Cranmore La.
KT24: W Hors ...6C 96
Little Cft. GU46: Yate ...1C 68
Littlecroft Rd. TW20: Egh ...6B 20
Littledale Cl. RG12: Brac ...2C 32
Little Dimocks SW12 ...3F 28
Little E. Fld. CR5: Coul ...8H 83
Little Elms UB3: Harl ...3E 8
Lit. Ferry Rd. TW1: Twick ...2H 25
Littlefield Cl. GU3: Worp ...8G 92
GU12: Ash ...3E 110
KT1: K Tham ...4K 203 (1L 41)
LITTLEFIELD COMMON ...7E 92
Littlefield Gdns.
GU12: Ash ...3E 110
Littlefield Ho.
KT1: K Tham ...4J 203
Littlefield Way GU3: Worp ...8F 92
Littleford La. GU4: B'eath ...2G 134
GU5: Sha G ...2G 134
Little Fryth RG40: Finch ...1B 48
Little Grebe RH12: Hors ...3J 197
Little Green TW9: Rich ...7K 11
Little Grn. La. GU9: Farnh ...4F 128
KT16: Chert ...9G 36
Little Gro. *RH4: Dork* ...*7J 119*
(off Stubs Hill)
Little Halliards
KT12: Wal T ...5H 39
Little Hatch RH12: Hors ...3M 197
LITTLE HAVEN ...3L 197
Littlehaven Station (Rail) ...3M 197
Littleheath La.
KT11: Cob, Sto D ...1A 78
Lit. Heath Rd. GU24: Chob ...5H 53
Littleheath Rd. CR2: Sels ...4E 64
Little Hide GU1: Guil ...1D 114
Lit. Holland Bungs.
CR3: Cate ...1A 104
Little Kiln GU7: Goda ...3H 133
Lit. King St. RH19: E Grin ...9A 166
LITTLE LONDON ...1A 136
Little London GU5: Alb ...1N 135
GU8: Wit ...5B 152
Lit. London Hill
RH12: Warn ...8G 179
Little Lullenden RH7: Ling ...6N 145
Lit. Manor Gdns.
GU6: Cranl ...8M 155
Little Mead GU6: Cranl ...8K 155
Littlemead GU21: Wok ...3J 73
KT10: Esh ...1D 58
Lit. Mead Ind. Est.
GU6: Cranl ...7K 155
Little Moor GU47: Sandh ...6H 49
Lit. Moreton Cl.
KT14: W By ...8K 55
Little Oaks *RH19: E Grin* ...*7N 165*
(off Springfield)
Lit. Oaks Cl. TW17: Shep ...3A 38
Little Orchard GU21: Wok ...1C 74
KT15: Wood ...7J 55
Little Orchards KT18: Eps ...8L 201
Lit. Orchard Way
GU4: Chil ...1A 134
Little Paddock GU15: Camb ...7E 50
Little Pk. Dr. TW13: Felt ...3M 23
LITTLE PARROCK ...7M 187
Little Platt GU2: Guil ...2G 112
Lit. Queen's Rd.
TW11: Tedd ...7F 24
Little Riding GU22: Wok ...3D 74
Little Ringdale RG12: Brac ...3C 32
Lit. Roke Av. CR8: Ken ...1M 83
Lit. Roke Rd. CR8: Ken ...1N 83
Littlers Cl. SW19 ...9B 28
Lit. St Leonard's
SW14 ...6B 12
LITTLE SANDHURST ...5F 48
Little St. GU2: Guil ...8L 93
Lit. Sutton La. SL3: Lang ...2D 6
(Brands Hill)
SL3: Lang ...1E 6
(Sutton)
Little Thatch GU7: Goda ...5J 133
Lit. Thurbans Cl.
GU9: Farnh ...5F 128
LITTLETON
GU3 ...8K 113
TW17 ...2B 38
LITTLETON COMMON ...8D 22
Littleton Ho. *RH2: Reig* ...*2M 121*
(off Somers Cl.)
Littleton La. GU3: Art ...8K 113
RH2: Reig ...5J 121
TW17: Shep ...6M 37
Littleton Rd. TW15: A'ford ...8D 22
Littleton St. SW18 ...3A 28
Lit. Tumners Ct.
GU7: Goda ...4H 133
Little Vigo GU46: Yate ...2A 68
Lit. Warkworth Ho.
TW7: Isle ...5H 11
Lit. Warren Cl. GU4: Guil ...5D 114
Lit. Wellington St.
GU11: Alde ...2M 109
LITTLEWICK ...3H 73
Littlewick Rd.
GU21: Knap, Wok ...3H 73
Littlewood GU6: Cranl ...7A 156
LITTLE WOODCOTE ...7F 62
Lit. Woodcote Est.
SM6: W'ton ...7F 62
Lit. Woodcote La. CR8: Pur ...8F 62
SM5: Cars ...8F 62
Little Woodlands SL4: W'sor ...6C 4
Lit. Wood St.
KT1: K Tham ...3H 203 (1K 41)
Littleworth Av. KT10: Esh ...2D 58
Littleworth Comn. Rd.
KT10: Esh ...9D 40
Littleworth La. KT10: Esh ...1D 58
Littleworth Pl. KT10: Esh ...1D 58
Littleworth Rd. GU10: Seal ...2C 130
KT10: Esh ...2D 58
Litttlehaven La.
RH12: Hors ...3M 197
Liverpool Rd. CR7: T Hea ...2N 45
KT2: K Tham ...8N 25
Livesey Cl.
KT1: K Tham ...5L 203 (2M 41)
Livingstone Cl. GU6: Cranl ...9A 156
Livingstone Ct. *TW19: Stan* ...*2N 21*
(off Explorer Av.)
Livingstone Mans.
W14 ...*2K 13*
(off Queen's Club Gdns.)
Livingstone Rd. CR3: Cate ...9A 84
CR7: T Hea ...1N 45
RH10: Craw ...5C 182
RH13: Hors ...7K 197
TW3: Houn ...7C 10
Livingwell Health Club
Purley ...3L 63
Llanaway Cl. GU7: Goda ...5J 133
Llanaway Ho. *GU7: Goda* ...*5J 133*
(off Meadrow)
Llanaway Rd. GU7: Goda ...5J 133
Llangar Gro. RG45: Crow ...2F 48
Llanthony Rd. SM4: Mord ...4B 44
Llanvair Cl. SL5: Asc ...5L 33
Llanvair Dr. SL5: Asc ...5K 33
Lloyd Av. CR5: Coul ...1E 82
SW16 ...9J 29
Lloyd Pk. Av. CR0: Croy ...1C 64
Lloyd Park Stop (CT) ...1C 64
Lloyd Rd. KT4: W Pk ...9H 43
Lloyds Ct. RH10: Craw ...9C 162
Lloyds Lanes Raynes Pk. ...2J 43
Lloyds Way BR3: Beck ...4H 47
Lobelia Rd. GU24: Bis ...2D 72
Locarno Ct. SW16 ...6G 29
Lochaline St. W6 ...2H 13
Lochinvar St. SW12 ...1F 28
Lochinver RG12: Brac ...6N 31
Lock Cl. KT15: Wood ...8G 55
Locke King Cl. KT13: Weybr ...4B 56
Locke King Rd.
KT13: Weybr ...4B 56
Lockesley Sq. KT6: Surb ...5K 41
Lockestone KT13: Weybr ...3A 56
Lockestone Cl.
KT13: Weybr ...3A 56
Lockets Cl. SL4: W'sor ...4A 4
Locke Way GU21: Wok ...4B 74
Lockfield Dr. GU21: Wok ...3H 73
Lockhart Rd. KT11: Cob ...9K 57
Lockhurst Hatch La.
GU5: Alb ...5N 135
Lockie Pl. SE25 ...2D 46
Lockites *GU7: Goda* ...*4F 132*
(off Duke's Dr.)
Lock La. GU22: Pyr ...3K 75
LOCKNER HOLT ...9H 115
Lock Path SL4: Dorn, E Wic ...2A 4
Lock Rd. GU1: Guil ...9N 93
GU11: Alde ...8B 90
TW10: Ham ...5J 25
Locks La. CR4: Mit ...9E 28
Locksley Dr. GU21: Wok ...4J 73
Locksmeade Rd.
TW10: Ham ...5J 25
Locks Mdw. RH7: Dorm ...1C 166
Locks Ride SL5: Asc ...9F 16
Lockswood GU24: B'wood ...7E 72
Lockton Chase SL5: Asc ...2H 33
Lockwood Cl. GU14: Cove ...6K 69
RH12: Hors ...3N 197
Lockwood Ct. RH10: Craw ...1D 182
Lockwood Path GU21: Wok ...9F 54
Lockwood Way
KT9: Ches ...2N 59
Lockyer Ho. SW15 ...6J 13
Locomotive Dr.
TW14: Felt ...2H 23
Loddon Cl. GU15: Camb ...9E 50
Loddon Rd. GU14: Cove ...8J 69
Loddon Way GU12: Ash ...3E 110
Loder Cl. GU21: Wok ...9F 54
Lodge, The RH7: Newc ...1H 165
SM7: Ban ...4A 82
Lodge Av. CR0: Wad ...9L 45
SW14 ...6D 12
Lodgebottom Rd.
KT18: Head ...5N 99
RH5: Mick ...5N 99
Lodge Cl. GU11: Alde ...4A 110
KT11: Sto D ...3N 77
KT17: Ewe ...6H 61
KT22: Fetc ...9D 78
RH5: Nth H ...9J 119
RH11: Craw ...3A 182
RH19: E Grin ...9M 165
SM6: W'ton ...7E 44
TW7: Isle ...4H 11
TW20: Eng G ...6N 19
Lodge Gdns. BR3: Beck ...4J 47
Lodge Gro. GU46: Yate ...9E 48
Lodge Hill CR8: Pur ...2L 83
Lodge Hill Cl.
GU10: L Bou ...5J 129
Lodge Hill Rd.
GU10: L Bou ...5J 129
Lodge La. CR0: N Add ...3K 65
RH1: Salf ...3C 142
RH5: Holm ...4L 139
TN16: Weste ...5L 107
Lodge Pl. SM1: Sut ...2N 61
Lodge Rd. CR0: Croy ...5M 45
KT22: Fetc ...9C 78
SM6: W'ton ...2F 62
Lodge Wlk. CR6: Warl ...3K 85
RH6: Horl ...*8D 142*
(off Thornton Pl.)
Lodge Way SL4: W'sor ...6B 4
TW15: A'ford ...3N 21
TW17: Shep ...1D 38
Lodkin Hill GU8: Hasc ...4N 153
Lodsworth GU14: Cove ...2J 89
Loft Ho. Pl. KT9: Ches ...3J 59
Lofts, The GU8: Worm ...1C 172
Logan Cl. TW4: Houn ...6N 9
Logmore La.
RH4: Dork, Westc ...7B 118
Lois Dr. TW17: Shep ...4C 38
Lollesworth La.
KT24: W Hors ...4D 96
Loman Rd. GU16: Mytc ...1E 90
Lomas Cl. CR0: N Add ...4M 65
Lombard Bus. Pk.
CR0: Croy ...6K 45
SW19 ...1N 43
Lombard Rd. SW19 ...1N 43
LOMBARD RDBT. ...6K 45
Lombard St. GU8: S'ford ...5K 131
Lombardy Cl. GU21: Wok ...4J 73
Lomond Gdns. CR2: Sels ...4H 65
Loncin Mead Av.
KT15: N Haw ...5L 55
London Apollo ...1H 13
LONDON - BIGGIN HILL AIRPORT
...8F 66
London Butterfly House ...4H 11
London Flds. Ho.
RH11: Craw ...8A 182
LONDON GATWICK AIRPORT,
NORTH TERMINAL ...2C 162
LONDON GATWICK AIRPORT,
SOUTH TERMINAL ...3E 162
LONDON-HEATHROW AIRPORT
...6B 8
London La. GU5: Shere ...7B 116
KT24: E Hor ...9G 97
London Rd.
CR0: Croy, T Hea
...1A 200 (4L 45)
CR3: Cate ...1A 104
CR4: Mit ...4C 44
(Bishopsford Rd.)
CR4: Mit ...6E 44
(Carshalton Rd.)
CR4: Mit ...1D 44
(Holborn Way)
CR7: T Hea ...9K 29
GU1: Guil ...4E 202 (4A 114)
(not continuous)
GU4: B'ham ...8D 94
(not continuous)
GU15: Camb ...9A 50
GU17: B'water, Min ...4D 68
GU19: Bag ...6F 50
GU20: Windl ...9M 33
GU23: Send ...4G 94
(not continuous)
GU25: V Wat ...2K 35
GU26: Hind ...5D 170
KT2: K Tham ...3L 203 (1M 41)
(not continuous)
KT17: Ewe ...5E 60
RG12: Bin ...1G 31
RG12: Brac ...1B 32
RG27: Min, B'water ...4A 68
RG40: W'ham ...2C 30
RG42: Bin ...9H 15
RH1: Red ...2D 122
RH2: Reig ...3M 121
RH4: Dork ...1L 201 (4H 119)
RH5: Dork ...3H 119
RH10: Craw, L Hea ...2B 182
RH12: Hors ...6J 197
RH18: F Row ...5G 186
RH19: E Grin ...6K 165
SL3: Dat ...3L 5
(not continuous)
SL3: Lang ...1A 6
SL5: Asc ...2E 32
SL5: Asc, S'hill ...2M 33
SL5: S'dale ...7B 34
SM3: Chea ...9J 43
SM4: Mord ...4M 43
SM6: W'ton ...1F 62
SW16 ...9K 29
SW17 ...8D 28
TN16: Weste ...1L 107
TW1: Twick ...1G 24
TW3: Houn ...6C 10
TW7: Brent, Isle ...5F 10
TW7: Isle, Twick ...8G 10
TW8: Brent ...3H 11
London Rd. TW14: Bedf ...4K 21
TW15: A'ford ...4K 21
TW18: Stain ...5J 21
TW20: Eng G ...2K 35
London Rd. Nth.
RH1: Mers ...4F 102
LONDON ROAD RDBT. ...9G 10
London Rd. Sth.
RH1: Mers, Red ...8E 102
London Road Station (Rail)
...3F 202 (3A 114)
London Scottish & Richmond RUFC
...6K 11
London Sq.
GU1: Guil ...3F 202 (3A 114)
London Stile W4 ...1N 11
London St. KT16: Chert ...6J 37
London Welsh RUFC ...6L 11
London Wetland Cen. ...4G 13
Loneacre GU20: Windl ...3B 52
Lone Oak RH6: Smal ...1M 163
LONESOME ...9G 28
Lonesome Cvn. Pk.
CR4: Mit ...9F 28
Lonesome La.
RH2: Reig, Sid ...7N 121
Lonesome Way SW16 ...9F 28
Long Acre RH10: Craw D ...1D 184
Longacre GU12: Ash ...2E 110
Longacre Pl. SM5: Cars ...3E 62
Long Beech Dr. GU14: Cove ...2H 89
Longbourn SL4: W'sor ...6D 4
Longbourne Grn.
GU7: Goda ...3H 133
Longbourne Way
KT16: Chert ...5H 37
Longboyds KT11: Cob ...2J 77
Long Bri. GU9: Farnh ...1H 129
Longbridge Ga. *RH6: Gat* ...*2C 162*
(off Gatwick Way)
Longbridge Rd. RH6: Horl ...1D 162
Longbridge Rdbt.
RH6: Horl ...9C 142
Longbridge Wlk.
RH6: Horl ...1D 162
Longbridge Way RH6: Gat ...1D 162
Longchamp Cl. RH6: Horl ...8G 143
Long Cl. RH10: Craw ...3H 183
Long Comn. GU5: Sha G ...8E 134
Long Copse Cl. KT23: Book ...1B 98
Longcroft Av. SM7: Ban ...1A 82
LONGCROSS ...9K 35
Long Cross Hill
GU35: Head ...4D 168
Longcross Rd. GU24: Chob ...9J 35
KT16: L'cross ...9A 36
Longcross Station (Rail) ...7J 35
Longdene Rd. GU27: Hasl ...2F 188
LONG DITTON ...7J 41
Longdon Wood BR2: Kes ...1G 66
Longdown GU52: Fleet ...7A 88
Longdown Chase Cotts.
GU26: Hind ...6E 170
Longdown Cl.
GU10: L Bou ...5H 129
Longdown La. Nth.
KT17: Eps ...1F 80
Longdown La. Sth.
KT17: Eps, Eps D ...1F 80
Longdown Lodge
GU47: Sandh ...7G 48
Longdown Rd. GU4: Guil ...6D 114
GU10: L Bou ...6G 128
GU47: Sandh ...7G 48
KT17: Eps ...1F 80
Long Dyke GU1: Guil ...1D 114
Longfellow Cl. RH12: Hors ...1L 197
Longfellow Rd. KT4: W Pk ...8F 42
Longfield Av. SM6: W'ton ...7E 44
Longfield Cl. GU14: Farnb ...6M 69
Longfield Cres. KT20: Tad ...7H 81
Longfield Dr. CR4: Mit ...9C 28
SW14 ...8A 12
Longfield Rd. GU12: Ash ...2E 110
RH4: Dork ...6F 118
RH12: Hors ...8G 196
Longfield St. SW18 ...1M 27
LONGFORD ...4K 7
Longford Av. TW14: Felt ...9F 8
TW19: Stan ...2N 21
Longford Cir. UB7: L'ford ...4K 7
Longford Cl. GU15: Camb ...2B 70
TW12: H Hill ...5A 24
TW13: Hanw ...4M 23
Longford Ct. KT19: Ewe ...1B 60
TW12: H Hill ...7B 24
Longford Gdns. SM1: Sut ...9A 44
Longford Ho. TW12: H Hill ...5A 24
Longford Ind. Est.
TW12: Hamp ...7B 24
LONGFORDMOOR ...4J 7
Longford Rd. TW2: Whitt ...2A 24
Longford Wlk. SW2 ...1L 29
Longford Way TW19: Stan ...2N 21
Long Gdn. M. *GU9: Farnh* ...*1G 129*
(off Long Garden Wlk.)
Long Gdn. Pl. GU9: Farnh ...9G 109
Long Gdn. Wlk.
GU9: Farnh ...1G 129
Long Gdn. Wlk. E.
GU9: Farnh ...9G 109
Long Gdn. Wlk. W.
GU9: Farnh ...9G 108

Long Gdn. Way—Lyndhurst Farm Cl.

Long Gdn. Way
GU9: Farnh 1G 128
Long Gore GU7: Goda 2H 133
Long Heath Dr. KT23: Book . . .2M 97
Longheath Gdns. CR0: Croy . . .4F 46
Long Hedges TW3: Houn 5A 10
Long Hill CR3: Wold 8G 85
GU10: Seal 2C 130
Long Hill Rd. SL5: Asc 1E 32
Longhope Dr. GU10: Wrec 5F 128
Long Ho's. GU24: Pirb 2A 92
Longhurst Rd. CR0: Croy 5E 46
KT24: E Hor 7F 96
RH11: Craw 8M 181
Longlands Av. CR5: Coul 1E 82
Longlands Ct. CR4: Mit 9E 28
Longlands Way
GU15: Camb 1H 71
Long La. CR0: Croy 5F 46
RG40: W'ham 7E 14
TW19: Stan 3A 22
Longleat Sq. GU14: Farnb 2C 90
Longleat Way TW14: Bedf 1E 22
Longley Rd. CR0: Croy 6M 45
GU9: Farnh 2J 129
SW17 . . . . .7C 28
Long Lodge Dr. KT12: Wal T . . .9K 39
Longmead GU1: Guil 3E 114
GU52: Fleet 7B 88
SL4: W'sor 4B 4
Longmead Bus. Cen.
KT19: Eps 7C 60
Longmead Cl. CR3: Cate 9B 84
Longmead Ho. SE27 . . . . .6N 29
Longmeadow GU16: Frim 3D 70
KT23: Book 3N 97
Long Mdw. Cl.
BR4: W Wick 6M 47
Long Mdw. Vs. RH6: Char 5K 161
Longmead Rd. KT7: T Dit 6E 40
KT19: Eps, Ewe 7C 60
SW17 . . . . .6D 28
Longmere Gdns. KT20: Tad 6H 81
Longmere Rd. RH10: Craw . . .1B 182
Long Mickle GU47: Sandh 6F 48
Longmoor Point *SW15* *2G 26*
(off Norley Vale)
Longmoors RG42: Brac 9K 15
Longmore Rd. KT12: Hers 1M 57
Long Orchards
KT20: K'wood 7K 81
Longpoles Rd. GU6: Cranl . . .8A 156
Long Reach GU23: Ockh 1B 96
KT24: W Hors 2C 96
Longridge Gro. GU22: Pyr 1H 75
Longridge Rd. SW5 . . . . .1M 13
Longridge Vw. CR5: Chip 7D 82
Long Rd., The GU10: Rowl . . .8E 128
Longroyd *KT24: E Hor* *4F 96*
(off Cobham Way)
Longs Cl. GU22: Pyr 3J 75
Longs Ct. TW9: Rich 7M 11
Longsdon Way CR3: Cate 2D 104
Longshaw KT22: Leat 7G 78
Longshot Ind. Est.
RG12: Brac 1K 31
Longshot La. RG12: Brac 2K 31
(not continuous)
Longside Cl. TW20: Egh 9E 20
Longstaff Cres. SW18 . . . . . . .9M 13
Longstaff Rd. SW18 . . . . .9M 13
Longstone Rd. SW17 . . . . .6F 28
Long's Way RG40: W'ham 1D 30
Longthornton Rd.
SW16 . . . . .1G 45
Long Wlk. GU4: E Cla 8N 95
KT3: N Mal 2B 42
KT14: W By 1L 75
KT18: Tat C 6H 81
SW13 . . . . .5D 12
TN8: C Hil 9K 107
Long Wlk., The SL4: W'sor 2G 19
Longwater Ho.
KT1: K Tham 6H 203
Longwater Rd. RG12: Brac 5A 32
Longwood Av. SL3: Lang 1D 6
Longwood Bus. Pk.
TW16: Sunb 4G 38
Longwood Dr. SW15 . . . . .9F 12
Longwood Rd. CR8: Ken 3A 84
(not continuous)
Longwood Vw.
RH10: Craw 6E 182
Longyard Ho. RH6: Horl 6F 142
Lonsdale Ct. KT6: Surb 6K 41
Lonsdale Gdns. CR7: T Hea . . .3K 45
Lonsdale M. TW9: Kew 4N 11
Lonsdale Pl. RH4: Dork 1L 201
Lonsdale Rd. KT13: Weybr 4B 56
RH4: Dork 1L 201 (4H 119)
SE25 . . . . .3E 46
SW13 . . . . .4E 12
Lonsdale Road Reservoir
Bird Sanctuary 3E 12
Look Out, The (Heritage Cen.)
. . . . .7B 32
Loop Rd. GU22: Wok 7B 74
KT18: Eps 3B 80
Loppets Rd. RH10: Craw 5D 182
Lorac Ct. SM2: Sut 4M 61
Loraine Gdns. KT21: A'tead 4L 79
Loraine Ho. SM6: W'ton 1F 62
Loraine Rd. W4 . . . . .2A 12
Lord Chancellor Wlk.
KT2: K Tham 9B 26
Lord Darby M. TN14: Cud 2M 87
Lordell Pl. SW19 . . . . .7H 27
Lord Knyvett Cl.
TW19: Stan 9M 7
Lord Knyvetts Ct.
TW19: Stan 9M 7
Lord Napier Pl. W6 . . . . .1F 12
Lord Raglan Ho. SL4: W'sor 6F 4
Lord Roberts M. SW6 . . . . .3N 13
Lordsbury Fld. SM6: W'ton 6G 62
Lords Cl. SE21 . . . . .3N 29
TW13: Hanw 3M 23
Lordsgrove Cl. KT20: Tad 7G 81
LORDSHILL COMMON 7F 134
Lords Hill Cotts.
GU5: Sha G 7E 134
Lordshill Rd. GU5: Sha G 6E 134
Lords Wood Ho. CR5: Coul 9H 83
Loretto Cl. GU6: Cranl 7A 156
Lorian Dr. RH2: Reig 2A 122
Loriners RH10: Craw 6B 182
Loriners Cl. KT11: Cob 1H 77
Loring Rd. SL4: W'sor 4C 4
TW7: Isle 5F 10
Lorne, The KT23: Book 4A 98
Lorne Av. CR0: Croy 6G 47
Lorne Gdns. CR0: Croy 6G 47
GU21: Knap 6G 72
Lorne Rd. TW10: Rich 8M 11
Lorraine Rd. GU15: Camb 7D 50
Lory Ridge GU19: Bag 3J 51
Loseberry Rd. KT10: Clay 2D 58
Loseley House 9H 113
LOSELEY PARK 9J 113
Loseley Rd. GU7: Goda 3H 133
Losfield Rd. SL4: W'sor 4B 4
Lothian Rd. GU24: B'wood 8L 71
Lothian Wood KT20: Tad 9G 80
Lots Rd. SW10 . . . . .3N 13
Lotus Cl. SE21 . . . . .4N 29
Lotus Pk. TW18: Stain 5F 20
Lotus Rd. TN16: B Hil 5H 87
Loubet St. SW17 . . . . .7D 28
Loudwater Cl. TW16: Sunb 3H 39
Loudwater Rd. TW16: Sunb . . .3H 39
Loughborough RG12: Brac 5C 32
Louisa Ct. TW2: Twick 3E 24
Louise Margaret Rd.
GU11: Alde 1A 110
Louis Flds. GU3: Worp 8F 92
Louisville Rd. SW17 . . . . .4E 28
Lovatt Ct. SW12 . . . . .2F 28
Lovat Wlk. TW5: Hest 3M 9
Loveday Ho. GU6: Cranl 5L 155
Lovedean Ct. RG12: Brac 5C 32
Lovejoy La. SL4: W'sor 5A 4
Lovekyn Cl.
KT2: K Tham 3L 203 (1L 41)
Lovelace Cl. KT24: E Jun 1H 97
Lovelace Dr. GU22: Pyr 3G 75
Lovelace Gdns. KT6: Surb 6K 41
KT12: Hers 2K 57
Lovelace Rd. KT6: Surb 6J 41
RG12: Brac 3K 31
SE21 . . . . .3N 29
Lovelace Vs. *KT7: T Dit* *6H 41*
(off Portsmouth Rd.)
Lovelands La. GU24: Chob 9F 52
KT20: Lwr K 5N 101
Love La. CR4: Mit 2C 44
(not continuous)
GU12: Ash 2F 110
KT6: Surb 8J 41
KT20: Wal H 5E 100
RH5: Ockl 6D 158
RH9: Gods 1F 124
SE25 . . . . .2E 46
(not continuous)
SM1: Sut 3L 61
SM3: Chea, Sut 3K 61
SM4: Mord 6M 43
Loveletts RH11: Craw 4M 181
Lovel La. SL4: Wink 5L 17
Lovell Path RH11: Ifi 4K 181
Lovell Rd. TW10: Ham 4J 25
Lovells Cl. GU18: Ligh 6M 51
Lovelock Cl. CR8: Ken 4N 83
Lovel Rd. SL4: Wink 5K 17
Lovers La. GU10: Fren 3H 149
RH13: Hors 9J 197
Lovett Dr. SM5: Cars 6A 44
Lovett Rd. TW18: Stain 5D 20
Lovibonds Av. BR6: Farnb 1K 67
Lowbury RG12: Brac 3C 32
Lowburys RH4: Dork 8H 119
Lowdell's Cl.
RH19: E Grin 6M 165
Lowdells Dr. RH19: E Grin . . .6M 165
Lowdell's La.
RH19: E Grin 6L 165
Lowe Cl. GU11: Alde 1L 109
RH11: Craw 9N 181
Lwr. Addiscombe Rd.
CR0: Croy 1F 200 (7B 46)
LOWER ASHTEAD 6K 79
Lwr. Barn Cl. RH12: Hors . . .3M 197
Lwr. Barn Rd. CR8: Pur 8N 63
LOWER BOURNE 4J 129
Lwr. Breache Rd.
GU6: Ewh 6H 157
Lower Bri. Rd. RH1: Red 3D 122
Lwr. Broadmoor Rd.
RG45: Crow 3H 49
Lwr. Charles St.
GU15: Camb 9A 50
Lwr. Church La.
GU9: Farnh 1G 129
Lwr. Church Rd.
GU47: Sandh 6D 48
Lwr. Church St.
CR0: Croy 3A 200 (8M 45)
Lower Comn. Sth.
SW15 . . . . .6G 13
Lwr. Coombe St.
CR0: Croy 6B 200 (1N 63)
Lower Ct. Rd. KT19: Eps 7B 60
Lower Dene RH19: E Grin 9C 166
Lwr. Downs Rd.
SW20 . . . . .9J 27
Lwr. Drayton Pl.
CR0: Croy 3A 200 (8M 45)
Lower Dunnymans
SM7: Ban 1L 81
LOWER EASHING 7C 132
Lower Eashing GU7: Eash 7B 132
Lwr. Edgeborough Rd.
GU1: Guil 4B 114
Lwr. Farm Rd. KT24: Eff 2J 97
Lwr. Farnham Rd.
GU11: Alde 5N 109
GU12: Alde 5N 109
LOWER FELTHAM 4G 23
Lwr. George St. TW9: Rich 8K 11
LOWER GREEN 8B 40
Lower Grn. Gdns.
KT4: W Pk 7F 42
Lower Grn. Rd. KT10: Esh 8B 40
Lower Grn. W. CR4: Mit 2C 44
Lower Gro. Rd.
TW10: Rich 9M 11
Lwr. Guildford Rd.
GU21: Knap 4G 72
LOWER HALLIFORD 5E 38
Lwr. Ham La. GU8: Els 7J 131
Lwr. Hampton Rd.
TW16: Sunb 2K 39
Lwr. Ham Rd.
KT2: K Tham 1J 203 (6K 25)
Lower Hanger GU27: Hasl 2A 188
Lwr. Hill Rd. KT19: Eps 8A 60
Lowerhouse La.
RH5: For G, W'wood 7K 157
Lwr. House Rd.
GU8: Bow G 9K 151
Lwr. King's Rd.
KT2: K Tham 1J 203 (9L 25)
LOWER KINGSWOOD 5L 101
Lower Lodge Shooting Grounds
. . . . .6G 194
Lower Mall W6 . . . . .1G 12
Lower Mnr. Rd.
GU7: Goda 5H 133
GU8: Mil 1B 152
Lwr. Marsh La.
KT1: K Tham . . .7L 203 (3M 41)
(not continuous)
Lower Mead RH1: Red 1D 122
Lower Mere RH19: E Grin 1B 186
Lower Mill KT17: Ewe 4E 60
Lwr. Mill Fld. GU19: Bag 5H 51
Lower Moor GU46: Yate 1C 68
Lwr. Morden La.
SM4: Mord 5H 43
Lwr. Mortlake Rd.
TW9: Rich 7L 11
Lwr. Moushill La.
GU8: Mil 1A 152
Lwr. Nelson St.
GU11: Alde 2M 109
Lwr. Newport Rd.
GU12: Alde 4B 110
Lower Northfield SM7: Ban 1L 81
Lower Nursery SL5: S'dale 4D 34
Lower Pk. Rd. CR5: Chip 5C 82
Lower Peryers KT24: E Hor 6F 96
Lwr. Pillory Down
CR5: Coul 9F 62
SM5: Cars 9F 62
Lwr. Pyrford Rd. GU22: Pyr . . .3K 75
Lwr. Richmond Rd.
SW14 . . . . .6A 12
SW15 . . . . .6G 13
TW9, Rich 6N 11
Lower Rd. CR8: Ken 9M 63
GU27: G'wood 7K 171
KT22: Fetc 1D 98
KT23: Book 3A 98
KT24: Eff 5L 97
RH1: Red 5B 122
RH18: F Row 6H 187
SM1: Sut 1A 62
Lower Sandfields
GU23: Send 2F 94
Lwr. Sand Hills KT6: Surb 6J 41
Lwr. Sandhurst Rd.
GU47: Sandh 5A 48
RG40: Finch 5A 48
Lower Sawleywood
SM7: Ban 1L 81
Lower Shott KT23: Book 4A 98
LOWER SOUTH PARK 9D 124
Lwr. South Pk.
RH9: S Gods 9D 124
Lwr. South St. GU7: Goda 7G 133
Lwr. South Vw.
GU9: Farnh 9H 109
Lower Sq. RH18: F Row 6H 187
TW7: Isle 6H 11
Lower Sq., The SM1: Sut 2N 61
Lower St. GU5: Shere 8B 116
GU27: Hasl 2F 188
Lwr. Sunbury Rd.
TW12: Hamp 1N 39
Lwr. Tanbridge Way
RH12: Hors 6H 197
Lwr. Teddington Rd.
KT1: H Wic 1G 203 (9K 25)
Lower Ter. *SE27* *6M 29*
(off Woodcote Pl.)
Lwr. Village Rd. SL5: S'hill . . .4M 33
Lwr. Weybourne La.
GU9: B Lea, Weybo 6L 109
Lwr. Wokingham Rd.
RG40: Finch 1C 48
RG45: Crow 1C 48
Lwr. Wood Rd. KT10: Clay 3H 59
Lowestoft Wlk.
RH10: Craw 5F 182
Loweswater Wlk.
GU15: Camb 2H 71
Lowfield Cl. GU18: Ligh 7L 51
LOWFIELD HEATH 5C 162
Lowfield Heath Ind. Est.
RH11: L Hea 5C 162
Lowfield Heath Rd.
RH6: Char 4L 161
Lowfield Rd. RH13: Slin 5L 195
Lowfield Way RH11: L Hea . . .5C 162
Lowicks Rd. GU10: Rush 4N 149
Lowlands Dr. TW19: Stan 8M 7
Lowlands Rd.
GU17: B'water 2H 69
Low La. GU9: B Lea 6N 109
Lowndes Bldgs.
GU9: Farnh 9G 108
Lowry Cl. GU47: C Tow 9J 49
Lowry Cres. CR4: Mit 1C 44
Lowther Rd.
KT2: K Tham . . .1M 203 (9M 25)
SW13 . . . . .4E 12
Lowthorpe GU21: Wok 5K 73
Loxford Ct. GU6: Cranl 8H 155
Loxford Ho.
KT17: Eps 5M 201 (8D 60)
Loxford Rd. CR3: Cate 3C 104
Loxford Way CR3: Cate 3C 104
LOXHILL 9A 154
Loxley Rd. SW18 . . . . .2B 28
TW12: Hamp 5N 23
Loxmeadows Cl. RH14: Ifo . . .5F 192
LOXWOOD 4H 193
Loxwood KT13: Weybr 9F 38
Loxwood Cl. TW14: Bedf 2E 22
Loxwood Farm Pl.
RH14: Loxw 5H 193
Loxwood Rd. GU6: Alf 9H 175
RH12: Rudg 4N 193
RH14: Loxw 5J 193
RH14: Plais 6B 192
Loxwood Wlk. RH11: Craw . . .1L 181
(not continuous)
Lucan Dr. TW18: Stain 8M 21
Lucas Cl. GU46: Yate 1C 68
RH10: Craw 6F 182
RH19: E Grin 9C 166
Lucas Dr. GU46: Yate 1C 68
Lucas Fld. GU27: Hasl 2C 188
Lucas Grn. Rd.
GU24: W End 2A 72
Lucas Ho. *SW10* *3N 13*
(off Coleridge Gdns.)
Lucas Rd. RH12: Warn 9E 178
Lucerne Cl. GU22: Wok 6A 74
Lucerne Dr. RH10: Craw 6H 183
Lucerne Rd. CR7: T Hea 4M 45
Lucie Av. TW15: A'ford 7C 22
Lucien Rd. SW17 . . . . .5E 28
SW19 . . . . .3N 27
Lucilina Dr. TN8: Eden 3L 147
Luckley Path RG40: W'ham 2B 30
Luckley Rd. RG41: W'ham 5A 30
Luckley Wood
RG41: W'ham 5A 30
Luddington Av.
GU25: V Wat 1B 36
Ludford Cl.
CR0: Wad 6A 200 (9M 45)
Ludgrove RG40: W'ham 5C 30
Ludlow RG12: Brac 6N 31
Ludlow Cl. GU16: Frim 7E 70
Ludlow Rd.
GU2: Guil 5A 202 (4L 113)
TW13: Felt 5H 23
Ludovick Wlk. SW15 . . . . .7D 12
Ludshott Gro.
GU35: H Dwn 4G 169
Ludshott Mnr.
GU30: Brams 8H 169
Luff Cl. SL4: W'sor 6B 4
Luffs Mdw. GU28: North 9D 190
Luke Rd. GU11: Alde 4K 109
Luke Rd. E. GU11: Alde 4K 109
Lullarook Cl. TN16: B Hil 3E 86
LULLENDEN 5H 167
Lulworth Av. TW5: Hest 4A 10
Lulworth Cl. GU14: Farnb 7M 69
RH11: Craw 6M 181
Lulworth Cres. CR4: Mit 1C 44
Lumiere Ct. SW17 . . . . .3E 28
Lumley Ct. RH6: Horl 7E 142
Lumley Gdns. SM3: Chea 2K 61
Lumley Rd. RH6: Horl 7E 142
SM3: Chea 2K 61
Lunar Cl. TN16: B Hil 3F 86
Luna Rd. CR7: T Hea 2N 45
Lundy Cl. RH11: Craw 6A 182
Lundy Dr. UB3: Harl 1F 8
Lunghurst Rd. CR3: Wold 7J 85
Lupin Cl. CR0: Croy 7G 46
GU19: Bag 6G 51
SW2 . . . . .3M 29
UB7: W Dray 1M 7
Lupin Ride RG45: Crow 8G 30
Lurgan Av. W6 . . . . .2J 13
Lushington Dr. KT11: Cob 1J 77
Lushington Ho.
KT12: Wal T 5K 39
Lusted Hall La.
TN16: B Hil, Tats 7E 86
Lusteds Cl. RH4: Dork 8J 119
Lutea Ho. *SM2: Sut* *4A 62*
(off Walnut M.)
Luther M. TW11: Tedd 6F 24
Luther Rd. TW11: Tedd 6F 24
Lutterworth Cl. RG42: Brac 8A 16
Luttrell Av. SW15 . . . . .8G 13
Lutyens Cl. RH11: Craw 5K 181
Luxford Cl. RH12: Hors 3M 197
Luxford's La.
RH19: E Grin 4D 186
LUXTED 1J 87
Luxted Rd. BR6: Dow 8J 67
Lyall Pl. GU9: U Hal 5G 108
Lychett Minster Cl.
RG12: Brac 4D 32
Lych Ga. Cl. GU47: Sandh 7E 48
Lych Way GU21: Wok 3N 73
Lyconby Gdns. CR0: Croy 6H 47
Lydbury RG12: Brac 2D 32
Lydden Gro. SW18 . . . . .1N 27
Lydden Rd. SW18 . . . . .1N 27
Lydele Cl. GU21: Wok 2B 74
Lydens La.
TN8: Eden, Hev 6N 147
Lydford Cl. GU14: Farnb 7M 69
GU16: Frim 7E 70
Lydger Rd. GU22: Wok 7D 74
Lydhurst Av. SW2 . . . . .3K 29
Lydia Ct. *KT1: K Tham* *6J 203*
(off Grove Cres.)
Lydney RG12: Brac 6N 31
Lydney Cl. SW19 . . . . .3K 27
Lydon Ho. RH11: Craw 9B 162
Lye, The KT20: Tad 9H 81
Lye Copse Av.
GU14: Farnb 6N 69
Lyefield La. RH5: For G 4K 157
Lyell Rd. SL4: W'sor 6A 4
Lyfield KT22: Oxs 1B 78
Lyford Rd. SW18 . . . . .1B 28
Lygon Ho. *SW6* *4K 13*
(off Fulham Pal. Rd.)
Lyham Cl. SW2 . . . . .1J 29
Lyham Rd. SW2 . . . . .1J 29
Lyle Cl. CR4: Mit 6E 44
Lyle Ct. SM4: Mord 5B 44
Lymbourne Cl. SM2: Sut 6M 61
Lymden Gdns. RH2: Reig 4N 121
Lyme Regis Rd. SM7: Ban 4L 81
Lymescote Gdns. SM1: Sut . . .8M 43
Lyminge Gdns. SW18 . . . . .2C 28
Lymington Av. GU46: Yate 1A 68
Lymington Cl. SW16 . . . . .1H 45
Lymington Ct. SM1: Sut 9N 43
Lymington Gdns. KT19: Ewe . . .2E 60
Lynchborough Rd.
GU30: Pass 9C 168
Lynchen Cl. TW5: C'ford 4J 9
Lynchford La. GU14: Farnb 5C 90
Lynchford Rd. GU12: A Va 5D 90
GU14: Farnb 6N 89
(not continuous)
Lynchmere Pl. GU2: Guil 9K 93
Lynch Rd. GU9: Farnh 1J 129
Lyncroft Gdns. KT17: Ewe 5E 60
TW3: Houn 8C 10
Lyndale KT7: T Dit 6E 40
Lyndale Ct. KT14: W By 9J 55
RH1: Red 9E 102
Lyndale Dr. GU51: Fleet 4E 88
Lyndale Rd. RH1: Red 9D 102
Lynde Ho. KT12: Wal T 5K 39
Lynden Hyrst CR0: Croy 8C 46
Lyndford Ter. GU52: Fleet 6A 88
Lyndhurst Av. GU11: Alde 6A 110
GU17: B'water 9H 49
KT5: Surb 7A 42
SW16 . . . . .1H 45
TW2: Whitt 2N 23
TW16: Sunb 2H 39
Lyndhurst Cl. BR6: Farnb 1K 67
CR0: Croy 9C 46
GU21: Wok 2N 73
RG12: Brac 2E 32
RH11: Craw 4B 182
Lyndhurst Ct. *SM2: Sut* *4M 61*
(off Grange Rd.)
Lyndhurst Dr. KT3: N Mal 6D 42
Lyndhurst Farm Cl.
RH19: Fel 6G 165

Lyndhurst Rd.—Manor Ho.

Lyndhurst Rd. CR5: Coul . . . 3E 82
CR7: T Hea . . . 3L 45
RH2: Reig . . . 6M 121
SL5: Asc . . . 3L 33
Lyndhurst Vs. RH1: Red . . . 9D 102
Lyndhurst Way KT16: Chert . . . 9G 36
SM2: Sut . . . 5M 61
Lyndon Av. SM6: W'ton . . . 9E 44
Lyndons, The GU30: Pass . . . 9C 168
Lyndon Yd. SW17 . . . 5A 28
Lyndsey Cl. GU14: Cove . . . 1G 88
Lyndum Pl. GU35: Lind . . . 4A 168
Lyndwood Dr. SL4: O Win . . . 9K 5
Lyndwood Pde. *SL4: O Win* . . . *9K 5*
(off St Luke's Rd.)
LYNE . . . 7C 36
Lyne Cl. GU25: V Wat . . . 5B 36
Lyne Crossing Rd.
KT16: Lyne . . . 5C 36
Lynegrove Av. TW15: A'ford . . . 6D 22
Lyneham Rd. RG45: Crow . . . 2G 48
Lyne La. GU25: V Wat . . . 5C 36
KT16: Lyne . . . 5C 36
Lyne Rd. GU25: V Wat . . . 5N 35
Lynford Ct. CR0: Croy . . . 7F 200
Lynhurst KT13: Weybr . . . 3C 56
Lynmead Cl. TN8: Eden . . . 8K 127
Lynmouth Av. SM4: Mord . . . 5J 43
Lynmouth Gdns. TW5: Hest . . . 3L 9
Lynn Cl. TW15: A'ford . . . 6E 22
Lynn Ct. CR3: Whyte . . . 5C 84
Lynne Cl. BR6: Chels . . . 3N 67
CR2: Sels . . . 7F 64
Lynne Ct. CR2: S Croy . . . 7F 200
Lynne Wlk. KT10: Esh . . . 2C 58
Lynn Rd. SW12 . . . 1F 28
Lynn Wlk. RH2: Reig . . . 6N 121
Lynn Way GU14: Cove . . . 7L 69
Lynscott Way CR2: S Croy . . . 5M 63
Lynstead Ct. BR3: Beck . . . 1H 47
Lynton Cl. GU9: Farnh . . . 4F 128
KT9: Ches . . . 1L 59
RH19: E Grin . . . 8B 166
TW7: Isle . . . 7F 10
Lynton Ct. KT17: Ewe . . . 7E 60
Lynton Pk. Av.
RH19: E Grin . . . 8B 166
Lynton Rd. CR0: Croy . . . 5L 45
KT3: N Mal . . . 4C 42
LYNWICK . . . 9B 176
Lynwick St. RH12: Rudg . . . 1C 194
Lynwood GU2: Guil . . . 4L 113
Lynwood Av. CR5: Coul . . . 2F 82
KT17: Eps . . . 1E 80
TW20: Egh . . . 7A 20
Lynwood Chase RG12: Brac . . . 8A 16
Lynwood Cl. GU21: Wok . . . 9F 54
GU35: Lind . . . 4B 168
Lynwood Ct. KT1: K Tham . . . 1A 42
KT17: Eps . . . 9E 60
RH12: Hors . . . 5J 197
Lynwood Cres. SL5: S'dale . . . 5B 34
Lynwood Dr. GU16: Mytc . . . 2E 90
KT4: W Pk . . . 8F 42
Lynwood Gdns. CR0: Wad . . . 1K 63
Lynwood Rd. KT7: T Dit . . . 8F 40
KT17: Eps . . . 1E 80
RH1: Red . . . 1E 122
SW17 . . . 4D 28
Lynx Hill KT24: E Hor . . . 6G 96
Lyon Cl. RH10: Craw . . . 7G 183
Lyon Ct. RH13: Hors . . . 6L 197
Lyon Oaks RG42: Warf . . . 7N 15
Lyon Rd. KT12: Wal T . . . 8M 39
RG45: Crow . . . 1H 49
SW19 . . . 9A 28
Lyons Cl. RH13: Slin . . . 5L 195
Lyons Ct.
RH4: Dork . . . 2K 201 (5H 119)
Lyonsdene KT20: Lwr K . . . 5L 101
Lyons Dr. GU2: Guil . . . 7K 93
Lyons Farm Est.
RH13: Slin . . . 6A 196
Lyons Rd. RH13: Slin . . . 5L 195
Lyon Way GU16: Frim . . . 5A 70
Lyon Way Ind. Est.
GU16: Frim . . . 5A 70
Lyric Cl. RH10: Craw . . . 5H 183
Lyric Rd. SW13 . . . 4E 12
Lyric Sq. *W6* . . . *1H 13*
(off King St.)
Lyric Theatre
Hammersmith . . . 1H 13
Lysander Dr. RG12: Brac . . . 3A 32
Lysander Gdns. KT6: Surb . . . 5M 41
Lysander Rd. CR0: Wad . . . 3K 63
Lysia Ct. *SW6* . . . *3J 13*
(off Lysia St.)
Lysias Rd. SW12 . . . 1F 28
Lysia St. SW6 . . . 3J 13
Lysons Av. GU12: A Va . . . 5D 90
Lyson's Rd. GU11: Alde . . . 3M 109
Lysons Wlk. SW15 . . . 7F 12
Lyster M. KT11: Cob . . . 9K 57
Lytchgate Cl. CR2: S Croy . . . 4B 64
Lytcott Dr. KT8: W Mole . . . 2N 39
Lytham RG12: Brac . . . 5K 31
Lytham Ct. SL5: S'hill . . . 4N 33
LYTHE HILL . . . 2L 189
Lythe Hill Pk. GU27: Hasl . . . 3J 189
Lytton Dr. RH10: Craw . . . 2H 183
Lytton Gdns. SM6: Bedd . . . 1H 63
Lytton Gro. SW15 . . . 8J 13
Lytton Pk. KT11: Cob . . . 8N 57
Lytton Rd. GU22: Wok . . . 3D 74
Lyveden Rd. SW17 . . . 7D 28
Lywood Cl. KT20: Tad . . . 9H 81

M

Mabbotts KT20: Tad . . . 8J 81
Mabel St. GU21: Wok . . . 5N 73
Maberley Rd. BR3: Beck . . . 2G 46
Mablethorpe Rd. SW6 . . . 3K 13
Macadam Av. RG45: Crow . . . 9H 31
McAlmont Ridge
GU7: Goda . . . 4G 132
Macaulay Av. KT10: H Wood . . . 8F 40
Macaulay Rd. CR3: Cate . . . 9B 84
Macbeth Ct. RG42: Warf . . . 9C 16
Macbeth St. W6 . . . 1G 13
McCarthy Rd. TW13: Hanw . . . 6L 23
McClaren Technology Cen.
GU21: Wok . . . 7C 54
Macclesfield Rd.
SE25 . . . 4F 46
Macdonald Rd.
GU9: U Hal . . . 5G 109
GU18: Ligh . . . 8K 51
McDonalds Almshouses
GU9: Farnh . . . 2F 128
McDonough Cl. KT9: Ches . . . 1L 59
McDougall Ct. TW9: Rich . . . 5N 11
Macdowall Rd. GU2: Guil . . . 7L 93
Mace La. TN14: Cud . . . 9M 67
Macfarlane La. TW7: Isle . . . 2F 10
Machahon Cl. GU24: Chob . . . 6H 53
McIndoe Rd. RH19: E Grin . . . 7N 165
McIntosh Cl. SM6: W'ton . . . 4J 63
McIver Cl. RH19: Fel . . . 6J 165
McKay Cl. GU11: Alde . . . 1A 110
McKay Rd. SW20 . . . 8G 27
McKay Trad. Est. SL3: Poy . . . 5G 7
Mackenzie Rd. BR3: Beck . . . 1F 46
McKenzie Way KT19: Eps . . . 5N 59
McKernan Ct. GU47: Sandh . . . 7E 48
Mackie Rd. SW2 . . . 1L 29
Mackies Hill GU5: P'lake . . . 4E 136
Mackrells RH1: Red . . . 6A 122
Maclaren Dr. RG42: Warf . . . 9D 16
Maclaren M. SW15 . . . 7H 13
Macleod Rd. RH13: Hors . . . 7L 197
(not continuous)
Macmillan Ho. *SM7: Ban* . . . *1L 81*
(off Basing Rd.)
Macmillan Way SW17 . . . 5F 28
Macnaghten Woods
GU15: Camb . . . 9C 50
McNaughton Cl.
GU14: Cove . . . 2H 89
Macphail Cl.
RG40: W'ham . . . 9D 14
McRae La. CR4: Mit . . . 6D 44
Macrae Rd. GU46: Yate . . . 9B 48
Madan Cl. TN16: Weste . . . 3N 107
Madan Rd. TN16: Weste . . . 3M 107
Madans Wlk.
KT18: Eps . . . 8K 201 (2C 80)
(not continuous)
Maddison Cl. TW11: Tedd . . . 7F 24
Maddox Dr. RH10: Wor . . . 4H 183
Maddox La. KT23: Book . . . 9M 77
Maddox Pk. KT23: Book . . . 1M 97
Madehurst Ct.
RH11: Craw . . . 6L 181
Madeira Av. RH12: Hors . . . 6J 197
Madeira Cl. KT14: W By . . . 9J 55
Madeira Cres. KT14: W By . . . 9H 55
Madeira Rd. CR4: Mit . . . 3D 44
KT14: W By . . . 9H 55
SW16 . . . 6J 29
Madeira Wlk. RH2: Reig . . . 2B 122
SL4: W'sor . . . 4G 5
Madeley Rd. GU52: C Cro . . . 7C 88
Madgehole La.
GU5: Sha G . . . 7J 135
Madingley RG12: Brac . . . 7N 31
Madison Cl. SM2: Sut . . . 4B 62
Madox Brown End
GU47: C Tow . . . 8K 49
Madrid Rd. GU2: Guil . . . 4L 113
SW13 . . . 4F 12
Maesmaur Rd. TN16: Tats . . . 8F 86
Mafeking Av. TW8: Brent . . . 2L 11
Mafeking Rd. TW19: Wray . . . 3D 20
Magazine Pl. KT22: Leat . . . 9H 79
Magazine Rd. CR3: Cate . . . 9M 83
Magdala Rd. CR2: S Croy . . . 4A 64
TW7: Isle . . . 6G 11
Magdalen Cl. KT14: Byf . . . 1N 75
Magdalen Cres. KT14: Byf . . . 1N 75
Magdalene Cl.
RH10: Craw . . . 9G 162
Magdalene Rd.
GU47: Owls . . . 5L 49
TW17: Shep . . . 3A 38
Magdalen Rd. SW18 . . . 2A 28
Magellan Ter. RH10: Craw . . . 8E 162
Magna Carta La.
TW19: Wray . . . 2N 19
Magna Carta Monument . . . 3N 19
Magna Rd. TW20: Eng G . . . 7L 19
Magnolia Cl. GU47: Owls . . . 6J 49
KT2: K Tham . . . 7A 26
RG42: Warf . . . 9E 16
Magnolia Ct. RH6: Horl . . . 8E 142
SM2: Sut . . . *4M 61*
(off Grange Rd.)
SM6: W'ton . . . 2F 62
TW9: Kew . . . 4A 12
TW13: Felt . . . *2H 23*
(off Plum Cl.)
Magnolia Dr. TN16: B Hil . . . 3F 86
Magnolia Pl. GU1: Guil . . . 9M 93
Magnolia Rd. W4 . . . 2A 12
Magnolia St. UB7: W Dray . . . 1M 7
Magnolia Way GU52: Fleet . . . 6B 88
KT19: Ewe . . . 2B 60
RH5: Nth H . . . 8K 119
Magpie Cl. CR5: Coul . . . 5G 83
GU10: Ews . . . 4C 108
Magpie Grn. *TN8: Eden* . . . *9M 127*
(off Woodland Dr.)
Magpie Wlk. RH10: Craw . . . 1D 182
Maguire Dr. GU16: Frim . . . 3G 71
TW10: Ham . . . 5J 25
Mahonia Cl. GU24: W End . . . 9C 52
Maida Rd. GU11: Alde . . . 9N 89
MAIDENBOWER . . . 5G 183
Maidenbower Bus. Pk.
RH10: Wor . . . 5J 183
Maidenbower Community
Sports Cen. . . . 5F 182
Maidenbower Dr.
RH10: Craw . . . 5G 182
Maidenbower La.
RH10: Craw . . . 4G 182
(Billinton Dr.)
RH10: Craw . . . 5F 182
(St Leonard's Dr.)
Maidenbower Pl.
RH10: Craw . . . 5G 183
Maidenbower Sq.
RH10: Craw . . . 5G 183
Maidenhead Rd.
RG40: W'ham . . . 6D 14
RG42: Warf . . . 3N 15
SL4: W'sor . . . 3A 4
Maiden La. RH11: Craw . . . 1A 182
MAIDEN'S GREEN . . . 3F 16
Maiden's Grn. SL4: Wink . . . 3F 16
Maidenshaw Rd.
KT19: Eps . . . 5J 201 (8C 60)
Maids of Honour Row
TW9: Rich . . . 8K 11
Main Dr. RG42: Warf . . . 8D 16
Mainprize Rd. RG12: Brac . . . 9C 16
Main Rd. BR2: Kes . . . 9E 66
GU10: B Oak . . . 2A 148
SL4: W'sor . . . 3A 4
TN8: C Hil, Eden . . . 6K 127
TN16: B Hil, Weste . . . 9E 66
Mainstone Cl. GU16: Deep . . . 7G 71
Mainstone Cres.
GU24: B'wood . . . 8A 72
Mainstone Rd. GU24: Bis . . . 3C 72
Main St. KT15: Addl . . . 9N 37
TW13: Hanw . . . 6L 23
Mainwaring Ct. CR4: Mit . . . 1E 44
Maisie Webster Cl.
TW19: Stan . . . 1M 21
Maisonettes, The
SM1: Sut . . . 2L 61
Maitland Cl. KT12: Wal T . . . 8M 39
KT14: W By . . . 9J 55
TW4: Houn . . . 6N 9
Maitland Rd. GU14: Farnb . . . 5N 89
Maitlands Cl. GU10: Tong . . . 6C 110
Maize Cft. RH6: Horl . . . 7G 142
Maize La. RG42: Warf . . . 7B 16
Majestic Way CR4: Mit . . . 1D 44
Majors Farm Rd. SL3: Dat . . . 3N 5
Major's Hill RH10: Wor . . . 4N 183
Makepiece Rd.
RG42: Brac . . . 8N 15
Malacca Farm GU4: W Cla . . . 5K 95
Malan Cl. TN16: B Hil . . . 4G 87
Malbrook Rd. SW15 . . . 7G 13
Malcolm Dr. KT6: Surb . . . 7L 41
Malcolm Gdns. RH6: Hook . . . 1B 162
Malcolm Rd. CR5: Coul . . . 2H 83
SE25 . . . 5D 46
SW19 . . . 7K 27
Malden Av. SE25 . . . 3E 46
Malden Cen., The . . . 3E 42
Malden Ct. SW20: N Mal . . . 2G 42
MALDEN GREEN . . . 7F 42
Malden Grn. Av.
KT4: W Pk . . . 7E 42
Malden Grn. M. KT4: W Pk . . . 7F 42
Malden Hill KT3: N Mal . . . 2E 42
Malden Hill Gdns.
KT3: N Mal . . . 2E 42
MALDEN JUNC. . . . 4E 42
Malden Manor Station (Rail)
. . . 6D 42
Malden Pk. KT3: N Mal . . . 5E 42
Malden Rd. KT3: N Mal . . . 4D 42
KT4: W Pk . . . 6E 42
SM3: Chea . . . 1J 61
MALDEN RUSHETT . . . 7J 59
Malden Way KT3: N Mal . . . 5C 42
Maldon Ct. SM6: W'ton . . . 2G 62
Maldon Rd. SM6: W'ton . . . 2F 62
Malet Cl. TW20: Egh . . . 7F 20
Maley Av. SE27 . . . 3M 29
Malham Cl. RH10: Craw . . . 6G 183
Malham Fell RG12: Brac . . . 3M 31
Mall, The
CR0: Croy . . . 2B 200 (8N 45)
KT6: Surb . . . 4K 41
KT12: Hers . . . *2L 57*
(off Hersham Grn. Shop. Cen.)
SW14 . . . 8B 12
TW8: Brent . . . 2K 11
Mallard Cl. GU12: Ash . . . 1D 110
GU27: Hasl . . . 2C 188
RH1: Red . . . 9E 102
RH6: Horl . . . 6E 142
RH12: Hors . . . 3J 197
TW2: Whitt . . . 1A 24
Mallard Ct. *GU11: Alde* . . . *5M 109*
(off Boxhalls La.)
RH4: Dork . . . 1J 201
Mallard Pl. GU14: Cove . . . 5M 69
RH19: E Grin . . . 1B 186
TW1: Twick . . . 4G 24
Mallard Rd. CR2: Sels . . . 6G 65
Mallards, The GU16: Frim . . . 4D 70
TW18: Lale . . . 1K 37
Mallards Reach
KT13: Weybr . . . 8E 38
Mallards Way GU18: Ligh . . . 7L 51
Mallard Wlk. BR3: Beck . . . 4G 47
Mallard Way GU46: Yate . . . 9A 48
SM6: W'ton . . . 5G 63
TN8: Eden . . . 9L 127
Malling Cl. CR0: Croy . . . 5F 46
Malling Gdns. SM4: Mord . . . 5A 44
Mallinson Rd. CR0: Bedd . . . 9H 45
Mallow Cl. CR0: Croy . . . 7G 46
GU35: Lind . . . 4B 168
KT20: Tad . . . 7G 81
RH12: Hors . . . 2L 197
Mallow Cres. GU4: B'ham . . . 9D 94
Mallowdale Rd. RG12: Brac . . . 6C 32
Mall Rd. W6 . . . 1G 13
Mall Vs. *W6* . . . *1G 13*
(off Mall Rd.)
Malmains Cl. BR3: Beck . . . 3N 47
Malmains Way BR3: Beck . . . 3M 47
Malmesbury Rd.
SM4: Mord . . . 6A 44
Malmstone Av. RH1: Mers . . . 6G 103
Malory Cl. BR3: Beck . . . 1H 47
Malta Rd. GU16: Deep . . . 6J 71
Maltby Rd. KT9: Ches . . . 3N 59
Malt Hill RG42: Warf . . . 5C 16
TW20: Egh . . . 6A 20
Malt Ho., The GU10: Til . . . 8A 130
Malt Ho. Cl. SL4: O Win . . . 1L 19
Malthouse Ct. GU24: W End . . . 8C 52
Malthouse Dr. TW13: Hanw . . . 6L 23
W4 . . . 2E 12
Malthouse La. GU3: Worp . . . 2F 92
GU8: Hamb . . . 9F 152
GU24: Pirb . . . 1E 92
GU24: W End . . . 9C 52
Malthouse Mead GU8: Wit . . . 5C 152
Malthouse Pas. *SW13* . . . *5E 12*
(off Maltings Cl.)
Malthouse Rd.
RH10: Craw . . . 5B 182
Malthouses, The
GU6: Cranl . . . 7N 155
Maltings W4 . . . 1N 11
Maltings, The KT14: Byf . . . 9A 56
RH8: Oxt . . . 9B 106
TW18: Stain . . . 5G 20
Maltings Cl. SW13 . . . 5E 12
Maltings Lodge *W4* . . . *2D 12*
(off Corney Reach Way)
Maltings Pl. SW6 . . . 4N 13
Malting Way TW7: Isle . . . 6F 10
Malus Cl. KT15: Addl . . . 4H 55
Malus Dr. KT15: Addl . . . 4H 55
Malva Cl. SW18 . . . 8N 13
Malvern Cl. CR4: Mit . . . 2G 44
KT6: Surb . . . 7L 41
KT16: Otter . . . 3E 54
SE20 . . . 1D 46
Malvern Ct.
KT18: Eps . . . 8K 201 (1C 80)
SL3: Lang . . . 2C 6
SM2: Sut . . . 4M 61
Malvern Dr. TW13: Hanw . . . 6L 23
Malvern Rd. CR7: T Hea . . . 3L 45
GU14: Cove . . . 7J 69
GU17: Min . . . 5E 68
KT6: Surb . . . 8L 41
RH11: Craw . . . 4A 182
TW12: Hamp . . . 8A 24
UB3: Harl . . . 3F 8
Malwood Rd. SW12 . . . 1F 28
Malyons, The TW17: Shep . . . 5E 38
Manatee Pl. SM6: Bedd . . . 9H 45
Manawey Bus. Units
GU12: Alde . . . 3C 110
Manbre Rd. W6 . . . 2H 13
Manchester Rd. CR7: T Hea . . . 2N 45
Mandalay *GU9: U Hal* . . . *5F 108*
(off Lawday Pl. La.)
Mandel Ho. SW18 . . . 7M 13
Mandeville Cl. GU2: Guil . . . 9K 93
SW20 . . . 8K 27
Mandeville Ct. TW20: Egh . . . 5C 20
Mandeville Dr. KT6: Surb . . . 7K 41
Mandeville Rd. TW7: Isle . . . 5G 10
TW17: Shep . . . 4B 38
Mandora Rd. GU11: Alde . . . 9N 89
Mandrake Rd. SW17 . . . 4D 28
Manfield Pk. GU6: Cranl . . . 5K 155
Manfield Rd. GU12: Ash . . . 2E 110
Manfred Rd. SW15 . . . 8L 13
Mangles Ct.
GU1: Guil . . . 4B 202 (4M 113)
Mangles Rd. GU1: Guil . . . 1N 113
Manitoba Gdns. BR6: Chels . . . 3N 67
Manley Bri. Rd.
GU10: Rowl, Wrec . . . 6D 128
Mannamead KT18: Eps D . . . 6D 80
Mannamead Cl.
KT18: Eps D . . . 6D 80
Mann Cl.
CR0: Croy . . . 4B 200 (9N 45)
RH11: Craw . . . 9N 181
Manning Cl. RH19: E Grin . . . 7N 165
Manning Gdns. CR0: Croy . . . 6E 46
Manning Pl. TW10: Rich . . . 9M 11
Mannings Cl. RH10: Craw . . . 9H 163
MANNINGS HEATH . . . 9B 198
Mannings Hill GU6: Cranl . . . 4M 155
Manningtree Cl. SW19 . . . 2K 27
Mann's Cl. TW7: Isle . . . 8F 10
Manny Shinwell Ho.
SW6 . . . *2L 13*
(off Clem Attlee Ct.)
Manoel Rd. TW2: Twick . . . 4C 24
Manor, The GU8: Mil . . . 1C 152
Manor Av. CR3: Cate . . . 2B 104
TW4: Houn . . . 6L 9
Manor Chase KT13: Weybr . . . 2C 56
MANOR CIRCUS . . . 6N 11
Manor Cl. CR6: Warl . . . 4H 85
GU10: Tong . . . 5D 110
GU22: Pyr . . . 4H 75
GU27: Hasl . . . 2C 188
KT4: W Pk . . . 7D 42
KT24: E Hor . . . 6F 96
RG42: Brac . . . 8M 15
RH6: Horl . . . 8D 142
RH9: S Gods . . . 7J 125
Manor Ct. BR4: W Wick . . . 7L 47
GU52: C Cro . . . 9B 88
KT2: K Tham . . . 9N 25
KT8: W Mole . . . 3A 40
KT13: Weybr . . . 1C 56
RH10: Craw . . . 9D 162
RH12: Hors . . . 3N 197
SM5: Cars . . . 9E 44
SW6 . . . 4N 13
SW16 . . . 4J 29
TW2: Twick . . . 3C 24
TW18: Stain . . . 6F 20
Manor Cres. GU2: Guil . . . 1L 113
GU24: B'wood . . . 7A 72
GU27: Hasl . . . 2C 188
KT5: Surb . . . 5N 41
KT14: Byf . . . 9A 56
KT19: Eps . . . 8N 59
Manorcrofts Rd. TW20: Egh . . . 7C 20
Manordene Cl. KT7: T Dit . . . 7G 40
Manor Dr. KT5: Surb . . . 5M 41
KT10: H Wood . . . 8F 40
KT15: N Haw . . . 6J 55
KT19: Ewe . . . 3D 60
RH6: Horl . . . 8D 142
TW13: Hanw . . . 6L 23
TW16: Sunb . . . 1H 39
Manor Dr., The KT4: W Pk . . . 7D 42
Manor Dr. Nth. KT3: N Mal . . . 6C 42
KT4: W Pk . . . 7D 42
Manor Farm GU3: Wan . . . 6N 111
Mnr. Farm Av. TW17: Shep . . . 5C 38
Mnr. Farm Bus. Cen.
GU10: Tong . . . 7D 110
Mnr. Farm Cl. GU3: Norm . . . 1M 111
GU12: Ash . . . 3D 110
KT4: W Pk . . . 7D 42
SL4: W'sor . . . 6C 4
Mnr. Farm Cotts.
GU3: Wan . . . 6N 111
SL4: O Win . . . 8K 5
Mnr. Farm Ct. TW20: Egh . . . 6C 20
Manor Farm Craft Cen. . . . 8F 110
MANOR FARM ESTATE . . . 1M 19
Mnr. Farm Ho. SL4: W'sor . . . 6C 4
Mnr. Farm La. TW20: Egh . . . 6C 20
Mnr. Farm Rd. SW16 . . . 1L 45
Manor Flds. GU8: Mil . . . 9B 132
GU10: Seal . . . 7F 110
RH13: Hors . . . 4N 197
SW15 . . . 9J 13
Manorfields RH11: Craw . . . 7J 181
Manor Gdns. CR2: S Croy . . . 3C 64
GU2: Guil . . . 1L 113
GU7: Goda . . . 4H 133
GU10: L Bou . . . 6J 129
KT24: Eff . . . 6L 97
SW20 . . . 1L 43
TW9: Rich . . . 7M 11
TW12: Hamp . . . 8B 24
TW16: Sunb . . . 9H 23
W4 . . . 1D 12
Manor Ga. RH10: Craw . . . 9D 162
Manorgate Rd.
KT2: K Tham . . . 9N 25
Manor Grn. GU8: Mil . . . 1B 152
Manor Grn. Rd. KT19: Eps . . . 9A 60
Manor Gro. BR3: Beck . . . 1L 47
TW9: Rich . . . 7N 11
Manor Hill SM7: Ban . . . 2D 82
Manor Ho. *SL4: Eton* . . . *2G 4*
(off Common La.)

Manor Ho., The—Martin Way

Manor Ho., The
GU15: Camb . . . 9B 50
KT20: K'wood . . . 1A 102
Manor Ho. Ct.
KT18: Eps . . . 7H 201 (9B 60)
TW17: Shep . . . 6C 38
Manor Ho. Dr. KT12: Hers . . . 2G 57
SL5: Asc . . . 8L 17
Manor Ho. Flats
GU10: Tong . . . 6C 110
Manor Ho. Gdns.
TN8: Eden . . . 2L 147
Manor Ho. La. KT23: Book . . . 4M 97
SL3: Dat . . . 3L 5
Manor Ho. Way TW7: Isle . . . 6H 11
Manor La. GU5: Sha G . . . 8G 134
KT20: Lwr K . . . 7M 101
RH13: Hors . . . 8A 198
SM1: Sut . . . 2A 62
TW13: Felt . . . 3H 23
TW16: Sunb . . . 1H 39
UB3: Harl . . . 2E 8
Manor Lea GU27: Hasl . . . 2C 188
Manor Lea Cl. GU8: Mil . . . 9B 132
Manor Lea Rd. GU8: Mil . . . 9B 132
Manor Leaze TW20: Egh . . . 6D 20
Manor Lodge GU2: Guil . . . 1L 113
Manor Pk. TW9: Rich . . . 7M 11
TW13: Felt . . . 3H 23
TW18: Stain . . . 4F 20
Manor Pk. Cl. BR4: W Wick . . . 7L 47
Manor Pk. Dr. GU46: Yate . . . 1C 68
Manor Pk. Ind. Est.
GU12: Alde . . . 3A 110
Manor Pk. Rd.
BR4: W Wick . . . 7L 47
SM1: Sut . . . 2A 62
Manor Pk. Village
GU2: Guil . . . 4H 113
Manor Pl. CR4: Mit . . . 2G 45
KT12: Wal T . . . 6G 39
(not continuous)
KT23: Book . . . 4A 98
SM1: Sut . . . 1N 61
TW14: Felt . . . 2H 23
TW18: Stain . . . 6K 21
Manor Rd. BR3: Beck . . . 1L 47
BR4: W Wick . . . 8L 47
CR4: Mit . . . 3G 44
GU2: Guil . . . 1L 113
GU9: Farnh . . . 8K 109
GU10: Tong . . . 4D 110
GU11: Alde . . . 4L 109
GU12: Ash . . . 4D 110
GU14: Farnb . . . 1B 90
GU21: Wok . . . 3M 73
GU23: Rip . . . 1H 95
KT8: E Mol . . . 3D 40
KT12: Wal T . . . 6G 39
RH1: Mers . . . 7G 102
RH2: Reig . . . 1L 121
RH12: Hors . . . 3N 197
RH19: E Grin . . . 8M 165
SE25 . . . 3D 46
SL4: W'sor . . . 5B 4
SM2: Chea . . . 4L 61
SM6: W'ton . . . 1F 62
SW20 . . . 1L 43
TN8: Eden . . . 2K 147
TN16: Tats . . . 7G 86
TW2: Twick . . . 3C 24
TW9: Rich . . . 7N 11
TW11: Tedd . . . 6G 25
(not continuous)
TW15: A'ford . . . 6A 22
Manor Rd. Nth. KT7: T Dit . . . 9F 40
KT10: H Wood, T Dit . . . 9F 40
SM6: W'ton . . . 1F 62
Manor Rd. Sth.
KT10: H Wood . . . 1E 58
Manor Royal RH10: Craw . . . 9C 162
Mnr. Royal Ind. Est.
RH10: Craw . . . 9C 162
Manor Ter. GU7: Goda . . . 5J 133
Manor Va. TW8: Brent . . . 1J 11
Manor Wlk. GU12: Alde . . . 3N 109
(not continuous)
KT13: Weybr . . . 2C 56
RH6: Horl . . . 8D 142
(off Manor Dr.)
Manor Way BR3: Beck . . . 1K 47
CR2: S Croy . . . 3B 64
CR4: Mit . . . 2G 44
CR8: Pur . . . 8J 63
GU2: Guil . . . 6H 113
GU19: Bag . . . 5J 51
GU22: Wok . . . 8D 74
KT4: W Pk . . . 7D 42
KT22: Oxs . . . 2C 78
SM7: Ban . . . 3D 82
TW20: Egh . . . 7B 20
Manor Way, The
SM6: W'ton . . . 1F 62
Mnr. Wood Rd. CR8: Pur . . . 9J 63
Mansard Beeches
SW17 . . . 6E 28
Manse Cl. UB3: Harl . . . 2E 8
Mansel Cl. GU2: Guil . . . 7L 93
Mansell Cl. SL4: W'sor . . . 4B 4
Mansell Way CR3: Cate . . . 9A 84
Mansel Rd. SW19 . . . 7K 27
Mansfield Cl. SL5: Asc . . . 9H 17
Mansfield Cres. RG12: Brac . . . 5N 31
Mansfield Dr. RH1: Mers . . . 6H 103
Mansfield Pl. CR2: S Croy . . . 3A 64
SL5: Asc . . . 1H 33
Mansfield Rd. CR2: S Croy . . . 3A 64
KT9: Ches . . . 2J 59
Manship Rd. CR4: Mit . . . 8E 28
Mansions, The SW5 . . . 1N 13
Manston Av. UB2: S'hall . . . 1A 10
Manston Cl. SE20 . . . 1F 46
Manston Dr. RG12: Brac . . . 5A 32
Manston Gro. KT2: K Tham . . . 6K 25
Manston Rd. GU4: B'ham . . . 8C 94
Mantilla Rd. SW17 . . . 5E 28
Mantle Ct. *SW18 . . . 9N 13*
(off Mapleton Rd.)
Mantlet Cl. SW16 . . . 8G 29
Manville Ct. GU4: Chil . . . 2A 134
Manville Gdns. SW17 . . . 4F 28
Manville Rd. SW17 . . . 3E 28
Manygate La. TW17: Shep . . . 6D 38
Manygate Mobile Home Est.
TW17: Shep . . . 5E 38
(off Mitre Cl.)
Manygates SW12 . . . 3F 28
Maori Rd. GU1: Guil . . . 3B 114
Maple Cl. CR3: Whyte . . . 4C 84
CR4: Mit . . . 9F 28
GU12: A Va . . . 6D 90
GU17: B'water . . . 1H 69
GU47: Sandh . . . 6E 48
RH11: Craw . . . 9A 162
RH12: Hors . . . 3N 197
TW12: Hamp . . . 7N 23
Maple Ct.
CR0: Croy . . . 6C 200 (1N 63)
(Lwr. Coombe St.)
CR0: Croy . . . 6B 200
(The Waldrons)
GU21: Wok . . . 3M 73
KT3: N Mal . . . 2C 42
KT22: Leat . . . 7F 78
RG12: Brac . . . 3D 32
SL4: W'sor . . . 6F 4
TW15: A'ford . . . 8E 22
TW20: Eng G . . . 7L 19
Mapledale Av. CR0: Croy . . . 8D 46
Mapledrakes Cl. GU6: Ewh . . . 5F 156
Mapledrakes Rd.
GU6: Ewh . . . 5F 156
Maple Dr. GU18: Ligh . . . 7K 51
KT23: Book . . . 3B 98
RG45: Crow . . . 9H 31
RH1: Red . . . 9D 122
RH19: E Grin . . . 9C 166
Maple Gdns. GU46: Yate . . . 1C 68
KT17: Eps . . . 6L 201
TW19: Stan . . . 3N 21
Maple Grn. RH11: Craw . . . 4A 182
Maple Gro. GU1: Guil . . . 1N 113
GU22: Wok . . . 8A 74
KT23: Book . . . 5A 98
TW8: Brent . . . 3H 11
Maple Gro. Bus. Cen.
TW4: Houn . . . 7K 9
Maplehatch Cl. GU7: Goda . . . 9H 133
Maple Ho. KT1: K Tham . . . 8J 203
RH1: Red . . . 3D 122
(off Chapel Rd.)
TW9: Kew . . . 4A 12
Maplehurst BR2: Brom . . . 1N 47
KT22: Fetc . . . 1D 98
Maplehurst Cl.
KT1: K Tham . . . 8J 203 (3L 41)
Maple Ind. Est. TW13: Felt . . . 4H 23
Maple Leaf Cl. GU14: Cove . . . 2L 89
TN16: B Hil . . . 3F 86
Mapleleaf Cl. CR2: Sels . . . 7G 64
Maple Lodge GU27: Hasl . . . 4J 189
Maple M. SW16 . . . 6K 29
Maple Pl. SM7: Ban . . . 1J 81
Maple Rd. CR3: Whyte . . . 4C 84
GU23: Rip . . . 2J 95
KT6: Surb . . . 8J 203 (5K 41)
KT21: A'tead . . . 6K 79
RH1: Red . . . 7D 122
SE20 . . . 1E 46
Maplers Dr. GU51: Fleet . . . 2A 88
Maples, The KT1: Tedd . . . 8J 25
KT10: Clay . . . 4G 59
KT16: Otter . . . 3D 54
SM7: Ban . . . 1N 81
Maple Silver Birch
GU14: Cove . . . 9J 69
Maplestead Rd. SW2 . . . 1K 29
Maplethorpe Rd.
CR7: T Hea . . . 3L 45
Mapleton Cres. SW18 . . . 9N 13
Mapleton Rd. SW18 . . . 9M 13
(not continuous)
TN16: Weste . . . 8N 107
Maple Wlk. GU12: Alde . . . 4B 110
SM2: Sut . . . 6N 61
Maple Way CR5: Coul . . . 8F 82
GU35: H Dwn . . . 3G 169
TW13: Felt . . . 4H 23
Marbeck Cl. SL4: W'sor . . . 4A 4
Marble Hill Cl. TW1: Twick . . . 1H 25
Marble Hill Gdns.
TW1: Twick . . . 1H 25
Marble Hill House . . . 1J 25
Marbles Way KT20: Tad . . . 6J 81
Marbull Way RG42: Warf . . . 7N 15
Marcellina Way BR6: Orp . . . 1N 67
Marchant's Hill (Activity Cen.)
. . . 2B 170
Marchbank Rd. W14 . . . 2L 13
March Ct. SW15 . . . 7G 12
Marcheria Cl.
RG12: Brac . . . 5N 31
Marches, The
RH12: K'fold . . . 4H 179
Marches Rd.
RH12: Warn, K'fold . . . 5D 178
Marchmont Gdns.
TW10: Rich . . . 8M 11
Marchmont Pl. RG12: Brac . . . 2A 32
Marchmont Rd.
SM6: W'ton . . . 4G 62
TW10: Rich . . . 8M 11
March Rd. KT13: Weybr . . . 2B 56
TW1: Twick . . . 1G 24
Marchside Cl. TW5: Hest . . . 4L 9
Marcus Ct. GU22: Wok . . . 5B 74
Marcuse Rd. CR3: Cate . . . 1A 104
Marcus St. SW18 . . . 9N 13
Marcus Ter. SW18 . . . 9N 13
Mardale GU15: Camb . . . 2G 71
Mardell Rd. CR0: Croy . . . 4G 46
Marden Cres. CR0: Croy . . . 5K 45
MARDEN PARK . . . 1H 105
Marden Rd. CR0: Croy . . . 5K 45
Mardens, The RH11: Craw . . . 2N 181
Mare La. GU8: Hasc . . . 6L 153
RG42: Bin . . . 1K 15
(not continuous)
Mareschal Rd.
GU2: Guil . . . 7A 202 (5M 113)
Maresfield CR0: Croy . . . 9B 46
Maresfield Ho. *GU1: Guil . . . 2F 114*
(off Merrow St.)
Mareshall Av. RG42: Warf . . . 7N 15
Mare St. GU8: Hasc . . . 6N 153
Mareth Cl. GU11: Alde . . . 2N 109
Marfleet Cl. SM5: Cars . . . 8C 44
Margaret Cl. TW18: Stain . . . 7M 21
Margaret Herbison Ho.
SW6 . . . 2L 13
(off Clem Attlee Ct.)
Margaret Ho. *W6 . . . 1H 13*
(off Queen Caroline St.)
Margaret Ingram Cl.
SW6 . . . 2L 13
Margaret Lockwood Cl.
KT1: K Tham . . . 7M 203 (3M 41)
Margaret Rd.
GU1: Guil . . . 4B 202 (4M 113)
Margaret Rutherford Pl.
SW12 . . . 2G 28
Margaret Way CR5: Coul . . . 6M 83
MARGERY . . . 7M 101
Margery Gro. KT20: Lwr K . . . 7K 101
Margery La. KT20: Lwr K . . . 7L 101
Margery Wood La.
KT20: Lwr K . . . 7L 101
Margin Dr. SW19 . . . 6J 27
Margravine Gdns. W6 . . . 1J 13
Margravine Rd. W6 . . . 1J 13
Marham Gdns. SM4: Mord . . . 5A 44
SW18 . . . 2C 28
Maria Ct. SE25 . . . 1B 46
Marian Ct. SM1: Sut . . . 2N 61
Marianne North Gallery . . . 5M 11
Marian Rd. SW16 . . . 9G 29
Maria Theresa Cl.
KT3: N Mal . . . 4C 42
Mariette Way SM6: W'ton . . . 5J 63
Marigold Cl. RG45: Crow . . . 9E 30
Marigold Ct. GU1: Guil . . . 9A 94
Marigold Dr. GU24: Bis . . . 2D 72
Marigold Way CR0: Croy . . . 7G 46
Marina Av. KT3: N Mal . . . 4G 42
Marina Cl. KT16: Chert . . . 7L 37
Marina Pl. *KT1: H Wic . . . 1K 41*
(off Old Bri. St.)
Marina Way TW11: Tedd . . . 8K 25
Marinefield Rd. SW6 . . . 5N 13
Mariner Bus. Cen.
CR0: Wad . . . 2L 63
Mariner Gdns.
TW10: Ham . . . 4J 25
Mariners Dr. GU3: Norm . . . 9M 91
GU14: Farnb . . . 8A 70
Marion Av. TW17: Shep . . . 4C 38
Marion M. SE21 . . . 4N 29
Marion Rd. CR7: T Hea . . . 4N 45
RH10: Craw . . . 5F 182
Marius Mans. SW17 . . . 3E 28
Marius Rd. SW17 . . . 3E 28
Marjoram Cl. GU2: Guil . . . 8K 93
GU14: Cove . . . 1G 89
Marjorie Fosters Way
GU24: B'wood . . . 6A 72
Marke Cl. BR2: Kes . . . 1G 66
Markedge La. CR5: Coul . . . 2D 102
RH1: Reig . . . 2D 102
Markenfield Rd.
GU1: Guil . . . 3C 202 (3N 113)
Markenhorn GU7: Goda . . . 4G 132
Market, The SM5: Sut . . . 7A 44
Market Cen., The
UB2: S'hall . . . 1J 9
Market Dr. W4 . . . 3D 12
Marketfield Rd. RH1: Red . . . 3D 122
Marketfield Way RH1: Red . . . 3D 122
Market Pde. SE25 . . . 3D 46
TW13: Hanw . . . 4M 23
Market Pl.
KT1: K Tham . . . 3H 203 (1K 41)
RG12: Brac . . . 1N 31
RG40: W'ham . . . 2B 30
SL3: Coln . . . 3E 6
TW8: Brent . . . 3J 11
Market Rd. TW9: Rich . . . 6N 11
Market Sq. GU21: Wok . . . 4A 74
KT1: K Tham . . . 4H 203
(off Market Pl.)
RH12: Hors . . . 7J 197
TN16: Weste . . . 4M 107
TW18: Stain . . . 6G 21
Market St.
GU1: Guil . . . 5C 202 (4N 113)
RG12: Brac . . . 1N 31
SL4: W'sor . . . 4G 5
Market Ter. *TW8: Brent . . . 2L 11*
(off Albany Rd.)
Market Way TN16: Weste . . . 4M 107
Markfield CR0: Sels . . . 6J 65
(not continuous)
Markfield Rd. CR3: Cate . . . 4E 104
Markham Ct. GU15: Camb . . . 9B 50
Markham M.
RG40: W'ham . . . 2A 30
Markham Rd. RH5: Cap . . . 5J 159
Markhole Cl. TW12: Hamp . . . 8N 23
Mark Oak La. KT22: Fetc . . . 9A 78
Marksbury Av. TW9: Rich . . . 6N 11
Marks Rd. CR6: Warl . . . 5H 85
Marks St. RH2: Reig . . . 2N 121
Markville Gdns. CR3: Cate . . . 3D 104
Mark Way GU7: Hurt . . . 3E 132
Markway TW16: Sunb . . . 1K 39
Markwick La. GU8: Loxh . . . 6L 153
Marlborough *SW19 . . . 2J 27*
(off Inner Pk. Rd.)
Marlborough Bus. Cen.
KT16: Chert . . . 8H 37
Marlborough Cl.
GU51: Fleet . . . 5E 88
KT12: Hers . . . 9L 39
RH11: Craw . . . 7A 182
RH12: Hors . . . 3K 197
SW19 . . . 7C 28
Marlborough Ct.
CR2: S Croy . . . 7F 200
RG40: W'ham . . . 1C 30
RH4: Dork . . . 3K 201 (5H 119)
SM6: W'ton . . . 4G 62
TN16: Weste . . . 4L 107
(off Croydon Rd.)
Marlborough Cres. UB3: Harl . . . 3E 8
Marlborough Dr.
KT13: Weybr . . . 9D 38
Marlborough Gdns.
KT6: Surb . . . 6K 41
Marlborough Hill
RH4: Dork . . . 3K 201 (5H 119)
Marlborough M. SM7: Ban . . . 2M 81
Marlborough Pl.
RH12: Hors . . . 5H 197
(off Rushams Rd.)
Marlborough Ri.
GU15: Camb . . . 9C 50
Marlborough Rd.
CR2: S Croy . . . 4N 63
GU21: Wok . . . 3C 74
RH4: Dork . . . 2K 201 (5H 119)
SL3: Lang . . . 1A 6
SM1: Sut . . . 9M 43
SW19 . . . 7C 28
TW7: Isle . . . 4H 11
TW10: Rich . . . 9M 11
TW12: Hamp . . . 7A 24
TW13: Felt . . . 3L 23
TW15: A'ford . . . 6M 21
W4 . . . 1B 12
Marlborough Vw.
GU14: Cove . . . 9H 69
Marld, The KT21: A'tead . . . 5M 79
Marles La. RH14: Have . . . 7D 194
Marley Av. GU27: Hasl . . . 5C 188
Marley Cl. KT15: Addl . . . 3H 55
Marley Combe Rd.
GU27: Hasl . . . 3D 188
MARLEY COMMON . . . 5D 188
Marley Hanger GU27: Hasl . . . 5E 188
Marley Hgts. GU27: K Grn . . . 8D 188
Marley La.
GU27: Hasl, K Grn . . . 3C 188
Marley Ri. RH4: Dork . . . 8G 119
Marlfield Cl. KT4: W Pk . . . 7F 42
Marlhurst TN8: Eden . . . 8K 127
Marlin Cl. TW16: Sunb . . . 7F 22
Marling Ct. TW12: Hamp . . . 7N 23
Marlingdene Cl.
TW12: Hamp . . . 7A 24
MARLING PARK . . . 8N 23
Marlings Cl. CR3: Whyte . . . 4B 84
Marlins Cl. SM1: Sut . . . 2A 62
Marlow Cl. SE20 . . . 2E 46
Marlow Ct. RH10: Craw . . . 2B 182
Marlow Cres. TW1: Twick . . . 9F 10
Marlow Dr. SM3: Chea . . . 8J 43
Marlowe Ho. KT1: K Tham . . . 8H 203
Marlowe Sq. CR4: Mit . . . 3G 44
Marlowe Way CR0: Bedd . . . 8J 45
Marlow Ho. KT5: Surb . . . 8K 203
TW11: Tedd . . . 5G 25
Marlow Rd. SE20 . . . 2E 46
Marlpit Av. CR5: Coul . . . 4J 83
Marlpit Cl. RH19: E Grin . . . 7A 166
TN8: Eden . . . 8L 127
MARLPIT HILL . . . 8K 127
Marlpit La. CR5: Coul . . . 3H 83
Marl Rd. SW18 . . . 7N 13
Marlyns Cl. GU4: B'ham . . . 9C 94
Marlyns Dr. GU4: B'ham . . . 8C 94
Marmot Rd. TW4: Houn . . . 6L 9
Marncrest Cl. KT12: Hers . . . 2J 57
Marnell Way TW4: Houn . . . 6L 9
Marneys Cl. KT18: Eps . . . 2N 79
Marnfield Cres. SW2 . . . 2L 29
Marnham Pl. KT15: Addl . . . 1L 55
Marqueen Towers
SW16 . . . 8K 29
Marquis Ct. KT1: K Tham . . . 8H 203
KT19: Eps . . . 6J 201 (9C 60)
TW19: Stan . . . 2N 21
Marrick Cl. SW15 . . . 7F 12
Marriott Cl. TW14: Felt . . . 9E 8
Marriott Lodge Cl.
KT15: Addl . . . 1L 55
Marrowbrook Cl.
GU14: Cove . . . 2M 89
Marrowbrook La.
GU14: Cove . . . 3L 89
Marrowells KT13: Weybr . . . 9G 38
Marrow Meade GU51: Fleet . . . 2A 88
Marryat Cl. TW4: Houn . . . 7N 9
Marryat Pl. SW19 . . . 5K 27
Marryat Rd. SW19 . . . 6J 27
Marryat Sq. SW6 . . . 4K 13
Marsden Way BR6: Orp . . . 1N 67
Marshall Cl. CR2: Sande . . . 9D 64
GU14: Cove . . . 7L 69
GU16: Frim . . . 4H 71
TW4: Houn . . . 8N 9
Marshall Hall *TW20: Eng G . . . 4M 19*
(off Coopers Hill La.)
Marshall Pde. GU22: Pyr . . . 2H 75
Marshall Pl. KT15: N Haw . . . 5L 55
Marshall Rd. GU7: Goda . . . 6H 133
GU47: C Tow . . . 8J 49
RH10: Craw . . . 5G 182
Marshalls Cl.
KT19: Eps . . . 6H 201 (9B 60)
Marshall's Rd. SM1: Sut . . . 1N 61
Marsham Ho. RG42: Brac . . . 8N 15
Marsh Av. CR4: Mit . . . 1D 44
KT19: Ewe . . . 6D 60
Marsh Cl. GU35: Bor . . . 6A 168
Marsh Ct. RH11: Craw . . . 8N 181
SW19 . . . 9A 28
Marsh Farm Rd. TW2: Twick . . . 2F 24
Marshfield SL3: Dat . . . 4M 5
MARSH GREEN . . . 6K 147
Marsh Grn. Rd.
TN8: M Grn . . . 7K 147
Marshlands Cotts.
RH5: Newd . . . 7B 160
Marsh La. KT15: Addl . . . 1K 55
Marshwood Rd. GU18: Ligh . . . 7A 52
Marston KT19: Eps . . . 7B 60
Marston Av. KT9: Ches . . . 3L 59
Marston Ct. KT12: Wal T . . . 7K 39
Marston Dr. CR6: Warl . . . 5H 85
GU14: Farnb . . . 7N 69
Marston Rd. GU9: Farnh . . . 1E 128
GU21: Wok . . . 4L 73
TW11: Tedd . . . 6H 25
Marston Way SE19 . . . 8M 29
SL5: Asc . . . 1J 33
Martel Cl. GU15: Camb . . . 8G 50
Martell Rd. SE21 . . . 4N 29
Martens Pl. GU7: Goda . . . 5H 133
Martin Cl. CR2: Sels . . . 7G 64
CR6: Warl . . . 3E 84
RH11: Craw . . . 1B 182
SL4: W'sor . . . 4A 4
Martin Ct. CR2: S Croy . . . 8F 200
Martin Cres. CR0: Croy . . . 7L 45
Martindale SW14 . . . 8B 12
Martindale Av. GU15: Camb . . . 2G 71
Martindale Cl. GU4: Guil . . . 1F 114
Martindale Rd. GU21: Wok . . . 5K 73
SW12 . . . 1F 28
TW4: Houn . . . 6M 9
Martineau Cl. KT10: Esh . . . 1D 58
Martineau Dr. RH4: Dork . . . 7H 119
TW1: Twick . . . 7H 11
Martingale Cl. TW16: Sunb . . . 3H 39
Martingale Ct. GU11: Alde . . . 2K 109
Martingales Cl. TW10: Ham . . . 4K 25
Martin Gro. SM4: Mord . . . 2M 43
Martin Rd. GU2: Guil . . . 1K 113
Martins, The
RH10: Craw D . . . 1F 184
Martins Cl. BR4: W Wick . . . 7N 47
GU1: Guil . . . 2E 114
GU17: B'water . . . 2J 69
Martin's Dr. RG41: W'ham . . . 9A 14
MARTIN'S HERON . . . 2D 32
Martin's Heron Station (Rail)
. . . 3D 32
Martin's La. RG12: Brac . . . 2C 32
Martins Pk. Cvn. Pk.
GU14: Cove . . . 7J 69
Martins Wood GU8: Mil . . . 3B 152
Martinsyde GU22: Wok . . . 4E 74
Martin Way GU16: Frim . . . 5C 70
GU21: Wok . . . 5K 73
SM4: Mord . . . 2K 43
SW20 . . . 1J 43

Martlands Ind. Est.—Melfort Av.

Martlands Ind. Est.
GU22: Wok ... 1K 93
Martlets, The RH10: Craw ... 3C 182
Martlets Cl. RH12: Hors ... 3J 197
Martletts Cnr.
RH12: Rudg ... 1E 194
Marts, The RH12: Rudg ... 1E 194
Martyns Pl. RH19: E Grin ... 1B 186
Martyr Rd.
GU1: Guil ... 5C 202 (4N 113)
Martyrs Av. RH11: Craw ... 9A 162
MARTYR'S GREEN ... 7E 76
Martyr's La. GU21: Wok ... 8D 54
Marvell Cl. RH10: Craw ... 1G 182
Marville Rd. SW6 ... 3L 13
Marwell TN16: Weste ... 4K 107
Mary Adelaide Cl.
SW15 ... 5D 26
Mary Drew Almshouses
TW20: Eng G ... 7N 19
Mary Flowers Hall
SL5: S'hill ... 2C 34
(off Buckhurst Rd.)
Mary Flux Ct. *SW5 ... 1N 13*
(off Bramham Gdns.)
Maryhill Cl. CR8: Ken ... 4N 83
Mary Holben Ho.
SW16 ... 6G 28
Mary Ho. *W6 ... 1H 13*
(off Queen Caroline St.)
Maryland Rd. CR7: T Hea ... 9M 29
Maryland Way
TW16: Sunb ... 1H 39
Marylebone Gdns.
TW9: Rich ... 7N 11
Mary Macarthur Ho.
W6 ... 2K 13
Mary Mead RG42: Warf ... 7B 16
Mary Rd.
GU1: Guil ... 4B 202 (4M 113)
Mary Rose Cl. TW12: Hamp ... 9A 24
Mary Smith Ct. *SW5 ... 1M 13*
(off Trebovir Rd.)
Mary's Ter. TW1: Twick ... 1G 24
(not continuous)
Mary Va. GU7: Goda ... 9G 133
Mary Wallace Theatre ... 2G 25
Marzell Ho. *W14 ... 1L 13*
(off North End Rd.)
Marzena Ct. TW3: Houn ... 9C 10
Masault Ct. *TW9: Rich ... 7L 11*
(off Kew Foot Rd.)
Mascotte Rd. SW15 ... 7J 13
Masefield Ct. KT6: Surb ... 6K 41
Masefield Gdns.
RG45: Crow ... 4G 48
Masefield Rd. RH11: Craw ... 6K 181
TW12: Hamp ... 5N 23
Masefield Way TW19: Stan ... 2A 22
Maskall Cl. SW2 ... 2L 29
Maskani Wlk. SW16 ... 8G 29
Maskell Rd. SW17 ... 4A 28
Maskell Way GU14: Cove ... 2H 89
Mason Cl. GU46: Yate ... 1D 68
RH19: E Grin ... 8A 166
SW20 ... 9J 27
TW12: Hamp ... 9N 23
Masonettes *KT19: Ewe ... 6C 60*
(off Sefton Rd.)
Masonic Hall Rd.
KT16: Chert ... 5H 37
Mason Pl. GU47: Sandh ... 7E 48
Mason Rd. GU14: Cove ... 8K 69
RH10: Craw ... 5C 182
SM1: Sut ... 2N 61
Mason's Av.
CR0: Croy ... 5C 200 (9N 45)
Mason's Bri. Rd.
RH1: Red, Salf ... 8F 122
Masons Fld. RH13: M Hea ... 9B 198
Masons Paddock
RH4: Dork ... 3G 118
Masons Pl. CR4: Mit ... 9D 28
Mason's Yd. SW19 ... 6J 27
Mason Way GU11: Alde ... 5N 109
Massetts Rd. RH6: Horl ... 9D 142
Massingberd Way
SW17 ... 5F 28
Master Cl. RH8: Oxt ... 7A 106
Masters Cl. SW16 ... 7G 29
MASWELL PARK ... 8C 10
Maswell Pk. Cres.
TW3: Houn ... 8C 10
Maswell Pk. Rd.
TW3: Houn ... 8B 10
Matcham Ct. *TW1: Twick ... 9K 11*
(off Clevedon Rd.)
Matham Rd. KT8: E Mol ... 4D 40
Matheson Rd. W14 ... 1L 13
Mathew Ter. GU11: Alde ... 2A 110
Mathias Cl.
KT18: Eps ... 7H 201 (9B 60)
Mathisen Way SL3: Poy ... 4G 7
Mathison Ho. *SW10 ... 3N 13*
(off Coleridge Gdns.)
Mathon Ct. GU1: Guil ... 3B 114
Matlock Cres. SM3: Chea ... 1K 61
Matlock Gdns. SM3: Chea ... 1K 61
Matlock Pl. SM3: Chea ... 1K 61
Matlock Rd. CR3: Cate ... 8B 84
Matlock Way KT3: N Mal ... 9C 26
Maton Ho. *SW6 ... 3L 13*
(off Estcourt Rd.)
Matthew Arnold Cl.
KT11: Cob ... 1H 77
TW18: Stain ... 7L 21
Matthew Arnold Sports Cen.
... 7L 21
Matthew Ct. CR4: Mit ... 4H 45
Matthew Rd. GU11: Alde ... 4K 109
Matthews Chase RG42: Bin ... 8L 15
Matthews Cl. GU14: Farnb ... 5B 90
Matthews Ct. SL5: S'hill ... 3A 34
Matthews Dr. RH10: Craw ... 7F 182
Matthews Gdns.
CR0: N Add ... 7N 65
Matthewsgreen Rd.
RG41: W'ham ... 9A 14
Matthews La. TW18: Stain ... 5H 21
Matthews Lodge
KT15: Addl ... 1M 55
Matthews Rd.
GU15: Camb ... 7A 50
Matthews St. RH2: Reig ... 7M 121
Matthews Way GU51: Fleet ... 3A 88
Matthews Yd. CR0: Croy ... 4B 200
Matthey Pl. RH10: Craw ... 9H 163
Maudit Ho. *GU51: Fleet ... 2A 88*
(off Rykmansford Rd.)
Maudsley Ho. TW8: Brent ... 1L 11
Maultway, The GU15: Camb ... 7F 50
Maultway Cl. GU15: Camb ... 7F 50
Maultway Cres.
GU15: Camb ... 7F 50
Maultway Nth. GU15: Camb ... 6E 50
Maunsell Pk. RH10: Craw ... 3F 182
Maureen Campbell Ct.
TW17: Shep ... 4C 38
(off Harrison Way)
Maureen Ct. BR3: Beck ... 1F 46
Maurice Av. CR3: Cate ... 9A 84
Maurice Ct. TW8: Brent ... 3K 11
Mausoleum ... 6J 5
Mauveine Gdns.
TW3: Houn ... 7A 10
Mavins Rd. GU9: Farnh ... 3J 129
Mavis Av. KT19: Ewe ... 2D 60
Mavis Cl. KT19: Ewe ... 2D 60
Mawbey Rd. KT16: Otter ... 3F 54
Mawson Cl. SW20 ... 1K 43
Mawson La. W4 ... 2E 12
Maxine Cl. GU47: Sandh ... 6G 48
Maxton Wlk. RH11: Craw ... 8N 181
Maxwell Cl. CR0: Wad ... 7J 45
Maxwell Dr. KT14: W By ... 7L 55
Maxwell Rd. SW6 ... 3N 13
TW15: A'ford ... 7D 22
Maxwell Way RH10: Craw ... 9E 162
May Bate Av.
KT2: K Tham ... 1H 203 (9K 25)
Maybelle Cl. RH5: B Grn ... 8K 139
Mayberry Pl. KT5: Surb ... 6M 41
Maybourne Ri. GU22: Wok ... 2N 93
Maybrick Cl. GU47: Sandh ... 6E 48
MAYBURY ... 3E 74
Maybury Cl. GU16: Frim ... 6B 70
KT20: Tad ... 6K 81
Maybury Ct. CR2: S Croy ... 8A 200
Maybury Est. GU22: Wok ... 3E 74
Maybury Hill GU22: Wok ... 3D 74
Maybury Rd. GU21: Wok ... 4B 74
Maybury Rough
GU22: Wok ... 4D 74
Maybury St. SW17 ... 6C 28
May Cl. GU7: Goda ... 9E 132
GU35: Head ... 5D 168
GU47: Owls ... 7J 49
KT9: Ches ... 3M 59
May Ct. *SW19 ... 9A 28*
(off Pincott Rd.)
May Cres. GU12: Ash ... 3C 110
Maycross Av. SM4: Mord ... 3L 43
Mayday Rd. CR7: T Hea ... 5M 45
Maydwell Av. RH13: Slin ... 6J 195
Mayell Cl. KT22: Leat ... 1J 99
Mayes Cl. CR6: Warl ... 5G 85
RH10: Craw ... 4G 182
MAYES GREEN ... 7M 157
Mayes La. RH12: Warn ... 7E 178
Mayfair Av. KT4: W Pk ... 7F 42
TW2: Whitt ... 1C 24
Mayfair Cl. KT6: Surb ... 7L 41
Mayfield GU10: Rowl ... 8E 128
KT22: Leat ... 8J 79
RH7: Dorm ... 1C 166
RH10: Wor ... 3H 183
Mayfield Av. KT15: N Haw ... 6K 55
W4 ... 1D 12
Mayfield Cl. GU9: B Lea ... 6N 109
KT7: T Dit ... 7H 41
KT12: Hers ... 1H 57
KT15: N Haw ... 6L 55
RH1: Red ... 9E 122
SE20 ... 1E 46
TW15: A'ford ... 7C 22
Mayfield Ct. RH1: Red ... 8D 122
Mayfield Cres. CR7: T Hea ... 3K 45
Mayfield Dr. SL4: W'sor ... 6D 4
Mayfield Gdns. KT12: Hers ... 1H 57
KT15: N Haw ... 6K 55
TW18: Stain ... 7H 21
Mayfield Grn. KT23: Book ... 5A 98
Mayfield Light Ind. Est.
SL4: Wink ... 4M 17
Mayfield Mans.
SW15 ... 8L 13
Mayfield Rd. CR2: Sande ... 5A 64
CR7: T Hea ... 3K 45
GU14: Cove, Farnb ... 7L 69
GU15: Camb ... 5N 69
KT12: Hers ... 1H 57
KT13: Weybr ... 2A 56
SM2: Sut ... 3B 62
SW19 ... 9L 27
Mayflower Cl. RH10: Craw ... 4H 183
Mayflower Dr. GU46: Yate ... 8A 48
MAYFORD ... 9M 73
Mayford Cl. BR3: Beck ... 2G 47
GU22: Wok ... 9N 73
SW12 ... 1D 28
Mayford Grn. GU22: Wok ... 9M 73
Mayford Rd. SW12 ... 1D 28
Mayhurst Av. GU22: Wok ... 3E 74
Mayhurst Cl. GU22: Wok ... 3E 74
Mayhurst Cres. GU22: Wok ... 3E 74
Mayhurst M. GU22: Wok ... 3E 74
Maynard Cl. RH10: Cop ... 6N 163
SW6 ... 3N 13
Maynard Ct. SL4: W'sor ... 4D 4
TW18: Stain ... 5J 21
Maynooth Gdns.
SM5: Cars ... 6D 44
Mayo Rd. CR0: Croy ... 4A 46
KT12: Wal T ... 6H 39
Maypole Rd.
RH19: Ash W ... 3G 186
RH19: E Grin ... 8N 165
May Rd. TW2: Twick ... 2E 24
Mayroyd Av. KT6: Surb ... 8N 41
Mays Cl. KT13: Weybr ... 6A 56
Mays Cft. RG12: Brac ... 3M 31
Maysfield Rd. GU23: Send ... 1F 94
MAY'S GREEN ... 7F 76
Mays Gro. GU23: Send ... 1F 94
Mays Rd. RG40: W'ham ... 2D 30
TW11: Tedd ... 6D 24
May St. W14 ... 1L 13
(North End Rd.)
W14 ... 1L 13
(Vereker Rd.)
Maytree Cl. GU1: Guil ... 8M 93
Maytree Ct. CR4: Mit ... 2E 44
Maytrees GU21: Knap ... 4F 72
Maytree Wlk. SW2 ... 3L 29
Maywater Cl. CR2: Sande ... 7A 64
Maywood Dr. GU15: Camb ... 8F 50
Maze Rd. TW9: Kew ... 3N 11
Meachen Ct. RG40: W'ham ... 2B 30
Mead, The BR3: Beck ... 1M 47
BR4: W Wick ... 7N 47
GU14: Farnb ... 2N 89
KT21: A'tead ... 6L 79
RH4: Dork ... 8J 119
SM6: W'ton ... 3H 63
Mead Av. RH1: Salf ... 2E 142
Mead Cl. GU6: Cranl ... 8N 155
RH1: Red ... 9E 102
TW20: Egh ... 7D 20
Mead Ct. GU21: Knap ... 3H 73
TW20: Egh ... 7E 20
Mead Cres. KT23: Book ... 3A 98
SM1: Sut ... 9C 44
Meade Cl. W4 ... 2N 11
Meade Ct. GU19: Bag ... 4K 51
KT20: Wal H ... 2F 100
Mead End KT21: A'tead ... 4M 79
Meades, The KT13: Weybr ... 3D 56
RH7: Dorm ... 1C 166
Meades Cl. RH7: Dorm ... 1D 166
Meadfoot Rd. SW16 ... 8G 28
Meadhurst Pk. TW16: Sunb ... 7F 22
Meadhurst Rd. KT16: Chert ... 7K 37
Meadhurst Sports Club ... 6G 22
Meadlands Dr. TW10: Ham ... 3K 25
Mead La. GU9: Farnh ... 1G 128
KT16: Chert ... 6K 37
Meadow, The RH10: Cop ... 7L 163
Meadow App. RH10: Cop ... 7L 163
Meadow Av. CR0: Croy ... 5G 47
Meadow Bank GU1: Guil ... 1M 113
GU9: Farnh ... 1G 128
KT24: E Hor ... 5G 96
Meadowbank KT5: Surb ... 5M 41
Meadowbank Cl. SW6 ... 3H 13
Meadowbank Gdns.
TW5: C'ford ... 4H 9
Meadowbank Rd.
GU18: Ligh ... 6N 51
Meadowbrook RH8: Oxt ... 8M 105
Meadowbrook Cl. SL3: Poy ... 4H 7
Meadowbrook Ct. TW7: Isle ... 6E 10
Meadow Brook Ind. Cen.
RH10: Craw ... 9E 162
Meadowbrook Rd.
RH4: Dork ... 1J 201 (4G 119)
Meadow Cl. CR8: Pur ... 9H 63
GU7: Goda ... 4H 133
GU8: Mil ... 1D 152
GU12: A Va ... 4D 90
GU17: Haw ... 2J 69
KT10: H Wood ... 9F 40
KT12: Hers ... 1N 57
RH10: Cop ... 7L 163
RH12: Hors ... 3N 197
SL4: O Win ... 8L 5
SM1: Sut ... 8A 44
SW20 ... 3H 43
TW4: Houn ... 9A 10
TW10: Ham ... 2L 25
Meadow Cotts.
GU24: W End ... 8C 52
Meadow Ct. GU14: Cove ... 1L 89
GU51: Fleet ... 4A 88
KT18: Eps ... 7H 201 (9B 60)
RH1: Mers ... 8G 103
RH19: E Grin ... 8A 166
TW3: Houn ... 9B 10
TW18: Stain ... 4G 20
Meadowcroft *W4 ... 1N 11*
(off Brooks Rd.)
Meadowcroft Cl.
RH6: Horl ... 2G 162
RH11: Craw ... 4L 181
RH19: E Grin ... 8M 165
Meadow Dr. GU23: Rip ... 1H 95
Meadow Farm La.
RH12: Hors ... 1M 197
Meadow Gdns.
TW18: Stain ... 6F 20
Meadow Ga.
KT21: A'tead ... 4L 79
Meadowgate *RH12: Hors ... 1M 197*
(off Giblets La.)
Meadow Ga. Av.
GU14: Farnb ... 3L 89
Meadow Hill CR5: Coul ... 1G 82
CR8: Pur ... 1G 82
KT3: N Mal ... 5D 42
Meadow Ho. *GU4: Guil ... 2F 114*
(off Merrow St.)
GU17: Haw ... 2K 69
Meadowlands
GU4: W Cla ... 8K 95
KT11: Cob ... 9H 57
RH8: Oxt ... 3C 126
RH11: Craw ... 3A 182
Meadowlands Pk.
KT15: Addl ... 9N 37
Meadow La. KT22: Fetc ... 9C 78
SL4: E Wic ... 2E 4
TN8: Eden ... 8K 127
Meadowlea Cl. UB7: Harm ... 2M 7
Meadow Pl. W4 ... 3D 12
Meadow Ri. CR5: Coul ... 9H 63
GU21: Knap ... 4F 72
Meadow Rd. GU4: B'ham ... 8C 94
GU14: Farnb ... 7N 69
GU25: V Wat ... 4H 35
KT10: Clay ... 3E 58
KT21: A'tead ... 4L 79
SM1: Sut ... 1C 62
SW19 ... 8A 28
TW13: Felt ... 3M 23
TW15: A'ford ... 6E 22
Meadows, The CR6: Warl ... 4G 85
GU2: Guil ... 8B 202 (6M 113)
GU10: Churt ... 9L 149
GU12: Ash ... 2F 110
(off Chester Rd.)
GU47: C Tow ... 1K 69
Meadows Bus. Pk., The
GU17: B'water ... 1K 69
Meadows End
TW16: Sunb ... 9H 23
Meadowside KT12: Wal T ... 8K 39
KT23: Book ... 1A 98
RH6: Horl ... 7F 142
TW1: Twick ... 1K 25
TW18: Stain ... 6J 21
Meadowside Pk.
RH7: Ling ... 5M 145
Meadowside Rd.
SM2: Chea ... 5K 61
Meadows Leigh Cl.
KT13: Weybr ... 9C 38
Meadow Stile
CR0: Croy ... 5C 200 (9N 45)
Meadowsweet Cl.
SW20 ... 3H 43
Meadow Va. GU27: Hasl ... 2E 188
Meadow Vw. GU35: Bor ... 6A 168
KT16: Chert ... 7L 37
RH6: Smal ... 8N 143
TW19: Stan M ... 8H 7
Meadow Vw. Rd.
CR7: T Hea ... 4M 45
Meadowview Rd.
KT19: Ewe ... 5D 60
Meadow Wlk. KT17: Ewe ... 3D 60
KT19: Ewe ... 3D 60
(not continuous)
KT20: Wal H ... 2G 100
SM6: W'ton ... 9F 44
Meadow Way
GU10: Rowl ... 8E 128
GU12: Alde ... 1D 110
GU17: B'water ... 1H 69
GU24: W End ... 8C 52
KT9: Ches ... 2L 59
KT15: Addl ... 1K 55
KT20: Tad ... 4K 81
KT23: Book ... 1B 98
KT24: W Hors ... 3E 96
RG42: Brac ... 8M 15
RH2: Reig ... 7N 121
SL4: O Win ... 9L 5
Meadow Waye
TW5: Hest ... 2M 9
Mead Path SW17 ... 5A 28
Mead Pl.
CR0: Croy ... 1A 200 (7N 45)
RH6: Smal ... 8N 143
Mead Rd. CR3: Cate ... 1C 104
GU6: Cranl ... 7N 155
GU26: Hind ... 5D 170
KT12: Hers ... 1M 57
RH10: Craw ... 2D 182
TN8: Eden ... 4M 147
TW10: Ham ... 4J 25
Meadrow GU7: Goda ... 6J 133
Meadrow Ct. GU7: Goda ... 5K 133
Meads, The GU27: Hasl ... 2D 188
RH19: E Grin ... 2A 186
SL4: W'sor ... 5D 4
SM3: Chea ... 9K 43
SM4: Mord ... 4C 44
Meadside *GU22: Wok ... 5B 74*
(off Park Dr.)
KT18: Eps ... 7J 201
Meads Rd. GU1: Guil ... 3D 114
MEAD VALE ... 5B 122
Meadvale RH12: Hors ... 6F 196
Meadvale Rd. CR0: Croy ... 6C 46
Mead Way CR0: Croy ... 8H 47
CR5: Coul ... 5J 83
GU4: B'ham ... 7E 94
Meadway BR3: Beck ... 1M 47
CR6: Warl ... 3F 84
GU16: Frim ... 4D 70
GU27: Hasl ... 2D 188
KT5: Surb ... 7B 42
KT10: Esh ... 5B 58
KT19: Eps ... 5G 201 (8B 60)
KT22: Oxs ... 1E 78
KT24: Eff ... 6M 97
SW20 ... 3H 43
TW2: Twick ... 2D 24
TW15: A'ford ... 5B 22
TW18: Stain ... 8J 21
Meadway, The RH6: Horl ... 8G 142
Meadway Cl. TW18: Stain ... 8H 21
Meadway Ct. TW11: Tedd ... 6J 25
Meadway Dr. GU21: Wok ... 3M 73
KT15: Addl ... 4L 55
Mead Way Path CR5: Coul ... 5K 83
Meare Cl. KT20: Tad ... 1H 101
MEATH GREEN ... 6D 142
Meath Grn. Av. RH6: Horl ... 6D 142
Meath Grn. La. RH6: Horl ... 3C 142
Mecca Bingo
Croydon ... 2B 200
Earlsfield ... 2N 27
Fulham Broadway ... 3M 13
(off Vanston Pl.)
Hounslow ... 5C 10
Rosehill ... 6A 44
Medawar Rd. GU2: Guil ... 4G 113
Medcroft Gdns. SW14 ... 7B 12
Mede Cl. TW19: Wray ... 2N 19
Mede Ct. TW18: Stain ... 4G 20
Mede Fld. KT22: Fetc ... 2D 98
Medfield St. SW15 ... 1F 26
Medhurst Cl. GU24: Chob ... 5J 53
Medieval Undercroft ... 6C 202
Medina Av. KT10: H Wood ... 9E 40
Medina Sq. KT19: Eps ... 5N 59
Medlake Pl. TW20: Egh ... 8E 20
Medlake Rd. TW20: Egh ... 7E 20
Medland Cl. SM6: W'ton ... 7E 44
Medlar Cl. GU1: Guil ... 1M 113
RH11: Craw ... 9A 162
Medlar Dr. GU17: Haw ... 3L 69
Medlars Ct. RH5: Newd ... 1A 160
Medonte Cl. GU51: Fleet ... 5C 88
Medora Rd. SW2 ... 1K 29
Medway RH10: T Hil ... 4D 184
Medway Cl. CR0: Croy ... 5F 46
Medway Ct. RH12: Hors ... 3A 198
Medway Dr. GU14: Cove ... 8K 69
RH18: F Row ... 7J 187
RH19: E Grin ... 3N 185
Medway Ho.
KT2: K Tham ... 1H 203 (9K 25)
Medway Rd. RH11: Craw ... 4L 181
Medway Vw. RH18: F Row ... 7J 187
Medwin Wlk. RH12: Hors ... 6J 197
Megabowl
Croydon ... 8K 45
Feltham ... 3J 23
Kingston upon Thames
... 3K 203
(in The Rotunda Cen.)
Streatham Hill ... 3J 29
Melancholy Wlk.
TW10: Ham ... 3J 25
Melbourne Cl. SM6: W'ton ... 2G 62
Melbourne Mans. *W14 ... 2K 13*
(off Musard Rd.)
Melbourne Rd. SM6: W'ton ... 2F 62
SW19 ... 9M 27
TW11: Tedd ... 7J 25
Melbourne Ter. *SW6 ... 3N 13*
(off Moore Pk. Rd.)
Melbourne Way
RH12: Hors ... 3M 197
Melbray M. SW6 ... 5L 13
Melbury Cl. KT10: Clay ... 3H 59
KT14: W By ... 1J 75
KT16: Chert ... 6J 37
Melbury Gdns. SW20 ... 9G 26
Meldon Cl. SW6 ... 4N 13
Meldone Cl. KT5: Surb ... 6A 42
Meldrum Cl. RH8: Oxt ... 1B 126
Melford Cl. KT9: Ches ... 2M 59
Melfort Av. CR7: T Hea ... 2M 45

Melfort Rd.—Mill La.

Melfort Rd. CR7: T Hea 2M 45
Melina Ct. SW15 . . . . .6F 12
Melksham Cl. GU47: Owls 6J 49
RH13: Hors 7L 197
Meller Cl. CR0: Bedd 9J 45
Mellersh Hill Rd.
GU5: Wone 4D 134
Mellifont Cl. SM5: Cars 6B 44
Mellison Rd. SW17 . . . . .6C 28
Melliss Av. TW9: Kew 4A 12
Mellor Cl. KT12: Wal T 6N 39
Mellor Wlk. *SL4: W'sor* *4G 4*
(off Batchelors Acre)
Mellow Cl. SM7: Ban 1A 82
Mellows Rd. SM6: W'ton 2H 63
Melody Rd. TN16: B Hil 5E 86
Melrose RG12: Brac 7N 31
Melrose Av. CR4: Mit 8F 28
GU14: Cove 9H 69
SW16 . . . . .2K 45
SW19 . . . . .3L 27
TW2: Whitt 1B 24
Melrose Cl. GU14: Cove 9H 69
Melrose Cres. BR6: Orp 1M 67
Melrose Gdns. KT3: N Mal 2C 42
KT12: Hers 2K 57
Melrose Rd. CR5: Coul 2F 82
KT13: Weybr 2B 56
SW13 . . . . .5E 12
SW18 . . . . .9L 13
SW19 . . . . .1M 43
TN16: B Hil 3E 86
Melrose Tudor *SM6: W'ton* *2J 63*
(off Plough La.)
Melsa Rd. SM4: Mord 5A 44
Melton Ct. SM2: Sut 4A 62
Melton Flds. KT19: Ewe 5C 60
Melton Pl. KT19: Ewe 5C 60
Melton Rd. RH1: Mers 8G 102
Melville Av. CR2: S Croy 2C 64
GU16: Frim 5D 70
SW20 . . . . .8F 26
Melville Ct.
GU2: Guil 8B 202 (6M 113)
W4 . . . .*1N 11*
(off Haining Cl.)
Melville Rd. SW13 . . . . .4F 12
Melville Ter. GU9: Farnh 1G 128
Melvinshaw KT22: Leat 8J 79
Membury Cl. GU16: Frim 7E 70
Membury Wlk. RG12: Brac 3C 32
Memorial Cl. RH8: Oxt 5N 105
TW5: Hest 2N 9
Memorial Gdns. 3C 182
Mendip Cl. KT4: W Pk 7H 43
SL3: Lang 1C 6
UB3: Harl 3E 8
Mendip Rd. GU14: Cove 7K 69
RG12: Brac 4C 32
Mendip Wlk. RH11: Craw 3N 181
Mendora Rd. SW6 . . . . .3K 13
Menin Way GU9: Farnh 2J 129
Menlo Gdns. SE19 . . . . .8N 29
Mentone Mans. *SW10* *3N 13*
(off Fulham Rd.)
Meon Cl. GU14: Cove 8J 69
KT20: Tad 9G 80
Meon Ct. TW7: Isle 5E 10
Meopham Rd. CR4: Mit 9G 28
Merantun Way SW19 . . . . .9N 27
Mercedes-Benz World 5A 56
Mercer Cl. KT7: T Dit 6F 40
RH10: Craw 6G 182
Mercer Rd. RH12: Hors 9J 179
Mercers Country Pk. 9H 103
Merchants Cl. GU21: Knap 4F 72
SE25 . . . . .3D 46
Mercia Ho. TW15: A'ford 9D 22
Mercia Wlk. GU21: Wok 4B 74
Mercier Rd. SW15 . . . . .8K 13
Mercury Cen. TW14: Felt 8H 9
Mercury Cl. GU35: Bor 6A 168
RH11: Craw 6K 181
Mercury Ho. *TW8: Brent* *2J 11*
(off Glenhurst Rd.)
Mercury Rd. TW8: Brent 2J 11
Merebank RH5: B Grn 7K 139
Merebank La. CR0: Wad 2K 63
Mere Cl. SW15 . . . . .1J 27
Meredyth Rd. SW13 . . . . .5F 12
Mere End CR0: Croy 6G 47
Merefield Gdns. KT20: Tad 6J 81
Mere Rd. KT13: Weybr 9E 38
KT20: Tad 2G 101
TW17: Shep 5C 38
Mereside Pk. TW15: A'ford 5D 22
Mereside Pl. GU25: V Wat 7K 35
Merevale Cres. SM4: Mord 5A 44
Mereway Rd. TW2: Twick 2D 24
Merewood Gdns. CR0: Croy . . .6G 46
Mereworth Dr.
RH10: Craw 1H 183
Merideth Ct.
KT1: K Tham . . .4M 203 (1M 41)
Meridian Cen. CR0: N Add 6A 66
Meridian Cl. RH11: Craw 6L 181
Meridian Ct. RH19: F Row 9A 186
SL5: Asc 7M 33
Meridian Gro. RH6: Horl 7G 143
Meridian Way
RH19: E Grin 7B 166
Merivale Rd. SW15 . . . . .7K 13
Merland Cl. KT20: Tad 7H 81
Merland Grn. KT20: Tad 7H 81
Merland Ri. KT18: Tat C 6H 81
KT20: Tad 6H 81
MERLE COMMON 5D 126
Merle Comn. Rd.
RH8: Oxt 4C 126
Merlewood RG12: Brac 4B 32
Merlewood Cl. CR3: Cate 7A 84
Merlin Cen. RH11: Craw 7B 162
Merlin Cl.
CR0: Croy 6F 200 (1B 64)
CR4: Mit 2C 44
RH11: Ifi 3K 181
SL3: Lang 2D 6
SM6: W'ton 3K 63
Merlin Clove RG42: Wink R . . .7F 16
Merlin Ct. GU16: Frim 5B 70
GU21: Wok 1E 74
Merling Cl. KT9: Ches 2J 59
Merlin Gro. BR3: Beck 3J 47
Merlins Cl. GU9: Farnh 2H 129
Merlin Way GU14: Cove 2J 89
RH19: E Grin 7C 166
Merredene St. SW2 . . . . .1K 29
Merrilands Rd. KT4: W Pk 7H 43
Merrilyn Cl. KT10: Clay 3G 58
Merrington Rd. SW6 . . . . .2M 13
Merrin Hill CR2: Sande 7B 64
Merritt Gdns. KT9: Ches 3J 59
(not continuous)
Merrivale Gdns.
GU21: Wok 4M 73
Merron Cl. GU46: Yate 1B 68
MERROW 2D 114
Merrow Bus. Pk. GU4: Guil 9F 94
Merrow Chase GU1: Guil 3E 114
Merrow Comn. Rd.
GU4: Guil 9E 94
Merrow Copse GU1: Guil 2D 114
Merrow Ct. CR4: Mit 1B 44
GU1: Guil 3F 114
Merrow Cft. GU1: Guil 2E 114
MERROW DOWNS 4F 114
Merrow La.
GU4: B'ham, Guil 7E 94
Merrow Pl. GU4: Guil 1F 114
Merrow Rd. SM2: Chea 5J 61
Merrow St. GU4: Guil 1F 114
Merrow Way CR0: N Add 3M 65
GU1: Guil 2F 114
Merrow Woods GU1: Guil 1D 114
Merryacres GU8: Wit 4B 152
Merrydene Ct. RG12: Bin 1H 31
Merryfield Dr. RH12: Hors . . .6G 197
Merryhill Rd. RG42: Brac 8M 15
Merryhills Cl. TN16: B Hil 3F 86
Merryhills La. RH14: Loxw . . .3J 193
Merrylands KT16: Chert 9G 37
Merrylands Rd.
KT23: Book 1N 97
Merryman Dr. RG45: Crow 1E 48
Merrymeet SM7: Ban 1D 82
Merryweather Ct.
KT3: N Mal 4D 42
Merrywood Gro.
KT20: Lwr K 8K 101
Merrywood Pk.
GU15: Camb 2D 70
RH2: Reig 1N 121
Merrywood Pk. Cvn. Site
KT20: Box H 8A 100
Merryworth Cl.
GU12: Ash 3D 110
Mersey Ct. KT2: K Tham 1H 203
Mersham Pl. *CR7: T Hea* *1A 46*
(off Livingstone Rd.)
Mersham Rd. CR7: T Hea 2A 46
MERSTHAM 6G 102
Merstham Rd. RH1: Blet 7L 103
Merstham Station (Rail) 6G 102
Merthyr Ter. SW13 . . . . .2G 13
MERTON 8A 28
Merton Abbey Mills
SW19 . . . . .9A 28
Merton Av. W4 . . . . .1E 12
Merton Cl. GU47: Owls 5L 49
Merton Gdns. KT20: Tad 6J 81
Merton Hall Gdns.
SW20 . . . . .9K 27
Merton Hall Rd.
SW19 . . . . .8K 27
Merton High St. SW19 . . . . . . .8N 27
Merton Ind. Pk. SW19 . . . . . . .9N 27
Merton Mans. SW20 . . . . .1J 43
MERTON PARK 1M 43
Merton Pk. Pde.
SW19 . . . . .9L 27
Merton Park Stop (CT) 9M 27
Merton Pl. *SW19* *9A 28*
(off Nelson Gro. Rd.)
Merton Rd. RH11: Craw 9N 181
SE25 . . . . .4C 46
SW18 . . . . .9M 13
SW19 . . . . .8N 27
Merton Wlk. KT22: Leat 5G 79
Merton Way KT8: W Mole 3B 40
KT22: Leat 6G 79
Mervyn Rd. TW17: Shep 6D 38
Merwin Way SL4: W'sor 5A 4
Meryton Ho. SL4: W'sor 6D 4
Messenger Cl.
RH11: Craw 1M 181
Metana Ho. RH10: Craw 7E 162
Metcalf Rd. TW15: A'ford 6C 22
Metcalf Wlk. TW13: Hanw 5M 23
Metcalf Way RH11: Craw 8B 162
Meteor Way SM6: W'ton 4J 63
Metro Ind. Cen. TW7: Isle 5E 10
Metropolitan Club, The 1N 27
Metropolitan Sta. Bldgs.
W6 . . . .*1H 13*
(off Beadon Rd.)
Meudon Av. GU14: Farnb 2N 89
Mews, The
GU1: Guil 4A 202 (4M 113)
GU8: Duns 4B 174
RH2: Reig 2N 121
RH12: Bro H *4D 196*
(off Old Guildford Rd.)
TW1: Twick 9H 11
TW20: Eng G *5N 19*
(off Coopers Hill La.)
Mews Ct. RH19: E Grin 3B 186
Mews End TN16: B Hil 5F 86
Mexfield Rd. SW15 . . . . .8L 13
Meyrick Cl. GU21: Knap 3H 73
Michael Cres. RH6: Horl 1E 162
Michael Flds.
RH18: F Row 7G 186
Michael La. GU2: Guil 7L 93
Michaelmas Cl.
GU46: Yate 2C 68
SW20 . . . . .2H 43
Michael Rd. SE25 . . . . .2B 46
SW6 . . . . .4N 13
Michael Stewart Ho.
SW6 . . . .*2L 13*
(off Clem Attlee Ct.)
Micheldever Way
RG12: Brac 5D 32
Michelet Cl. GU18: Ligh 6M 51
Michelham Gdns.
KT20: Tad 7H 81
TW1: Twick 4F 24
Michell Cl. RH12: Hors 6G 197
Michelsdale Dr. TW9: Rich 7L 11
Michel's Row *TW9: Rich* *7L 11*
(off Michelsdale Dr.)
MICKLEHAM 6J 99
Mickleham By-Pass
RH5: Mick 5H 99
MICKLEHAM DOWNS 4K 99
Mickleham Dr. RH5: Mick 4J 99
Mickleham Gdns.
SM3: Chea 3K 61
Mickleham Way
CR0: N Add 4N 65
Mickle Hill GU47: Sandh 6F 48
Micklethwaite Rd.
SW6 . . . . .2M 13
Mick Mill's Race
RH13: Col 4E 198
Midas Metropolitan Ind. Est.
SM4: Mord 6H 43
Mid City Lanes
Croydon 3L 63
Middle Av. GU9: Farnh 3J 129
MIDDLE BOURNE 4H 129
Middle Bourne La.
GU10: L Bou 5G 129
Middle Church La.
GU9: Farnh 1G 129
Middle Cl. CR5: Coul 7L 83
GU15: Camb 9F 50
KT17: Eps 8D 60
Middle Farm Cl. KT24: Eff 5L 97
Middle Farm Pl. KT24: Eff 5K 97
Middlefield GU9: Farnh 4F 128
(not continuous)
RH6: Horl 7G 143
Middlefield Cl. GU9: Farnh . . .3F 128
Middlefields CR0: Sels 5H 65
Middle Gordon Rd.
GU15: Camb 1A 70
Middle Grn. RH3: Brock 5A 120
TW18: Stain 8M 21
Middle Grn. Cl. KT5: Surb 5M 41
Middle Hill GU11: Alde 1M 109
TW20: Egh, Eng G 5M 19
Middle La. KT17: Eps 8D 60
TW11: Tedd 7F 24
Middlemarch GU8: Wit 5B 152
Middlemead Cl.
KT23: Book 3A 98
Middlemead Rd.
KT23: Book 3N 97
Middle Mill Halls of Residence
KT1: K Tham . . .6K 203 (2M 41)
Middlemoor Rd.
GU16: Frim 5C 70
Middle Old Pk. GU9: Farnh . . .8E 108
Middle Rd. KT22: Leat 8H 79
SW16 . . . . .1H 45
Middle Row RH19: E Grin 1B 186
Middlesex Ct. *KT15: Addl* *2L 55*
(off Marnham Pl.)
W4 . . . . .1E 12
Middlesex Rd. CR4: Mit 4J 45
Middle St.
CR0: Croy 3C 200 (8N 45)
(not continuous)
GU5: Shere 8B 116
RH3: Betch, Brock 4A 120
RH12: Hors 6J 197
Middleton Gdns.
GU14: Cove 8K 69
Middleton Rd. GU15: Camb . . .9C 50
KT11: Down 6J 77
KT19: Ewe 6C 60
RH12: Hors 6G 197
SM4: Mord 5N 43
SM5: Cars 6B 44
Middleton Way RH11: Ifi 4K 181
Middle Vw. Dr. GU3: Norm . . .9A 92
Middle Wlk. GU21: Wok 4A 74
Middle Way SW16 . . . . .1H 45
Midgarth Cl. KT22: Oxs 1C 78
Midgeley Rd. RH10: Craw . . .1D 182
Midholm Rd. CR0: Croy 8H 47
MID HOLMWOOD 2H 139
Mid Holmwood La.
RH5: Mid H 2H 139
Midhope Cl. GU22: Wok 6A 74
Midhope Gdns.
GU22: Wok 6A 74
Midhope Rd. GU22: Wok 6A 74
Midhurst Av. CR0: Croy 6L 45
Midhurst Cl. RH11: Craw 2M 181
Midhurst Rd.
GU27: Fern, K Grn 7F 188
(not continuous)
GU27: Hasl 4E 188
Midleton Cl. GU8: Mil 9C 132
Midleton Ind. Est.
GU2: Guil 3L 113
Midleton Ind. Est. Rd.
GU2: Guil 1A 202 (2L 113)
Midleton Rd. GU2: Guil 2L 113
KT3: N Mal 2B 42
Midmoor Rd. SW12 . . . . .2G 29
SW19 . . . . .9J 27
Mid St. RH1: Sth N 6K 123
Midsummer Av. TW4: Houn 7N 9
Midsummer Wlk.
GU21: Wok 3N 73
Midway KT12: Wal T 8J 39
SM3: Sut 6L 43
Midway Av. KT16: Chert 2J 37
TW20: Thor 2D 36
Midway Cl. TW18: Stain 4K 21
Miena Way KT21: A'tead 4K 79
Mike Hawthorn Dr.
GU9: Farnh 9H 109
Milbanke Ct. RG12: Brac 1L 31
Milbanke Way RG12: Brac 1L 31
Milborne Rd. RH10: Craw 7G 182
Milbourne La. KT10: Esh 3C 58
Milbrook KT10: Esh 3C 58
Milburn Wlk. KT18: Eps 2D 80
Milbury Grn. CR6: Warl 5N 85
Milcombe Cl. GU21: Wok 5M 73
Milden Cl. GU16: Frim G 8E 70
Milden Gdns. GU16: Frim G . . .8D 70
Mildred Ct. CR0: Croy 7D 46
Mile Path GU22: Wok 8J 73
(not continuous)
Mile Rd. SM6: Bedd, W'ton 7F 44
(not continuous)
Miles Ct. CR0: Croy 3A 200
Miles La. KT11: Cob 9M 57
RH8: Tand 5J 125
RH9: Tand 5J 125
Miles Pl. GU18: Ligh 8K 51
KT5: Surb 8L 203 (3M 41)
Miles Rd. CR4: Mit 2C 44
GU12: Ash 1F 110
KT19: Eps 8C 60
Miles's Hill RH5: H Mary 8K 137
Milestone Cl. GU23: Rip 9J 75
SM2: Sut 3B 62
Milestone Dr. CR8: Pur 1K 83
MILESTONE GREEN 7B 12
Milestone Ho.
KT1: K Tham 6H 203
Mileswood Farm Ind. Est.
RG40: W'ham 7G 31
MILFORD 1C 152
Milford By-Pass Rd.
GU8: Mil 2A 152
Milford Gdns. CR0: Croy 4F 46
Milford Gro. SM1: Sut 1A 62
Milford Heath Rd.
GU8: Mil 2B 152
Milford Lodge GU8: Mil 2C 152
Milford M. SW16 . . . . .4K 29
Milford Rd. GU8: Els, Mil 7H 131
Milford Station (Rail) 3D 152
Milkhouse Ga.
GU1: Guil 6D 202 (5N 113)
Milking La. BR2: Kes 7F 66
BR6: Dow 8G 67
Mill, The KT13: Weybr 9B 38
Millais RH13: Hors 5N 197
Millais Cl. RH11: Craw 7L 181
Millais Ct. RH13: Hors 4N 197
Millais Cres. KT19: Ewe 2D 60
Millais Rd. KT3: N Mal 6D 42
Millais Way KT19: Ewe 1B 60
Millan Cl. KT15: N Haw 6K 55
Millbank SM6: W'ton 2H 63
Millbank, The
RH11: Craw 3L 181
Millbay La. RH12: Hors 7H 197
MILL BOTTOM 4K 139
Millbottom La. RH5: Holm . . .4K 139
Millbourne Rd.
TW13: Hanw 5M 23
MILLBRIDGE 9J 129
Millbridge Rd. GU46: Yate 7A 48
Millbrook
GU1: Guil 6B 202 (5N 113)
KT13: Weybr 1F 56
Millbrook Way SL3: Poy 5G 7
Mill Chase Leisure Cen. *6A 168*
(off Mill Chase Rd.)
Mill Chase Rd. GU35: Bor 5A 168
Mill Cleave *KT14: W By* *8J 55*
(off Claremont Rd.)
Mill Cl. GU19: Bag 4H 51
GU27: Hasl 2C 188
KT23: Book 2A 98
RH6: Horl 7C 142
RH19: E Grin 2A 186
SM5: Cars 8E 44
Mill Copse Rd.
GU27: Hasl 4F 188
Mill Cnr. GU51: Fleet 1D 88
Mill Cotts. RH12: Rudg 3E 194
RH19: E Grin 2A 186
Mill Ct. RH10: Craw 4D 182
Millennium Cen., The
GU9: Farnh 2F 128
Millennium Cotts.
GU5: Alb 8L 115
Millennium Ho.
RH11: Craw *6L 181*
(off Meridian Cl.)
Millennium Way
RG12: Brac 9N 15
Miller Cen., The 2D 104
Miller Cl. CR4: Mit 6D 44
Miller Rd. CR0: Croy 7K 45
GU4: Guil 9E 94
SW19 . . . . .7B 28
Millers Cl. TW18: Stain 6K 21
Millers Copse KT18: Eps D 6C 80
RH1: Out 4M 143
Millers Ct. TW20: Egh 7F 20
Millers Ga. RH12: Hors 3K 197
Miller's La. RH1: Out 4M 143
SL4: O Win 9J 5
Millers Thumb RG12: Brac 9C 16
Mill Farm Av. TW16: Sunb 8F 22
Mill Farm Bus. Pk.
TW4: Houn 1M 23
Mill Farm Cres. TW4: Houn . . .2M 23
Mill Farm Rd. RH13: Hors 4N 197
MILLFIELD 7L 177
Mill Fld. GU19: Bag 4H 51
Millfield
KT1: K Tham . . .5L 203 (2M 41)
TW16: Sunb 9E 22
Millfield La. KT20: K'wood . . .3L 101
Millfield Rd. TW4: Houn 2M 23
Millfields Cres. RH6: Char . . .4J 161
Millford GU21: Wok 4L 73
Millgate Ct. GU9: Farnh 9J 109
Mill Grn. CR4: Mit 6E 44
RG42: Bin 8K 15
Mill Grn. Bus. Pk. CR4: Mit . . .6E 44
Mill Grn. Rd. CR4: Mit 6D 44
Millhedge Cl. KT11: Cob 3M 77
Mill Hill RH3: Brock 4B 120
SW13 . . . . .5F 12
TN8: Eden, M Grn 3L 147
Mill Hill La. RH3: Brock 3A 120
Mill Hill Rd. SW13 . . . . .5F 12
Millholme Wlk.
GU15: Camb 2G 71
Mill Ho. La. KT16: Chert 3D 36
TW20: Thor 3D 36
Millhouse Pl. SE27 . . . . .5M 29
Milliners Ho. SW18 . . . . .7M 13
Millins Cl. GU47: Owls 6K 49
Mill La. BR6: Dow 6J 67
CR0: Wad 9K 45
GU1: Guil 6C 202 (5N 113)
GU3: P'marsh 2M 133
GU4: Guil 8H 115
GU5: Braml 5B 134
GU7: Goda 7G 132
GU8: Chid 7D 172
GU8: Duns 4A 174
GU8: Wit 5C 152
GU10: Fren 3G 148
GU23: Rip 6M 75
GU24: Pirb 2A 92
GU27: Hasl 4G 188
GU30: Pass 8C 168
GU35: Lind 5B 168
GU46: Yate 7C 48
KT14: Byf 9A 56
KT17: Ewe 5E 60
KT22: Fetc 9G 78
RG12: Brac 3L 31
RH1: Mers 9G 103
RH4: Dork 1K 201 (4H 119)
RH5: For G 3L 157
RH5: Newd 7C 140
RH6: Hook 8B 142
RH7: Ling 1B 166
RH8: Limp 9H 107
RH8: Oxt 1B 126
RH11: Ifi 1M 181
RH13: Itch 8B 196
RH19: Fel 5H 165
SL3: Hort 6D 6
SL4: W'sor 3D 4
SL5: S'hill 1C 34
SM5: Cars 1D 62
TN16: Weste 5L 107
TW20: Thor 3E 36

Mill La. Trad. Est.—Moor Pk. Gdns.

Mill La. Trad. Est.
CR0: Wad 9K **45**
Mill Mead TW18: Stain 5H **21**
Millmead
GU2: Guil 6B **202** (5M **113**)
KT10: Esh 8A **40**
KT14: Byf 8A **56**
Millmead Ct.
GU2: Guil 7B **202** (5M **113**)
Millmead Ter.
GU2: Guil 7B **202** (5M **113**)
Millmere GU46: Yate 8C **48**
Mill Pl.
KT1: K Tham . . .5K **203** (2M **41**)
SL3: Dat 5N **5**
Mill Pl. Cvn. Pk. SL3: Dat 5M **5**
Mill Plat TW7: Isle 5G **11**
(not continuous)
Mill Plat Av. TW7: Isle 5G **10**
Millpond Ct. KT15: Addl 2N **55**
Millpond Pl. SM5: Cars 9E **44**
Mill Pond Rd.
GU20: Windl 1M **51**
Mill Reach GU4: Guil 7H **115**
Mill Ride SL5: Asc 9G **17**
Mill Rd. GU3: P'marsh 2M **133**
KT10: Esh 8A **40**
KT11: Cob 2K **77**
KT17: Eps 5M **201** (8E **60**)
KT20: Tad 1J **101**
RH5: Holm 4J **139**
RH10: Craw 2F **182**
SW19 . . . . .8A **28**
TW2: Twick 3C **24**
Mills Cl. RH13: Hors 7M **197**
Mill Shaw RH8: Oxt 1B **126**
Millshot Cl. SW6 . . . . .4H **13**
Millside SM5: Cars 8D **44**
Millside Ct. KT23: Book 3A **98**
Millside Pk. SL4: Wink 2K **17**
Millside Pl. TW7: Isle 5H **11**
Mills Rd. KT12: Hers 2K **57**
Mills Row W4 . . . . .1C **12**
Mills Spur SL4: O Win 1L **19**
Millstead Cl. KT20: Tad 9G **81**
Mill Stream GU9: Weybo 6K **109**
Millstream, The
GU27: Hasl 3C **188**
Mill St.
KT1: K Tham 5K **203** (2L **41**)
RH1: Red 4C **122**
SL3: Coln 3F **6**
TN16: Weste 5M **107**
Millthorpe Rd.
RH12: Hors 4M **197**
Mill Vw. Cl. KT17: Ewe 4E **60**
Millview Cl. RH2: Reig 1B **122**
Mill Vw. Gdns. CR0: Croy 9G **46**
Mill Way KT18: Head, Leat 3N **99**
KT22: Leat 2M **99**
RH19: E Grin 2A **186**
TW14: Felt 8J **9**
Millway RH2: Reig 3B **122**
Millwood RH10: T Hil 4H **185**
Millwood Rd. TW3: Houn 8C **10**
Milman Cl. RG12: Brac 1E **32**
Milne Cl. RH11: Craw 6K **181**
Milne Pk. E. CR0: N Add 7N **65**
Milne Pk. W. CR0: N Add 7N **65**
Milner App. CR3: Cate 8D **84**
Milner Cl. CR3: Cate 9C **84**
Milner Dr. KT11: Cob 8N **57**
TW2: Whitt 1D **24**
Milner Pl. SM5: Cars 1E **62**
Milner Rd. CR3: Cate 9D **84**
CR7: T Hea 2A **46**
KT1: K Tham 6H **203** (2K **41**)
SM4: Mord 4B **44**
SW19 . . . . .9N **27**
Milnthorpe Rd. W4 . . . . .2C **12**
Milnwood Rd. RH12: Hors . . .5J **197**
Milton Av. CR0: Croy 6A **46**
RH4: Westc 6D **118**
SM1: Sut 9B **44**
Milton Cl. GU3: Norm 9M **91**
RG12: Brac 5N **31**
SL3: Hort 6C **6**
SM1: Sut 9B **44**
Milton Ct. RG40: W'ham 1A **30**
RH4: Dork 5E **118**
SW18 . . . . .8M **13**
TW2: Twick 4E **24**
Milton Ct. La.
RH4: Dork 2G **201** (5E **118**)
Milton Cres. RH19: E Grin . . .1M **185**
Milton Dr. RG40: W'ham 1A **30**
TW17: Shep 3N **37**
Milton Gdns.
KT18: Eps 8L **201** (1D **80**)
RG40: W'ham 2A **30**
TW19: Stan 2A **22**
Milton Grange GU12: A Va 8E **90**
Milton Ho. SM1: Sut 9M **43**
Milton Lodge TW2: Twick 1F **24**
Milton Mans. *W14* *2K 13*
(off Queen's Club Gdns.)
Milton Mt. RH10: Craw 9H **163**
Milton Mt. Av.
RH10: Craw 1G **183**
Milton Mount Gdns. 9H **163**
Milton Rd. CR0: Croy 6A **46**
CR3: Cate 8A **84**
CR4: Mit 8E **28**
Milton Rd. KT12: Wal T 9L **39**
KT15: Addl 3J **55**
RG40: W'ham 9A **14**
RH10: Craw 2G **182**
RH12: Hors 5J **197**
SM1: Sut 9M **43**
SM6: W'ton 3G **63**
SW14 . . . . .6C **12**
SW19 . . . . .7A **28**
TW12: Hamp 8A **24**
TW20: Egh 6B **20**
Miltons Cres. GU7: Goda 9E **132**
Milton St. RH4: Westc 6D **118**
Miltons Yd. *GU8: Wit* *6C 152*
(off Petworth Rd.)
Milton Way KT22: Fetc 3C **98**
UB7: W Dray 1A **8**
Milward Gdns. RG12: Bin 1H **31**
MIMBRIDGE 9K **53**
Mimosa Cl. GU35: Lind 4B **168**
Mimosa St. SW6 . . . . .4L **13**
Mina Rd. SW19 . . . . .9M **27**
Minchin Cl. KT22: Leat 9G **79**
Minchin Grn. RG42: Bin 6H **15**
Mincing La. GU24: Chob 4J **53**
Mindelheim Av.
RH19: E Grin 8D **166**
Minden Rd. SM3: Sut 8K **43**
Minehead Rd. SW16 . . . . .6K **29**
Minehurst Rd. GU16: Mytc 1D **90**
Minerva Cl. TW19: Stan M 8J **7**
Minerva Rd.
KT1: K Tham . . .3L **203** (1M **41**)
Minimax Cl. TW14: Felt 9H **9**
Mink Ct. TW4: Houn 5K **9**
MINLEY 5C **68**
Minley Cl. GU14: Cove 1K **89**
Minley Ct. RH2: Reig 2M **121**
Minley Gro. GU51: Fleet 2C **88**
Minley La. GU17: Min 4C **68**
Minley Link Rd.
GU14: Cove 1G **88**
Minley Rd. GU14: Cove 8H **69**
GU17: Min 6E **68**
(Minley La.)
GU17: Min 7B **68**
(Yateley Dr.)
GU51: Fleet 7B **68**
Minniedale
KT5: Surb 8M **203** (4M **41**)
Minorca Av. GU16: Deep 4J **71**
Minorca Rd. GU16: Deep 5J **71**
KT13: Weybr 1B **56**
Minoru Pl. RG42: Bin 6J **15**
Minstead Cl. RG12: Brac 2D **32**
Minstead Dr. GU46: Yate 1B **68**
Minstead Gdns. SW15 . . . . .1E **26**
Minstead Way KT3: N Mal 5D **42**
Minster Av. SM1: Sut 8M **43**
Minster Cl. GU14: Farnb 4B **90**
Minster Ct. GU15: Camb 2L **69**
(Tuscam Way)
GU15: Camb 8B **50**
(York Rd.)
Minster Dr. CR0: Croy 1B **64**
Minster Gdns. KT8: W Mole . . .3N **39**
Minsterley Av. TW17: Shep 3F **38**
Minster Rd. GU7: Goda 9H **133**
Minstrel Gdns.
KT5: Surb 8M **203** (3M **41**)
Minstrels Cl. TN8: Eden 1L **147**
Mint, The GU7: Goda 7G **132**
Mint Gdns.
RH4: Dork 1J **201** (4G **119**)
Mint La. KT20: Lwr K 7M **101**
Mint Rd. SM6: W'ton 1F **62**
SM7: Ban 3A **82**
Mint St. GU7: Goda 7G **133**
Mint Wlk.
CR0: Croy 4C **200** (9N **45**)
CR6: Warl 4G **85**
GU21: Knap 4H **73**
Mintwater Cl. KT17: Ewe 6F **60**
Mirabel Rd. SW6 . . . . .3L **13**
Miranda Wlk. RH11: Craw . . .5K **181**
Misbrooks Grn. Rd.
RH5: B Grn, Cap 1L **159**
Missenden Cl. TW14: Felt 2G **23**
Missenden Gdns.
SM4: Mord 5A **44**
Mission Sq. TW8: Brent 2L **11**
Mistletoe Cl. CR0: Croy 7G **46**
Mistletoe Rd. GU46: Yate 2C **68**
Mistley Ct. KT18: Eps 7K **201**
Mistley Gdns. RH6: Hook 9B **142**
Misty's Fld. KT12: Wal T 7K **39**
MITCHAM 2D **44**
Mitcham Ct. GU15: Camb 6F **50**
Mitcham Gdn. Village
CR4: Mit 4E **44**
Mitcham Ind. Est. CR4: Mit 9E **28**
Mitcham Junction Station (Rail & CT)
. . . . .4E **44**
Mitcham La. SW16 . . . . .7G **28**
Mitcham Pk. CR4: Mit 3C **44**
Mitcham Rd.
CR0: Croy 1A **200** (5J **45**)
GU15: Camb 6E **50**
SW17 . . . . .6D **28**
Mitcham Stop (CT) 3C **44**
Mitchell Gdns. RH13: Slin 5L **195**
Mitchell Pk. Farm Cotts.
GU28: North 8G **190**
Mitchell Rd. BR6: Orp 1N **67**
Mitchells Cl. GU4: Chil 9A **114**
Mitchells Rd.
RH10: Craw 3D **182**
Mitchells Row GU4: Chil 1A **134**
Mitchener's La. RH1: Blet 3A **124**
Mitchley Av. CR2: Sande 9N **63**
CR8: Pur 9N **63**
Mitchley Gro. CR2: Sande 9D **64**
Mitchley Hill CR2: Sande 9C **64**
Mitchley Vw. CR2: Sande 9D **64**
Mitford Bldgs. *SW6* *3M 13*
(off Dawes Rd.)
Mitford Cl. KT9: Ches 3J **59**
Mitford Wlk. RH11: Craw 6M **181**
Mitre Cl. SM2: Sut 4A **62**
TW17: Shep 5E **38**
Mitre Ct. RH12: Hors 6H **197**
Mitre Pl. RG42: Warf 7N **15**
Mixbury Gro. KT13: Weybr 3E **56**
Mixnams La. KT16: Chert 2J **37**
Mizen Cl. KT11: Cob 1L **77**
Mizen Way KT11: Cob 2K **77**
Moat, The KT3: N Mal 9D **26**
Moat Ct. KT16: Otter 3E **54**
KT21: A'tead 4L **79**
Moated Farm Dr.
KT15: Addl, N Haw 4L **55**
Moat La. KT8: E Mol 2F **40**
Moat Lodge GU6: Cranl 7M **155**
Moat Rd. RH19: E Grin 8A **166**
Moat Side TW13: Hanw 5K **23**
Moats La. RH1: Sth N 1J **143**
Moat Wlk. RH10: Craw 2G **183**
Moberly Rd. SW4 . . . . .1H **29**
Moberly Way CR8: Ken 7A **84**
Mocatta M. RH1: Mers 9G **103**
Mockford M. RH1: Mers 9G **102**
Modder Pl. SW15 . . . . .7J **13**
Model Cotts. GU24: Pirb 8A **72**
SW14 . . . . .7B **12**
Moffat Ct. SW19 . . . . .6M **27**
Moffat Rd. CR7: T Hea 1N **45**
SW17 . . . . .5D **28**
Moffats Cl. GU47: Sandh 7F **48**
MOGADOR 6K **101**
Mogador Rd. KT20: Lwr K 6K **101**
Mogden La. TW7: Isle 8F **10**
Moir Cl. CR2: Sande 5D **64**
Mole Abbey Gdns.
KT8: W Mole 2B **40**
Mole Bus. Pk. KT22: Leat 8G **78**
Mole Cl. GU14: Cove 8J **69**
RH11: Craw 1N **181**
Mole Ct. KT19: Ewe 1B **60**
Molember Ct. KT8: E Mol 3E **40**
Molember Rd. KT8: E Mol 4E **40**
Mole Rd. KT12: Hers 2L **57**
KT22: Fetc 8D **78**
Moles Cl. RG40: W'ham 3C **30**
Molesey Av. KT8: W Mole 4N **39**
Molesey Cl. KT12: Hers 1M **57**
Molesey Dr. SM3: Chea 8K **43**
Molesey Pk. Av.
KT8: W Mole 4B **40**
Molesey Pk. Cl. KT8: E Mol . . .4C **40**
Molesey Pk. Rd.
KT8: W Mole, E Mol 4B **40**
Molesey Rd. KT8: W Mole 6M **39**
KT12: Hers, Wal T, W Mole
. . . . .2L **57**
Molesford Rd. SW6 . . . . .4M **13**
Molesham Cl. KT8: W Mole 2B **40**
Molesham Way
KT8: W Mole 2B **40**
Moles Hill KT22: Oxs 7D **58**
Moles Mead TN8: Eden 1L **147**
Mole St. RH5: Ockl 3A **158**
Molesworth Rd. KT11: Cob 9H **57**
Mole Valley Pl.
KT21: A'tead 6K **79**
Molins Ct. *RH11: Craw* *6M 181*
(off Brideake Cl.)
Mollison Dr. SM6: W'ton 4H **63**
Mollison Sq. *SM6: W'ton* *4H 63*
(off Mollison Dr.)
Molloy Ct. GU21: Wok 3C **74**
Molly Huggins Cl.
SW12 . . . . .1G **28**
Molly Millars Bri.
RG41: W'ham 4A **30**
Molly Millars Cl.
RG41: W'ham 4A **30**
Molly Millars La.
RG41: W'ham 4A **30**
Molyneux Dr. SW17 . . . . .5F **28**
Molyneux Rd. GU7: Goda 4J **133**
GU20: Windl 3A **52**
KT13: Weybr 2B **56**
Monahan Av. CR8: Pur 8K **63**
Monarch Cl. BR4: W Wick 1B **66**
RH11: Craw 6M **181**
TW14: Felt 1F **22**
Monarch M. SW16 . . . . .6L **29**
Monarch Pde. CR4: Mit 1D **44**
Monaveen Gdns.
KT8: W Mole 2B **40**
Moncks Row SW18 . . . . .9L **13**
Mondial Way UB3: Harl 3D **8**
Money Av. CR3: Cate 9B **84**
Money Rd. CR3: Cate 9A **84**
Mongers La. KT17: Ewe 6E **60**
(not continuous)
Monkey Puzzle Rdbt.
GU14: Cove 2K **89**
Monkleigh Rd. SM4: Mord 2K **43**
Monks All. RG42: Bin 6G **14**
Monks Av. KT8: W Mole 4N **39**
Monks Cl. GU14: Farnb 1A **90**
(not continuous)
SL5: Asc 5M **33**
Monks Ct. RH2: Reig 3N **121**
Monks Cres. KT12: Wal T 7J **39**
KT15: Addl 2K **55**
Monksdene Gdns.
SM1: Sut 9N **43**
Monks Dr. SL5: Asc 5M **33**
Monksfield RH10: Craw 3D **182**
Monks Grn. KT22: Fetc 8C **78**
Monks Gro. GU3: Comp 8B **112**
Monkshanger GU9: Farnh 1K **129**
Monks Hill Sports Cen. 4G **65**
Monkshood Cl.
RG40: W'ham 1D **30**
Monks La. RH5: Oak 4N **177**
TN8: Eden 6F **126**
MONKS ORCHARD 6H **47**
Monks Orchard Rd.
BR3: Beck 7K **47**
Monks Path GU14: Farnb 9B **70**
Monks Pl. CR3: Cate 9E **84**
Monks Rd. GU25: V Wat 3N **35**
SL4: W'sor 5A **4**
SM7: Ban 4M **81**
Monks Wlk. GU9: Farnh 4L **129**
KT16: Chert 3G **37**
RH2: Reig 3N **121**
SL5: Asc 5M **33**
TW20: Thor 2F **36**
Monks Way BR3: Beck 5K **47**
TW18: Stain 8M **21**
UB7: Harm 2N **7**
Monks Well GU10: Farnh 2N **129**
Monkswell La. CR5: Coul 2N **101**
Monkton La.
GU9: Farnh, Hale 7K **109**
Monkton Pk. GU9: Farnh 8L **109**
Monmouth Av. KT1: H Wic 8J **25**
Monmouth Cl. CR4: Mit 3J **45**
Mono La. TW13: Felt 3J **23**
Monro Dr. GU2: Guil 9K **93**
Monroe Dr. SW14 . . . . .8A **12**
Monro Pl. KT19: Eps 5N **59**
Mons Barracks GU11: Alde 8A **90**
Mons Cl. GU11: Alde 6C **90**
Monsell Gdns. TW18: Stain . . .6G **21**
Monson Rd. RH1: Red 9D **102**
Mons Wlk. TW20: Egh 6E **20**
Montacute Cl. GU14: Farnb 1B **90**
Montacute Rd. CR0: N Add . . .5M **65**
SM4: Mord 5B **44**
Montague Av. CR2: Sande 8B **64**
Montague Cl. GU15: Camb 1N **69**
GU18: Ligh 6L **51**
KT12: Wal T 6J **39**
RG40: W'ham 9D **14**
Montague Dr. CR3: Cate 9N **83**
Montague Rd.
CR0: Croy 1A **200** (7M **45**)
SW19 . . . . .8N **27**
TW3: Houn 6B **10**
TW10: Rich 9L **11**
Montagu Gdns. SM6: W'ton . . .1G **62**
Montagu Rd. SL3: Dat 4L **5**
Montana Cl. CR2: Sande 6A **64**
Montana Gdns. SM1: Sut 2A **62**
Montana Rd. SW17 . . . . .4E **28**
SW20 . . . . .9H **27**
Monteagle La. GU46: Yate 1A **68**
Montem Rd. KT3: N Mal 3D **42**
Montford Rd. TW16: Sunb 3H **39**
Montfort Pl. SW19 . . . . .2J **27**
Montfort Ri. RH1: Salf 2D **142**
Montgomerie Dr. GU2: Guil . . .7K **93**
Montgomery Av.
KT10: H Wood 8E **40**
Montgomery Cl. CR4: Mit 3J **45**
GU47: Sandh 7G **49**
Montgomery Ct.
CR2: S Croy 8F **200**
KT22: Leat *7H 79*
(off Levett Rd.)
W4 . . . . .3B **12**
Montgomery Gdns.
SM2: Sut 4B **62**
Montgomery of Alamein Ct.
RG12: Brac 9B **16**
Montgomery Path
GU14: Cove 2L **89**
Montgomery Rd.
GU14: Cove 2L **89**
GU22: Wok 5A **74**
Montgomery Way CR8: Ken . . .7A **84**
Montholme Rd. SW11 . . . . .1D **28**
Montolieu Gdns.
SW15 . . . . .8G **13**
Montpelier Ct. SL4: W'sor 5F **4**
Montpelier Rd. CR8: Pur 6M **63**
SM1: Sut 1A **62**
Montpelier Row TW1: Twick . . .1J **25**
Montpellier Ct. KT12: Wal T . . .5H **39**
Montreal Ct. GU11: Alde 3L **109**
Montrell Rd. SW2 . . . . .2J **29**
Montreux Ct. RH11: Craw 3N **181**
Montrose Av. SL3: Dat 3M **5**
TW2: Whitt 1B **24**
Montrose Cl. GU16: Frim 4C **70**
GU51: Fleet 5C **88**
TW15: A'ford 7D **22**
Montrose Gdns. CR4: Mit 1D **44**
KT22: Oxs 8D **58**
SM1: Sut 8N **43**
Montrose Rd. TW14: Bedf 9E **8**
Montrose Wlk. KT13: Weybr . . .9C **38**
Montrose Way SL3: Dat 4N **5**
Montrouge Cres.
KT17: Eps D 3H **81**
Mont St Aignan Way
TN8: Eden 2L **147**
Montserrat Rd. SW15 . . . . .7K **13**
Monument Bri. Ind. Est. E.
GU21: Wok 2D **74**
Monument Bri. Ind. Est. W.
GU21: Wok 2C **74**
Monument Bus. Cen.
GU21: Wok 2D **74**
Monument Grn.
KT13: Weybr 9C **38**
Monument Hill
KT13: Weybr 1C **56**
Monument Rd. GU21: Wok 1C **74**
KT13: Weybr 1C **56**
Monument Way E.
GU21: Wok 2D **74**
Monument Way W.
GU21: Wok 2C **74**
Moon Hall Rd. GU6: Ewh 1D **156**
Moons, The RH1: Mers 9G **102**
Moons Hill GU10: Fren 9G **129**
Moons La. RH7: Dorm 3F **166**
RH13: Hors 7L **197**
MOOR, THE 3F **20**
Moor Cl. GU47: Owls 6K **49**
Moorcroft Cl. RH11: Craw 2N **181**
Moorcroft Rd. SW16 . . . . .4J **29**
Moordale Av. RG42: Brac 9K **15**
Moore Cl. CR4: Mit 1F **44**
GU10: Tong 4D **110**
GU52: C Cro 8B **88**
KT15: Addl 2K **55**
SW14 . . . . .6B **12**
Moore Ct. RH12: Hors 7G **196**
Moore Gro. Cres.
TW20: Egh 7B **20**
Moore Pk. Ct. *SW6* *3N 13*
(off Fulham Rd.)
Moore Pk. Rd. SW6 . . . . .3M **13**
Moore Rd. GU24: B'wood 8M **71**
GU52: C Cro 8B **88**
SE19 . . . . .7N **29**
Moores Grn. RG40: W'ham 9D **14**
Moores La. SL4: E Wic 1C **4**
Moore's Rd.
RH4: Dork 1L **201** (4H **119**)
Moore Way SM2: Sut 5M **61**
Moorfield GU27: Hasl 3D **188**
RH5: Holm 4K **139**
Moorfield Cen., The
GU1: Guil 8N **93**
Moorfield Point GU1: Guil 8A **94**
Moorfield Rd. GU1: Guil 8N **93**
KT9: Ches 2L **59**
Moorfields Cl. TW18: Stain . . .9G **21**
Moorhayes Dr. TW18: Lale 2L **37**
Moorhead Rd. RH12: Hors . . .3A **198**
Moorhead Rdbt.
RH12: Hors 1A **198**
Moorholme GU22: Wok 6A **74**
MOORHOUSE 5H **107**
MOORHOUSE BANK 6J **107**
Moorhouse Rd.
RH8: Limp, Weste 9H **107**
TN16: Weste 9H **107**
Moorhurst La. RH5: Holm 7G **138**
Moorings, The GU26: Hind 6C **170**
KT14: W By 8L **55**
KT23: Book 3A **98**
RH19: E Grin 7K **165**
Moorings Ho. TW8: Brent 3J **11**
MOOR JUNC. 3K **7**
Moorland Cl. TW2: Whitt 1A **24**
Moorland Rd. RH10: Craw 6G **183**
UB7: Harm 2L **7**
Moorlands *KT12: Wal T* *9H 39*
(off Ashley Pk. Rd.)
Moorlands, The
GU22: Wok 8B **74**
Moorlands Cl. GU26: Hind 5C **170**
GU51: Fleet 5C **88**
Moorlands Pl. GU15: Camb . . .1M **69**
Moorlands Rd.
GU15: Camb 2M **69**
Moor La. GU22: Wok 9A **74**
KT9: Ches 1L **59**
RG12: Bin 2H **31**
RH7: Dorm 9D **146**
TN8: Dorm, M Grn 9D **146**
TW18: Stain 4G **20**
TW19: Stain 2F **20**
UB7: Harm 2L **7**
Moormead Dr. KT19: Ewe 2D **60**
Moor Mead Rd. TW1: Twick 9G **11**
Moormede Cres.
TW18: Stain 5H **21**
Moor Pk. *RH6: Horl* *9F 142*
(off Aurum Cl.)
Moor Pk. Cres. RH11: Ifi 4J **181**
Moor Pk. Gdns.
KT2: K Tham 8D **26**

Moor Pk. Ho.—Nell Gwynne Cl.

Moor Pk. Ho. RG12: Brac ... 5K 31
(off St Andrews)
Moor Pk. La. GU9: Farnh ... 9K 109
(not continuous)
GU10: Farnh ... 1M 129
Moor Pk. Way GU9: Farnh ... 1L 129
Moor Pl. GU20: Windl ... 2M 51
RH19: E Grin ... 8N 165
Moor Rd. GU14: Farnb ... 6H 69
GU16: Frim ... 6D 70
GU27: Hasl ... 3A 188
Moors, The GU10: Tong ... 5C 110
Moorside Cl. GU14: Cove ... 5M 69
Moors La. GU8: Els ... 8G 130
Moorsom Way CR5: Coul ... 4H 83
Moral Rd. GU17: Min ... 5E 68
Moray Av. GU47: C Tow ... 7J 49
(not continuous)
Moray Ct. CR2: S Croy ... 8B 200
Morcote Cl. GU4: Chil ... 1A 134
Mordaunt Dr. RG45: Crow ... 4G 48
MORDEN ... 2N 43
Morden Cl. KT20: Tad ... 7J 81
RG12: Brac ... 3D 32
Morden Ct. SM4: Mord ... 3N 43
Morden Ct. Pde.
SM4: Mord ... 3N 43
Morden Gdns. CR4: Mit ... 3B 44
Morden Hall Rd.
SM4: Mord ... 2N 43
Morden Ho. SM4: Mord ... 3M 43
MORDEN PARK ... 5K 43
Morden Pk. Pool ... 5L 43
Morden Rd. CR4: Mit ... 3A 44
SM4: Mord ... 3A 44
SW19 ... 9N 27
Morden Road Stop (CT) ... 1N 43
Morden South Station (Rail)
... 4M 43
Morden Station (Tube) ... 2N 43
Morden Way SM3: Sut ... 6M 43
More Circ. GU7: Goda ... 4H 133
More Cl. CR8: Pur ... 7L 63
Morecombe Cl.
RH11: Craw ... 5L 181
Morecoombe Cl.
KT2: K Tham ... 8A 26
Moreland Av. SL3: Coln ... 3E 6
Moreland Cl. SL3: Coln ... 3E 6
More La. KT10: Esh ... 8B 40
Morella Cl. GU25: V Wat ... 3N 35
Morella Rd. SW12 ... 1D 28
More Rd. GU7: Goda ... 4H 133
Moresby Av. KT5: Surb ... 6A 42
Moretaine Rd.
TW15: A'ford ... 4M 21
Moreton Almshouses
TN16: Weste ... 4M 107
Moreton Av. TW7: Isle ... 4E 10
Moreton Cl. GU10: Churt ... 9K 149
GU52: C Cro ... 9A 88
Moreton Rd.
CR2: S Croy ... 8E 200 (2A 64)
KT4: W Pk ... 8F 42
Morgan Ct. GU14: Cove ... 1H 89
(off Whetstone Rd.)
SM5: Cars ... 1D 62
TW15: A'ford ... 6C 22
Morgan Ho. RH10: Craw ... 2F 182
(off Trafalgar Gdns.)
MORGAN'S GREEN ... 7D 194
Morgan Wlk. BR3: Beck ... 3L 47
Morie St. SW18 ... 8N 13
Moring Rd. SW17 ... 5E 28
Morland Av. CR0: Croy ... 7B 46
Morland Cl. CR4: Mit ... 2C 44
TW12: Hamp ... 6N 23
Morland Rd. CR0: Croy ... 7B 46
GU11: Alde ... 5N 109
SM1: Sut ... 2A 62
Morland's Rd. GU11: Alde ... 8B 90
Morley Cl. GU46: Yate ... 1A 68
Morley Ct. KT22: Fetc ... 8D 78
Morley Rd. CR2: Sande ... 6C 64
GU9: Farnh ... 2H 129
SM3: Sut ... 7L 43
TW1: Twick ... 9K 11
Morningside Rd. KT4: W Pk ... 8H 43
Mornington Av. W14 ... 1L 13
Mornington Av. Mans.
W14 ... 1L 13
(off Mornington Av.)
Mornington Cl. TN16: B Hil ... 4F 86
Mornington Cres.
TW5: C'ford ... 4J 9
Mornington Rd.
TW15: A'ford ... 6D 22
Mornington Wlk.
TW10: Ham ... 5J 25
Morrell Av. RH12: Hors ... 3M 197
Morris Cl. CR0: Croy ... 4H 47
Morris Ct. SL4: W'sor ... 4B 4
Morris Gdns. SW18 ... 1M 27
Morrish Rd. SW2 ... 1J 29
Morrison Ct. RH11: Craw ... 8N 181
Morrison Ho. SW2 ... 2L 29
(off High Trees)
Morris Rd. GU14: Farnb ... 5B 90
RH1: Sth N ... 5J 123
TW7: Isle ... 6F 10
Morston Cl. KT20: Tad ... 7G 81
Morth Gdns. RH12: Hors ... 7J 197
Mortimer Cl. SW16 ... 3H 29
Mortimer Cres. KT4: W Pk ... 9C 42
Mortimer Ho. W14 ... 1K 13
(off North End Rd.)
Mortimer Rd. CR4: Mit ... 9D 28
RH5: Cap ... 4K 159
TN16: B Hil ... 8E 66
MORTLAKE ... 6C 12
Mortlake Cl. CR0: Bedd ... 9J 45
Mortlake Crematorium
TW9: Rich ... 5A 12
Mortlake Dr. CR4: Mit ... 9C 28
Mortlake High St.
SW14 ... 6C 12
Mortlake Rd.
TW9: Kew, Rich ... 3N 11
Mortlake Station (Rail) ... 6B 12
Mortlake Ter. TW9: Kew ... 3N 11
(off Mortlake Rd.)
Morton KT20: Tad ... 8J 81
Morton Cl. GU16: Frim ... 7D 70
GU21: Wok ... 2M 73
RH11: Craw ... 9N 181
SM6: W'ton ... 4K 63
Morton Gdns. SM6: W'ton ... 2G 62
Morton M. SW5 ... 1N 13
Morton Rd. GU21: Wok ... 2N 73
RH19: E Grin ... 2A 186
SM4: Mord ... 4B 44
Morval Cl. GU14: Cove ... 1K 89
Morven Rd. SW17 ... 4D 28
Moselle Cl. GU14: Cove ... 9J 69
Moselle Rd. TN16: B Hil ... 5G 87
Mosford Cl. RH6: Horl ... 6D 142
Mospey Cres. KT17: Eps ... 2E 80
Mosquito Cl. SM6: W'ton ... 4J 63
(off Mollison Dr.)
MOSS END ... 3N 15
Mossfield KT11: Cob ... 9H 57
Moss Gdns. CR2: Sels ... 4G 64
TW13: Felt ... 3H 23
Moss La. GU7: Goda ... 7G 133
Mosslea Rd. CR3: Whyte ... 3C 84
Mossville Gdns. SM4: Mord ... 2L 43
Moston Cl. UB3: Harl ... 1G 8
Mostyn Ho. RG42: Brac ... 8N 15
(off Merryhill Rd.)
Mostyn Rd. SW19 ... 9L 27
Mostyn Ter. RH1: Red ... 4E 122
Moth Cl. SM6: W'ton ... 4J 63
MOTSPUR PARK ... 5F 42
Motspur Pk. KT3: N Mal ... 5E 42
Motspur Park Station (Rail)
... 4G 42
Motts Hill La.
KT20: Tad, Wal H ... 1F 100
Mouchotte Cl. TN16: B Hil ... 8D 66
Moulsham Copse La.
GU46: Yate ... 8A 48
Moulsham Grn. GU46: Yate ... 8A 48
Moulsham La. GU46: Yate ... 8A 48
Moulton Av. TW3: Houn ... 5M 9
Mount, The CR2: S Croy ... 8C 200
CR5: Coul ... 2E 82
CR6: Warl ... 6D 84
GU2: Guil ... 8A 202 (5M 113)
GU6: Cranl ... 8N 155
GU6: Ewh ... 4F 156
GU21: Knap ... 6F 72
GU21: Wok ... 5N 73
(off Elm Rd.)
GU21: Wok ... 6K 73
(St Johns Ct.)
GU25: V Wat ... 5N 35
GU27: G'wood ... 7K 171
GU35: Head ... 3F 168
GU51: Fleet ... 3B 88
KT3: N Mal ... 2E 42
KT4: W Pk ... 1G 61
KT10: Esh ... 3A 58
KT13: Weybr ... 8F 38
KT17: Ewe ... 6E 60
KT20: Lwr K ... 4L 101
KT22: Fetc ... 1E 98
RH11: Ifi ... 1G 180
Mt. Angelus Rd. SW15 ... 1E 26
Mt. Ararat Rd. TW10: Rich ... 8L 11
Mount Av. CR3: Cate ... 2N 103
Mountbatten Cl.
RH11: Craw ... 7A 182
Mountbatten Ct.
GU11: Alde ... 2M 109
(off Birchett Rd.)
Mountbatten Gdns.
BR3: Beck ... 3H 47
Mountbatten Lodge
GU9: Farnh ... 1G 128
(off The Hart)
Mountbatten M.
GU15: Camb ... 8A 50
SW18 ... 1A 28
Mountbatten Ri.
GU47: Sandh ... 6E 48
Mountbatten Sq. SL4: W'sor ... 4F 4
Mount Cl. CR8: Ken ... 3A 84
GU6: Ewh ... 5F 156
GU22: Wok ... 8M 73
KT22: Fetc ... 1E 98
RH10: Craw ... 2H 183
SM5: Cars ... 5E 62
Mount Cl., The
GU25: V Wat ... 5N 35
Mountcombe Cl. KT6: Surb ... 6L 41
Mount Cotts. RH11: Ifi ... 2H 181
Mount Ct. BR4: W Wick ... 8N 47
GU2: Guil ... 6B 202 (5M 113)
SW15 ... 6K 13
Mount Dr., The
RH2: Reig ... 1B 122
Mountearl Gdns.
SW16 ... 4K 29
Mt. Ephraim La.
SW16 ... 4H 29
Mt. Ephraim Rd.
SW16 ... 4H 29
Mount Felix KT12: Wal T ... 7G 38
MOUNT HERMON ... 6M 73
Mt. Hermon Cl. GU22: Wok ... 6N 73
Mt. Hermon Rd.
GU22: Wok ... 6N 73
Mount Holme KT7: T Dit ... 6H 41
Mount La. RG12: Brac ... 2A 32
RH10: T Hil ... 5D 184
Mount Lee TW20: Egh ... 6B 20
Mount M. TW12: Hamp ... 9B 24
Mount Noddy ... 8A 166
Mt. Nod Rd. SW16 ... 4K 29
Mount Pk. SM5: Cars ... 4E 62
Mount Pk. Av. CR2: S Croy ... 5M 63
Mount Pl.
GU2: Guil ... 6B 202 (5M 113)
Mt. Pleasant
GU2: Guil ... 7B 202 (5M 113)
GU9: Farnh ... 2F 128
GU47: Sandh ... 6F 48
KT13: Weybr ... 9B 38
KT17: Ewe ... 6E 60
KT24: Eff ... 6M 97
KT24: W Hors ... 7C 96
RG12: Brac ... 2A 32
RG41: W'ham ... 2A 30
RH5: A Ham ... 9G 116
SE27 ... 5N 29
TN16: B Hil ... 4F 86
Mt. Pleasant Cl. GU18: Ligh ... 6L 51
Mt. Pleasant Rd.
CR3: Cate ... 1D 104
GU12: Alde ... 2A 110
GU35: Lind ... 4A 168
KT3: N Mal ... 2B 42
RH7: Ling ... 7M 145
Mount Ri. RH1: Red ... 5B 122
Mount Rd. CR4: Mit ... 1B 44
GU6: Cranl ... 8N 155
GU22: Wok ... 8L 73
GU24: Chob ... 8L 53
KT3: N Mal ... 2C 42
KT9: Ches ... 2M 59
SW19 ... 3M 27
TW13: Hanw ... 4M 23
Mountsfield Cl.
TW19: Stan M ... 9J 7
Mounts Hill SL4: Wink ... 3N 17
Mountside CR3: Cate ... 2C 104
GU2: Guil ... 7A 202 (5L 113)
Mt. Side Pl. GU22: Wok ... 5B 74
Mount St.
RH4: Dork ... 2H 201 (5G 118)
Mount Vw. GU11: Alde ... 3M 109
Mountview Cl. RH1: Red ... 5C 122
Mountview Dr. RH1: Red ... 5C 122
Mount Vw. Rd. KT10: Clay ... 4H 59
Mount Vs. SE27 ... 4M 29
Mount Way SM5: Cars ... 5E 62
Mountwood KT8: W Mole ... 2B 40
Mountwood Cl. CR2: Sande ... 6E 64
Moushill La. GU8: Mil ... 2B 152
Mowat Ct. KT4: W Pk ... 8E 42
(off The Avenue)
Mowatt Rd. GU26: G'hott ... 7B 170
Mowbray Av. KT14: Byf ... 9N 55
Mowbray Cres. TW20: Egh ... 6C 20
Mowbray Dr. RH11: Craw ... 5L 181
Mowbray Gdns. RH4: Dork ... 3H 119
Mowbray Rd. TW10: Ham ... 4J 25
Mower Cl. RG40: W'ham ... 1E 30
Mower Pl. GU6: Cranl ... 6N 155
MOWSHURST ... 8N 127
Moxey Cl. TN16: B Hil ... 9E 66
Moylan Rd. W6 ... 2K 13
Moyne Ct. GU21: Wok ... 5J 73
Moyne Rd. RH11: Craw ... 7A 182
Moys Cl. CR0: Croy ... 5J 45
Moyser Rd. SW16 ... 6F 28
Muchelney Rd. SM4: Mord ... 5A 44
Muckhatch La. TW20: Thor ... 2D 36
Muggeridge Cl.
CR2: S Croy ... 8E 200 (2A 64)
Muggeridges Hill
RH12: Cap ... 1L 179
MUGSWELL ... 3N 101
Muirdown Av. SW14 ... 7C 12
Muirfield Cl. RH11: Ifi ... 4J 181
Muirfield Ho. RG12: Brac ... 5K 31
(off St Andrews)
Muirfield Rd. GU21: Wok ... 5K 73
Mulberries, The
GU9: Farnh ... 8L 109
Mulberry Av. SL4: W'sor ... 6J 5
TW19: Stan ... 2N 21
Mulberry Cl. GU12: A Va ... 9E 90
GU21: Wok ... 1A 74
GU47: Owls ... 7J 49
KT13: Weybr ... 9C 38
RG45: Crow ... 3H 49
RH12: Hors ... 3J 197
SW16 ... 5G 28
Mulberry Ct. GU4: Guil ... 1F 114
KT6: Surb ... 6K 41
RG12: Brac ... 4C 32
RG40: W'ham ... 2B 30
TW1: Twick ... 4F 24
Mulberry Cres. TW8: Brent ... 3H 11
Mulberry Dr. SL3: Lang ... 1A 6
Mulberry Gdns.
RH12: Bro H ... 5E 196
Mulberry Ga. SM7: Ban ... 3L 81
Mulberry Ho. BR2: Brom ... 1N 47
Mulberry La. CR0: Croy ... 7C 46
Mulberry M. SM6: W'ton ... 3G 62
Mulberry Pl. RH5: Newd ... 9B 140
W6 ... 1F 12
Mulberry Rd. RH11: Craw ... 9N 161
Mulberry Trees TW17: Shep ... 6E 38
Mulberry Way GU14: Cove ... 9J 69
Mulgrave Ct. SM2: Sut ... 3N 61
(off Mulgrave Rd.)
Mulgrave Rd.
CR0: Croy ... 5D 200 (9A 46)
GU16: Frim ... 4D 70
SM2: Sut ... 4L 61
SW6 ... 2L 13
Mulgrave Way GU21: Knap ... 5H 73
Mulholland Cl. CR4: Mit ... 1F 44
Mullards Cl. CR4: Mit ... 7D 44
Mullein Wlk. RH11: Craw ... 7M 181
Mullens Rd. TW20: Egh ... 6D 20
Muller Rd. SW4 ... 1H 29
Mullins Path SW14 ... 6C 12
Mulroy Dr. GU15: Camb ... 9E 50
Multon Rd. SW18 ... 1B 28
Muncaster Cl. TW15: A'ford ... 5B 22
Muncaster Rd.
TW15: A'ford ... 6C 22
Munday Ct. RG42: Bin ... 8K 15
Munday's Boro GU3: Put ... 8L 111
Munday's Boro Rd.
GU3: Put ... 8L 111
Mund St. W14 ... 1L 13
Mundy Ct. SL4: Eton ... 2G 4
Munnings Dr. GU47: C Tow ... 9J 49
Munnings Gdns. TW7: Isle ... 8D 10
Munro Ho. KT11: Cob ... 8L 57
Munro Way GU11: Alde ... 5B 90
Munslow Gdns. SM1: Sut ... 1B 62
Munstead Heath Rd.
GU5: Braml ... 9K 133
GU8: Bus ... 9K 133
Munstead Pk. GU8: Bus ... 8M 133
Munstead Vw. GU3: Art ... 7L 113
Munstead Vw. Rd.
GU5: Braml ... 6N 133
Munster Av. TW4: Houn ... 8M 9
Munster Ct. SW6 ... 5L 13
TW11: Tedd ... 7J 25
Munster M. SW6 ... 3K 13
Munster Rd. SW6 ... 3K 13
TW11: Tedd ... 7H 25
Murdoch Cl. TW18: Stain ... 6J 21
Murdoch Rd. RG40: W'ham ... 3B 30
Murfett Cl. SW19 ... 3K 27
Murray Av. TW3: Houn ... 8B 10
Murray Ct. RH11: Craw ... 8M 181
RH13: Hors ... 4A 198
SL5: S'hill ... 5N 33
TW2: Twick ... 3D 24
Murray Grn. GU21: Wok ... 1E 74
Murray Ho. KT16: Otter ... 3E 54
Murray Rd. GU14: Cove ... 2L 89
KT16: Otter ... 3E 54
SW19 ... 7J 27
TW10: Ham ... 3H 25
W5 ... 1J 11
Murray's La.
KT14: W By, Byf ... 1M 75
Murrays Rd. GU11: Alde ... 7B 90
Murrell Hill La. RG42: Bin ... 8H 15
Murrell Rd. GU12: Ash ... 1E 110
Murrells La. GU15: Camb ... 3N 69
Murrell's Wlk. KT23: Book ... 1A 98
Murreys, The KT21: A'tead ... 5J 79
Murreys Ct. KT21: A'tead ... 5K 79
Murtmead La. GU3: Put ... 9L 111
Musard Rd. W6 ... 2K 13
Muscal W6 ... 2K 13
(off Field Rd.)
Muschamp Rd. SM5: Cars ... 8C 44
Museum Hill GU27: Hasl ... 2H 189
Mus. of Eton Life ... 2G 5
Mus. of Richmond ... 8K 11
Mus. of Rugby, The ... 9E 10
Musgrave Av.
RH19: E Grin ... 2A 186
Musgrave Cres. SW6 ... 3M 13
Musgrave Rd. TW7: Isle ... 4F 10
Mushroom Castle
RG42: Wink R ... 7F 16
Musquash Way TW4: Houn ... 5K 9
Mustard Mill Rd.
TW18: Stain ... 5H 21
Mustians SL4: Eton ... 2F 4
(off Eton Wick Rd.)
Mustow Pl. SW6 ... 5L 13
Mutton Hill RG12: Bin ... 9H 15
RH7: Dorm ... 3C 166
Mutton Oaks RG12: Bin ... 9J 15
Muybridge Rd. KT3: N Mal ... 1B 42
Muybridge Yd. KT6: Surb ... 6M 41
Myers Way GU16: Frim ... 4H 71
Mylne Cl. W6 ... 1F 12
Mylne Sq. RG40: W'ham ... 2C 30
Mylor Cl. GU21: Wok ... 1A 74
Mynn's Cl. KT18: Eps ... 1A 80
MYNTHURST ... 4G 141
Mynthurst RH2: Leigh ... 4G 141
MYRKE ... 1J 5
Myrke, The SL3: Dat ... 1J 5
Myrna Cl. SW19 ... 8C 28
Myrtle Av. TW14: Felt ... 8F 8
Myrtle Cl. GU18: Ligh ... 7M 51
SL3: Poy ... 4G 6
Myrtle Dr. GU17: B'water ... 1J 69
Myrtle Gro. KT3: N Mal ... 1B 42
Myrtle Pas. RH4: Dork ... 2J 201
Myrtle Rd. CR0: Croy ... 9K 47
RH4: Dork ... 1J 201 (4G 119)
SM1: Sut ... 2A 62
TW3: Houn ... 5C 10
TW12: H Hill ... 7C 24
MYTCHETT ... 1D 90
Mytchett Farm Cvn. Pk.
GU16: Mytc ... 3D 90
Mytchett Heath GU16: Mytc ... 3E 90
Mytchett Lake Rd.
GU16: Mytc ... 4E 90
Mytchett Pl. Rd. GU12: A Va ... 4F 90
GU16: Mytc ... 2E 90
GU24: Pirb ... 4F 90
Mytchett Rd. GU16: Mytc ... 1D 90
Myton Rd. SE21 ... 4N 29

N

Naafi Rdbt. GU11: Alde ... 2N 109
Nadine Ct. SM6: W'ton ... 5G 62
Nailsworth Cres.
RH1: Mers ... 7H 103
Nairn Cl. GU16: Frim ... 4C 70
NALDERSWOOD ... 4H 141
Naldrett Cl. RH12: Hors ... 4M 197
Naldretts La. RH12: Rudg ... 3E 194
Nallhead Rd. TW13: Hanw ... 6K 23
Namba Roy Cl. SW16 ... 5K 29
Namton Dr. CR7: T Hea ... 3K 45
Napier Av. SW6 ... 6L 13
Napier Cl. GU11: Alde ... 6C 90
RG45: Crow ... 2H 49
Napier Ct. CR3: Cate ... 9B 84
GU21: Wok ... 3A 74
SW6 ... 6L 13
(off Ranelagh Gdns.)
Napier Dr. GU15: Camb ... 8E 50
Napier Gdns. GU1: Guil ... 2D 114
Napier La. GU12: A Va ... 9E 90
Napier Lodge TW15: A'ford ... 7E 22
Napier Rd. CR2: S Croy ... 4A 64
RG45: Crow ... 3H 49
SE25 ... 3E 46
TW7: Isle ... 7G 10
TW15: A'ford ... 8E 22
Napier Wlk. TW15: A'ford ... 8E 22
Napier Way RH10: Craw ... 9D 162
Napoleon Av. GU14: Farnb ... 8N 69
Napoleon Rd. TW1: Twick ... 1H 25
Napper Cl. SL5: Asc ... 1G 33
Napper Pl. GU6: Cranl ... 9N 155
Nappers Wood GU27: Fern ... 9E 188
Narborough St. SW6 ... 5N 13
Narrow La. CR6: Warl ... 6E 84
Narwhal Inuit Art Gallery ... 1C 12
Naseby RG12: Brac ... 7N 31
Naseby Cl. TW7: Isle ... 4E 10
Naseby Ct. KT12: Wal T ... 8K 39
NASH ... 3C 66
Nash Cl. GU14: Cove ... 1L 89
SM1: Sut ... 9B 44
Nash Dr. RH1: Red ... 1D 122
Nash Gdns. RH1: Red ... 1D 122
SL5: Asc ... 1J 33
Nashlands Cotts.
RH17: Hand ... 6N 199
Nash La. BR2: Kes ... 4C 66
Nash Pk. RG42: Bin ... 7G 15
Nash Rd. RH10: Craw ... 6C 182
SL3: Lang ... 1B 6
Nassau Rd. SW13 ... 4E 12
Nasturtium Dr. GU24: Bis ... 2D 72
Natalie Cl. TW14: Bedf ... 1E 22
Natalie M. TW2: H Hill ... 4D 24
Natal Rd. CR7: T Hea ... 2A 46
SW16 ... 7H 29
National Archives, The ... 3N 11
National Walks TW4: Houn ... 6N 9
Natural History Mus.
Eton ... 2G 4
Navigation Ho. KT15: Addl ... 1N 55
Navigator Pk. UB2: S'hall ... 1K 9
Neale Cl. RH19: E Grin ... 7L 165
Neath Gdns. SM4: Mord ... 5A 44
Neb La. RH8: Oxt ... 9M 105
Needham Cl. SL4: W'sor ... 4B 4
Needles Bank RH9: Gods ... 9E 104
(not continuous)
Needles Cl. RH12: Hors ... 7H 197
Neil Cl. TW15: A'ford ... 6D 22
Neil Wates Cres. SW2 ... 2L 29
Nella Rd. W6 ... 2J 13
Nell Ball RH14: Plais ... 6A 192
Nell Gwynne Av. SL5: S'hill ... 3A 34
TW17: Shep ... 5E 38
Nell Gwynne Cl. KT19: Eps ... 7N 59
SL5: S'hill ... 3A 34

266 A-Z Surrey

Nelson Cl.—Norley Va.

Nelson Cl.
CR0: Croy 1A **200** (7M **45**)
GU9: H End 4J **109**
GU12: Alde 3A **110**
KT12: Wal T 7J **39**
RG12: Brac 9C **16**
RH10: Craw 4G **183**
TN16: B Hil 4G **86**
TW14: Felt 2G **23**
Nelson Ct. KT16: Chert 7J **37**
Nelson Gdns. GU1: Guil 2C **114**
TW3: Houn 9A **10**
Nelson Gro. Rd. SW19 . . . . .9N **27**
Nelson Rd. CR3: Cate 1A **104**
GU9: H End 4J **109**
KT3: N Mal 4C **42**
RH12: Hors 5H **197**
SL4: W'sor 6C **4**
SW19 . . . . .8N **27**
TW2: Whitt 1B **24**
TW3: Houn 9A **10**
TW6: Lon A 4A **8**
TW15: A'ford 6N **21**
Nelson Rd. M. *SW19 . . . . .8N 27*
(off Nelson Rd.)
Nelson's La. RG10: Hurst 4A **14**
Nelson St. GU11: Alde 2M **109**
Nelson Trad. Est.
SW19 . . . . .9N **27**
Nelson Wlk. KT19: Eps 5N **59**
Nelson Way GU15: Camb 2L **69**
Nene Gdns. TW13: Hanw 4N **23**
Nene Rd. TW6: Lon A 4C **8**
Nene Rd. Rdbt. TW6: Lon A 4C **8**
Nepean St. SW15 . . . . .9F **12**
Neptune Cl. RH11: Craw 5K **181**
Neptune Rd. GU35: Bor 7A **168**
TW6: Lon A 4E **8**
Nero Ct. TW8: Brent 3K **11**
Nesbit Ct. RH11: Craw 6K **181**
Nescot Sports Cen. 7F **60**
Netheravon Rd. W4 . . . . .1E **12**
Netheravon Rd. Sth.
W4 . . . . .1E **12**
Netherby Pk. KT13: Weybr 2F **56**
Nethercote Av. GU21: Wok 4J **73**
Netherfield Rd. SW17 . . . . .4E **28**
Netherlands, The CR5: Coul . . .6G **83**
Netherleigh Pk.
RH1: Sth N 6J **123**
Nether Mt. GU2: Guil 5L **113**
Nethern Ct. Rd.
CR3: Wold 1K **105**
Netherne Dr. CR5: Coul 8F **82**
Netherne La. CR5: Coul 8G **83**
RH1: Coul 1G **102**
NETHERNE-ON-THE-HILL 9H **83**
Netherton RG12: Brac 3M **31**
Netherton Rd. TW1: Twick 8G **11**
Nether Vell-Mead
GU52: C Cro 9A **88**
Netherwood RH11: Craw 5N **181**
Netley Cl. CR0: N Add 4M **65**
GU5: Gorn 7D **116**
RH11: Craw 9A **182**
SM3: Chea 2J **61**
Netley Dr. KT12: Wal T 6N **39**
Netley Gdns. SM4: Mord 6A **44**
Netley Rd. SM4: Mord 6A **44**
TW8: Brent 2L **11**
Netley St. GU14: Farnb 5N **89**
Nettlecombe RG12: Brac 5B **32**
Nettlecombe Cl. SM2: Sut 5N **61**
Nettlefold Pl. SE27 . . . . .4M **29**
Nettlefold Wlk. KT12: Wal T . . .7G **39**
Nettles Ter.
GU1: Guil 3C **202** (3N **113**)
Nettleton Rd. TW6: Lon A 4C **8**
Nettlewood Rd. SW16 . . . . . . .8H **29**
Neuman Cres. RG12: Brac 5M **31**
Nevada Cl. GU14: Cove 2J **89**
KT3: N Mal 3B **42**
Nevelle Cl. RG42: Bin 9J **15**
Nevern Mans. *SW5 . . . . .1M 13*
(off Nevern Sq.)
Nevern Pl. SW5 . . . . .1M **13**
Nevern Rd. SW5 . . . . .1M **13**
Nevern Sq. SW5 . . . . .1M **13**
Nevile Cl. RH11: Craw 6M **181**
Neville Av. KT3: N Mal 9C **26**
Neville Cl. KT10: Esh 3N **57**
SM7: Ban 1N **81**
TW3: Houn 5B **10**
Neville Duke Rd.
GU14: Cove 6L **69**
Neville Gill Cl. SW18 . . . . .9M **13**
Neville Ho. Yd.
KT1: K Tham 3J **203** (1L **41**)
Neville Rd. CR0: Croy 6A **46**
KT1: K Tham 1N **41**
TW10: Ham 4J **25**
Neville Wlk. SM5: Cars 6C **44**
Nevis Rd. SW17 . . . . .3E **28**
New Acres Mobile Home Pk.
RG40: W'ham 9D **30**
NEW ADDINGTON 6M **65**
New Addington Pools & Fitness Cen.
. . . . .6M **65**
New Addington Stop (CT) 6M **65**
Newall Rd. TW6: Lon A 4D **8**
Newark Cl. GU4: B'ham 7D **94**
GU23: Rip 8J **75**
Newark Cotts. GU23: Rip 8J **75**
Newark Ct. KT12: Wal T 7K **39**
Newark La. GU22: Pyr 6H **75**
GU23: Rip 6H **75**
Newark Rd. CR2: S Croy 3A **64**
GU17: Min 5D **68**
GU20: Windl 1M **51**
RH10: Craw 1D **182**
New Ashgate Gallery 1G **129**
New Barn Cl. SM6: W'ton 3K **63**
New Barn La. CR3: Whyte 3B **84**
RH5: Newd 9B **140**
RH5: Ockl 7A **158**
TN14: Cud 5L **87**
TN16: Cud, Weste 5L **87**
New Barns Av. CR4: Mit 3H **45**
(not continuous)
New Battlebridge La.
RH1: Mers 8F **102**
Newberry Cres. SL4: W'sor 5A **4**
New Berry La. KT12: Hers 2L **57**
Newbolt Av. SM3: Chea 2H **61**
Newborough Grn.
KT3: N Mal 3C **42**
Newbridge Cl. RH12: Bro H . . .5C **196**
New Bri. Cotts.
GU6: Cranl 7K 155
(off Elmbridge Rd.)
Newbridge Ct. GU6: Cranl 7K **155**
New Bri. Rdbt.
RH12: Bro H 5C **196**
New B'way. TW12: H Hill 6D **24**
Newbury Gdns. KT19: Ewe 1E **60**
Newbury Rd. RH10: Craw 3H **183**
TW6: Lon A 4A **8**
New C'way. RH2: Reig 6N **121**
NEWCHAPEL 1H **165**
Newchapel Rd. RH7: Ling 1J **165**
New Chapel Sq. TW13: Felt 2J **23**
New Chiswick Pool 3D **12**
New Cl. SW19 . . . . .2A **44**
TW13: Hanw 6M **23**
New Colebrooke Ct.
SM5: Cars 4D 62
(off Stanley Rd.)
Newcombe Gdns.
SW16 . . . . .5J **29**
TW4: Houn 7N **9**
Newcome Pl. GU12: Alde 5B **110**
Newcome Rd.
GU9: Weybo 6K **109**
New Coppice GU21: Wok 6H **73**
New Cotts. GU24: Pirb 9A **72**
RH10: T Hil 5D **184**
New Ct. KT15: Addl 9L **37**
New Cross Rd. GU2: Guil 1K **113**
New Dawn Cl. GU14: Cove 2J **89**
NEWDIGATE 1A **160**
Newdigate Rd. RH2: Leigh . . .1D **140**
RH5: B Grn 9K **139**
RH12: Rusp 1B **180**
NEWELL GREEN 6B **16**
Newell Grn. RG42: Warf 6A **16**
New England Hill
GU24: W End 8A **52**
Newenham Rd. KT23: Book . . .4A **98**
Newent Cl. SM5: Cars 7D **44**
New Farm Cl. TW18: Stain 9L **21**
New Farthingdale
RH7: Dorm 2C **166**
Newfield Av. GU14: Cove 8K **69**
Newfield Cl. TW12: Hamp 9A **24**
Newfield Rd. GU12: A Va 7E **90**
New Forest Ride
RG12: Brac 3D **32**
Newfoundland Rd.
GU16: Deep 6H **71**
Newgate CR0: Croy 7N **45**
Newgate Cl. TW13: Hanw 3M **23**
Newhache RH7: Dorm 1C **166**
Newhall Gdns. KT12: Wal T 8K **39**
Newhaven Cres.
TW15: A'ford 6E **22**
Newhaven Rd. SE25 . . . . .4A **46**
NEW HAW 4L **55**
New Haw Rd. KT15: Addl 2L **55**
New Heston Rd. TW5: Hest 3N **9**
Newholme Ct. KT13: Weybr 9F **38**
New Horizons Ct.
TW8: Brent 2G **11**
Newhouse Bus. Cen.
RH12: Fay 1B **198**
Newhouse Cl. KT3: N Mal 6D **42**
Newhouse Cotts.
RH5: Newd 6B **160**
New Ho. Farm La.
GU3: Wood V 2F **112**
New Ho. La. RH1: Salf 2H **143**
Newhouse Ter. TN8: Eden 9L **127**
Newhouse Wlk. SM4: Mord 6A **44**
Newhurst Gdns.
RG42: Warf 6B **16**
New Inn La. GU4: B'ham 8D **94**
New Kelvin Av. TW11: Tedd 7E **24**
New Kings Rd. SW6 . . . . .5L **13**
Newlands GU52: Fleet 7B **88**
Newlands, The KT7: T Dit 7E **40**
SM6: W'ton 4G **63**
Newlands Av. GU22: Wok 8B **74**
KT7: T Dit 7E **40**
Newlands Cl. GU46: Yate 1C **68**
KT12: Hers 1M **57**
RH6: Horl 6D **142**
UB2: S'hall 1M **9**
NEWLANDS CORNER 5J **115**
Newlands Corner Countryside Cen.
. . . . .5J **115**
Newlands Ct. *CR3: Cate 8N 83*
(off Coulsdon Rd.)
KT15: Addl 2K 55
(off Addlestone Pk.)
Newlands Cres. GU1: Guil . . .5B **114**
RH19: E Grin 8N **165**
Newlands Dr. GU12: A Va 9F **90**
SL3: Poy 6G **7**
Newlands Est. GU8: Wit 5C **152**
Newlands Farm Ind. Est.
RG40: W'ham 7G **31**
Newlands Flats *GU1: Guil 2B 114*
(off Buckingham Cl.)
Newlands Pk. RH10: Cop 7B **164**
Newlands Pl.
RH18: F Row 6H **187**
Newlands Rd. GU15: Camb . . .5N **69**
RH11: Craw 4A **182**
RH12: Hors 4J **197**
SW16 . . . . .1J **45**
Newlands Way KT9: Ches 2J **59**
Newlands Wood CR0: Sels 5J **65**
New La. GU4: Sut G 9A **74**
New Lodge Dr. RH8: Oxt 6B **106**
Newlyn KT13: Weybr 1G **56**
NEW MALDEN 3D **42**
New Malden Station (Rail) . . .2D **42**
Newman Cl. RH10: Craw 5G **182**
Newman Rd. CR0: Croy 7K **45**
Newman Rd. Ind. Est.
CR0: Croy 6K **45**
Newmans Ct. GU9: U Hal 5F **108**
Newmans La. KT6: Surb 5K **41**
Newmans Pl. SL5: S'dale 6E **34**
Newmarket Rd.
RH10: Craw 6E **182**
New Mdw. SL5: Asc 9H **17**
New Mile Rd. SL5: Asc 1M **33**
New Mill Cotts.
GU27: Hasl 2B **188**
Newminster Rd. SM4: Mord . . .5A **44**
New Moorhead Dr.
RH12: Hors 2B **198**
Newnes Path SW15 . . . . .7G **12**
Newnham Cl. CR7: T Hea 1N **45**
New North Rd. RH2: Reig 6L **121**
New Pde. KT23: Book 3C **98**
TW15: A'ford 5A **22**
New Pk. Pde. *SW2 . . . . .1J 29*
(off New Pk. Rd.)
New Pk. Rd. GU6: Cranl 7N **155**
SW2 . . . . .2H **29**
TW15: A'ford 6D **22**
New Pl. CR0: A'ton 3K **65**
New Pl. Gdns. RH7: Ling 7A **146**
New Pond Rd.
GU3: Art, Comp 1G **132**
GU7: Goda 1G **132**
New Poplars Ct.
GU12: Ash 3E **110**
Newport Dr. RG42: Warf 7N **15**
Newport Rd. GU12: Alde 3A **110**
SW13 . . . . .4F **12**
TW6: Lon A 4B **8**
New Rd. CR4: Mit 7D **44**
GU4: Chil, Guil 1D **134**
GU4: E Cla 9N **95**
GU5: Alb 8M **115**
GU5: Gorn 8D **116**
GU5: Wone 3D **134**
GU8: Hamb 4H **153**
GU8: Mil 1B **152**
GU8: Worm 1D **172**
GU10: Tong 6D **110**
GU17: Haw 2K **69**
GU19: Bag 4K **51**
GU20: Bag, Windl 4K **51**
GU27: Hasl 3D **188**
GU47: Sandh 7F **48**
GU52: C Cro 7C **88**
KT2: K Tham 8N **25**
KT8: W Mole 3A **40**
KT10: Esh 9C **40**
KT13: Weybr 2D **56**
KT20: Tad 1H **101**
KT22: Oxs 7F **58**
RG12: Brac 1B **32**
RG45: Crow 2H **49**
RH5: Dork 6K **119**
RH5: For G 4M **157**
RH6: Smal 8M **143**
RH8: Limp 8D **106**
RH8: Tand 5K **125**
SL3: Dat 4N **5**
SL5: Asc 8J **17**
TW3: Houn 7B **10**
TW8: Brent 2K **11**
TW10: Ham 5J **25**
TW13: Hanw 6M **23**
TW14: Bedf 9E **8**
TW14: Felt 2J **23**
TW17: Shep 2B **38**
TW18: Stain 6E **20**
UB3: Harl 3D **8**
New Rd. Hill BR2: Kes 5G **67**
BR6: Dow 5G **67**
Newry Rd. TW1: Twick 8G **11**
Newsham Rd. GU21: Wok 4J **73**
New Sq. TW14: Bedf 2D **22**
New Sq. Pk. TW14: Bedf 2D **22**
Newstead Cl. GU7: Goda 5G **132**
Newstead Hall RH6: Horl 9H **143**
Newstead Ho. CR3: Cate 4E **104**
Newstead Ri. CR3: Cate 4E **104**
Newstead Wlk. SM5: Cars 6A **44**
Newstead Way
SW19 . . . . .5J **27**
New St. RH10: Craw 2E **182**
RH13: Hors 7K **197**
TN16: Weste 5L **107**
TW18: Stain 5J **21**
Newton Av. RH19: E Grin 3B **186**
Newton Ct. SL4: O Win 9K **5**
Newton La. SL4: O Win 9L **5**
Newton Mans. *W14 . . . . .2K 13*
(off Queen's Club Gdns.)
Newton Rd. CR8: Pur 8G **63**
GU14: Farnb 8B **70**
RH10: Craw 8D **162**
SW19 . . . . .8K **27**
TW7: Isle 5F **10**
Newtonside Orchard
SL4: O Win 9K **5**
Newton's Yd. SW18 . . . . .8M **13**
Newton Way GU10: Tong 5C **110**
Newton Wood Rd.
KT21: A'tead 3M **79**
NEW TOWN 7K **197**
New Town RH10: Cop 7M **163**
Newtown Ct. RH13: Hors 7K **197**
Newtown Rd. GU47: Sandh 7G **48**
New Victoria Theatre *4A 74*
(in The Ambassadors)
New Way GU7: Goda 7E **132**
New Wickham La.
TW20: Egh 8C **20**
NEW WINDSOR 6G **4**
New Wokingham Rd.
RG40: W'ham 9F **30**
RG45: Crow 9F **30**
New Zealand Av.
KT12: Wal T 7G **38**
Nexus Pk. GU12: A Va 5D **90**
Nicholas Ct. *W4 . . . . .2D 12*
(off Corney Reach Way)
Nicholas Gdns. GU22: Pyr 3H **75**
Nicholas Lodge KT10: Esh 8A **40**
Nicholas M. W4 . . . . .2D **12**
Nicholas Rd. CR0: Bedd 1J **63**
Nicholes Rd. TW3: Houn 7A **10**
Nicholls SL4: W'sor 6A **4**
Nicholls Cl. CR3: Cate 9N **83**
Nicholls Wlk. SL4: W'sor 6A **4**
Nichols Cl. KT9: Ches 3J **59**
Nicholsfield RH14: Loxw 4H **193**
Nicholson M.
KT1: K Tham 7K **203** (3L **41**)
TW20: Egh 6C 20
(off Nicholson Wlk.)
Nicholson Rd. CR0: Croy 7C **46**
Nicholson Wlk. TW20: Egh 6C **20**
Nickols Wlk. SW18 . . . . .7N **13**
Nicola Cl. CR2: S Croy 3N **63**
Nicol Cl. TW1: Twick 9H **11**
Nicosia Rd. SW18 . . . . .1C **28**
Nigel Fisher Way KT9: Ches . . .4J **59**
Nigel Playfair Av. W6 . . . . . . .1G **12**
Nightingale Av.
KT24: W Hors 2E **96**
Nightingale Cl. GU14: Cove . . .8H **69**
GU27: Fern 9E **188**
KT11: Cob 7L **57**
KT19: Eps 8N **59**
RH11: Craw 1A **182**
RH19: E Grin 2N **185**
SM5: Cars 8E **44**
TN16: B Hil 2E **86**
W4 . . . . .2B **12**
Nightingale Ct. GU21: Wok 5H **73**
RH1: Red 2E 122
(off St Anne's Mt.)
SM1: Sut 2A **62**
SW6 . . . . .4N 13
(off Maltings Pl.)
Nightingale Cres.
KT24: W Hors 3D **96**
RG12: Brac 4A **32**
Nightingale Dr. GU16: Mytc . . .2E **90**
KT19: Ewe 3A **60**
Nightingale Gdns.
GU47: Sandh 7G **48**
Nightingale Ho.
KT17: Eps 5L **201** (8D **60**)
Nightingale Ind. Est.
RH12: Hors 5K **197**
Nightingale La.
RH10: T Hil 4F **184**
SW12 . . . . .1D **28**
TW10: Rich 1L **25**
Nightingale M.
KT1: K Tham 5H **203**
Nightingale Rd. CR2: Sels 7G **64**
GU1: Guil 2D **202** (3N **113**)
GU7: Goda 6H **133**
GU12: Ash 1G **111**
KT8: W Mole 4B **40**
KT10: Esh 2N **57**
KT12: Wal T 6K **39**
KT24: E Hor 3G **96**
RH12: Hors 5K **197**
SM5: Cars 9D **44**
TW12: Hamp 6A **24**
Nightingales GU6: Cranl 9N **155**
Nightingales, The
TW19: Stan 2A **22**
Nightingales Cl.
RH13: Hors 6M **197**
Nightingale Shott
TW20: Egh 7B **20**
Nightingale Sq. SW12 . . . . . . .1E **28**
Nightingale Wlk.
SL4: W'sor 6F **4**
Nightingale Way RH1: Blet . . .3B **124**
Nightjar Cl. GU10: Ews 4C **108**
Nimbus Rd. KT19: Eps 6C **60**
Nimrod Ct. *RH10: Craw 9H 163*
(off Wakehams Grn. Dr.)
Nimrod Rd. SW16 . . . . .7F **28**
Nineacres Way CR5: Coul 3J **83**
Nine Elms Cl. TW14: Felt 2G **23**
Ninehams Cl. CR3: Cate 7A **84**
Ninehams Gdns. CR3: Cate 7A **84**
Ninehams Rd. CR3: Cate 8A **84**
TN16: Tats 8E **86**
Nine Mile Ride RG12: Brac 7A **32**
RG40: Finch, W'ham 1A **48**
RG45: Brac 7L **31**
SL5: Asc 6J **33**
Nineteenth Rd. CR4: Mit 3J **45**
Ninfield Ct. RH11: Craw 7L **181**
Ninhams Wood BR6: Farnb 1J **67**
Ninth Av. KT20: Lwr K 3L **101**
Niton Rd. TW9: Rich 6N **11**
Niton St. SW6 . . . . .3J **13**
Niven Cl. RH10: Craw 4H **183**
Noah's Ct. RH10: T Hil 5D **184**
Nobel Dr. UB3: Harl 4E **8**
Noble Cnr. TW5: Hest 4A **10**
Noble Ct. CR4: Mit 1B **44**
Noble St. KT12: Wal T 9K **39**
Nobles Way TW20: Egh 7A **20**
Noel Ct. TW4: Houn 6N **9**
Noke Dr. RH1: Red 2E **122**
Nokes Ct. RH10: Craw 4D **182**
Nomad Theatre 6G **96**
Nonsuch Ct. Av. KT17: Ewe . . .6G **60**
Nonsuch Ho. SW19 . . . . .9B **28**
Nonsuch Pl. *SM3: Chea 4J 61*
(off Ewell Rd.)
Nonsuch Trad. Est.
KT17: Eps 7D **60**
Nonsuch Wlk. SM2: Chea 6H **61**
(not continuous)
Nook, The GU47: Sandh 7F **48**
Noons Cnr. Rd.
RH5: A Com 3N **137**
NORBITON 1N **41**
Norbiton Av. KT1: K Tham 9N **25**
Norbiton Comn. Rd.
KT1: K Tham 2A **42**
Norbiton Hall
KT2: K Tham . . .3M **203** (1M **41**)
Norbiton Station (Rail) 9N **25**
NORBURY 1K **45**
Norbury Av. CR7: T Hea 9K **29**
SW16 . . . . .9K **29**
TW3: Houn 7D **10**
Norbury Cl. SW16 . . . . .9L **29**
Norbury Ct. Rd.
SW16 . . . . .2J **45**
Norbury Cres. SW16 . . . . .9K **29**
Norbury Cross SW16 . . . . .2J **45**
Norbury Hill SW16 . . . . .8L **29**
NORBURY PARK 4H **99**
Norbury Ri. SW16 . . . . .2J **45**
Norbury Rd. CR7: T Hea 1N **45**
RH2: Reig 3L **121**
TW13: Felt 4G **22**
Norbury Station (Rail) 9K **29**
Norbury Trad. Est.
SW16 . . . . .1K **45**
Norbury Way KT23: Book 3C **98**
Norcutt Rd. TW2: Twick 2E **24**
Norfolk Av. CR2: Sande 6C **64**
Norfolk Chase RG42: Warf 8D **16**
Norfolk Cl. RH6: Horl 9E **142**
RH11: Craw 7K **181**
TW1: Twick 9H **11**
Norfolk Ct. RH5: Nth H 9K **119**
RH12: Hors 3A **198**
Norfolk Farm Cl. GU22: Pyr . . .3F **74**
Norfolk Farm Rd.
GU22: Pyr 2F **74**
Norfolk Gdns. TW4: Houn 8N **9**
Norfolk Ho. Rd. SW16 . . . . . . .4H **29**
Norfolk La. RH5: Mid H 2H **139**
Norfolk Rd. CR7: T Hea 2N **45**
KT10: Clay 2E **58**
RH4: Dork 3J **201** (5G **119**)
RH5: Holm 5J **139**
RH12: Hors 6K **197**
SW19 . . . . .8C **28**
TW13: Felt 2K **23**
Norfolk Ter. RH12: Hors 6K **197**
W6 . . . . .1K **13**
Norgrove St. SW12 . . . . .1E **28**
Norheads La. CR6: B Hil 6C **86**
TN16: B Hil 5C **86**
Norhyrst Av. SE25 . . . . .2C **46**
NORK 2J **81**
Nork Gdns. SM7: Ban 1K **81**
Nork Ri. SM7: Ban 3J **81**
Nork Way SM7: Ban 3H **81**
Norlands La. TW20: Thor 2G **36**
Norley La. GU5: Sha G 6D **134**
Norley Va. SW15 . . . . .2F **26**

Norman Av.—Oak Dell

Norman Av. CR2: Sande 6N 63
KT17: Eps 8E 60
TW1: Twick 1J 25
TW13: Hanw 3M 23
Normanby Cl. SW15 8L 13
Norman Cl. GU35: Bor 6A 168
KT18: Tat C 6G 81
Norman Colyer Ct.
KT19: Eps 6C 60
Norman Ct. GU9: Farnh 2H 129
TN8: Eden 1K 147
Norman Cres. TW5: Hest 3L 9
Normand Gdns. W14 2K 13
(off Greyhound Rd.)
Normand Mans. W14 2K 13
(off Normand M.)
Normand M. W14 2K 13
Normand Rd. W14 2L 13
NORMANDY 9M 91
Normandy RH12: Hors 7J 197
Normandy Cl. GU16: Deep 6J 71
RH10: Craw 5F 182
RH19: E Grin 1B 186
NORMANDY COMMON 9L 91
Normandy Comn. La.
GU3: Norm 9M 91
Normandy Gdns.
RH12: Hors 7J 197
Normandy Wlk. TW20: Egh 6E 20
Norman Hay Trad. Est., The
UB7: Sip 3A 8
Norman Ho. TW13: Hanw 3N 23
(off Watermill Way)
Normanhurst TW15: A'ford 6B 22
Normanhurst Cl.
RH10: Craw 3D 182
Normanhurst Dr.
TW1: Twick 8G 11
Normanhurst Rd.
KT12: Wal T 8L 39
SW2 3K 29
Norman Keep RG42: Warf 9D 16
Norman Rd. CR7: T Hea 4M 45
SM1: Sut 2M 61
SW19 8A 28
TW15: A'ford 7E 22
Normansfield Av.
TW11: Tedd 8J 25
Normans Gdns.
RH19: E Grin 9A 166
Normans La. TN8: Eden 4G 147
Norman's Rd. RH1: Out 6N 143
RH6: Smal 6N 143
Normanton Av. SW19 3M 27
Normanton Rd.
CR2: S Croy 8F 200 (2B 64)
Normington Cl. SW16 6L 29
NORNEY 5B 132
Norney GU8: S'ford 5B 132
Norrels Dr. KT24: E Hor 4G 96
(not continuous)
Norrels Ride KT24: E Hor 3G 97
Norreys Av. RG40: W'ham 2C 30
Norris Cl. KT19: Eps 7A 60
Norris Hill Rd. GU51: Fleet 5D 88
GU52: Fleet 5D 88
Norris Rd. TW18: Stain 5H 21
Norroy Rd. SW15 7J 13
Norstead Pl. SW15 3F 26
North Acre SM7: Ban 3L 81
Northampton Cl.
RG12: Brac 2B 32
Northampton Rd. CR0: Croy 8D 46
Northanger Rd. SW16 7J 29
NORTH ASCOT 9H 17
North Ash RH12: Hors 4J 197
North Av. GU9: H End 5J 109
KT12: Whit V 5F 56
SM5: Cars 4E 62
TW9: Kew 4N 11
Northborough Rd.
SW16 2H 45
Northbourne GU7: Goda 3J 133
Nth. Breache Rd.
GU6: Ewh 4H 157
NORTH BRIDGE 3F 172
Northbrook Copse
RG12: Brac 5D 32
Northbrook Rd. CR0: Croy 4A 46
GU11: Alde 4N 109
NORTH CAMP 7A 90
North Camp Station (Rail) 5D 90
Nth. Camp Sta. Rdbt.
GU14: Farnb 5C 90
NORTHCHAPEL 9D 190
NORTH CHEAM 9H 43
North Cheam Sports Club 9J 43
Northcliffe Cl. KT4: W Pk 9D 42
North Cl. GU12: Alde 3C 110
GU14: Farnb 6M 69
RH5: Nth H 9J 119
RH10: Craw 2D 182
SL4: W'sor 4C 4
SM4: Mord 3K 43
TW14: Bedf 9E 8
North Comn. KT13: Weybr 1D 56
Northcote KT15: Addl 1M 55
Northcote Av. KT5: Surb 6A 42
TW7: Isle 8G 10
Northcote Cl. KT24: W Hors 3D 96
Northcote Cres.
KT24: W Hors 3D 96
Northcote La. GU5: Sha G 5F 134
Northcote Pk. KT22: Oxs 1C 78
Northcote Rd. CR0: Croy 5A 46
GU12: A Va 6D 90
GU14: Cove 8L 69
KT3: N Mal 2B 42
KT24: W Hors 3D 96
TW1: Twick 8G 11
Northcott RG12: Brac 7M 31
Northcott Gdns. GU14: Cove 9J 69
North Ct. GU7: Goda 4E 132
Northcroft Cl. TW20: Eng G 6L 19
Northcroft Gdns.
TW20: Eng G 6L 19
Northcroft Rd. KT19: Ewe 4D 60
TW20: Eng G 6L 19
Northcroft Vs. TW20: Eng G 6L 19
Northdale Ct. SE25 2C 46
North Dene TW3: Houn 4B 10
North Down CR2: Sande 7B 64
Northdown Cl.
RH12: Hors 4M 197
Northdown La.
GU1: Guil 8F 202 (6A 114)
Northdown Rd. CR3: Wold 2K 105
SM2: Sut 6M 61
Northdowns GU6: Cranl 9N 155
Nth. Downs Cres.
CR0: N Add 5L 65
(not continuous)
Nth. Downs Rd. CR0: N Add 6L 65
Northdown Ter.
RH19: E Grin 7N 165
North Dr. BR3: Beck 3L 47
BR6: Orp 1N 67
GU24: B'wood 8N 71
GU25: V Wat 5H 35
SW16 5G 28
TW3: Houn 5C 10
North E. Surrey Crematorium
SM4: Mord 5H 43
NORTH END 7L 165
North End
CR0: Croy 2B 200 (8N 45)
RH19: E Grin 7L 165
North End Cres. W14 1L 13
North End Ho. W14 1K 13
North End La. BR6: Dow 7J 67
SL5: S'dale 6E 34
North End Pde. W14 1K 13
(off North End Rd.)
North End Rd. SW6 2L 13
W14 1K 13
Northerams Woods Nature Reserve
3K 31
Northernhay Wlk.
SM4: Mord 3K 43
Northern Perimeter Rd.
TW6: Lon A 4C 8
Northern Perimeter Rd. (West)
TW6: Lon A 4M 7
Northey Av. SM2: Chea 6J 61
Nth. Eyot Gdns. W6 1E 12
Nth. Farm Rd. GU14: Cove 6L 69
NORTH FARNBOROUGH 1N 89
NORTH FELTHAM 9J 9
Nth. Feltham Trad. Est.
TW14: Felt 8J 9
Northfield GU4: Chil 2A 134
GU8: Wit 6C 152
GU18: Ligh 7M 51
Northfield Cl. GU12: Alde 3B 110
GU52: C Cro 7D 88
Northfield Ct. TW18: Stain 9K 21
Northfield Cres. SM3: Chea 1K 61
Northfield Farm M.
KT11: Cob 9H 57
Northfield Pl. KT13: Weybr 4C 56
Northfield Rd. GU52: C Cro 7C 88
KT11: Cob 9H 57
TW5: Hest 2L 9
TW18: Stain 9K 21
Northfields KT17: Eps 7D 60
KT21: A'tead 5L 79
(not continuous)
SW18 7M 13
Northfields Prospect Bus. Cen.
SW18 7M 13
Northfleet Lodge
GU22: Wok 6A 74
North Fryerne GU46: Yate 7C 48
North Gdns. SW19 8B 28
NORTHGATE 2C 182
Northgate Av. RH10: Craw 3C 182
Northgate Dr. GU15: Camb 8E 50
Northgate Pl. RH10: Craw 2C 182
Nth. Gate Rd. GU14: Farnb 3A 90
Northgate Rd. RH6: Gat 2D 162
(off Racecourse Rd.)
RH10: Craw 3B 182
North Grn. RG12: Brac 9B 16
North Gro. KT16: Chert 5H 37
Nth. Hatton Rd. TW6: Lon A 4E 8
Nth. Heath Cl. RH12: Hors 3K 197
Nth. Heath Est.
RH12: Hors 2K 197
Nth. Heath La.
RH12: Hors 4K 197
Nth. Holmes Cl.
RH12: Hors 3A 198
NORTH HOLMWOOD 9H 119
North Ho. GU6: Cranl 5L 155
Nth. Hyde La. TW5: Hest 1M 9
UB2: S'hall 1L 9
Northington Cl. RG12: Brac 5D 32
Northlands Av. BR6: Orp 1N 67
Northlands Bungs.
RH5: Newd 2A 160
Northlands Bus. Pk.
RH12: Warn 5C 178
Northlands Cotts.
RH12: Warn 5D 178
Northlands Rd.
RH12: Hors 1L 197
RH12: Warn 6D 178
North La. GU12: Alde 1B 110
TW11: Tedd 7F 24
Nth. Lodge Cl. SW15 8J 13
Nth. Lodge Dr. SL5: Asc 1G 33
NORTH LOOE 9H 61
North Mall GU51: Fleet 4A 88
SW18 8N 13
(off Buckhold Rd.)
TW18: Stain 5H 21
(in Elmsleigh Shop. Cen.)
North Mead RH1: Red 9D 102
RH10: Craw 1C 182
Northmead GU14: Farnb 1N 89
North Moors GU1: Guil 8A 94
NORTH MUNSTEAD 2L 153
Nth. Munstead La.
GU7: Bus 1K 153
GU8: Bus 1K 153
Northolt Rd. TW6: Lon A 4M 7
North Pde. KT9: Ches 2M 59
RH12: Hors 3J 197
North Pk. La. RH9: Gods 7D 104
North Pas. SW18 8M 13
Nth. Perimeter Rd.
RH6: Gat 4B 162
(off Old Control Tower Rd.)
North Pl. CR4: Mit 8D 28
TW11: Tedd 7F 24
Northpoint Cl. SM1: Sut 9A 44
Nth. Pole La. BR2: Kes 3B 66
North Rd. BR4: W Wick 7L 47
GU2: Guil 9L 93
GU12: A Va 9D 90
GU21: Wok 3C 74
KT6: Surb 5K 41
KT12: Hers 2K 57
RH2: Reig 6L 121
RH10: Craw 1E 182
SL5: Asc 9F 16
SW19 7A 28
TW5: Hest 2K 9
TW8: Brent 2L 11
TW9: Kew 4N 11
TW9: Rich 6N 11
TW14: Bedf 9E 8
Northrop Rd. TW6: Lon A 4F 8
NORTH SHEEN 6N 11
North Sheen Station (Rail) 7N 11
North Side GU10: Tong 5D 110
North Side Ct GU10: Tong 5E 110
Northspur Rd. SM1: Sut 9M 43
Nth. Station App.
RH1: Sth N 5K 123
Northstead Rd. SW2 3L 29
North St.
GU1: Guil 5C 202 (4N 113)
GU7: Goda 4H 133
KT22: Leat 8G 79
RH1: Red 2D 122
RH4: Dork 2J 201 (5G 119)
RH10: T Hil 5D 184
RH12: Hors 6K 197
SL4: Wink 5K 17
SM5: Cars 9D 44
TW7: Isle 6G 11
TW20: Egh 6B 20
Nth. Terminal App.
RH6: Gat 2D 162
North Ter. SL4: W'sor 3G 5
NORTH TOWN 1C 110
Northtown Trad. Est.
GU12: Alde 2C 110
Northumberland Av.
TW7: Isle 4F 10
Northumberland Cl.
RG42: Warf 8D 16
TW19: Stan 9N 7
Northumberland Cres.
TW14: Felt 9F 8
Northumberland Gdns.
CR4: Mit 4H 45
TW7: Isle 3G 11
Northumberland Pl.
TW10: Rich 8K 11
Nth. Verbena Gdns.
W6 1F 12
North Vw. RG12: Bin 2H 31
SW19 6H 27
North Vw. Cres. KT18: Tat C 4H 81
North Wlk. CR0: N Add 3L 65
(not continuous)
Northway GU2: Guil 1K 113
GU7: Goda 4E 132
RH6: Gat 2D 162
(off Gatwick Way)
SM4: Mord 2K 43
SM6: W'ton 1G 63
Northway Rd. CR0: Croy 5C 46
Northweald La.
KT2: K Tham 6K 25
Nth. Weylands Ind. Est.
KT12: Wal T 8M 39
Northwood Av. CR8: Pur 8L 63
GU21: Knap 5G 72
Nth. Wood Ct. SE25 2D 46
Northwood Ho.
KT2: K Tham 3M 203
Northwood Pk.
RH10: Craw 8E 162
Northwood Rd. SM5: Cars 3E 62
TW6: Lon A 4M 7
Nth. Worple Way
SW14 6C 12
Norton Av. KT5: Surb 6A 42
Norton Cl. GU3: Worp 5G 93
Norton Ct. BR3: Beck 1J 47
Norton Gdns. SW16 1J 45
Norton La. KT11: Cob 6G 77
Norton Pk. SL5: S'hill 4N 33
Norton Rd. GU15: Camb 2G 71
RG40: W'ham 3B 30
Norwich Av. GU15: Camb 3C 70
Norwich Rd. CR7: T Hea 2N 45
RH10: Craw 5E 182
Norwood Cl. KT24: Eff 6M 97
TW2: Twick 3D 24
UB2: S'hall 1A 10
Norwood Farm La.
KT11: Cob 7H 57
Norwood Grn. Rd.
UB2: S'hall 1A 10
Norwood High St.
SE27 4M 29
NORWOOD HILL 7J 141
Norwood Hill RH6: N Hil 9H 141
Norwood Hill Rd.
RH6: Char, N Hil 8K 141
Norwood Junction Station (Rail)
3D 46
NORWOOD NEW TOWN 7N 29
Norwood Pk. Rd. SE27 6N 29
Norwood Rd. KT24: Eff 6M 97
SE24 2M 29
SE27 3M 29
UB2: S'hall 1A 10
Norwood Ter. UB2: S'hall 1B 10
Notley End TW20: Eng G 8M 19
Notson Rd. SE25 3E 46
Nottingham Cl. GU21: Wok 5J 73
Nottingham Ct. GU21: Wok 5J 73
(off Nottingham Cl.)
Nottingham Rd.
CR2: S Croy 7B 200 (1N 63)
SW17 2D 28
TW7: Isle 5F 10
Nova M. SM3: Sut 7K 43
Nova Rd. CR0: Croy 7M 45
Novello St. SW6 4M 13
Novello Theatre 4A 34
Nowell Rd. SW13 2F 12
Nower Cl. E. RH4: Dork 6F 118
Nower Cl. W. RH4: Dork 6F 118
Nower Rd.
RH4: Dork 3H 201 (5G 118)
Nowhurst Bus. Pk.
RH12: Bro H 2A 196
Nowhurst La.
RH12: Bro H 3N 195
Noyna Rd. SW17 4D 28
Nuffield Ct. TW5: Hest 3N 9
Nuffield Dr. GU47: Owls 6L 49
Nugee Ct. RG45: Crow 2G 49
Nugent Cl. GU8: Duns 3B 174
Nugent Rd. GU2: Guil 3G 112
SE25 2C 46
Numa Ct. TW8: Brent 3K 11
Nunappleton Way
RH8: Oxt 1C 126
Nuneaton Rd. RG12: Brac 5C 32
Nunns Fld. RH5: Cap 5J 159
Nuns Wlk. GU25: V Wat 4N 35
RH5: Ran C 8B 98
NUPTOWN 2D 16
Nuptown La. RG42: Warf 2D 16
Nursery Av. CR0: Croy 8G 46
Nursery Cl. CR0: Croy 8G 46
GU16: Frim G 7D 70
GU21: Wok 3M 73
GU51: Fleet 5E 88
KT15: Wood 6H 55
KT17: Ewe 6D 60
KT20: Wal H 3G 100
RH5: Cap 5J 159
SW15 7J 13
TW14: Felt 1J 23
(not continuous)
Nursery Gdns. GU4: Guil 9D 114
TW4: Houn 8N 9
TW12: Hamp 5N 23
TW16: Sunb 1G 39
TW18: Stain 7K 21
Nursery Hill GU5: Sha G 6F 134
Nurserylands
RH11: Craw 3M 181
Nursery La. RH6: Hook 9B 142
SL5: Asc 9J 17
Nursery Pl. SL4: O Win 9L 5
Nursery Rd. CR4: Mit 2C 44
CR7: T Hea 3A 46
GU7: Goda 4J 133
GU21: Knap 4G 73
KT20: Wal H 3F 100
SM1: Sut 1A 62
SW19 8K 27
(Elm Gro.)
Nursery Rd. SW19 1N 43
(Parkleigh Rd.)
TW16: Sunb 1F 38
Nursery Way RH8: Oxt 7A 106
TW19: Wray 9N 5
Nutbourne GU9: Weybo 5K 109
Nutbourne Cotts.
GU8: Hamb 2H 173
Nutbourne Ct.
RH12: Hors 3K 197
(off Woodstock Cl.)
TW18: Stain 8H 21
NUTCOMBE 7C 170
Nutcombe La. GU26: Hind 9C 170
RH4: Dork 2G 201 (5F 118)
Nutcroft Gro. KT22: Fetc 8E 78
NUTFIELD 2K 123
Nutfield Cl. SM5: Cars 9C 44
Nutfield Ct. GU15: Camb 8B 50
RH1: Nut 1K 123
Nutfield Marsh Rd.
RH1: Nut 9H 103
NUTFIELD PARK 6L 123
Nutfield Pas. CR7: T Hea 3M 45
(off Nutfield Rd.)
Nutfield Priory 3H 123
Nutfield Rd. CR5: Coul 3E 82
CR7: T Hea 3M 45
RH1: Mers 7G 102
RH1: Red, Nut 3F 122
Nutfield Station (Rail) 5J 123
Nuthatch Cl. GU10: Ews 5C 108
TW19: Stan 2A 22
Nuthatch Gdns. RH2: Reig 7A 122
Nuthatch Way RH10: T Hil 4F 184
RH12: Hors 1K 197
Nuthurst RG12: Brac 4C 32
Nuthurst Av. GU6: Cranl 7N 155
SW2 3K 29
Nuthurst Cl. RH11: Craw 2M 181
Nutley RG12: Brac 7M 31
Nutley Cl. GU46: Yate 1C 68
Nutley Ct. RH2: Reig 3L 121
(off Nutley La.)
Nutley Dean Bus. Pk.
RH6: N Hil 5K 141
Nutley Gro. RH2: Reig 3M 121
Nutley La. RH2: Reig 2L 121
Nutmeg Ct. GU14: Cove 9H 69
Nutshell La. GU9: U Hal 6H 109
Nuttall Gdns. GU6: Cranl 5N 155
Nutty La. TW17: Shep 2D 38
Nutwell St. SW17 6C 28
Nutwood GU7: Goda 5G 133
(off Frith Hill Rd.)
Nutwood Av. RH3: Brock 4B 120
Nutwood Cl. RH3: Brock 4B 120
Nye Bevan Ho. SW6 3L 13
(off St Thomas's Way)
Nyefield Pk. KT20: Wal H 4F 100
Nylands Av. TW9: Kew 4N 11
Nymans Cl. RH12: Hors 1N 197
Nymans Ct. RH10: Craw 6F 182
Nymans Gdns. SW20 2G 42

O

Oakapple Cl. CR2: Sande 1E 84
RH11: Craw 8N 181
Oak Av. CR0: Croy 7K 47
GU47: Owls 6J 49
TW5: Hest 3L 9
TW12: Hamp 6M 23
TW20: Egh 8E 20
Oak Bank CR0: N Add 3M 65
Oakbank GU22: Wok 6A 74
KT22: Fetc 1C 98
Oakbank Av. KT12: Wal T 6N 39
Oakbark Ho. TW8: Brent 3J 11
(off High St.)
Oakbury Rd. SW6 5N 13
Oak Cl. GU6: Ewh 4F 156
GU7: Goda 3H 133
GU8: Chid 5D 172
KT20: Box H 8A 100
RH10: Cop 7L 163
SM1: Sut 8A 44
Oakcombe Cl. KT3: N Mal 9D 26
Oak Cnr. RH5: B Grn 7J 139
Oak Cott. Cl. GU3: Wood V 2F 112
Oak Cotts. GU27: Hasl 2C 188
(not continuous)
RH17: Hand 5N 199
Oak Ct. GU9: Farnh 2G 129
GU14: Farnb 4C 90
RH10: Craw 8B 162
RH19: E Grin 8N 165
(off Newlands Cres.)
Oak Cft. RH19: E Grin 1C 186
Oakcroft Bus. Cen.
KT9: Ches 1M 59
Oakcroft Cl. KT14: W By 1H 75
Oakcroft Rd. KT9: Ches 1M 59
KT14: W By 1H 75
Oakcroft Vs. KT9: Ches 1M 59
Oakdale RG12: Brac 5B 32
Oakdale La. TN8: C Hil 2L 127
Oakdale Rd. KT13: Weybr 9B 38
KT19: Ewe 5C 60
SW16 6J 29
Oakdale Way CR4: Mit 6E 44
Oak Dell RH10: Craw 2G 183

268 A-Z Surrey

Oakdene—Olden La.

Oakdene GU24: Chob 6J 53
KT20: Tad 7K 81
SL5: S'dale 5C 34
Oakdene Av. KT7: T Dit 7G 40
Oakdene Cl. KT23: Book 5C 98
RH3: Brock 5B 120
Oakdene Ct. KT12: Wal T 9J 39
KT13: Weybr 1B 56
Oakdene Dr. KT5: Surb 6B 42
Oakdene M. SM3: Sut 7L 43
Oakdene Pde. KT11: Cob 1J 77
Oakdene Pl.
GU3: P'marsh 2M 133
Oakdene Rd.
GU3: P'marsh 2M 133
GU7: Goda 8G 133
KT11: Cob 1J 77
KT23: Book 2N 97
RH1: Red 3D 122
RH3: Brock 5A 120
Oak Dr. KT20: Box H 8A 100
Oake Ct. SW15 8K 13
Oaken Coppice
KT21: A'tead 6N 79
Oaken Copse GU52: C Cro 9C 88
Oaken Copse Cres.
GU14: Farnb 7N 69
Oak End RH5: B Grn 8J 139
Oaken Dr. KT10: Clay 3F 58
Oak End Way KT15: Wood 8G 55
Oakengates RG12: Brac 7M 31
Oakengate Wood
KT20: Box H 9B 100
Oaken La. KT10: Clay 1E 58
Oakenshaw Cl. KT6: Surb 6L 41
Oakey Dr. RG40: W'ham 3A 30
Oak Farm Cl.
GU17: B'water 1H 69
Oakfield GU21: Wok 4H 73
RH14: Plais 6A 192
Oakfield Cl. KT3: N Mal 4E 42
KT13: Weybr 1D 56
Oakfield Cotts.
GU27: Hasl 7M 189
Oakfield Ct. KT13: Weybr 1D 56
RH6: Horl 8E 142
(off Consort Way)
Oakfield Dr. RH2: Reig 1M 121
Oakfield Gdns. BR3: Beck 4L 47
SM5: Cars 7C 44
Oakfield Glade
KT13: Weybr 1D 56
Oakfield La. BR2: Kes 1E 66
Oakfield Pl. GU14: Cove 1H 89
Oakfield Rd.
CR0: Croy 1B 200 (7N 45)
GU17: Haw 2K 69
KT11: Cob 1J 77
KT21: A'tead 4K 79
SW19 4J 27
TN8: Eden 7K 127
TW15: A'ford 6C 22
Oakfields GU3: Guil 1H 113
GU15: Camb 1N 69
KT12: Wal T 7H 39
KT14: W By 1K 75
RH5: W'wood 1L 177
RH10: Craw 1H 183
Oakfield St. SW10 2N 13
Oakfield Way
RH19: E Grin 7B 166
Oak Gdns. CR0: Croy 8K 47
Oak Glade KT19: Eps 8N 59
Oak Grange Rd. GU4: W Cla 7K 95
OAK GROVE 9K 49
Oak Gro. BR4: W Wick 7M 47
GU6: Cranl 9A 156
RH14: Loxw 4J 193
TW16: Sunb 8J 23
Oak Gro. Cres. GU15: Camb 9L 49
Oak Gro. Rd. SE20 1F 46
Oakhall Dr. TW16: Sunb 6G 22
Oakhaven RH10: Craw 5B 182
OAKHILL 7L 197
Oak Hill GU3: Wood V 1E 112
GU4: B'ham 7E 94
KT6: Surb 6L 41
KT18: Eps 3C 80
Oakhill KT10: Clay 3G 58
Oakhill Chase
RH10: Craw 2H 183
Oakhill Cl. KT21: A'tead 5J 79
Oakhill Cotts. RH5: Oak 1N 177
Oakhill Ct. SW19 8J 27
Oak Hill Cres. KT6: Surb 6L 41
Oakhill Dr. KT6: Surb 6L 41
Oakhill Gdns. KT13: Weybr 8F 38
Oak Hill Gro. KT6: Surb 5L 41
Oak Hill Path KT6: Surb 5L 41
Oakhill Pl. SW15 8M 13
Oak Hill Rd. KT6: Surb 5L 41
Oakhill Rd. BR3: Beck 1M 47
GU35: H Dwn 4G 169
KT15: Addl 3H 55
KT21: A'tead 5J 79
RH2: Reig 4N 121
RH13: Hors 6L 197
SM1: Sut 9N 43
SW15 8L 13
SW16 9J 29
Oak Ho. KT22: Leat 7F 78
RH10: Craw 8B 162
TW9: Kew 4A 12
Oakhurst GU21: Wok 3N 73
GU24: Chob 5H 53
GU26: G'hott 6B 170
Oakhurst Cl. TW11: Tedd 6E 24
Oakhurst Cottage 1F 172
Oakhurst Gdns.
RH19: E Grin 8M 165
Oakhurst La. RH14: Loxw 2G 193
Oakhurst M. RH13: Hors 4N 197
Oakhurst Ri. SM5: Cars 6C 62
Oakhurst Rd. KT19: Ewe 3B 60
Oakington Av. UB3: Harl 1E 8
Oakington Cl. TW16: Sunb 1K 39
Oakington Dr. TW16: Sunb 1K 39
Oakland Av. GU9: Weybo 5K 109
Oakland Cl. RH13: Hors 8L 197
Oakland Ct. KT15: Addl 9K 37
Oaklands CR8: Ken 1N 83
GU6: Cranl 9M 155
GU27: Hasl 1G 188
GU46: Yate 9C 48
KT22: Fetc 2D 98
RH6: Horl 8G 143
RH9: S Gods 6H 125
RH13: Hors 6L 197
Oaklands Av. BR4: W Wick 9L 47
CR7: T Hea 3L 45
KT10: Esh 7D 40
TW7: Isle 2F 10
Oaklands Cl. GU4: Chil 2A 134
KT9: Ches 1J 59
SL5: Asc 8K 17
Oaklands Dr. RH1: Red 5F 122
SL5: Asc 8K 17
TW2: Whitt 1C 24
Oaklands Est. SW4 1G 29
Oaklands Gdns. CR8: Ken 1N 83
Oaklands La. RG45: Crow 1F 48
TN16: B Hil 9D 66
Oaklands Rd. SW14 6C 12
Oaklands Way KT20: Tad 9H 81
SM6: W'ton 4H 63
Oakland Way KT19: Ewe 3D 60
Oak La. GU22: Wok 3D 74
RH12: Bro H 5E 196
SL4: W'sor 4D 4
TW1: Twick 1G 25
TW7: Isle 7E 10
TW20: Eng G 4M 19
Oaklawn Rd. KT22: Leat 5E 78
Oaklea GU12: A Va 8E 90
Oak Leaf Cl. GU2: Guil 2G 113
KT19: Eps 5G 201 (8B 60)
Oak Leaf Ct. SL5: Asc 9H 17
Oaklea Pas.
KT1: K Tham 5H 203 (2K 41)
Oakleigh
KT18: Eps 8L 201 (1D 80)
RH9: Gods 8F 104
Oakleigh Av. KT6: Surb 7N 41
Oakleigh Ct. RH8: Oxt 7A 106
Oakleigh Gdns. BR6: Orp 1N 67
Oakleigh Rd. RH12: Hors 4M 197
Oakleigh Way CR4: Mit 9F 28
KT6: Surb 7N 41
Oakley Av. CR0: Bedd 1K 63
Oakley Cl. KT15: Addl 1M 55
RH19: E Grin 2D 186
TW7: Isle 4D 10
Oakley Ct. CR4: Mit 6E 44
RH1: Red 2E 122
(off St Anne's Ri.)
Oakley Dell GU4: Guil 1E 114
Oakley Dr. GU51: Fleet 5B 88
Oakley Gdns. RH3: Betch 9B 120
SM7: Ban 2N 81
Oakley Ho. GU7: Goda 3H 133
Oakley Rd. CR6: Warl 5D 84
GU15: Camb 2N 69
SE25 4E 46
Oakley Wlk. W6 2J 13
Oak Lodge GU27: Hasl 4J 189
KT11: Cob 2K 77
(off Leigh Cnr.)
RG45: Crow 2H 49
SM1: Sut 1A 62
TW16: Sunb 8G 22
(off Forest Dr.)
Oak Lodge Cl. KT12: Hers 2K 57
Oak Lodge Dr. BR4: W Wick 6L 47
RH1: Salf 2E 142
Oak Lodge La.
TN16: Weste 3M 107
Oakman Ho. SW19 2J 27
Oak Mead GU7: Goda 3G 133
Oakmead Grn. KT18: Eps 2B 80
Oakmead Pl. CR4: Mit 9C 28
Oakmead Rd. CR0: Croy 5H 45
SW12 2E 28
Oakmede Pl. RG42: Bin 7H 15
Oak Pk. KT14: W By 9G 55
Oak Pk. Gdns. SW19 2J 27
Oak Pl. SW18 8N 13
Oak Ridge RH4: Dork 8H 119
Oakridge GU24: W End 9C 52
Oak Rd. CR3: Cate 9B 84
GU14: Farnb 2A 90
KT3: N Mal 1C 42
KT11: Cob 2L 77
KT22: Leat 5G 79
RH2: Reig 2N 121
RH11: Craw 4A 182
TN16: Weste 3M 107
Oak Row SW16 1G 45
Oaks, The GU8: Chid 5E 172
GU14: Cove 2J 89
GU46: Yate 1C 68
KT14: W By 1J 75
KT18: Eps 8M 201 (1E 80)
KT20: Tad 1H 101
RG12: Brac 1B 32
RH4: Dork 8H 119
RH19: E Grin 1C 186
SM4: Mord 3K 43
TW18: Stain 5H 21
Oaks Av. KT4: W Pk 9G 43
TW13: Felt 3M 23
Oaks Cvn. Pk., The
KT9: Ches 9J 41
Oaks Cl. GU27: Fern 9F 188
KT22: Leat 8G 79
RH12: Hors 2A 198
Oaksend Cl. KT22: Oxs 7C 58
Oakshade Rd. KT22: Oxs 1C 78
Oakshaw RH8: Oxt 5N 105
Oakshaw Rd. SW18 1N 27
Oaks Ho. Cvn. Pk., The
RH5: B Grn 1K 159
Oakside Ct. RH6: Horl 7G 143
Oakside La. RH6: Horl 7G 143
Oaks La. CR0: Croy 9E 46
RH5: Mid H 3H 139
Oaks Rd. CR0: Croy 2E 64
CR8: Ken 1M 83
GU21: Wok 4A 74
RH2: Reig 2B 122
TW19: Stan 9M 7
Oaks Sports Cen. 7C 62
Oaks Sq., The
KT19: Eps 6K 201
Oaks Track SM5: Cars 7D 62
SM6: W'ton 6E 62
Oaks Way CR8: Ken 1N 83
GU23: Rip 2J 95
KT6: Surb 7K 41
KT18: Tat C 6G 80
SM5: Cars 4D 62
Oak Tree Cl. GU4: B'ham 7E 94
GU4: J Wel 6N 93
GU12: A Va 4D 90
GU12: Alde 4C 110
GU21: Knap 5E 72
GU25: V Wat 5N 35
GU35: Head 5D 168
RH19: E Grin 7M 165
Oak Tree Dr. GU1: Guil 8M 93
TW20: Eng G 6M 19
Oaktree Dr. SL3: Lang 1D 6
Oak Tree Gdns.
GU1: Guil 9D 94
Oak Tree La. GU27: Hasl 2B 188
Oak Tree M. RG12: Brac 2B 32
Oak Tree Rd. GU8: Mil 1B 152
GU21: Knap 5E 72
Oaktrees GU9: U Hal 6G 109
GU12: Ash 3D 110
Oaktrees Ct. *GU12: Ash 3D 110*
(off Oaktrees)
Oak Tree Vw. GU9: H End 6K 109
Oaktree Wlk. CR3: Cate 9B 84
Oak Tree Way
GU47: Sandh 6F 48
Oaktree Way RH13: Hors 4M 197
Oak Vw. RG40: W'ham 4A 30
TN8: Eden 1K 147
Oakview Apartments
SM1: Sut 1B 62
Oakview Gro. CR0: Croy 7H 47
Oak Wlk. RH12: Fay 8E 180
Oak Way CR0: Croy 5G 47
GU12: Alde 4C 110
KT21: A'tead 3N 79
RH2: Reig 4B 122
RH10: Craw 2C 182
RH13: M Hea 9B 198
SM6: W'ton 7E 44
(off Helios Rd.)
TW14: Felt 2F 22
Oakway BR2: Brom 1N 47
GU21: Wok 6H 73
SW20 3H 43
Oakway Dr. GU16: Frim 5C 70
Oakwood GU2: Guil 7K 93
GU52: C Cro 9B 88
KT18: Eps 8L 201
Oakwood Av. BR3: Beck 1M 47
CR4: Mit 1B 44
CR8: Pur 8M 63
KT19: Eps 5N 59
Oakwood Cl. KT24: E Hor 5F 96
RH1: Red 3E 122
RH1: Sth N 5K 123
Oakwood Ct. GU24: Bis 3D 72
RH11: Craw 9N 181
Oakwood Dr. KT24: E Hor 5F 96
Oakwood Gdns.
GU21: Knap 5D 72
SM1: Sut 8M 43
Oakwood Grange
KT13: Weybr 9F 38
Oakwood Hall
KT20: K'wood 1A 102
OAKWOODHILL 2A 178
Oakwood Ind. Pk.
RH10: Craw 9E 162
Oakwood Pk.
RH18: F Row 7H 187
Oakwood Pl. CR0: Croy 5L 45
RG45: Crow 3F 48
Oakwood Ri. CR3: Cate 3B 104
Oakwood Rd. CR0: Croy 5L 45
GU20: Windl 3B 52
GU21: Wok 6H 73
GU25: V Wat 4M 35
RG12: Brac 1C 32
RH1: Mers 7L 103
RH6: Horl 7E 142
SW20 9F 26
Oakwood Sports Cen. 8G 142
Oareborough RG12: Brac 3C 32
Oarsman Pl. KT8: E Mol 3E 40
Oast Ho. Cl. TW19: Wray 1A 20
Oast Ho. Cres. GU9: Hale 6H 109
Oasthouse Dr. GU51: Fleet 1D 88
Oast Ho. La. GU9: Hale 7J 109
Oast La. GU11: Alde 5N 109
Oast Lodge *W4 3D 12*
(off Corney Reach Way)
Oast Rd. RH8: Oxt 9B 106
Oates Cl. BR2: Brom 2N 47
Oates Wlk. RH10: Craw 6D 182
Oatfield Rd. KT20: Tad 7G 80
Oatlands RH6: Horl 7G 142
RH11: Craw 4M 181
Oatlands Av. KT13: Weybr 2E 56
Oatlands Chase
KT13: Weybr 9F 38
Oatlands Cl. KT13: Weybr 1D 56
Oatlands Dr. KT13: Weybr 1D 56
Oatlands Grn. KT13: Weybr 9E 38
Oatlands Mere
KT13: Weybr 9E 38
OATLANDS PARK 9E 38
Oatlands Rd. KT20: Tad 6K 81
Oatsheaf Pde. GU51: Fleet 5A 88
Oban Rd. SE25 3A 46
Obelisk Ride TW20: Eng G 7H 19
Obelisk Way GU15: Camb 9A 50
(not continuous)
Oberon Way RH11: Craw 6K 181
TW17: Shep 2N 37
Oberursel Way GU11: Alde 2L 109
Observatory Rd. SW14 7B 12
Observatory Wlk.
RH1: Red 3D 122
Observer Ct. RH12: Hors 7J 197
Occam Ct. GU2: Guil 3G 113
Occam Rd. GU2: Guil 3G 112
Ocean Ho. RG12: Brac 1N 31
Ockenden Cl. GU22: Wok 5B 74
Ockenden Gdns.
GU22: Wok 5B 74
Ockenden Rd. GU22: Wok 5B 74
Ockfields GU8: Mil 1C 152
Ockford Ct. GU7: Goda 7G 132
Ockford Dr. GU7: Goda 8F 132
OCKFORD RIDGE 8E 132
Ockford Ridge GU7: Goda 8E 132
Ockford Rd. GU7: Goda 8F 132
OCKHAM 8C 76
Ockham Dr. KT24: W Hors 2E 96
Ockham La. GU23: Ockh 8B 76
KT11: Cob 7F 76
Ockham Rd. Nth.
GU23: Ockh 7N 75
KT24: E Hor, W Hors 2D 96
Ockham Rd. Sth.
KT24: E Hor 4F 96
OCKLEY 5D 158
Ockley Ct. GU4: B'ham 7D 94
SM1: Sut 1A 62
Ockley Rd. CR0: Croy 6K 45
GU6: Ewh 4F 156
RH5: B Grn 1H 159
RH5: For G, Ockl 2M 157
SW16 5J 29
Ockleys Mead RH9: Gods 7F 104
Ockley Station (Rail) 4G 159
O'Connor Rd. GU11: Alde 6C 90
Octagon, The *SW10 3N 13*
(off Coleridge Gdns.)
Octagon Rd. KT12: Whit V 5F 56
Octavia RG12: Brac 7M 31
Octavia Cl. CR4: Mit 4C 44
Octavia Rd. TW7: Isle 6E 10
Octavia Way TW18: Stain 7J 21
Odard Rd. KT8: W Mole 3A 40
Odeon Cinema
Beckenham 1J 47
Bracknell *1N 39*
(within The Point Leisure Cen.)
Epsom 6L 201 (9D 60)
Esher 1B 58
Guildford 5B 202 (4M 113)
Hill St. 8K 11
Kingston upon Thames
3K 203
Putney 6K 13
Richmond 8K 11
Streatham 4J 29
Sutton 2N 61
Wimbledon 7L 27
Odiham Rd. GU10: U Hal 5E 108
Offers Ct.
KT1: K Tham 5L 203 (2M 41)
Office Pk., The KT22: Leat 6F 78
Offley Pl. TW7: Isle 5D 10
Off Up. Manor Rd.
GU7: Goda 4H 133
(off Up. Manor Rd.)
Ogden Ho. TW13: Hanw 4M 23
Ogden Pk. RG12: Brac 2C 32
Oglethorpe Ct. *GU7: Goda 7G 133*
(off High St.)
O'Gorman Av. GU14: Farnb 3N 89
Oil Mill La. W6 1F 12
Okeburn Rd. SW17 6E 28
Okehurst La.
RH14: Bill, Have 9B 194
OKEWOODHILL 2A 178
Okewood Hill RH5: Oak 2A 178
Okingham Cl. GU47: Owls 5J 49
Old Acre GU22: Pyr 1J 75
Oldacre GU24: W End 8C 52
Oldacre M. SW12 1E 28
Old Av. KT13: Weybr 4D 56
KT14: W By 9G 54
Old Av. Cl. KT14: W By 9G 54
Old Bakery Ct. GU6: Ewh 5F 156
Old Bakery M. GU5: Alb 8K 115
RG42: Warf 6B 16
Old Barn Cl. SM2: Chea 4K 61
Old Barn Cotts.
RH12: K'fold 2J 179
Old Barn Dr. RH5: Cap 4K 159
Old Barn La. CR8: Ken 3C 84
GU10: Churt 8N 149
Old Barn Rd. KT18: Eps 4B 80
Old Barn Vw. GU7: Goda 9F 132
Old Bisley Rd. GU16: Frim 4E 70
Old Bracknell Cl.
RG12: Brac 2N 31
Old Bracknell La. E.
RG12: Brac 2N 31
Old Bracknell La. W.
RG12: Brac 2M 31
OLD BRENTFORD 3K 11
Old Brewery Ct. RH4: Dork 2K 201
Old Brickfield Rd.
GU11: Alde 5N 109
Old Bri. Rd. GU10: Run 8N 109
Old Bri. St.
KT1: H Wic 3G 203 (1K 41)
Old Brighton Rd.
RH11: P Pot 3N 199
Old Brighton Rd. Sth.
RH11: L Hea 6C 162
Old Brompton Rd.
SW5 1M 13
Oldbury RG12: Brac 2L 31
Oldbury Cl. GU16: Frim 6D 70
RH12: Hors 1N 197
OLD BURY HILL 7E 118
Old Bury Hill Ho.
RH4: Westc 7E 118
Oldbury Rd. KT16: Chert 6G 36
Old Chapel La. GU12: Ash 2E 110
Old Charlton Rd.
TW17: Shep 4D 38
Old Char Wharf
RH4: Dork 1G 201 (4F 118)
Old Chertsey Rd.
GU24: Chob 6L 53
Old Chestnut Av. KT10: Esh 3A 58
Old Chiswick Yd. *W4 2D 12*
(off Pumping Sta. Rd.)
Old Church La. GU9: Farnh 4K 129
Old Church Path KT10: Esh 1C 58
Old Claygate La.
KT10: Clay 3G 58
Old Coach Rd. KT16: Chert 4F 36
OLD COMMON 9J 57
Old Comn. Rd. KT11: Cob 8J 57
Old Compton La.
GU9: Farnh 1K 129
Old Control Twr. Rd.
RH6: Gat 4B 162
Old Convent RH19: E Grin 8A 166
Old Convent, The
GU10: Dock 7C 148
Old Corn M. GU7: Goda 5J 133
Old Cote Dr. TW5: Hest 2A 10
OLD COULSDON 6L 83
Old Ct. KT21: A'tead 6L 79
Old Ct. Rd. GU2: Guil 4K 113
Old Courtyard, The
TW20: Egh 7B 20
Old Cove Rd. GU51: Fleet 2C 88
Old Crawley Rd.
RH12: Fay 2B 198
Old Cross Tree Way
GU12: A Grn 4G 111
Old Dairy Cl. GU51: Fleet 4B 88
Old Dairy M. SW12 2E 28
Old Dean Rd. GU15: Camb 8B 50
Old Deer Pk. 5J 11
Old Deer Pk. Gdns.
TW9: Rich 6L 11
Old Denne Gdns.
RH12: Hors 7J 197
Old Devonshire Rd.
SW12 1F 28
Old Dock Cl. TW9: Kew 2N 11
Old Dorking Rd.
RH12: Warn 2H 197
Old Dr. GU5: Gorn 7D 116
Olde Farm Dr.
GU17: B'water 9G 48
Old Elstead Rd. GU8: Mil 9B 132
Olden La. CR8: Pur 8L 63

Old Epsom Rd.—Osborne Ct.

Old Epsom Rd. GU4: E Cla 9M **95**
Old Esher Cl. KT12: Hers 2L **57**
Old Esher Rd. KT12: Hers 2L **57**
Old Farleigh Rd. CR2: Sels 6F **64**
CR6: Warl 9H **65**
Old Farm Cl. SW17 3C **28**
TW4: Houn 7N **9**
Old Farm Dr. RG12: Brac 8A **16**
Old Farm Ho. Dr. KT22: Oxs 2D **78**
Old Farm Pas. TW12: Hamp 9C **24**
Old Farm Pl. GU12: A Va 9D **90**
Old Farm Rd. GU1: Guil 9N **93**
TW12: Hamp 7N **23**
(not continuous)
Old Farnham La.
GU9: Farnh 3H **129**
GU10: Farnh 2A **128**
Old Ferry Dr. TW19: Wray 9M **5**
Oldfield Cl. RH6: Horl 1D **162**
Oldfield Ct. KT5: Surb 8L **203**
Oldfield Gdns. KT21: A'tead 6K **79**
Oldfield Ho. *W4 1D 12*
(off Devonshire Rd.)
Oldfield Rd. RH6: Horl 1D **162**
SW19 7K **27**
TW12: Hamp 9N **23**
Oldfields Rd. SM1: Sut 9L **43**
Oldfields Trad. Est.
SM1: Sut 9M **43**
Oldfield Wood GU22: Wok 4D **74**
Old Forge, The RH13: Slin 5L **195**
Old Forge Cl. RH12: Fay 8E **180**
Old Forge Ct. GU4: Chil 9B **114**
Old Forge Cres.
TW17: Shep 5C **38**
Old Forge End GU47: Sandh 8G **49**
Old Fox Cl. CR3: Cate 8M **83**
Old Frensham Rd.
GU10: L Bou 5J **129**
Old Glebe GU27: Fern 9F **188**
Old Green La. GU15: Camb 8A **50**
Old Guildford Rd.
GU16: Frim G 9F **70**
GU24: Pirb 1H **91**
RH12: Bro H 4D **196**
Old Harrow La.
TN16: Weste 6L **87**
Old Haslemere Rd.
GU27: Hasl 3G **189**
Old Heath Rd. KT13: Weybr 3B **56**
Old Heath Way GU9: U Hal 5H **109**
Old Hill BR6: Dow 3M **67**
GU22: Wok 7N **73**
Old Hill Est. GU22: Wok 7N **73**
Old Holbrook RH12: Hors 9L **179**
Old Hollow
RH10: Craw, Wor 3K **183**
Old Horsham Rd.
RH5: B Grn, Holm 6J **139**
RH11: Craw 5N **181**
Old Hospital Cl. SW12 2D **28**
Old Ho. Cl. KT17: Ewe 6E **60**
SW19 6K **27**
Old Ho. Gdns. TW1: Twick 9J **11**
Oldhouse La. GU20: Windl 4M **51**
(not continuous)
GU24: Bis 1D **72**
Old House M. RH12: Hors 6J **197**
OLD ISLEWORTH 6H **11**
Old Ively Rd. GU14: Farnb 5F **88**
Old Kiln Cl. GU10: Churt 8L **149**
Old Kiln La. GU10: Churt 7L **149**
RH3: Brock 3B **120**
Old Kiln Mus. & Rural Life Cen.
8L **129**
Old Kings Head Ct.
RH4: Dork 2K **201**
Old Kingston Rd.
KT4: W Pk 8B **42**
Old Lands Hill RG12: Brac 9B **16**
Old La. GU10: Dock 5F **148**
GU11: Alde 5M **109**
GU12: Alde 1C **110**
KT11: Cob 4C **76**
RH8: Oxt 7B **106**
(not continuous)
TN16: Tats 7F **86**
Old La., The GU10: Churt 1L **169**
Old La. Gdns. KT11: Cob 9H **77**
Old Lodge Cl. GU7: Goda 8E **132**
Old Lodge La.
CR8: Ken, Pur 4M **83**
CR8: Pur 9K **63**
Old Lodge Pl. TW1: Twick 9H **11**
Old London Rd.
KT2: K Tham 3K **203** (1L **41**)
KT18: Eps D 6F **80**
(not continuous)
KT24: E Hor 4H **97**
RH5: Mick 5J **99**
OLD MALDEN 7D **42**
Old Malden La. KT4: W Pk 8C **42**
Old Malt Way GU21: Wok 4N **73**
Old Manor Cl.
RH11: Craw 1M **181**
Old Manor Ct.
RH11: Craw 1M **181**
Old Manor Dr. TW7: Isle 9C **10**
Old Manor Gdns.
GU4: Guil 9E **114**
Old Manor Ho. M.
TW17: Shep 2B **38**
Old Manor La. GU4: Guil 9E **114**
Old Manor Yd. SW5 1N **13**
Old Market Ct. SM1: Sut 1N **61**
Old Martyrs RH11: Craw 9B **162**
Old Merrow St. GU4: Guil 9F **94**
Old Mill La. RH1: Mers 6F **102**
Old Millmeads
RH12: Hors 3J **197**
Old Mill Pl. GU27: Hasl 1D **188**
TW19: Wray 9D **6**
Old Monteagle La.
GU46: Yate 9A **48**
Old Mus. Ct. GU27: Hasl 2H **189**
Old Nursery Pl.
TW15: A'ford 6C **22**
Old Oak Av. CR5: Chip 6C **82**
Old Oak Cl. KT9: Ches 1M **59**
KT11: Cob 9J **57**
Old Orchard KT14: Byf 8A **56**
TW16: Sunb 1K **39**
Old Orchard, The
GU9: Farnh 4E **128**
Old Orchards RH10: Wor 3J **183**
Old Overthorpe
RH6: Smal 1M **163**
OLD OXTED 8N **105**
Old Palace La. TW9: Rich 8J **11**
Old Palace Rd.
CR0: Croy 4A **200** (9M **45**)
GU2: Guil 4K **113**
KT13: Weybr 9C **38**
Old Palace Ter. TW9: Rich 8K **11**
Old Palace Yd. TW9: Rich 8J **11**
Old Park Av. SW12 1E **28**
Old Park Cl. GU9: U Hal 6F **108**
Old Park La. GU9: Farnh 7F **108**
GU10: U Hal 5E **108**
(not continuous)
Old Park M. TW5: Hest 3N **9**
Old Parvis Rd. KT14: W By 8L **55**
Old Pasture Rd.
GU16: Frim 4D **70**
Old Pharmacy Ct.
RG45: Crow 3G **49**
Old Pond Cl. GU15: Camb 5A **70**
Old Portsmouth Rd.
GU3: Art, P'marsh 3L **133**
GU7: Art, Goda, P'marsh
3L **133**
GU8: Thur 6H **151**
GU15: Camb 1E **70**
Old Post Cotts.
RH12: Bro H 5E 196
(off Wickhurst La.)
Old Pottery Cl. RH2: Reig 5N **121**
Old Pound Cl. TW7: Isle 4G **10**
Old Pound Cotts. RH11: Ifi 2J **181**
Old Priory La. RG42: Warf 7B **16**
Old Pumphouse Cl.
GU51: Fleet 3C **88**
Old Quarry, The
GU27: Hasl 4D **188**
Old Rectory, The
KT23: Book 5N **97**
Old Rectory Cl.
GU5: Braml 5B **134**
KT20: Wal H 2F **100**
Old Rectory Dr. GU12: Ash 2F **110**
Old Rectory Gdns.
GU7: Bus 9J **133**
GU14: Farnb 1B **90**
Old Rectory La. KT24: E Hor 4F **96**
Old Redstone Dr.
RH1: Red 4E **122**
Old Reigate Rd.
RH3: Betch 3A **120**
RH4: Dork 3L **119**
Oldridge Rd. SW12 1E **28**
Old Rd. KT15: Addl 4H **55**
RH3: Buck 3D **120**
RH19: E Grin 9B **166**
Old Rope Wlk. TW16: Sunb 2J **39**
Old Row Ct. RG40: W'ham 2B **30**
Old St Mary's KT24: W Hors 7C **96**
Old Sawmill La.
RG45: Crow 1H **49**
Old School Cl. BR3: Beck 1G **47**
GU1: Guil 3C **202** (3N **113**)
GU12: Ash 1E **110**
(not continuous)
GU51: Fleet 4B **88**
SW19 1M **43**
Old School Ct. KT22: Leat 9H **79**
TW19: Wray 1A **20**
Old School Ho. *TN8: Eden 2L 147*
(off Lingfield Rd.)
Old School La. GU46: Yate 9B **48**
RH3: Brock 6A **120**
Old School M. KT13: Weybr 1E **56**
TW18: Stain 6F **20**
Old School Pl. CR0: Wad 1L **63**
GU22: Wok 8A **74**
RH7: Ling 7N **145**
Old Schools La. KT17: Ewe 5E **60**
Old School Sq. KT7: T Dit 5F **40**
Old School Ter. *GU51: Fleet 4B 88*
(off Old School Cl.)
SM3: Chea 4J **61**
Old School Yd. RH1: Nut 2K **123**
Old Slade La. SL0: R Pk 1H **7**
SL3: Coln 1H **7**
Old Station App. KT22: Leat 8G **78**
Old Station Cl.
RH10: Craw D 2E **184**
Old Station Gdns.
TW11: Tedd 7G 24
(off Victoria Rd.)
Old Station Way
GU7: Goda 6H **133**
Oldstead RG12: Brac 4B **32**
Old Stede Cl. KT21: A'tead 4M **79**
Old St., The KT22: Fetc 1D **98**
Old Studio Cl. CR0: Croy 6A **46**
OLD SURREY HALL 5G **167**
Old Swan Yd. SM5: Cars 1D **62**
Old Tilburstow Rd.
RH9: S Gods 3F **124**
Old Town
CR0: Croy 4A **200** (9M **45**)
Old Tye Av. TN16: B Hil 3G **87**
Old Water Yd.
RH4: Dork 1H **201** (4G **118**)
Old Welmore GU46: Yate 1D **68**
Old Westhall Cl. CR6: Warl 6F **84**
Old Wharf Way
KT13: Weybr 1A **56**
Old Wickhurst La.
RH12: Bro H 7D **196**
OLD WINDSOR 9K **5**
Old Windsor Lock
SL4: O Win 8M **5**
OLD WOKING 8D **74**
Old Wokingham Rd.
RG40: W'ham 6G **31**
RG45: Crow 9H **31**
Old Woking Rd.
GU22: Wok, Pyr 6D **74**
KT14: W By 9H **55**
Oldwood Chase
GU14: Cove 2G **89**
Old Yard, The RH1: Blet 2N **123**
Old York Rd. SW18 8N **13**
Oleander Cl. BR6: Farnb 2M **67**
RG45: Crow 9E **30**
Oliver Av. SE25 2C **46**
Oliver Cl. KT15: Addl 1J **55**
W4 2A **12**
Oliver Gro. SE25 3C **46**
Olive Rd. SW19 8A **28**
Oliver Rd. KT3: N Mal 1B **42**
RH12: Hors 7G **197**
SL5: Asc 3L **33**
SM1: Sut 1B **62**
Olivette St. SW15 6J **13**
Olivia Ct. RG41: W'ham 2A **30**
Olivia Dr. SL3: Lang 1B **6**
Olivier Rd. RH10: Craw 4H **183**
Ollerton RG12: Brac 7M **31**
Olley Cl. SM6: W'ton 4J **63**
Olveston Wlk. SM5: Cars 5B **44**
O'Mahoney Ct. SW17 4A **28**
Omega Rd. GU21: Wok 3C **74**
Omega Way TW20: Thor 9E **20**
Omnibus Bldg.
RH2: Reig 4N **121**
One Tree Hill Rd.
GU4: Guil 4D **114**
Ongar Cl. KT15: Addl 3H **55**
Ongar Hill KT15: Addl 3J **55**
Ongar Pde. KT15: Addl 3J **55**
Ongar Pl. KT15: Addl 3J **55**
Ongar Rd. KT15: Addl 2J **55**
SW6 2M **13**
Onslow Av. SM2: Chea 6L **61**
TW10: Rich 8L **11**
Onslow Cl. GU22: Wok 4C **74**
KT7: T Dit 7E **40**
Onslow Ct. RH10: Craw 9E **162**
Onslow Cres. GU22: Wok 4C **74**
Onslow Dr. SL5: Asc 8L **17**
Onslow Gdns. CR2: Sande 8D **64**
KT7: T Dit 7E **40**
SM6: W'ton 3G **62**
Onslow Ho. KT2: K Tham 1L **203**
Onslow M. KT16: Chert 5H **37**
Onslow Rd. CR0: Croy 6K **45**
GU1: Guil 3D **202** (3N **113**)
KT3: N Mal 3F **42**
KT12: Hers 1G **57**
SL5: S'dale 6E **34**
TW10: Rich 8L **11**
Onslow St.
GU1: Guil 5B **202** (4M **113**)
ONSLOW VILLAGE 5J **113**
Onslow Way GU22: Pyr 2H **75**
KT7: T Dit 7E **40**
Ontario Cl. RH6: Smal 9L **143**
Openfields GU35: Head 4D **168**
Openview SW18 2A **28**
Ophelia Ho. *W6 1J 13*
(off Fulham Pal. Rd.)
Opladen Way RG12: Brac 4A **32**
Opossum Way TW4: Houn 6K **9**
Opus Pk. GU1: Guil 8N **93**
Orange Ct. La. BR6: Dow 5J **67**
Orangery, The TW10: Ham 3J **25**
Orange Tree Theatre 7L **11**
Orbain Rd. SW6 3K **13**
Orchard, The GU18: Ligh 7L **51**
GU21: Wok 3L **73**
GU22: Wok 9A **74**
GU25: V Wat 4A **36**
KT13: Weybr 1C **56**
KT17: Ewe 4E **60**
(Meadow Wlk.)
KT17: Ewe 6E **60**
(Tayles Hill Dr.)
Orchard, The RH5: Nth H 9J **119**
RH6: Horl 8E **142**
RH12: Bro H 5D **196**
RH13: Hors 4A **198**
SM7: Ban 2M **81**
TW3: Houn 5C **10**
Orchard Av. CR0: Croy 8H **47**
CR4: Mit 7E **44**
KT3: N Mal 1D **42**
KT7: T Dit 7G **41**
KT15: Wood 7H **55**
SL4: W'sor 4D **4**
TW5: Hest 3M **9**
TW14: Felt 8E **8**
TW15: A'ford 7D **22**
Orchard Bus. Cen.
RH1: Salf 3F **142**
Orchard Cl. GU1: Guil 3D **114**
GU3: Flex 3M **111**
GU8: Els 7H **131**
GU9: B Lea 6N **109**
GU12: A Va 8E **90**
GU17: Haw 5L **69**
GU22: Wok 3D **74**
GU24: W End 9A **52**
GU27: Hasl 3D **188**
KT7: T Dit 7H **41**
KT12: Wal T 6J **39**
KT19: Ewe 3A **60**
KT22: Fetc 9D **78**
KT22: Leat 6F **78**
KT24: E Hor 2G **97**
RG40: W'ham 2C **30**
RH6: Horl 7D **142**
SM7: Ban 1N **81**
SW20 3H **43**
TN8: Eden 1K **147**
TW15: A'ford 7D **22**
TW20: Egh 6D **20**
Orchard Cotts. GU4: Guil 9G **114**
KT2: K Tham 2M **203** (9M **25**)
RH6: Char 3L **161**
Orchard Ct. CR3: Cate 2C **104**
GU15: Camb 4N 69
(off Orchard Way)
KT4: W Pk 7F **42**
KT12: Wal T 7G 39
(off Bridge St.)
RG12: Brac 1A **32**
RH7: Ling 8N **145**
SM6: W'ton 2F **62**
TW2: Twick 3D **24**
TW7: Isle 4D **10**
UB7: L'ford 3L **7**
Orchard Dene *KT14: W By 9J 55*
(off Madeira Rd.)
Orchard Dr. GU21: Wok 2A **74**
GU35: Lind 5B **168**
KT21: A'tead 7K **79**
TN8: Eden 1K **147**
TW17: Shep 2F **38**
Orchard End CR3: Cate 9B **84**
GU10: Rowl 8E **128**
KT13: Weybr 8F **38**
KT22: Fetc 2C **98**
Orchard Fld. Rd.
GU7: Goda 4J **133**
Orchard Flds. GU51: Fleet 4A **88**
Orchard Gdns. GU6: Cranl 8A **156**
GU12: Alde 4A **110**
KT9: Ches 1L **59**
KT18: Eps 1B **80**
KT24: Eff 6M **97**
RH12: Hors 4J **197**
SM1: Sut 2M **61**
Orchard Ga. GU47: Sandh 7G **49**
KT10: Esh 7D **40**
Orchard Gro. CR0: Croy 6H **47**
Orchard Hill GU20: Windl 4A **52**
RH12: Rudg 1D **194**
SM5: Cars 2D **62**
Orchard Ho. *GU4: Guil 2F 114*
(off Merrow St.)
GU10: Tong 5C **110**
SW6 3L 13
(off Varna Rd.)
Orchard La. KT8: E Mol 5D **40**
SW20 9G **27**
Orchard Lea Cl. GU22: Pyr 2G **75**
Orchardleigh KT22: Leat 9H **79**
Orchard Mains GU22: Wok 6M **73**
Orchard M. GU21: Knap 5E **72**
SW17 4A **28**
Orchard Mobile Home Pk.
KT20: Box H 8A **100**
Orchard Pk. Cvn. Site
RH1: Out 3K **143**
Orchard Pl. BR2: Kes 5E **66**
RG40: W'ham 2B **30**
Orchard Ri. CR0: Croy 7H **47**
KT2: K Tham 9B **26**
TW10: Rich 7A **12**
Orchard Rd. BR6: Farnb 2K **67**
CR2: Sande 1E **84**
CR4: Mit 7E **44**
GU2: Guil 5J **113**
GU4: B'ham 8D **94**
GU4: Chil 9A **114**
GU5: Shere 8B **116**
GU9: B Lea 6M **109**
GU14: Farnb 1M **89**
KT1: K Tham 4J **203** (1L **41**)
KT9: Ches 1L **59**
Orchard Rd. RH2: Reig 3N **121**
RH4: Dork 6H **119**
RH6: Smal 8N **143**
RH13: Hors 7L **197**
SL4: O Win 9L **5**
SM1: Sut 2M **61**
TW1: Twick 8G **11**
TW4: Houn 8N **9**
TW8: Brent 2J **11**
TW9: Rich 6N **11**
TW12: Hamp 8N **23**
TW13: Felt 2H **23**
TW16: Sunb 8J **23**
Orchards, The RH11: Ifi 4J **181**
RH12: Hors 3M **197**
Orchards Cl. KT14: W By 1J **75**
Orchard Sq. W14 1L **13**
Orchard St. RH11: Craw 3B **182**
Orchard Vw. KT16: Chert 5J **37**
Orchard Wlk.
KT2: K Tham 2M **203**
Orchard Way BR3: Beck 7H **47**
CR0: Croy 7H **47**
GU3: Flex 3M **111**
GU3: Worp 2G **92**
GU12: Alde 4A **110**
GU15: Camb 4N **69**
GU23: Send 3E **94**
KT10: Esh 3C **58**
KT15: Addl 2K **55**
KT20: Lwr K 4L **101**
RH2: Reig 6N **121**
RH4: Dork 6H **119**
RH8: Oxt 2C **126**
RH19: E Grin 9A **166**
SM1: Sut 1B **62**
TW15: A'ford 3A **22**
Orchid Cl. KT9: Ches 4J **59**
Orchid Ct. TW20: Egh 5D **20**
Orchid Dr. GU24: Bis 2D **72**
Orchid Gdns. TW3: Houn 7N **9**
Orchid Mead SM7: Ban 1N **81**
Orde Cl. RH10: Craw 9H **163**
Ordnance Cl. TW13: Felt 3H **23**
Ordnance Rd.
GU11: Alde 2N **109**
Ordnance Rdbt.
GU11: Alde 2N **109**
Oregano Way GU2: Guil 7K **93**
Oregon Cl. KT3: N Mal 3B **42**
Orestan La. KT24: Eff 5J **97**
Orewell Gdns. RH2: Reig 5N **121**
Orford Ct. SE27 3M **29**
Orford Gdns. TW1: Twick 3F **24**
ORGAN CROSSROADS 4F **60**
Oriel, The RH6: Horl 9E **142**
Oriel Cl. CR4: Mit 3H **45**
RH10: Craw 9G **162**
Oriel Ct.
CR0: Croy 1D **200** (7A **46**)
Oriel Dr. SW13 2H **13**
Oriel Hill GU15: Camb 2B **70**
Oriental Cl. GU22: Wok 4B **74**
Oriental Rd. GU22: Wok 4B **74**
SL5: S'hill 3A **34**
Orion RG12: Brac 7M **31**
Orion Cen., The CR0: Bedd 8J **45**
Orion Ct. RH11: Craw 5J **181**
Orlando Gdns. KT19: Ewe 6C **60**
Orleans Cl. KT10: Esh 8D **40**
Orleans Ct. KT12: Wal T 8K **39**
TW1: Twick 1H **25**
Orleans House Gallery 2H **25**
Orleans Pk. School Sports Cen.
1H **25**
Orleans Rd. TW1: Twick 1H **25**
Orltons La. RH12: Rusp 8E **160**
Ormathwaites Cnr.
RG42: Warf 8C **16**
Ormeley Rd. SW12 2F **28**
Orme Rd. KT1: K Tham 1A **42**
SM1: Sut 3N **61**
Ormerod Gdns. CR4: Mit 1E **44**
Ormesby Wlk. RH10: Craw 5F **182**
Ormond Av. TW10: Rich 8K **11**
TW12: Hamp 9B **24**
Ormond Cres. TW12: Hamp 9B **24**
Ormond Dr. TW12: Hamp 8B **24**
Ormonde Av. KT19: Ewe 6C **60**
Ormonde Ct. SW15 7H **13**
Ormonde Pl. KT13: Weybr 3E **56**
Ormonde Rd. GU7: Goda 5H **133**
GU21: Wok 3M **73**
RG41: W'ham 3A **30**
SW14 6B **12**
Ormond Rd. TW10: Rich 8K **11**
Ormsby SM2: Sut 4N **61**
Ormside Way RH1: Red 8F **102**
Orpen Ho. *SW5 1M 13*
(off Trebovir Rd.)
Orpheus Cen., The 8D **104**
Orpin Rd. RH1: Mers 8F **102**
Orpwood Cl. TW12: Hamp 7N **23**
Orwell Cl. GU14: Cove 8K **69**
SL4: W'sor 6G **4**
Osborne Av. TW19: Stan 2N **21**
Osborne Cl. BR3: Beck 3H **47**
GU16: Frim 6D **70**
TW13: Hanw 6L **23**
Osborne Ct. GU14: Farnb 5A **90**
GU51: Fleet 5A **88**
RH11: Craw 7N **181**
SL4: W'sor 5F **4**

270 A-Z Surrey

Osborne Dr.—Park Ct.

Osborne Dr. GU18: Ligh 7L 51
GU52: Fleet 6C 88
Osborne Gdns. CR7: T Hea 1N 45
Osborne La. RG42: Warf 6A 16
Osborne M. SL4: W'sor 5F 4
Osborne Pl. SM1: Sut 2B 62
Osborne Rd. CR7: T Hea 1N 45
GU14: Farnb 4A 90
KT2: K Tham 8L 25
KT12: Wal T 7H 39
RG40: W'ham 2B 30
RH1: Red 9E 102
SL4: W'sor 5F 4
TW3: Houn 6N 9
TW20: Egh 7B 20
Osborne Ter. SW17 ......6D 28
(off Church La.)
Osborne Way KT9: Ches 2M 59
(off Bridge Rd.)
Osborn Rd. GU9: Farnh 8J 109
Osbourne Ho. TW2: Twick 3C 24
Oscar Cl. CR8: Pur 6L 63
Osgood Av. BR6: Chels 2N 67
Osier Ct. TW8: Brent 2L 11
(off Ealing Rd.)
Osier M. W4 ......2D 12
Osier Pl. TW20: Egh 7E 20
Osiers Ct. KT1: K Tham 2H 203
Osiers Est., The
SW18 ......7M 13
Osiers Rd. SW18 ......7M 13
Osier Way CR4: Mit 4D 44
SM7: Ban 1K 81
Osman's Cl. RG42: Wink R 8F 16
Osmond Gdns. SM6: W'ton 2G 62
Osmunda Bank
RH19: D Pk 4A 166
Osmund Cl. RH10: Wor 3J 183
Osnaburgh Hill
GU15: Camb 1N 69
Osney Cl. RH11: Craw 4A 182
Osney Wlk. SM5: Cars 5B 44
Osprey Av. RG12: Brac 3J 31
Osprey Cl. KT22: Fetc 9C 78
SM1: Sut 2L 61
Osprey Gdns. CR2: Sels 6H 65
GU11: Alde 5M 109
Ostade Rd. SW2 ......1K 29
OSTERLEY 3D 10
Osterley Av. TW7: Isle 3D 10
Osterley Cl. RG40: W'ham 3E 30
Osterley Ct. TW7: Isle 4D 10
Osterley Cres. TW7: Isle 4E 10
Osterley Gdns. CR7: T Hea 1N 45
Osterley La. TW7: Isle 1C 10
UB2: S'hall 1A 10
(not continuous)
Osterley Lodge TW7: Isle 3E 10
(off Church Rd.)
Osterley Pk. 2C 10
Osterley Pk. House (NT) 2C 10
Osterley Rd. TW7: Isle 3E 10
Osterley Station (Tube) 3D 10
Ostlers Dr. TW15: A'ford 6D 22
Oswald Cl. KT22: Fetc 9C 78
RG42: Warf 8C 16
Oswald Rd. KT22: Fetc 9C 78
Osward CR0: Sels 5J 65
(not continuous)
Osward Rd. SW17 ......3D 28
Otford Cl. RH11: Craw 9A 182
Othello Gro. RG42: Warf 9C 16
Otho Ct. TW8: Brent 3K 11
Otterbourne Pl.
RH19: E Grin 9L 165
Otterbourne Rd.
CR0: Croy 2B 200 (8N 45)
Otterburn Gdns.
TW7: Isle 3G 10
Otterburn St. SW17 ......7D 28
Otter Cl. GU12: Alde 1B 110
KT16: Otter 3D 54
RG45: Crow 9F 30
Otterden Cl. BR6: Orp 1N 67
Ottermead La. KT16: Otter 3E 54
Otter Mdw. KT22: Leat 6F 78
OTTERSHAW 3E 54
Ottershaw Pk. KT16: Otter 4C 54
(not continuous)
Ottway's Av. KT21: A'tead 6K 79
Ottways La. KT21: A'tead 7K 79
Otway Cl. RH11: Craw 5L 181
Oulton Wlk. RH10: Craw 5F 182
Ouseley Lodge
SL4: O Win 1M 19
(off Ouseley Rd.)
Ouseley Rd. SL4: O Win 1M 19
(not continuous)
SW12 ......2D 28
TW19: Wray 1M 19
Outdowns KT24: Eff 8J 97
Outram Pl. KT13: Weybr 2D 56
Outram Rd. CR0: Croy 8C 46
OUTWOOD 3N 143
OUTWOOD COMMON 3N 143
Outwood Ho. SW2 ......1K 29
(off Deepdene Gdns.)
Outwood La.
CR5: Chip, K'wood 7C 82
KT20: K'wood 9N 81
RH1: Blet, Sth N 2A 124
RH1: Out 3A 144
Outwood Post Windmill 3A 144
Oval, The GU2: Guil 4K 113
GU3: Wood V 2E 112
GU7: Goda 4J 133
SM7: Ban 1M 81
Oval Ho. CR0: Croy 1F 200
Oval Rd.
CR0: Croy 2E 200 (8A 46)
Overbrook GU7: Goda 6K 133
KT24: W Hors 7C 96
Overbury Av. BR3: Beck 2L 47
Overbury Cres. CR0: N Add 6M 65
Overdale KT21: A'tead 2L 79
RH1: Blet 2N 123
RH5: Dork 4J 119
Overdale Av. KT3: N Mal 1B 42
Overdale Ri. GU16: Frim 3C 70
Overdene Dr. RH11: Craw 3M 181
Overford Cl. GU6: Cranl 8M 155
Overford Dr. GU6: Cranl 8N 155
Overhill CR6: Warl 6F 84
Overhill Rd. CR8: Pur 5L 63
Overhill Way BR3: Beck 4N 47
Overlord Cl. GU15: Camb 7A 50
Overlord Ct. KT22: Fetc 8D 78
Overstand Cl. BR3: Beck 4K 47
Overstone Gdns. CR0: Croy 6J 47
Overthorpe Cl. GU21: Knap 4H 73
Overton Cl. GU11: Alde 6A 110
TW7: Isle 4F 10
Overton Ct. GU10: Tong 6D 110
RH19: E Grin 9A 166
SM2: Sut 4M 61
Overton Ho. SW15 ......1E 26
(off Tangley Gro.)
Overton Rd. SM2: Sut 3M 61
Overton Shaw
RH19: E Grin 6A 166
Overton's Yd.
CR0: Croy 4B 200 (9N 45)
Oveton Way KT23: Book 4A 98
Ovington Ct. GU21: Wok 3J 73
Owen Cl. CR0: Croy 5A 46
SL3: Lang 1B 6
Owen Ho. TW1: Twick 1H 25
TW14: Felt 1H 23
Owen Mans. W14 ......2K 13
(off Queen's Club Gdns.)
Owen Pl. KT22: Leat 9H 79
Owen Rd. GU7: Goda 5J 133
GU20: Windl 2A 52
Owers Cl. RH13: Hors 6L 197
Owlbeech Ct. RH13: Hors 4A 198
Owlbeech Pl. RH13: Hors 4A 198
Owlbeech Way
RH13: Hors 4A 198
Owl Cl. CR2: Sels 6G 65
Owletts RH10: Craw 2H 183
Owlscastle Cl. RH12: Hors 3K 197
OWLSMOOR 6K 49
Owlsmoor Rd.
GU47: C Tow, Owls 7J 49
(not continuous)
Ownstead Gdns.
CR2: Sande 7C 64
Ownsted Hill CR0: N Add 6M 65
Oxberry Av. SW6 ......5K 13
Oxdowne Cl. KT11: Sto D 1B 78
Oxenden Ct. GU10: Tong 4C 110
Oxenden Rd. GU10: Tong 4C 110
Oxenhope RG12: Brac 3M 31
Oxfield TN8: Eden 9M 127
(off Rowfield)
Oxford Av. SW20 ......1K 43
TW5: Hest 1A 10
UB3: Harl 3G 8
Oxford Cl. CR4: Mit 2G 44
TW15: A'ford 8D 22
Oxford Ct.
KT18: Eps 8L 201 (1D 80)
TW13: Hanw 5L 23
W4 ......1A 12
Oxford Cres. KT3: N Mal 5C 42
Oxford Gdns. W4 ......1N 11
Oxford Rd.
GU1: Guil 6D 202 (5N 113)
GU14: Farnb 4A 90
GU47: Owls 5K 49
RG41: W'ham 2A 30
RH1: Red 2C 122
RH10: Craw 7C 182
RH13: Hors 6K 197
SL4: W'sor 4F 4
SM5: Cars 3C 62
SM6: W'ton 2G 62
SW15 ......7K 13
TW11: Tedd 6D 24
Oxford Rd. E. SL4: W'sor 4F 4
Oxford Rd. Nth. W4 ......1A 12
Oxford Rd. Sth. W4 ......1N 11
Oxfordshire Pl. RG42: Warf 8D 16
Oxford Ter.
GU1: Guil 6D 202 (5N 113)
Oxford Way TW13: Hanw 5L 23
Ox La. KT17: Ewe 5F 60
Oxleigh Cl. KT3: N Mal 4D 42
Oxlip Cl. CR0: Croy 7G 46
OXSHOTT 9D 58
Oxshott Ri. KT11: Cob 9L 57
Oxshott Rd. KT22: Leat 3E 78
Oxshott Station (Rail) 9C 58
Oxshott Village Sports Club
......1C 78
Oxshott Way KT11: Cob 2M 77
OXTED 7A 106
Oxted Cl. CR4: Mit 2B 44
Oxted Grn. GU8: Mil 3B 152
Oxted Rd. RH9: Gods 8F 104
Oxted Station (Rail) 7A 106
Oxtoby Way SW16 ......9H 29
Oyster La. KT14: Byf 6M 55
(not continuous)

P

Pachesham Dr. KT22: Leat 3F 78
PACHESHAM PARK 3F 78
Pachesham Pk. KT22: Leat 3G 78
Pacific Cl. TW14: Felt 2G 23
Packer Cl. RH19: E Grin 6C 166
Packham Ct. KT4: W Pk 9H 43
Packway GU9: Farnh 4K 129
Padbrook RH8: Limp 7C 106
(not continuous)
Padbrook Cl. RH8: Limp 7C 106
Padbury Cl. TW14: Bedf 2E 22
Padbury Oaks
UB7: L'ford 4K 7
Paddock, The GU1: Guil 2F 114
GU6: Cranl 7M 155
GU6: Ewh 6F 156
GU7: Goda 8H 133
GU18: Ligh 7M 51
GU26: G'hott 5M 169
GU27: Hasl 9E 170
GU35: Head 4D 168
RG45: Crow 1F 48
RH4: Westc 6B 118
RH10: Craw 2H 183
SL3: Dat 4L 5
SL4: Wink 1J 17
(Crouch La.)
SL4: Wink 2M 17
(Squirrel La.)
TN16: Weste 4L 107
Paddock Cl. BR6: Farnb 1K 67
GU8: Hamb 9F 152
GU15: Camb 9E 50
KT4: W Pk 7D 42
RH5: B Grn 7K 139
RH7: Ling 8M 145
RH8: Oxt 9B 106
TN8: Eden 9L 127
Paddock Gdns.
RH19: E Grin 2A 186
Paddock Gro. RH5: B Grn 7K 139
Paddock Ho. GU4: Guil 2F 114
(off Merrow St.)
Paddockhurst Rd.
RH10: T Hil 9K 183
RH11: Craw 4M 181
Paddock Mobile Home Pk.
BR2: Kes 5G 67
Paddocks, The CR0: A'ton 3K 65
GU3: Flex 3N 111
GU25: V Wat 5A 36
KT13: Weybr 9F 38
KT15: N Haw 6K 55
KT23: Book 4B 98
Paddocks Cl. KT11: Cob 1K 77
KT21: A'tead 5L 79
Paddocks Mead GU21: Wok 3H 73
Paddocks Rd. GU4: B'ham 8C 94
Paddocks Way KT16: Chert 7K 37
KT21: A'tead 5L 79
Paddock Wlk. CR6: Warl 6E 84
Paddock Way GU21: Wok 1D 74
GU27: G'wood 7L 171
RH8: Oxt 9B 106
SW15 ......1H 27
Padley Cl. KT9: Ches 2M 59
Padstow Wlk. RH11: Craw 5K 181
TW14: Felt 2G 22
Padwick Rd. RH13: Hors 6N 197
Pageant Wlk.
CR0: Croy 4F 200 (9B 46)
Page Cl. TW12: Hamp 7M 23
Page Ct. RH10: Craw 4D 182
RH13: Hors 7K 197
Page Cres. CR0: Wad 2M 63
Page Cft. KT15: Addl 8K 37
Pagehurst Rd. CR0: Croy 6E 46
Pageites GU7: Goda 4E 132
Page Rd. TW14: Bedf 9E 8
Page's Cft. RG40: W'ham 3C 30
Pages Yd. W4 ......2E 12
Paget Av. SM1: Sut 9B 44
Paget Cl. GU15: Camb 8F 50
RH13: Hors 8L 197
TW12: H Hill 5D 24
Paget La. TW7: Isle 6D 10
Paget Pl. KT2: K Tham 7B 26
KT7: T Dit 7F 40
PAGEWOOD 3J 161
Pagewood Cl. RH10: Craw 5H 183
Pagoda Av. TW9: Rich 6M 11
Pagoda Gro. SE27 ......3N 29
Paice Grn. RG40: W'ham 1C 30
Painesfield Dr. KT16: Chert 7J 37
Pain's Cl. CR4: Mit 1F 44
PAINS HILL
KT11 ......1G 76
RH8 ......9E 106
PAINSHILL 9G 56
Pains Hill RH8: Limp 1E 126
Pains Hill Ho. KT11: Cob 1G 76
Painshill Pk. 1G 76
Paisley Rd. SM5: Cars 7B 44
Paisley Ter. SM5: Cars 6B 44
Pakenham Cl. SW12 ......2E 28
Pakenham Dr.
GU11: Alde 1L 109
Pakenham Rd. RG12: Brac 6B 32
Palace Ct. GU21: Wok 3C 74
(off Maybury Rd.)
Palace Dr. KT13: Weybr 9C 38
Palace Grn. CR0: Sels 4J 65
Palace Mans.
KT1: K Tham 8H 203
Palace M. SW6 ......3M 13
Palace Rd.
KT1: K Tham 8H 203 (3K 41)
KT8: E Mol 2C 40
SW2 ......2K 29
TN16: Weste 8J 87
Palace Vw. CR0: Croy 1J 65
Palace Way GU22: Wok 7D 74
KT13: Weybr 9C 38
Palace Wharf W6 ......3H 13
(off Rainville Rd.)
Palemead Cl. SW6 ......4J 13
Palestine Gro. SW19 ......9B 28
Palewell Comn. Dr.
SW14 ......8C 12
Palewell Pk. SW14 ......8C 12
Palgrave Ho. TW2: Whitt 1C 24
Palladino Ho. SW17 ......6C 28
(off Laurel Cl.)
Pallant Way BR6: Farnb 1J 67
Pallingham Dr.
RH10: Craw 6G 182
Palliser Ct. W14 ......1K 13
(off Palliser Rd.)
Palliser Rd. W14 ......1K 13
Palmer Av. SM3: Chea 1H 61
Palmer Cl. BR4: W Wick 9N 47
RG40: W'ham 8F 30
RH1: Red 4E 122
RH6: Horl 6D 142
TW5: Hest 4A 10
Palmer Ct. RG40: W'ham 2B 30
Palmer Cres.
KT1: K Tham 5J 203 (2L 41)
KT16: Otter 3F 54
Palmer Rd. RH10: Craw 6G 182
Palmer School Rd.
RG40: W'ham 2B 30
PALMERS CROSS 4F 154
Palmersfield Rd. SM7: Ban 1M 81
Palmers Gro. KT8: W Mole 3A 40
Palmers Lodge GU2: Guil 4K 113
Palmers Pas. SW14 ......6B 12
(off Palmers Rd.)
Palmers Rd. SW14 ......6B 12
SW16 ......1K 45
Palmerston Cl. GU14: Cove 2J 89
GU21: Wok 1C 74
RH1: Red 6E 122
Palmerston Ct. KT6: Surb 6K 41
Palmerstone Ct.
GU25: V Wat 4A 36
(off Sandhills La.)
Palmerston Gro.
SW19 ......8M 27
Palmerston Ho. SM7: Ban 2L 81
(off Basing Rd.)
Palmerston Mans.
W14 ......2K 13
(off Queen's Club Gdns.)
Palmerston Rd. BR6: Farnb 1L 67
CR0: Croy 4A 46
SM1: Sut 2A 62
SM5: Cars 1D 62
SW14 ......7B 12
SW19 ......8M 27
TW2: Twick 9E 10
TW3: Houn 4C 10
Palm Gro. GU1: Guil 7M 93
Pampisford Rd.
CR2: S Croy 5M 63
CR8: Pur 7L 63
Pams Way KT19: Ewe 2C 60
Pankhurst Cl. TW7: Isle 6F 10
Pankhurst Ct. RH11: Craw 8N 181
Pankhurst Dr. RG12: Brac 4B 32
Pankhurst Rd. KT12: Wal T 6K 39
Panmuir Rd. SW20 ......9G 27
Pannell Cl. RH19: E Grin 1N 185
Pannells GU10: L Bou 6J 129
Pannells Ash RH14: Ifo 5E 192
Pannells Cl. KT16: Chert 7H 37
Pannells Ct.
GU1: Guil 5D 202 (4N 113)
Pan's Gdns. GU15: Camb 2D 70
Pantile Rd. KT13: Weybr 1E 56
Pantiles Cl. GU21: Wok 5L 73
Panton Cl.
CR0: Croy 1A 200 (7M 45)
Papercourt La. GU23: Rip 9H 75
Papercourt Sailing Club 9H 75
Paper M.
RH4: Dork 1L 201 (4H 119)
Papermill Cl. SM5: Cars 1E 62
Papworth Way SW2 ......1L 29
Parade, The CR0: Croy 5J 45
GU2: Guil 7L 93
(off Burden Rd.)
GU12: A Va 9E 90
GU16: Frim 6B 70
Parade, The GU25: V Wat 5N 35
GU46: Yate 9D 48
KT2: K Tham 3K 203
KT4: W Pk 1E 60
KT10: Clay 3E 58
KT18: Eps 1N 79
(off Spa Dr.)
KT18: Eps 7K 201 (9C 60)
(The Parade)
KT20: Tad 6K 81
KT22: Leat 7G 79
(off Kingston Rd.)
RH1: Red 4E 122
RH10: Craw 2C 182
RH12: Hors 5G 197
(off Caterways)
RH19: E Grin 7L 165
SL4: W'sor 4A 4
SM1: Sut 9L 43
SM5: Cars 2D 62
(off Beynon Rd.)
TN16: Tats 8E 86
(off Ship Hill)
TW12: Tedd 6D 24
TW16: Sunb 8G 23
TW18: Stain 6F 20
(off Thorpe Rd.)
Parade Ct. KT24: E Hor 4F 96
Parade M. SE27 ......3M 29
Paradise Rd. TW9: Rich 8K 11
Paragon TW8: Brent 1J 11
(off Boston Pk. Rd.)
Paragon Cotts. GU4: E Cla 9M 95
Paragon Gro. KT5: Surb 5M 41
Paragon Pl. KT5: Surb 5M 41
Parbury Ri. KT9: Ches 3L 59
Parchmore Rd.
CR7: T Hea 1M 45
Parchmore Way
CR7: T Hea 1M 45
Pares Cl. GU21: Wok 3N 73
Parfitts Cl. GU9: Farnh 1F 128
Parfour Dr. CR8: Ken 3N 83
Parfrey St. W6 ......2H 13
Parham Rd. RH11: Craw 2L 181
Parish Cl. GU9: U Hal 6F 108
GU12: Ash 3F 110
Parish Ct. KT6: Surb 4L 41
Parish Ho. RH11: Craw 4B 182
Parish Rd. GU14: Farnb 5A 90
Park, The KT23: Book 1A 98
RH4: Dork 7G 118
SM5: Cars 2D 62
Park & Ride
Artington 8M 113
Spectrum 1B 114
Hop Oast 9G 196
Kingston-upon-Thames
(November-mid. January)
......5J 59
Ladymead 1B 202 (2M 113)
University 3K 113
Windsor (Home Park) 2H 5
Windsor (Legoland) 8B 4
Park Av. BR4: W Wick 8M 47
CR3: Cate 2B 104
CR4: Mit 8F 28
GU8: P Har 6N 131
GU15: Camb 2A 70
RG40: W'ham 3A 30
(not continuous)
RH1: Salf 2D 142
SM5: Cars 3E 62
SW14 ......7C 12
TN8: Eden 1K 147
TW3: Houn 9B 10
TW17: Shep 2F 38
TW18: Stain 7H 21
TW19: Wray 8N 5
TW20: Egh 7E 20
Park Av. E. KT17: Ewe 3F 60
Park Av. M. CR4: Mit 8F 28
Park Av. W. KT17: Ewe 3F 60
PARK BARN 2H 113
Park Barn Dr. GU2: Guil 1H 113
Park Barn E. GU2: Guil 2J 113
Park Barn Way GU2: Guil 3H 113
(off Southway)
Park Chase
GU1: Guil 3E 202 (3A 114)
GU7: Goda 9H 133
Park Cl. GU27: G'wood 8K 171
KT2: K Tham 1M 203 (9N 25)
KT10: Esh 3A 58
KT12: Wal T 8G 38
KT15: N Haw 6K 55
KT22: Fetc 2D 98
RH3: Brock 8A 120
RH8: Oxt 6B 106
SL4: W'sor 5G 5
SM5: Cars 3D 62
TW3: Houn 8C 10
TW12: Hamp 9C 24
W4 ......2C 12
Park Copse RH5: Dork 5K 119
Park Cnr. SL4: W'sor 6B 4
Park Cnr. Dr. KT24: E Hor 6F 96
Park Cotts. RH5: For G 2L 157
Park Ct. CR2: S Croy 8B 200
GU9: Farnh 9J 109
GU22: Wok 5B 74
KT1: H Wic 9J 25
KT3: N Mal 3C 42

Park Ct.—Peascod Pl.

Park Ct. KT14: W By 9J 55
SE21 4N 29
SM6: W'ton 2J 63
Park Crematorium, The
GU12: Alde 6B 110
Park Cres. RH18: F Row 7J 187
SL5: S'dale 5C 34
TW2: Twick 2D 24
Parkdale Cres. KT4: W Pk 9C 42
Park Dr. GU5: Braml 5B 134
GU6: Cranl 6A 156
GU22: Wok 5B 74
KT13: Weybr 2C 56
KT21: A'tead 5N 79
SL5: S'dale 5C 34
SW14 8C 12
Parker Cl. RH10: Craw 4H 183
SM5: Cars 3D 62
Parke Rd. SW13 4F 12
TW16: Sunb 3H 39
Parker Rd.
CR0: Croy 6C 200 (1N 63)
Parker's Cl. KT21: A'tead 6L 79
Parkers Ct. GU19: Bag 4J 51
Parker's Hill KT21: A'tead 6L 79
Parkers La. KT21: A'tead 6L 79
RG42: Wink R 4F 16
Park Farm Cl. RH12: Hors 1K 197
Park Farm Ind. Est.
GU16: Camb 5A 70
Park Farm Rd.
KT2: K Tham 8L 25
RH12: Hors 1K 197
Parkfield GU7: Bus 9H 133
RH12: Hors 5J 197
TW7: Isle 4E 10
Parkfield Av. SW14 7D 12
TW13: Felt 4H 23
Parkfield Cl. RH11: Craw 4L 181
Parkfield Cres. TW13: Felt 4H 23
Parkfield Ho. RG45: Crow 3H 49
(off Cambridge Rd.)
Parkfield Pde. TW13: Felt 4H 23
Parkfield Rd. TW13: Felt 4H 23
Parkfields CR0: Croy 7J 47
GU46: Yate 1C 68
KT22: Oxs 7D 58
SW15 7H 13
Parkfields Av. SW20 9G 26
Parkfields Cl. SM5: Cars 1E 62
Parkfields Rd.
KT2: K Tham 6M 25
Park Gdns. KT2: K Tham 6M 25
PARKGATE 7C 140
Parkgate Cl. KT2: K Tham 7A 26
Park Ga. Cotts.
GU6: Cranl 7K 155
Park Ga. Ct. GU22: Wok 5A 74
TW12: H Hill 7C 24
Parkgate Gdns. SW14 8C 12
Parkgate Rd. RH2: Reig 4N 121
RH5: Newd 9A 140
SM6: W'ton 2E 62
Park Grn. KT23: Book 2A 98
Park Hall Rd. RH2: Reig 1M 121
SE21 4N 29
Park Hall Trad. Est.
SE21 4N 29
Park Hgts. GU22: Wok 5A 74
(off Constitution Hill)
KT18: Eps 8J 201 (1C 80)
Park Hill GU52: C Cro 8A 88
SM5: Cars 3C 62
TW10: Rich 9M 11
Parkhill KT10: Esh 1C 58
Park Hill Cl. SM5: Cars 2C 62
Parkhill Cl. GU17: B'water 2J 69
Park Hill Ct. SW17 4D 28
Park Hill M.
CR2: S Croy 8E 200 (2A 64)
Park Hill Ri. CR0: Croy 8B 46
Park Hill Rd. BR2: Brom 1N 47
CR0: Croy 3F 200 (8B 46)
KT17: Ewe 7E 60
SM6: W'ton 4F 62
Parkhill Rd. GU17: B'water 2J 69
Park Horsley KT24: E Hor 7H 97
Park Ho. Dr. RH2: Reig 5L 121
Park Ho. Gdns. TW1: Twick 8J 11
Parkhurst KT19: Eps 6B 60
Parkhurst Flds.
GU10: Churt 9L 149
Parkhurst Gro. RH6: Horl 7C 142
Parkhurst Rd. GU2: Guil 2K 113
RH6: Horl 7C 142
SM1: Sut 1B 62
Parkland Av. SL3: Lang 1N 5
Parkland Dr. RG12: Brac 9C 16
Parkland Gdns. SW19 2J 27
Parkland Gro. GU9: Weybo 4L 109
TW15: A'ford 5B 22
Parkland Rd. TW15: A'ford 5B 22
PARKLANDS 1A 136
Parklands GU2: Guil 8K 93
KT5: Surb 4M 41
KT15: Addl 2L 55
KT23: Book 1A 98
RH1: Red 1E 122
RH5: Nth H 9H 119
RH8: Oxt 9A 106
Parklands Cl. SW14 8B 12
Parklands Cotts.
GU5: Shere 1A 136
Parklands Ct. TW5: Hest 5L 9
Parklands Gro. TW7: Isle 4F 10
Parklands Pde. TW5: Hest 5L 9
(off Parklands Ct.)
Parklands Pl. GU1: Guil 3D 114
Parklands Rd. SW16 6F 28
Parklands Way KT4: W Pk 8D 42
Park La.
CR0: Croy 3D 200 (9A 46)
CR5: Coul 8H 83
GU4: Guil 9F 94
GU8: Brook 2J 171
GU10: Churt 9G 149
GU15: Camb 1A 70
KT21: A'tead 5M 79
RG42: Bin 8K 15
RH2: Reig 4K 121
RH5: B Grn, Ockl 4F 158
RH19: Ash W 3F 186
SL3: Hort 6C 6
SL4: Wink 2M 17
SM3: Chea 3K 61
SM5: Cars 1E 62
SM6: W'ton 2E 62
TW5: C'ford 3H 9
TW9: Rich 7K 11
TW11: Tedd 7F 24
Park La. E. RH2: Reig 6L 121
Park La. Mans.
CR0: Croy 5D 200
PARK LANGLEY 3M 47
Parklawn Av. KT18: Eps 9A 60
RH6: Horl 6D 142
Park Lawn Rd.
KT13: Weybr 1D 56
Parkleigh Rd. SW19 1N 43
Park Ley Rd. CR3: Wold 7G 85
Parkleys TW10: Ham 5K 25
Parkleys Pde.
TW10: K Tham 5K 25
Park Mnr. SM2: Sut 4A 62
(off Christchurch Pk.)
Parkmead GU6: Cranl 6A 156
SW15 9G 12
Park M. SE24 1N 29
TW19: Stan 1A 22
Parkpale La.
RH3: Betch, Brock 8N 119
Park Pl. GU17: Haw 3L 69
GU22: Wok 5B 74
(off Hill Vw. Rd.)
GU52: C Cro 8A 88
RH12: Hors 7J 197
TW12: H Hill 7C 24
Park Ride SL4: W'sor 1A 18
Park Ri. KT22: Leat 8H 79
RH12: Hors 4H 197
Park Ri. Cl. KT22: Leat 8H 79
Park Rd. CR3: Cate 1B 104
CR6: Warl 1A 86
CR8: Ken 2M 83
GU1: Guil 3C 202 (3N 113)
GU5: Alb 9N 115
GU7: Goda 9H 133
GU9: Farnh 8J 109
GU11: Alde 4N 109
GU14: Farnb 4C 90
GU15: Camb 3N 69
GU22: Wok 4B 74
(not continuous)
GU27: Hasl 2G 188
GU47: Sandh 8H 49
KT1: H Wic 9J 25
KT2: K Tham 1M 203 (6M 25)
KT3: N Mal 3C 42
KT5: Surb 5M 41
KT8: E Mol 3C 40
KT10: Esh 1B 58
KT21: A'tead 5L 79
RG12: Brac 1B 32
RG40: W'ham 2A 30
RH1: Red 1D 122
(not continuous)
RH6: Smal 1N 163
RH7: Ling 9A 126
RH8: Oxt 6B 106
RH12: Fay 8E 180
RH13: Slin 5L 195
RH17: Hand 9N 199
RH18: F Row 7H 187
RH19: D Pk 4A 166
RH19: E Grin 9N 165
SE25 3B 46
SM3: Chea 3K 61
SM6: W'ton 2F 62
(Clifton Rd.)
SM6: W'ton 8F 44
(Elmwood Cl.)
SM7: Ban 2N 81
SW19 7B 28
TW1: Twick 9J 11
TW3: Houn 8B 10
TW7: Isle 4H 11
TW10: Rich 9M 11
TW11: Tedd 7F 24
TW12: H Hill 5B 24
TW13: Hanw 5L 23
TW15: A'ford 6C 22
TW16: Sunb 8J 23
TW17: Shep 7B 38
TW19: Stan, Stan M 9K 7
TW20: Egh 5C 20
W4 3B 12
Park Rd. Ho.
KT2: K Tham 1M 203 (8N 25)
Park Rd. Nth. W4 1C 12
Park Rd. Rdbt.
GU14: Farnb 5C 90
Park Row GU9: Farnh 9G 109
SW2 1L 29
Parkshot TW9: Rich 7K 11
Parkside GU9: U Hal 6H 109
KT15: N Haw 7K 55
RH10: Craw 3C 182
RH19: E Grin 9M 165
SM3: Chea 3K 61
SW19 4J 27
TW12: H Hill 6D 24
Parkside Av. SW19 6J 27
Parkside Cl. KT24: E Hor 3G 96
Parkside Cotts.
GU4: W Cla 1J 115
Parkside Ct. KT13: Weybr 1B 56
RH1: Red 8D 102
Parkside Cres. KT5: Surb 5B 42
Parkside Gdns. CR5: Coul 4F 82
SW19 5J 27
Parkside M. CR6: Warl 3K 85
RH12: Hors 6K 197
Parkside Pl. KT24: E Hor 3G 96
TW18: Stain 7J 21
Parkside Rd. SL5: S'dale 5D 34
TW3: Houn 8B 10
Parkside Ter. BR6: Farnb 1K 67
(off Willow Wlk.)
Park Sq. KT10: Esh 1B 58
SL4: Wink 2M 17
Parkstead Rd. SW15 8F 12
Parkstone Dr. GU15: Camb 2A 70
PARK STREET 5K 195
Park St.
CR0: Croy 3C 200 (8N 45)
GU1: Guil 6B 202 (5M 113)
GU15: Camb 9A 50
GU19: Bag 4J 51
RH12: Hors 6K 197
RH13: Slin 5K 195
SL3: Coln 4F 6
SL4: W'sor 4G 5
TW11: Tedd 7E 24
Park Ter. KT4: W Pk 7F 42
SM5: Cars 9C 44
Park Ter. Courtyard
RH12: Hors 7K 197
(off Park Ter. W.)
Park Ter. E. RH13: Hors 7K 197
Park Ter. W. RH12: Hors 7K 197
Parkthorne Rd. SW12 1H 29
Park Vw. CR3: Cate 3D 104
GU19: Bag 4H 51
KT3: N Mal 2E 42
KT15: Addl 2L 55
(off Hollies Ct.)
KT23: Book 3A 98
RH6: Horl 8E 142
RH11: Craw 4A 182
Park Vw. Cl. TN8: Eden 1K 147
Parkview Cl. SM5: Cars 4D 62
Park Vw. Ct. GU22: Wok 6B 74
SE20 1E 46
Parkview Ct. SW6 5K 13
SW18 9M 13
Park Vw. Dr. CR4: Mit 1B 44
Park Vw. Gdns.
RH19: E Grin 7N 165
Park Vw. Ho. GU11: Alde 2M 109
(off High St.)
Park Vw. Rd. CR3: Wold 9H 85
KT22: Leat 7F 78
RH1: Salf 1E 142
Parkview Rd. CR0: Croy 7D 46
Parkview Va. GU4: Guil 9E 94
Park Vs. GU17: Haw 4L 69
Parkville Rd. SW6 3L 13
Park Wlk. KT21: A'tead 6M 79
Park Way KT8: W Mole 2B 40
KT23: Book 1A 98
RH6: Horl 8E 142
RH10: Craw 2F 182
RH12: Hors 6J 197
TW14: Felt 1J 23
Parkway CR0: N Add 5L 65
GU1: Guil 1D 202 (2N 113)
GU15: Camb 3A 70
KT13: Weybr 1E 56
RG45: Crow 2F 48
RH4: Dork 1J 201 (4G 119)
SW20 3J 43
Parkway, The TW4: C'ford 5J 9
TW5: C'ford 1H 9
UB2: S'hall 1H 9
Parkway Trad. Est.
TW5: Hest 2K 9
Parkwood Av. KT10: Esh 7C 40
Parkwood Cl. SM7: Ban 2J 81
Parkwood Gro. TW16: Sunb 2H 39
Parkwood Rd. RH1: Nut 2J 123
SM7: Ban 2J 81
SW19 6L 27
TN16: Tats 8G 87
TW7: Isle 4F 10
Parkwood Vw. SM7: Ban 3H 81
Park Works Rd. RH1: Nut 2K 123
Parley Dr. GU21: Wok 4M 73
Parliamentary Rd.
GU24: B'wood 8L 71
Parliament M. SW14 5B 12
Parnell Cl. RH10: Craw 5H 183
Parnell Gdns. KT13: Weybr 7B 56
Parnham Av. GU18: Ligh 7A 52
Parr Av. KT17: Ewe 5G 61
Parr Cl. KT22: Leat 7F 78
Parr Ct. GU21: Knap 6F 72
(off Tudor Way)
TW13: Hanw 5K 23
Parrington Ho. SW4 1H 29
Parris Cft. RH4: Dork 8J 119
Parrock La. TN7: U Har 8M 187
Parrs Cl. CR2: Sande 5A 64
Parrs Pl. TW12: Hamp 8A 24
Parry Cl. KT17: Ewe 4G 60
RH13: Hors 4B 198
Parry Dr. KT13: Weybr 6B 56
Parry Rd. SE25 2B 46
Parsley Gdns. CR0: Croy 7G 46
Parsonage Bus. Pk.
RH12: Hors 4L 197
Parsonage Cl. CR6: Warl 3J 85
RH4: Westc 7C 118
Parsonage La. RH4: Westc 6C 118
SL4: W'sor 4D 4
Parsonage Rd. GU6: Cranl 7M 155
RH12: Hors 4K 197
TW20: Eng G 6N 19
Parsonage Sq. RH4: Dork 2H 201
Parsonage Way GU16: Frim 5C 70
RH12: Hors 4L 197
Parsons Cl. GU11: Alde 2A 110
GU27: Hasl 9G 171
GU52: C Cro 8A 88
RH6: Horl 7C 142
SM1: Sut 9N 43
Parsons Cotts. GU12: Ash 1G 111
Parsons Fld. GU47: Sandh 7G 49
Parsonsfield Cl. SM7: Ban 2J 81
Parsonsfield Rd. SM7: Ban 3J 81
PARSONS GREEN 5L 13
Parsons Grn. GU1: Guil 1N 113
GU27: Hasl 9G 171
SW6 4M 13
Parsons Grn. Ct. GU1: Guil 9N 93
Parson's Grn. La. SW6 4M 13
Parsons Green Station (Tube) 4M 13
Parsons La. GU26: Hind 3A 170
Parsons Mead
CR0: Croy 1A 200 (7M 45)
KT8: E Mol 2C 40
Parson's Ride RG12: Brac 6D 32
Parsons Rd. SL3: Lang 1B 6
Parsons Wlk. RH12: Hors 8F 196
Parthenia Rd. SW6 4M 13
Parthia Cl. KT20: Tad 6G 81
Parthings La. RH13: Hors 9E 196
Partridge Av. GU46: Yate 9A 48
Partridge Cl. GU10: Ews 4C 108
GU16: Frim 5C 70
RG12: Brac 3K 31
Partridge Knoll CR8: Pur 8M 63
Partridge La. RH5: Newd 7C 140
RH12: Rusp 8C 160
Partridge Mead SM7: Ban 2H 81
Partridge Pl. RH10: T Hil 3F 184
Partridge Rd. TW12: Hamp 7N 23
Partridge Way GU4: Guil 1F 114
Parvis Rd. KT14: W By, Byf 9K 55
Paschal Rd. GU15: Camb 7D 50
Passage, The TW9: Rich 8L 11
PASSFIELD 8E 168
Passfield Ent. Cen.
GU30: Pass 9C 168
Passfield Mill Bus. Pk.
GU30: Pass 8C 168
Passfield Rd. GU30: Pass 9D 168
Passfields W14 1L 13
(off Star St.)
Passingham Ho. TW5: Hest 2A 10
Pastens Rd. RH8: Limp 9E 106
Paston Cl. SM6: W'ton 9G 44
Pasture, The RH10: Craw 3G 182
Pasture Wood Rd.
RH5: A Com, H Mary 6K 137
Patching Cl. RH11: Craw 2L 181
Patchings RH13: Hors 5M 197
Paterson Rd. TW15: A'ford 6M 21
Pates Mnr. Dr. TW14: Bedf 1E 22
Path, The SW19 9N 27
Pathfield GU8: Chid 5E 172
Pathfield Cl. GU8: Chid 5E 172
RH12: Rudg 1E 194
Pathfield Rd. RH12: Rudg 1E 194
SW16 7H 29
Pathfields GU5: Shere 9B 116
GU27: Hasl 1G 189
Pathfields Cl. GU27: Hasl 1G 189
Pathfinders, The
GU14: Cove 2H 89
Path Link RH10: Craw 2C 182
Pathway, The GU23: Send 3H 95
RG42: Bin 6H 15
Patmore La. KT12: Hers 3G 56
Patricia Gdns. SM2: Sut 7M 61
Patrick Gdns. RG42: Warf 8C 16
Patrington Cl. RH11: Craw 6M 181
Patten All. TW10: Rich 8K 11
Patten Ash Dr.
RG40: W'ham 1D 30
Patten Av. GU46: Yate 1B 68
Patten Rd. SW18 1C 28
Patterdale Cl. RH11: Craw 5N 181
Patterson Cl. GU16: Frim 3G 71
Paul Cl. GU11: Alde 4K 109
Paul Ct. TW20: Egh 6F 20
Paulet Cl. GU51: Fleet 2A 88
Paul Gdns. CR0: Croy 8C 46
Pauline Cres. TW2: Whitt 2C 24
Paul Robeson Theatre, The 6B 10
Pauls Mead RH7: Ling 6A 146
Paul's Pl. KT21: A'tead 6A 80
Paul Vanson Ct. KT12: Hers 3L 57
Paved Ct. TW9: Rich 8K 11
Pavement, The RH10: Craw 3C 182
TW7: Isle 6G 11
(off South St.)
Pavement Sq. CR0: Croy 7D 46
Pavilion, The
KT20: K'wood 1A 102
RH2: Reig 1C 122
Pavilion Ct. GU6: Cranl 7L 155
(off East Vw. La.)
Pavilion Gdns. TW18: Stain 8K 21
(not continuous)
Pavilion La. GU11: Alde 1K 109
Pavilion Rd. GU11: Alde 3K 109
Pavilions, The
RH11: P Pot 2N 199
Pavilions End, The
GU15: Camb 3B 70
Pavilions in the Pk., The 5J 197
Pavilion Sports & Fitness Club, The 2C 40
Pavilion Sq. SW17 4D 28
Pavilion Way RH19: E Grin 1A 186
Paviours GU9: Farnh 9G 109
Pawley Cl. GU10: Tong 5D 110
Pawsons Rd. CR0: Croy 5N 45
Pax Cl. RH11: Craw 5K 181
Paxton Cl. KT12: Wal T 6K 39
TW9: Kew 5M 11
Paxton Ct. CR4: Mit 1D 44
(off Armfield Cres.)
Paxton Gdns. GU21: Wok 8F 54
Paxton Rd. W4 2D 12
Payley Dr. RG40: W'ham 9D 14
Payne Cl. RH10: Craw 1H 183
Paynesfield Av. SW14 6C 12
Paynesfield Rd. TN16: Tats 8E 86
(not continuous)
PAYNES GREEN 1D 178
Paynes Wlk. W6 2K 13
Paynetts Ct. KT13: Weybr 2E 56
Peabody Cl. CR0: Croy 7F 46
Peabody Est. SE24 1M 29
SW6 2M 13
(off Lillie Rd.)
W6 1H 13
Peabody Hill SE21 2M 29
Peabody Rd. GU14: Farnb 4B 90
Peace Cl. SE25 3B 46
Peacemaker Cl.
RH11: Craw 5K 181
Peaches Cl. SM2: Chea 4K 61
Peach Rd. TW13: Felt 2H 23
Peach St. RG40: W'ham 2B 30
Peach Tree Cl.
GU14: Farnb 7M 69
Peacock Av. TW14: Bedf 2E 22
Peacock Cotts. RG12: Brac 3H 31
Peacock Gdns. CR2: Sels 6H 65
Peacock La. RG12: Brac 4G 31
RG40: W'ham 4G 31
Peacocks Shop. Cen., The
GU21: Wok 4A 74
Peacock Wlk.
RH4: Dork 4J 201 (6G 119)
RH11: Craw 6M 181
PEAKED HILL 1A 110
Peakfield GU10: Fren 3H 149
Peak Rd. GU2: Guil 9K 93
Peaks Hill CR8: Pur 6H 63
Peaks Hill Ri. CR8: Pur 6J 63
Peall Rd. CR0: Croy 5K 45
Peall Rd. Ind. Est.
CR0: Croy 5K 45
Pearce Cl. CR4: Mit 1E 44
Pearl Ct. GU21: Wok 3H 73
Pearmain Cl. TW17: Shep 4C 38
Pears Av. TW17: Shep 2F 38
Pearscroft Ct. SW6 4N 13
Pearscroft Rd. SW6 4N 13
Pearson Cl. CR8: Pur 7M 63
Pearson Rd. RH10: Craw 2G 182
Pearson Way CR4: Mit 9E 28
Pears Rd. TW3: Houn 6C 10
Pear Tree Av. GU51: Fleet 3A 88
Peartree Av. SW17 4A 28
Pear Tree Cl. CR4: Mit 1C 44
GU35: Lind 5A 168
KT9: Ches 2N 59
KT15: Addl 2J 55
Peartree Cl. CR2: Sande 1E 84
Pear Tree Ct. GU15: Camb 7F 50
Peartree Grn. GU8: Duns 2N 173
Pear Tree Hill RH1: Salf 3E 142
Pear Tree La. GU10: Rowl 8E 128
Pear Tree Rd. GU35: Lind 5A 168
KT15: Addl 2J 55
TW15: A'ford 6D 22
Peary Cl. RH12: Hors 2K 197
Peascod Pl. SL4: W'sor 4G 4
(off Peascod St.)

272 A-Z Surrey

Peascod St.—Pine Cl.

Peascod St. SL4: W'sor . . . 4F 4
PEASE POTTAGE . . . 2N 199
Pease Pottage Hill
RH11: Craw . . . 8A 182
PEASE POTTAGE SERVICE AREA
. . . 9A 182
PEASLAKE . . . 5E 136
Peaslake La. GU5: P'lake . . . 5E 136
Peaslake Rd. GU6: Ewh . . . 2E 156
PEASMARSH . . . 2M 133
Peat Comn. GU8: Els . . . 9G 131
Peat Cotts. GU8: Els . . . 9G 131
Peatmoor Cl. GU51: Fleet . . . 3A 88
Peatmore Av. GU22: Pyr . . . 3J 75
Peatmore Cl. GU22: Pyr . . . 3J 75
Peatmore Dr.
GU24: B'wood . . . 8N 71
Pebble Cl. KT20: Wal H . . . 7D 100
Pebble Hill Rd.
RH3: Betch . . . 7D 100
Pebble La. KT18: Eps D . . . 9N 79
KT22: Leat . . . 2M 99
(not continuous)
Pebworth Ct. RH1: Red . . . 1E 122
Peddlars Gro. GU46: Yate . . . 9D 48
Peeble Hill KT24: W Hors . . . 2D 116
Peek Cres. SW19 . . . 6J 27
Peeks Brook La.
RH6: S Bri, Horl . . . 4J 163
Peel Av. GU16: Frim . . . 7E 70
Peel Cen., The RG12: Brac . . . 1M 31
Peel Cl. SL4: W'sor . . . 6E 4
Peel Ct. GU14: Farnb . . . 5A 90
Peel Rd. BR6: Farnb . . . 2L 67
Pegasus Av. GU12: Alde . . . 1C 110
Pegasus Cl. GU27: Hasl . . . 3B 188
Pegasus Ct. CR3: Cate . . . 1C 104
GU12: Alde . . . 3C 110
GU51: Fleet . . . 3A 88
KT1: K Tham . . . 6H 203 (2K 41)
KT22: Leat . . . 8J 79
(off Epsom Rd.)
RH11: Craw . . . 5K 181
SM7: Ban . . . 2M 81
TW8: Brent . . . 1M 11
TW20: Egh . . . 6D 20
Pegasus Pl. SW6 . . . 4M 13
Pegasus Rd. CR0: Wad . . . 3L 63
GU14: Cove . . . 7L 69
Pegasus Way
RH19: E Grin . . . 7D 166
Peggotty Pl. GU47: Owls . . . 5K 49
Pegg Rd. TW5: Hest . . . 3L 9
Pegler Way RH11: Craw . . . 3B 182
Pegwell Cl. RH11: Craw . . . 5L 181
Peket Cl. TW18: Stain . . . 9G 21
Pelabon Ho. *TW1: Twick . . . 9K 11*
(off Clevedon Rd.)
Peldon Ct. TW9: Rich . . . 7M 11
Peldon Pas. TW10: Rich . . . 7M 11
Pelham Ct. RH11: Craw . . . 7N 181
RH12: Hors . . . 6H 197
TW18: Stain . . . 6K 21
(off Kingston Rd.)
Pelham Dr. RH11: Craw . . . 7M 181
Pelham Ho. CR3: Cate . . . 2C 104
W14 . . . 1L 13
(off Mornington Av.)
Pelham Pl. GU10: Wrec . . . 7F 128
RH11: Craw . . . 7N 181
Pelham Rd. BR3: Beck . . . 1F 46
SW19 . . . 8M 27
Pelham's Cl. KT10: Esh . . . 1A 58
Pelham's Wlk. KT10: Esh . . . 1A 58
Pelham Way KT23: Book . . . 4B 98
Pellant Rd. SW6 . . . 3K 13
Pelling Hill SL4: O Win . . . 1L 19
Pelman Way KT19: Eps . . . 6A 60
Pelton Av. SM2: Sut . . . 6N 61
Pemberley Chase
KT19: Ewe . . . 2A 60
Pemberley Cl. KT19: Ewe . . . 2A 60
Pemberley Ho. *KT19: Ewe . . . 2A 60*
(off Pemberley Chase)
Pemberley Lodge SL4: W'sor . . . 6D 4
Pemberton Pl. KT10: Esh . . . 9C 40
Pemberton Rd. KT8: E Mol . . . 3C 40
Pembley Grn. RH10: Cop . . . 7A 164
Pembridge Av. TW2: Whitt . . . 2N 23
Pembridge Pl. SW15 . . . 8M 13
Pembroke RG12: Brac . . . 6L 31
W14 . . . 1L 13
(off Mornington Av.)
Pembroke Av. KT5: Surb . . . 4A 42
KT12: Hers . . . 1L 57
Pembroke B'way.
GU15: Camb . . . 1A 70
Pembroke Cl. SL5: S'hill . . . 4A 34
SM7: Ban . . . 4N 81
Pembroke Gdns.
GU22: Wok . . . 5C 74
Pembroke M. SL5: S'hill . . . 4A 34
Pembroke Pde. GU46: Yate . . . 8D 48
Pembroke Pl. TW7: Isle . . . 5E 10
Pembroke Rd. CR4: Mit . . . 1E 44
GU22: Wok . . . 5C 74
RH10: Craw . . . 9G 163
SE25 . . . 3B 46
Pembroke Vs. TW9: Rich . . . 7K 11
Pembury Av. KT4: W Pk . . . 7F 42
Pembury Cl. CR5: Coul . . . 1E 82
Pembury Ct. UB3: Harl . . . 2E 8
Pembury Pl. GU12: Alde . . . 3A 110
Pembury Rd. SE25 . . . 3D 46
Pemdevon Rd. CR0: Croy . . . 6L 45
Pemerich Cl. UB3: Harl . . . 1G 8
Penart Ct. SM2: Sut . . . 4A 62
Penates KT10: Esh . . . 1D 58
Penbury Rd. UB2: S'hall . . . 1N 9
Pendarves Rd. SW20 . . . 9H 27
Pendarvis Ct.
GU26: G'hott . . . 6A 170
Pendell Av. UB3: Harl . . . 3G 8
Pendell Rd. RH1: Blet . . . 9M 103
Pendennis Cl. KT14: W By . . . 1J 75
Pendennis Rd. SW16 . . . 5J 29
Pendenza KT11: Cob . . . 3M 77
Penderel Rd. TW3: Houn . . . 8A 10
Pendine Pl. RG12: Brac . . . 4N 31
Pendlebury RG12: Brac . . . 6M 31
Pendlebury Ct. KT5: Surb . . . 8K 203
Pendle Rd. SW16 . . . 7F 28
Pendleton Cl. RH1: Red . . . 4D 122
Pendleton Rd. RH1: Red . . . 6A 122
RH2: Reig . . . 6A 122
Pendragon Way
GU15: Camb . . . 2H 71
Pendry's La. RG42: Warf . . . 1M 15
Penfold Cl. CR0: Wad . . . 9L 45
Penfold Cft. GU9: Farnh . . . 8L 109
(not continuous)
Penfold Mnr. GU27: Hasl . . . 2H 189
Penfold Rd. RH10: Craw . . . 7F 182
Penfurzen La. RG42: Warf . . . 1B 16
Penge Rd. SE20 . . . 2D 46
SE25 . . . 2D 46
Pengilly Ho. GU1: Guil . . . 3E 114
Pengilly Rd. GU9: Farnh . . . 1G 128
Penhurst GU21: Wok . . . 1B 74
Peninsular Cl. GU15: Camb . . . 8F 50
TW14: Felt . . . 9E 8
Peninsular Pl. RG45: Crow . . . 3H 49
Penistone Rd. SW16 . . . 8J 29
Penlee Cl. TN8: Eden . . . 1L 147
Pennards, The TW16: Sunb . . . 2K 39
Penn Cl. RH11: Craw . . . 9B 162
Penn Ct. RH11: Craw . . . 3L 181
Pennefather's Rd.
GU11: Alde . . . 1L 109
Penner Cl. SW19 . . . 3K 27
Penners Gdns. KT6: Surb . . . 6L 41
Penn Ho. *SL4: Eton . . . 1G 4*
(off Common La.)
Pennine Cl. RH11: Craw . . . 3N 181
Pennine Way GU14: Cove . . . 7J 69
UB3: Harl . . . 3E 8
Pennings Av. GU2: Guil . . . 1J 113
Pennington Dr. KT13: Weybr . . . 9F 38
Pennington Lodge
KT5: Surb . . . 8K 203
Penn Rd. SL3: Dat . . . 4N 5
Penns Wood GU14: Farnb . . . 4B 90
Pennycroft CR0: Sels . . . 5H 65
Penny Dr. GU3: Wood V . . . 2E 112
Pennyfield KT11: Cob . . . 9H 57
Penny Hill Cvn. Pk.
GU17: Min . . . 4B 68
PENNYHILL PARK . . . 5F 50
Penny La. TW17: Shep . . . 6F 38
Pennymead Dr. KT24: E Hor . . . 5G 96
Pennymead Pl. KT10: Esh . . . 3N 57
Pennymead Ri.
KT24: E Hor . . . 5G 96
Penny M. SW12 . . . 1F 28
PENNY POT . . . 8F 52
Pennypot La. GU24: Chob . . . 9E 52
Penny Royal SM6: W'ton . . . 3H 63
Penrhyn Cl. CR3: Cate . . . 7A 84
GU12: Alde . . . 3N 109
Penrhyn Cres. SW14 . . . 7B 12
Penrhyn Gdns.
KT1: K Tham . . . 7H 203 (3K 41)
Penrhyn Rd.
KT1: K Tham . . . 7J 203 (3L 41)
Penrith Cl. RH2: Reig . . . 2C 122
SW15 . . . 8K 13
Penrith Pl. SE27 . . . 3M 29
Penrith Rd. CR7: T Hea . . . 1N 45
KT3: N Mal . . . 3C 42
Penrith St. SW16 . . . 7G 28
Penrose Ct. TW20: Eng G . . . 7N 19
(not continuous)
Penrose Dr. KT19: Eps . . . 7N 59
Penrose Gdns. GU12: A Va . . . 7E 90
Penrose Rd. KT22: Fetc . . . 9C 78
Penryn Dr. GU35: H Dwn . . . 4H 169
Penryn Ho. *RH1: Red . . . 1E 122*
(off London Rd.)
Pensfold La. RH12: Rudg . . . 3F 194
Pensford Av. TW9: Kew . . . 5N 11
Pensford Cl. RG45: Crow . . . 9G 30
Penshurst Cl. RH10: Craw . . . 2H 183
Penshurst Ri. GU16: Frim . . . 6D 70
Penshurst Rd. CR7: T Hea . . . 4M 45
Penshurst Way SM2: Sut . . . 4M 61
Penstock M. GU7: Goda . . . 6K 133
Pentelow Gdns. TW14: Felt . . . 9H 9
Pentire Cl. GU21: Wok . . . 1A 74
Pentland Av. TW17: Shep . . . 4B 38
Pentland Gdns. SW18 . . . 9N 13
Pentland Pl. GU14: Cove . . . 7K 69
Pentlands Cl. CR4: Mit . . . 2F 44
Pentland St. SW18 . . . 9N 13
Pentlow St. SW15 . . . 6H 13
Pentney Rd. SW12 . . . 2G 28
SW19 . . . 9K 27
Penton Av. TW18: Stain . . . 8H 21
Penton Ct. TW18: Stain . . . 7H 21
Penton Hall TW18: Stain . . . 9J 21
Penton Hall Dr. TW18: Stain . . . 9J 21
Penton Hook Marina . . . 2J 37
Penton Hook Rd.
TW18: Stain . . . 8J 21
Penton Pk. KT16: Chert . . . 2K 37
Penton Rd. TW18: Stain . . . 8H 21
Pentreath Av. GU2: Guil . . . 4J 113
Penwerris Av. TW7: Isle . . . 3C 10
Penwerris Ct. TW5: Hest . . . 3C 10
Penwith Dr. GU27: Hasl . . . 4B 188
Penwith Rd. SW18 . . . 3M 27
Penwith Wlk. GU22: Wok . . . 6N 73
Penwood End GU22: Wok . . . 8L 73
Penwood Gdns. RG12: Brac . . . 5J 31
Penwood Ho. SW15 . . . 9E 12
Penwortham Rd.
CR2: Sande . . . 6N 63
SW16 . . . 7F 28
Pen-y-Bos Track
GU27: Hasl . . . 5K 189
Penywern Rd. SW5 . . . 1M 13
Peperham Ho. GU27: Hasl . . . 1G 189
Peperham Rd. GU27: Hasl . . . 9G 171
PEPER HAROW . . . 6N 131
Peper Harow La.
GU8: S'ford . . . 5N 131
Peperharow Rd.
GU7: Goda . . . 5E 132
Peppard Rd. RH10: Craw . . . 5H 183
Pepperbox La. GU5: Braml . . . 5F 154
Pepper Cl. CR3: Cate . . . 3B 104
Peppercorn Cl. CR7: T Hea . . . 1A 46
Peppermint Cl. CR0: Croy . . . 6J 45
Peppers Yd. RH12: Hors . . . 5K 197
Pepys Cl. KT21: A'tead . . . 4N 79
SL3: Lang . . . 2D 6
Pepys Rd. SW20 . . . 9H 27
Percheron Cl. TW7: Isle . . . 6F 10
Percheron Dr. GU21: Knap . . . 6F 72
Percival Cl. KT22: Oxs . . . 7B 58
Percival Rd. SW14 . . . 7B 12
TW13: Felt . . . 3G 22
Percival Way KT19: Ewe . . . 1C 60
Percy Av. TW15: A'ford . . . 6B 22
Percy Bryant Rd.
TW16: Sunb . . . 8F 22
Percy Gdns. KT4: W Pk . . . 7C 42
TW7: Isle . . . 6G 11
Percy Laurie Ho.
SW15 . . . 7J 13
(off Nursery Cl.)
Percy Pl. SL3: Dat . . . 4L 5
Percy Rd. CR4: Mit . . . 6E 44
GU2: Guil . . . 1L 113
RH12: Hors . . . 5H 197
SE20 . . . 1G 46
SE25 . . . 4D 46
TW2: Whitt . . . 2B 24
TW7: Isle . . . 7G 11
TW12: Hamp . . . 8A 24
Percy Way TW2: Whitt . . . 2C 24
Peregrine Cl. GU6: Cranl . . . 6N 155
RG12: Brac . . . 5C 32
Peregrine Ct. SW16 . . . 5K 29
Peregrine Gdns. CR0: Croy . . . 8H 47
Peregrine Rd. TW16: Sunb . . . 1G 38
Peregrine Way SW19 . . . 8H 27
Perham Rd. W14 . . . 1K 13
Perifield SE21 . . . 2N 29
Perimeter Rd. RH6: Gat . . . 3F 162
Perimeter Rd. E. RH6: Gat . . . 5E 162
Perimeter Rd. Nth.
RH6: Gat . . . 2B 162
Perimeter Rd. Sth.
RH6: Gat . . . 5A 162
Periwinkle Cl. GU35: Lind . . . 4B 168
Perkin Cl. TW3: Houn . . . 7A 10
Perkins Ct. TW15: A'ford . . . 6A 22
Perkstead Ct. *RH11: Craw . . . 6M 181*
(off Waddington Cl.)
Perleybrooke La.
GU21: Wok . . . 4K 73
Perotts Wood Nature Reserve
. . . 5A 82
Perowne St. GU11: Alde . . . 2L 109
Perran Rd. SW2 . . . 2M 29
Perran Wlk. TW8: Brent . . . 1L 11
Perrin Cl. TW15: A'ford . . . 6A 22
Perrin Ct. GU21: Wok . . . 2D 74
TW15: A'ford . . . 5B 22
Perring Av. GU14: Cove . . . 6K 69
Perring Rd. GU14: Farnb . . . 4M 89
Perrior Rd. GU7: Goda . . . 4H 133
Perry Av. RH19: E Grin . . . 7A 166
Perry Cl. GU7: Goda . . . 6K 133
Perry Ct. KT2: K Tham . . . 3K 203
Perrycroft SL4: W'sor . . . 6B 4
Perryfield Ho. *RH11: Craw . . . 4B 182*
(off Perryfield Rd.)
Perryfield Rd. RH11: Craw . . . 4A 182
Perryfield Way TW10: Ham . . . 4H 25
Perry Hill GU3: Worp . . . 5H 93
(not continuous)
Perryhill Dr. GU47: Sandh . . . 6E 48
Perry How KT4: W Pk . . . 7E 42
Perrylands RH6: Char . . . 3L 161
Perrylands La. RH6: Horl . . . 9K 143
Perrymead St. SW6 . . . 4M 13
Perryn Ct. TW1: Twick . . . 9G 10
Perry Oaks RG12: Brac . . . 1C 32
Perry Way GU9: U Hal . . . 5G 109
GU18: Ligh . . . 8K 51
GU35: Head . . . 5E 168
RG12: Brac . . . 1C 32
Perrywood Bus. Pk.
RH1: Salf . . . 2F 142
Perseverance Cotts.
GU23: Rip . . . 8L 75
Perseverance Pl. TW9: Rich . . . 7L 11
Persfield Cl. KT17: Ewe . . . 6E 60
Persfield M. KT17: Ewe . . . 6E 60
Pershore Gro. SM5: Cars . . . 5B 44
Perth Cl. RH11: Craw . . . 9B 162
SW20 . . . 1E 42
Perth Rd. BR3: Beck . . . 1M 47
Perth Way RH12: Hors . . . 4M 197
Petavel Rd. TW11: Tedd . . . 7E 24
Peter Av. RH8: Oxt . . . 7N 105
Peterborough M. SW6 . . . 5M 13
Peterborough Rd.
GU2: Guil . . . 1J 113
RH10: Craw . . . 7C 182
SM5: Cars . . . 5C 44
SW6 . . . 5M 13
Peterborough Vs. SW6 . . . 4N 13
Peterhead M. SL3: Lang . . . 1C 6
Peterhouse Cl. GU47: Owls . . . 5L 49
Peterhouse Pde.
RH10: Craw . . . 9G 162
Peter Kennedy Ct.
CR0: Croy . . . 5J 47
Peterlee Wlk. RH11: Craw . . . 7K 181
Peter Scott Vis. Cen., The . . . 4G 12
Petersfield Av. TW18: Stain . . . 6L 21
Petersfield Cres. CR5: Coul . . . 2J 83
Petersfield Ri. SW15 . . . 2G 26
Petersfield Rd. TW18: Stain . . . 6L 21
PETERSHAM . . . 2L 25
Petersham Av. KT14: Byf . . . 8N 55
Petersham Cl. KT14: Byf . . . 8N 55
SM1: Sut . . . 2M 61
TW10: Ham . . . 3K 25
Petersham Rd.
TW10: Rich, Ham . . . 9K 11
Petersham Ter. *CR0: Bedd . . . 9J 45*
(off Richmond Grn.)
Petersmead Cl. KT20: Tad . . . 1H 101
Peterstow Cl. SW19 . . . 3K 27
Peters Wood RH5: Cap . . . 5J 159
Peterwood Pk. CR0: Wad . . . 8K 45
Peterwood Way CR0: Wad . . . 8K 45
Petley Rd. W6 . . . 2J 13
Petridge Rd. RH1: Red . . . 8D 122
PETRIDGE WOOD COMMON
. . . 8D 122
Petters Rd. KT21: A'tead . . . 3M 79
Pettiward Cl. SW15 . . . 7H 13
Petts La. TW17: Shep . . . 3B 38
Petworth Cl. CR5: Coul . . . 6G 82
GU16: Frim . . . 6D 70
Petworth Ct. *GU15: Camb . . . 2D 70*
(off Portsmouth Rd.)
GU27: Hasl . . . 2H 189
RH11: Craw . . . 6L 181
SL4: W'sor . . . 4D 4
Petworth Dr. RH12: Hors . . . 1M 197
Petworth Gdns. SW20 . . . 2G 42
Petworth Rd. GU8: Chid . . . 2C 190
(Cripplecrutch Hill)
GU8: Chid . . . 4C 190
(Fisher St.)
GU8: Hasl . . . 2H 189
GU8: Mil, Wit, Worm . . . 3B 152
GU8: Worm . . . 8C 152
GU27: Hasl . . . 2H 189
Pevensey Cl. RH10: Craw . . . 4G 182
TW7: Isle . . . 3C 10
Pevensey Ct. SW16 . . . 4L 29
Pevensey Rd. SW17 . . . 5B 28
TW13: Felt . . . 2M 23
Pevensey Way GU16: Frim . . . 6D 70
Peverel Rd. RH11: Ifi . . . 4K 181
Peveril Dr. TW11: Tedd . . . 6D 24
Pewley Bank
GU1: Guil . . . 6F 202 (5A 114)
Pewley Hill
GU1: Guil . . . 6D 202 (5N 113)
Pewley Point
GU1: Guil . . . 7F 202 (5A 114)
Pewley Way
GU1: Guil . . . 6F 202 (5A 114)
Pewsey Va. RG12: Brac . . . 4D 32
Peyton's Cotts. RH1: Nut . . . 1K 123
Pharaoh Cl. CR4: Mit . . . 6D 44
Pharaoh's Island
TW17: Shep . . . 8A 38
Pheasant Cl. CR8: Pur . . . 9M 63
Pheasant Vw. RG12: Brac . . . 3J 31
Phelps Way UB3: Harl . . . 1G 9
Philanthropic Rd.
RH1: Red . . . 4E 122
Philbeach Gdns. SW5 . . . 1M 13
Philip Gdns. CR0: Croy . . . 8J 47
Philip Rd. TW18: Stain . . . 7M 21
Philips Cl. SM5: Cars . . . 7E 44
Philips Ho. GU26: G'hott . . . 6N 169
Phillip Copse RG12: Brac . . . 6B 32
Phillippines Cl. TN8: Eden . . . 3M 147
Phillips Cl. GU7: Goda . . . 9G 132
GU10: Tong . . . 4C 110
GU35: Head . . . 4E 168
RH10: Craw . . . 8F 182
Phillips Cres. GU35: Head . . . 4E 168
Phillips Hatch GU5: Wone . . . 3E 134
Phillip's Quad. GU22: Wok . . . 5A 74
Philpot La. GU24: Chob . . . 9L 53
Philpot Sq. SW6 . . . 6N 13
Phipps Bri. Rd. CR4: Mit . . . 1A 44
SW19 . . . 1A 44
Phipps Bridge Stop (CT) . . . 2B 44
Phoenix Bus. Pk.
RG12: Brac . . . 1H 31
Phoenix Cen. . . . 4J 63
Phoenix Cl. BR4: W Wick . . . 8N 47
KT19: Eps . . . 8N 59
Phoenix Ct. CR2: S Croy . . . 2C 64
GU1: Guil . . . 6C 202 (5N 113)
GU11: Alde . . . 3M 109
KT3: N Mal . . . 2E 42
KT17: Eps . . . 6L 201
TW4: Houn . . . 8L 9
TW8: Brent . . . 1L 11
TW13: Felt . . . 5F 22
Phoenix Dr. BR2: Kes . . . 1F 66
Phoenix Ho. SM1: Sut . . . 1N 61
Phoenix La. RH19: Ash W . . . 3G 186
Phoenix Trad. Pk.
TW8: Brent . . . 1K 11
Phoenix Way TW5: Hest . . . 2L 9
Phyllis Av. KT3: N Mal . . . 4G 42
Phyllis Ho. CR0: Wad . . . 7A 200
Piccards, The GU2: Guil . . . 7M 113
Pickering RG12: Brac . . . 3M 31
Pickering Gdns. CR0: Croy . . . 5C 46
Pickering Pl. GU2: Guil . . . 1K 113
Picket Post Cl. RG12: Brac . . . 2D 32
Pickets St. SW12 . . . 1F 28
Picketts Hill
GU35: Head, Slea . . . 9A 148
Picketts La. RH1: Salf . . . 2G 142
RH6: Gat . . . 4H 163
Pickford Ho. *GU11: Alde . . . 2N 109*
(off Pickford St.)
Pickford St. GU11: Alde . . . 2N 109
Pickhurst Ri. BR4: W Wick . . . 6M 47
Pickhurst Rd. GU8: Chid . . . 6F 172
Pickins Piece SL3: Hort . . . 5C 6
Pickwick Cl. TW4: Houn . . . 8M 9
Pickwick Gdns. GU15: Camb . . . 2F 70
Picquets Way SM7: Ban . . . 3K 81
Picton Cl. GU15: Camb . . . 8G 50
Picton Mt. CR6: Warl . . . 6D 84
Picton Pl. KT6: Surb . . . 7N 41
Picts Hill RH13: Hors . . . 9G 197
Picture Ho. SW16 . . . 3J 29
Pieris Ho. *TW13: Felt . . . 3H 23*
(off Highfield Rd.)
Pierrefonde's Av.
GU14: Farnb . . . 9M 69
Pier Rd. TW14: Felt . . . 8J 9
Pierson Rd. SL4: W'sor . . . 4A 4
Pier Ter. SW18 . . . 7N 13
Pigbush La. RH14: Loxw . . . 1H 193
Pigeon Gro. RG12: Brac . . . 3J 31
Pigeon Ho. La. CR5: Coul . . . 3A 102
Pigeonhouse La. SL4: Wink . . . 4H 17
Pigeon La. TW12: Hamp . . . 5A 24
Pigeon Pass RH10: T Hil . . . 4F 184
Piggott Ct. RH13: Hors . . . 7L 197
Pigott Rd. RG40: W'ham . . . 9C 14
Pig Pound Wlk.
RH17: Hand . . . 6N 199
Pike Cl. GU11: Alde . . . 2A 110
KT10: H Wood . . . 8F 40
Pikes Hill
KT17: Eps . . . 6M 201 (9D 60)
Pikes La. RH7: Ling . . . 2A 146
Pilgrim Cl. SM4: Mord . . . 6N 43
Pilgrim Ct. GU8: Mil . . . 2C 152
Pilgrim Hill SE27 . . . 5N 29
Pilgrims Cl. GU5: Shere . . . 8B 116
GU9: Farnh . . . 3F 128
RH5: Westh . . . 9G 99
Pilgrims La. CR3: Cate . . . 4K 103
RH8: T'sey . . . 3D 106
TN16: Tats . . . 1G 106
Pilgrims Pl. RH2: Reig . . . 1M 121
Pilgrims Vw. GU12: A Grn . . . 4G 111
Pilgrims Way CR2: S Croy . . . 3C 64
GU4: Guil . . . 7N 113
(not continuous)
GU5: Alb . . . 6H 115
GU5: Shere . . . 8B 116
GU24: Bis . . . 3D 72
GU35: Head . . . 4D 168
RH2: Reig . . . 1L 121
RH5: Westh . . . 9H 99
TN16: Weste, Brast . . . 1H 107
Pilgrims Way Cotts.
RH3: Betch . . . 2B 120
Pilsden Cl. SW19 . . . 2J 27
Pilton Est., The
CR0: Croy . . . 2A 200 (8M 45)
Pimms Cl. GU4: B'ham . . . 8C 94
Pinckards GU8: Chid . . . 4D 172
Pincott La. KT24: W Hors . . . 7C 96
Pincott Rd. SW19 . . . 8A 28
Pine Av. BR4: W Wick . . . 7L 47
GU15: Camb . . . 2B 70
Pine Bank GU26: Hind . . . 5C 170
Pine Cl. CR8: Ken . . . 4A 84
GU12: A Va . . . 7E 90
GU15: Camb . . . 8K 49
GU21: Wok . . . 3M 73
KT15: N Haw . . . 7K 55
RH11: Craw . . . 9A 162

Pine Coombe CR0: Croy 1G **64**
Pinecote Dr. SL5: S'dale 6C **34**
Pine Ct. GU11: Alde 2M **109**
GU16: Mytc 2E **90**
KT13: Weybr 2D **56**
RG12: Brac 3C **32**
Pine Cres. SM5: Cars 7B **62**
Pinecrest Gdns. BR6: Farnb 1K **67**
Pine Cft. *KT13: Weybr* *3E* ***56***
(off St George's Rd.)
Pine Dean KT23: Book 3B **98**
Pine Dr. GU17: Haw 3K **69**
Pinefields *KT15: Addl* *1K* ***55***
(off Church Rd.)
Pinefields Cl. RG45: Crow 2G **48**
Pine Gdns. KT5: Surb 5N **41**
RH6: Horl 9E **142**
Pine Glade BR6: Farnb 1H **67**
Pine Gro. GU10: L Bou 5K **129**
GU20: Windl 3A **52**
GU52: C Cro 8C **88**
(not continuous)
KT13: Weybr 2C **56**
RH19: E Grin 7L **165**
SW19 6L **27**
TN8: Eden 1K **147**
Pine Gro. M. KT13: Weybr 2D **56**
Pine Hill KT18: Eps 2C **80**
Pinehill Ri. GU47: Sandh 7H **49**
Pinehill Rd. RG45: Crow 3G **49**
Pinehurst *GU22: Wok* *5B* ***74***
(off Park Dr.)
RH12: Hors 4J **197**
SL5: S'hill 4A **34**
TW20: Eng G 8M **19**
Pinehurst Av. GU14: Farnb 3N **89**
Pinehurst Cl. KT20: K'wood 9M **81**
Pinehurst Cotts.
GU14: Farnb 3N **89**
Pinehurst Pas. GU14: Farnb 3N **89**
Pinehurst Rd. GU14: Farnb 3M **89**
Pinehurst Rdbt.
GU14: Farnb 2N **89**
Pinel Cl. GU25: V Wat 3A **36**
Pine Lodge *KT11: Cob* *2K* ***77***
(off Leigh Cnr.)
Pinemount Rd.
GU15: Camb 2B **70**
Pine Pk. GU3: Worp 7D **92**
Pine Pl. SM7: Ban 1J **81**
Piner Cotts. SL4: W'sor 6B **4**
Pine Ridge SM5: Cars 4E **62**
Pineridge Cl. KT13: Weybr 1F **56**
Pine Ridge Dr.
GU10: L Bou 6G **129**
Pine Ridge Mobile Home Pk.
RG40: W'ham 9D **30**
Pine Rd. GU22: Wok 7M **73**
Pines, The CR5: Coul 5F **82**
CR8: Pur 9N **63**
GU15: Camb 8D **50**
GU21: Wok 1B **74**
KT9: Ches 9L **41**
RH4: Dork 6H **119**
RH10: Wor 3H **183**
RH12: Hors 3B **198**
SE19 7M **29**
TW16: Sunb 2H **39**
Pine Shaw RH10: Craw 2H **183**
Pines Rd. GU51: Fleet 3A **88**
Pines Trad. Est., The
GU3: Guil 1H **113**
Pinetops RH12: Hors 3B **198**
Pine Tree Cl. TW5: C'ford 4J **9**
Pine Tree Hill GU22: Pyr 3F **74**
Pine Trees Bus. Pk.
TW18: Stain 6G **20**
Pinetrees Cl. RH10: Cop 7M **163**
Pine Vw. GU35: H Dwn 3H **169**
Pine Vw. Cl. GU4: Guil 9H **115**
GU9: B Lea 7M **109**
GU27: Hasl 9G **170**
Pine Wlk. CR3: Cate 9B **84**
KT5: Surb 5N **41**
KT11: Cob 1L **77**
KT23: Book 3B **98**
KT24: E Hor 6G **97**
SM5: Cars 6B **62**
SM7: Ban 4D **82**
Pine Wlk. E. SM5: Cars 7B **62**
Pine Wlk. W. SM5: Cars 6B **62**
Pine Way TW20: Eng G 7L **19**
Pine Way Cl. RH19: E Grin 2A **186**
PINEWOOD 1G **48**
Pine Wood TW16: Sunb 9H **23**
Pinewood Av. KT15: N Haw 5L **55**
RG45: Crow 1H **49**
Pinewood Cvn. Pk.
RG40: W'ham 8H **31**
Pinewood Cl. CR0: Croy 9H **47**
GU21: Wok 2C **74**
GU47: Sandh 7E **48**
RH12: Bro H 5D **196**
Pinewood Ct. GU51: Fleet 3B **88**
KT15: Addl 1M **55**
Pinewood Cres.
GU14: Cove 9H **69**
Pinewood Dr. BR6: Orp 2N **67**
TW18: Stain 6J **21**
Pinewood Gdns. GU19: Bag 4G **50**
Pinewood Gro.
KT15: N Haw 6K **55**
Pinewood Hill GU51: Fleet 3B **88**

Pinewood Leisure Cen. 8G **31**
Pinewood M. TW19: Stan 9M **7**
Pinewood Pk. GU14: Cove 7H **69**
KT15: N Haw 7K **55**
Pinewood Pl. KT19: Ewe 1C **60**
Pinewood Rd. GU12: Ash 1H **111**
GU25: V Wat 3K **35**
TW13: Felt 4J **23**
Pinfold Rd. SW16 5J **29**
Pinglestone Cl. UB7: Harm 3N **7**
Pinkcoat Cl. TW13: Felt 4J **23**
Pinkerton Pl. SW16 5H **29**
Pinkham Mans. W4 1N **11**
Pinkhurst La. RH13: Slin 6A **196**
PINKS HILL 2F **112**
Pinova Cl. RH11: Ifi 9M **161**
Pioneer Pl. CR0: Sels 5K **65**
Pioneers Ind. Pk.
CR0: Bedd 7J **45**
Piper Rd.
KT1: K Tham 5M **203** (2N **41**)
Pipers Cl. KT11: Cob 2L **77**
Pipers Cft. GU52: C Cro 9B **88**
Pipers End GU25: V Wat 2N **35**
RH13: Slin 5M **195**
Piper's Gdns. CR0: Croy 6H **47**
Pipers La. GU28: North 8D **190**
Pipers Patch GU14: Farnb 1N **89**
Pipewell Rd. SM5: Cars 5C **44**
PIPPBROOK 1L **201** (4J **119**)
Pippbrook Gdns.
RH4: Dork 1L **201** (4H **119**)
Pippin Cl. CR0: Croy 7J **47**
Pippin Link RH11: Ifi 9M **161**
Pippins Ct. TW15: A'ford 7C **22**
Pipson La. GU46: Yate 1C **68**
Pipsons Cl. GU46: Yate 9C **48**
Piquet Rd. SE20 1F **46**
PIRBRIGHT 1C **92**
PIRBRIGHT CAMP 8M **71**
Pirbright Cres. CR0: N Add 3M **65**
Pirbright Grn. GU24: Pirb 1C **92**
Pirbright Rd. GU3: Norm 1J **111**
GU14: Farnb 2A **90**
SW18 2L **27**
Pirbright Ter. GU24: Pirb 1C **92**
Piries Pl. *RH12: Hors* *6J* ***197***
(off East St.)
Pisley La. RH5: Ockl 6N **157**
Pitcairn Rd. CR4: Mit 8D **28**
Pitchfont La.
RH8: Limp, T'sey 3B **106**
PITCH HILL 1D **156**
PITCH PLACE
GU2 7K **93**
GU8 7E **150**
Pitch Pl. RG42: Bin 6J **15**
Pit Farm Rd. GU1: Guil 3C **114**
Pit Farm Tennis Club 3C **114**
Pitfold Av. GU27: Hasl 2B **188**
Pitfold Cl. GU27: Hasl 2C **188**
Pitlake CR0: Croy 2A **200** (8M **45**)
PITLAND STREET 6K **137**
Pitland St. RH5: H Mary 6K **137**
Pit La. TN8: Eden 8L **127**
Pitson Cl. KT15: Addl 1M **55**
Pitt Cres. SW19 5N **27**
Pitt La. GU10: Fren 4F **148**
Pitt Pl. KT17: Eps 8M **201** (1D **80**)
Pitt Rd. BR6: Farnb 1L **67**
CR0: Croy 4N **45**
CR7: T Hea 4N **45**
KT17: Eps 8M **201** (1D **80**)
Pitts Cl. RG42: Bin 7J **15**
Pitts Rd. GU11: Alde 9N **89**
Pittville Gdns. SE25 2D **46**
Pitt Way GU14: Cove 9L **69**
Pitwood Grn. KT20: Tad 7H **81**
Pitwood Pk. Ind. Est.
KT20: Tad 7G **81**
PIXHAM 3K **119**
Pixham End RH4: Dork 2J **119**
Pixham La. RH4: Dork 2J **119**
Pixholme Gro. RH4: Dork 3J **119**
PIXTON HILL 5K **187**
Pixton Way CR0: Sels 5H **65**
Place Ct. GU11: Alde 5A **110**
Place Farm Rd. RH1: Blet 8A **104**
Placehouse La. CR5: Coul 6K **83**
Plain Ride SL4: W'sor 2N **17**
PLAISTOW 6A **192**
Plaistow Rd. GU8: Chid 4C **190**
GU8: Duns 1M **191**
RH14: Kird 8D **192**
RH14: Plais, Loxw 5D **192**
Plaistow St. RH7: Ling 7N **145**
Plane Ho. BR2: Brom 1N **47**
Planes, The KT16: Chert 6L **37**
Plane Tree Cres. TW13: Felt 4J **23**
Plantagenet Cl. KT4: W Pk 1C **60**
Plantagenet Pk.
RG42: Warf 9D **16**
Plantain Cres.
RH11: Craw 7M **181**
Plantation La.
CR3: Warl, Wold 6H **85**
CR6: Warl 6H **85**
Plantation Row
GU15: Camb 1N **69**
Plas Newydd RH19: D Pk 4B **166**
Plat, The RH12: Hors 5G **197**
TN8: Eden 2M **147**
Plateau, The RG42: Warf 8E **16**

Platt, The RH7: Dorm 1C **166**
SW15 6J **13**
Platt Mdw. GU4: Guil 9F **94**
Plaws Hill GU5: P'lake 5E **136**
Playden Ct. RH11: Craw 6L **181**
Playfair Mans. *W14* *2K* ***13***
(off Queen's Club Gdns.)
Playfair St. W6 1H **13**
Playground Cl. BR3: Beck 1G **47**
Playhouse, The *7G* *38*
(off Hurst Gro.)
Playing Fld. Cl.
GU27: Hasl 9G **171**
Polygon Bus. Cen. SL3: Poy 5H **7**
Playscape Pro Racing Karting Track
6H **29**
Plaza, The RG40: W'ham 3B **30**
Pleasance, The SW15 7G **12**
Pleasance Rd. SW15 8G **12**
Pleasant Gro. CR0: Croy 9J **47**
Pleasant Pl. KT12: Hers 3K **57**
Pleasant Vw. Pl.
BR6: Farnb 2K **67**
Pleasure Pit Rd.
KT21: A'tead 5A **80**
Plesman Way SM6: W'ton 5J **63**
Plevna Rd. TW12: Hamp 9B **24**
Plough Cl. RH11: Ifi 1L **181**
Plough Ind. Est. KT22: Leat 7G **79**
Ploughlands RG42: Brac 9L **15**
Plough La. CR8: Pur 5J **63**
GU6: Ewh 6G **156**
KT11: Cob 4H **77**
RG40: W'ham 1E **30**
RH12: Hors 3L **197**
SM6: Bedd 1J **63**
SW17 6N **27**
SW19 6N **27**
TW11: Tedd 6G **24**
Plough La. Cl. SM6: Bedd 2J **63**
Ploughmans End TW7: Isle 8D **10**
Plough Rd. GU46: Yate 1C **68**
KT19: Ewe 5C **60**
RH6: Smal 8M **143**
RH7: Dorm 9C **146**
Plough Wlk. *TN8: Eden* *9L* ***127***
(off Fircroft Way)
Plover Cl. RH11: Craw 1A **182**
TN8: Eden 9M **127**
TW18: Stain 4H **21**
Plovers Ri. GU24: B'wood 7B **72**
Plovers Rd. RH13: Hors 5M **197**
Plum Cl. TW13: Felt 2H **23**
Plum Gth. TW8: Brent 1K **11**
Plummer La. CR4: Mit 1D **44**
Plummer Rd. SW4 1H **29**
Plumpton Way SM5: Cars 9C **44**
Plumtree Cl. SM6: W'ton 4H **63**
Plymen Ho. KT8: W Mole 4A **40**
Plymouth Ct. KT5: Surb 8K **203**
Pocket Cl. RG12: Bin 1J **31**
Pockford Rd. GU8: Chid 5F **172**
Pocklington Ct. SW15 2F **26**
Pococks La. SL4: Eton 1H **5**
Podmore Rd. SW18 7N **13**
Poels Ct. RH19: E Grin 8A **166**
Point, The *GU21: Wok* *3B* ***74***
(off Chertsey Rd.)
Pointers, The KT21: A'tead 7L **79**
Pointers Cotts. TW10: Ham 3J **25**
POINTERS GREEN 5H **77**
Pointers Hill RH4: Westc 7C **118**
Pointers Rd. KT11: Cob 3D **76**
Point Leisure Cen., The 1N **31**
Point Pleasant SW18 7M **13**
Point Wharf TW8: Brent 3L **11**
Point Wharf La. TW8: Brent 3K **11**
Polar Pk. UB7: Harm 3A **8**
Polden Cl. GU14: Cove 7K **69**
POLECAT 8D **170**
Polecat Hill GU26: Hind 8D **170**
GU27: Hasl 8D **170**
Polecat Valley GU26: Hind 8D **170**
Polehamptons, The
TW12: Hamp 8C **24**
Polesden Gdns. SW20 1G **42**
POLESDEN LACEY 8C **98**
Polesden Lacey 8B **98**
Polesden La. GU23: Rip 1H **95**
Polesden Rd. KT23: Book 7B **98**
Polesden Vw. KT23: Book 5B **98**
Poles La. RH11: L Hea 6A **162**
Polesteeple Hill TN16: B Hil 4F **86**
Police Sta. Rd. KT12: Hers 3K **57**
Polkerris Way GU52: C Cro 9C **88**
Pollard Cl. SL4: O Win 8L **5**
Pollard Gro. GU15: Camb 2G **71**
Pollard Ho. KT4: W Pk 1H **61**
Pollard Rd. GU22: Wok 3D **74**
SM4: Mord 4B **44**
Pollardrow Av. RG42: Brac 9L **15**
(not continuous)
Pollards RH11: Craw 4M **181**
Pollards Cres. SW16 2J **45**
Pollards Dr. RH13: Hors 5L **197**
Pollards Hill E. SW16 2K **45**
Pollards Hill Nth.
SW16 2J **45**
Pollards Hill Sth.
SW16 2J **45**
Pollards Hill W. SW16 2K **45**
Pollards Oak Cres.
RH8: Oxt 1C **126**
Pollards Oak Rd. RH8: Oxt 1C **126**

Pollards Wood Hill
RH8: Oxt 8D **106**
Pollards Wood Rd.
RH8: Oxt 9D **106**
SW16 2J **45**
Pollocks Path GU26: Hind 7B **170**
Polmear Cl. GU52: C Cro 9C **88**
Polsted La. GU3: Comp 1E **132**
Poltimore Rd. GU2: Guil 5K **113**
Polworth Rd. SW16 6J **29**
Polyanthus Way
RG45: Crow 8G **30**
Pomeroy Cl. TW1: Twick 7H **11**
Pond Cl. KT12: Hers 3G **57**
(not continuous)
RH14: Loxw 4H **193**
Pond Copse La.
RH14: Loxw 3H **193**
Pond Cott. La. BR4: Beck 7K **47**
Pond Cft. GU46: Yate 9D **48**
Pond Farm Cl.
KT20: Wal H 2G **100**
Pondfield Ho. SE27 6N **29**
Pondfield Rd. CR8: Ken 3M **83**
GU7: Goda 4J **133**
RH12: Rudg 9F **176**
Pond Head La.
RH5: For G, Ockl 6L **157**
Pond Hill Gdns. SM3: Chea 3K **61**
Pond Ho. KT16: Chert 6K **37**
Pond La. GU5: P'lake 4D **136**
GU10: Churt 6H **149**
Pond Mdw. GU2: Guil 3H **113**
Pond Moor Rd. RG12: Brac 4N **31**
Pond Piece KT22: Oxs 9B **58**
Pond Pl. KT21: A'tead 4L **79**
Pond Rd. GU22: Wok 7K **73**
GU35: H Dwn 5F **168**
TW20: Egh 7E **20**
Ponds, The KT13: Weybr 3E **56**
Pondside Cl. UB3: Harl 2E **8**
Ponds La. GU5: Alb 2N **135**
(not continuous)
PONDTAIL
GU51, Edenbridge 5M **167**
GU51, Fleet 4D **88**
Pondtail Cl. GU51: Fleet 5D **88**
RH12: Hors 2K **197**
Pondtail Copse
RH12: Hors 2K **197**
Pondtail Dr. RH12: Hors 1K **197**
Pondtail Gdns. GU51: Fleet 5D **88**
Pondtail Pk. RH12: Hors 2K **197**
Pondtail Rd. GU51: Fleet 5D **88**
RH12: Hors 3J **197**
Pondview Cl. GU51: Fleet 3C **88**
Pond Way RH19: E Grin 9D **166**
TW11: Tedd 7J **25**
Pond Wood Rd.
RH10: Craw 1E **182**
Ponsonby Rd. SW15 1G **26**
Pony Chase KT11: Cob 9N **57**
Pook Hill GU8: Chid, Hasl 5B **172**
Pool Cl. KT8: W Mole 4N **39**
Poole Ct. TW4: Houn 5M **9**
Poole Ct. Rd. TW4: Houn 5M **9**
POOL END 4B **38**
Pool End Cl. TW17: Shep 4B **38**
Poole Rd. GU21: Wok 5A **74**
KT19: Ewe 3C **60**
Pooles Cotts. TW10: Ham 3K **25**
Pooley Av. TW20: Egh 6D **20**
Pooley Dr. SW14 6B **12**
POOLEY GREEN 6E **20**
Pooley Grn. Cl. TW20: Egh 6E **20**
Pooley Grn. Rd. TW20: Egh 6D **20**
Pool in the Pk. 6B **74**
Poolmans Rd. SL4: W'sor 6A **4**
Pool Rd. GU11: Alde 5A **110**
KT8: W Mole 4N **39**
Pools on the Pk. 7K **11**
POOTINGS 5N **127**
Pootings Rd. TN8: C Hil 3M **127**
Pope Cl. SW19 7B **28**
TW14: Felt 2G **22**
Popes Av. TW2: Twick 3E **24**
Popes Cl. SL3: Coln 3D **6**
Popes Ct. TW2: Twick 3E **24**
Popes Gro. CR0: Croy 9J **47**
TW1: Twick 3E **24**
TW2: Twick 3F **24**
Popes La. RH8: Oxt 3A **126**
Popes Mead GU27: Hasl 1G **189**
POPESWOOD 8J **15**
Popeswood Rd. RG42: Bin 8J **15**
Popeswood Rdbt. RG42: Bin 9J **15**
Popham Cl. RG12: Brac 4D **32**
TW13: Hanw 4N **23**
Popham Gdns. TW9: Rich 6N **11**
Popinjays Row *SM3: Chea* *2J* ***61***
(off Netley Cl.)
Poplar Av. CR4: Mit 9D **28**
GU20: Windl 1L **51**
KT22: Leat 9H **79**
Poplar Cl. GU14: Cove 9H **69**
GU16: Mytc 2E **90**
RG12: Brac 2B **32**
RH11: Craw 9A **162**
SL3: Poy 4G **7**
Poplar Cotts. GU3: Guil 9H **93**
Poplar Ct. SW19 6M **27**
TW1: Twick 9J **11**

Poplar Cres. KT19: Ewe 3B **60**
Poplar Dr. SM7: Ban 1J **81**
Poplar Farm Cl. KT19: Ewe 3B **60**
Poplar Gdns. KT3: N Mal 1C **42**
Poplar Gro. GU22: Wok 6A **74**
KT3: N Mal 1C **42**
Poplar Ho. SL3: Lang 1B **6**
Poplar La. RH18: F Row 8G **187**
Poplar Rd. GU4: Chil 1A **134**
KT22: Leat 9H **79**
SM3: Sut 7L **43**
SW19 1M **43**
TW15: A'ford 6D **22**
Poplar Rd. Sth. SW19 2M **43**
Poplars, The RH13: Hors 5L **197**
SL5: Asc 4L **33**
Poplar Vs. *GU16: Frim G* *8D* ***70***
(off Beech Rd.)
Poplar Wlk.
CR0: Croy 1B **200** (8N **45**)
CR3: Cate 1B **104**
GU9: H End 5J **109**
Poplar Way TW13: Felt 4H **23**
Poppy Cl. SM6: W'ton 7E **44**
Poppyhills Rd. GU15: Camb 7D **50**
Poppy La. CR0: Croy 6F **46**
Poppy Pl. RG40: W'ham 2A **30**
Porchester SL5: Asc 3L **33**
Porchester Rd.
KT1: K Tham 1A **42**
Porchfield Cl. SM2: Sut 6N **61**
Porridge Pot All.
GU1: Guil 7C **202** (5N **113**)
GU2: Guil 7B **202** (5N **113**)
Portal Cl. SE27 4L **29**
Porters Lodge, The
SW10 *3N* ***13***
(off Coleridge Gdns.)
Portesbery Hill Dr.
GU15: Camb 9C **50**
Portesbery Rd.
GU15: Camb 9B **50**
Portia Gro. RG42: Warf 9C **16**
Portinscale Rd. SW15 8K **13**
Portland Av. KT3: N Mal 6E **42**
Portland Bus. Cen. *SL3: Dat* *4L* ***5***
(off Manor Ho. La.)
Portland Cl. KT4: W Pk 6G **42**
Portland Cotts. CR0: Bedd 6H **45**
Portland Cres. TW13: Felt 5E **22**
Portland Dr. GU52: C Cro 9A **88**
RH1: Mers 7H **103**
Portland Ho. RH1: Mers 7G **103**
Portland Pl. KT17: Eps 8D **60**
SE25 *3D* ***46***
(off Sth. Norwood Hill)
Portland Rd. CR4: Mit 1C **44**
KT1: K Tham 6K **203** (2L **41**)
RH4: Dork 1J **201** (4G **119**)
RH19: E Grin 1A **186**
SE25 3D **46**
TW15: A'ford 4N **21**
Portland Ter. TW9: Rich 7K **11**
Portley La. CR3: Cate 8B **84**
Portley Wood Rd.
CR3: Whyte 7C **84**
Portman Av. SW14 6C **12**
Portman Cl. RG42: Brac 9M **15**
Portman Rd.
KT1: K Tham 4M **203** (1M **41**)
Portmore Pk. Rd.
KT13: Weybr 1B **56**
Portmore Pl. *KT13: Weybr* *9E* ***38***
(off Oatlands Dr.)
Portmore Quays
KT13: Weybr 1A **56**
Portmore Way KT13: Weybr 9B **38**
Portnall Dr. GU25: V Wat 4J **35**
Portnall Ri. GU25: V Wat 4J **35**
Portnall Rd. GU25: V Wat 4J **35**
Portnalls Cl. CR5: Coul 3F **82**
Portnalls Ri. CR5: Coul 3G **82**
Portnalls Rd. CR5: Coul 5F **82**
Porton Ct. KT6: Surb 5J **41**
Portsmouth Av. KT7: T Dit 6G **40**
Portsmouth Rd.
GU2: Guil 8B **202** (7M **113**)
GU7: Goda 1D **152**
GU8: Goda, Mil 1D **152**
GU8: Mil, Thur 5E **170**
GU15: Camb 9E **50**
GU16: Frim 5B **70**
GU23: Rip 8M **75**
GU23: Send, Rip 3H **95**
GU26: Brams, Lip 9M **169**
KT1: K Tham 8G **203** (6G **41**)
KT6: Surb 8G **203** (6G **41**)
KT7: T Dit 8G **203** (6G **41**)
KT10: Esh 3A **58**
(Old Chestnut Av.)
KT10: Esh 1C **58**
(Sandown Rd.)
KT11: Cob 9G **57**
SW15 1G **27**
Portswood Pl. SW15 9E **12**
Portugal Gdns. TW2: Twick 3C **24**
Portugal Rd. GU21: Wok 3B **74**
Port Way GU24: Bis 3D **72**
Portway KT17: Ewe 5F **60**
Portway Cres. KT17: Ewe 5F **60**
Post Boys Row KT11: Cob 1H **77**
Postford Farm Cotts.
GU5: Alb 1J **135**

Postford Mill Cotts.—Putney Bridge Station (Tube)

Postford Mill Cotts.
GU4: Guil 7H 115
Post Horn Cl.
RH18: F Row 8K 187
Post Horn La.
RH18: F Row 8J 187
Post Ho. La. KT23: Book 3A 98
Post La. TW2: Twick 2D 24
Postmill Cl. CR0: Croy 9F 46
Post Office All. *W4 2A 12*
(off Thames Rd.)
Post Office Row
RH8: Limp 9G 107
Potbury Cl. SL4: Wink 7M 17
POT COMMON 8G 131
Potkiln Ho. GU51: Fleet 1A 88
Potley Hill Rd. GU46: Yate 9E 48
Potter Cl. CR4: Mit 1F 44
Potteries, The GU14: Cove 8J 69
KT16: Otter 3G 54
Potteries La. GU16: Mytc 2D 90
Potterne Cl. SW19 1J 27
Potters Cl. CR0: Croy 7H 47
GU8: Mil 9C 132
Potters Ct. *SM1: Sut 3L 61*
(off Rosebery Rd.)
Potters Cres. GU12: Ash 1F 110
Potter's Cft. RH13: Hors 6L 197
Pottersfield RH10: Craw 2B 182
Potters Ga. GU9: Farnh 1F 128
Potters Gro. KT3: N Mal 3B 42
Potter's Hill GU8: Ent G 5F 152
Potters Ind. Pk.
GU52: C Cro 8D 88
Potters La. GU23: Send 1D 94
SW16 7H 29
Potters Pl. RH12: Hors 6J 197
Potters Way RH2: Reig 7A 122
Pottery Ct. GU10: Wrec 5E 128
Pottery La. GU10: Wrec 5E 128
Pottery Rd. TW8: Brent 2L 11
Poulcott TW19: Wray 9A 6
Poulett Gdns. TW1: Twick 2G 24
Poulters Wood BR2: Kes 2F 66
Poulton Av. SM1: Sut 9B 44
Pound Cl. GU7: Goda 7H 133
GU35: Head 4E 168
KT6: Surb 7J 41
KT19: Eps 7C 60
RH14: Loxw 3H 193
Pound Ct. GU3: Wood V 2E 112
KT21: A'tead 5M 79
Pound Cres. KT22: Fetc 8D 78
Pound Farm Cl. KT10: Esh 7D 40
Pound Farm La.
GU12: Ash, A Grn 2H 111
Pound Fld.
GU1: Guil 2C 202 (2N 113)
Poundfield Ct. GU22: Wok 8E 74
Poundfield Gdns.
GU22: Wok 7E 74
(not continuous)
Poundfield La.
RH14: Plais 4D 192
POUND HILL 3G 183
Pound Hill GU3: Wood V 2E 112
Pound Hill Pde.
RH10: Craw 2G 183
Pound Hill Pl. RH10: Craw 3G 183
Pound La. GU3: Wood V 2E 112
GU7: Goda 7H 133
(not continuous)
GU20: Windl 3N 51
KT19: Eps 5G 201 (8B 60)
RH10: Hurst 4A 14
Pound La. Cvn. Site
GU3: Wood V 2E 112
Pound Pl. GU4: Chil 9B 114
RG42: Bin 6H 15
Pound Pl. Cl. GU4: Chil 9B 114
Pound Rd. GU12: Alde 3A 110
KT16: Chert 6K 37
SM7: Ban 4L 81
Pound St. SM5: Cars 2D 62
POVEY CROSS 1B 162
Povey Cross Rd.
RH6: Horl 1B 162
Powderham Ct. GU21: Knap 5G 72
Powder Mill La. TW2: Whitt 1N 23
Powell Cl. GU2: Guil 5J 113
KT9: Ches 2K 59
RH6: Horl 7C 142
SM6: W'ton 4J 63
Powell Ct. CR2: S Croy 7A 200
Powells Cl. RH4: Dork 8J 119
Powell's Wlk. W4 2D 12
Power Cl.
GU1: Guil 1B 202 (2M 113)
Powerleague Soccer Cen.
Norbury 9J 29
Purley 3K 63
Power Rd. W4 1N 11
Powers Ct. TW1: Twick 1K 25
Pownall Gdns. TW3: Houn 7B 10
Pownall Rd. TW3: Houn 7B 10
POYLE 5G 7
Poyle Cl. SL3: Poy 5G 6
Poyle Gdns. RG12: Brac 9B 16
Poyle Ho. *GU4: Guil 2F 114*
(off Merrow St.)
Poyle Ind. Est. SL3: Poy 6H 7
Poyle New Cotts. SL3: Poy 5H 7
Poyle Pk. SL3: Poy 6G 6
Poyle Rd.
GU1: Guil 7E 202 (5A 114)
GU10: Tong 6D 110
SL3: Poy 6G 6
Poyle Technical Cen.
SL3: Poy 5G 7
Poyle Ter.
GU1: Guil 6D 202 (5N 113)
Poyle Trad. Est. SL3: Poy 6G 7
Poynders Ct. SW4 1G 29
Poynders Gdns. SW4 1G 29
Poynders Rd. SW4 1G 28
Poynes Rd. RH6: Horl 6C 142
Poynings Rd. RH11: Ifi 4J 181
Prairie Cl. KT15: Addl 9K 37
Prairie Rd. KT15: Addl 9K 37
Pratts La. KT12: Hers 1L 57
Pratts Pas.
KT1: K Tham 4J 203 (1L 41)
Prebend Gdns. W4 1E 12
Prebend Mans. *W4 1E 12*
(off Chiswick High Rd.)
Precinct, The GU6: Cranl 6N 155
TW20: Egh 6C 20
Precincts, The SM4: Mord 5M 43
Premier Ho.
RH10: Craw 8B 162
Premier Pde. *RH6: Horl 8F 142*
(off High St.)
Premier Pl. SW15 7K 13
Prentice Ct. GU14: Farnb 6N 69
Prentice Ct. SW19 6L 27
Prentis Rd. SW16 5H 29
Presburg Rd. KT3: N Mal 4D 42
Presbury Ct. GU21: Wok 5K 73
Prescott RG12: Brac 6L 31
Prescott Cl. SW16 8J 29
Prescott Rd. SL3: Poy 5G 6
Presentation M. SW2 3K 29
Preshaw Cres. CR4: Mit 2C 44
Prestbury Cres. SM7: Ban 3D 82
Preston Cl. TW2: Twick 4E 24
Preston Ct. KT12: Wal T 7K 39
Preston Dr. KT19: Ewe 3D 60
Preston Gro. KT21: A'tead 4J 79
Preston La. KT20: Tad 8G 81
Preston Pl. TW10: Rich 8L 11
Preston Rd. SE19 7M 29
SW20 8E 26
TW17: Shep 4B 38
Prestwick Cl. RH11: Ifi 4J 181
UB2: S'hall 1M 9
Prestwick La. GU8: Chid 7L 171
GU27: G'wood, Chid 7L 171
Prestwood Cl. RH11: Craw 9N 161
Prestwood Gdns.
CR0: Croy 6N 45
Prestwood La. RH11: Ifi 9H 161
RH12: Rusp 9F 160
Pretoria Rd. KT16: Chert 7H 37
SW16 7F 28
Pretty La. CR5: Coul 8G 82
Prewetts Mill RH12: Hors 7H 197
Prey Heath Cl. GU22: Wok 2M 93
Prey Heath Rd. GU22: Wok 2L 93
Preymead Ind. Est.
GU9: B Lea 5N 109
Price Cl. SW17 4D 28
Price Gdns. RG42: Warf 7N 15
Price Rd.
CR0: Wad 8A 200 (2M 63)
Prices La. RH2: Reig 6M 121
Price Way TW12: Hamp 7M 23
Priddy Pl. RH1: Mers 9G 102
Priddy's Yd.
CR0: Croy 3B 200 (8N 45)
Prideaux Gdns. RH5: Ockl 6D 158
Prides Crossing SL5: Asc 8L 17
Pridham Rd. CR7: T Hea 3A 46
Priest Av. RG40: W'ham 3E 30
Priestcroft Cl.
RH11: Craw 3M 181
Priest Hill RH8: Limp 7D 106
SL4: O Win 4M 19
TW20: Eng G, O Win 4M 19
Priestlands Cl. RH6: Horl 7D 142
Priest La. GU24: W End 9N 51
Priestley Gdns. GU22: Wok 7C 74
Priestley Rd. CR4: Mit 1E 44
GU2: Guil 3G 112
Priestley Way RH10: Craw 8E 162
Priest's Bri. SW14 6D 12
PRIESTWOOD 9M 15
Priestwood Av. RG42: Brac 9L 15
Priestwood Ct. Rd.
RG42: Brac 9M 15
Priestwood Sq. RG42: Brac 9L 15
Primrose Av. RH6: Horl 1F 162
Primrose Cl. RH11: Craw 6N 181
SM6: W'ton 6F 44
Primrose Copse
RH12: Hors 1K 197
Primrose Ct. GU12: Ash 2E 110
SW12 1H 29
Primrose Dr. GU24: Bis 2D 72
Primrose Gdns. GU14: Cove 2K 89
Primrose La. CR0: Croy 7F 46
RH18: F Row 8J 187
Primrose Pl. GU7: Goda 9E 132
TW7: Isle 5F 10
Primrose Ridge
GU7: Goda 9E 132
Primrose Rd. KT12: Hers 2K 57
Primrose Wlk. GU46: Yate 9A 48
GU51: Fleet 3A 88
KT17: Ewe 4E 60
RG12: Brac 4A 32
Primrose Way GU5: Braml 6N 133
GU47: Sandh 6G 49
Primula Rd. GU35: Bor 6A 168
Prince Albert Ct.
TW16: Sunb 8F 22
Prince Albert Dr. SL5: Asc 3H 33
Prince Albert Sq.
RH1: Red 8D 122
Prince Albert's Wlk.
SL4: W'sor 4K 5
Prince Andrew Way
SL5: Asc 1H 33
Prince Charles Cres.
GU14: Farnb 6N 69
Prince Charles Way
SM6: W'ton 9F 44
Prince Consort Cotts.
SL4: W'sor 5G 4
Prince Consort Dr. SL5: Asc 3H 33
Prince Consort's Dr.
SL4: W'sor 9C 4
Prince Dr. GU47: Sandh 6F 48
Prince George's Av.
SW20 1H 43
Prince George's Rd.
SW19 9B 28
Prince of Wales Ct.
GU11: Alde 2L 109
(off Queen Elizabeth Dr.)
Prince of Wales Rd.
RH1: Out 2L 143
SM1: Sut 8B 44
Prince of Wales Ter.
W4 1D 12
Prince of Wales Wlk.
GU15: Camb 9A 50
Prince Regent Rd.
TW3: Houn 6C 10
Prince Rd. SE25 4B 46
Princes Av. CR2: Sande 2E 84
GU7: Goda 4F 132
GU11: Alde 8N 89
KT6: Surb 7N 41
SM5: Cars 4D 62
Princes Cl. CR2: Sande 2E 84
SL4: E Wic 1C 4
TW11: Tedd 5D 24
Princes Ct. GU1: Guil 2C 202
KT13: Weybr 2C 56
(off Princes Rd.)
Prince's Dr. KT22: Oxs 8E 58
Princes Hall 2L 109
Princes Mead (Shop. Cen.)
GU14: Farnb 1N 89
Princes M. TW3: Houn 7A 10
W6 1G 13
(off Down Pl.)
Princes Rd. KT2: K Tham 8N 25
KT13: Weybr 2C 56
RH1: Red 5D 122
SW14 6C 12
SW19 7M 27
TW9: Kew 4M 11
TW10: Rich 8M 11
TW11: Tedd 5D 24
TW13: Felt 3G 22
TW15: A'ford 6A 22
TW20: Egh 7B 20
Princess Anne Rd.
RH12: Rudg 1E 194
Princess Av. SL4: W'sor 6E 4
Princess Ct. KT1: K Tham 6L 203
Princess Gdns. GU22: Wok 3D 74
Princess Ho. RH1: Red 2E 122
Princess Margaret Rd.
RH12: Rudg 1E 194
Princess Mary Cl. GU2: Guil 8K 93
Princess Marys Rd.
KT15: Addl 1L 55
Princess M.
KT1: K Tham 6L 203 (2M 41)
Princess Pde. BR6: Farnb 1J 67
Princess Pct. *RH6: Horl 8E 142*
(off High St.)
Princess Rd. CR0: Croy 5N 45
GU22: Wok 3D 74
RH11: Craw 3A 182
Princess Sq. RG12: Brac 1N 31
Princes St. SM1: Sut 1B 62
TW9: Rich 7L 11
Princess Way GU15: Camb 9A 50
RH1: Red 2E 122
Princes Way BR4: W Wick 1B 66
CR0: Wad 2K 63
GU11: Alde 2M 109
GU19: Bag 6J 51
SW19 1J 27
Princeton Ct. SW15 6J 13
Princeton M.
KT2: K Tham 2M 203 (9N 25)
Prince William Ct.
TW15: A'ford 6A 22
(off Princes Rd.)
Pringle Gdns. CR8: Pur 6K 63
SW16 5G 28
(not continuous)
Prior Av. SM2: Sut 4C 62
Prior Cft. Cl. GU15: Camb 2E 70
Prior End GU15: Camb 1E 70
Prioress Rd. SE27 4M 29
Prior Rd. GU15: Camb 1E 70
Priors, The KT21: A'tead 6K 79
Priors Cl. GU14: Farnb 6M 69
Priors Ct. GU12: Ash 3D 110
GU21: Wok 5K 73
Prior's Cft. GU22: Wok 7C 74
Priorsfield Rd. GU3: Comp 9C 112
GU7: Hurt 9C 112
Priors Hatch La.
GU7: Hurt 2C 132
Priors Keep GU52: Fleet 5C 88
Prior's La. GU17: B'water 1F 68
Priors Mead KT23: Book 3C 98
Priors Rd. SL4: W'sor 6A 4
Priors Wlk. RH10: Craw 3C 182
Priors Wood GU27: Hasl 2D 188
KT10: H Wood 8F 40
RG45: Crow 3C 48
Priorswood GU3: Comp 1C 132
Priory, The CR0: Wad 1L 63
KT22: Leat 9H 79
RH9: Gods 9E 104
Priory Av. SM3: Chea 1J 61
Priory Cl. BR3: Beck 2H 47
GU21: Wok 9F 54
KT12: Wal T 9H 39
RH4: Dork 7G 119
RH6: Horl 7D 142
SL5: S'dale 6D 34
SW19 9N 27
TW12: Hamp 9N 23
TW16: Sunb 8H 23
Priory Ct. GU2: Guil 7M 113
GU15: Camb 1L 69
KT1: K Tham 5J 203
KT17: Ewe 5E 60
RH4: Dork 7H 119
SM3: Chea 1K 61
TW3: Houn 6B 10
TW20: Egh 7E 20
Priory Cres. SE19 8N 29
SM3: Chea 1J 61
Priory Dr. RH2: Reig 5M 121
Priory Gdns. SE25 3C 46
SW13 6E 12
TW12: Hamp 8N 23
TW15: A'ford 6E 22
Priory Grn. TW18: Stain 6K 21
Priory La. GU10: Fren 2K 149
KT8: W Mole 3B 40
RG42: Brac 8A 16
SW15 9D 12
TW9: Kew 3N 11
Priory Lodge *W4 1N 11*
(off Kew Bri. Ct.)
Priory M. TW18: Stain 6K 21
Priory Pl. KT12: Wal T 9H 39
Priory Retail Pk.
SW19 8B 28
Priory Rd. CR0: Croy 6L 45
KT9: Ches 9L 41
RH2: Reig 5M 121
RH18: F Row 9D 186
SL5: Asc 9F 16
SL5: S'dale 6D 34
SM3: Chea 1J 61
SW19 8B 28
TW3: Houn 8C 10
TW9: Kew 2N 11
TW12: Hamp 8N 23
Priory St. GU14: Farnb 1B 90
Priory Ter. TW16: Sunb 8H 23
Priory Wlk. RG12: Brac 3D 32
Priory Way SL3: Dat 3L 5
UB7: Harm 2N 7
Privet Rd. GU35: Lind 4B 168
Probyn Rd. SW2 3M 29
Proctor Cl. CR4: Mit 9E 28
RH10: Craw 5G 183
Proctor Gdns. KT23: Book 3B 98
Proctors Cl. TW14: Felt 2H 23
Proctors Rd. RG40: W'ham 2E 30
Proffits Cotts. KT20: Tad 9J 81
Profumo Rd. KT12: Hers 2L 57
Progress Bus. Pk.
CR0: Wad 8K 45
Progress Way CR0: Wad 8K 45
Prologis Pk. CR0: Bedd 6H 45
TW4: Houn 7K 9
Promenade, The W4 5D 12
Promenade App. Rd.
W4 3D 12
Promenade de Verdun
CR8: Pur 7H 63
Prospect Av. GU14: Farnb 8N 69
Prospect Cl. TW3: Houn 4N 9
Prospect Cotts. GU12: A Va 9E 90
SW18 7M 13
Prospect Cres. TW2: Whitt 9C 10
Prospect Hill GU35: Head 1D 168
Prospect Ho. KT19: Eps 5A 60
SW19 9B 28
(off Chapter Way)
Prospect La. TW20: Eng G 6K 19
Prospect Pl.
KT17: Eps 6L 201 (8D 60)
RH11: Craw 3A 182
SL4: W'sor 6G 4
(off Osbourne Rd.)
SW20 8G 27
TW18: Stain 6H 21
W4 1C 12
Prospect Quay *SW18 7M 13*
(off Lightermans Wlk.)
Prospect Rd. GU10: Rowl 8D 128
GU12: A Va 8E 90
GU14: Cove, Farnb 1M 89
KT6: Surb 5J 41
Prossers KT20: Tad 8J 81
Prothero Rd. SW6 3K 13
Providence La. UB3: Harl 3E 8
Providence Pl. GU22: Pyr 1J 75
KT17: Eps 5M 201 (8D 60)
Providence Ter.
RH10: T Hil 5D 184
Prudence La. BR6: Farnb 1J 67
Prune Hill TW20: Egh, Eng G 8N 19
Prunus Cl. GU24: W End 9B 52
Pryors Wood RH12: K'fold 3J 179
Ptarmigan Hgts. RG12: Brac 3J 31
Puckridge Hill Rd.
GU11: Alde 7K 89
Pucks Hill GU21: Knap 4G 73
Puckshott Way GU27: Hasl 9H 171
Puddenhole Cotts.
RH3: Betch 2N 119
Pudding La. RH6: Char 2K 161
Puffin Cl. BR3: Beck 4G 46
Puffin Hill RH10: T Hil 4F 184
Puffin Rd. RH11: Ifi 4J 181
Pulborough Rd. SW18 1L 27
Pulborough Way TW4: Houn 7K 9
Pullman Ct. SW2 2J 29
Pullman Gdns. SW15 9H 13
Pullman La. GU7: Goda 9F 132
Pullman Pl. *RH1: Mers 6G 102*
(off Station Rd.)
Pullmans Pl. TW18: Stain 6J 21
Pulteney Cl. TW7: Isle 6G 10
Pulton Pl. SW6 3M 13
Pump All. TW8: Brent 3K 11
Pumping Sta. Rd. W4 3D 12
Pump La. SL5: Asc 9B 18
Pump Pail Nth.
CR0: Croy 5B 200 (9N 45)
Pump Pail Sth.
CR0: Croy 5B 200 (9N 45)
Punchbowl La. RH5: Dork 4K 119
Punch Copse Rd.
RH10: Craw 2D 182
Punnetts Ct. RH11: Craw 6L 181
Purbeck Av. KT3: N Mal 5E 42
Purbeck Cl. RH1: Mers 6H 103
(not continuous)
Purbeck Ct. GU2: Guil 3H 113
Purbeck Dr. GU21: Wok 1B 74
Purberry Gro. KT17: Ewe 6E 60
Purbrook Ct. RG12: Brac 5C 32
Purcell Cl. CR8: Ken 1N 83
Purcell Cres. SW6 3J 13
(not continuous)
Purcell Mans. *W14 2K 13*
(off Queen's Club Gdns.)
Purcell Rd. RG45: Crow 9G 30
RH11: Craw 6L 181
Purcell's Cl. KT21: A'tead 5M 79
Purdy Ct. KT4: W Pk 8F 42
PURLEY 7L 63
Purley Bury Av. CR8: Pur 7N 63
Purley Bury Cl. CR8: Pur 7N 63
Purley Cl. RH10: Craw 6H 183
PURLEY CROSS 7L 63
Purley Downs Rd.
CR2: Sande 6N 63
CR8: Pur 6N 63
Purley Hill CR8: Pur 8M 63
Purley Knoll CR8: Pur 7K 63
Purley Oaks Rd.
CR2: Sande 5A 64
Purley Oaks Station (Rail) 5A 64
Purley Pde. CR8: Pur 7L 63
Purley Pk. Rd. CR8: Pur 6M 63
Purley Pool 7L 63
Purley Ri. CR8: Pur 8K 63
Purley Rd. CR2: S Croy 4A 64
CR8: Pur 7L 63
Purley Station (Rail) 7L 63
Purley Va. CR8: Pur 9M 63
Purley Vw. Ter. *CR2: S Croy 4A 64*
(off Sanderstead Rd.)
Purley Way CR0: Croy, Wad 6K 45
CR8: Pur 7L 63
GU16: Frim 6C 70
Purley Way Cen., The
CR0: Wad 8L 45
Purley Way Cnr. CR0: Croy 6K 45
Purmerend Cl. GU14: Cove 9H 69
Purser Ho. *SW2 1L 29*
(off Tulse Hill)
Pursers Cross Rd. SW6 4L 13
(not continuous)
Pursers La. GU5: P'lake 2E 136
Pursers Lea GU5: P'lake 4E 136
Purslane RG40: W'ham 3C 30
Purton Rd. RH12: Hors 4H 197
Purvis Ho. CR0: Croy 6A 46
PUTNEY 7J 13
Putney Arts Theatre 7J 13
Putney Bri. SW6 6K 13
SW15 6K 13
Putney Bri. App. SW6 6K 13
Putney Bri. Rd. SW15 7K 13
SW18 7K 13
Putney Bridge Station (Tube)
6L 13

Putney Comn.—Raleigh Gdns.

Putney Comn. SW15 6H 13
Putney Exchange Shop. Cen. SW15 7J 13
PUTNEY HEATH 9H 13
Putney Heath SW15 1G 26
Putney Heath La. SW15 9J 13
Putney High St. SW15 7J 13
Putney Hill SW15 1J 27 (not continuous)
Putney Leisure Cen. 7H 13
Putney Pk. Av. SW15 7F 12
Putney Pk. La. SW15 7G 12 (not continuous)
Putney Pier (Riverbus) 6K 13
Putney Station (Rail) 7K 13
PUTNEY VALE 4F 26
Putney Va. Crematorium SW15 3F 26
Putney Wharf SW15 6K 13
PUTTENHAM 8N 111
Puttenham Heath Rd. GU3: Comp, Put 8A 112
Puttenham Hill GU3: Put 7N 111
Puttenham La. GU8: S'ford 2N 131
Puttenham Rd. GU10: Seal 8F 110
Puttocks Cl. GU27: Hasl 3B 188
Pye Cl. CR3: Cate 1A 104
Pyecombe Ct. RH11: Craw 6L 181
Pyegrove Chase RG12: Brac 6C 32
PYESTOCK 4G 88
Pyestock Cres. GU14: Cove 1H 89
Pyke Cl. RG40: W'ham 2C 30
Pylbrook Rd. SM1: Sut 9M 43
PYLE HILL 2N 93
Pyle Hill GU22: Wok 2N 93
Pylon Way CR0: Bedd 7J 45
Pymers Mead SE21 2N 29
Pyne Rd. KT6: Surb 7N 41
Pyramid Ct. *KT1: K Tham* 4M 203 (off Cambridge Rd.)
Pyramid Ho. TW4: Houn 5M 9
Pyrcroft La. KT13: Weybr 2C 56
Pyrcroft Rd. KT16: Chert 6G 36
PYRFORD 3J 75
Pyrford Comn. Rd. GU22: Pyr 3F 74
Pyrford Ct. GU22: Pyr 4G 75
PYRFORD GREEN 4K 75
Pyrford Heath GU22: Pyr 3H 75
Pyrford Rd. GU22: Pyr 9J 55
KT14: W By 9J 55
PYRFORD VILLAGE 5J 75
Pyrford Wood Est. GU22: Pyr 3H 75
Pyrford Woods GU22: Pyr 2G 75
Pyrford Woods Cl. GU22: Pyr 2H 75
Pyrian Cl. GU22: Wok 3F 74
Pyrland Rd. TW10: Rich 9M 11
Pyrmont Gro. SE27 4M 29
Pyrmont Rd. W4 2N 11
Pytchley Cres. SE19 7N 29

Q

QUABROOK 8L 187
Quadrangle, The GU2: Guil 4K 113
GU16: Frim 6A 70
RH6: Horl 8E 142
SW6 3K 13
Quadrant, The GU1: Guil 5B 202
GU12: A Va 9E 90
KT13: Weybr 1B 56 (off Church St.)
KT17: Eps 6L 201 (9D 60)
SM2: Sut 3A 62
SW20 9K 27
TW9: Rich 7K 11
Quadrant Ct. RG12: Brac 2C 32
Quadrant Rd. CR7: T Hea 3M 45
TW9: Rich 7K 11
Quadrant Way KT13: Weybr 1B 56
Quadrum Pk. GU3: P'marsh 1L 133
Quail Cl. RH12: Hors 1K 197
Quail Cnr. RG12: Brac 3K 31
Quail Gdns. CR2: Sels 6H 65
Quain Mans. *W14* 2K 13 (off Queen's Club Gdns.)
Quakers La. TW7: Isle 3G 10 (not continuous)
Quakers Way GU3: Worp 8F 92
Qualitas RG12: Brac 7L 31
Quality St. RH1: Mers 6F 102
Quantock Cl. RH11: Craw 3N 181
SL3: Lang 1C 6
UB3: Harl 3E 8
Quantock Dr. KT4: W Pk 8H 43
Quarrendon St. SW6 5M 13
Quarr Rd. SM5: Cars 5B 44
Quarry, The RH3: Betch 1C 120
Quarry Bank GU18: Ligh 7L 51
Quarry Cl. KT22: Leat 8K 79
RH8: Oxt 8A 106
RH12: Hors 2M 197
Quarry Cotts. RH2: Reig 9N 101
Quarry Gdns. KT22: Leat 8K 79
Quarry Hill GU7: Goda 8E 132
Quarry Hill Pk. RH2: Reig 9A 102
Quarry La. GU46: Yate 1D 68
Quarry Pk. Rd. SM1: Sut 3L 61
Quarry Path RH8: Oxt 9A 106
Quarry Ri. RH19: E Grin 7C 166
SM1: Sut 3L 61
Quarry Rd. GU7: Hurt 4D 132
RH8: Oxt 8A 106
RH9: Gods 6F 104
Quarryside Bus. Pk. RH1: Red 9F 102
Quarry St. GU1: Guil 6C 202 (5N 113)
Quarterbrass Farm Rd. RH12: Hors 1K 197
Quartermaine Av. GU22: Wok 9B 74
Quartermile Rd. GU7: Goda 9H 133
Quarters Rd. GU14: Farnb 3N 89
Quayside Wlk. *KT1: K Tham* 4H 203 (off Wadbrook St.)
Quebec Av. TN16: Weste 4M 107
Quebec Cl. RH6: Smal 8L 143
Quebec Cotts. TN16: Weste 5M 107
Quebec Gdns. GU17: Haw 2J 69
Quebec House 4M 107
Quebec Sq. TN16: Weste 4M 107
Queen Adelaide's Ride SL4: Wink 9A 4
Queen Alexandra's Ct. SW19 6L 27
Queen Alexandra's Way KT19: Eps 7N 59
Queen Anne Dr. KT10: Clay 4E 58
Queen Anne's Cl. SL4: W'sor 4E 18
TW2: Twick 4D 24
Queen Anne's Gdns. CR4: Mit 2D 44
KT22: Leat 8H 79
Queen Anne's Ga. GU9: H End 5J 109
Queen Anne's Ride SL4: W'sor 6D 18
Queen Anne's Rd. SL4: W'sor 7F 4 (not continuous)
Queen Anne's Ter. KT22: Leat 8H 79
Queen Ann's Ct. *SL4: W'sor* 4G 4 (off Peascod St.)
Queen Caroline St. W6 1H 13 (not continuous)
Queen Catherine Ho. *SW6* 3N 13 (off Wandon Rd.)
Queen Charlotte's Cottage 5K 11
Queen Charlotte St. *SL4: W'sor* 4G 5 (off High St.)
Queendale Ct. GU21: Wok 3J 73
Queen Eleanor's Rd. GU2: Guil 4J 113
Queen Elizabeth Cl. GU12: Ash 2E 110
Queen Elizabeth Dr. GU11: Alde 2L 109
Queen Elizabeth Gdns. SM4: Mord 3M 43
Queen Elizabeth Ho. SW12 1E 28
QUEEN ELIZABETH PARK 8K 93
Queen Elizabeth Rd. GU15: Camb 6B 50
KT2: K Tham 3L 203 (1M 41)
RH12: Rudg 1E 194
Queen Elizabeth's Dr. CR0: N Add 5N 65
Queen Elizabeth's Gdns. CR0: N Add 6N 65
Queen Elizabeth's Wlk. SL4: W'sor 5H 5
SM6: Bedd 1H 63 (off Croydon Rd.)
SM6: Bedd 1H 63 (Sandhills)
Queen Elizabeth Wlk. SW13 4F 12
Queen Elizabeth Way GU22: Wok 6B 74
Queenhill Rd. CR2: Sels 6E 64
Queenhythe Cres. GU4: J Wel 6N 93
Queenhythe Rd. GU4: J Wel 6N 93
Queen Mary Av. GU15: Camb 1M 69
SM4: Mord 4J 43
Queen Mary Cl. GU22: Wok 3E 74
GU51: Fleet 2A 88
KT6: Ches 9N 41
KT6: Surb 9A 42
Queen Mary Ct. TW19: Stan 2N 21
Queen Mary Rd. SE19 7M 29
TW17: Shep 1D 38
Queen Mary's Av. SM5: Cars 4D 62
Queen Mary's Dr. KT15: N Haw 6H 55
Queens Acre SL4: W'sor 7G 4
SM3: Chea 4J 61
Queens Acre Ho. SL4: W'sor 6G 4
Queens Av. GU11: Alde 1M 109
KT14: Byf 8M 55
TW13: Hanw 5K 23
Queensberry Ho. TW9: Rich 8J 11
Queensberry Pl. *TW9: Rich* 8K 11 (off Retreat Rd.)
Queensbridge Pk. TW7: Isle 8E 10
Queensbury Pl. GU17: Haw 3H 69
Queens Cl. GU14: Farnb 5N 89
GU24: Bis 3D 72
KT10: Esh 1B 58
KT20: Wal H 2F 100
SL4: O Win 8K 5
SL5: Asc 9J 17
SM6: W'ton 2F 62
Queen's Club Gdns. W14 2K 13
Queen's Club, The (Tennis Courts) 1K 13
Queens Club Ter. *W14* 2L 13 (off Normand Rd.)
Queens Ct. CR2: S Croy 8C 200
CR7: T Hea 4L 45
GU1: Guil 3D 202 (3N 113)
GU9: U Hal 5G 109
GU14: Farnb 5A 90
GU22: Wok 5B 74
KT13: Weybr 2E 56
KT19: Ewe 6D 60
RH1: Red 2E 122 (off St Anne's Mt.)
RH6: Horl 8E 142
SM2: Sut 7M 61
TN8: Eden 2M 147
TW10: Rich 9M 11
TW18: Stain 7M 21
Queens Ct. Ride KT11: Cob 9H 57
Queen's Cres. RH4: Dork 4J 201 (6G 119)
TW10: Rich 8M 11
Queens Dr. GU2: Guil 9K 93
GU7: Goda 4E 132
KT5: Surb 6N 41
KT7: T Dit 5G 41
KT22: Oxs 7C 58
Queensfield Ct. SM3: Chea 1H 61
Queen's Gdns. TW5: Hest 4M 9
Queens Ga. *GU7: Goda* 7H 133 (off Queen St.)
RH6: Gat 3E 162
Queensgate KT11: Cob 8L 57
Queens Ga. Cotts. SL4: W'sor 7G 4
Queens Ga. Gdns. SW15 7G 13
Queen's Ga. Rd. GU14: Farnb 5N 89
Queens Hill Ri. SL5: Asc 2N 33
Queens Ho. TW11: Tedd 7F 24
Queen's Keep TW1: Twick 9J 11
Queensland Av. SW19 9N 27
Queens La. GU9: U Hal 5G 109
Queen's Mead GU8: Chid 5E 172
Queensmead GU14: Farnb 1N 89
KT22: Oxs 7C 58
SL3: Dat 3L 5
Queensmead Av. KT17: Ewe 6G 61
Queensmere Cl. SW19 3J 27
Queensmere Ct. SW13 3E 12
Queensmere Rd. SW19 3J 27
Queensmill Rd. SW6 3J 13
Queens Pde. *RH13: Hors* 7K 197 (off Queen St.)
Queen's Pde. Path GU11: Alde 7N 89
Queen's Pk. Gdns. TW13: Felt 4G 23
Queen's Pk. Rd. CR3: Cate 1B 104
Queens Pine RG12: Brac 5C 32
Queens Pl. SL5: Asc 2L 33
SM4: Mord 3M 43
Queen's Prom. KT1: K Tham, Surb 8G 203 (3K 41)
Queens Reach KT1: K Tham 4G 203 (1K 41)
KT8: E Mol 3E 40
Queens Ride RG45: Crow 9F 30
SW13 6F 12
SW15 6F 12
Queens Ri. TW10: Rich 9M 11
Queens Rd. BR3: Beck 1H 47
CR0: Croy 5M 45
CR4: Mit 2B 44
GU1: Guil 3D 202 (3N 113)
GU9: U Hal 6H 109
GU11: Alde 3L 109
GU14: Farnb 5A 90
GU15: Camb 2N 69
GU21: Knap 5F 72
GU24: Bis, B'wood 7B 72
GU52: Fleet 6B 88
KT2: K Tham 8N 25
KT3: N Mal 3E 42
KT7: T Dit 5F 40
KT12: Hers 1G 57
KT13: Weybr 1D 56
RH6: Horl 8E 142
RH19: E Grin 1A 186
SL3: Dat 3L 5
SL4: E Wic 1C 4
Queens Rd. SL4: W'sor 5F 4
SL5: S'hill 4A 34
SM2: Sut 6M 61
SM4: Mord 3M 43
SM6: W'ton 2F 62
SW14 6C 12
SW19 7L 27
TW1: Twick 2G 24
TW3: Houn 6B 10
TW10: Rich 1M 25
TW11: Tedd 7F 24
TW12: H Hill 5B 24
TW13: Felt 2J 23
TW20: Egh 6B 20
Queen's Rdbt. GU11: Alde 6N 89
Queen's Royal Surrey Regiment Mus., The 1J 115
Queens Sports Cen. 4E 132
Queen's Sq. RH10: Craw 3B 182
Queens St. TW15: A'ford 5A 22
Queens Ter. *KT7: T Dit* 5G 41 (off Queens Dr.)
SL4: W'sor 6G 5
TW7: Isle 7G 11
Queen St. CR0: Croy 6B 200 (1N 63)
GU5: Gorn 8D 116
GU12: Alde 2B 110
KT16: Chert 7J 37
RH13: Hors 7K 197
Queensville Rd. SW12 1H 29
Queens Wlk. RH19: E Grin 9A 166
TW15: A'ford 5M 21
Queens Way GU24: B'wood 6A 72
TW13: Hanw 5K 23
Queensway BR4: W Wick 1A 66
CR0: Wad 3K 63
GU6: Cranl 8A 156
GU16: Frim G 7E 70
RG42: Brac 9L 15
RH1: Red 2D 122
RH10: Craw 3C 182
RH13: Hors 7J 197
RH19: E Grin 9A 166
TW16: Sunb 1J 39
Queensway Nth. KT12: Hers 1K 57 (not continuous)
Queensway Sth. KT12: Hers 2K 57 (not continuous)
Queens Wharf W6 1H 13
Queenswood Av. CR7: T Hea 4L 45
SM6: Bedd 1H 63
TW3: Houn 5N 9
TW12: Hamp 7B 24
Queenswood Rd. GU21: Wok 6G 73
QUEEN VICTORIA 1H 61
Queen Victoria Ct. GU14: Farnb 9N 69
Queen Victoria Rd. GU24: B'wood 6A 72
Queen Victoria's Wlk. GU15: Camb 9L 49
Queen Victoria Wlk. SL4: W'sor 4H 5
Quell La. GU27: Hasl 9L 189
Quelmans Head Ride SL4: W'sor 3A 18
Quelm La. RG42: Brac 8N 15
RG42: Warf 7N 15
Quennell Cl. KT21: A'tead 6M 79
Quennells Hill GU10: Wrec 5D 128
Quentins Dr. TN16: B Hil 3K 87
Quentins Wlk. *TN16: B Hil* 3K 87 (off St Anns Way)
Quentin Way GU25: V Wat 3L 35
Querrin St. SW6 5N 13
Questen M. RH10: Craw 1H 183
Quetta Pk. GU52: C Cro 2C 108
Quiberon Ct. TW16: Sunb 2H 39
Quick Rd. W4 1D 12
Quicks Rd. SW19 8N 27
Quiet Cl. KT15: Addl 1J 55
Quiet Nook BR2: Kes 1F 66
Quill La. SW15 7J 13
Quillot, The KT12: Hers 2G 56
Quince Cl. SL5: S'hill 3N 33
Quince Dr. GU24: Bis 2E 72
Quincy Rd. TW20: Egh 6C 20
Quinney's GU14: Farnb 4A 90
Quintet, The KT12: Wal T 7H 39
Quintilis RG12: Brac 7L 31 (not continuous)
Quintin Av. SW20 9L 27
Quinton Cl. BR3: Beck 2M 47
SM6: W'ton 1F 62
TW5: C'ford 3J 9
Quinton Rd. KT7: T Dit 7G 41
Quinton St. SW18 3A 28
Quintrell Cl. GU21: Wok 4L 73

R

Rabbit La. KT12: Hers 4H 57
Rabies Heath Rd. RH1: Blet 2B 124
Raby Rd. KT3: N Mal 3C 42
Raccoon Way TW4: Houn 5K 9
Racecourse Rd. RH6: Gat 2D 162
RH7: Dorm, Ling 8A 146
Racecourse Way *RH6: Gat* 2D 162 (off Nth. Terminal App.)
Rachael's Lake Vw. RG42: Warf 8C 16
Rackfield GU27: Hasl 1B 188
Rackham Cl. RH11: Craw 5B 182
Rackham M. SW16 7G 29
Rack's Ct. GU1: Guil 7D 202 (5N 113)
Rackstraw Rd. GU47: C Tow, Owls 6H 49
Racquets & Fitness Spa, The 4A 24
Racquets Ct. Hill GU7: Goda 5F 132
Racton Rd. SW6 2M 13
Radbourne Rd. SW12 1G 29
Radcliffe Cl. GU16: Frim 7D 70
Radcliffe Gdns. SM5: Cars 5C 62
Radcliffe M. TW12: H Hill 6C 24
Radcliffe Rd. CR0: Croy 8C 46
Radcliffe Sq. SW15 9J 13
Radcliffe Way RG42: Brac 9K 15
Radford Cl. GU9: Hale 7K 109
Radford Rd. RH10: Craw 6F 162
Radipole Rd. SW6 4L 13
Radius Pk. TW14: Felt 7G 9
Rad La. GU5: P'lake 2E 136 (not continuous)
Radley Cl. TW14: Felt 2G 23
Radnor Cl. CR4: Mit 3J 45
Radnor Ct. RH1: Red 3C 122
Radnor Gdns. TW1: Twick 3F 24
Radnor Ho. SW16 1K 45
Radnor La. RH5: H Mary 9H 137 (Three Mile Rd.)
RH5: H Mary 4H 137 (Woodhouse La.)
Radnor Rd. GU5: P'lake 5E 136
KT13: Weybr 9B 38
RG12: Brac 2D 32
TW1: Twick 2F 24
Radnor Ter. SM2: Sut 4M 61
Radnor Wlk. CR0: Croy 5H 47
Radnor Way SL3: Lang 1A 6
Radolphs KT20: Tad 9J 81
Radstock Way RH1: Mers 6H 103
Radstone Ct. GU22: Wok 5B 74
Raeburn Av. KT5: Surb 7A 42
Raeburn Cl. KT1: H Wic 1G 203 (8K 25)
Raeburn Ct. GU21: Wok 6K 73
Raeburn Gro. GU21: Wok 5K 73
Raeburn Way GU47: C Tow 9J 49
RAFBOROUGH 2K 89
Rafborough Footpath GU14: Cove 2M 89
GU14: Farnb 2M 89
Rafdene Copse GU22: Wok 6M 73
Rag Hill Cl. TN16: Tats 8G 86
Rag Hill Rd. TN16: Tats 8F 86
Raglan Cl. GU12: Alde 3A 110
GU16: Frim 6E 70
RH2: Reig 1B 122
TW4: Houn 8N 9
Raglan Ct. CR2: S Croy 8A 200 (2M 63)
Raglan Pct. CR3: Cate 9B 84
Raglan Rd. GU21: Knap 5H 73
RH2: Reig 9N 101
Raikes Hollow RH5: A Ham 2J 137
Raikes La. RH5: A Ham 2J 137
Railey Rd. RH10: Craw 2C 182
Railpit La. CR6: Warl 2A 86
Railshead Rd. TW7: Isle 7H 11
Rails La. GU24: Pirb 3N 91
Railton Rd. GU2: Guil 8L 93
Railway App. KT16: Chert 7H 37
RH19: E Grin 9A 166
SM6: W'ton 2F 62
TW1: Twick 1G 24
Railway Cotts. GU19: Bag 3J 51
SW19 5N 27
Railway Pas. TW11: Tedd 7G 24
Railway Rd. TW11: Tedd 5E 24
Railway Side SW13 6D 12 (not continuous)
Railway Ter. *CR5: Coul* 2H 83 (off Station App.)
TN16: Weste 3M 107
TW13: Felt 2H 23
TW18: Stain 6F 20
Rainbow Ct. GU21: Wok 3H 73
Rainbow Ind. Est. SW20 1G 43
Rainbow Leisure Cen. 5L 201 (8D 60)
Rainforest Wlk. *RG12: Brac* 4N 31 (off Pond Moor Rd.)
Rainville Rd. W6 2H 13
Rake La. GU8: Mil 3C 152
Rakers Ridge RH12: Hors 3K 197
Raleigh Av. SM6: Bedd 1H 63
Raleigh Ct. RH10: Craw 7E 162
SM6: W'ton 3F 62
TW18: Stain 5J 21
Raleigh Dr. KT5: Surb 7B 42
KT10: Clay 2D 58
RH6: Smal 8L 143
Raleigh Gdns. CR4: Mit 2D 44 (not continuous)

276 A-Z Surrey

Raleigh Rd.—Regents M.

Raleigh Rd. TW9: Rich 6M **11**
TW13: Felt 4G **22**
UB2: S'hall 1M **9**
Raleigh Wlk. RH10: Craw 5C **182**
Raleigh Way GU16: Frim 3D **70**
TW13: Hanw 6K **23**
Ralliwood Rd. KT21: A'tead ...6N **79**
Ralph Perring Ct.
BR3: Beck 3K **47**
Ralph's Ride RG12: Brac 2C **32**
(Broad La., not continuous)
RG12: Brac 4C **32**
(Mendip Rd.)
Ralston Ct. *SL4: W'sor 4G 4*
(off Russell St.)
Rama Cl. SW16 ....8J **29**
Rambler Cl. SW16 ....5G **28**
Ramblers Way
RH11: Craw 9N **181**
Rame Cl. SW17 ....6E **28**
Ramillies Cl. GU11: Alde 6C **90**
RAMILLIES PARK 7B **90**
Ramin Ct. GU1: Guil 9M **93**
Ramones Ter. *CR4: Mit 3J 45*
(off Yorkshire Rd.)
Ramornie Cl. KT12: Hers 1N **57**
Ram Pas.
KT1: K Tham 4H **203** (1K **41**)
Rampling Ct. RH10: Craw 4D **182**
Ramsay Cl. GU15: Camb 8F **50**
Ramsay Ct. RH11: Craw 8N **181**
Ramsay Rd. GU20: Windl 2B **52**
Ramsbury Cl. RG12: Brac 5K **31**
Ramsdale Rd. SW17 ....6E **28**
Ramsden Rd. GU7: Goda 8G **133**
SW12 ....1E **28**
Ramsey Cl. RH6: Horl 8D **142**
RH12: Hors 3K **197**
Ramsey Ct. CR0: Croy 3A **200**
Ramsey Pl. CR3: Cate 9N **83**
Ramsey Rd. CR7: T Hea 5K **45**
Ramslade Cotts.
RG12: Brac 2A **32**
Rams La. GU8: Duns 7C **174**
RAMSNEST COMMON 1D **190**
Ramster Cotts.
GU8: Chid 1C **190**
Ram St. SW18 ....8N **13**
Ramuswood Av. BR6: Chels ...2N **67**
Ranald Ct. SL5: Asc 7K **17**
Rances La. RG40: W'ham 2D **30**
Randal Cres. RH2: Reig 5M **121**
Randall Cl. SL3: Lang 1B **6**
Randall Ct. *SL4: O Win 9K 5*
(off Lyndwood Dr.)
Randall Mead RG42: Bin 7G **15**
Randall Scholfield Ct.
RH10: Craw 2E **182**
Randalls Cres. KT22: Leat 7G **78**
Randalls Pk. Av. KT22: Leat ...7G **78**
Randalls Pk. Crematorium
KT22: Leat 7E **78**
Randalls Pk. Dr. KT22: Leat ...8G **78**
Randalls Rd. KT22: Leat 6E **78**
Randalls Way KT22: Leat 8G **78**
Randell Cl. GU17: Haw 5K **69**
Randell Ho. GU17: Haw 5K **69**
Randle Rd. TW10: Ham 5J **25**
Randolph Cl. GU21: Knap 4H **73**
KT2: K Tham 6B **26**
KT11: Sto D 2A **78**
Randolph Dr. GU14: Cove 2H **89**
Randolph Rd.
KT17: Eps 8M **201** (1E **80**)
SL3: Lang 1B **6**
Randolph's La.
TN16: Weste 4K **107**
Ranelagh SL4: Wink 3M **17**
Ranelagh Av. SW6 ....6L **13**
SW13 ....5F **12**
Ranelagh Cres. SL5: Asc 9G **17**
Ranelagh Dr. RG12: Brac 2A **32**
TW1: Twick 7H **11**
Ranelagh Gdns. SW6 ....6K **13**
(not continuous)
W4 ....3B **12**
Ranelagh Gdns. Mans.
SW6 ....6K 13
(off Ranelagh Gdns.)
Ranelagh Pl. KT3: N Mal 4D **42**
Ranelagh Rd. RH1: Red 3C **122**
Ranfurly Rd. SM1: Sut 8M **43**
Range, The GU5: Braml 7C **134**
Range Ride GU15: Camb 8L **49**
Range Rd. GU14: Farnb 5J **89**
RG40: Finch 9A **30**
Ranger Wlk. KT15: Addl 2K **55**
Range Vw. GU47: C Tow 7K **49**
Range Way TW17: Shep 6B **38**
Rankine Cl. GU9: B Lea 6M **109**
Ranmere St. SW12 ....2F **28**
Ranmore Av. CR0: Croy 9C **46**
Ranmore Cl. RH1: Red 9E **102**
RH11: Craw 9A **182**
RANMORE COMMON 3D **118**
Ranmore Comn. Rd.
RH5: Ran C, Westh 3M **117**
Ranmore Pk. RH4: Dork 3G **118**
Ranmore Pl. KT13: Weybr 2D **56**
Ranmore Rd.
RH4: Dork 1H **201** (3C **118**)
SM2: Chea 5J **61**
Rannoch Rd. W6 ....2H **13**

Ransome Cl. RH11: Craw 6K **181**
Ranyard Cl. KT9: Ches 9M **41**
Rapallo Cl. GU14: Farnb 1A **90**
Rapeland Hill RH12: Hors 7M **179**
Raphael Dr. KT7: T Dit 6F **40**
Rapley Cl. GU15: Camb 7D **50**
Rapley Grn. RG12: Brac 5A **32**
Rapley's Fld. GU24: Pirb 1B **92**
Rapsley La. GU21: Knap 5E **72**
Rashleigh Ct. GU52: C Cro 9C **88**
Rastell Av. SW2 ....3H **29**
Ratcliffe Rd. GU14: Cove 6L **69**
Rathbone Ho. RH11: Craw 8N **181**
Rathbone Sq.
CR0: Croy 6B **200** (1N **63**)
Rathgar Cl. RH1: Red 8E **122**
Rathlin Rd. RH11: Craw 6N **181**
Rathmell Dr. SW4 ....1H **29**
Ravelin Cl. GU51: Fleet 1A **88**
Raven Cl. GU46: Yate 9A **48**
RH10: T Hil 4F **184**
RH12: Hors 2L **197**
Ravendale Rd. TW16: Sunb ...1G **38**
Ravendene Ct.
RH11: Craw 4B **182**
Ravenfield TW20: Eng G 7M **19**
Ravenfield Rd. SW17 ....4D **28**
Raven La. RH11: Craw 1A **182**
Ravenna Rd. SW15 ....8J **13**
Ravensbourne Av.
TW19: Stan 2N **21**
Ravensbourne Rd.
TW1: Twick 9J **11**
Ravensbourne Ter.
TW19: Stan 2N **21**
Ravensbury Av. SM4: Mord 4A **44**
Ravensbury Ct. *CR4: Mit 3B 44*
(off Ravensbury Gro.)
Ravensbury Gro. CR4: Mit 3B **44**
Ravensbury La. CR4: Mit 3B **44**
Ravensbury Path CR4: Mit 3B **44**
Ravensbury Rd.
SW18 ....3M **27**
Ravensbury Ter. SW18 ....3N **27**
Ravenscar Rd. KT6: Surb 8M **41**
Ravens Cl. GU21: Knap 3F **72**
KT6: Surb 5K **41**
RH1: Red 2D **122**
Ravens Ct. KT1: K Tham 8H **203**
Ravenscourt TW16: Sunb 9G **23**
Ravenscourt Av. W6 ....1F **12**
Ravenscourt Pl. W6 ....1G **12**
Ravenscroft Cl. GU12: Ash ...1G **111**
Ravenscroft Ct.
RH12: Hors 5J **197**
Ravenscroft Rd. BR3: Beck 1F **46**
KT13: Weybr 7D **56**
Ravensdale Cotts.
GU26: Hind 9A **170**
Ravensdale Gdns.
TW4: Houn 6M **9**
Ravensdale M. TW18: Stain ...7K **21**
Ravensdale Rd. SL5: Asc 4L **33**
TW4: Houn 6M **9**
Ravensfield Gdns.
KT19: Ewe 2D **60**
Ravenshead Cl. CR2: Sels 7F **64**
Ravenside KT1: K Tham 8G **203**
Ravenslea Rd. SW12 ....1D **28**
Ravensmede Way W4 ....1E **12**
Ravenstone Rd.
GU15: Camb 1H **71**
Ravenstone St. SW12 ....2E **28**
Ravenswold CR8: Ken 2N **83**
Ravenswood Av.
BR4: W Wick 7M **47**
KT6: Surb 8M **41**
RG45: Crow 2D **48**
Ravenswood Cl. KT11: Cob 2L **77**
Ravenswood Ct.
GU22: Wok 5B **74**
KT2: K Tham 7A **26**
Ravenswood Cres.
BR4: W Wick 7M **47**
Ravenswood Dr.
GU15: Camb 1E **70**
Ravenswood Gdns.
TW7: Isle 4E **10**
Ravenswood Rd.
CR0: Wad 5A **200** (9M **45**)
SW12 ....1F **28**
Ravensworth Ct. *SW6 ....3M 13*
(off Fulham Rd.)
Rawchester Cl. SW18 ....2L **27**
Rawdon Ri. GU15: Camb 1F **70**
Rawlings Cl. BR3: Beck 4M **47**
Rawlins Cl. CR2: Sels 4H **65**
Rawlinson Rd. GU11: Alde 8A **90**
GU15: Camb 9L **49**
RH10: Craw 5H **183**
Rawnsley Av. CR4: Mit 4B **44**
Raworth Cl. RH10: Craw 5F **182**
Rawsthorne Ct. TW4: Houn 7N **9**
Raybell Ct. TW7: Isle 5F **10**
Ray Cl. KT9: Ches 3J **59**
RH7: Ling 6M **145**
Ray La. RH7: Blin H, Ling 4J **145**
Rayleigh Av. TW11: Tedd 7E **24**
Rayleigh Ct.
KT1: K Tham 3M **203** (1N **41**)
Rayleigh Ri. CR2: S Croy 3B **64**
Rayleigh Rd. SW19 ....9L **27**
Raymead Av. CR7: T Hea 4L **45**

Raymead Cl. KT22: Fetc 9E **78**
Raymead Pas. *CR7: T Hea 4L 45*
(off Raymead Av.)
Raymead Way KT22: Fetc 9E **78**
Raymer Wlk. RH6: Horl 7G **142**
Raymond Cl. SL3: Poy 4G **7**
Raymond Cres. GU2: Guil 4J **113**
Raymond Rd. BR3: Beck 3H **47**
SW19 ....7K **27**
Raymond Way KT10: Clay 3G **59**
Raynald Ho. SW16 ....4J **29**
Rayne Ho. SW12 ....1E **28**
Rayners Cl. SL3: Coln 3E **6**
Rayners Rd. SW15 ....8K **13**
RAYNES PARK 3H **43**
Raynes Pk. Bri. SW20 ....1H **43**
Raynes Pk. School Sports Cen.
..................2G **42**
Raynes Park Station (Rail)
..................1H **43**
Ray Rd. KT8: W Mole 4B **40**
Ray's Av. SL4: W'sor 3C **4**
Rays Rd. BR4: W Wick 6M **47**
Raywood Cl. UB3: Harl 3D **8**
Read Cl. KT7: T Dit 6G **40**
Readens, The SM7: Ban 3C **82**
Reading Arch Rd.
RH1: Red 3D **122**
Reading Rd. GU14: Farnb 4A **90**
GU17: B'water 8A **48**
GU46: Yate 8A **48**
RG41: Win 1A **30**
SM1: Sut 2A **62**
Reading Rd. Nth.
GU51: Fleet 4A **88**
Reading Rd. Sth.
GU51: Fleet 5A **88**
GU52: C Cro, Fleet 5A **88**
Read Rd. KT21: A'tead 4K **79**
Reads Rest La. KT20: Tad 7M **81**
Reapers Cl. RH12: Hors 3K **197**
Reapers Way TW7: Isle 8D **10**
Reckitt Rd. W4 ....1D **12**
Recovery St. SW17 ....6C **28**
Recreation Cl. GU14: Cove 5L **69**
Recreation Rd.
GU1: Guil 2B **202** (3N **113**)
GU10: Rowl 8D **128**
Recreation Way CR4: Mit 2H **45**
Rectory Cl. GU4: Guil 1F **114**
GU6: Ewh 5F **156**
GU7: Bus 9J **133**
GU47: Sandh 7E **48**
KT6: Surb 7J **41**
KT14: Byf 9M **55**
KT21: A'tead 6M **79**
RG12: Brac 4N **31**
RG40: W'ham 2B **30**
RH5: Ockl 7C **158**
SL4: W'sor 4D **4**
SW20 ....2H **43**
TW17: Shep 2B **38**
Rectory Ct. SM6: W'ton 1G **63**
TW13: Felt 5K **23**
Rectory Flats RH11: Ifi 1L **181**
Rectory Gdn. GU6: Cranl 7M **155**
Rectory Grn. BR3: Beck 1J **47**
Rectory Gro.
CR0: Croy 3A **200** (8M **45**)
TW12: Hamp 5N **23**
Rectory La. GU5: Shere 8B **116**
GU20: Windl 3A **52**
KT6: Surb 7H **41**
KT14: Byf 9N **55**
KT21: A'tead 6M **79**
KT23: Book 4N **97**
RG12: Brac 4N **31**
RH3: Buck 9E **100**
RH6: Char 3J **161**
RH11: Ifi 1L **181**
SM6: W'ton 1G **63**
SM7: Ban 2L **81**
SW17 ....7E **28**
TN16: Tats 1G **106**
Rectory Orchard SW19 ....5K **27**
Rectory Pk. CR2: Sande 9B **64**
Rectory Rd. BR2: Kes 4F **66**
BR3: Beck 1K **47**
CR5: Coul 3A **102**
GU14: Farnb 1A **90**
RG40: W'ham 2B **30**
SM1: Sut 9M **43**
SW13 ....5F **12**
TW4: C'ford 5K **9**
Rectory Row RG12: Brac 3N **31**
Red Admiral St.
RH12: Hors 2L **197**
Redan Gdns. GU12: Alde 2A **110**
REDAN HILL 2B **110**
Redan Hill Ind. Est.
GU12: Alde 2A **110**
Redan Rd. GU12: Alde 2A **110**
Redbarn Cl. CR8: Pur 7M **63**
Redcliffe Cl. *SW5 ....1N 13*
(off Old Brompton Rd.)
Redcliffe Gdns. SW10 ....1N **13**
W4 ....3A **12**
Redcliffe M. SW10 ....1N **13**
Redcliffe Sq. SW10 ....1N **13**
Redcliffe St. SW10 ....2N **13**
Redclose Av. SM4: Mord 4M **43**
Redcote Pl. RH4: Dork 3K **119**
Red Cotts. GU27: G'wood 7J **171**

Redcourt
CR0: Croy 5F **200** (9B **46**)
GU22: Pyr 2F **74**
Redcrest Gdns.
GU15: Camb 1D **70**
Redcroft Wlk. GU6: Cranl 8N **155**
Red Deer Cl. RH13: Hors 5A **198**
Reddington Cl.
CR2: Sande 5A **64**
Redding Way GU21: Knap 6E **72**
Redditch RG12: Brac 6B **32**
Redditch Cl. RH11: Craw 7K **181**
Reddown Rd. CR5: Coul 5H **83**
Rede Ct. GU14: Farnb 4A **90**
KT13: Weybr 9C 38
(off Old Palace Rd.)
Redehall Rd. RH6: Smal 8M **143**
Redenham Ho. *SW15 ....1F 26*
(off Ellisfield Dr.)
Redesdale Gdns. TW7: Isle ...3G **10**
Redfern Av. TW4: Houn 1A **24**
Redfields La. GU52: C Cro 1A **108**
Redfields Pk. GU52: C Cro 1A **108**
Redford Av. CR5: Coul 2F **82**
CR7: T Hea 3K **45**
RH12: Hors 4H **197**
SM6: W'ton 3J **63**
Redford Cl. TW13: Felt 3G **22**
Redford Rd. SL4: W'sor 4A **4**
Redgarth Ct. RH19: E Grin 7L **165**
Redgate Ter. SW15 ....9J **13**
Redgrave Cl. CR0: Croy 5C **46**
Redgrave Ct. GU12: Ash 2D **110**
Redgrave Dr. RH10: Craw 4H **183**
Redgrave Rd. SW15 ....6J **13**
Redhall Ct. CR3: Cate 1A **104**
Redhearn Flds.
GU10: Churt 8K **149**
Redhearn Grn.
GU10: Churt 8K **149**
RED HILL 1L **109**
REDHILL 2D **122**
Redhill Aerodrome and Heliport
..................8H **123**
Redhill Ct. SW2 ....3L **29**
Redhill Distribution Cen.
RH1: Salf 2E **142**
Redhill Ho. RH1: Red 1D **122**
Redhill Rd. KT11: Cob 8C **56**
Redhill Station (Rail) 2E **122**
Redhill Tennis Club 1D **122**
Red Ho. La. GU8: Els 8G **131**
KT12: Wal T 8H **39**
Redhouse Rd. CR0: Croy 5H **45**
TN16: Tats 7E **86**
Redkiln Cl. RH13: Hors 5M **197**
Redkiln Cl. Ind. Est.
RH13: Hors 4M **197**
Redkiln Way RH13: Hors 4M **197**
Redknap Ho. TW10: Ham 4J **25**
Redlake La. RG40: W'ham 6E **30**
Redland Gdns.
KT8: W Mole 3N **39**
REDLANDS
GU10 ....5A **108**
RH5 ....5G **139**
Redlands CR5: Coul 3J **83**
TW11: Tedd 7G **25**
Redlands, The BR3: Beck 1L **47**
Redlands Cotts.
RH5: Mid H 2H **139**
Redlands La.
GU10: Cron, Ews 5A **108**
RH5: Mid H 2G **139**
Redlands Way SW2 ....1K **29**
Red La. GU35: H Dwn 2G **168**
KT10: Clay 3G **58**
RH5: Holm 1L **139**
RH8: Oxt 3D **126**
Redleaf Cl. KT22: Fetc 2D **98**
Redleaves Av. TW15: A'ford 7C **22**
Redlees Cl. TW7: Isle 7G **10**
Redlin Ct. RH1: Red 1D **122**
Red Lion Bus. Pk.
KT6: Surb 9M **41**
Red Lion La. GU9: Farnh 2G **129**
GU24: Chob 5H **53**
Red Lion Rd. GU24: Chob 5H **53**
KT6: Surb 8M **41**
Red Lion Sq. SW18 ....8M **13**
Red Lion St. TW9: Rich 8K **11**
Red Lodge BR4: W Wick 7M **47**
Red Lodge Rd.
BR4: W Wick 7M **47**
Redmayne Cl. GU15: Camb 2G **71**
Red River Ct. RH12: Hors 3H **197**
Red Rd. GU15: Ligh 9H **51**
GU18: Ligh 9H **51**
KT20: Betch, Box H 1A **120**
Red Rose RG42: Bin 6H **15**
RED ROVER 7F **12**
Redruth Gdns. KT10: Clay 4F **58**
Redruth Ho. SM2: Sut 4N **61**
Redshank Ct. *RH11: Ifi 4J 181*
(off Stoneycroft Wlk.)
Redstart Cl. CR0: N Add 6N **65**
Redstone Hill RH1: Red 3E **122**
Redstone Hollow
RH1: Red 4E **122**
Redstone Mnr. RH1: Red 3E **122**
Redstone Pk. RH1: Red 3E **122**
Redstone Rd. RH1: Red 4E **122**
Red Tiles Gdns. CR8: Ken 2M **83**

Redvers Buller Rd.
GU11: Alde 6A **90**
Redvers Ct. *CR6: Warl 5G 84*
(off Redvers Rd.)
Redvers Rd. CR6: Warl 5G **84**
RG12: Brac 4N **31**
Redway Dr. TW2: Whitt 1C **24**
Redwing Av. GU7: Goda 2G **133**
Redwing Cl. CR2: Sels 7G **64**
RH13: Hors 5M **197**
Redwing Gdns. KT14: W By 8K **55**
Redwing Ri. GU4: Guil 1F **114**
Redwing Rd. SM6: W'ton 4J **63**
Redwood TW20: Thor 1G **37**
Redwood Cl. CR8: Ken 1N **83**
RH10: Craw 1C **182**
Redwood Ct. KT6: Surb 6K **41**
KT17: Ewe 7E **60**
KT22: Leat 7F 78
(off Park Vw. Rd.)
Redwood Dr. GU15: Camb 2H **71**
SL5: S'dale 5E **34**
Redwood Est. TW5: C'ford 2J **9**
Redwood Gro. GU4: Guil 9E **114**
Redwood Ho. TN16: Weste ...1K **107**
Redwood Mnr. GU27: Hasl ...1G **188**
Redwood M. *TW15: A'ford 8E 22*
(off Staines Rd. W.)
Redwood Mt. RH2: Reig 9M **101**
Redwoods KT15: Addl 3J **55**
SW15 ....2F **26**
Redwoods, The SL4: W'sor 6G **4**
Redwoods Way
GU52: C Cro 8C **88**
Redwood Wlk. KT6: Surb 7K **41**
Reed Cl. GU11: Alde 7B **90**
Reed Dr. RH1: Red 6E **122**
Reed Hall *TW20: Eng G 4M 19*
(off Coopers Hill La.)
Reedham Dr. CR8: Pur 9K **63**
Reedham Pk. Av. CR8: Pur 3L **83**
Reedham Station (Rail) 9K **63**
Reedings RH11: Ifi 5J **181**
Reed Pl. KT14: W By 9G **54**
TW17: Shep 7A **38**
REEDS, THE 8L **129**
Reedsfield Cl. TW15: A'ford 4C **22**
Reedsfield Rd.
TW15: A'ford 5C **22**
Reed's Hill RG12: Brac 4N **31**
Reeds Mdw. RH1: Mers 8G **102**
Reeds Rd., The
GU10: Fren, Til 1J **149**
Rees Gdns. CR0: Croy 5C **46**
Reeve Ct. *GU2: Guil 8K 93*
(off Tarragon Rd.)
Reeve Rd. RH2: Reig 7A **122**
Reeves Cnr.
CR0: Croy 3A **200** (8M **45**)
Reeves Corner Stop (CT)
..........3A **200** (8M **45**)
Reeves Ho. *RH10: Craw 3F 182*
(off Trafalgar Gdns.)
Reeves Rd. GU12: Alde 3A **110**
Refectory Hall
TW20: Eng G 4M 19
(off Coopers Hill La.)
Regal Ct. GU1: Guil 2D **202**
Regal Cres. SM6: W'ton 9F **44**
Regal Dr. RH19: E Grin 1B **186**
Regalfield Cl. GU2: Guil 8J **93**
Regal Pl. SW6 ....3N **13**
Regan Cl. GU2: Guil 7L **93**
Regatta Ho. TW11: Tedd 5G **25**
Regatta Point TW8: Brent 2M **11**
Regency Cl. TW12: Hamp 6N **23**
Regency Ct. *KT15: Addl 9M 37*
(off Albert Rd.)
SM1: Sut 1A **62**
TW11: Tedd 7H **25**
Regency Dr. KT14: W By 9H **55**
Regency Gdns. KT12: Wal T ...7K **39**
Regency Lodge
KT13: Weybr 9F 38
(off Oatlands Chase)
Regency M. TW7: Isle 8E **10**
Regency Wlk. CR0: Croy 5J **47**
TW10: Rich 8L 11
(off Grosvenor Av.)
TW10: Rich 8L 11
(off The Vineyard)
Regent Cl. GU51: Fleet 5B **88**
KT15: N Haw 5M **55**
RH1: Mers 7G **102**
TW4: C'ford 4J **9**
Regent Ct. GU2: Guil 1L **113**
GU19: Bag 5K **51**
SL4: W'sor 4G **5**
Regent Cres. RH1: Red 1D **122**
Regent Ho. KT17: Eps 7D **60**
RH1: Red 2D **122**
Regent Pde. SM2: Sut 3A **62**
Regent Pk. KT22: Leat 5G **78**
Regent Pl. CR0: Croy 7C **46**
SW19 ....6A **28**
Regent Rd. KT5: Surb 4M **41**
Regents Cl. CR2: S Croy 3B **64**
CR3: Whyte 5B **84**
RH11: Craw 7A **182**
Regents Ct. KT2: K Tham 2J **203**
KT13: Weybr 3C **56**
Regents Dr. BR2: Kes 2F **66**
Regents M. RH6: Horl 8E **142**

Regents Pl.—Riverside Arts Cen.

Regents Pl. GU47: Sandh 7H 49
Regent St. GU51: Fleet 5B 88
W4 . . . . .1N 11
Regents Wlk. SL5: Asc 5N 33
Regent Way GU16: Frim 5D 70
Regiment Cl. GU14: Cove 2H 89
Regina Rd. SE25 . . . . .2D 46
UB2: S'hall 1M 9
Regis Ct. CR4: Mit 9C 28
Regnolruf Ct. KT12: Wal T 6H 39
Reid Av. CR3: Cate 8A 84
Reid Cl. CR5: Coul 3F 82
Reidonhill Cotts.
GU21: Knap 5E 72
REIGATE 3M 121
Reigate Av. SM1: Sut 7M 43
Reigate Bus. M.
RH2: Reig 2L 121
Reigate Cl. RH10: Craw 9H 163
REIGATE HEATH 3J 121
Reigate Heath Postmill 3H 121
Reigate Hill RH2: Reig 8A 102
Reigate Hill Cl. RH2: Reig . . .9M 101
REIGATE HILL INTERCHANGE
. . . . .7N 101
Reigate Priory Mus. 4M 121
Reigate Rd.
KT17: Eps D, Tad 7F 60
KT17: Eps, Ewe 6E 60
KT20: Tad 7F 60
KT22: Leat 9J 79
RH1: Red 3N 121
RH2: Buck 2D 120
RH2: Reig 3N 121
RH2: Sid 1N 141
RH3: Betch, Buck 4J 119
RH4: Dork 1L 201 (4J 119)
RH6: Hook, Horl 9B 142
Reigate Station (Rail) 2M 121
Reigate Way SM6: W'ton 2J 63
Reindorp Cl. GU2: Guil 4K 113
Relko Ct. KT19: Eps 7C 60
Relko Gdns. SM1: Sut 2B 62
Rembrandt Ct. KT19: Ewe 3E 60
Rembrandt Way
KT12: Wal T 8J 39
Renaissance Ct. SM5: Sut 7A 44
TW3 . . . . .6C 10
Renaissance Ho.
KT17: Eps 6M 201
Rendel Ho. SM7: Ban 5A 82
Rendle Cl. CR0: Croy 4C 46
Renfree Way TW17: Shep 6B 38
Renfrew Ct. TW4: Houn 5M 9
Renfrew Rd. KT2: K Tham 8A 26
TW4: Houn 5L 9
Renmans, The
KT21: A'tead 3M 79
Renmuir St. SW17 . . . . .7D 28
Rennels Way TW7: Isle 5E 10
Rennie Cl. TW15: A'ford 4M 21
Rennie Ter. RH1: Red 4E 122
Renown Cl.
CR0: Croy 1A 200 (7M 45)
Renton Cl. SW2 . . . . .1K 29
Replingham Rd. SW18 . . . . . . .2L 27
Reporton Rd. SW6 . . . . .3K 13
Repton Av. UB3: Harl 1E 8
Repton Cl. SM5: Cars 2C 62
Reris Grange Cl. GU8: Mil . . .9C 132
Reservoir Cl. CR7: T Hea 2A 46
Restavon Cvn. Site
TN16: B Hil 3K 87
Restmor Way SM6: W'ton 8E 44
Restormel Cl. TW3: Houn 8A 10
Restwell Av. GU6: Cranl 4K 155
Results Healthclub
Bracknell 4C 32
Retreat, The CR7: T Hea 3A 46
GU6: Cranl 6L 155
GU51: C Cro 7A 88
KT4: W Pk 8G 43
KT5: Surb 5M 41
SW14 . . . . .6D 12
TW20: Eng G 6N 19
Retreat Rd. TW9: Rich 8K 11
Reubens Ct. W4 . . . . .1A 12
(off Chaseley Dr.)
Revell Cl. KT22: Fetc 9B 78
Revell Dr. KT22: Fetc 9B 78
Revell Rd. KT1: K Tham 1A 42
SM1: Sut 3L 61
Revelstoke Av. GU14: Farnb . . .9N 69
Revelstoke Rd. SW18 . . . . .3L 27
Revere Way KT19: Ewe 5D 60
Revesby Cl. GU24: W End 9A 52
Revesby Rd. SM5: Cars 5B 44
Rewell St. SW6 . . . . .3N 13
Rewley Rd. SM5: Cars 5B 44
Rex Av. TW15: A'ford 7B 22
Rex Ct. GU27: Hasl 2D 188
Reynard Cl. RH12: Hors 3A 198
Reynard Mills Trad. Est.
TW8: Brent 1J 11
Reynolds Av. KT9: Ches 4L 59
Reynolds Cl. SM5: Cars 7D 44
SW19 . . . . .9B 28
Reynolds Grn. GU47: C Tow 9J 49
Reynolds Pl. RH11: Craw 2A 182
TW10: Rich 9M 11
Reynolds Rd. GU14: Farnb 5G 89
KT3: N Mal 6C 42
RH11: Craw 2A 182
Reynolds St. GU51: Fleet 1A 88
Reynolds Way CR0: Croy 1B 64
Rheingold Way SM6: W'ton . . .5J 63
Rhine Banks GU14: Cove 9J 69
Rhoda McGaw Theatre and Cinema
. . . . .4A 74
(in The Ambassadors)
Rhodes Cl. TW20: Egh 6D 20
Rhodes Ct. TW20: Egh 6E 20
(off Pooley Grn. Cl.)
Rhodes Moorhouse Ct.
SM4: Mord 5M 43
Rhodes Way RH10: Craw 6D 182
Rhododendron Cl. SL5: Asc . . .8J 17
Rhododendron Ride
TW20: Eng G 7J 19
Rhododendron Rd.
GU16: Frim 5E 70
Rhododendron Wlk.
SL5: Asc 8J 17
Rhodrons Av. KT9: Ches 2L 59
Rhyll Gdns. GU11: Alde 3L 109
Rialto Rd. CR4: Mit 1E 44
Ribble Pl. GU14: Cove 8K 69
Ribblesdale RH4: Dork 7H 119
Ribblesdale Rd. SW16 . . . . . . .7F 28
Ricardo Ct. GU5: Braml 6B 134
Ricards Rd. SL4: O Win 9L 5
Ricards Rd. SW19 . . . . .6L 27
Ricebridge La. RH2: Reig 6G 120
Rices Cnr. GU4: Chil 2C 134
Rices Hill RH19: E Grin 9B 166
Richard Burbidge Mans.
SW13 . . . . .2H 13
(off Brasenose Dr.)
Richard Meyjes Rd.
GU2: Guil 4H 113
Richards Cl. GU12: A Va 8E 90
UB3: Harl 2E 8
Richards Fld. KT19: Ewe 5C 60
Richard Sharples Ct.
SM2: Sut 4A 62
Richardson Ct. RH11: Craw . . .8N 181
Richards Rd. KT11: Sto D 1B 78
Richbell Cl. KT21: A'tead 5K 79
Richborough Ct.
RH11: Craw 3A 182
Richens Cl. TW3: Houn 5D 10
Richland Av. CR5: Coul 1E 82
Richlands Av. KT17: Ewe 1F 60
Rich La. SW5 . . . . .1N 13
RICHMOND 8K 11
Richmond Av. SW20 . . . . .9K 27
TW14: Felt 9F 8
Richmond Bri. TW1: Twick 9K 11
RICHMOND CIRCUS 7L 11
Richmond Cl. GU14: Cove 2J 89
GU16: Frim 5D 70
GU52: Fleet 7A 88
KT18: Eps 8L 201 (1D 80)
KT22: Fetc 2C 98
TN16: B Hil 6D 86
Richmond Ct. CR4: Mit 2B 44
GU51: Fleet 5A 88
RH10: Craw 4C 182
Richmond Cres.
TW18: Stain 6H 21
Richmond Cricket Club 6L 11
Richmond Dr. TW17: Shep 5E 38
Richmond Filmhouse 8K 11
Richmond Grn. CR0: Bedd 9J 45
Richmond Gro. KT5: Surb 5M 41
Richmond Hill TW10: Rich 9L 11
Richmond Hill Ct.
TW10: Rich 9L 11
Richmond Ho. CR3: Cate 2C 104
GU47: C Tow 8K 49
Richmond Mans. SW5 . . . . . . .1N 13
(off Old Brompton Rd.)
TW1: Twick 9K 11
Richmond M. TW11: Tedd 6F 24
Richmond Pde. TW1: Twick 9J 11
(off Richmond Rd.)
Richmond Pk. 2N 25
Richmond Pk. Rd.
KT2: K Tham 1J 203 (9L 25)
SW14 . . . . .8B 12
Richmond Rd. CR0: Bedd 9J 45
CR5: Coul 2F 82
CR7: T Hea 2M 45
GU7: Goda 5G 133
GU47: C Tow 7K 49
KT2: K Tham 1J 203 (6K 25)
RH12: Hors 4J 197
SW20 . . . . .9G 26
TW1: Twick 1H 25
TW7: Isle 6G 11
TW18: Stain 6H 21
Richmond RUFC 6K 11
Richmond Station (Rail & Tube)
. . . . .7L 11
Richmond Theatre 7K 11
Richmond University 1L 25
Richmond Way KT22: Fetc 1B 98
(not continuous)
RH19: E Grin 1B 186
Richmondwood SL5: S'dale 7E 34
Rickard Cl. SW2 . . . . .2L 29
Rickards Cl. KT6: Surb 8L 41
Ricketts Hill Rd. TN16: Tats . . .5F 86
Rickett St. SW6 . . . . .2M 13
Rickfield RH11: Craw 4M 181
Rickford GU3: Worp 4G 92
Rickford Hill GU3: Worp 4G 93
Rickman Cl. RG12: Brac 5A 32
Rickman Ct. KT15: Addl 9K 37
Rickman Cres. KT15: Addl 9K 37
Rickman Hill CR5: Coul 5F 82
Rickman Hill Rd.
CR5: Chip, Coul 5F 82
(not continuous)
RICKMANS GREEN 7H 163
Rickman's La.
RH14: Plais, Kird 6B 192
Ricksons La. KT24: W Hors . . .5C 96
Rickwood RH6: Horl 7F 142
Rickwood Pk. RH5: B Grn 1K 159
Rickyard GU2: Guil 3G 113
Riddings, The CR3: Cate 3C 104
RIDDLESDOWN 9N 63
Riddlesdown Av. CR8: Pur 7N 63
Riddlesdown Rd. CR8: Ken . . .1B 84
CR8: Pur 6N 63
Riddlesdown Station (Rail) . . .9N 63
Ride, The RH14: Ifo 5D 192
TW8: Brent 1H 11
Ride La. GU5: Alb 4M 135
(not continuous)
Riders Way RH9: Gods 9F 104
Ride Way GU6: Ewh 9C 136
Rideway Cl. GU15: Camb 2N 69
Ridge, The CR3: Wold 4K 105
CR5: Coul 1J 83
CR6: Warl 4K 105
CR8: Pur 6G 63
GU22: Wok 4D 74
KT5: Surb 4N 41
KT18: Eps 5B 80
KT22: Fetc 2D 98
RH12: Rudg 9F 176
SL5: S'dale 6D 34
TW2: Whitt 1D 24
RIDGEBRIDGE HILL 1H 155
Ridge Cl. GU22: Wok 8L 73
RH3: Brock 7A 120
Ridge Ct. CR6: Warl 5D 84
SL4: W'sor 6F 4
Ridgegate Cl. RH2: Reig 1B 122
RIDGE GREEN 6J 123
Ridge Grn. RH1: Sth N 6J 123
Ridge Grn. Cl. RH1: Sth N 6J 123
Ridgehurst Dr. RH12: Hors 7F 196
Ridgelands KT22: Fetc 2D 98
Ridge Langley CR2: Sande 6D 64
Ridgemead Rd.
TW20: Eng G 4K 19
Ridgemoor Cl. GU26: Hind . . .4C 170
Ridgemount GU2: Guil 4L 113
KT13: Weybr 8F 38
Ridgemount Av. CR0: Croy 7G 47
CR5: Coul 4F 82
Ridgemount Est.
GU16: Deep 7G 70
Ridgemount Rd.
SL5: S'dale 7D 34
Ridgemount Way
RH1: Red 5B 122
Ridge Pk. CR8: Pur 6H 63
Ridge Rd. CR4: Mit 8F 28
SM3: Sut 7K 43
RIDGES, THE 3A 48
Ridges, The GU3: Art 8M 113
Ridgeside RH10: Craw 3D 182
(not continuous)
Ridges Yd.
CR0: Croy 4A 200 (9M 45)
Ridge Way GU25: V Wat 4A 36
TN8: Eden 8L 127
TW13: Hanw 4M 23
Ridge Way, The CR2: Sande . . .5B 64
Ridgeway GU21: Wok 2N 73
KT19: Eps 5G 201 (8B 60)
RH19: E Grin 2A 186
TW10: Rich 9L 11
Ridgeway, The CR0: Wad 9K 45
GU1: Guil 4C 114
GU6: Cranl 7A 156
GU18: Ligh 6M 51
GU24: B'wood 7C 72
KT12: Wal T 7G 38
KT22: Fetc 1D 98
KT22: Oxs 1C 78
RG12: Brac 2A 32
RH6: Horl 1E 162
RH12: Hors 4H 197
Ridgeway Cl. GU6: Cranl 7B 156
GU18: Ligh 7L 51
GU21: Wok 2N 73
KT22: Fetc 2E 98
KT22: Oxs 1C 78
RH4: Dork 7G 118
Ridgeway Ct. RH1: Red 4D 122
Ridgeway Cres. BR6: Orp 1N 67
Ridgeway Dr. RH4: Dork 8G 119
Ridgeway Gdns.
GU21: Wok 2N 73
Ridgeway Ho. RH6: Horl 1E 162
(off The Crescent)
Ridgeway Pde.
GU52: C Cro 8B 88
Ridgeway Rd. RH1: Red 3D 122
RH4: Dork 7G 118
TW7: Isle 3E 10
Ridgeway Rd. Nth.
TW7: Isle 2E 10
Ridgewood Dr. GU16: Frim 3H 71
Ridgley Rd. GU8: Chid 5D 172
Ridgmount Rd.
SW18 . . . . .8N 13
RIDGWAY 2J 75
Ridgway GU22: Pyr 2J 75
SW19 . . . . .8H 27
Ridgway, The SM2: Sut 4B 62
Ridgway Ct. SW19 . . . . .7J 27
Ridgway Gdns. SW19 . . . . .8J 27
Ridgway Hill Rd.
GU9: Farnh 3H 129
Ridgway Pde. GU9: Farnh 4H 129
(off Ridgway Rd.)
Ridgway Pl. SW19 . . . . .7K 27
Ridgway Rd. GU9: Farnh 4H 129
GU22: Pyr 2H 75
Riding, The GU6: Cranl 6N 155
GU21: Wok 1D 74
Riding Ct. Farm SL3: Dat 2L 5
Riding Ct. Rd.
SL3: Dat, Lang 3M 5
Riding Hill CR2: Sande 9D 64
Ridings, The GU16: Frim 3F 70
GU23: Rip 1J 95
KT5: Surb 4N 41
KT11: Cob 8A 58
KT15: Addl 3G 55
KT17: Ewe 5E 60
KT18: Eps 2D 80
KT20: Tad 7L 81
KT21: A'tead 4K 79
KT24: E Hor 3F 96
RH2: Reig 1B 122
RH10: Craw 2H 183
SL4: W'sor 3A 4
TN16: B Hil 4G 86
TW16: Sunb 9H 23
Ridings La. GU23: Ockh 1C 96
Ridlands Gro. RH8: Limp 8G 106
Ridlands La. RH8: Limp 8F 106
Ridlands Ri. RH8: Limp 8G 106
Ridley Cl. GU52: Fleet 6A 88
Ridley Ct. RH10: Craw 9H 163
SW16 . . . . .7J 29
Ridley Rd. CR6: Warl 5F 84
SW19 . . . . .8N 27
Ridleys Cnr. Rdbt.
RH10: Craw 1H 183
Ridsdale Rd. GU21: Wok 4L 73
Riesco Dr. CR0: Croy 3F 64
Rifle Butts All. KT18: Eps 1E 80
Rifle Way GU14: Cove 2H 89
Rigault Rd. SW6 . . . . .5K 13
Rigby Cl. CR0: Wad 9L 45
Riggindale Rd. SW16 . . . . .6H 29
Riley Cl. KT19: Eps 7A 60
Rillside RH10: Craw 6E 182
Rill Wlk. RH19: E Grin 9D 166
Rimbault Cl. GU11: Alde 6B 90
Rimmer Cl. RH11: Craw 9N 181
Rinaldo Rd. SW12 . . . . .1F 28
Rindle Cl. GU14: Cove 1H 89
Ring, The RG12: Brac 1N 31
Ringford Rd. SW18 . . . . .8L 13
Ringley Av. RH6: Horl 8E 142
Ringley Oak RH12: Hors 4M 197
Ringley Pk. Av. RH2: Reig 4B 122
Ringley Pk. Rd. RH2: Reig . . .3A 122
Ringley Rd. RH12: Hors 4L 197
Ringmead RG12: Brac 4K 31
(not continuous)
Ringmer Av. SW6 . . . . .4K 13
Ringmore Dr. GU4: Guil 9E 94
Ringmore Rd. KT12: Wal T 9K 39
Ring Rd. Nth. RH6: Gat 2F 162
Ring Rd. Sth. RH6: Gat 3G 162
Ringside TN8: Eden 1L 147
Ringstead Rd. SM1: Sut 1B 62
Ringway UB2: S'hall 1L 9
Ringwood RG12: Brac 6L 31
Ringwood Av. CR0: Croy 6J 45
RH1: Red 9D 102
Ringwood Cl. RH10: Craw . . .5C 182
SL5: Asc 3M 33
Ringwood Gdns. SW15 . . . . . . .2F 26
Ringwood Lodge RH1: Red . . .9E 102
Ringwood Rd. GU14: Farnb . . .7A 70
GU17: B'water 9H 49
Ringwood Way TW12: H Hill . . .5A 24
RIPLEY 8L 75
Ripley Av. TW20: Egh 7A 20
Ripley By-Pass GU23: Rip 1L 95
Ripley Cl. CR0: N Add 3M 65
Ripley Ct. CR4: Mit 1B 44
Ripley Gdns. SM1: Sut 1A 62
(not continuous)
SW14 . . . . .6C 12
Ripley La. GU23: Rip 1N 95
KT24: W Hors 3B 96
Ripley Rd. GU4: E Cla 7M 95
GU23: Send 4L 95
TW12: Hamp 8A 24
RIPLEY SPRINGS 7A 20
Ripley Way KT19: Eps 7N 59
Ripon Cl. GU2: Guil 1J 113
GU15: Camb 3H 71
Ripon Gdns. KT9: Ches 2K 59
Ripon Rd. GU17: Min 5E 68
Ripplesmere RG12: Brac 3B 32
Ripplesmore Cl.
GU47: Sandh 7G 48
Ripston Rd. TW15: A'ford 6E 22
Risborough Dr. KT4: W Pk 6F 42
Rise, The CR2: Sels 5F 64
KT17: Ewe 6E 60
KT20: Tad 7H 81
KT24: E Hor 4F 96
RG42: Warf 9E 16
RG45: Crow 2E 48
RH10: Craw 3G 183
RH19: E Grin 1B 186
Rise Rd. SL5: S'dale 4B 34
Ritchie Cl. RH10: Craw 7G 182
Ritchie Rd. CR0: Croy 5E 46
Ritherdon Rd. SW17 . . . . .3E 28
Riva Bingo 2J 29
RIVER ASH ESTATE 6G 39
River Av. KT7: T Dit 6G 41
River Bank KT7: T Dit 4F 40
KT8: E Mol 2E 40
TW12: Hamp 2A 40
Riverbank RH4: Westc 5B 118
TW18: Stain 7H 21
Riverbank, The SL4: W'sor 3E 4
Riverbank Way TW8: Brent 2J 11
River Bourne Health Club 6J 37
River Cl. GU1: Guil 1M 113
River Ct. GU21: Wok 1E 74
KT6: Surb 8H 203
TW17: Shep 6D 38
Rivercourt Rd. W6 . . . . .1G 12
River Crane Way
TW13: Hanw 3N 23
(off Watermill Way)
Riverdale GU10: Wrec 4D 128
Riverdale Dr. GU22: Wok 8B 74
SW18 . . . . .2N 27
Riverdale Gdns.
TW1: Twick 9J 11
Riverdale Rd. TW1: Twick 9J 11
TW13: Hanw 5M 23
Riverdene Ind. Est.
KT12: Hers 2L 57
Riverfield Rd. TW18: Stain 7H 21
River Gdns. SM5: Cars 8E 44
TW14: Felt 8J 9
River Gdns. Bus. Cen.
TW14: Felt 8J 9
River Gro. Pk. BR3: Beck 1J 47
Riverhead Dr. SM2: Sut 6N 61
River Hill KT11: Cob 2J 77
Riverhill KT4: W Pk 8C 42
Riverhill M. KT4: W Pk 9C 42
Riverhill Mobile Home Pl.
KT4: W Pk 8C 42
Riverholme Dr. KT19: Ewe 5C 60
Riverhouse Barn 6G 39
River Island Cl. KT22: Fetc 8D 78
River La. GU9: Farnh 4D 128
KT11: Cob 3M 77
KT22: Fetc, Leat 8D 78
TW10: Ham 1K 25
River Mead RH11: Ifi 9M 161
RH12: Hors 7H 197
Rivermead
KT1: K Tham 8H 203 (4K 41)
KT8: W Mole 2C 40
KT14: Byf 9A 56
Rivermead Cl. KT15: Addl 4L 55
TW11: Tedd 6H 25
Rivermead Ct. SW6 . . . . .6L 13
Rivermead Ho. TW16: Sunb 2K 39
(off Thames St.)
Rivermead Rd.
GU15: Camb 4N 69
River Meads Av.
TW2: Twick 4A 24
Rivermede GU35: Bor 5A 168
River Mole Bus. Pk.
KT10: Esh 8A 40
River Mt. KT12: Wal T 6G 38
Rivermount Gdns.
GU2: Guil 8B 202 (6M 113)
Rivernook Cl. KT12: Wal T 4K 39
River Pk. Av. TW18: Stain 5F 20
River Reach TW11: Tedd 6J 25
River Rd. GU46: Yate 7A 48
SL4: W'sor 3A 4
TW18: Stain 9H 21
River Row GU9: Farnh 4E 128
River Row Cotts.
GU9: Farnh 3E 128
Rivers Cl. GU14: Farnb 4C 90
Riversdale Rd. KT7: T Dit 4G 40
Riversdell Cl. KT16: Chert 6H 37
Rivers Ho. TW7: Isle 7H 11
(off Richmond Rd.)
W4 . . . . .1N 11
(off Chiswick High Rd.)
Riverside GU1: Guil 1N 113
KT16: Chert 1J 37
RH4: Dork 3K 119
RH6: Horl 1E 162
RH12: Hors 6G 196
RH18: F Row 6G 187
TN8: Eden 2L 147
TW1: Twick 2H 25
TW9: Rich 8K 11
TW16: Sunb 2L 39
TW17: Shep 6F 38
TW18: Stain 9H 21
TW19: Wray 1M 19
TW20: Egh 4C 20
Riverside, The KT8: E Mol 2D 40
Riverside Arts Cen. 2K 39
(off Thames St.)

Riverside Av.—Rosevine Rd.

Riverside Av. GU18: Ligh 7N 51
KT8: E Mol 4D 40
Riverside Bus. Cen.
GU1: Guil 3A 202 (3M 113)
SW18 . . . . .2N 27
Riverside Bus. Pk.
GU9: Farnh 9J 109
SW19 . . . . .9A 28
Riverside Cl. GU14: Cove 9L 69
GU24: B'wood 7C 72
KT1: K Tham 7H 203 (3K 41)
SM6: W'ton 9F 44
TW18: Stain 9H 21
Riverside Ct. GU9: Farnh 9H 109
KT22: Fetc 9G 78
RH4: Dork 3K 119
TN8: Eden 2M 147
TW7: Isle 5F 10
(off Woodlands Rd.)
TW14: Felt 1F 22
Riverside Dr. CR4: Mit 4C 44
GU5: Braml 4C 134
KT10: Esh 1A 58
TW10: Ham 4H 25
TW18: Stain 6G 21
W4 . . . . .3C 12
Riverside Gdns.
GU22: Wok 8D 74
W6 . . . . .1G 13
Riverside Health & Raquets Club
. . . . .4D 12
Riverside Ind. Pk.
GU9: Farnh 9J 109
Riverside M. CR0: Bedd 9J 45
Riverside Pk. GU9: Farnh 9J 109
KT13: Addl 2N 55
SL3: Poy 5G 6
Riverside Pk. (Watchmoor Pk.)
GU15: Camb 3M 69
Riverside Pl. TW19: Stan 9M 7
Riverside Rd. KT12: Hers 1L 57
SW17 . . . . .5N 27
TW18: Stain 8H 21
TW19: Stan 8M 7
(not continuous)
Riverside Studios 1H 13
Riverside Vs. KT6: Surb 5J 41
Riverside Wlk.
BR4: W Wick 7L 47
GU7: Goda 6G 133
KT1: K Tham . . .3G 203 (2K 41)
SL4: W'sor 3G 5
(off Thames Side)
SW6 . . . . .6K 13
TW7: Isle 6E 10
W4 . . . . .2E 12
(off Chiswick Wharf)
Riverside Way
GU15: Camb 3M 69
Riverside Yd. SW17 . . . . .5A 28
Riverstone Ct.
KT2: K Tham . . .2L 203 (9M 25)
River St. SL4: W'sor 3G 4
River Ter. W6 . . . . .1H 13
River Thames Vis. Cen. 8K 11
(within Mus. of Richmond)
River Vw. KT15: Addl 2L 55
Riverview
GU1: Guil 2A 202 (3M 113)
River Vw. Gdns. TW1: Twick . . .3F 24
Riverview Gdns. KT11: Cob 9H 57
SW13 . . . . .2G 13
Riverview Gro. W4 . . . . .2A 12
Riverview Rd. KT19: Ewe 1B 60
W4 . . . . .3A 12
River Wlk. KT12: Wal T 5H 39
W6 . . . . .3H 13
River Way KT19: Ewe 2C 60
TW2: Twick 3B 24
Riverway TW18: Stain 9K 21
Riverway Est.
GU3: P'marsh 3M 133
Riverwood Ct. GU1: Guil 1M 113
Rivett Drake Cl. GU2: Guil 8L 93
Rivey Cl. KT14: W By 1H 75
RLC Mus. 6H 71
Road Ho. Est. GU22: Wok 8C 74
Roakes Av. KT15: Addl 8J 37
Roan Ind. Est. CR4: Mit 9D 28
(off Lavender Av.)
Roasthill La. SL4: Dorn 2A 4
Robert Cl. KT12: Hers 2J 57
Robert Gentry Ho.
W14 . . . . .1K 13
(off Gledstanes Rd.)
Robert Owen Ho. SW6 . . . . . . .4J 13
Robertsbridge Rd.
SM5: Cars 7A 44
Roberts Cl. CR7: T Hea 2A 46
SM3: Chea 4J 61
TW19: Stan 9L 7
Roberts Ct. KT9: Ches 2K 59
Robertson Ct. GU21: Wok 5H 73
Robertson Gro. SW17 . . . . .6C 28
Robertson Way GU12: Ash . . .3D 110
Roberts Rd. GU12: Alde 3A 110
GU15: Camb 9M 49
Robert St.
CR0: Croy 4C 200 (9N 45)
Roberts Way GU6: Cranl 6N 155
TW20: Eng G 8M 19
Robert Way GU16: Mytc 2D 90
RH12: Hors 1M 197
Robin Cl. GU12: A Va 7E 90
KT15: Addl 2M 55
RH11: Craw 1A 182
RH19: E Grin 8B 166
TW12: Hamp 6M 23
Robin Ct. SM6: W'ton 2G 63
Robin Gdns. RH1: Red 1E 122
Robin Gro. TW8: Brent 2J 11
Robin Hill GU7: Goda 4G 133
Robin Hill Dr. GU15: Camb 3E 70
ROBIN HOOD 4D 26
Robin Hood Cl.
GU14: Farnb 7M 69
GU21: Wok 5J 73
Robinhood Cl. CR4: Mit 2G 45
Robin Hood Cres.
GU21: Knap 4H 73
Robin Hood La.
GU4: Sut G 2B 94
RH12: Warn 3E 196
SM1: Sut 2M 61
SW15 . . . . .4D 26
Robinhood La. CR4: Mit 2G 45
Robin Hood Rd.
GU21: Knap, Wok 4G 73
(not continuous)
SW19 . . . . .6F 26
Robin Hood Rdbt.
RH12: Warn 3H 197
Robin Hood Way
SW15 . . . . .4D 26
SW20 . . . . .4D 26
Robin Hood Works
GU21: Knap 4H 73
Robinites GU7: Goda 4E 132
Robin La. GU47: Sandh 7G 49
(not continuous)
Robin Row RH10: T Hil 4F 184
Robin's Bow GU15: Camb 2N 69
Robins Ct. BR3: Beck 1N 47
CR2: S Croy 7F 200
Robins Dale GU21: Knap 4F 72
Robins Gro. Cres.
GU46: Yate 9A 48
Robinson Cl. GU22: Wok 7E 74
Robinson Ct. CR7: T Hea 5M 45
TW9: Rich 7M 11
Robinson Ho. RH11: Craw . . .4B 182
Robinson Rd. SW17 . . . . .7C 28
Robinsway KT12: Hers 1K 57
Robinswood Ct.
RH12: Hors 4M 197
Robin Way GU2: Guil 8L 93
TW18: Stain 4H 21
Robin Willis Way
SL4: O Win 9K 5
Robinwood Pl. SW15 . . . . .5C 26
Robson Rd. SE27 . . . . .4M 29
Roby Dr. RG12: Brac 6B 32
Robyns Way TN8: Eden 3M 147
Roche Rd. SW16 . . . . .9K 29
Rochester Av. TW13: Felt 3G 23
Rochester Cl. SW16 . . . . .8J 29
Rochester Gdns. CR0: Croy . . .9B 46
CR3: Cate 9B 84
Rochester Gro. GU51: Fleet . . .5B 88
Rochester Pde. TW13: Felt 3H 23
Rochester Rd. SM5: Cars 1D 62
TW18: Stain 7F 20
Rochester Wlk. RH2: Reig . . .8N 121
Roche Wlk. SM5: Cars 5B 44
Rochford Way CR0: Croy 5J 45
Rock Av. SW14 . . . . .6C 12
Rock Cl. CR4: Mit 1B 44
Rockdale Dr. GU26: G'hott . . .6B 170
Rockdale Ho.
GU26: G'hott 6B 170
Rockdene Cl.
RH19: E Grin 9C 166
Rockery, The GU14: Cove 2J 89
Rockfield Cl. RH8: Oxt 9B 106
Rockfield Rd. RH8: Oxt 7B 106
Rockfield Way
GU47: C Tow 7J 49
Rock Gdns. GU11: Alde 3L 109
Rockhampton Cl. SE27 . . . . . . .5L 29
Rockhampton Rd.
CR2: S Croy 3B 64
SE27 . . . . .5L 29
Rock Hill GU8: Hamb 8G 152
Rock Ho. La. GU10: Farnh . . .9L 109
Rockingham Cl. SW15 . . . . . . .7E 12
Rockland Rd. SW15 . . . . .7K 13
Rock La. GU10: Wrec 6F 128
Rocks, The RH19: Ash W 3E 186
Rockshaw Rd. RH1: Mers 5G 102
Rocks La. SW13 . . . . .4F 12
ROCKWOOD PARK 4M 185
Rocky La. RH2: Reig 6D 102
Rocque Ho. SW6 . . . . .3L 13
(off Estcourt Rd.)
Rodale Mans. SW18 . . . . .9N 13
Rodborough Hill Cotts.
GU8: Mil 3N 151
Rodd Est. TW17: Shep 4D 38
Roden Gdns. CR0: Croy 5B 46
Rodenhurst Rd. SW4 . . . . .1G 29
Rodgate La. GU27: Hasl 3A 190
Rodgers Ho. SW4 . . . . .1H 29
(off Clapham Pk. Est.)
Roding Cl. GU6: Cranl 8H 155
Rodmel Ct. GU14: Farnb 4C 90
Rodmill La. SW2 . . . . .1J 29
Rodney Cl.
CR0: Croy 1A 200 (7M 45)
KT3: N Mal 4D 42
KT12: Wal T 7K 39
Rodney Gdns. BR4: W Wick . . .1C 66
Rodney Grn. KT12: Wal T 8K 39
Rodney Pl. SW19 . . . . .9A 28
Rodney Rd. CR4: Mit 2C 44
KT3: N Mal 4D 42
KT12: Wal T 8K 39
TW2: Whitt 9A 10
Rodney Way GU1: Guil 2C 114
SL3: Poy 4G 7
Rodona Rd. KT13: Weybr 7E 56
Rodsall La. GU3: Put 3K 131
Rodway Rd. SW15 . . . . .1F 26
Rodwell Ct. KT12: Wal T 9J 39
KT15: Addl 1L 55
Roebuck Cl. KT21: A'tead 7L 79
RH2: Reig 3M 121
RH13: Hors 4A 198
TW13: Felt 5J 23
Roebuck Est. RG42: Bin 8H 15
Roebuck Rd. KT9: Ches 2N 59
Roedean Cres. SW15 . . . . .9D 12
Roedeer Copse
GU27: Hasl 2C 188
ROEHAMPTON 1F 26
Roehampton Cl. SW15 . . . . . . .7F 12
Roehampton Ga.
SW15 . . . . .9D 12
Roehampton High St.
SW15 . . . . .1F 26
ROEHAMPTON LANE 2G 27
Roehampton La. SW15 . . . . . . .7F 12
Roehampton Recreation Cen.
. . . . .1F 26
Roehampton Va. SW15 . . . . . . .4E 26
Roe Way SM6: W'ton 3J 63
Roffe's La. CR3: Cate 2A 104
ROFFEY 4N 197
Roffey Cl. CR8: Pur 3M 83
RH6: Horl 8D 142
ROFFEY PARK 2E 198
Roffey Pk. RH12: Col 2D 198
Roffey's Cl. RH10: Cop 6L 163
Roffey Social and Sports Club
. . . . .3N 197
(off Spooners Rd.)
Roffords GU21: Wok 4L 73
Roffye Ct. RH12: Hors 4N 197
Rogers Cl. CR3: Cate 9E 84
CR5: Coul 5M 83
Roger Simmons Ct.
KT23: Book 2N 97
Rogers La. CR6: Warl 5J 85
Rogers Mead RH9: Gods 1E 124
Rogers Rd. SW17 . . . . .5B 28
ROGER'S TOWN 6N 167
Rokeby Cl. RG12: Brac 9B 16
Rokeby Ct. GU21: Wok 4J 73
Rokeby Ho. SW12 . . . . .1F 28
(off Lochinvar St.)
Rokeby Pl. SW20 . . . . .8G 27
Roke Cl. CR8: Ken 1N 83
GU8: Wit 5B 152
Roke La. GU8: Wit 6N 151
Roke Lodge Rd. CR8: Pur 9M 63
Roke Rd. CR8: Ken 2N 83
Rokers La. GU8: S'ford 4A 132
(not continuous)
Rokewood Dr. RH11: Ifi 9M 161
Roland Way KT4: W Pk 8E 42
Rolinsden Way BR2: Kes 2F 66
Rollesby Rd. KT9: Ches 3N 59
Rolleston Rd. CR2: S Croy 4A 64
Rollit Cres. TW3: Houn 8A 10
Rolls Royce Cl. SM6: W'ton . . .4J 63
Rolston Ho. GU27: Hasl 2D 188
Romana Ct. TW18: Stain 5J 21
Romanby Ct. RH1: Red 4D 122
Roman Cl. TW14: Felt 8K 9
Roman Ct. TN8: Eden 2L 147
Roman Farm Way
GU2: Guil 2G 113
Romanfield Rd. SW2 . . . . .1K 29
Romanhurst Gdns.
BR2: Brom 3N 47
Roman Ind. Est. CR0: Croy 6B 46
Roman Ride RG45: Crow 2C 48
Roman Rd. RH4: Dork 7G 119
TN8: M Grn 5M 147
Romans Bus. Pk.
GU9: Farnh 9J 109
Romans Way GU22: Pyr 2J 75
Roman Way
CR0: Croy 2A 200 (8M 45)
GU9: Farnh 8K 109
RG42: Warf 9D 16
SM5: Cars 5D 62
Romany, The GU14: Farnb 4F 88
Romany Gdns. SM3: Sut 6M 43
Romany Rd. GU21: Knap 2F 72
Roma Read Cl. SW15 . . . . .1G 26
Romayne Cl. GU14: Cove 9M 69
Romberg Rd. SW17 . . . . .4E 28
Romeo Hill RG42: Warf 9D 16
Romeyn Rd. SW16 . . . . .4K 29
Romily Ct. SW6 . . . . .5L 13
Romley Ct. GU9: Farnh 2J 129
Romney Cl. KT9: Ches 1L 59
TW15: A'ford 6D 22
Romney Ho. RG12: Brac 3C 32
Romney Lock SL4: W'sor 2H 5
Romney Lock Rd.
SL4: W'sor 3G 5
Romney Rd. KT3: N Mal 5C 42
Romney Wlk. SL4: W'sor 3G 5
Romola Rd. SE24 . . . . .2M 29
Romsey Cl. BR6: Farnb 1K 67
GU11: Alde 6A 110
GU17: B'water 9H 49
Romulus Ct. TW8: Brent 3K 11
Rona Cl. RH11: Craw 6N 181
Ronald Cl. BR3: Beck 3J 47
Ronald Ross Rd.
GU2: Guil 4H 113
Ronelean Rd. KT6: Surb 8M 41
Ronneby Cl. KT13: Weybr 9F 38
Ronson Way KT22: Leat 8G 78
Roof of the World Cvn. Pk.
KT20: Box H 9A 100
Rookeries Cl. TW13: Felt 4J 23
Rookery, The RH4: Westc 7A 118
Rookery Cl. KT22: Fetc 2E 98
Rookery Dr. RH4: Westc 7A 118
Rookery Hill KT21: A'tead 5N 79
RH1: Out 4L 143
RH6: Out 4L 143
Rookery La.
RH6: Out, Smal 6L 143
Rookery Mead CR5: Coul 9H 83
Rookery Rd. BR6: Dow 6H 67
TW18: Stain 6K 21
Rookery Way KT20: Lwr K 5L 101
Rook La. CR3: Cate 3K 103
Rookley Cl. SM2: Sut 5N 61
Rooks Hill GU5: Braml 9D 134
Rooksmead Rd.
TW16: Sunb 1G 39
ROOKS NEST 8H 105
Rookstone Rd. SW17 . . . . .6D 28
Rookswood RG42: Brac 8N 15
Rook Way RH12: Hors 2M 197
Rookwood Av. GU47: Owls 5K 49
KT3: N Mal 3F 42
SM6: Bedd 1H 63
Rookwood Cl. RH1: Mers 7F 102
Rookwood Ct.
GU2: Guil 8A 202 (6M 113)
Rookwood Pk. RH12: Hors 5F 196
Rookwood Pl. RH1: Mers 6F 102
(off London Rd. Sth.)
Roosthole Hill RH13: Col 8C 198
Roothill La. RH3: Betch 1N 139
Ropeland Way RH12: Hors 1L 197
Ropers Wlk. SW2 . . . . .1L 29
Roper Way CR4: Mit 1E 44
Rope Wlk. TW16: Sunb 2K 39
Rorkes Drift GU16: Mytc 1D 90
Rosa Av. TW15: A'ford 5B 22
Rosalind Franklin Cl.
GU2: Guil 4H 113
Rosaline Rd. SW6 . . . . .3K 13
Rosaline Ter. SW6 . . . . .3K 13
(off Rosaline Rd.)
Rosamund Cl.
CR2: S Croy 7E 200 (1A 64)
Rosamund Rd.
RH10: Craw 5F 182
Rosamun St. UB2: S'hall 1M 9
Rosary Cl. TW3: Houn 5M 9
Rosary Gdns. GU46: Yate 9C 48
TW15: A'ford 5C 22
Rosaville Rd. SW6 . . . . .3L 13
Roseacre RH8: Oxt 3C 126
Roseacre Cl. SM1: Sut 8A 44
TW17: Shep 4B 38
Roseacre Gdns. GU4: Guil . . .9H 115
Rose & Crown Pas.
TW7: Isle 4G 11
Rose Av. CR4: Mit 9D 28
SM4: Mord 4A 44
Rosebank
KT18: Eps 8H 201 (1B 80)
SW6 . . . . .3H 13
Rosebank Cl. TW11: Tedd 7G 25
Rose Bank Cotts.
GU22: Wok 9A 74
Rosebay RG40: W'ham 9D 14
Roseberry Gdns. BR6: Orp 1N 67
Rosebery Av. CR7: T Hea 1N 45
KT3: N Mal 1E 42
KT17: Eps 8M 201 (1D 80)
Rosebery Cl. SM4: Mord 5J 43
Rosebery Cres. GU22: Wok 7B 74
Rosebery Gdns. SM1: Sut 1N 61
Rosebery Rd. KT1: K Tham 1A 42
KT18: Eps D 6C 80
SM1: Sut 3L 61
TW3: Houn 8C 10
Roseberys, The KT18: Eps 1D 80
Rosebery Sq. KT1: K Tham 1A 42
Rosebine Av. TW2: Twick 1D 24
Rosebriar Cl. GU22: Pyr 3J 75
Rosebriars CR3: Cate 7B 84
KT10: Esh 2C 58
(not continuous)
Rosebury Dr. GU24: Bis 2D 72
Rosebury Rd. SW6 . . . . .5N 13
Rose Bushes KT17: Eps D 3G 81
Rose Cotts. BR2: Kes 7E 66
GU8: Worm 8D 152
RH12: Fay 9H 181
RH18: F Row 6G 187
Rose Ct. RG40: W'ham 2B 30
Rosecourt Rd. CR0: Croy 5K 45
Rosecroft Cl. TN16: B Hil 5H 87
Rosecroft Gdns.
TW2: Twick 2D 24
Rosedale CR3: Cate 1B 104
GU12: Alde 2A 110
KT21: A'tead 5J 79
RG42: Bin 6H 15
Rosedale Cl. RH11: Craw . . .5M 181
Rosedale Gdns.
RG12: Brac 4M 31
Rosedale Pl. CR0: Croy 6G 47
Rosedale Rd. KT17: Ewe 2F 60
TW9: Rich 6L 11
Rosedene Av. CR0: Croy 6J 45
SM4: Mord 4M 43
SW16 . . . . .4K 29
Rosedene Gdns.
GU51: Fleet 3A 88
Rosedene La.
GU47: C Tow 9J 49
Rosedew Rd. W6 . . . . .2J 13
Rose End KT4: W Pk 7J 43
Rosefield Cl. SM5: Cars 2C 62
Rosefield Gdns.
KT16: Otter 3F 54
Rosefield Rd. TW18: Stain 5J 21
Rose Gdns. GU14: Cove 2K 89
RG40: W'ham 2B 30
TW13: Felt 3H 23
TW19: Stan 1M 21
Roseheath Rd. TW4: Houn 8N 9
ROSE HILL 3K 201 (5G 119)
ROSEHILL 6A 44
Rose Hill RG42: Bin 6H 15
RH4: Dork 3J 201 (5G 119)
SM1: Sut 8N 43
Rosehill KT10: Clay 3G 58
RH2: Reig 2B 122
TW12: Hamp 9A 24
Rose Hill Arch M.
RH4: Dork 2K 201
Rose Hill Av. SM5: Sut 7A 44
Rosehill Av. GU21: Wok 3M 73
Rosehill Ct. SM4: Mord 6A 44
(off St Helier Av.)
Rosehill Ct. Pde.
SM4: Mord 6A 44
(off St Helier Av.)
Rosehill Farm Mdw.
SM7: Ban 2N 81
Rosehill Gdns. SM1: Sut 8N 43
Rose Hill Pk. W. SM1: Sut 7A 44
Rosehill Rd. SW18 . . . . .9N 13
TN16: B Hil 4E 86
ROSE HILL RDBT. 6A 44
Rose La. GU23: Rip 8L 75
Roseleigh Cl. TW1: Twick 9K 11
Rosemary Av. GU12: A Va 5E 90
KT8: W Mole 2A 40
TW4: Houn 5L 9
Rosemary Cl. CR0: Croy 5J 45
GU14: Cove 9J 69
RH8: Oxt 2C 126
Rosemary Ct. GU27: Hasl 1G 188
RH6: Horl 7C 142
Rosemary Cres. GU2: Guil 8J 93
Rosemary Gdns.
GU17: B'water 1H 69
KT9: Ches 1L 59
SW14 . . . . .6B 12
Rosemary Ga. KT10: Esh 2C 58
Rosemary La. GU6: Alf 9E 174
GU10: Rowl 7D 128
GU17: B'water 9H 49
RH6: Char 3K 161
RH6: Horl 9F 142
SW14 . . . . .6B 12
TW20: Thor 2D 36
Rosemary Rd. SW17 . . . . .4A 28
Rosemead KT16: Chert 6K 37
Rosemead Av. CR4: Mit 2G 45
TW13: Felt 3G 22
Rosemead Cl. RH1: Red 5B 122
Rosemead Gdns.
RH10: Craw 4C 182
(off Richmond Ct.)
Rose Mdw. GU24: W End 9D 52
Rosemont Rd. KT3: N Mal 2B 42
TW10: Rich 9L 11
Rosemount SM6: W'ton 3G 62
(off Clarendon Rd.)
Rosemount Av.
KT14: W By 9J 55
Rosendale Rd. SE21 . . . . .4N 29
SE24 . . . . .1N 29
Roseneath Ct. CR3: Cate 3D 104
Roseneath Dr. GU8: Chid 5E 172
Roseneath Pl. SW16 . . . . .5K 29
(off Curtis Fld. Rd.)
Rose Pk. KT15: Otter 5G 54
Rosery, The CR0: Croy 5G 46
TW20: Thor 1G 36
Rose's Cotts. RH4: Dork 2J 201
(off Junction Rd.)
Roses La. SL4: W'sor 5A 4
Rose St. RG40: W'ham 2B 30
Rosethorn Cl. SW12 . . . . .1H 29
Rosetrees GU1: Guil 4C 114
Rose Vw. KT15: Addl 2L 55
Roseville Av. TW3: Houn 8A 10
Roseville Rd. UB3: Harl 1H 9
Rosevine Rd. SW20 . . . . .9H 27

Rose Wlk.—Ruxley Cl.

Rose Wlk. BR4: W Wick 8M 47
CR8: Pur 7H 63
GU51: Fleet 3A 88
KT5: Surb 4A 42
RH11: Craw 5N 181
Rosewarne Cl. GU21: Wok 5K 73
Rosewood GU22: Wok 6C 74
KT7: T Dit 8G 40
SM2: Sut 6A 62
Rosewood Ct. KT2: K Tham 8N 25
Rosewood Dr. TW17: Shep 4A 38
Rosewood Gro. SM1: Sut 8A 44
Rosewood Rd. GU35: Lind 4B 168
Rosewood Way GU24: W End 9B 52
Roshni Ho. SW17 7C 28
Roskell Rd. SW15 6J 13
Roslan Ct. RH6: Horl 9F 142
Roslyn Cl. CR4: Mit 1B 44
Roslyn Ct. GU21: Wok 5K 73
Ross Cl. RH10: Craw 6D 182
Ross Ct. RH6: Horl 8F 142
SW15 1J 27
Rossdale SM1: Sut 2C 62
Rossdale Rd. SW15 7H 13
Rossett Cl. RG12: Brac 3N 31
Rossetti Gdns. CR5: Coul 5K 83
Rossignol Gdns. SM5: Cars 8E 44
Rossindel Rd. TW3: Houn 8A 10
Rossiter Lodge GU1: Guil 4C 114
Rossiter Rd. SW12 2F 28
Rosslare Cl. TN16: Weste 3M 107
Rosslea GU20: Windl 1L 51
Rosslyn Av. SW13 6D 12
TW14: Felt 9H 9
Rosslyn Cl. TW16: Sunb 7F 22
Rosslyn Pk. KT13: Weybr 1E 56
Rosslyn Pk. RUFC 7E 12
Rosslyn Rd. TW1: Twick 9J 11
Rossmore Cl. RH10: Craw 8H 163
Rossmore Gdns. GU11: Alde 3K 109
Ross Pde. SM6: W'ton 3F 62
Ross Rd. KT11: Cob 9K 57
SE25 2A 46
SM6: W'ton 2G 62
TW2: Whitt 2B 24
Rosswood Gdns. SM6: W'ton 3G 62
Rostella Rd. SW17 5B 28
Rostrevor Gdns. UB2: S'hall 1M 9
Rostrevor M. SW6 4L 13
Rostrevor Rd. SW6 4L 13
SW19 6M 27
Rothbury Gdns. TW7: Isle 3G 10
Rothbury Wlk. GU15: Camb 2G 71
Rother Cl. GU47: Sandh 7H 49
Rother Cres. RH11: Craw 4L 181
Rotherfield Rd. SM5: Cars 1E 62
Rotherhill Av. SW16 7H 29
Rother Rd. GU14: Cove 8K 69
Rothervale RH6: Horl 5E 142
Rotherwick Ct. GU14: Farnb 5A 90
Rotherwood Cl. SW20 9K 27
Rotherwood Rd. SW15 6J 13
Rothesay Av. SW20 1K 43
TW10: Rich 7A 12
Rothesay Rd. SE25 3A 46
Rothes Rd. RH4: Dork 1K 201 (4H 119)
Rothsay Ct. KT13: Weybr 3E 56
Rothschild St. SE27 5M 29
Rothwell Ho. RG45: Crow 3H 49
TW5: Hest 2A 10
Rotunda Cen., The 3K 203 (1L 41)
Rotunda Est. GU11: Alde 2N 109
Rougemont Av. SM4: Mord 5M 43
Rough, The GU22: Wok 4F 74
ROUGHETS, THE 7C 104
Roughets La. RH1: Blet 7B 104
Rough Fld. RH19: E Grin 6N 165
Roughgrove Copse RG42: Bin 7G 15
Roughlands GU22: Pyr 2G 75
Rough Rew RH4: Dork 8H 119
Rough Rd. GU22: Wok 9F 72
Rough Way RH12: Hors 3M 197
Rounce La. GU24: W End 9A 52
Roundabout Rd. RH10: Cop 6A 164
Roundacre SW19 3J 27
Roundals La. GU8: Hamb 1H 173
Round Cl. GU46: Yate 1E 68
Round Gro. CR0: Croy 6G 47
ROUND HILL 1K 109
Roundhill GU22: Wok 6D 74
Roundhill Dr. GU22: Wok 5D 74
Roundhill Way GU2: Guil 3J 113
KT11: Cob 7B 58
ROUNDHURST 7M 189
Round Oak Rd. KT13: Weybr 1A 56
ROUNDSHAW 4J 63
Roundshead Dr. RG42: Warf 9B 16
ROUNDS HILL 9L 15
Rounds Hill RG12: Brac 9K 15
Roundthorn Way GU21: Wok 3J 73
Roundway GU15: Camb 9G 50
TN16: B Hil 3E 86
TW20: Egh 6E 20
Roundway, The KT10: Clay 3F 58
Roundway Cl. GU15: Camb 9G 50
Roundway Ct. RH10: Craw 1B 182
Roundwood Vw. SM7: Ban 2J 81
Roundwood Way SM7: Ban 2J 81
Rounton Rd. GU52: C Cro 7B 88
Roupell Ho. KT2: K Tham 1M 203
Roupell Rd. SW2 2K 29
Routh Ct. TW14: Bedf 2E 22
Routh Rd. SW18 1C 28
Row, The TN8: Eden 8K 127
Rowallan Rd. SW6 3K 13
Rowan RG12: Brac 4D 32
Rowan Av. TW20: Egh 6E 20
Rowan Chase GU10: Wrec 6F 128
Rowan Cl. GU1: Guil 9L 93
GU15: Camb 7D 50
GU51: Fleet 4D 88
KT3: N Mal 1D 42
RH2: Reig 5A 122
RH10: Craw 3D 182
RH12: Hors 3A 198
SW16 9G 29
TW15: A'ford 5M 21
Rowan Ct. SW11 1D 28
Rowan Cres. SW16 9G 29
Rowan Dale GU52: C Cro 8A 88
Rowan Dr. RG45: Crow 9H 31
Rowan Gdns. CR0: Croy 9C 46
Rowan Grn. KT13: Weybr 1E 56
Rowan Gro. CR5: Coul 8F 82
Rowan Hall *TW20: Eng G 4M 19*
(off Coopers Hill La.)
Rowan Mead KT20: Tad 6G 81
Rowan Rd. SW16 1G 45
TW8: Brent 3H 11
UB7: W Dray 1M 7
Rowans, The GU22: Wok 5A 74
GU26: Hind 7B 170
TW16: Sunb 6G 23
Rowans Cl. GU14: Cove 5K 69
Rowanside Cl. GU35: H Dwn 5H 169
Rowan Wlk. RH10: Craw D 1F 184
Rowan Way RH12: Hors 3A 198
Rowbarns Way KT24: E Hor 8G 97
Rowberry Cl. SW6 3H 13
Rowbury GU7: Goda 3K 133
Rowcliffe Springs GU8: Hasc 6A 154
Rowcroft Cl. GU12: A Va 7E 90
Rowden Rd. KT19: Ewe 1A 60
Rowdown Cres. CR0: N Add 5N 65
Rowe La. GU24: Pirb 2D 92
Rowena Ho. *RH11: Craw 9B 162*
(off Dobson Rd.)
ROWFANT 2A 184
Rowfant Bus. Cen. RH10: Row 3A 184
Rowfant Cl. RH10: Wor 3J 183
Rowfant Rd. SW17 2E 28
Rowfield TN8: Eden 9M 127
ROWHILL 3H 55
Rowhill KT15: Addl 3H 55
Rowhill Av. GU11: Alde 3L 109
Rowhill Cl. GU14: Cove 1H 89
Rowhill Cres. GU11: Alde 4L 109
Rowhill Nature Reserve 4K 109
Rowhills GU9: H End 4J 109
Rowhills Cl. GU9: Weybo 5L 109
ROWHOOK 8M 177
Rowhook Hill RH12: Rowh 8M 177
Rowhook Rd. RH12: Rowh, Bro H 9N 177
(not continuous)
Rowhurst Av. KT15: Addl 3K 55
KT22: Leat 4F 78
Rowland Cl. RH10: Cop 5B 164
SL4: W'sor 6A 4
Rowland Hill Almshouses *TW15: A'ford 6B 22*
(off Feltham Hill Rd.)
Rowland Ho. GU6: Cranl 7M 155
Rowland Rd. GU6: Cranl 7M 155
Rowlands Rd. RH12: Hors 2N 197
Rowland Way SW19 9N 27
TW15: A'ford 8E 22
Row La. GU5: Alb 8N 135
(not continuous)
ROWLEDGE 8D 128
ROWLEY 4K 155
Rowley Cl. GU22: Pyr 3K 75
RG12: Brac 2C 32
Rowley Ct. CR3: Cate 9A 84
Rowlls Rd. KT1: K Tham 5M 203 (2M 41)
Rowly Dr. GU6: Cranl 5J 155
Rowly Edge GU6: Cranl 4J 155
Rowntree Rd. TW2: Twick 2E 24
Rowplatt Cl. RH19: Fel 6H 165
Rowplatt La. RH19: Fel 7H 165
ROW TOWN 3J 55
Row Town KT15: Addl 4H 55
Roxbee Cox Rd. GU14: Farnb 3E 88
Roxborough Av. TW7: Isle 3F 10
Roxburgh Cl. GU15: Camb 2G 71
Roxburgh Rd. SE27 6M 29
Roxby Pl. SW6 2M 13
Roxeth Ct. TW15: A'ford 6B 22
Roxford Cl. TW17: Shep 4F 38
Roxton Gdns. CR0: A'ton 2K 65
Royal Aerospace Establishment Rd. GU14: Farnb 4N 89
Royal Army Medical Corps Mus. 4F 90
Royal Ascot Golf Course 1L 33
Royal Av. KT4: W Pk 8D 42
Royal Botanic Gdns. 4L 11
Royal Cir. SE27 4L 29
Royal Cl. BR6: Farnb 1L 67
KT4: W Pk 8D 42
SW19 4J 27
Royal County of Berkshire Racquets and Health Club, The 7B 32
Royal Dr. KT18: Tat C 5G 80
Royal Duchess M. SW12 1F 28
Royal Earlswood Pk. RH1: Red 6E 122
Royale Cl. GU11: Alde 4A 110
Royal Free Ct. *SL4: W'sor 4G 4*
(off Batchelors Acre)
Royal Holloway University of London 7N 19
Royal Holloway University Sports Cen. 8A 20
Royal Horticultural Society Cotts. GU23: Wis 3N 75
Royal Horticultural Society Gardens, The (Wisley) 5N 75
Royal Huts Av. GU26: Hind 5D 170
Royal Mausoleum 6H 5
Royal M. KT8: E Mol 2E 40
SL4: W'sor 4G 5
Royal Mid Surrey Golf Course 6K 11
Royal Military Academy Sandhurst 8M 49
Royal Oak Cl. GU46: Yate 9D 48
Royal Oak Dr. RG45: Crow 8G 30
Royal Oak Ho. RH10: Craw D 2E 184
Royal Oak M. TW11: Tedd 6G 25
Royal Oak Rd. GU21: Wok 5M 73
Royal Orchard Cl. SW18 1K 27
Royal Pde. GU26: Hind 5D 170
SW6 3K 13
TW9: Kew 4N 11
(off Station App.)
Royal Quarter KT2: K Tham 2H 203 (9L 25)
Royal Rd. TW11: Tedd 6D 24
Royals, The GU1: Guil 5E 202 (4N 113)
Royal Victoria Gdns. SL5: Asc 4L 33
Royal Wlk. SM6: W'ton 8F 44
Royal Windsor Racecourse 2B 4
Royce Rd. RH10: Craw 7E 162
Roycroft Cl. SW2 2L 29
Roydon Ct. KT12: Hers 1H 57
TW20: Egh 7F 20
Roy Gro. TW12: Hamp 7B 24
Roymount Ct. TW2: Twick 4E 24
Royston Av. KT14: Byf 8N 55
SM1: Sut 9B 44
SM6: Bedd 1H 63
Royston Cen., The GU12: A Va 5D 90
Royston Cl. KT12: Wal T 7H 39
RH10: Craw 8E 162
TW5: C'ford 4J 9
Royston Ct. KT10: H Wood 8F 40
SE24 1N 29
TW9: Kew 4M 11
Royston Pk. KT14: Byf 8N 55
Royston Rd. KT14: Byf 8N 55
TW10: Rich 8L 11
Roystons, The KT5: Surb 4A 42
Rozeldene GU26: Hind 6C 170
Rozel Ter. CR0: Croy 4B 200
RQ33 SW18 7M 13
RSPB Great Bramshot Reserve 1G 88
Rubus Cl. GU24: W End 9B 52
Ruckmans La. RH5: Oak 3A 178
Rudd Hall Ri. GU15: Camb 3B 70
Ruddlesway SL4: W'sor 5A 4
(not continuous)
Ruden Way KT17: Eps D 3G 80
Rudge Ri. KT15: Addl 2H 55
RUDGWICK 9E 176
Rudgwick Keep *RH6: Horl 7G 142*
(off Langshott La.)
Rudgwick Rd. RH11: Ifi 2L 181
Rudloe Rd. SW12 1G 28
Rudsworth Cl. SL3: Coln 4F 6
Ruffetts, The CR2: Sels 4E 64
Ruffetts Cl. CR2: Sels 4E 64
Ruffetts Way KT20: Tad 5K 81
Rufford Cl. GU52: Fleet 7B 88
Rufus Bus. Cen. SW18 3N 27
Rufwood RH10: Craw D 1D 184
Rugby Cl. GU47: Owls 6K 49
Rugby La. SM2: Chea 5J 61
Rugby Rd. TW1: Twick 8E 10
Ruggles-Brise Rd. TW15: A'ford 6M 21
Rugosa Rd. GU24: W End 9B 52
Ruislip St. SW17 5D 28
Rumbold Rd. SW6 3N 13
Rumsey Cl. TW12: Hamp 7N 23
RUN COMMON 1G 155
Runcorn Cl. RH11: Craw 7K 181
Runes Cl. CR4: Mit 3B 44
RUNFOLD 8A 110
Runfold St George GU10: B Lea 7N 109
Runnemede Rd. TW20: Egh 5B 20
Running Horse Yd. TW8: Brent 2L 11
RUNNYMEDE 3N 19
Runnymede 3N 19
Runnymede SW19 9A 28
Runnymede Cl. TW2: Whitt 9B 10
Runnymede Ct. GU14: Farnb 7M 69
SM6: W'ton 3F 62
SW15 2F 26
TW20: Egh 5C 20
Runnymede Cres. SW16 9H 29
Runnymede Gdns. TW2: Whitt 9B 10
Runnymede Ho. *KT16: Chert 6J 37*
(off Heriot Rd.)
Runnymede Rd. TW2: Whitt 9B 10
Runnymede Rdbt. TW20: Egh 5D 20
Runshooke Ct. RH11: Craw 6M 181
Runtley Wood La. GU4: Sut G 3B 94
Runwick La. GU10: Farnh 3A 128
Rupert Ct. *KT8: W Mole 3A 40*
(off St Peters Rd.)
Rupert Ho. *SW5 1M 13*
(off Nevern Sq.)
Rupert Rd. GU2: Guil 5A 202 (4M 113)
Rural Cl. GU9: Farnh 5E 128
Rural Way RH1: Red 3E 122
SW16 8F 28
Ruscoe Dr. GU22: Wok 4C 74
Ruscombe Gdns. SL3: Dat 3K 5
Ruscombe Way TW14: Felt 1G 22
Rush, The *SW19 9L 27*
(off Kingston Rd.)
Rusham Ct. TW20: Egh 7C 20
Rusham Pk. Av. TW20: Egh 7B 20
Rusham Rd. SW12 1D 28
TW20: Egh 7B 20
Rushams Rd. RH12: Hors 6H 197
Rushbury Ct. TW12: Hamp 9A 24
Rush Comn. M. SW2 1K 29
(Cotherstone Rd.)
SW2 1J 29
(New Pk. Rd.)
Rush Cft. GU7: Goda 3K 133
Rushdene Wlk. TN16: B Hil 4F 86
Rushden Way GU9: H End 5J 109
Rushen Wlk. SM5: Cars 7B 44
RUSHETT 5K 127
Rushett Cl. KT7: T Dit 7H 41
RUSHETT COMMON 1E 154
Rushett Dr. RH4: Dork 8H 119
Rushett La. KT9: Ches 7J 59
Rushett Rd. KT7: T Dit 6H 41
RUSHETTS FARM 7A 122
Rushetts Pl. RH11: Craw 9A 162
Rushetts Rd. RH2: Reig 7A 122
RH11: Craw 9N 161
Rushey Cl. KT3: N Mal 3C 42
Rushfords RH7: Ling 6A 146
Rushley Cl. BR2: Kes 1F 66
Rushmead TW10: Ham 4H 25
Rushmead Cl. CR0: Croy 1C 64
Rushmere Ct. KT4: W Pk 8F 42
Rushmere Pl. SW19 6J 27
TW20: Eng G 6A 20
Rushmon Gdns. KT12: Wal T 9J 39
Rushmon Pl. SM3: Chea 3K 61
Rushmon Vs. KT3: N Mal 3E 42
RUSHMOOR 4A 150
Rushmoor Arena 9K 89
Rushmoor Cl. GU2: Guil 9J 93
GU52: Fleet 6B 88
Rushmoor Ct. GU14: Farnb 5A 90
Rushmoor Gym 5A 110
Rushmoor Rd. GU11: Alde 8J 89
Rushmore Ho. SW15 1F 26
Rusholme Rd. SW15 9J 13
Rushton Av. RH9: S Gods 7F 124
Rushworth Rd. RH2: Reig 2M 121
Rushy Mdw. La. SM5: Cars 8C 44
Ruskin Av. TW9: Kew 3N 11
(not continuous)
TW14: Felt 9G 9
Ruskin Cl. RH10: Craw 9G 163
Ruskin Ct. RG45: Crow 3E 48
Ruskin Dr. KT4: W Pk 8G 43
Ruskin Ho. CR2: S Croy 8D 200
Ruskin Mans. *W14 2K 13*
(off Queen's Club Gdns.)
Ruskin Pde. CR2: S Croy 8D 200
Ruskin Rd. CR0: Croy 2A 200 (8M 45)
SM5: Cars 2D 62
TW7: Isle 6F 10
TW18: Stain 7H 21
Ruskin Way SW19 9B 28
Rusmon Ct. KT16: Chert 6H 37
RUSPER 2C 180
Rusper Ct. Cotts. RH12: Rusp 3D 180
Rusper Rd. RH5: Cap 6J 159
RH5: Newd 2A 160
RH11: Ifi 2H 181
RH12: Hors 4M 197
RH12: Ifi 2F 180
RH12: Newd, Rusp 9C 160
Rusper Rd. Rdbt. RH12: Hors 1M 197
Ruspers Keep RH11: Ifi 2L 181
Russell Cl. BR3: Beck 2L 47
GU21: Wok 2M 73
KT20: Wal H 3F 100
RG12: Brac 7B 32
W4 2E 12
Russell Ct. CR8: Pur 6L 63
GU1: Guil 9M 93
GU17: B'water 1J 69
GU26: Hind 5D 170
KT22: Leat 9H 79
SM6: W'ton 2G 63
(off Ross Rd.)
SW16 6K 29
Russell Dr. TW19: Stan 9M 7
Russell Gdns. TW10: Ham 3J 25
UB7: Sip 1B 8
Russell Grn. Cl. CR8: Pur 6L 63
Russell Hill CR8: Pur 6K 63
Russell Hill Pl. CR8: Pur 7L 63
Russell Hill Rd. CR8: Pur 7L 63
Russell Kerr Cl. W4 3B 12
Russell Pl. SM2: Sut 4N 61
Russell Rd. CR4: Mit 2C 44
GU21: Wok 2M 73
KT12: Wal T 5H 39
SW19 8M 27
TW2: Twick 9F 10
TW17: Shep 6D 38
Russells KT20: Tad 9J 81
Russells Cres. RH6: Horl 9E 142
Russell's Footpath SW16 6J 29
Russell St. SL4: W'sor 4G 4
Russell Wlk. TW10: Rich 9M 11
Russell Way RH10: Craw 4E 182
SM1: Sut 2N 61
Russell Yd. SW15 7K 13
Russet Av. TW17: Shep 2F 38
Russet Cl. GU10: Tong 5C 110
KT12: Hers 9L 39
RH6: Horl 8G 143
TW19: Stan M 9H 7
Russet Ct. RH13: Hors 4N 197
Russet Dr. CR0: Croy 7H 47
Russet Gdns. GU15: Camb 3B 70
Russet Glade GU11: Alde 4J 109
Russets KT20: Tad 1H 101
Russett Ct. CR3: Cate 3D 104
Russetts Cl. GU21: Wok 2B 74
Russetts Dr. GU51: Fleet 5B 88
Russet Way RH5: Nth H 8K 119
RUSS HILL 5G 161
Russ Hill RH6: Char 5F 160
Russ Hill Rd. RH6: Char 4J 161
Russington Rd. TW17: Shep 5E 38
Rusthall Cl. CR0: Croy 5F 46
Rustic Av. SW16 8F 28
Rustic Glen GU52: C Cro 8A 88
Rustington Wlk. SM4: Mord 6L 43
Ruston Av. KT5: Surb 6A 42
Ruston Cl. RH10: Craw 6G 182
Ruston Way SL5: Asc 1H 33
Rutford Rd. SW16 6J 29
Ruth Cl. GU14: Cove 9H 69
Ruthen Cl. KT18: Eps 1A 80
Rutherford Cl. SL4: W'sor 4C 4
SM2: Sut 3B 62
Rutherford Way RH10: Craw 7E 162
Rutherford Way Ind. Est. RH10: Craw 7E 162
Rutherwick Cl. RH6: Horl 8D 142
Rutherwick Ri. CR5: Coul 4J 83
Rutherwick Twr. RH6: Horl 8D 142
Rutherwyke Cl. KT17: Ewe 3F 60
Rutherwyk Rd. KT16: Chert 6G 36
Rutland Cl. GU11: Alde 1M 109
KT9: Ches 3M 59
KT19: Ewe 6C 60
KT21: A'tead 4L 79
RH1: Red 2D 122
SW14 6A 12
SW19 8C 28
Rutland Ct. KT1: K Tham 8H 203
Rutland Dr. SM4: Mord 5L 43
TW10: Ham 2K 25
Rutland Gdns. CR0: Croy 1B 64
Rutland Gro. W6 1G 13
Rutland Rd. SW19 8C 28
TW2: Twick 3D 24
UB3: Harl 1E 8
Rutland Ter. GU11: Alde 1M 109
Rutlish Rd. SW19 9M 27
Rutson Rd. KT14: Byf 1A 76
Rutter Gdns. CR4: Mit 3A 44
Rutton Hill Rd. GU8: Bow G 2H 171
Ruvigny Gdns. SW15 6J 13
Ruxbury Ct. TW15: A'ford 4N 21
Ruxbury Rd. KT16: Chert 5E 36
Ruxley Cl. KT19: Ewe 2A 60

280 A-Z Surrey

Ruxley Ct.—St John's Cres.

Ruxley Ct. *GU22: Wok* 6N **73**
(off W. Hill Rd.)
KT19: Ewe 2B **60**
Ruxley Cres. KT10: Clay 3H **59**
Ruxley Gdns. TW17: Shep 4D **38**
Ruxley La. KT19: Ewe 3A **60**
Ruxley M. KT19: Ewe 2A **60**
Ruxley Ridge KT10: Clay 4G **58**
Ruxley Towers KT10: Clay 4G **59**
Ruxton Cl. CR5: Coul 2G **83**
Ryan Ct. SW16 8J **29**
Ryan Dr. TW8: Brent 2G **11**
Ryan Mt. GU47: Sandh 7F **48**
Ryarsh Cres. BR6: Orp 1N **67**
Rybrook Dr. KT12: Wal T 8K **39**
Rycroft SL4: W'sor 6C **4**
Rydal Cl. CR8: Pur 9A **64**
GU14: Cove 2J **89**
GU15: Camb 1H **71**
RH11: Ifi 5J **181**
Rydal Dr. GU52: C Cro 8A **88**
Rydal Gdns. SW15 6D **26**
TW3: Houn 9B **10**
Rydal Pl. GU18: Ligh 7M **51**
Rydal Rd. SW16 5H **29**
Rydal Way TW20: Egh 8D **20**
Ryde, The TW18: Stain 9K **21**
Ryde Cl. GU23: Rip 8L **75**
Ryde Ct. GU12: Alde 3A **110**
Ryde Gdns. GU46: Yate 9A **48**
Ryde Heron GU21: Knap 4H **73**
Ryde Lands GU6: Cranl 6A **156**
RYDENS 9K **39**
Rydens Av. KT12: Wal T 8J **39**
Rydens Cl. KT12: Wal T 8K **39**
Rydens Gro. KT12: Hers 1L **57**
Rydens Pk. KT12: Wal T 8L **39**
Rydens Rd. KT12: Wal T 9J **39**
Rydens Way GU22: Wok 7C **74**
Ryde Pl. TW1: Twick 9K **11**
Ryders Way RH12: Hors 1M **197**
Rydes Av. GU2: Guil 9J **93**
Rydes Cl. GU22: Wok 7E **74**
RYDESHILL 1H **113**
Ryde's Hill Cres. GU2: Guil 8J **93**
Ryde's Hill Rd. GU2: Guil 1J **113**
Ryde Va. Rd. SW12 3G **28**
Rydings SL4: W'sor 6C **4**
Rydon Bus. Cen.
KT22: Leat 7H **79**
Rydon M. SW19 8H **27**
Rydon's La. CR5: Coul 7N **83**
Rydons Way RH1: Red 4D **122**
Rydon's Wood Cl.
CR5: Coul 7N **83**
Rye Ash RH10: Craw 2E **182**
(not continuous)
Ryebeck Rd. GU52: C Cro 8B **88**
Ryebridge Cl. KT22: Leat 5G **79**
Ryebrook KT22: Leat 7G **79**
Ryebrook Rd. KT22: Leat 5G **79**
Rye Cl. GU2: Guil 1H **113**
GU14: Cove 8K **69**
GU51: Fleet 9D **68**
RG12: Brac 8B **16**
Ryecroft Av. TW2: Whitt 1B **24**
Ryecroft Dr. RH12: Hors 5G **196**
Ryecroft Gdns.
GU17: B'water 2K **69**
Ryecroft Rd. SW16 7L **29**
Ryecroft St. SW6 4N **13**
Rye Fld. KT21: A'tead 3K **79**
Ryefield Path SW15 2F **26**
Ryefield Rd. SE19 7N **29**
Rye Gro. GU6: Cranl 7J **155**
GU18: Ligh 4C **52**
Ryehurst La. RG42: Bin 5K **15**
Ryeland Cl. GU51: Fleet 9D **68**
Ryelands RH6: Horl 7G **142**
RH11: Craw 4M **181**
Ryelands Cl. CR3: Cate 8B **84**
Ryelands Ct. KT22: Leat 5G **79**
Ryelands Pl. KT13: Weybr 9F **38**
Ryelaw Rd. GU52: C Cro 8B **88**
Ryemead La. SL4: Wink 5G **17**
Ryersh La. RH5: Cap 3H **159**
Rye Wlk. SW15 8J **13**
Ryfold Rd. SW19 4M **27**
Rykens La. RH3: Betch 8B **120**
Rykmansford Rd.
GU51: Fleet 1A **88**
Ryland Cl. TW13: Felt 5G **23**
Rylandes Rd. CR2: Sels 5E **64**
Ryle Rd. GU9: Farnh 3G **128**
Rylston Rd. SW6 2L **13**
Rylton Ho. KT12: Wal T 7H **39**
Rymer Rd. CR0: Croy 6B **46**
Rysted La. TN16: Weste 4L **107**
Ryst Wood Rd.
RH18: F Row 7K **187**
Rythe, The KT10: Esh 6B **58**
Rythe Cl. KT9: Ches 4J **59**
KT10: Clay 2E **58**
Rythe Ct. KT7: T Dit 6G **41**
Rythe Rd. KT10: Clay 2D **58**
Ryves Av. GU46: Yate 1A **68**

S

Sabah Ct. TW15: A'ford 5B **22**
Sable Cl. TW4: Houn 6K **9**
Sabre Ct. GU11: Alde 2K **109**
Sachel Ct. Dr. GU6: Alf 7H **175**
Sachel Ct. M. GU6: Alf 7G **174**
Sachel Ct. Rd. GU6: Alf 6F **174**
Sachel Hill La. GU6: Alf 7F **174**
Sackville Cl. RH19: E Grin 7M **165**
Sackville College 9B **166**
Sackville Cotts. RH1: Blet 2A **124**
Sackville Ct. RH19: E Grin 1B **186**
Sackville Gdns.
RH19: E Grin 7M **165**
(not continuous)
Sackville Ho. SW16 4J **29**
Sackville La. RH19: E Grin 7L **165**
Sackville Rd. SM2: Sut 4M **61**
Saco Ct. *GU14: Farnb* 4A **90**
(off Reading Rd.)
Saddleback Rd.
GU15: Camb 7C **50**
Saddleback Way
GU51: Fleet 1C **88**
Saddlebrook Pk.
TW16: Sunb 8F **22**
Saddler Cnr. GU47: Sandh 8G **49**
Saddler Row RH10: Craw 6B **182**
Saddlers Cl. GU4: Guil 2F **114**
Saddlers Ct.
KT18: Eps 7J **201** (9B **60**)
Saddlers M. KT1: H Wic 9J **25**
Saddlers Scarp
GU26: G'hott 5M **169**
Saddlers Way KT18: Eps D 6C **80**
Saddlewood GU15: Camb 2A **70**
Sadler Cl. CR4: Mit 1D **44**
Sadlers Ride KT8: W Mole 1C **40**
Sadlers Way GU27: Hasl 1H **189**
Saffron Cl. CR0: Croy 5J **45**
RH11: Craw 6M **181**
SL3: Dat 4L **5**
Saffron Ct. GU14: Cove 1H **89**
TW14: Bedf 1D **22**
Saffron Ho. SM2: Sut 4N **61**
TW9: Kew 4A **12**
Saffron M. SW19 8K **27**
Saffron Platt GU2: Guil 8K **93**
Saffron Rd. RG12: Brac 3N **31**
Saffron Way KT6: Surb 7K **41**
Sage Wlk. RG42: Warf 8B **16**
Sailors La. GU8: Thur 8D **150**
Sainfoin Rd. SW17 3E **28**
Sainsbury Cen., The
KT16: Chert 6J **37**
St Agatha's Dr.
KT2: K Tham 7M **25**
St Agatha's Gro. SM5: Cars 7D **44**
St Agnes Rd. RH19: E Grin 8A **166**
St Albans Av. KT13: Weybr 9B **38**
TW13: Hanw 6L **23**
St Albans Cl.
GU3: Wood V 2E **112**
SL4: W'sor 4G **5**
St Albans Farm TW4: Houn 8K **9**
St Alban's Gdns.
TW11: Tedd 6G **25**
St Alban's Gro. SM5: Cars 6C **44**
St Alban's Rd. KT2: K Tham 7L **25**
RH2: Reig 1M **121**
SM1: Sut 1L **61**
St Albans Rdbt.
GU14: Farnb 5A **90**
St Alban's St. SL4: W'sor 4G **5**
St Albans Ter. W6 2K **13**
St Andrews GU6: Cranl 6K **155**
RG12: Brac 5K **31**
RH6: Horl 9F **142**
(off Aurum Cl.)
St Andrew's Av. SL4: W'sor 5C **4**
St Andrews Cl. GU21: Wok 4M **73**
KT7: T Dit 7H **41**
RG45: Crow 1E **48**
RH2: Reig 4N **121**
SL4: O Win 9K **5**
SW19 7N **27**
TW7: Isle 4E **10**
TW17: Shep 3E **38**
TW19: Wray 9A **6**
St Andrews Cotts.
SL4: W'sor 5D **4**
(off Cross Oak)
St Andrews Ct. SM1: Sut 9C **44**
SW18 3A **28**
St Andrew's Cres.
SL4: W'sor 5C **4**
St Andrews Gdns.
KT11: Cob 9K **57**
St Andrew's Ga. GU22: Wok 5B **74**
St Andrews Mans.
W14 2K **13**
(off St Andrews Rd.)
St Andrews M. SW12 2H **29**
St Andrews Rd.
CR0: Croy 6B **200** (1N **63**)
CR5: Coul 3E **82**
KT6: Surb 5K **41**
RH11: Ifi 4J **181**
SM5: Cars 9C **44**
W14 2K **13**
St Andrew's Sq. KT6: Surb 5K **41**
St Andrew's Wlk. KT11: Cob 2J **77**
St Andrews Way
GU16: Frim 7D **70**
RH8: Limp 9G **107**
St Anne's Av. TW19: Stan 1M **21**
St Annes Blvd. RH1: Red 1F **122**
St Anne's Ct. BR4: W Wick 1A **66**
St Annes Dr. RG40: W'ham 2F **30**
RH1: Red 2E **122**
St Annes Dr. Nth.
RH1: Red 1E **122**
St Annes Glade GU19: Bag 4H **51**
St Anne's Mt. RH1: Red 2E **122**
St Anne's Ri. RH1: Red 2E **122**
St Annes Rd. GU7: Goda 6K **133**
RH10: Craw 9G **163**
(not continuous)
St Annes Way *RH1: Red* 2E **122**
(off St Annes Mt.)
St Anns GU22: Wok 5A **74**
St Ann's Cl. KT16: Chert 5H **37**
St Ann's Cres. SW18 9N **13**
St Ann's Hill SW18 8N **13**
St Ann's Hill Rd.
KT16: Chert 5E **36**
ST ANN'S PARK 3A **36**
St Ann's Pk. Rd. SW18 1A **28**
St Ann's Pas. SW13 6D **12**
St Ann's Rd. KT16: Chert 5G **36**
(Pyrcroft Rd.)
KT16: Chert 5H **37**
(Staines Rd.)
SW13 5E **12**
St Anns Way CR2: S Croy 3M **63**
TN16: B Hil 3K **87**
St Anselms Ct. SW16 6J **29**
St Anthonys Cl. RG42: Brac 9M **15**
SW17 3C **28**
St Anthony's Ct. SW17 3E **28**
St Anthony's Way TW14: Felt 7G **9**
St Arvan's Cl. CR0: Croy 9B **46**
St Aubin Cl. RH11: Craw 7L **181**
St Aubyns RH4: Dork 7G **119**
St Aubyn's Av. SW19 6L **27**
TW3: Houn 8A **10**
St Augustine's Av.
CR2: S Croy 3N **63**
St Augustine's Cl.
GU12: Alde 3B **110**
St Austins GU26: G'hott 6B **170**
St Barnabas Cl. BR3: Beck 1M **47**
St Barnabas Ct.
RH10: Craw 2G **182**
St Barnabas Gdns.
KT8: W Mole 4A **40**
St Barnabas Rd. CR4: Mit 8E **28**
SM1: Sut 2B **62**
St Bartholomews Ct.
GU1: Guil 5B **114**
St Benedicts Cl.
GU11: Alde 3M **109**
SW17 6E **28**
St Benet's Cl. SW17 3C **28**
St Benet's Gro. SM5: Cars 6A **44**
St Bernards
CR0: Croy 5F **200** (9B **46**)
St Brelades Cl. RH4: Dork 7G **119**
St Brelade's Mobile Home Pk.
TN8: Eden 9J **127**
St Brelades Rd.
RH11: Craw 7L **181**
St Catherines GU22: Wok 6M **73**
KT13: Weybr 9C **38**
(off Thames St.)
St Catherines Cl. KT9: Ches 3K **59**
SW17 3C **28**
St Catherines Ct.
GU5: Braml 4B **134**
RH19: E Grin 8N **165**
TW13: Felt 2H **23**
(off Orchard Rd.)
TW18: Stain 5J **21**
St Catherine's Cross
RH1: Blet 3B **124**
St Catherine's Dr.
GU2: Guil 7L **113**
St Catherine's Hill
GU2: Guil 7M **113**
St Catherines Pk.
GU1: Guil 5B **114**
St Catherines Pl.
TW20: Egh 6C **20**
St Catherines Rd.
GU16: Frim 5D **70**
(not continuous)
RH10: Craw 9G **163**
St Catherines Wood
GU15: Camb 2A **70**
St Cecilia's Cl. SM3: Sut 7K **43**
St Chads Cl. KT6: Surb 6J **41**
St Charles Ct. KT13: Weybr 2B **56**
St Charles Pl. KT13: Weybr 2B **56**
St Christopher's RH7: Ling 7N **145**
St Christophers Cl.
GU12: Alde 2B **110**
GU27: Hasl 2E **188**
RH12: Hors 4J **197**
TW7: Isle 4E **10**
St Christophers Ct.
KT12: Wal T 8K **39**
(off Rydens Av.)
St Christophers Gdns.
CR7: T Hea 2L **45**
SL5: Asc 9H **17**
St Christopher's Grn.
GU27: Hasl 2E **188**
St Christopher's M.
SM6: W'ton 2G **62**
St Christopher's Pl.
GU14: Cove 2L **89**
St Christopher's Rd.
GU14: Cove 2M **89**
GU27: Hasl 2E **188**
St Clair Cl. RH2: Reig 3A **122**
RH8: Oxt 8M **105**
St Clair Dr. KT4: W Pk 9G **42**
St Claire Cotts.
RH7: Dorm 1D **166**
St Clair's Rd.
CR0: Croy 3F **200** (8B **46**)
St Clare Bus. Pk.
TW12: H Hill 7C **24**
St Clement Rd.
RH11: Craw 7L **181**
St Clements Ct.
GU14: Farnb 7N **69**
St Clements Mans. *SW6* 2J **13**
(off Lillie Rd.)
St Cloud Rd. SE27 5N **29**
St Crispin's Leisure Cen. 2C **30**
St Crispins Way
KT16: Otter 5E **54**
St Cross Rd. GU9: Farnh 9H **109**
GU16: Frim 7E **70**
St Cuthberts Cl.
TW20: Eng G 7N **19**
St Cyprian's St. SW17 5D **28**
St David's CR5: Coul 4K **83**
St David's Cl. BR4: W Wick 6L **47**
GU9: Weybo 5K **109**
GU14: Cove 6L **69**
RH2: Reig 2A **122**
St Davids Ct. TW15: A'ford 3A **22**
St Davids Dr. TW20: Eng G 8M **19**
St Denis Rd. SE27 5N **29**
St Denys Cl. CR8: Pur 6M **63**
GU21: Knap 5F **72**
St Dionis Rd. SW6 5L **13**
St Dominic Cl.
GU14: Farnb 6M **69**
ST DUNSTAN'S 3L **61**
St Dunstan's Cl. UB3: Harl 1G **8**
St Dunstan's Hill SM1: Sut 2K **61**
St Dunstan's La. BR3: Beck 5M **47**
St Dunstan's Rd. SE25 3C **46**
TW4: C'ford 5J **9**
(not continuous)
TW13: Felt 4G **23**
W6 1J **13**
St Edith Cl.
KT18: Eps 8H **201** (1B **80**)
St Edmund Cl. RH11: Craw 9B **162**
St Edmund's Cl. SW17 3C **28**
St Edmund's La.
TW2: Whitt 1B **24**
St Edmunds Sq. SW13 2H **13**
St Edmund's Steps
GU7: Goda 7G **133**
St Edward's Cl. CR0: N Add 7N **65**
RH19: E Grin 9M **165**
St Elizabeth Dr.
KT18: Eps 8H **201** (1B **80**)
St Faith's Rd. SE21 2M **29**
St Francis Cl. RG45: Crow 3D **48**
St Francis Gdns.
RH10: Cop 6M **163**
St Francis Pl. SW12 1F **28**
St Francis Wlk.
RH11: Craw 5K **181**
St George Ga. KT15: Addl 9M **37**
St Georges RH6: Horl 9F **142**
St George's Av.
KT13: Weybr 3C **56**
St Georges Bus. Pk.
KT13: Weybr 5B **56**
St Georges Chapel 4G **5**
St Georges Cl. GU9: B Lea 6N **109**
KT13: Weybr 2D **56**
RH6: Horl 8F **142**
SL4: W'sor 4B **4**
St Georges Ct. GU47: Owls 5K **49**
KT13: Weybr 3D **56**
KT15: Addl 1L **55**
RH10: Craw 2B **182**
RH19: E Grin 7M **165**
SW15 7L **13**
St George's Gdns.
KT6: Surb 8A **42**
KT17: Eps 1E **80**
RH13: Hors 4L **197**
St George's Gro.
SW17 4B **28**
ST GEORGE'S HILL 6C **56**
St George's Hill RH1: Salf 2H **143**
St George's Ind. Est.
GU15: Camb 3N **69**
KT2: K Tham 6K **25**
St George's La. SL5: Asc 2M **33**
St George's M. *GU9: Farnh* 9G **109**
(off Bear La.)
St George's Pl. TW1: Twick 2G **25**
St Georges Rd. BR3: Beck 1L **47**
CR4: Mit 2F **44**
GU9: B Lea 6N **109**
(not continuous)
GU9: Farnh 2J **129**
GU10: B Lea 6N **109**
GU12: Alde 3N **109**
GU15: Camb 9B **50**
KT2: K Tham 1M **203** (8N **25**)
KT13: Weybr 3E **56**
KT15: Addl 1L **55**
RH1: Salf 2H **143**
St Georges Rd. SM6: W'ton 2F **62**
SW19 8L **27**
(not continuous)
TW1: Twick 8H **11**
TW9: Rich 6M **11**
TW13: Hanw 5L **23**
St George's Rd. E.
GU12: Alde 3N **109**
St George's Sq. KT3: N Mal 2D **42**
St George's Wlk.
CR0: Croy 3C **200** (9N **45**)
St George's Yd.
GU9: Farnh 1G **129**
(off Castle St.)
St Giles Cl. BR6: Farnb 2M **67**
TW5: Hest 3M **9**
St Gothard Rd. SE27 5N **29**
(not continuous)
St Helens KT7: T Dit 6F **40**
St Helens Cres.
GU47: Sandh 7G **48**
SW16 9K **29**
St Helen's Rd. SW16 9K **29**
ST HELIER 6C **44**
St Helier Av. SM4: Mord 6A **44**
St Helier Cl. RG41: W'ham 5A **30**
RH11: Craw 7M **181**
St Helier's Av. TW3: Houn 8A **10**
St Hilda's Av. TW15: A'ford 6N **21**
St Hilda's Cl. GU21: Knap 4G **73**
RH6: Horl 8F **142**
RH10: Craw 8G **163**
SW17 3C **28**
St Hilda's Rd. SW13 2G **12**
SAINT HILL 5N **185**
Saint Hill Grn.
RH19: E Grin 5N **185**
Saint Hill Manor 5M **185**
Saint Hill Rd.
RH19: E Grin 3L **185**
St Hughes Cl. SW17 3C **28**
St Hughs Cl. RH10: Craw 9G **163**
St Ives RH10: Craw 2G **182**
St James Av. GU9: Farnh 8J **109**
KT17: Ewe 7E **60**
SM1: Sut 2M **61**
St James Cl. GU21: Wok 5K **73**
KT3: N Mal 4E **42**
KT18: Eps 8L **201** (1D **80**)
St James Ct. CR0: Croy 6M **45**
GU9: Farnh 9H **109**
KT21: A'tead 4K **79**
RH19: E Grin 9N **165**
St James Ga. SL5: S'dale 6D **34**
St James Ho.
RH19: E Grin 9A **166**
St James M. KT13: Weybr 1C **56**
St James Rd. CR4: Mit 8E **28**
CR8: Pur 9M **63**
GU51: Fleet 5A **88**
KT6: Surb 5K **41**
RH19: E Grin 9N **165**
SM1: Sut 2M **61**
SM5: Cars 9C **44**
St James's Av. BR3: Beck 2H **47**
TW12: H Hill 6C **24**
St James's Cl. SW17 3D **28**
St James's Cotts.
TW9: Rich 8K **11**
St James's Ct.
KT1: K Tham 6J **203** (2L **41**)
St James's Dr. SW17 2D **28**
St James's Pk. CR0: Croy 6N **45**
St James's Pl.
GU6: Cranl 7L **155**
St James's Rd. CR0: Croy 6M **45**
KT1: K Tham 4H **203** (1K **41**)
TW12: H Hill 6B **24**
St James St. W6 1H **13**
St James Ter. GU9: Farnh 9H **109**
SW12 2E **28**
St James Wlk.
RH11: Craw 8A **182**
St Joan Cl. RH11: Craw 9B **162**
St John Cl. RH13: Hors 7L **197**
ST JOHNS
GU21 6K **73**
RH1 5C **122**
St Johns RH1: Red 5C **122**
RH5: Nth H 9J **119**
St John's Av. KT17: Eps 8F **60**
KT22: Leat 8H **79**
SW15 8J **13**
St Johns Chu. Rd.
RH5: Wott 8N **117**
St Johns Cl. GU2: Guil 4K **113**
KT22: Leat 8J **79**
RH19: E Grin 8A **166**
SW6 3M **13**
TN16: B Hil 3K **87**
St John's Cnr. *RH1: Red* 5D **122**
(off St John's Rd.)
St Johns Ct. GU14: Cove 9J **69**
GU21: Wok 6K **73**
GU24: B'wood 7C **72**
KT1: K Tham 7K **203**
RH4: Westc 6C **118**
(off St John's Rd.)
RH9: S Gods 7J **125**
TW7: Isle 5F **10**
TW20: Egh 6C **20**
St John's Cres.
RH12: Bro H 5E **196**

St Johns Dr. KT12: Wal T 7K 39
SL4: W'sor 5D 4
SW18 ....2N 27
St John's Gdns. GU21: Wok 5K 73
(off St John's Rd.)
St Johns Gro. GU9: Farnh 3G 129
SW13 ....5E 12
TW9: Rich 7L 11
St John's Hill CR5: Coul 4L 83
St John's Hill Rd.
GU21: Wok 6K 73
St Johns Lodge GU21: Wok 6K 73
St John's Lye GU21: Wok 6J 73
St John's Mdw.
RH7: Blin H 3G 145
St John's M. GU21: Wok 6K 73
KT1: H Wic 1J 41
St John's Pas. SW19 ....7K 27
St Johns Ri. GU21: Wok 6L 73
TN16: B Hil 3K 87
St John's Rd.
CR0: Croy 4A 200 (9M 45)
GU2: Guil 4J 113
GU9: Farnh 3G 129
GU14: Cove 1J 89
GU21: Wok 6J 73
GU47: Sandh 8G 49
KT1: H Wic 1J 41
KT3: N Mal 2B 42
KT8: E Mol 3D 40
KT22: Leat 8J 79
RH1: Red 5D 122
RH4: Westc 6C 118
RH11: Craw 3A 182
RH19: E Grin 8A 166
SL4: W'sor 5D 4
SL5: Asc 8K 17
(not continuous)
SM1: Sut 8N 43
SM5: Cars 9C 44
SW19 ....8K 27
TW7: Isle 5F 10
TW9: Rich 7L 11
TW13: Hanw 5M 23
St Johns St. GU7: Goda 5J 133
RG45: Crow 2G 49
St John's Ter. SW15 ....4D 26
(off Kingston Va.)
St John's Ter. Rd.
RH1: Red 5D 122
St Johns Waterside
GU21: Wok 5J 73
(off Copse Rd.)
St Johns Way KT16: Chert 7J 37
TN8: Eden 9K 127
St Joseph's Cl. BR6: Orp 1N 67
St Joseph's College Sports Cen.
....7M 29
St Joseph's Rd.
GU12: Alde 3M 109
St Jude's Cl. TW20: Eng G 6M 19
St Jude's Cotts.
TW20: Eng G 6M 19
St Judes Rd. TW20: Eng G 4M 19
St Julian's Cl. SW16 ....5L 29
St Julian's Farm Rd.
SE27 ....5L 29
St Katherines Rd.
CR3: Cate 3D 104
St Lawrence Bus. Cen.
TW13: Felt 3J 23
St Lawrence Ct.
GU24: Chob 7H 53
St Lawrence Ho.
GU24: Chob 7H 53
(off Bagshot Rd.)
St Lawrence's Way
RH2: Reig 3M 121
St Lawrence Way
CR3: Cate 1N 103
St Leonard's Av. SL4: W'sor 5F 4
St Leonards Ct. SW14 ....6B 12
St Leonard's Dr.
RH10: Craw 5E 182
ST LEONARDS FOREST 3C 198
St Leonard's Gdns.
TW5: Hest 3M 9
St Leonard's Hill SL4: W'sor 7A 4
ST LEONARD'S PARK 5A 198
St Leonards Pk.
RH19: E Grin 9A 166
St Leonard's Ri. BR6: Orp 1N 67
St Leonard's Rd. CR0: Wad 9M 45
KT6: Surb 4K 41
KT7: T Dit 5G 40
KT10: Clay 3F 58
KT18: Tat C 6H 81
RH13: Hors 8L 197
SL4: Wink 9A 4
SL4: W'sor 6D 4
SW14 ....6A 12
St Leonards Sq. KT6: Surb 4K 41
St Leonard's Wlk. SW16 ....8K 29
St Louis Rd. SE27 ....5N 29
St Luke's Cl. SE25 ....5E 46
St Lukes Ct. GU21: Wok 1E 74
St Luke's Pas.
KT2: K Tham 1L 203 (9M 25)
St Luke's Rd. CR3: Whyte 5C 84
SL4: O Win 9K 5
St Lukes Sq. GU1: Guil 4B 114
St Margaret Dr.
KT18: Eps 8H 201 (1B 80)
ST MARGARETS 9H 11
St Margarets GU1: Guil 3B 114
St Margarets Av.
RH19: D Pk 4A 166
SM3: Chea 9K 43
TN16: B Hil 3K 87
TW15: A'ford 6C 22
St Margarets Bus. Cen.
TW1: Twick 9H 11
St Margarets Cotts.
GU27: Fern 9F 188
St Margarets Ct.
SW15 ....7G 12
St Margaret's Cres.
SW15 ....8G 13
St Margaret's Dr.
TW1: Twick 8H 11
St Margaret's Gro.
TW1: Twick 9G 11
St Margarets Rd. CR5: Coul 8F 82
RH19: E Grin 7B 166
TW1: Twick 9H 11
TW7: Isle 7H 11
ST MARGARETS RDBT. 9H 11
St Margrets Ct. RH4: Dork 4J 201
St Marks Cl. GU14: Farnb 4A 90
SW6 ....4M 13
St Mark's Ct. GU22: Wok 6A 74
(off Brooklyn Rd.)
St Mark's Gro. SW10 ....3N 13
St Mark's Hill KT6: Surb 5L 41
St Mark's La. RH12: Hors 2L 197
St Marks Pl. GU9: U Hal 5G 109
SL4: W'sor 5F 4
SW19 ....7L 27
St Marks Rd. CR4: Mit 1D 44
KT18: Tat C 5H 81
RG42: Bin 8H 15
SE25 ....3D 46
SL4: W'sor 5F 4
TW11: Tedd 8H 25
St Martha's Av. GU22: Wok 8B 74
St Marthas Ct. GU4: Guil 9D 114
St Martin Cl. RH17: Hand 9N 199
St Martin's Av.
KT18: Eps 8L 201 (1D 80)
St Martins Cl.
KT17: Eps 7M 201 (9E 60)
KT24: E Hor 7F 96
St Martin's Ct. KT24: E Hor 7F 96
TW15: A'ford 6L 21
St Martins Dr. KT12: Wal T 9K 39
St Martins Est. SW2 ....2L 29
St Martin's La. BR3: Beck 4L 47
St Martins M. GU22: Pyr 3J 75
RH4: Dork 2J 201 (5G 119)
St Martin's Wlk.
RH4: Dork 1K 201 (4H 119)
St Martins Way SW17 ....4A 28
St Mary Av. SM6: W'ton 9E 44
St Marys KT13: Weybr 9E 38
St Mary's Av. TW11: Tedd 7F 24
TW19: Stan 1M 21
St Mary's Av. Central
UB2: S'hall 1B 10
St Mary's Av. Sth.
UB2: S'hall 1B 10
St Mary's Cl. GU47: Sandh 7H 49
KT9: Ches 4M 59
KT17: Ewe 4E 60
KT22: Fetc 1D 98
RH8: Oxt 7A 106
TW16: Sunb 3H 39
TW19: Stan 1M 21
St Mary's Copse KT4: W Pk 8D 42
St Mary's Ct. SM6: W'ton 1G 62
TN16: Weste 4M 107
St Mary's Cres. TW7: Isle 3D 10
TW19: Stan 1M 21
St Mary's Dr. RH10: Craw 1F 182
TW14: Bedf 1D 22
St Marys Gdn. GU3: Worp 5H 93
St Mary's Gdns. GU19: Bag 4J 51
RH12: Hors 7J 197
St Mary's Grn. TN16: B Hil 5E 86
St Mary's Gro. SW13 ....6G 12
TN16: B Hil 5E 86
TW9: Rich 7M 11
W4 ....2A 12
St Mary's Hill SL5: S'hill 5N 33
St Mary's Ho. RH12: Hors 7J 197
(off Normandy)
St Mary's La. SL4: Wink 4H 17
St Marys M. TW10: Ham 3J 25
St Marys Mill GU8: Chid 6E 172
St Mary's Mt. CR3: Cate 2C 104
St Marys Pl. GU9: Farnh 9H 109
St Mary's Rd. CR2: Sande 6A 64
GU12: A Va 8E 90
GU15: Camb 9A 50
GU21: Wok 4M 73
KT4: W Pk 8D 42
KT6: Surb 6J 41
(St Chads Cl.)
KT6: Surb 5K 41
(Victoria Rd.)
KT8: E Mol 4D 40
KT13: Weybr 1E 56
KT22: Leat 9H 79
RH2: Reig 4N 121
SE25 ....2B 46
SL5: Asc 6M 33
SW19 ....6K 27
St Mary's Ter. GU1: Guil 6C 202
St Mary's University College
Sports Cen. 5F 24
St Mary's Wlk. RH1: Blet 2A 124
RH12: Hors 7J 197
St Marys Way GU2: Guil 1H 113
St Matthew's Av.
KT6: Surb 7L 41
St Matthew's Ct.
TW15: A'ford 5B 22
(off Feltham Rd.)
St Matthew's Rd.
RH1: Red 2D 122
St Maur Rd. SW6 ....4L 13
St Michael's RH8: Limp 8C 106
St Michael's Av. GU3: Worp 7F 92
St Michaels Cl.
GU28: North 9D 190
GU51: Fleet 5D 88
KT4: W Pk 8E 42
KT12: Wal T 8K 39
St Michaels Cotts.
RG40: W'ham 8H 31
St Michael's Ct. CR0: Croy 1B 200
KT13: Weybr 2D 56
(off Pine Gro.)
St Michaels Rd.
CR0: Croy 1C 200 (7N 45)
CR3: Cate 9A 84
GU12: Alde 3N 109
GU14: Farnb 8N 69
GU15: Camb 1N 69
GU21: Wok 1F 74
GU47: Sandh 7E 48
RH19: E Grin 8A 166
SM6: W'ton 3G 62
TW15: A'ford 6B 22
St Mildred's Rd.
GU1: Guil 2B 114
St Monica's Rd.
KT20: K'wood 8L 81
St Nazaire Cl. TW20: Egh 6E 20
St Nicholas Av. KT23: Book 3B 98
St Nicholas Cen. SM1: Sut 2N 61
St Nicholas Cl. GU51: Fleet 4A 88
St Nicholas Ct.
KT1: K Tham 8J 203
RH10: Craw 2G 182
St Nicholas Cres. GU22: Pyr 3J 75
St Nicholas Dr. TW17: Shep 6B 38
St Nicholas Glebe
SW17 ....6E 28
St Nicholas Hill KT22: Leat 9H 79
St Nicholas M. KT7: T Dit 5F 40
St Nicholas Rd. KT7: T Dit 5F 40
SM1: Sut 2N 61
St Nicholas Way SM1: Sut 1N 61
St Nicolas Av. GU6: Cranl 7N 155
St Nicolas Cl. GU6: Cranl 7N 155
St Normans Way KT17: Ewe 6F 60
St Olaf's Rd. SW6 ....3K 13
St Olaves Cl. TW18: Stain 8H 21
St Olaves Wlk. SW16 ....1G 45
St Omer Ridge GU1: Guil 4C 114
St Omer Rd. GU1: Guil 4C 114
St Oswald's Rd.
SW16 ....9M 29
St Oswalds Studios
SW6 ....2M 13
(off Sedlescombe Rd.)
St Pauls Cl. GU10: Tong 5D 110
KT9: Ches 1K 59
KT15: Addl 2J 55
SM5: Cars 7C 44
TW3: Houn 5M 9
TW15: A'ford 6D 22
UB3: Harl 1E 8
St Paul's Ct. TW4: Houn 6M 9
St Paul's Ga. RG41: W'ham 2A 30
St Pauls M.
RH4: Dork 4L 201 (6H 119)
St Paul's Rd. CR7: T Hea 2N 45
GU22: Wok 4C 74
TW8: Brent 2K 11
TW9: Rich 6M 11
TW18: Stain 6F 20
St Paul's Rd. E.
RH4: Dork 3L 201 (5H 119)
St Paul's Rd. W.
RH4: Dork 4J 201 (6G 119)
St Paul's Studios W14 ....1K 13
(off Talgarth Rd.)
St Paul's Wlk. KT2: K Tham 8N 25
St Peters KT16: Chert 9E 36
St Peters Av. TN16: B Hil 3K 87
St Peter's Cl. GU22: Wok 7E 74
SL4: O Win 8K 5
SW17 ....3C 28
TW18: Stain 7H 21
St Peters Ct. KT8: W Mole 3A 40
St Peters Gdns.
GU10: Wrec 5E 128
GU46: Yate 9C 48
SE27 ....4L 29
St Peter's Gro. W6 ....1F 12
St Peters Mead GU12: Ash 2F 110
St Peters Pk. GU11: Alde 4K 109
St Peters Rd.
CR0: Croy 6D 200 (1A 64)
GU22: Wok 8D 74
KT1: K Tham 1N 41
KT8: W Mole 3A 40
RH11: Craw 3A 182
St Peters Rd. SL4: O Win 8K 5
TW1: Twick 8H 11
W6 ....1F 12
St Peter's Sq. W6 ....1E 12
St Peter's St.
CR2: S Croy 8E 200 (2A 64)
St Peter's Ter. SW6 ....3L 13
St Peter's Vs. W6 ....1F 12
St Peters Way GU16: Frim 7D 70
KT15: Addl 1F 54
KT16: Chert 1F 54
UB3: Harl 1E 8
St Peter's Wharf W4 ....1F 12
St Philip's Av. KT4: W Pk 8G 42
St Philip's Ga. KT4: W Pk 8G 43
St Philips Rd. KT6: Surb 5K 41
St Phillips Ct. GU51: Fleet 4B 88
St Pier's La. RH7: Ling 8B 146
TN8: Ling 8B 146
St Pinnock Av. TW18: Stain 9J 21
St Richard's M.
RH10: Craw 3D 182
(off Broomdashers Rd.)
St Sampson Rd.
RH11: Craw 7L 181
St Saviour's Ct. CR8: Pur 9K 63
(off Lodge La.)
St Saviours Pl.
GU1: Guil 3B 202 (3M 113)
St Saviour's Rd. CR0: Croy 5M 45
Saints Cl. SE27 ....5M 29
St Sebastian's Cl.
RG40: W'ham 9D 30
St Simon's Av. SW15 ....8H 13
Saints M. CR4: Mit 2C 44
St Stephen Cl.
RH11: Craw 9B 162
St Stephen's Av.
KT21: A'tead 3L 79
St Stephens Cl.
GU27: Hasl 2D 188
St Stephens Ct.
RH9: S Gods 7H 125
(off Oaklands)
St Stephen's Cres.
CR7: T Hea 2L 45
St Stephen's Gdns.
SW15 ....8L 13
TW1: Twick 9J 11
St Stephen's Pas.
TW1: Twick 9J 11
St Stephen's Rd.
TW3: Houn 9A 10
St Swithun's Cl.
RH19: E Grin 9B 166
St Theresa Cl.
KT18: Eps 8H 201 (1B 80)
St Theresa's Rd. TW14: Felt 7G 9
St Thomas Cl. GU4: Guil 9E 114
GU21: Wok 4M 73
KT6: Surb 7M 41
St Thomas Dr. GU4: E Cla 9N 95
St Thomas Rd. W4 ....2B 12
St Thomas's M. GU1: Guil 5B 114
St Thomas's Way SW6 ....3L 13
St Thomas Wlk. SL3: Coln 3F 6
St Vincent Cl. RH10: Craw 4H 183
SE27 ....6M 29
St Vincent Rd. KT12: Wal T 9J 39
TW2: Whitt 9C 10
St Winifreds CR8: Ken 2N 83
St Winifred's Rd.
TN16: B Hil 5H 87
TW11: Tedd 7H 25
Salamanca RG45: Crow 2D 48
Salamander Cl.
KT2: K Tham 6J 25
Salamander Quay
KT1: H Wic 2G 203 (9K 25)
Salbrook Rd. RH1: Salf 2E 142
Salcombe Dr. SM4: Mord 7J 43
Salcombe Rd. TW15: A'ford 4N 21
Salcombe Vs. TW10: Rich 8L 11
Salcot Cres. CR0: N Add 6M 65
Salcott Rd. CR0: Bedd 9J 45
Sale Gdn. Cotts.
RG40: W'ham 3B 30
Salehurst Rd. RH10: Wor 3J 183
Salem Pl.
CR0: Croy 5B 200 (9N 45)
Salerno Cl. GU11: Alde 1M 109
Sales Ct. GU11: Alde 3L 109
Salesian Gdns. KT16: Chert 7J 37
Salesian Vw. GU14: Farnb 5C 90
Salford Rd. SW2 ....2H 29
SALFORDS 2E 142
Salfords Ind. Est.
RH1: Salf 3E 142
Salfords Station (Rail) 2F 142
Salisbury Av. SM1: Sut 3L 61
Salisbury Cl. KT4: W Pk 9E 42
Salisbury Ct. SM5: Cars 2D 62
Salisbury Gdns.
SW19 ....8K 27
Salisbury Gro. GU16: Mytc 1D 90
Salisbury Ho. SM6: W'ton 2F 62
Salisbury M. SW6 ....3L 13
Salisbury Pas. SW6 ....3L 13
(off Dawes Rd.)
Salisbury Pavement
SW6 ....3L 13
(off Dawes Rd.)
Salisbury Pl. KT14: W By 7L 55
Salisbury Rd. GU12: Ash 1E 110
GU14: Farnb 1A 90
GU17: B'water 1H 69
GU22: Wok 6A 74
KT3: N Mal 2C 42
KT4: W Pk 1C 60
RH9: Gods 9F 104
RH10: Craw 7C 182
(not continuous)
RH13: Hors 8G 196
SE25 ....5D 46
SM5: Cars 3D 62
SM7: Ban 1N 81
SW19 ....8K 27
TW4: Houn 6K 9
TW6: Lon A 9D 8
(not continuous)
TW9: Rich 7L 11
TW13: Felt 2K 23
Salisbury Ter. GU16: Mytc 2E 90
Salix Cl. KT22: Fetc 1B 98
TW16: Sunb 8J 23
Salliesfield TW2: Whitt 9D 10
Salmons La. CR3: Whyte 7B 84
CR3: Whyte, Cate 7B 84
Salmons La. W. CR3: Cate 7B 84
Salmons Rd. KT9: Ches 3L 59
KT24: Eff 7J 97
Saltash Cl. SM1: Sut 1L 61
Saltbox Hill TN16: B Hil 9D 66
Salt Box Rd. GU3: Guil 7J 93
GU4: Guil 7J 93
Saltdean Cl. RH10: Craw 6B 182
Salterford Rd. SW17 ....7E 28
Salterns Rd. RH10: Craw 6G 182
Salter's Hill SE19 ....6N 29
Saltire Gdns. RG42: Brac 9M 15
Salt La. GU8: Hamb 4G 153
Saltram Rd. GU14: Farnb 3C 90
Salvador SW17 ....6D 28
Salvation Pl. KT22: Fetc 2G 98
Salvia Ct. GU24: Bis 3D 72
Salvington Rd.
RH11: Craw 6L 181
Salvin Rd. SW15 ....6J 13
Salwey Cl. RG12: Brac 5N 31
Samaritan Cl. RH11: Craw 5K 181
Samarkand Cl. GU15: Camb 2F 70
Samels Ct. W6 ....1F 12
Samian Pl. RG42: Bin 8K 15
Sammi Ct. CR7: T Hea 3N 45
Samos Rd. SE20 ....1E 46
Samphire Cl. RH11: Craw 6M 181
Sampleoak La.
GU4: B'eath, Guil 9G 114
Sampson Ct. TW17: Shep 4D 38
Sampson Pk. RG42: Bin 9J 15
Sampson's Almshouses
GU9: Farnh 2E 128
Samuel Gray Gdns.
KT2: K Tham 1H 203 (9K 25)
Samuel Johnson Cl.
SW16 ....5K 29
Samuel Lewis Trust Dwellings
SW6 ....3M 13
(off Vanston Pl.)
Samuel Richardson Ho.
W14 ....1L 13
(off North End Cres.)
San Carlos App.
GU11: Alde 2A 110
Sanctuary, The SM4: Mord 5M 43
Sanctuary Rd. TW6: Lon A 9B 8
Sandal Rd. KT3: N Mal 4C 42
Sandalwood GU2: Guil 4L 113
Sandalwood Av.
KT16: Chert 9G 36
Sandalwood Rd. TW13: Felt 4J 23
Sandbanks TW14: Felt 2F 22
Sandbourne Av. SW19 ....1N 43
Sandcross La. RH2: Reig 6L 121
Sandell's Av. TW15: A'ford 5D 22
Sandeman Way
RH13: Hors 8L 197
Sanders Cl. TW12: H Hill 6C 24
Sandersfield Gdns.
SM7: Ban 2M 81
Sandersfield Rd. SM7: Ban 2N 81
SANDERSTEAD 8D 64
Sanderstead Cl. SW12 ....1G 29
Sanderstead Ct. Av.
CR2: Sande 9D 64
Sanderstead Hill
CR2: Sande 7B 64
Sanderstead Rd.
CR2: Sande, S Croy 4A 64
Sanderstead Station (Rail) 5A 64
Sandes Pl. KT22: Leat 5G 79
Sandfield Ct. GU1: Guil 4C 202
Sandfield Gdns.
CR7: T Hea 2M 45
Sandfield Pas. CR7: T Hea 2N 45
Sandfield Pl. CR7: T Hea 2N 45
Sandfield Rd. CR7: T Hea 2M 45
Sandfields GU23: Send 2F 94
Sandfield Ter.
GU1: Guil 4C 202 (4N 113)
Sandford Ct. GU11: Alde 3L 109
Sandford Down RG12: Brac 4D 32
Sandford Rd. GU9: U Hal 5G 109
GU11: Alde 3L 109
Sandford St. SW6 ....3N 13
Sandgate La. SW18 ....2C 28

Sandgates—Selwyn Ct.

Sandgates KT16: Chert 8G 37
Sandhawes Hill
RH19: E Grin 6C 166
Sandheath Rd.
GU26: Hind 2A 170
Sand Hill GU14: Farnb 7N 69
Sand Hill Ct. GU14: Farnb 7N 69
Sandhill La.
RH10: Craw D 2E 184
SANDHILLS 9A 152
Sandhills SM6: Bedd 1H 63
Sandhills Ct. GU25: V Wat 4A 36
Sandhills La. GU25: V Wat 4A 36
Sandhills Mdw.
TW17: Shep 6D 38
Sandhills Rd. RH2: Reig 4M 121
SANDHURST 8G 49
Sandhurst Av. KT5: Surb 6A 42
Sandhurst Cl. CR2: Sande 5B 64
Sandhurst La.
GU17: B'water 9G 48
Sandhurst Rd. GU46: Yate 8E 48
RG40: Finch 8A 30
RG45: Crow 4G 49
Sandhurst Sports Cen. 7K 49
Sandhurst Station (Rail) 8F 48
Sandhurst Way CR2: Sande ...4B 64
Sandiford Rd. SM3: Sut 8L 43
Sandilands CR0: Croy 8D 46
Sandilands Rd. SW6 ....4N 13
Sandilands Stop (CT) 8C 46
Sandlands Gro.
KT20: Wal H 1F 100
Sandlands Rd.
KT20: Wal H 1F 100
Sandmartin Way SM6: Mit 7E 44
Sandon Cl. KT10: Esh 6D 40
Sandown Av. KT10: Esh 2C 58
Sandown Cl. GU17: B'water ...1J 69
TW5: C'ford 4H 9
Sandown Ct. RH1: Red 2C 122
(off Station Rd.)
RH10: Craw 3H 183
SM2: Sut 4N 61
Sandown Cres.
GU11: Alde 5N 109
Sandown Dr. GU16: Frim 4B 70
SM5: Cars 5E 62
Sandown Ga. KT10: Esh 9D 40
Sandown Ind. Pk.
KT10: Esh 8A 40
Sandown Lodge KT18: Eps 1C 80
Sandown Pk. Racecourse 9C 40
Sandown Rd. CR5: Coul 3E 82
KT10: Esh 1C 58
SE25 ....4E 46
Sandown Sports Cen. 9B 40
Sandpiper Cl. RH11: Ifi 5J 181
Sandpiper Rd. CR2: Sels 7G 64
SM1: Sut 2L 61
Sandpit Cotts. GU24: Pirb 9B 72
Sandpit Hall Rd.
GU24: Chob 8K 53
Sandpit Heath GU3: Worp 8G 92
Sandpit La. GU21: Knap 1E 72
(not continuous)
Sandpit Rd. RH1: Red 4C 122
Sandpits Rd. CR0: Croy 1G 64
TW10: Ham 3K 25
Sandra Cl. TW3: Houn 8B 10
Sandra Ct. CR4: Mit 7D 28
Sandra Ho. KT8: E Mol 4D 40
Sandringham Av.
SW20 ....9K 27
Sandringham Cl. GU22: Pyr ...3J 75
RH19: E Grin 1C 186
SW19 ....2J 27
Sandringham Ct.
KT2: K Tham 1H 203
(off Skerne Wlk.)
SM2: Sut 5M 61
Sandringham Dr.
TW15: A'ford 5M 21
Sandringham Gdns.
KT8: W Mole 3A 40
TW5: C'ford 4H 9
Sandringham M.
TW12: Hamp 9N 23
Sandringham Pk.
KT11: Cob 8A 58
Sandringham Rd.
CR7: T Hea 4N 45
KT4: W Pk 9F 42
RH11: Craw 7N 181
TW6: Lon A 8N 7
Sandringham Way
GU16: Frim 6D 70
Sandrock GU27: Hasl 2G 188
Sandrock Cotts.
GU28: North 9D 190
Sandrock Hill Rd.
GU10: Wrec 5E 128
Sandrock Pl. CR0: Croy 1G 64
Sandrock Rd. RH4: Westc 7B 118
Sandroyd Way KT11: Cob 9A 58
SANDS, THE 2C 130
Sands Cl. GU10: Seal 1B 130
SANDS END 4N 13
Sand's End La. SW6 ....4N 13
Sands Rd. GU10: Run 9A 110
Sandy Bury BR6: Orp 1M 67
Sandy Cl. GU22: Wok 4E 74
RH10: Craw D 1D 184
Sandycombe Rd.
TW9: Kew, Rich 6M 11
TW14: Felt 2H 23
Sandycoombe Rd.
TW1: Twick 9J 11
Sandy Ct. KT11: Cob 9N 57
Sandy Cft. KT17: Ewe 6H 61
SANDY CROSS 8C 110
Sandy Dr. KT11: Cob 7A 58
TW14: Felt 2F 22
Sandy Hill Rd. GU9: U Hal ...5F 108
SM6: W'ton 5G 62
Sandy Holt KT11: Cob 9N 57
Sandy La. CR4: Mit 9E 28
(not continuous)
GU3: Art 8K 113
GU3: Art, Comp 8G 112
GU3: Norm, Wood V 9B 92
GU5: Alb 1L 135
GU5: Shere 8B 116
GU7: Goda 5G 133
GU8: Mil 2B 152
GU10: Rush 4M 149
GU14: Cove 8H 69
GU15: Camb 9C 50
GU22: Pyr 4J 75
(not continuous)
GU22: Wok 4D 74
GU23: Send 1E 94
GU24: Chob 5H 53
GU25: V Wat 3A 36
GU27: G'wood, Hasl 8J 171
GU27: Lip 1A 188
GU47: Sandh 6E 48
GU52: C Cro 9B 88
KT1: H Wic 8H 25
KT11: Cob 8N 57
KT12: Wal T 5J 39
KT20: K'wood 2L 101
KT22: Oxs 8N 57
RG12: Brac 9A 16
RH1: Blet 1M 123
RH1: Sth N 4H 123
RH2: Reig 4G 120
RH3: Betch 4D 120
RH8: Limp 5D 106
RH8: Oxt 7M 105
RH10: Craw D 1C 184
RH19: E Grin 9A 166
SL5: Asc 9F 16
SL5: S'dale 4D 34
SM2: Chea 4K 61
SM6: W'ton 3H 63
TN16: Weste 3M 107
TW10: Ham 3J 25
TW11: Tedd 8G 24
Sandy La. Nth. SM6: W'ton ...3H 63
Sandy La. Sth. SM6: W'ton ...5G 62
Sandy Mead KT19: Eps 6N 59
Sandy Ride SL5: S'hill 3B 34
Sandy Rd. KT15: Addl 3J 55
Sandy Way CR0: Croy 9J 47
GU22: Wok 4E 74
KT11: Cob 8A 58
KT12: Wal T 7G 38
San Feliu Ct. RH19: E Grin ...8D 166
Sanger Av. KT9: Ches 2L 59
Sanger Dr. GU23: Send 1E 94
Sangers Dr. RH6: Horl 8D 142
Sangers Wlk. RH6: Horl 8D 142
Sangley Rd. SE25 ....3B 46
Sankey La. GU51: Fleet 1E 88
Santina Cl. GU9: H End 4J 109
Santos Rd. SW18 ....8M 13
SANWAY 1N 75
Sanway Cl. KT14: Byf 1N 75
Sanway Rd. KT14: Byf 1N 75
Saphora Cl. BR6: Farnb 2M 67
Sappho Ct. GU21: Wok 3H 73
Sapte Cl. GU6: Cranl 7B 156
Saracen Cl. CR0: Croy 5A 46
Sarah Way GU14: Farnb 1N 89
Sarel Way RH6: Horl 6F 142
Sargent Cl. RH10: Craw 7D 182
Sarjant Path SW19 ....3J 27
(off Blincoe Cl.)
Sarjeant Ct. BR4: W Wick 8N 47
(off Bencurtis Pk.)
Sark Cl. RH11: Craw 7M 181
TW5: Hest 3A 10
Sarsby Dr. TW19: Wray 3C 20
Sarsen Av. TW3: Houn 5A 10
Sarsfeld Rd. SW12 ....2D 28
Sarum RG12: Brac 7L 31
Sarum Cres. RG40: W'ham 1C 30
Sarum Grn. KT13: Weybr 9F 38
Satellite Bus. Village
RH10: Craw 8C 162
Satis Ct. KT17: Ewe 7E 60
Satis Ho. SL3: Dat 3M 5
Saturn Cl. RH11: Craw 5K 181
Saturn Cft. RG42: Wink R 7F 16
Saunderites GU7: Goda 4F 132
Saunders Cl. RH10: Craw 3F 182
Saunders Copse GU22: Wok ...9L 73
Saunders La. GU22: Wok 9H 73
Saunton Av. UB3: Harl 3G 8
Saunton Gdns.
GU14: Farnb 8M 69
Savernake Wlk.
RH10: Craw 6D 182
Savernake Way RG12: Brac ...5C 32
Savery Dr. KT6: Surb 6H 41
Savile Cl. KT3: N Mal 4D 42
KT7: T Dit 7F 40
Savile Gdns. CR0: Croy 8C 46
Saville Cl. KT19: Eps 7A 60
Saville Cres.
TW15: A'ford 7E 22
Saville Gdns. GU15: Camb 1F 70
Saville Rd. TW1: Twick 2F 24
Savill Garden, The 7H 19
Savill Gdns. SW20 ....2F 42
Savill Ho. SW4 ....1H 29
Savill M. TW20: Eng G 7N 19
Savin Lodge SM2: Sut 4A 62
(off Walnut M.)
Savona Cl. SW19 ....8J 27
Savory Wlk. RG42: Bin 7G 15
Savoy Av. UB3: Harl 1F 8
Savoy Gro. GU17: Haw 3J 69
Sawkins Cl. SW19 ....3K 27
Sawpit La. GU4: E Cla 9N 95
Sawtry Cl. SM5: Cars 6C 44
Sawyers Cl. SL4: W'sor 3B 4
Sawyer's Hill TW10: Rich 1M 25
Saxby Rd. SW2 ....1J 29
Saxby's La. RH7: Ling 7N 145
Saxley RH6: Horl 7G 142
Saxon Av. TW13: Hanw 3M 23
Saxonbury Av. TW16: Sunb 2J 39
Saxonbury Cl. CR4: Mit 2B 44
Saxonbury Gdns.
KT6: Surb 7J 41
Saxon Bus. Cen.
SW19 ....1A 44
Saxon Cl. KT6: Surb 5K 41
Saxon Cres. RH12: Hors 4H 197
Saxon Cft. GU9: Farnh 2H 129
Saxon Dr. RG42: Warf 9D 16
Saxonfield Cl. SW2 ....1K 29
Saxon Ho.
KT1: K Tham ...7M 203 (3M 41)
TW13: Hanw 3N 23
Saxon Lodge CR0: Croy 1C 200
Saxon Rd.
KT2: K Tham 1J 203 (9L 25)
KT12: Wal T 9L 39
RH10: Wor 4J 183
SE25 ....4A 46
TW15: A'ford 7E 22
Saxons KT20: Tad 8J 81
Saxon Way RH2: Reig 2L 121
SL4: O Win 9L 5
UB7: Harm 2L 7
Saxon Way Ind. Est.
UB7: Harm 2L 7
Saxony Way GU46: Yate 2B 68
Sayers, The RH19: E Grin ...9M 165
Sayers Cl. GU16: Frim G 7C 70
KT22: Fetc 1C 98
RH13: Hors 6L 197
Sayer's Wlk. TW10: Rich 1M 25
Sayes Ct. KT15: Addl 2L 55
Sayes Ct. Farm Dr.
KT15: Addl 2K 55
Scallows Cl. RH10: Craw 2E 182
Scallows Rd. RH10: Craw 2E 182
Scania Wlk. RG42: Wink R 7F 16
Scarborough Cl. SM2: Chea ...7L 61
TN16: B Hil 5E 86
Scarborough Rd.
TW6: Lon A 9D 8
Scarbrook Rd.
CR0: Croy 5B 200 (9N 45)
Scarlet Oaks GU15: Camb 3C 70
Scarlett Cl. GU21: Wok 5J 73
Scarlette Mnr. Way
SW2 ....1L 29
Scarlett's Rd. GU11: Alde ...1M 109
Scarth Rd. SW13 ....6E 12
Scawen Cl. SM5: Cars 1E 62
Schaffer Ct. RH10: Craw 5G 183
Schlumberger Ho.
RH6: Gat 3G 163
Scholars Rd. SW12 ....2G 28
Scholars Wlk. GU2: Guil 4L 113
GU14: Farnb 8M 69
School All. TW1: Twick 2G 25
School Allotment Ride
SL4: Wink 1M 17
School Cl. GU1: Guil 9N 93
GU24: Bis 2C 72
RH12: Hors 2N 197
School Cotts. GU22: Wok 9M 73
School Fld. TN8: Eden 1L 147
School Hill GU10: Seal 8F 110
GU10: Wrec 4E 128
GU47: Sandh 6F 48
RG45: Crow 3J 49
(not continuous)
RH1: Mers 6G 102
RH12: Warn 9F 178
School Ho. La. TW11: Tedd ...8H 25
School La. CR3: Cate 4C 104
GU3: Norm 9K 91
GU3: Put 8N 111
GU4: E Cla 9N 95
GU8: Chid 5E 172
GU8: S'ford 5B 132
GU10: Ews 4C 108
GU10: L Bou 5J 129
GU19: Bag 5H 51
GU20: Windl 2A 52
GU23: Ockh 9C 76
GU24: Pirb 9B 72
School La. GU46: Yate 9A 48
KT1: H Wic 9J 25
KT6: Surb 7N 41
KT15: Addl 2J 55
KT20: Wal H 3F 100
KT22: Fetc 9D 78
KT24: W Hors 7C 96
RH4: Westc 6D 118
RH5: Mick 5J 99
RH5: Ockl 6D 158
RH18: F Row 7H 187
RH19: Ash W 3F 186
SL5: Asc 9H 17
TW17: Shep 5C 38
TW20: Egh 6C 20
School Mdw. GU2: Guil 1G 113
School Pas.
KT1: K Tham ...4M 203 (1M 41)
School Rd. GU10: Rowl 8D 128
GU20: Windl 1L 51
GU26: G'hott 6N 169
GU27: Hasl 3D 188
KT1: H Wic 9J 25
KT8: E Mol 3D 40
RG40: W'ham 2C 30
SL5: S'hill 4A 34
TW3: Houn 6C 10
TW12: H Hill 7C 24
TW15: A'ford 7C 22
UB7: Harm 2M 7
School Rd. Av. TW12: H Hill ...7C 24
SCHOOL ROAD JUNC. 8C 22
School Wlk. RH6: Horl 8C 142
TW16: Sunb 3G 38
Schroder Ct. TW20: Eng G 6L 19
Schroders Av. RH1: Red 1F 122
Schubert Rd. SW15 ....8L 13
Scillonian Rd. GU2: Guil 4K 113
SCILLY ISLES 8E 40
Scizdons Climb GU7: Goda ...7J 133
Scoles Cres. SW2 ....2M 29
Scope Way
KT1: K Tham 7K 203 (3L 41)
Scory Cl. RH11: Craw 6M 181
Scotia Rd. SW2 ....1L 29
Scotland Bri. Rd.
KT15: N Haw 7J 55
Scotland Cl. GU12: A Va 8E 90
Scotland Farm Rd.
GU12: A Va 8E 90
Scotland Hill GU47: Sandh 6F 48
Scotland La. GU27: Hasl 3F 188
Scotlands Cl. GU27: Hasl 3F 188
Scotlands Dr. GU27: Hasl 3F 188
(not continuous)
Scotney Cl. BR6: Farnb 1J 67
Scots Cl. TW19: Stan 2M 21
Scotsdale Cl. SM3: Chea 4K 61
Scotshall La. CR6: Warl 2M 85
Scotswood Pk. GU21: Wok 1F 74
Scott Av. SW18 ....9K 13
Scott Cl. GU2: Guil 1K 113
KT19: Ewe 2B 60
SW16 ....9K 29
Scott Farm Cl. KT7: T Dit 7H 41
Scott Gdns. TW5: Hest 3L 9
Scott Rd. RH10: Craw 6D 182
Scotts Av. BR2: Brom 1N 47
TW16: Sunb 8F 22
Scott's Ct. GU14: Farnb 7N 69
Scotts Dr. TW12: Hamp 8B 24
Scotts Farm Rd. KT19: Ewe 3B 60
Scott's Gro. Cl. GU24: Chob ...9G 52
Scott's Gro. Rd.
GU24: Chob 9E 52
Scott's Hill RH1: Out 5A 144
Scotts La. BR2: Brom 2N 47
KT12: Hers 1L 57
Scotts M. SL5: Asc 9F 16
Scotts Way TW16: Sunb 8F 22
Scott Ter. RG12: Brac 9C 16
Scott Trimmer Way
TW3: Houn 5M 9
Screen, The
Reigate 3M 121
Scrutton Cl. SW12 ....1H 29
Scutley La. GU18: Ligh 5B 52
GU20: Windl 5B 52
Scylla Cres. TW6: Lon A 1C 22
(not continuous)
Scylla Pl. GU21: Wok 6K 73
Scylla Rd. TW6: Lon A 9C 8
Seabrook Dr. BR4: W Wick 8N 47
Seaford Ct. RG40: W'ham 2C 30
(not continuous)
Seaford Rd. RG40: W'ham 2C 30
RH11: Craw 8M 181
TW6: Lon A 8M 7
Seaforth Av. KT3: N Mal 4G 42
Seaforth Gdns. KT19: Ewe 1E 60
Seagrave Lodge SW6 ....2M 13
(off Seagrave Rd.)
Seagrave Rd. SW6 ....2M 13
Sealand Rd. TW6: Lon A 9B 8
SEALE 8F 110
Seale Hill RH2: Reig 5M 121
Seale La. GU3: Put 8J 111
GU10: Seal 8B 110
(not continuous)
Seale Rd. GU8: Els 3F 130
GU10: Seal 3F 130
Searchwood Rd. CR6: Warl 5E 84
Searle Rd. GU9: Farnh 3H 129
Searle's Vw. RH12: Hors 3L 197
Seaton Cl. SW15 ....2G 27
TW2: Whitt 9D 10
Seaton Dr. TW15: A'ford 3N 21
Seaton Rd. CR4: Mit 1C 44
GU15: Camb 1N 69
TW2: Whitt 9C 10
Sebastopol La.
GU8: Worm 9A 152
Sebastopol Rd.
GU11: Alde 2N 109
Secombe Theatre 2N 61
Second Av. KT12: Wal T 5J 39
KT20: Lwr K 3K 101
SW14 ....6D 12
Second Cl. KT8: W Mole 3C 40
Second Cross Rd.
TW2: Twick 3E 24
Seddon Ct. RH11: Craw 8N 181
Seddon Hill RG42: Warf 7N 15
Seddon Rd. SM4: Mord 4B 44
Sedgefield Cl. RH10: Craw ...2J 183
Sedgemoor GU14: Farnb 7N 69
Sedgewick Cl.
RH10: Craw 3G 183
Sedgwick La. RH13: Hors ...9M 197
Sedleigh Rd. SW18 ....9L 13
Sedlescombe Rd.
SW6 ....2M 13
Seebys Oak GU47: C Tow 9J 49
Seely Rd. SW17 ....7E 28
SEETHING WELLS 5J 41
Seething Wells La.
KT6: Surb 5J 41
Sefton Cl. GU24: W End 9C 52
Sefton Ct. TW3: Houn 4B 10
Sefton Rd. CR0: Croy 7D 46
KT19: Ewe 6C 60
Sefton St. SW15 ....6H 13
Sefton Vs. RH5: Nth H 9H 119
Segrave Cl. KT13: Weybr 4B 56
Segsbury Gro. RG12: Brac 3C 32
Sekhon Ter. TW13: Hanw 4A 24
Selborne Av. GU11: Alde 5N 109
Selborne Cl. GU17: B'water ...9H 49
Selborne Gdns.
GU9: Farnh 4F 128
Selborne Rd. CR0: Croy 9B 46
KT3: N Mal 1D 42
Selbourne Av. KT6: Surb 8M 41
KT15: N Haw 5K 55
Selbourne Cl. KT15: N Haw ...5K 55
RH10: Craw 8H 163
Selbourne Rd. GU4: B'ham ...9C 94
Selbourne Sq. RH9: Gods 8F 104
Selby Cl. KT9: Ches 4L 59
Selby Grn. SM5: Cars 6C 44
Selby Rd. SE20 ....1D 46
SM5: Cars 6C 44
TW15: A'ford 7D 22
Selbys RH7: Ling 6A 146
Selby Wlk. GU21: Wok 5L 73
Selcroft Rd. CR8: Pur 8M 63
Selham Cl. RH11: Craw 2M 181
SELHURST 5B 46
Selhurst Cl. GU21: Wok 2B 74
SW19 ....2J 27
SELHURST COMMON 3C 154
Selhurst New Rd.
SE25 ....5B 46
Selhurst Pk. 3B 46
Selhurst Pl.
SE25: Croy, Lon 5B 46
Selhurst Rd. SE25 ....5B 46
Selhurst Station (Rail) 4B 46
Selkirk Rd. SW17 ....5C 28
TW2: Twick 3C 24
Sellar's Hill GU7: Goda 4G 132
Sellincourt Rd. SW17 ....6C 28
Sells, The GU1: Guil 5B 114
SELSDON 6F 64
Selsdon Av. CR2: S Croy 3A 64
Selsdon Cl. KT6: Surb 4L 41
Selsdon Cres. CR2: Sels 5F 64
Selsdon Pk. Rd. CR0: Sels 5G 65
CR2: Sels 5G 65
Selsdon Rd.
CR2: S Croy 8D 200 (2A 64)
KT15: N Haw 7J 55
SE27 ....4L 29
Selsdon Wood Nature Reserve
..........................7H 65
Selsey Ct. RH11: Craw 7N 181
Selsey Rd. RH11: Craw 7M 181
SELSFIELD COMMON 8E 184
Selsfield Rd.
RH10: T Hil, Sharp 6D 184
RH19: W Hoa 8E 184
Seltops Cl. GU6: Cranl 8A 156
Selwin Ct. KT12: Wal T 7K 39
Selwood Cl. TW19: Stan 9L 7
Selwood Gdns. TW19: Stan 9L 7
Selwood Rd. CR0: Croy 8E 46
GU22: Wok 7D 74
KT9: Ches 1K 59
SM3: Sut 7L 43
Selwoods SW2 ....1L 29
Selwyn Av. TW9: Rich 6L 11
Selwyn Cl. RH10: Craw 9G 163
SL4: W'sor 5A 4
TW4: Houn 7M 9
Selwyn Ct. TW10: Rich 8M 11
(off Church Rd.)

Selwyn Dr.—Shirley Pl.

Selwyn Dr. GU46: Yate 9A 48
Selwyn Rd. KT3: N Mal 4C 42
Semaphore Rd.
GU1: Guil 7E 202 (5A 114)
Semley Rd. SW16 . . . . .1J 45
Semper Cl. GU21: Knap 4H 73
Sen Cl. RG42: Warf 7A 16
SEND 2F 94
Send Barns La.
GU23: Send 2F 94
Send Cl. GU23: Send 1E 94
Send Hill GU23: Send 3E 94
SEND MARSH 1H 95
Send Marsh Grn. GU23: Rip . . .1H 95
Send Marsh Rd.
GU23: Rip, Send 2F 94
Send Pde. Cl. GU23: Send 1E 94
Send Rd. GU23: Send 1D 94
Seneca Rd. CR7: T Hea 3N 45
Sener Ct. CR2: S Croy 3N 63
Senga Rd. SM6: W'ton 7E 44
Senhouse Rd. SM3: Chea 9J 43
Sentamu Cl. SE24 . . . . .2M 29
Sepen Meade GU52: C Cro 9A 88
Sequoia Pk. RH11: Craw 5B 182
Sergeant Ind. Est.
SW18 . . . . .9N 13
Sergeants Pl. CR3: Cate 9N 83
Serpentine Grn.
RH1: Mers 7H 103
Serrin Way RH12: Hors 3L 197
Servite Ho. BR3: Beck 1J 47
GU21: Knap 4G 73
KT4: W Pk 8E 42
(off The Avenue)
RH4: Dork 7G 119
(off Harrow Rd. W.)
Servius Ct. TW8: Brent 3K 11
Setley Way RG12: Brac 2D 32
Sett, The GU46: Yate 1A 68
Setter Combe RG42: Warf 7B 16
Settrington Rd. SW6 . . . . .5N 13
Seven Acres SM5: Cars 8C 44
Seven Arches App.
KT13: Weybr 4A 56
Seven Hills Cl.
KT12: Whit V 5F 56
Seven Hills Rd. KT11: Cob 6F 56
KT12: Hers, Whit V 6F 56
Seven Hills Rd. Sth.
KT11: Cob 9F 56
Seven Kings Way
KT2: K Tham 1J 203 (9L 25)
Sevenoaks Cl. SM2: Sut 6M 61
Sevenoaks Rd.
BR6: Chels, Orp 2N 67
BR6: P Bot 4N 67
Sevenseas Rd. TW6: Lon A 9D 8
Seventh Av. KT20: Lwr K 3K 101
Severells Copse 4N 137
Severn Cl. GU47: Sandh 7H 49
Severn Ct. KT2: K Tham 1H 203
Severn Cres. SL3: Lang 1D 6
Severn Dr. KT10: H Wood 8G 41
KT12: Wal T 8L 39
Severn Rd. GU14: Cove 8K 69
RH10: Craw 4G 182
Seward Rd. BR3: Beck 1G 47
Sewell Av. RG41: W'ham 9A 14
Sewer's Farm Rd.
RH5: A Com 5N 137
Sewill Cl. RH6: Char 3L 161
Seymour Av. CR3: Cate 1N 103
KT17: Ewe 5G 61
SM4: Mord 6J 43
Seymour Cl. KT8: E Mol 4C 40
Seymour Ct. GU51: Fleet 3B 88
KT11: Cob 9G 57
KT19: Ewe 5D 60
RG45: Crow 3D 48
Seymour Dr. GU15: Camb 7F 50
Seymour Gdns. KT5: Surb 4M 41
TW1: Twick 1H 25
TW13: Hanw 5K 23
Seymour Ho. SM2: Sut 3N 61
(off Mulgrave Rd.)
Seymour M. KT17: Ewe 6F 60
Seymour Pl. GU22: Wok 7L 73
SE25 . . . . .3E 46
Seymour Rd. CR4: Mit 6E 44
GU7: Goda 8E 132
GU35: H Dwn 5H 169
KT1: H Wic 2G 203 (9K 25)
KT8: W Mole, E Mol 4C 40
RH11: Craw 7M 181
SM5: Cars 2E 62
SW18 . . . . .1L 27
SW19 . . . . .4J 27
TW12: H Hill 6C 24
Seymour Ter. SE20 . . . . .1E 46
Seymour Vs. SE20 . . . . .1E 46
Seymour Way TW16: Sunb 8G 22
Shabden Cotts. CR5: Chip 8D 82
SHACKLEFORD 4A 132
Shackleford Rd.
GU8: Els, S'ford 7L 131
GU8: S'ford 4A 132
GU22: Wok 7C 74
Shacklegate La.
TW11: Tedd 5E 24
Shackleton Cl. GU12: A Va 8D 90
Shackleton Ct. TW19: Stan 9N 7
(off Whitley Cl.)
Shackleton Rd.
RH10: Craw 6C 182
Shackleton Wlk. GU2: Guil . . .3H 113
(off Chapelhouse Cl.)
Shackstead La. GU7: Goda 8F 132
Shadbolt Cl. KT4: W Pk 8E 42
Shadyhanger GU7: Goda 5H 133
Shady Nook GU9: U Hal 6G 108
Shaef Way TW11: Tedd 8G 25
Shaftesbury Av. TW14: Felt 9H 9
Shaftesbury Cl. RG12: Brac . . .4B 32
Shaftesbury Ct.
GU14: Farnb 5A 90
RG40: W'ham 1C 30
SW6 . . . . .4N 13
(off Maltings Pl.)
SW16 . . . . .4H 29
Shaftesbury Cres.
TW18: Stain 8M 21
Shaftesbury Ho. CR5: Coul 9H 83
Shaftesbury Mt. GU17: Haw 3H 69
Shaftesbury Rd. BR3: Beck 1J 47
GU22: Wok 4D 74
GU24: Bis 3C 72
RH10: Craw 5H 183
SM5: Cars 6B 44
TW9: Rich 6L 11
Shaftesbury Way
TW2: Twick 4D 24
Shakespeare Av. TW14: Felt 9H 9
Shakespeare Gdns.
GU14: Cove 9J 69
Shakespeare Rd.
KT15: Addl 1M 55
Shakespeare Way
RG42: Warf 8C 16
TW13: Hanw 5K 23
Shalbourne Ri.
GU15: Camb 1B 70
Shalden Ho. SW15 . . . . .9E 12
Shalden Rd. GU12: Alde 4B 110
Shaldon Dr. SM4: Mord 4K 43
Shaldon Way KT12: Wal T 9K 39
Shale Grn. RH1: Mers 7H 103
Shalesbrook La.
RH18: F Row 8H 187
SHALFORD 9A 114
Shalford Cl. BR6: Farnb 1L 67
Shalford Hill GU27: K Grn 8G 189
Shalford Mill 8A 114
Shalford Rd.
GU1: Guil 8D 202 (6N 113)
GU4: Guil 6N 113
Shalford Station (Rail) 9A 114
Shalstone Rd. SW14 . . . . .6A 12
Shalston Vs. KT6: Surb 5M 41
Shambles, The
GU1: Guil 6C 202 (5N 113)
SHAMLEY GREEN 7G 134
Shamrock Cl. GU16: Frim 6B 70
KT22: Fetc 8D 78
Shamrock Cotts. GU3: Worp . . .6L 93
Shamrock Rd. CR0: Croy 5K 45
Shandys Cl. RH12: Hors 7G 196
Shanklin Ct. GU12: Alde 3A 110
Shannon Cl. UB2: S'hall 1L 9
Shannon Commercial Cen.
KT3: N Mal 3F 42
SHANNON CORNER 3F 42
Shannon Cnr. Retail Pk.
KT3: N Mal 3F 42
Shannon Ct. CR0: Croy 1C 200
Shanti Ct. SW18 . . . . .2M 27
Shap Cres. SM5: Cars 7D 44
Sharland Cl. CR7: T Hea 5L 45
Sharman Row SL3: Lang 1B 6
Sharnbrook Ho. W14 . . . . .2M 13
Sharon Cl. KT6: Surb 7J 41
KT19: Eps 6H 201 (9B 60)
KT23: Book 2A 98
RH10: Craw 6E 182
Sharon Ct. CR2: S Croy 8C 200
Sharon Rd. W4 . . . . .1C 12
Sharp Ho. TW1: Twick 9K 11
Sharpthorne Cl. RH11: Ifi 3L 181
Shaw Cl. CR2: Sande 8C 64
KT16: Otter 3E 54
KT17: Ewe 7E 60
Shaw Ct. CR3: Cate 8A 84
SL4: O Win 8K 5
SM4: Mord 6A 44
Shaw Cres. CR2: Sande 8C 64
Shaw Dr. KT12: Wal T 6K 39
SHAW FARM 7H 5
Shawfield Cotts.
GU12: Ash 2D 110
Shawfield La. GU12: Ash 2D 110
Shawfield Rd. GU12: Ash 3D 110
Shawford Ct. SW15 . . . . .1F 26
Shawford Rd. KT19: Ewe 3C 60
Shaw Gdns. SL3: Lang 1B 6
Shaw Ho. SM7: Ban 6A 82
Shawley Cres. KT18: Tat C 5H 81
Shawley Way KT18: Tat C 5G 81
Shaw Pk. RG45: Crow 4G 48
Shaw Rd. TN16: Tats 7E 86
Shaws Cotts. GU2: Guil 7J 93
(off Worplesdon Rd.)
Shaws Path KT1: H Wic 9J 25
(off Bennett Cl.)
Shaws Rd. RH10: Craw 2D 182
Shaw Way SM6: W'ton 4J 63
Shaxton Cres. CR0: N Add 5M 65
Sheaf Cotts. KT7: T Dit 7E 40
(off Weston Grn.)
Shearing Dr. SM5: Cars 6A 44
SHEARS, THE 8F 22
Shears Ct. TW16: Sunb 8F 22
Shears Way TW16: Sunb 9F 22
Shearwater Ct. RH11: Ifi 4J 181
(off Stoneycroft Wlk.)
Shearwater Rd. SM1: Sut 2L 61
Sheath Cotts. KT7: T Dit 5H 41
(off Ferry Rd.)
Sheath's La. KT22: Oxs 9B 58
Sheen Comn. Dr.
TW10: Rich 7N 11
Sheen Ct. TW10: Rich 7N 11
Sheen Ct. Rd. TW10: Rich 7N 11
Sheendale Rd. TW9: Rich 7M 11
Sheen Ga. Gdns.
SW14 . . . . .7B 12
Sheengate Mans.
SW14 . . . . .7C 12
Sheen La. SW14 . . . . .8B 12
Sheen Pk. TW9: Rich 7M 11
Sheen Rd. TW9: Rich 8L 11
TW10: Rich 8L 11
Sheen Sports & Fitness Cen.
. . . . .7D 12
Sheen Way SM6: W'ton 2K 63
Sheen Wood SW14 . . . . .8B 12
Sheepbarn La. CR6: B Hil 8B 66
Sheepcote Cl. TW5: C'ford 3H 9
Sheepcote Rd. SL4: E Wic 1D 4
SL4: W'sor 5B 4
Sheepfold Rd. GU2: Guil 9J 93
SHEEP GREEN 3C 158
Sheephatch La.
GU10: Til 6N 129
Sheep Ho. GU9: Farnh 3H 129
Sheephouse Grn.
RH5: Wott 9N 117
Sheephouse La.
RH5: A Com, Wott 8N 117
(not continuous)
Sheephouse Way
KT3: N Mal 7C 42
Sheeplands Av. GU1: Guil 1E 114
Sheepmoor Dr. GU51: Fleet . . .2A 88
Sheep Wlk. KT18: Eps D 8C 80
RH2: Reig 9L 101
TW17: Shep 6A 38
Sheep Wlk., The
GU22: Wok 5F 74
Sheepwalk La.
KT24: E Hor 3G 116
RH5: Ran C 3H 117
Sheep Wlk. M. SW19 . . . . .7J 27
SHEERWATER 1F 74
Sheerwater Av.
KT15: Wood 8G 55
Sheerwater Bus. Cen.
GU21: Wok 2E 74
Sheerwater Rd. GU21: Wok 8G 54
KT14: W By 9G 55
KT15: Wood 8G 54
Sheet's Heath La.
GU24: B'wood 6D 72
Sheet St. SL4: W'sor 5G 5
Sheet St. Rd. SL4: W'sor 5A 18
Sheffield Cl. GU14: Cove 1L 89
RH10: Craw 5F 182
Sheffield Rd. TW6: Lon A 9D 8
Sheffield Way TW6: Lon A 8E 8
Shefford Cres.
RG40: W'ham 9C 14
Shelburne Dr. TW4: Houn 9A 10
Sheldon Cl. RH2: Reig 4N 121
RH10: Craw 4H 183
Sheldon Ct. GU1: Guil 4B 114
Sheldon St.
CR0: Croy 5B 200 (9N 45)
Sheldrick Cl. SW19 . . . . .1B 44
Shelford KT1: K Tham 1N 41
Shelley Av. RG12: Brac 1C 32
Shelley Cl. CR5: Coul 4K 83
GU51: Fleet 5B 88
RH10: Craw 1G 182
SL3: Lang 1B 6
SM7: Ban 2J 81
Shelley Ct. GU15: Camb 1A 70
Shelley Cres. TW5: Hest 4L 9
Shelley Dr. RH12: Bro H 5C 196
Shelley Ri. GU14: Farnb 8L 69
Shelley Rd. RH12: Hors 5H 197
RH19: E Grin 9M 165
Shelleys Ct. RH13: Hors 4N 197
Shelley Wlk. GU46: Yate 1A 68
Shelley Way SW19 . . . . .6B 28
Shellfield Cl. TW19: Stan M 8J 7
SHELLWOOD CROSS 4D 140
Shellwood Dr. RH5: Nth H 9J 119
Shellwood Rd. RH2: Leigh 1B 140
Shelson Av. TW13: Felt 4G 22
Shelton Av. CR6: Warl 4F 84
Shelton Cl. CR6: Warl 4F 84
GU2: Guil 7K 93
Shelton Rd. SW19 . . . . .9M 27
Shelvers Grn. KT20: Tad 8H 81
Shelvers Hill KT20: Tad 8G 81
Shelvers Spur KT20: Tad 8H 81
Shelvers Way KT20: Tad 8H 81
Shenfield Cl. CR5: Coul 6G 82
Shenley Cl. CR2: Sande 6C 64
Shenley Rd. TW5: Hest 4M 9
Shenston Ct. SL4: W'sor 4G 4
(off James St.)
Shenstone Ho. SW16 . . . . .6G 29
Shenstone Pk. SL5: S'hill 3B 34
Shepherd & Flock Rdbt.
GU9: Farnh 9K 109
Shepherd Cl. RH10: Craw 6C 182
TW13: Hanw 5M 23
Shepherds Chase
GU19: Bag 5J 51
Shepherds Cl. TW17: Shep 5C 38
Shepherds Ct. GU9: Farnh 3H 129
SL4: W'sor 5B 4
Shepherds Gro. La.
RH19: E Grin 5H 167
Shepherds Hill GU2: Guil 1K 113
GU27: Hasl 2G 188
RG12: Brac 9A 16
RH1: Mers 4G 102
TN7: C Hat 8M 187
Shepherd's Hill Bungs.
GU27: Hasl 2G 189
(off Shepherd's Hill)
Shepherds La. GU2: Guil 9J 93
GU20: Windl 2C 52
RG42: Brac 8M 15
Shepherds Wlk.
GU14: Cove 7K 69
KT18: Eps D 8A 80
Shepherds Way CR2: Sels 4G 64
GU4: Guil 7A 114
(not continuous)
GU10: Til 7A 130
RG45: Crow 3D 48
RH12: Hors 3N 197
Shepiston La. UB3: Harl 1C 8
Shepley Cl. SM5: Cars 9E 44
Shepley Dr. SL5: S'dale 5F 34
Shepley End SL5: S'dale 4F 34
Sheppard Cl.
KT1: K Tham 8K 203 (3L 41)
Sheppard Ho. SW2 . . . . .2L 29
SHEPPERTON 5C 38
Shepperton Bus. Pk.
TW17: Shep 4D 38
Shepperton Ct. TW17: Shep . . .5C 38
Shepperton Ct. Dr.
TW17: Shep 4C 38
Shepperton Film Studios 2A 38
SHEPPERTON GREEN 3B 38
Shepperton Rd.
TW18: Lale, Shep 2L 37
Shepperton Station (Rail) 4D 38
Sheppey Cl. RH11: Craw 6N 181
Sheraton Cl. GU17: Haw 2K 69
Sheraton Dr.
KT19: Eps 6H 201 (9B 60)
Sheraton Wlk.
RH11: Craw 8N 181
Sherborne Cl. KT18: Tat C 4H 81
SL3: Poy 4G 7
Sherborne Ct.
GU2: Guil 6B 202 (5M 113)
Sherborne Cres. SM5: Cars . . .6C 44
Sherborne Gdns.
TW17: Shep 6F 38
Sherborne La. GU5: Ewh 1G 157
RH5: H Mary 1G 157
Sherborne Rd. GU14: Farnb . . .4B 90
KT9: Ches 2L 59
SM3: Sut 8M 43
TW14: Bedf 2E 22
(not continuous)
Sherborne Wlk. KT22: Leat 8J 79
Sherbourne GU5: Alb 8M 115
Sherbourne Cotts.
GU5: Alb 7N 115
Sherbourne Ct. SM2: Sut 3A 62
Sherbourne Dr. SL4: W'sor 7C 4
SL5: S'dale 4G 34
Sherbrooke Rd. SW6 . . . . .3K 13
Sherbrooke Ter. SW6 . . . . . . .3K 13
(off Sherbrook Rd.)
Sherbrooke Way KT4: W Pk 6G 42
SHERE 8B 116
Shere Av. SM2: Chea 6H 61
Shere Cl. KT9: Ches 2K 59
RH5: Nth H 9J 119
Shere La. GU5: Shere 8B 116
Shere Mus. 8B 116
Shere Rd.
GU4: Guil, W Cla 4J 115
GU5: Alb, Gorn, Shere 7N 115
GU6: Ewh 2E 156
KT24: W Hors 8C 96
(not continuous)
Sherfield Cl. KT3: N Mal 3A 42
Sherfield Gdns. SW15 . . . . . . .9E 12
Sheridan Cl. GU11: Alde 4M 109
Sheridan Ct. CR0: Croy 6F 200
SW5 . . . . .1N 13
(off Barkston Gdns.)
TW4: Houn 8M 9
Sheridan Dr. RH2: Reig 1N 121
Sheridan Grange
SL5: S'dale 5D 34
Sheridan Ho. KT22: Leat 8G 78
Sheridan Pl. RH19: E Grin . . .9M 165
SW13 . . . . .6E 12
Sheridan Rd. GU16: Frim 6B 70
SW19 . . . . .9L 27
TW10: Ham 4J 25
Sheridans Rd. KT23: Book 4C 98
Sheridan Wlk. SM5: Cars 2D 62
Sheridan Way BR3: Beck 1J 47
Sheriden Pl. TW12: Hamp 9B 24
Sheringham Av. TW2: Whitt . . .2N 23
TW13: Felt 4H 23
Sheringham Ct. TW13: Felt 4H 23
(off Sheringham Av.)
Sheringham Rd. SE20 . . . . . . .2F 46
Sherington Cl. GU14: Farnb . . .8N 69
Sherland Rd. TW1: Twick 2F 24
Sherlocks Ct RH4: Dork 1J 201
Shermanbury Ct.
RH12: Hors 4K 197
(off Blenheim Rd.)
Shernden La. TN8: M Grn 5L 147
Sherriff Cl. KT10: Esh 8B 40
Sherring Cl. RG42: Brac 8A 16
Sherrydon GU6: Cranl 6A 156
Sherwin Cres. GU14: Farnb . . .6N 69
Sherwood KT6: Surb 8K 41
Sherwood Av. SW16 . . . . .8H 29
Sherwood Cl. KT22: Fetc 1C 98
RG12: Brac 1E 32
SW13 . . . . .6G 13
Sherwood Ct. CR2: S Croy . . .8B 200
SL3: Lang 1B 6
Sherwood Cres. RH2: Reig . . .7N 121
Sherwood Pk. Rd. CR4: Mit . . .3G 44
SM1: Sut 2M 61
Sherwood Rd. CR0: Croy 6E 46
CR5: Coul 3G 82
GU21: Knap 4H 73
SW19 . . . . .8L 27
TW12: H Hill 6C 24
Sherwood Wlk.
RH10: Craw 6D 182
Sherwood Way
BR4: W Wick 8M 47
Shetland Cl. GU4: B'ham 7D 94
RH10: Craw 2J 183
Shetland Rd. TW6: Lon A 9D 8
Shetland Way GU51: Fleet 1C 88
Shewens Rd. KT13: Weybr 1E 56
Shey Copse GU22: Wok 4E 74
Shield Dr. TW8: Brent 2G 11
Shield Rd. TW15: A'ford 5D 22
Shilburn Way GU21: Wok 5K 73
Shildon Cl. GU15: Camb 3H 71
SHILLINGLEE 3G 190
Shillinglee Rd.
GU8: Chid, Plais 4G 190
RH14: Plais 4G 190
Shimmings, The GU1: Guil 2C 114
Shinners Cl. SE25 . . . . .4D 46
Shinwell Wlk. RH11: Craw 8N 181
Ship All. GU14: Farnb 8A 70
W4 . . . . .2N 11
Shipfield Cl. TN16: Tats 8E 86
Ship Hill TN16: Tats 8E 86
Shipka Rd. SW12 . . . . .2F 28
Shiplake Ho. RG12: Brac 3D 32
Ship La. GU14: Farnb 8A 70
SW14 . . . . .6B 12
SHIPLEY BRIDGE 4K 163
Shipley Bri. La.
RH6: S Bri 5K 163
RH10: S Bri 5K 163
Shipley Rd. RH11: Craw 2M 181
Ship St. RH19: E Grin 1A 186
Ship Yd. KT13: Weybr 9C 38
Shire Av. GU51: Fleet 1D 88
Shire Cl. GU19: Bag 5J 51
RG42: Warf 8D 16
Shire Ct. GU11: Alde 2K 109
KT17: Ewe 4E 60
Shire Horse Way TW7: Isle 6F 10
Shire La. BR2: Kes 5G 67
BR6: Chels, Dow 4K 67
(not continuous)
Shire M. TW2: Whitt 9C 10
Shire Pde. RH10: Craw 2H 183
Shire Pl. RH1: Red 5D 122
RH10: Craw 2H 183
(off The Ridings)
SW18 . . . . .1A 28
TW8: Brent 3K 11
Shires, The TW10: Ham 5L 25
Shires Cl. KT21: A'tead 6K 79
Shires Ho. KT14: Byf 9N 55
Shires Wlk. TN8: Eden 9K 127
Shires Way GU46: Yate 8C 48
SHIRLEY 8F 46
Shirley Av. CR0: Croy 7F 46
CR5: Coul 6M 83
RH1: Red 8D 122
SL4: W'sor 4C 4
SM1: Sut 1B 62
SM2: Chea 5L 61
Shirley Chu. Rd. CR0: Croy 9G 46
Shirley Cl. RH11: Craw 7J 181
TW3: Houn 8C 10
Shirley Ct. GU1: Guil 4D 202
SW16 . . . . .8J 29
Shirley Cres. BR3: Beck 3H 47
Shirley Dr. TW3: Houn 8C 10
Shirley Hgts. SM6: W'ton 5G 62
Shirley Hills Rd. CR0: Croy 2F 64
Shirleyhyrst KT13: Weybr 3E 56
SHIRLEY OAKS 7G 46
Shirley Oaks Rd. CR0: Croy 7G 46
Shirley Pk. CR0: Croy 8F 46
Shirley Pk. Rd. CR0: Croy 7E 46
Shirley Pl. GU21: Knap 4F 72

Shirley Rd.—Sorrel Cl.

Shirley Rd. CR0: Croy . . . 6E 46
SM6: W'ton . . . 5G 62
Shirley Way CR0: Croy . . . 9H 47
Shirley Windmill . . . 9F 46
Shoe Bridges TN8: Cow . . . 5M 167
Shoe La. GU11: Alde . . . 7M 89
Sholto Rd. TW6: Lon A . . . 8A 8
Shophouse La. GU5: Alb . . . 4M 135
Shoppe Hill GU8: Duns . . . 4A 174
Shops, The GU5: Wone . . . 3D 134
Shord Hill CR8: Ken . . . 3A 84
Shore Cl. TW12: Hamp . . . 7M 23
TW14: Felt . . . 1H 23
Shore Gro. TW13: Hanw . . . 3N 23
Shoreham Cl. CR0: Croy . . . 5F 46
SW18 . . . 8N 13
Shoreham Rd.
RH10: Craw . . . 6G 183
Shoreham Rd. E.
TW6: Lon A . . . 8N 7
Shoreham Rd. W.
TW6: Lon A . . . 8N 7
Shores Rd. GU21: Wok . . . 1A 74
Shorland Oaks RG42: Brac . . . 7A 16
Shorrold's Rd. SW6 . . . 3L 13
Shortacres RH1: Nut . . . 2K 123
Short Cl. RH11: Craw . . . 9B 162
Shortcroft Rd. KT17: Ewe . . . 4E 60
Shortdale Rd. GU11: Alde . . . 6A 110
SHORTFIELD COMMON . . . 1H 149
Shortfield Rd. GU10: Fren . . . 1H 149
Short Gallop RH10: Craw . . . 2H 183
SHORTHEATH . . . 5F 128
Shortheath Crest
GU9: Farnh . . . 5E 128
Shortheath Rd. GU9: Farnh . . . 5F 128
Short Hedges TW3: Houn . . . 4A 10
Shortlands GU10: Fren . . . 1G 149
UB3: Harl . . . 2E 8
W6 . . . 1J 13
Shortlands Gro. BR2: Brom . . . 2N 47
Shortlands Rd. BR2: Brom . . . 2N 47
KT2: K Tham . . . 1M 203 (8M 25)
Short La. RH8: Limp . . . 1D 126
TW19: Stan . . . 1A 22
Short Rd. TW6: Lon A . . . 9N 7
W4 . . . 2D 12
Shortsfield Cl. RH12: Hors . . . 3J 197
Shorts Rd. SM5: Cars . . . 1C 62
Short St. GU11: Alde . . . 2M 109
Short Way TW2: Whitt . . . 1C 24
Shortwood *GU22: Wok* . . . *6N 73*
(off Mt. Hermon Rd.)
Shortwood Av. TW18: Stain . . . 4K 21
Shotfield SM6: W'ton . . . 3F 62
Shott Cl. SM1: Sut . . . 2A 62
Shottendane Rd. SW6 . . . 4M 13
SHOTTERMILL . . . 1D 188
Shottermill RH12: Hors . . . 1N 197
Shottermill Pk.
GU27: Hasl . . . 1C 188
Shottermill Pond
GU27: Hasl . . . 3C 188
Shottermill Rd.
GU27: Hasl . . . 3C 188
Shottfield Av. SW14 . . . 7D 12
Shovelstrode La.
RH19: Ash W, E Grin . . . 1E 186
Shrewsbury Av. SW14 . . . 7B 12
Shrewsbury Cl. KT6: Surb . . . 8L 41
Shrewsbury Rd. BR3: Beck . . . 2H 47
RH1: Red . . . 3C 122
SM5: Cars . . . 5C 44
TW6: Lon A . . . 9D 8
(not continuous)
Shrewsbury Wlk. TW7: Isle . . . 6G 11
Shrewton Rd. SW17 . . . 8D 28
Shrivenham Cl.
GU47: C Tow . . . 7J 49
Shropshire Cl. CR4: Mit . . . 3J 45
Shropshire Gdns.
RG42: Warf . . . 8D 16
Shrubbery, The GU14: Cove . . . 2J 89
KT6: Surb . . . 7L 41
Shrubbery Rd. SW16 . . . 5J 29
Shrubbs Hill GU24: Chob . . . 5F 52
Shrubbs Hill La. SL5: S'dale . . . 5F 34
Shrubbs La. GU10: Rowl . . . 7E 128
Shrubland Ct. *SM7: Ban* . . . *3L 81*
(off Garratts La.)
Shrubland Gro. KT4: W Pk . . . 9H 43
Shrubland Rd. SM7: Ban . . . 3L 81
Shrublands Av. CR0: Croy . . . 9K 47
Shrublands Dr. GU18: Ligh . . . 7M 51
SHRUBS HILL . . . 5F 34
Shulbrede Priory . . . 8B 188
Shurlock Dr. BR6: Farnb . . . 1L 67
SHURLOCK ROW . . . 1F 14
Shute End RG40: W'ham . . . 2A 30
Shuters Sq. W14 . . . 1L 13
Sian Cl. GU52: C Cro . . . 8C 88
Sibley Ct. BR2: Brom . . . 1N 47
Sibthorp Rd. CR4: Mit . . . 1D 44
Sibton Rd. SM5: Cars . . . 6C 44
Sickle Rd. GU27: Hasl . . . 3D 188
Sidbury Cl. SL5: S'dale . . . 4D 34
Sidbury St. SW6 . . . 4K 13
Siddeley Dr. TW4: Houn . . . 6M 9
Siddons Rd. CR0: Wad . . . 9L 45
Sideways La. RH6: Hook . . . 1A 162
Sidings, The GU11: Alde . . . 1A 110
RH12: Rudg . . . 1E 194
TW18: Stain . . . 5K 21
Sidlaws Rd. GU14: Cove . . . 7J 69
SIDLOW . . . 1N 141
Sidmouth Av. TW7: Isle . . . 5E 10
Sidney Gdns. TW8: Brent . . . 2K 11
Sidney Rd. BR3: Beck . . . 1H 47
KT12: Wal T . . . 6H 39
SE25 . . . 4D 46
SL4: W'sor . . . 6A 4
TW1: Twick . . . 9G 11
TW18: Stain . . . 5J 21
Siebel Ct. TW20: Egh . . . 5D 20
Sienna Cl. KT9: Ches . . . 3K 59
Sienna Dr. RH10: Craw . . . 8H 163
Signal Ct. RH7: Ling . . . 6A 146
Sigrist Sq.
KT2: K Tham . . . 2K 203 (9L 25)
Silbury Av. CR4: Mit . . . 9C 28
Silchester Ct. CR7: T Hea . . . 3L 45
TW15: A'ford . . . 3N 21
Silchester Dr. RH11: Craw . . . 6N 181
Silent Pool . . . 6M 115
Silistria Cl. GU21: Knap . . . 5F 72
Silkham Rd. RH8: Oxt . . . 5N 105
Silkin Wlk. RH11: Craw . . . 8M 181
Silkmore La. KT24: W Hors . . . 3B 96
Silk Pl. RG40: W'ham . . . 1C 30
Silo Cl. GU7: Goda . . . 3J 133
Silo Dr. GU7: Goda . . . 3J 133
Silo Rd. GU7: Goda . . . 3J 133
Silverbeck Way
TW19: Stan M . . . 8J 7
Silver Birch Cvn. Site
KT16: Lyne . . . 6F 36
Silver Birch Cl.
GU52: C Cro . . . 8A 88
KT15: Wood . . . 8G 55
Silver Birch Cotts.
GU10: Churt . . . 9B 150
Silver Birches Way
GU8: Els . . . 8J 131
Silver Birch Ho.
RH11: Craw . . . 8A 182
Silver Cl. KT20: K'wood . . . 2K 101
Silver Ct. KT22: Leat . . . 7H 79
RH19: E Grin . . . 8M 165
Silver Cres. W4 . . . 1A 12
Silverdale GU52: Fleet . . . 7B 88
Silverdale Av. KT12: Wal T . . . 8G 38
KT22: Oxs . . . 1C 78
Silverdale Cl. RH3: Brock . . . 7A 120
SM1: Sut . . . 1L 61
Silverdale Ct. TW18: Stain . . . 5K 21
Silverdale Dr. TW16: Sunb . . . 1J 39
Silver Dr. GU16: Frim . . . 3G 70
Silvergate KT19: Ewe . . . 2B 60
Silverglade Bus. Pk.
KT9: Ches . . . 8J 59
Silver Glades GU46: Yate . . . 2B 68
Silverhall St. TW7: Isle . . . 6G 11
Silver Hill GU47: C Tow . . . 7K 49
Silver Jubilee Way
TW4: C'ford . . . 5J 9
Silverlands Cl. KT16: Chert . . . 9F 36
Silver La. BR4: W Wick . . . 8N 47
CR8: Pur . . . 8H 63
Silverlea Gdns. RH6: Horl . . . 9G 142
Silverleigh Rd. CR7: T Hea . . . 3K 45
Silvermere Ct. CR3: Cate . . . 2C 104
CR8: Pur . . . 8L 63
Silver Pk. Cl. GU52: C Cro . . . 7C 88
Silversmiths Way
GU21: Wok . . . 5M 73
Silverstead La.
TN16: Weste . . . 8M 87
Silverstone Cl. RH1: Red . . . 1D 122
Silverton Rd. W6 . . . 2J 13
Silver Tree Cl. KT12: Wal T . . . 9H 39
Silver Wing Ind. Est.
CR0: Wad . . . 3K 63
Silverwood GU6: Cranl . . . 4K 155
Silverwood Cl. CR0: Sels . . . 5J 65
Silverwood Cotts.
GU5: Alb . . . 7N 115
Silver Wood Ct. GU51: Fleet . . . 3A 88
Silverwood Dr. GU15: Camb . . . 8E 50
Silverwood Ind. Est.
RH10: Craw D . . . 7C 164
Silwood RG12: Brac . . . 7K 31
Silwood Cl. SL5: Asc . . . 3L 33
Silwood Pk. . . . 2B 34
Silwood Rd.
SL5: S'dale, S'hill . . . 3C 34
Simkin's Cl. RG42: Wink R . . . 7F 16
Simmil Rd. KT10: Clay . . . 2E 58
Simmonds Cl. RG42: Brac . . . 9K 15
Simmond's Cotts.
GU7: Goda . . . 7E 132
Simmonds Ct. *GU9: Farnh* . . . *1H 129*
(off Victoria Rd.)
SW5 . . . *1N 13*
(off Earl's Ct. Gdns.)
Simmondstone La.
GU10: Churt . . . 8J 149
Simmons Cl. KT9: Ches . . . 3J 59
SL3: Lang . . . 1C 6
Simmons Ga. KT10: Esh . . . 2C 58
Simmons Pl. TW18: Stain . . . 6G 21
Simms Cl. SM5: Cars . . . 8C 44
Simonds M. *GU14: Farnb* . . . *5A 90*
(off Queen's Rd.)
Simone Dr. CR8: Ken . . . 3N 83
Simons Cl. KT16: Otter . . . 3E 54
Simons Wlk. TW20: Eng G . . . 8M 19
Simplemarsh Ct.
KT15: Addl . . . 1K 55
Simplemarsh Rd.
KT15: Addl . . . 1J 55
Simpson Rd. TW4: Houn . . . 9N 9
TW10: Ham . . . 5J 25
Simpson Way KT6: Surb . . . 5J 41
Simrose Ct. SW18 . . . 8M 13
Sinclair Cl. RH10: Craw . . . 5G 182
Sinclair Ct. CR0: Croy . . . 8B 46
Sinclair Dr. SM2: Sut . . . 5N 61
Sinclair Rd. SL4: W'sor . . . 6F 4
Sincots Rd. RH1: Red . . . 3D 122
Sine Cl. GU14: Farnb . . . 6N 69
SINGLE STREET . . . 2K 87
Single St. TN16: B Hil . . . 2K 87
Singleton Cl. CR0: Croy . . . 6N 45
CR4: Mit . . . 8D 28
SW17 . . . 8D 28
Singleton Rd.
RH12: Bro H . . . 5C 196
Sinhurst Rd. GU15: Camb . . . 2N 69
Sion Ct. TW1: Twick . . . 2H 25
Sion Rd. TW1: Twick . . . 2H 25
SIPSON . . . 2B 8
Sipson Cl. UB7: Sip . . . 2B 8
Sipson La. UB3: Harl . . . 2B 8
UB7: Sip . . . 2B 8
Sipson Rd. UB7: Sip, W Dray . . . 1A 8
(not continuous)
Sipson Way UB7: Sip . . . 3B 8
Sir Abraham Dawes Cotts.
SW15 . . . 7K 13
Sir Cyril Black Way
SW19 . . . 8M 27
Sirdar Rd. CR4: Mit . . . 7E 28
Sir Oswald Stoll Foundation, The
SW6 . . . *3N 13*
(off Fulham Rd.)
Sir Oswald Stoll Mans.
SW6 . . . *3N 13*
(off Fulham Rd.)
Sir Robert M. SL3: Lang . . . 1C 6
Sir Sydney Camm Ho.
SL4: W'sor . . . 4E 4
Sir William Atkins Ho.
KT18: Eps . . . 7K 201 (9C 60)
Sir William Powell's Almshouses
SW6 . . . 5K 13
Sir William Siemens Sq.
GU16: Frim . . . 5C 70
Siskin Av. RH10: T Hil . . . 4F 184
Siskin Cl. RH12: Hors . . . 3L 197
Sispara Gdns. SW18 . . . 9L 13
Sissinghurst Cl.
RH10: Craw . . . 2H 183
Sissinghurst Rd. CR0: Croy . . . 6D 46
Sistova Rd. SW12 . . . 2F 28
Siward Rd. SW17 . . . 4A 28
Six Acres RH13: Slin . . . 5L 195
Six Bells Rdbt. GU9: Farnh . . . 7K 109
Six Penny Cl. TN8: Eden . . . 3L 147
Sixteenth Av. KT20: Lwr K . . . 4K 101
Sixth Av. KT20: Lwr K . . . 3K 101
Sixth Cross Rd. TW2: Twick . . . 4C 24
Skeena Hill SW18 . . . 1K 27
Skelbrook St. SW18 . . . 3A 28
Skelgill Rd. SW15 . . . 7L 13
Skelmersdale Wlk.
RH11: Craw . . . 7K 181
Skelton Flds. RG42: Warf . . . 8A 16
Skelwith Rd. W6 . . . 2H 13
Skerne Rd.
KT2: K Tham . . . 2H 203 (9K 25)
Skerne Wlk.
KT2: K Tham . . . 1H 203 (9K 25)
Skeynes Rd. TN8: Eden . . . 2K 147
Skid Hill La. CR6: Warl . . . 8B 66
Skiffington Cl. SW2 . . . 2L 29
Skiff La.
RH14: W Grn, Loxw . . . 9H 193
Skimmington Cotts.
RH2: Reig . . . 4J 121
SKIMPED HILL . . . 1M 31
Skimped Hill La.
RG12: Brac . . . 1M 31
Skinners La. GU8: Chid . . . 4G 172
KT21: A'tead . . . 5K 79
TN8: Eden . . . 9M 127
TW5: Hest . . . 4B 10
Skipsea Ho. SW18 . . . 1C 28
Skipton Way RH6: Horl . . . 6F 142
Sky Bus. Cen. TW20: Thor . . . 1E 36
Skylark Vw. RH12: Hors . . . 1K 197
Skyline Ct. CR0: Croy . . . 5D 200
Skyport Dr. UB7: Harm . . . 3M 7
Skyview Apartments
CR0: Croy . . . 3C 200
Skyway SL3: Poy . . . 6H 7
Skyway Trad. Est. SL3: Poy . . . 6H 7
Slade Ct. KT16: Otter . . . 3F 54
Slade Ho. TW4: Houn . . . 9N 9
Slade La. GU12: Ash . . . 9H 91
Slade Rd. GU24: B'wood . . . 7A 72
KT16: Otter . . . 3F 54
Slade Way CR4: Mit . . . 9E 28
Slaidburn Grn. RG12: Brac . . . 6C 32
Slapleys GU22: Wok . . . 7A 74
Slattery Rd. TW13: Felt . . . 2L 23
Slaugham Ct. RH11: Craw . . . 6L 181
SLEAFORD . . . 9A 148
Sledmere Ct. TW14: Bedf . . . 2F 22
Sleets Rd. RH12: Bro H . . . 5E 196
Slim Cl. GU11: Alde . . . 6C 90
Slim Rd. GU15: Camb . . . 8N 49
Slines Oak Rd. CR3: Wold . . . 1K 105
CR6: Warl, Wold . . . 6K 85
SLINFOLD . . . 5L 195
Slinfold Wlk. RH11: Craw . . . 3M 181
(not continuous)
Slip, The TN16: Weste . . . 4L 107
Slip of Wood GU6: Cranl . . . 6N 155
Slipshatch Rd. RH2: Reig . . . 7J 121
Slipshoe St. RH2: Reig . . . 3L 121
Sloane Ct. TW7: Isle . . . 4E 10
Sloane Wlk. CR0: Croy . . . 5J 47
Slocock Hill GU21: Wok . . . 4M 73
Sloughbrook Cl.
RH12: Hors . . . 2M 197
Slough La. KT18: Head . . . 3B 100
RH3: Buck . . . 1F 120
Slough Rd. SL3: Dat . . . 1K 5
SL4: Eton . . . 2G 4
Slyfield Ct. GU1: Guil . . . 9A 94
SLYFIELD GREEN . . . 9N 93
Slyfield Grn. GU1: Guil . . . 8A 94
Slyfield Ind. Est.
GU1: Guil . . . 8A 94
Smallberry Av. TW7: Isle . . . 5F 10
SMALLFIELD . . . 8M 143
Smallfield Rd. RH6: Horl . . . 8F 142
(not continuous)
RH6: Horn, Smal . . . 8A 144
Smallmead RH6: Horl . . . 8F 142
Smalls Hill Rd. RH2: Leigh . . . 1F 140
RH6: N Hil . . . 5H 141
Small's La. RH11: Craw . . . 3A 182
Smalls Mead RH11: Craw . . . 3A 182
Smallwood Rd. SW17 . . . 5B 28
Smart's Heath La.
GU22: Wok . . . 1K 93
Smart's Heath Rd.
GU22: Wok . . . 1J 93
Smeaton Cl. KT9: Ches . . . 3K 59
Smeaton Dr. GU22: Wok . . . 7D 74
Smeaton Rd. SW18 . . . 1M 27
Smeeds Cl. RH19: E Grin . . . 7C 166
Smitham Bottom La.
CR8: Pur . . . 7G 63
Smitham Downs Rd.
CR8: Pur . . . 9H 63
Smitham Station (Rail) . . . 2J 83
Smithbarn RH13: Hors . . . 5N 197
Smithbarn Cl. RH6: Horl . . . 7F 142
SMITHBROOK . . . 7E 154
Smithbrook Ga. GU6: Cranl . . . 6F 154
Smithbrook Kilns
GU6: Cranl . . . 7F 154
Smith Cl. RH10: Craw . . . 6B 182
Smith Ct. GU21: Wok . . . 9F 54
Smithers, The RH3: Brock . . . 5A 120
Smithers Cotts.
RH12: Rudg . . . 1G 195
Smithers La. RH19: E Grin . . . 5J 167
Smithfield La.
GU35: H Dwn . . . 8F 148
Smith Hill TW8: Brent . . . 2L 11
Smith Rd. RH2: Reig . . . 6L 121
Smiths La. SL4: W'sor . . . 5B 4
TN8: C Hil . . . 2L 127
Smith's Lawn (Polo Pitch) . . . 8G 19
Smiths Path RG45: Crow . . . 3E 48
Smith Sq. RG12: Brac . . . 1B 32
Smith St. KT5: Surb . . . 5M 41
Smiths Yd. CR0: Croy . . . 4C 200
SW18 . . . 3A 28
Smithwood Av. GU6: Cranl . . . 3K 155
Smithwood Cl. SW19 . . . 2K 27
SMITHWOOD COMMON . . . 2L 155
Smithwood Comn. Rd.
GU6: Cranl . . . 2J 155
Smithy Cl. KT20: Lwr K . . . 4L 101
Smithyfield TN8: Eden . . . 9M 127
Smithy La. GU10: Dock . . . 8C 148
KT20: Lwr K . . . 5L 101
Smithy's Grn. GU20: Windl . . . 3A 52
Smock Wlk. CR0: Croy . . . 5N 45
Smokejack Hill
RH5: W'wood . . . 2L 177
Smoke La. RH2: Reig . . . 5N 121
SMOKY HOLE . . . 4E 136
Smolletts RH19: E Grin . . . 1M 185
Smoothfield Cl. TW3: Houn . . . 7A 10
Smugglers La. RH5: Ockl . . . 2E 178
RH12: Rusp . . . 3F 180
Smugglers Way GU10: Til . . . 3B 130
(not continuous)
SW18 . . . 7N 13
Snag La. BR6: Cud, P Bot . . . 7N 67
TN14: Cud . . . 8M 67
Snailslynch GU9: Farnh . . . 1J 129
Snakey La. TW13: Felt . . . 5H 23
Snatts Hill RH8: Oxt . . . 7B 106
Snelgate Cotts. GU4: E Cla . . . 9M 95
Snell Hatch RH11: Craw . . . 3N 181
Snellings Rd. KT12: Hers . . . 2K 57
Snipe Rd. GU27: K Grn . . . 7E 188
Snodland Cl. BR6: Dow . . . 6J 67
Snowbury Rd. SW6 . . . 5N 13
Snowden Cl. SL4: W'sor . . . 7A 4
Snowdenham La.
GU5: Braml . . . 6A 134
Snowdenham Links Rd.
GU5: Braml . . . 5N 133
Snowdon Rd. GU14: Cove . . . 7K 69
TW6: Lon A . . . 9D 8
Snowdrop Cl. RH11: Craw . . . 7M 181
TW12: Hamp . . . 7A 24
Snowdrop Wlk. *GU51: Fleet* . . . *3A 88*
(off Stockton Av.)
Snowdrop Way GU24: Bis . . . 4D 72
Snowerhill Rd.
RH3: Betch . . . 5D 120
SNOW HILL . . . 6D 164
Snow Hill RH10: Craw D . . . 7C 164
Snowhill Bus. Cen.
RH10: Cop . . . 6D 164
Snowhill La.
RH10: Cop, Craw D . . . 5C 164
Snows Paddock
GU20: Windl . . . 9M 33
Snow's Ride GU20: Windl . . . 2M 51
Snowy Fielder Waye
TW7: Isle . . . 5H 11
Snoxhall Fld. GU6: Cranl . . . 8M 155
Soames Wlk. KT3: N Mal . . . 9D 26
Soane Cl. RH11: Craw . . . 5K 181
Soaphouse La. TW8: Brent . . . 3L 11
Sobraon Ho. KT2: K Tham . . . 1L 203
Solaris Ho. GU17: Min . . . 7H 69
Solartron Retail Pk.
GU14: Farnb . . . 2M 89
Solartron Rd. GU14: Farnb . . . 2N 89
Soldiers Ri. RG40: Finch . . . 9C 30
Solecote KT23: Book . . . 3A 98
Sole Farm Av. KT23: Book . . . 3N 97
Sole Farm Cl. KT23: Book . . . 2N 97
Sole Farm Rd. KT23: Book . . . 3N 97
Solent Ct. SW16 . . . 1K 45
Solna Av. SW15 . . . 8H 13
Soloms Ct. Rd. SM7: Ban . . . 4B 82
(not continuous)
Solway Cl. TW4: Houn . . . 6M 9
Sol-y-Vista GU7: Goda . . . 5G 133
Sombourne Ho. *SW15* . . . *1F 26*
(off Fontley Way)
Somer Ct. *SW6* . . . *2M 13*
(off Anselm Rd.)
Somerfield Cl. KT20: Tad . . . 6K 81
Somergate RH12: Hors . . . 6F 196
Somersbury La. GU6: Ewh . . . 8G 156
RH12: Ewh, Rudg . . . 8G 156
Somers Cl. RH2: Reig . . . 2M 121
Somerset Av. KT9: Ches . . . 1K 59
SW20 . . . 1G 42
Somerset Cl. KT3: N Mal . . . 5D 42
KT12: Hers . . . 2J 57
KT19: Ewe . . . 5C 60
Somerset Ct. GU14: Farnb . . . 4A 90
Somerset Gdns. SW16 . . . 2K 45
TW11: Tedd . . . 6E 24
Somerset Gro. RG42: Warf . . . 8D 16
Somerset Ho. RH1: Red . . . 2D 122
SW19 . . . 4J 27
Somerset Lodge
TW8: Brent . . . 2K 11
Somerset Rd. GU14: Farnb . . . 4A 90
KT1: K Tham . . . 4M 203 (1M 41)
RH1: Red . . . 5B 122
SW19 . . . 4J 27
TW8: Brent . . . 2J 11
TW11: Tedd . . . 6E 24
Somerset Waye TW5: Hest . . . 2M 9
Somers Pl. RH2: Reig . . . 2M 121
SW2 . . . 1K 29
Somers Rd. RH2: Reig . . . 2M 121
SW2 . . . 1K 29
Somerswey GU4: Chil . . . 2A 134
Somerton Av. TW9: Rich . . . 6A 12
Somerton Cl. CR8: Pur . . . 2L 83
Somertons Cl. GU2: Guil . . . 9K 93
Somerville Av. SW13 . . . 2G 13
Somerville Ct. *RH1: Red* . . . *2C 122*
(off Oxford Rd.)
Somerville Cres.
GU46: Yate . . . 9D 48
Somerville Dr.
RH10: Craw . . . 9G 163
Somerville Ri. RG12: Brac . . . 4N 31
Somerville Rd. KT11: Cob . . . 1A 78
SL4: Eton . . . 1F 4
Sondes Farm
RH4: Dork . . . 3G 201 (5F 118)
Sondes Pl. Dr. RH4: Dork . . . 5F 118
Songhurst Cl. CR0: Croy . . . 5K 45
Sonia Gdns. TW5: Hest . . . 3A 10
Sonic Ct.
GU1: Guil . . . 1B 202 (2M 113)
Sonnet Wlk. TN16: B Hil . . . 5D 86
Sonninge Cl. GU47: C Tow . . . 7J 49
Sonning Gdns.
TW12: Hamp . . . 7M 23
Sonning Rd. SE25 . . . 5D 46
Sontan Ct. TW2: Twick . . . 2D 24
Soper Dr. CR3: Cate . . . 1A 104
Sophia Ho. *W6* . . . *1H 13*
(off Queen Caroline St.)
Sopwith Av. KT9: Ches . . . 2L 59
Sopwith Cl. KT2: K Tham . . . 6M 25
TN16: B Hil . . . 3F 86
Sopwith Dr. KT13: Weybr . . . 7N 55
Sopwith Rd. TW5: Hest . . . 3K 9
Sopwith Way
KT2: K Tham . . . 2J 203 (9L 25)
Sorbie Cl. KT13: Weybr . . . 3E 56
Sorrel Bank CR0: Sels . . . 6H 65
Sorrel Cl. GU14: Cove . . . 9H 69
RG40: W'ham . . . 9D 14
RH11: Craw . . . 7M 181

Sorrel Dr.—Spring Av.

Sorrel Dr. GU18: Ligh 8K 51
Sorrell Cl. TN8: Eden 9M 127
Sorrell Rd. RH12: Hors 3L 197
Sorrento Rd. SM1: Sut 9M 43
Sotheron Rd. SW6 . . . . .3N 13
Sth. Albert Rd. RH2: Reig 2L 121
Southall La. TW5: C'ford 2J 9
UB2: S'hall 2J 9
Southam Ho. *KT15: Addl 2K 55*
(off Addlestone Pk.)
Southampton Cl.
GU17: B'water 9H 49
Southampton Gdns.
CR4: Mit 4J 45
Southampton Rd. E.
TW6: Lon A 9A 8
Southampton Rd. W.
TW6: Lon A 9N 7
(not continuous)
Southampton St.
GU14: Farnb 5N 89
SOUTH ASCOT 5L 33
Sth. Atlantic Dr.
GU11: Alde 1A 110
South Av. GU9: H End 6J 109
KT12: Whit V 6F 56
KT13: Weybr 6B 56
SM5: Cars 4E 62
TW9: Kew 5N 11
TW20: Egh 7E 20
South Bank KT6: Surb 5L 41
TN16: Weste 4M 107
Southbank KT7: T Dit 6H 41
Sth. Bank Ter. KT6: Surb 5L 41
SOUTH BEDDINGTON 3H 63
Sth. Black Lion La. W6 . . . . . . .1F 12
Sth. Bolton Gdns.
SW5 . . . . .1N 13
Sth. Border, The CR8: Pur 7H 63
SOUTHBOROUGH 7L 41
Southborough Cl. KT6: Surb . . .7K 41
Southborough Rd.
KT6: Surb 7L 41
Southbridge Pl.
CR0: Croy 6B 200 (1N 63)
Southbridge Rd.
CR0: Croy 6B 200 (1N 63)
Southbrook RH11: Craw 8A 182
Southbrook Rd. SW16 . . . . .9J 29
Southbury GU2: Guil 7B 202
Southby Dr. GU51: Fleet 4C 88
SOUTH CAMP 9A 90
Sth. Circular Rd.
SW15 . . . . .7F 12
South Cl. GU21: Wok 3M 73
RG40: W'ham 2B 30
(Peach St.)
RG40: W'ham 4B 30
(South Dr.)
RH10: Craw 2D 182
SM4: Mord 5M 43
TW2: Twick 4A 24
South Cl. Grn. RH1: Mers 7F 102
Southcote GU21: Wok 2N 73
Southcote Av. KT5: Surb 6A 42
TW13: Felt 3G 23
Southcote Dr. GU15: Camb 1E 70
Southcote Ho. KT15: Addl 8M 37
Southcote Pk. GU15: Camb 2E 70
Southcote Rd. CR2: Sande 6B 64
RH1: Mers 8G 102
SE25 . . . . .4E 46
Southcroft TW20: Eng G 6L 19
Southcroft Av.
BR4: W Wick 8M 47
Southcroft Rd. SW16 . . . . .7E 28
SW17 . . . . .7E 28
SOUTH CROYDON 2A 64
South Croydon Sports Club . . .2B 64
South Croydon Station (Rail)
. . . . .8E 200 (2A 64)
Southdean Gdns.
SW19 . . . . .3L 27
Southdown Cl.
RH12: Hors 3N 197
Southdown Dr. SW20 . . . . .8J 27
Southdown Rd. CR3: Wold 9J 85
KT12: Hers 1M 57
SM5: Cars 5E 62
SW20 . . . . .9J 27
South Dr. BR6: Orp 2N 67
CR5: Coul 2H 83
GU24: B'wood 8N 71
GU25: V Wat 7K 35
RG40: W'ham 3B 30
RH5: Dork . . .2M 201 (5J 119)
SM2: Chea 6K 61
SM7: Ban 9C 62
Sth. Ealing Rd. W5 . . . . .1K 11
Sth. Eden Pk. Rd.
BR3: Beck 5L 47
South End
CR0: Croy 6C 200 (1N 63)
KT23: Book 4B 98
Southerland Cl.
KT13: Weybr 1D 56
Southern Av. RH1: Salf 1E 142
SE25 . . . . .2C 46
TW14: Felt 2H 23
Southern Bungs.
GU4: Guil 1D 134
Southern Cotts.
TW19: Stan M 8J 7
SOUTHERN INDUSTRIAL AREA
. . . . .2K 31
Southern Perimeter Rd.
TW6: Lon A 8K 7
(Stanwell Moor Rd.)
TW6: Lon A 8D 8
(Swindon Rd.)
TW19: Stan 8K 7
(not continuous)
Southern Rd. GU15: Camb 9A 50
Southerns La. CR5: Coul 3A 102
Southern Way GU9: Farnh . . .2H 129
GU14: Cove 2J 89
Southey Ct. KT23: Book 2B 98
Southey Rd. SW19 . . . . .8M 27
Sth. Farm La. GU19: Ligh 5L 51
SOUTH FARNBOROUGH 4B 90
Southfield Gdns.
TW1: Twick 5F 24
Southfield Pl. KT13: Weybr . . .4C 56
SOUTHFIELDS 2L 27
Southfields KT8: E Mol 5E 40
Southfields Av.
TW15: A'ford 7C 22
Southfields Ct. SM1: Sut 8M 43
Southfields M. SW18 . . . . .9M 13
Southfields Pas.
SW18 . . . . .9M 13
Southfields Rd. CR3: Wold 9L 85
SW18 . . . . .9M 13
Southfields Station (Tube) 2L 27
Southfleet Rd. BR6: Orp 1N 67
South Gdns. SW19 . . . . .8B 28
SOUTHGATE 5B 182
Southgate Av. RH10: Craw . . .6B 182
TW13: Felt 5E 22
Southgate Dr. RH10: Craw . . .5B 182
Southgate Pde.
RH10: Craw 5B 182
Southgate Rd. RH10: Craw . . .5B 182
Southgate Rdbt.
RH11: Craw 6A 182
SOUTH GODSTONE 7H 125
South Gro. GU51: Fleet 1D 88
KT16: Chert 5H 37
RH13: Hors 7K 197
Sth. Guildford St.
KT16: Chert 7H 37
South Hill
GU1: Guil 6D 202 (5N 113)
GU7: Goda 7H 133
South Hill Pk. Arts Cen. 6A 32
South Hill Rd. BR2: Brom 2N 47
RG12: Brac 5M 31
Sth. Holmes Rd.
RH13: Hors 4A 198
SOUTH HOLMWOOD 5J 139
Southlands RH6: Horl 8D 142
RH19: E Grin 2A 186
Southlands Av. BR6: Orp 1M 67
RH6: Horl 7D 142
Southlands Cl. CR5: Coul 4K 83
GU12: Ash 3E 110
RG40: W'ham 3C 30
Southlands Dr. SW19 . . . . .3J 27
Southlands La.
RH8: Oxt, Tand 3L 125
Southlands Rd. GU12: Ash . . .3E 110
RG40: W'ham 4C 30
Southland Way TW3: Houn 8D 10
South La. GU12: Ash 3F 110
KT1: K Tham 6H 203 (2K 41)
(not continuous)
KT3: N Mal 3C 42
South La. W. KT3: N Mal 3C 42
South Lawn *SL4: Eton 2F 4*
(off South Mdw. La.)
SOUTHLEA 5L 5
Southlea Rd. SL3: Dat 4L 5
SL4: W'sor 7K 5
South Lodge TW2: Whitt 9C 10
Sth. Lodge Av. CR4: Mit 3J 45
Sth. Lodge Rd. KT12: Hers 5H 57
Sth. London Crematorium
CR4: Mit 1G 44
South London Theatre . . . . . . *.4M 29*
(off Norwood High St.)
Sth. Lynn Cres. RG12: Brac . . .4N 31
South Mall GU51: Fleet 4A 88
SW18 . . . . .9N 13
TW18: Stain 5H 21
(in Elmsleigh Shop. Cen.)
South Mead KT19: Ewe 4E 60
RH1: Red 9D 102
South Mdw. RG45: Crow 4J 49
South Mdw. La. SL4: Eton 2F 4
Southmead Rd. GU11: Alde . . .4N 109
SW19 . . . . .2K 27
SOUTH MERSTHAM 7H 103
South Merton Station (Rail)
. . . . .2L 43
Southmont Rd.
KT10: H Wood 8E 40
SOUTH MUNSTEAD 4M 153
Sth. Munstead La.
GU8: Bus 3L 153
SOUTH NORWOOD 3C 46
South Norwood Country Pk.
. . . . .3F 46
South Norwood Country Pk.
Vis. Cen. 3E 46
Sth. Norwood Hill
SE25 . . . . .1B 46
South Norwood Pools &
Fitness Cen. 4E 46
SOUTH NUTFIELD 5K 123
Sth. Oak Rd. SW16 . . . . .5K 29
South Pde. RH1: Mers 6G 102
RH6: Horl 7D 142
SM6: W'ton 3G 62
SOUTH PARK
RH1 . . . . .6D 124
RH2 . . . . .6M 121
South Pk. Gro. KT3: N Mal 3B 42
South Pk. Hill Rd.
CR2: S Croy 8E 200 (2A 64)
South Pk. La. RH1: Blet 5D 124
South Pk. M. SW6 . . . . .6N 13
South Pk. Rd. SW19 . . . . .7M 27
South Path SL4: W'sor 4F 4
Sth. Perimeter Track
RH6: Gat 5N 161
Sth. Pier Rd. RH6: Gat 3F 162
South Pl. KT5: Surb 6M 41
South Ridge KT13: Weybr 6C 56
Southridge Pl. SW20 . . . . .8J 27
South Ri. SM5: Cars 5C 62
South Rd. GU2: Guil 1L 113
GU12: A Va 9E 90
GU21: Wok 2M 73
GU24: Bis 3C 72
GU47: Owls 4K 49
KT13: Weybr 2D 56
(Queens Rd.)
KT13: Weybr 5C 56
(West Rd.)
RG40: W'ham 6J 31
RG45: Crow 4K 49
RH2: Reig 4N 121
SW19 . . . . .7A 28
TW2: Twick 4D 24
TW5: Hest 2K 9
TW12: Hamp 7M 23
TW13: Hanw 6L 23
TW20: Eng G 7M 19
Southsea Rd.
KT1: K Tham 7J 203 (3L 41)
South Side GU10: Tong 5D 110
KT16: Chert 2J 37
Southside Comn.
SW19 . . . . .7H 27
Southside House 7H 27
Southside Shop. Cen.
SW18 . . . . .9N 13
Sth. Station App.
RH1: Sth N 5J 123
SOUTH STREET 6J 87
South St. GU7: Goda 7G 133
(not continuous)
GU9: Farnh 1H 129
GU14: Farnb 4C 90
KT18: Eps 7J 201 (9C 60)
RH4: Dork 4J 201 (6G 119)
RH12: Hors 7J 197
TW7: Isle 6G 10
TW18: Stain 6H 21
South Ter. KT6: Surb 5L 41
RH4: Dork 4K 201 (6H 119)
SL4: W'sor 4H 5
South Vw. KT19: Eps 6N 59
RG12: Bin 2J 31
SL4: Eton, E Wic 1E 4
SW19 . . . . .7J 27
Southview GU10: Fren 1J 149
Southview Cl. RH10: Cop 7B 164
SW17 . . . . .6E 28
South Vw. Ct. GU22: Wok 5A 74
SE19 . . . . .8N 29
Southview Gdns.
SM6: W'ton 4G 63
South Vw. Rd. KT21: A'tead 6K 79
Southview Rd. CR3: Wold 2L 105
CR6: Warl 6D 84
(not continuous)
GU35: H Dwn 4G 168
Southviews CR2: Sels 6G 65
Southville Cl. KT19: Ewe 5C 60
TW14: Bedf, Felt 2F 22
TW14: Felt 2F 22
Southville Cres. TW14: Felt 2F 22
Southville Rd. KT7: T Dit 6G 41
TW14: Felt 2F 22
South Wlk. GU12: Alde 2B 110
RH2: Reig 3N 121
Southwark Cl. GU46: Yate 9B 48
RH11: Craw 7N 181
Southwater Cl.
RH11: Craw 3M 181
South Way CR0: Croy 9H 47
SM5: Cars 6B 62
Southway GU2: Guil 3H 113
GU15: Camb 2N 69
SM6: W'ton 1G 63
SW20 . . . . .4H 43
Southway Ct. GU2: Guil 3H 113
Southways Pk.
RH10: L Hea 7B 162
Southwell Cotts.
RH6: Char 3K 161
Southwell Pk. Rd.
GU15: Camb 1N 69
Southwell Rd. CR0: Croy 5L 45
Sth. Western Rd.
TW1: Twick 9G 11
South W. Middlesex Crematorium
TW13: Felt 2M 23
Southwick GU19: Bag 6J 51
Southwick Cl.
RH19: E Grin 8N 165
Southwick Ct. RG12: Brac 5C 32
SOUTH WIMBLEDON 7N 27
South Wimbledon Station (Tube)
. . . . .8N 27
Southwold RG12: Brac 7K 31
SOUTHWOOD 2H 89
Southwood RG40: W'ham 4C 30
SL5: S'hill 2C 34
(off Buckhurst Rd.)
Southwood Av. CR5: Coul 2G 83
GU21: Knap 5G 73
KT2: K Tham 9B 26
KT16: Otter 4E 54
Southwood Bus. Cen.
GU14: Cove 1J 89
Southwood Chase
GU6: Cranl 9A 156
Southwood Cl. KT4: W Pk 7J 43
Southwood Ct. KT13: Weybr . . .2C 56
Southwood Cres.
GU14: Cove 1J 89
Southwood Dr. KT5: Surb 6B 42
Southwood Gdns.
KT10: H Wood 9G 40
Southwood La. GU14: Cove 2J 89
GU51: Fleet 2E 88
Southwood Rd. GU14: Cove 2J 89
GU17: Min 5D 68
Southwood Village Cen.
GU14: Cove 2J 89
Sth. Worple Av. SW14 . . . . . . .6D 12
Sth. Worple Way
SW14 . . . . .6C 12
Sovereign Cl. CR8: Pur 6K 63
Sovereign Ct. CR2: S Croy 8C 200
GU51: Fleet 4A 88
(off Victorian Rd.)
KT8: W Mole 3N 39
SL5: S'dale 6E 34
TW3: Houn 6A 10
Sovereign Dr. GU15: Camb 8F 50
Sovereign Flds.
RG12: Brac 5M 31
Sovereign Hgts. SL3: Dat 2C 6
Sovereign Ho. TW15: A'ford . . .5N 21
Soyer Ct. GU21: Wok 5H 73
Spa at Beckenham, The 1J 47
Space Waye TW14: Felt 8H 9
Spa Cl. SE25 . . . . .1B 46
Spa Ct. SW16 . . . . .5K 29
Spa Dr. KT18: Eps 1N 79
Spa Hill SE19 . . . . .9N 29
Spalding Rd. SW17 . . . . .6F 28
Sparc Ho. GU17: Min 7H 69
Sparks Cl. TW12: Hamp 7M 23
Sparrow Cl. TW12: Hamp 7M 23
Sparrow Farm Dr.
TW14: Felt 1K 23
(not continuous)
Sparrow Farm Rd.
KT17: Ewe 1F 60
Sparrowhawk Cl.
GU10: Ews 5C 108
SPARROW ROW 3E 52
Sparrow Row GU24: Chob 3E 52
Sparrows Mead RH1: Red 9E 102
Spartan Cl. SM6: W'ton 4J 63
Spartan Way RH11: Ifi 9M 161
Sparvell Rd. GU21: Knap 6E 72
Sparvell Way GU15: Camb 9A 50
Spats La. GU35: H Dwn 1E 168
Speakers Ct.
CR0: Croy 1D 200 (7A 46)
Spear M. SW5 . . . . .1M 13
Speart La. TW5: Hest 3M 9
Spectrum Leisure Complex
. . . . .1F 202 (2A 114)
Speedbird Way UB7: Harm 3K 7
Speedwell Cl. GU4: Guil 9E 94
TN8: Eden 9M 127
(off Woodpecker Cl.)
Speedwell Way
RH12: Hors 3L 197
Speer Rd. KT7: T Dit 5F 40
Speirs Cl. KT3: N Mal 5E 42
Speke Rd. CR7: T Hea 1A 46
Spelthorne Gro.
TW16: Sunb 8G 22
Spelthorne La.
TW15: A'ford 9D 22
Spelthorne Leisure Cen. 6J 21
Spelthorne Mus. 6H 21
Spence Av. KT14: Byf 1N 75
Spencer Cl. GU16: Frim G 8C 70
GU21: Wok 9E 54
GU52: C Cro 8D 88
KT18: Eps D 6D 80
Spencer Ct. BR6: Farnb 2L 67
KT22: Leat 1J 99
SW20 . . . . .9G 27
Spencer Gdns. SW14 . . . . .8B 12
TW20: Eng G 6N 19
Spencer Hill SW19 . . . . .7K 27
Spencer Hill Rd.
SW19 . . . . .8K 27
Spencer Mans. *W14 . . . . .2K 13*
(off Queen's Club Gdns.)
Spencer M. W6 . . . . .2K 13
Spencer Pk. KT8: E Mol 4C 40
Spencer Pl. CR0: Croy 6A 46
Spencer Rd. CR2: S Croy 2B 64
CR3: Cate 8A 84
CR4: Mit 2E 44
(Commonside E.)
CR4: Mit 6E 44
(Wood St.)
KT8: E Mol 3C 40
KT11: Cob 2J 77
RG42: Brac 9L 15
SW20 . . . . .9G 27
TW2: Twick 4E 24
TW7: Isle 4C 10
W4 . . . . .3B 12
Spencers La. RH6: Char 1L 161
Spencers Pl. RH12: Hors 4H 197
Spencers Rd. RH11: Craw 4A 182
RH12: Hors 5H 197
Spencer Wlk. SW15 . . . . .7J 13
Spencer Way RH1: Red 8E 122
Spenser Av. KT13: Weybr 5B 56
Spiceall GU3: Comp 1E 132
Spicer Cl. KT12: Wal T 5K 39
Spicers Fld. KT22: Oxs 9D 58
Spice's Yd.
CR0: Croy 6C 200 (1N 63)
Spiers Way RH6: Horl 1F 162
Spindle Way RH10: Craw 4D 182
Spindlewood Gdns.
CR0: Croy 6F 200 (1B 64)
Spindlewoods KT20: Tad 9G 81
Spinis RG12: Brac 7K 31
Spinnaker Ct. KT1: H Wic 2G 203
Spinner Grn. RG12: Brac 4N 31
Spinners Wlk. SL4: W'sor 4F 4
Spinney, The CR8: Pur 7M 63
GU2: Guil 2K 113
GU15: Camb 9G 51
GU23: Send 5L 95
GU26: G'hott 5M 169
GU27: Hasl 3B 188
(Hammer La.)
GU27: Hasl 9G 171
(Weycombe Rd.)
GU46: Yate 8B 48
KT18: Head 4B 100
KT18: Tat C 6G 81
KT22: Oxs 8C 58
KT23: Book 2B 98
RH6: Horl 6E 142
RH11: Craw 5N 181
SL5: S'dale 4B 34
SM3: Chea 1H 61
SW13 . . . . .3G 12
SW16 . . . . .4G 29
TW16: Sunb 9H 23
Spinney Cl. BR3: Beck 3L 47
KT3: N Mal 4D 42
KT4: W Pk 8E 42
KT11: Cob 7A 58
RH10: Craw D 1F 184
RH12: Hors 2A 198
Spinneycroft KT22: Oxs 2D 78
Spinney Dr. TW14: Bedf 1D 22
Spinney Hill KT15: Addl 2G 55
Spinney La. SL4: Wink 2M 17
Spinney Oak KT16: Otter 3F 54
Spinney Way TN14: Cud 7M 67
Spinning Wlk., The
GU5: Shere 8B 116
Spinningwheel La.
RG42: Bin 1H 15
(not continuous)
Spire Ct. *BR3: Beck 1L 47*
(off Crescent Rd.)
Spire Pl. CR6: Warl 5H 85
SPITAL 6E 4
Spital Heath
RH4: Dork 1M 201 (4J 119)
SPITALS CROSS 9L 127
SPITALS CROSS ESTATE 9M 127
Spitfire Bus. Pk. CR0: Wad 3L 63
Spitfire Cl. SL3: Lang 1C 6
Spitfire Est., The
TW5: C'ford 1K 9
Spitfire Rd. SM6: W'ton 4J 63
TW6: Lon A 9D 8
Spitfire Way TW5: C'ford 1K 9
Splash, The RG42: Warf 7N 15
Spoil La. GU10: Tong 5D 110
Spokane Cl. GU11: Alde 4L 109
Spook Hill RH5: Nth H 1H 139
Spooner Ho. TW5: Hest 2A 10
Spooners Indoor Bowls Club
. . . . .3A 186
Spooners Rd. RH12: Hors . . .4N 197
Spooner Wlk. SM6: W'ton 2J 63
Spottiswood Ct. *CR0: Croy 5N 45*
(off Harry Cl.)
Spout Hill CR0: A'ton 2K 65
Spout La. TN8: C Hil 3L 127
TW19: Stan M 8J 7
Spout La. Nth.
TW19: Stan M 7K 7
Spratts All. KT16: Otter 3G 54
Spratts La. KT16: Otter 3G 54
Spray La. TW2: Whitt 9E 10
Spreadbury Dr. GU51: Fleet 2A 88
Spread Eagle Wlk.
KT19: Eps 6K 201 (9C 60)
SPREAKLEY 2G 149
Spreighton Rd.
KT8: W Mole 3B 40
Spring Av. TW20: Egh 7A 20

Springbok Cotts.—Station App.

Springbok Cotts. GU6: Alf 7F 174
Springbok Est. GU6: Alf 7F 174
Springbottom La.
RH1: Blet 5L 103
Spring Cl. GU7: Goda 3H 133
RH11: Craw 4B 182
Springclose La.
SM3: Chea 3K 61
Spring Copse RH10: Cop 7N 163
RH19: E Grin 7B 166
Spring Copse Bus. Pk.
RH13: Slin 5K 195
Springcopse Rd.
RH2: Reig 5A 122
Spring Cnr. TW13: Felt 4H 23
Spring Cotts. KT6: Surb 4K 41
RH5: Holm 6J 139
Spring Ct. GU2: Guil 8L 93
KT17: Ewe 5E 60
Springcross Av. GU17: Haw 3J 69
Springfarm Rd.
GU27: Hasl 3C 188
Springfield GU8: Els 7H 131
GU18: Ligh 7A 52
RH8: Oxt 8N 105
RH19: E Grin 6N 165
SE25 2D 46
Springfield Av. SW20 2L 43
TW12: Hamp 7B 24
Springfield Cl. GU21: Knap 5H 73
SL4: W'sor 5E 4
Springfield Ct.
KT1: K Tham 6J 203
RH11: Craw 4B 182
RH12: Hors 6J 197
SM6: W'ton 2F 62
Springfield Cres.
RH12: Hors 6H 197
Springfield Dr. KT22: Leat 6E 78
Springfield Gdns.
BR4: W Wick 8L 47
Springfield Gro.
TW16: Sunb 9G 23
Springfield La. GU51: Fleet 4A 88
KT13: Weybr 1C 56
RH12: Col 5F 198
Springfield Mdws.
KT13: Weybr 1C 56
Springfield Pk.
RH12: Hors 5J 197
Springfield Pk. Rd.
RH12: Hors 6H 197
Springfield Pl. KT3: N Mal 3B 42
Springfield Rd. CR7: T Hea 9N 29
GU1: Guil 4E **202** (4A 114)
GU12: A Va 8E 90
GU15: Camb 1E 70
KT1: K Tham 6K **203** (2L 41)
KT17: Ewe 6H 61
KT22: Leat 6F 78
RG12: Bin 1H 31
RH4: Westc 6B 118
RH11: Craw 4A 182
RH12: Hors 6H 197
(not continuous)
SL3: Lang 3D 6
SL4: W'sor 5E 4
SM6: W'ton 2F 62
SW19 6L 27
TN8: Eden 2K 147
TW2: Whitt 2A 24
TW11: Tedd 6G 24
TW15: A'ford 6A 22
Springfields Cl. KT16: Chert 7K 37
Springfield Way GU8: Els 8J 131
Springflower Cotts.
GU3: Worp 9F 92
Spring Gdns. GU14: Farnb 7M 69
GU15: Camb 1E 70
KT8: W Mole 4B 40
RH4: Dork 2H **201** (5G 118)
RH10: Cop 7N 163
RH12: Hors 5J 197
SL5: Asc 8J 17
(New Rd.)
SL5: Asc 3M 33
(Ringwood Cl.)
SM6: W'ton 2G 62
TN16: B Hil 5E 86
SPRING GROVE 4E 10
Spring Gro. CR4: Mit 9E 28
GU7: Goda 3H 133
KT22: Fetc 1B 98
TW12: Hamp 9B 24
W4 1N 11
Spring Gro. Cres.
TW3: Houn 4C 10
Spring Gro. Rd.
TW3: Houn, Isle 4B 10
TW7: Isle 4B 10
TW10: Rich 8M 11
Springhaven *GU8: Els 8J 131*
(off Up. Springfield)
Springhaven Cl. GU1: Guil 3C 114
Spring Health Leisure Club
Richmond 7K 11
(in Pools on the Pk.)
Springhill GU8: Els 8J 131
Springhill Ct. RG12: Brac 3N 31
Springholm Cl.
GU9: B Lea 6N 109
TN16: B Hil 5E 86
Springhurst Cl. CR0: Croy 1J 65
Springlakes Ind. Est.
GU12: Alde 1C 110
Spring La. GU9: U Hal 5F 108
RH8: Oxt 9N 105
RH13: Slin 5K 195
SE25 5E 46
Spring La. W. GU9: U Hal 6F 108
Springmead Ct.
GU27: Hasl 3B 188
(off Copse Rd.)
GU47: Owls 6K 49
Spring Mdw. RG12: Brac 9B 16
RH18: F Row 8H 187
Spring M. KT17: Ewe 5E 60
SPRING PARK 9K 47
Spring Pk. Av. CR0: Croy 8G 47
Springpark Dr. BR3: Beck 2M 47
Spring Pk. Rd. CR0: Croy 8G 47
Spring Pas. SW15 6J 13
Spring Plat RH10: Craw 3G 183
Spring Plat Ct.
RH10: Craw 3G 183
Spring Ri. TW20: Egh 7A 20
Spring Rd. TW13: Felt 4G 23
Springside Ct.
GU1: Guil 1B **202** (2M 113)
Spring St. KT17: Ewe 5E 60
Spring Ter. TW9: Rich 8L 11
Springvale Av. TW8: Brent 1K 11
Springvale Cl. KT23: Book 3B 98
Spring Wlk. RH6: Horl 8D 142
Spring Way RH19: E Grin 6C 166
Springwell Cl. SW16 5K 29
Springwell Rd.
RH5: B Grn 8K 139
SW16 5L 29
TW4: Houn 5L 9
TW5: Hest 5L 9
Springwood GU8: Mil 1D 152
Springwood Ct.
CR2: S Croy 7F 200
(off Birdhurst Rd.)
Springwood Pl.
KT13: Weybr 4C 56
Spring Woods GU25: V Wat 3L 35
GU47: Sandh 6H 49
GU52: Fleet 6A 88
Sprint Ind. Est. KT14: Byf 7M 55
Sproggit Ind. Est.
TW19: Stan 9A 8
Spruce Cl. RH1: Red 2D 122
Sprucedale Gdns.
CR0: Croy 1G 64
SM6: W'ton 5J 63
Spruce Dr. GU18: Ligh 8L 51
Spruce Rd. TN16: B Hil 3F 86
Spruce Way GU51: Fleet 4E 88
Spur, The GU21: Knap 5E 72
KT12: Wal T 8K 39
Spurfield KT8: W Mole 2B 40
Spurgeon Cl. RH11: Craw 2A 182
Spurgeon Rd. SE19 9N 29
Spur Rd. TW7: Isle 3G 11
TW14: Felt 7J 9
Spurs Ct. GU11: Alde 2K 109
Spy La. RH14: Loxw 3H 193
Square, The CR3: Cate 2D 104
GU2: Guil 5J 113
GU5: Shere 8B 116
GU10: Rowl 8D 128
GU14: Farnb 3N 89
GU18: Ligh 6N 51
GU19: Bag 4J 51
GU23: Wis 3N 75
GU26: G'hott 6B 170
KT13: Weybr 1D 56
RG12: Brac 3C 32
RH7: Ling 7M 145
RH10: Craw 3B 182
SM5: Cars 2E 62
TN16: Tats 7E 86
TW9: Rich 8K 11
UB7: L'ford 4K 7
W6 1H 13
Square Dr. GU27: K Grn 7F 188
Squarey St. SW17 4A 28
Squerryes TN16: Weste 6L 107
Squerryes, The CR3: Cate 8B 84
Squerryes Court Manor House & Garden 6L 107
Squerryes Mede
TN16: Weste 5L 107
Squerryes Pk. Cotts.
TN16: Weste 5L 107
Squire's Bri. Rd.
TW17: Shep 3A 38
Squires Cl. RH10: Craw D 1D 184
Squires Ct. KT16: Chert 7K 37
SW19 5M 27
Squires Hill La. GU10: Til 6A 130
Squire's Rd. TW17: Shep 3A 38
Squires Wlk. TW15: A'ford 8E 22
(not continuous)
Squirrel Cl. GU47: Sandh 7G 48
RH11: Craw 9N 161
TW4: Houn 6K 9
Squirrel Ct. GU12: Alde 1C 110
Squirrel Dr. SL4: Wink 2M 17
Squirrel Keep KT14: W By 8K 55
Squirrel La. GU14: Cove 9M 69
SL4: Wink 2M 17
Squirrel Ridge
RH10: Craw D 2E 184
Squirrel's Cl. GU7: Goda 2G 133
Squirrels Ct. *KT4: W Pk 8E 42*
(off The Avenue)
Squirrels Drey *BR2: Brom 1N 47*
(off Park Hill Rd.)
RG45: Crow 2E 48
Squirrels Grn. KT4: W Pk 8E 42
KT23: Book 1A 98
RH1: Red 2D 122
Squirrels Way KT18: Eps 1C 80
Squirrel Wood KT14: W By 8K 55
Stable Cl. KT2: K Tham 7M 25
KT18: Eps D 6D 80
RH10: Craw 6H 183
Stable Cotts. GU7: Goda 4K 133
RH11: P Pot 9M 181
Stable Ct. CR3: Cate 9D 84
SM6: W'ton 9E 44
Stable Cft. GU19: Bag 5H 51
Stable Flats RH11: P Pot 9M 181
Stable M. RH2: Reig 3M 121
Stables, The GU1: Guil 9N 93
KT11: Cob 1N 77
Stables M. SE27 6N 29
Stables Yd. SW18 9M 13
Stable Vw. GU46: Yate 8C 48
Stable Yd. SW15 6H 13
Stableyard M. TW11: Tedd 7F 24
Stace Way RH10: Craw 1J 183
Stacey Ct. RH1: Mers 7G 102
Stacey's Farm Rd.
GU8: Els 8H 131
Staceys Mdw. GU8: Els 7H 131
Stackfield TN8: Eden 9M 127
Stackfield Rd. RH11: Ifi 4K 181
Stack Ho. RH8: Oxt 8A 106
Staddon Cl. BR3: Beck 3H 47
Staff College Rd.
GU15: Camb 9M 49
Staffhurst Wood Nature Reserve
6E 126
Staffhurst Wood Rd.
TN8: Limp 6E 126
Stafford Cl. CR3: Cate 1C 104
SM3: Chea 3K 61
Stafford Cripps Ho.
SW6 2L 13
(off Clem Attlee Ct.)
Stafford Cross Bus. Pk.
CR0: Wad 2K 63
Stafford Gdns. CR0: Wad 2K 63
Stafford Ho. GU11: Alde 2N 109
STAFFORDLAKE 5C 72
Stafford Lake GU21: Knap 5C 72
Stafford Pl. TW10: Rich 1M 25
Stafford Rd. CR0: Wad 1L 63
CR3: Cate 1C 104
KT3: N Mal 2B 42
RH11: Craw 9M 161
SM6: W'ton 3G 62
Staffordshire Cft.
RG42: Warf 7D 16
Staffords Pl. RH6: Horl 1F 162
Stafford Sq. KT13: Weybr 1E 56
Staff Rd. GU12: Alde 2A 110
Stagbury Av. CR5: Chip 5C 82
Stagbury Cl. CR5: Chip 6C 82
Stagbury Ho. CR5: Chip 6C 82
Stag Ct. KT2: K Tham 2M 203
Stagelands RH11: Craw 1N 181
Stagelands Ct.
RH11: Craw 1A 182
Stag Hill GU2: Guil 4K 113
Stag Hill Ct. GU2: Guil 3L 113
STAG LANE 3E 26
Stag La. SW15 4E 26
Stag Leys KT21: A'tead 7L 79
Stag Leys Cl. SM7: Ban 2C 82
Stag Meadow 7E 4
Stags Way TW7: Isle 2F 10
Stainash Cres. TW18: Stain 6K 21
Stainash Pde. *TW18: Stain 6K 21*
(off Kingston Rd.)
Stainbank Rd. CR4: Mit 2F 44
STAINES 5H 21
Staines Av. SM3: Chea 8J 43
Staines Bri. TW18: Stain 6G 20
Staines By-Pass
TW15: A'ford 5K 21
TW18: Stain 5K 21
TW19: Stain 3E 20
Staines La. KT16: Chert 5H 37
Staines La. Cl. KT16: Chert 5H 37
Staines Moor Nature Reserve
2G 21
Staines Reservoirs (Bird Sanctuary)
3L 21
Staines Rd. KT16: Chert 1H 37
TW2: Twick 4A 24
TW3: Houn 9J 9
TW4: Houn 9J 9
TW14: Bedf, Felt 2B 22
(not continuous)
TW18: Lale, Stain 9K 21
TW19: Wray 1A 20
Staines Rd. E. TW16: Sunb 8H 23
Staines Rd. W.
TW15: A'ford 7C 22
TW16: Sunb 7C 22
Staines Station (Rail) 6J 21
Staines Town FC 8J 21
Stainford Cl. TW15: A'ford 6E 22
Stainton Wlk. GU21: Wok 5M 73
Staiths Way KT20: Tad 7G 81
Stake La. GU14: Cove 1M 89
Stakescorner Rd. GU3: Art 2K 133
Stalisfield Pl. BR6: Dow 6J 67
Stambourne Way
BR4: W Wick 8M 47
Stamford Av. GU16: Frim 5D 70
Stamford Bridge 3N 13
Stamford Bri. Studios
SW6 3N 13
(off Wandon Rd.)
Stamford Cotts. *SW6 3N 13*
(off Billing St.)
Stamford Ga. SW6 3N 13
STAMFORD GREEN 9A 60
Stamford Grn. Rd.
KT18: Eps 9A 60
Stamford Ho. *GU24: Chob 7H 53*
(off Bagshot Rd.)
Stamford Rd. KT12: Wal T 9L 39
Stammerham Bus. Cen.
RH12: Rusp 2L 179
Stanacre Ct. KT20: K'wood 8L 81
Stanborough Cl.
TW12: Hamp 7N 23
Stanborough Rd.
TW3: Houn 6D 10
Stanbridge Cl. RH11: Ifi 3K 181
Stanbridge Rd. SW15 6H 13
TN8: Eden 1K 147
Standard Rd. BR6: Dow 6J 67
TW4: Houn 6M 9
Standen 5N 185
Standen Cl. RH19: E Grin 7K 165
Standen Pl. RH12: Hors 1N 197
Standen Rd. SW18 1L 27
Standford Hill
GU35: Stand 8B 168
Standford La. GU30: Pass 8B 168
GU35: Head, Stand 5B 168
GU35: Stand 8B 168
STANDFROD 8B 168
Standinghall La.
RH10: T Hil 6L 183
Standish Ho. *W6 1F 12*
(off St Peter's Gro.)
Standish Rd. W6 1F 12
Standon Cotts. RH5: Ockl 7B 158
Standon La. RH5: Ockl 8M 157
Stane Cl. SW19 8N 27
Stane St. RH5: Ockl 9B 158
RH13: Slin 9H 195
RH14: Bill 9H 195
Stane St. Cotts.
RH12: Rowh 8M 177
Stane Way KT17: Ewe 6F 60
Stanford Cl. TW12: Hamp 7N 23
STANFORD COMMON 4B 92
Stanford Cotts. GU24: Pirb 4B 92
Stanford Ct. *RH10: Craw 5G 183*
(off Maidenbower Pl.)
SW6 4N 13
Stanford Orchard
RH12: Warn 9F 178
Stanford Rd. SW16 1H 45
Stanfords, The *KT17: Eps 8E 60*
(off East St.)
Stanfords Pl. RH7: Ling 8N 145
Stanford Way RH12: Bro H 5D 196
SW16 1H 45
Stanger Rd. SE25 3D 46
Stangrove Lodge
TN8: Eden 2L 147
Stangrove Pde. *TN8: Eden 2L 147*
(off Stangrove Rd.)
Stangrove Rd. TN8: Eden 2L 147
(not continuous)
Stan Hill RH6: Char 1H 161
Stanhope Ga. GU15: Camb 1M 69
Stanhope Gro. BR3: Beck 4J 47
Stanhope Heath TW19: Stan 9L 7
Stanhope Rd.
CR0: Croy 4F **200** (9B 46)
GU15: Camb 2L 69
SM5: Cars 4E 62
Stanhopes RH8: Limp 6D 106
Stanhope Ter. TW2: Twick 1F 24
Stanhope Way TW19: Stan 9L 7
Stanier Cl. RH10: Craw 4F 182
W14 1L 13
Staniland Dr. KT13: Weybr 7A 56
Stanley Av. BR3: Beck 1M 47
KT3: N Mal 4F 42
Stanley Bri. Studios
SW6 3N 13
(off King's Rd.)
Stanley Cen. RH10: Craw 9D 162
Stanley Cl. CR5: Coul 4K 83
RH10: Craw 5C 182
Stanley Ct. SM2: Sut 4N 61
SM5: Cars 4E 62
Stanleycroft Cl. TW7: Isle 4E 10
Stanley Dr. GU14: Cove 2H 89
Stanley Gdns. CR2: Sande 8D 64
CR4: Mit 7E 28
KT12: Hers 3K 57
SM6: W'ton 3G 62
Stanley Gdns. Rd.
TW11: Tedd 6E 24
Stanley Gro. CR0: Croy 5L 45
Stanley Hill GU24: Pirb 9N 71
Stanley Ho. *SW10 3N 13*
(off Coleridge Gdns.)
Stanley M. *SW10 3N 13*
(off Coleridge Gdns.)
Stanley Pk. Rd. SM5: Cars 4C 62
SM6: W'ton 3F 62
Stanley Picker Gallery 6K 203
(within Kingston University)
Stanley Rd. CR0: Croy 6L 45
CR4: Mit 8E 28
GU21: Wok 3B 74
RG40: W'ham 2D 30
SM2: Sut 3N 61
SM4: Mord 3M 43
SM5: Cars 4E 62
SW14 7A 12
SW19 7M 27
TW2: Twick 4D 24
TW3: Houn 7C 10
TW11: Tedd 5E 24
TW15: A'ford 6N 21
Stanley Sq. SM5: Cars 5D 62
Stanley St. CR3: Cate 9N 83
Stanley Wlk. RG12: Brac 1A 32
RH13: Hors 6K 197
Stanmore Cl. SL5: Asc 3L 33
Stanmore Gdns. SM1: Sut 9A 44
TW9: Rich 6M 11
Stanmore Rd. TW9: Rich 6M 11
Stanmore Ter. BR3: Beck 1K 47
STANNERS HILL 4N 53
Stannet Way SM6: W'ton 1G 62
Stansfield Rd. TW4: C'ford 5J 9
Stanstead Mnr. SM1: Sut 3M 61
Stanstead Rd. CR3: Cate 5A 104
Stansted Rd. TW6: Lon A 9A 8
Stan's Way RH12: Hors 6J 197
Stanthorpe Cl. SW16 6J 29
Stanthorpe Rd. SW16 6J 29
Stanton Av. TW11: Tedd 7E 24
Stanton Cl. GU6: Cranl 7J 155
KT4: W Pk 7J 43
KT19: Ewe 2A 60
Stanton Ct. CR2: S Croy 8F 200
Stanton Dr. GU51: Fleet 5A 88
Stanton Rd. CR0: Croy 6N 45
SW13 5E 12
SW20 9J 27
Stantons Wharf
GU5: Braml 4C 134
Stanton Way SL3: Lang 1A 6
STANWELL 9M 7
Stanwell Cl. TW19: Stan 9M 7
Stanwell Gdns. TW19: Stan 9M 7
STANWELL MOOR 8J 7
Stanwell Moor Rd.
TW18: Stain 4J 21
TW19: L'ford, Stan M 7K 7
TW19: Stain, Stan M 4K 21
UB7: L'ford 7K 7
Stanwell New Rd.
TW18: Stain 4J 21
Stanwell Rd. SL3: Hort 6C 6
TW14: Bedf 1C 22
TW15: A'ford 3N 21
Stanwick Rd. W14 1L 13
Stanworth Ct. TW5: Hest 3N 9
Staplecross Ct.
RH11: Craw 6M 181
Staplefield Cl. SW2 2J 29
Stapleford Cl. KT1: K Tham 1N 41
SW19 1K 27
Staple Hill Rd. GU24: Chob 3G 53
Staplehurst RG12: Brac 6K 31
Staplehurst Cl. RH2: Reig 7A 122
Staplehurst Rd. RH2: Reig 7A 122
SM5: Cars 4C 62
Staple La. GU4: E Cla 1M 115
GU5: Shere 3A 116
Stapleton Gdns. CR0: Wad 2L 63
Stapleton Rd. SW17 4E 28
Star & Garter Hill
TW10: Rich 2L 25
Starborough Rd.
TN8: Eden, M Grn 5F 146
Star Cl. RH13: Hors 4N 197
Star Hill GU10: Churt 8J 149
Star Hill Dr. GU10: Churt 7J 149
Star La. CR5: Coul 8E 82
GU12: Ash 2D 110
Starling Cl. CR0: Croy 5H 47
Starlings, The KT22: Oxs 9C 58
Starling Wlk. TW12: Hamp 6M 23
Starmead Dr. RG40: W'ham 3C 30
Star Post Rd. GU15: Camb 7C 50
Star Rd. TW7: Isle 5D 10
W14 2L 13
Starrock La. CR5: Chip 7D 82
Starrock Rd. CR5: Coul 6F 82
Starts Hill Av. BR6: Farnb 1K 67
Starts Hill Rd. BR6: Farnb 1K 67
Starwood Cl. KT14: W By 7L 55
State Farm Av. BR6: Farnb 1K 67
Staten Gdns. TW1: Twick 2F 24
Statham Ct. RG42: Brac 9K 15
Station App. BR4: W Wick 6M 47
CR0: Croy 3E 200
CR2: Sande 5A 64
CR3: Whyte 4D 84
CR5: Chip 5D 82
CR5: Coul 3H 83
CR8: Pur 7L 63
GU1: Guil 4E **202** (4A 114)
GU3: Flex 3M 111
GU4: Chil 9A 114

Station App.—Stratton Ct.

Station App. GU5: Gorn 8E 116
GU7: Goda 7G 132
GU8: Worm 1C 172
GU12: A Va 6E 90
GU14: Farnb 9N 69
GU16: Frim 6B 70
GU17: B'water 2K 69
GU22: Wok 5B 74
GU25: V Wat 3N 35
GU51: Fleet 2C 88
KT1: K Tham 9N 25
KT4: W Pk 7F 42
KT10: H Wood 9F 40
KT13: Weybr 3B 56
KT14: W By 8J 55
KT17: Ewe 6G 60
(Cheam Rd.)
KT17: Ewe 5E 60
(Fennels Mead)
KT19: Eps 6J 201 (9C 60)
KT19: Ewe 2F 60
KT20: Tad 9H 81
KT22: Leat 8G 78
(not continuous)
KT22: Oxs 8C 58
KT24: E Hor 4F 96
RG40: W'ham 2A 30
RH1: Red 2E 122
(off Redstone Hill)
RH4: Dork 3J 119
RH5: Ockl 5H 159
RH6: Horl 8F 142
RH8: Oxt 7A 106
SM2: Chea 4K 61
SM2: Sut 6N 61
SM5: Cars 1D 62
SW6 6K 13
SW14 6B 12
SW16 7H 29
(Estreham Rd.)
SW16 6H 29
(Gleneagle Rd.)
SW20 1G 43
TN8: Eden 1L 147
TW8: Brent 2J 11
(off Sidney Gdns.)
TW9: Kew 4N 11
TW12: Hamp 9A 24
TW15: A'ford 5A 22
TW16: Sunb 9H 23
TW17: Shep 4D 38
TW18: Stain 6J 21
Station App. E. RH1: Red 5D 122
Station App. Rd. CR5: Coul 2H 83
RH6: Gat 2F 162
W4 3B 12
Station App. W. RH1: Red 5D 122
Station Av. CR3: Cate 2D 104
KT3: N Mal 2D 42
KT12: Wal T 1H 57
KT19: Ewe 5D 60
TW9: Kew 4N 11
Station Bldgs.
KT1: K Tham 3J 203
Station Cl. RH13: Hors 6K 197
TW12: Hamp 9B 24
Station Cotts. RH13: Hors 9D 196
Station Cres. TW15: A'ford 4M 21
Station Est. BR3: Beck 2G 47
Station Est. Rd. TW14: Felt 2J 23
Station Garage M.
SW16 7H 29
Station Gdns. W4 3B 12
Station Hill GU9: Farnh 1H 129
RH10: Craw 2F 182
SL5: Asc 2L 33
Station Ind. Est.
RG41: W'ham 2A 30
Station La.
GU8: Ent G, Hamb, Mil
1D 152
GU8: Worm 9B 152
Station Pde. GU25: V Wat 3N 35
KT24: E Hor 4F 96
(not continuous)
SL5: S'dale 6D 34
SM2: Sut 3A 62
(off High St.)
SW12 2E 28
TW9: Kew 4N 11
TW14: Felt 2J 23
TW15: A'ford 5A 22
W4 3B 12
Station Path SW6 6L 13
TW18: Stain 5H 21
Station Pl. GU7: Goda 4J 133
Station Ri. SE27 3M 29
Station Rd. BR4: W Wick 7M 47
CR0: Croy 1B 200 (7N 45)
CR3: Whyte 5C 84
CR3: Wold 9H 85
CR8: Ken 1N 83
GU4: Chil 9A 114
GU5: Braml 5B 134
GU5: Gorn 8D 116
GU7: Goda 4J 133
(Grays Rd.)
GU7: Goda 7G 132
(Station App.)
GU11: Alde 2N 109
GU14: Farnb 1N 89
GU16: Frim 5A 70
GU19: Bag 3J 51
Station Rd. GU24: Chob 7J 53
KT1: H Wic 1G 203 (9J 25)
KT2: K Tham 9N 25
KT3: N Mal 4G 42
KT7: T Dit 6F 40
KT9: Ches 2L 59
KT10: Clay 3E 58
KT10: Esh 8D 40
KT11: Sto D 4M 77
KT14: W By 8J 55
KT15: Addl 1L 55
KT16: Chert 7H 37
KT22: Leat 8G 79
RG12: Brac 1N 31
RG40: W'ham 2A 30
RH1: Mers 6G 102
RH1: Red 2C 122
(not continuous)
RH3: Betch 9D 100
(not continuous)
RH4: Dork 1H 201 (4G 118)
RH6: Horl 8F 142
RH7: Ling 6A 146
RH9: S Gods 7K 125
RH10: Craw 4B 182
RH10: Craw D 1E 184
RH12: Cranl, Rudg 6C 176
RH12: Rudg 1E 194
RH12: Warn 9G 179
RH13: Hors 9D 196
(Christs Hospital Rd.)
RH13: Hors 6K 197
(Station Cl.)
RH14: Loxw 5H 193
RH18: F Row 6H 187
RH19: E Grin 9N 165
SE25 3C 46
SL5: S'dale 5D 34
SM2: Sut 6M 61
SM5: Cars 1D 62
SW13 5E 12
SW19 9A 28
TN8: Eden 9L 127
TW1: Twick 2F 24
TW3: Houn 7B 10
TW11: Tedd 7G 24
TW12: Hamp 9A 24
TW15: A'ford 5A 22
TW16: Sunb 8H 23
TW17: Shep 4D 38
TW19: Wray 9B 6
TW20: Egh 6C 20
Station Rd. E. GU12: A Va 6D 90
RH8: Oxt 7A 106
Station Rd. Nth.
RH1: Mers 6G 102
TW20: Egh 6C 20
Station Rd. Sth.
RH1: Mers 6G 102
Station Rd. W. GU12: A Va 5D 90
RH8: Oxt 7A 106
Station Row GU4: Chil 9A 114
Station Ter.
RH4: Dork 1H 201 (4G 118)
Station Vw.
GU1: Guil 4A 202 (4M 113)
GU12: A Va 5E 90
Station Way KT10: Clay 3E 58
KT19: Eps 6J 201 (9C 60)
RG12: Brac 1A 32
RH10: Craw 4B 182
SM3: Chea 3K 61
Station Yd. CR8: Pur 8M 63
TW1: Twick 1G 24
Staunton Rd. KT2: K Tham 7L 25
Staveley Gdns. W4 4C 12
Staveley Rd. TW15: A'ford 7E 22
W4 2B 12
Staveley Way GU21: Knap 4H 73
Staverton Cl. RG40: W'ham 2E 30
RG42: Brac 8N 15
Stavordale Rd. SM5: Cars 6A 44
Stayne End GU25: V Wat 3K 35
Stayton Rd. SM1: Sut 9M 43
Stbale M. TW1: Twick 2F 24
Steadfast Rd.
KT1: K Tham 2H 203 (9K 25)
Steam Farm La. TW14: Felt 7G 8
Steele Rd. TW7: Isle 7G 11
Steele's Rd. GU11: Alde 9N 89
(not continuous)
Steel's La. KT22: Oxs 1B 78
Steep Hill
CR0: Croy 6F 200 (1B 64)
GU24: Chob 4F 52
SW16 4H 29
Steeple Cl. SW6 5K 13
SW19 6K 27
Steeple Gdns. KT15: Addl 2K 55
Steeple Hgts. Dr.
TN16: B Hil 4F 86
Steeple Point SL5: Asc 2M 33
Steepways GU26: Hind 3N 169
Steeres Hill RH12: Rusp 3B 180
Steerforth Copse
GU47: Owls 5K 49
Steerforth St. SW18 3A 28
Steer Pl. RH1: Salf 3E 142
Steers La. RH10: Craw 6G 162
Steers Mead CR4: Mit 9D 28
Stella Rd. SW17 7D 28
Stembridge Rd. SE20 1E 46
Stem Ct. KT16: Chert 7L 37
Stennings, The
RH19: E Grin 8M 165
Stents La. KT11: Sto D 7N 77
Stepbridge Path
GU21: Wok 4N 73
Stepgates KT16: Chert 6K 37
Stepgates Cl. KT16: Chert 6K 37
Stephanie Chase Ct.
RG40: W'ham 1C 30
Stephen Cl. BR6: Orp 1N 67
TW20: Egh 7E 20
Stephendale Rd.
GU9: Farnh 8J 109
SW6 6N 13
Stephen Fox Ho. *W4 1D 12*
(off Chiswick La.)
Stephenson Ct. *SM2: Chea 4K 61*
(off Station App.)
Stephenson Dr.
RH19: E Grin 2B 186
SL4: W'sor 3E 4
Stephenson Pl. *RH1: Mers 6G 102*
(off Station Rd. Nth.)
RH10: Craw 3F 182
Stephenson Rd. GU2: Guil 3G 112
TW2: Whitt 1A 24
Stephenson Way
RH10: Craw 3E 182
Stephenson Way Ind. Est.
RH10: Craw 3F 182
Stephyns Dr. GU51: Fleet 1A 88
Stepney Cl. CR4: Mit 9E 28
RH10: Craw 5G 182
Sterling Bldgs.
RH12: Hors 6J 197
(off Carfax)
Sterling Cen. RG12: Brac 1B 32
Sterling Ct. KT16: Chert 6J 37
Sterling Gdns. GU47: C Tow 7K 49
Sterling Pk. RH10: Craw 7F 162
Sterling Pl. KT13: Weybr 1F 56
W5 1L 11
Sternhold Av. SW2 3H 29
Sterry Dr. KT7: T Dit 5E 40
KT19: Ewe 1D 60
Steve Biko Way TW3: Houn 6A 10
Stevenage Rd.
RH11: Craw 6K 181
SW6 3J 13
Stevens Cl.
KT17: Eps 6M 201 (8D 60)
TW12: Hamp 7N 23
Stevens Hill GU46: Yate 1D 68
Stevens La. KT10: Clay 4G 59
Stevenson Dr. RG42: Bin 6H 15
Stevens Pl. CR8: Pur 9M 63
Stewards Ri. GU10: Wrec 4E 128
Stewart KT20: Tad 8J 81
Stewart Av. TW17: Shep 3B 38
Stewart Cl. GU21: Wok 4J 73
TW12: Hamp 7M 23
Stewart Ho.
KT1: K Tham 6L 203 (2M 41)
Steyning Cl. CR8: Ken 3M 83
RH10: Craw 1C 182
Steyning Way TW4: Houn 7K 9
St Helier Station (Rail) 5M 43
Stickle Down GU16: Deep 6H 71
Stile Footpath RH1: Red 3D 122
Stile Gdns. GU27: Hasl 2D 188
Stile Hall Gdns. W4 1N 11
Stile Hall Pde. W4: Brent 1N 11
Stile Ho. *GU1: Guil 2F 114*
(off Merrow St.)
Stile Path TW16: Sunb 2H 39
Stillers GU8: Chid 5E 172
Stillingfleet Rd. SW13 2F 12
Stilwell Cl. GU46: Yate 9D 48
Stirling Av. SM6: W'ton 4J 63
TW17: Shep 2F 38
Stirling Cl. GU12: A Va 8D 90
GU14: Cove 2M 89
GU16: Frim 4C 70
RH10: Craw 4F 182
SL4: W'sor 5A 4
SM7: Ban 4L 81
SW16 9H 29
Stirling Dr. CR3: Cate 8N 83
Stirling Gro. TW3: Houn 5C 10
Stirling Ho. RH1: Red 3D 122
Stirling Pl. RH12: Bro H 5D 196
Stirling Rd. GU2: Guil 3G 113
TW2: Whitt 1A 24
TW6: Lon A 9A 8
Stirling Wlk. KT5: Surb 5A 42
Stirling Way CR0: Bedd 6J 45
RH13: Hors 6L 197
RH19: E Grin 7D 166
Stirrup Way RH10: Craw 2H 183
Stites Hill Rd. CR5: Coul 7M 83
St Margarets Station (Rail) 9H 11
Stoatley Hollow
GU27: Hasl 9E 170
Stoatley Ri. GU27: Hasl 9E 170
Stoats Nest Rd. CR5: Coul 1J 83
Stoats Nest Village
CR5: Coul 2J 83
Stockbridge Dr.
GU11: Alde 6A 110
Stockbridge Way
GU46: Yate 2C 68
Stockbury Rd. CR0: Croy 5F 46
Stockdales Rd. SL4: E Wic 1C 4
Stockers La. GU22: Wok 7B 74
(not continuous)
Stockfield RH6: Horl 7F 142
Stockfield Rd. KT10: Clay 2E 58
SW16 4K 29
Stockham's Cl.
CR2: Sande 6A 64
Stock Hill TN16: B Hil 3F 86
Stockhurst Cl. SW15 5H 13
Stocklund Sq. GU6: Cranl 7L 155
Stockport Rd. SW16 9H 29
Stocks Cl. RH6: Horl 9F 142
Stockton Av. GU51: Fleet 2A 88
Stockton Pk. GU51: Fleet 3A 88
Stockton Rd. RH2: Reig 6M 121
Stockwell Cen.
RH10: Craw 3E 182
Stockwell Rd.
RH19: E Grin 3A 186
Stockwood Ri. GU15: Camb 1D 70
Stockwood Way
GU9: Weybo 5L 109
Stocton Cl.
GU1: Guil 1B 202 (2M 113)
Stocton Rd.
GU1: Guil 1B 202 (2N 113)
Stoford Cl. SW19 1K 27
Stoke Cl. KT11: Sto D 3N 77
STOKE D'ABERNON 4M 77
Stoke Flds.
GU1: Guil 4C 202 (3N 113)
(Church Rd.)
GU1: Guil 3C 202
(Drummond Rd.)
Stokeford Cl. RG12: Brac 4D 32
Stoke Gro.
GU1: Guil 3D 202 (3N 113)
Stoke Hills GU9: Farnh 9H 109
Stoke Hospital GU1: Guil 3D 202
Stoke M.
GU1: Guil 4D 202 (4N 113)
Stoke Mill Cl. GU1: Guil 1N 113
Stokenchurch St. SW6 4N 13
Stoke Pk. Ct.
GU1: Guil 3D 202 (3N 113)
Stoke Rd.
GU1: Guil 1D 202 (2N 113)
KT2: K Tham 8B 26
KT11: Cob, Sto D 2K 77
KT12: Wal T 9K 39
Stoke Rd. Cotts. KT22: Fetc 8D 78
Stokers Cl. RH6: Gat 2C 162
Stokesby Rd. KT9: Ches 3M 59
Stokes Cl. RH10: Craw 5G 183
Stokesheath Rd. KT22: Oxs 7C 58
Stoke Sq. GU1: Guil 3C 202
Stokes Ridings KT20: Tad 1J 101
Stokes Rd. CR0: Croy 5G 47
Stompond La. KT12: Wal T 8H 39
Stonards Brow GU5: Sha G 7E 134
Stonebanks KT12: Wal T 6H 39
STONEBRIDGE 8K 119
Stonebridge Ct.
RH11: Craw 7A 182
RH12: Hors 6G 197
Stonebridge Fld. SL4: Eton 1E 4
Stonebridge Flds.
GU4: Chil 1N 133
Stonebridge Wharf
GU4: Chil 1N 133
Stonecot Cl. SM3: Sut 7K 43
Stonecot Hill SM3: Sut 7K 43
Stone Ct. CR3: Cate 3B 104
RH10: Craw 3H 183
Stonecourt Cl. RH6: Horl 8G 143
Stone Cres. TW14: Felt 1G 22
Stonecroft Way CR0: Croy 6J 45
Stonecrop Cl. RH11: Craw 6N 181
Stonecrop Rd. GU4: Guil 1E 114
Stonedene Cl.
GU35: H Dwn 5G 169
RH18: F Row 7K 187
Stonefield Cl. RH10: Craw 4B 182
Stonegate GU15: Camb 9G 50
Stone Hatch GU6: Alf 6J 175
STONEHILL 3A 54
Stone Hill RH19: E Grin 7M 185
Stonehill Cl. KT23: Book 3A 98
SW14 8C 12
Stonehill Cres. KT16: Otter 3A 54
Stonehill Ga. SL5: S'hill 5A 34
Stonehill Pk.
GU35: H Dwn 5G 169
Stone Hill Rd. W4 1N 11
Stonehill Rd. GU18: Ligh 6L 51
GU24: Chob 6M 53
GU35: H Dwn 5H 169
KT16: Otter 2B 54
SW14 8B 12
Stone Ho. Gdns.
CR3: Cate 3B 104
Stonehouse Ri. GU16: Frim 5C 70
STONELEIGH 2F 60
Stoneleigh Av. KT4: W Pk 1F 60
Stoneleigh B'way.
KT17: Ewe 2F 60
Stoneleigh Cl.
RH19: E Grin 9B 166
Stoneleigh Ct. GU16: Frim 5D 70
KT11: Sto D 4M 77
Stoneleigh Cres. KT19: Ewe 2E 60
Stoneleigh Pk.
KT13: Weybr 2D 56
Stoneleigh Pk. Av.
CR0: Croy 5G 47
Stoneleigh Pk. Rd.
KT19: Ewe 3E 60
Stoneleigh Rd. RH8: Limp 8G 107
SM5: Cars 6C 44
Stoneleigh Station (Rail) 2F 60
Stone Pk. Av. BR3: Beck 3K 47
Stonepark Dr.
RH18: F Row 7J 187
Stonepit Cl. GU7: Goda 7E 132
Stone Pl. KT4: W Pk 8F 42
STONEQUARRY 6C 166
Stones La. RH4: Westc 6C 118
(not continuous)
Stone's Rd. KT17: Eps 8D 60
Stone St. GU12: Alde 4B 110
Stoneswood Rd.
RH8: Limp 8D 106
Stoney Bottom
GU26: G'hott 6A 170
Stoney Brook GU2: Guil 2H 113
Stoneybrook RH12: Hors 7F 196
Stoney Cl. GU46: Yate 2C 68
Stoney Cft. CR5: Coul 9G 83
Stoneycroft Wlk. RH11: Ifi 4J 181
Stoneydeep TW11: Tedd 5G 25
Stoneyfield Rd. CR5: Coul 4K 83
Stoneyfields GU9: Farnh 2K 129
Stoneylands Ct. TW20: Egh 6B 20
Stoneylands Rd. TW20: Egh 6B 20
Stoney Rd. RG42: Brac 9M 15
Stonny Cft. KT21: A'tead 4M 79
Stonor Rd. W14 1L 13
Stonyfield TN8: Eden 9M 127
Stony Hill KT10: Esh 4N 57
Stookes Way GU46: Yate 2A 68
Stoop Ct. KT14: W By 8K 55
Stoop Memorial Ground 1E 24
Stopham Rd. RH10: Craw 6G 182
Stormont Way KT9: Ches 2J 59
Storrington Ct.
RH11: Craw 2M 181
Storrington Rd. CR0: Croy 7C 46
Storr's La. GU3: Worp 2F 92
STOUGHTON 9K 93
Stoughton Av. SM3: Chea 2J 61
Stoughton Cl. SW15 2F 26
Stoughton Rd. GU1: Guil 9K 93
GU2: Guil 9K 93
Stour Cl. BR2: Kes 1E 66
Stourhead Cl. GU14: Farnb 1B 90
SW19 1J 27
Stourhead Gdns.
SW20 2F 42
Stourton Av. TW13: Hanw 5N 23
Stovell Rd. SL4: W'sor 3E 4
Stovolds Hill GU6: Cranl 9E 154
Stovold's Way GU11: Alde 4L 109
Stowell Av. CR0: N Add 6N 65
Stowting Rd. BR6: Orp 1N 67
Strachan Pl. SW19 7H 27
Strachey Ct. RH11: Craw 8N 181
Stradella Rd. SE24 1N 29
Strafford Rd. TW1: Twick 1G 25
TW3: Houn 6N 9
Straight Mile, The
RG10: S Row, Twy 1C 14
RG40: W'ham 1C 14
Straight Rd. SL4: O Win 8K 5
Strand Cl. KT18: Eps D 6C 80
RH10: Craw 5H 183
Strand Dr. TW9: Kew 3A 12
STRAND ON THE GREEN 2N 11
Strand on the Grn. W4 2N 11
Strand School App.
W4 2N 11
Strata Ct. KT12: Wal T 7G 39
Stratfield RG12: Brac 7K 31
Stratford Ct. GU9: Farnh 2H 129
KT3: N Mal 3C 42
Stratford Gro. SW15 7J 13
Stratford Rd. CR7: T Hea 3L 45
GU12: A Va 5D 90
TW6: Lon A 9C 8
Strathan Cl. SW18 9K 13
Strathavon Cl. GU6: Cranl 3K 155
Strathbrook Rd. SW16 8K 29
Strathcona Av. KT23: Book 6M 97
Strathcona Gdns.
GU21: Knap 5G 72
(not continuous)
Strathdale SW16 6K 29
Strathdon Dr. SW17 4B 28
Strathearn Av. TW2: Whitt 2B 24
UB3: Harl 3G 9
Strathearn Rd. SM1: Sut 2M 61
SW19 6M 27
Strathmore Cl. CR3: Cate 8B 84
Strathmore Ct. GU15: Camb 9B 50
Strathmore Rd. CR0: Croy 6A 46
RH11: Ifi 9M 161
SW19 4M 27
TW11: Tedd 5E 24
Strathville Rd. SW18 3M 27
(not continuous)
Strathyre Av. SW16 2L 45
STRATTON 1F 124
Stratton Av. SM6: W'ton 5H 63
Stratton Cl. KT12: Wal T 7K 39
SW19 1M 43
TW3: Houn 4A 10
Stratton Ct. GU2: Guil 1K 113

Stratton Rd.—Sutherland Dr.

Stratton Rd. SW19 ... 1M 43
TW16: Sunb ... 1G 38
Stratton Ter. TN16: Weste ... 5L 107
Stratton Wlk. GU14: Farnb ... 7M 69
Strawberry Cl.
GU24: B'wood ... 8A 72
Strawberry Ct. GU16: Deep ... 6H 71
Strawberry Flds.
BR6: Farnb ... 2K 67
GU24: Bis ... 2D 72
STRAWBERRY HILL ... 4F 24
Strawberry Hill RG42: Warf ... 7C 16
TW1: Twick ... 4F 24
Strawberry Hill Cl.
TW1: Twick ... 4F 24
Strawberry Hill House ... 4F 24
(within St Mary's College)
Strawberry Hill Rd.
TW1: Twick ... 4F 24
Strawberry Hill Station (Rail)
... 4F 24
Strawberry La. SM5: Cars ... 9E 44
Strawberry Ri. GU24: Bis ... 2D 72
Strawberry Va. TW1: Twick ... 4G 24
(not continuous)
Straw Cl. CR3: Cate ... 1N 103
Strawson Ct. RH6: Horl ... 7D 142
Stream Banks
GU3: Wood V ... 2E 112
(off Pound Ct.)
Stream Cl. KT14: Byf ... 8M 55
Stream Cotts. GU16: Frim ... 5B 70
(off Grove Cross Rd.)
Stream Farm Cl.
GU10: L Bou ... 4J 129
Stream Pk. RH19: E Grin ... 7K 165
Streamside GU51: Fleet ... 5B 88
Stream Valley Rd.
GU10: L Bou ... 5H 129
Streatfield TN8: Eden ... 2M 147
STREATHAM ... 6J 29
Streatham Cl. SW16 ... 3J 29
STREATHAM COMMON ... 7J 29
Streatham Comn. Nth.
SW16 ... 6J 29
Streatham Comn. Sth.
SW16 ... 7J 29
Streatham Common Station (Rail)
... 7H 29
Streatham Ct. SW16 ... 4J 29
Streatham High Rd.
SW16 ... 5J 29
STREATHAM HILL ... 3J 29
Streatham Hill SW2 ... 3J 29
Streatham Hill Station (Rail)
... 3J 29
Streatham Ice Arena ... 6H 29
Streatham Leisure Cen. ... 6J 29
STREATHAM PARK ... 6G 29
Streatham Pl. SW2 ... 1J 29
Streatham Rd. CR4: Mit ... 9E 28
SW16 ... 9E 28
Streatham Station (Rail) ... 6H 29
STREATHAM VALE ... 8G 29
Streatham Va. SW16 ... 9G 29
Streathbourne Rd.
SW17 ... 3E 28
Street, The GU3: Comp ... 9D 112
GU3: Put ... 8M 111
GU4: Chil ... 8N 113
GU4: E Cla ... 9M 95
GU4: W Cla ... 6J 95
GU5: Alb ... 8K 115
GU5: Wone ... 4C 134
GU6: Ewh ... 4F 156
(not continuous)
GU8: Hasc ... 4N 153
GU8: S'ford ... 3N 131
GU8: Thur ... 7G 150
GU10: Dock ... 4D 148
GU10: Fren ... 3H 149
GU10: Tong ... 5D 110
GU10: Wrec ... 5D 128
KT21: A'tead ... 6L 79
KT22: Fetc ... 9D 78
KT24: Eff ... 5L 97
KT24: W Hors ... 7C 96
RH3: Betch ... 4D 120
RH5: Cap ... 5J 159
RH6: Char ... 3K 161
RH13: Slin ... 5K 195
RH14: Plais ... 6A 192
Streeters Cl. GU7: Goda ... 5K 133
Streeters La. SM6: Bedd ... 9H 45
Streetfield Rd. RH13: Slin ... 5L 195
Street Hill RH10: Wor ... 4J 183
Streets Heath GU24: W End ... 8C 52
(not continuous)
Stretton Rd. CR0: Croy ... 6B 46
TW10: Ham ... 3J 25
Strickland Cl. RH11: Ifi ... 4K 181
Strickland Row SW18 ... 1B 28
Strides Ct. KT16: Otter ... 3E 54
(off Brox Rd.)
Stringer's Av. GU4: J Wel ... 6N 93
STRINGERS COMMON ... 7M 93
Stringhams Copse
GU23: Rip ... 2H 95
Strode Rd. SW6 ... 3K 13
Strode's Coll. La.
TW20: Egh ... 6B 20
(off High St.)
Strode's Cres. TW18: Stain ... 6L 21
Strode St. TW20: Egh ... 5C 20
Stronsay Cl. GU26: Hind ... 4C 170
STROOD GREEN
RH3 ... 7B 120
RH12 ... 2B 196
Strood La.
RH12: Bro H, Warn ... 1B 196
SL4: Wink ... 7N 17
STROUD ... 6L 171
Stroud Cl. SL4: W'sor ... 6A 4
STROUD COMMON ... 9H 135
Stroud Comn. GU5: Sha G ... 8H 135
Stroud Cres. SW15 ... 4F 26
STROUDE ... 2A 36
Stroude Rd. GU25: V Wat ... 4A 36
TW20: Egh ... 7C 20
Stroudes Cl. KT4: W Pk ... 6D 42
Stroud Grn. Gdns.
CR0: Croy ... 6F 46
Stroud Grn. Way CR0: Croy ... 6E 46
Stroud La. GU5: Sha G ... 9J 135
GU17: B'water ... 2F 68
Stroudley Cl. RH10: Craw ... 4F 182
Stroudley Ct. RH19: E Grin ... 8B 166
(off Badger's Way)
Stroud Rd. SE25 ... 5D 46
SW19 ... 4M 27
Stroudwater Pk.
KT13: Weybr ... 3C 56
Stroud Way TW15: A'ford ... 7C 22
Struan Gdns. GU21: Wok ... 2A 74
Strudgate Cl. RH10: Craw ... 5F 182
Strudwicks Fld.
GU6: Cranl ... 6A 156
Stuart Av. KT12: Wal T ... 7J 39
Stuart Cl. GU14: Cove ... 9M 69
RH10: Craw ... 4G 183
SL4: W'sor ... 5C 4
Stuart Ct. CR0: Croy ... 4A 200
GU7: Goda ... 7H 133
RH1: Red ... 2E 122
(off St Anne's Ri.)
Stuart Cres. CR0: Croy ... 9J 47
RH2: Reig ... 6M 121
Stuart Gro. TW11: Tedd ... 6E 24
Stuart Ho. RG42: Brac ... 9L 15
(off Windlesham Rd.)
Stuart Lodge KT18: Eps ... 7K 201
Stuart Pl. CR4: Mit ... 9D 28
Stuart Rd. CR6: Warl ... 7E 84
CR7: T Hea ... 3N 45
RH2: Reig ... 6M 121
SW19 ... 4M 27
TW10: Ham ... 3H 25
Stuart Way GU25: V Wat ... 3K 35
RH19: E Grin ... 2B 186
SL4: W'sor ... 5B 4
TW18: Stain ... 7K 21
Stubbs Ct. W4 ... 1A 12
(off Chaseley Dr.)
Stubbs Folly GU47: C Tow ... 8J 49
Stubbs Hill RG42: Bin ... 5K 15
Stubbs La. KT20: Lwr K ... 6L 101
Stubbs Moor Rd.
GU14: Cove ... 9L 69
Stubbs Way SW19 ... 9B 28
Stubfield RH12: Hors ... 5G 196
Stubpond La. RH7: Newc ... 2F 164
(not continuous)
RH19: Fel ... 2F 164
Stubs Cl. RH4: Dork ... 7J 119
Stubs Hill RH4: Dork ... 7J 119
Stucley Rd. TW5: Hest ... 3C 10
Studdridge St. SW6 ... 5M 13
(not continuous)
Studio Arts & Media Cen., The
... 1H 47
Studio Plaza KT12: Wal T ... 7H 39
Studios Rd. TW17: Shep ... 2A 38
Studio Theatre ... 1E 62
Studland Rd. KT2: K Tham ... 7L 25
KT14: Byf ... 9A 56
Studland St. W6 ... 1G 12
Stumblets RH10: Craw ... 2G 183
Stumps La. CR3: Whyte ... 4C 84
(not continuous)
Sturdee Cl. GU16: Frim ... 5C 70
Sturges Rd. RG40: W'ham ... 3B 30
Sturmey Dr. GU51: Fleet ... 1A 88
Sturt Av. GU27: Hasl ... 3D 188
Sturt Ct. GU4: Guil ... 1D 114
Sturt Mdw. Cotts.
GU27: Hasl ... 3D 188
Sturt Rd. GU9: U Hal ... 5G 109
GU16: Frim G ... 9D 70
GU27: Hasl ... 2D 188
Sturt's La. KT20: Wal H ... 5E 100
Stychens Cl. RH1: Blet ... 2N 123
Stychens La. RH1: Blet ... 9N 103
Styles End KT23: Book ... 5B 98
Styles Way BR3: Beck ... 3M 47
Styventon Pl. KT16: Chert ... 6H 37
Subrosa Cvn. Site
RH1: Mers ... 8F 102
Subrosa Dr. RH1: Mers ... 8F 102
Succombs Hill CR3: Warl ... 7E 84
CR6: Warl ... 7E 84
Succombs Pl. CR6: Warl ... 6E 84
Sudbrooke Rd. SW12 ... 1D 28
Sudbrook Gdns.
TW10: Ham ... 4K 25
Sudbrook La. TW10: Ham ... 2L 25
Sudbury Gdns. CR0: Croy ... 1B 64
Sudbury Ho. SW18 ... 8N 13
Sudlow Rd. SW18 ... 8M 13
Suffield Cl. CR2: Sels ... 8G 64
Suffield La.
GU8: Els, Put, S'ford ... 4H 131
Suffield Rd. SE20 ... 1F 46
Suffolk Cl. GU19: Bag ... 5J 51
RH6: Horl ... 9E 142
Suffolk Combe RG42: Warf ... 8D 16
Suffolk Ct. GU16: Deep ... 6H 71
Suffolk Dr. GU4: B'ham ... 7D 94
Suffolk Ho. CR0: Croy ... 3D 200
Suffolk Rd. KT4: W Pk ... 8E 42
SE25 ... 3C 46
SW13 ... 3E 12
Sugden Rd. KT7: T Dit ... 7H 41
Sulina Rd. SW2 ... 1J 29
Sulivan Ct. SW6 ... 5M 13
Sulivan Ent. Cen. SW6 ... 6N 13
Sulivan Rd. SW6 ... 6M 13
Sullington Hill
RH11: Craw ... 5B 182
Sullington Mead
RH12: Bro H ... 5E 196
Sullivan Cl. GU14: Farnb ... 1N 89
KT8: W Mole ... 2B 40
Sullivan Dr. RH11: Craw ... 6K 181
Sullivan Rd. GU15: Camb ... 1M 69
Sullivans Reach
KT12: Wal T ... 6G 39
Sultan St. BR3: Beck ... 1G 47
Sulzers Rdbt. GU14: Farnb ... 2N 89
Summer Av. KT8: E Mol ... 4E 40
Summer Crossing
KT7: E Mol ... 4E 40
Summerene Cl. SW16 ... 8G 29
Summerfield KT21: A'tead ... 6K 79
Summerfield Cl.
KT15: Addl ... 2H 55
Summerfield La.
GU10: Fren ... 9F 128
KT6: Surb ... 8K 41
Summerfield Pl.
KT16: Otter ... 3F 54
Summerfold RH12: Rudg ... 9F 176
Summer Gdns.
GU15: Camb ... 1G 71
KT8: E Mol ... 4E 40
Summerhayes Cl.
GU21: Wok ... 1A 74
Summerhays KT11: Cob ... 9L 57
Summerhill GU7: Goda ... 5G 132
Summerhill Cl. BR6: Orp ... 1N 67
Summerhill Way CR4: Mit ... 9E 28
Summer Ho. RH11: Craw ... 4A 182
(off Oak Rd.)
Summerhouse Av.
TW5: Hest ... 4M 9
Summerhouse Cl.
GU7: Goda ... 8G 133
Summerhouse Ct.
GU26: G'hott ... 6B 170
Summerhouse La.
UB7: Harm ... 2M 7
Summerhouse Rd.
GU7: Goda ... 8G 133
Summerlands GU6: Cranl ... 6N 155
Summerlands Lodge
BR6: Farnb ... 1J 67
Summerlay Cl. KT20: Tad ... 7K 81
Summerleigh KT13: Weybr ... 3E 56
(off Gower Rd.)
Summerley St. SW18 ... 3N 27
Summerly Av. RH2: Reig ... 2M 121
Summer Pl. RG12: Brac ... 9M 15
Summer Rd. KT7: T Dit ... 4E 40
KT8: E Mol ... 4D 40
(not continuous)
Summersbury Dr.
GU4: Chil ... 2A 134
Summersbury Hall
GU4: Chil ... 2A 134
Summersby Cl. GU7: Goda ... 4J 133
Summers Cl. KT13: Weybr ... 7B 56
SM2: Sut ... 4M 61
Summers La. GU7: Hurt ... 3D 132
Summer's Rd. GU7: Goda ... 4J 133
SUMMERSTOWN ... 4A 28
Summerstown SW17 ... 4A 28
Summersvere Cl.
RH10: Craw ... 9E 162
Summerswood Cl.
CR8: Ken ... 3A 84
Summer Trees TW16: Sunb ... 9J 23
Summerville Gdns.
SM1: Sut ... 3L 61
Summerwood Rd. TW7: Isle ... 8F 10
Summit Av. GU14: Cove ... 1G 88
Summit Bus. Pk.
TW16: Sunb ... 8H 23
Summit Pl. KT13: Weybr ... 4B 56
Sumner Cl. BR6: Farnb ... 1L 67
KT22: Fetc ... 2D 98
Sumner Ct. GU9: Farnh ... 9H 109
Sumner Gdns. CR0: Croy ... 7L 45
Sumner Pl. KT15: Addl ... 2J 55
Sumner Rd. CR0: Croy ... 7L 45
GU9: Farnh ... 9H 109
Sumner Rd. Sth. CR0: Croy ... 7L 45
Sun All. TW9: Rich ... 7L 11
Sun Brow GU27: Hasl ... 3D 188
SUNBURY ... 2K 39
Sunbury Av. SW14 ... 7C 12
Sunbury Av. Pas.
SW14 ... 7D 12
Sunbury Bus. Cen.
TW16: Sunb ... 9G 22
Sunbury Cl. KT12: Wal T ... 5H 39
SUNBURY COMMON ... 8G 23
Sunbury Ct. SL4: Eton ... 2G 4
Sunbury Ct. Island
TW16: Sunb ... 2L 39
Sunbury Ct. M. TW16: Sunb ... 1L 39
Sunbury Ct. Rd.
TW16: Sunb ... 1K 39
Sunbury Cres. TW13: Felt ... 5G 23
SUNBURY CROSS ... 8H 23
Sunbury Cross Cen.
TW16: Sunb ... 8G 23
Sunbury Ho. TW16: Sunb ... 9F 22
(off Windmill Rd. W.)
Sunbury La. KT12: Wal T ... 5H 39
Sunbury Leisure Cen. ... 9G 23
Sunburylock Ait KT12: Sunb ... 3J 39
Sunbury Pk. Walled Garden
... 2J 39
Sunbury Rd. SL4: Eton ... 2G 4
SM3: Chea ... 9J 43
TW13: Felt ... 4G 23
Sunbury Station (Rail) ... 9H 23
Sunbury Way TW13: Hanw ... 6K 23
Sun Cl. SL4: Eton ... 2G 4
Sundale Av. CR2: Sels ... 6F 64
Sundeala Cl. TW16: Sunb ... 8H 23
Sunderland Ct. TW19: Stan ... 9N 7
(off Whitley Cl.)
Sundew Cl. GU18: Ligh ... 7A 52
RG40: W'ham ... 1D 30
RH11: Craw ... 7M 181
Sundial Av. SE25 ... 2C 46
Sundials Cvn. Site
RH6: Hook ... 9B 142
Sundon Cres. GU25: V Wat ... 4L 35
Sundown Av. CR2: Sande ... 7C 64
Sundown Rd. TW15: A'ford ... 6D 22
Sundridge Pl. CR0: Croy ... 7D 46
Sundridge Rd. CR0: Croy ... 6C 46
GU22: Wok ... 6C 74
Sun Hill GU22: Wok ... 8K 73
Sun Inn Rd. GU8: Duns ... 4B 174
Sunken Rd. CR0: Croy ... 2F 64
Sunkist Way SM6: W'ton ... 5J 63
Sun Life Trad. Est.
TW14: Felt ... 6H 9
Sunlight Cl. SW19 ... 7A 28
Sunmead Cl. KT22: Fetc ... 9F 78
Sunmead Rd. TW16: Sunb ... 2H 39
Sunna Gdns. TW16: Sunb ... 1J 39
Sunna Lodge TW16: Sunb ... 8G 22
Sunniholme Ct.
CR2: S Croy ... 8B 200
Sunning Av. SL5: S'dale ... 6B 34
SUNNINGDALE ... 6D 34
Sunningdale Av.
TW13: Hanw ... 3M 23
Sunningdale Cl. KT6: Surb ... 8L 41
Sunningdale Ct.
RH10: Craw ... 5B 182
TW7: Isle ... 9D 10
(off Whitton Dene)
Sunningdale Golf Course ... 8E 34
Sunningdale Pk. ... 4C 34
Sunningdale Rd. SM1: Sut ... 9L 43
Sunningdale Station (Rail) ... 6D 34
SUNNINGHILL ... 4A 34
Sunninghill Cl. SL5: S'hill ... 3A 34
Sunninghill Ct. SL5: S'hill ... 3A 34
SUNNINGHILL PARK ... 8A 18
Sunninghill Rd.
GU20: Windl ... 9L 33
SL4: Wink ... 6A 18
SL5: Asc ... 6A 18
SL5: S'hill ... 4A 34
Sunningvale Av. TN16: B Hil ... 2E 86
Sunningvale Cl. TN16: B Hil ... 3F 86
Sunny Av. RH10: Craw D ... 1D 184
Sunny Bank CR6: Warl ... 4H 85
SE25 ... 2D 46
Sunnybank KT18: Eps ... 3B 80
SL5: Asc ... 3L 33
Sunnybank Rd. GU14: Cove ... 8J 69
(not continuous)
Sunnybank Vs. RH1: Blet ... 1C 124
Sunnycroft Rd. SE25 ... 2D 46
TW3: Houn ... 5B 10
Sunnydell La. GU10: Wrec ... 5F 128
(not continuous)
Sunnydene Rd. CR8: Pur ... 9M 63
Sunnydown GU8: Wit ... 5B 152
Sunnyhill GU8: Wit ... 5B 152
Sunnyhill Cl.
RH10: Craw D ... 1D 184
Sunny Hill Rd. GU11: Alde ... 2J 109
Sunnyhill Rd. SW16 ... 5J 29
Sunnyhurst Cl. SM1: Sut ... 9M 43
Sunnymead RH10: Craw D ... 1E 184
(not continuous)
RH11: Craw ... 3B 182
Sunnymead Av. CR4: Mit ... 2H 45
Sunnymead Rd. SW15 ... 8G 12
SUNNYMEADS ... 7A 6
Sunnymeads Station (Rail) ... 6A 6
Sunnymede Av. KT19: Ewe ... 5D 60
SM5: Cars ... 7B 62
Sunny Nook Gdns.
CR2: S Croy ... 3A 64
Sunny Ri. CR3: Cate ... 2A 104
SUNNYSIDE ... 2A 186
Sunnyside GU21: Knap ... 6E 72
GU51: Fleet ... 3A 88
KT12: Wal T ... 4K 39
SW19 ... 7K 27
TN8: Eden ... 9K 127
Sunnyside Cotts.
RH5: H Mary ... 6K 137
Sunnyside Pas. SW19 ... 7K 27
Sunnyside Pl. SW19 ... 7K 27
Sunnyside Rd.
GU35: H Dwn ... 5H 169
TW11: Tedd ... 5D 24
Sunnyview Cl. GU12: Alde ... 3A 110
Sunoak Rd. RH13: Hors ... 6B 198
Sun Pas. SL4: W'sor ... 4G 4
Sunray Av. KT5: Surb ... 8A 42
Sunray Est. GU47: Sandh ... 7F 48
Sunrise Cl. TW13: Hanw ... 4N 23
Sun Rd. W14 ... 1L 13
Sunset Gdns. SE25 ... 1C 46
Sunset Rd. SW19 ... 6G 26
Sunshine Way CR4: Mit ... 1D 44
Sunstone Gro. RH1: Mers ... 7H 103
Sunvale Av. GU27: Hasl ... 2B 188
Sunvale Cl. GU27: Hasl ... 2B 188
Superior Dr. BR6: Chels ... 3N 67
SURBITON ... 5K 41
Surbiton Ct. KT6: Surb ... 5J 41
Surbiton Cres.
KT1: K Tham ... 8J 203 (3L 41)
Surbiton Hall Cl.
KT1: K Tham ... 8J 203 (3L 41)
Surbiton Hill Pk. KT5: Surb ... 4M 41
Surbiton Hill Rd.
KT6: Surb ... 8J 203 (3L 41)
Surbiton Pde. KT6: Surb ... 5L 41
Surbiton Rd. GU15: Camb ... 6E 50
KT1: K Tham ... 7H 203 (3K 41)
Surbiton Station (Rail) ... 5L 41
Surly Hall Wlk. SL4: W'sor ... 4C 4
Surrenden Ri. RH11: Craw ... 9A 182
Surrey & Sussex Crematorium
RH10: Craw ... 8H 163
Surrey Av. GU15: Camb ... 2M 69
Surrey Cloisters
GU7: Goda ... 5J 133
Surrey County Council
Smallholdings Rd.
KT17: Eps ... 8H 61
(not continuous)
Surrey County Cricket Cen.
... 1C 114
Surrey Ct. GU2: Guil ... 3L 113
RG42: Warf ... 8D 16
Surrey Cres. W4 ... 1N 11
Surrey Gdns. KT24: E Jun ... 9H 77
Surrey Golf & Fitness ... 4L 55
Surrey Gro. SM1: Sut ... 9B 44
Surrey Guild Craft Gallery ... 2B 152
Surrey Heath Mus. ... 9B 50
Surrey Hills Av.
KT20: Box H ... 8B 100
Surrey Hills Bus. Pk.
RH5: Wott ... 8A 118
Surrey Hills Pk. GU3: Norm ... 9B 92
Surrey Hills Res. Pk.
KT20: Box H ... 8B 100
Surrey History Cen. ... 5N 73
Surrey Lodge KT12: Hers ... 2J 57
(off Queens Rd.)
Surrey Research Pk., The
GU2: Guil ... 3G 112
Surrey Rd. BR4: W Wick ... 7L 47
Surrey St.
CR0: Croy ... 3B 200 (8N 45)
Surrey Technology Cen.
GU2: Guil ... 4G 113
Surrey Towers KT15: Addl ... 2L 55
(off Garfield Rd.)
Surrey Way GU2: Guil ... 2L 113
Surridge Ct. GU19: Bag ... 5J 51
Sury Basin
KT2: K Tham ... 1H 203 (9L 25)
Sussex Av. TW7: Isle ... 6E 10
Sussex Cl. GU21: Knap ... 5F 72
KT3: N Mal ... 3D 42
RH2: Reig ... 4B 122
TW1: Twick ... 9H 11
Sussex Ct. GU21: Knap ... 4F 72
KT15: Addl ... 2L 55
RH13: Hors ... 7K 197
Sussex Gdns. GU51: Fleet ... 1C 88
KT9: Ches ... 3K 59
Sussex Lodge RH12: Hors ... 4J 197
Sussex Mnr. Bus. Pk.
RH10: Craw ... 8E 162
Sussex Pl. GU21: Knap ... 5F 72
KT3: N Mal ... 3D 42
W6 ... 1H 13
Sussex Rd. BR4: W Wick ... 7L 47
CR2: S Croy ... 3A 64
CR4: Mit ... 4J 45
GU21: Knap ... 5F 72
KT3: N Mal ... 3D 42
SM5: Cars ... 3D 62
Sutherland Av. GU4: J Wel ... 6A 94
TN16: B Hil ... 4F 86
TW16: Sunb ... 1G 39
Sutherland Chase SL5: Asc ... 9J 17
Sutherland Dr. GU4: B'ham ... 9B 94
SW19 ... 9B 28

A-Z Surrey 289

Sutherland Gdns.—Teddington Bus. Pk.

Sutherland Gdns.
KT4: W Pk 7G 42
SW14 6D 12
TW16: Sunb 1G 39
Sutherland Grange
SL4: W'sor 3A 4
Sutherland Gro. SW18 9K 13
TW11: Tedd 6E 24
Sutherland Rd. CR0: Croy 6L 45
W4 2D 12
SUTTON
SL3 1E 6
SM1 2N 61
SUTTON ABINGER 3H 137
Sutton Arena Leisure Cen. 6A 44
Sutton Av. GU21: Wok 6H 73
Sutton Comn. Rd. SM1: Sut 6L 43
SM3: Sut 6L 43
Sutton Common Station (Rail) 8N 43
Sutton Ct. KT8: W Mole 4N 39
SM2: Sut 3A 62
W4 2B 12
Sutton Ct. Rd. SM1: Sut 3A 62
W4 3B 12
Sutton Dene TW3: Houn 4B 10
Sutton Ecology Cen. 1D 62
Sutton Gdns. CR0: Croy 4C 46
RH1: Mers 7H 103
SUTTON GREEN 4B 94
Sutton Grn. Rd. GU4: Sut G 4A 94
Sutton Gro. SM1: Sut 1B 62
Sutton Hall Rd. TW5: Hest 3A 10
Sutton Hgts. SM2: Sut 4B 62
Sutton Hill GU4: B'ham 7E 94
Sutton Junior Tennis Cen. 7N 43
Sutton La.
RH5: A Com, A Ham 3J 137
SL3: Lang 2D 6
SM2: Sut 7N 61
SM7: Ban 7N 61
TW3: Houn 6N 9
Sutton La. Nth. W4 1B 12
Sutton La. Sth. W4 2B 12
Sutton Lodge GU1: Guil 3F 202
SUTTON PARK 4B 94
Sutton Pk. Rd. SM1: Sut 3N 61
Sutton Pl. RH5: A Ham 3G 136
SL3: Lang 2D 6
Sutton Rd. GU15: Camb 6E 50
TW5: Hest 4A 10
Sutton Sq. TW5: Hest 4N 9
Sutton Station (Rail) 3A 62
Sutton Superbowl 2N 61
Sutton United FC 1M 61
Sutton Way TW5: Hest 4N 9
Swaby Rd. SW18 2A 28
Swaffield Rd. SW18 1N 27
Swail Ho.
KT18: Eps 7K 201 (9C 60)
Swain Cl. SW16 7F 28
Swain Rd. CR7: T Hea 4N 45
Swains Rd. SW17 8D 28
Swaledale RG12: Brac 4M 31
Swaledale Cl. RH11: Craw 6A 182
Swaledale Gdns.
GU51: Fleet 1C 88
Swale Rd. GU14: Cove 8K 69
Swallow Cl. GU8: Mil 3B 152
GU46: Yate 9A 48
TW18: Stain 5H 21
Swallowdale CR2: Sels 5G 65
Swallowfield RH7: Dorm 1C 166
TW20: Eng G 7L 19
Swallowfields RH6: Horl 8F 142
(off Rosemary La.)
Swallow Gdns. SW16 6H 29
Swallow La. RH5: Mid H 2H 139
Swallow Pk. KT6: Surb 9M 41
Swallow Ri. GU21: Knap 4F 72
Swallow Rd. RH11: Craw 1A 182
Swallow St. RH10: T Hil 4F 184
Swallowtail Rd.
RH12: Hors 2L 197
SWAN, THE 8M 47
Swanage Rd. SW18 1A 28
Swan Barn Rd.
GU27: Hasl 2H 189
Swan Cen., The KT22: Leat 8H 79
SW17 4N 27
Swan Cl. CR0: Croy 6B 46
TW13: Hanw 5M 23
Swancote Grn. RG12: Brac 4N 31
Swan Ct. GU1: Guil 1N 113
GU17: Haw 2K 69
(off Toad La.)
KT22: Leat 9H 79
SW6 3M 13
(off Fulham Rd.)
TW7: Isle 6H 11
(off Swan St.)
Swandon Way SW18 8N 13
Swandrift TW18: Stain 8H 21
Swan Island TW1: Twick 4G 24
Swan La.
GU1: Guil 5C 202 (4N 113)
GU47: Sandh 8G 48
RH6: Char 3L 161
TN8: Eden 8L 127
Swan M. CR4: Mit 9D 28
SW6 4L 13
Swan Mill Gdns.
RH4: Dork 3J 119
Swann Ct. TW7: Isle 6G 11
(off South St.)
Swanns Mdw. KT23: Book 4A 98
Swann Way RH12: Bro H 5E 196
Swan Pl. SW13 5E 12
Swan Ridge TN8: Eden 8M 127
Swan Rd. TW13: Hanw 6M 23
Swan Sanctuary, The 5F 38
Swanscombe Rd. W4 1D 12
Swansea Rd. TW14: Felt 9D 8
Swans Ghyll
RH18: F Row 6G 187
Swan Sq. RH12: Hors 6J 197
Swan St. TW7: Isle 6H 11
Swansway, The
KT13: Weybr 9B 38
Swan Ter. SL4: W'sor 3E 4
Swanton Gdns. SW19 2J 27
Swan Wlk. RH12: Hors 6J 197
TW17: Shep 6F 38
Swanwick Cl. SW15 1E 26
Swanworth La. RH5: Mick 6G 99
Swathling Ho. SW15 9E 12
(off Tunworth Cres.)
Swaynesland Rd.
TN8: C Hil 3H 127
Swayne's La. GU1: Guil 3G 114
Sweeps Ditch Cl.
TW18: Stain 8J 21
Sweeps La. TW20: Egh 6B 20
Sweetbriar RG45: Crow 9F 30
Sweet Briar La.
KT18: Eps 8J 201 (1C 80)
Sweet La. GU5: P'lake 3F 136
Sweetwater Cl.
GU5: Sha G 7F 134
Sweetwater La.
GU5: Sha G 7F 134
GU8: Worm 7D 152
Sweetwell Rd. RG12: Brac 1K 31
Swievelands Rd.
TN16: B Hil 6D 86
Swift Cen. CR0: Wad 4K 63
Swift Ct. GU51: Fleet 4B 88
SM2: Sut 4N 61
Swift La. GU19: Bag 4K 51
RH11: Craw 1A 182
Swift La. Cvn. Site
GU19: Bag 4L 51
Swift La. Ind. Est.
GU19: Bag 4L 51
Swift Rd. GU9: U Hal 5H 109
TW13: Hanw 4M 23
Swift's Cl. GU10: Farnh 2N 129
Swift St. SW6 4L 13
Swinburne Cres. CR0: Croy 5F 46
Swinburne Rd. SW15 7F 12
Swindon Rd. RH12: Hors 4H 197
TW6: Lon A 9B 8
Swinfield Cl. TW13: Hanw 4M 23
Swingate Rd. GU9: Farnh 3J 129
Swinley Rd. GU19: Bag 1H 51
SL5: Asc 2G 32
Swires Shaw BR2: Kes 1F 66
Swiss Cl. GU10: Wrec 7F 128
Swissland Hill RH19: D Pk 4N 165
Switchback La.
GU10: Rowl 7E 128
(not continuous)
Swithin Chase RG42: Warf 8C 16
Swithins Rd. GU51: Fleet 1A 88
Swordsmans Rd.
GU16: Deep 5H 71
Swyncombe Av. W5 1H 11
Sybil Thorndike Casson Ho.
SW5 1M 13
(off Kramer M.)
Sycamore Av. RH12: Hors 2B 198
Sycamore Cl.
CR2: S Croy 8F 200 (2B 64)
GU16: Frim 5C 70
GU47: Sandh 8G 48
KT22: Fetc 1F 98
RH11: Craw 9A 162
SM5: Cars 1D 62
TW13: Felt 4H 23
Sycamore Cotts.
GU15: Camb 3N 69
(off Frimley Rd.)
Sycamore Ct. GU1: Guil 5F 202
(off Harvey Rd.)
GU7: Goda 3J 133
KT3: N Mal 2D 42
KT13: Weybr 9G 38
RH8: Oxt 7A 106
SL4: W'sor 6F 4
TW4: Houn 7M 9
Sycamore Dr. GU10: Wrec 5F 128
GU12: A Va 6E 90
GU16: Frim 4C 70
RH19: E Grin 9C 166
Sycamore Gdns. CR4: Mit 1B 44
Sycamore Gro. KT3: N Mal 2C 42
Sycamore Ho. CR6: Warl 2L 85
Sycamore Lodge
TW16: Sunb 8G 22
Sycamore Ri. RG12: Brac 2N 31
SM7: Ban 1J 81
Sycamore Rd.
GU1: Guil 2C 202 (3N 113)
GU14: Farnb 3A 90
(not continuous)
SW19 7H 27
Sycamores, The
GU14: Farnb 2B 90
GU17: B'water 1G 68
KT23: Book 2C 98
Sycamore Wlk. RH2: Reig 6A 122
TW20: Eng G 7L 19
Sycamore Way CR7: T Hea 4L 45
TW11: Tedd 7J 25
Sydcote SE21 2N 29
Sydenham Ct. CR0: Croy 1D 200
Sydenham Pl. SE27 4M 29
Sydenham Rd.
CR0: Croy 2C 200 (7N 45)
GU1: Guil 6D 202 (5N 113)
Sydney Av. CR8: Pur 8K 63
Sydney Cl. RG45: Crow 9H 31
Sydney Cres.
TW15: A'ford 7C 22
Sydney Loader Pl.
GU17: B'water 9F 48
Sydney Pl. GU1: Guil 4B 114
Sydney Rd. GU1: Guil 4B 114
SM1: Sut 1M 61
SW20 1J 43
TW9: Rich 7L 11
TW11: Tedd 6F 24
TW14: Felt 2H 23
Sydney Ter. KT10: Clay 3F 58
(off The Green)
Sykes Dr. TW18: Stain 6K 21
Sylvan Cl. CR2: Sels 6E 64
GU22: Wok 4D 74
RH8: Limp 7D 106
Sylvan Ct. GU14: Farnb 4B 90
Sylvan Est. SE19 1C 46
Sylvan Gdns. KT6: Surb 6K 41
Sylvan Ridge GU47: Sandh 6F 48
Sylvan Rd. RH10: Craw 5E 182
Sylvanus RG12: Brac 6L 31
Sylvan Way BR4: W Wick 1A 66
GU52: C Cro 8A 88
RH1: Red 4E 122
(not continuous)
Sylvaways Cl. GU6: Cranl 7B 156
Sylverdale Rd.
CR0: Croy 4A 200 (9M 45)
CR8: Pur 9M 63
Sylverns Ct. RG42: Warf 8B 16
Sylvestrus Cl. KT1: K Tham 9N 25
Symonds Ho. RH11: Ifi 9M 161
Symondson M. RG42: Bin 5H 15
Syon Ga. Way TW8: Brent 3G 11
Syon House 4J 11
Syon La. TW7: Isle 2E 10
Syon Lane Station (Rail) 3G 11
Syon Pk. 4H 11
Syon Pk. Gdns. TW7: Isle 3F 10
Syon Pl. GU14: Farnb 1B 90
Sythwood GU21: Wok 4L 73
Szabo Cres. GU3: Flex 3M 111

T

Tabarin Way KT17: Eps D 3H 81
Tabor Ct. SM3: Chea 3K 61
Tabor Gdns. SM3: Chea 3L 61
Tabor Gro. SW19 8L 27
Tachbrook Rd. TW14: Felt 1G 23
Tadlow KT1: K Tham 5M 203
Tadmor Cl. TW16: Sunb 3G 39
Tadorne Rd. KT20: Tad 8H 81
Tadpole La. GU10: Ews 3C 108
TADWORTH 9H 81
Tadworth Av. KT3: N Mal 3E 42
Tadworth Cl. KT20: Tad 9J 81
Tadworth Ct. KT20: Tad 8J 81
TADWORTH PARK 8J 81
Tadworth Station (Rail) 9H 81
Tadworth St. KT20: Tad 1H 101
Taff Ho. KT2: K Tham 1H 203
(off Henry Macaulay Av.)
Taffy's Row CR4: Mit 2C 44
Taggs Ho. KT1: K Tham 4H 203
(off Wadbrook St.)
Taggs Island TW12: Hamp 1D 40
Tait Rd. CR0: Croy 6B 46
Tait Rd. Ind. Est. CR0: Croy 6B 46
(off Tait Rd.)
Talavera Cl. RG45: Crow 3E 48
Talavera Pk. GU11: Alde 1M 109
Talbot Cl. GU16: Mytc 1E 90
RH2: Reig 4N 121
Talbot Ct. SL4: W'sor 6E 4
Talbot La. RH12: Hors 7J 197
Talbot Lodge KT10: Esh 2A 58
Talbot Pl. GU19: Bag 3J 51
SL3: Dat 4M 5
Talbot Rd. CR7: T Hea 3A 46
GU9: Farnh 3G 128
RH7: Ling 8N 145
SM5: Cars 2E 62
TW2: Twick 2E 24
TW7: Isle 7G 11
TW15: A'ford 6N 21
Talcott Path SW2 2L 29
Taleworth Cl. KT21: A'tead 7K 79
Taleworth Pk. KT21: A'tead 7K 79
Taleworth Rd. KT21: A'tead 6K 79
Talfourd Way RH1: Red 6D 122
Talgarth Dr. GU14: Farnb 3B 90
Talgarth Mans. W14 1K 13
(off Talgarth Rd.)
Talgarth Rd. W6 1J 13
W14 1J 13
Talina Cen. SW6 4N 13
Talisman Cl. RG45: Crow 2C 48
Talisman Way KT17: Eps D 3H 81
Tallis Cl. RH11: Craw 6L 181
Tallow Rd. TW8: Brent 2J 11
Tall Pines KT17: Eps 7E 60
Tall Trees RH19: E Grin 1B 186
SL3: Coln 4F 6
SW16 2K 45
Tally Rd. RH8: Limp 9G 107
Talma Gdns. TW2: Twick 9E 10
Talman Cl. RH11: Ifi 4K 181
Tamar Cl. RH10: Craw 4G 182
Tamarind Cl. GU2: Guil 7K 93
Tamarind Ct. TW20: Egh 6B 20
Tamarisk Ri. RG40: W'ham 1B 30
Tamar Way SL3: Lang 1D 6
Tamerton Sq. GU22: Wok 6A 74
Tamesis Gdns. KT4: W Pk 8D 42
Tamian Ind. Est. TW4: Houn 7K 9
Tamian Way TW4: Houn 7K 9
Tamworth RG12: Brac 6B 32
Tamworth Dr. GU51: Fleet 1C 88
Tamworth La. CR4: Mit 1F 44
Tamworth Pk. CR4: Mit 3F 44
Tamworth Pl.
CR0: Croy 3B 200 (8N 45)
Tamworth Rd.
CR0: Croy 3A 200 (8M 45)
Tamworth St. SW6 2M 13
Tamworth Vs. CR4: Mit 3F 44
Tanbridge Ho. RH12: Hors 7H 197
Tanbridge Pk. RH12: Hors 7G 197
Tanbridge Pl. RH12: Hors 7H 197
Tanbridge Retail Pk.
RH12: Hors 7H 197
Tandem Cen. SW19 9B 28
Tandem Way SW19 9B 28
TANDRIDGE 2K 125
Tandridge Ct. CR3: Cate 9D 84
Tandridge Gdns.
CR2: Sande 9C 64
Tandridge Golf Course 9M 105
Tandridge Hill La.
RH9: Gods 6J 105
Tandridge La. RH7: Ling 4K 145
RH8: Tand 1K 125
Tandridge Leisure Cen. 7A 106
Tandridge Rd. CR6: Warl 6G 84
Tanfield Ct. RH12: Hors 6H 197
Tanfield Rd.
CR0: Croy 6B 200 (1N 63)
Tangier Ct. GU11: Alde 2L 109
SL4: Eton 2G 5
Tangier La. SL4: Eton 2G 4
Tangier Rd. GU1: Guil 4C 114
TW10: Rich 7N 11
Tangier Way KT20: Tad 4K 81
Tangier Wood KT20: Tad 5K 81
Tangle Oak RH19: Fel 6H 165
Tanglewood Cl. CR0: Croy 9F 46
GU22: Pyr 3F 74
KT16: L'cross 9L 35
Tanglewood Ride
GU24: W End 8A 52
Tanglewood Way TW13: Felt 4J 23
Tangley Dr. RG41: W'ham 4A 30
Tangley Gro. SW15 9E 12
Tangley La. GU3: Guil 8J 93
Tangley Pk. Rd.
TW12: Hamp 6N 23
Tanglyn Av. TW17: Shep 4C 38
Tangmere Gro.
KT2: K Tham 6K 25
Tangmere Rd. RH11: Craw 3L 181
Tanhouse Rd. RH8: Oxt 1N 125
Tanhurst Ho. SW2 1K 29
(off Redlands Way)
Tanhurst La. RH5: H Mary 2M 157
Tankerton Rd. KT6: Surb 8M 41
Tankerton Ter. CR0: Croy 5K 45
Tankerville Ct. TW3: Houn 6C 10
Tankerville Rd. SW16 8H 29
Tank Rd. GU47: C Tow 1L 69
Tanners Cl. KT12: Wal T 5J 39
Tanners Ct. RH3: Brock 4A 120
(Middle St.)
RH3: Brock 7B 120
(Tanners Mdw.)
Tanners Dean KT22: Leat 9J 79
Tannersfield GU4: Chil 2A 134
Tanner's Hill RH3: Brock 5A 120
Tanners La. GU27: Hasl 1G 188
Tanners Mdw. RH3: Brock 7A 120
Tanners M. TN8: Eden 2L 147
Tanners Yd. GU19: Bag 4H 51
Tannery, The RH1: Red 3D 122
Tannery Cl. BR3: Beck 4G 46
RH13: Slin 5L 195
Tannery Ct. RH13: Hors 7K 197
(off Boxall Wlk.)
Tannery La. GU5: Braml 3B 134
GU23: Send 1F 94
Tansy Cl. GU4: Guil 1E 114
Tantallon Rd. SW12 2E 28
Tanyard Av. RH19: E Grin 1C 186
Tanyard Cl. RH10: Craw 6G 182
RH13: Hors 7L 197
Tanyard Ho. TW8: Brent 3J 11
(off High St.)
Tanyard Way RH6: Horl 6F 142
Tapestries Hall SL4: O Win 8K 5
Tapestry Cl. SM2: Sut 4N 61
Taplow Ct. CR4: Mit 3C 44
Tapner's Rd. RH2: Leigh 9E 120
RH3: Betch 8E 120
Tapping Cl. KT2: K Tham 8N 25
Tara Arts Cen. 2N 27
(off Garratt La.)
Tara Ct. BR3: Beck 1L 47
Tarbat Ct. GU47: C Tow 7J 49
Target Cl. TW14: Felt 9F 8
Target Hill RG42: Warf 8B 16
Tarham Cl. RH6: Horl 6C 142
Tarmac Way UB7: Harm 3K 7
Tarnbrook Way RG12: Brac 6C 32
Tarn Cl. GU14: Cove 3K 89
Tarn Rd. GU26: Hind 6B 170
Tarragon Cl. GU14: Cove 1H 89
RG12: Brac 8B 16
Tarragon Ct. GU2: Guil 8K 93
Tarragon Dr. GU2: Guil 7K 93
Tarragon Rd. GU2: Guil 8K 93
Tarrant Grn. RG42: Warf 8A 16
Tarrington Cl. SW16 4H 29
Tartar Hill KT11: Cob 9K 57
Tartar Rd. KT11: Cob 9K 57
Tasker Cl. UB3: Harl 3D 8
Tasman Ct. TW16: Sunb 8F 22
Tasso Rd. W6 2K 13
Tasso Yd. W6 2K 13
(off Tasso Rd.)
Tatchbury Ho. SW15 9E 12
(off Tunworth Cres.)
Tate Cl. KT22: Leat 1J 99
Tate Rd. SM1: Sut 2M 61
Tates Way RH12: Rudg 1E 194
Tatham Ct. RH11: Craw 8N 181
TATSFIELD 8E 86
TATSFIELD GREEN 8G 86
Tatsfield La. TN16: Tats 8H 87
TATTENHAM CORNER 5G 80
Tattenham Cnr. Rd.
KT18: Eps D, Tat C 4E 80
Tattenham Corner Station (Rail) 5G 80
Tattenham Cres.
KT18: Tat C 5F 80
Tattenham Gro. KT18: Tat C 5G 80
Tattenham Way KT20: Tad 5J 81
Tattersall Cl. RG40: W'ham 3D 30
Taunton Av. CR3: Cate 1C 104
SW20 1G 42
TW3: Houn 5C 10
Taunton Cl. RH10: Craw 2H 183
SM3: Sut 7M 43
Taunton La. CR5: Coul 6L 83
Tavern Cl. SM5: Cars 6C 44
Tavistock Cl. TW18: Stain 8M 21
Tavistock Ct. CR0: Croy 7A 46
(off Tavistock Rd.)
Tavistock Cres. CR4: Mit 3J 45
Tavistock Gdns.
GU14: Farnb 7N 69
Tavistock Ga.
CR0: Croy 1D 200 (7A 46)
Tavistock Gro. CR0: Croy 6A 46
Tavistock Rd.
CR0: Croy 1D 200 (7A 46)
SM5: Cars 7B 44
Tavistock Wlk. SM5: Cars 7B 44
Tawfield RG12: Brac 6K 31
Tawny Cl. TW13: Felt 4H 23
Tawny Cft. GU47: C Tow 7K 49
Tayben Av. TW2: Twick 9E 10
Tay Cl. GU14: Cove 8K 69
Tayles Hill Dr. KT17: Ewe 6E 60
Taylor Av. TW9: Kew 5A 12
Taylor Cl. KT19: Eps 7N 59
TW3: Houn 4C 10
TW12: H Hill 6C 24
Taylor Ct. SE20 1F 46
(off Elmers End Rd.)
Taylor Rd. CR4: Mit 8C 28
GU11: Alde 6B 90
KT21: A'tead 4K 79
SM6: W'ton 2F 62
Taylor's Bushes Ride
SL4: W'sor 3N 17
Taylors Cl. GU35: Lind 4A 168
Taylors Ct. TW13: Felt 3H 23
Taylors Cres. GU6: Cranl 7A 156
Taylors La. GU35: Lind 4A 168
Taylor Wlk. RH11: Craw 3A 182
Taymans Track
RH17: Hand 8L 199
Taynton Dr. RH1: Mers 8H 103
Teal Cl. CR2: Sels 7G 64
RH12: Hors 3J 197
Teal Ct. RH4: Dork 1J 201
SM6: W'ton 2G 63
Tealing Dr. KT19: Ewe 1C 60
Teal Pl. SM1: Sut 2L 61
Teasel Cl. CR0: Croy 7G 46
RH11: Craw 6N 181
Teazlewood Pk. KT22: Leat 4G 78
Tebbit Cl. RG12: Brac 1B 32
Teck Cl. TW7: Isle 5G 11
Tedder Cl. KT9: Ches 2J 59
Tedder Rd. CR2: Sels 4F 64
TEDDINGTON 6G 24
Teddington Bus. Pk.
TW11: Tedd 7F 24
(off Station Rd.)

Teddington Cl.—Tilehouse Rd.

Teddington Cl. KT19: Eps 6C **60**
Teddington Pk. TW11: Tedd 6F **24**
Teddington Pk. Rd.
TW11: Tedd 5F **24**
Teddington Pool & Fitness Cen.
..................6G **24**
Teddington Sports Cen. 7K **25**
Teddington Station (Rail) 7G **24**
Tedham La. RH9: S Gods 3E **144**
Tees Cl. GU14: Cove 8K **69**
Teesdale RH11: Craw 6A **182**
Teesdale Av. TW7: Isle 4G **11**
Teesdale Gdns. SE25 ....1B **46**
TW7: Isle 4G **11**
Tees Ho. Ga. GU14: Farnb 3N **89**
Teevan Cl. CR0: Croy 6D **46**
Teevan Rd. CR0: Croy 7D **46**
Tegan Cl. SM2: Sut 4M **61**
Tegg's La. GU22: Pyr 3H **75**
Tekels Av. GU15: Camb 1B **70**
Tekels Pk. GU15: Camb 1C **70**
Tekels Way GU15: Camb 3C **70**
Telconia Cl. GU35: H Dwn 5H **169**
Telegraph La. KT10: Clay 1F **58**
Telegraph Pas. *SW2* *1J 29*
(off New Pk. Rd.)
Telegraph Rd. SW15 ....1G **27**
Telegraph Track SM5: Cars 7E **62**
Telephone Pl. SW6 ....2L **13**
Telferscot Rd. SW12 ....2H **29**
Telford Av. RG45: Crow 9H **31**
SW2 ....2H **29**
Telford Ct. GU1: Guil 3B **114**
Telford Dr. KT12: Wal T 6K **39**
Telford Pl. RH10: Craw 4C **182**
Telford Rd. TW2: Whitt 1A **24**
Telham Ct. RH11: Craw 6L **181**
Tellisford KT10: Esh 1B **58**
Temeraire Pl. TW8: Brent 1M **11**
Temperley Rd. SW12 ....1E **28**
Tempest M. RG12: Brac 3B **32**
Tempest Rd. TW20: Egh 7E **20**
Templar Av. GU9: Farnh 3G **129**
Templar Cl. GU47: Sandh 7F **48**
Templar Ct. *TN8: Eden* *9L 127*
(off Farmstead Dr.)
Templar Pl. TW12: Hamp 8A **24**
Temple Av. CR0: Croy 8J **47**
Temple Bar Rd. GU21: Wok 6J **73**
Temple Cl.
KT19: Eps 5J **201** (8C **60**)
RH10: Craw 4H **183**
Templecombe M.
GU22: Wok 3D **74**
Templecombe Way
SM4: Mord 4K **43**
Temple Ct. KT13: Weybr 1C **56**
KT19: Eps 8C **60**
Templecroft TW15: A'ford 7E **22**
Templedene Av.
TW18: Stain 8K **21**
Temple Fld. Cl. KT15: Addl 3K **55**
Temple Gdns. TW18: Stain 9H **21**
Temple La. RH5: Cap 4L **159**
Templeman Cl. CR8: Pur 3M **83**
Templemere KT13: Weybr 9E **38**
Temple Pk. Rdbt.
RG42: Bin 7L **15**
Templer Av. GU14: Farnb 3L **89**
Temple Rd.
CR0: Croy 6D **200** (1A **64**)
KT19: Eps 5J **201** (8C **60**)
SL4: W'sor 5F **4**
TN16: B Hil 4F **86**
TW3: Houn 7B **10**
TW9: Rich 5M **11**
Temple's Cl. GU10: Farnh 2A **130**
Temple Sheen SW14 ....7B **12**
Temple Sheen Rd.
SW14 ....7A **12**
Templeton Cl. SE19 ....1A **46**
Templeton Pl. SW5 ....1M **13**
Temple Way RG42: Bin 9K **15**
SM1: Sut 9B **44**
Temple Wood Dr.
RH1: Red 9D **102**
Ten Acre GU21: Wok 5K **73**
Ten Acre La. TW20: Thor 1E **36**
Ten Acres KT22: Fetc 2D **98**
Ten Acres Cl. KT22: Fetc 2D **98**
Ten Acre Wlk.
GU10: Fren, Rowl 7E **128**
Tenbury Ct. SW2 ....2H **29**
Tenby Dr. SL5: S'hill 4A **34**
Tenby Rd. GU16: Frim 6E **70**
Tenchley's La. RH8: Limp 9E **106**
Tenham Av. SW2 ....2H **29**
Tenniel Cl. GU2: Guil 1L **113**
Tennis Ct. La. KT8: E Mol 2F **40**
Tennison Cl. CR5: Coul 7M **83**
Tennison Rd. SE25 ....3C **46**
Tennyson Av. KT3: N Mal 4G **43**
TW1: Twick 2F **24**
Tennyson Cl. RH10: Craw 1F **182**
RH12: Hors 2L **197**
TW14: Felt 9G **9**
Tennyson Ct. GU26: Hind 5D **170**
SW6 ....*4N 13*
(off Imperial Rd.)
Tennyson Mans. *W14* *2L 13*
(off Queen's Club Gdns.)
Tennyson Ri.
RH19: E Grin 9M **165**
Tennyson Rd. KT15: Addl 1N **55**
SW19 ....7A **28**
TW3: Houn 5C **10**
TW15: A'ford 6N **21**
Tennyson's La.
GU27: Hasl 3H **189**
Tennyson's Ridge
GU27: Hasl 3H **189**
Tensing Ct. TW19: Stan 2N **21**
Tentelow La. UB2: S'hall 1A **10**
Tenterden Gdns. CR0: Croy 6D **46**
Tenterden Rd. CR0: Croy 6D **46**
Tenth Av. KT20: Lwr K 4K **101**
Teresa Va. RG42: Warf 7C **16**
Terminal Four Rdbt.
TW6: Lon A 9D **8**
Terminal 5 Rdbt. TW6: L'ford ...5K **7**
Tern Rd. RH11: Ifi 4J **181**
Terrace, The GU14: Farnb 2C **90**
GU15: Camb 1L **69**
GU22: Wok 7C **74**
KT15: Addl 2N **55**
RG40: W'ham 2A **30**
RG45: Crow 2J **49**
RH5: Dork 6J **119**
SL5: S'hill 4A **34**
SW13 ....5D **12**
Terrace Gdns. SW13 ....5E **12**
Terrace Hill CR0: Croy 5A **200**
Terrace La. TW10: Rich 9L **11**
Terrace Rd. KT12: Wal T 6H **39**
Terrace Rd. Nth. RG42: Bin ...6H **15**
Terrace Rd. Sth. RG42: Bin ...7H **15**
Terra Cotta Ct.
GU10: Wrec 5E **128**
Terracotta Rd.
RH9: S Gods 7F **124**
Terrano Ho. TW9: Kew 3A **12**
Terrapin Rd. SW17 ....4F **28**
Terrent Ct. SL4: W'sor 4D **4**
Terry Rd. RH11: Craw 8N **181**
Tersha St. TW9: Rich 7M **11**
Testard Rd.
GU2: Guil 6A **202** (5M **113**)
Tester's Cl. RH8: Oxt 9D **106**
Testwood Rd. SL4: W'sor 4A **4**
Teviot Cl. GU2: Guil 9K **93**
Tewkesbury Cl. KT14: Byf 7M **55**
Tewkesbury Rd. SM5: Cars 7B **44**
Textile Est. GU46: Yate 8C **48**
Teynham Ct. BR3: Beck 2L **47**
Thackeray Cl. SW19 ....8J **27**
TW7: Isle 5G **11**
Thackeray Lodge TW14: Bedf ...9E **8**
Thames Av. KT16: Chert 2J **37**
SL4: W'sor 3G **4**
Thames Bank SW14 ....5B **12**
Thames Cl. GU14: Cove 8K **69**
KT16: Chert 6K **37**
TW12: Hamp 1B **40**
Thames Cotts. KT7: T Dit 5H **41**
Thames Ct. KT8: W Mole 1B **40**
Thames Cres. W4 ....3D **12**
THAMES DITTON 5G **40**
Thames Ditton Miniature Railway
..........................7G **41**
Thames Ditton Station (Rail)
..........................6F **40**
Thames Edge Ct.
TW18: Stain *5G 21*
(off Clarence St.)
Thames Eyot TW1: Twick 2G **24**
Thamesfield Ct.
TW17: Shep 6D **38**
Thamesfield M.
TW17: Shep 6D **38**
Thames Ga. TW18: Stain 1K **37**
Thamesgate Cl.
TW10: Ham 5H **25**
Thames Haven KT6: Surb 4K **41**
Thames Ho. KT1: K Tham 7H **203**
Thameside KT8: W Mole 2B **40**
KT16: Chert 3L **37**
TW11: Tedd 8K **25**
TW18: Lale 1K **37**
TW18: Stain 6H **21**
Thameside Cen.
TW8: Brent 2M **11**
Thameside Pl.
KT1: H Wic 1G **203** (9K **25**)
Thames Lock KT12: Wal T 2K **39**
KT13: Weybr 9B **38**
Thames Mead SL4: W'sor 4B **4**
Thamesmead KT12: Wal T 5H **39**
Thames Mdw. KT8: W Mole 1A **40**
TW17: Shep 7E **38**
Thames Pl. SW15 ....6J **13**
(not continuous)
Thamespoint TW11: Tedd 8K **25**
Thames Reach *W6* *2H 13*
(off Rainville Rd.)
Thames Rd. W4 ....2N **11**
Thames Side
KT1: K Tham 2H **203** (9K **25**)
KT7: T Dit 5H **41**
SL4: W'sor 3G **4**
Thames St.
KT1: K Tham 3H **203** (1K **41**)
(not continuous)
KT12: Wal T 6G **39**
KT13: Weybr 8C **38**
SL4: W'sor 4G **4**
TW12: Hamp 9B **24**
Thames St. TW16: Sunb 3H **39**
TW18: Stain 6H **21**
Thames Va. Cl. TW3: Houn ...6A **10**
Thames Valley Athletics Cen.
..........................1H **5**
Thames Valley University
Paragon Campus *1J 11*
(off Boston Mnr. Rd.)
Thamesview Ho's.
KT12: Wal T 5H **39**
Thames Village W4 ....4B **12**
Thames Wharf Studios *W6* *2H 13*
(off Rainville Rd.)
Thanescroft Gdns.
CR0: Croy 9B **46**
Thanet Dr. BR2: Kes 1F **66**
Thanet Ho. CR0: Croy 6C **200**
Thanet Pl.
CR0: Croy 6C **200** (1N **63**)
Tharp Rd. SM6: W'ton 2H **63**
Thatcher Cl. RH10: Craw 6B **182**
Thatchers Cl. RH6: Horl 6F **142**
RH12: Hors 4L **197**
Thatchers La. GU3: Worp 5G **93**
Thatchers Way TW7: Isle 8D **10**
Thaxted Pl. SW20 ....8J **27**
Thaxton Rd. W14 ....2L **13**
Thayers Farm Rd.
BR3: Beck 1H **47**
The ....
Names prefixed with 'The' for example 'The Acorns' are indexed under the main name such as 'Acorns, The'
Theal Cl. GU47: C Tow 7J **49**
Theatre Ct.
KT18: Eps 7J **201** (9C **60**)
Theatrerites 3N **27**
Theatre Royal
Windsor 3G **5**
Thelma Gro. TW11: Tedd 7G **24**
Thelton Av. RH12: Bro H 5D **196**
Theobald Rd.
CR0: Croy 2A **200** (8M **45**)
Theobalds Way GU16: Frim 3G **71**
Thepps Cl. RH1: Sth N 6K **123**
Therapia La. CR0: Bedd 6H **45**
CR0: Croy 5J **45**
Therapia Lane Stop (CT) 6J **45**
Theresa Rd. W6 ....1F **12**
Theresa's Wlk. CR2: Sande 5A **64**
Thetford Rd. KT3: N Mal 5C **42**
TW15: A'ford 5N **21**
Thetford Wlk. RH11: Craw ...7K **181**
Thetis Ter. TW9: Kew 2N **11**
Theydon Cl. RH10: Craw 5E **182**
Theydon Ct. GU6: Cranl 8J **155**
Thibet Rd. GU47: Sandh 7H **49**
Thicket Cres. SM1: Sut 1A **62**
Thicket Rd. SM1: Sut 1A **62**
Thickthorne La.
TW18: Stain 8L **21**
Third Av. KT20: K'wood 3K **101**
Third Cl. KT8: W Mole 3C **40**
Third Cross Rd. TW2: Twick ...3D **24**
Thirlmere Cl. GU14: Cove 1K **89**
TW20: Egh 8D **20**
Thirlmere Cres.
GU52: C Cro 8A **88**
Thirlmere Ho. TW7: Isle 8F **10**
Thirlmere Rd. RH11: Ifi 5J **181**
SW16 ....5H **29**
Thirlmere Wlk.
GU15: Camb 2H **71**
Thirsk Ct. GU12: Alde 2B **110**
Thirsk Rd. CR4: Mit 8E **28**
SE25 ....3A **46**
Thirteenth Av. KT20: Lwr K 4L **101**
Thistlecroft Rd. KT12: Hers 1K **57**
Thistledene KT7: T Dit 5E **40**
KT14: W By 9N **55**
Thistledown Va. RH14: Ifo 4F **192**
Thistles, The KT22: Leat 9J **79**
Thistle Way RH6: Smal 8N **143**
Thistlewood Cres.
CR0: N Add 8N **65**
Thistleworth Cl. TW7: Isle 3D **10**
Thistleworth Marina
TW7: Isle *7H 11*
(off Railshead Rd.)
Thistley Cl. CR5: Coul 9H **83**
Thistley La. GU6: Cranl 6N **155**
Thomas Av. CR3: Cate 8N **83**
Thomas Dr. RG42: Warf 8C **16**
Thomas Ho. SM2: Sut 4N **61**
Thomas Moore Ho.
RH2: Reig *3A 122*
(off Reigate Rd.)
Thomas Rd. GU11: Alde 6B **90**
Thomas Turner Path
CR0: Croy 3C **200**
Thomas Wall Cl. SM1: Sut 2N **61**
Thompson Av. TW9: Rich 6N **11**
Thompson Cl. SL3: Lang 1C **6**
SM3: Sut 7M **43**
Thompson Rd. TW3: Houn 7B **10**
Thompson's Cl. GU24: Pirb 1A **92**
Thompson's La.
GU24: Chob 5G **53**
Thomson Ct. RH11: Craw 8N **181**
Thomson Cres. CR0: Croy 7L **45**
Thorburn Chase
GU47: C Tow 9K **49**
Thorburn Way SW19 ....9B **28**
Thorkhill Gdns. KT7: T Dit 7G **41**
Thorkhill Rd. KT7: T Dit 7G **41**
Thorley Cl. KT14: W By 1J **75**
Thorley Gdns. GU22: Pyr 2J **75**
Thornash Cl. GU21: Wok 2M **73**
Thornash Rd. GU21: Wok 2M **73**
Thornash Way GU21: Wok 2M **73**
Thorn Bank GU2: Guil 5K **113**
Thornbank Cl.
TW19: Stan M 8J **7**
Thornberry Way GU1: Guil 8B **94**
Thornbury Av. TW7: Isle 3D **10**
Thornbury Cl. RG45: Crow 2G **48**
Thornbury Ct. CR2: S Croy 8E **200**
CR3: Whyte 7C **84**
TW7: Isle 3E **10**
Thornbury Rd. SW2 ....1J **29**
TW7: Isle 3D **10**
Thorncliffe Rd. SW2 ....1J **29**
UB2: S'hall 1N **9**
Thorn Cl. GU10: Wrec 7E **128**
THORNCOMBE STREET 1N **153**
Thorncombe St.
GU5: Braml 1A **154**
Thorncroft TW20: Eng G 8M **19**
Thorncroft Cl. CR5: Coul 6L **83**
Thorncroft Dr. KT22: Leat 1H **99**
Thorncroft Rd. SM1: Sut 2N **61**
Thorndean St. SW18 ....3A **28**
Thorndon Gdns. KT19: Ewe 2D **60**
Thorndown La.
GU20: Windl 4A **52**
Thorndyke Cl. RH10: Craw ...4H **183**
Thorne Cl. KT10: Clay 4G **59**
RG45: Crow 9F **30**
TW15: A'ford 8D **22**
Thorneloe Gdns.
CR0: Wad 8A **200** (2L **63**)
Thorne Pas. SW13 ....5D **12**
Thornes Cl. BR3: Beck 2M **47**
Thorne St. SW13 ....6D **12**
Thorneycroft Cl.
KT12: Wal T 5K **39**
Thorney Hedge Rd.
W4 ....1A **12**
Thornfield Grn. GU17: Haw 3L **69**
Thornfield Rd. SM7: Ban 4M **81**
Thornhill RG12: Brac 3C **32**
RH11: Craw 5N **181**
Thornhill Av. KT6: Surb 8L **41**
Thornhill Ho. *W4* *1D 12*
(off Wood St.)
Thornhill M. SW15 ....7L **13**
Thornhill Rd. CR0: Croy 6N **45**
GU11: Alde 9B **90**
KT6: Surb 8L **41**
Thornhill Way TW17: Shep 4B **38**
Thornlaw Rd. SE27 ....5L **29**
Thornleas Pl. KT24: E Hor 4F **96**
Thorn Rd. GU10: Wrec 6F **128**
Thornsett Pl. SE20 ....1E **46**
Thornsett Rd. SE20 ....1E **46**
SW18 ....2N **27**
Thornsett Ter. *SE20* *1E 46*
(off Croydon Rd.)
Thornton Av. CR0: Croy 5K **45**
SW2 ....2H **29**
W4 ....1D **12**
Thornton Cl. GU2: Guil 9K **93**
RH6: Horl 8C **142**
Thornton Cres. CR5: Coul 6L **83**
Thornton Dene BR3: Beck 1K **47**
Thornton Gdns. SW12 ....2H **29**
Thornton Health Leisure Cen.
..........................3N **45**
THORNTON HEATH 3N **45**
THORNTON HEATH POND 4L **45**
Thornton Heath Station (Rail)
..........................3N **45**
Thornton Hill SW19 ....8K **27**
Thornton M. RG45: Crow 3H **49**
Thornton Pl. RH6: Horl 8C **142**
Thornton Rd. CR0: Croy 6K **45**
CR7: T Hea 6K **45**
SM5: Cars 7B **44**
SW12 ....1H **29**
SW14 ....7C **12**
SW19 ....7J **27**
Thornton Rd. E. SW19 ....7J **27**
Thornton Rd. Ind. Est.
CR0: Croy 5K **45**
Thornton Row CR7: T Hea 4L **45**
Thornton Side RH1: Mers 9F **102**
Thornton Wlk. RH6: Horl 8C **142**
Thornville Gro. CR4: Mit 1B **44**
Thornycroft Ho. *W4* *1D 12*
(off Fraser St.)
Thornyhurst Rd.
GU16: Mytc 1E **90**
Thorold Cl. CR2: Sels 6G **65**
Thorold Rd. GU9: Farnh 9H **109**
Thoroughfare, The
KT20: Wal H 2F **100**
Thorp Cl. RG42: Bin 6H **15**
THORPE 2D **36**
Thorpe By-Pass
TW20: Thor 1D **36**
Thorpe Cl. CR0: N Add 7M **65**
RG41: W'ham 5A **30**
THORPE GREEN 3C **36**
Thorpe Ind. Pk. TW20: Thor 9E **20**
THORPE LEA 7E **20**
Thorpe Lea Rd.
TW20: Egh, Thor 7D **20**
Thorpe Pk. 3G **37**
Thorpe Rd.
KT2: K Tham 1K **203** (8L **25**)
KT16: Chert 4F **36**
TW18: Stain 7F **20**
Thorpe's Cl. GU2: Guil 9K **93**
Thorpeside Cl. TW18: Stain ...1G **37**
Thorsden Cl. GU22: Wok 6A **74**
Thorsden Ct. GU22: Wok 5A **74**
Thrale Rd. SW16 ....5G **28**
Three Acres RH12: Hors 7G **197**
Three Arch Bus. Pk.
RH1: Red 7E **122**
Three Arches Pk.
RH1: Red 7D **122**
Three Arch Rd. RH1: Red 7D **122**
THREE BRIDGES 2E **182**
Three Bridges Rd.
RH10: Craw 3D **182**
Three Bridges Station (Rail)
..........................3F **182**
Three Gates GU1: Guil 2E **114**
Three Gates La.
GU27: Hasl 1H **189**
Three Mile Rd.
RH5: H Mary 9H **137**
Three Pears Rd. GU1: Guil 3G **114**
Threestile Rd. RH12: Warn ...8F **178**
Three Stiles Rd.
GU9: Farnh 9E **108**
Threshers Cnr. GU51: Fleet 1D **88**
Threshfield RG12: Brac 4M **31**
Thrift La. TN14: Cud 4N **87**
Thrift Va. GU4: Guil 9F **94**
Thrigby Rd. KT9: Ches 3M **59**
Throgmorton Rd.
GU46: Yate 1A **68**
Thrower Pl. RH5: Dork 7J **119**
Throwley Rd. SM1: Sut 2N **61**
Throwley Way SM1: Sut 1N **61**
Thrupp Cl. CR4: Mit 1F **44**
Thrupp Ho. *GU4: Guil* *2F 114*
(off Merrow St.)
Thrupp's Av. KT12: Hers 2L **57**
Thrupp's La. KT12: Hers 2L **57**
Thundery Hill GU10: Seal 8D **110**
Thurbans Rd. GU9: Farnh 4F **128**
Thurbarns Hill RH5: B Grn ...1L **159**
Thurlby Rd. SE27 ....5L **29**
Thurleigh Ct. SW12 ....1E **28**
Thurleigh Rd. SW12 ....1D **28**
Thurleston Av. SM4: Mord 4K **43**
Thurlestone Cl.
TW17: Shep 5D **38**
Thurlestone Pde.
TW17: Shep *5D 38*
(off High St.)
Thurlestone Rd. SE27 ....4L **29**
Thurlow Hill SE21 ....2N **29**
Thurlow Ho. SW16 ....4J **29**
Thurlow Pk. Rd. SE21 ....3M **29**
Thurlow Wlk. GU6: Cranl 9N **155**
Thurlton Ct. GU21: Wok 3A **74**
Thurnby Ct. TW2: Twick 4E **24**
Thurne Way RH12: Rudg 1E **194**
Thurnham Way KT20: Tad 7J **81**
Thursby Rd. GU21: Wok 5K **73**
THURSLEY 6G **150**
Thursley Common National
Nature Reserve 4H **151**
Thursley Cres. CR0: N Add 4M **65**
Thursley Gdns. SW19 ....3J **27**
Thursley Ho. *SW2* *1K 29*
(off Holmewood Gdns.)
Thursley Rd. GU8: Els 4F **150**
GU8: Thur 7A **150**
GU10: Churt 7A **150**
Thurso St. SW17 ....5B **28**
Thurstan Rd. SW20 ....8G **26**
Thyer Cl. BR6: Farnb 1L **67**
Thyme Ct. GU4: B'ham 9D **94**
GU14: Cove 9H **69**
Tibbet's Cl. SW19 ....2J **27**
TIBBET'S CORNER 1J **27**
Tibbet's Ride SW15 ....1J **27**
Ticehurst Cl. RH10: Wor 3J **183**
Tichborne Cl. GU16: Frim 3D **70**
GU17: B'water 1J **69**
Tichborne Pl. GU12: Alde 4B **110**
Tichmarsh KT19: Eps 6B **60**
TICKLEBACK ROW 3N **15**
Tickleback Row RG42: Warf 3N **15**
TICKNERS HEATH 6F **174**
Tidenham Gdns. CR0: Croy 9B **46**
Tides End Ct. GU15: Camb 2D **70**
Tideswell Rd. CR0: Croy 9K **47**
SW15 ....7H **13**
Tideway Cl. TW10: Ham 5H **25**
Tidwells Lea RG42: Warf 9C **16**
Tierney Ct. CR0: Croy 8B **46**
Tierney Rd. SW2 ....2J **29**
Tiffany Hgts. SW18 ....1M **27**
Tiffin School Sports Hall
..............3M **203** (1M **41**)
Tilburstow Hill Rd.
RH9: Gods 1F **124**
RH9: S Gods 4F **124**
Tildesley Rd. SW15 ....9H **13**
Tile Barn Cl. GU14: Farnb 9M **69**
Tile Farm Rd. BR6: Orp 1M **67**
Tilehouse Rd. GU4: Guil 7A **114**

Tilehurst La.—Treyford Cl.

Tilehurst La. RG42: Bin 6H 15
RH5: Dork 6L 119
Tilehurst Rd. SM3: Chea 2K 61
SW18 .....2B 28
Tilers Cl. RH1: Mers 9G 103
Tiler's Wlk. RH2: Reig 7A 122
Tiler's Way RH2: Reig 7A 122
TILFORD 8A 130
Tilford Av. CR0: N Add 5M 65
TILFORD COMMON 1A 150
Tilford Gdns. SW19 .....2J 27
Tilford Ho. *SW2* *1K 29*
(off Holmewood Gdns.)
Tilford Rd. GU9: Farnh 2J 129
GU10: Churt, Rush 7A 150
GU10: Til 8A 130
GU26: Hind 2B 170
Tilford St. GU10: Til 8A 130
TILGATE 6C 182
Tilgate Comn. RH1: Blet 2N 123
Tilgate Dr. RH10: Craw 7B 182
(Brighton Rd.)
RH10: Craw 4E 182
(Water Lea)
Tilgate Forest (Forest Ga.) Bus. Cen.
RH11: Craw 8B 182
Tilgate Forest Lodge
RH11: P Pot 4N 199
Tilgate Forest Pk. 8C 182
TILGATE FOREST ROW 3N 199
Tilgate Forest Row
RH11: P Pot 3N 199
Tilgate Forest Theatre 8C 182
Tilgate Mans. RH10: Craw 8C 182
Tilgate Pde. RH10: Craw 6C 182
Tilgate Pk. Nature Reserve
.....8C 182
Tilgate Pl. RH10: Craw 6C 182
Tilgate Way RH10: Craw 6C 182
Tilia Cl. SM1: Sut 2L 61
Tilletts La. RH12: Warn 9E 178
Tilley La.
KT18: Eps D, Head 9B 80
Tilley Rd. TW13: Felt 2H 23
Tillingbourne Rd.
GU4: Chil 9A 114
Tillingdown Hill
CR3: Cate, Wold 9E 84
Tillingdown La.
CR3: Wold, Cate 2E 104
(not continuous)
Tillotson Cl. RH10: Craw 4H 183
Tillys La. TW18: Stain 5H 21
Tilney Cl. KT22: Leat 7G 78
Tilson Gdns. SW2 .....1J 29
Tilson Ho. SW2 .....1J 29
Tilstone Av. SL4: E Wic 1B 4
Tilstone Cl. SL4: E Wic 1B 4
Tilt Cl. KT11: Cob 3M 77
Tilthams Cnr. Rd.
GU5: Braml 3L 133
GU7: Goda 3L 133
Tilthams Grn. GU7: Goda 3L 133
Tilt Mdw. KT11: Cob 3M 77
Tilton St. SW6 .....2K 13
Tilt Rd. KT11: Cob, Sto D 2K 77
Tiltview KT11: Cob 2K 77
Tiltwood Dr. RH10: Craw D 9F 164
Timber Bank
GU16: Frim G 8E 70
Timber Cl. *GU9: Farnh* *1G 128*
(off The Hart)
GU22: Pyr 1H 75
KT23: Book 4C 98
Timber Ct. RH12: Hors 5J 197
Timbercroft KT19: Ewe 1D 60
Timberham Farm Rd.
RH6: Gat 2B 162
Timberham Way RH6: Gat 2C 162
Timberhill KT21: A'tead 6L 79
Timber Hill Cl. KT16: Otter 4E 54
Timber Hill Rd. CR3: Cate 2D 104
Timberlands RH11: Craw 8N 181
Timber La. CR3: Cate 2D 104
Timberley Pl. RG45: Crow 3D 48
Timberling Gdns.
CR2: Sande 5A 64
Timbermill Ct. GU27: Hasl 2D 188
Timbers, The
RH13: M Hea 9B 198
RH19: E Grin 8M 165
SM3: Chea 3K 61
Timberslip Dr. SM6: W'ton 5H 63
Timbertop Rd. TN16: B Hil 5E 86
Timbralls *SL4: Eton* *1G 4*
(off Slough Rd.)
Times Sq. SM1: Sut 2N 61
Timline Grn. RG12: Brac 1D 32
Timothy Pl. KT8: W Mole 4N 39
Timperley Ct. *RH1: Red* *1C 122*
(off Timperley Gdns.)
SW19 .....2K 27
Timperley Gdns. RH1: Red 1C 122
Timsbury Wlk. SW15 .....2F 26
Timsway TW18: Stain 6H 21
Tindal Cl. GU46: Yate 9C 48
Tindale Cl. CR2: Sande 7A 64
Tinderbox All. SW14 .....6C 12
Tinefields KT20: Tad 6K 81
Tinkers La. SL4: W'sor 5A 4
SL5: S'dale 5E 34
Tinmans Row KT11: Down 5K 77
Tinsey Cl. TW20: Egh 6D 20
Tinsley Cl. RH10: Craw 9E 162
SE25 .....2E 46
TINSLEY GREEN 6F 162
Tinsley Grn. RH10: Craw 6F 162
Tinsley La. RH10: Craw 8E 162
Tinsley La. Nth.
RH10: Craw 7F 162
Tinsley La. Sth.
RH10: Craw *1E 182*
(off Hazelwick Av.)
Tintagel Cl.
KT17: Eps 8M 201 (1E 80)
Tintagel Ct. RH13: Hors 7K 197
Tintagel Dr. GU16: Frim 5D 70
Tintagel Rd. RG40: Finch 8A 30
Tintagel Way GU22: Wok 3C 74
Tintells La. KT24: W Hors 6C 96
Tintern Cl. SW15 .....8K 13
SW19 .....7A 28
Tintern Rd. RH11: Craw 5M 181
SM5: Cars 7B 44
Tippits Mead RG42: Brac 9J 15
Tipton Dr. CR0: Croy 1B 64
Tiree Path RH11: Craw 6N 181
Tirlemont Rd. CR2: S Croy 4N 63
Tirrell Rd. CR0: Croy 5N 45
Tisbury Rd. SW16 .....1J 45
TISMAN'S COMMON 2A 194
Tismans Comn.
RH12: Rudg 2A 194
Titan Ct. TW8: Brent 1M 11
Titchfield Rd. SM5: Cars 7B 44
Titchfield Wlk. SM5: Cars 6B 44
Titchwell Rd. SW18 .....2B 28
Tite Hill TW20: Egh, Eng G 6N 19
Tithe, The RH11: Ifi 9M 161
Tithe Barn Cl.
KT2: K Tham 2L 203 (9M 25)
Tithebarns La. GU23: Send 4J 95
Tithe Cl. GU25: V Wat 5N 35
KT12: Wal T 5J 39
Tithe Ct. RG40: W'ham 1B 30
Tithe La. TW19: Wray 9C 6
Tithe Mdws. GU25: V Wat 5M 35
Tithe Orchard RH19: Fel 6H 165
Tithepit Shaw La.
CR6: Warl 4E 84
Tithing Rd. GU51: Fleet 1A 88
Titlarks Hill SL5: S'dale 8E 34
Titmus Dr. RH10: Craw 6D 182
Titness Pk. SL5: S'hill 2D 34
TITSEY 3D 106
Titsey Hill RH8: T'sey 1C 106
Titsey Place & Gdns. 2D 106
Titsey Rd.
RH8: Limp, T'sey 3D 106
Tiverton Cl. CR0: Croy 6C 46
Tiverton Rd. TW3: Houn 5C 10
Tiverton Way GU16: Frim 5D 70
KT9: Ches 2K 59
Tivoli Rd. SE27 .....6N 29
TW4: Houn 7M 9
Toad Hall Adventure 3K 73
Toad La. GU17: Haw 2K 69
TW4: Houn 7N 9
Toat Hill RH13: Slin 8N 195
Tobermory Cl. SL3: Lang 1A 6
Tobin Cl. KT19: Eps 7A 60
Toby Way KT5: Surb 8A 42
Tocker Gdns. RG42: Warf 7N 15
Tockington Ct. GU46: Yate 9C 48
Todds Cl. RH6: Horl 6C 142
Toftwood Cl. RH10: Craw 4G 183
Token Yd. SW15 .....7K 13
Toland Sq. SW15 .....8F 12
Tolgate Ct. RH1: Red 8D 122
Toll Bar Ct. SM2: Sut 5N 61
Tolldene Cl. GU21: Knap 4H 73
Tollers La. CR5: Coul 5K 83
Toll Gdns. RG12: Brac 2D 32
Tollgate GU1: Guil 3F 114
Tollgate Av. RH1: Red 8D 122
Tollgate Ct.
CR2: S Croy 8E 200 (2A 64)
Tollgate Hill RH11: Craw 9A 182
Tollgate Hill Rdbt.
RH11: Craw 9N 181
Tollgate Pl. *RH19: E Grin* *1B 186*
(off Lewes Rd.)
Tollgate Rd. RH4: Dork 8H 119
Tollhouse La. SM6: W'ton 5G 63
Tolpuddle Way GU46: Yate 1E 68
Tolson Rd. TW7: Isle 6G 10
Tolvaddon Cl. GU21: Wok 4K 73
Tolverne Rd. SW20 .....9H 27
TOLWORTH 8A 42
Tolworth B'way. KT6: Surb 7A 42
Tolworth Cl. KT6: Surb 7A 42
TOLWORTH JUNC. (TOBY JUG)
.....8A 42
Tolworth Pk. Rd. KT6: Surb 8M 41
Tolworth Recreation Cen. 9M 41
Tolworth Ri. Nth. KT5: Surb 7A 42
Tolworth Ri. Sth. KT5: Surb 8A 42
Tolworth Rd. KT6: Surb 8L 41
Tolworth Station (Rail) 8A 42
Tolworth Twr. KT6: Surb 8A 42
Tomlin Cl. KT19: Eps 7C 60
Tomlin Ct. KT19: Eps 7C 60
RH10: Craw 3D 182
Tomlins All. TW1: Twick 2G 24
Tomlins Av. GU16: Frim 4D 70
Tomlinscote Sports Cen. 4D 70
Tomlinscote Way
GU16: Frim 4E 70
Tomlinson Cl. W4 .....1A 12
Tomlinson Dr. RG40: Finch 9A 30
TOMPSET'S BANK 9H 187
Tompset's Bank
RH18: F Row 9H 187
Tomtit Cres. RH10: T Hil 4F 184
Tom Tits La. RH18: F Row 8G 187
(not continuous)
Tom Williams Ho. *SW6* *2L 13*
(off Clem Attlee Ct.)
Tonbridge Cl. SM7: Ban 1D 82
Tonbridge Rd. KT8: W Mole 3N 39
Tonfield Rd. SM3: Sut 7L 43
Tonge Cl. BR3: Beck 4K 47
TONGHAM 6D 110
Tongham Mdws.
GU10: Tong 5C 110
Tongham Rd. GU10: B Lea 7B 110
GU10: Run 8A 110
(not continuous)
GU12: Alde 4B 110
Tonsley Hill SW18 .....8N 13
Tonsley Pl. SW18 .....8N 13
Tonsley Rd. SW18 .....8N 13
Tonsley St. SW18 .....8N 13
Tonstall Rd. CR4: Mit 1E 44
KT19: Eps 6C 60
Tony Law Ho. SE20 .....1E 46
Toogood Pl. RG42: Warf 6B 16
TOOTING 6C 28
TOOTING BEC 4D 28
Tooting Bec Gdns.
SW16 .....5H 29
(not continuous)
Tooting Bec Lido 5G 29
Tooting Bec Rd. SW16 .....4E 28
SW17 .....4E 28
Tooting Bec Station (Tube) 4E 28
Tooting B'way. SW17 .....6C 28
Tooting Broadway Station (Tube)
.....6C 28
TOOTING GRAVENEY 7D 28
Tooting Gro. SW17 .....6C 28
Tooting High St. SW17 .....7C 28
Tooting Leisure Cen. 5B 28
Tooting Mkt. SW17 .....5D 28
Tooting Station (Rail) 7D 28
Topcliffe Dr. BR6: Farnb 1M 67
Top Comn. RG42: Warf 8B 16
Topiary, The GU14: Cove 2K 89
KT21: A'tead 7L 79
Topiary Sq. TW9: Rich 6M 11
Toplady Pl. GU9: U Hal 5H 109
Top Pk. BR3: Beck 4N 47
Topsham Rd. SW17 .....4D 28
Torin Ct. TW20: Eng G 6M 19
Torland Dr. KT22: Oxs 9D 58
Tor La. KT13: Weybr 7D 56
Tormead Cl. SM1: Sut 3M 61
Tormead Rd. GU1: Guil 3B 114
Toronto Dr. RH6: Smal 9L 143
Torrens Cl. GU2: Guil 9K 93
Torre Wlk. SM5: Cars 7C 44
Torridge Rd. CR7: T Hea 4M 45
SL3: Lang 2D 6
Torridon Cl. GU21: Wok 4L 73
Torrington Cl. GU35: Lind 4B 168
KT10: Clay 3E 58
Torrington Rd. KT10: Clay 3E 58
Torrington Sq. CR0: Croy 6A 46
Torrington Way
SM4: Mord 5M 43
Tor Rd. GU9: Farnh 1E 128
(not continuous)
Torwood La. CR3: Whyte 7C 84
Torwood Rd. SW15 .....8F 12
Totale Ri. RG42: Warf 7N 15
Totford La. GU10: Seal 9J 111
TOT HILL 4B 100
Totland Cl. GU14: Farnb 8M 69
Tottenham Rd. GU7: Goda 5H 133
Tottenham Wlk.
GU47: Owls 6J 49
Totterdown St. SW17 .....5D 28
Totton Rd. CR7: T Hea 2L 45
Toulouse Cl. GU15: Camb 8F 50
Tourist Info. Cen.
Bracknell 7B 32
Croydon 4C 200 (9N 45)
Edenbridge 1L 147
Farnham 1G 128
Fleet 4A 88
Gatwick 3F 162
Guildford 6D 202 (5N 113)
Heathrow Central 6C 8
Horsham 7J 197
Hounslow 6B 10
Kingston upon Thames
.....4H 203 (1K 41)
London-Heathrow Airport
Terminal 1 .....5C 8
Terminal 2 .....6C 8
Terminal 3 .....6B 8
Richmond 8K 11
Twickenham 2H 25
Windsor 4G 5
Woking 4B 74
Tournai Cl. GU11: Alde 6C 90
Tournay Rd. SW6 .....3L 13
Tovil Cl. SE20 .....1E 46
Tower App. Rd. RH6: Gat 4C 162
Tower Cl. GU21: Wok 4N 73
GU26: Hind 5C 170
RH6: Horl 8D 142
RH13: Hors 8G 196
RH19: E Grin 8A 166
Tower Ct. RH13: Hors 7J 197
RH19: E Grin *8A 166*
(off Tower Cl.)
Tower Gdns. KT10: Clay 4G 59
Towergate Bus. Cen.
GU8: Worm 2C 172
Tower Gro. KT13: Weybr 8F 38
TOWER HILL
RH4 .....7H 119
RH13 .....8G 196
Tower Hill GU14: Cove 2M 89
RH4: Dork 7H 119
RH13: Hors 9F 196
Towerhill GU5: Gorn 9D 116
Towerhill La. GU5: Gorn 8D 116
(not continuous)
Towerhill Ri. GU5: Gorn 9D 116
Tower Hill Rd. RH4: Dork 7H 119
Tower Ho. *KT14: Byf* *8N 55*
(off High Rd.)
Tower La. RH2: Reig 6C 102
Tower Pl. CR6: Warl 2K 85
Tower Ride SL4: W'sor 4B 18
Tower Ri. TW9: Rich 6L 11
Tower Rd. GU26: Hind 5C 170
KT20: Tad 1H 101
RH12: Fay, Col 9E 180
TW1: Twick 4F 24
Towers, The CR8: Ken 2N 83
Towers Dr. RG45: Crow 3G 48
Towers Pl. TW9: Rich 8L 11
Towers Wlk. KT13: Weybr 3C 56
Tower Vw. CR0: Croy 6H 47
Tower Yd. TW10: Rich 8M 11
Towfield Ct. TW13: Hanw 3N 23
Towfield Rd. TW13: Hanw 3N 23
Town & Crown Exhibition 4G 5
Town Barn Rd.
RH11: Craw 3A 182
Town End CR3: Cate 9B 84
Town End Cl. CR3: Cate 9B 84
GU7: Goda 7H 133
Town End Pde.
KT1: K Tham 5H 203
Town End St. GU7: Goda 7H 133
Town Farm Way
TW19: Stan 1M 21
Townfield Ct.
RH4: Dork 4J 201 (6G 119)
Townfield Rd.
RH4: Dork 4J 201 (6G 119)
Town Fld. Way TW7: Isle 5G 11
Towngate KT11: Cob 2M 77
Town Hall Av. W4 .....1C 12
Town Hill RH7: Ling 7N 145
Town La. TW19: Stan 9M 7
(not continuous)
Town Mead RH1: Blet 2A 124
RH11: Craw 2B 182
Townmead Bus. Cen.
SW6 .....6N 13
Town Mdw. TW8: Brent 2K 11
Town Mdw. Rd. TW8: Brent 3K 11
Townmead Rd. SW6 .....6N 13
TW9: Rich 5A 12
Townquay *TW18: Lale* *2K 37*
(off Blacksmiths La.)
Townsend Cl. RG12: Brac 4C 32
Townsend La. GU22: Wok 8D 74
Townsend M. SW18 .....3A 28
Townsend Rd.
TW15: A'ford 6N 21
Townsend Way
RH10: Craw 5H 183
Townshend Rd. TW9: Rich 7M 11
Townshend Ter. TW9: Rich 7M 11
Townshott Cl. KT23: Book 3A 98
Townside Pl. GU15: Camb 9B 50
Townslow La. GU23: Wis 3L 75
Town Sq. GU15: Camb 9A 50
GU21: Wok 4A 74
RG12: Brac 1A 32
TW7: Isle *6H 11*
(off Swan St.)
Town Tree Rd. TW15: A'ford 6B 22
Town Wharf TW7: Isle 6H 11
Towpath KT12: Wal T 4H 39
TW17: Shep 7A 38
Towpath Way CR0 .....5C 46
Towton Rd. SE27 .....3N 29
Toynbee Rd. SW20 .....9K 27
Tozer Wlk. SL4: W'sor 6A 4
Tracery, The SM7: Ban 2N 81
Tracious Cl. GU21: Wok 3L 73
Tracious La. GU21: Wok 3L 73
Tracy Av. SL3: Lang 1B 6
Trade City KT13: Weybr 6N 55
Trafalgar Av. KT4: W Pk 7J 43
Trafalgar Ct. GU9: Farnh 2G 129
KT11: Cob 9H 57
Trafalgar Dr. KT12: Wal T 9J 39
Trafalgar Gdns.
RH10: Craw 2F 182
Trafalgar Rd. RH12: Hors 4J 197
SW19 .....8N 27
TW2: Twick 3D 24
Trafalgar Vs. *GU14: Cove* *1H 89*
(off Brownsover Rd.)
Trafalgar Way CR0: Wad 8L 45
GU15: Camb 2L 69
Trafford Rd. CR7: T Hea 4K 45
GU16: Frim 6B 70
Traherne Lodge TW11: Tedd 6F 24
Tramlink, The SW19 .....1A 44
Tramsheds, The CR0: Bedd 6H 45
Tramway Cl. SE20 .....1F 46
Tramway Path CR4: Mit 3C 44
(not continuous)
Tranmere Ct. SM2: Sut 4A 62
Tranmere Rd. SW18 .....3A 28
TW2: Whitt 1B 24
Tranquil Dale RH3: Buck 1E 120
Transport Av. TW8: Brent 1G 11
Trap La. RH5: Ockl 8N 157
Traps La. KT3: N Mal 9D 26
Traq Motor Racing 5F 44
Trasher Mead RH4: Dork 7J 119
Travellers Way TW4: C'ford 5K 9
Travis La. GU47: Sandh 8H 49
Treadcroft Dr. RH12: Hors 3L 197
Treadwell Rd. KT18: Eps 3D 80
Treasury Cl. SM6: W'ton 2H 63
Treaty Cen. TW3: Houn 6B 10
Trebor Av. GU9: Farnh 2J 129
Trebovir Rd. SW5 .....1M 13
Tredenham Cl. GU14: Farnb 5A 90
Tredwell Cl. SW2 .....3K 29
Tredwell Rd. SE27 .....5M 29
Treebourne Rd. TN16: B Hil 4E 86
Treebys Av. GU4: J Wel 6N 93
Tree Cl. TW10: Ham 2K 25
Treelands RH5: Nth H 8J 119
Treemount Ct.
KT17: Eps 6M 201 (9D 60)
Treen Av. SW13 .....6E 12
Treeside Dr. GU9: Weybo 5K 109
Treetops CR3: Warl 5D 84
RH9: S Gods 6H 125
Tree Tops Av. GU15: Camb 7E 50
Tree Tops Cvn. Pk.
GU5: Alb 6N 135
Treeview RH11: Craw 8A 182
Treeview Ct. *RH2: Reig* *3B 122*
(off Wray Comn. Rd.)
Tree Way RH2: Reig 9N 101
Trefoil Cl. RG40: W'ham 1D 30
RH12: Hors 3L 197
Trefoil Cres. RH11: Craw 7M 181
Trefusis Ct. TW5: C'ford 4J 9
Tregaron Gdns. KT3: N Mal 3D 42
Tregarthen Pl. KT22: Leat 8J 79
Tregarth Pl. GU21: Wok 4J 73
Tregloss Ct. KT13: Weybr 7F 38
Tregolls Dr. GU14: Farnb 2A 90
Tregunter Rd. SW10 .....2N 13
Trehaven Pde. RH2: Reig 6N 121
Treherne Ct. SW17 .....5E 28
Trehern Rd. SW14 .....6C 12
Trelawn Cl. KT16: Otter 4E 54
Trelawne Dr. GU6: Cranl 8N 155
Trelawney Av. SL3: Lang 1B 6
Trelawney Gro.
KT13: Weybr 3B 56
Tremaine Rd. SE20 .....1E 46
Trematon Pl. TW11: Tedd 8J 25
Tremayne Wlk.
GU15: Camb 2G 70
Trenance GU21: Wok 4K 73
Trenchard Cl. KT12: Hers 2K 57
Trenchard Ct. SM4: Mord 5M 43
Trenear Cl. RH13: Hors 6L 197
Trenham Dr. CR6: Warl 3F 84
Trenholme Ct. CR3: Cate 1D 104
Trent Cl. GU14: Cove 8K 69
RH11: Craw 5L 181
Trent Ct. CR2: S Croy 8B 200
Trentham Cres. GU22: Wok 8C 74
Trentham Rd. RH1: Red 5D 122
Trentham St. SW18 .....2M 27
Trent Ho.
KT2: K Tham 1H 203 (9K 25)
Trenton Cl. GU16: Frim 4E 70
Trent Rd. SL3: Lang 2D 6
Trent Vs. *SL3: Dat* *4L 5*
(off Datchet Pl.)
Trent Way KT4: W Pk 9H 43
Treport St. SW18 .....1N 27
Tresham Cres. GU46: Yate 9A 48
Tresidder Ho. SW4 .....1H 29
Tresillian Way GU21: Wok 3K 73
Tresta Wlk. GU21: Wok 3K 73
Trevanion Rd. W14 .....1K 13
Trevanne Plat RH10: Craw 2H 183
Trevelyan RG12: Brac 6K 31
Trevelyan Ct. KT3: N Mal 6D 42
SL4: W'sor 5E 4
Trevelyan Rd. SW17 .....6C 28
Trevereux Hill
RH8: C Hil, Limp 9H 107
Treville St. SW15 .....1G 26
Trevithick Cl. TW14: Felt 2G 23
Trevone Ct. *SW2* *1J 29*
(off Doverfield Rd.)
Trevor Cl. TW7: Isle 8F 10
Trevor Rd. SW19 .....8K 27
Trevose Av. KT14: W By 1H 75
Trewaren Ct. RH11: Craw 3N 181
Trewenna Dr. KT9: Ches 2K 59
Trewince Rd. SW20 .....9H 27
Trewint St. SW18 .....3A 28
Treyford Cl. RH11: Craw 3L 181

Triangle, The—Up. Hale Rd.

Triangle, The GU21: Wok 5M 73
KT1: K Tham 1A 42
Trickett Ho. SM2: Sut 5N 61
Trident Bus. Cen.
SW17 . . . . .6D 28
Trident Ho. TW19: Stan 1N 21
(off Clare Rd.)
Trident Ind. Est. SL3: Poy 6G 7
Triffins Girls Community Sports Cen.
. . . . .7L 25
Trigg's Cl. GU22: Wok 6N 73
Trigg's La. GU21: Wok 6M 73
GU22: Wok 6M 73
Trigo Ct. KT19: Eps 7C 60
Trig St. RH5: B Grn, Newd 1L 159
Trilakes Country Pk. 7E 48
Trimmers GU9: Farnh 2F 128
Trimmers Cl. GU9: U Hal 5G 109
Trimmers Fld. GU9: Farnh . . .2K 129
Trimmers Wood
GU26: Hind 3B 170
Trimmer Wlk. TW8: Brent 2L 11
Trinder M. TW11: Tedd 6G 25
Trindledown RG42: Brac 7M 15
Trindles Rd. RH1: Sth N 5K 123
Tring Ct. TW1: Twick 5G 24
Tringham Cl. GU21: Knap 5F 72
KT16: Otter 2E 54
Tringham Cotts.
GU24: W End 8C 52
Trinity GU47: Owls 5K 49
Trinity Chu. Pas.
SW13 . . . . .2G 13
Trinity Chu. Rd. SW13 . . . . . . .2G 13
Trinity Chyd.
GU1: Guil 6D 202 (5N 113)
Trinity Cl. CR2: Sande 5B 64
RH10: Craw 1G 183
TW4: Houn 7M 9
TW19: Stan 9L 7
Trinity Cotts. TW9: Rich 6M 11
Trinity Ct.
CR0: Croy 2C 200 (8N 45)
RG12: Brac 1L 31
RH12: Hors 5J 197
SE25 . . . . .5B 46
Trinity Cres. SL5: S'dale 4D 34
SW17 . . . . .3D 28
Trinity Flds. GU9: U Hal 5F 108
Trinity Ga. GU1: Guil 5E 202
Trinity Hill GU9: U Hal 5F 108
Trinity M. SE20 . . . . .1E 46
Trinity Pl. SL4: W'sor 5F 4
Trinity Ri. SW2 . . . . .2L 29
Trinity Rd. GU21: Knap 5E 72
SW17 . . . . .2C 28
SW18 . . . . .1B 28
SW19 . . . . .7M 27
TW9: Rich 6M 11
Trinity Sq. RH13: Hors 6K 197
Trist Way RH11: Craw 1M 181
Tritton Av. CR0: Bedd 1J 63
Trittons KT20: Tad 8J 81
Triumph Cl. UB3: Harl 4D 8
Trodd's La. GU1: Guil 2F 114
GU4: Guil 2F 114
Trojan Way CR0: Wad 9K 45
Troon Cl. RH11: Ifi 4J 181
Troon Ct. SL5: S'hill 4N 33
Troston Ct. TW18: Stain 6H 21
Trotsford Mdw.
GU17: B'water 2H 69
Trotsworth Av. GU25: V Wat . . .3A 36
Trotsworth Ct. GU25: V Wat . . .3N 35
Trotters La. GU24: Chob 8L 53
Trotter Way KT19: Eps 8N 59
Trotton Cl. RH10: Craw 6G 182
Trotts La. TN16: Weste 5L 107
Trotwood Cl. GU47: Owls 5K 49
Troutbeck Wlk.
GU15: Camb 3H 71
Trout Rd. GU27: Hasl 2C 188
Trouville Rd. SW4 . . . . .1G 29
Trowers Way RH1: Red 9F 102
Trowlock Av. TW11: Tedd 7J 25
Trowlock Island TW11: Tedd . . .7K 25
Trowlock Way TW11: Tedd 7K 25
Troy Cl. KT20: Tad 7G 81
Troy La. TN8: Eden 8H 127
TROY TOWN 8H 127
Trueman Rd. CR8: Ken 7A 84
Truggers RH17: Hand 8N 199
Trumble Gdns. CR7: T Hea 3M 45
Trumbull Rd. RG42: Brac 8M 15
Trumpets Hill Rd.
RH2: Reig 4G 120
TRUMPS GREEN 5N 35
Trumpsgreen Av.
GU25: V Wat 5N 35
Trumps Grn. Cl.
GU25: V Wat 4A 36
Trumpsgreen Rd.
GU25: V Wat 7M 35
Trumps Mill La.
GU25: V Wat 5B 36
Trundle Mead RH12: Hors 3J 197
Trunk Rd. GU14: Cove 1H 89
Trunley Heath Rd.
GU5: Braml 4M 133
Truslove Rd. SE27 . . . . .6L 29
Truss Hill Rd. SL5: S'hill 4N 33
Trust Wlk. SE21 . . . . .2M 29
Trystings Cl. KT10: Clay 3G 59
Tubbenden Dr. BR6: Orp 1M 67
Tubbenden La. BR6: Orp 1M 67
Tubbenden La. Sth.
BR6: Farnb 2M 67
Tucker Rd. KT16: Otter 3F 54
Tuckers Cnr. GU6: Cranl 7K 155
Tuckers Dr. GU6: Cranl 7K 155
Tuckey Gro. GU23: Rip 1H 95
Tucklow Wlk. SW15 . . . . .1E 26
Tudor Av. KT4: W Pk 9G 42
TW12: Hamp 7A 24
Tudor Circ. GU7: Goda 4H 133
Tudor Cl. CR2: Sande 2E 84
CR5: Coul 5L 83
GU22: Wok 4C 74
GU26: G'hott 7B 170
KT9: Ches 2L 59
KT11: Cob 9N 57
KT17: Ewe 6E 60
KT23: Book 2N 97
(not continuous)
RG40: W'ham 3E 30
RH6: Smal 8M 143
RH10: Craw 4H 183
RH19: E Grin 1B 186
SM3: Chea 2J 61
SM6: W'ton 4G 63
SM7: Ban 2K 81
SW2 . . . . .1K 29
TW12: H Hill 6C 24
TW15: A'ford 5N 21
Tudor Ct. GU12: Ash 3D 110
GU21: Knap 4G 72
RH1: Red 2E 122
(off St Anne's Ri.)
TN16: B Hil 5G 86
TW11: Tedd 7F 24
TW13: Hanw 5K 23
TW19: Stan 9N 7
TW20: Egh 6C 20
Tudor Dr. GU46: Yate 2C 68
KT2: K Tham 6K 25
KT12: Wal T 7L 39
SM4: Mord 5J 43
Tudor Gdns. BR4: W Wick 9M 47
SW13 . . . . .6D 12
TW1: Twick 2F 24
Tudor Grange KT13: Weybr 8F 38
Tudor Hall GU15: Camb 9D 50
Tudor Ho. KT13: Weybr 3B 56
RG12: Brac 4N 31
Tudor La. SL4: O Win 1M 19
Tudor Lodge KT20: K'wood 8L 81
Tudor Pl. CR4: Mit 8C 28
Tudor Rd. BR3: Beck 2M 47
GU7: Goda 4H 133
KT2: K Tham 8N 25
SE25 . . . . .4E 46
TW3: Houn 7D 10
TW12: Hamp 8A 24
TW15: A'ford 7E 22
Tudors, The RH2: Reig 9A 102
Tudor Wlk. KT13: Weybr 9C 38
KT22: Leat 7F 78
Tudor Way GU21: Knap 6F 72
GU52: C Cro 9B 88
SL4: W'sor 4B 4
TUESLEY 1F 152
Tuesley Cnr. GU7: Goda 8G 132
Tuesley La. GU7: Goda 8G 133
Tufton Gdns. KT8: W Mole 1B 40
Tugela Rd. CR0: Croy 5A 46
Tuggles Plat RH12: Warn 1E 196
Tugmutton Cl. BR6: Farnb 1K 67
Tugwood Cl. CR5: Coul 8H 83
Tulip Cl. CR0: Croy 7G 46
TW12: Hamp 7N 23
Tulip Ct. RH12: Hors 4J 197
Tulip Tree Ct. SM2: Sut 7M 61
Tulk Ho. KT16: Otter 4D 54
Tullett Rd. RH10: Craw 7F 182
Tulleys Farm 5A 184
Tulls La. GU35: Stand 7C 168
Tull St. CR4: Mit 6D 44
Tulse Cl. BR3: Beck 2M 47
TULSE HILL 2M 29
Tulse Hill SW2 . . . . .1L 29
Tulse Hill Est. SW2 . . . . .1L 29
Tulse Hill Station (Rail) 3M 29
Tulse Ho. SW2 . . . . .1L 29
Tulsemere Rd. SE27 . . . . .3N 29
Tulyar Cl. KT20: Tad 7G 81
Tumber Cl. GU12: Ash 2E 110
Tumber St. KT18: Head 3B 100
Tumblewood Rd. SM7: Ban 3K 81
Tumbling Bay KT12: Wal T 5H 39
Tummons Gdns. SE25 . . . . .1B 46
Tunbridge La.
GU30: Brams 8F 168
Tunley Rd. SW17 . . . . .2E 28
Tunnel Link Rd. TW6: Lon A 8B 8
Tunnel Rd. RH2: Reig 3M 121
RH6: Gat 2C 162
Tunnel Rd. E. TW6: Lon A 4C 8
Tunnel Rd. W. TW6: Lon A 4B 8
Tunnmeade RH11: Ifi 4K 181
Tunsgate
GU1: Guil 6D 202 (5N 113)
Tunsgate Sq. GU1: Guil 6C 202
Tunstall Cl. BR6: Orp 1N 67
Tunstall Rd. CR0: Croy 7B 46
Tunstall Wlk. TW8: Brent 2L 11
Tunworth Cres. SW15 . . . . .9E 12
Tupwood Ct. CR3: Cate 2D 104
Tupwood La. CR3: Cate 4D 104
Tupwood Scrubbs Rd.
CR3: Cate 6D 104
Turbary St. GU51: Fleet 1A 88
Turf Hill Rd. GU15: Camb 7D 50
Turfhouse La. GU24: Chob 5H 53
Turing Dr. RG12: Brac 5M 31
Turks Boatyard
KT1: K Tham 2H 203 (9K 25)
Turks Head Ct. SL4: Eton 3G 4
Turle Rd. SW16 . . . . .1J 45
Turnberry RG12: Brac 5K 31
Turner Av. CR4: Mit 9D 28
TN16: B Hil 8E 66
TW2: Twick 4C 24
Turner Cl. GU4: B'ham 9B 94
Turner Ct. KT22: Leat 8G 78
(off Highbury Dr.)
RH19: E Grin 7C 166
Turner Ho. RH5: B Grn 7J 139
TW1: Twick 9K 11
(off Clevedon Rd.)
Turner M. SM2: Sut 4N 61
Turner Pl. GU47: C Tow 9J 49
Turner Rd. KT3: N Mal 6C 42
Turners Cl. TW18: Stain 6K 21
TURNERS HILL 5D 184
Turners Hill Pk.
RH10: T Hil 4F 184
Turners Hill Rd.
RH10: Craw D 7B 164
RH10: Craw, Wor 3H 183
RH10: T Hil 4C 184
RH19: E Grin 4J 185
Turners La. KT12: Hers 3J 57
Turners Mead GU8: Chid 6F 172
Turners Mdw. Way
BR3: Beck 1J 47
Turner's Way CR0: Wad 8L 45
Turner Wlk. RH10: Craw 6D 182
Turneville Rd. W14 . . . . .2L 13
Turney Rd. SE21 . . . . .1N 29
Turnham Cl. GU2: Guil 7M 113
Turnham Grn. Ter. W4 . . . . . . .1D 12
Turnham Grn. Ter. M.
W4 . . . . .1D 12
Turnoak Av. GU22: Wok 7A 74
Turnoak La. GU22: Wok 7A 74
Turnoak Pk. SL4: W'sor 7B 4
Turnpike La. SM1: Sut 2A 62
Turnpike Link
CR0: Croy 3F 200 (8B 46)
Turnpike Pl. RH11: Craw 1B 182
Turnpike Rd. RG42: Brac 1J 31
Turnpike Way TW7: Isle 4G 10
Turnstone Cl. CR2: Sels 6H 65
Turnstone End GU46: Yate 9A 48
Turnville Cl. GU18: Ligh 6L 51
Turpin Rd. TW14: Felt 9G 9
Turpins Ri. GU20: Windl 1M 51
Turpin Way SM6: W'ton 4F 62
Turret Ct. RH19: E Grin 7M 165
Turtledove Av. RH10: T Hil 4F 184
Turville Ct. KT23: Book 3B 98
Tuscam Way GU15: Camb 2L 69
Tuscany Gdns.
RH10: Craw 9C 162
Tuscany Way GU46: Yate 2B 68
Tushmore Av. RH10: Craw 9C 162
Tushmore Ct. RH10: Craw 1C 182
Tushmore Cres.
RH10: Craw 9B 162
Tushmore La. RH10: Craw 1C 182
Tushmore Rdbt.
RH10: Craw 1B 182
Tussock Cl. RH11: Craw 5M 181
Tuxford Cl. RH10: Craw 5G 182
Tweed Cl. GU14: Cove 8K 69
Tweeddale Rd. SM5: Cars 7B 44
Tweed La. RH3: Brock 7N 119
RH11: Ifi 9L 161
Tweed Rd. SL3: Lang 2D 6
Tweedsmuir Cl. GU14: Cove 2J 89
Twelfth Av. KT20: Lwr K 4K 101
Twelve Acre Cl. KT23: Book 2N 97
Twelve Acre Cres.
GU14: Cove 9J 69
Twelve Trees Ho.
RG45: Crow 3H 49
(off Cambridge Rd.)
Tweseldown Race Course 8D 88
Tweseldown Rd.
GU52: C Cro 9C 88
TWICKENHAM 2G 25
Twickenham Baths 2G 25
Twickenham Bri.
TW1: Twick 8J 11
TW9: Rich 8J 11
Twickenham Cl. CR0: Bedd 9K 45
Twickenham Pl. KT7: T Dit 8F 40
(off Woodfield Rd.)
Twickenham Rd. TW7: Isle 8G 10
TW9: Rich 7J 11
TW11: Tedd 5G 24
(not continuous)
TW13: Hanw 4N 23
Twickenham Rugby Union
Football Ground 9E 10
Twickenham Station (Rail) 1G 24
Twickenham Trad. Est.
TW1: Twick 9F 10
Twilley St. SW18 . . . . .1N 27
Twin Bridges Bus. Pk.
CR2: S Croy 3A 64
Twining Av. TW2: Twick 4C 24
Twinoaks KT11: Cob 9A 58
Twitten, The RH11: Craw 3A 182
Twitten La. RH19: Fel 6H 165
Two Rivers Retail Pk.
TW18: Stain 5G 21
Two Ways RH14: Loxw 4J 193
Twycross Rd. GU7: Goda 4G 132
Twyford Ct. GU2: Guil 3K 113
Twyford La. GU10: Wrec 5G 128
Twyford Rd. RG40: W'ham 9A 14
RG42: Bin 1H 15
SM5: Cars 7B 44
Twyhurst Ct. RH19: E Grin 7N 165
Twyne Cl. RH11: Craw 5L 181
Twyner Cl. RH6: Horl 7H 143
Twynersh Av. KT16: Chert 5H 37
Twynholm Mans. SW6 . . . . .3K 13
(off Lillie Rd.)
Tybenham Rd. SW19 . . . . .2M 43
Tychbourne Dr. GU4: Guil 9E 94
Tydcombe Rd. CR6: Warl 6F 84
Tye La. BR6: Farnb 2L 67
KT18: Head 5D 100
Tylden Way RH12: Hors 2M 197
Tylecroft Rd. SW16 . . . . .1J 45
Tylehost GU2: Guil 8K 93
Tylehurst Dr. RH1: Red 4D 122
Tyle Pl. SL4: O Win 8K 5
Tyler Gdns. KT15: Addl 1L 55
Tyler Rd. RH10: Craw 6B 182
Tylers Cl. RH9: Gods 8E 104
Tylers Ct. GU6: Cranl 7M 155
(off Rowland Rd.)
TYLER'S GREEN 7E 104
Tylers Path SM5: Cars 1D 62
Tyler Wlk. SL3: Lang 1B 6
Tymperley Ct. RH13: Hors 5L 197
(off King's Rd.)
Tynamara KT1: K Tham 7H 203
Tynan Cl. TW14: Felt 2H 23
Tyndalls GU26: Hind 5D 170
Tyne Cl. GU14: Cove 8K 69
RH10: Craw 4G 183
Tynedale Rd. RH3: Brock 7A 120
Tyne Ho.
KT2: K Tham 1H 203 (9K 25)
Tynemouth Rd. CR4: Mit 8E 28
Tynemouth St. SW6 . . . . .5N 13
Tynley Gro. GU4: J Wel 6N 93
Typhoon Cl. RG12: Brac 2B 32
Typhoon Way SM6: W'ton 4J 63
Tyrawley Rd. SW6 . . . . .4N 13
Tyrell Ct. SM5: Cars 1D 62
Tyrell Gdns. SL4: W'sor 6C 4
Tyrells Pl. GU1: Guil 4B 114
Tyrrell Sq. CR4: Mit 9C 28
TYRRELL'S WOOD 2N 99
Tyrwhitt Ct. GU2: Guil 8L 93
(off Grange Rd.)
Tythebarn Cl. GU4: B'ham 7D 94
Tytherton RG12: Brac 1A 32
Tyting Cotts. GU4: Guil 6E 114

U

Uckfield Gro. CR4: Mit 8E 28
Udney Pk. Rd. TW11: Tedd 7G 25
Uffington Dr. RG12: Brac 3C 32
Uffington Rd. SE27 . . . . .5L 29
Ujima Ct. SW16 . . . . .5J 29
Ullathorne Rd. SW16 . . . . .5G 28
Ullswater RG12: Brac 6K 31
Ullswater Av. GU14: Cove 2K 89
Ullswater Bus. Pk. CR5: Coul . . .3J 83
Ullswater Cl. GU9: U Hal 6F 108
GU18: Ligh 6M 51
SW15 . . . . .5C 26
Ullswater Ct. GU12: A Va 8D 90
(off Lakeside Cl.)
Ullswater Cres. CR5: Coul 3H 83
SW15 . . . . .5C 26
Ullswater Rd. GU18: Ligh 6M 51
SE27 . . . . .3M 29
SW13 . . . . .3F 12
Ulric Ho. GU51: Fleet 9A 68
Ulstan Cl. CR3: Wold 1K 105
Ulva Rd. SW15 . . . . .8J 13
Ulverstone Rd. SE27 . . . . .3M 29
Ulwin Av. KT14: Byf 9N 55
Umberstones GU25: V Wat 5N 35
Umbria St. SW15 . . . . .9F 12
Underhill Cl. GU7: Goda 8H 133
Underhill La. GU10: L Bou 4G 129
Underhill Pk. Rd.
RH2: Reig 9M 101
Underhill Rd. RH5: Newd 1A 160
Underwood CR0: N Add 2M 65
RG12: Brac 5K 31
Underwood Av. GU12: Ash 3C 110
Underwood Cl.
RH10: Craw D 1E 184
Underwood Ct. CR3: Cate 3B 104
RG42: Bin 7H 15
Underwood Ho.
KT8: W Mole 4A 40
(off Approach Rd.)
Underwood Rd. CR3: Cate 4B 104
GU27: Hasl 1D 188
Undine St. SW17 . . . . .6D 28
Unicorn Trad. Est.
GU27: Hasl 1F 188
Union Cl. GU47: Owls 5K 49
Union Ct. TW9: Rich 8L 11
Union Rd. CR0: Croy 6N 45
GU9: Farnh 1H 129
GU16: Deep 6H 71
Union St. GU11: Alde 2M 109
GU14: Farnb 1M 89
GU24: B'wood 8L 71
KT1: K Tham 3H 203 (1K 41)
Union Ter. GU11: Alde 2M 109
Unisport 3K 113
Unitair Cen. TW14: Bedf 9D 8
Unity Cl. CR0: N Add 5L 65
SE19 . . . . .6N 29
University College for the
Creative Arts
Epsom Campus
. . . . .8K 201 (1D 80)
University Ct.
GU2: Guil 3A 202 (3L 113)
University of Surrey
Austin Pearce Building
. . . . .3A 202 (3K 113)
St Mary's College 4F 24
University of Surrey Gallery
. . . . .3K 113
(in University of Surrey)
University Rd. SW19 . . . . .7B 28
Unstead La. GU5: Braml 4M 133
Unstead Wood
GU3: P'marsh 2M 133
UNSTED 6N 133
Unwin Av. TW14: Felt 8E 8
Unwin Mans. W14 . . . . .2L 13
(off Queen's Club Gdns.)
Unwin Rd. TW7: Isle 6E 10
Upavon Gdns. RG12: Brac 4D 32
Upcroft SL4: W'sor 6E 4
Updown Hill GU20: Windl 3A 52
Upfield CR0: Croy 9E 46
RH6: Horl 9E 142
Upfield Cl. RH6: Horl 1E 162
Upfold Cl. GU6: Cranl 4K 155
Upfold La. GU6: Cranl 5K 155
Upfolds Grn. GU4: B'ham 8E 94
Upgrove Mnr. Way
SW2 . . . . .1L 29
Upham Pk. Rd. W4 . . . . .1D 12
Upland Rd.
CR2: S Croy 8D 200 (2A 64)
CR3: Warl, Wold 7K 85
GU15: Camb 8B 50
SM2: Sut 4B 62
Uplands BR3: Beck 1K 47
CR6: Warl 5J 85
KT21: A'tead 7K 79
Uplands Cl. GU27: Hasl 9H 171
GU47: Sandh 7G 48
SW14 . . . . .8A 12
Uplands Dr. KT22: Oxs 1D 78
Uplands Rd. CR8: Ken 3N 83
GU9: Farnh 2K 129
Upland Way KT18: Tat C 5H 81
Uppark Gdns. RH12: Hors 2M 197
Up. Bourne La.
GU10: Wrec 6F 128
Up. Bourne Va.
GU10: Wrec 6F 128
Upper Bri. Rd. RH1: Red 3C 122
Up. Brighton Rd. KT6: Surb 5K 41
Up. Broadmoor Rd.
RG45: Crow 2H 49
Upper Butts TW8: Brent 2J 11
Up. Charles St.
GU15: Camb 9A 50
Up. Chobham Rd.
GU15: Camb 3E 70
Up. Church La.
GU9: Farnh 1G 129
Upper Cl. RH18: F Row 7H 187
Up. College Ride
GU15: Camb 7C 50
Upper Ct. Rd. CR3: Wold 1K 105
KT19: Eps 7B 60
Upper Dr. TN16: B Hil 5E 86
Upper Dunnymans
SM7: Ban 1L 81
UPPER EASHING 7D 132
Up. Edgeborough Rd.
GU1: Guil 4B 114
UPPER ELMERS END 4J 47
Up. Elmers End Rd.
BR3: Beck 3H 47
Up. Elms Rd. GU11: Alde 3M 109
Up. Fairfield Rd.
KT22: Leat 8H 79
Up. Farm Rd. KT8: W Mole 3N 39
UPPER GATTON 5B 102
Up. Gordon Rd.
GU15: Camb 1B 70
Upper Grn. E. CR4: Mit 2D 44
Upper Grn. W. CR4: Mit 1D 44
(not continuous)
Up. Grotto Rd. TW1: Twick 3F 24
Upper Gro. SE25 . . . . .3B 46
Up. Guildown Rd.
GU2: Guil 8A 202 (6L 113)
UPPER HALE 6H 109
Up. Hale Rd.
GU9: Hale, U Hal 5F 108

A-Z Surrey 293

Upper Halliford—Vincent Av.

UPPER HALLIFORD 3F 38
Up. Halliford By-Pass
TW17: Shep 4F 38
Up. Halliford Grn.
TW17: Shep 3F 38
Up. Halliford Rd.
TW17: Shep 2F 38
Upper Halliford Station (Rail) 1F 38
Up. Ham Rd. TW10: Ham 5K 25
Upper Harestone
CR3: Cate 5D 104
Up. High St.
KT17: Eps 6L 201 (9D 60)
Up. House La.
GU5: Sha G 1H 155
UPPER IFOLD 1B 192
Upper Kiln RH4: Dork 7J 119
(off Stubs Hill)
Up. Lodge Way CR5: Coul 9H 83
Upper Mall W6 1F 12
(not continuous)
Up. Manor Rd. GU7: Goda 4H 133
GU8: Mil 1B 152
Upper Mt. GU27: G'wood 8K 171
Up. Mulgrave Rd.
SM2: Chea 4K 61
UPPER NORWOOD 1A 46
Upper Nursery SL5: S'dale 4D 34
Up. Old Pk. La.
GU9: Farnh 7E 108
Upper Pk. Rd. GU15: Camb 1B 70
KT2: K Tham 7N 25
UPPER PARROCK 7N 187
Upper Path RH4: Dork 7H 119
Up. Pillory Down SM5: Cars 9E 62
Upper Pines SM7: Ban 4D 82
Up. Pinewood Rd.
GU12: Ash 1H 111
Up. Queen St. GU7: Goda 7H 133
(not continuous)
Up. Richmond Rd.
SW15 7E 12
Up. Richmond Rd. W.
SW14 7N 11
TW10, Rich 7N 11
Upper Rd. SM6: W'ton 2H 63
Up. Rose Hill
RH4: Dork 4K 201 (6H 119)
Up. St Michael's Rd.
GU11: Alde 4N 109
Upper Sawleywood
SM7: Ban 1L 81
Up. School Dr. GU27: Hasl 3D 188
Up. Selsdon Rd.
CR2: Sande, Sels 4C 64
UPPER SHIRLEY 1G 64
Up. Shirley Rd. CR0: Croy 8J 65
Up. South Vw. GU9: Farnh 9H 109
Upper Springfield GU8: Els 8J 131
Upper Sq. RH18: F Row 6H 187
TW7: Isle 6G 11
Upper Stanford GU24: Pirb 3C 92
Up. Star Post Ride
RG12: Brac 9N 31
Upper St. GU5: Shere 7A 116
(not continuous)
GU51: Fleet 4A 88
Up. Sunbury Rd.
TW12: Hamp 9M 23
Up. Sutton La. TW5: Hest 3A 10
Up. Teddington Rd.
KT1: H Wic 8J 25
Upperton Rd.
GU2: Guil 6A 202 (4M 113)
UPPER TOOTING 5D 28
Up. Tooting Pk. SW17 3D 28
Up. Tooting Rd. SW17 5D 28
Up. Tulse Hill SW2 1K 29
Up. Union St.
GU11: Alde 2M 109
Up. Union Ter.
GU11: Alde 2M 109
UPPER VANN 8J 153
Up. Vann La. GU8: Hamb 9K 153
Up. Vernon Rd. SM1: Sut 2B 62
Up. Verran Rd.
GU15: Camb 3B 70
Up. Village Rd. SL5: S'hill 4N 33
Upper Wlk. GU25: V Wat 3A 36
Upper Warlingham Station (Rail) 5D 84
Upper Way GU9: Farnh 4F 128
Up. West St. RH2: Reig 3L 121
Up. Weybourne La.
GU9: H End 4J 109
Up. Woodcote Village
CR8: Pur 8H 63
Upshire Gdns. RG12: Brac 3D 32
Upshot La. GU22: Pyr 4H 75
Upton GU21: Wok 4L 73
Upton Cl. GU14: Farnb 2B 90
Upton Dene SM2: Sut 4N 61
Upton Rd. CR7: T Hea 1A 46
TW3: Houn 6A 10
Upwood Rd. SW16 9J 29
Urmston Dr. SW19 2K 27
Usherwood Cl.
KT20: Box H 9A 100
Uvedale Cl. CR0: N Add 7N 65
Uvedale Cres. CR0: N Add 7N 65
Uvedale Rd. RH8: Oxt 8B 106
Uxbridge Ct. KT1: K Tham 8H 203
Uxbridge Rd.
KT1: K Tham 8G 203 (3K 41)
TW12: Hamp, H Hill 5A 24
TW13: Felt 3K 23

V

Vachery La. GU6: Cranl 2N 175
Vaillant Rd. KT13: Weybr 1D 56
Vale, The CR0: Croy 8G 47
CR5: Coul 1H 83
TW5: Hest 2M 9
TW14: Felt 9J 9
TW16: Sunb 7H 23
Vale Border CR0: Sels 7G 65
CR2: Sels 7G 65
Vale Cl. BR6: Farnb 1J 67
CR5: Coul 1J 83
GU10: L Bou 7H 129
GU21: Wok 3A 74
KT13: Weybr 9E 38
TW1: Twick 4G 24
Vale Cotts. SW15 4D 26
Vale Ct. GU12: A Va 6E 90
KT13: Weybr 9E 38
Vale Cres. SW15 5D 26
Vale Cft. KT10: Clay 5F 58
Vale Dr. RH12: Hors 6H 197
Vale Farm Rd. GU21: Wok 4A 74
Vale Ho. GU21: Wok 4A 74
Valentines RH14: Plais 3N 191
Valentines Lea
GU28: North 8D 190
Valentyne Cl. CR0: N Add 7A 66
Vale Pde. SW15 4D 26
Valerie Ct. SM2: Sut 4N 61
Vale Rd. CR4: Mit 2H 45
GU12: A Va 6E 90
GU15: Camb 2M 69
(not continuous)
KT4: W Pk 9E 42
KT10: Clay 5E 58
KT13: Weybr 9E 38
KT19: Ewe 1E 60
SL4: W'sor 3C 4
SM1: Sut 1N 61
Vale Rd. Nth. KT6: Surb 8L 41
Vale Rd. Sth. KT6: Surb 8L 41
Valery Pl. TW12: Hamp 8A 24
Vale St. SE27 4N 29
Vale Wood Dr. GU10: L Bou 7J 129
Vale Wood La.
GU26: G'hott 5A 170
(not continuous)
Valewood Rd. GU27: Hasl 4G 188
Valiant Pl. RG12: Brac 2A 32
Vallance By-Ways Gatwick
RH6: Char 4L 161
Valley, The GU2: Guil 7M 113
Valley Ct. CR3: Cate 9D 84
VALLEY END 3D 52
Valley End Rd. GU24: Chob 3D 52
Valleyfield Rd. SW16 6K 29
Valley Gdns., The 1H 35
Valley Gdns. SW19 8B 28
Valley La. GU10: L Bou 5H 129
Valley Leisure Pk. CR0: Wad 7J 45
Valley M. TW1: Twick 3F 24
Valley Point Ind. Est.
CR0: Bedd 6J 45
Valley Rd. CR8: Ken 2A 84
GU16: Deep, Frim 6E 70
SW16 6K 29
Valley Trade Pk. CR0: Bedd 6J 45
(off Therapia La.)
Valley Vw. GU7: Goda 7G 132
GU47: Sandh 8F 48
TN16: B Hil 5E 86
Valley Vw. Gdns. CR8: Ken 2B 84
Valley Wlk. CR0: Croy 8F 46
Vallis Way KT9: Ches 1K 59
Valnay St. SW17 6D 28
Valonia Gdns. SW18 9L 13
Valroy Cl. GU15: Camb 9B 50
Vanbrugh Cl. RH11: Craw 6K 181
Vanbrugh Dr. KT12: Wal T 6K 39
Vanbrugh M. KT12: Wal T 6K 39
Vancouver Cl. KT19: Eps 7B 60
Vancouver Ct. RH6: Smal 8L 143
Vancouver Dr. RH11: Craw 9B 162
Vancouver Rd. TW10: Ham 5J 25
Vanderbilt Rd. SW18 2N 27
Van Dyck Av. KT3: N Mal 6C 42
Vandyke RG12: Brac 5K 31
Vandyke Cl. RH1: Red 9D 102
SW15 1J 27
Van Gogh Cl. TW7: Isle 6G 10
Vanguard Cl.
CR0: Croy 1A 200 (7M 45)
Vanguard Way SM6: W'ton 4J 63
TW6: Lon A 5F 8
VANN COMMON 9E 188
Vanneck Sq. SW15 8F 12
Vanners RH10: Craw 2C 182
Vanners Pde. KT14: Byf 9N 55
Vann Farm Rd. RH5: Ockl 6E 158
Vann Lake RH5: Ockl 6F 158
Vann Lake Rd. RH5: Ockl 7F 158
Vann La. GU8: Chid, Hamb 9G 152
Vann Rd. GU27: Fern 9E 188
Vanquish Cl. TW2: Whitt 1A 24
Vansittart Est. SL4: W'sor 3F 4
Vansittart Rd. SL4: W'sor 4E 4
Vanston Pl. SW6 3M 13
Vantage Ct. GU21: Wok 4N 73
Vantage Pl. TW14: Felt 9H 9
Vantage Point CR2: Sande 5A 64
Vantage W. TW8: Brent 1M 11
Vant Rd. SW17 6D 28
Vapery La. GU24: Pirb 8A 72
Varley Way CR4: Mit 1B 44
Varna Rd. SW6 3K 13
TW12: Hamp 9B 24
Varney Cl. GU14: Cove 9K 69
Varsity Dr. TW1: Twick 8E 10
Varsity Row SW14 5B 12
Vaughan Almshouses
TW15: A'ford 6C 22
(off Feltham Hill Rd.)
Vaughan Cl. TW12: Hamp 7M 23
Vaughan Copse SL4: Eton 1G 4
Vaughan Ct. GU2: Guil 8L 93
(off Grange Rd.)
Vaughan Gdns. SL4: E Wic 1C 4
Vaughan Ho. SW4 1G 29
Vaughan Rd. KT7: T Dit 6H 41
Vaughan Way
RH4: Dork 2H 201 (5G 118)
Vaux Cres. KT12: Hers 3J 57
Vauxhall Gdns.
CR2: S Croy 3N 63
Veals Mead CR4: Mit 9C 28
Vectis Gdns. SW17 7F 28
Vectis Rd. SW17 7F 28
Vector Point RH10: Craw 8D 162
Vegal Cres. TW20: Eng G 6L 19
Veitch Cl. TW14: Felt 1G 23
Vellum Dr. SM5: Cars 9E 44
Velmead Cl. GU52: Fleet 6C 88
Velmead Rd. GU52: Fleet 6B 88
Vencourt Pl. W6 1F 12
Ventnor Rd. SM2: Sut 4N 61
Ventnor Ter. GU12: Alde 3A 110
Venton Cl. GU21: Wok 4L 73
Venus M. CR4: Mit 2C 44
Vera Rd. SW6 4K 13
Verbania Way
RH19: E Grin 9D 166
Verbena Cl. UB7: W Dray 1M 7
Verbena Gdns. W6 1F 12
Verdayne Av. CR0: Croy 8G 47
Verdayne Gdns.
CR6: Warl 3F 84
Verdun Rd. SW13 2F 12
Vereker Dr. TW16: Sunb 2H 39
Vereker Rd. W14 1K 13
Verge Wlk. GU11: Alde 5M 109
Verites GU7: Goda 4F 132
Vermont Rd. SM1: Sut 9N 43
SW18 9N 13
Verne, The GU52: C Cro 8B 88
Verner Cl. GU35: Head 5D 168
Vernon Av. SW20 1J 43
Vernon Cl. KT16: Otter 3F 54
KT19: Ewe 3B 60
RH12: Hors 4N 197
TW19: Stan 2N 21
Vernon Ct. GU9: Farnh 1F 128
SL5: Asc 2H 33
Vernon Dr. CR3: Cate 9N 83
SL5: Asc 1H 33
Vernon Mans. W14 2L 13
(off Queen's Club Mans.)
Vernon Rd. SM1: Sut 2A 62
SW14 6C 12
TW13: Felt 3G 22
Vernon Wlk. KT20: Tad 7J 81
Vernon Way GU2: Guil 2J 113
Vern Pl. TN16: Tats 8E 86
Verona Ct. TW15: A'ford 5C 22
W4 1D 12
Verona Dr. KT6: Surb 8L 41
Veronica Gdns. SW16 9G 28
Veronica Rd. SW17 3F 28
Verralls GU22: Wok 4D 74
(not continuous)
Verran Rd. GU15: Camb 3B 70
SW12 1F 28
Verulam Av. CR8: Pur 8G 63
Veryan GU21: Wok 4K 73
Vesey Cl. GU14: Farnb 9M 69
Vevers Rd. RH2: Reig 6A 122
Vibart Gdns. SW2 1K 29
Vibia Cl. TW19: Stan 1M 21
Viburnum Ct. GU24: W End 9B 52
Vicarage Av. TW20: Egh 6D 20
Vicarage Cl. GU9: Farnh 4J 129
KT4: W Pk 7D 42
KT20: K'wood 2K 101
KT23: Book 3A 98
RH7: Ling 7N 145
RH12: Col 2H 199
Vicarage Ct. BR3: Beck 2H 47
TW14: Bedf 1D 22
TW20: Egh 7D 20
Vicarage Cres. TW20: Egh 6D 20
Vicarage Dr. BR3: Beck 1K 47
SW14 8C 12
Vicarage Farm Ct.
TW5: Hest 3N 9
Vicarage Farm Rd.
TW3: Houn 5M 9
TW4: Houn 5M 9
TW5: Hest 4M 9
Vicarage Flds. KT12: Wal T 5K 39
Vicarage Gdns. CR4: Mit 2C 44
GU26: G'hott 6A 170
GU52: C Cro 9A 88
SL5: Asc 4L 33
SW14 8B 12
Vicarage Ga. GU2: Guil 5K 113
Vicarage Ga. M.
KT20: K'wood 2K 101
Vicarage Hill GU9: Farnh 4J 129
GU10: L Bou 4J 129
RH14: Loxw 5J 193
TN16: Weste 4M 107
Vicarage Ho.
KT1: K Tham 3M 203
Vicarage La. GU9: Farnh 1G 129
(Lwr. Church La.)
GU9: Farnh 4J 129
(Vicarage Hill)
GU9: U Hal 5H 109
GU19: Bag 2E 50
GU23: Send 4E 94
GU27: Hasl 2D 188
GU46: Yate 8B 48
KT17: Ewe 5F 60
(not continuous)
KT20: K'wood 1K 101
KT22: Leat 9H 79
RH5: Cap 4K 159
RH6: Horl 7D 142
TW18: Lale 2L 37
TW19: Wray 2A 20
Vicarage Rd. CR0: Wad 9L 45
GU17: Haw 2K 69
GU19: Bag 3G 50
GU22: Wok 8B 74
GU24: Chob 7G 53
GU46: Yate 8A 48
KT1: H Wic 9J 25
KT1: K Tham 3H 203 (1K 41)
RH7: Ling 7N 145
RH10: Craw D 2D 184
SM1: Sut 9N 43
SW14 8B 12
TW2: Twick 3E 24
TW2: Whitt 9C 10
TW11: Tedd 6G 24
TW16: Sunb 6G 23
TW18: Stain 4G 20
TW20: Egh 6C 20
Vicarage Wlk. GU7: Goda 6G 132
(off Borough Rd.)
KT12: Wal T 6H 39
RH19: E Grin 9B 166
Vicarage Way SL3: Coln 3E 6
Viceroy Ct.
CR0: Croy 1D 200 (7A 46)
Vickers Cl. SM6: W'ton 4K 63
Vickers Ct. TW19: Stan 9N 7
(off Whitley Cl.)
Vickers Dr. Nth.
KT13: Weybr 6N 55
Vickers Dr. Sth.
KT13: Weybr 7N 55
Vickers Rd. GU12: A Va 8D 90
Vickers Way TW4: Houn 8M 9
Victor Ct. RH10: Craw 9H 163
Victoria Almshouses
RH1: Red 9E 102
RH2: Reig 3A 122
Victoria Av. CR2: Sande 6N 63
GU15: Camb 1M 69
KT6: Surb 5K 41
KT8: W Mole 2B 40
SM6: W'ton 9E 44
TW3: Houn 8A 10
Victoria Cl. KT8: W Mole 2A 40
KT13: Weybr 9E 38
RH6: Horl 8E 142
TN8: Eden 3L 147
Victoria Cotts. TW9: Kew 4M 11
Victoria Ct. GU1: Guil 4C 202
GU4: Chil 9A 114
(off Station Row)
GU19: Bag 6J 51
GU51: Fleet 4A 88
RH1: Red 6E 122
RH13: Hors 6K 197
Victoria Cres. SW19 8L 27
Victoria Dr. GU17: B'water 2H 69
SW19 1J 27
Victoria Gdns. GU14: Cove 1J 89
GU51: Fleet 4A 88
RG40: W'ham 9D 14
TN16: B Hil 2E 86
TW5: Hest 4M 9
Victoria Ho. KT22: Leat 8J 79
Victoria La. UB3: Harl 1E 8
Victoria Mans. W14 2L 13
(off Queen's Club Mans.)
Victoria M. KT13: Weybr 1B 56
(off Balfour Rd.)
RH11: Craw 3B 182
SW18 2A 28
TW20: Eng G 7M 19
Victoria Pde. TW9: Kew 4N 11
(off Sandycombe Rd.)
Victoria Pl. GU21: Wok 3C 74
(off North Rd.)
KT10: Esh 1B 58
(off Esher Pk. Av.)
KT11: Cob 1J 77
KT17: Eps 5M 201 (8D 60)
TW9: Rich 8K 11
Victoria Rd. CR4: Mit 8C 28
CR5: Coul 2H 83
GU1: Guil 3E 202 (3A 114)
GU6: Cranl 7M 155
GU7: Goda 7H 133
GU9: Farnh 1H 129
GU11: Alde 2M 109
GU14: Farnb 1M 89
GU21: Knap 4G 72
GU22: Wok 4A 74
GU47: Owls 6K 49
GU51: Fleet 4A 88
KT1: K Tham 4L 203 (1M 41)
KT6: Surb 5K 41
KT13: Weybr 9E 38
KT15: Addl 1M 55
RH1: Red 4E 122
RH6: Horl 8E 142
RH11: Craw 3A 182
SL4: E Wic 1B 4
SL5: Asc 4L 33
SM1: Sut 2B 62
SW14 6C 12
TN8: Eden 3L 147
TW1: Twick 1H 25
TW11: Tedd 7G 24
TW13: Felt 2J 23
TW18: Stain 4G 20
Victoria Sq. RH6: Horl 8E 142
(off Consort Way)
Victoria St. RH13: Hors 6K 197
SL4: W'sor 4G 4
TW20: Eng G 7M 19
Victoria Ter. GU26: G'hott 6A 170
(off Crossways Rd.)
RH4: Dork 3J 201 (5G 119)
RH19: E Grin 7A 166
Victoria Vs. TW9: Rich 6M 11
Victoria Wlk.
RG40: W'ham 9D 14
Victoria Way GU21: Wok 4A 74
KT13: Weybr 9E 38
RH19: E Grin 2B 186
Victor Rd. SL4: W'sor 6F 4
TW11: Tedd 5E 24
Victors Dr. TW12: Hamp 7M 23
Victor Wlk. RG12: Brac 2B 32
Victor Way GU14: Farnb 5J 89
Victory Av. SM4: Mord 4A 44
Victory Bus. Cen. TW7: Isle 7F 10
Victory Cl. TW19: Stan 2N 21
Victory Cotts. KT24: Eff 6M 97
Victory Pk. Rd. KT15: Addl 9L 37
(not continuous)
Victory Rd. KT16: Chert 7J 37
RH12: Hors 5H 197
SW19 8A 28
Victory Rd. M. SW19 8A 28
(off Victory Rd.)
Victory Way TW5: C'ford 1K 9
Vidler Cl. KT9: Ches 3J 59
View Cl. TN16: B Hil 3E 86
Viewfield Rd. SW18 9L 13
Viewlands Av. TN16: Weste 7N 87
View Ter. RH7: Dorm 2C 166
Viggory La. GU21: Wok 2M 73
Vigo La. GU46: Yate 2B 68
Viking RG12: Brac 4K 31
Viking Ct. SW6 2M 13
Viking Ho. RH6: L Hea 5B 162
VILLAGE, THE 4D 18
Village, The GU6: Ewh 4E 156
Village Cl. KT13: Weybr 9E 38
Village Ct. KT13: Weybr 1E 56
(off Oatlands Dr.)
Village Gdns. KT17: Ewe 6E 60
Village Ga. TW17: Shep 4C 38
Village Grn. Av.
TN16: B Hil 4G 87
Village Grn. Way
TN16: B Hil 4G 87
Village Health Club, The 9N 83
Village Rd. TW20: Thor 2E 36
Village Row SM2: Sut 4M 61
Village Sq., The
CR5: Coul 9H 83
Village St. RH5: Newd 1A 160
Village Way BR3: Beck 1K 47
CR2: Sande 9D 64
GU6: Cranl 7M 155
GU46: Yate 8C 48
TW15: A'ford 5A 22
Villas, The RH7: Blin H 3H 145
Villiers, The
KT13: Weybr 3E 56
Villiers Av.
KT5: Surb 8L 203 (4M 41)
TW2: Whitt 2N 23
Villiers Cl.
KT5: Surb 8M 203 (3M 41)
Villiers Ct. SL4: W'sor 3D 4
Villiers Gro. SM2: Chea 5J 61
Villiers Ho. SL4: Eton 1F 4
(off Common La.)
Villiers Path KT6: Surb 4L 41
Villiers Rd. BR3: Beck 1G 47
KT1: K Tham 7L 203 (3M 41)
TW7: Isle 5E 10
Vimy Cl. TW4: Houn 8N 9
Vinall Gdns. RH12: Bro H 4D 196
Vincam Cl. TW2: Whitt 1A 24
Vincent Av. KT5: Surb 8B 42
SM5: Cars 7B 62

Vincent Cl.—Warltersville Way

Vincent Cl. CR5: Chip 7D **82**
KT10: Esh 9B **40**
KT16: Chert 6G **37**
KT22: Fetc 1B **98**
RH13: Hors 6M **197**
UB7: Sip 2B **8**
Vincent Ct. GU51: Fleet 4B **88**
Vincent Dr.
RH4: Dork 4H **201** (6G **118**)
TW17: Shep 2F **38**
Vincent La.
RH4: Dork 2H **201** (5G **118**)
Vincent Ri. RG12: Brac 2C **32**
Vincent Rd. CR0: Croy 6B **46**
CR5: Coul 3G **82**
KT1: K Tham 2N **41**
KT11: Sto D 3M **77**
KT16: Chert 6G **37**
RH4: Dork 3H **201** (5G **118**)
TW4: Houn 5L **9**
TW7: Isle 4D **10**
Vincent Row TW12: H Hill 7C **24**
Vincent Sq. TN16: B Hil 9E **66**
Vincent Wlk. *RH4: Dork* *2J 201*
(off South St.)
Vincent Works
RH4: Dork 3H **201** (5G **118**)
Vine Cl. GU3: Worp 4G **93**
GU10: Wrec 7F **128**
GU11: Alde 7M **89**
KT5: Surb 5M **41**
RH5: Holm 4J **139**
SM1: Sut 9A **44**
TW19: Stan M 8J **7**
UB7: W Dray 1B **8**
Vine Cotts. GU6: Cranl 7K **155**
GU28: North 8D **190**
Vine Ct. KT12: Hers 3K **57**
Vine Ho. Cl. GU16: Mytc 2E **90**
Vine La. GU10: Wrec 6F **128**
Vine Pl. TW3: Houn 7B **10**
Viner Cl. KT12: Wal T 5K **39**
Vineries Cl. UB7: Sip 2B **8**
Vine Rd. KT8: E Mol 3C **40**
SW13 ....6E **12**
Vine Sq. *W14* *1L 13*
(off Star Rd.)
Vine St. GU11: Alde 3M **109**
Vine Way GU10: Wrec 6F **128**
Vineyard, The TW10: Rich 8L **11**
Vineyard Cl.
KT1: K Tham ...5L **203** (2M **41**)
Vineyard Hill Rd.
SW19 ....5L **27**
Vineyard M. TW10: Rich 8L **11**
Vineyard Pas. TW10: Rich 8L **11**
Vineyard Path *SW14* *6C 12*
(off Church Path)
SW14 ....6C **12**
(Sheen La.)
Vineyard Rd. TW13: Felt 4H **23**
Vineyard Row KT1: H Wic 9J **25**
Vineyards, The *TW13: Felt* *4H 23*
(off High St.)
TW16: Sunb 2H **39**
Viney Bank CR0: Sels 5J **65**
Vinter Ct. TW17: Shep 4B **38**
Viola Av. TW14: Felt 9K **9**
TW19: Stan 2M **21**
Viola Cft. RG42: Warf 9D **16**
Violet Cl. SM3: Sut 7K **43**
SM6: W'ton 7E **44**
Violet Gdns.
CR0: Wad 8A **200** (2M **63**)
Violet La.
CR0: Wad 8A **200** (3M **63**)
Virgin Active 2B 182
Virgin Active TW16: Sunb 9H **23**
Virginia Av. GU25: V Wat 4M **35**
Virginia Beeches
GU25: V Wat 2L **35**
Virginia Cl. KT3: N Mal 3B **42**
KT13: Weybr 3D **56**
KT21: A'tead 5K **79**
TW18: Lale 2L **37**
Virginia Ct. GU25: V Wat 3N **35**
Virginia Dr. GU25: V Wat 4M **35**
Virginia Gdns. GU14: Farnb ...3A **90**
Virginia Ho. TW11: Tedd 6H **25**
Virginia Pk. GU25: V Wat 3A **36**
Virginia Pl. KT11: Cob 1H **77**
Virginia Rd. CR7: T Hea 9M **29**
Virginia Wlk. SW2 ....1K **29**
VIRGINIA WATER 4A **36**
Virginia Water 2H 35
Virginia Water Station (Rail)
..........4A **36**
Viscount Cl. GU12: A Va 8D **90**
Viscount Ct. SL4: W'sor 4F **4**
Viscount Gdns. KT14: Byf 8N **55**
Viscount Ind. Est. SL3: Poy 6G **6**
Viscount Rd. TW19: Stan 2N **21**
Viscount Way TW6: Lon A 7F **8**
Vista Ho. *SW19* *9B 28*
(off Chapter Way)
Vivenne Ho. TW18: Stain 6J **21**
Vivian Cl. GU52: C Cro 7C **88**
Vivien Cl. KT9: Ches 4L **59**
Vivienne Cl. RH11: Craw 9B **162**
TW1: Twick 9K **11**
Vixen Dr. GU12: Alde 1C **110**
Voewood Cl. KT3: N Mal 5E **42**
Vogan Cl. RH2: Reig 6N **121**
Volta Way CR0: Wad 7K **45**
Voss Ct. SW16 ....7J **29**
Vowels La. RH19: E Grin 8F **184**
Vue Cinema
Croydon, Hesterman Way
..........7K 45
Croydon, High St.
..........4C 200 (9N 45)
Fulham Broadway 3M 13
Staines 5G 21
Vulcan Bus. Cen.
CR0: N Add 5A **66**
Vulcan Cl. GU47: Sandh 8F **48**
RH11: Craw 7A **182**
Vulcan Ct. GU47: Sandh 8F **48**
Vulcan Dr. RG12: Brac 2A **32**
Vulcan Way CR0: N Add 6A **66**
GU47: Sandh 8F **48**
SM6: W'ton 5J **63**

W

Wadbrook St.
KT1: K Tham ...4H **203** (1K **41**)
Waddington Av. CR5: Coul 7L **83**
Waddington Cl. CR5: Coul 6M **83**
RH11: Craw 6M **181**
Waddington Way SE19 ......8N **29**
WADDON 9L **45**
Waddon Cl. CR0: Wad 9L **45**
Waddon Ct. Rd. CR0: Wad 9L **45**
Waddon Marsh Stop (CT) 8L **45**
Waddon Marsh Way
CR0: Wad 7K **45**
Waddon New Rd.
CR0: Croy 4A **200** (9M **45**)
Waddon Pk. Av. CR0: Wad 1L **63**
Waddon Rd.
CR0: Croy, Wad
..........4A **200** (9L **45**)
Waddon Station (Rail) 1L **63**
Waddon Way CR0: Wad 3L **63**
Wades La. TW11: Tedd 6G **24**
Wadham GU47: Owls 6L **49**
Wadham Cl. RH10: Craw 9G **162**
TW17: Shep 6D **38**
Wadham Rd. SW15 ....7K **13**
Wadhurst Cl. SE20 ....1E **46**
Wadlands Brook Rd.
RH19: E Grin 5N **165**
Wagbullock Ri. RG12: Brac ...5A **32**
Wagg Cl. RH19: E Grin 9C **166**
Waggon Cl. GU2: Guil 2H **113**
Waggoners Hollow
GU19: Bag 5J **51**
WAGGONERS RDBT. 4J **9**
Waggoners Way
GU26: G'hott 6M **169**
Waggoners Wells La.
GU26: G'hott 6M **169**
Wagner M. *KT6: Surb* *4L 41*
(off Avenue Elmers)
Wagon Yd. GU9: Farnh 1G **129**
Wagtail Cl. RH12: Hors 1K **197**
Wagtail Gdns. CR2: Sels 6H **65**
Wagtail Wlk. BR3: Beck 4M **47**
Waight's Ct.
KT2: K Tham ...1K **203** (9L **25**)
Wain End RH12: Hors 3K **197**
Wainford Cl. SW19 ....2J **27**
Wainhouse Cl. TN8: Eden ...9M **127**
Wainscot SL5: S'dale 5C **34**
Wainwright Cl.
RG40: W'ham 2F **30**
Wainwright Gro. TW7: Isle 7D **10**
Wainwrights RH10: Craw 6B **182**
Wait Ct. *CR0: Croy* *5M 45*
(off Goodman Ct.)
Wake Cl. GU2: Guil 7L **93**
Wake Ct. GU2: Guil 9L **93**
Wakefield Cl. KT14: Byf 8N **55**
Wakefield Ct. RH12: Hors ...6H **197**
Wakefield Rd. TW10: Rich 8K **11**
Wakefords Cl. GU11: Alde 7B **90**
Wakefords Copse
GU52: C Cro 1C **108**
Wakefords Pk. GU52: C Cro ...1C **108**
(not continuous)
Wakehams Grn. Dr.
RH10: Craw 9H **163**
Wakehurst Dr. RH10: Craw 6B **182**
Wakehurst M. RH12: Hors 7F **196**
Wakehurst Path GU21: Wok ...1E **74**
Wakely Cl. TN16: B Hil 5E **86**
Walburton Rd. CR8: Pur 9G **63**
Walbury RG12: Brac 3C **32**
Waldby Ct. RH11: Craw 6M **181**
Waldeck Gro. SE27 ....4M **29**
Waldeck Rd. SW14 ....6B **12**
W4 ....2N **11**
Waldeck Ter. *SW14* *6B 12*
(off Waldeck Rd.)
Waldegrave Gdns.
TW1: Twick 3F **24**
Waldegrave Pk. TW1: Twick ...5F **24**
Waldegrave Rd. TW1: Twick ...5F **24**
TW11: Tedd 5F **24**
Waldegrove CR0: Croy 9C **46**
Waldemar Av. SW6 ....4K **13**
Waldemar Rd. SW19 ....6M **27**
Walden Cotts. GU3: Norm 1L **111**
Walden Gdns. CR7: T Hea 2K **45**
Waldens Pk. Rd.
GU21: Wok 3M **73**
Waldens Rd. GU21: Wok 4N **73**
Waldo Pl. CR4: Mit 8C **28**
Waldorf Cl. CR2: S Croy 5M **63**
Waldorf Hgts. GU17: Haw 3J **69**
Waldron Gdns. BR2: Brom 2N **47**
Waldron Hill RG12: Brac 9D **16**
Waldronhyrst
CR2: S Croy 7A **200** (1M **63**)
Waldron Rd. SW18 ....4A **28**
Waldrons, The
CR0: Croy 7A **200** (1M **63**)
RH8: Oxt 9B **106**
Waldron's Path
CR2: S Croy 7B **200** (1N **63**)
Waldy Ri. GU6: Cranl 6N **155**
Waleron Rd. GU51: Fleet 1A **88**
Wales Av. SM5: Cars 2C **62**
Walesbeech RH10: Craw 4E **182**
Waleton Acres
SM6: W'ton 3G **63**
Waley's La. RH5: Ockl 8C **158**
Walford Rd. RH5: Nth H 9H **119**
WALHAM GREEN 4M **13**
Walham Grn. Ct. *SW6* *3N 13*
(off Waterford Rd.)
Walham Gro. SW6 ....3M **13**
Walham Ri. SW19 ....7K **27**
Walham Yd. SW6 ....3M **13**
Walhatch Cl. RH18: F Row ...7H **187**
Walk, The RH8: Tand 2K **125**
SL4: E Wic 1D **4**
TW16: Sunb 8G **22**
Walker Cl. TW12: Hamp 7N **23**
TW14: Felt 1G **22**
Walker Cres. SL3: Lang 1B **6**
Walker Rd. RH10: Craw 5F **182**
Walkerscroft Mead
SE21 ....2N **29**
Walkers Pl. SW15 ....7K **13**
Walker's Ridge
GU15: Camb 2C **70**
Walkfield Dr. KT18: Tat C 4G **81**
Walking Bottom
GU5: P'lake 5D **136**
Wallace Cl. GU3: Worp 9F **92**
TW17: Shep 3E **38**
Wallace Cres. SM5: Cars 2D **62**
Wallace Flds. KT17: Eps 9F **60**
Wallace Sq. CR5: Coul 9H **83**
Wallace Wlk. KT15: Addl 1L **55**
SL4: Eton 1J **5**
Wallace Way GU11: Alde 1L **109**
Wallage La. RH10: Row 3N **183**
Wallbrook Bus. Cen.
TW4: Houn 6J **9**
Wallcroft Cl. RG42: Bin 8K **15**
Walldown Rd.
GU35: White 8A **168**
Walled Gdn., The KT20: Tad ...9J **81**
RH3: Betch 4C **120**
RH14: Loxw 1H **193**
Walled Gdn. Cl. BR3: Beck 3L **47**
Waller La. CR3: Cate 1C **104**
WALL HILL 5G **186**
Wall Hill Rd.
RH19: Ash W, F Row 4F **186**
Wallingford Cl. RG12: Brac ...3C **32**
WALLINGTON 3F **62**
Wallington Cnr. *SM6: W'ton* ...*1F 62*
(off Manor Rd. Nth.)
Wallington Ct. *SM6: W'ton* ...*3F 62*
(off Stanley Pk. Rd.)
WALLINGTON GREEN 1F **62**
Wallington Rd.
GU15: Camb 6E **50**
Wallington Sq. SM6: W'ton 3F **62**
Wallington Station (Rail) 3F **62**
Wallis Ct. RH10: Craw 8D **162**
Wallis Ho. *RH19: E Grin* *9A 166*
(off Orchard Way)
Wallis M. KT22: Leat 9G **78**
Wallis's Cotts. SW2 ....1J **29**
Wallis Way RH13: Hors 4N **197**
WALLISWOOD 9L **157**
Wallis Wood Nature Reserve
..........8M 157
Wallner Way RG40: W'ham ...3D **30**
Wallorton Gdns. SW14 ....7C **12**
Walls Ct. GU16: Frim 6C **70**
Walmer Cl. BR6: Farnb 1M **67**
GU16: Frim 7E **70**
RG45: Crow 2H **49**
Walmer Ct. KT5: Surb 8K **203**
Walnut Cl. GU11: Alde 4M **109**
GU46: Yate 2C **68**
KT18: Eps 2E **80**
SM5: Cars 2D **62**
Walnut Ct. RH13: Hors 7L **197**
Walnut Dr. KT20: K'wood 2K **101**
Walnut Flds. KT17: Ewe 5E **60**
Walnut Gro. SM7: Ban 1J **81**
Walnut Ho. RH2: Reig 5A **122**
Walnut La. RH11: Craw 9N **161**
Walnut M. SM2: Sut 4A **62**
Walnuts, The RH12: Hors 4J **197**
Walnut Tree Av. *CR4: Mit* *2C 44*
(off Dearn Gdns.)
Walnut Tree Cl.
GU1: Guil 2A **202** (3M **113**)
SM7: Ban 8K **61**
SW13 ....4E **12**
Walnut Tree Cl.
TN16: Weste 4M **107**
TW17: Shep 2D **38**
Walnut Tree Cotts.
SW19 ....6K **27**
Walnut Tree Gdns.
GU7: Goda 4H **133**
Walnut Tree Ho. *SW10* *2N 13*
(off Tregunter Rd.)
Walnut Tree La. KT14: Byf 8M **55**
Walnut Tree Pk.
GU1: Guil 2A **202** (3M **113**)
Walnut Tree Pl.
GU23: Send 1F **94**
Walnut Tree Rd. TW5: Hest 2N **9**
TW8: Brent 2L **11**
TW17: Shep 1D **38**
Walpole Av. CR5: Chip 6D **82**
TW9: Kew 5M **11**
Walpole Ct. TW2: Twick 3E **24**
Walpole Cres. TW11: Tedd 6F **24**
Walpole Gdns. TW2: Twick 3E **24**
W4 ....1B **12**
Walpole Ho. *KT8: W Mole* *4A 40*
(off Approach Rd.)
SL4: Eton *2F 4*
(off Eton Wick Rd.)
Walpole M. SW19 ....7B **28**
Walpole Pk. KT13: Weybr 4B **56**
Walpole Pl. TW11: Tedd 6F **24**
Walpole Rd.
CR0: Croy 2D **200** (8A **46**)
KT6: Surb 6L **41**
SL4: O Win 1L **19**
SW19 ....7B **28**
TW2: Twick 3E **24**
TW11: Tedd 6F **24**
Walsham Rd. TW14: Felt 1J **23**
Walsh Av. RG42: Warf 8C **16**
Walsh Cres. CR0: N Add 8A **66**
Walsingham Gdns.
KT19: Ewe 1D **60**
Walsingham Lodge
SW13 ....4F **12**
Walsingham Mans.
SW6 ....*3N 13*
(off Fulham Rd.)
Walsingham Rd.
CR0: N Add 6M **65**
CR4: Mit 4D **44**
Walstead Ct. RH10: Craw 4B **182**
Walstead Ho. RH10: Craw 4B **182**
Walters Mead KT21: A'tead 4L **79**
Walters Rd. SE25 ....3B **46**
Walter St.
KT2: K Tham 2J **203** (9L **25**)
Waltham Av. GU2: Guil 8L **93**
Waltham Cl. GU47: Owls 6J **49**
Waltham Rd. CR3: Cate 9E **84**
SM5: Cars 6B **44**
Walton & Hersham FC 8H 39
Walton Av. KT3: N Mal 3E **42**
SM3: Chea 9L **43**
Walton Bri. KT12: Wal T 6F **38**
TW17: Shep 6F **38**
Walton Bri. Rd.
TW17: Shep 6F **38**
Walton Cl. GU51: Fleet 5A **88**
Walton Ct. CR2: S Croy 8C **200**
GU21: Wok 3C **74**
Walton Dr. RH13: Hors 4A **198**
SL5: Asc 9K **17**
Walton Gdns. TW13: Felt 5G **22**
Walton Grn. CR0: N Add 5L **65**
WALTON HEATH 5E **100**
Walton Heath RH10: Craw ...1H **183**
Walton Heath Golf Course
..........4G 101
Walton La. KT13: Weybr 8C **38**
TW17: Shep 6E **38**
WALTON-ON-THAMES 7H **39**
Walton-on-Thames Station (Rail)
..........1H **57**
WALTON ON THE HILL 2F **100**
Walton Pk. KT12: Wal T 8L **39**
Walton Pk. La. KT12: Wal T ...8L **39**
Walton Rd. GU21: Wok 3B **74**
KT8: W Mole, E Mol 3N **39**
KT12: Wal T 4K **39**
KT18: Eps D 4E **80**
KT18: Eps D, Head 8B **80**
Walton Screen Cinema 7H 39
Walton St. KT20: Wal H 2F **100**
Walton Ter. GU21: Wok 2D **74**
Walton Way CR4: Mit 3G **44**
WANBOROUGH 6N **111**
Wanborough Bus. Cen.
GU3: Flex 4B **112**
WANBOROUGH COMMON ...9C **112**
Wanborough Dr.
SW15 ....2G **26**
Wanborough Hill
GU3: Wan 6N **111**
Wanborough La.
GU6: Cranl 6B **156**
Wanborough Station (Rail)
..........3N **111**
Wandle Bank CR0: Bedd 9J **45**
SW19 ....8B **28**
Wandle Cl. GU12: Ash 3E **110**
RH10: Craw 4G **182**
Wandle Ct. CR0: Bedd 9J **45**
KT19: Ewe 1B **60**
Wandle Ct. Gdns.
CR0: Bedd 9J **45**
Wandle Industrial Mus.
(within The Vestry Hall Annexe)
..........2D 44
Wandle Meadow Nature Pk.
..........6A 28
Wandle Park Stop (CT) 8L **45**
Wandle Pk. Trad. Est., The
CR0: Croy 7M **45**
Wandle Recreation Cen. 9N 13
Wandle Rd. CR0: Bedd 9J **45**
CR0: Croy 5C **200** (9N **45**)
SM4: Mord 3A **44**
SM6: W'ton 9F **44**
SW17 ....3C **28**
Wandle Side CR0: Wad 9K **45**
SM6: W'ton 9F **44**
Wandle Technology Pk.
CR4: Mit 6D **44**
Wandle Trad. Est. CR4: Mit 6D **44**
Wandle Way CR4: Mit 4D **44**
SW18 ....2N **27**
Wandon Rd. SW6 ....3N **13**
(not continuous)
Wandsdown Pl. SW6 ....3N **13**
WANDSWORTH 8N **13**
Wandsworth Bri. SW6 ....6N **13**
Wandsworth Bri. Rd.
SW6 ....4N **13**
WANDSWORTH COMMON 2D **28**
Wandsworth Common Station (Rail)
..........2D **28**
WANDSWORTH GYRATORY
..........8N **13**
Wandsworth High St.
SW18 ....8M **13**
Wandsworth Mus. 8N 13
Wandsworth Plain
SW18 ....8N **13**
Wandsworth Town Station (Rail)
..........7N **13**
Wanmer Ct. *RH2: Reig* *2M 121*
(off Birkheads Rd.)
Wansdyke Cl. GU16: Frim 6D **70**
Wansford Grn. GU21: Wok 4J **73**
Wanstraw Gro. RG12: Brac 6C **32**
Wantage Cl. RG12: Brac 4C **32**
RH10: Craw 6G **182**
Wantage Rd. GU47: C Tow 7J **49**
Waplings, The
KT20: Wal H 2G **100**
Wapses Lodge CR3: Wold 7E **84**
WAPSES LODGE RDBT. 7E **84**
Wapshott Rd. TW18: Stain 7G **20**
Warbank Cl. CR0: N Add 6A **66**
Warbank Cres. CR0: N Add 6A **66**
Warbank La. KT2: K Tham 8E **26**
Warbeck Ho. *KT13: Weybr* *2E 56*
(off Queens Rd.)
Warbler's Grn. KT11: Cob 1N **77**
Warbleton Ho.
RH11: Craw *6L 181*
(off Salvington Rd.)
Warboys App. KT2: K Tham 7A **26**
Warboys Rd. KT2: K Tham 7A **26**
Warburton Cl.
RH19: E Grin 9C **166**
Warburton Rd. TW2: Whitt 2B **24**
Warbury La. GU21: Knap 2E **72**
War Coppice Rd. CR3: Cate ...5A **104**
Ward Cl. CR2: S Croy 3B **64**
RG40: W'ham 9C **14**
Wardens Fld. Cl.
BR6: Chels 3N **67**
Ward La. CR6: Warl 3F **84**
Wardle Cl. GU19: Bag 4J **51**
Wardley St. SW18 ....1N **27**
Wardo Av. SW6 ....4K **13**
Ward Rd. SW19 ....9A **28**
Wardrobe, The *TW9: Rich* *8K 11*
(off Old Palace Rd.)
Ward Royal SL4: W'sor 4F **4**
Ward Royal Pde. *SL4: W'sor* *4F 4*
(off Alma Rd.)
Ward's Pl. TW20: Egh 7E **20**
Wards Stone Pk.
RG12: Brac 6C **32**
Ward St.
GU1: Guil 5D **202** (4N **113**)
Ware Ct. SM1: Sut 1L **61**
Wareham Cl. TW3: Houn 7B **10**
Wareham Rd. RG12: Brac 4D **32**
Warehouse Theatre
..........2E 200 (8A 46)
Warenne Rd. KT22: Fetc 9C **78**
WARFIELD 4C **16**
WARFIELD PARK 8E **16**
Warfield Rd. RG12: Brac 7A **16**
RG42: Brac 7A **16**
TW12: Hamp 9B **24**
TW14: Felt 1F **22**
Warfield St. RG42: Warf 6A **16**
Wargrove Dr. GU47: C Tow 7J **49**
Warham Rd.
CR2: S Croy 8A **200** (2M **63**)
Waring St. SE27 ....5N **29**
Warkworth Gdns. TW7: Isle 3G **10**
WARLINGHAM 5G **84**
Warlingham Rd.
CR7: T Hea 3M **45**
Warltersville Way
RH6: Horl 1G **162**

Warminster Gdns.—Wellesley Dr.

Warminster Gdns. SE25 1D 46
Warminster Rd. SE25 1C 46
Warminster Sq. SE25 1D 46
Warminster Way CR4: Mit 9F 28
Warner Av. SM3: Chea 8K 43
Warner Cl. RH10: Craw 7G 182
TW12: Hamp 6N 23
UB3: Harl 3E 8
Warner Ct. GU47: C Tow 8K 49
Warners La. GU5: Alb 1N 135
KT2: K Tham 5K 25
Warnford Ho. *SW15* 9D 12 (off Tunworth Cres.)
WARNHAM 9F 178
Warnham Ct. RH12: Warn 1F 196
Warnham Ct. M. RH12: Warn 1F 196
Warnham Ct. Rd. SM5: Cars 4D 62
Warnham Ho. *SW2* 1K 29 (off Up. Tulse Hill)
Warnham Mnr. RH12: Warn 1C 196
Warnham Nature Reserve 3H 197
Warnham Pk. 2F 196
Warnham Rd. RH10: Craw 5E 182
RH12: Bro H 4D 196
RH12: Warn, Hors 3H 197
Warnham Station (Rail) 9J 179
Warramill Rd. GU7: Goda 6K 133
Warre Ho. *SL4: Eton* 1F 4 (off Common La.)
WARREN, THE
GU6 1C 156
RG12 3D 32
Warren, The GU9: H End 4K 109
GU11: Alde 3L 109
GU30: Pass 9D 168
KT4: W Pk 1C 60
KT20: K'wood 1K 101
KT21: A'tead 6L 79
KT22: Oxs 8C 58
KT24: E Hor 8G 96
RG12: Brac 3D 32
SM5: Cars 5B 62
TW5: Hest 3N 9
Warren Av. BR6: Chels 2N 67
CR2: Sels 4G 64
SM2: Chea 6L 61
TW10: Rich 7A 12
Warren Cl. GU47: Sandh 7F 48
GU52: Fleet 6C 88
KT10: Esh 1B 58
RH19: Fel 7H 165
SE21 1N 29
WARREN CORNER 5C 108
Warren Cnr. GU10: Ews 5B 108
Warren Cotts. RH17: Hand 8N 199
Warren Ct. CR0: Croy 7B 46
KT13: Weybr 2B 56
Warren Cutting KT2: K Tham 8C 26
Warren Down RG42: Brac 9K 15
Warren Dr. KT20: K'wood 9L 81
RH11: Craw 2M 181
Warren Dr. Nth. KT5: Surb 7A 42
Warren Dr. Sth. KT5: Surb 7B 42
Warreners La. KT13: Weybr 4E 56
Warren Farm Mobile Home Pk. GU22: Pyr 6K 75
Warren Footpath TW1: Twick 2J 25
Warren Hill KT18: Eps 3C 80
Warren Ho. Rd. RG40: W'ham 9B 14
Warrenhyrst GU1: Guil 4C 114
Warren La. GU5: Alb 8L 115
GU22: Pyr 5J 75
KT22: Oxs 7C 58
RH8: Oxt 3C 126
Warren Lodge KT20: K'wood 2K 101
Warren Lodge Dr. KT20: K'wood 2K 101
Warren Mead SM7: Ban 2H 81
Warrenne Hgts. RH1: Red 5B 122
Warrenne Rd. RH3: Brock 5B 120
Warrenne Way RH2: Reig 3M 121
Warren Pk. CR6: Warl 5G 84
GU8: Thur 5K 151
KT2: K Tham 7B 26
KT20: Box H 9B 100
Warren Pk. Rd. SM1: Sut 3B 62
Warren Ri. GU16: Frim 4C 70
KT3: N Mal 9C 26
Warren Rd. BR6: Chels 2N 67
CR0: Croy 7B 46
CR8: Pur 8M 63
GU1: Guil 4B 114
GU7: Goda 4H 133
KT2: K Tham 7B 26
KT15: N Haw 6J 55
RH2: Reig 2N 121
SM7: Ban 1H 81
SW19 7C 28
TW2: Whitt 9C 10
TW15: A'ford 8F 22
Warren Row SL5: Asc 1H 33
Warren Way KT13: Weybr 2D 56
Warrington Cl. RH11: Craw 7K 181
Warrington Ct. CR0: Wad 5A 200
Warrington M. GU11: Alde 4K 109
Warrington Rd. CR0: Wad 5A 200 (9M 45)
TW10: Rich 8K 11
Warrington Spur SL4: O Win 1L 19
Warsop Trad. Est. TN8: Eden 3M 147
Warwark Ct. KT6: Surb 8L 41
Warwick RG12: Brac 5C 32
W14 1L 13 (off Kensington Village)
Warwick Av. TW18: Stain 7L 21
TW20: Egh 9E 20
Warwick Cl. GU11: Alde 4A 110
GU15: Camb 3F 70
RH5: Holm 4H 139
TW12: Hamp 8C 24
Warwick Ct. BR2: Brom 1N 47
KT13: Weybr 2B 56
SL4: W'sor 5F 4 (off Alma Rd.)
Warwick Deeping KT16: Otter 2E 54
Warwick Dr. SW15 6G 12
Warwick Gdns. CR7: T Hea 2L 45
KT7: T Dit 4F 40
KT21: A'tead 4J 79
Warwick Gro. KT5: Surb 6M 41
Warwick Ho. KT2: K Tham 1K 203
Warwick La. GU21: Wok 6K 73
Warwick Lodge TW2: Twick 4B 24
Warwick Pl. KT7: T Dit 5G 40
Warwick Quad. RH1: Red 2E 122
Warwick Rd. CR5: Coul 1G 83
CR7: T Hea 2L 45
GU12: A Va 5E 90
KT1: H Wic 9J 25
KT3: N Mal 2B 42
KT7: T Dit 4F 40
RH1: Red 2D 122
RH5: Holm 5J 139
SE20 2E 46
SM1: Sut 1A 62
SW5 1M 13
TW2: Twick 2E 24
TW4: Houn 6J 9
TW15: A'ford 6N 21
Warwicks Bench GU1: Guil 7D 202 (5N 113)
Warwick's Bench La. GU1: Guil 6B 114
Warwick's Bench Rd. GU1: Guil 8E 202 (6A 114)
Warwick Vs. TW20: Egh 9E 20
WARWICK WOLD 7L 103
Warwick Wold Rd. RH1: Mers 7L 103
Wasdale Cl. GU47: Owls 5J 49
Washford Cl. GU35: Bor 5A 168
Washford La. GU35: Lind 4A 168
Washington Cl. RH2: Reig 1M 121
Washington Ct. SL4: W'sor 6B 4
Washington Rd. KT1: K Tham 4M 203 (1N 41)
KT4: W Pk 8G 42
RH11: Craw 6K 181
SW13 3F 12
Washpond La. CR6: Warl 5M 85
WASP GREEN 3N 143
Wasp Grn. La. RH1: Out 3N 143
Wassand Cl. RH10: Craw 3E 182
Watchetts Dr. GU15: Camb 4A 70
Watchetts Lake Cl. GU15: Camb 3B 70
Watchetts Rd. GU15: Camb 2N 69
Watchfield Ct. W4 1B 12
Watchmoor Point GU15: Camb 2M 69
Watchmoor Rd. GU15: Camb 3M 69
Watchmoor Trade Cen. GU15: Camb 2M 69
Watcombe Cotts. TW9: Kew 2N 11
Watcombe Pl. SE25 4E 46
Watcombe Rd. SE25 4E 46
Waterbourne Way CR8: Ken 1A 84
Watercress Pl. RH13: Hors 5M 197
Watercress Way GU21: Wok 4L 73
Waterden Cl. GU1: Guil 4B 114
Waterden Rd. GU1: Guil 4F 202 (4A 114)
Waterer Gdns. KT20: Tad 5J 81
Waterer Ri. SM6: W'ton 3H 63
Waterers Ri. GU21: Knap 4G 72
Waterfall Cl. GU25: V Wat 2K 35
Waterfall Cotts. SW19 7B 28
Waterfall Rd. SW19 7B 28
Waterfall Ter. SW17 7C 28
Waterfield KT20: Tad 7G 81 (Campion Dr.)
KT20: Tad 7G 81 (Watermead)
Waterfield Cl. RH13: Hors 5L 197
Waterfield Dr. CR6: Warl 6F 84
KT18: Tat C 6G 81
KT20: Tad 6G 81
Waterfield Gdns. RH11: Craw 5K 181
SE25 3A 46
Waterfield Grn. KT20: Tad 7G 81
Waterfields KT22: Leat 6H 79
Waterford Cl. KT11: Cob 7M 57
Waterford Rd. SW6 3N 13 (not continuous)
Waterford Way RG40: W'ham 2B 30
Waterfront Bus. Pk. GU51: Fleet 2C 88
Watergardens, The KT2: K Tham 7B 26
Waterham Rd. RG12: Brac 5N 31
Waterhouse Cl. W6 1J 13
Waterhouse La. CR8: Ken 6N 83
KT20: K'wood 8K 81
RH1: Blet 1C 124
Waterhouse Mead GU47: C Tow 8J 49
Waterlakes TN8: Eden 3L 147
Waterlands La. RH12: Rowh 9M 177
Water La. GU5: Alb 6K 115
GU8: Ent G 7D 152
GU9: Farnh 8K 109
GU14: Farnb 7M 69
GU24: Bis 6B 72
GU24: Chob 5E 52
KT1: K Tham 2H 203 (9K 25)
KT11: Cob 2M 77
KT23: Book 3L 97
RH1: Blet 8M 103
RH5: A Ham 3J 137
RH8: Limp 4C 106
RH9: S Gods 7G 124
TN8: Eden 4F 146
TN16: Weste 5M 107
TW1: Twick 2G 25
TW9: Rich 8K 11
Water Lea RH10: Craw 4E 182
Waterloo Cl. GU15: Camb 8F 50
RG40: W'ham 3D 30
TW14: Felt 2G 23
Waterloo Cres. RG40: W'ham 3D 30
WATERLOO PARK 1N 109
Waterloo Pl. RG45: Crow 3G 49
SM5: Cars 9D 44 (off Wrythe La.)
TW9: Kew 2N 11
TW9: Rich 7L 11
Waterloo Rd. GU12: Alde 3A 110
KT19: Eps 5K 201 (8C 60)
RG40: W'ham 3D 30
RG45: Crow 3F 48
SM1: Sut 2B 62
Waterloo Ter. *KT13: Weybr* 1C 56 (off Baker St.)
Waterlow Rd. RH2: Reig 4A 122
Waterman Cl. GU35: Bor 7A 168
Watermans Art Cen., Cinema & Theatre 2L 11
Watermans Bus. Pk. TW18: Stain 5G 20
Watermans Cl. KT2: K Tham 8L 25
Watermans Ct. *TW8: Brent* 2K 11 (off High St.)
Waterman St. SW15 6J 13
Water Mead CR5: Chip 4D 82
Watermead GU21: Wok 3J 73
KT20: Tad 8G 81
TW14: Felt 2F 22
Watermead La. SM5: Cars 6D 44
Watermill Cl. TW10: Ham 4J 25
Water Mill Ho. TW13: Hanw 3A 24
Watermill Way SW19 9A 28
TW13: Hanw 3N 23
Waterperry La. GU24: Chob 6J 53
Water Rede GU52: C Cro 1A 108
Waters Dr. TW18: Stain 4H 21
Water's Edge *SW6* 4H 13 (off Palemead Cl.)
Watersedge KT19: Ewe 1B 60
WATERSIDE 4A 146
Waterside KT20: Tad 7G 81
RH6: Horl 6E 142
RH19: E Grin 9D 166
UB7: Harm 3L 7
Waterside Av. *BR3: Beck* 4M 47 (off Adamson Way)
Waterside Bus. Cen. TW7: Isle 7H 11
Waterside Cen., The 1M 113
Waterside Cl. GU7: Goda 6K 133
GU35: Bor 5A 168
KT6: Surb 8L 41
RH11: Craw 5K 181
Waterside Ct. GU51: Fleet 2C 88
SM5: Cars 9E 44 (off Millpond Pl.)
Waterside Dr. KT12: Wal T 4H 39
Waterside La. GU7: Goda 8F 132
Waterside M. GU1: Guil 1M 113
GU51: Fleet 2C 88
Waterside Pk. Ind. Est. RG12: Brac 9L 15 (not continuous)
Waterside Rd. GU1: Guil 9N 93
Waterside Trad. Est. KT15: Addl 1N 55
Waterside Way GU21: Wok 5L 73
SW17 5A 28
Waterslade RH1: Red 3C 122
Watersmeet Cl. GU4: B'ham 7C 94
Waters Pl. SW15 5H 13
Watersplash Cl. KT1: K Tham 5J 203 (2L 41)
Watersplash La. RG42: Warf 7N 15
SL5: Asc 9A 18
TW5: C'ford 1J 9
UB3: Harl 1H 9
Watersplash Rd. TW17: Shep 4B 38
Waters Rd. KT1: K Tham 1A 42
Waters Sq. KT1: K Tham 2A 42
Water Twr. Hill CR0: Croy 6E 200 (1A 64)
Water Vw. RH6: Horl 8H 143
Waterway Rd. KT22: Leat 9G 78
Waterworks Cl. RH18: F Row 5H 187
Waterworks Yd. *CR0: Croy* 4B 200 (off Surrey St.)
Watery La. GU24: Chob 6G 52
KT16: Lyne 6F 36
SW20 1L 43
UB3: Harl 1F 8
Wates Way CR4: Mit 5D 44
Watford Cl. GU1: Guil 3B 114
Wathen Rd. RH4: Dork 1L 201 (4H 119)
Watlings Cl. CR0: Croy 5H 47
Watney Cl. CR8: Pur 9K 63
Watney Cotts. SW14 6B 12
Watney Rd. SW14 6B 12
Watney's Rd. CR4: Mit 4H 45
Watson Av. SM3: Chea 8K 43
Watson Cl. RH10: Craw 5G 182
SW19 7C 28
Watson Ho. RH2: Reig 2M 121
Watson Rd. RH4: Westc 6C 118
Wattendon Rd. CR8: Ken 3M 83
Wattlehurst Farm 2H 179
Watt's Cl. KT20: Tad 9J 81
Watts Farm Pde. *GU24: Chob* 6J 53 (off Barnmead)
Watts Gallery, The 8E 112
Watts La. KT20: Tad 9J 81
TW11: Tedd 6G 24
Watts Lea GU21: Wok 2K 73
Watt's Mead KT20: Tad 9J 81
Watts Rd. GU14: Cove 9L 69
KT7: T Dit 6G 40
Wavel Ct. CR0: Croy 8E 200
Wavell-Cody Community Campus (Leisure Cen.) 6N 89
Wavendene Av. TW20: Egh 8D 20
Wavendon Av. W4 1C 12
Waveney Wlk. RH10: Craw 5F 182
Waverleigh Rd. GU6: Cranl 9N 155
Waverley RG12: Brac 4K 31
Waverley Av. CR8: Ken 3B 84
GU51: Fleet 2A 88
KT5: Surb 5A 42
SM1: Sut 8N 43
TW2: Whitt 2N 23
Waverley Cl. GU9: Farnh 1J 129
GU15: Camb 2D 70
KT8: W Mole 4A 40
Waverley Cotts. GU10: Til 3B 130
Waverley Ct. GU22: Wok 5A 74
RH12: Hors 6H 197
Waverley Dr. GU12: A Va 7E 90
GU15: Camb 1C 70
GU25: V Wat 2K 35
KT16: Chert 9F 36
Waverley Gdns. GU12: A Va 7E 90
Waverley Hgts. GU9: Farnh 2K 129
Waverley La. GU9: Farnh 1J 129
GU10: Farnh, Til 1J 129
Waverley Pl. KT22: Leat 9H 79
Waverley Rd. GU14: Farnb 2B 90
GU19: Bag 4J 51
KT11: Sto D, Oxs 1B 78
KT13: Weybr 2B 56
KT17: Ewe 2G 60
KT22: Oxs 1B 78
SE25 2E 46
Waverley Way SM5: Cars 3C 62
Waverton Rd. SW18 1A 28
Wavertree Ct. *RH6: Horl* 9D 142 (off Massetts Rd.)
SW2 2J 29
Wavertree Rd. SW2 2K 29
Way, The RH2: Reig 2B 122
Waye Av. TW5: C'ford 4H 9
Wayland Cl. RG12: Brac 3D 32
Waylands TW19: Wray 9A 6
Waylands Mead BR3: Beck 1L 47
Waylett Pl. SE27 4M 29
Wayman Rd. GU14: Cove 6K 69
Wayneflete Pl. KT10: Esh 9A 40
Wayneflete Twr. Av. KT10: Esh 9A 40
Waynflete *SL4: Eton* 2F 4 (off Common La.)
Waynflete Av. CR0: Wad 5A 200 (9M 45)
Waynflete Ho. *KT10: Esh* 1B 58 (off High St.)
Waynflete La. GU9: Farnh 1E 128
Waynflete St. SW18 3A 28
Ways End GU15: Camb 2C 70
Wayside CR0: N Add 3L 65
RH5: Cap 4K 159
RH11: Ifi 5K 181
SW14 8B 12
Wayside Cotts. GU10: Churt 7J 149
RH5: H Mary 5K 137
RH12: Rudg 5G 177
Wayside Ct. GU21: Wok 3H 73
TW1: Twick 9J 11
Wayside Dr. TN8: Eden 9M 127
Weald, The RH19: E Grin 6B 166
Weald Cl. GU4: Chil 9A 114
RH13: Hors 8L 197
Weald Dr. RH10: Craw 4E 182
Wealden Ho. RH19: E Grin 3E 186
Wealdon Ct. GU2: Guil 3J 113
Wealdstone Rd. SM3: Sut 8L 43
Weald Way CR3: Cate 6B 104
RH2: Reig 7A 122
Weall Cl. CR8: Pur 8K 63
Weare St. RH5: Cap, Ockl 5G 158
RH5: Ockl 2C 178
Weasdale Ct. GU21: Wok 3J 73
Weatherall Cl. KT15: Addl 2K 55
WEATHERHILL 8L 143
Weatherhill Cl. RH6: Horl 8K 143
Weatherhill Rd. RH6: Horl, Smal 8K 143
Weather Way RG12: Brac 1A 32
Weaver Cl. CR0: Croy 1C 64
RH11: Ifi 4K 181
Weaver Moss GU47: Sandh 8G 49
Weavers Cl. TW7: Isle 7E 10
Weavers Gdns. GU9: Farnh 4E 128
Weavers Ter. *SW6* 2M 13 (off Micklethwaite Rd.)
Weavers Yd. GU9: Farnh 1G 129
Weaver Wlk. SE27 5N 29
Webb Cl. GU19: Bag 6J 51
RG42: Bin 8K 15
RH11: Craw 8N 181
Webb Ct. RG40: W'ham 9D 14
Webb Ho. TW13: Hanw 4M 23
Webb Rd. GU8: Mil, Wit 3N 151
Webster Cl. KT22: Oxs 1B 78
Webster Ct. *GU5: Braml* 4B 134 (off Horsham Rd.)
Websters Cl. GU22: Wok 7L 73
Weddell Rd. RH10: Craw 6D 182
Wedgwood Pl. KT11: Cob 9H 57
Wedgwoods TN16: Tats 8E 86
Wedgwood Way SE19 8N 29
Weighton M. SE20 1E 46
Weighton Rd. SE20 1E 46
Weihurst Ct. SM1: Sut 2C 62
Weihurst Gdns. SM1: Sut 2B 62
Weimar St. SW15 6K 13
Weint, The SL3: Coln 3E 6
Weir Av. GU14: Cove 2M 89
Weirbrook RH10: Craw 6E 182
Weir Cl. GU14: Cove 2M 89
Weir Ct. KT13: Weybr 8C 38
Weir Pl. TW18: Stain 9G 21
Weir Rd. KT12: Wal T 5H 39
KT16: Chert 6K 37
SW12 1G 28
SW19 4N 27
WEIR WOOD 7D 186
Weir Wood Reservoir 7B 186
Weiss Rd. SW15 6J 13
Welbeck RG12: Brac 4K 31
Welbeck Cl. GU14: Cove 2L 89
KT3: N Mal 4E 42
KT17: Ewe 4F 60
Welbeck Rd. SM1: Sut 8B 44
SM5: Cars 8B 44
Welbeck Wlk. SM5: Cars 7B 44
Welcomes Cotts. CR3: Wold 1K 105
Welcomes Rd. CR8: Ken 4A 84
Welcomes Ter. CR3: Ken 3C 84
Weldon Cl. GU52: C Cro 8C 88
Weldon Dr. KT8: W Mole 3N 39
Weldon Way RH1: Mers 7H 103
Welford Pl. SW19 5K 27
Welham Rd. SW16 7F 28
SW17 6E 28
Welhouse Rd. SM5: Cars 7C 44
Welland Cl. SL3: Lang 2D 6
Wellbrook Rd. BR6: Farnb 1J 67
Wellburn Cl. GU47: Sandh 8G 49
Well Cl. GU15: Camb 2N 69
GU21: Wok 4M 73
SW16 5K 29
Weller Cl. RH10: Wor 4H 183
Weller Dr. GU15: Camb 3A 70
Weller Pl. BR6: Dow 7J 67
Wellers Cl. TN16: Weste 5L 107
Wellers Ct. GU5: Shere 8B 116
Weller's La. RG42: Warf 3A 16
Wellesford Cl. SM7: Ban 4L 81
Wellesley Cl. GU12: A Va 6D 90
GU19: Bag 4G 51
Wellesley Ct. RG45: Crow 3E 48
SM3: Sut 7K 43
Wellesley Ct. Rd. CR0: Croy 3D 200 (8A 46)
Wellesley Cres. TW2: Twick 3E 24
Wellesley Dr. RG45: Crow 2D 48

296 A-Z Surrey

Wellesley Gdn.—W. Norwood Crematorium

Wellesley Gdn.
GU9: U Hal 5H 109
Wellesley Ga.
GU12: Alde 3N 109
Wellesley Gro.
CR0: Croy 3D 200 (8A 46)
Wellesley Ho. SL4: W'sor 4E 4
(off Vansittart Rd.)
Wellesley Mans. W14 1L 13
(off Edith Vs.)
Wellesley Pde. TW2: Twick 4E 24
Wellesley Pas.
CR0: Croy 2C 200 (8N 45)
Wellesley Rd.
CR0: Croy 1C 200 (7N 45)
GU10: Rush 4N 149
GU11: Alde 1J 109
(not continuous)
GU12: A Va 6D 90
(not continuous)
SM2: Sut 3A 62
(not continuous)
TW2: Twick 4D 24
W4 1N 11
Wellesley Road Stop (CT) 2D 200 (8A 46)
Welley Av. TW19: Wray 7A 6
Welley Rd. SL3: Hort 9A 6
TW19: Wray 9A 6
Well Farm Rd. CR6: Warl 6D 84
Wellfield RH19: E Grin 2E 186
Wellfield Gdns. SM5: Cars 5C 62
Wellfield Rd. SW16 5J 29
Wellfield Wlk. SW16 6K 29
(not continuous)
Well Ho. SM7: Ban 2N 81
Wellhouse La. RH3: Betch 7B 120
Wellhouse Rd. BR3: Beck 3K 47
Wellingham Way
RH12: Fay 7H 181
Wellington Av.
GU11: Alde 2K 109
GU25: V Wat 4L 35
GU51: Fleet 3C 88
KT4: W Pk 9H 43
TW3: Houn 8A 10
Wellington Bus. Pk.
RG45: Crow 3D 48
Wellington Cen., The
GU11: Alde 2M 109
Wellington Cl.
GU47: Sandh 7H 49
KT12: Wal T 7G 39
RH10: Craw 9J 163
Wellington College Sports Club, The 3E 48
Wellington Cotts.
KT24: E Hor 7F 96
Wellington Ct. SW6 4N 13
(off Maltings Pl.)
TW12: Tedd 6D 24
TW15: A'ford 6N 21
TW19: Stan 1N 21
Wellington Cres.
KT3: N Mal 2B 42
Wellington Dr. CR8: Pur 6K 63
RG12: Brac 4B 32
Wellington Gdns.
GU11: Alde 3L 109
TW2: Twick 5D 24
Wellingtonia Av.
GU15: Camb 1H 71
RG45: Crow 3A 48
Wellingtonia Ho.
KT15: Addl 2J 55
Wellingtonia Pl.
RH2: Reig 2M 121
Wellingtonia Rdbt.
RG45: Crow 3D 48
Wellingtonias RG42: Warf 8E 16
Wellingtonia Way
TN8: Eden 1L 147
Wellington La. GU9: H End 5J 109
Wellington Lodge
SL4: Wink 3M 17
Wellington Mans. W14 2L 13
(off Queen's Club Mans.)
Wellington M. SW16 4H 29
Wellington Monument 1K 109
Wellington Pl. GU12: A Va 9D 90
KT11: Cob 8A 58
Wellington Rd. CR0: Croy 6M 45
CR3: Cate 9N 83
GU47: Sandh 7G 48
RG40: W'ham 2A 30
RG45: Crow 3H 49
RH12: Hors 6K 197
SW19 3M 27
TW2: Twick 6D 24
TW12: H Hill 6D 24
TW14: Felt 8F 8
TW15: A'ford 6N 21
Wellington Rd. Nth.
TW4: Houn 6N 9
Wellington Rd. Sth.
TW4: Houn 7N 9
Wellington Rdbt.
GU11: Alde 2K 109
Wellington St. GU11: Alde 2M 109
Wellington Ter. GU21: Knap 5H 73
GU47: Sandh 7H 49
Wellington Town Rd.
RH19: E Grin 8N 165
Wellington Way
KT13: Weybr 6A 56
RH6: Horl 6D 142
Well La. GU8: Worm 1A 172
GU21: Wok 4M 73
GU27: Hasl 2H 189
SW14 8B 12
Wellow Wlk. SM5: Cars 7B 44
Well Path GU21: Wok 4M 73
WELLS, THE 1N 79
Wells Cl. CR2: S Croy 2B 64
KT23: Book 2C 98
RH12: Hors 6F 196
SL4: W'sor 4D 4
Wells Cotts. GU9: Farnh 4F 128
Wells Ct. BR2: Brom 1N 47
Wells Ho. KT18: Eps 1N 79
Wellside Gdns. SW14 7B 12
Wells La. GU3: Norm 9N 91
SL5: Asc 2M 33
Wells Lea RH19: E Grin 7N 165
Wells Mdw. RH19: E Grin 7N 165
Wells Pl. RH1: Mers 8F 102
SW18 1A 28
TN16: Weste 5L 107
Wells Pl. Ind. Est.
RH1: Mers 7F 102
Wells Rd. GU4: Guil 9E 94
KT18: Eps 1N 79
RH10: Craw 7C 182
Wellswood SL5: Asc 2M 33
Well Way KT18: Eps 2N 79
Wellwood Cl. CR5: Coul 1J 83
RH13: Hors 4A 198
Wellwynds Rd. GU6: Cranl 8N 155
Weltje Rd. W6 1F 12
Welwyn Av. TW14: Felt 9G 8
Welwyn Cl. RH11: Craw 7K 181
Wembley Rd. TW12: Hamp 9A 24
Wembury Pk. RH7: Newc 1H 165
Wend, The CR5: Coul 1H 83
Wendela Cl. GU22: Wok 5B 74
Wenderholme CR2: S Croy 8E 200
Wendley Dr. KT15: N Haw 6H 55
Wendling Rd. SM1: Sut 7B 44
Wendover Dr. GU16: Frim 3G 70
KT3: N Mal 5E 42
Wendover Pl. TW18: Stain 6F 20
Wendover Rd. TW18: Stain 6E 20
Wendron Cl. GU21: Wok 5K 73
Wendy Cres. GU2: Guil 1K 113
Wenlock Cl. RH11: Craw 5M 181
Wenlock Edge RH4: Dork 7J 119
Wensleydale RH11: Craw 6A 182
Wensleydale Dr.
GU15: Camb 1H 71
Wensleydale Gdns.
TW12: Hamp 8B 24
Wensleydale Pas.
TW12: Hamp 9A 24
Wensleydale Rd.
TW12: Hamp 7A 24
Wensley Dr. GU51: Fleet 2B 88
WENTWORTH 4H 35
Wentworth Av. SL5: Asc 1G 33
Wentworth Cl. BR6: Farnb 2N 67
GU9: Weybo 6L 109
GU12: A Va 6E 90
GU23: Rip 8K 75
GU46: Yate 1C 68
KT6: Surb 8K 41
RG45: Crow 1E 48
SM4: Mord 6M 43
TW15: A'ford 5C 22
Wentworth Ct. SW18 9N 13
(off Garratt La.)
TW2: Twick 4E 24
W6 2K 13
(off Paynes Wlk.)
Wentworth Cres.
GU12: A Va 7E 90
(not continuous)
Wentworth Dene
KT13: Weybr 2C 56
Wentworth Dr. GU25: V Wat 3J 35
RH10: Craw 2H 183
Wentworth Golf Course
(East Course) 4K 35
Wentworth Golf Course
(West Course) 4K 35
Wentworth Ho. KT15: Addl 1K 55
Wentworth Pl. GU15: Camb 2M 69
(off Vale Rd.)
Wentworth Rd. CR0: Croy 6L 45
UB2: S'hall 1L 9
Wentworth Tennis &
Health Club, The 4K 35
Wentworth Way CR2: Sande 1D 84
SL5: Asc 1G 33
Werndee Rd. SE25 3D 46
Werter Rd. SW15 7K 13
Wesco Ct. GU21: Wok 3C 74
Wescott Rd. RG40: W'ham 2C 30
Wesley Av. TW3: Houn 5M 9
Wesley Cl. RH2: Reig 4L 121
RH6: Horl 6E 142
RH11: Craw 6K 181
Wesley Dr. TW20: Egh 7C 20
Wesley Pl. SL4: Wink 3M 17
Wessels KT20: Tad 8J 81
Wessex Av. SW19 2M 43
Wessex Cl. KT1: K Tham 9A 26
KT7: T Dit 8F 40
Wessex Ct. TW19: Stan 9N 7
Wessex Pl. GU9: Farnh 2H 129
West Acres KT10: Esh 4N 57
West Av. GU9: H End 6J 109
KT12: Whit V 6F 56
RH1: Red 9E 122
RH10: Craw 1E 182
SM6: W'ton 2J 63
West Bank
RH4: Dork 4G 201 (6F 118)
Westbank Rd. TW12: H Hill 7C 24
WEST BARNES 4G 42
W. Barnes La. KT3: N Mal 3G 43
SW20: N Mal 2G 42
WEST BEDFONT 9A 8
WESTBOROUGH 2J 113
Westbourne Av. SM3: Chea 8K 43
Westbourne Ho. TW5: Hest 2A 10
Westbourne Rd. CR0: Croy 5C 46
GU47: C Tow 8K 49
TW13: Felt 4G 22
TW18: Stain 8K 21
West Brompton Station (Rail & Tube) 2M 13
WESTBROOK 6F 132
Westbrook RH18: F Row 6G 187
Westbrook Av. TW12: Hamp 8N 23
Westbrook Gdns.
RG12: Brac 9A 16
Westbrook Hill GU8: Els 7F 130
Westbrook Rd. CR7: T Hea 1A 46
GU7: Goda 6F 132
TW5: Hest 3N 9
TW18: Stain 6H 21
Westbury SL4: Eton 2F 4
(off Eton Wick Rd.)
Westbury Av. GU51: Fleet 5E 88
KT10: Clay 3F 58
Westbury Cl. CR3: Whyte 5C 84
GU51: Fleet 5D 88
RG45: Crow 1G 48
TW17: Shep 5C 38
Westbury Gdns.
GU9: Farnh 8K 109
GU51: Fleet 5E 88
Westbury Pl. TW8: Brent 2K 11
Westbury Rd. BR3: Beck 2H 47
CR0: Croy 5A 46
KT3: N Mal 3C 42
SE20 1G 46
TW13: Felt 2L 23
Westbury Ter.
TN16: Weste 5L 107
Westbury Way GU12: Alde 2B 110
WEST BYFLEET 9J 55
West Byfleet Station (Rail) 8J 55
Westcar La. KT12: Hers 3J 57
WEST CLANDON 6K 95
West Cl. GU9: H End 5J 109
GU27: Fern 9F 188
TW12: Hamp 7M 23
TW15: A'ford 5N 21
Westcombe Av. CR0: Croy 6J 45
Westcombe Cl. RG12: Brac 6C 32
West Comn. Rd. BR2: Hay 1D 66
BR2: Kes 1D 66
Westcoombe Av.
SW20 9E 26
Westcote Rd. KT19: Eps 7A 60
SW16 6G 29
WESTCOTT 6C 118
Westcott Cl. CR0: N Add 5L 65
RH11: Craw 9A 182
WESTCOTT COMMON 7B 118
Westcott Keep RH6: Horl 7G 142
(off Langshott La.)
Westcott Rd.
RH4: Dork 3G 201 (6D 118)
Westcotts Grn. RG42: Warf 7B 16
Westcott St. RH4: Westc 6B 118
Westcott Way SM2: Chea 6H 61
West Ct. GU4: B'ham 8C 94
TW7: Isle 3C 10
West Cres. SL4: W'sor 4C 4
Westcroft Gdns. SM4: Mord 2L 43
Westcroft Leisure Cen. 1E 62
Westcroft Rd. SM5: Cars 1E 62
SM6: W'ton 1E 62
W. Cromwell Rd. SW5 1M 13
W14 1L 13
W. Cross Cen. TW8: Brent 2G 11
W. Cross Way TW8: Brent 2H 11
West Croydon Station (Rail & CT) 1B 200 (7N 45)
Westdean Cl. SW18 9N 13
West Dene SM3: Chea 3K 61
Westdene KT12: Hers 1J 57
Westdene Mdws.
GU6: Cranl 7J 155
Westdene Way KT13: Weybr 9F 38
West Down KT23: Book 5B 98
West Dr. GU25: V Wat 6H 35
KT15: N Haw 6K 55
KT20: Tad 5J 81
SL5: S'dale, V Wat 4G 34
SM2: Chea 5J 61
SM5: Cars 6B 62
SW16 5G 28
WEST DULWICH 3N 29
WEST END
GU24 8C 52
KT10 2N 57
RG42 6N 15
W. End Cen. GU11: Alde 2L 109
(off Queen's Rd.)
West End Gdns. KT10: Esh 2N 57
West End Gro. GU9: Farnh 1F 128
West End La. GU10: Fren 1D 148
GU27: Hasl 9A 172
KT10: Esh 4N 57
RG42: Warf 6N 15
UB3: Harl 3D 8
Westerdale Dr. GU16: Frim 3F 70
Westerfolds Cl. GU22: Wok 4E 74
Westergate Ho.
KT1: K Tham 8H 203
WESTERHAM 4M 107
Westerham Cl. KT15: Addl 3L 55
SM2: Sut 6M 61
WESTERHAM HILL 7J 87
Westerham Hill
TN16: Weste 8K 87
Westerham Rd. BR2: Kes 3F 66
RH8: Limp, Weste, Oxt 7B 106
TN16: Weste 7B 106
Westerham Trade Cen.
TN16: Weste 3M 107
Westerley Ware TW9: Kew 2N 11
(off Waterloo Pl.)
Westermain KT15: N Haw 6L 55
Western Av. KT16: Chert 2J 37
TW20: Thor 2D 36
Western Cen., The
RG12: Brac 1L 31
Western Cl. KT16: Chert 2J 37
Western Dr. TW17: Shep 5E 38
WESTERN INDUSTRIAL AREA 1L 31
Western Intl. Mkt.
UB2: S'hall 1J 9
Western La. SW12 1E 28
Western Pde. RH2: Reig 6N 121
Western Perimeter Rd.
TW6: Lon A 5K 7
TW6: Lon A, L'ford 5K 7
UB7: L'ford 5K 7
Western Pl. RH4: Dork 3J 201
Western Rd. CR4: Mit 9B 28
GU11: Alde 3K 109
RG12: Brac 9K 15
SM1: Sut 2M 61
SW19 9B 28
Western Ter. W6 1F 12
(off Chiswick Mall)
WEST EWELL 5C 60
W. Farm Av. KT21: A'tead 5J 79
W. Farm Cl. KT21: A'tead 6J 79
W. Farm Dr. KT21: A'tead 6K 79
WESTFIELD 8A 74
Westfield KT21: A'tead 5M 79
RH2: Reig 9N 101
RH5: A Ham 3G 136
Westfield Av. CR2: Sande 9A 64
GU22: Wok 8A 74
Westfield Cl. SM1: Sut 1L 61
SW10 3N 13
Westfield Comn.
GU22: Wok 9A 74
Westfield Ct. GU51: Fleet 4A 88
KT6: Surb 8H 203
(off Portsmouth Rd)
Westfield Dr. KT23: Book 9A 78
Westfield Gdns.
RH4: Dork 2H 201 (5G 118)
Westfield Gro. GU22: Wok 7A 74
Westfield Ho. SW18 2N 27
Westfield La. GU10: Wrec 5D 128
Westfield Pde.
KT15: N Haw 6M 55
Westfield Rd. BR3: Beck 1J 47
CR0: Croy 2A 200 (8M 45)
CR4: Mit 1C 44
GU1: Guil 8A 94
GU15: Camb 4N 69
GU22: Wok 9N 73
KT6: Surb 4K 41
KT12: Wal T 6M 39
RH11: Craw 3N 181
SM1: Sut 1L 61
Westfields GU8: Wit 5C 152
SW13 6E 12
Westfields Av. SW13 6D 12
Westfield Sq. GU22: Wok 9A 74
Westfield Way GU22: Wok 9A 74
W. Flexford La.
GU3: Flex, Wan 3N 111
West Fryerne GU46: Yate 7C 48
West Gdns. KT17: Ewe 6D 60
SW17 7C 28
Westgate Cl. KT18: Eps 2C 80
Westgate Est. TW14: Bedf 2C 22
Westgate Ho. KT18: Eps 2C 80
(off Chalk La.)
TW7: Isle 5D 10
Westgate Rd. BR3: Beck 1M 47
SE25 3E 46
Westgate Ter. SW10 2N 13
West Glade GU14: Cove 1J 89
WEST GREEN 2A 182
West Grn. GU46: Yate 8A 48
West Grn. Dr. RH11: Craw 2A 182
West Green Pk. 2A 182
West Gro. KT12: Hers 2J 57
Westhall Pk. CR6: Warl 6F 84
W. Hall Rd. TW9: Kew 4A 12
Westhall Rd. CR6: Warl 5D 84
Westhatch La. RG42: Warf 5N 15
Westhay Gdns. SW14 8A 12
WEST HEATH
GU14 9L 69
RH8 8C 106
West Heath GU24: Pirb 1A 92
(not continuous)
W. Heath Rd. GU14: Cove 1L 89
WEST HILL 9L 13
West Hill BR6: Dow 8H 67
CR2: Sande 6B 64
GU8: Els 8G 131
KT19: Eps 6G 201 (9A 60)
RH8: Oxt 8N 105
RH19: D Pk 4A 166
RH19: E Grin 1N 185
SW15 1J 27
SW18 1J 27
W. Hill Av.
KT19: Eps 5G 201 (9A 60)
W. Hill Bank RH8: Oxt 8N 105
W. Hill Cl. GU8: Els 8G 131
GU24: B'wood 7E 72
W. Hill Ct. KT19: Eps 6H 201
W. Hill Rd. GU22: Wok 6N 73
SW18 9L 13
W. Hoathly Rd.
RH19: E Grin 5M 185
(not continuous)
Westhorpe Rd. SW15 6H 13
WEST HORSLEY 7C 96
West Ho. GU6: Cranl 5L 155
West Ho. Cl. SW19 2K 27
WESTHUMBLE 9H 99
Westhumble St.
RH5: Westh 9H 99
W. Kensington Ct.
W14 1L 13
(off Edith Vs.)
W. Kensington Mans.
W14 1L 13
(off Beaumont Cres.)
West Kensington Station (Tube) 1L 13
Westland Cl. TW19: Stan 9N 7
Westland Ct. GU14: Cove 1J 89
Westlands RH13: Hors 5L 197
Westlands Ct. KT8: E Mol 3D 40
KT18: Eps 2B 80
Westlands Way RH8: Oxt 5N 105
West La. RH5: Wott 8L 117
RH19: E Grin 1N 185
Westleas RH6: Horl 6C 142
Westlees Cl. RH5: N Holm 8K 119
West Leigh RH19: E Grin 2A 186
Westleigh Av. CR5: Coul 3E 82
SW15 8G 13
Westleigh Ct. CR2: S Croy 7F 200
Westley Mill RG42: Bin 1K 15
Westmacott Dr. TW14: Felt 2G 22
Westmark Point SW15 2G 26
(off Norley Vale)
West Mead KT19: Ewe 3D 60
Westmead GU9: Farnh 1G 128
GU14: Farnb 2N 89
GU21: Wok 4L 73
SL4: W'sor 6E 4
SW15 9G 12
Westmead Cnr. SM5: Cars 1C 62
Westmead Dr. RH1: Salf 2E 142
Westmead Ho. SM1: Sut 1B 62
Westmead Rd. SM1: Sut 1B 62
West Meads GU2: Guil 4J 113
RH6: Horl 8G 143
Westminster Av.
CR7: T Hea 1M 45
Westminster Cl.
GU51: Fleet 3B 88
TW11: Tedd 6G 24
TW14: Felt 2H 23
Westminster Ct.
GU1: Guil 5E 202 (4A 114)
GU22: Wok 8D 74
Westminster Rd.
RH10: Craw 4G 182
SM1: Sut 8B 44
WEST MOLESEY 3A 40
Westmont Rd.
KT10: H Wood 8E 40
Westmore Ct. SW15 8K 13
Westmore Grn. TN16: Tats 7E 86
Westmoreland Dr.
SM2: Sut 4N 61
Westmoreland Rd.
SW13 4E 12
Westmore Rd. TN16: Tats 8E 86
Westmorland Cl.
KT19: Ewe 6D 60
TW1: Twick 9H 11
Westmorland Ct. KT6: Surb 6K 41
Westmorland Dr.
GU15: Camb 3F 70
RG42: Warf 7D 16
Westmorland Sq. CR4: Mit 4J 45
(off Westmorland Way)
Westmorland Way CR4: Mit 3H 45
West Mt.
GU2: Guil 7A 202 (5M 113)
(not continuous)
WEST NORWOOD 5N 29
W. Norwood Crematorium
SE27 4N 29

West Norwood Station (Rail)—Whittingham Ct.

West Norwood Station (Rail) . . . 5M 29
Weston Av. KT7: T Dit . . . 6E 40
KT8: W Mole . . . 2M 39
KT15: Addl . . . 1K 55
Weston Cl. CR5: Coul . . . 7K 83
GU7: Goda . . . 5H 133
Weston Ct. GU7: Goda . . . 5H 133
KT1: K Tham . . . 6J 203
Weston Dr. CR3: Cate . . . 9N 83
Weston Farm Cotts.
GU5: Alb . . . 8K 115
Westonfields GU5: Alb . . . 8L 115
Weston Gdns. GU22: Pyr . . . 3G 75
TW7: Isle . . . 4E 10
WESTON GREEN . . . 7E 40
Weston Grn. KT7: T Dit . . . 8E 40
(Hampton Ct. Way)
KT7: T Dit . . . 7E 40
(Weston Grn. Rd.)
Weston Grn. Rd.
KT7: T Dit . . . 7E 40
KT10: Esh . . . 7D 40
Weston Gro. GU19: Bag . . . 5K 51
Weston Lea KT24: W Hors . . . 3E 96
Weston Pk.
KT1: K Tham . . . 3J 203 (1L 41)
KT7: T Dit . . . 7E 40
Weston Pk. Cl. KT7: T Dit . . . 7E 40
Weston Rd. GU2: Guil . . . 2K 113
(not continuous)
KT7: T Dit . . . 7E 40
KT17: Eps . . . 7D 60
Westons Cl. RH12: Hors . . . 1K 197
Westons Yd. SL4: Eton . . . 2G 4
Weston Way GU22: Pyr . . . 3G 75
Weston Yd. GU5: Alb . . . 8L 115
Westover Cl. SM2: Sut . . . 5N 61
Westover Rd. GU51: Fleet . . . 4C 88
SW18 . . . 1A 28
West Pal. Gdns.
KT13: Weybr . . . 9C 38
West Pde. RH12: Hors . . . 4J 197
West Pk. Av. TW9: Kew . . . 4N 11
West Pk. Cl. TW5: Hest . . . 2N 9
West Pk. Rd. KT19: Eps . . . 8M 59
RH7: Newc . . . 6C 164
RH10: Cop, Newc . . . 6C 164
(not continuous)
RH17: Hand . . . 9N 199
TW9: Kew . . . 4N 11
West Parkside CR6: Warl . . . 2K 85
West Pl. SW19 . . . 6H 27
W. Point Cl. TW4: Houn . . . 6N 9
(off Grosvenor Rd.)
West Ramp TW6: Lon A . . . 4B 8
West Ridge GU10: Seal . . . 7C 110
West Ring GU10: Tong . . . 5D 110
West Rd.
GU1: Guil . . . 4F 202 (4A 114)
GU14: Farnb . . . 6N 69
GU15: Camb . . . 1B 70
KT2: K Tham . . . 9B 26
KT9: Ches . . . 8J 59
KT13: Weybr . . . 5C 56
RG40: W'ham . . . 6G 31
RH2: Reig . . . 4N 121
TW14: Bedf . . . 9E 8
Westrow SW15 . . . 9H 13
W. Sheen Va. TW9: Rich . . . 7M 11
W. Side Comn. SW19 . . . 6H 27
Westside Ct. GU24: W End . . . 9B 52
Westside Ho. RH1: Salf . . . 1F 142
West St.
CR0: Croy . . . 6C 200 (1N 63)
GU9: Farnh . . . 2E 128
GU21: Wok . . . 4B 74
GU27: Hasl . . . 1G 189
KT17: Ewe . . . 6D 60
KT18: Eps . . . 7H 201 (9B 60)
(not continuous)
RH2: Reig . . . 3K 121
RH4: Dork . . . 2J 201 (5G 119)
RH7: Dorm . . . 1C 166
RH11: Craw . . . 4B 182
RH12: Hors . . . 6J 197
RH19: E Grin . . . 1A 186
SM1: Sut . . . 2N 61
SM5: Cars . . . 9D 44
TW8: Brent . . . 2J 11
West St. La. SM5: Cars . . . 1D 62
(not continuous)
West St. Pl. CR0: Croy . . . 6C 200
West Sutton Station (Rail) . . . 1M 61
W. Temple Sheen
SW14 . . . 8A 12
West Vw. KT21: A'tead . . . 6J 79
TW14: Bedf . . . 1D 22
Westview GU22: Wok . . . 5B 74
(off Park Dr.)
West Vw. Av.
CR3: Whyte . . . 5C 84
Westview Cl. RH1: Red . . . 5C 122
West Vw. Cotts.
RH5: Newd . . . 2A 160
West Vw. Gdns.
RH19: E Grin . . . 1A 186
West Vw. Rd.
GU35: H Dwn . . . 5H 169
Westview Rd. CR6: Warl . . . 6E 84
Westville Rd. KT7: T Dit . . . 7G 41
Westward Ho. GU1: Guil . . . 1B 114
Westwates Cl. RG12: Brac . . . 9B 16
West Way BR4: W Wick . . . 5N 47
CR0: Croy . . . 8H 47
RH10: Craw . . . 2E 182
RH13: Slin . . . 5L 195
SM5: Cars . . . 6B 62
TW5: Hest . . . 4N 9
TW17: Shep . . . 5E 38
Westway CR3: Cate . . . 9A 84
GU2: Guil . . . 1J 113
GU8: Worm . . . 1C 172
RH6: Gat . . . 3F 162
RH10: Cop . . . 7K 163
SW20 . . . 2G 43
Westway Cl. SW20 . . . 2G 43
Westway Ct. CR3: Cate . . . 1A 104
W. Way Gdns. CR0: Croy . . . 8G 47
Westway Gdns.
RH1: Red . . . 9E 102
Westways KT19: Ewe . . . 1E 60
TN8: Eden . . . 1L 147
TN16: Weste . . . 4L 107
Westwell M. SW16 . . . 7J 29
Westwell Rd. SW16 . . . 7J 29
Westwell Rd. App.
SW16 . . . 7J 29
Westwick KT1: K Tham . . . 4M 203
(off Chesterton Ter.)
Westwick Gdns. TW4: C'ford . . . 5J 9
WEST WICKHAM . . . 7M 47
West Wickham Pools . . . 7M 47
West Wickham Station (Rail)
. . . 6M 47
Westwood Av. KT15: Wood . . . 8H 55
SE19 . . . 9N 29
Westwood Cl. KT10: Esh . . . 9D 40
Westwood Ct. GU2: Guil . . . 2J 113
Westwood Gdns.
SW13 . . . 6E 12
Westwood La. GU3: Norm . . . 1L 111
Westwood Rd. CR5: Coul . . . 5H 83
GU20: Windl . . . 8B 34
SW13 . . . 6E 12
Wetherby Gdns.
GU14: Farnb . . . 5A 90
SW5 . . . 1N 13
Wetherby Mans. SW5 . . . 1N 13
(off Earls Ct. Sq.)
Wetherby M. SW5 . . . 1N 13
Wetherby Way KT9: Ches . . . 4L 59
Wettern Cl. CR2: Sande . . . 6B 64
Wetton Pl. TW20: Egh . . . 6B 20
Wexfenne Gdns.
GU22: Pyr . . . 3K 75
Wexford Rd. SW12 . . . 1D 28
Wey and Arun Junction Canal
. . . 7D 134
Wey Av. KT16: Chert . . . 2J 37
Weybank GU23: Wis . . . 3N 75
Weybank Cl. GU9: Farnh . . . 1H 129
Wey Barton KT14: Byf . . . 9A 56
WEYBOURNE . . . 6K 109
Weybourne Pl. CR2: Sande . . . 6A 64
Weybourne Rd.
GU9: Farnh . . . 7K 109
Weybourne St. SW18 . . . 3A 28
WEYBRIDGE . . . 1B 56
Weybridge Bus. Pk.
KT15: Addl . . . 1N 55
Weybridge Ho.
KT13: Weybr . . . 2E 56
Weybridge Mead
GU46: Yate . . . 8D 48
Weybridge Pk. KT13: Weybr . . . 2B 56
Weybridge Rd. CR7: T Hea . . . 3L 45
KT13: Weybr . . . 1N 55
KT15: Addl . . . 1N 55
Weybridge Station (Rail) . . . 3B 56
Weybrook Dr. GU4: B'ham . . . 7D 94
Wey Cl. GU12: Ash . . . 3E 110
GU15: Camb . . . 1N 69
KT14: W By . . . 9K 55
Weycombe Rd.
GU27: Hasl . . . 1G 189
(not continuous)
Wey Ct.
GU1: Guil . . . 4B 202 (4M 113)
GU7: Goda . . . 5K 133
KT15: N Haw . . . 5M 55
KT19: Ewe . . . 1B 60
Wey Ct. Cl. GU7: Goda . . . 5J 133
Weycrofts RG42: Brac . . . 8L 15
Weydon Farm La.
GU9: Farnh . . . 3G 128
Weydon Hill Cl.
GU9: Farnh . . . 3G 129
Weydon Hill Rd.
GU9: Farnh . . . 3G 129
Weydon La. GU9: Farnh . . . 4E 128
Weydon Mill La.
GU9: Farnh . . . 2G 128
Weydown Cl. GU2: Guil . . . 7K 93
SW19 . . . 2K 27
Weydown Cotts.
GU27: Hasl . . . 8G 170
Weydown Ct. GU27: Hasl . . . 1F 188
Weydown Ind. Est.
GU27: Hasl . . . 1F 188
(not continuous)
Weydown La. GU2: Guil . . . 7K 93
Weydown Rd. GU27: Hasl . . . 2F 188
Wey Gdns. GU27: Hasl . . . 3D 188
Wey Hill GU27: Hasl . . . 2E 188
Weylands Cl. KT12: Wal T . . . 7N 39
Weylands Ct. KT15: Addl . . . 1M 55
(off Corrie Rd.)
Weylands Pk. KT13: Weybr . . . 3E 56
Weylea Av. GU4: B'ham . . . 9C 94
Wey Mnr. Rd. KT15: N Haw . . . 5M 55
Weymead Cl. KT16: Chert . . . 7L 37
Wey Mdws. KT13: Addl . . . 2N 55
Weymede KT14: Byf . . . 8A 56
Weymouth Ct. SM2: Sut . . . 4M 61
Wey Retail Pk. KT14: Byf . . . 8N 55
Wey Rd. GU7: Goda . . . 6K 133
KT13: Weybr . . . 9A 38
Weyside GU9: Farnh . . . 1H 129
Weyside Cl. KT14: Byf . . . 8A 56
Weyside Gdns. GU1: Guil . . . 1M 113
Weyside Pk. GU7: Goda . . . 6K 133
Weyside Rd. GU1: Guil . . . 1L 113
Weysprings GU27: Hasl . . . 1D 188
Weystone Rd. KT13: Addl . . . 1A 56
Weyvern Pk. GU3: P'marsh . . . 2L 133
Weyvern Pl. GU3: P'marsh . . . 2L 133
Weyview Cl. GU1: Guil . . . 1M 113
Wey Vw. Ct.
GU1: Guil . . . 4A 202 (4M 113)
Weywood Cl. GU9: Weybo . . . 5L 109
Weywood La. GU9: Weybo . . . 5K 109
Whaley Rd. RG40: W'ham . . . 9C 14
Wharf, The GU7: Goda . . . 6H 133
KT13: Weybr . . . 8B 38
Wharfedale Gdns.
CR7: T Hea . . . 3K 45
Wharfedale St. SW10 . . . 1N 13
Wharfenden Way
GU16: Frim G . . . 8D 70
Wharf La. GU23: Rip . . . 5M 75
GU23: Send . . . 1E 94
TW1: Twick . . . 2G 24
Wharf Rd.
GU1: Guil . . . 3B 202 (3M 113)
GU12: A Va . . . 9E 90
GU16: Frim G . . . 8D 70
TW19: Wray . . . 1M 19
Wharf St. GU7: Goda . . . 7H 133
Wharf Way GU16: Frim G . . . 8E 70
Wharncliffe Gdns.
SE25 . . . 1B 46
Wharncliffe Rd. SE25 . . . 1B 46
Whateley Cl. GU2: Guil . . . 7L 93
Whatley Av. SW20 . . . 2J 43
Whatley Grn. RG12: Brac . . . 5N 31
Whatmore Cl. TW19: Stan M . . . 9J 7
Wheatash Rd. KT15: Addl . . . 8K 37
Wheatbutts, The SL4: E Wic . . . 1C 4
Wheatcroft Ct. SM1: Sut . . . 7N 43
(off Cleeve Way)
Wheatfield Way
KT1: K Tham . . . 5J 203 (1L 41)
RH6: Horl . . . 6F 142
Wheathill Ho. SE20 . . . 1E 46
(off Croydon Rd.)
Wheathill Rd. SE20 . . . 2E 46
Wheat Knoll CR8: Ken . . . 3N 83
Wheatlands TW5: Hest . . . 2A 10
Wheatlands Rd. SW17 . . . 4E 28
Wheatley RG12: Brac . . . 4K 31
Wheatley Ho. SW15 . . . 1F 26
(off Ellisfield Dr)
Wheatley Rd. GU11: Alde . . . 1L 109
TW7: Isle . . . 6F 10
Wheatley's Eyot
TW16: Sunb . . . 4H 39
Wheatsheaf Cl. GU21: Wok . . . 3A 74
KT16: Otter . . . 3F 54
RH12: Hors . . . 3L 197
Wheatsheaf Ct.
GU35: Head . . . 3E 168
Wheatsheaf La. SW6 . . . 3H 13
TW18: Stain . . . 8H 21
Wheatsheaf Pde. SL4: O Win . . . 8K 5
(off St Luke's Rd.)
Wheatsheaf Pk. . . . 9J 21
Wheatsheaf Ter. SW6 . . . 3L 13
Wheatstone Cl. CR4: Mit . . . 9C 28
RH10: Craw . . . 7F 162
Wheeler Av. RH8: Oxt . . . 7N 105
Wheeler La. GU8: Wit . . . 4B 152
Wheeler Rd. RH10: Craw . . . 5F 182
Wheelers La.
KT18: Eps . . . 8G 201 (1A 80)
RH3: Brock . . . 5A 120
RH6: Smal . . . 9L 143
Wheeler's St. SM1: Sut . . . 9M 43
WHEELERSTREET . . . 4C 152
Wheelerstreet GU8: Wit . . . 4C 152
Wheelers Way RH19: Fel . . . 7H 165
Wheelwright Ct.
RH5: Ockl . . . 5D 158
Wheelwrights La.
GU26: G'hott . . . 5M 169
Wheelwrights Pl. SL3: Coln . . . 3E 6
Whelan Way SM6: Bedd . . . 9H 45
Wherwell Rd.
GU2: Guil . . . 6A 202 (5M 113)
Whetstone Rd. GU14: Cove . . . 1H 89
Whimbrel Cl. CR2: Sande . . . 7A 64
Whinfell Cl. SW16 . . . 6H 29
Whin Holt GU52: Fleet . . . 7B 88
Whins Cl. GU15: Camb . . . 2N 69
Whins Dr. GU15: Camb . . . 2N 69
Whinshill Ct. SL5: S'dale . . . 7D 34
Whipley Cl. GU4: B'ham . . . 7D 94
Whistler Cl. RH10: Craw . . . 6D 182
Whistler Gro. GU47: C Tow . . . 9J 49
Whistley Cl. RG12: Brac . . . 2C 32
Whitby Cl. GU14: Farnb . . . 4C 90
TN16: B Hil . . . 6D 86
Whitby Gdns. SM1: Sut . . . 8B 44
Whitby Rd. SM1: Sut . . . 8B 44
Whitchurch Cl.
GU11: Alde . . . 6B 110
Whitcombe M. TW9: Kew . . . 4A 12
Whitcome M. TW9: Kew . . . 4A 12
White Acres Rd.
GU16: Mytc . . . 1D 90
Whitebeam Dr. RH2: Reig . . . 6N 121
Whitebeam Gdns.
GU14: Cove . . . 2H 89
White Beam Way
KT20: Tad . . . 8F 80
White Beech La.
GU8: Chid . . . 4K 173
Whiteberry Rd.
RH5: A Com, Cold . . . 3B 138
Whitebines GU9: Farnh . . . 1J 129
White Bri. Av. CR4: Mit . . . 2B 44
Whitebridge Cl. TW14: Felt . . . 9G 9
WHITE BUSHES . . . 8E 122
Whitebushes RH1: Red . . . 7E 122
White City RG45: Crow . . . 2J 49
(not continuous)
White Cott. Cl. GU9: Hale . . . 6J 109
White Ct. GU2: Guil . . . 9K 93
Whitecroft RH6: Horl . . . 7F 142
Whitecroft Cl. BR3: Beck . . . 3N 47
Whitecroft Way BR3: Beck . . . 4M 47
White Down La.
RH5: Ran C . . . 4K 117
Whitefield Av. CR8: Pur . . . 3L 83
Whitefield Cl. SW15 . . . 9K 13
White Ga. GU22: Wok . . . 7B 74
White Gates KT7: T Dit . . . 6G 40
Whitegates CR3: Warl . . . 6D 84
Whitegate Way KT20: Tad . . . 7G 81
WHITEGROVE . . . 7B 16
Whitehall . . . 3K 61
Whitehall Cres. KT9: Ches . . . 2K 59
Whitehall Dr. RH11: Ifi . . . 3K 181
Whitehall Farm La.
GU25: V Wat . . . 1A 36
(not continuous)
Whitehall Gdns. W4 . . . 2A 12
Whitehall La. RH2: Reig . . . 7L 121
TW19: Wray . . . 9C 6
TW20: Egh . . . 8B 20
Whitehall Pde.
RH19: E Grin . . . 9A 166
(off London Rd.)
Whitehall Pk. Rd. W4 . . . 2A 12
Whitehall Pl. SM6: W'ton . . . 1F 62
Whitehall Rd. CR7: T Hea . . . 4L 45
White Hart Cl. UB3: Harl . . . 2E 8
White Hart Ct. GU23: Rip . . . 8L 75
RH12: Hors . . . 4J 197
White Hart Ind. Est.
GU17: B'water . . . 2K 69
White Hart La.
GU3: Wood V . . . 2D 112
SW13 . . . 6D 12
White Hart Mdws.
GU23: Rip . . . 8L 75
White Hart Row KT16: Chert . . . 6J 37
Whitehead Cl. SW18 . . . 1A 28
White Hermitage
SL4: O Win . . . 8M 5
White Heron M.
TW11: Tedd . . . 7F 24
White Hill CR2: Sande . . . 6A 64
CR5: Chip . . . 1C 102
GU20: Windl . . . 1M 51
Whitehill Cl. GU15: Camb . . . 8B 50
White Hill La. RH1: Blet . . . 5A 104
Whitehill La. KT11: Cob . . . 1D 96
Whitehill Pk.
GU35: White . . . 9A 168
Whitehill Pl. GU25: V Wat . . . 4A 36
Whitehill Rd. GU35: Stand . . . 8A 168
White Horse Dr.
KT18: Eps . . . 8G 201 (1B 80)
White Horse La. GU23: Rip . . . 8L 75
Whitehorse La. SE25 . . . 3A 46
White Horse Rd.
SL4: W'sor . . . 6A 4
Whitehorse Rd. CR0: Croy . . . 6N 45
CR7: T Hea . . . 6N 45
RH12: Hors . . . 2A 198
White Ho. KT15: Addl . . . 1L 55
SW4 . . . 1H 29
(off Clapham Pk. Est.)
White Ho., The
RH10: Craw . . . 7B 162
Whitehouse Cl.
GU14: Farnb . . . 8N 69
White Ho. Dr. GU1: Guil . . . 3D 114
White Ho. Gdns.
GU46: Yate . . . 8B 48
White Ho. La. GU4: J Wel . . . 7N 93
(not continuous)
White Ho. Wlk.
GU9: H End . . . 5J 109
White Knights Rd.
KT13: Weybr . . . 4D 56
White Knobs Way
CR3: Cate . . . 3D 104
Whitelands Cres.
SW18 . . . 1K 27
Whitelands Dr. SL5: Asc . . . 9H 17
White La. GU4: Guil . . . 5E 114
GU5: Alb . . . 5E 114
GU10: Tong . . . 7G 110
GU12: A Grn . . . 3G 110
RH8: T'sey . . . 1D 106
TN16: Tats, T'sey . . . 1D 106
Whiteley SL4: W'sor . . . 3B 4
Whiteley's Way
TW13: Hanw . . . 4A 24
WHITELEY VILLAGE . . . 5F 56
White Lillies Island
SL4: W'sor . . . 3D 4
White Lion Ct. TW7: Isle . . . 6H 11
White Lion Ga. KT11: Cob . . . 1H 77
White Lion Wlk.
GU1: Guil . . . 6C 202 (4N 113)
White Lion Way GU46: Yate . . . 8C 48
White Lodge KT21: A'tead . . . 7L 79
SE19 . . . 8M 29
White Lodge Cl. SM2: Sut . . . 4A 62
TW7: Isle . . . 5G 11
White Lodge Ct.
TW16: Sunb . . . 9K 23
White Lodge Gdns.
RH1: Salf . . . 2E 142
WHITELY HILL . . . 8K 183
Whitely Hill RH10: Wor . . . 8K 183
Whitemore Rd. GU1: Guil . . . 8N 93
White Oak Dr. BR3: Beck . . . 1M 47
Whiteoaks SM7: Ban . . . 9N 61
White Pillars GU22: Wok . . . 7L 73
WHITE POST . . . 2B 124
Whitepost Hill RH1: Red . . . 3C 122
(not continuous)
White Post La.
GU10: Wrec . . . 7F 128
White Rd. GU15: Camb . . . 9L 49
KT20: Betch, Box H . . . 2N 119
RH3: Betch . . . 2N 119
White Rose La.
GU10: L Bou . . . 4G 129
GU22: Wok . . . 5B 74
Whites La. GU24: Pirb . . . 2D 92
SL3: Dat . . . 2L 5
Whites Rd. GU14: Farnb . . . 4C 90
Whitestile Rd. TW8: Brent . . . 1J 11
White Swan M. W4 . . . 1D 12
Whitethorn Av. CR5: Coul . . . 2E 82
Whitethorn Cl. GU12: Ash . . . 3F 110
Whitethorn Cotts.
GU6: Cranl . . . 5K 155
Whitethorn Gdns.
CR0: Croy . . . 8E 46
Whitethorns GU9: H End . . . 4J 109
(off Lwr. Weybourne La.)
Whitewalls RH11: Craw . . . 3L 181
(off Rusper Rd.)
Whitewater Rd. GU51: Fleet . . . 1A 88
Whiteway KT23: Book . . . 4B 98
Whiteways Ct. TW18: Stain . . . 8K 21
WHITEWOOD . . . 5D 144
Whitewood Cotts.
TN16: Tats . . . 7E 86
Whitewood La. RH6: Horn . . . 5D 144
RH9: S Gods . . . 5D 144
Whitfield Cl. GU2: Guil . . . 9K 93
GU27: Hasl . . . 8G 171
Whitfield Rd. GU27: Hasl . . . 9G 171
Whitford Gdns. CR4: Mit . . . 2D 44
Whitgift Av.
CR2: S Croy . . . 8A 200 (2M 63)
Whitgift Cen.
CR0: Croy . . . 2C 200 (8N 45)
Whitgift Ct. CR2: S Croy . . . 8C 200
Whitgift Sq.
CR0: Croy . . . 3C 200 (8N 45)
Whitgift St.
CR0: Croy . . . 5B 200 (9N 45)
Whitgift Wlk. RH10: Craw . . . 6B 182
Whitland Rd. SM5: Cars . . . 7B 44
Whitlet Cl. GU9: Farnh . . . 2G 128
Whitley Cl. TW19: Stan . . . 9N 7
Whitley Rd. GU46: Yate . . . 2C 68
Whitlock Dr. SW19 . . . 1K 27
Whitmead Cl. CR2: S Croy . . . 3B 64
Whitmead La. GU10: Til . . . 6C 130
Whitmoor La. GU4: Sut G . . . 4N 93
Whitmoor Rd. GU19: Bag . . . 4K 51
Whitmoor Va.
GU26: G'hott . . . 2K 169
Whitmoor Va. Rd.
GU26: G'hott, Hind . . . 2L 169
Whitmore Cl. GU47: Owls . . . 7J 49
Whitmore Grn.
GU9: H End . . . 6K 109
Whitmore La.
SL5: S'dale, S'hill . . . 4D 34
Whitmore Rd. BR3: Beck . . . 2J 47
Whitmores Cl. KT18: Eps . . . 2B 80
Whitmore Vale Rd.
GU26: G'hott . . . 5M 169
Whitmore Way RH6: Horl . . . 7C 142
Whitnell Way SW15 . . . 8H 13
Whitstable Cl. BR3: Beck . . . 1J 47
Whitstable Pl.
CR0: Croy . . . 7C 200 (1N 63)
Whitstone La. BR3: Beck . . . 4L 47
Whittaker Av. TW9: Rich . . . 8K 11
Whittaker Ct. KT21: A'tead . . . 4K 79
Whittaker Pl. TW9: Rich . . . 8K 11
(off Whittaker Av.)
Whittaker Rd. SM3: Sut . . . 9L 43
Whittingham Ct. W4 . . . 3D 12

Whittingstall Rd.—Windermere Ho.

Whittingstall Rd. SW6 . . . . . . .4L 13
Whittington Rd.
RH10: Craw 6B 182
Whittlebury Cl. SM5: Cars 4D 62
Whittle Cl. GU12: A Va 8D 90
GU47: Sandh 6F 48
Whittle Cres. GU14: Cove 7L 69
Whittle Rd. TW5: Hest 3K 9
Whittle Way RH10: Craw 6E 162
WHITTON 1C 24
Whitton Dene TW3: Houn 8C 10
TW7: Isle 9D 10
Whitton Mnr. Rd. TW7: Isle . . .9C 10
Whitton Rd. RG12: Brac 2D 32
TW1: Twick 9F 10
TW2: Twick 9E 10
TW3: Houn 7B 10
WHITTON ROAD RDBT. 9F 10
Whitton Sports & Fitness Cen. 3B 24
Whitton Station (Rail) 1C 24
Whitton Waye TW3: Houn 9A 10
Whitwell Hatch
GU27: Hasl 3H 189
Whitworth Rd.
RH11: Craw 8B 162
SE25 . . . . .2B 46
Whopshott Av. GU21: Wok 3M 73
Whopshott Cl. GU21: Wok 3M 73
Whopshott Dr. GU21: Wok 3M 73
Whynstones Rd. SL5: Asc 5L 33
Whyteacre CR3: Warl 7E 84
Whyte Av. GU12: Alde 4B 110
Whytebeam Vw.
CR3: Whyte 5C 84
Whytecliffe Rd. Nth.
CR8: Pur 7M 63
Whytecliffe Rd. Sth.
CR8: Pur 7L 63
Whytecroft TW5: Hest 3L 9
WHYTELEAFE 5C 84
Whyteleafe Bus. Village
CR3: Whyte 4C 84
Whyteleafe Hill CR3: Whyte . . .7B 84
(not continuous)
Whyteleafe Rd. CR3: Cate 7B 84
Whyteleafe South Station (Rail) 6D 84
Whyteleafe Station (Rail) 4C 84
Whyte M. SM3: Chea 4K 61
Wicket, The CR0: A'ton 2K 65
Wicket Hill GU10: Wrec 5F 128
Wickets, The TW15: A'ford 5N 21
Wickham Av. CR0: Croy 8H 47
SM3: Chea 2H 61
Wickham Chase
BR4: W Wick 7N 47
Wickham Cl. GU52: C Cro 7A 88
KT3: N Mal 5E 42
RH6: Horl 7D 142
Wickham Ct. KT5: Surb 8L 203
Wickham Ct. Rd.
BR4: W Wick 8M 47
Wickham Cres.
BR4: W Wick 8M 47
Wickham La. TW20: Egh 8C 20
Wickham Pl. GU52: C Cro 7A 88
Wickham Rd. BR3: Beck 1L 47
CR0: Croy 8G 46
GU15: Camb 7C 50
GU52: C Cro 7A 88
Wickham Theatre Cen. 8N 47
Wickham Va. RG12: Brac 5K 31
Wickham Way BR3: Beck 3M 47
WICK HILL 8B 16
Wick Hill La. RG40: Finch 1A 48
Wick Ho. KT1: H Wic 1G 203
Wickhurst Gdns.
RH12: Bro H 5E 196
Wickhurst La.
RH12: Bro H 5E 196
Wickland Ct. RH10: Craw 6B 182
Wick La. TW20: Eng G 7J 19
Wick Rd. TW11: Tedd 8H 25
TW20: Eng G 9K 19
Wick's Grn. RG42: Bin 5H 15
Wicks La. RG10: S Row 1D 14
Wicksteed Ho. TW8: Brent 1M 11
Wide Way CR4: Mit 2H 45
Widewing Cl. TW11: Tedd 8H 25
Widgeon Way RH12: Hors 3J 197
Widmer Ct. TW3: Houn 5M 9
Wiggett Gro. RG42: Bin 7H 15
Wiggie La. RH1: Red 1E 122
Wiggington Ho. *SL4: Eton* *3G 4*
(off High St.)
Wiggins La. TW10: Ham 3J 25
Wiggins Yd. GU7: Goda 7H 133
Wight Ho. KT1: K Tham 6H 203
Wighton M. TW7: Isle 5E 10
Wigley Rd. TW13: Felt 3L 23
Wigmore La. RH5: B Grn 9J 139
Wigmore Rd. SM5: Cars 8B 44
Wigmore Wlk. SM5: Cars 8B 44
Wilberforce Cl.
RH11: Craw 9A 182
Wilberforce Ct. BR2: Kes 4F 66
KT18: Eps 8K 201
Wilberforce Way
RG12: Brac 4B 32
SW19 . . . . .7J 27
Wilbury Av. SM2: Chea 6L 61
Wilbury Rd. GU21: Wok 4N 73
Wilcot Cl. GU24: Bis 3D 72
Wilcot Gdns. GU24: Bis 3D 72
Wilcox Gdns. TW17: Shep 2N 37
Wilcox Rd. SM1: Sut 1N 61
TW11: Tedd 5D 24
Wildacre Cl. RH14: Ifo 5F 192
Wild Acres KT14: W By 7L 55
Wildbank Ct. GU22: Wok 5B 74
Wildcroft Dr. RH5: Nth H 8K 119
Wildcroft Mnr. SW15 . . . . .1H 27
Wildcroft Rd. SW15 . . . . .1H 27
Wildcroft Wood GU8: Wit 4A 152
Wilde Pl. SW18 . . . . .1B 28
Wilderness, The
KT8: W Mole, E Mol 4C 40
TW12: H Hill 5B 24
Wilderness Ct. GU2: Guil 5J 113
Wilderness Island Nature Reserve 8E 44
Wilderness Ri.
RH19: D Pk 5C 166
Wilderness Rd. GU2: Guil 5J 113
GU16: Frim 4C 70
RH8: Oxt 8N 105
Wilders Cl. GU16: Frim 3C 70
GU21: Wok 5M 73
RG42: Brac 8M 15
Wilderwick Rd.
RH7: E Grin 3C 166
RH19: E Grin 3C 166
Wilde Theatre 6A 32
Wildfield Cl. GU3: Wood V 2E 112
Wildgoose Dr. RH12: Hors . . .5F 196
Wildmoor Heath Local
Nature Reserve 5H 49
WILDRIDINGS 3M 31
Wildridings Rd. RG12: Brac . . .3L 31
Wildridings Sq.
RG12: Brac 3M 31
Wild Wood RH12: Hors 5F 196
Wildwood Cl. GU6: Cranl 9A 156
GU22: Pyr 2H 75
KT24: E Hor 3G 96
Wildwood Ct. CR8: Ken 2A 84
Wildwood Gdns.
GU46: Yate 2B 68
Wildwood La.
GU6: Alf, Cranl 4J 175
Wilford Rd. CR0: Croy 5N 45
Wilfred Owen Cl.
SW19 . . . . .7A 28
Wilfred St. GU21: Wok 5N 73
Wilhelmina Av. CR5: Coul 6G 83
Wilkes Rd. TW8: Brent 2L 11
Wilkins Cl. CR4: Mit 9C 28
UB3: Harl 1G 9
Wilkinson Ct. RH11: Craw 8N 181
SW17 . . . . .5B 28
Wilkinson Gdns. SE25 . . . . . . .1B 46
Wilks Gdns. CR0: Croy 7H 47
Willard Way RH19: E Grin 7K 165
Willats Cl. KT16: Chert 5H 37
Willcocks Cl. KT9: Ches 9L 41
Willems Av. GU11: Alde 2L 109
Willems Rdbt. GU11: Alde 2L 109
Willerton Lodge
KT13: Weybr 3E 56
Willett Pl. CR7: T Hea 4L 45
Willett Rd. CR7: T Hea 4L 45
Willetts Way RH14: Loxw 5H 193
Willey Broom La.
CR3: Cate 3L 103
Willey Farm La. CR3: Cate 4N 103
WILLEY GREEN 9A 92
Willey La. CR3: Cate 3A 104
William Banfield Ho.
SW6 . . . . .5L 13
(off Munster Rd.)
William Ct. *GU14: Farnb 4A 90*
(off Cambridge Rd. W.)
William Dyce M.
SW16 . . . . .5H 29
William Ellis Cl. SL4: O Win . . .8K 5
William Evans Rd.
KT19: Eps 7N 59
William Evelyn Ct.
RH5: Wott 8N 117
William Farm La.
SW15 . . . . .6G 13
William Farthing Cl.
GU11: Alde 2M 109
William Gdns. SW15 . . . . .8G 13
William Harvey Ho.
SW19 . . . . .2K 27
(off Whitlock Dr.)
William Hitchcock Ho.
GU14: Farnb 7N 69
William Hunt Mans.
SW13 . . . . .2H 13
William Morris Ho.
W6 . . . . .2J 13
William Morris Way
RH11: Craw 9N 181
SW6 . . . . .6N 13
William Penney Hall
SL5: S'hill 2C 34
(off Buckhurst Rd.)
William Rd. CR3: Cate 9A 84
GU1: Guil 3B 202 (3M 113)
SM1: Sut 2A 62
SW19 . . . . .8K 27
William Russell Ct.
GU21: Wok 5H 73
Williams Cl. KT15: Addl 2K 55
SW6 . . . . .3K 13
Williams Dr. TW3: Houn 7A 10
Williams Gro. KT6: Surb 5J 41
Williams Hall *TW20: Eng G . . .4M 19*
(off Coopers Hill La.)
William Sim Wood
RG42: Wink R 7F 16
Williams La. SM4: Mord 4A 44
SW14 . . . . .6B 12
Williamson Cl.
GU27: G'wood 8K 171
Williams Pl. GU6: Ewh 5F 156
Williams Rd. UB2: S'hall 1M 9
Williams Ter. CR0: Wad 3L 63
William St. SL4: W'sor 4G 4
SM5: Cars 9C 44
William's Wlk. GU2: Guil 8L 93
Williams Way GU51: Fleet 4D 88
RH10: Craw 3F 182
Willian Pl. GU26: Hind 3C 170
Willingham Way
KT1: K Tham 2N 41
Willington Cl. GU15: Camb 9N 49
Willis Av. SM2: Sut 3C 62
Willis Cl. KT18: Eps 1A 80
Willis Ct. BR4: W Wick 8N 47
CR7: T Hea 5L 45
Willis Rd. CR0: Croy 6N 45
Will Miles Ct. SW19 . . . . .8A 28
Willmore End SW19 . . . . .9N 27
Willoughby Av. CR0: Bedd 1K 63
Willoughby Rd.
KT2: K Tham . . .1M 203 (9M 25)
RG12: Brac 2L 31
TW1: Twick 8J 11
(not continuous)
Willoughbys, The
SW14 . . . . .6D 12
Willow Av. SW13 . . . . .5E 12
Willow Bank GU22: Wok 9A 74
SW6 . . . . .6K 13
TW10: Ham 4H 25
Willowbank CR5: Coul 1J 83
Willowbank Gdns.
KT20: Tad 9G 81
Willowbank Pl.
CR8: S Croy 5M 63
Willow Brean RH6: Horl 7C 142
Willowbrook SL4: Eton 1G 5
TW12: H Hill 6B 24
Willowbrook Rd.
TW19: Stan 3N 21
Willow Bus. Cen., The
CR4: Mit 5D 44
Willow Cl. GU16: Mytc 1C 90
KT15: Wood 7H 55
KT16: Chert 8G 36
RH5: B Grn 7J 139
RH10: Craw 1C 182
RH19: E Grin 7N 165
SL3: Coln 3E 6
TW8: Brent 2J 11
Willow Cnr. RH6: Char 3L 161
Willow Cotts. TW9: Kew 2N 11
TW13: Hanw 4M 23
Willow Ct. GU12: A Va 6E 90
GU16: Frim 5B 70
(off Grove Cross Rd.)
RH6: Horl 5F 142
TW16: Sunb 8F 22
(off Staines Rd. W.)
W4 . . . . .3D 12
(off Corney Reach Way)
Willow Cres. GU14: Farnb 7N 69
Willowdene Cl. TW2: Whitt 1C 24
Willow Dr. GU3: Flex 3N 111
GU23: Rip 2J 95
RG12: Brac 9A 16
Willow End KT6: Surb 7L 41
Willowfield RH11: Craw 4A 182
Willow Flds. GU12: A Grn 3F 110
Willowford GU46: Yate 9C 48
Willow Gdns. TW3: Houn 4A 10
Willow Glade RH2: Reig 6A 122
Willow Grn. GU24: W End 9C 52
RH5: Nth H 9H 119
Willowhayne Ct.
KT12: Wal T 6J 39
(off Willowhayne Dr.)
Willowhayne Dr.
KT12: Wal T 6J 39
Willowhayne Gdns.
KT4: W Pk 9H 43
Willowherb Cl.
RG40: W'ham 1D 30
Willow Ho. CR6: Warl 2L 85
Willow La. CR4: Mit 4D 44
GU1: Guil 2C 114
GU17: Haw 2J 69
Willow Lodge SW6 . . . . .4J 13
TW16: Sunb 8G 23
(off Forest Dr.)
Willow Mead GU8: Wit 5B 152
RH4: Dork 1J 201 (4G 119)
RH19: E Grin 1B 186
Willowmead TW18: Stain 9K 21
Willowmead Cl. GU21: Wok . . .3K 73
Willowmere KT10: Esh 1C 58
Willow M. GU8: Wit 5C 152
Willow Mt. CR0: Croy 9B 46
Willow Pk. GU12: Ash 2D 110
Willow Pl. SL4: Eton 2F 4
Willow Ridge RH10: T Hil 6D 184
Willow Rd. GU7: Goda 3J 133
KT3: N Mal 3B 42
RH1: Red 6A 122
RH12: Hors 3A 198
SL3: Poy 5G 7
SM6: W'ton 4F 62
Willows, The *GU2: Guil 7K 93*
(off Worplesdon Rd.)
GU4: Guil 1E 114
GU8: Chid 5D 172
GU10: Run 8A 110
GU18: Ligh 6A 52
KT10: Clay 3E 58
KT13: Weybr 9B 38
KT14: Byf 9N 55
RG12: Brac 3D 32
RH1: Red 4D 122
RH12: Hors 3K 197
SL4: W'sor 3A 4
Willows Av. SM4: Mord 4N 43
Willows End GU47: Sandh 7G 48
Willows Lodge SL4: W'sor 3A 4
Willows Mobile Home Pk., The
GU3: Norm 9A 92
Willows Path KT18: Eps 1A 80
SL4: W'sor 4A 4
Willow Tree Cl. SW18 . . . . . . .2N 27
Willowtree Way CR7: T Hea . . .9L 29
Willow Va. KT22: Fetc 1B 98
(not continuous)
Willow Vw. SW19 . . . . .9B 28
Willow Wlk. BR6: Farnb 1K 67
GU5: Shere 8B 116
KT16: Chert 6J 37
KT20: Box H 8A 100
RH1: Red 5F 122
SM3: Sut 9L 43
TW20: Eng G 6M 19
Willow Way GU1: Guil 8L 93
GU9: Hale 6J 109
GU12: Alde 4C 110
GU22: Wok 8A 74
GU47: Sandh 6E 48
KT14: W By 7L 55
KT19: Ewe 3C 60
RH9: Gods 1E 124
TW2: Twick 3B 24
TW16: Sunb 3H 39
Willow Wood Cres.
SE25 . . . . .5B 46
Wills Cres. TW3: Houn 9B 10
Willson Rd. TW20: Eng G 6L 19
Wilmar Gdns. BR4: W Wick . . .7L 47
Wilmer Cl. KT2: K Tham 6M 25
Wilmer Cres. KT2: K Tham . . .6M 25
Wilmerhatch La. KT18: Eps . . .5A 80
Wilmington Av. W4 . . . . .3C 12
Wilmington Cl.
RH11: Craw 8N 181
Wilmington Ct. SW16 . . . . .8J 29
Wilmot Cl. RG42: Bin 7H 15
Wilmot Cotts. SM7: Ban 2N 81
Wilmot Rd. CR8: Pur 8L 63
SM5: Cars 2D 62
Wilmots Cl. RH2: Reig 2A 122
Wilmot's La. RH1: Horn 4A 144
RH6: Horn 4A 144
Wilmot Way GU15: Camb 3D 70
SM7: Ban 1M 81
Wilna Rd. SW18 . . . . .1A 28
Wilson Av. CR4: Mit 8C 28
Wilson Cl.
CR2: S Croy 8D 200 (2A 64)
RH10: Craw 6H 183
Wilson Dr. KT16: Otter 2D 54
Wilson Rd. GU12: Alde 3B 110
GU14: Cove 2L 89
KT9: Ches 3M 59
Wilsons KT20: Tad 8J 81
Wilsons Rd. GU35: H Dwn 4G 169
W6 . . . . .1J 13
Wilson Way GU21: Wok 3N 73
Wilstrode Av. RG42: Bin 8L 15
Wilton Av. W4 . . . . .1D 12
Wilton Cl. UB7: Harm 2M 7
Wilton Ct. GU14: Farnb 2B 90
Wilton Cres. SL4: W'sor 7A 4
SW19 . . . . .8L 27
Wilton Gdns. KT8: W Mole 2A 40
KT12: Wal T 7L 39
Wilton Gro. KT3: N Mal 5E 42
SW19 . . . . .9L 27
Wilton Ho. CR2: S Croy 8B 200
RH11: Craw 3A 182
Wilton Pde. TW13: Felt 3H 23
Wilton Pl. KT15: N Haw 5M 55
Wilton Rd. GU15: Camb 3N 69
RH1: Red 4D 122
SW19 . . . . .8C 28
TW4: Houn 6L 9
Wiltshire Av. RG45: Crow 1G 48
Wiltshire Cl.
CR2: S Croy 8C 200 (2N 63)
Wiltshire Dr. RG40: W'ham 1C 30
Wiltshire Gdns. TW2: Twick . . .2C 24
Wiltshire Gro. RG42: Warf 7D 16
Wiltshire Rd. CR7: T Hea 2L 45
RG40: W'ham 9B 14
Wilverley Cres. KT3: N Mal . . .5D 42
Wilwood Rd. RG42: Brac 9K 15
Wimbart Rd. SW2 . . . . .1K 29
WIMBLEDON 6J 27
Wimbledon
All England Lawn Tennis &
Croquet Club 5K 27
Wimbledon Bri. SW19 . . . . . . .7L 27
Wimbledon Chase Station (Rail) 1K 43
Wimbledon Cl. GU15: Camb . . .6D 50
SW20 . . . . .8J 27
Wimbledon Common 5E 26
Wimbledon Greyhound &
Speedway Stadium 5A 28
Wimbledon Hill Rd.
SW19 . . . . .7K 27
Wimbledon Lawn Tennis Mus. 4K 27
Wimbledon Leisure Cen. 7N 27
Wimbledon Mus. of Local History 7K 27
WIMBLEDON PARK 4M 27
Wimbledon Pk. Ct.
SW19 . . . . .2L 27
Wimbledon Pk. Rd.
SW18 . . . . .3K 27
SW19 . . . . .3K 27
Wimbledon Pk. Side
SW19 . . . . .4J 27
Wimbledon Park Station (Tube) 4M 27
Wimbledon Rd.
GU15: Camb 6D 50
SW17 . . . . .5A 28
Wimbledon Stadium Bus. Cen.
SW17 . . . . .4N 27
Wimbledon Station (Rail, Tube & CT) 7L 27
Wimbledon Theatre 8M 27
Wimbledon Windmill Mus. . . .3G 27
WIMBLE HILL 1A 128
Wimblehurst Ct.
RH12: Hors 4J 197
Wimblehurst Rd.
RH12: Hors 4J 197
Wimborne Av. RH1: Red 8D 122
Wimborne Cl. KT4: W Pk 7H 43
KT17: Eps 7M 201 (9D 60)
Wimborne Ct. SW12 . . . . .4G 28
Wimborne Ho. GU14: Farnb . . .3B 90
SW12 . . . . .4G 28
Wimborne Way BR3: Beck 2G 47
Wimbourne Ho.
RH11: Craw 3A 182
Wimland Hill RH12: Fay 7C 180
Wimland Rd.
RH12: Rusp, Fay 4A 180
Wimlands La. RH12: Fay 7C 180
Wimpole Cl.
KT1: K Tham . . .4M 203 (1M 41)
Wimshurst Cl. CR0: Wad 7J 45
Wincanton Cl. RH10: Craw . . .2H 183
Wincanton Rd. SW18 . . . . .1L 27
Winch Cl. RG42: Bin 6H 15
Winchcombe Cl.
GU51: Fleet 5B 88
Winchcombe Rd.
SM5: Cars 6B 44
Winchelsea Cl. SW15 . . . . .8J 13
Winchelsey Ri. CR2: S Croy . . .3C 64
Winchendon Rd. SW6 . . . . .4L 13
TW11: Tedd 5D 24
Winches, The RH13: Col 2H 199
Winchester Av. TW5: Hest 2N 9
Winchester Cl.
KT2: K Tham 8A 26
KT10: Esh 1A 58
SL3: Poy 4G 7
Winchester Ho. *KT19: Eps 8N 59*
(off Phoenix Cl.)
Winchester M. KT4: W Pk 8J 43
Winchester Rd.
GU10: Rush 3N 149
GU12: Ash 1E 110
KT12: Wal T 7H 39
RH10: Craw 7C 182
TW1: Twick 9H 11
TW13: Hanw 4N 23
UB3: Harl 3F 8
Winchester St.
GU14: Farnb 5A 90
Winchester Way
GU17: B'water 9H 49
Winchet Wlk. CR0: Croy 5F 46
Winchfield Ho. SW15 . . . . .9E 12
Winchgrove Rd.
RG42: Brac 8M 15
Winchilsea Cres.
KT8: W Mole 1C 40
Winchstone Cl. TW17: Shep . . .3A 38
Windborough Rd.
SM5: Cars 4E 62
Windermere Av. SW19 . . . . . . .2N 43
Windermere Cl.
GU14: Cove 2K 89
TW14: Felt 2G 22
TW19: Stan 2N 21
TW20: Egh 8D 20
Windermere Ct. CR8: Ken 2M 83
GU12: A Va 9D 90
(off Lakeside Cl.)
GU21: Wok 5K 73
(off St John's Rd.)
SM5: Cars 9E 44
SW13 . . . . .2E 12
Windermere Ho. TW7: Isle 8F 10

Windermere Rd.—Woodcrest Wlk.

Windermere Rd. CR0: Croy 7C 46
CR5: Coul 2J 83
GU18: Ligh 6M 51
SW15 5D 26
SW16 9G 29
Windermere Wlk.
GU15: Camb 1H 71
Windermere Way
GU9: U Hal 6F 108
RH2: Reig 2C 122
Windfield KT22: Leat 8H 79
Windgates GU4: Guil 9E 94
Windham Av. CR0: N Add 6N 65
Windham Rd. TW9: Rich 6M 11
Windings, The
CR2: Sande 7C 64
Winding Wood Dr.
GU15: Camb 2F 70
Windlebrook Grn.
RG42: Brac 9M 15
Windle Cl. GU20: Windl 3A 52
WINDLESHAM 3A 52
Windlesham Ct.
GU20: Windl 9N 33
Windlesham Ct. Dr.
GU20: Windl 1N 51
Windlesham Gro.
SW19 2J 27
Windlesham Rd.
GU24: Chob 4D 52
GU24: W End 7B 52
RG42: Brac 9L 15
Windmill Av. KT17: Ewe 7E 60
Windmill Bri. Ho.
CR0: Croy 7B 46
(off Freemasons Rd.)
Windmill Bus. Village
TW16: Sunb 9F 22
Windmill Cl. CR3: Cate 8N 83
KT6: Surb 7J 41
KT17: Eps 8E 60
RH6: Horl 8F 142
RH13: Hors 4N 197
SL4: W'sor 5E 4
TW16: Sunb 8F 22
Windmill Ct. RH4: Dork 8H 119
RH10: Craw 1B 182
Windmill Dr. BR2: Kes 1E 66
GU35: H Dwn 3G 168
KT22: Leat 1J 99
RH2: Reig 1B 122
Windmill End KT17: Eps 8E 60
Windmill Fld.
GU20: Windl 3N 51
Windmill Grn. *TW17: Shep 6F 38*
(off Walton La.)
Windmill Gro. CR0: Croy 5N 45
Windmill Hill GU12: Alde 3A 110
Windmill La. KT6: Surb 5H 41
KT17: Eps 8E 60
RH19: E Grin 2E 186
(Lewes Rd.)
RH19: E Grin 7N 165
(Lowdell's La.)
TW7: Isle 1E 10
Windmill M. W4 1D 12
Windmill Pas. W4 1D 12
Windmill Ri.
KT2: K Tham 8A 26
Windmill Rd. CR0: Croy 6N 45
CR4: Mit 4G 44
GU12: Alde 3A 110
RG42: Brac 9L 15
SW19 3G 27
TW8: Brent 1J 11
TW12: H Hill 6B 24
TW16: Sunb 9F 22
W4 1D 12
W5 1J 11
Windmill Rd. W.
TW16: Sunb 1F 38
Windmill Shott
TW20: Egh 7B 20
Windmill Ter. TW17: Shep 6F 38
Windmill Way RH2: Reig 1B 122
Windrum Cl. RH12: Hors 8F 196
Windrush KT3: N Mal 3A 42
Windrush Cl. GU5: Braml 5B 134
RH11: Craw 5L 181
W4 4B 12
Wind Rushes CR3: Cate 3D 104
Windrush Hgts.
GU47: Sandh 7F 48
WINDSOR 4G 4
Windsor & Eton FC 7E 4
Windsor & Eton Relief Rd.
SL4: Eton, W'sor 4E 4
Windsor Av. KT3: N Mal 4B 42
KT8: W Mole 2A 40
SM3: Chea 9K 43
SW19 9A 28
Windsor Boys School Sports Cen.
4E 4
Windsor Brass Rubbing Cen. 4G 5
(off High St.)
Windsor Bus. Cen.
SL4: W'sor 3F 4
Windsor Castle 3H 5
Windsor Cl. GU2: Guil 5J 113
GU14: Farnb 1N 89
RH11: Craw 7A 182
SE27 5N 29
TW8: Brent 2H 11
Windsor Ct. CR3: Whyte 5C 84
GU11: Alde 2L 109
(off Queen Elizabeth Dr.)
GU24: Chob 5H 53
GU51: Fleet 4B 88
KT1: K Tham 8H 203
RG12: Brac 3A 32
RH13: Hors 5M 197
TW16: Sunb 8H 23
Windsor Ct. Rd.
GU24: Chob 5H 53
Windsor Cres.
GU9: U Hal 6G 108
Windsor Dr. TW15: A'ford 5M 21
Windsor & Eton Central Station
(Rail) 4G 4
Windsor & Eton Riverside Station
(Rail) 3G 5
Windsor Fitness & Rackets Club, The
4E 4
Windsor Forest Ct.
SL5: Asc 9H 17
Windsor Gdns. CR0: Bedd 9J 45
GU12: Ash 2D 110
Windsor Great Pk. 4E 18
Windsor Gro. SE27 5N 29
Windsor Leisure Cen. 3E 4
Windsor M. *SW18 1A 28*
(off Wilna Rd.)
Windsor Pk. Rd. UB3: Harl 3G 8
Windsor Pl. KT16: Chert 5J 37
RH10: Craw 8D 162
RH19: E Grin 1C 186
Windsor Ride GU15: Camb 7M 49
(not continuous)
RG12: Brac 5D 32
(New Forest Ride)
RG12: Brac 4A 50
(Up. Star Post Ride)
SL5: Asc 4F 32
Windsor Rd. CR7: T Hea 1M 45
GU14: Farnb 4B 90
GU24: Chob 1F 52
GU35: Lind 4A 168
KT2: K Tham 8L 25
KT4: W Pk 8F 42
SL3: Dat 3K 5
SL4: O Win 2M 19
SL4: Wink 8L 17
SL4: W'sor 4A 4
SL5: Asc 2J 33
TW4: C'ford 5J 9
TW9: Kew 5M 11
TW11: Tedd 6D 24
TW16: Sunb 7H 23
TW19: Wray 9A 6
TW20: Egh 2M 19
Windsor St. KT16: Chert 5J 37
Windsor Wlk. GU35: Lind 4A 168
KT12: Wal T 7L 39
KT13: Weybr 2C 56
Windsor Way GU11: Alde 2N 109
GU16: Frim 6D 70
GU22: Wok 3E 74
Winds Ridge GU23: Send 3E 94
Windways GU8: Duns 2B 174
Windycroft Cl. CR8: Pur 9H 63
Windy Gap 3M 169
Windyridge RH11: Craw 4M 181
Windy Ridge Cl. SW19 6J 27
Windy Wood GU7: Goda 8F 132
Winern Glebe KT14: Byf 9M 55
Winery La.
KT1: K Tham 5L 203 (2M 41)
Winey Cl. KT9: Ches 4J 59
Winfield Gro. RH5: Newd 1N 159
Winfrith Rd. SW18 1A 28
Wingate Ct. GU11: Alde 2L 109
Wingate Cres. CR0: Croy 5J 45
Wingfield Cl. KT15: N Haw 6K 55
Wingfield Ct. SM7: Ban 2M 81
Wingfield Gdns.
GU16: Frim 3H 71
Wingfield Rd. KT2: K Tham 7M 25
Wingford Rd. SW2 1J 29
Wingrave Rd. W6 2H 13
Wings Cl. GU9: U Hal 6G 109
SM1: Sut 1M 61
Wings Rd. GU9: U Hal 6G 109
Winifred Rd. CR5: Coul 3E 82
SW19 9M 27
TW12: H Hill 5A 24
WINKFIELD 4H 17
Winkfield Cl. RG41: W'ham 5A 30
Winkfield La. SL4: Wink 3F 16
Winkfield Mnr. SL5: Asc 8H 17
Winkfield Rd. SL4: Wink 2N 17
SL5: Asc 7L 17
WINKFIELD ROW 6F 16
Winkfield Row
RG42: Wink R 5E 16
WINKFIELD STREET 3G 16
Winkfield St. SL4: Wink 3F 16
Winkworth Arboretum 3M 153
Winkworth Pl. SM7: Ban 1L 81
Winkworth Rd. SM7: Ban 1M 81
Winnards GU21: Wok 5K 73
Winnington Way
GU21: Wok 5L 73
Winnipeg Dr. BR6: Chels 3N 67
Winscombe RG12: Brac 4K 31
Winslow Rd. W6 2H 13
Winslow Way KT12: Wal T 9K 39
TW13: Hanw 4L 23
Winstanley Cl. KT11: Cob 1J 77
Winstanley Wlk. *KT11: Cob 1J 77*
(off Winstanley Cl.)
Winston Churchill Sports Cen., The
5H 73
Winston Cl. GU16: Frim G 8D 70
Winston Dr. KT11: Sto D 3M 77
TN16: B Hil 4F 86
Winston Wlk. GU10: L Bou 5H 129
Winston Way GU22: Wok 7D 74
Winta Dr. GU51: Fleet 1A 88
Winterborne Av. BR6: Orp 1M 67
Winterbourne RH12: Hors 1M 197
Winterbourne Ct.
RG12: Brac 1A 32
Winterbourne Gro.
KT13: Weybr 3D 56
Winterbourne M.
RH8: Oxt 8M 105
Winterbourne Rd.
CR7: T Hea 3L 45
Winterbourne Wlk.
GU16: Frim 6D 70
Winter Box Wlk.
TW10: Rich 8M 11
Winterbrook Rd. SE24 1N 29
Winter Cl. GU12: A Va 5E 90
Winterdown Gdns.
KT10: Esh 3N 57
Winterdown Rd. KT10: Esh 3N 57
Winterfold RH10: Craw 6E 182
Winterfold Cl. SW19 3K 27
Winterfold Cotts. GU5: Alb 7N 135
WINTERFOLD HEATH 1N 155
Winter Gdns. RH11: Craw 4A 182
Winterhill Way GU4: B'ham 8D 94
Wintersells Ind. Est.
KT14: Byf 6N 55
Wintersells Rd. KT14: Byf 6M 55
Winters Rd. KT7: T Dit 6H 41
Winterton Ct. KT1: H Wic 1G 203
RH13: Hors 6K 197
SE20 1D 46
TN16: Weste 5M 107
(off Market Sq.)
Winthorpe Rd. SW15 7K 13
Winton Cres. GU46: Yate 1C 68
Winton Rd. BR6: Farnb 1K 67
GU9: Farnh 9J 109
GU11: Alde 3M 109
Winton Way SW16 6L 29
Winwood SL4: W'sor 4C 4
Wire Cut GU10: Fren 1J 149
Wireless Rd. TN16: B Hil 2F 86
Wire Mill La. RH7: Newc 2H 165
Wisbeach Rd. CR0: Croy 4A 46
Wisborough Ct.
RH11: Craw 6L 181
Wisborough Rd.
CR2: Sande 5C 64
Wisdom Ct. *TW7: Isle 6G 11*
(off South St.)
Wise La. UB7: W Dray 1M 7
Wiseton Rd. SW17 2C 28
Wishanger La.
GU10: Churt 8F 148
Wishbone Way GU21: Wok 3J 73
Wishford Ct. KT21: A'tead 5M 79
Wishmoor Cl. GU15: Camb 7C 50
Wishmoor Rd. GU15: Camb 7C 50
WISLEY 3N 75
WISLEY COMMON 3B 76
Wisley Ct. CR2: Sande 6A 64
RH1: Red 2D 122
(off Clarendon Rd.)
Wisley Gdns. 5N 75
Wisley Gdns. GU14: Cove 2J 89
WISLEY INTERCHANGE 3D 76
Wisley La. GU23: Wis 3L 75
Wistaria La. GU46: Yate 1B 68
Wiston Ct. RH11: Craw 6L 181
RH12: Hors 3K 197
(off Woodstock Cl.)
Witham Ct. SW17 4D 28
Witham Rd. SE20 2F 46
TW7: Isle 4D 10
Witherby Cl. CR0: Croy 2B 64
Wither Dale RH6: Horl 7C 142
Withers Cl. KT9: Ches 3J 59
Witherslack Cl.
GU35: H Dwn 5G 169
Withey Brook RH6: Hook 1B 162
Withey Cl. SL4: W'sor 4B 4
Witheygate Av. TW18: Stain 7K 21
Withey Mdws. RH6: Hook 1B 162
Withies, The GU21: Knap 4H 73
KT22: Leat 7H 79
Withies La. GU3: Comp 1F 132
Withybed Cnr.
KT20: Wal H 1G 100
Withy Cl. GU18: Ligh 6N 51
Withycombe Rd. SW19 1J 27
Withypitts RH10: T Hil 6D 184
Withypitts E. RH10: T Hil 6D 184
WITLEY 6C 152
Witley Cres. CR0: N Add 3M 65
Witley Ho. SW2 1J 29
WITLEY PARK 7L 151
Witley Point *SW15 2G 26*
(off Wanborough Dr.)
Witley Station (Rail) 1C 172
Wittenham Rd. RG12: Brac 9D 16
Wittering Cl. KT2: K Tham 6K 25
Wittmead Rd. GU16: Mytc 1D 90
Witts Ho. KT1: K Tham 5L 203
Wivenhoe Ct. TW3: Houn 7N 9
Wix Hill KT24: W Hors 8C 96
Wix Hill Cl. KT24: W Hors 9C 96
Woburn Av. CR8: Pur 7L 63
GU14: Farnb 1B 90
Woburn Cl. GU16: Frim 5E 70
SW19 7A 28
Woburn Ct.
CR0: Croy 1C 200 (7N 45)
Woburn Hill KT15: Addl 8L 37
WOBURN PARK 8M 37
Woburn Rd.
CR0: Croy 1C 200 (7N 45)
RH11: Craw 5M 181
SM5: Cars 7C 44
Wodeland Av.
GU2: Guil 7A 202 (5L 113)
Woffington Cl. KT1: H Wic 9J 25
WOKING 4B 74
Woking Bus. Pk.
GU21: Wok 2D 74
Woking Cl. SW15 7E 12
Woking Crematorium
GU21: Wok 6H 73
Woking FC 7B 74
WOKINGHAM 2A 30
Wokingham Rd.
GU47: Sandh 3D 48
RG42: Brac 9K 15
RG45: Crow 3D 48
Wokingham Station (Rail) 2A 30
Wokingham Theatre 9A 14
WOKINGHAM WITHOUT 8E 30
Woking Leisure Cen. 6B 74
Woking Rd. GU1: Guil 6M 93
(not continuous)
GU4: J Wel 6M 93
Woking Station (Rail) 4B 74
Wold, The CR3: Wold 9K 85
Wold Cl. RH11: Craw 5L 181
Woldhurstlea Cl.
RH11: Craw 5M 181
WOLDINGHAM 1K 105
WOLDINGHAM GARDEN VILLAGE
7H 85
Woldingham Nature Reserve
4L 105
Woldingham Rd. CR3: Wold 7E 84
Woldingham Station (Rail) 9G 85
Wolds Dr. BR6: Farnb 1J 67
Wolesley Ct. *GU21: Knap 5F 72*
(off Tudor Way)
Wolfe Cotts. TN16: Weste 5M 107
Wolfe Rd. GU12: Alde 3A 110
Wolfington Rd. SE27 5M 29
Wolf La. SL4: W'sor 6A 4
Wolf's Hill RH8: Oxt 9C 106
Wolf's Rd. RH8: Limp 8D 106
Wolf's Row RH8: Limp 7D 106
Wolfs Wood RH8: Oxt 1C 126
Wolseley Av. SW19 3M 27
Wolseley Gdns. W4 2A 12
Wolseley Rd. CR4: Mit 6E 44
GU7: Goda 5H 133
GU11: Alde 3M 109
Wolsey Av. KT7: T Dit 4F 40
Wolsey Cl. KT2: K Tham 9A 26
KT4: W Pk 1F 60
SW20 8G 26
TW3: Houn 7C 10
Wolsey Cres. CR0: N Add 5M 65
SM4: Mord 6K 43
Wolsey Dr. KT2: K Tham 6L 25
KT12: Wal T 7L 39
Wolsey Gro. KT10: Esh 1B 58
Wolsey Pl. Shop. Cen.
GU21: Wok 4A 74
Wolsey Rd. KT8: E Mol 3D 40
KT10: Esh 1B 58
TW12: H Hill 7B 24
TW15: A'ford 5N 21
TW16: Sunb 8G 23
Wolsey Wlk. GU21: Wok 4A 74
Wolsey Way KT9: Ches 2N 59
Wolstonbury Cl.
RH11: Craw 5A 182
Wolvens La. RH4: Dork 9A 118
RH5: A Com, Cold 2B 138
Wolverton Av. KT2: K Tham 9N 25
Wolverton Cl. RH6: Horl 1D 162
Wolverton Gdns.
RH6: Horl 9D 142
Wolves Hill RH5: Cap 6J 159
Wondesford Dale
RG42: Bin 5H 15
WONERSH 4D 134
WONERSH COMMON 2D 134
Wonersh Comn. Rd.
GU5: Wone 2D 134
Wonersh Pk. GU5: Wone 5D 134
Wonersh Way SM2: Chea 5J 61
Wonford Cl. KT2: K Tham 9D 26
KT20: Wal H 4F 100
Wonham La. RH3: Betch 4D 120
Wonham Pl. RH9: Tand 4J 125
Wonham Way
GU5: Gorn, P'lake 8E 116
(not continuous)
Wontford Rd. CR8: Pur 2L 83
Wontner Rd. SW17 3D 28
Woodall Cl. KT9: Ches 4J 59
Woodbarn, The
GU9: Farnh 2H 129
Woodberry Cl. GU8: Chid 4D 172
TW16: Sunb 7H 23
Woodbine Cl. GU47: Sandh 8H 49
TW2: Twick 3D 24
Woodbine La. KT4: W Pk 9G 43
Woodbines Av.
KT1: K Tham 6H 203 (2K 41)
Woodborough Rd.
SW15 7G 12
Woodbourne GU9: Weybo 5K 109
Woodbourne Av.
SW16 4H 29
Woodbourne Cl. GU46: Yate 9C 48
SW16 4J 29
Woodbourne Dr. KT10: Clay 3F 58
Woodbourne Gdns.
SM6: W'ton 4F 62
Woodbridge Av. KT22: Leat 5G 79
Woodbridge Bus. Pk.
GU1: Guil 1A 202 (2M 113)
Woodbridge Cnr.
KT22: Leat 5G 78
Woodbridge Ct.
RH12: Hors 3N 197
Woodbridge Dr.
GU15: Camb 8B 50
Woodbridge Gro. KT22: Leat 5G 79
WOODBRIDGE HILL 2L 113
Woodbridge Hill GU2: Guil 2L 113
Woodbridge Hill Gdns.
GU2: Guil 2K 113
Woodbridge Mdws.
GU1: Guil 1A 202 (2M 113)
Woodbridge Rd.
GU1: Guil 1A 202 (2M 113)
(not continuous)
GU17: B'water 1G 69
Woodbury Av. RH19: E Grin 1D 186
Woodbury Cl. CR0: Croy 8C 46
RH19: E Grin 1C 186
(not continuous)
TN16: B Hil 5H 87
Woodbury Dr. SM2: Sut 6A 62
Woodbury St. SW17 6C 28
Woodby Dr. SL5: S'dale 6C 34
Wood Cl. RH1: Salf 3E 142
SL4: W'sor 7F 4
Woodcock Bottom & Whitmore Vale
4N 169
Woodcock Chase
RG12: Brac 3J 31
Woodcock Dr. GU24: Chob 4F 52
Woodcock Hill RH19: Fel 4J 165
Woodcock La. GU24: Chob 4E 52
WOODCOTE
CR8 8H 63
KT18 3B 80
Woodcote GU2: Guil 7L 113
GU6: Cranl 6K 155
GU7: Goda 5G 133
(off Frith Hill Rd.)
RH6: Horl 7F 142
Woodcote Av. CR7: T Hea 3M 45
SM6: W'ton 5F 62
Woodcote Cl. KT2: K Tham 6M 25
KT18: Eps 8J 201 (1C 80)
Woodcote Dr. CR8: Pur 6H 63
Woodcote End KT18: Eps 2C 80
WOODCOTE GREEN 5G 62
Woodcote Grn. SM6: W'ton 5G 62
Woodcote Grn. Rd.
KT18: Eps 2B 80
WOODCOTE GROVE 9F 62
Woodcote Gro. Rd.
CR5: Coul 2H 83
Woodcote Hall
KT18: Eps 8J 201 (1C 80)
Woodcote Ho. KT18: Eps 2B 80
Woodcote Ho. Ct.
KT18: Eps 2C 80
Woodcote Hurst KT18: Eps 3B 80
Woodcote La. CR8: Pur 7H 63
Woodcote Lodge KT18: Eps 2B 80
Woodcote M. SM6: W'ton 3F 62
WOODCOTE PARK 4B 80
Woodcote Pk. Av. CR8: Pur 8G 63
Woodcote Pk. Rd.
KT18: Eps 3B 80
Woodcote Pl. SE27 6M 29
SL5: Asc 9K 17
Woodcote Rd. CR8: Pur 6G 62
KT18: Eps 8J 201 (1C 80)
RH18: F Row 7G 187
SM6: W'ton 3F 62
Woodcote Side KT18: Eps 2A 80
Woodcote Valley Rd.
CR8: Pur 9H 63
Woodcote Vs. *SE27 6N 29*
(off Woodcote Pl.)
Woodcot Gdns. GU14: Cove 1J 89
Woodcott Ter. GU12: Alde 4B 110
Wood Ct. GU2: Guil 1L 113
Woodcourt RH11: Craw 8A 182
Woodcray La.
RG40: W'ham 6A 30
Wood Crest *SM2: Sut 4A 62*
(off Christchurch Pk.)
Woodcrest Rd. CR8: Pur 9J 63
Woodcrest Wlk. RH2: Reig 1C 122

Woodcroft Rd.—Worple Rd.

Woodcroft Rd. CR7: T Hea . . . 4M 45
RH11: Ifi . . . 5J 181
Woodcut Rd. GU10: Wrec . . . 5E 128
WOOD END . . . 7M 17
Wood End GU14: Farnb . . . 2B 90
RH12: Hors . . . 3B 198
Wood End, The SM6: W'ton . . . 5F 62
Woodend KT10: Esh . . . 8C 40
KT22: Leat . . . 3J 99
SE19 . . . 7N 29
SM1: Sut . . . 8A 44
Woodend Cl. GU21: Wok . . . 6K 73
RH10: Craw . . . 1E 182
SL5: Asc . . . 9J 17
Woodend Dr. SL5: S'hill . . . 4M 33
Woodend Pk. KT11: Cob . . . 2L 77
Woodend Ride SL4: Wink . . . 8M 17
SL5: Asc . . . 8M 17
Woodend Rd. GU16: Deep . . . 7G 71
Woodenhill RG12: Brac . . . 6K 31
Wooderson Cl. SE25 . . . 3B 46
Woodfield KT21: A'tead . . . 4K 79
Woodfield Av. SM5: Cars . . . 3E 62
SW16 . . . 4H 29
Woodfield Cl. CR5: Coul . . . 6G 82
KT21: A'tead . . . 4K 79
RH1: Red . . . 1C 122
RH10: Craw . . . 2C 182
SE19 . . . 8N 29
Woodfield Gdns.
KT3: N Mal . . . 4E 42
Woodfield Gro. SW16 . . . 4H 29
Woodfield Hill CR5: Coul . . . 6F 82
Woodfield Ho. KT7: T Dit . . . 8F 40
(off Woodfield Rd.)
Woodfield La. KT21: A'tead . . . 4L 79
SW16 . . . 4H 29
Woodfield Lodge
RH10: Craw . . . 1E 182
Woodfield Rd. KT7: T Dit . . . 8F 40
KT21: A'tead . . . 4K 79
RH10: Craw . . . 2C 182
RH12: Rudg . . . 1E 194
TW4: C'ford . . . 5J 9
Woodfields, The
CR2: Sande . . . 7C 64
Woodfield Way RH1: Red . . . 1C 122
Woodforde Ct. UB3: Harl . . . 1E 8
Woodford Grn. RG12: Brac . . . 3D 32
Woodgate GU51: Fleet . . . 2D 88
Woodgate Av. KT9: Ches . . . 2K 59
Woodgate Cl. KT11: Cob . . . 9J 57
Woodgate Dr. SW16 . . . 8H 29
Woodgates Cl.
RH13: Hors . . . 5M 197
Woodgavil SM7: Ban . . . 3L 81
Woodger Cl. GU4: Guil . . . 1E 114
Woodhall La. SL5: S'dale . . . 8B 34
WOODHAM . . . 6J 55
Woodham Hall Farm
GU21: Wok . . . 1D 74
Woodham La. GU21: Wok . . . 1D 74
KT15: Wok . . . 1D 74
KT15: Wood, N Haw . . . 8G 55
Woodham Lock KT14: W By . . . 8H 55
Woodham Pk. Rd.
KT15: Wood . . . 5H 55
Woodham Pk. Way
KT15: Wood . . . 7H 55
Woodham Pl. GU21: Wok . . . 1B 74
Woodham Ri. GU21: Wok . . . 1B 74
Woodham Rd. GU21: Wok . . . 2A 74
Woodham Waye
GU21: Wok . . . 9D 54
WOODHATCH . . . 6N 121
Woodhatch Rd. RH1: Red . . . 6N 121
RH2: Reig . . . 6N 121
Woodhatch Spinney
CR5: Coul . . . 3J 83
Woodhaven M. KT12: Wal T . . . 1H 57
Woodhaw TW20: Egh . . . 5D 20
Woodhayes RH6: Horl . . . 7F 142
Woodhayes Rd. SW19 . . . 8H 27
Woodhill GU23: Send . . . 4F 94
Woodhill Ct. GU23: Send . . . 3F 94
Woodhill La. GU5: Sha G . . . 7G 135
GU10: Fren . . . 2D 148
Woodhouse La.
RH5: H Mary . . . 3H 137
Woodhouse St. RG42: Bin . . . 8K 15
Woodhurst La. RH8: Oxt . . . 8A 106
Woodhurst Pk. RH8: Oxt . . . 8A 106
Woodhyrst Gdns. CR8: Ken . . . 2M 83
Woodies Cl. RG42: Bin . . . 8H 15
Wooding Gro. RH11: Craw . . . 8N 181
Woodland Av. GU6: Cranl . . . 7A 156
SL4: W'sor . . . 7C 4
Woodland Cl. KT13: Weybr . . . 1E 56
KT19: Ewe . . . 3D 60
KT24: E Hor . . . 5G 97
RH13: Hors . . . 4A 198
Woodland Ct. GU52: C Cro . . . 9A 88
KT17: Eps . . . 8E 60
RH8: Oxt . . . 6N 105
Woodland Craft Cen. . . . 8C 62
Woodland Cres.
GU14: Farnb . . . 8A 70
RG42: Brac . . . 8A 16
Woodland Dr. GU10: Wrec . . . 5G 128
KT24: E Hor . . . 5G 96
RH5: Ockl . . . 5G 159
RH10: Craw D . . . 1E 184
TN8: Eden . . . 9M 127
Woodland Gdns. CR2: Sels . . . 7F 64
TW7: Isle . . . 6E 10
Woodland Gro.
KT13: Weybr . . . 1E 56
Woodland La. RH13: Col . . . 6G 198
Woodland M. SW16 . . . 4J 29
Woodland Ri.
GU52: C Cro . . . 8A 88
RH8: Oxt . . . 8A 106
Woodland Rd. CR7: T Hea . . . 3L 45
WOODLANDS . . . 5E 10
Woodlands GU22: Wok . . . 5B 74
GU23: Send . . . 3H 95
GU46: Yate . . . 3C 68
GU51: Fleet . . . 3A 88
KT15: Addl . . . 9N 37
KT21: A'tead . . . 5L 79
RH6: Horl . . . 7G 143
RH10: Craw . . . 1H 183
SW20 . . . 3H 43
Woodlands, The GU1: Guil . . . 2E 114
KT10: Esh . . . 8C 40
RH6: Smal . . . 8M 143
SE19 . . . 8N 29
SM6: W'ton . . . 5F 62
TW7: Isle . . . 5F 10
Woodlands Av.
GU9: Weybo . . . 5L 109
KT3: N Mal . . . 9B 26
KT4: W Pk . . . 8E 42
KT14: W By . . . 9H 55
RH1: Red . . . 4D 122
Woodlands Cvn. Pk.
GU12: Ash . . . 3D 110
Woodlands Cl. GU1: Guil . . . 8A 94
GU6: Cranl . . . 7A 156
GU12: A Va . . . 8E 90
GU17: Haw . . . 5K 69
KT10: Clay . . . 4F 58
KT16: Otter . . . 6D 54
RH10: Craw D . . . 2E 184
SL5: Asc . . . 5K 33
Woodlands Copse
KT21: A'tead . . . 3K 79
Woodlands Cotts.
RH5: Newd . . . 7B 160
Woodlands Ct. GU21: Wok . . . 5K 73
GU22: Wok . . . 6A 74
GU47: Owls . . . 6L 49
RH1: Red . . . 5D 122
Woodlands Dr.
RH9: S Gods . . . 6H 125
TW16: Sunb . . . 1K 39
Woodlands Gdns.
KT18: Tat C . . . 4H 81
Woodlands Ga. SW15 . . . 8L 13
(off Woodlands Way)
Woodlands Gro. CR5: Coul . . . 4E 82
TW7: Isle . . . 5E 10
Woodlands Ho. GU21: Wok . . . 1E 74
Woodlands La.
GU20: Windl . . . 3A 52
GU27: Hasl . . . 1D 188
KT11: Leat, Sto D . . . 4A 78
Woodlands Pde.
TW15: A'ford . . . 7D 22
Woodlands Pk. GU1: Guil . . . 2D 114
GU21: Wok . . . 1E 74
KT15: Addl . . . 2H 55
KT20: Box H . . . 9A 100
Woodlands Ride SL5: Asc . . . 5K 33
Woodlands Rd. GU1: Guil . . . 8N 93
GU8: Hamb . . . 9G 152
GU14: Cove . . . 8J 69
GU15: Camb . . . 1N 69
GU25: V Wat . . . 3M 35
KT6: Surb . . . 6K 41
KT14: W By . . . 1H 75
KT18: Eps . . . 2N 79
KT22: Leat . . . 4D 78
KT23: Book . . . 6M 97
RH1: Red . . . 5D 122
RH19: E Grin . . . 6C 166
SW13 . . . 6E 12
TW7: Isle . . . 6D 10
Woodlands Rd. E.
GU25: V Wat . . . 3M 35
Woodlands Rd. W.
GU25: V Wat . . . 3M 35
Woodlands Vw.
RH5: Mid H . . . 2H 139
Woodlands Wlk.
GU17: Haw . . . 5K 69
Woodlands Way
KT21: A'tead . . . 3N 79
SW15 . . . 8L 13
Woodland Vw.
GU7: Goda . . . 2H 133
Woodland Wlk.
GU12: Alde . . . 1B 110
KT19: Ewe . . . 3N 59
Woodland Way
BR4: W Wick . . . 1L 65
CR0: Croy . . . 7H 47
CR3: Cate . . . 6B 104
CR4: Mit . . . 8E 28
CR8: Pur . . . 9L 63
KT5: Surb . . . 8A 42
KT13: Weybr . . . 2E 56
KT20: Box H . . . 8B 100
KT20: K'wood . . . 9K 81
RH13: Hors . . . 4N 197
SM4: Mord . . . 3L 43
Wood La. CR3: Cate . . . 2A 104
GU10: Seal . . . 8F 110
GU14: Cove . . . 2M 89
GU21: Knap . . . 5G 72
GU51: Fleet . . . 4D 88
KT13: Weybr . . . 5D 56
KT20: Tad . . . 4L 81
RG42: Bin . . . 6J 15
TW7: Isle . . . 2E 10
Woodlark Glade
GU15: Camb . . . 8B 50
Woodlawn Cl. SW15 . . . 8L 13
Woodlawn Cres.
TW2: Whitt . . . 3B 24
Woodlawn Dr. TW13: Felt . . . 3L 23
Woodlawn Gro.
GU21: Wok . . . 2B 74
Woodlawn Rd. SW6 . . . 3J 13
Woodlawns KT19: Ewe . . . 4C 60
Wood Lea Cotts.
RH12: Bro H . . . 1N 195
Woodlee Cl. GU25: V Wat . . . 1M 35
Woodleigh GU51: Fleet . . . 5B 88
Woodleigh Gdns.
SW16 . . . 4J 29
Woodley Cl. SW17 . . . 8D 28
Woodley Ho. GU7: Goda . . . 3H 133
Woodley La. SM5: Cars . . . 9C 44
Woodlodge KT21: A'tead . . . 4L 79
Wood Lodge La.
BR4: W Wick . . . 9M 47
Woodmancote Ct.
RH12: Hors . . . 3K 197
(off Blenheim Rd.)
Woodmancote Gdns.
KT14: W By . . . 9J 55
Woodmancott Cl.
RG12: Brac . . . 5D 32
Woodman Ct. GU51: Fleet . . . 5A 88
Woodmancourt
GU7: Goda . . . 3F 132
Woodman M. TW9: Kew . . . 4A 12
Woodman Rd. CR5: Coul . . . 2G 83
Woodmans Hill
RH11: Craw . . . 8A 182
WOODMANSTERNE . . . 2D 82
Woodmansterne La.
SM5: Cars . . . 8D 62
SM6: W'ton . . . 8D 62
SM7: Ban . . . 2N 81
Woodmansterne Rd.
CR5: Coul . . . 2G 83
SM5: Cars . . . 8D 62
SW16 . . . 8G 29
Woodmansterne Station (Rail)
. . . 3F 82
Woodmansterne St.
SM7: Ban . . . 2C 82
Woodmere RG12: Brac . . . 3C 32
Woodmere Av. CR0: Croy . . . 6F 46
Woodmere Cl. CR0: Croy . . . 6G 47
Woodmere Gdns.
CR0: Croy . . . 6G 46
Woodmere Way BR3: Beck . . . 4N 47
Woodmill Ct. SL5: Asc . . . 2H 33
Woodnook Rd. SW16 . . . 6F 28
Woodpecker Cl.
GU10: Ews . . . 4C 108
KT11: Cob . . . 8M 57
TN8: Eden . . . 9M 127
Woodpecker La.
RH5: Newd . . . 9B 140
Woodpecker Mt. CR0: Sels . . . 5H 65
Woodpeckers GU8: Mil . . . 3B 152
RG12: Brac . . . 3N 31
(off Crowthorne Rd.)
Woodpecker Way
GU22: Wok . . . 2N 93
RH10: T Hil . . . 4F 184
Woodplace Cl. CR5: Coul . . . 6G 83
Woodplace La. CR5: Coul . . . 5G 83
Woodridge Cl. RG12: Brac . . . 2A 32
Wood Riding GU22: Pyr . . . 2G 75
Woodridings KT13: Weybr . . . 3B 56
Wood Ri. GU3: Guil . . . 1H 113
Wood Rd. GU7: Goda . . . 4J 133
GU9: U Hal . . . 5H 109
GU15: Camb . . . 5N 69
GU26: Hind . . . 3B 170
TN16: B Hil . . . 5E 86
TW17: Shep . . . 3B 38
Woodroffe Benton Ho.
RH11: Craw . . . 3L 181
(off Rusper Rd.)
Woodrough Copse
GU5: Braml . . . 6C 134
Woodrough La. GU5: Braml . . . 5B 134
(off High St.)
Woodrow Dr.
RG40: W'ham . . . 2D 30
Woodroyd Av. RH6: Horl . . . 9D 142
Woodroyd Gdns.
RH6: Horl . . . 1D 162
Woodruff Av. GU1: Guil . . . 9C 94
Woods Hill Cl.
RH19: Ash W . . . 3F 186
Woods Hill La.
RH19: Ash W . . . 3F 186
Woodshore Cl.
GU25: V Wat . . . 5L 35
WOODSIDE
SE25 . . . 5D 46
SL4 . . . 6N 17
Woodside GU14: Farnb . . . 7N 69
GU15: Camb . . . 8L 49
GU17: Haw . . . 4H 69
KT12: Wal T . . . 7H 39
KT20: Lwr K . . . 6L 101
KT22: Fetc . . . 9B 78
KT24: W Hors . . . 4D 96
RH13: Hors . . . 4A 198
SW19 . . . 7L 27
Woodside Av. KT10: Esh . . . 6E 40
KT12: Hers . . . 1J 57
SE25 . . . 5E 46
Woodside Cl. CR3: Cate . . . 2B 104
GU8: Chid . . . 5E 172
GU21: Knap . . . 4G 73
KT5: Surb . . . 6B 42
Woodside Cotts.
CR3: Wold . . . 1K 105
GU8: Els . . . 8G 131
Woodside Ct. GU14: Cove . . . 9J 69
(off Guillemont Flds.)
Woodside Ct. Rd.
CR0: Croy . . . 6D 46
Woodside Cres.
RH6: Smal . . . 8L 143
Woodside Gdns.
GU51: Fleet . . . 4D 88
Woodside Grn. SE25 . . . 5D 46
(not continuous)
Woodside Ho. SW19 . . . 7L 27
Woodside La. SL4: Wink . . . 6N 17
Woodside Pk. SE25 . . . 5E 46
Woodside Pk. Est.
GU7: Goda . . . 7J 133
Woodside Rd. CR8: Pur . . . 9H 63
GU2: Guil . . . 2J 113
GU8: Chid . . . 4C 172
GU9: Weybo . . . 5K 109
GU14: Farnb . . . 6L 89
KT2: K Tham . . . 8L 25
KT3: N Mal . . . 1C 42
KT11: Cob . . . 9A 58
RH5: B Grn . . . 8K 139
RH10: Craw . . . 1D 182
SE25 . . . 5E 46
SL4: Wink . . . 6M 17
SM1: Sut . . . 9A 44
Woodside Rd. Flats
GU8: Chid . . . 5E 172
(off Woodside Rd.)
Woodside Stop (CT) . . . 5E 46
Woodside Way CR0: Croy . . . 5F 46
CR4: Mit . . . 9F 28
GU25: V Wat . . . 2L 35
RH1: Red . . . 4E 122
(Redstone Hollow)
RH1: Red . . . 9E 122
(West Av.)
Woodsome Lodge
KT13: Weybr . . . 3D 56
Woodspring Rd. SW19 . . . 3K 27
WOODSTOCK, THE . . . 6L 43
Woodstock GU4: W Cla . . . 6K 95
RH19: E Grin . . . 8M 165
Woodstock Av. SL3: Lang . . . 1N 5
SM3: Sut . . . 6L 43
TW7: Isle . . . 8G 10
Woodstock Cl. GU6: Cranl . . . 9A 156
GU21: Wok . . . 3A 74
RH12: Hors . . . 3K 197
Woodstock Ct.
KT19: Eps . . . 5K 201 (9C 60)
Woodstock Gro.
GU7: Goda . . . 4G 133
Woodstock La. KT9: Ches . . . 1H 59
Woodstock La. Nth.
KT6: Surb . . . 8J 41
Woodstock La. Sth.
KT9: Ches . . . 2H 59
KT10: Clay . . . 2H 59
Woodstock Ri. SM3: Sut . . . 6L 43
Woodstock Rd.
CR0: Croy . . . 5D 200 (9A 46)
CR5: Coul . . . 3F 82
SM5: Cars . . . 2E 62
Woodstocks GU14: Farnb . . . 8A 70
Woodstock Way CR4: Mit . . . 1F 44
Woodstone Av. KT17: Ewe . . . 2F 60
Wood St. CR4: Mit . . . 6E 44
GU12: A Va . . . 7E 90
KT1: K Tham . . . 3H 203 (1K 41)
(not continuous)
RH1: Mers . . . 7G 103
RH19: E Grin . . . 9N 165
W4 . . . 1D 12
Wood St. Grn.
GU3: Wood V . . . 1D 112
WOOD STREET VILLAGE . . . 1E 112
Woodsway KT22: Oxs . . . 1E 78
Woodthorpe Rd.
SW15 . . . 7G 13
TW15: A'ford . . . 7M 21
Woodvale Av. SE25 . . . 2C 46
Woodvale Wlk. SE27 . . . 6N 29
Woodview KT9: Ches . . . 7J 59
Woodview Cl. CR2: Sande . . . 1E 84
KT21: A'tead . . . 3N 79
SW15 . . . 5C 26
Woodview Ct. KT13: Weybr . . . 2D 56
Woodville Cl.
GU17: B'water . . . 1G 68
TW11: Tedd . . . 5G 24
Woodville Ct. KT22: Leat . . . 7H 79
Woodville Gdns. KT6: Surb . . . 6K 41
Woodville Rd. CR7: T Hea . . . 3N 45
SM4: Mord . . . 3M 43
TW10: Ham . . . 4H 25
Woodvill Rd. KT22: Leat . . . 7H 79
Woodward Cl. KT10: Clay . . . 3F 58
Woodwards RH11: Craw . . . 8N 181
Woodward's Footpath
TW2: Whitt . . . 9C 10
Woodway GU1: Guil . . . 2D 114
GU15: Camb . . . 1N 69
Woodyers Cl. GU5: Wone . . . 4D 134
Woolacombe Way UB3: Harl . . . 1G 8
Woolborough Cl.
RH10: Craw . . . 2C 182
Woolborough La. RH1: Out . . . 3K 143
RH10: Craw . . . 9D 162
Woolborough Rd.
RH10: Craw . . . 2B 182
Wooldridge Cl. TW14: Bedf . . . 2D 22
Woolf Dr. RG40: W'ham . . . 1A 30
Woolford Cl. RG42: Wink R . . . 8F 16
Woolfords La. GU8: Els . . . 3E 150
Woolhampton Way
RG12: Brac . . . 4B 32
Woolhams CR3: Cate . . . 4D 104
Woollards Rd. GU12: A Va . . . 9F 90
Woolmead, The
GU9: Farnh . . . 9H 109
Woolmead Rd. GU9: Farnh . . . 9H 109
Woolmead Wlk.
GU9: Farnh . . . 9H 109
(off Woolmead Rd.)
WOOLMER HILL . . . 1A 188
Woolmer Hill Rd.
GU27: Hasl . . . 9A 170
Woolmer La. GU30: Brams . . . 8F 168
(not continuous)
Woolmer Vw. GU26: G'hott . . . 6B 170
Woolneigh St. SW6 . . . 6N 13
Wool Rd. SW20 . . . 7G 27
Woolsack Ct. GU2: Guil . . . 9K 93
Woolsack Way GU7: Goda . . . 7H 133
Wootton KT10: Esh . . . 1C 58
Wootton Cl. KT18: Eps . . . 3E 80
Wootton Grange GU22: Wok . . . 6A 74
(off Langley Wlk.)
Worbeck Rd. SE20 . . . 1E 46
Worcester Cl. CR0: Croy . . . 8K 47
CR4: Mit . . . 1E 44
GU14: Farnb . . . 7N 69
Worcester Ct. GU51: Fleet . . . 2A 88
(off King John St.)
KT4: W Pk . . . 9D 42
KT12: Wal T . . . 8K 39
RH1: Red . . . 1C 122
(off Timperley Gdns.)
Worcester Dr. TW15: A'ford . . . 6C 22
Worcester Gdns. KT4: W Pk . . . 9D 42
WORCESTER PARK . . . 7F 42
Worcester Pk. Rd.
KT4: W Pk . . . 9C 42
Worcester Park Station (Rail)
. . . 7F 42
Worcester Rd. GU2: Guil . . . 1J 113
RH2: Reig . . . 2L 121
RH10: Craw . . . 7C 182
SM2: Sut . . . 4M 61
SW19 . . . 6L 27
Worcestershire Lea
RG42: Warf . . . 8D 16
Wordsworth RG12: Brac . . . 4K 31
Wordsworth Av. CR8: Ken . . . 2A 84
GU46: Yate . . . 1A 68
Wordsworth Cl.
RH10: Craw . . . 1F 182
Wordsworth Dr. SM3: Chea . . . 1H 61
Wordsworth Mans.
W14 . . . 2L 13
(off Queens Club Gdns.)
Wordsworth Mead
RH1: Red . . . 1E 122
Wordsworth Pl.
RH12: Hors . . . 1L 197
Wordsworth Ri.
RH19: E Grin . . . 9M 165
Wordsworth Rd.
KT15: Addl . . . 1M 55
SM6: W'ton . . . 3G 63
TW12: Hamp . . . 5N 23
Wordsworth Way
UB7: W Dray . . . 1N 7
Workshop Gym, The
. . . 1D 202 (2N 113)
World Bus. Cen. TW6: Lon A . . . 4D 8
World's End KT11: Cob . . . 1H 77
Worlds End Hill RG12: Brac . . . 5D 32
Worleys Dr. BR6: Orp . . . 1M 67
Worlidge St. W6 . . . 1H 13
WORMLEY . . . 9C 152
Wormley La. GU8: Worm . . . 9D 152
Worple, The TW19: Wray . . . 9B 6
Worple Av. SW19 . . . 8J 27
TW7: Isle . . . 8G 10
TW18: Stain . . . 7K 21
Worple Rd.
KT18: Eps . . . 8K 201 (2C 80)
KT22: Leat . . . 9H 79
(Orchard Leigh, not continuous)
KT22: Leat . . . 1H 99
(The Driftway, not continuous)
SW19 . . . 1H 43
SW20 . . . 1H 43

HOSPITALS and HOSPICES
covered by this atlas.

N.B. Where Hospitals and Hospices are not named on the map, the reference
given is for the road in which they are situated.

ABRAHAM COWLEY UNIT 9F **36**
Holloway Hill
Lyne
CHERTSEY
KT16 0AE
Tel: 01932 872010

ALPHA HOSPITAL, WOKING 5G **72**
Redding Way
Knaphill
WOKING
GU21 2QS
Tel: 01483 795100

ASHFORD HOSPITAL 3N **21**
London Road
ASHFORD
TW15 3AA
Tel: 01784 884488

ASHTEAD CAPIO HOSPITAL 6L **79**
The Warren
ASHTEAD
KT21 2SB
Tel: 01372 221400

BARNES HOSPITAL 6D **12**
South Worple Way
LONDON
SW14 8SU
Tel: 020 88784981

BECKENHAM HOSPITAL 1J **47**
379 Croydon Road
BECKENHAM
BR3 3QL
Tel: 01689 863000

BETHLEM ROYAL HOSPITAL 6K **47**
Monks Orchard Road
BECKENHAM
BR3 3BX
Tel: 020 32286000

BRITISH HOME, THE 6M **29**
Crown Lane
LONDON
SW16 3JB
Tel: 020 8670 8261

BROADMOOR HOSPITAL 2K **49**
Kentigern Drive
CROWTHORNE
RG45 7EG
Tel: 01344 754520

CANE HILL FORENSIC MENTAL HEALTH UNIT
.................................5G **82**
Brighton Road
COULSDON
CR5 3YL
Tel: 01737 758300

CARSHALTON WAR MEMORIAL HOSPITAL
.................................3D **62**
The Park
CARSHALTON
SM5 3DB
Tel: 020 8647 5534

CASSEL HOSPITAL, THE 5K **25**
1 Ham Common
RICHMOND
TW10 7JF
Tel: 020 8940 8181

CASUALTY PLUS WALK-IN CENTRE
(BRENTFORD) 1J **11**
1010 Great West Road
BRENTFORD
TW8 9BA
Tel: 0845 677 7999

CATERHAM DENE HOSPITAL 1C **104**
Church Road
CATERHAM
CR3 5RA
Tel: 01883 837500

CHARING CROSS HOSPITAL 2J **13**
Fulham Palace Road
LONDON
W6 8RF
Tel: 020 88461234

CHASE CHILDREN'S HOSPICE
(CHRISTOPHER'S) 8M **113**
Old Portsmouth Road
Artington
GUILDFORD
GU3 1LP
Tel: 01483 230960

CHILDREN'S TRUST, THE 8J **81**
Tadworth Court
TADWORTH
KT20 5RU
Tel: 01737 365000

CLARE PARK CLASSIC HOSPITAL 8A **108**
Crondall Lane
FARNHAM
GU10 5XX
Tel: 01252 850216

COBHAM COMMUNITY HOSPITAL 9J **57**
Portsmouth Road
COBHAM
KT11 1HT
Tel: 020 8296 2000

CRANLEIGH VILLAGE HOSPITAL 8M **155**
6 High Street
CRANLEIGH
GU6 8AE
Tel: 01483 782000

CRAWLEY HOSPITAL 3A **182**
West Green Drive
CRAWLEY
RH11 7DH
Tel: 01293 600300

DORKING COMMUNITY HOSPITAL 6H **119**
Horsham Road
DORKING
RH4 2AA
Tel: 01306 887150

EAST SURREY HOSPITAL 7E **122**
Canada Avenue
REDHILL
RH1 5RH
Tel: 01737 768511

EDENBRIDGE & DISTRICT WAR
MEMORIAL HOSPITAL 4L **147**
Mill Hill
EDENBRIDGE
TN8 5DA
Tel: 01732 863164 / 862137

EPSOM DAY SURGERY UNIT 9E **60**
The Old Cottage Hospital
Alexandra Road
EPSOM
KT17 4BL
Tel: 01372 739002

EPSOM GENERAL HOSPITAL 2B **80**
Dorking Road
EPSOM
KT18 7EG
Tel: 01372 735735

FARMFIELD 1N **161**
Farmfield Drive
Charlwood
HORLEY
RH6 0BN
Tel: 01293 787500

FARM PLACE 2C **178**
Stane Street
Ockley
DORKING
RH5 5NG
Tel: 01306 627742

FARNHAM HOSPITAL & CENTRE FOR HEALTH
.................................9K **109**
Hale Road
FARNHAM
GU9 9QL
Tel: 01483 782000

FARNHAM ROAD HOSPITAL
.................6A **202** (5L **113**)
Farnham Road
GUILDFORD
GU2 7LX
Tel: 01483 443535

FLEET COMMUNITY HOSPITAL 3A **88**
Church Road
FLEET
GU51 4LZ
Tel: 01483 782700

FRIMLEY PARK HOSPITAL 4B **70**
Portsmouth Road
Frimley
CAMBERLEY
GU16 7UJ
Tel: 01276 604604

GATWICK PARK BUPA HOSPITAL 9C **142**
Povey Cross Road
HORLEY
RH6 0BB
Tel: 01293 785511

GUILDFORD NUFFIELD HOSPITAL 3H **113**
Stirling Road
GUILDFORD
GU2 7RF
Tel: 01483 555800

HARLINGTON HOSPICE
(THE REG HOPKINS DAY CARE HOSPICE)
.................................1E **8**
St Peters Way
HAYES
UB3 5AB
Tel: 020 8759 0453 / 1700

HASLEMERE COMMUNITY HOSPITAL ...1H **189**
Church Lane
HASLEMERE
GU27 2BJ
Tel: 01483 782000

HEATHERWOOD HOSPITAL 2J **33**
London Road
ASCOT
SL5 8AA
Tel: 01344 623333

HENDERSON HOSPITAL 5N **61**
2 Homeland Drive
SUTTON
SM2 5LY
Tel: 020 86611611

HOLY CROSS HOSPITAL 1D **188**
Hindhead Road
HASLEMERE
GU27 1NQ
Tel: 01428 643311

HORSHAM HOSPITAL 5J **197**
Hurst Road
HORSHAM
RH12 2DR
Tel: 01403 227000

KING EDWARD VII HOSPITAL 6F **4**
St Leonard's Road
WINDSOR
SL4 3DP
Tel: 01753 860 441

KINGSTON HOSPITAL 9A **26**
Galsworthy Road
KINGSTON UPON THAMES
KT2 7QB
Tel: 020 8546 7711

LEATHERHEAD HOSPITAL 9J **79**
Poplar Road
LEATHERHEAD
KT22 8SD
Tel: 01372 384384

MACMILLAN HOUSE DAY THERAPY UNIT
(HOSPICE) 3A **30**
Wokingham Community Hospital,
Barkham Road
WOKINGHAM
RG41 2RE
Tel: 0118 949 5030

MARIE CURIE HOSPICE, CATERHAM, THE
.................................3C **104**
Harestone Drive
CATERHAM
CR3 6YQ
Tel: 01883 832600

MAYDAY UNIVERSITY HOSPITAL 5M **45**
530 London Road
THORNTON HEATH
CR7 7YE
Tel: 020 8401 3000

MCINDOE SURGICAL CENTRE 7B **166**
Holtye Road
EAST GRINSTEAD
RH19 3EB
Tel: 01342 330300

MEDICAL RECEPTION STATION (SANDHURST)
.................................7M **49**
Royal Military Academy Sandhurst
Egerton Road
CAMBERLEY
GU15 4PQ
Tel: 01276 412234

MILFORD HOSPITAL 2F **152**
Tuesley Lane
GODALMING
GU7 1UF
Tel: 01483 782000

MOLESEY HOSPITAL 4A **40**
High Street
WEST MOLESEY
KT8 2LU
Tel: 020 8941 4481

MOUNT ALVERNIA BMI HOSPITAL
.................6F **202** (5A **114**)
46 Harvey Road
GUILDFORD
GU1 3LX
Tel: 01483 570122

NELSON HOSPITAL 1L **43**
Kingston Road
LONDON
SW20 8DB
Tel: 020 8251 1111

NEW EPSOM & EWELL COMMUNITY HOSPITAL
.................................7L **59**
West Park
Horton Lane
EPSOM
KT19 8PB
Tel: 01372 734834

NEW VICTORIA HOSPITAL 9D **26**
184 Coombe Lane West
KINGSTON UPON THAMES
KT2 7EG
Tel: 020 8949 9000

NHS WALK-IN CENTRE (ASHFORD) 3N **21**
Ashford Hospital
London Road
ASHFORD
TW15 3AA
Tel: 01784 884488

NHS WALK-IN CENTRE (CHARING CROSS)
.................................1J **13**
Charing Cross Hospital
Fulham Palace Road
LONDON
W6 8RF
Tel: 020 8846 1234

NHS WALK-IN CENTRE (CRAWLEY) 3A **182**
Crawley Hospital
West Green Drive
CRAWLEY
RH11 7DH
Tel: 01293 600300

NHS WALK-IN CENTRE (CROYDON)
.................4C **200** (9N **45**)
45 High Street
CROYDON
CR0 1QD
Tel: 020 8666 0555

NHS WALK-IN CENTRE (PARSONS GREEN)
.................................4M **13**
5-7 Parsons Green
LONDON
SW6 4UL
Tel: 020 8846 6758

NHS WALK-IN CENTRE (TEDDINGTON) ...7E **24**
Teddington Memorial Hospital
Hampton Road
TEDDINGTON
TW11 0JL
Tel: 020 8714 4004

NHS WALK-IN CENTRE (TOOTING) 6C **28**
St. George's Hospital
Blackshaw Road
LONDON
SW17 0QT
Tel: 020 8700 0505

NHS WALK-IN CENTRE (WEYBRIDGE)
.................................1B **56**
Weybridge Community Hospital
22 Church Street
WEYBRIDGE
KT13 8DY
Tel: 01932 826013

NHS WALK-IN CENTRE (WOKING) 5B **74**
Woking Community Hospital
Heathside Road
WOKING
GU22 7HS
Tel: 01483 776080

NORTH DOWNS CAPIO HOSPITAL 3C **104**
46 Tupwood Lane
CATERHAM
CR3 6DP
Tel: 01883 348981

PARKSIDE HOSPITAL 4J **27**
53 Parkside
LONDON
SW19 5NX
Tel: 020 8971 8000

PHYLLIS TUCKWELL HOSPICE 2K **129**
Waverley Lane
FARNHAM
GU9 8BL
Tel: 01252 729400

PRINCESS ALICE HOSPICE, THE 2A **58**
West End Lane
ESHER
KT10 8NA
Tel: 01372 468811

PRINCESS MARGARET BMI HOSPITAL ...5G **4**
Osborne Road
WINDSOR
SL4 3SJ
Tel: 01753 743434

PRINCESS ROYAL UNIVERSITY HOSPITAL, THE
......................................1J **67**
Farnborough Common
ORPINGTON
BR6 8ND
Tel: 01689 863000

PURLEY WAR MEMORIAL HOSPITAL 7L **63**
856 Brighton Road
PURLEY
CR8 2YL
Tel: 020 8401 3000

QUEEN MARY'S HOSPITAL FOR CHILDREN
.................................7A **44**
Wrythe Lane
CARSHALTON
SM5 1AA
Tel: 020 8296 2000

QUEEN MARY'S HOSPITAL, ROEHAMPTON
.................................9F **12**
Roehampton Lane
LONDON
SW15 5PN
Tel: 020 8487 6000

QUEEN VICTORIA HOSPITAL 7B **166**
Holtye Road
EAST GRINSTEAD
RH19 3DZ
Tel: 01342 414000

REDWOOD BUPA DIAGNOSIS &
     TREATMENT CENTRE 7F **122**
Canada Drive
REDHILL
RH1 5BY
Tel: 01737 277277

RICHMOND ROYAL HOSPITAL 6L **11**
Kew Foot Road
RICHMOND
TW9 2TE
Tel: 020 8940 3331

RIDGEWOOD CENTRE, THE 3G **71**
Old Bisley Road
CAMBERLEY
GU16 9QE
Tel: 01276 692919

ROEHAMPTON HUNTERCOMBE HOSPITAL
.................................1F **26**
Holybourne Avenue
LONDON
SW15 4JL
Tel: 020 8780 6155

ROEHAMPTON PRIORY HOSPITAL 7E **12**
Priory Lane
LONDON
SW15 5JJ
Tel: 020 8876 8261

ROYAL HOSPITAL FOR NEURO-DISABILITY
.................................9K **13**
West Hill
LONDON
SW15 3SW
Tel: 020 8780 4500

ROYAL MARSDEN HOSPITAL (SUTTON), THE
.................................6A **62**
Downs Road
SUTTON
SM2 5PT
Tel: 020 8642 6011

ROYAL SURREY COUNTY HOSPITAL ...3H **113**
Egerton Road
GUILDFORD
GU2 7XX
Tel: 01483 571122

RUNNYMEDE BMI HOSPITAL 9F **36**
Guildford Road
Ottershaw
CHERTSEY
KT16 0RQ
Tel: 01932 877800

ST ANTHONY'S HOSPITAL 7J **43**
London Road
SUTTON
SM3 9DW
Tel: 020 8337 6691

ST CATHERINE'S HOSPICE 5B **182**
Malthouse Road
CRAWLEY
RH10 6BH
Tel: 01293 447333

ST EBBA'S 5B **60**
Hook Road
EPSOM
KT19 8QJ
Tel: 01883 388300

ST GEORGE'S HOSPITAL (TOOTING) ...6C **28**
Blackshaw Road
LONDON
SW17 0QT
Tel: 020 8672 1255

ST HELIER HOSPITAL 7A **44**
Wrythe Lane
CARSHALTON
SM5 1AA
Tel: 020 8296 2000

ST JOHN'S AND AMYAND HOUSE 1G **25**
Strafford Road
TWICKENHAM
TW1 3AD
Tel: 020 8744 9943

ST PETER'S HOSPITAL 9F **36**
Guildford Road
CHERTSEY
KT16 0PZ
Tel: 01932 872000

ST RAPHAEL'S HOSPICE 8J **43**
St. Anthony's Hospital
London Road
SUTTON
SM3 9DX
Tel: 020 8335 4575

SAM BEARE HOSPICE 1B **56**
in Weybridge Hospital
22 Church Street
WEYBRIDGE
KT13 8DY
Tel: 01932 826095

SHIRLEY OAKS BMI HOSPITAL 6F **46**
Poppy Lane
CROYDON
CR9 8AB
Tel: 020 8655 5500

SHOOTING STAR HOUSE, CHILDREN'S
     HOSPICE 7N **23**
The Avenue
HAMPTON
TW12 3RA
Tel: 020 8783 2000

SLOANE BMI HOSPITAL, THE 1N **47**
125 Albemarle Road
BECKENHAM
BR3 5HS
Tel: 020 8466 4000

SPRINGFIELD UNIVERSITY HOSPITAL ..4C **28**
61 Glenburnie Road
LONDON
SW17 7DJ
Tel: 020 8682 6000

STURT HOUSE PRIORY HOSPITAL 5F **100**
Sturts Lane
Walton on the Hill
TADWORTH
KT20 7RQ
Tel: 01737 817610

SURBITON HOSPITAL 5L **41**
Ewell Road
SURBITON
KT6 6EZ
Tel: 020 8399 7111

SUTTON HOSPITAL 6N **61**
Cotswold Road
SUTTON
SM2 5NF
Tel: 020 8296 2000

TEDDINGTON MEMORIAL HOSPITAL ...7E **24**
Hampton Road
TEDDINGTON
TW11 0JL
Tel: 020 8714 4000

THAMES HOSPICECARE (ASCOT) 2J **33**
Paul Bevan House
King's Ride
ASCOT
SL5 7RD
Tel: 08456 128812

THAMES HOSPICECARE (WINDSOR) ...6D **4**
Hatch Lane
WINDSOR
SL4 3RW
Tel: 08456 128812

TOLWORTH HOSPITAL 8N **41**
Red Lion Road
SURBITON
KT6 7QU
Tel: 020 8390 0102

UNSTED PARK NEURO REHABILITATION
     CENTRE 6M **133**
Munstead Heath Road
GODALMING
GU7 1UW
Tel: 01483 892061

WALTON COMMUNITY HOSPITAL 8J **39**
Rodney Road
WALTON-ON-THAMES
KT12 3LD
Tel: 01932 220060

WEALD DAY HOSPITAL 3A **182**
Crawley Hospital
West Green Drive
CRAWLEY
RH11 7DH
Tel: 01293 600300

WEST MIDDLESEX UNIVERSITY HOSPITAL
.................................5G **11**
Twickenham Road
ISLEWORTH
TW7 6AF
Tel: 020 8560 2121

WEST PARK HOSPITAL SITE 8L **59**
Horton Lane
EPSOM
KT19 8PB
Tel: 01883 388300

WEYBRIDGE COMMUNITY HOSPITAL ...1B **56**
22 Church Street
WEYBRIDGE
KT13 8DY
Tel: 01932 852931

WOKING COMMUNITY HOSPITAL 5B **74**
Heathside Road
WOKING
GU22 7HS
Tel: 01483 715911

WOKINGHAM COMMUNITY HOSPITAL
.................................2A **30**
41 Barkham Road
WOKINGHAM
RG41 2RE
Tel: 0118 949 5000

WOKING HOSPICE 5B **74**
5 Hill View Road
WOKING
GU22 7HW
Tel: 01483 881750

WOKING NUFFIELD HOSPITAL 1A **74**
Shores Road
WOKING
GU21 4BY
Tel: 01483 227800

WOKING PRIORY HOSPITAL 3F **72**
Chobham Road
Knaphill
WOKING
GU21 2QF
Tel: 01483 489211